A Piero
con amicizia e stima
perenne

Daniele Ce...

THE ULTIMATE GUIDE TO ITALIAN WINE 2017

DANIELE CERNILLI

Editor: Daniele Cernilli

Executive Editor: Stefania Vinciguerra

Technical Supervision: Dario Cappelloni, Riccardo Viscardi

Editorial Assistant: Iolanda Maggio

Contributors: Antonella Amodio, Francesco Annibali, Livia Belardelli, Alessandro Brizi, Luigi Buonanno, Fabrizio Carrera, Fabio Casamassima, Goffredo D'Andrea, Sandra Furlan, Chiara Giannotti, Chiara Giovoni, Andrea Gori, Mirka Guberti, Federico Latteri, Luciano Lombardi, Marco Manzoli, Luca Miorandi, Alessandra Ruggi, Fiorenzo Sartore

With the participation to the tastings of: Filippo Casamassima, Sergio Ceccarelli, Rosanna Ferraro, Luca Gardini, Vito Intini, Nereo Pederzolli, Silvano Prompicai, Federica Randazzo, Luciano Rappo, Flavia Rendina, Katiuscia Rotoloni.

A special thanks for the cooperation given: Associazione Grandi Cru della Costa Toscana, Assoenologi, Assovini Sicilia, Best Italian Wine Award (BIWA), Camera di Commercio di Bolzano, Camera di Commercio di Verona, Comune di Neoneli (OR), Campania Stories, Concours Mondial de Bruxelles, Consorzio di Tutela Bardolino, Consorzio di Tutela Brunello di Montalcino, Consorzio di Tutela Carmignano, Consorzio di Tutela Chianti, Consorzio di Tutela Chianti Classico, Consorzio di Tutela Chianti Rufina, Consorzio di Tutela Colline Lucchesi e Montecarlo, Consorzio di Tutela Colline Pisane, Consorzio di Tutela Custoza, Consorzio di Tutela Franciacorta, Consorzio di Tutela Lugana, Consorzio di Tutela Montecucco, Consorzio di Tutela Morellino di Scansano, Consorzio di Tutela Oltrepò Pavese, Consorzio di Tutela Orcia, Consorzio di Tutela Prosecco Conegliano Valdobbiadene, Consorzio di Tutela Sangrantino di Montefalco, Consorzio di Tutela Sicilia Doc, Consorzio di Tutela del Soave, Consorzio di Tutela Vini Orvieto, Consorzio di Tutela Vini Piceni, Consorzio di Tutela Vino Nobile di Montepulciano, Consorzio ViniVeri, Convito di Romagna, Decanter World Wine Awards (DWWA), Enoteca Il Goccetto di Roma, Enoteca Regionale Emilia Romagna, Enoteca Trimani, Ente Fiera Verona - Vinitaly, Ersa Friuli Venezia Giulia, Istituto Marchigiano Tutela Vini (IMT), Istituto Trentodoc, Italia in Rosa, Nebbiolo Prima, Onav, Perfero Caffè di Marina di Altidona (FM), Ristoranti Baccano, La Ciambella, La Regola e Zanzara di Roma, Trattoria Visconti di Ambivere (BG), Unione Produttori Vini Albesi-Albeisa

Translation & Editing: Luigi Buonanno, Ron Fangel, Iolanda Maggio, Walter Tassa

Piazza SS. Apostoli 81 - 00187 Roma
redazione@doctorwine.it - www.doctorwine.it
 redazionedw DoctorWine DoctorWine1

Design and production: Stefania Serra

The ultimate guide to Italian wine
by Daniele Cernilli

INDEX

THE REGIONS

THE ULTIMATE GUIDE TO ITALIAN WINE 2017

Three is the charm and here is the third edition of our *The Ultimate Guide to Italian Wine* which this time is published directly by Doctor Wine, which makes its debut in the printed media after existing as a website-magazine that I invite all to visit. Mondadori, which played an important role in the first two editions, is no longer involved in the project and we thank them for all they have done as well as for our cordial and consensual separation during which there were no personal bad feelings, something that we are pleased about.

But lets get back to us. For those who have just now discovered our guide, we want, first of all, to say that it's a very different guide from all the others on the market. It's different because it's 'essential,' which means it doesn't strive to be encyclopedic but instead has as its goal a rigorous selection: the best and most interesting Italian wineries and wines admitted for evaluation within its pages.

It goes without saying that such a selection must begin with the creation of a team of highly experienced wine professionals. The team that contributed to the writing of this guide comprises people with great confidence and skill in tasting and evaluating wines, and the majority of them have a long and wide curriculum. That team began with the leader of our group, which is to say the present author. His experience is paramount: for twenty-four years he coordinated the guide that, up to now, had been the most prestigious Italian wine guide. During those years he tasted and evaluated about 150,000 wines, making him very likely the one person who contributed the most to the classification of the highest number of Italian wines. Experience profiles of such a level have made it possible to limit to almost 1,000 the number of wineries selected to be part of The Ultimate Guide to Italian Wine, and to about 2,500 the number of labels evaluated. The average is 2.5 labels per winery, the two most prestigious ones and the one that has the best quality/price ratio, in order to give useful information to those who want to drink good bottles of wine at reasonable prices.

THE TASTINGS

Having produced two previous editions, the organization of tastings was an established procedure. We did not ask for samples from producers, except in exceptional cases. We again preferred to take advantage of tastings open to the public held both at home and abroad, both the 'institutional' ones of producer associations or agencies and the more or less private ones organized by various associations, clubs and other groups. We exploited the Anteprime (Preview) tastings in Tuscany, Emilia Romagna, Umbria, Veneto and Sicily as well as Nebbiolo Prima and Campania Stories. We attended tastings organized at the headquarters of producer associations and chambers of commerce and at the international contests we were invited to, like the Best Italian Wine Award (BIWA), Decanter Wine World Award (DWWA), Concours Mondial de Bruxelles and the Douja d'Or di Asti. We also tasted wines at leading trade fairs, like Vinitaly in Verona where we had our own stand. We visited wineries, tasted wines with various enologists, frequented wine bars, compared opinions and discussed ratings. When we had to request samples, we asked producers for only one bottle, nothing more to avoid any questions over what happens to leftover bottles. In the end we were able to put together an impressive book working with calm and complete independence.

As you can observe, there is some advertising in this guide but none involving individual wine producers. This in order to avoid any interference or sensation of feeling obligated. Producer associations did advertise, this is true, but not individual producers and there is big difference.

THE CONTRIBUTORS

The *editor-in-chief* of this guide is me, Daniele Cernilli (aka Doctor Wine). Working with me is the person we jokingly refer to as our *artistic director*, Stefania Vinciguerra, who DoctorWine readers also know as Shedoctor and who is the managing editor of the site. She is the one who coordinated the work of our various collaborators, was in charge of all the editing and putting the guide together. Besides all this, she also found time to do some tasting and write evaluations. Working with her was the irreplaceable Iolanda Maggio who, thanks to her masters in gastronomic journalism from Gambero Rosso, contributed to the project not only in regard to organization but was a key component of our staff also in regard to the English edition, now in its second year. Completing the editorial Holy Trinity was our graphic artist Stefania Serra. Special mention also goes to those involved in organizing and coordinating the publication, promotion and distribution of the guide: Marina Thompson, who is also my wife, and Elisabetta Solinas.

In regard to the tasting we benefitted from to *fine palates* of our co-editors editors: Dario Cappelloni and Riccardo Viscardi, both old colleagues of mine from our Gambero Rosso days producing their Wine Guide. While both are wine experts, they have very different personalities. Dario 'wraps up' his work by mid-June so he can retire to his beloved Sardinia from where he keeps in touch from a distance. Riccardo, on the other hand, worked up to the last minute tasting, writing, correcting and revising. This year he also lent a hand as proof-reader.

We refer to our other collaborators as *the drinkers* because while it is true that they tasted and evaluated wines it is also true that they enjoy drinking wine on their own and are thus not just interested in evaluating them. Women are an important component at DoctorWine and our 'drinkers' included (in alphabetical order): the shy Antonella Amodio; the delicate Livia Belardelli; Mondadori manager Sandra Furlan; the cheerful Chiara Giannotti; the volcanic *Madame Perlage* Chiara Giovoni; the overwhelming Emilia sommelier Mirka Guberti, formerly of Bologna's *Di Vinis* and currently the co-owner of the Rome Restaurant *La Ciambella*; and, last but not least, the phlegmatic ONAV (National Wine Tasters Association) advisor Alessandra Ruggi, who some of you may remember was my co-presenter on my 'Wine Protagonists' show on the Gambero Rosso Channel ten or so years ago. Among the men are the jolly Francesco Annibali, who also works at ONAV; *new entry* Alessandro Brizi, my co-editor at the ONAV magazine *L'Assaggiatore*; our correspondent in London Luigi Buonanno; 'The' Sicilian journalist Fabrizio Carrera, the editor of the *Cronache di Gusto* site with which we sometimes exchange articles; the energetic director of the *Baccano* and *La Zanzara* restaurants in Rome Fabio Casamassima; the ex-director of *Grapes* in Isernia Goffredo D'Andrea who, after trying London, returned to Italy to give us a hand (a *new entry*) and is responsible for wine at the *Da Burde* restaurant in Florence as well as a *blogger* and historic collaborator for Andrea Gori's *Intravino* site; the meticulous Federico Latteri of *Cronache di Gusto*; the *social-media-addicted* Vigna del Mar Luciano Lombardi; biologist Marco Manzoli (aka Vinogodi); *new entry* Luca Miorandi, head of ONAV in Trento; and finally the owner of the Genoa wine shop *La Botta Piena*, as well as collaborator from the start of *Intravino*, Fiorenzo Sartore. There we also some young tasters – all from ONAV – who took part in the tastings but did not write for us: Filippo Casamassima, Flavia Rendina and Federica Randazzo.

I forgot to mention that I, too, am a member of ONAV, an organization that has existed since 1951 and includes members qualified to make a sensorial analyses of wines and organizes wine appreciation courses throughout Italy and is renowned for its great professionalism.

We are many and many more will be part of next year's edition. One last observation, as you can see there is an important, majority feminine presence at DoctorWine and it includes Katiuscia Rotoloni who writes our weekly column offering recipes. The fact that women are a majority is more unique than rare for a publication dedicated to wine, a sector that has

7

traditionally been dominated by men. And it is something that I am and everyone should be proud of. This is something else makes our guide different from the others. And i was about to forget the 'mythical Prompi', historical friend, incredibly good adviser and wine critic. But don't ask him to write…

THE EVALUATIONS

The evaluation system is structured on three levels. The first one is for the winery itself, with a score that goes from zero to three stars. The second is for individual wines, and rated by the 100-point scale. The third is for the quality/price ratio, which is expressed with the 'like' or 'thumbs up' symbol.

The stars, a sign of excellence

They range from zero to three, and the rating is an overall evaluation of the winery, not directly connected with the wines listed and evaluated in the present edition of the guide, but connected to other factors. First of all, the importance of the brand, its strategic role in the area. Then its development in recent years, its reputation for consistent quality and its international image. The number of produces with wines that were award the top three-star rating this year totaled 90 in all Italy, with four new entries to this exclusive club. You will have to discover who they are on your own when you look through our guide.

The points

Each wine has been evaluated according to the 100-point scale commonly used in international wine writing. Scoring wine is always subjective, always difficult. Conveying quality judgments through numerical scores is always very difficult, which is something we are always mindful of. Sometimes it's not only hard but also wrong to use the same evaluation system for different wines. But there is still the need to summarize numerically a judgment that often is challenging to express in words alone. This is a method used in many fields, for the football players after the matches or for movies, books or music c.d.'s or even for the scores given in schools at any age. So, if it's possible to give a score in points to a graduating student, why not do the same with wines? Usually the criteria is to use a scheme that gives up to ten points to the color, forty points to the aromatic profile and fifty points to the taste and aftertaste. We have to say, though, that often all this is calibrated on the responsiveness of each wine to its variety.

DoctorWine Faces

Wines scored between 95 and 100 are assigned a symbol called the DoctorWine 'faces'. (DoctorWine is my pseudonym.) That means that 'I put my face on it' – I stand behind the rating; I guarantee it whether the score was awarded by me personally or a member of my team. DoctorWine Faces were awarded to 219 wines in this edition. They are valid solely for this edition.

While they may seem to be many, the fact is they represent less than 10% of the wines reviewed, which already represent a restricted selection of the best wines Italy has to offer.

The prices of the wines

Calculating precise prices for wines in the Guide's English version was impossible due to all the international market variables including transportation costs, taxes, currency exchange rates and mark-up polices. For this reason we have created system of price categories to give a general idea of a wine's price. The categories are:

A – inexpensive
B – reasonable
C – expensive
D – luxury
E – priceless

The thumbs-up symbol

Indicating a favorable good quality/price ratio, it's awarded only to the so called everyday wines, wines belonging to the first category, the A.

SPECIAL PRIZES

We have focused on several wines and on the work of certain individuals to give our Guide a point of view on the world of Italian wine. Of eleven special prizes, six are for wines and five for people - or for wineries, which are teams of people. Now let's proceed.

The prize for the best red wine of the year went to Perillo's Taurasi Riserva 2007, a truly extraordinary wine that came on the market after ten years of aging. Among the whites, the best, in our view, was Castelli di Jesi Verdicchio Classico Villa Bucci Riserva 2013, produced by the wine world institution Ampelio Bucci. The prize for sparkling wine went to that great classic Trentodoc Giulio Ferrari Riserva del Fondatore 2005 from Cantine Ferrari. There is nothing to add to recall the role that the Lunelli brothers have in the production of quality Italian bubbly.

The sweet wine of the year, which is not sweet but a wine you have to think about, is the greatest that has every come on the market. We're talking about Marco De Bartoli's Vecchio Samperi. We are quite moved to give this award to Marco considering what he has represented for winemaking in his area. The wine with the best quality/price ratio this time was from the region of Lazio: Tellus Syrah 2015 from Falesco, a modern estate that combines high production with top quality and good prices.

We also have a prize for a top-quality wine that is produced in quantity. This year's winner was practically the only one running, a wine famous the world over and which for decades has been emblematic for a land the whole world knows: Chianti Classico Grand Selezione Riserva Ducale Oro from Ruffino.

And lets ahead with the estates. Alto Adige's Cantina Terlano/Terlan was the estate of the year. This is an estate that every year amazes us with the high level of quality of all its wines and we had to make an effort to limit the number of 'faccini' hedcuts, this year three, we give them. The prize for the up-and-coming estate came from a more than classic area but one where it is always possible to find something new and interesting. The winner was the Vallepicciola estate in Chianti Classico, a corner of paradise in the province of Siena where "even the angels drink wine". The prize for the best wine cooperative went to a giant of this sector: Cavit. The Trentino cooperative produces over 60 million bottle a year, or three-quarters of all the wine produced in the province of Trento, with great skill and professionalism.

The enologist of the year was Doctor Lorenzo Landi, a Tuscan from Pescia who, while he been established for years, continues to travel the world to study and update himself, especially in France. And the results are self-evident: the wines he produces are always well-made and reflect the area where they are made as well as the philosophy of the pro-

INTRODUCTION

ducer without emphasizing the contribution the enologist made. This is something we see as a plus.

Our last prize was for sustainable winemaking, which this year went to Professor Attilio Scienza for the work he has done in applying the principles of cis-genetics to winegrowing. In medicine this involves altering genes in the human genome that cause disease. In winegrowing, this technique can be used to correct the genome of the vine to produce plants that have a greater natural resistance to certain diseases, like powdery and downy mildew. This is not transgenetics, or GMO, but cis-genetics that does not add but modifies genes that are already present in the plant's DNA.

Conclusions

There is not much to add. Even though we no longer have the name Mondadori on the cover we believe we have done a good job and hope you do, too. Like other guides, ours has a limited time period it can be produced in, one that depends on when wines come out on the market and thus when they can be tasted, as well as the time needed to write and publish it. The guide is the result of two months of crazy and desperate work, made even worse by the fact that these were July and August. But despite the summer heat we pulled it off. We hope you like it because we gave it all we had.

Daniele Cernilli aka DoctorWine

The introduction of the wineries, apart from all the usual information, also offers social media connections, contacts for direct sales, hospitality and extra virgin olive oil production.

Evaluation of the winery, from zero to three stars, an "historical" evaluation based on the reliability and the prestige of the winery.

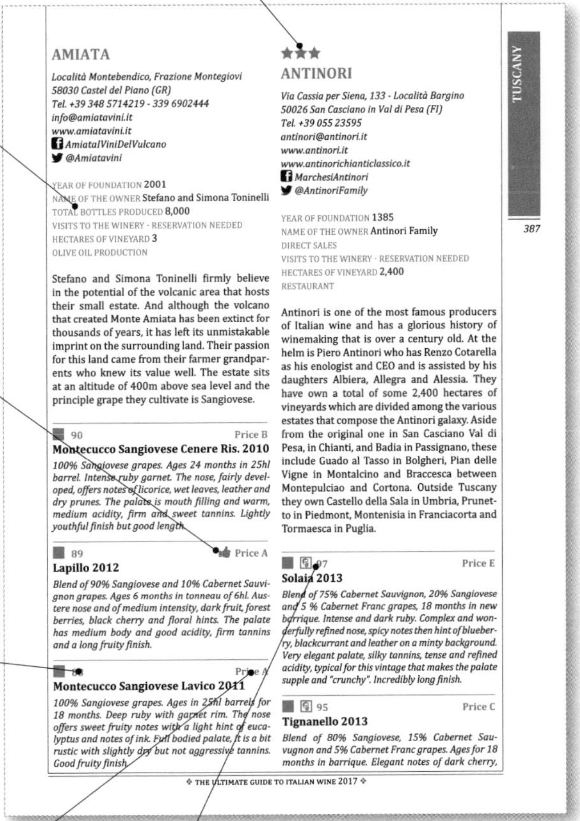

AMIATA

Località Montebendico, Frazione Montegiovi
58030 Castel del Piano (GR)
Tel. +39 348 5714219 - 339 6902444
info@amiatavini.it
www.amiatavini.it
AmiatalViniDelVulcano
@Amiatavini

YEAR OF FOUNDATION **2001**
NAME OF THE OWNER **Stefano and Simona Toninelli**
TOTAL BOTTLES PRODUCED **8,000**
VISITS TO THE WINERY - RESERVATION NEEDED
HECTARES OF VINEYARD **3**
OLIVE OIL PRODUCTION

Stefano and Simona Toninelli firmly believe in the potential of the volcanic area that hosts their small estate. And although the volcano that created Monte Amiata has been extinct for thousands of years, it has left its unmistakable imprint on the surrounding land. Their passion for this land came from their farmer grandparents who knew its value well. The estate sits at an altitude of 400m above sea level and the principle grape they cultivate is Sangiovese.

90 — Price B
Montecucco Sangiovese Cenere Ris. 2010
100% Sangiovese grapes. Ages 24 months in 25hl barrel. Intense ruby garnet. The nose, fairly developed, offers notes of licorice, wet leaves, leather and dry prunes. The palate is mouth filling and warm, medium acidity, firm and sweet tannins. Lightly youthful finish but good length.

89 — Price A
Lapillo 2012
Blend of 90% Sangiovese and 10% Cabernet Sauvignon grapes. Ages 6 months in tonneau of 6hl. Austere nose and of medium intensity, dark fruit, forest berries, black cherry and floral hints. The palate has medium body and good acidity, firm tannins and a long fruity finish.

88 — Price A
Montecucco Sangiovese Lavico 2011
100% Sangiovese grapes. Ages in 25hl barrels for 18 months. Deep ruby with garnet rim. The nose offers sweet fruity notes with a light hint of eucalyptus and notes of ink. Full bodied palate, it is a bit rustic with slightly dry but not aggressive tannins. Good fruity finish.

★★★
ANTINORI

Via Cassia per Siena, 133 - Località Bargino
50026 San Casciano in Val di Pesa (FI)
Tel. +39 055 23595
antinori@antinori.it
www.antinori.it
www.antinorichianticlassico.it
MarchesiAntinori
@AntinoriFamily

YEAR OF FOUNDATION **1385**
NAME OF THE OWNER **Antinori Family**
DIRECT SALES
VISITS TO THE WINERY - RESERVATION NEEDED
HECTARES OF VINEYARD **2,400**
RESTAURANT

Antinori is one of the most famous producers of Italian wine and has a glorious history of winemaking that is over a century old. At the helm is Piero Antinori who has Renzo Cotarella as his enologist and CEO and is assisted by his daughters Albiera, Allegra and Alessia. They have own a total of some 2,400 hectares of vineyards which are divided among the various estates that compose the Antinori galaxy. Aside from the original one in San Casciano Val di Pesa, in Chianti, and Badia in Passignano, these include Guado al Tasso in Bolgheri, Pian delle Vigne in Montalcino and Braccesca between Montepulciao and Cortona. Outside Tuscany they own Castello della Sala in Umbria, Prunetto in Piedmont, Montenisia in Franciacorta and Tormaesca in Puglia.

97 — Price E
Solaia 2013
Blend of 75% Cabernet Sauvignon, 20% Sangiovese and 5 % Cabernet Franc grapes, 18 months in new barrique. Intense and dark ruby. Complex and wonderfully refined nose, spicy notes then hint of blueberry, blackcurrant and leather on a minty background. Very elegant palate, silky tannins, tense and refined acidity, typical for this vintage that makes the palate supple and "crunchy". Incredibly long finish.

95 — Price C
Tignanello 2013
Blend of 80% Sangiovese, 15% Cabernet Sauvignon and 5% Cabernet Franc grapes. Ages for 18 months in barrique. Elegant notes of dark cherry,

TUSCANY
387

❖ THE ULTIMATE GUIDE TO ITALIAN WINE 2017 ❖

The 'like' symbol 👍 indicating a favorable good quality/price ratio, it's awarded only to the so called everyday wines, wines belonging to the first category, the A.

- Red Wine
- White Wine
- Rosé Wine
- Sweet Wine
- Sparkling Wine

The **prices** of the **wines**:
A – inexpensive
B – reasonable
C – expensive
D – luxury
E – priceless

Evaluation of the single **wines**, in cents, from a minimum of 80 to a maximum of 100. Those that have over 95 points get the DoctorWine 'face'.

ABBREVIATIONS	
AA	Alto Adige
FCO	Friuli Colli Orientali
OP	Oltrepò Pavese
Class.	Classico
Ris.	Riserva
Sup.	Superiore

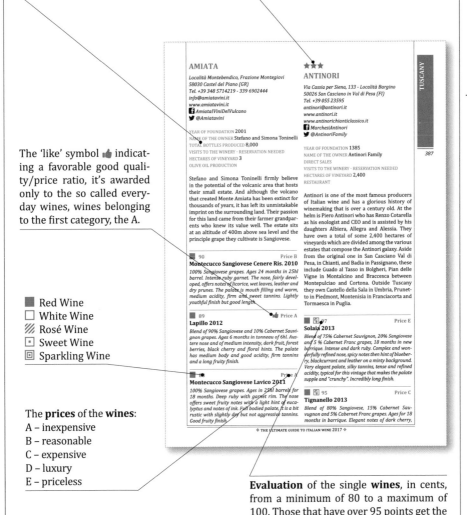

★★★ THE 3 STARS

Allegrini, Veneto
Elio Altare, Piemonte
Antinori, Toscana
Antoniolo, Piemonte
Argiolas, Sardegna
Barone Ricasoli - Castello di Brolio, Toscana
Bellavista, Lombardia
Bertani, Veneto
Biondi Santi - Tenuta Il Greppo, Toscana
Borgogno, Piemonte
Brovia, Piemonte
Bucci, Marche
Ca' del Bosco, Lombardia
Cantina San Michele Appiano, Alto Adige
Cantina Terlano / Terlan, Alto Adige
Cantine Ferrari, Trentino
Capezzana, Toscana
Caprai, Arnaldo, Umbria
Casanova di Neri, Toscana
Castel Juval Unterortl, Alto Adige
Castellare di Castellina, Toscana
Castello della Sala, Umbria
Castello di Ama, Toscana
Castello di Fonterutoli, Toscana
Castello di Monsanto, Toscana
Cerbaiona, Toscana
Còlpetrone, Umbria
Conterno, Giacomo, Piemonte
Coppo, Piemonte
Cottanera, Sicilia
Cusumano, Sicilia
Romano Dal Forno, Veneto
Marco De Bartoli, Sicilia
Falesco, Lazio
Fattoria Zerbina, Emilia Romagna
Livio Felluga, Friuli Venezia Giulia
Gianfranco Fino, Puglia
Fontanafredda, Piemonte
Fontodi, Toscana
Gabbas, Sardegna
Gaja, Piemonte
Gioacchino Garofoli, Marche
Bruno Giacosa, Piemonte
Elio Grasso, Piemonte
Gravner, Friuli Venezia Giulia

Il Pollenza, Marche
Illuminati, Abruzzo
Isole e Olena, Toscana
Jermann, Friuli Venezia Giulia
Koefererhof, Alto Adige
Lungarotti, Umbria
Bartolo Mascarello, Piemonte
Masciarelli, Abruzzo
Masi - Serego Alighieri, Veneto
Massolino, Piemonte
Mastroberardino, Campania
Miani, Friuli Venezia Giulia
Monsupello, Lombardia
Montevetrano, Campania
Muri-Gries, Alto Adige
Nino Negri, Lombardia
Oasi degli Angeli, Marche
Palari, Sicilia
Pieropan, Veneto
Pietracupa, Campania
Pio Cesare, Piemonte
Planeta, Sicilia
Poggio di Sotto, Toscana
Poliziano, Toscana
Produttori del Barbaresco, Piemonte
Querciabella, Toscana
Giuseppe Quintarelli, Veneto
Roagna I Paglieri, Piemonte
San Leonardo, Trentino
San Patrignano, Emilia Romagna
Luciano Sandrone, Piemonte
Schiopetto, Friuli Venezia Giulia
Tasca d'Almerita, Sicilia
Tenuta dell'Ornellaia, Toscana
Tenuta San Guido, Toscana
Tenuta Sette Ponti, Toscana
Franco Toros, Friuli Venezia Giulia
Umani Ronchi, Marche
Valentini, Abruzzo
Venica & Venica, Friuli Venezia Giulia
Vie di Romans, Friuli Venezia Giulia
Vietti, Piemonte
Roberto Voerzio, Piemonte
Volpe Pasini, Friuli Venezia Giulia
Elena Walch, Alto Adige

🪧 DOCTORWINE FACES

99

Barbaresco Crichet Pajé 2006, Roagna I Paglieri, Piemonte

Brunello di Montalcino Cerretalto 2010, Casanova di Neri, Toscana

Brunello di Montalcino Il Greppo Riserva 2010, Biondi Santi - Tenuta Il Greppo, Toscana

Chianti Classico Riserva 2013, Querciabella, Toscana

Taurasi Riserva 2007, Perillo, Campania (Red Wine of the Year)

98

AA Terlano Nova Domus Riserva 2013, Cantina Terlano / Terlan, Alto Adige

Barbaresco Sorì San Lorenzo 2013, Gaja, Piemonte

Barolo Casa Mirafiore Riserva 2007, Fontanafredda, Piemonte

Barolo Ester Canale Rosso Poderi dell'Antica Vigna Rionda 2012, Giovanni Rosso, Piemonte

Bolgheri Sassicaia 2013, Tenuta San Guido, Toscana

Castelli di Jesi Verdicchio Riserva Classico Villa Bucci 2013, Bucci, Marche (White Wine of the Year)

Cervaro della Sala 2014, Castello della Sala, Umbria

Collio Friulano M 2015, Schiopetto, Friuli Venezia Giulia

Kupra 2013, Oasi degli Angeli, Marche

Ugo Contini Bonacossi 2013, Capezzana, Toscana

Vecchio Samperi, Marco De Bartoli, Sicilia (Sweet Wine of the Year)

97

AA Terlano I (Primo) Grande Cuvée 2013, Cantina Terlano / Terlan, Alto Adige

Amarone della Valpolicella Classico 2008, Bertani, Veneto

Amarone della Valpolicella Vigneto di Monte Lodoletta 2010, Romano Dal Forno, Veneto

Barbaresco Asili Riserva 2011, Bruno Giacosa, Piemonte

Barbaresco Sorì Tildin 2013, Gaja, Piemonte

Barolo 2012, Bartolo Mascarello, Piemonte

Bolgheri Superiore Grattamacco 2013, Grattamacco, Toscana

Brunello di Montalcino Madonna del Piano 2010, Valdicava, Toscana

Brunello di Montalcino Riserva 2010, Capanna, Toscana

Brunello di Montalcino Riserva 2010, Caprili, Toscana

Brunello di Montalcino Ugolaia 2010, Lisini, Toscana

Brunello di Montalcino Vigna di Pianrosso Santa Caterina d'Oro Riserva 2010, Ciacci Piccolomini d'Aragona, Toscana

Chianti Classico Gran Selezione Castello di Fonterutoli 2012, Castello di Fonterutoli, Toscana

Chianti Classico Gran Selezione Sergio Zingarelli 2012, Rocca delle Macìe, Toscana

Chianti Classico Riserva 2013, Val delle Corti, Toscana

Contea di Sclafani Rosso del Conte 2012, Tasca d'Almerita, Sicilia

Costabate 2010, Uccelliera, Toscana

Cupo 2013, Pietracupa, Campania

Etna Rosso Zottorinoto Riserva 2012, Cottanera, Sicilia

Faro Palari 2011, Palari, Sicilia

FCO Merlot Filip 2012, Miani, Friuli Venezia Giulia

Gioia del Colle Primitivo Riserva 2011, Chiaromonte, Puglia

Masseto 2013, Tenuta dell'Ornellaia, Toscana

Montepulciano d'Abruzzo 2012, Valentini, Abruzzo

Recioto della Valpolicella 2004, Giuseppe Quintarelli, Veneto

Ribolla Gialla 2008, Gravner, Friuli Venezia Giulia

San Leonardo 2011, San Leonardo, Trentino

Solaia 2013, Antinori, Toscana

Solo MM12 2012, Vodopivec, Friuli Venezia Giulia

Tenores 2012, Dettori, Sardegna

Trentodoc Giulio Ferrari Riserva del Fondatore 2005, Cantine Ferrari, Trentino (Sparkling Wine of the Year)

Valtellina Superiore Sfursat 5 Stelle 2013, Nino Negri, Lombardia

Vino Nobile di Montepulciano Asinone 2012, Poliziano, Toscana

96

AA Terlano Pinot Bianco Vorberg Riserva 2013, Cantina Terlano / Terlan, Alto Adige

Amarone della Valpolicella 2007, Giuseppe Quintarelli, Veneto

Amarone della Valpolicella 2012, Roccolo Grassi, Veneto

Amarone della Valpolicella Classico La Fabriseria Riserva 2011, Tedeschi, Veneto

Amarone della Valpolicella La Mattonara Riserva 2006, Zymè, Veneto

Amarone della Valpolicella Mazzano 2009, Masi - Serego Alighieri, Veneto

Amarone della Valpolicella Mithas 2010, Corte Sant'Alda, Veneto

Barbaresco Angelo 2013, Albino Rocca, Piemonte

Barbaresco Asili Riserva 2011, Ca' del Baio, Piemonte

Barbaresco Camp Gros Martinenga Riserva 2011, Tenute Cisa Asinari dei Marchesi di Gresy, Piemonte

Barbaresco Cottà 2013, Sottimano, Piemonte

Barbaresco Pajé Vecchie Viti 2010, Roagna I Paglieri, Piemonte

Barbaresco Rio Sordo Cascina Bruciata Riserva 2011, Marchesi di Barolo, Piemonte

Barbera d'Asti Superiore Nizza 2013, Olim Bauda, Piemonte

Barbera d'Asti Superiore Nizza La Court Vigna Veja 2011, Michele Chiarlo, Piemonte

Barbera d'Asti Superiore Nizza Riserva della Famiglia 2007, Coppo, Piemonte

Barolo Brunate 2011, Elio Altare, Piemonte

Barolo Brunate 2012, Roberto Voerzio, Piemonte

Barolo Francia 2012, Giacomo Conterno, Piemonte

Barolo Gran Bussia Riserva 2008, Aldo Conterno, Piemonte

Barolo Liste 2011, Borgogno, Piemonte

Barolo Monprivato 2011, Giuseppe Mascarello & Figlio, Piemonte

Barolo Vigna Elena Riserva 2010, Elvio Cogno, Piemonte

Brunello di Montalcino Poggio all'Oro Riserva 2010, Castello Banfi, Toscana

Brunello di Montalcino PS Riserva 2010, Siro Pacenti, Toscana

Brunello di Montalcino Riserva 2010, Castello Romitorio, Toscana

Cannonau di Sardegna Classico Dule 2013, Gabbas, Sardegna

Castelli di Jesi Verdicchio Riserva Classico 2013, Pievalta, Marche

Castello del Terriccio 2011, Castello del Terriccio, Toscana

Chianti Classico Gran Selezione Castello di Brolio 2013, Barone Ricasoli - Castello di Brolio,
 Toscana

Chianti Classico Il Campitello Riserva 2013, Monteraponi, Toscana

Collio Friulano 2015, Ronco Blanchis, Friuli Venezia Giulia

Collio Friulano 2015, Schiopetto, Friuli Venezia Giulia

Costa d'Amalfi Furore Bianco Fiorduva 2014, Marisa Cuomo, Campania

Duemani 2013, Duemani, Toscana

Etna Bianco Contrada Calderara 2014, Cottanera, Sicilia

FCO Sauvignon Zuc di Volpe 2015, Volpe Pasini, Friuli Venezia Giulia

Fontalloro 2013, Fèlsina, Toscana

Franciacorta EBB Extra Brut 2011, Mosnel, Lombardia

Franciacorta Vintage Collection Dosage Zéro Noir Riserva 2007, Ca' del Bosco, Lombardia

Friuli Isonzo Rive Alte Pinot Grigio Sot Lis Rivis 2015, Ronco del Gelso, Friuli Venezia Giulia

Friuli Isonzo Sauvignon Piere 2014, Vie di Romans, Friuli Venezia Giulia

Gambellara Classico Vin Santo Nostra Historia 2010, Menti, Veneto

Ghemme Le Blanque 2011, Vigneti Valle Roncati, Piemonte

Ghemme Vigna Pelizzane 2010, Torraccia del Piantavigna, Piemonte

I Sodi di San Niccolò 2012, Castellare di Castellina, Toscana

Kurni 2014, Oasi degli Angeli, Marche

Matarocchio 2012, Guado al Tasso, Toscana

Orma 2013, Orma, Toscana

Pecorino Il Frontone 2013, Cataldi Madonna, Abruzzo

Primitivo di Manduria Es 2014, Gianfranco Fino, Puglia

Romagna Albana Passito Scaccomatto 2013, Fattoria Zerbina, Emilia Romagna

Rosso Piceno Superiore Roggio del Filare 2013, Velenosi, Marche

Saffredi 2013, Fattoria Le Pupille, Toscana

Sicilia Carricante Eruzione 1614 2015, Planeta, Sicilia

Soave Classico Calvarino 2014, Pieropan, Veneto

Syrah Collezione de Marchi 2009, Isole e Olena, Toscana

Taurasi Selezione Hamilton Riserva 2008, Di Meo, Campania

Taurasi Vigna Grande Cerzito Riserva 2010, Quintodecimo, Campania

Taurasi Vigne d'Alto 2011, Contrade di Taurasi, Campania

Torgiano Rosso Riserva Vigna Monticchio 2011, Lungarotti, Umbria

Verdicchio dei Castelli di Jesi Classico Superiore Podium 2014, Gioacchino Garofoli, Marche

95

AA Gewürztraminer Vigna Kastelaz 2015, Elena Walch, Alto Adige

AA Gewürztraminer Nussbaumer 2014, Cantina Tramin, Alto Adige

AA Lagrein Mauns Riserva 2012, Ritterhof, Alto Adige

AA Lagrein Mirell 2013, Waldgries, Alto Adige

AA Müller Thurgau Feldmarschall von Fenner 2014, Tiefenbrunner, Alto Adige

AA Pinot Nero Trattmann Mazon Riserva 2013, Cantina Girlan, Alto Adige

AA Pinot Nero Zeno Riserva 2013, Cantina Meran Burggraefler, Alto Adige

AA Sauvignon Riserva 2014, Cantina Bolzano / Bozen, Alto Adige

AA Sauvignon Sanct Valentin 2015, Cantina San Michele Appiano, Alto Adige

AA Terlano Pinot Bianco Eichhorn 2015, Manincor, Alto Adige

AA Valle Venosta Riesling Windbichel 2014, Castel Juval Unterortl, Alto Adige

Aglianico del Vulture Re Manfredi 2012, Re Manfredi Terre degli Svevi, Basilicata

Alghero Marchese di Villamarina 2011, Sella & Mosca, Sardegna

Amarone della Valpolicella Campo dei Gigli 2012, Tenuta Sant'Antonio, Veneto

Amarone della Valpolicella Classico Monte Ca' Bianca 2011, Lorenzo Begali, Veneto

Amarone della Valpolicella Classico Sergio Zenato Riserva 2010, Zenato, Veneto

Amarone della Valpolicella Riserva Cent'anni Alberto Trabucchi 1907 2008, Trabucchi d'Illasi, Veneto

Arshura 2014, Valter Mattoni, Marche

Barbaresco Il Bricco 2012, Pio Cesare, Piemonte

Barbaresco Rabajà 2013, Rocca Rabajà, Bruno, Piemonte

Barbaresco Rombone 2012, Fiorenzo Nada, Piemonte

Barolo Bricco delle Viole 2012, G.D. Vajra, Piemonte

Barolo Bricco Rocche 2012, Ceretto, Piemonte

Barolo Briccolina 2012, Batasiolo, Piemonte

Barolo Bussia Riserva 2010, Barale Fratelli, Piemonte

Barolo Bussia Vigna Colonnello Riserva 2010, Prunotto, Piemonte

Barolo Essenze Riserva 2007, Vite Colte, Piemonte

Barolo Falletto 2012, Bruno Giacosa, Piemonte

Barolo Lazzarito 2012, Vietti, Piemonte

Barolo Parafada 2012, Massolino, Piemonte

Barolo San Bernardo Riserva 2010, Palladino, Piemonte

Bolgheri Camarcanda 2013, Ca' Marcanda, Toscana

Bolgheri Superiore Ornellaia 2013, Tenuta dell'Ornellaia, Toscana

Brunello di Montalcino 2011, Giodo, Toscana

Brunello di Montalcino 2011, Le Potazzine, Toscana

Brunello di Montalcino Riserva 2010, Argiano, Toscana

Brunello di Montalcino Riserva 2010, Canalicchio di Sopra, Toscana

Brunello di Montalcino Riserva 2010, La Fortuna, Toscana

Brunello di Montalcino Vigna Schiena d'Asino 2010, Mastrojanni, Toscana

Capichera 2014, Capichera, Sardegna

Casa Romana 2012, Principe Pallavicini, Lazio

Castel del Monte Aglianico Bocca di Lupo 2012, Tormaresca, Puglia

Castel del Monte Rosso Vigna Pedale Riserva 2013, Torrevento, Puglia

Castelli di Jesi Verdicchio Riserva Utopia 2013, Montecappone, Marche

Centomoggia 2012, Terre del Principe, Campania

Centosassi 2012, Amastuola, Puglia

Chianti Classico Gran Selezione Solatìo 2012, Castello d'Albola, Toscana

Chianti Classico Novecento Riserva 2013, Dievole, Toscana

Chianti Classico Vigneto La Selvanella Riserva 2012, Melini, Toscana

Colli Tortonesi Derthona Timorasso Sterpi 2013, Vigneti Massa, Piemonte

Collio Friulano 2015, Franco Toros, Friuli Venezia Giulia

Collio Sauvignon Ronco delle Mele 2015, Venica & Venica, Friuli Venezia Giulia

Collio Sauvignon Segre 2015, Castello di Spessa, Friuli Venezia Giulia

Conero Campo San Giorgio Riserva 2011, Umani Ronchi, Marche

Contessa Entellina Mille e una notte 2011, Donnafugata, Sicilia

Controguerra Lumen Riserva 2011, Illuminati, Abruzzo

Core Bianco 2015, Montevetrano, Campania

Do ut des 2013, Carpineta Fontalpino, Toscana

Dogliani Papà Celso 2015, Marziano Abbona, Piemonte

Etna Bianco Superiore Pietra Marina 2012, Benanti, Sicilia

Etna Rosso Feudo di Mezzo 2014, Girolamo Russo, Sicilia

FCO Bianco Pomédes 2014, Roberto Scubla, Friuli Venezia Giulia

FCO Friulano Vigne Cinquant'Anni 2015, Le Vigne di Zamò, Friuli Venezia Giulia

FCO Sauvignon Liende 2015, La Viarte, Friuli Venezia Giulia

Fiano di Avellino 2014, Rocca del Principe, Campania

Fiorano Rosso 2011, Tenuta di Fiorano, Lazio

Flaccianello della Pieve 2013, Fontodi, Toscana

Franciacorta Sansevé Satèn, Monte Rossa, Lombardia

Frascati Superiore Luna Mater Riserva 2015, Fontana Candida, Lazio

Friuli Isonzo Pinot Grigio Gris 2014, Lis Neris, Friuli Venezia Giulia

Gioia del Colle Primitivo 14 Vigneto Marchesana 2013, Polvanera, Puglia

Grave di Stecca 2012, Nino Franco, Veneto

Habemus Etichetta Rossa 2013, San Giovenale, Lazio

I Capitelli 2012, Roberto Anselmi, Veneto

Il Pollenza 2013, Il Pollenza, Marche

K'un 2013, Clara Marcelli, Marche

Mamuthone 2014, Giuseppe Sedilesu, Sardegna

Montecucco Sangiovese Poggio Lombrone Riserva 2012, ColleMassari, Toscana

Montefalco Sagrantino 25 Anni 2012, Arnaldo Caprai, Umbria

Montello Colli Asolani Il Rosso dell'Abazia 2011, Serafini & Vidotto, Veneto

Moscato Passito di Saracena 2015, Cantine Viola, Calabria

Nuracada 2014, Audarya, Sardegna

Ograde Bianco 2013, Skerk, Friuli Venezia Giulia

Olmaia 2012, Col d'Orcia, Toscana

OP Barbera La Maga 2013, Castello di Cigognola, Lombardia

Orvieto Classico Superiore Pourriture Noble 2014, Decugnano dei Barbi, Umbria

Paleo Rosso 2013, Le Macchiole, Toscana

Roero Mompissano Riserva 2013, Cascina Ca' Rossa, Piemonte

Roero Printi Riserva 2012, Monchiero Carbone, Piemonte

Romagna Sangiovese Predappio di Predappio Vigna del Generale Riserva 2013, Fattoria Ni-colucci, Emilia Romagna

Romagna Sangiovese Superiore Avi Riserva 2012, San Patrignano, Emilia Romagna

Rosso In Correggio 2005, Lini 910, Emilia Romagna

Secco Bertani Original Vintage 2013, Bertani, Veneto

Sicilia Sàgana 2014, Cusumano, Sicilia

Sicilia Saia 2014, Feudo Maccari, Sicilia

Soave Classico Monte Fiorentine 2015, Ca' Rugate, Veneto

Soente 2015, Falesco, Lazio

Stellato Nature 2015, Pala, Sardegna

Taurasi Radici Riserva 2009, Mastroberardino, Campania

Terre di Pisa Nambrot 2013, Tenuta di Ghizzano, Toscana

Tignanello 2013, Antinori, Toscana

Trebbiano d'Abruzzo Castello di Semivicoli 2014, Masciarelli, Abruzzo

Trentodoc Altemasi Graal Brut Riserva 2009, Cavit, Trentino

Trentodoc Ororosso Dosaggio Zero, Cembra Cantina di Montagna, Trentino

Val d'Arno di Sopra Sangiovese Vigneto di Bòggina 2013, Petrolo, Toscana

Verdicchio di Matelica Cambrugiano Riserva 2013, Belisario, Marche

Stellato Nature 2015, Pala, Sardegna

Vernaccia di San Gimignano Albereta Riserva 2013, Il Colombaio di Santa Chiara, Toscana

Vino Nobile di Montepulciano Simposio 2011, Tenuta Tre Rose, Toscana

Vintage Tunina 2014, Jermann, Friuli Venezia Giulia

SPECIAL PRIZES

RED WINE OF THE YEAR

Taurasi Riserva 2007, Perillo, Campania (pag. 113)

WHITE WINE OF THE YEAR

Castelli di Jesi Verdicchio Riserva Classico Villa Bucci 2013, Bucci, Marche (pag. 232)

SPARKLING WINE OF THE YEAR

Trentodoc Giulio Ferrari Riserva del Fondatore 2005, Cantine Ferrari, Trentino (pag. 371)

SWEET WINE OF THE YEAR

Vecchio Samperi, Marco De Bartoli, Sicilia (pag. 348)

BEST QUALITY/PRICE RATIO

Tellus Syrah 2015, Falesco, Lazio (pag. 183)

WIDESPREAD QUALITY

Chianti Classico Gran Selezione Riserva Ducale Oro, Ruffino, Toscana (pag. 468)

WINERY OF THE YEAR

Cantina Terlano / Terlan, Alto Adige (pag. 44)

EMERGING PRODUCER

Vallepicciola, Toscana (pag. 486)

COOPERATION PRIZE

Cavit, Trentino (pag. 372)

OENOLOGIST OF THE YEAR

Doctor Lorenzo Landi

AWARD FOR SUSTAINABLE VITICULTURE

Professor Attilio Scienza

ABRUZZO

A bruzzo has an ancient winemaking tradition that was introduced to the region by the Etruscans already in the VII-VI centuries BC. In the IV century BC the Apianae grape, which was very sweet and probably similar to today's Moscato, was cultivated in vast areas of the region and the wines it made were quite famous and praised by Greek and Latin poets and scholars. Perhaps the most famous was Ovid, who was from the Abruzzo town of Sulmona and knew his region well.

Beginning in the Middle Ages and right up to modern times many of the area's winemaking traditions were lost due to the depopulation of the countryside and mountainous areas.

Only in the past 20 years that winemaking has seen an important renaissance, this mainly thanks to the many cooperatives that sprouted up, above all in the central-eastern province of Chieti. The some 3.5 million hl of wine produced in Abruzzo, of which one million are DOC or DOCG classified, make the region one of the most important for winemaking in Italy. Many of the wines, however, have not yet been appreciated and are sold bulk without the recognition they deserve. It is a fate that wines from other southern Italian regions share but things are slowly changing. This is particularly true in Abruzzo where

the DOC wines may be few in number but their quality has been constantly improving. The leading white wine, Trebbiano d'Abruzzo, is probably the best wine made from the Trebbiano grape, a variety that is unjustly underrated but that here produces wines with unique body and concentration. But the region's truly outstanding wine is Montepulciano d'Abruzzo, a red with an excellent body and the wines some from certain producers are among the best in Italy. Although the grape's name recalls the Tuscan city famous for Vino Nobile, it has little to do with the Sangiovese that makes it although they do share some ancient similarities.

The Apennine mountain chain is dominated by the Gran Sasso massif where Monte Corno reaches an altitude of close to 3,000m asl and it is the highest point in the range. Some 30km south is the region's second massif, Majella, which has peaks that are only 200m lower. The soil of the region is chalky and morainal and winegrowing is only possible in the gorges and valleys created by the rivers that run perpendicular to the coast, the plains along the coast and at lower altitudes on the mountains and foothills.

The vines are trained using the traditional high trellis tendone abruzzese method. The region's geography is quite diverse. In some winegrowing areas, like San Martino sulla Marrucina and Guardiagrele, you can ski on the Majella during the day, which is only 10km away, and then have dinner by the sea which is 20km away. In the radius of 30km there are significant climactic differences and between summer and winter, during harvest, between night and day. Daytime temperatures in September can easily rise above 30°C to then plummet to 10°C at night. Rainfall is almost always scare between June and October and sometimes drought can cause problems.

Controlled and Guaranteed Designation of Origin (DOCG)

- Montepulciano d'Abruzzo Colline Teramane

Controlled Designation of Origin (DOC)

- Abruzzo
- Cerasuolo d'Abruzzo
- Controguerra, annoso allowed (for passito)
- Montepulciano d'Abruzzo, with or without Casauria, Terre di Casauria, Terre dei Vestini, Alto Tirino, Terre dei Peligni, Teate
- Ortona
- Trebbiano d'Abruzzo
- Terre Tollesi, Tullum
- Villamagna

BOSCO NESTORE

Contrada Casali, 147
65010 Nocciano (PE)
Tel. 085 847345
info@nestorebosco.com
www.nestorebosco.com
f *CantineBoscoNestore*
🐦 *@BoscoNestore*

YEAR OF FOUNDATION **1897**
NAME OF THE OWNER **Nestore and Stefania Bosco**
BOTTLES PRODUCED **650,000**
DIRECT SALES
VISITS TO THE WINERY
HECTARS OF VINEYARD **75**
OLIVE OIL PRODUCTION

An historic producer in Abruzzo, the estate of the Bosco siblings has been in the limelight for some years now. Situated in the Pescara hills, their wines are able to express the character of the land using an approach that is both traditional and innovative. The wines are clean and, at the same time, full of personality and very consistent over the years.

■ 88   **Price B**

Montepulciano d'Abruzzo Pan Riserva 2012

100% Montepulciano grapes. Matures for 18 months in barrique. Black ruby red. Notes of nutmeg, slightly woody (coconut, vanilla), macerated red fruits in the background. No dought about the richness on the palate, the tannin is grainy and it anticipates a woody finish. Very good, it only lacks a hint of elegance.

☐ 88   **👍 Price A**

Pecorino 2015

100% Pecorino grapes. Stainless steel. Straw yellow color. Not very rich in the beginning, then it opens to notes of bread, camphor, yellow flowers. On the palate all the saltiness of this fantastic grape variety. Simple but very good.

■ 87   **Price A**

Montepulciano d'Abruzzo Linea Storica 2013

100% Montepulciano grapes. Matures in big barrels. Dark ruby red. Sweet nose of strawberry, spontaneous, ferrous. Medium richeness on the palate, with pleasantly rustic tannins. An every day wine to pair with food.

★

CANTINA TOLLO

Via Garibaldi, 68
66010 Tollo (CH)
Tel. +39 0871 96251
Fax +39 0871 962122
info@cantinatollo.it
www.cantinatollo.it
f *cantinatollo*
🐦 *@cantinatollo*

YEAR OF FOUNDATION **1960**
NAME OF THE OWNER **Tonino Verna**
BOTTLES PRODUCED **11,500,000**
DIRECT SALES
VISITS TO THE WINERY - RESERVATION NEEDED
HECTARS OF VINEYARD **3,200**
CERTIFIED ORGANIC VITICULTURE

Considered to be one of the best wine cooperatives in Italy, Tollo has become the winemaking backbone of the region with thousands of members most of whom are small farmers who without this outlet would more than likely have disappeared. The cooperative thus has a social as well as productive function. Cantina Tollo offers dozens of different and good wines some of which are excellent and many of which at an honest price. The range of regional wines is complete, even though the most interesting wines continue to come from the reds.

■ 89   **Price B**

Abruzzo Rosso 2011

100% Montepulciano grapes. Matures in big barrels for 2 years. Dense and dark ruby. Black cherry, violets, slightly smoky, chocolate on the nose. Impressive concentration on the palate, tannic, black fruits and chocolate. Incredible structure.

☐ 88   **👍 Price A**

Pecorino 2015

100% Pecorino grapes. 6 months in stainless steel on the yeasts. Bright straw yellow, simple but clear notes of aromatic herbs and white flowers. On the palate, instead, it's rich and electric, with tropical notes and a tasty finish. One of the best Pecorino 2015 of the region.

■ 87   **👍 Price A**

Montepulciano d'Abruzzo Riserva 2012

100% Montepulciano grapes. 2 years in big barrels.

Dark ruby. Notes of black cherry, violes, choccolate and very rich on the palate, almost creamy with fat tannins. A very pleasant wine, even if it lacks a little bit of complexity for a riserva.

CATALDI MADONNA

Località Piano
67025 Ofena (AQ)
Tel. +39 0862 954252
cataldimadonna@virgilio.it
www.cataldimadonna.com
Azienda-Agricola-Luigi-Cataldi-Madonna

YEAR OF FOUNDATION 1920
NAME OF THE OWNER Luigi Cataldi Madonna
BOTTLES PRODUCED 230,000
DIRECT SALES
VISITS TO THE WINERY - RESERVATION NEEDED
HECTARS OF VINEYARD 30

Luigi Cataldi Madonna is a baron as well as a philosophy professor, a cultured and intelligent man but above all one of the greatest producers of Abruzzo wine and year after year his splendid estate turns out some true wine gems. He has been able to bring out the best from the area around Capestrano and Ofena, between the provinces of L'Aquila and Pescara, which has incredible temperature variations between night and day, and the quality of his wines are difficult to match. The new Pecorino Frontone since its first vintage is one of the top Italian white wines.

 96   👍 Price B

Pecorino Frontone 2013

100% Pecorino grapes. Stainless steel on the yeasts. Very bright straw yellow, rich of light and greenish hints. Beautiful notes of peach, nettle, pink grapefruit. Impressive on the palate for salinity and incredible length, of grapefruit, nettle and a hint of flint. Without any doubt one of the best Pecorino ever produced, not only in Abruzzo.

 90   Price B

Cerasuolo d'Abruzzo Pie' delle Vigne 2014

100% Montepulciano grapes. Matures on the yeasts. Bright cherry color, almost red. Usual incredible fresh and fragrant notes on the nose with a uniquely bitter palate. Magnificent as always.

■ 88   Price A

Montepulciano d'Abruzzo Malandrino 2014

100% Montepulciano grapes. Matures in stainless steel and concrete. Dark ruby red. Very smoky notes, almost phenolic, very austere on the nose. Dry on the palate, lively, easy to drink, it only lacks a hint of fruit.

CENTORAME

Via delle Fornaci, sn - Casoli
64030 Atri (TE)
Tel. +39 085 8709115
Ⓢ *vini centorame*
info@centorame.it
www.centorame.it
Vini-Centorame
🐦 *@LambertoVannucc*

YEAR OF FOUNDATION 1987
NAME OF THE OWNER Lamberto Vannucci
BOTTLES PRODUCED 100,000
DIRECT SALES
VISITS TO THE WINERY
HECTARS OF VINEYARD 12
OLIVE OIL PRODUCTION

For just over a decade, Lamberto Vannucci has been the owner, factotum and soul of this small, organic winery. It is located in the DOCG appellation of Colline Teramane, more precisely in Val Vomano in the southernmost part of the district. The reds are bold and the whites soft and full-bodied with an unmistakable personality.

□ 88   Price A

Trebbiano d'Abruzzo Castellum Vetus 2014

100% Trebbiano d'Abruzzo grapes. Matures 10 months in tonneau. Light but bright straw yellow. Notes of alfalfa and hints of yeast (bread dough), celery. Very elegant palate and in line with the persistent finish. A really elegant wine that could get better in the next 2-3 years.

 87   Price A

Montepulciano d'Abruzzo Liberamente 2015

100% Montepulciano grapes. Stainless steel. Dark ruby. Very open on the nose with notes of leather and black cherry. Easy to drink and pleasant, extremely fresh. No added sulfites. Drink it fresh and don't let it age: it won't disappoint you!

☐ 85   Price A
Montepulciano d'Abruzzo Castellum Vetus 2013

100% Montepulciano grapes. Matures 15 months in barrique. Dark ruby. Closed on the nose in the beginning, rustic aromas with leather and licorice and animal notes on a black cherry background. Very rich and compact on the palate with an astringent and tannic finish. It needs time.

CIAVOLICH

Contrada Salmacina, 11
65014 Loreto Aprutino (PE)
Tel. +39 085 8289002
ciavolich@ciavolich.com
www.ciavolich.com
 Ciavolich-Vini-dAbruzzo
🐦 *@ciavolichwinery*

YEAR OF FOUNDATION 1853
NAME OF THE OWNER Chiara Ciavolich
BOTTLES PRODUCED 200,000
DIRECT SALES
VISITS TO THE WINERY - RESERVATION NEEDED
HECTARS OF VINEYARD 44
HOSPITALITY
RESTAURANT
OLIVE OIL PRODUCTION

If you are among those who love the wonderful wine Montepulciano d'Abruzzo and you are willing to spend to get the best, then here at Ciavolich you will find one you cannot miss: Fosso Cancelli. But their whole line of wines is also impressive. A new (even if founded in 1983) source in one of the best towns for Abruzzo wine.

■ 91   Price C
Montepulciano d'Abruzzo Fosso Cancelli 2008

100% Montepulciano grapes. Matures in concrete. Incredible dark ruby red. Very young. Spectacular notes of fur, dry mushroom, eucalyptus hints, blackberry and tobacco. Great wine on the palate: wide and deep at the same time, rich shades of mushroom and tobacco with just a little bit short in the finish.

☐ 87   Price A
Pecorino Aries 2015

100% Pecorino grapes. Matures part in stainless steel and part in tonneau. Straw yellow. Clear notes of coriander, malt, pennyroyal. Lively and agile on the palate and yeasts on the finish (bread, pennyroyal). Good body.

CONTESA

Strada delle Vigne, 28 - Contrada Caparrone
65010 Collecorvino (PE)
Tel. +39 085 8205078
Fax +39 085 8205902
info@contesa.it
www.contesa.it
📘 *ViniContesa*
🐦 *@ViniContesa*

YEAR OF FOUNDATION 1999
NAME OF THE OWNER Rocco Pasetti
BOTTLES PRODUCED 240,000
DIRECT SALES
VISITS TO THE WINERY - RESERVATION NEEDED
HECTARS OF VINEYARD 40

Franco Pasetti is one of Abruzzo's most famous producers. His specialty is Pecorino and it has become an icon in its category. He has some 40 hectares of vineyards in Collecorvino and Casalincontrada which for the most part have a southwest exposure and many of the vines grow in rows as opposed to the traditional pergola abruzzese.

☐ 88   Price A
Abruzzo Pecorino 2015

100% Pecorino grapes. One third of the mass matures for 6 months in barrique, the rest in stainless steel. Deep greenish straw yellow. Typical nose with light notes of citrus and hints of sweet spices and exotic fruits. Saline, strong flavor, great body, long and persistent.

DE FERMO

Contrada Cordano
65014 Loreto Aprutino (PE)
Tel. +39 085 8289136
Fax +39 085 76474
info@defermo.it

www.defermo.it
f *defermo.societaagricola*

YEAR OF FOUNDATION 2005
NAME OF THE OWNER Stefano Papetti
BOTTLES PRODUCED 15,000
DIRECT SALES
VISITS TO THE WINERY - RESERVATION NEEDED
HECTARS OF VINEYARD 17
CERTIFIED ORGANIC VITICULTURE
OLIVE OIL PRODUCTION

Known since ancient times for its olive oil, Loreto Apruntino became famous for its Montepulciano d'Abruzzo thanks to the great Edorardo Valentini. De Fermo has a magnificent vineyard with an exceptional exposure in the area of Cordano. With the help of Professor Leonardo Seghetti, Stefano Papetti is creating wines that are extremely respectful of tradition.

◼ 88   Price B
Montepulciano d'Abruzzo 2015

100% Montepulciano grapes. Stainless steel only. Bright ruby red, not too deep. Light aromas, notes of cherry and violets. Very vivid on the palate, with a little rustic tannins that make it easy to drink. Very straightforward.

☐ 87   Price B
Abruzzo Pecorino Don Carlino 2015

100% Pecorino grapes. Stainless steel. Bright straw yellow. Closed in the beginning, then it opens with artisanal aromas of cereals and malt, the winemaking style prevails on the variety. Then dried red flowers. Agile on the palate, taste like beer, in the finish it opens clearly on malt and marzipan.

FEUDO ANTICO

Via Perruna, 35
66010 Tollo (CH)
Tel. 0871 969128
info@feudoantico.it
www.feudoantico.it
f *feudoanticotullum*

YEAR OF FOUNDATION 2008
NAME OF THE OWNER Vittorio di Carlo
BOTTLES PRODUCED 80,000
DIRECT SALES
VISITS TO THE WINERY - RESERVATION NEEDED

HECTARS OF VINEYARD 20
CERTIFIED ORGANIC VITICULTURE
OLIVE OIL PRODUCTION

This young estate (2008) is in the 'super-wine' town of Tollo and has already made a name for itself among those who love the region's wines. The estate is young in every way and its wines unite a clear technical approach with the characteristics of the land while keep a close eye on new trends. A winery to watch.

☐ 89   Price A
Tullum Pecorino Biologico 2015

100% Pecorino grapes. Matures in concrete for 6 months on the yeasts. Bright golden straw yellow. Clear aromas with a very pleasant pink grapefruit note. Tense, very fresh on the palate, with a slightly gingery finish. Delicious.

◼ 87   Price A
Tullum Rosso 2012

100% Montepulciano grapes. Matures on concrete for 14 months. Dark ruby red with an impressive intensity. Earthy notes, rustic, wet soil, rosolio. Great on the palate, dynamic, pressing tannins. Not a thin wine but with great expressiveness.

FRATELLI BARBA

Strada Rotabile per Casoli - Frazione Scerne
64025 Pineto (TE)
Tel. +39 085 9461020
cantina@fratellibarba.it
www.fratellibarba.it
f *barbavini*
🐦 *@CantinaBarba*

YEAR OF FOUNDATION 1991
NAME OF THE OWNER Vincenzo, Giovanni and Domenico Barba
BOTTLES PRODUCED 250,000
DIRECT SALES
VISITS TO THE WINERY - RESERVATION NEEDED
HECTARS OF VINEYARD 68
HOSPITALITY
OLIVE OIL PRODUCTION

The estate is an enormous farm in the area of Teramano with over 680 hectares of land of which 400 are dedicated to livestock raising and milk production and 68 to cultivating wine grapes and other produce. The vineyards are situated in the most favorable areas of Colle Morino, Casal Thaulero and San Lorenzo. The farm is the fiefdom of Vincenzo, Giovanni and Domenico Barba who consistently offer us well-made wines some of which are excellent and have a surprising quality/price ratio.

■ 85   Price A
Montepulciano d'Abruzzo Vigna Franca 2013

100% Montepulciano grapes. Matures 14 months in barrique. Almost black color. Not very thin on the nose, with nice aromas of black cherry and oregano. On the palate it lacks a little fruit (common characteristic to 2013 wines), but it is a serious wine with a little dry tannin in the finish. Austere.

☐ 84   Price B
Trebbiano d'Abruzzo 2013

100% Trebbiano d'Abruzzo grapes. 70% vinified without the skins and matured 9 months in barrique. 30% is vinified with skin contact and matured in tonneau. Matt, deep golden yellow. Almost late harvest aromas on the nose, very intense, honey and white truffle. Then varietal notes of white flowers, slightly vegetal. Wide on the palate, very horizontal, with a vigorous finish, pleasantly dry. To drink not too cold.

I FAURI

Strada Corta, 9
66100 Chieti (CH)
Tel. +39 0871 332627
info@tenutaifauri.it
www.tenutaifauri.it
 tenuta.ifauri
 @TenutaiFauri

YEAR OF FOUNDATION 1978
NAME OF THE OWNER Luigi Di Camillo
BOTTLES PRODUCED 150,000
DIRECT SALES
VISITS TO THE WINERY - RESERVATION NEEDED
HECTARS OF VINEYARD 35
OLIVE OIL PRODUCTION

While they may not stand out for their complexity, the wines from Luigi Di Camillo's lovely winery are well-made and pleasing. And most of all they are not excessively expensive, a factor that makes them preferable to others. The winery is near the hill on which Chieti is situated.

■ 90   👍 Price A
Montepulciano d'Abruzzo Ottobre Rosso 2015

100% Pecorino grapes. Stainless steel only. Nice bright and shiny straw yellow. Stingy notes in the beginning on the nose, then peach and yellow flowers. Gritty and spontaneous on the palate, with a pleasantly citrusy finish.

☐ 87   Price A
Abruzzo Pecorino 2015

100% Pecorino grapes. Stainless steel only. Nice bright and shiny straw yellow. Stingy notes in the beginning on the nose, then peach and yellow flowers. Gritty and spontaneous on the palate, with a pleasantly citrusy finish.

IL FEUDUCCIO

Via Feuduccio, 2
66036 Orsogna (CH)
Tel. +39 0871 891646
info@ilfeuduccio.it
www.ilfeuduccio.it
 ilfeuduccio
 @IlFeuduccio

YEAR OF FOUNDATION 1996
NAME OF THE OWNER Lamaletto Family
BOTTLES PRODUCED 130,000
DIRECT SALES
VISITS TO THE WINERY - RESERVATION NEEDED
HECTARS OF VINEYARD 54
OLIVE OIL PRODUCTION

The Lamaletto family estate is situated in the Ortona hinterland, the heart of winemaking in Abruzzo, more precisely in Orsogna at an altitude of 450m above sea level. Their wines have a modern imprint that brings together significant fruity consistency with characteristics typical to the region. The level of quality is high for the whole line of wines has been consistent over the years. A place to go.

■ 92   👍 Price A
Montepulciano d'Abruzzo Feuduccio 2012

100% Montepulciano grapes. 12 months in stain-

less steel then another 12 months in different type of barrels. Intense garnet ruby color. Complex notes of dry flowers, black cherry, black pepper and a slate smoky hint. Vivid on the palate, rustic tannins and the usual power of the variety. Splendid.

---

 88   Price A

Montepulciano d'Abruzzo Fonte Venna 2014

100% Montepulciano grapes. 6 months in stainless steel, then another 6 months in different type of barrels. Light ruby red. Spicy, with cloves, pink pepper and black cherry. Pleasantly rough tannin on the palate, really good, with a flowery finish. Great quality/price ratio.

---

 86   Price A

Cerasuolo d'Abruzzo 2015

100% Montepulciano grapes. Stainless steel. Very bright cherry pink, clean aromas, fruity with pomegranate juice notes. Rich and dry on the palate. Nice freshness and most of all no sugar residual (not an easy task for the Cerasuolo 2015). Well-made and great.

 ★★★

ILLUMINATI

Contrada San Biagio, 18
64010 Controguerra (TE)
Tel. +39 0861 808008
Fax +39 0861 810004
info@illuminativini.it
www.illuminativini.it
f *IlluminatiVini*

YEAR OF FOUNDATION 1890
NAME OF THE OWNER Dino Illuminati
BOTTLES PRODUCED 1,150,000
DIRECT SALES
VISITS TO THE WINERY - RESERVATION NEEDED
HECTARS OF VINEYARD 130

We like to underline the great reliability of the winery of Dino Illuminati and his offspring Stefano, Anna and Lorenzo and the efforts made over the past 20 years to bring its bottles to tables around the world. This has been possible also thanks to a pricing policy of rare honesty and foresight, something which resulted in its Montepulciano d'Abruzzo Illuminati that we awarded last year for being the Italian wine with the best quality/price ratio. The estate

is in Controguerra, on the Abruzzo side of the Valle del Tronto, on the border with the Marche region, where there is a specific appellation which allows for the use of grapes other than just Montepulciano. The vineyards, from which one can see the port of Ascoli and the Adriatic Sea, produce majestic reds than can age long.

---

 95   Price B

Controguerra Lumen Riserva 2011

70% Montepulciano and 30% Cabernet Sauvignon grapes. Matures 18 months in barrique. Dark ruby red. Very complex aromas, eucalyptus, red fruits jam, oriental spices. Powerful on the palate and great finish that keep the wine dynamic. It will last a lot of years.

■ 91   Price B

Montepulciano d'Abruzzo Colline Teramane Zanna Riserva 2011

100% Montepulciano grapes. Matures 2 years in big barrels. Dark ruby red. Not very complex on the nose, red fruits and smokey notes. Not very deep on the palate but with a fat tannin that gives great drinkability. Powerful: very good.

■ 90   Price A

Montepulciano d'Abruzzo Ilico 2014

100% Montepulciano grapes. 10 months in big barrels. Intense ruby red and typical notes of black cherry, vanilla and spices with flowery hints. Agile structure, more than in other vintages. Tense and well sustained by the acidity and with a warm and persistent finish.

■ 90   Price A

Montepulciano d'Abruzzo Riparosso 2015

100% Montepulciano grapes. Matures 6 months in big barrels. As always one of the best easy to drink Montepulciano d'Abruzzo. Ruby red with violet hints. Fragrant notes of violet. Delicious on the palate. The tannins are a little too thick for its kind but ever ending finish. Excellent.

JASCI & MARCHESANI

Via Colli II, 3
66054 Vasto (CH)
Tel. +39 0873 364315
Fax +39 0873 380044
info@jasciemarchesani.it
www.jasciemarchesani.it
f *Jasci-Marchesani-Vini-Biologici-Fan-Page*

YEAR OF FOUNDATION 1978
NAME OF THE OWNER Ludovico Jasci
BOTTLES PRODUCED 150,000
DIRECT SALES
VISITS TO THE WINERY - RESERVATION NEEDED
HECTARS OF VINEYARD 33
CERTIFIED ORGANIC VITICULTURE

Champions of organic farming in the region long before this became trendy, in fact they began in 1978, the Jasci family estate is one of the few in the region that produces white wines that are on the level of their reds. Located near the sea in Vasto, this year they offered two exemplary wines: a Montepulciano, which was good despite the difficult 2014 harvest, and an excellent 2015 Pecorino.

 89   Price A
Montepulciano d'Abruzzo 2014

100% Montepulciano grapes. Matures 6 months in durmast barrels. Dark ruby red. Rustic notes, foxy shades than wet tobacco, black cherry. Lively palate, nice tannins and a finish that reminds a Sangiovese: vibrant. Very tasty.

 88   Price A
Abruzzo Pecorino Superiore Bio 2015

100% Pecorino grapes. Stainless steel. Straw yellow. Nice fruity aromas, typical hints of chamomile and alfalfa. Thick on the palate and very agile at the same time, with all the vibrations you would expect from a top level Pecorino. Really excellent.

LA VALENTINA

Via Torretta, 52
65010 Spoltore (PE)
Tel. +39 085 4478158
Fax +39 085 4478158
lavalentina@fattorialavalentina.it
www.lavalentina.it
 La-Valentina
🐦 *@FLaValentina*

YEAR OF FOUNDATION 1990
NAME OF THE OWNER Sabatino Di Properzio
BOTTLES PRODUCED 350,000
DIRECT SALES
VISITS TO THE WINERY - RESERVATION NEEDED
HECTARS OF VINEYARD 40

This modern winery is nicely run by Sabatino Di Properzio and his brothers Andrea and Roberto. The vineyards are situated on the hills overlooking the lower Valle del Pescara in the townships of Spoltore, Scafa and San Valentino. Their wines are made with in a modern and measured style, all to enhance their drinkability. Their Cerasuolo is simply irresistible.

 92   👍 Price B
Montepulciano d'Abruzzo Spelt Ris. 2012

100% Montepulciano grapes. Matures part in barrique and part in big barrels. Dark ruby red. Very flowery and fragrant with a palate that demonstrates the grit of Montepulciano. No wood on the finish on leather notes. One of the best versions ever.

■ 90   Price B
Montepulciano d'Abruzzo Bellovedere Riserva 2012

100% Montepulciano grapes. Matures part in barrique and part in big barrel, then concrete. Intense ruby red. Notes of morello cherry, smoky and cocoa. Powerful on the palate, still a little tied up, very long. It needs to rest some years in the bottle.

□ 89   Price B
Montepulciano d'Abruzzo Binomio Riserva 2012

100% Montepulciano grapes. Matures in new and used barrique. Very fresh color, dark ruby red. Fragrant on the nose with notes of strawberry. Neat on the palate with a tannic finish. Not very agile but with strong personality.

LEPORE

Contrada Civita, 29
64010 Colonnella (TE)
Tel. +39 0861 70860
info@vinilepore.it
www.vinilepore.it

YEAR OF FOUNDATION 1992
NAME OF THE OWNER Gaspare Lepore
BOTTLES PRODUCED 330,000
DIRECT SALES
VISITS TO THE WINERY - RESERVATION NEEDED
HECTARS OF VINEYARD 40

In production since the 1990s in Colonnella, a stone's throw from the Adriatic and the Marche region, Gaspare Lepore's winery has had its ups and downs. Over the past few years, however, there can be no doubts over the quality of his wines. This year there was a wine that shot to the top – and could only have give its name Colline Teramare Re (King). This is simply one of the best reds the region produced this year.

 93   👍 **Price A**

Montepulciano d'Abruzzo Colline Teramane Re 2012

100% Montepulciano grapes. Matures 8 months in barrique. Garnet ruby red. Complex aromas: as it happens in the Colline Teramane that look like Tuscany: cigar and wet soil on shades of violet. Elegant on the palate, wide, nicely dry tannin and agile finish on notes of leather and tobacco. Fantastic.

91   **Price B**

Montepulciano d'Abruzzo Colline Teramane Luigi Lepore Riserva 2011

100% Montepulciano grapes. Matures 8 months in barrique. Garnet ruby red. Complex aromas: as it happens in the Colline Teramane that look like Tuscany: cigar and wet soil on shades of violet. Elegant on the palate, wide, nicely dry tannin and agile finish on notes of leather and tobacco. Fantastic.

84   **Price A**

Montepulciano d'Abruzzo 2014

100% Montepulciano grapes. Matures part in big barrels and part in barrique. Dark ruby red. Simple but clean aromas on notes of cherry, not very rich, you can feel it wasn't a great vintage. Not very thick tannins on the palate, then hint of herbs, average finish, slightly slippery but good.

★★★

MASCIARELLI

*Via Gamberale, 1
66010 San Martino Sulla Marrucina (CH)
Tel. +39 0871 85241
info@masciarelli.it
www.masciarelli.it*
📘 *Masciarelli-Tenute-Agricole*
🐦 *@MasciarelliVini*

YEAR OF FOUNDATION **1981**
NAME OF THE OWNER **Marina Cvetic**
BOTTLES PRODUCED **2,500,000**
DIRECT SALES

VISITS TO THE WINERY - RESERVATION NEEDED
HECTARS OF VINEYARD **320**
OLIVE OIL PRODUCTION

The estate founded by Gianni Masciarelli has for some years now been run by his wife Marina Cvetic who continues her late husband's work with great dedication and rigor. The estate's over 300 hectares of vineyards produce some true enological gems that have become famous worldwide and are produced using a modern style that respects origins, varieties and terroirs. The winery, which was totally revamped less than ten years ago, is one of the most functional and efficient in Italy.

☐ 🍴 **95**   **Price B**

Trebbiano d'Abruzzo Castello di Semivicoli 2014

100% Trebbiano grapes. 1 year in stainless steel on the yeasts. Bright greenish straw yellow. Complex nose, with smoky notes, white peach, grapefruit, alfalfa and flint. Elegant flavor, tense, agile, with good body structure balanced by fresh and salty acidity. Incredibly long finish.

93   **Price C**

Montepulciano d'Abruzzo Villa Gemma Riserva 2011

100% Montepulciano grapes. 1 year in big barrels and 18 months in barrique. Very intense garnet ruby red. Vanilla, sweet spices dominate the aromatic bouquet, then macerated black cherry, cocoa and tamarind. Rich flavor, tense, warm, powerful, enveloping, well balanced by acidity. Very long finish.

91   **Price B**

Montepulciano d'Abruzzo Marina Cvetic San Martino Riserva 2014

100% Montepulciano grapes. 2 years in barrique and stainless steel. Intense ruby red. Black cherry, plum, hints of cocoa and vanilla dominate the nose. Full flavor, tense, less powerful compared to other versions, more agile and easy to drink with a warm and persistent finish.

90   **Price B**

Iskra 2011

100% Montepulciano grapes. 2 years in barrique and stainless steel. Intense ruby red. Enveloping and ethereal on the nose, notes of black cherry, cocoa, eucalyptus hints. Rich and agile flavor, nice tannins, saline and warm.

🎗 87   Price A
Cerasuolo d'Abruzzo Villa Gemma 2015

100% Montepulciano grapes. Stainless steel. Bright pink. Fragrant and interesting fruit on the nose with notes of peach and strawberry on fermentative hints. Saline and tense flavor, easy to drink, simple but very good.

CAMILLO MONTORI

Via Piane Tronto, 80
64010 Controguerra (TE)
Tel. +39 0861 809900 - 809943
🅢 *Montori_Rn*
info@montorivini.it
www.montorivini.it
🅵 *Azienda-Agricola-Camillo-Montori*
🐦 *@MontoriWines*

YEAR OF FOUNDATION 1960
NAME OF THE OWNER Camillo Montori
BOTTLES PRODUCED 600,000
DIRECT SALES
VISITS TO THE WINERY - RESERVATION NEEDED
HECTARS OF VINEYARD 55
HOSPITALITY
RESTAURANT
OLIVE OIL PRODUCTION

An historic winery in the north of the region where its vineyards are for the most part in the DOCG district of Colle Teramane. It has been run for decades by Camillo Montori, a point of reference for the area thanks to his professionalism and fine results, which over the years have been well made and consistent. This year his Trebbiano stood out and even surpassed his always dependable Montepulciano Fonte Cupa.

🎗 88   Price A
Cerasuolo d'Abruzzo Fonte Cupa 2015

100% Montepulciano grapes. Stainless steel. Bright light pink. Notes of white flowers and pomegranate juice. Fresh on the palate, riche and slightly tannic finish. Very agile and good.

☐ 86   Price A
Trebbiano d'Abruzzo Fonte Cupa 2015

100% Trebbiano d'Abruzzo grapes. Stainless steel. Straw yellow. Yeast (bread dough) and pear on the nose, vegetal shades. A little simple on the palate

but very pleasant and most of all nicely dynamic, very classy.

NICODEMI

Contrada Veniglio
64024 Notaresco (TE)
Tel. +39 085 895493
fattoria.nicodemi@tin.it
www.nicodemi.com

YEAR OF FOUNDATION 1970
NAME OF THE OWNER Elena and
Alessandro Nicodemi
BOTTLES PRODUCED 250,000
DIRECT SALES
VISITS TO THE WINERY - RESERVATION NEEDED
HECTARS OF VINEYARD 30

Alessandro and Elena Nicodemi, who are Romans by birth but have chosen Abruzzo as their home, have been successfully running their family winery for some years now. It is located in Notaresco, in Val Vomano, a stone's throw from Roseto and the beaches of the Adriatic Riviera but with the Grand Sasso behind it. This area produces some fantastic reds with bold bodies and impenetrable colors and is the heart of the best Montepulciano d'Abruzzo Colline Teramano, a DOCG appellation which has a producers' association of which Alessandro is its outstanding president.

◼ 93   Price B
Montepulciano d'Abruzzo Colline Teramane Neromoro Riserva 2012

100% Montepulciano grapes. Matures 18 months in barrique. Intense and dark ruby red. Great impact on the nose with macerated black cherry, cocoa, plum, sweet spices, very typical. Enveloping flavor, warm, thick but elegant tannins, great body, rich but agile and incredible long finish.

☐ 86   👍 Price A
Trebbiano d'Abruzzo 2015

100% Trebbiano grapes. Stainless steel. Light straw yellow. Fragrant, fruity, maybe simple but very clear and balanced with notes of white peach and golden apple. Fresh, saline, pleasant, easy to drink and thin but good length in the finish.

PASETTI

Via San Paolo, 21
66023 Francavilla al Mare (CH)
Tel. +39 085 61875
Fax +39 085 4519292
info@pasettivini.it
www.pasettivini.it
 f *pasettivini*
 y *@PASETTIWINERY*

YEAR OF FOUNDATION 1960
NAME OF THE OWNER Domenico Pasetti
BOTTLES PRODUCED 600,000
DIRECT SALES
VISITS TO THE WINERY - RESERVATION NEEDED
HECTARS OF VINEYARD 70
HOSPITALITY
OLIVE OIL PRODUCTION

Do not let the location of Domenico Pasetti's winery fool you because even if its headquarters are in Francavilla al Mare, a seaside resort outside Pescara, the vineyards are between Val Tirino and the upper Aterno-Pescara River, between the Gran Sasso and Majella massifs. Here temperatures differ greatly between day and night during harvest and many of the vines are situated at a high altitude, including in the town of Pescosansonesco in the Monti Vestini.

■ 90	Price B

Montepulciano d'Abruzzo Testarossa 2011

100% Montepulciano grapes. About 20 months in barrique. Very dark garnet ruby. Macerated black cherry, tamarind and plum hints, then vanilla, cocoa and cardamom. Full, warm, tense flavor with great body well sustained by acidity. Very persistent finish.

■ 87	👍 Price A

Montepulciano d'Abruzzo 2013

100% Montepulciano grapes. 8 months in big barrels. Intense ruby red. A lot of macereted red fruit on the nose, slight spicy notes in the background. Strong, warm, tense flavor with good acidity that balances the powerful body. Good length in the finish.

☐ 86	Price B

Abruzzo Pecorino Collecivetta 2014

100% Pecorino grapes. Stainless steel only. Intense straw yellow. Citrucy on the nose and slightly flowery. Pleasantly saline and fresh with a good length in the finish.

PETTINELLA

Contrada San Silvestro, 16
64028 Silvi (TE)
Tel. +39 338 8279506
giuliano.pettinella@libero.it

YEAR OF FOUNDATION 2011
NAME OF THE OWNER Giuliano Pettinella
BOTTLES PRODUCED 1,800
VISITS TO THE WINERY SU PRENOTAZIONE
HECTARS OF VINEYARD 0.5

It takes a lot of determination to make wine but Giuliano Pettinella, a lawyer from the Marche region, had to overcome a thousand bureaucratic obstacles in order to restore an old Abruzzo farmhouse his family had owned for decades and begin producing the most visceral and loved – at least by the locals – Abruzzo wine, Cerasuolo. Even if he has only produced a few vintages, the first was a 2011, the resultsare already excellent.

⧄ 88	Price B

Tauma 2015

100% Montepulciano grapes. Matures in small used barrels and stainless steel. Cherry ruby with karkadè shades. Rustic notes, then raspberry, white pepper. Nice on the palate but less important than the previous vintages due to the vintage not so easy to deal with. None the less at the region top levels.

★

ITALO PIETRANTONJ

Via San Sebastiano, 38
67030 Vittorito (AQ)
Tel. +39 0864 727102
info@vinipietrantonj.it
www.vinipietrantonj.it

YEAR OF FOUNDATION 1830
NAME OF THE OWNER Nicola Pietrantonj
BOTTLES PRODUCED 650,000
DIRECT SALES
VISITS TO THE WINERY - RESERVATION NEEDED
HECTARS OF VINEYARD 60

Valle Peligna is one of those places that restores depth and personality to Montepulciano. Here the grapes' primary and typical notes of black cherry combine with scents of fur and tobacco while the tannins are more lively than usual. The Pietrantoni estate has been active for well over a century, with production starting in the 19th century, and has perfected exalting the area's characteristics. These are all perfectly expressed in the Cerano 2010, a wine not to be missed.

 93   Price B

Montepulciano d'Abruzzo Cerano Riserva 2010

100% Montepulciano grapes. Matures 16 months in tonneau. Dark ruby red. Beautiful nose of black truffle and wet tobacco, smoke and black cherry. Nice on the palate, fruity and smoky, full bodied and long finish, still with a little wood to integrate. Fantastic.

 88   Price A*

Terre Aquilane Passito Rosso 2012

*100% Montepulciano grapes. Stainless steel. Bright dark ruby. Notes of barbeque, cloves and black cherry in the background. A typical sweet wine even if not so long. *50 cl bottle.*

■ **87**   👍 Price A

Montepulciano d'Abruzzo Arbòreo 2012

100% Montepulciano grapes. Matures in big barrels. Intense ruby red, very young. Notes of chery, cinchona, a hint of tobacco. Average on the palate, delicate tannins and a hint of tobacco. Non very powerful but very well balanced. Easy to drink.

★

PRAESIDIUM

Via Nazareno Giovannucci, 24
67030 Prezza (AQ)
Tel. +39 0864 45103
info@vinipraesidium.it
www.vinipraesidium.it
🔲 *vinipraesidium*

YEAR OF FOUNDATION **1988**
NAME OF THE OWNER **Enzo Pasquale**
BOTTLES PRODUCED **25,000**
DIRECT SALES
VISITS TO THE WINERY - RESERVATION NEEDED
HECTARS OF VINEYARD **5**

The small hamlet of Prezza is in the province of L'Aquila, in the middle of the Apennines in the Peligna Valley. And it is here that the Praesidium winery of Enzo Pasquale and his children Ottaviano and Antonia, has its vineyards. Their wines have been constantly improving, above all from winemaking profile, and now have the characteristics and technical consistency to be evaluated in a positive way.

■ **93**   Price B

Montepulciano d'Abruzzo Riserva 2011

100% Montepulciano grapes. Matures 2 years in big barrels. Intense ruby red. Intensly spicy on the nose, with notes of vanilla, black cherry and cocoa hints. Clean flavor, elegant, nice tannins, good acidity, nice saltiness and average body. Great persistent finish.

TERZINI

Via Roma, 52
65028 Tocco da Casauria (PE)
Tel. +39 0859 158147
🅢 *Cantina Terzini*
info@cantinaterzini.it
www.cantinaterzini.it
🔲 *Cantina-Terzini*
🐦 *@Cantina_Terzini*

YEAR OF FOUNDATION 2009
NAME OF THE OWNER Domenico Terzini
BOTTLES PRODUCED **200,000**
DIRECT SALES
VISITS TO THE WINERY
HECTARS OF VINEYARD **22**
OLIVE OIL PRODUCTION

While not really known among wine lovers, the area of Tocco da Casauria has nothing the more famouas ones in the region don't have. The vineyards are at the foot of the mountains and the wines, while not losing an iota of richness, are distinctly fresh. The whole line of wines produced by Domenico Terzini is impressive. Hats off.

■ **91**   Price B

Montepulciano d'Abruzzo Vigna Vetum 2013

100% Montepulciano. Matures in barrique. Dark ruby. Complex nose, with smoky notes, soil, coffee liquor, really good. Rich, nicely rustic tannin and fruity and long finish. Great wine.

☐ 90   👍 Price A

Abruzzo Pecorino Terzini 2015

100% Pecorino grapes. Stainless steel on the skins. Bright straw yellow. Very typical notes of peach, alfalfa, coriander. Gritty on the palate, rich and juicy. One of the best Pecorino 2015 from Abruzzo.

■ 89   Price A

Montepulciano d'Abruzzo Terzini 2015

100% Montepulciano grapes. Stainless steel. Dark and bright color. Notes of strawberry and sweet licorice. Smoky notes on the palate (coffee, barbeque) and bitter, tannic finish.

★★
TORRE DEI BEATI

Contrada Poggioragone, 56
65014 Loreto Aprutino (PE)
Tel. +39 085 4916069
🇸 *fausto.albanesi*
info@torredeibeati.it
www.torredeibeati.it
🇫 *Torre-dei-Beati*

YEAR OF FOUNDATION **1999**
NAME OF THE OWNER **Adriana Galassio and Fausto Albanesi**
BOTTLES PRODUCED **100,000**
DIRECT SALES
VISITS TO THE WINERY - RESERVATION NEEDED
HECTARS OF VINEYARD **21**
CERTIFIED ORGANIC VITICULTURE

The estate of Adriana and Fausto Albanesi is one to remember. They are passionate and skilled who restore our faith in the world of winemaking which in recent years has become a little too glamourous. They are a lovely and kind couple with a humility that only authentic people have. They almost get embarrassed if you tell them their wines are fantastic, which they are, the product of hard work, passion and a love for what one does. If you go and visit them they will welcome you as old friends and our advice is to buy all wine you can, this year's lot is fantastic.

■ 90   Price B

Montepulciano d'Abruzzo Mazzamurello 2013

100% Montepulciano grapes. Matures 20 months

in barrique with a short skin contact. Intense ruby. Notes of vanilla, cocoa, eucalyptus and black cherry hints. Not too full bodied, cocoa tannins and slightly woody in the finish. Personality and muscles but a little bit too short but always good. Will it get better?

☐ 87   Price A

Abruzzo Pecorino Bianchi Grilli 2014

100% Pecorino grapes. Matures in barrique for 9 months. Bright straw yellow. Clean, yellow flowers. Rich and salty on the palate. Nice finish. Very balanced. It could get better with a few years of bottle.

☐ 86   Price A

Abruzzo Pecorino Giocheremo con i Fiori 2015

100% Pecorino grapes. Stainless steel on the skins. Very bright color, greenish straw yellow. Notes of yeasts and coriander. Average body with the acidity that isolates itself in the finish. Easy to drink.

★★★
VALENTINI

Via del Baio, 2
65014 Loreto Aprutino (PE)
Tel. +39 085 8291138

YEAR OF FOUNDATION **1650**
NAME OF THE OWNER **Francesco Paolo Valentini**
BOTTLES PRODUCED **32,000**
VISITS TO THE WINERY
HECTARS OF VINEYARD **70**

There are no tours of this winery and no onsite sales. Francesco Paolo Valentini, just like his father Edoardo, is not a showman and lets his wines, about which much has been written, do the talking. All Valentini's wines have an incredible lifespan and are a fine work of craftsmanship and need to age long in the bottle to be fully appreciated. Anyone without the patience or desire to wait should drink something else, they will not like these wines. Those who know the wines well don't mind waiting and we are proud to be among them.

■ 97   Price D

Montepulciano d'Abruzzo 2012

100% Montepulciano grapes. Matures in big barrels. Dark, deep, matt ruby red. Clear notes on cof-

fee cream, black olives, blueberry puree, slightly earthy. Wide and rich on the palate, slightly less tannic than usual but incredibly elegant. With 2012 vintage Francesco Paolo opted for a more delicate extraction (6-7 days of maceration and hand fulling). Open it many hours before drinking.

VALLE REALE

Località San Calisto
65026 Popoli (PE)
Tel. +39 085 9871039
info@vallereale.it
www.vallereale.it

YEAR OF FOUNDATION **1999**
NAME OF THE OWNER **Leonardo Pizzolo**
BOTTLES PRODUCED **250,000**
DIRECT SALES
VISITS TO THE WINERY - RESERVATION NEEDED
HECTARS OF VINEYARD **49**
CERTIFIED ORGANIC VITICULTURE

Leonardo Pizzolo, a descendant of a famous Veneto winegrowing family, is seeing his dream come true. Valle, as he refers to it, is more than ever his winery where he employs spontaneous fermentation and passionately cultivates his grapes organically. This different and original approach from that of his family and has allowed him to produce some very personal wines which improve year after year for both their character and how they express the land.

☐ **94**   Price B
Trebbiano d'Abruzzo Vigneto di Popoli 2014

100% Trebbiano d'Abruzzo. Stainless steel on the yeasts. Bright golden yellow, slightly matt. The aromas open slowly on pear, jasmine, yellow flowers, mustard, chalk and resin. Marvelous on the palate, with fantastic saltiness and really persistent finish, slightly fruity. Really a top level white wine.

☐ **93**   Price B
Trebbiano d'Abruzzo Vigna del Convento di Capestrano 2014

100% Trebbiano d'Abruzzo. Stainless steel on the yeasts. Matt and bright golden yellow. Explosive aromas with notes that remind a late harvest wine: ripe apricots, honey, salt, pistachios. Correspondent palate, slightly tannic, salty finish, very agile.

Sapidity more of a Pecorino then of a Trebbiano. Marvellous.

■ **91**   Price B
Montepulciano d'Abruzzo Vigna del Convento 2011

100% Montepulciano grapes. 2 years in big barrels. Intense ruby red. Almost delicate and neat on the nose with notes of black cherry, currant and red berries on smoky hints. Full taste but not heavy, young tannins, slightly rough and nice length in the finish.

■ **88**   Price A
Montepulciano d'Abruzzo 2015

100% Montepulciano grapes. Stainless steel only. Dark ruby red. Typical nose, irony, tobacco, truffle. Not very tannic on the palate, but very good to be an entry level wine. Simple finish on violet notes.

VALORI

Via Torquato al Salinello, 8
64027 Sant'Omero (TE)
Tel. +39 0861 88461
info@masciarellidistribuzione.it
www.masciarellidistribuzione.it

YEAR OF FOUNDATION **1998**
NAME OF THE OWNER **Luigi Valori**
BOTTLES PRODUCED **200,000**
DIRECT SALES
VISITS TO THE WINERY - RESERVATION NEEDED
HECTARS OF VINEYARD **40**
CERTIFIED ORGANIC VITICULTURE

Luigi Valori's smile is already a guarantee and if you add to this his joint-venture with Masciarelli then you understand that everything is on a first-name basis. Although his vineyards are in the southern part of Colline Teramane, Valori does not make a Montepulciano DOCG and prefers to make a DOC which has always been more than just good.

■ **94**   Price B
Montepulciano d'Abruzzo Vigna Sant'Angelo Riserva 2011

100% Montepulciano grapes. 12 months in barrique. Intense garnet ruby red. Enveloping and very typical notes on the nose with black cherry and co-

coa, then vanilla, plum and slightly smoky. Strong flavors, full bodied but tense, elegant, with neat and elegant tannins. Persistent finish.

VILLA MEDORO

Contrada Medoro, 1
64030 Atri (TE)
Tel. +39 085 8708139
info@villamedoro.it
www.villamedoro.it
villa.medoro

YEAR OF FOUNDATION **1995**
NAME OF THE OWNER **Federica Morricone**
BOTTLES PRODUCED **600.000**
DIRECT SALES
VISITS TO THE WINERY - RESERVATION NEEDED
HECTARS OF VINEYARD **102**

Federica Morricone is a young lady of Abruzzo wine and skilled businesswoman who has created a model winemaking estate in the heart of Val Vomano, near Atri, in the southern area of Colline Teramane. There she produces bold, typical wines that are technically well-made.

---

 93   Price B

Montepulciano d'Abruzzo Colline Teramane Adrano 2013

100% Montepulciano grapes. 12 months in barrique. Intense garnet ruby red. Enveloping and very typical notes on the nose with black cherry and cocoa, then vanilla, plum and slightly smoky. Strong flavors, full bodied but tense, elegant, with neat and elegant tannins. Persistent finish.

---

 90   Price A

Montepulciano d'Abruzzo Villa Medoro 2014

100% Montepulciano grapes. Stainless steel. Violet ruby red. Spicy aromas, reminds a Syrah, then violets. Fragrant palate, delicious and slightly tannic finish. Again an incredible quality/price wine.

---

 88   Price A

Cerasuolo d'Abruzzo Villa Medoro 2015

100% Montepulciano grapes. Stainless steel. Very bright cherry pink. Clear notes of orange juice on the nose. Dynamic and dry on the palate, a little tannic in the finish. One of the best Cerasuolo 2015.

ZACCAGNINI

Contrada Pozzo, 4
65020 Bolognano (PE)
Tel. +39 085 8880195
info@cantinazaccagnini.it
www.cantinazaccagnini.it
CantinaZaccagniniOfficial
@Zaccagninivini

YEAR OF FOUNDATION **1978**
NAME OF THE OWNER **Marcello Zaccagnini**
BOTTLES PRODUCED **3,000,000**
DIRECT SALES
VISITS TO THE WINERY - RESERVATION NEEDED
HECTARS OF VINEYARD **300**
OLIVE OIL PRODUCTION

An historic Abruzzo wine producer that combines quantity with good quality. Owned by Marcello Zaccagnini, the estate uses grapes from 300 hectares of vineyards which it either owns or leases. The wines are technical and full of personality at the same time, very precise yet rich in vibrations and this year they produced a world-class red Passito: Clematis.

---

93   Price C*

Clematis Passito 2011

*100% Montepulciano grapes dried on the shoots. 3 years in small barrels. Dark ruby red with violet shades. Dense. Nougat, nuts, black figs, very sweet mouth balanced by powerful tannins and nutty finish. Less woody and better than the last vintage! *37.5 cl bottle.*

---

88   Price B

Montepulciano d'Abruzzo San Clemente 2013

100% Montepulciano grapes. Matures in barrique. Very dark ruby red. Flowery, black cherry, slightly smoky. It doesn't lack structure and it's agile, Nebbiolo style tannins and a tasty finish. Great version, even though a little less fruity than usual.

---

87   Price A

Abruzzo Pecorino Yamada 2015

100% Pecorino grapes. Stainless steel. Very bright greenish straw yellow. Notes of green olives and grapefruit. Electric palate, with green olives and smoky notes on the finish. Very tasty. Not great complexity but easy to drink.

ALTO ADIGE

The sub-region of Alto Adige has a winemaking tradition that is thousands of years old and even pre-dates the Romans. Over the centuries, the vocation of produces to make and export their wines has not changed and their natural markets remain those of Germany and Austria thanks also to a common language (the majority of Alto Adige's population is German-speaking).

The DOC area in Alto Adige/Sudtirol is relatively small and the best zone is that of Trentino. It is for the most part in the valleys of the Adige and Isarco Rivers, with some small but important exceptions. The Alto Adige/Sudtirol appellation is a kind of legislative umbrella which governs production for some 80% of the area's total output, which is something more than 500,000 hectoliters a year.

Alto Adige is a bi-lingual, German-Italian speaking area and this is evident in the names of the denominations and the wines themselves, which are sometimes difficult to understand if you don't speak German. Often you will find on the label, alongside the Italian or French ones, the German name for the grape which can be totally different. For example, Pinot Bianco can be called Weissburgunder, Pinot Grigio is Rulander, Pinot Nero is Blauburgunder, Traminer Aromatico becomes Gewürztraminer, Lagrein Scuro is Lagre-

in Dunkel while the Chiaro or Rosato is Lagrein Kretzer (the common term for a rosé), Schiava is Vernatsche, Moscato Giallo is Goldmuskateller and the Rosato is Rosenmuskateller. The Cooperative Winery (Cantina Cooperativa) or Producers' Winery (Cantina Produttori) is Kellereigenossenschaft and towns usually have double names with Cornaiano also referred to as Girlan, Termeno is Tramin, Caldaro is Kaltern, Cortaccia is Kurtatsch, Appiano is Eppan and so on. With a little practice one can get the hang of it but it's not easy.

Among the white wines, the most widespread are Pinot Bianco/Weissburgunder followed by Riesling, Sauvignon, Pinot Grigio/Rulander and Traminer Aromatico/Gewürztraminer. The most popular red is Schiava/Vernatsche, a delicious, young red that is light and easy to drink and pairs splendidly with local cured meats like speck ham. It represents 20% of total red wine production and can be found almost everywhere. Schiava is also blended with other varieties to produce some fine wines like Lago di Caldoro/Kalterersee and Santa Maddalena, the latter being produced just outside Bolzano. Both wines are, obviously, DOC, with the second having the DOC subzone Alto Adige/Sudtirol. Also made near Bolzano, mostly in the suburb of Gries, is Lagrein, a red that is very similar to Teroldego Trentino, which is made from a grape of the same name. The reserve wines are quite interesting and are among the boldest and most full-bodied in the area and have a dark, almost impenetrable color. Other important reds include those made with international varieties like Pinot Nero/Blauburgunder, Cabernet Sauvignon and Merlot. Alto Adige has a continental climate to which the more northern grapes adapt well and produce wines on par with their French or Californian cousins.

Along with the Alto Adige/Sudtirol appellation there are also some important sub-zones which include Terlano/Terlan, Valle Isarco/Eisacktaler and Valle Ventoso. You often find their names alongside those of the DOC wines when they come from specific areas. The difference has minimum and one must keep in mind that the subzone are more to the north and thus produce wines that have less body but, especially in the case of the whites, are more fragrant and slightly more aromatic.

Among the more famous are Sylvaner and Veltlner from Valle Isarco, Pinot Bianco/Weissburgunder from the area of Terlano and the wonderful Rheinriesling from Val Ventosa.

The vine-training methods are quite uniform and are basically two. The most used is the pergola trentino system which in Alto Adige is less expansive with vegetation thicker on vines. The second is the famous Guyot method which is increasingly being employed at the expense of the former.

Controlled Designation of Origin (DOC)

- Alto Adige o dell'Alto Adige / Südtirol o Südtiroler, with or without the sub-areas
  - Colli di Bolzano / Bozner Leiten
  - Meranese di Collina o Meranese / Meraner Hügel o Meraner, with or without Küchelberg, Gneid, Rosengarten, Lebenberg, Labers, del Burgraviato, Burggräfler
  - Santa Maddalena / St. Magdalener, with or without Santa Giustina / St. Justina, Leitago / Leitach, San Pietro / St. Peter, Guncina / Guntschna, San Giorgio / St. Georgen, Rencio / Rentsch, Rena / Sand; with or without Classico
  - Terlano / Terlaner, with or without Classico
  - Valle Isarco / Eisacktal o Eisacktaler, with or without Bressanone / Brixner
  - Val Venosta / Vinschgau
- Lago di Caldaro o Caldaro / Kalterersee o Kalterer, with or without the sub-areas Classico / Klassisches Ursprungsgebiet o Klassisch; allowed to use Alto Adige designation in addition for wines Lago di Caldaro, Caldaro Classico, Caldaro Classico Superiore
- Valdadige / Etschtaler

★★
ABBAZIA DI NOVACELLA

Via Abbazia, 1
39040 Varna (BZ)
Tel. +39 0472 836189
Fax +39 0472 837305
info@abbazianovacella.it
www.abbazianovacella.it
🄵 *klosterneustift.abbazianovacella*

YEAR OF FOUNDATION **1142**
NAME OF THE OWNER **Order of St. Augustine**
TOTAL BOTTLES PRODUCED **750,000**
DIRECT SALES
VISITS TO THE WINERY - RESERVATION NEEDED
HECTARES OF VINEYARD **75**
RESTAURANT

For years now this has been a top producer both in Alto Adige and Italy. Director Urban Von Klebesberg and enologist Celestino Lucin are without a doubt the driving force behind the success of this winery that belongs to the Order of St. Augustine and is located in the Novacella Abbey that dates back to 1142 and which alone is worth a visit. The wines produced are the classic ones of Valle Isarco: Sylvaner, Kerner, Veltliner and Riesling, along with some interesting Pinot Grigio and, among the reds, Lagrein and Pinot Nero.

■ 93	Price B

AA Pinot Nero Praepositus Riserva 2012

100% Pinot Nero grapes. Aged in barrique. Lively ruby. Varietal and fascinating aromas. The palate is round, rich and gentle with juicy tannins and a supple, savory and vertical finish.

☐ 92	Price B

AA Valle Isarco Sylvaner Praepositus 2015

100% Sylvaner grapes. Stainless steel. Deep straw yellow. Complex nose of fine herbs and camomile. The palate is fresh, rich and with a wonderful balanced acidity. Long and smooth finish.

☐ 90	Price B

AA Valle Isarco Riesling Praepositus 2014

100% Riesling grapes. Ages in large casks. Deep straw yellow. Fruity and smoky nose. The palate is rich, round, tense and with a flavorful and supple finish.

⬛ 89	Price B*

AA Moscato Rosa Praepositus 2014

*100% Moscato Rosa grapes. Stainless steel. Intense ruby. Varietal and well defined nose. The palate is characterised by refined sweetness and well balanced acidity. Savory and rich finish. *37.5 cl bottle.*

☐ 88	Price B

AA Valle Isarco Kerner Praepositus 2015

100% Kerner grapes. Stainless steel. Shiny straw yellow. Aromatic and fascinating nose. The palate is supple and juicy with a fresh and savory finish.

BRUNNENHOF

Via degli Alpini, 5
39044 Egna (BZ)
Tel. +39 0471 820687
info@brunnenhof-mazzon.it
www.brunnenhof-mazzon.it

YEAR OF FOUNDATION **1987**
NAME OF THE OWNER **Rottensteiner Family**
TOTAL BOTTLES PRODUCED **20,000**
DIRECT SALES
VISITS TO THE WINERY - RESERVATION NEEDED
HECTARES OF VINEYARD **4**

This small winery of Kurt and Johanna Rottensteiner is situated in the heart of Mazzon and they have been operating it for the past 30 year with a passion equal only to their discretion. The wines are the classic Pinot Nero along with some whites that have surprising personality and stylistic definition. The grapes are carefully grown without the use of pesticides or herbicides and fermentation is done only with wild yeasts. The wines are austere and certainly need to age to bring out their best characteristics but the results are noteworthy.

☐ 91	👍 Price A

Eva 2015

100% Manzoni Bianco grapes. Stainless steel. Straw yellow. Complex and fascinating nose with notes of chocolate and passion fruit. The palate is fresh and supple, dynamic with a pleasant and savory long tail.

☐ 88	Price B

AA Gewürztraminer 2015

100% Gewürztraminer grapes. Stainless steel only.

Deep straw yellow. Multi-layered nose of rosehip, tropical fruit and wet leaves. The palate is refined, austere and vertical.

 88 Price A

AA Lagrein Alte Reben 2014

100% Lagrein grapes. Ages in large casks. Deep ruby red. Fragrant and fruity nose. The palate has good structure with a light herbaceous hint. Pleasant and supple finish.

CANTINA ANDRIANO / ANDRIAN

Via Silberleiten, 7
39018 Terlano (BZ)
Tel. +39 0471 257156
office@cantina-andriano.com
www.kellerei-andrian.com
 Kellerei-Cantina-Andrian
 @KellereiAndrian

YEAR OF FOUNDATION **1893**
TOTAL BOTTLES PRODUCED **300,000**
VISITS TO THE WINERY - RESERVATION NEEDED
HECTARES OF VINEYARD **105**

This small cooperative since many years is under the technical supervision of Cantina di Terlano. It did not take long for Andriano to become one of the more interesting winemaking realities in Valdadige. The white wines stand out with their Pinot Bianco, Sauvignon and Gewürztraminer bringing out the best from the land while in a good year their tasty reds should not be overlooked.

 94 Price B*

AA Gewürztraminer Passito Juvelo 2014

100% Gewürztraminer grapes. Ages in barrique. Amber color. Captivating nose of saffron, sea breeze and botrytis. The palate is rich and powerful, the sweetness is well balanced by refreshing acidity. Very long and rich finish.*37.5 cl bottle.

 91 Price B

AA Gewürztraminer Movado 2014

100% Gewürztraminer grapes. Stainless steel. Deep straw yellow. The nose offers captivating hints of tropical fruits and blossoms. Powerful and meaty palate yet tense and dynamic. Rich and supple finish.

 91 Price B

AA Pinot Nero Anrar Riserva 2013

100% Pinot Nero grapes. Ages in barrique. Lively ruby. The nose is elegant and refined. The palate delivers what promises on the nose; juicy tannins with a savory and supple tail.

 90 Price A

AA Pinot Bianco Finado 2015

100% Pinot Bianco grapes. Stainless steel only. Straw yellow with green hues. Nose of fine herbs and fresh almonds. Juicy palate, rich and savory finish.

CANTINA BOLZANO / BOZEN

Piazza Gries, 2
39100 Bolzano (BZ)
Tel. +39 0471 270909
info@cantinabolzano.com
www.cantinabolzano.com
 KellereiBozen
 @CantinaBolzano

YEAR OF FOUNDATION **2001**
TOTAL BOTTLES PRODUCED **3,000,000**
DIRECT SALES
VISITS TO THE WINERY - RESERVATION NEEDED
HECTARES OF VINEYARD **330**

Considered one of the most important winemaking realities in Alto Adige for both its history and the quality of its wines, this winery was created in 2001 through the merger of the Gries winery (founded in 1908) and Santa Maddalena (1930). The latter, which since 1988 has been run by Stephan Filippi, is the proud custodian of Bolzano's winemaking traditions. They produce various types of Lagrein and Santa Maddalena, first among them is the legendary Huck am Bach. The more important white produced is a Sauvignon.

 95 Price B

AA Sauvignon Riserva 2014

100% Sauvignon grapes. Ages in barrique for almost 6 months. Pale yellow with greenish hues. Extremely refined and complex nose: gooseberry, elderflower and fine herbs then hints of sweet spices. Tense and supple palate, very savory with a wonderful balanced acidity. Very slim and long finish.

□ 92   Price B*

AA Moscato Giallo Passito Vinalia 2012

*Moscato giallo grapes. Stainless steel. Golden yellow. Wonderful nose of saffron, quince and delicate botrytis hints. The palate is concentrated, balanced and fresh. Long and firm finish. *37.5 cl bottle.*

□ 90   Price B

AA Sauvignon Mock 2015

100% Sauvignon grapes. Stainless steel only. Shiny straw yellow with greenish hues. Clean citrusy and tropical fruit notes. The palate is fresh, supple and with a fairly long sea breeze finish.

■ 89   Price B

AA Lagrein Taber Riserva 2014

100% Lagrein grapes. Ages in different sized casks. Deep ruby. Fruity nose with hints of black pepper. The palate is juicy, supple and with fine tannins. Firm and fresh finish.

■ 89   Price A

AA Santa Maddalena Classico Huck am Bach 2015

Blend of Schiava and a small percentage of Lagrein grapes. Ages in large casks. Intense ruby red. Fragrant and fruity nose. The palate is rich, supple and crunchy. A great classic that never lets you down.

CANTINA COLTERENZIO / SCHRECKBICHL

Strada del Vino, 8 - Cornaiano
39057 Appiano (BZ)
Tel. +39 0471 664246
info@colterenzio.it
www.colterenzio.it
 colterenzio
 @Colterenzio

YEAR OF FOUNDATION 1960
TOTAL BOTTLES PRODUCED 1,600,000
DIRECT SALES
VISITS TO THE WINERY - RESERVATION NEEDED
HECTARES OF VINEYARD 300

Schreckbichl has become a monument in the winemaking history of Alto Adige and Italy, as demonstrated by the Sauvignon and Cabernet Sauvignon of the Lafóa line, which are universally recognized as some of the best wines in Italy. A new winery and new wines have pumped fresh blood into the whole line of wines which have achieved a high standard both for their quality and the way they express the land. The estate also has a very intelligent pricing policy.

□ 92   Price B

AA Sauvignon Lafóa 2014

100% Sauvignon grapes. Ages in different sized casks. Shiny straw yellow. The nose shows hints of tomato leaf and tropical fruit. Thin palate, savory and with a wonderfully controlled acidity. Vertical and elegant with a long savory finish.

■ 89   Price B

AA Pinot Nero St. Daniel Riserva 2013

100% Pinot Nero grapes. Ages in barrique. Lively ruby. Varietal nose. The palate is elegant, supple with fine grain tannins and a pleasantly vertical finish.

□ 88   Price B

AA Chardonnay Formigar 2014

100% Chardonnay grapes. Ages in barrique and casks. Warm straw yellow. The nose is complex and intense with light woody notes. The palate is pleasant, juicy and tense.

■ 88   Price B

AA Merlot-Cabernet Sauvignon Cornelius 2013

Blend of Merlot and Cabernet Sauvignon grapes. Ages in barrique. Intense garnet. Intense and well composed nose, the palate is fresh, meaty with soft tannins. Good weight and length.

CANTINA CORTACCIA / KURTATSCH

Strada del Vino, 23
39040 Cortaccia (BZ)
Tel. +39 0471 880115
info@kellerei-kurtatsch.it
www.kellerei-kurtatsch.it
 kellereikurtatsch.cantinacortaccia
 @KURTATSCHwine

YEAR OF FOUNDATION 1900
TOTAL BOTTLES PRODUCED 1,100,000
DIRECT SALES
VISITS TO THE WINERY
HECTARES OF VINEYARD 190

42

Cantina Cortaccia was one of the lead players in the rebirth of Alto Adige wines. Situated in Bassa Atesina (South Tyrolean Unterland) along the Strada del Vino (Wine Road), it benefits from a warm climate cooled by constant evening breezes. Many of the wines, both the reds and whites, have achieved cult status thanks to their unmistakable character. After declining for a few years, the winery is making a swift comeback to excellence thanks to its management and technical teams.

Tel. +39 0471 963149
info@kellereikaltern.com
www.kellereikaltern.com
f *KellereiKaltern*
y *@KellereiKaltern*

YEAR OF FOUNDATION **1906**
TOTAL BOTTLES PRODUCED **1,200,000**
DIRECT SALES
VISITS TO THE WINERY - RESERVATION NEEDED
HECTARES OF VINEYARD **300**

☐ 91   Price B
AA Gewürztraminer Brenntal Ris. 2014
100% Gewürztraminer grapes. Ages in casks and stainless steel tanks. Aromas of tropical fruits, rosehip and spices. The palate is powerful, rich, well executed and supple. Vertical and savory finish.

▣ 89   Price B*
Cuvée Bianco Passito Aruna 2014
*Blend of 70% Gewürztraminer with Moscato Giallo grapes. Ages in casks. Deep amber. Intense nose of dry figs and dates. The palate is round but supple, tense and with a firm and fresh finish.*37.5 cl bottle.*

■ 89   Price B
AA Merlot Brenntal Riserva 2013
100% Merlot grapes. Ages in barrique. Intense ruby. Aromas of ripe raspberry and spice. The palate is austere, savory but with a pleasant lift on the finish.

☐ 89   Price A
AA Pinot Grigio Penoner 2015
100% Pinot Grigio grapes. Ages in barrique and stainless steel tanks. Deep straw yellow. Multi-layered nose: fascinating and fruity with a hint of smoke. Rich palate, firm with a long juicy tail.

☐ 88   Price A
AA Müller Thurgau Graun 2015
100% Müller Thurgau grapes. Stainless steel only. Pale yellow. Fruity and floral nose. The palate is fresh and supple. It has excellent drinkability.

CANTINA DI CALDARO / KALTERN
Via Cantine, 12
39052 Caldaro (BZ)

This cooperative is one of the two greatest cooperative in the area, now casting with Erste+Neue, and produces wines from the typical grapes in the district, starting with Lago di Caldaro in various versions all very expressive. The cooperative has some 400 members who follow the indications given to them by the Kellermeister who monitors their actions throughout the year.

☐ 93   Price A
AA Sauvignon Premstaler 2015
100% Sauvignon grapes. Stainless steel only. Deep straw yellow. Classic aromas of tomato leaf and white stone fruit. Round palate, supple and dynamic; vertical with a fresh and savory finish.

☐ 91   Price B
AA Sauvignon Castel Giovanelli 2014
100% Sauvignon grapes. Ages in casks and stainless steel. Straw yellow with greenish hues. The nose offers neat notes of white peach, tropical fruit and boxwood. The palate is slightly thin but overall it is elegant and balanced. Long finish.

☐ 87   Price A
AA Pinot Bianco Vial 2015
100% Pinot Bianco grapes. Stainless steel only. Pale straw yellow. Fruity nose with hints of tropical fruits. Medium bodied on the palate but savory and pleasantly easy drinking.

CANTINA GIRLAN
Via San Martino, 24 - Cornaiano
39057 Appiano (BZ)
Tel. +39 0471 662403
info@girlan.it
www.girlan.it
f *CantinaGirlan*

YEAR OF FOUNDATION 1923
TOTAL BOTTLES PRODUCED 1,300,000
DIRECT SALES
VISITS TO THE WINERY - RESERVATION NEEDED
HECTARES OF VINEYARD 230

The team of Gerhard Kofler and Oscar Lorandi, respectively the kellermeister and the director of this historic cooperative, have in just a matter of years been able to transform this sleepy enterprise into one of the most interesting and expanding productive realties in the province of Bolzano. The wines are becoming more elegant and defined and are achieving the success they deserve. Production includes Pinot Bianco, Sauvignon and Pinot Nero, while their versions of Schiava are among the greatest produced in Alto Adige and are becoming the cooperative's leading product.

■ 🍷 95   Price B
AA Pinot Nero Trattmann Mazon Ris. 2013

100% Pinot Nero grapes. Ages in barrique. Dense ruby red. Multi-layered nose: notes of currant and black pepper. Rich and round palate, refined with juicy and elegant tannins.

☐ 93   Price B
AA Sauvignon Flora 2015

100% Sauvignon grapes. Ages in barrels and stainless steel tanks. Straw yellow with greenish hues. The nose is complex and captivating: hints of spices, citrus and flint. Mouth filling palate, tense, elegant and vertical. Savory and intense finish.

☐ 92   👍 Price A
AA Pinot Bianco Plattenriegl 2015

100% Pinot Bianco grapes. Stainless steel only. Warm straw yellow. Complex nose with notes of white peach and aromatic herbs. The palate is tense and supple with a savory and juicy finish.

▪ 90   Price B*
AA Gewürztraminer Pasithea Oro Riserva 2014

*100% Gewürztraminer grapes. Aged in barrels. Light amber. Intense nose of saffron and botrytis. Good weight on the palate: rich but supple with a long finish.*37.5 cl bottle.*

■ 90   Price B
AA Schiava Gschleier-Alte Reben 2014

100% Schiava grapes. Aged in barrels. Intense ruby.

Austere nose: hints of cherry and black pepper. The palate is dark, lightly tannic; it has a small body but great character.

CANTINA MERAN BURGGRÄFLER

Via Cantina, 9
39020 Marlengo (BZ)
Tel. +39 0473 447137
Fax +39 0473 445216
info@cantinamerano.it
www.cantinamerano.it
🔲 *Kellerei-Meran-Burggräfler*

YEAR OF FOUNDATION 1901
TOTAL BOTTLES PRODUCED 1,000,000
DIRECT SALES
VISITS TO THE WINERY - RESERVATION NEEDED
HECTARES OF VINEYARD 250

This solid cooperative in Burgraviato, which also extends to Val Ventosa, has for years been a 'go to' place for those seeking well-made, typical wines at the right price. This thanks to its over 100 members and the skill of their historic kellermeister Stefan Kapfinger, who continues to give the cooperative's wines a defined and convincing style. A vast array of wines are offered at prices that are more than just economical.

■ 🍷 95   Price B
AA Pinot Nero Zeno Riserva 2013

100% Pinot Nero grapes. Ages in barrique. Lively ruby. The nose is fascinating, fresh and elegant. The palate offers lively acidity, mouth filling, refined with juicy tannins and a dynamic body. The finish is complex, savory and vertical.

▪ 94   Price B*
AA Moscato Giallo Passito Sissi 2014

*100% Moscato Giallo grapes. Ages in barrique. Golden yellow. Complex nose of botrytis, saffron and apricot. The palate is powerful but with great acidity and elegance. The finish composed, of good weight and long finish. *37.5 cl bottle.*

☐ 91   Price B
AA Sauvignon Mervin 2014

100% Sauvignon grapes. Stainless steel only. Straw

yellow with green hues. Clean aromas of white peach, tropical fruit and spices. Mouth coating palate, juicy and tense. The finish is flavorful and fresh.

☐ 91 👍 Price A

AA Valle Venosta Pinot Bianco Sonnenberg 2015

100% Pinot Bianco grapes. Stainless steel only. Straw yellow with greenish hues. The nose offers fresh and captivating notes of white stone fruits and citrus hints. The palate is supple, fresh and elegant; long and deep finish.

■ 89 👍 Price A

AA Schiava Schickenburg Graf von Meran 2015

100% Schiava grapes. Ages in large casks. Light ruby. The nose shows refined fruity notes; fragrant and pleasant palate; very typical.

CANTINA SAN MICHELE APPIANO

Via Circonvallazione, 17/19
39057 Appiano (BZ)
Tel. +39 0471 664466
Fax +39 0471 660764
kellerei@stmichael.it
www.stmichael.it
 SanMicheleAppiano

YEAR OF FOUNDATION 1907
TOTAL BOTTLES PRODUCED 2,100,000
DIRECT SALES
VISITS TO THE WINERY - RESERVATION NEEDED
HECTARES OF VINEYARD 380

If Alto Adige wines are now known and respected throughout the world much of the credit goes to this estate and its historic kellermeister Hans Terzer. This is where the revolution began to uproot winemaking traditions that were outdated and provided little income for producers. The large cooperative does not just rest on its laurels and keeps up with the times and every year presents of full range of excellent products made with all the grape varieties typical to Alto Adige. Few wineries in Italy are as solid and unique as this one. Two years ago, Hans Terzer officially retired but he didn't just walk away.

☐ 🔲 95 Price B

AA Sauvignon Sanct Valentin 2015

100% Sauvignon grapes. Ages in different sized casks. Warm straw yellow. Rich nose with tropical fruits and delicate spicy notes. Round palate, very aromatic and vertical. The finish is meaty, savory and long.

☐ 92 Price B

AA Pinot Bianco Sanct Valentin 2014

100% Pinot Bianco grapes. Ages in tonneau and barrique. Shiny straw yellow. Intense and captivating nose of white stone fruit and smoky hints. The palate is juicy, supple and vibrant. The finish is long and with good depth.

☐ 91 Price D

AA Bianco Appius 2011

Blend of Sauvignon, Pinot Grigio, Chardonnay and Pinot Bianco grapes. Ages in barrique. Captivating aromas of ripe fruit and fine herbs. The palate is round and meaty; with a long flavorful finish.

☐ 89 Price B

AA Chardonnay Sanct Valentin 2013

100% Chardonnay grapes. Aged in barrels. Pale straw yellow. Intense fruity nose; the palate is rich, savory and with a dynamic and well defined finish.

★★★

CANTINA TERLANO / TERLAN

Via Silberleiten, 7
39018 Terlano (BZ)
Tel. +39 0471 257135
Fax +39 0471 256224
office@cantina-terlano.com
www.cantina-terlano.com
 Kellerei-Terlan-Cantina-Terlano
 @kellereiterlan

YEAR OF FOUNDATION 1893
TOTAL BOTTLES PRODUCED 1,400,000
DIRECT SALES
VISITS TO THE WINERY - RESERVATION NEEDED
HECTARES OF VINEYARD 170

Here at Cantina Terlano the wines produced are among the best white wines of the world and this fact, which is confirmed every year, is the reason why we proclaimed it 'Winery of the year'. Terlano's terroir is certainly one of the most interesting in Italy but extraordinary results can only be achieved through professionalism, maniacal care and a desire to accept new challenges and all this is what makes this cooperative unique. Production ranges from classic simple wines, which are anything but simple, to select and vintage ones and the latest novelty Terlaner I, is a Terlano that can challenge any international rival. Few can match the line which Rudi Kofler and Klaus Gasser offer every year and their Pinot Bianco, Terlano, Sauvignon and Chardonnay are absolute models for character and style.

☐ 🍇 98   **Price B**

AA Terlano Nova Domus Riserva 2013

Blend of Pinot Bianco, Chardonnay and Sauvignon grapes. Ages in barrels. Warm straw yellow with green hues. Multi-layered and complex nose: white chocolate, green plum, lightly peaty then hints of field blossoms. The palate is explosive for its elegance and dynamism; very good weight. The finish is vibrant, complex and endless.

☐ 🍇 97   **Price D**

AA Terlano I (Primo) Grande Cuvée 2013

Blend of Pinot Bianco, Chardonnay and Sauvignon grapes. Ages in casks. Intense straw yellow. Very complex nose: white chocolate, winter melon, spices and light sea breeze notes. The palate is still austere, powerful with a mouth coating texture yet with a wonderful dynamic sip. Incredibly long and savory finish.

☐ 🍇 96   **Price B**

AA Terlano Pinot Bianco Vorberg Riserva 2013

100% Pinot Bianco grapes. Ages in barrels. Intense straw yellow. Complex nose of white peach, fresh almond and delicate spicy notes. The palate is both rich and fresh; elegant. The savory and peat notes give tension and dynamism. Very long and austere finish.

☐ 94   **Price B**

AA Terlano Sauvignon Quarz 2014

100% Sauvignon grapes. Stainless steel. Straw yellow with greenish hues. Fascinating nose: boxwood, then citrus and spices. The palate is agile, balanced with good weight. The finish is very long with a sea breeze character, fresh and satisfying.

☐ 93   👍 **Price A**

AA Terlaner 2015

Blend of Pinot Bianco, Chardonnay and Sauvignon

---

grapes. Stainless steel. Rich, mouth filling with a fresh and savory character that reminds sea breeze. A smashing value for money wine; impeccable as previous vintages. What else can you say?

CANTINA TRAMIN

Strada del Vino, 144
39040 Termeno (BZ)
Tel. +39 0471 096633
info@cantinatramin.it
www.cantinatramin.it
🇫 *CantinaTramin*
🐦 *@CantinaTramin*

YEAR OF FOUNDATION **1898**
TOTAL BOTTLES PRODUCED **1,800,000**
DIRECT SALES
VISITS TO THE WINERY - RESERVATION NEEDED
HECTARES OF VINEYARD **250**

Some claim that Cantina Tramin 'rhymes' with Gewürztraminer. This may be true because the Nussbaumer is the best wine of its kind in Italy, in large part thanks to the contribution of the great and equally modest kellermeister Willi Sturz. Tramin's full line has an amazing stylistic definition as exemplified by the outstanding Pinot Grigio Unterebner, close second to Gewürztraminer Nussbaumer.

☐ 🍇 95   **Price B**

AA Gewürztraminer Nussbaumer 2014

100% Gewürztraminer grapes. Stainless steel only. Warm straw yellow. Intense nose of spices, tropical fruit and field blossoms. The palate is powerful but balanced; elegant and fragrant long finish.

☐ 93   **Price B**

AA Pinot Grigio Unterebner 2014

100% Pinot Grigio grapes. Ages in barrique and large casks. Rich straw yellow. Ripe fruit aromas well balanced with woody notes; rich and full bodied palate; juicy, dynamic and balanced. Long and supple finish.

☐ 92   👍 **Price A**

AA Gewürztraminer Selida 2015

100% Gewürztraminer grapes. Stainless steel only. Golden yellow. Complex nose with distinctive notes of rosehip and candied orange rind. The palate is rich, mouth coating and well balanced with the residual sugar. Long and vertical finish.

91　　　　　　　　　　Price B

AA Lagrein Urban Riserva 2014

100% Lagrein grapes. Ages in casks and barrique. Deep ruby red of great concentration. Intense and refined aromas on the nose. The palate is rich, mouth coating and with pencil lead notes. Long and juicy finish.

☐ **89**　　　　　　　　　　Price B

AA Bianco Stoan 2014

Blend of 60% Chardonnay, 22% Sauvignon, 11% Pinot Bianco and 7% Gewürztraminer grapes. Ages in casks. Shiny straw yellow. Clean notes of gooseberry, green plum and fine herbs. Medium bodied but very expressive and dynamic with a long and flavorful finish.

CANTINA VALLE ISARCO

Via Croste, 50
39043 Chiusa (BZ)
Tel. +39 0472 847553
info@eisacktalerkellerei.it
www.eisacktalerkellerei.it
 eisacktal.valleisarco

YEAR OF FOUNDATION 1956
TOTAL BOTTLES PRODUCED 750,000
DIRECT SALES
VISITS TO THE WINERY - RESERVATION NEEDED
HECTARES OF VINEYARD 140

The history of this winery is relatively recent and began with its foundation in 1956. In recent years, it has with great ability been able to take advantage of the growing success and interest for white wines from the Valle Isarco. Its best wines are in the Aristos line but one should not overlook its so-called 'classic' line that has a truly economical quality/price ratio.

☐ **92**　　　　　　　　　　Price A

AA Valle Isarco Grüner Veltliner Aristos 2015

100% Veltliner grapes. Ages in acacia wood casks and stainless steel tanks. Straw yellow with green hues. Fascinating nose of white pepper and loquat. The palate is rich, firm, savory and with juicy acidity. Long and flavorful finish.

☐ **92**　　　　　　　　　　Price A

AA Valle Isarco Müller Thurgau Aristos 2015

100% 100% Müller Thurgau grapes. Stainless steel only. Straw yellow with green hues. Aromatic and fragrant nose. The palate is juicy, flavorful and vertical. Good meaty length.

☐ **91**　　　　　　　　　　Price A

AA Valle Isarco Kerner Aristos 2015

100% Kerner grapes. Stainless steel only. Straw yellow with greenish hues. Fascinating nose with notes of fine herbs, passion fruit and hawthorn. The palate is rich and juicy, savory and it has great drinkability.

☐ **89**　　　　　　　　　　Price A

AA Valle Isarco Sylvaner Aristos 2015

100% Sylvaner grapes. Stainless steel only. Straw yellow with greenish hues. The nose offers note of fine herbs and white stone fruit. The palate is juicy, fresh and with a savory finish.

CARLOTTO

Via Clauser, 19
39040 Ora (BZ)
Tel. +39 0471 810407
michelacarlotto@gmail.com
www.fws.it/it/viticoltore-f-carlotto

YEAR OF FOUNDATION 2000
NAME OF THE OWNER Carlotto Family
TOTAL BOTTLES PRODUCED 20,000
DIRECT SALES
VISITS TO THE WINERY - RESERVATION NEEDED
HECTARES OF VINEYARD 4

Michela Carlotto is a shy, tenacious and skilled winemaker who has a burning passion for Pinot Nero. All her energy can be found in her Pinot Nero which are saline and fine with a strong personality and are impeccably made from a technical point of view. Her father Ferruccio also helps out and together they make other wines.

88　　　　　　　　　　Price B

AA Pinot Nero 2014

100% Pinot Nero grapes. Ages in casks and barrique. Delicate notes of wild strawberry and light smoky notes. Refined palate, well extracted tannins and lively acidity. Long flavorful finish.

CASTEL JUVAL UNTERORTL

Frazione Juval, 1b
39020 Castelbello Ciardes (BZ)
Tel. +39 0473 667580
info@unterortl.it
www.unterortl.it

YEAR OF FOUNDATION 1992
NAME OF THE OWNER Aurich Family
TOTAL BOTTLES PRODUCED 33,000
DIRECT SALES
VISITS TO THE WINERY - RESERVATION NEEDED
HECTARES OF VINEYARD 4

Martin Aurich is originally from Berlin and has not only become one of Italy's best winemakers but is also a professor of enology at Istituto Agrario di San Michele all'Adige-Edmund Mach Foundation. His small estate, where he works with his wife Gisela, is in a strikingly beautiful location where the vineyards on the steep sides of a valley have a pitch of as much as 60%. Over the years his white wines have achieved a level of quality that few can match. Their crystalline purity are the result of the skill and hard work of a true artist.

☐ 🥂 95   Price B
AA Valle Venosta Riesling Windbichel 2014

100% Riesling grapes. Stainless steel only. Intense straw yellow. Complex nose of grapefruit and delicate peat notes. The palate is slim but with good weight. Very good balance on the palate with savory and vertical finish.

☐ 91   👍 Price A
AA Valle Venosta Riesling Unterortl 2015

100% Riesling grapes. Stainless steel only. Straw yellow with green hues. Classic aromas of citrus and white stone fruit, then lightly smoky. On the palate is incredibly fresh and lively, sharp and tense with a savory and vibrant tail.

☐ 88   Price A
AA Valle Venosta Müller Thurgau 2015

100% 100% Müller Thurgau grapes. Stainless steel. Straw yellow with green hues. Well-defined notes of fine herbs and rennet apple. The palate is fresh and juicy with a delicate smoky note on the finish.

☐ 88   Price A
AA Valle Venosta Pinot Bianco 2015

100% Pinot Bianco grapes. Ages in stainless steel tanks and acacia wood casks. Light straw yellow. Refined nose, delicate with notes of hawthorn and fresh almond. The palate is elegant, medium bodied with a dynamic and tense finish.

☐ 88   Price A
AA Valle Venosta Riesling Gletscherschliff 2015

100% Riesling grapes. Stainless steel only. Light straw yellow with greenish hues. The nose shows prominent notes of anise and a delicate citrus and smoky notes. The palate is refined, slim, but balanced and dynamic.

PETER DIPOLI

Via Ortler Friedrich, 5
39044 Egna (BZ)
Tel. +39 0471 813400
Fax +39 0471 813444
peterdipoli@finewines.it
www.peterdipoli.com

YEAR OF FOUNDATION 1987
NAME OF THE OWNER Peter Dipoli
TOTAL BOTTLES PRODUCED 40,000
DIRECT SALES
VISITS TO THE WINERY - RESERVATION NEEDED
HECTARES OF VINEYARD 4.6

Aside from being a skilled winemaker, Peter Dipoli is also an excellent and extraordinarily passionate taster who travels the world to discover and promote interesting winemaking areas, although he has a blatant passion for Burgundy. And while he can be anything diplomatic, his positions are never boring. His Sauvignon Voglar is consistently considered one of Italy's best as is his Merlot Cabernet Sauvignon Iugum, a red with an elegant and refined style, when released.

☐ 91   Price B
AA Sauvignon Voglar 2014

100% Sauvignon grapes. Ages in acacia wood casks. Straw yellow with greenish hues. Well-defined notes of tropical fruit and cut grass. Supple structure, tense and with a vertical and long finish.

EBNER

Frazione Campodazzo, 18
39054 Renon (BZ)
Tel. +39 0471 353386
info@weingutebner.it
www.weingutebner.it

YEAR OF FOUNDATION 2013
NAME OF THE OWNER Florian and Brigitte
Unterthiner Family
TOTAL BOTTLES PRODUCED 15,000
DIRECT SALES
VISITS TO THE WINERY
HECTARES OF VINEYARD 4.5

The small and young estate of Florian and Brigitte is situated on the sunny Remon plateau in the southern part of the Iscarco valley, more precisely a rocky cliff that sits at an altitude of some 500m above sea level in the district if Campodazzo. Their wines are very expressive and impeccably made. The reds are produced from grapes grown in a volcanic soil, while the vineyards for the whites have a southeast exposure and are more ventilated. This small area is a rare mix of the Alpine and Mediterranean worlds without either dominating over the other.

☐ 94	👍 Price A

AA Valle Isarco Veltliner 2015

100% Veltliner grapes. Stainless steel only. Straw yellow with golden hues. Rich nose with hints of white pepper, loquat and fine herbs. Good weight on the palate; well balanced and dynamic.

☐ 92	Price B

AA Gewürztraminer 2015

100% Gewürztraminer grapes. Stainless steel only. Golden yellow. The nose is varietal and well-defined. Rich palate, powerful but balanced; elegant with a very long finish.

☐ 89	Price A

AA Pinot Bianco 2015

100% Pinot Bianco grapes. Stainless steel only. Intense straw yellow. Typical aromas of fine herbs and white stone fruit. Mouth filling palate, balanced acidity and long savory finish.

■ 88	Price A

AA Schiava 2015

100% Schiava grapes. Ages in casks. Light ruby red.

Fragrant and delicate aromas. Crunchy palate, very pleasant and typical.

ERBHOF UNTERGANZNER

Via Campiglio, 15 - Frazione Cardano
39053 Bolzano (BZ)
Tel. +39 0471 365582
mayr.unterganzner@dnet.it
www.fws.it/it/erbhof-unterganzner

YEAR OF FOUNDATION 1629
NAME OF THE OWNER Josephus Mayr
TOTAL BOTTLES PRODUCED 65,000
DIRECT SALES
VISITS TO THE WINERY - RESERVATION NEEDED
HECTARES OF VINEYARD 8.5
OLIVE OIL PRODUCTION

Josephus Mayr is the epitome of an Alto Adige winemaker: passionate, tenacious and always striving to outdo himself with every harvest, firmly convinced of his skill and experience. His winemaking method strongly respects nature and he only uses a very limited amount of chemical products. He adds a little 'madness' to his wines (he also produces olive oil in one of Bolzano's closest areas) that have an unmistakable style and distinct personality. He produces Lagrein, Cabernet and Santa Maddalena as well as a unique Sauvignon.

■ 91	Price B

AA Lagrein Riserva 2013

100% Lagrein grapes. Ages in barrique. Very deep ruby. Intense aromas of red jammy fruit. Rich palate, concentrated with ripe and firm tannins; supple. The captivating finish reminds earthy notes.

■ 91	Price B

AA Lamarein 2013

100% lighty dried Lagrein grapes. Stainless steel only. Very deep ruby. Well defined nose of blueberry jam and spices. The palate is powerful, firm tannins, but with great balanced acidity and a very good dynamic finish.

☐ 88	Price A

AA Sauvignon Platt & Pignat 2015

100% Sauvignon grapes. Ages in barrels and stainless steel tanks. Light straw yellow. Well defined and varietal nose: tomato leaf and hawthorn. The palate is fresh and balanced with a good weight finish.

ERSTE+NEUE

Via delle Cantine, 5/10
39052 Caldaro (BZ)
Tel. +39 0471 963122
Fax +39 0471 964368
info@erste-neue.it
www.erste-neue.it
 ErsteNeue

YEAR OF FOUNDATION 1900
TOTAL BOTTLES PRODUCED 1,400,000
DIRECT SALES
VISITS TO THE WINERY - RESERVATION NEEDED
HECTARES OF VINEYARD 264

This is the second-largest cooperative in Caldaro even if today is casting with Cantina di Caldaro and is famous for its Lago di Caldaro wine. The cooperative also produces some excellent Pinot Bianco and Sauvignon whites. These wines have an elegant style that is extremely respectful of the variety of grape and the land thanks to extreme care in the vineyard and top-notch methods in the winery.

☐ 92 🔶 Price A
AA Pinot Bianco Prunar 2015
100% Pinot Bianco grapes. Stainless steel only. Warm straw yellow. Fascinating nose of tropical fruit and fine herbs. The palate is dense, but harmonic and savory with a vertical and savory finish.

■ 88 🔶 Price A
AA Lago di Caldaro Classico Superiore Leuchtenburg 2015
100% Schiava grapes. Ages in large casks. Light ruby. Floral nose with a hints of red forest berries. The palate is fresh, juicy and supple with a pleasant meaty finish.

☐ 88 Price B
AA Sauvignon Puntay 2014
100% Sauvignon grape. Ages in large casks and stainless steel tanks. Shiny straw yellow. Nose of cut grass and ripe fruit. Decent weight on the palate, fresh and dynamic. Savory and juicy finish.

FALKENSTEIN

Via Castello, 15
39025 Naturno (BZ)
Tel. +39 0473 666054
Fax +39 0473 420256
info@falkenstein.bz
www.fws.it/it/falkenstein

YEAR OF FOUNDATION 1995
NAME OF THE OWNER Franz Pratzner
TOTAL BOTTLES PRODUCED 90,000
DIRECT SALES
VISITS TO THE WINERY - RESERVATION NEEDED
HECTARES OF VINEYARD 12
HOSPITALITY
RESTAURANT

The winery's name translates 'Falcons Rock' and Franz Pratzner produces wines that in less than 20 years have made him a star among wine lovers in Italy and abroad. He is a winemaker of few words who prefers actions, some of which buck the trends like the density of his vineyards that is unique for the region. The results are wines with great class and strong personality but which are undoubtedly elegant.

☐ 92 Price B
AA Valle Venosta Riesling 2014
100% Riesling grapes. Ages in casks and stainless steel tanks. Intense straw yellow. The nose offers citrusy notes, white stone fruit and smoky hint. The palate is rich, elegant, very fresh with a long juicy finish.

■ 89 Price B
AA Valle Venosta Pinot Nero 2013
100% Pinot Nero grapes. Ages in different sized barrels. Intense garnet. Delicate fruity nose with a lightly smoky hint. The palate is austere, refined and elegant, medium length.

☐ 87 Price B
AA Valle Venosta Pinot Bianco 2014
100% Pinot Bianco grapes. Stainless steel only. Light straw yellow with greenish hues. Delicate aromas of white peach with a smoky hint. The palate is thin with a refreshing and savory finish.

GLÖGGLHOF - GOJER

Via Rivellone, 1
39100 Bolzano (BZ)
Tel. +39 0471 978775
info@gojer.it
www.gojer.it

YEAR OF FOUNDATION **1982**
NAME OF THE OWNER **Franz Gojer**
TOTAL BOTTLES PRODUCED **55,000**
DIRECT SALES
VISITS TO THE WINERY - RESERVATION NEEDED
HECTARES OF VINEYARD **7.5**

The Gojer family's Glogglhof winery is one of the best in the district of Santa Maddalena and Franz and his talented son Florian are recognized by all to be top-rate winemakers. They produce three of the best Santa Maddalena in existence and their Lagreins are typical and consistent and all made with a tradition based on intelligence and foresight while their pricing policy is the right one.

■ **90** 👍 Price A
AA Santa Maddalena Class. Rondell 2015

Blend of Schiava with a little percentage of Lagrein grapes. Ages in casks. Lively ruby red. Intese fruity aromas with a light spicy hint. The palate is rich, meaty with a long earthy finish.

☐ **89** Price A
AA Sauvignon Karneid 2015

100% Sauvignon grapes. Stainless steel only. Relatively varietal nose with notes of nettle and tomato leaf. The palate is austere, but vertical and it has good drinkability.

■ **88** Price A
AA Santa Maddalena Classico 2015

Blend of Schiava with a little percentage of Lagrein grapes. Ages in casks. Lively ruby red. Intense fruity nose. The palate is fresh, fragrant and it has great drinkability.

GUMPHOF

Località Novale di Presule, 8
39050 Fiè allo Sciliar (BZ)

Tel. +39 0471 601190
Fax +39 0471 601190
S *Gumphof*
info@gumphof.it
www.gumphof.it

YEAR OF FOUNDATION **2000**
NAME OF THE OWNER **Markus Prackwieser**
TOTAL BOTTLES PRODUCED **45,000**
DIRECT SALES
VISITS TO THE WINERY - RESERVATION NEEDED
HECTARES OF VINEYARD **5**

The vineyards of Markus Prackwieser are among the steepest in all Alto Adige but it is here that the young and shy producer from Novale di Presule, at the entrance of Valle Isarco, is year after year building a career that is becoming one of the most important in the region. His Pinot Bianco Praesulis has always been one of the best, his Sauvignon is excellent, his magnificent Schiava and interesting other wines, all combined by great elegance, distinct personality and honest prices.

☐ **94** 👍 Price A
AA Pinot Bianco Praesulis 2015

100% Pinot Bianco grapes. Ages in barrels and stainless steel tanks. Straw yellow with green hues. Well defined aromas of white stone fruit and hints of spices. The palate very refined; juicy, supple and refreshing. Long peppery finish.

☐ **93** Price B
AA Sauvignon Praesulis 2015

100% Sauvignon grapes. Ages in barrels and stainless steel tanks. Straw yellow with greenish hues. Complex nose: grapefruit, flint and spices. Vertical palate yet with good weight. Tense finish with a long savory tail.

☐ **92** 👍 Price A
AA Pinot Bianco Mediaevum 2015

100% Pinot Bianco grapes. Ages in barrels and stainless steel tanks. Warm straw yellow. Well defined and well expressed fruity nose. The palate is savory, fresh, supple and with a good length.

■ **88** 👍 Price A
AA Schiava Mediaevum 2015

100% Schiava grapes. Ages in barrels. Shiny ruby. Fragrant nose of forest berries and floral hints. Fresh palate, supple and captivating finish.

FRANZ HAAS

Via Villa, 6
39040 Montagna (BZ)
Tel. +39 0471 812280
info@franz-haas.it
www.franz-haas.it
 Franz-Haas-Winery
 @FranzHaasWinery

YEAR OF FOUNDATION **1880**
NAME OF THE OWNER **Franz Haas**
TOTAL BOTTLES PRODUCED **300,000**
DIRECT SALES
VISITS TO THE WINERY - RESERVATION NEEDED
HECTARES OF VINEYARD **50**

The wines of Franziscus (Franz) Haas are known throughout the world. This thanks to seven generations of tireless hard work although undoubtedly Franz and his wife Luisa Manna have made a fundamental contribution and achieved important results. Franz Haas is always ready to question what he does and he is one of the most determined and passionate winemakers you will ever meet, traits that sometimes can rub people the wrong way.

---

 91   Price B
AA Moscato Rosa 2014

100% Moscato Rosa grapes. Stainless steel only. Intense ruby. Aromatic and fascinating nose. Juicy palate; the sweetness is well balanced by the acidity. Very pleasant finish.

---

 89   Price B
AA Pinot Nero 2014

100% Pinot Nero grapes. Ages in barrique. Ruby with garnet rim. Well defined flavor of forest berries and light smoky hints. The palate is thin, with fine tannins and a fresh, savory and juicy finish.

KETTMEIR

Via Cantine, 4
39052 Caldaro (BZ)
Tel. +39 0471 963135
info@kettmeir.com
www.kettmeir.com
 Kettmeir
 @Kettmeir

YEAR OF FOUNDATION **1919**
NAME OF THE OWNER **Santa Margherita Gruppo Vinicolo**
TOTAL BOTTLES PRODUCED **330,000**
DIRECT SALES
VISITS TO THE WINERY - RESERVATION NEEDED
HECTARES OF VINEYARD **40**
HOSPITALITY

Almost a century of history unites this winery founded by Giuseppe Kettmeir and the Alto Adige hills in Caldaro. They were pioneers in tackling international markets but most of all had a steadfast belief in the potential of sparkling wine, opting for the long Charmat Method. Their propensity for top quality and innovation was bolstered when they became part of Santa Margherita Group in 1986 and began producing wines using the traditional method. The line's strong link with the territory reinforces the estate's clear dedication to the typical characteristics of the various local grape varieties and they produce two excellent Maso (Alto Adige cru) made with Pinot Nero, Müller Thurgau and Chardonnay.

---

 91   Price B*
AA Moscato Rosa Athesis 2012

*100% Moscato Rosa grapes, dried for 6 weeks; ages in second and third fill barrique. Delicate ruby with orange hues. Intense and elegant nose, aromatic: hints of hibiscus, rose water, peach and delicately spicy. Soft and captivating sip, good acidity balanced by vibrant energy. *37.5 cl bottle.*

---

 90   👍 Price A
AA Metodo Classico Brut Rosè Athesis

100% Pinot Nero grapes from Caldaro hills. Matures in bottle with the lees for 30 months. Powder pink with peachy hues and fine bubbles. Fresh and citrusy nose, juicy notes of red fruit: pomegranate and blood orange. Vibrant palate with good balance between fruit and acidity; vertical and fragrant.

---

 89   Price B
AA Pinot Nero Maso Reiner 2013

100% Pinot Nero grapes from the Maso Reiner vineyard in Caldaro. Ages in 30hl casks for 15 months. Ruby red with garnet hues. Forest berries notes, wet leaves, floral: rosehip and anise with shades of vanilla and mint. Rich and fresh palate, satisfying and supple finish.

★★★
KÖFERERHOF

Via Pusteria, 3
39040 Varna (BZ)
Tel. +39 347 4778009
Fax +39 0472 863014
info@koefererhof.it
www.koefererhof.it

YEAR OF FOUNDATION **1995**
NAME OF THE OWNER **Günther Kerschbaumer**
TOTAL BOTTLES PRODUCED **80,000**
DIRECT SALES
VISITS TO THE WINERY - RESERVATION NEEDED
HECTARES OF VINEYARD **10**
RESTAURANT

In recent years, Günther Kerschbaumer has lifted the fame of Valle Isarco whites to levels that were unimaginable only ten years ago. This not only thanks to the great terroir but also his professionalism (he is also a great connoisseur), pure passion and tenacity. The wines not only express the typical characteristics of the area – acidity upheld by salinity – but also have a certain something that is rare to find elsewhere.

☐ **92**   Price B
AA Valle Isarco Riesling 2014

100% Riesling grapes. Ages in large casks and stainless steel tanks. Straw yellow with green hues. The nose offers notes of citrus and fine herbs. Austere palate, savory and wonderfully dynamic. Vibrant finish.

☐ **90**   👍 Price A
AA Valle Isarco Sylvaner 2015

100% Sylvaner grapes. Stainless steel only. Straw yellow with green hues. Classic notes of fine herbs. Tense palate with thin body. Sea breeze finish.

☐ **89**   Price B
AA Valle Isarco Pinot Grigio 2015

100% Pinot Grigio grapes. Ages in barrels and stainless steel tanks. Well defined and fruity nose. Juicy palate, lightly warm with a good savory length.

☐ **88**   Price B
AA Valle Isarco Sylvaner R 2014

100% Sylvaner grapes. Ages in barrels and stainless steel tanks. Shiny straw yellow. Intense nose of

fine herbs and sea breeze. The palate is thin, tense but with decent weight. Medium length finish.

★
KORNELL

Frazione Settequerce - Via Bolzano, 23
39018 Terlano (BZ)
Tel. +39 0471 917507
info@kornell.it
www.kornell.it

YEAR OF FOUNDATION **2001**
NAME OF THE OWNER **Florian Brigl**
TOTAL BOTTLES PRODUCED **100,000**
DIRECT SALES
VISITS TO THE WINERY - RESERVATION NEEDED
HECTARES OF VINEYARD **15**

Florian Brigl's estate is in a small hamlet of Terlano that is famous for its ancient winemaking traditions. Although the estate's first wine was bottle in 2001, the Brigl family has a much older winemaking history. The white grape vineyards are situated around the estate while the other varieties are grown in plots in Appiano Alta and Gries. The wines are distinguished by their very precise and consistent style and are technically impeccable with a firm and expanding personality.

■ **93**   Price B
AA Lagrein Staves Riserva 2013

100% Lagrein grapes. Ages in different sized barrels. Deep garnet. Minty and complex nose; fruity and spicy hint. Meaty palate with good acidity and juicy tannins. Long and vertical finish.

■ **91**   👍 Price A
AA Lagrein Greif 2015

100% Lagrein grapes. Ages in barrels. Very deep ruby. Minty nose with hints of blueberry and cassis. Rich palate, meaty with juicy and soft tannins. It has pleasant drinkability.

☐ **91**   Price B
AA Sauvignon Oberberg 2015

100% Sauvignon grapes. Ages in barrels and stainless steel tanks. Straw yellow with green hues. Elegant nose of ripe fruit and white pepper. Rich palate, elegant, very fresh and dynamic with a savory and chalky finish.

90 Price B

AA Merlot Staves Riserva 2013

100% Merlot grapes. Aged in barrique and tonneau. Intense ruby. Well defined and refined nose of forest berries and pencil lead. Typical palate, supple and juicy with a fresh and dynamic finish.

☐ **88** Price A

AA Pinot Bianco Eich 2015

100% Pinot Bianco grapes. Stainless steel only. Warm straw yellow. Delicate nose of white peach and smoky hint. The palate is refined and elegant; good weight. The finish is slim but very long.

★★

KUENHOF

*Località Mara, 110
39042 Bressanone (BZ)
Tel. +39 0472 850546
pliger.kuenhof@rolmail.net
www.fws.it/it/kuenhof*

YEAR OF FOUNDATION **1990**
NAME OF THE OWNER **Peter Pliger**
TOTAL BOTTLES PRODUCED **40,000**
DIRECT SALES
VISITS TO THE WINERY
HECTARES OF VINEYARD **6**

Peter Pilger and his wife Brigitte are undoubtedly among the leaders for the rebirth and growing success of Valle Isarco wines. Their wines are unmistakable, whispered yet strong, intriguing and pleasing. They are the product of an almost magical winegrowing method and bold, severe decisions in the winery which are always made with an open mind and heart. Tasting their wines is always an emotional experience.

☐ **94** Price B

AA Valle Isarco Riesling Kaiton 2015

100% Riesling grapes. Ages in acacia wood barrels. Shiny straw yellow. Fascinating nose: citrus, anise and aromatic herbs. Incredibly thin palate, but with great tension and incredible dynamism.

☐ **92** Price B

AA Valle Isarco Veltliner 2015

100% Veltliner grapes. Ages in acacia wood barrels.

Shiny straw yellow with green hues. Classic notes of white pepper, loquat and a hints of aromatic herbs. The palate is sharp and vibrant and a finish that reminds sea breeze.

☐ **91** Price B

AA Valle Isarco Sylvaner 2015

100% Sylvaner grapes. Ages in acacia wood barrels. Shiny straw yellow with greenish hues. Intense nose of fine herbs and white plum. The palate is elegant, thin but with good tension; very savory finish.

★★

MANINCOR

*Località San Giuseppe al Lago, 4
39052 Caldaro (BZ)
Tel. +39 0471 960230
info@manincor.com
www.manincor.com*
 Manincor

YEAR OF FOUNDATION **1996**
NAME OF THE OWNER **Michael Goëss-Enzenberg**
TOTAL BOTTLES PRODUCED **300,000**
DIRECT SALES
VISITS TO THE WINERY - RESERVATION NEEDED
HECTARES OF VINEYARD **50**
CERTIFIED BIODYNAMIC VITICULTURE

This young (1996) Caldaro estate belongs to Count Goëss-Enzenberg and is managed and run according to biodynamic methods by the talented enologist Helmut Zozin who wasted no time in placing it among the élite in Alto Adige. This was possible thanks to a style that leans more towards *chiaroscuro* that flashy colors, with elegance and finesses becoming the estate's creed.

☐ 🔲 **95** Price B

AA Terlano Pinot Bianco Eichhorn 2015

100% Pinot Bianco grapes. Ages in barrels. Warm straw yellow. Complex nose of fine herbs, white chocolate and the classic smoky hint. The palate is mouth coating but supple and dynamic; great acidity and wonderfully balanced. Very long and elegant finish.

☐ ▪ **94** Price B*

Le Petit 2014

100% Petit Manseng grapes. Ages in barrels. Warm

golden yellow. Aromas of saffron, custard and botrytis. Elegant palate, rich and well balanced by perfect acidity. Tense finish, long and vigorous. *37.5 cl bottle.

 94   Price B
AA Pinot Nero Mason di Mason 2013

100% Pinot Nero grapes. Ages in barrique. Intense ruby red. Fascinating nose of cassis and field blossoms; lightly smoky hints. The palate is juicy, rich and of wonderful finesse. Tense finish, firm and savory.

☐ 90   👍 Price A
AA Terlano Réserve della Contessa 2015

Blend of Pinot Bianco, Chardonnay and Sauvignon grapes. Ages in barrels. Warm straw yellow with greenish hues. The nose is fascinating and shows notes of field blossoms and camomile. Delicate palate, apparently thin with great tension and acidity. Long and slightly spicy finish.

★
LORENZ MARTINI

Via Pranzoll, 2d - Cornaiano
39057 Appiano (BZ)
Tel. +39 0471 664136
Fax +39 0471 664136
lorenz.martini@rolmail.net
www.lorenz-martini.com

YEAR OF FOUNDATION 1985
NAME OF THE OWNER Martini Family
TOTAL BOTTLES PRODUCED 15,000
VISITS TO THE WINERY - RESERVATION NEEDED
HECTARES OF VINEYARD 2

Lorenz Martini is one of the most esteemed experts in the province of Bolzano and has collaborated with a number of estates in Alto Adige. His passion, aside from vintage cars, has always been sparkling wines and his tiny winery consistently produces some very interesting ones. In recent years we have seen his wines leap in quality in regard to finesse and complexity.

 93   Price C
AA Comitissa Gold Brut Gran Riserva 2006

Blend of Chardonnay and Pinot Bianco grapes. Light straw yellow. Plenty of refined bubbles. Complex nose and delicately smoky. Creamy palate, rich and with prominent freshness. Long and satisfying finish.

 88   Price B
AA Comitissa Brut Riserva 2011

Blend of Chardonnay, Pinot Bianco and Pinot Nero grapes, refined bubbles. Fresh and well defined aromas of white stone fruits. The palate is juicy, dynamic and with a good weight palate, savory finish.

★★★
MURI-GRIES

Piazza Gries, 21
39100 Bolzano (BZ)
Tel. +39 0471 282287
Fax +39 0471 273448
info@muri-gries.com
www.muri-gries.com
f CantinaMuriGries

YEAR OF FOUNDATION 1845
TOTAL BOTTLES PRODUCED 700,000
DIRECT SALES
VISITS TO THE WINERY - RESERVATION NEEDED
HECTARES OF VINEYARD 50

The Benedictine Muri-Gries convent is one of Italy's most fascinating productive realities. Here Gries not only represents centuries of history but also an ability to manage nature and its fruits in a truly special way. The current protagonist of this story is Christian Werth, who became the convent's Kellermeister in 1988 taking the place of his father. His skill, passion and perfectionism make him the most severe critic of his own wines and are only equaled by his modesty. Lagrein Abtei Muri Riserva became a wine loved and respected by all, a true model for this type of wine but this year has not been produced. Each and every bottle produced is an example of maniacal attention to every detail.

☐ 93   👍 Price A
AA Terlano Pinot Bianco 2015

100% Pinot Bianco grapes. Ages in large casks. Straw yellow with green hues. Fascinating hints of white chocolate, aromatic herbs. The palate is rich and complex but also supple and juicy. Very long and savory finish.

☐ **89**   Price A

AA Pinot Grigio 2015

100% Pinot Grigio grapes. Ages in barrels and stainless steel tanks. Intense straw yellow. Clear notes of pear. The palate is fascinating, rich but with wonderful tension and freshness. Long and savory finish.

☐ **88**   Price A

AA Bianco Abtei Muri 2014

Blend of 60% Pinot Bianco and 40% Pinot Grigio grapes. Aged in barrels. Intense straw yellow. Fascinating nose of ripe white stone fruit and white chocolate. Thin palate but balanced and with a good tension. Medium length and savory finish.

 88   Price A

AA Lagrein 2015

100% Lagrein grapes. Ages in barrels. Ruby with purple hues. Fascinating nose offering notes of blueberry and black currant. The palate is fresh, meaty and it has wonderful drinkability.

★★
NALS MARGREID

Via Heiligenberg, 2
39010 Nalles (BZ)
Tel. +39 0471 678626
info@kellerei.it
www.kellerei.it
 Nals.Margreid

YEAR OF FOUNDATION **1932**
TOTAL BOTTLES PRODUCED **950,000**
DIRECT SALES
VISITS TO THE WINERY - RESERVATION NEEDED
HECTARES OF VINEYARD **150**

This important estate in the past ten years has made amazing progress with an impressive line of wines that stand out for their increasing quality and stylistic precision. Much of this is thanks to its director Gottfried Pollinger and the young star of Alto Adige winemaking Harald Schraffl. Pinot Bianco Sirmian has become a must and each year becomes more fine and complex.

☐ **92**   Price B

AA Pinot Bianco Sirmian 2015

100% Pinot Bianco grapes. Ages in large casks and stainless steel tanks. Warm straw yellow. Fascinating nose of white stone fruit and spice. The palate is still austere but rich, juicy and of good weight. Very long savory finish.

☐ **91**   👍 Price A

AA Pinot Grigio Punggl 2015

100% Pinot Grigio grapes. Ages in barrels. Intense straw yellow. Well defined and fascinating nose. Very good weight on the palate and wonderfully balanced by savory acidity. Long flavorful finish.

☐ **90**   Price B

AA Chardonnay Baron Salvadori Riserva 2013

100% Chardonnay grapes. Ages in tonneau. Shiny straw yellow. Intense fruity notes with a smoky hint. The palate is powerful, savory and with a good long sea breeze finish.

☐ **90**   Price B

AA Sauvignon Mantele 2015

100% Sauvignon grapes. Stainless steel only. Straw yellow with intense green hues. The nose offers hints of flint and citrus. The palate is composed, fresh; it has good structure and a long dynamic and savory finish.

 90   👍 Price A

AA Schiava Galea 2015

100% Schiava grapes. Ages in barrels. Light ruby-purple. Intense fruity and spicy notes. The palate is juicy, fresh and with a delicate pencil lead note. Long and juicy finish.

★
IGNAZ NIEDRIST

Via Ronco, 5 - Cornaiano
39057 Appiano (BZ)
Tel. +39 0471 664494
ignazniedrist@rolmail.net
www.fws.it/it/az-agr-niedrist

YEAR OF FOUNDATION **1990**
NAME OF THE OWNER **Ignaz Niedrist**
TOTAL BOTTLES PRODUCED **45,000**
DIRECT SALES
VISITS TO THE WINERY - RESERVATION NEEDED
HECTARES OF VINEYARD **10**

A rare intellectual winemaker (his library of wine technology is amazing), Ignaz Niedrist is a leading authority in Alto Adige and his wines have made leaps and bounds in recent years, which with the acquisition of new vineyards in Appiano Alta will surely increase even further. His Pinot Bianco, Sauvignon and Riesling have become points of reference. They are full yet elegant, briny and packed with energy and dynamism and all have a distinct personality. This year we're not missing an excellent version of Pinot Nero.

☐ 91　　　　　　　　　　　　Price B
AA Pinot Bianco Berg 2015

100% Pinot Bianco grapes. Stainless steel only. Light straw yellow. Varietal and well defined nose. Supple, elegant and delicately savory. Long juicy finish.

■ 90　　　　　　　　　　　　Price B
AA Pinot Nero 2013

100% Pinot Nero grapes. Ages in barrique. Intense ruby. The nose is fruity yet wrapped by good spiciness. The palate is solid, the tannins are firm and balanced by lively acidity. Long and savory finish.

☐ 90　　　　　　　　　　　　Price B
AA Terlano Sauvignon 2015

100% Sauvignon grapes. Stainless steel only. Warm straw yellow with green hues. Well defined nose: hawthorn and anise. The palate is elegant, soft, medium-bodied yet with fresh and savory finish.

OBERMOSER

Località Santa Maddalena di Sotto, 35
39100 Bolzano (BZ)
Tel. +39 0471 973549
info@obermoser.it
www.obermoser.it

YEAR OF FOUNDATION **1890**
NAME OF THE OWNER **Thomas Rottensteiner**
TOTAL BOTTLES PRODUCED **35,000**
DIRECT SALES
VISITS TO THE WINERY - RESERVATION NEEDED
HECTARES OF VINEYARD **3.5**

The young Thomas Rottensteiner represents the latest generation of one of the most classic, family-run estates in the area of Bolzano. The line of products as been reduced to the more typical of the area, most of all Lagrein and Santa Maddale-

na. The wines have a very classic style and the quality has been consistent over the years, the result of unusual passion and skill.

■ 91　　　　　　　　　　　👍 Price A
AA Santa Maddalena Classico 2015

Mainly Schiava grapes with a little percentage of Lagrein. Ages in barrels. Lively ruby. The nose offers typical fruity and spicy notes. The palate is mouth coating yet fresh and supple with a wonderful savory finish.

☐ 91　　　　　　　　　　　👍 Price A
AA Sauvignon 2015

100% Sauvignon grapes. Stainless steel only. Warm yellow with green hues. Notes of grapefruit and spices. Supple palate, juicy acidity and a long definitively sea breeze finish.

PACHERHOF

Casali Pacher, 1 - Novacella
39040 Varna (BZ)
Tel. +39 0472 835717
wein@pacherhof.com
www.pacherhof.com

YEAR OF FOUNDATION **XII secolo**
NAME OF THE OWNER **Andreas Huber**
TOTAL BOTTLES PRODUCED **80,000**
DIRECT SALES
VISITS TO THE WINERY - RESERVATION NEEDED
HECTARES OF VINEYARD **8**
HOSPITALITY
RESTAURANT

The Pacher farm dates back to 1142 and Andreas Huber's grandfather, Josef, was one of the pioneers of winemaking in Valle Isarco. The wines are the ones typical for the area and the whites have great personality and elegance. The vineyards are situated at an altitude of 600m above sea level and are among the oldest in the area. Cultivation is very natural and the estate is in the process of converting to biodynamic methods.

☐ 94　　　　　　　　　　　　Price B
AA Valle Isarco Pinot Grigio 2015

100% Pinot Grigio grapes. Ages in large casks and

stainless steel tanks. Warm straw yellow. Multy-layered and well defined fruity nose, smoky hint. The palate is tense, elegant and juicy with a flavorful finish.

---

 91   👍 Price A

AA Valle Isarco Kerner 2015

100% Kerner grapes. Stainless steel only. Straw yellow with greenish hues. The nose shows predominant sea breeze notes with citrusy hints. The palate is supple, agile and with good tension with a juicy acidity and a very good length.

☐ 90   Price B

AA Valle Isarco Riesling 2015

100% Riesling grapes. Ages in barrels and stainless steel tanks. Defined nose of grapefruit and aromatic herbs. Fresh palate, supple and juicy with a long and savory finish.

☐ 89   Price A

AA Valle Isarco Veltliner 2015

100% Veltliner grapes. Ages in casks and stainless steel tanks. Light straw yellow. Tropical nose. The palate is juicy and with a good weight. Supple finish.

★

PFANNENSTIELHOF

*Via Pfannenstiel, 9
39100 Bolzano (BZ)
Tel. +39 0471 970884
Fax +39 0471 970884
info@pfannenstielhof.it
www.pfannenstielhof.it*
🔲 *Pfannenstielhof*

YEAR OF FOUNDATION 1561
NAME OF THE OWNER Johannes Pfeiffer
TOTAL BOTTLES PRODUCED 43,000
DIRECT SALES
VISITS TO THE WINERY - RESERVATION NEEDED
HECTARES OF VINEYARD 4

Johannes Pfeifer is without a doubt one of the best producers of Santa Maddalena. His wines stand out for their simplicity, drinkability, typicity and surprising ability to age. Pfannenstielhof, located on the eastern edge of the Bolzano basin, naturally also produces other interesting wines starting with a classic Lagrein.

---

 92   Price B

AA Lagrein Riserva 2013

100% Lagrein grapes. Ages in different sized casks and stainless steel tanks. Concentrated ruby-purple. Intense and compact nose of forest berries and spices. The palate shows good structure and at the same time supple and fresh; it has pleasant is drinkability.

---

 92   👍 Price A

AA Santa Maddalena Classico 2015

Blend of Schiava with a little percentage of Lagrein grapes. Ages in barrels. Lively ruby. One of the best expression in its category. Delicate fruity and spicy nose. Fresh palate, fragrant and blissful. A safe bet.

🔲 88   Price A

AA Lagrein vom Boden 2015

100% Lagrein grapes. Ages in large casks. Deep ruby. It's a fresh wine, fragrant and with a wonderful personality. Classic fruity aromas on the nose; then a sea breeze hint. The palate is juicy, fresh and of good length.

★

RITTERHOF

*Strada del Vino, 1
39052 Caldaro (BZ)
Tel. +39 0471 963298
Fax +39 0471 961088
info@ritterhof.it
www.ritterhof.it*
🔲 *ritterhof.tenuta*

YEAR OF FOUNDATION 1968
NAME OF THE OWNER Roner Family
TOTAL BOTTLES PRODUCED 290,000
DIRECT SALES
VISITS TO THE WINERY - RESERVATION NEEDED
HECTARES OF VINEYARD 42

This lovely Caldaro estate belongs to the Roner family, famous distillers who have truly believed in this project and invested significant resources in it. The new winery seems to be making it easier for the talented Kellermeister Bernhard Hannes to produce wines that are well-defined and rich in personality. The principle wines produced are Gewürztraminer, Sauvignon and Lagrein although the Pinot Nero is quite ambitious.

🎖 95   Price B
AA Lagrein Mauns Riserva 2012

100% Lagrein grapes. Ages for 18 months in used barrique. Ruby with garnet rim. Fascinating and typical nose of forest berries, black pepper and pencil lead. Mouth filling and complex palate, with juicy tannins and a deep tense finish.

▪ 94   Price B*
Gewürztraminer Passito Sonus 2013

*100% Gewürztraminer grapes. Ages in casks. Shiny golden yellow. Distinctive aromas of saffron, botrytis, quince and apricot. The palate is creamy and powerful yet supple and with a pleasant acidity. Very long and elegant finish. *37.5 cl bottle.*

☐ 93   Price B
AA Gewürztraminer Auratus 2015

100% Gewürztraminer grapes. Stainless steel only. Straw yellow with golden hues. Multy-layered nose with hints of rosehip, tropical fruit and saffron. The palate is rich, mouth coating and with distinctive savory tension. The finish is meaty, long and very satisfying.

■ 88   Price A
AA Lago di Caldaro Classico Superiore Novis 2015

100% Schiava grapes. Ages in large casks. Light ruby. Well defined nose of forest berries and delicate spicy aromas. Juicy palate, supple and fresh.

STACHLBURG

Via Peter Mitterhofer, 2
39020 Parcines (BZ)
Tel. + 39 0473 968014
sigmund.kripp@stachlburg.com
www.stachlburg.com
 📘 *stachlburg*

YEAR OF FOUNDATION **1990**
NAME OF THE OWNER **Sigmund Kripp**
TOTAL BOTTLES PRODUCED **35,000**
DIRECT SALES
VISITS TO THE WINERY
HECTARES OF VINEYARD **7.5**
CERTIFIED ORGANIC VITICULTURE
CERTIFIED BIODYNAMIC VITICULTURE

Stachlburg is located in Parcines at the beginning of the Venosta Valley and is a typical 13th century Tyrolean reality. This is the kingdom of Baron Sigmund Kripp, a passionate and volcanic winemaker and wine lover. His vineyards are in Parcines and Naturno, at an altitude of over 600m, and in Andriano near Terlano. The estate has consistently practiced organic farming and work in the winery is anything but interventionist. The result are wines that have elegance, finesse and unmistakable character.

☐ 93   👍 Price A
AA Terlano Sauvignon 2015

100% Sauvignon grapes. Ages in casks and stainless steel tanks. Straw yellow with greenish hues. Typical and fascinating nose. Refined palate, elegant and dynamic. The finish is long and juicy with delicate smoky hints.

■ 91   👍 Price A
AA Pinot Nero 2012

100% Pinot Nero grapes. Aged in barrique. Intense ruby red. Classic notes of cassis, spices and delicate smoky hints. The palate is austere but well structured, balanced with ripe and firm tannins. Long and savory finish.

STRASSERHOF

Via Unterrain, 8 - Novacella
39040 Varna (BZ)
Tel. +39 348 3976680
Fax +39 0472 830804
info@strasserhof.info
www.strasserhof.info
 📘 *Strasserhof-NeustiftNovacella*

YEAR OF FOUNDATION **2003**
NAME OF THE OWNER **Hannes Baumgartner**
TOTAL BOTTLES PRODUCED **45,000**
DIRECT SALES
VISITS TO THE WINERY
HECTARES OF VINEYARD **5.5**
HOSPITALITY

The vineyards of the Baumgartner family are perhaps the northernmost in the Valle Isarco and the province of Bolzano and the young Hannes has demonstrated his skill at expressing the spirit of this frontier zone. The progress this estate has made is quite impressive, especially considering how little time it took. The whites have a strong personality and are austere to the point of being severe but undoubtedly have charm and stylistic rigor.

☐ 92 — Price B
AA Valle Isarco Sylvaner Anjo 2015

100% Sylvaner grapes. Ages in acacia wood barrels. Lively straw yellow. Fascinating nose of fine herbs, white stone fruits, sea breeze. The palate is round, flavorful and vibrant. The finish is fresh, juicy and very long.

☐ 90 — 👍 Price A
AA Valle Isarco Sylvaner 2015

100% Sylvaner grapes. Ages in acacia wood casks. Shiny straw yellow. The nose offers hints of passion fruits and fine herbs. The palate is juicy, well-structured and with a fresh and vibrant finish.

☐ 88 — Price A
AA Valle Isarco Kerner 2015

100% Kerner grapes. Ages in acacia wood casks. Straw yellow with greenish hues. Intense nose of fine herbs and field blossoms. Medium bodied with a supple and pleasant finish.

☐ 88 — Price A
AA Valle Isarco Riesling 2015

100% Riesling grapes. Ages in acacia wood casks. Shiny straw yellow. Austere nose, sea breeze and grapefruit hints. The palate is fresh, tense and vibrant. Medium bodied with a firm and savory finish.

STROBLHOF

Via Piganò, 25
39057 Appiano (BZ)
Tel. +39 0471 662250
weingut@stroblhof.it
www.stroblhof.it
f Hotel-Weingut-Stroblhof

YEAR OF FOUNDATION 1840
NAME OF THE OWNER Rosi and Andreas Nicolussi-Leck
TOTAL BOTTLES PRODUCED 38,000
DIRECT SALES
VISITS TO THE WINERY - RESERVATION NEEDED
HECTARES OF VINEYARD 5.2
HOSPITALITY
RESTAURANT

Andreas Nicolussi-Leck has been running this established Appiano estate since 1996 and is one of the best producers of Pinot Nero in Alto Adige, even if his vineyards are not in the famed area of Mazzon. For him this has represented a true challenge and the results are there for all to see and his Pinot Nero are classic, elegant and full of personality. He also produces a great Pinot Bianco, Strahler, but it needs to age.

■ 90 — Price B
AA Pinot Nero Pigeno 2013

100% Pinot Nero grapes. Ages in barrique. Light garnet. Intense and well-defined nose. Austere palate, savory with well extracted tannins and a juicy acidity. Long and fragrant finish.

☐ 89 — Price A
AA Pinot Bianco Strahler 2015

100% Pinot Bianco grapes. Stainless steel only. Shiny straw yellow. Intense and well-defined nose of white stone fruit and light smoky notes. The palate is tense, agile and elegant; good length.

☐ 89 — Price B
AA Sauvignon Nico 2015

100% Sauvignon grapes. Ages in casks. Light straw yellow. Nose of tropical fruit and hawthorn. Thin palate yet with good weight and a fresh finish. Elegant and savory.

☐ 88 — Price A
AA Chardonnay Schwarzhaus 2015

100% Chardonnay grapes. Ages in barrels. Intense straw yellow. The nose offers well defined fruity notes. Fragrant palate, vertical and a savory medium length.

TASCHLERHOF

Località La Mara, 107
39042 Bressanone (BZ)
Tel. +39 0472 851091
info@taschlerhof.com
www.taschlerhof.com

YEAR OF FOUNDATION 2000
NAME OF THE OWNER Peter Wachtler
TOTAL BOTTLES PRODUCED 30,000
DIRECT SALES
VISITS TO THE WINERY - RESERVATION NEEDED
HECTARES OF VINEYARD 4.2

Peter Wachtler began to bottle his wines in the mid-1990s. His small estate is in the Isarco Valley in the town of Mara outside Bressanone with vineyards on steep slopes that rise to over 500m above sea level. The soil is meagre and rocky and gives Taschlerhof wines the salinity typical of the valley. Great care is paid both in the vineyards and the winery and 60% of the wine is aged in acacia wood barrels and the rest in stainless steel.

☐ 91   Price B
AA Valle Isarco Sylvaner Lahner 2015

100% Sylvaner grapes. Ages in acacia wood casks and stainless steel tanks. Straw yellow with intense greenish hues. Expressive nose: fine herbs and white peach. The palate is fresh and fragrant with juicy acidity and long tense finish.

☐ 90   Price B
AA Valle Isarco Kerner 2015

100% Kerner grapes. Ages in acacia wood casks and stainless steel tanks. Warm straw yellow. Intense nose of green apple and smoky hints. The palate is composed, juicy and with a savory finish.

☐ 89   Price A
AA Valle Isarco Sylvaner 2015

100% Sylvaner grapes. Ages in acacia wood casks and stainless steel tanks. Warm straw yellow. Well defined and typical nose. The palate is fresh, juicy and dynamic.

TIEFENBRUNNER

Via Castello, 4
39040 Cortaccia (BZ)
Tel. +39 0471 880122
Fax +39 0471 880433
info@tiefenbrunner.com
www.tiefenbrunner.com
 Turmhof.Tiefenbrunner

YEAR OF FOUNDATION 1848
NAME OF THE OWNER Christof Tiefenbrunner
TOTAL BOTTLES PRODUCED 750,000
DIRECT SALES
VISITS TO THE WINERY - RESERVATION NEEDED
HECTARES OF VINEYARD 25
RESTAURANT

Tiefenbrunner were the first Alto Adige wines be marketed outside the region. Over the past ten years, Christof Tiefenbrunner has been able to impose a precise style to the full range of wines which include all those typical to the area. These are wines that play on *chiaroscuro*, they are elegant, delicate and absolutely recognizable even when trends dictated may be otherwise. At the same time, they have made some courageous decisions including bottling the estate's leading wine, Feldmarschall, with a screw-on cap.

☐ 95   Price B
AA Müller Thurgau Feldmarschall von Fenner 2014

100% Müller Thurgau grapes. Ages in casks and stainless steel tanks. Wonderful version of this unique wine. Light straw yellow with greenish hues. Captivating nose of saffron, camomile and fine herbs. Rocky palate, solid and elegant; juicy and vertical. The finish is refreshing, savory and very long.

■ 92   Price B
AA Lagrein Linticlarus Riserva 2013

100% Lagrein grapes. Ages in barrique and large casks. Deep ruby red. Intense and delicate nose. The palate is juicy, round and balanced with soft tannins and vertical finish.

■ 90   Price B
AA Pinot Nero Linticlarus Riserva 2013

100% Pinot Nero grapes. Ages in barrique. Lively ruby. Refined and typical nose. The palate has good weight, well defined and vertical. Ripe tannins and with a fresh and dynamic finish.

★★★
ELENA WALCH

Via A. Hofer, 1
39040 Termeno (BZ)
Tel. +39 0471 860172
Fax +39 0471 860781
info@elenawalch.it
www.elenawalch.it
 Walch.Elena
 @ElenaWalch

YEAR OF FOUNDATION 1988
NAME OF THE OWNER Elena Walch
TOTAL BOTTLES PRODUCED 500,000

DIRECT SALES
VISITS TO THE WINERY - RESERVATION NEEDED
HECTARES OF VINEYARD **55**
RESTAURANT

By now this has become a point of reference for Oltreadige wineries. It has its headquarters in Termeno, where the Kastelaz vineyards are terraced and overlook the ancient town, while a significant part of the estate is situated in Castel Ringberg, in the township of Caldaro. At the helm of the winery are Elena and Werner Walch but their daughter Giulia has now been working with them on a continual basis. The estate's specialty is Gewürztraminer but all the wines they produce have an exemplary reliability and a very high level of quality.

 95 — Price B
AA Gewürztraminer Vigna Kastelaz 2015
100% Gewürztraminer grapes. Stainless steel only. Light golden yellow. Elegant and delicate aromatic nose: rose and lychee, very typical and varietal, lightly smoky hints. Composed palate, warm, captivating and savory with good acidity well balanced with the smooth texture; barely perceptible residual sugar. Very long length.

☐ **93** — Price B
AA Pinot Bianco Kristalberg 2015
100% Pinot Bianco grapes. Stainless steel only. Pale yellow. Very varietal nose, notes of hawthorn, white peach and fresh almond. The palate is tense, savory, fresh, supple, juicy; it has good drinkability enhanced by great acidity. Thin and long finish.

☐ **91** — Price B
AA Bianco Beyond the Clouds 2014
Blend of Chardonnay with a little percentage of Gewürztraminer, Pinot Bianco and Sauvignon grapes. Part of the wine ages in barrique for 1 year and the rest matures in stainless steel tank. Multy-layered nose, vanilla, toasted bread then aromatic notes of rose petals and white peach. Rich palate, full bodied but supple; refreshing and savory acidity. Warm and long finish.

☐ **90** — Price B
AA Sauvignon Castel Ringberg 2015
100% Sauvignon grapes. Stainless steel only. Intense green yellow. Aromas of mango, elderflower, white peach, fragrant and well defined. Fresh palate, refined, very typical and with a wonderful drinkability.

 ★★
WALDGRIES

Località S. Giustina, 2
39100 Bolzano (BZ)
Tel. +39 0471 323603
info@waldgries.it
www.waldgries.it
f *AnsitzWaldgries*

YEAR OF FOUNDATION **1930**
NAME OF THE OWNER **Christian Plattner**
TOTAL BOTTLES PRODUCED **70,000**
DIRECT SALES
VISITS TO THE WINERY - RESERVATION NEEDED
HECTARES OF VINEYARD **8**

Christian Plattner is not only one of the best winemakers in the area of Santa Maddalena, he is also someone who is always looking for new challenges to stimulate his passion for making wine. This is what led to the creation of Santa Maddalena Antheos which recovers local grape varieties used over one hundred years ago. If we add that his Santa Maddalena is the absolute champion of its kind and the Lagrein are always among the best, then you get a pretty clear picture of this estate.

■ **95** — Price B
AA Lagrein Mirell 2013
100% Lagrein grapes. Ages in large casks. Deep ruby. Captivating notes of ripe fruits, spices and licorice. The palate is powerful, austere but supple and tense with juicy tannins and good freshness. Long and tense finish.

☐ **94** — Price B
AA Pinot Bianco Isos 2014
100% Pinot Bianco grapes. Matures in stainless steel tanks and tonneau. Warm straw yellow. Classic notes of hawthorn and white peach. The palate is tense, elegant and very expressive. The finish is firm, savory and of good depth.

☐ **94** — Price B
AA Sauvignon Myra 2015
100% Sauvignon grapes, 90% matures in stainless steel tanks and the rest in barrique. Warm straw yellow with greenish hues. The nose is definitively expressive with notes of grapefruit, spices and ripe fruits. The palate is rich, well-structured and dynamic with an impressive savory length.

93 👍 Price A

AA Santa Maddalena Classico 2015

Blend of Schiava and little percentage of Lagrein grapes. Ages in large casks. Intense ruby red. Expressive nose with well-defined notes of forest berries, spices and dried blossoms. The palate combines a good structure with fragrant and fresh drinkability.

WASSERERHOF

Via Völserried, 21 - Novale di Fiè
39050 Fiè allo Sciliar (BZ)
Tel. +39 0471 724114
info@wassererhof.com
www.wassererhof.com
f *wassererhof*

YEAR OF FOUNDATION 2013
NAME OF THE OWNER Christoph and Andreas Mock
TOTAL BOTTLES PRODUCED 16,000
DIRECT SALES
VISITS TO THE WINERY - RESERVATION NEEDED
HECTARES OF VINEYARD 1.5
HOSPITALITY
RESTAURANT

The estate of twins Christoph and Andreas Mock is relatively new and the first wine produced was a vintage 2013. It is situated at the entrance to Valle Isarco in a beautiful farmhouse that their parents bought in 1996 and then restored. The vineyards are beautiful and sit at an altitude of between 350 and 450m above sea level. Christoph is the farmer and winemaker while Andreas is the chef at one of the best restaurants in the province of Bolzano. From the very beginning the wines were well-made with a strong personality and great purity.

92 👍 Price A

AA Pinot Bianco 2015

100% Pinot Bianco grapes. Ages in tonneau and stainless steel tanks. Straw yellow with greenish hues. Captivating and aromatic nose enhanced by smoky notes. The palate is firm, fresh, vertical but with good weight. The finish is savory and dynamic.

92 👍 Price A

AA Sauvignon 2015

100% Sauvignon grapes, 95% matures in stainless

steel tanks and 5% in tonneau. Intense straw yellow. Spicy nose, citrusy and hints of white truffle. The palate is flavorful, vertical, elegant and tense with a long and very savory finish.

88 Price A

AA Santa Maddalena Classico Mumelterhof 2015

Blend of Schiava with a little percentage of Lagrein grapes. Ages in barrels. Lively ruby red. The nose is floral and spicy. The palate is refined, delicate and juicy, meaty and fresh finish.

APULIA

pulia produces an average of six million hectoliters of wine a year and 60% of this is either classified as controlled designation origin (DOC) or typical geographic indication (IGT) made from 85,000 hectares of vineyards, 15% of the national total. The region can be divided into three distinct zones: the province of Foggia and Capitanta; the province of Bari and the Murge; and Salento. In the first zone the principle DOC wines are San Severo, Cacc'e Mmitte di Lucera, Orta Nova and Rosso di Cerignola. San Severo can be a white wine, made from Bombino and Trebbiano, or a red or rosé made using Montepulciano and Sangiovese grapes. These are wines that have a medium structure and are more similar to DOC wines from Abruzzo than the other wines of the region. Cacc'e Mmitte di Lucera takes its name from an ancient winemaking method (which translates 'take off and put on') and is made with Troia, Montepulciano and other red grapes. It is a rare wine to find and is very traditional and a bit rustic. Orta Nova is either a red or a rosé and is made with Montepulciano and Troia grapes as is Rosso di Cerignola, which can also be made with Negroamaro. Overall they are all similar wines that have organoleptic profiles similar to the wines of Campania and Abruzzo than the bold reds of Salento. The same is true of the wines from the area of Bari, Rosso Barletta and Rosso Canosa.

Further to the south is the vast zone of Castel del Monte, the most important appellation in central-northern Apulia which was recently upgraded to DOCG. Here instead of Bombino they use Pampanuto grapes and together with Troia they use Aglianico as opposed to Sangiovese or Montepulciano. These grapes are used to make a delicate white wine and soft reds and rosés. Aglianico is also used to make a varietal red. But the Castel del Monte appellation also allows for a series of innovative wines wisely made using international varieties. Among these is a soft Chardonnay, a distinct Sauvignon and a delicate Pinot Bianco. In the area of Bari they also produce a delicious sweet white, Moscato di Trani, which is one of the most interesting dessert wines in all of southern Italy, the so-called Mezzogiorno.

The hilly area of the Murge produces Gravina, a delicate white made from Malvasia Bianco and Greco. The area straddling this zone and the beginning of that of Taranto is home to various versions of Gioia del Colle and a grape that is fundamental grape in Apulia winemaking: Primitivo. This grape is used in red blends or to make a varietal wine which is by far the most interesting wine in the area made in the province of Taranto. Locorotondo and Martina Franca are twin whites made from Verdeca and Bianco d'Alessano grapes close the selection of wines made in the provinces of Taranto and Brindisi.

Salento, the 'heel' of the Italian boot, is the land of Negroamaro, a grape with extraordinary potential which is the base of almost all the reds and rosés of this area, with the exception of Primitivo di Manduria, another outstanding Apulia wine. Alezio, Salice Salentino Rosso, Lizzano, Brindisi, Squinzano, Copertino, Nardò,

Leverano and Matino, in other words all the leading Salento wines made in the provinces of Brindisi and Lecce, are made with Negroamaro with small additions of Malvasia Nera. These are reds with an explosive potential, wines that almost seem to stain the glass. In the area of Salice Salentino, the more important DOC zone in this part of the region, several innovative wines are having a critical success. This is particularly true of Salice Salentino Bianco, made primarily with Chardonnay, and Salice Salentino Pinot Bianco. Both are soft wines with nice bodies.

CONTROLLED AND GUARANTEED DESIGNATION OF ORIGIN (DOCG)

- Primitivo di Manduria Dolce Naturale
- Castel del Monte Bombino Nero, geographic references allowed
- Castel del Monte Nero di Troia Riserva, geographic references allowed
- Castel del Monte Rosso Riserva, geographic references allowed

CONTROLLED DESIGNATION OF ORIGIN (DOC)

- Aleatico di Puglia
- Alezio
- Barletta
- Brindisi
- Cacc'e Mmitte di Lucera
- Castel del Monte, geographic references allowed
- Colline Joniche Tarantine
- Copertino
- Galatina
- Gioia del Colle
- Gravina
- Leverano, geographic references allowed
- Lizzano
- Locorotondo
- Martina o Martina Franca
- Matino
- Moscato di Trani
- Nardò
- Negroamaro di Terra d'Otranto
- Orta Nova
- Ostuni
- Primitivo di Manduria
- Rosso di Cerignola
- Salice Salentino
- San Severo
- Squinzano
- Tavoliere delle Puglie or Tavoliere, geographic references allowed
- Terra d'Otranto

AGRICOLE VALLONE

Via XXV Luglio, 7
73100 Lecce (LE)
Tel. +39 0832 308041
info@agricolevallone.it
www.agricolevallone.it
 agricolevallone

YEAR OF FOUNDATION 1934
NAME OF THE OWNER Vittoria, Maria Teresa and Francesco Vallone
TOTAL BOTTLES PRODUCED 400,000
VISITS TO THE WINERY - RESERVATION NEEDED
HECTARES OF VINEYARD 160

Situated in the sun-drenched and hot heart of Salento, this winery has written some of the most important pages in Puglia winemaking history. It has 40 hectares of vineyards in its Tenuta di Castelserranova estate, 90 in the Tenuta di Flaminio and 30 hectares in Tenuta di Iore, where they cultivate grapes typical to the area. Their Graticciaia wine consistently wins prizes and other recognitions but all their wines are capable of efficiently communicating to those who drink them how this region has some hidden jewels.

■ 94   Price C
Graticciaia 2012

100%Negroamarograpes from an old Alberello-trained vineyard. Straw matt dried grapes, matures 1 year in barrique. Intense ruby red with garnet shades. Complex and aristocratic nose with blackberry, tobacco, licorice. Impressive on the palate, warm with a hint of sweetness and great acidity. A real champion in the finish.

■ 92   👍 Price A
Susumaniello 2015

100% Susumaniello grapes. Matures in concrete vats. Purple red color. Intense and elegant on the nose but crunchy with notes of morello cherry and red berries, then laurel and spices. Complex and rich on the palate but most of all easy to drink and a really convincing finish.

☐ 90   Price B
Fiano Tenuta Serranova 2015

100% Fiano grapes. Matures 4 months in stainless steel. Light straw yellow color. Very clear aromas of

---

herbs, flowers and citrusy hints. Interesting on the palate with great freshness and savory with a typical almond note in the finish.

AMASTUOLA

Via Martina Franca, 80
74016 Massafra (TA)
Tel. +39 099 8805668
🔵 *amastuola*
info@amastuola.it
www.amastuola.it
 amastuola
🐦 *@Amastuola*

YEAR OF FOUNDATION 2003
NAME OF THE OWNER Montanaro Family
TOTAL BOTTLES PRODUCED 800,000
DIRECT SALES
VISITS TO THE WINERY - RESERVATION NEEDED
HECTARES OF VINEYARD 101
HOSPITALITY
RESTAURANT
CERTIFIED ORGANIC VITICULTURE
OLIVE OIL PRODUCTION

Peppino Montanaro, with his children Filippo, Illaria and Donato, together with his son-in-law Giuseppe Sportelli, has restored this splendid masseria farm estate to its ancient glory. Wine has been made here for at least four centuries and the main building of the masseria will soon house the center of production. Not far away is the Masseria Accetta Grande where one can stay and bike to Amastuola. Of particular interest are the 'wave' vineyards that wind along following the line of the hills and that were designed by garden architect Fernando Caruncho.

■ 🅖 95   Price B
Centosassi 2012

100% Primitivo grapes. Maturs for 30 months in barrique. Intense ruby red color. Very complex in the nose with aromas of blackberry, mulberry, dry figs, licorice and eucalyptus notes. Full, rich palate but very elegant thanks to his high acidity that give it harmony. Integrated tannins and long finish.

■ 91   👍 Price A
Primitivo 2014

100% Primitivo grapes. Matures 18 months in big

barrels. Intense ruby color. Nice confirmation for a "base" Primitivo that offers black cherry and cassis aromas, eucalyptus notes and tobacco hints. Very typical on the palate, sweet, rich and warm but balanced by perfect acidity.

---

 90   Price B
Aglianico 2013

100% Aglianico grapes. A brand new wine for the producer. Matures in barrique for 24 months in big barrels. Intense ruby color. Complex and clear aromas of ripe red fruits, eucalyptus notes with aromas of spices, pepper, cinnamon and nutmeg. Very powerful mouth, with evident tannins but with a long finish.

---

 89   👍 Price A
Ondarosa 2015

100% Aglianico grapes. Pink color. Stainless steel only. interesting nose with rose, cherry and strawberry aromas. The palate is fresh but it feels the strength of the grape, clear savory note that makes it tasty, balanced and slightly tannin on the finish.

ANTICA MASSERIA JORCHE

Contrada Jorche
74020 Torricella (TA)
Tel. +39 099 9573232
Fax +39 099 9573232
jorche@jorche.it
www.jorche.it
f anticamasseria.jorche
🐦 @Jorche_masseria

YEAR OF FOUNDATION **1935**
NAME OF THE OWNER **Dalila and Emanuela Gianfreda**
TOTAL BOTTLES PRODUCED **80,000**
DIRECT SALES
VISITS TO THE WINERY - RESERVATION NEEDED
HECTARES OF VINEYARD **31**
HOSPITALITY
RESTAURANT
OLIVE OIL PRODUCTION

The winery was recently built in a modern and technically advanced style. The vineyards that surround it are young, eight years old, and the estate also owns another 17 hectares that are 40 years old a few hundred meters from the sea. Only native grapes are cultivated including Primitivo (70% of the total) and Negroamaro for the reds and Fiano Minutolo and Bianco d'Alessano for the whites. The grapes are en-

tirely picked by hand and collected into baskets and every step of the winemaking process is organized to bring out the best quality possible.

▪ **90**   Price B
Primitivo di Manduria Dolce Naturale
Lo Apu 2014

From 70 years old Primitivo grapes. Matures 5 months in barrique. Very impressive, dark red color, almost black. Prominent chocolate note, but are also present spices, tobacco and plum aromas. Very soft, sweet mouth, balanced and assisted by a vivid acidity.

■ **90**   Price B
Primitivo di Manduria Riserva 2012

100% Primitivo grapes. 90% matures 12 months in barrique and 10% in amphorae. Deep red color, impenetrable. Aromas of cherry jam, rhubarb, dry morello cherry, ripe plum, cinchona, spices and sweet tobacco. Prominent coffee aroma. Wide and full of red fruits on the palate ,soft , big structure and gentle tannins.

BOTROMAGNO

Via Archimede, 24
70024 Gravina In Puglia (BA)
Tel. +39 080 3265865
Fax +39 080 3269026
S botromagno
info@botromagno.it
www.botromagno.it
f botromagno.vignetiecantine
🐦 @BOTROMAGNOVIGNE

YEAR OF FOUNDATION **1991**
NAME OF THE OWNER **D'Agostino Family**
TOTAL BOTTLES PRODUCED **300,000**
DIRECT SALES
VISITS TO THE WINERY - RESERVATION NEEDED
HECTARES OF VINEYARD **45**
RESTAURANT

Beniamino and Alberto D'Agostino a few years back acquired a wine cooperative in Gravina and turned it into a modern winery with an eye on producing wines for export. Today, Botromagno is a well-known brand known around the world.

90   Price B
Pier delle Vigne 2012

Blend of Aglianico and Montepulciano grapes. Matures 2 years in barrique. Intense ruby red color. Very clean in the nose, at first with sour cherries, plum and mulberry aromas, then leather with vanilla and coffee. The mouth is powerful, thick and very complex that closes with a long outstretched final.

MICHELE CALÒ E FIGLI

Via Masseria Vecchia, 1
73058 Tuglie (LE)
Tel. +39 0833 596242
Fax +39 0833 381612
info@michelecalo.it
www.michelecalo.it
🇫 *vinimichelecalo*

YEAR OF FOUNDATION **1954**
NAME OF THE OWNER **Giovanni and Fernando Calò**
TOTAL BOTTLES PRODUCED **150,000**
DIRECT SALES
VISITS TO THE WINERY - RESERVATION NEEDED
HECTARES OF VINEYARD **35.7**
OLIVE OIL PRODUCTION

This famous winery in the deep Salento town of Tuglie recently turned 60 and continues to use the 'a lacrima' (teardrop) winemaking method for their rosé wines, which is the estate's specialty. But this year we have been impressed by the quality of the reds.

90   👍 Price A
Grecàntico 2013

70% of Negroamaro and 30% Malvasia Nera grapes. Matures in stainless steel for 6 months. Purple color with a very clean nose and blackberry and blueberry aromas. On the palate it's tasty, fresh and crispy, perfectly made with red fruits that come back on the finish.

88   Price A
Primiter 2013

100% Primitivo grapes. 60% of it matures in stainless steel and 40% for 12 months in barrique. Intense ruby color, very classic nose with plum, violet and tobacco aromas. The mouth is powerful with nice tannins and good complex balance.

86   👍 Price A
Mjere 2013

Blend of Negramaro and Malvasia grapes. Most of it matures in stainless steel for 1 year but a small amount of grapes mature in barrique. intense purple color with aromas of cherry, violet and spices. The mouth is lean with good acidity, tense and with a good finish.

★
CANDIDO

Via A. Diaz, 46
72025 San Donaci (BR)
Tel. +39 0831 635674
Fax +39 0831 634695
candido@candidowines.it
www.candidowines.it
🇫 *candidowines.it*

YEAR OF FOUNDATION **1929**
NAME OF THE OWNER **Alessandro and Giacomo Candido**
TOTAL BOTTLES PRODUCED **1.600,000**
DIRECT SALES
VISITS TO THE WINERY - RESERVATION NEEDED
HECTARES OF VINEYARD **140**

This is one of the most important and historic wine estates in Salento and its products have made winemaking history in Puglia. Their production is quite vast and over the years they have been able to offer good quality to a vast public.

92   Price B
Salice Salentino Immensum Riserva 2012

100% Negramaro grapes. Matures 8 months in barrique. Intense ruby red color with purple hues. Complex and rich nose with blackberry, mulberry and sweet spicy aromas. Powerful but soft mouth, fresh and with not too strong tannins. Wonderful outstretched finish and perfect persistence.

90   👍 Price A
Cappello di Prete 2012

100% Negramaro grapes. Matures in barrique. Intense ruby red color. Aromas of mulberry, tobacco, chocolate and vanilla. The mouth is balanced and compact, also warm, savory and very persistent.

90   Price A

Salice Salentino La Carta Riserva 2012

Blend of 95% Negramaro and 5% Malvasia Nera grapes. Stainless steel only. Dark ruby red color with aromas of tamarind, tobacco, leather and cocoa. Intense on the palate, full and warm, with light tannins, very persistent.

★★

CANTELE

S.P. 365, Km 1
73010 Guagnano (LE)
Tel. +39 0832 705010
Fax +39 0832 705003
cantele@cantele.it
www.cantelevini.com
🅵 *cantelevini*
🆇 *@CanteleWines*

YEAR OF FOUNDATION **1979**
NAME OF THE OWNER **Cantele Family**
TOTAL BOTTLES PRODUCED **1.600,000**
DIRECT SALES
VISITS TO THE WINERY - RESERVATION NEEDED
HECTARES OF VINEYARD **200**
RESTAURANT

The Cantele winery in Guagnano is less than 40 years old but for some time now it has been a leading force in Salento winemaking. This thanks to its founders Giovan Battista and Teresa and, today, their grandchildren and heirs, first among them Gianni Cantele who is responsible for the technical side of winemaking.

■ **93**   Price B

Fanòi 2011

100% Primitivo grapes. Matures in new and used barrique for 14 months. Purple and intense ruby red color. Rich nose with very harmonic and clean aromas of plum, laurel leafs, cinchona and tobacco. Powerful mouth but with a typical and rich tasty finish.

☐ **92**   👍 Price A

Teresa Manara Chardonnay 2015

Very lucky vintage for the most popular white wines from Puglia. 100% Chardonnay grapes. Matures in barrique for 8 months. Intense straw yellow color. Very intriguing olfactory imprint, aromas of yellow flowers and ripe exotic fruits. Important on the pal-

ate, clean and very pleasant, savory and with good acidity that makes it very interesting to drink.

 90   👍 Price A

Teresa Manara Negroamaro 2014

100% Negramaro grapes. Matures 14 months in barrique. Intense garnet ruby color. Clean and typical nose with aromas of blueberry jam, cassis and Mediterranean woods. Full, rich and savory on the plate with nice tannins and an outstretched and persistent finish.

★

CANTINE DUE PALME

Via San Marco, 130
72020 Cellino San Marco (BR)
Tel. +39 0831 617865
Fax +39 0831 617866
segreteria@cantineduepalme.it
www.cantineduepalme.it
🅵 *Cantine-Due-Palme*
🆇 *@CantineDuePalme*

YEAR OF FOUNDATION **1989**
NAME OF THE OWNER
TOTAL BOTTLES PRODUCED **10,000,000**
DIRECT SALES
VISITS TO THE WINERY - RESERVATION NEEDED
HECTARES OF VINEYARD **2,500**
CERTIFIED ORGANIC VITICULTURE

Angelo Maci is one of the saviors of winemaking in Salento. In just 15 years he has created a wine empire through the Due Palme cooperatives, one of the best examples of this form of wine production in Italy. They produce simple and everyday wines as well as some prestigious ones that have become famous the world over.

■ **92**   👍 Price A

Serre 2014

100% Susumaniello grapes. Stainless steel only. Intense ruby color. Very powerful and rich nose with aromas of currant, blackberry, spices and eucalyptus notes. Very nice on the palate, lithe and elegant, soft but fresh with a very interesting finish.

■ **90**   👍 Price A

Primitivo di Manduria Ettamiano Riserva 2013

100% Primitivo grapes. Matures 9 months in Amer-

ican durmast barrique. Purple color. Aromas of ripe fruits and roasted chocolate and vanilla. The mouth is powerful and smooth, warm but with extremely balanced.

■ 88 **Price B**

Salice Salentino Selvarossa Riserva 2013

Blend of Negroamaro and Malvasia Nera grapes. Matures for 9 months in barrique. Intense garnet red color. Warm nose with aromas of ripe red fruits, rhubarb and intense eucalyptus scents. The palate is rich and powerful with the good balance between alcohol and acidity.

CANTINE FERRI

Via Bari, 347
70010 Valenzano (BA)
Tel. +39 080 4671753
info@cantineferri.it
www.cantineferri.it
📘 *cantineferri*

YEAR OF FOUNDATION 1976
NAME OF THE OWNER Nicola Ferri
TOTAL BOTTLES PRODUCED 40,000
DIRECT SALES
VISITS TO THE WINERY
HECTARES OF VINEYARD 4
OLIVE OIL PRODUCTION

The Ferri family has been growing grapes and making wine since the start of the 20th century in the agricultural area of Adelfia, in the province of Bari. In the 1970s they moved near Valenzano where they built their current winery and cellars, which can hold up to some 6,000 hectoliters, not far from the 11th century Romanesque abbey of Ognissanti di Cuti. They mostly work with native grapes like Primitivo, Negroamaro, Nero di Troia, Bombino Nero and Bianco, Verdeca and Moscato but also cultivate and make wines from Chardonnay, Garganega, Cabernet Sauvignon, Montepulciano and Sangiovese.

■ 91 **Price B**

Gioia del Colle Primitivo Memor 2012

100% Primitivo grapes from centenarian vineyard. Stainless steel only. Intense red color, almost impenetrable. Very intense and warm aromas of plum, morello, cherry compote. On the palate results full, warm and complete. Impressively powerful.

■ 89 **Price A**

Oblivio Nero di Troia 2011

100% Nero di Troia grapes from very old vineyards. Bright scarlet red. Rich and multicolored nose that reminds the wines from the north: herbs, ripe black cherry, nice eucalyptus hint. Powerful on the palate, with nice silky tannins, agile and elegant. One of the best versions ever.

CARVINEA

Via per Serranova, 1
72012 Carovigno (BR)
Tel. + 39 080 5862345
Fax + 39 080 5322247
info@carvinea.com
www.carvinea.com
📘 *Carvinea*
🐦 *@carvinea*

YEAR OF FOUNDATION 2002
NAME OF THE OWNER Beppe di Maria
TOTAL BOTTLES PRODUCED 50,000
DIRECT SALES
VISITS TO THE WINERY - RESERVATION NEEDED
HECTARES OF VINEYARD 9
OLIVE OIL PRODUCTION

A new entry in the guide for this estate that produces wine in Carovigno, in the province of Brindisi. It is the brainchild of the wise and foresighted businessman Beppe Di Maria who had the patience to wait and build, with the help of Riccardo Cotarella, a solid winemaking reality. The Ottavianello grape is at the center of production and the results are truly encouraging.

■ 93 **Price B**

Otto 2014

100% Ottavianello grapes. Matures 12 months in big barrels and barrique. Intense ruby color. Light aromatic impact. Clean aromas of cherry with red fruits and sweet spices. Rich on the palate but easy to drink and harmonic and fresh, perfect balance, with a long finish and good persistence.

▨ 90 **Price B**

MerulaRosa 2015

100% Montepulciano grapes. Matures in stainless steel. Bright cherry color. At the nose is intriguing with a predominant spicy aroma. The mouth is intriguing, very fresh, simple but not trivial.

90   **Price A**

Primitivo 2014

100% Primitivo grape. Matures in French durmast barrique for 12 months. Intense purple color. Sweet spices and red fruit aromas. Thick on the palate, rich and perfectly made, savory with light tannins, with balanced acidity, good persistence and good finish.

★

CASTELLO MONACI

Via Case Sparse - Contrada Monaci
73015 Salice Salentino (LE)
Tel. +39 0831 665700
castello.monaci@giv.it
www.castellomonaci.it
 Cantine-Castello-Monaci
 @castellomonaci

YEAR OF FOUNDATION 1480
NAME OF THE OWNER Gruppo Italiano Vini
TOTAL BOTTLES PRODUCED 2,000,000
DIRECT SALES
VISITS TO THE WINERY - RESERVATION NEEDED
HECTARES OF VINEYARD 200
HOSPITALITY
RESTAURANT

Vitantonio Seracca Guerrieri and his wife Lina Memmo, the last descendent of the ancient proprietors, are the lucky owners of this castle in this incredible setting near Salice Salentino. Castello Monaci is a 16th century fortress that has been restored several times. It is surrounded by vineyards as far as the eye can see, some 200 hectares, and today is part of the Gruppo Italiano Vini which handles the winemaking and sales.

 92   **Price A**

Salice Salentino Aiace Riserva 2013

Blend of Negramaro and Malvasia Nera grapes. Matures in new and used barrique. Intense garnet color. Aromas of macerated cherry, carob , spices and eucalyptus hints. The palate is soft and savory with a great balance.

 90   **Price A**

Maru 2015

100% Negramaro grapes. Matures for 6 months in barrique and part in stainless steel. Very dark color with aromas of plum and black cherry, complex eu-

calyptus and spicy notes. Warm, powerful but really rich and persistent.

☐ **88** **Price A**

Petraluce 2015

100% Verdeca grapes. Matures in stainless steel. Light golden yellow color. Clean and interesting nose with aromas of pineapple, white peach and citrus. Balanced, fresh and savory mouth, pleasant to drink with a nice aromatic finish.

★

CHIAROMONTE

Contrada Borgo Annunziata (Z.I.)
70021 Acquaviva delle Fonti (BA)
Tel. +39 080 3050432
Fax +39 080 3050432
 tenutechiaromonte
info@tenutechiaromonte.com
www.tenutechiaromonte.com
 tenutechiaromonte1
 @NicolaTenute

YEAR OF FOUNDATION 1826
NAME OF THE OWNER Nicola Chiaromonte
TOTAL BOTTLES PRODUCED 60,000
DIRECT SALES
VISITS TO THE WINERY - RESERVATION NEEDED
HECTARES OF VINEYARD 27
RESTAURANT

This winery is in Gioia del Colle and area that had the first DOC for Primitivo, which was then followed by Manduria in the province of Taranto. Nicola Chiaromonte likes to surprise and provoke. The exasperated organoleptic characteristics of his wines are never an end to themselves but are unique and describe how he sees and likes to convey his beloved land. He has come a long way in 18 years and we are convinced he will still go far.

■ 🍷 **97** **Price C**

Gioia del Colle Primitivo Riserva 2011

100% Primitivo grapes. Matures in barrique and big barrels. Very dark ruby color. Wonderful nose with amazing aromas of ripe fruits, blueberry, morello, carob and tamarind, Mediterranean woods, cinnamon and nutmeg. The palate has a strong impact, very rich and amazing to drink. Gorgeous.

■ 93   Price B

Gioia del Colle Primitivo Muro Sant'Angelo Contrada Barbatto 2013

100% Primitivo grapes. Matures in stainless steel. Very typical dark color. Intense nose with aromas of sour cherry, dry figs, chocolate and ink. The palate is powerful and elegant with an evident fruit note and very typical. Very long finish.

■ 90   👍 Price A

Primitivo Elè 2014

100% Primitivo grapes. Matures in stainless steel. Black color with shades of purple. Classic aromas of plum, spices an licorice, very balanced mouth, well made, full but tense with an hint of sweetness at the end.

COLLI DELLA MURGIA

Contrada Zingariello
70024 Gravina In Puglia (BA)
Tel. +39 080 3261271
info@collidellamurgia.it
www.collidellamurgia.it
f colli.dellamurgia

YEAR OF FOUNDATION 1998
NAME OF THE OWNER Enrico Malgi
TOTAL BOTTLES PRODUCED 125,000
DIRECT SALES
VISITS TO THE WINERY - RESERVATION NEEDED
HECTARES OF VINEYARD 15
CERTIFIED ORGANIC VITICULTURE

The Colli della Murgia borders with the Bosco Difesa Grande nature reserve and is among the first to make organic wines exploiting the area's typical, earthy and chalky soil, rich in iron, and with an agricultural approach that allows the vines to have deep roots and obtain everything needed for the grapes to express their full potential. These strong and healthy vines produce a lively wine that represents in the best way the relationship between the land and local culture.

☐ 90   👍 Price A

Tufjano 2015

100% Fiano Minutolo grapes. Matures in stainless steel. Golden yellow color. Typical nose with complex aromas of exotic fruits, yellow flowers and honey. Juicy mouth, elegant, fresh and savory.

☐ 88   Price A

Erbaceo 2015

Blend of Fiano Minutolo and Greco grapes. Matures in stainless steel. Straw yellow color. Aromas of white fruits, flowers and cut grass. The palate is tasty and crisp, fresh and elegant with a nice savory in the finish.

★★
CONTI ZECCA

Via Cesarea
73045 Leverano (LE)
Tel. +39 0832 925613
Fax +39 0832 922606
S conti.zecca
info@contizecca.it
www.contizecca.it
f conti.zecca
@conti_zecca

YEAR OF FOUNDATION 1935
NAME OF THE OWNER Conti Zecca
TOTAL BOTTLES PRODUCED 2.800,000
DIRECT SALES
VISITS TO THE WINERY - RESERVATION NEEDED
HECTARES OF VINEYARD 320
OLIVE OIL PRODUCTION

This winery has been operating for 80 years maintaining consistent quality in all its wines, which are for the most part made with local grapes. Their top wine is Nero, a blend of Negroamaro and Cabernet Sauvignon which has an international by territorial style. The winery has decided to postpone the release of 2013 vintage so their Nero skips this edition of the guide.

■ 90   Price B

Terra 2013

Blend of 85% Aglianico and Negroamaro grapes. Matures for 14 months in barrique and 16 months in 30hl oak barrels. Very dark ruby color. Typical and complex nose with aromas of sour cherry, tamarind, vanilla and leather. On the palate it is perfectly made, elegant and easy to drink with a long and outstretched finish.

☐ 88   Price A

Luna 2015

Blend of Chardonnay and Malvasia grapes. Matures

6 months in barrique. Intense straw yellow color. The nose is clean and elegant with aromatic notes and citrus, fruits and honey. The palate is fresh, easy to drink but important.

■ 86   👍 Price A
Cantalupi Negroamaro 2014

100% Negramaro grapes. Matures for 12 months in 30 hl barrels and then in underground concrete vats. Intense garnet ruby red color. Aromas of sour cherry and aromatic herbs. Smooth on the palate for a wine that confirms the clean, honest style of the producer. Perfect to drink.

COPPADORO

Via Marzio Tremaglia, 30
71016 San Severo (FG)
Tel. +39 0882 223174
Fax +39 0882 405111
info@tenutacoppadoro.it
www.tenutacoppadoro.it
🅵 CapitanataAgricolaSanSevero

YEAR OF FOUNDATION 2001
NAME OF THE OWNER Pisante and Sannella Families
TOTAL BOTTLES PRODUCED 600,000
DIRECT SALES
VISITS TO THE WINERY - RESERVATION NEEDED
HECTARES OF VINEYARD 148
OLIVE OIL PRODUCTION

This splendid estate in northern Puglia has risen from the ashes with new owners and the same enologist, Riccardo Cotarella. The wines have a new imprint characterized by a pleasing drinkability and a good quality/price ratio.

☐ 88   👍 Price A
Ratino Bombino 2015

100% Bombino Bianco grapes. Matures in stainless steel only. Light straw yellow color. Clear fruity aromas with notes of cedar and fragrant fermentative notes. Savory, fresh with a nice acidity that makes it easier to drink. Thin finish.

☐ 87   👍 Price A
Diomede Vermentino 2015

100% Vermentino grapes. Shiny straw yellow color. Aromas of citrus and grapefruit, tense and savory on the palate, very pleasant and easy to drink.

D'ALFONSO DEL SORDO

Contrada Sant'Antonino
71016 San Severo (FG)
Tel. +39 0882 221444
info@dalfonsodelsordo.it
www.dalfonsodelsordo.it
🅵 cantinedalfonsodelsordo

YEAR OF FOUNDATION 1957
NAME OF THE OWNER Gianfelice and Celeste D'Alfonso del Sordo
TOTAL BOTTLES PRODUCED 300,000
DIRECT SALES
VISITS TO THE WINERY - RESERVATION NEEDED
HECTARES OF VINEYARD 45
HOSPITALITY
RESTAURANT
OLIVE OIL PRODUCTION

An authentic prototype of a family history that is also the history of wine. It brought together what was created by Baron Alfonso del Sordo, when the estate was founded in the middle of the 19th century, and the winemaking skills of Ludovico D'Alfonso. At the beginning of the 20th century, in fact, the two families joined forces to create the D'Alfono del Sordo whose heir, Antonio del Sordo, in the middle of the 20th century, created the conditions to expand the historic estate. It is situated in the farmlands of San Severo and composed of three farms with different vineyards and grapes typical to the area. Ample attention is also paid to study and research, in collaboration with the University of Foggia, which seeks to enhance the value of Nero di Troia, an historic local varietal.

■ 90   👍 Price A
Guado San Leo 2013

100% Nero di Troia grapes from Coppanetta estate. Matures in barrique for at least 9 months. Clean aromas of morello, blueberry and violet, with an hint of pepper and cinnamon. Full and outstretched palate, tannic but soft. Intense and fruity finish.

■ 88   👍 Price A
Casteldrione 2014

100% Nero di Troia grapes from Coppanetta estate. Matures in barrique for at least 9 months. Clean aromas of morello, blueberry and violet, with an hint of pepper and cinnamon. Full and outstretched palate, tannic but soft. Intense and fruity finish.

D'ARAPRÌ

Via Michele Zannotti, 30
71016 San Severo (FG)
Tel. +39 0882 227643
info@darapri.it
www.darapri.it
f *dAraprì-Spumante-Metodo-Classico-San-Severo*
𝕏 *@dAapriSpumanti*

YEAR OF FOUNDATION **1979**
NAME OF THE OWNER **Girolamo D'Amico, Louis Rapini and Ulrico Priore**
TOTAL BOTTLES PRODUCED **80,000**
DIRECT SALES
VISITS TO THE WINERY - RESERVATION NEEDED
HECTARES OF VINEYARD **7**

The d'Araprì winery is at the center of northern Tavoliere and its name is composed of the first letters of the surnames of its three partner: Girolamo, Luis and Ulrico. In 1979, when these 'bubbly' friends were in their mid-20s, they decided to unite their passions for jazz and wine. And they had the courageous and brilliant idea, which was unusual for the area and the times, of making sparkling wines out of the traditional grapes using the traditional or 'Champenoise' method. While this at first seem extravagant, the results were unique and paid off. Their cellars are in a very suggestive place, a wonderful cavern that in part dates back to the end of the 16th century.

🔲 **92** Price B
Spumante Metodo Classico Gran Cuvèe XXI Secolo 2009

Blend of Bombino Bianco, Pinot Nero and Montepulciano grapes that lie on yeast for 60 months. Intense gold color with light perlage. Very complex at the nose, aromas of citrus and honey, bread and hazelnut. Creamy on the palate, savory and fresh, with a very elegant carbonic feeling. Another amazing sparkling wine this year.

🔲 **90** Price B
Spumante Metodo Classico Riserva Nobile 2011

100% Bombino Bianco grapes. Classic method. The color is bright light gold and the perlage is thick and long. At the nose is complex with aromas of yeast, fruits and yellow plum. the mouth is lively with a very long and surprising finish.

DUCA CARLO GUARINI

Largo Frisari, 1
73020 Scorrano (LE)
Tel. +39 0836 460288
info@ducacarloguarini.it
www.ducacarloguarini.it
f *duca.guarini*

YEAR OF FOUNDATION **1065**
NAME OF THE OWNER **Guarini Family**
TOTAL BOTTLES PRODUCED **300,000**
DIRECT SALES
VISITS TO THE WINERY
HECTARES OF VINEYARD **70**
CERTIFIED ORGANIC VITICULTURE
OLIVE OIL PRODUCTION

Substance reigns behind the lofty name of this estate. Historic substance because the Guarini family moved from Normandy to Puglia, more specifically Salento, soon after the year 1000. And productive substance because the wines are for the most part made from native grapes including Primitivo and Negroamaro. Special mention should be made of his pricing policy which has kept them low.

◼ **90** 👍 Price A
Nativo Bio 2013

100% Negroamaro grapes. Matures in stainless steel. Intense garnet ruby color. Rich and ethereal nose with aromas of plum and dark cherry. Compact, rich and warm on the palate. Reallly persistent.

◼ **88** Price A
Malìa Bio 2013

100% Malvasia Nera grapes. Matures in stainless steel. Purple color with a very rich aroma of ripe red fruits and spices. Soft, fresh and easy to drink on the palate with the pepper notes that come back in the finish.

FATALONE

Strada Vicinale Spinomarino, 291
70023 Gioia del Colle (BA)
Tel. +39 080 3448037
Ⓢ *ppetrera-fatalonewine*
info@fatalone.it
www.fatalone.it
f *FataloneWines*
𝕏 *@FataloneWines*

YEAR OF FOUNDATION **1987**
NAME OF THE OWNER **Orfino Rosa and Petrera Family**
TOTAL BOTTLES PRODUCED **50,000**
DIRECT SALES
VISITS TO THE WINERY - RESERVATION NEEDED
HECTARES OF VINEYARD **8.5**
CERTIFIED ORGANIC VITICULTURE
OLIVE OIL PRODUCTION

The estate's brand name is a reference to Filippo Petrera who in his time was nicknamed Il Fatalone, which in local dialect meant The Seducer. Great attention is paid to the vineyards where the artisan winemaker, as Pasquale Petrera like to define himself, takes maniacal care of his plants to have grapes that he can pay the same attention to in the winery. He uses mostly stainless steel vats but allows his wine to age for two-three months in large barrels of Slovenian oak accompanied by classical and new age music along with sounds of nature as a means of improving, with pleasing vibrations, the living microflora in the wine and the micro-oxidation through the wood.

---

 93   Price B

Gioia del Colle Primitivo Riserva 2010

100% Primitivo grapes. Matures 1 year in stainless steel and 1 year in 750 l Slavonia barrels. Dark ruby color. Very intense typical aromas: plum, mulberry, carob and smoky aromas. Very strong in the mouth, balanced and soft, with a deep and long finish and light eucalyptus aromas.

■ 91   Price B

Gioia del Colle Primitivo Riserva 2009

100% Primitivo grapes. Matures for 6 months in stainless steel and for another 6 moths in Slavonia durmast barrels. Very dark color. The nose presents aromas of red fruits, violet and chocolate. Fat and deep mouth, very typical, with good freshness and balance, the tannins are well absorbed.

★★★

GIANFRANCO FINO

Via Piave, 12
74028 Sava (TA)
Tel. +39 099 7773970
Fax +39 099 7773970
🇸 *gianfrancofinoviticultore*
info@gianfrancofino.it

www.gianfrancofino.it
🇫 *gianfranco.fino.3*
🐦 *@gianfrancofino*

YEAR OF FOUNDATION **2004**
NAME OF THE OWNER **Gianfranco Fino**
TOTAL BOTTLES PRODUCED **20,000**
VISITS TO THE WINERY - RESERVATION NEEDED
HECTARES OF VINEYARD **14.5**

Up until a few years ago, the winemaking aristocracy in Puglia thought they had had nothing to worry about, perhaps too much so, then, suddenly, young producers began emerging who in a very short time climbed up the rankings and surpassed the old wines and territories. If one had to name just one of these producers and one wine then it would without a doubt be that of Gianfranco Fino and his Es.

■ 96   Price C

Primitivo di Manduria Es 2014

100% Primitivo grapes. Matures in barrique for 9 months. Very intense ruby color. Clean and full-flavored in the nose. Mon-cherrie aromas, with sour cherry compote and strawberry. Firm and rich taste with less residual sugar of other versions, strong but agile body with a warm long finish.

■ 92   Price B

Negroamaro Jo 2014

100% Negramaro grapes. Matures 1 year in barrique. Intense garnet ruby color. On the nose it is spicy, varietal, with tamarind, dry plum aromas as well as raspberry and wild strawberry. Full-flavored, warm, stretch taste with a good savory body.

★★

SEVERINO GAROFANO - TENUTA MONACI

Località Tenuta Monaci
73043 Copertino (LE)
Tel. +39 0832 947512
Fax +39 0832 1830364
vini@aziendamonaci.com
garofano.aziendamonaci.com
🇫 *AziendaMonaci.Vini*
🐦 *@girofles*

YEAR OF FOUNDATION **1995**
NAME OF THE OWNER **Garofano Family**

TOTAL BOTTLES PRODUCED **220,000**
DIRECT SALES
VISITS TO THE WINERY - RESERVATION NEEDED
HECTARES OF VINEYARD **36**

Severino Garofano is an enologist who in the past decades has created the greatest Puglia wines, so much so that the history of Puglia winemaking can be divided into before and after him. For a few years now he has stopped working for other estates and set up his own in Salento, in Copertino, where his is joined by his son Stefano and daughter Renata. Needless to say, production is dominated by Negroamaro and the results are often exhilarating.

 92   Price B
Le Braci 2010

100% overripe Negroamaro grapes. Matures in barrique. Intense ruby color with purple reflexes. The bouquet is complex, thick and intense with aromas of fruits as well as chocolate, vanilla, cinchona and mint. Graceful and strong mouth, of big impact and elegant, sweet on the finish.

 90   Price A
Girofle 2015

100% Negramaro grapes. Matures in stainless steel. Bright and full coral pink color. Intense aromas of flower and wild strawberry. Rich, fresh and fragrant mouth, savory and balanced taste. A quality pleadge rosé wine year after year.

 88   Price A
Copertino Negroamaro Eloquenzia 2011

100% Negramaro grapes. Matures in stainless steel. Intense ruby color. Clean on the nose with aromas of black cherry, coffee beans and leather. The mouth is powerful, pleasant to drink with a long convincing finish.

ROMALDO GRECO

Via Santa Maria, 14
73050 Seclì (LE)
Tel. +39 0836 554895
info@romaldogreco.it
www.romaldogreco.it
 f *romaldogreco*
 𝕏 *@RomaldoGreco*

YEAR OF FOUNDATION **1973**
NAME OF THE OWNER **Greco Family**

TOTAL BOTTLES PRODUCED **60,000**
DIRECT SALES
VISITS TO THE WINERY - RESERVATION NEEDED
HECTARES OF VINEYARD **13**

A small estate that has made its debut on the new Puglia winemaking scene where research is aimed at achieving elegance even in areas where, while there is no lack of alcohol or sugars, the flavor and aromas of the wines tend to be heavy. The aim of father Romaldo and, above all, his son Antongiulio is to avoid this excessive tendency. The result is Era, the estate's top Primitivo, which attentively unites boldness with elegance. The vineyards are all spur and cordon trained with a density of some 4,500 vines per hectare. Aside from local varietals like Negroamaro and Primitivo, they also cultivate 'foreign' varieties like Syrah, Cabernet and Merlot. The quality/price ration of the wines is very good.

 90   Price B
Era 2012

100% Primitivo grapes. Matures in barrique. Dark ruby color. Clean and intense with light aromas of spices, underbrush, fur and eucalyptus hints. The taste is rich and intense but never sickly, an unexpected elegance for the area. The tannin is polite with the right acidy. Elegant and savory. Firm finish.

   89   Price A
Duodecim 2015

100% Negramaro grapes. Stainless steel only. Bright cherry red color. Clean and intense on the nose with light aromas of red fruits and aromatic herbs. Very punchy and pleasant. Savory taste with an elegant tannin and a wide and pleasant body. Tasty and savory finish.

LEONE DE CASTRIS

Via Senatore De Castris, 26
73015 Salice Salentino (LE)
Tel. +39 0832 731112
Fax +39 0832 731114
 S *leonedecastris*
marketing@leonedecastris.com
www.leonedecastris.com
 f *LeoneDeCastrisSrl*
 𝕏 *@leonedecastris*

YEAR OF FOUNDATION 1665
NAME OF THE OWNER Piernicola Leone De Castris
TOTAL BOTTLES PRODUCED 2.500,000
DIRECT SALES
VISITS TO THE WINERY - RESERVATION NEEDED
HECTARES OF VINEYARD 300
RESTAURANT
OLIVE OIL PRODUCTION

Piernicola Leone De Castris is a descendent of Salento winemakers whose origins go back three centuries and who made a decisive and contribution to winegrowing and winemaking in Puglia. Today he heads a modern and efficient winery producing prestigious wines that do honor to his historic roots.

■ 93 👍 Price A
Salice Salentino 50° Vendemmia Riserva 2014

100% Negramaro and Malvasia Nera grapes. Matures 1 year in barrique. Very powerful, complex and convincing nose with aromas of balck cherry, nutmeg, tobacco and leather. The mouth is imposing, rich and full but with a good balance and acidity that makes it harmonic. Very good finish.

▥ 90 👍 Price A
Rosato Five Roses 72° Anniversario 2015

Blend of 80% Negramaro and Malvasia Nera grapes. Matures in stainless steel. Coral color. Clean aromas of cherry, raspberries and ash. The palate is fresh, tasty, crispy and full with a little hint of savory.

ALBERTO LONGO

S.P. 5 - Lucera-Pietra - Km 4
71036 Lucera (FG)
Tel. +39 0881 539057
🔵 *alberto.longo58*
info@albertolongo.it
www.albertolongo.it
📘 *vinialbertolongo*
🐦 *@CantineLongo*

YEAR OF FOUNDATION 2000
NAME OF THE OWNER Alberto Longo
TOTAL BOTTLES PRODUCED 180,000
DIRECT SALES
VISITS TO THE WINERY - RESERVATION NEEDED
HECTARES OF VINEYARD 35

HOSPITALITY
RESTAURANT
OLIVE OIL PRODUCTION

Say what you will about producer Alberto Longo but not that he hasn't made great economic and technological investments in his estate in Lucera. The location is enchanting and he expanded an ancient structure making it a thoroughly contemporary one. The intermingling between the old and the new is a common thread that runs through all his production and is evidenced in his wines.

☐ 91 👍 Price A
Le Valli 2015

Belnd of 90% Bombino Bianco and Moscato grapes. Matures in stainless steel. Intense straw yellow color. Very clean nose. Elegant and slightly aromatic with aromas of flowers and fruits. The palate is soft with a semi structured body, fresh and savory finish.

☐ 90 👍 Price A
Falanghina Le Fossette 2015

100% Falanghina grapes. Matures 4 months on yeast in stainless steel. Intense straw yellow color. Very good confirmation for a white that ,this year as well, we really appreciated. The nose has aromas of white fruits, pineapple and grapefruit, wild flowers and rosemary. Fresh and savory on the palate.

■ 88 Price A
Cacc'e mmitte di Lucera 2014

Blend of Nero di Troia, Montepucliano with a hint of Bombino Bianco grapes. Matures in concrete vats. Intense ruby color. Morello cherry and tobacco notes. The mouth is intense, typical, a little rustic but very pleasant.

■ 88 Price A
Capoposto 2013

100% Negroamaro grapes. Matures in concrete vats for almost 8 months. Intense ruby color. Aromas of dry figs and chocolate. Fresh on the palate with sweet tannins and soft finish, very well balanced.

MASSERIA L'ASTORE

Via G. Di Vittorio, 1
73020 Cutrofiano (LE)
Tel. +39 0836 542020

Fax +39 0836 541525
🅢 *lastoremasseria*
info@lastoremasseria.it
www.lastoremasseria.it
🅕 *lastoremasseria*
🐦 *@lastoremasseria*

YEAR OF FOUNDATION 1936
NAME OF THE OWNER Benegiamo Family
TOTAL BOTTLES PRODUCED 90,000
DIRECT SALES
VISITS TO THE WINERY
HECTARES OF VINEYARD 15
HOSPITALITY
RESTAURANT
CERTIFIED ORGANIC VITICULTURE
OLIVE OIL PRODUCTION

The Benegiamo family has owned this ancient masseria farm complex since 1935 but only relatively recently did they decide to produce quality wine, embarking on a virtuous path of growth which, in turn, led them to make some important changes. Now that their direction is clear, we can confirm that they have opted for indigenous grapes and a traditional approach.

---

90   Price B
Alberelli di Negroamaro 2012

100% Negroamaro grapes. Matures in stainless steel. Dark red color with purple shades. Dynamic and intense on the nose with typical fruits aromas as well as macerated cherries, violet, sweet tobacco and cinnamon. The mouth has a strong body and is very rich, persistent and convincing in the finish.

☐ **85**   👍 Price A
Krita 2014

100% Malvasia Bianca grapes. Matures in stainless steel. Light straw yellow color. The nose is elegant, clean and very aromatic with notes of pineapple, yellow peach and melon. The mouth is fresh with the sweetness and savory that lead to a perfect finish.

★

MASSERIA LI VELI

S.P. Cellino-Campi, km 1
72020 Cellino San Marco (BR)
Tel. +39 0831 618259
Fax +39 0831 616657
🅢 *masserialiveli*

info@liveli.it
www.liveli.it
🅕 Masseria-Li-Veli

YEAR OF FOUNDATION 1999
NAME OF THE OWNER Falvo Family
TOTAL BOTTLES PRODUCED 350,000
DIRECT SALES
VISITS TO THE WINERY - RESERVATION NEEDED
HECTARES OF VINEYARD 33
CERTIFIED ORGANIC VITICULTURE

The Falvo family have found in this masseria farm house in Cellino San Marco the ideal location to continue their winemaking activities after the important experience they gained in other areas of Italy known for quality wine production. In order to produce their modern-style wines, they have focused on local grapes from vineyards in the areas that are traditionally the best for them. This mix of modernity and tradition has struck a proper balance.

---

92   👍 Price A
Askos Susumaniello 2015

100% Susumaniello grapes. Matures in durmast barrels for 9 months. Intense purple color. Very complex nose with aromas of cherry, morello, then aromas of carob, cassis, leather and tobacco. Juicy, elegant and fresh on the palate, perfectly balanced by the richness of the nose. A very nice suprise.

---

92   Price B
Salice Salentino Pezzo Morgana Riserva 2014

100% Negroamaro grapes. Matures in French barrique for over 12 months. Dark red ruby color. It presents very intense aromas of black cherry, toasted aromas and tobacco. The mouth is powerful and warm. Very deep and persistent finish.

---

91   Price B
MLV Masseria Li Veli 2013

Blend of 85% of Negroamaro and Cabernet Sauvignon grapes. Matures in new barrique for 18 months. This is the label dedicated to the founder of the estate. Very dark ruby color. On the nose very intense aromas of spices, vanilla and eucalyptus note. The mouth is well structured but well balanced and pleasant with a persistent and a long final.

---

90   👍 Price A
Rosato Li Veli 2015

100% Negramaro grapes. Matures in stainless

steel. Salmon pink color. The nose is intense and pleasant, very fresh with aromas of fruits, very whole and composed to drink, the finish is fruity, very attractive.

MASSERIA TRULLO DI PEZZA

Contrada Trullo di Pezza
74020 Torricella (TA)
Tel. +39 099 9872011
info@trullodipezza.com
www.trullodipezza.com
Trullo-Di-Pezza-Vini
@Trullodipezza

YEAR OF FOUNDATION 2012
NAME OF THE OWNER Marika and Simona Lacaita
TOTAL BOTTLES PRODUCED 60,000
DIRECT SALES
VISITS TO THE WINERY - RESERVATION NEEDED
HECTARES OF VINEYARD 50
HOSPITALITY
RESTAURANT
CERTIFIED ORGANIC VITICULTURE
OLIVE OIL PRODUCTION

This young estate has only been bottling its wine since 2012 and is named after the name of the Lacaita family's 'masseria' farm. And it fully reflects its historic characteristics and solid foundation with character and typicity in an area filled with the typical Trullo circular farmhouses and memories of a farming past. All the wines are organically produced using native grapes that grow in sunny vineyards near the sea, where the soil is rich in iron minerals, and they are as elegant as the land they are made in.

☐ 90   👍 Price A
Dieci Grana 2015
100% fiano grapes. Matures in stainless steel. Delicate straw yellow color. Fresh on the nose with aromas of white flowers, with peach and mulberries, an hint of mint. On the palate the freshness comes back with aromas of white fruits, juicy peach, melon, and wild herbs. Savory, tense with a perfect acidity and a good finish

■ 90   👍 Price A
Mezza Pezza 2014
100% Primitivo grapes that matures in stainless steel. Purple ruby red color. On the nose it offers clear and typical aromas of the grape with mature

plum, dry figs, and cinnamon. The mouth is full with a pleasant sweetness as well as a good acidity that support the full body.

■ 88   Price A
Primitivo di Manduria Licurti 2014
100% Primitivo grapes. Matures in barrique for 6 months. Intense garnet color. The nose has a good impact with aromas of morello, cinchona, toasted notes. The palate is thick, full-flavored, warm and soft with the presence of tannins. The finish has a good persistance.

PIETRAVENTOSA

Strada Vicinale Latta
70023 Gioia del Colle (BA)
Tel. +39 335 5730274
Fax +39 080 5034436
info@pietraventosa.it
www.pietraventosa.it
Agricole.Pietraventosa
@pietraventosa

YEAR OF FOUNDATION 2005
NAME OF THE OWNER Marianna Annio
TOTAL BOTTLES PRODUCED 16,000
VISITS TO THE WINERY - RESERVATION NEEDED
HECTARES OF VINEYARD 5.4
CERTIFIED ORGANIC VITICULTURE
OLIVE OIL PRODUCTION

The Pietraventosa winery is west of Gioia del Colle and has five and a half hectares of land in the heart of the rocky area of Murgiana to produce great wines even using young grapes. Young because Marianna Annio, the owner of this winery is a woman 'in a hurry' who aspires to obtain great results and has the patience to get them. The vineyard is cord-trained and spur-pruned and she has another older one that is a hectare in size and only grows Primitivo, which as tradition dictates is alberello trained.

■ 92   Price B
Ossimoro 2012
Blend of Primitivo and Aglianico grapes that matures, in equal parts, in stainless steel as well as in barrique. Intense ruby red color. Aromas of morello, chocolate, black pepper and nutmeg. The fruit is very present and of a great quality and balance , that gives to the wine a soft and attractive finish.

PIETREGIOVANI

Via O. Marzano, 34
70125 Bari (BA)
Tel. +39 080 9752924
customer@pietregiovani.com
ww.pietregiovani.com
 az.agr.pietregiovani

YEAR OF FOUNDATION 2009
NAME OF THE OWNER Fabio Pietrogiovanni
TOTAL BOTTLES PRODUCED 12,000
DIRECT SALES
VISITS TO THE WINERY - RESERVATION NEEDED
HECTARES OF VINEYARD 3.5
OLIVE OIL PRODUCTION

Fabio Pietrogiovanni is the 'architect' of Pietregiovani who returned to Salentino and his cultural roots and set up and estate in 2009. It is distinguished by its young freshness and imagination both in its products and management. While 'young', the estate is as solid as a rock (pietra).

 92   Price A
Primitivo 2013

Great debut for this 100% Primitivo grapes wine. Matures 12 months in stainless steel. Clean, fine and very typical nose with aromas of red plum, figs, cinnamon and licorice. The palate is full-flavored and structured but balanced with light tannins and a very persistent finish.

 91   Price A
Negroamaro 2013

100% Negramaro grapes that mature in stainless steel. Intense ruby red. The nose is clearly aromatic, with fruits, flowers and spices aroma in great harmony between them. The mouth is juicy and rich, easy to drink with an hint of briny that completes the aromatic profile.

PLANTAMURA

Via Santa Candida, 1
70023 Gioia del Colle (BA)
Tel. +39 347 4711027
info@viniplantamura.it
www.viniplantamura.it

YEAR OF FOUNDATION 2002
NAME OF THE OWNER Plantamura Family

TOTAL BOTTLES PRODUCED **48,000**
DIRECT SALES
VISITS TO THE WINERY - RESERVATION NEEDED
HECTARES OF VINEYARD **8**
CERTIFIED ORGANIC VITICULTURE

There are very few estates in Puglia that are run by women but Mariangela Plantamura has a great passion for her land and for her Primitivo. Her husband Vincenzo plays an important role and together they run every phase of production, from the vineyards to the cellar. And they do this by respecting the environment and following simple and traditional rules that were handed down from her grandparents, using an old, wooden press to ensure a soft pressing. After years of producing bulk wine, in 2005 they decided to bottle their wine and embark on a great, new adventures with excellent results.

 94   Price A
Gioia del Colle Primitivo Contrada San Pietro Riserva 2013

100% Primitivo grapes. Matures 1 year in stainless steel. Very dark ruby color. Aromas of great impact: black cherry, mulberries, tamarind, spices aromas with eucalyptus taste underneath. The palate is typically sweet but rich and very well balanced even if is a full body wine with a strong presence of alcohol. Simply delicious.

 92   Price A
Gioia del Colle Primitivo Parco Largo 2015

100% Primitivo grapes matured in stainless steel. Strong ruby color. On the nose is very typical with plum, red fruits, black pepper and cinnamon aromas. The mouth is soft, warm but very harmonic and sweet, it is well balance by a great acidity with a long finish and very pleasant.

POLVANERA

Strada Vicinale Lamie Marchesana, 601
70023 Gioia del Colle (BA)
Tel. +39 080 758900
Fax +39 080 2140523
info@cantinepolvanera.it
www.cantinepolvanera.it
 Cantine-Polvanera

YEAR OF FOUNDATION 2002
NAME OF THE OWNER Filippo Cassano
TOTAL BOTTLES PRODUCED 200,000
DIRECT SALES
VISITS TO THE WINERY
HECTARES OF VINEYARD 70
RESTAURANT
CERTIFIED ORGANIC VITICULTURE
OLIVE OIL PRODUCTION

Filippo Cassano, the estate owner and enologist is one of the 'young lions' of Puglia winemaking, one who has very clear ideas of what he wants: all his 70 hectares of vineyards must be organic and the wines they produce must communicate the land they were made in. Naturally, the best are the Primitivo ones but the estate's vast range of whites are also making a name for themselves.

---

 95   Price A

Gioia del Colle Primitivo 14 Vigneto Marchesana 2013

100% Primitivo grapes. Matures in stainless steel for 16 months. Very dark ruby red color. The nose is strong, elegant and very rich with aromas of mature fruits as well as pepper, nutmeg, cinnamon and dry figs. The mouth is a triumph, of strong impact and typicality ,warm soft and with an hint of sweetness that makes the wine delicious. Great finish, great wine.

---

94   Price B

Gioia del Colle Primitivo 17 Vigneto Montevella 2013

100% Primitivo grapes that mature in steel for 18 months. The color is very dark. Very powerful aromas of blackberry, sour cherry, tobacco, licorice, and spices. The mouth is rich and warm, it is full and alcoholic but magically well balanced by a persistent freshness.

---

93   Price B

Gioia del Colle Primitivo 16 Vigneto San Benedetto 2013

100% Primitivo grapes. Matures in stainless steel for 16 months. The color is very dark. The nose is fruity with aromas of sour cherry compote and figs in the background. The mouth is firm, warm, powerful but very tense and wide. Long and persistent finish.

 ★★

RIVERA

S.P. 231, km 60,500
76123 Andria (BT)
Tel. +39 0883 569510
info@rivera.it
www.rivera.it
f *Vini-Rivera*
y *@CantineRivera*

YEAR OF FOUNDATION 1950
NAME OF THE OWNER De Corato Family
TOTAL BOTTLES PRODUCED 1.200,000
DIRECT SALES
VISITS TO THE WINERY - RESERVATION NEEDED
HECTARES OF VINEYARD 75

To speak of Rivera and the De Corato family is to talk about the history of quality wine in Puglia. Better yet that wonderful winemaking area around the legendary Castel del Monte and the DOC appellation of the same name. Just the name Il Falcone brings memories of one of the first great southern wines that had a capacity to age and achieved a level of quality unimaginable for wines from this area.

---

92   Price B

Castel del Monte Puer Apuliae 2012

100% Nero di Troia grapes. Matures 14 months in barrique. Very dark ruby color. The nose is very intense with aromas of mulberry, licorice and cocoa. The mouth is thick and soft, very interesting with fruits taste. The tannin is soft and well absorbed.

---

90   Price A

Bombino Nero Pungirosa 2015

100% Bombino Nero grapes. Matures in stainless steel. Clean and bright pink color. The nose is elegant with aromas of ripe cherry, peach and myrtle, the mouth is fragrant, very fresh and balanced, savory and harmonic finish.

ROSA DEL GOLFO

Via Garibaldi, 18
73011 Alezio (LE)
Tel. +39 0833 281045
calo@rosadelgolfo.com
www.rosadelgolfo.com
f *Rosa-del-Golfo/138352306283242*

YEAR OF FOUNDATION 1930
NAME OF THE OWNER Damiano Calò
TOTAL BOTTLES PRODUCED 300,000
DIRECT SALES
VISITS TO THE WINERY - RESERVATION NEEDED
HECTARES OF VINEYARD 40
OLIVE OIL PRODUCTION

The name of the estate, Rose of the Gulf, is a clear indication of the wine the estate makes and where it is located. In fact, they produce excellent rosé wines using native grapes grown near the Gulf of Gallipoli, in the heart of Salento. The Calò family naturally does not limit itself to making rosé but it is their leading product, often with results that defining them as good would be a gross understatement.

 91 Price B

Vigna Mazzì 2014

Blend of Negramaro and Malvasia Nera grapes. Most of it matures in stainless steel but a small quantity matures in tonneau. Coral pink color. Beautiful intensity on the nose, with aromas of dark fruits, hazelnut and honey. The mouth, coherent, confirms the structure of the body but with a fresh, savory taste, very easy drink.

 90 👍 Price A

Portulano 2013

Blend of Negramaro and Malvasia Nera grapes. Matures for 12 months in big durmast barrels. Intense ruby color with garnet hues. The nose has aromas of macerated cherries, cocoa, spices and eucalyptus notes. Warm, full and alcoholic, but stretch by a good acidity on the palate.

COSIMO TAURINO

S.P. 365, km 1,400
73010 Guagnano (LE)
Tel. +39 832 706490
Fax +39 832 706242
info@taurinovini.it
www.taurinovini.it
 taurinovini
 @TaurinoVini

YEAR OF FOUNDATION 1970
NAME OF THE OWNER Rosanna and Rita Taurino
TOTAL BOTTLES PRODUCED 900,000
DIRECT SALES

VISITS TO THE WINERY - RESERVATION NEEDED
HECTARES OF VINEYARD 90

Cosimo Taurino is one of the most farsighted producers Puglia has ever had and putting his trust in the young enologist Severino Garofano led to the creation of Patriglione, an authentic wine legend, which sparked a sea change in the production of quality wines in Puglia. His absence has been sorely felt for many, too many years but his daughter is doing all she can to continue in his footsteps. In the past few years the results have not always been consistent but this year they were good once again.

 92 👍 Price A

Salice Salentino Rosso Riserva 2011

Belnd of Negramaro and Malvasia Nera grapes. Matures in barrique for 6 months. Very thick ruby color, impenetrable. The nose is very rich with aromas of morello, toasted notes together with black cherry and sweet spices. Intense and balanced on the palate with the acidity that gives freshness.

 91 👍 Price A

Notarpanaro 2011

100 % Negroamaro grapes. Matures 6 months in used barrique. Dark ruby color. On the nose aromas of carob, chocolate and licorice. The mouth is full, intense and elegant with taste of morello cherry. Nice acidity well blended with the tannins.

 90 Price C

Patriglione 2011

100 % Negramaro grapes. Matures 12 months in French durmast barrique. Intense ruby red color. The nose offers typical notes of the Negramaro with ethereal and elegant scents: spices, dark cherry and blackberries. The mouth is rich, comfortable and juicy, good acidity and an hint of savory.

TENUTA VIGLIONE

Via Carlo Marx, 44
70029 Santeramo In Colle (BA)
Tel. +39 080 212366
info@tenutaviglione.it
www.tenutaviglione.it
 tenutaviglione
 @tenutaviglione

YEAR OF FOUNDATION 1937
NAME OF THE OWNER Zullo Family

TOTAL BOTTLES PRODUCED **250,000**
DIRECT SALES
VISITS TO THE WINERY - RESERVATION NEEDED
HECTARES OF VINEYARD **55**
HOSPITALITY
RESTAURANT
CERTIFIED ORGANIC VITICULTURE
OLIVE OIL PRODUCTION

Tenuta Viglione is in the heart of the Murgia near Bari, a hilly area with an altitude of 450m above sea level which is the highest point of the Gioia del Colle DOC appellation. It is here where the Zullo family, driven by a desire to boost the zone's winemaking potential, have for three generations been producing quality wines using the most modern and advanced production methods and technology available. They recently completed building a modern winery in Viglione as well as a new structure to host guests wishing to visit this enchanted area.

■ **90**   👍 **Price A**
Primitivo 2013

Made with Primitivo grapes. Matures 12 months in big barrels and for another 12 months in barrique. Intense ruby red color. Complex and very spicy scents on the nose with aromas of red fruits, myrtle and carob. The mouth is powerful with a soft pleasant finish.

■ **88**   **Price A**
Gioia del Colle Pri-mi-tivo 2013

100% Primitvo grapes. Matures in big barrels. Dark ruby color. Very expressive nose with aromas of red fruits compote, myrtle, coffee, dry figs. The plate is rich with the tannins in evidence.

TENUTE AL BANO CARRISI

Contrada Bosco, 13
72020 Cellino San Marco (BR)
Tel. +39 0831 619211
vinicola@albanocarrisi.com
www.vinicolacarrisi.com
 tenute.albanocarrisi
 @TenuteAlbano

YEAR OF FOUNDATION **2000**
NAME OF THE OWNER **Al Bano Carrisi**
TOTAL BOTTLES PRODUCED **800,000**
DIRECT SALES

VISITS TO THE WINERY - RESERVATION NEEDED
HECTARES OF VINEYARD **65**
HOSPITALITY
RESTAURANT
OLIVE OIL PRODUCTION

Al Bano Carrisi is a famous Italian singer who is very popular in Russia and abroad. He is also a wine producer, from a family of winemakers, and it took him just over 15 years to be making quality wines in the northern area of Salento, which is in the in the province of Brindisi and no longer that of Lecce. His estate also hosts a beautiful resort and an excellent restaurant.

■ **91**   **Price C**
Platone 2010

Blend Negramaro and Primitivo grapes. Matures 8 months in barrique. Intense and dark garnet color. The nose is warm with aromas of sweet spices, sour cherry compote, tamarind and carob. Full flavored, alcoholic, opulent with a thick intense body. A muscular wine made of the sun. Immense.

★★

TORMARESCA

Contrada Torre d'Isola - Località Tofano
76013 Minervino Murge (BA)
Tel. +39 0883 692631
tormaresca@tormaresca.it
www.tormaresca.it
 Tormaresca
 @Tormaresca

YEAR OF FOUNDATION **1997**
NAME OF THE OWNER **Marchesi Antinori**
TOTAL BOTTLES PRODUCED **3.200,000**
DIRECT SALES
VISITS TO THE WINERY - RESERVATION NEEDED
HECTARES OF VINEYARD **380**
CERTIFIED ORGANIC VITICULTURE
OLIVE OIL PRODUCTION

This vast Antinori estate is composed of two distinct bodies. One is in Minervino Murge and is called Bocca di Lupo and here they cultivate Nero di Troia and Aglianico as well as some international varieties like Chardonnay. The other is Masseria Maime and is situated in the heart of Salento and is best suited for growing Negroamaro, Primitivo and Fiano.

95   Price B

Castel del Monte Aglianico Bocca di Lupo 2012

100% overripe Aglianico. Matures 18 months in French durmast barrels. Very intense garnet ruby color. Very complex nose, rich, warm with aromas of black cherries, spices and kirsch. Very firm mouth, the tannins are thick but elegant and fine. The taste in warm, sour, full-flavored and young with a perfect finish.

92   Price B

Castel del Monte Chardonnay Pietrabianca 2015

100% Chardonnay grapes. Matures 10 months in barrique. Intense straw yellow color. Aromas of yellow plums, pineapple, wild flowers and cedar, in the background an hint of vanilla. The wine is savory and tense, warm and full-flavored, very easy to drink even with a full body.

90   Price B

Masseria Maime 2013

100% Negramaro grapes. Matures for 12 month in barrique. Dark and intense garnet ruby color. Very spicy with aromas of raspberries compote and an hint of tamarind. Firm, warm and savory taste. Good persistence.

★★

TORREVENTO

S.P. 234, km 10,600 (ex S.S. 170)
70033 Corato (BA)
Tel. +39 080 8980923
 torreventoufficio
info@torrevento.it
www.torrevento.it
torrevento

YEAR OF FOUNDATION 1920
NAME OF THE OWNER Francesco Liantonio
TOTAL BOTTLES PRODUCED 2.500,000
DIRECT SALES
VISITS TO THE WINERY - RESERVATION NEEDED
HECTARES OF VINEYARD 450
HOSPITALITY
RESTAURANT
OLIVE OIL PRODUCTION

The vineyards are right below Castel del Monte and the silhouette of that mysterious citadel build by Frederick II dominated the surrounding landscape. Francesco Liantonio and his partners must surly fee a great responsibility, perhaps more than others given the estate's location, of transmitting the magic of that area and the grape Nero di Troia, which is the fundamental one in their production.

95   Price A

Castel del Monte Rosso Vigna Pedale Riserva 2013

This year Vigna Pedale won over Ottagono even if for just one point becaming the new star. 100% Nero di Troia grapes. Matures for 8 months in stainless steel and 12 months in big barrels. Dark ruby color. The nose is very rich with an infinite range of scents as blackberries, mulberries, pepper, leather and eucalyptus notes. The mouth is powerful and elegant but incredible to drink and a very persistence finish.

94   Price B

Castel del Monte Nero di Troia Ottagono Riserva 2014

100% Nero di Troia grapes. Matures in big barrels for 24 months. Very dark ruby red color. Very intense on the nose with aromas of carob, tamarind, spices and vanilla. The mouth has a great impact, very warm and soft, with a very solid fruit and a well integrate tannin.

91   Price A

Since 1913 2015

100% Primitivo grapes. Matures for 10 months in stainless steel and then 6 months in barrique. Intense ruby color. The nose offers a range of typical aromas as plum, violet and cocoa. The mouth is powerful and warm but with a nice acidity that makes the wine very balanced to drink.

VARVAGLIONE VIGNE & VINI

Contrada Santa Lucia
74021 Leporano (TA)
Tel. +39 099 5315370
Fax +39 099 5315739
info@varvaglione.com
www.varvaglione.com
Varvaglione
@Varvaglione

YEAR OF FOUNDATION 1921
NAME OF THE OWNER Cosimo Varvaglione

TOTAL BOTTLES PRODUCED 3,000,000
DIRECT SALES
VISITS TO THE WINERY - RESERVATION NEEDED
HECTARES OF VINEYARD 155
CERTIFIED ORGANIC VITICULTURE

YEAR OF FOUNDATION 2014
NAME OF THE OWNER Bruno Vespa
TOTAL BOTTLES PRODUCED 60,000
VISITS TO THE WINERY
HECTARES OF VINEYARD 13

A scrupulous selection of typical Salentino grapes and advanced winemaking technology that respect tradition are the chief characteristics of this estate that has been operating since 1921 and managed by the same family for three generations. It is situated in Leporano, in the province of Taranto, what was once part of Magna Grecia where the first Greek colonists trained their vines alberello-style to allow the grapes to reap the best benefits of the sun.

The merger of his passion for wine and love of Salento was for Bruno Vespa the driving force behind this winemaking project, which became even more ambitious after he consulted with Riccardo Cotarella. It is so ambitious, in fact, that it has involved even the sons of the well-known TV journalist: Federico and Alessandro. This very young wine initiative centers its production on Puglia's number one grape: Primitivo.

 92   Price B

Primitivo di Manduria Papale 2014

100% Primitivo grapes. Matures in French and American barrique for 10 months. Very dark ruby color. Very complex nose of great expression, aromas of black cherry, blackberries and sweet notes, after follows aromas of coffee, licorice and leather. powerful mouth, light tannins, great persistence.

 93   Price B

Raccontami 2014

This wine improves year by year. 100% Primitivo grapes. Matures 1 year in barrique. The color is the classic dark ruby, typical of the Primitivo. The nose is strong and very complex with aromas of plum, carob, violet, tobacco and cinnamon. The palate is full, velvety with elegant, sweet harmonic taste. Elegant tannin. Easy to drink and great body.

☐ 91   👍 Price A

Margrande 2015

100% Fiano grapes. Matures in stainless steel. Light yellow color with green hues. The nose offers aromas of white fruits, citrus and almonds. The mouth has a strong acidity that balances an elegant savory, harmonic and long finish.

 90   Price A

Il Rosso dei Vespa 2015

100% Primitivo grapes. Matures 6 month in barrique. Deep red ruby color. Fine and attractive nose, very typical, with aromas of plum, violet and carob, eucalyptus and spicy aromas. Rich and very fluid on the palate, harmonic, with a nice fruity taste and an elegant tannin.

■ 90   👍 Price A

12 e mezzo 2015

100% Negroamaro grapes. Matures 6 months in French tonneau. Amaranth color. Aromas of raspberries, coffee, licorice. The mouth is fine, graceful and sweet with a particular long finish.

▨ 88   👍 Price A

Il Bruno dei Vespa 2015

Blend of Negroamaro and Aleatico grapes. Matures in stainless steel. Nice coral pink color. It present good aromatic notes of rose and crispy cherry that makes everyone love this win. Fresh and savory on the palate. The Aleatico grapes give the final touch with a very pleasant finish.

VESPA VIGNAIOLI
PER PASSIONE

S.P. Manduria-Avetrana km 3
74024 Manduria (TA)
Tel. +39 06 37514609
Fax +39 06 37517625
info@bvfutura14.it
www.vespavignaioli.it
 VespaVignaioli
🐦 *@VespaVignaioli*

BASILICATA

asilicata does not produce much wine, some 190,000 hectoliters from just under 4,500 hectares of vineyards, 30% of which are DOC classified. The only DOCG wine is an Aglianico del Vulture Superiore which was first produced in 2001. The reasons for this are understandable. The land is arid and mountainous and so not suitable for wine-growing. The climate does not help either and Potenza, for example, is one of the coldest cities in Italy. This situation may seem unusual for those who are used to considering the southern, Mezzogiorno half of Italy as being sub-tropical, a place where the sun always shines and where the temperatures are always high, even in winter.

The district of Vulture is to the far north of the region, between Irpinia and Capitanata, in other words between the regions of Campania and Puglia, just across the Ofanto River. Monte Vulture is an ancient, extinct volcano as is evidenced by the small, circular lakes of Monticchio. Aglianico del Vulture is produced in this area, near the towns of Melfi, Rionero, Lavello, Venosa, Barile and a dozen or so other small villages. It is a bold and full-bodied red that should be allowed to age a few years in order to be appreciated. The standard wine ages for at least a year, while the Superiore is not sent to market until it has aged for four years.

CONTROLLED AND GUARANTEED DESIGNATION OF ORIGIN (DOCG)

- Aglianico del Vulture Superiore, geographic references allowed

CONTROLLED DESIGNATION OF ORIGIN (DOC)

- Aglianico del Vulture, geographic references allowed
- Grottino di Roccanova
- Matera
- Terre dell'Alta Val d'Agri

BASILISCO

Via delle Cantine, 22
85022 Barile (PZ)
Tel. +39 0972 771033
Fax +39 0972 771033
basiliscovini@gmail.com
www.basiliscovini.it

f *basiliscovini*
🐦 *@basiliscovini*

YEAR OF FOUNDATION 1992
NAME OF THE OWNER Feudi di San Gregorio
BOTTLES PRODUCED 50,000
DIRECT SALES
VISITS TO THE WINERY - RESERVATION NEEDED
HECTARS OF VINEYARD 27
CERTIFIED ORGANIC VITICULTURE

Founded by Michele Cutolo, this estate has for some years now belonged to Feudi di San Gregorio, the famous Irpinia winery. They produce wines with a modern style using selected grape and the use of new-wood barrels for their top wine. Of the estate's 27 hectares of vineyards, 20 are directly owned and seven are leased.

---

 93   Price B
Aglianico del Vulture Basilisco 2012

100% Aglianico grapes. Matures for 10 months in used barrique. Deep ruby red. A clean and fruity nose, black cherry, plum, then very neat spicy hints. Saline and tense flavor, warm, agile, elegant, with good length in the finish.

★★

CANTINE DEL NOTAIO

Via Roma, 159
85028 Rionero In Vulture (PZ)
Tel. +39 0972 723689
Fax +39 0972 725435
🅢 *cantine.del.notaio*
info@cantinedelnotaio.it
www.cantinedelnotaio.com

f *cantinedelnotaio*
🐦 *@Cantine_Notaio*

YEAR OF FOUNDATION 1998
NAME OF THE OWNER Gerardo Giuratrabocchetti
BOTTLES PRODUCED 240,000
DIRECT SALES

VISITS TO THE WINERY - RESERVATION NEEDED
HECTARS OF VINEYARD 30
RESTAURANT
CERTIFIED ORGANIC VITICULTURE
CERTIFIED BIODYNAMIC VITICULTURE
OLIVE OIL PRODUCTION

The winery is incredibly beautiful and is carved out of volcanic tuff stone and looks like a cathedral packed with barrels and sacred images. Gerardo Giuratrabocchetti puts his heart and soul into his passion and his wines are always extraordinary and full of personality. Each wine has the name of a notary function in honor of the profession of his ancestors.

---

 90   Price B
Aglianico del Vulture Il Repertorio 2013

100% Aglianico grapes. Matures for 1 year in barrique. Fruity aromas of black cherry, plum, tamarind, then sweet spices and slight flowery notes. Strong, tense taste, saline, young and with evident tannins. Good acidity and appropriate persistence in the finish.

■ 88   Price A
Aglianico del Vulture L'Atto 2014

100% Aglianico grapes. Matures 6 months in used barrique. Intensly fruity, with fragrant notes of black cherry and plum: very pleasant and easy to drink, saline, agile, fresh and with good persistent finish.

★★

ELENA FUCCI

Contrada Solagna del Titolo
85022 Barile (PZ)
Tel. +39 0972 770736
🅢 *FucciElena*
info@elenafuccivini.com
www.elenafuccivini.com

f *elena.fucci*
🐦 *@elena_fucci*

YEAR OF FOUNDATION 2000
NAME OF THE OWNER Elena Fucci
BOTTLES PRODUCED 18,000
DIRECT SALES
VISITS TO THE WINERY - RESERVATION NEEDED
HECTARS OF VINEYARD 6

Elena Fucci is a young enologist and winemaker who has become the whiz kid of Vulture. She makes only one wine in her new winery but does it with great skill and passion, so much so it is known around the world despite her small production.

■ 92   Price B
Aglianico del Vulture Titolo 2014

100% Aglianico grapes. Matures 1 year in barrique. Intense garnet ruby red. Black cherry, sweet spices, blond tobacco, slight tamarind on the nose. Agile, tense, with a thinner body compared to the previous versions, tannins are a little bit more woody. Excellent acidity and good length in the finish.

GRIFALCO

Località Pian di Camera
85029 Venosa (PZ)
Tel. +39 0972 31002
grifalcodellalucania@email.it
www.grifalco.com
🅕 *Grifalco-Vini*
🐦 *@GrifalcoVini*

YEAR OF FOUNDATION 2004
NAME OF THE OWNER Fabrizio Piccin and Cecilia Naldoni
BOTTLES PRODUCED 45,000
DIRECT SALES
VISITS TO THE WINERY - RESERVATION NEEDED
HECTARS OF VINEYARD 15
CERTIFIED ORGANIC VITICULTURE

The estate is run by Fabrizio and Ceclia Piccin who have some 15 hectares of vineyards in the best areas of the district – in the towns of Venosa, Ginesta and Maschito – and produce a wine that is a true Vulture cru. Each single vineyards plot is vinified separately according to the area and the age of the vines (some plots were acquired already operational and they sought out old vines). The winery operates with an eye on nature and unites a low environmental footprint with excellent functionality.

■ 92   Price B
Aglianico del Vulture Damaschito 2012

100% Aglianico grapes. Matures for about two years in different types of wood. Intense garnet ruby red. Black cherry, tamarind, black tobacco and a hint of

---

sweet spices on the nose. Tannic flavor, with a little bit of young edges, rich, warm, persistent.

MASTRODOMENICO

Viale Europa, 5
85022 Barile (PZ)
Tel. +39 0972 770108
🅢 *giuseppe.mastrodomenico*
info@vignemastrodomenico.com
www.vignemastrodomenico.com
🅕 *VigneMastrodomenico*
🐦 *@manulikos*

YEAR OF FOUNDATION 2004
NAME OF THE OWNER Giuseppe Mastrodomenico
BOTTLES PRODUCED 30,000
DIRECT SALES
VISITS TO THE WINERY - RESERVATION NEEDED
HECTARS OF VINEYARD 8
CERTIFIED ORGANIC VITICULTURE

This tiny winery has existed for decades but its wines did not reach the market until 2004. Initially, they either sold their grapes or made bulk wine. Donato Mastrodomenico for a while now has been assisted by his offspring Giuseppe and Emanuela and they are producing some marvelous, traditional wines made with first-rate techniques.

■ 91   👍 Price A
Aglianico del Vulture Likos 2012

100% Aglianico grapes, 10 months in barrique. Concentrated ruby. Ethereal nose, with notes of plum jam and blackberries, followed by spicy tones of vanilla and some cinnamon. Rich, powerful flavor, with youthful but ripe, well-integrated tannins. Saline, also on the persistent finish.

■ 91   Price D
Mos 2013

100% Aglianico grapes. Matures in stainless steel. Deep, bright ruby. Cherries, strawberries, plums and blackberries on the nose, with spicy hints of white pepper. Very attractive flavor: easy-todrink, saline, lively, fresh and really quite long.

MUSTO CARMELITANO

Via Pietro Nenni, 23
85020 Maschito (PZ)

Tel. +39 0972 33312
info@mustocarmelitano.it
www.mustocarmelitano.it
f *AZ-Agricola-Musto-Carmelitano*
𝕏 *@MustoCarmelitan*

YEAR OF FOUNDATION 2007
NAME OF THE OWNER Elisabetta Musto
Carmelitano
BOTTLES PRODUCED 23,000
DIRECT SALES
VISITS TO THE WINERY - RESERVATION NEEDED
HECTARS OF VINEYARD 9
CERTIFIED ORGANIC VITICULTURE
OLIVE OIL PRODUCTION

Although new, this tiny winery has attracted the attention of wine lovers thanks to the sober and elegant style of its products. It is run by a young woman, Elisabetta Musto Carmelitano, who with determination and talent has created her own personal interpretation of Aglianico del Vulture without relying on too much texture or super-ripe grapes.

■ 91   Price B
Aglianico del Vulture Serra del Prete 2012

100% Aglianico grapes. Concrete and stainless steel. Deep ruby-garnet. The nose is dominated by spicy notes, followed by hints of plums and sour cherries, and then undergrowth. Rich, saline flavor, with youthful tannins that are beginning to soften; alcoholic, very persistent finish.

■ 90   Price B
Aglianico del Vulture Pian del Moro 2012

100% Aglianico grapes. Matures 1 year in tonneau. Dark garnet ruby. Rich and articulated nose with notes of violet, tamarind, black cherry and plum jam. Firm to the palate, with strong tannins, very young and a bit edgy. Very warm and persistent finish.

■ 83   Price A
Aglianico del Vulture Maschitano Rosso 2013

100% Aglianico grapes. Stainless steel. Deep bright ruby. Strawberries, fresh cherries and blackcurrants on the nose. Lively, acidulous, saline and quite alcoholic flavor. Not very tannic.

PATERNOSTER

Contrada Valle del Titolo
85022 Barile (PZ)
Tel. +39 0972 770224
info@paternostervini.it
www.paternostervini.it
f *paternostervini*
𝕏 *@PaternosterVini*

YEAR OF FOUNDATION 1925
NAME OF THE OWNER Paternoster Family
BOTTLES PRODUCED 130,000
DIRECT SALES
VISITS TO THE WINERY - RESERVATION NEEDED
HECTARS OF VINEYARD 20
CERTIFIED ORGANIC VITICULTURE

This is a winery of great prestige which for decades has been among the best for quality in the district. The fact that it is family run by no means that it lacks in professionalism or modern approaches, quite the contrary. They produce wines that are both traditional and modern, seeking ways to interpret the land and the Aglianico grape in the best way possible often achieving very great and interesting results.

■ 92   Price B
Aglianico del Vulture Don Anselmo 2012

100% Aglianico grapes. 50% matures in big barrels and 50% in barrique for different periods of time. Intense garnet color. Smoky notes and tamarind on the nose, followed by eucalyptus hints, almost resinous and of wild cherry jam. Warm and tense on the palate, strong but not aggressive tannins, very persistent finish.

■ 90   Price B
Aglianico del Vulture Rotondo 2012

100% Aglianico grapes. Matures 18 months in barrique. Intense ruby red with garnet hues. Deep on the nose with notes of anise, fresh almond and the classic aromas of red fruits, then tobacco and plums. Powerful on the palate, thick and progressive body with young tannins that give taste and deepness.

RE MANFREDI
TERRE DEGLI SVEVI

Località Pian di Camera
85029 Venosa (PZ)
Tel. +39 0972 31263
terredeglisvevi@giv.it
www.cantineremanfredi.com
 Cantine-Re-Manfredi-Venosa

YEAR OF FOUNDATION 1998
NAME OF THE OWNER Gruppo Italiano Vini
BOTTLES PRODUCED 230,000
DIRECT SALES
VISITS TO THE WINERY - RESERVATION NEEDED
HECTARS OF VINEYARD 120
RESTAURANT

The largest estate in the area of Vulture, with over 100 hectares of vineyards, is in reality one of average size and is part of the Gruppo Italiano Vini, a vast empires of wineries that together form the biggest winemaking enterprise in Italy.

---

 95   Price B
Aglianico del Vulture Re Manfredi 2012

100% Aglianico grapes. Matures 1 year in barrique. Intense garnet. Very ethereal on the nose, eucalyptus notes of resins and rhubarb, then black cherry and slight sweet spices. Intense flavors, well balanced tannins, velvety body, great acidity and extremely long persistence.

---

 91   Price A
Aglianico del Vulture Taglio del Tralcio 2013

100% Aglianico grapes left on the vine after cutting the shoot, thus becoming slightly over-ripe. Matures 1 year in barrique. Intense garnet. Licorice notes, macerated black cherry and slight tamarind. Enveloping flavor, tense and with good acidity and tidy tannins.

---

 88   Price B
Aglianico del Vulture Serpara 2011

100% Aglianico grapes. Matures 2 years in barrique. Dark and concentrated garnet color. Notes of dried plum, tamarind, wild cherry jam and eucalyptus hints in the background. Very warm on the palate, alcoholic, rich, even a little bit heavy and bitter in the finish.

CALABRIA

The principle wine production areas and almost all those for the DOC wines are located in central-northern Calabria All the reds have the Gaglioppo grape in common, which is native to the area, and almost all the whites are produced with the Greco grape.

The wines which by far represents the region is Cirò. It is produced as a red which can also be Superiore if it has an alcoholic content of over 13.5%, a Riserva if it ages for at least two years or a Classico if the grapes come from the zone where it has bene cultivated since ancient times. Cirò Rosso is a bold wine with a high alcoholic content and while the tannins by seem old-style they are a guarantee.

The Rosato is a rosé made from Gaglioppo grapes while the white Bianco is made with Greco.

Almost all the other DOC wines are similar to Cirò and while produced in other areas all use the same grapes. Among these are Sant'Anna Isola Capo Rizzuto, Melissa, Savuto, Scavigna and Donnici, which recently became a sub-appellation of the DOC Terre di Cosenza, as are San Vito di Luzzi, Verbicaro, Pollino, Condoleo, Colline del Crati and Esaro.

Lamezia is an exception and the white wine is a blend of Greco, Trebbiano and Malvasia, while the red is a blend of Nerello Mascalese, Greco Nero and Gaglioppo.

Completing the panorama is the rare but delicious sweet wine produced on the Locride coast, Greco di Bianco.

CONTROLLED DESIGNATION OF ORIGIN (DOC)

- Sant'Anna di Isola Capo Rizzuto
- Bivongi
- Cirò, accompagnata o no dalla sottozona Classico (Classico, Classico Superiore, Classico Superiore Riserva only for Cirò rosso)
- Greco di Bianco
- Lamezia
- Melissa
- Savuto, with or without Classico
- Scavigna
- Terre di Cosenza, with or without Condoleo, Donnici, Esaro, Pollino, San Vito di Luzzi, Colline del Crati, Verbicaro

'A VITA

S.S. 106, km 279,8
88811 Cirò Marina (KR)
Tel. +39 329 0732473
avita.info@gmail.com
www.avitavini.it
f *avitavini*
𝕏 *@avita_ciro*

YEAR OF FOUNDATION **2008**
NAME OF THE OWNER Francesco De Franco and
Laura Violino
BOTTLES PRODUCED **10,000**
DIRECT SALES
VISITS TO THE WINERY
HECTARS OF VINEYARD **8**
CERTIFIED ORGANIC VITICULTURE

Francesco and Laura produce their wines with
determination and passion just south of Cirò
Marina and for years have been cultivating
their vineyards following strict, organic methods. Their wines have great personality, are
very territorial and decidedly authentic and
are just rustic enough to be unmistakable.

■ 92   Price B
Cirò Rosso Classico Superiore Riserva 2012

100% Gaglioppo grapes. Matures 1 year in big
barrels and 2 in stainless steel. Light ruby red with
garnet highlights. Clear notes of rose petals and
morello cherry, light spicy notes. Great structure on
the palate with evident acidity well balanced by the
tannins of good extraction. A wine with personality
and respect of the terroir.

CANTINE LENTO

Via del Progresso, snc
88040 Amato (CZ)
Tel. +39 0961 993031
info@cantinelento.it
www.cantinelento.it
f *Cantine-Lento*

YEAR OF FOUNDATION **1972**
NAME OF THE OWNER Salvatore Lento
BOTTLES PRODUCED **500,000**
DIRECT SALES

VISITS TO THE WINERY - RESERVATION NEEDED
HECTARS OF VINEYARD **70**
HOSPITALITY
OLIVE OIL PRODUCTION

The Lento family has tied its name to the Lamezia DOC appellation and for it they have exalted indigenous grapes like Magliocco. Salvatore
Lento took control of his family's estate in the
1960s and since then has always paid great
attention to the land and tradition. Today his
children are running the estate following in
their father's footsteps.

■ 91   Price B
Magliocco 2011

100% Magliocco grapes. Matures in French oak
barrique for 12 months. Ruby red with garnet high-
lights. Mediterranean notes on the nose with aro-
mas of rosemary, juniper and wild strawberry. The
palate is austere with great thick tannin extraction
never overwhelming and sustained by a nice acid-
ity. Long finish that goes back to Mediterranean
notes. It's a very Mediterranean wine with person-
ality and structure.

■ 90   Price B
Lamezia Rosso Riserva 2011

Magliocco, Greco Nero and Nerello grapes. Matures
2 years in stainless steel then 1 year in french oak
barrique. Concentrated ruby red. Notes of licorice,
chincona, mulberry and black wild berries. The pal-
ate is soft and enveloping with a good body and a
good tannic plot, sustained by nice acidity. The per-
sistence reminds of notes of licorice and black wild
berries.

CANTINE VIOLA

Via Roma, 18
87010 Saracena (CS)
Tel. +39 0981 349099
Fax +39 0981 349099
info@cantineviola.it
www.cantineviola.it
f *CantineViola*

YEAR OF FOUNDATION **1999**
NAME OF THE OWNER Luigi Viola
BOTTLES PRODUCED **10,000**
DIRECT SALES
VISITS TO THE WINERY - RESERVATION NEEDED

HECTARS OF VINEYARD 3
CERTIFIED ORGANIC VITICULTURE
OLIVE OIL PRODUCTION

The tale of this winery seems to go back thousands of years. Their Moscato di Saracena, in particular, seems like a wine straight out of the Odyssey. Produced using ancestral methods with a partial cooking of the must (which is creating no few problems with EU regulations), their wines are a cultural heritage as well as being excellent. Theirs is the only Passito made without using carbon dioxide.

 95   Price B*
Moscato Passito di Saracena 2015
*Guarnaccia, Malvasia and Moscadello di Saracena grapes. Matures in stainless steel for 1 year on the yeasts. Bright amber. Usual sensational notes of dried apricots, honey, spices, candied orange peels, date and tamarind. Sweet and enveloping flavor, very saline, never too sweet, warm and never ending finish. This is like ancient Grece wines must have been 2000 years ago. In the heart of Magna Grecia the Viola produce this incredible wine with a millenary tradition. *50 cl bottle.*

☐ 92   👍 Price A
Bianco Margherita 2015
65% white Guarnacca and 35% white Mantonico grapes. 15% of the mass matures for 6 months in used barrique, the rest in stainless steel. Intense straw yellow. Medlar, yellow plum and slight vanilla on the nose. Saline flavor, great body, tense, warm, very persistent.

 91   Price B
Rosso Viola 2013
Sweet Magliocco grapes. Matures 1 year in barrique. Intense garnet ruby red. Black cherry, red myrtle, slight hints of cocoa and spices on the nose. Strong flavor, with some tannic edge due to the young age and warm and persistent finish.

CAPARRA & SICILIANI

S.S. 106
88811 Cirò Marina (KR)
Tel. +39 0962 373319
Fax +39 0962 379000
info@caparraesiciliani.it
www.caparraesiciliani.it
🅕 *caparraesiciliani*

YEAR OF FOUNDATION 1963
NAME OF THE OWNER Caparra and Siciliani Families
BOTTLES PRODUCED 800,000
DIRECT SALES
VISITS TO THE WINERY - RESERVATION NEEDED
HECTARS OF VINEYARD 217

This famous winery just recently turned 50 and for many years has represented one of the few established points of reference in the area of Cirò. Today it continues to produce wines that are well-made and economical.

 89   Price A
Cirò Rosso Classico Superiore Volvito Riserva 2013
100% Gaglioppo grapes. Matures in barrique for 1 year. Intense garnet ruby. Varietal notes, typical, ethereal, with a little stinging alcoholic note and aromas of macerated black cherry and sweet spices. Neat flavor, nice lively tannins but a little bit dry in the finish.

★
CERAUDO

Contrada Dattilo
88815 Strongoli (KR)
Tel. +39 0962 865613
Fax +39 0962 865696
info@dattilo.it
www.dattilo.it
🅕 *aziendaceraudoroberto.ceraudo*

YEAR OF FOUNDATION 1973
NAME OF THE OWNER Maria Assunta Ceraudo
BOTTLES PRODUCED 70,000
DIRECT SALES
VISITS TO THE WINERY - RESERVATION NEEDED
HECTARS OF VINEYARD 20
HOSPITALITY
RESTAURANT
CERTIFIED ORGANIC VITICULTURE

Although small, the quality of this winery near Crotone has been growing significantly. It is run by the Ceraudo family who have followed the dictates of organic farming for over 20 years. They mostly cultivate local grapes and their winemaking method seeks to exalt their best characteristics.

■ 90   Price B
Petraro 2010

100% Gaglioppo grapes, 30% Black Greco, 20% Cabernet Sauvignon. 18 months in barrique. Intense garnet ruby. Dinamyc on the nose with eucalyptus aromas, plum and black cherry. Rich, concentrated flavor, composed tannins, saline notes, warm and persistent finish.

FEUDO DEI SANSEVERINO

Via Vittorio Emanuele, 100
87010 Saracena (CS)
Tel. +39 0981 21461
info@feudodeisanseverino.it
www.feudodeisanseverino.it
 feudodeisanseverino

YEAR OF FOUNDATION 1999
NAME OF THE OWNER Roberto Bisconte
BOTTLES PRODUCED 15,000
DIRECT SALES
VISITS TO THE WINERY - RESERVATION NEEDED
HECTARS OF VINEYARD 5
OLIVE OIL PRODUCTION

Roberto and Maurizio Bisconte have run this small five-hectare estate since 1999. Its family gem is without a doubt their Moscato Passito al Governo di Saracena while they also produce a Passito made with only Moscato Bianco that is very interesting. Donna Marianna is a wine that they describe as "from a bygone era" when red and wine grapes were fermented together. The estate practices biodynamic methods and its wines are authentic and full of character.

□ 94   Price B
Moscato Passito Mastro Terenzio 2012

100% white Moscato grapes. Amber yellow. Complex and elegant nose. Aromas of toasted almond, sweet tobacco, dried figs, dried flowers. Sweet on the palate and balanced by great acidity. The finish reminds the toasted almond and barley candies.

□ 93   Price B
Moscato Passito al Governo di Saracena 2009

Guarnaccia, Malvasia and Moscato grapes. Bright amber yellow. Notes of dried apricot, honey, dried figs and dater hints. The palate is fascinating, sweet and soft but sustained by great acidity which makes it easy to drink. Long persistence that reminds notes of honey and dried apricot.

■ 90   👍 Price A
Donna Marianna 2013

60% Gaglioppo with Malvasia and Guarnaccia grapes. Matures in stainless steel with a little passage in used French barrique. Light and bright ruby red. Notes of apple peels on the nose, eucalyptus hints and Mediterranean woods that remind of rosemary. Lively on the palate, pleasantly fresh and with little tannins. A wine like it used to be that has authenticity and a rustic character.

■ 89   Price A
Lacrima Nera 2011

100% black Lacrima grapes. Matures for 12/16 months in used french barrique. Light ruby red. Balck cherry, mulberry, rosemary, sage on the nose. Agile on the palate, fresh and with good tannic extraction. The finish reminds notes of mulberry and black cherry. Good persistence.

IGRECO

Via Magenta, 33
87062 Cariati (CS)
Tel. +39 0983 969441
Fax +39 0983 96020
info@igreco.it
www.igreco.it
 azienda.igreco
 @aziendaigreco

YEAR OF FOUNDATION 1963
NAME OF THE OWNER Greco Family
BOTTLES PRODUCED 250,000
DIRECT SALES
VISITS TO THE WINERY - RESERVATION NEEDED
HECTARS OF VINEYARD 80
HOSPITALITY
RESTAURANT
CERTIFIED ORGANIC VITICULTURE
OLIVE OIL PRODUCTION

The Greco family is famous most of all for their excellent extra-virgin olive oil which they have been producing for decades. However, for several years now they have also been producing quality wines with positive results. Their vineyards are located between Cirò and Carlati and the grapes are for the most part the indigenous varieties while their enologist consultant is the renowned Riccardo Cotarella.

90   👍 Price A
Masino 2014

100% Calabrese grapes. Matures 12 months in French oak barrique. Intense ruby red. Notes of black cherry in syrup, dried rose petals, hints of cocoa. Mediterranean on the palate, warm and juicy, well extracted tannins and great salty finish. Good persistence.

89   Price B
Tumasu 2014

Gaglioppo and Calabrese grapes. Matures for 12 months in French oak barrique. Intense ruby red with garnet shadows. Black wild berries on the nose, cassis, leather, sweet tobacco and licorice root. Warm and rich palate and great structure. Evident tannins well blended, good acidity and long finish that reminds notes of cassis.

87   👍 Price A
Catà 2014

100% Gaglioppo grapes. Matures 6 months in French oak barrique. Almost garnet ruby red. Notes of plum, dried rose petals, black cherry and cocoa. Soft and warm palate; thick tannins but not edgy. Long finish that reminds notes of black cherry and cocoa.

★★
LIBRANDI

Contrada San Gennaro
88811 Cirò Marina (KR)
Tel. +39 0962 31518
Fax +39 0962 370542
librandi@librandi.it
www.librandi.it
🔲 *WineLibrandi*
🐦 *@LibrandiWine*

YEAR OF FOUNDATION 1950
NAME OF THE OWNER Antonio and Nicodemo Librandi
BOTTLES PRODUCED 2,200,000
DIRECT SALES
VISITS TO THE WINERY - RESERVATION NEEDED
HECTARS OF VINEYARD 232
RESTAURANT
CERTIFIED ORGANIC VITICULTURE
OLIVE OIL PRODUCTION

This is by far the most famous and successful Calabrian winery for quality. Today it is in the sure hands of Nicodemo Librandi, an esteemed wine entrepreneur. The wines are made with a technical skill that make them reliable and easy to appreciate around the world.

90   👍 Price A
Cirò Rosso Classico Superiore Duca di San Felice Riserva 2014

100% Gaglioppo grapes. Matures in stainless steel. Ruby red with garnet shadow. Elegant Mediterranean nose. Notes of wild blackberry and licorice root, slightly smoky. Fresh and agile on the palate, light tannins and a pleasantly saline finish. Good persistence.

89   👍 Price A
Cirò Rosso Classico 2014

100% Gaglioppo grapes. Stainless steel. Ruby red. Mediterranean nose with hints of rosemary and dried tomatoes. Soft and agile on the palate with a light tannin and freshness that gives drinkability. Good persistence.

ODOARDI

Viale della Repubblica, 143
87100 Cosenza (CS)
Tel. +39 0984 29961
Fax +39 0984 28503
info@cantineodoardi.it
www.cantineodoardi.it

YEAR OF FOUNDATION 1994
NAME OF THE OWNER Gregorio Odoardi
BOTTLES PRODUCED 300,000
DIRECT SALES
VISITS TO THE WINERY - RESERVATION NEEDED
HECTARS OF VINEYARD 70
OLIVE OIL PRODUCTION

Originally from Germany, the Odoardi family settled in Nocera Terinese in 1480. While they have always worked the land, it was not until 1994 that Gregorio and Giovanni Battista dedicated themselves to producing quality wines. The vineyards, which are a stone's throw from the sea, are subject to distinct temperature variations. Gregorio Lillo Odoardi's ambition is to enhance the value of the local appellations Scavigna and Savuto while at the same time experimenting with 'international' varietals.

89   Price B
Odoardi GB 2013

Gaglioppo, Magliocco, Nerello Cappuccio and black Greco grapes. Matures 12 months in barrique. Deep ruby red. Notes of black cherry and dried flowers, hints of vanilla and leather. Rich and enveloping palate, sweet and round tannins with pleasant freshness. Good persistence.

88   👍 Price A
Savuto Rosso 2014

Gaglioppo, Aglianico, Magliocco Canino, black Greco and Nerello Cappuccio grapes. Stainless steel only. Ruby red. Intense notes of morello cherry, smoky aromas and licorice. Good structure on the palate with velvety tannins and pleasant finish of morello cherry.

88   Price A
Terre Damia Rosso 2014

Gaglioppo, Magliocco, Nerello Cappuccio and black Greco grapes. Matures in stainless steel with a little passage in used barrique. Deep ruby. Notes of morello cherry, cocoa and coffee beans; slightly smoky. Soft and round mouth-feel with sweet tannins and good saltiness. Nice acidity and finish that reminds of vanilla and coffee.

www.doctorwine.it is the first **totally bi-lingual (Italian-English)** web-magazine published in Italy and thus offers an Italian point of view to a global public. It is not a blog but an authentic **on-line magazine** which deals with wine and related subjects. The magazine was created and is run by **Daniele Cernilli**, internationally considered to be one of Italy's most authoritative wine critics, who used his nickname as the magazine's name.

From February 2016 DoctorWine is on line with a completely new site. We realized we have an impressive archive that is constantly expanding and which we wanted to make as accessible as possible. Thus the key feature in the change is related to the research of information within the site: making it easier for anyone to find a particular wine we have taste.

CAMPANIA

Campania is one of the regions that has made the most progress in wine-making in recent years and it appears to be striving to regain its position as a leader in quality production that it had in centuries past. The region stands out for its variety of soils and microclimates which allows it to produce a multitude of types of wine and organoleptic characteristics even when using the same grapes. The grape varieties are almost entirely indigenous and offer an element of uniformity in a complex webs of appellations which the regions hosts today. Greco, Fiano, Biancolella and Falanghina for the white wines and Piedirosso and Aglianico for the reds are the grapes used to make vast number of DOC and DOCG wines which, however, only represent 15% of a total wine production of over one and a half million hectoliters a year.

The Falanghina-based wines Falerno del Massico Bianco and Sant'Agata dei Goti Bianco, along with Falanghina Sant'Agata dei Goti, Solopaca Falanghina, Guardia Sanframondi Falanghina and Taburno Falanghina today are all grouped together in the DOC Falanghina del Sannio appellation and represent its sub-zones. Then there are Campi Flegrei Bianco, and Sorrentina Bianco. Greco grapes are used for Greco di Tufo and Capri Bianco, while Fiano is used for Fiano di Avellino and Cilento Bianco.

Among the reds, Aglianico is grape used to make Taurasi, Cilento Rosso, Aglianico Taburno, Sannio Santi'Agata dei Goti rosso, Sannio Solopaca Aglianico and Falerno del Massico Rosso. Pieirosso (AKA Per'e Palummo) is the grape used for Vesuvio Rosso, Campi Fregrei Rosso, Capi Rosso and Ischia Rosso.

Thus there are a vast number of types of wines from different areas. Some of these are coastal, others are from the interior where the climate is anything but southern and Mediterranean. In Irpinia, for example, the weather in September and October is often more like that of Piedmont, while on the Amalfi Coast it is more like Sicily. In order to get a clear picture of the situation, one needs to almost be an expert in geography as well as wine. This allows you to understand why Falanghina wines are deliciously soft and often fragrant when they come from near the sea and yet a bit tart away from the coast. Aglianico always makes great reds for aging but there is a distinct difference between gritty tannins of a Taurasi from the Avellino hill and the velvety reliability of a Falerno del Massicio Rosso, the vineyards for which are close to the sea. Piedirosso wines are typical coastal reds which are soft and at the same time, as in the case of Gragnano and Lettere della Penisola Sorrentina, can also be sparkling reds perfect to pair with tasty seafood dishes (Polpi alla Lucina) or typical Neapolitan cuisine (Sartù di Riso). Among the more unique wines are Asprino di Aversa, produced in the province of Caserta where the vine are 'tree-trained' and climb as high as three meters. This is a light and sometimes sparkling wine that tradition dictates should be paired with Pizza Napolitana.

CONTROLLED AND GUARANTEED DESIGNATION OF ORIGIN (DOCG)

- Aglianico del Taburno
- Fiano di Avellino
- Greco di Tufo
- Taurasi

CONTROLLED DESIGNATION OF ORIGIN (DOC)

- Aversa
- Campi Flegrei
- Capri
- Casavecchia di Pontelatone
- Castel San Lorenzo, allowed the use of Lambiccato (Moscato variety)
- Cilento
- Costa d'Amalfi, with or without Furore, Ravello, Tramonti
- Falanghina del Sannio, with or without Guardia Sanframondi, Guardiolo, Sant'Agata dei Goti, Solopaca, Taburno
- Falerno del Massico
- Galluccio
- Irpinia, accompagnata o no dalla sottozona Campi Taurasini
- Ischia
- Penisola Sorrentina, with or without Gragnano, Lettere o Sorrento
- Sannio, with or without Guardia Sanframondi, Guardiolo, Sant'Agata dei Goti, Solopaca, Solopaca Classico, Taburno
- Vesuvio

AGNANUM

Via Vicinale Abbandonata agli Astroni, 3
80125 Napoli (NA)
Tel. +39 081 2303507
info@agnanum.it
www.agnanum.it
moccia.azagricolaagnanum

YEAR OF FOUNDATION **1960**
NAME OF THE OWNER **Raffaele Moccia**
TOTAL BOTTLES PRODUCED **13,000**
DIRECT SALES
VISITS TO THE WINERY - RESERVATION NEEDED
HECTARES OF VINEYARD **3.5**

Raffaele Moccia is truly a heroic winemaker who grows his grapes in the Naples suburb of Campi Flegrei, right above the industrial area of Bagnoli and inside the Astroni Park where the soil is volcanic. Given the steep pitch of his land, the vineyards have all been terraced by hand. He cultivates only Piedirosso and Falanghina grapes, which are native to the area, and his vines have not been grafted. Thanks to his exemplary passion and dedication, along with hard work, he offers us some truly moving wines.

 90 Price B

Campi Flegrei Piedirosso Vigna delle Volpi 2014

100% Piedirosso grapes. Ages for 8 months in casks. Ruby. Neat and intense nose of red fruits, violet and geranium. The palate is fresh and savory with thin tannins and long finish that reminds sour cherries and blackberry.

 88 Price B

Campi Flegrei Piedirosso 2014

100% Piedirosso grapes. Matures in stainless steel tanks. Vivid Ruby. Nose of cherry, crunchy plum and rosehip. The palate is rustic but with a pleasant and balanced freshness.

ASTRONI

Via Sartania, 48
80126 Napoli (NA)
Tel. +39 081 5884182
info@cantineastroni.com

www.cantineastroni.com
cantineastroni
@CantineAstroni

YEAR OF FOUNDATION **1999**
NAME OF THE OWNER **Varchetta Family**
TOTAL BOTTLES PRODUCED **300,000**
DIRECT SALES
VISITS TO THE WINERY - RESERVATION NEEDED
HECTARES OF VINEYARD **25**
CERTIFIED ORGANIC VITICULTURE

The Varchetta family has been making wine in the heart of Campi Flegrei for over 100 years and have always worked to protect and enhance the value of the whole area. The winery is on the slopes of the Astroni Crater, a dead volcano that is part of the volcanic area bordering with the WWF nature reserve that borders with what once was the hunting reserve of the Bourbon kings. The wines they produce have an unmistakable style and character thanks to the Mediterranean climate and the composition of the soil which includes lapillus, ash and sand. Their 25 hectares of vineyards are planted with Falanghina and Piedirosso.

 93 Price B

Campi Flegrei Piedirosso Tenuta Camaldoli Riserva 2012

100% Piedirosso grapes. Ages in different sized casks. Lively Ruby-garnet. The nose is complex and offers notes of black cherry, cardamom, lightly smoky and hints of tobacco leaf. Firm palate with a good balanced acidity, savory and tense finish. Very good length.

ANTONIO CAGGIANO

Contrada Sala
83030 Taurasi (AV)
Tel. +39 0827 74723
Fax +39 0827 74723
info@cantinecaggiano.it
www.cantinecaggiano.it
cantinecaggiano

YEAR OF FOUNDATION **1990**
NAME OF THE OWNER **Antonio and Giuseppe Caggiano**
TOTAL BOTTLES PRODUCED **155,000**

DIRECT SALES
VISITS TO THE WINERY - RESERVATION NEEDED
HECTARES OF VINEYARD 25

Antonio Caggiano and his son Pino are among the most famous producers of Taurasi and their Vigna Macchia dei Goti is a recognized great classic. The winery, built in 1990 in Contrada Sala, a hamlet in Taurasi, is a small museum of farmer culture full of tools and equipment together with barrels and barriques.

☐ 90 👍 Price A

Fiano di Avellino Bechar 2015

100% Fiano grapes. Matures in stainless steel tanks. Straw yellow. The nose offers herbaceous and floral notes. The palate is supple and savory with wonderful freshness that reminds lemon peel and thyme. Long finish.

☐ 89 👍 Price A

Fiagre 2015

Blend of 70% Fiano and 30% Greco. Matures in stainless steel tanks. Straw yellow with greenish hues. Citrusy nose, cedar, grapesfruit and sage. The palate is savory, tense and with great acidity. The depth brings notes of anise and eucalyptus.

■ 89 Price B

Taurasi Vigna Macchia dei Goti 2012

100% Aglianico grapes. Ages in barrique for 18 months. Deep Ruby. Nose of red fruit like plum and blackberry, then floral notes of rose and violet. The palate offers a youthful tannin but well extracted, savory and firm. Long firm finish.

CANTINE DELL'ANGELO

Via Santa Lucia, 32
83010 Tufo (AV)
Tel. +39 0825 998073
info@cantinedellangelo.com
www.cantinedellangelo.com

YEAR OF FOUNDATION 2006
NAME OF THE OWNER Muto Family
TOTAL BOTTLES PRODUCED 22,000
DIRECT SALES
VISITS TO THE WINERY - RESERVATION NEEDED
HECTARES OF VINEYARD 5

Angelo Muto has been running the winery he inherited from his father in Tufo since 2006. He is an excellent example of an honest and humble winegrower who knows and protects his land. His five hectares of vineyards are planted with Greco and some of them are near an old sulfur mine. Angelo works his own land using traditional farming methods, while his wine consultant is Luigi Sarno. His annual production is about 22,000 bottles and the two wines he produces stand out for their character and complexity.

☐ 90 Price B

Greco di Tufo 2014

100% Greco grapes. Matures in stainless steel tanks for 10 months. Golden yellow. Complex nose of nectarine, quince, sage, black pepper and flint. The palate is citrusy, tense with great freshness. Wonderful finish with savory notes and flint.

CAUTIERO

Contrada Arbusti
82030 Frasso Telesino (BN)
Tel. +39 338 7640641
info@cautiero.it
www.cautiero.it
 cautiero.aziendaagricola

YEAR OF FOUNDATION 2002
NAME OF THE OWNER Fulvio and Imma Cautiero
TOTAL BOTTLES PRODUCED 16,000
DIRECT SALES
VISITS TO THE WINERY - RESERVATION NEEDED
HECTARES OF VINEYARD 4
HOSPITALITY
CERTIFIED ORGANIC VITICULTURE

Fulvio and Imma escaped from the urban chaos of Naples in 2002 for a country life in the green hills of Frasso Telesino on the slopes of Taburno. They bought the Donna Candida estate and engaged in organic farming. They have four hectares of vineyards with the native grapes Falanghina, Greco, Fiano, Aglianico and Piedirosso.

☐ 92 👍 Price A

Falanghina Fois 2015

100% Falanghina grapes. Stainless steel tanks. Straw yellow with green hues. Very expressive and floral nose, white stone fruit and light aromas of thyme and sage. Savory palate, supple and fresh. Long sea breeze finish.

90 Price B
Donna Candida 2011

100% Aglianico grapes. Ages in barrique for 24 months. Ruby with garnet rim. Intense nose of geranium, violet, blackberry and cherry. Rich palate, savory, vertical and with smooth tannins. Long finish.

★
COLLI DI LAPIO

Via Arianello, 47
83030 Lapio (AV)
Tel. +39 0825 982184
info@collidilapio.it
www.collidilapio.it
Colli-di-lapio

YEAR OF FOUNDATION 1994
NAME OF THE OWNER Clelia Romano
TOTAL BOTTLES PRODUCED 50,000
DIRECT SALES
VISITS TO THE WINERY - RESERVATION NEEDED
HECTARES OF VINEYARD 6
CERTIFIED ORGANIC VITICULTURE

Clelia Romano founded this small yet now legendary winery some 20 years ago and it is specialized in producing Fiano di Avellino. It is located in Lapio, at the heart of the appellation (before it was given its official name of Fiano di Avellino was called Fiano di Lapio). The vineyards are situated at an altitude of over 500m above sea level and the wine are briny and much more northern than one would expect at that latitude.

☐ **91** Price A
Greco di Tufo Alexandros 2015

100% Greco grapes. Matures in stainless steel. Straw yellow with green hues. The nose offers savory notes, pencil shavings, lemongrass and mint. The palate is dominated by freshness and savoriness, tense and the finish reminds citrusy notes.

☐ **89** Price A
Fiano di Avellino 2015

100% Fiano grapes. Matures in stainless steel tanks. Captivating nose of lemon peel, thyme, sage, sea breeze. The palate is savory, fresh with a wonderful sea line minerality aftertaste. Good length.

 ★
CONTRADE DI TAURASI

Via Municipio, 39
83030 Taurasi (AV)
Tel. +39 0827 74483
info@contradeditaurasi.it
www.contradeditaurasi.it

YEAR OF FOUNDATION 1998
NAME OF THE OWNER Enza Lonardo
TOTAL BOTTLES PRODUCED 15,000
DIRECT SALES
VISITS TO THE WINERY - RESERVATION NEEDED
HECTARES OF VINEYARD 5.5
CERTIFIED ORGANIC VITICULTURE

If you are looking for a real Taurasi from Taurasi then go no further than the tiny winery of the Lonardo brothers, who considered to be among the best producers of this wine. These authentic Campania winemakers, better yet Taurasi-makers, produce only a few thousand bottles of their wine, which has an incredible typicity wine, from their six hectares of vineyards.

■ 🍇 **96** Price B
Taurasi Vigne d'Alto 2011

100% Aglianico grapes. Ages in oak barrels for 24 months. The nose is an explosion of flavors, black fruits, violet and rose, eucalyptus, pencil shavings and wet leaves. Rich and bold palate, it had refined and solid tannins; supple and firm. It is a sleek wine. The finish is long and reminds notes of tobacco and licorice.

■ **93** Price B
Taurasi Coste 2011

100% Aglianico grapes. Ages in oak barrels for 24 months. Very traditional and elegant; nose of cassis, black cherry, black pepper and a light woody notes. The palate is savory, velvety, fresh with a wet leaves and musk notes. Great length.

☐ **89** Price B
Burlesque Grecomusc' 2015

100% Ravello grapes. Matures in stainless steel tanks for 8 months. First vintage for this single vineyard pre phylloxera Cru. Green yellow. Nose of cedar, white plum and green apple. Supple palate, juicy with sea line character. Long finish.

★★
MARISA CUOMO

Via G.B. Lama, 16/18
84010 Furore (SA)
Tel. +39 089 830348
Fax +39 089 8304014
info@marisacuomo.com
www.marisacuomo.com
 CantineMarisaCuomo
 @CuomoMarisa

YEAR OF FOUNDATION 1980
NAME OF THE OWNER Marisa Cuomo
TOTAL BOTTLES PRODUCED 110,000
DIRECT SALES
VISITS TO THE WINERY - RESERVATION NEEDED
HECTARES OF VINEYARD 19

The vineyards are literally hanging off the coast, small trellised plots of grapes that alternate with those of lemons and olives. Marina Cuomo is the Queen of Amalfi Coast wines, a champion of ancient and heroic winemaking methods and producer of wines that are deeply Mediterranean and, at the same time, extremely good and comprehensible, deeply connected with this magnificent land.

☐ 96   Price B
Costa d'Amalfi Furore Bianco Fiorduva 2014
Blend of Ripoli, Fenile and Ginestra grapes. Ages in barrique for 6 months. Austere and refined nose; sea breeze, citrusy and floral. Round palate, savory and supple; wonderful acidity and depth with peppery notes, eucalyptus and sea-line minerality. Very long finish.

█ 92   Price B
Ravello Rosso Riserva 2012
Blend of 70% Piedirosso and 30% Ravello grapes. Ages in oak barrels for 12 months. Garnet. Intense nose of blackberry, violet and rhubarb. Rich and juicy palate. It is smooth and fresh with elegant tannins and a wonderful sea breeze notes. The finish is very long.

☐ 89   Price A
Costa d'Amalfi Ravello bianco 2015
Blend of 60% Falanghina and 40% Biancolella grapes. Ages for 4 months in stainless steel tanks. Green yellow. Notes of peach, white plum, fresh al-

mond; then aromas of tomato leaf and sage. The palate is definitively fresh, savory and supple. Long finish with a sea breeze note.

★
D'AMBRA

Via Mario D'Ambra, 16
80075 Forio D'Ischia (NA)
Tel. +39 081 907246
Fax +39 081 908190
info@dambravini.com
www.dambravini.com
 dambravini
 @ViniDAmbra

YEAR OF FOUNDATION 1888
NAME OF THE OWNER Andrea D'Ambra
TOTAL BOTTLES PRODUCED 500,000
DIRECT SALES
VISITS TO THE WINERY - RESERVATION NEEDED
HECTARES OF VINEYARD 12

This estate is the ancient and traditional symbol of winemaking on the island of Ischia and has existed for over a century, founded by the ancestors of the current owners. Today it is an important winemaking reality that makes impeccable wines from grapes grown on magnificent terraced vineyards on the slopes of Monte Epomeo, which are in part owned by the winery and the rest from by historic suppliers. Their leading wine is made with grapes from the Frassitelli vineyard that has green tuff stone in its soil and is surrounded by stone walls.

█ 93   Price B
Ischia Piedirosso La Vigna dei Mille Anni 2013
A blend of Piedirosso, Cabernet Sauvignon and 100% Aglianico that ages in Allier oak barrels for at least 18 months. Complex bouquet, distinct and sweet scents of red fruit (especially raspberry), floral tones and notes of pistachio and hazelnut, then hints of chocolate and white pepper. The mouthfeel is bold and elegant, wiht great finesses and promises of a long life.

☐ 92   Price A
Ischia Biancolella Frassitelli 2015
Biancolella grapes. Matures in stainless steel tanks. Green yellow. Interesting nose of broom blossoms, cedar, banana and Mediterranean scrub. The pal-

ate is round, fresh and savory with notes white blossoms and lightly aromatic; very good length.

■ 90   Price B

Mario D'Ambra 2013

Blend of 50% guarnaccia, 50% per'e' palumm grapes. Ages in different sized oak barrels. Deep Ruby. Nose of black cherry, clove, white tobacco. The palate is tense, juicy, warm and elegant, good depth and length.

DE CONCILIIS

Località Querce, 1
84060 Prignano Cilento (SA)
Tel. +39 0974 831090
info@viticoltorideconciliis.it
www.viticoltorideconciliis.it
❤ *Viticoltori-De-Conciliis*

YEAR OF FOUNDATION 1996
NAME OF THE OWNER Paola, Bruno, Luigi De Conciliis
TOTAL BOTTLES PRODUCED 180,000
DIRECT SALES
VISITS TO THE WINERY SU PRENOTAZIONE
HECTARES OF VINEYARD 25
CERTIFIED ORGANIC VITICULTURE
OLIVE OIL PRODUCTION

Bruno De Conciliis is a talented, skilled and passionate winemaker who for some years now has struck out on his own personal quest to gain recognition for the wines made in Cilento, which is more known for its beaches. He produces bold reds and whites that are deeply Mediterranean with an unmistakable style and winegrowing practices that respect nature and the environment.

☐ 88   Price A

Donnaluna 2015

100% Fiano grapes. Matures in stainless steel tank. The nose is surprisingly neat and clean: citrus leaves, hazelnut, thyme, sage and sea breeze. Round and pleasant palate with notes of cedar and lemon. Good acidity and long finish.

DI MARZO

Via Gaetano di Marzo, 2
83010 Tufo (AV)
Tel. +39 0825 998022

info@cantinedimarzo.it
www.cantinedimarzo.it

YEAR OF FOUNDATION 1648
NAME OF THE OWNER di Somma Family
TOTAL BOTTLES PRODUCED 150,000
DIRECT SALES
VISITS TO THE WINERY - RESERVATION NEEDED
HECTARES OF VINEYARD 23

The di Marzo family has played an important role in Italy's political and economic life, especially during the 19th century. But the winery became a reality many centuries before, in 1648, thanks to Scipione di Marzo. Since 2009, the direct descendants of the di Marzo family, Ferrante and Maria Giovanna di Somma, have run the winery with excellent results. Their wines are very interesting quality-wise and are made with the consultancy of Paolo Caciorgna and Maurizio Baldi. The estate is comprised of 50 hectares of land of which 23 are vineyards of Aglianico and Greco.

■ 91   Price A

Irpinia Aglianico Cantine Stroriche 2013

100% Aglianico grapes. Ages 4 months in casks. Ruby with garnet rim. The nose offers notes of tamarind, rose petals, violet and lightly smoky. The palate offers youth tannins, savory, fresh and easy drinking. The finish is supple and long.

☐ 89   Price A

Greco di Tufo Franciscus 2015

100% Greco grapes. Matures for 7 months in stainless steel tanks on the lees. Golden yellow. Nose lightly rustic that offers notes of resin, anise, lemongrass and apple. The palate is fresh, savory and vertical. Good length.

DI MEO

Contrada Coccovoni, 1
83050 Salza Irpina (AV)
Tel. +39 0825 981419
info@dimeo.it
www.dimeo.it
❤ *Di-Meo-Vini*

YEAR OF FOUNDATION 1986
NAME OF THE OWNER Di Meo Brothers

TOTAL BOTTLES PRODUCED **450,000**
DIRECT SALES
VISITS TO THE WINERY - RESERVATION NEEDED
HECTARES OF VINEYARD **30**
RESTAURANT

Last year we were happily surprised by the amazing Fiano di Avellino Ermina Di Meo 2003. This year it is a great Taurasi Riserva Selezione Hamilton 2008 that deserves the 'DoctorWine face', confirming the good quality of the winery. Roberto, Erminia and Generoso Di Meo continue to consistently offer us delicious wines but have now achieved a level of quality that deserves to be recognized.

---

 96   Price B
Taurasi Selezione Hamilton Riserva 2008

100% Aglianico grapes. Matures for 18 months in tonneau and barrique. Deep ruby. Wonderful nose: aromatic herbs, red fruits, wet leaves, licorice and tobacco. Tense palate, savory and extraordinary acidity; smooth tannins. This is a great wine, sleek and complex. Wonderful long finish.

---

 93   Price B
Taurasi Vigna Olmo Riserva 2008

100% Aglianico grapes. Matures for 18 months in tonneau and barrique. Deep ruby. Wonderful nose: aromatic herbs, red fruits, wet leaves, licorice and tobacco. Tense palate, savory and extraordinary acidity; smooth tannins. This is a great wine, sleek and complex. Wonderful long finish.

---

 90   Price B
Fiano di Avellino Colle dei Cerri 2006

100% Fiano grapes, matures for 10 months in barrique and then 12 months in stainless steel tanks. Deep golden yellow. Nose of almond, petrol and woody notes. Savory and rich palate, supple and pleasant. Long finish.

DI PRISCO

Contrada Rotole, 27
83040 Fontanarosa (AV)
Tel. +39 0825 475738
cantinadiprisco@libero.it
www.cantinadiprisco.it
 Cantinadiprisco

YEAR OF FOUNDATION **1995**
NAME OF THE OWNER **Pasqualino Di Prisco**

TOTAL BOTTLES PRODUCED **120,000**
DIRECT SALES
VISITS TO THE WINERY - RESERVATION NEEDED
HECTARES OF VINEYARD **10**

This estate has vineyards situated at over 600m above sea level and produces wines of great character with a natural predilection for whites, which are often among the best found in the region. The estate of Pasqualino Di Prisco is located in Fontanarosa, northeast of Taurasi, but it gets its white grapes from Montefusco, which produces bulk wines that are agile and mineral and could be considered Mediterranean Chablis.

---

 91   👍 Price A
Greco di Tufo 2015

100% Greco grapes. Matures in stainless steel tanks. Green yellow. The nose offer note of pear, apricot, almond and mint. The palate shows wonderful freshness, tense and savory. Long finish of good depth that reminds notes of mint and sage.

---

 89   Price B
Fiano di Avellino Rotole 2015

100% Fiano grapes. Matures in stainless steel tanks. Deep Straw yellow. Intriguing nose; peach, quince, thyme, sage and Mediterranean scrub. The palate is tense and supple, fresh and very pleasant. Long finish with a pleasant savory note.

DONNACHIARA

Via Stazione - Località Pietracupa
83030 Montefalcione (AV)
Tel. +39 0825 977135
info@donnachiara.it
www.donnachiara.it
 Donnachiara-Concept-Winery
 @DonnaChiara

YEAR OF FOUNDATION **2005**
NAME OF THE OWNER **Petitto Family**
TOTAL BOTTLES PRODUCED **200,000**
DIRECT SALES
VISITS TO THE WINERY - RESERVATION NEEDED
HECTARES OF VINEYARD **27**

Illaria Petitto is young and cute and is still a wine 'girl', in the totally affectionate sense of the word. And yet she is becoming very passionate about wine and is doing some good work. The wines from her family's estate keep getting better year after year and we are convinced that soon everyone will be talking about this small Irpinia winery. This year, side from the Taurasi, we have also included their Fiano and Aglianico.

 90   Price B

Taurasi di Umberto 2012

100% Aglianico grapes. Ages in barrique for 12 months. Ruby with garnet rim. Intense nose of black cherry, plum, redcurrant, wet leaves and Indian spices. The palate is tense with exuberant tannins, it's savory and austere, good length with resin and minty finish.

 89   Price A

Irpinia Aglianico 2013

100% Aglianico grapes. Ages 6 months in barrique. Deep ruby. The nose offers aromas of red fruits, violet, pomegranate and plum. The palate is spicy, savory with firm tannins and good balanced acidity. The finish is long and reminds notes of clove.

☐ **88**   Price A

Greco di Tufo 2015

100% Greco grapes. Matures in stainless steel tanks. Straw yellow of good depth. Nose of thyme, cedar and peat. The palate is vertical, fresh and savory. It has good depth and long finish.

★★

BENITO FERRARA

Frazione San Paolo, 14
83010 Tufo (AV)
Tel. +39 0825 998194
info@benitoferrara.it
www.benitoferrara.it
 f *aziendaagricola.benitoferrara*

YEAR OF FOUNDATION 1860
NAME OF THE OWNER Gabriella Ferrara and Sergio Ambrosino
TOTAL BOTTLES PRODUCED 45,000
DIRECT SALES
VISITS TO THE WINERY - RESERVATION NEEDED
HECTARES OF VINEYARD 10

Gabriella Ferrara and Sergio Ambrosino own this winery that is among the most classic for Greco di Tufo. They have vineyards that sit at over 500m meters above sea level and include Vigna Cicogna, a true grand cru for the area with vines that are decades old and produce wines that have an extraordinary capacity to age. In fact, the wines that are over ten years old are still perfectly drinkable.

☐ **91**   Price B

Greco di Tufo Vigna Cicogna 2015

100% Greco grapes. Matures on the lees in stainless steel. Straw yellow. Complex nose: white plum, hazelnut, rosemary and fennel. Tense and vibrant palate; wonderful acidity. The finish is pleasant and long with fruity and yellow blossom aftertaste.

FEUDI DI SAN GREGORIO

Località Cerza Grossa
83050 Sorbo Serpico (AV)
Tel. +39 0825 986683
Fax +39 0825 986230
info@feudi.it
www.feudi.it
 f *feudisg*
 🐦 *@FeudiDSGregorio*

YEAR OF FOUNDATION 1986
NAME OF THE OWNER Capaldo Family
TOTAL BOTTLES PRODUCED 3,500,000
DIRECT SALES
VISITS TO THE WINERY - RESERVATION NEEDED
HECTARES OF VINEYARD 250
RESTAURANT
CERTIFIED ORGANIC VITICULTURE

This is a leading winery in the Campania and was founded almost 30 years ago by the Ecolino family. It was later acquired by the Capaldo family that is expanding and promoting to it in a decisive way thanks to the efforts of its young and talented president Antonio Capaldo and CEO Pierpaolo Sirch, who look more like winemaker. Production is varied and vast and includes all the types of wine produced in Irpinia, wines that are more technical than they were in the past but strive to be pleasing and to exalt specific territorial characteristics. All the grapes are organically grown, an approach which is no simple feat for an estate of this size.

91 👍 **Price A**

Greco di Tufo Cutizzi 2015

100% Greco grapes. Matures for 5 months on the lees in stainless steel tanks. Complex flavors of loquat, white plum, cedar, camomile and almond. Very savory palate, fresh, slim and round. Citrusy finish.

90 **Price B**

Serpico 2010

100% Aglianico grapes. Ages in barrique for 18 months. Deep garnet. Flavorsome nose of violet, cassis, plum and licorice. Tense and juicy palate with light tannins. Lightly smoky and fine herbs notes. The finish is rich and long.

88 **Price A**

Fiano di Avellino Pietracalda 2015

100% Fiano grapes. Matures in stainless steel tank for 5 months. Straw yellow. Citrusy, floral and fruity nose. The palate is savory, supple, fresh and tense with lively acidity. Pleasant finish.

FONTANAVECCHIA

*Via Fontanavecchia
82030 Torrecuso (BN)
Tel. +39 0824 876275
info@fontanavecchia.info
www.fontanavecchia.info*

YEAR OF FOUNDATION 1980
NAME OF THE OWNER Libero Rillo
TOTAL BOTTLES PRODUCED 160,000
DIRECT SALES
VISITS TO THE WINERY - RESERVATION NEEDED
HECTARES OF VINEYARD 18

Libero Rillo is one of the 'fathers' of Falanghina del Sannio, a wine which he is very dedicated to and he often produces some outstanding versions. His winery also makes several versions of Aglianico del Taburno, which was recently classified DOCG, and Fiano del Sannio. Rillo and his Fontanavecchia winery can be found in Torrecuso, west of Benevento.

91 **Price B**

Aglianico del Taburno Vigna Cataratte Riserva 2008

100% Aglianico grapes. Ages in French barrique. Lively garnet. Complex nose of blackberry, plum, vio-

let and black pepper. Then offers notes of eucalyptus and cocoa. Balanced. The palate shows firm and refined tannins; good length with a coffee aftertaste.

88 **Price A**

Falanghina del Sannio Taburno 2014

100% Falanghina grapes. Matures in stainless steel tanks. Straw yellow with green hues. The wine excels for its captivating and clean aromas. The palate is supple, savory, juicy and vigorous.

★★

GALARDI

*Frazione San Carlo
81037 Sessa Aurunca (CE)
Tel. +39 0823 708900
Fax +39 0823 708034
info@terradilavoro.it
www.terradilavoro.com*

YEAR OF FOUNDATION 1991
NAME OF THE OWNER Francesco and Dora Catello, Arturo Celentano and Maria Luisa Murena
TOTAL BOTTLES PRODUCED 33,000
DIRECT SALES
VISITS TO THE WINERY - RESERVATION NEEDED
HECTARES OF VINEYARD 10
CERTIFIED ORGANIC VITICULTURE
OLIVE OIL PRODUCTION

This tiny and legendary estate is the creation of four 'visionaries': Francesco and Dora Catello, Arturo Celentano and Maria Luisa Murena. It is located in Terra di Lavoro in the northern part of Campania, in the district of Roccamonfina, a volcanic area with a very particular soil. Thanks also the consultancy of renowned enologist Riccardo Cotarella, they have produced a great red, a blend of Aglianico and a little Piedirosso, a wine the whole world is talking about and that has become an international icon.

93 **Price C**

Terra di Lavoro 2014

Blend of 80% Aglianico and 20% Piedirosso grapes. Ages 1 year in barrique. Deep ruby. Rich nose of red fruits, violet, juniper and wet leaves. Sleek and with great personality. The nose offers shades of sea breeze, resin and pine. It's still young and the lively tannins are there to confirm it; savory, warm and with great body. Long finish with woody notes.

GUASTAFERRO

Via Gramsci, 2
83030 Taurasi (AV)
Tel. +39 334 1551543
info@guastaferro.it
www.guastaferro.it
Raffaele Guastaferro

YEAR OF FOUNDATION **2007**
NAME OF THE OWNER **Raffaele Guastaferro**
TOTAL BOTTLES PRODUCED **10,000**
DIRECT SALES
VISITS TO THE WINERY - RESERVATION NEEDED
HECTARES OF VINEYARD **7**

In 2002, Raffaele Guastaferro earned his degree in enology and inherited 10 hectares of vineyards from his grandfather with over 100-year-old vines trained using the old starseto (pergola Avellinese) method. Raffaele's training and the experience of Antoine Gaita were key in creating a very interesting style for the wines that were also rooted in tradition. The excellent quality of the grapes comes from the fact that the vineyards are situated in select areas like Contrada Piano d'Angelo and Contrada Pozzillo. Just over 10,000 bottles are produced a year, mostly Aglianico and Taurasi with a limited amount of Fiano and Greco.

---

92   Price B

Taurasi Primum Riserva 2008

100% Aglianico grapes, 24 months in oak barrels. Ruby with garnet hues. The nose is predominantly fruity with hint of black cherry, plum and blackcurrant. On the palate is more elegant than powerful. It's savory, earthy, fresh and it has a long finish. Produced only with grapes from centenarian vines.

---

91   Price B

Taurasi Primum 2011

100% Aglianico grapes. Ages in oak barrels for 18 months. Dense Ruby. Nutty nose, wet leaves and spices. The palate is rich, earthy and with great depth. Warm and balanced. Great body and tannic structure.

★

I FAVATI

Piazza Di Donato, 41
83020 Cesinali (AV)

Tel. +39 0825 666898
info@cantineifavati.it
www.cantineifavati.it
Cantine-I-Favati
@IFavati

YEAR OF FOUNDATION **1996**
NAME OF THE OWNER **Piersabino, Giancarlo Favati and Rosanna Petrozziello**
TOTAL BOTTLES PRODUCED **80,000**
DIRECT SALES
VISITS TO THE WINERY - RESERVATION NEEDED
HECTARES OF VINEYARD **10**

Piersabino and Giancarlo Favati and Rosanna Petrozziello, the wife of the latter, are 'I' (The) Favati. For almost 20 years they have been making wine just south of Atripalda and Avellino. Their prestigious line of production is distinguished by their white labels and include Greco and Fiano, the estate's specialty.

☐ **93**   👍 Price A

Fiano di Avellino Pietramara 2015

100% Fiano grapes. Unfiltered, matures in stainless steel tanks on the lees. Green yellow. Wine of great impact and personality, unripe apricot, lime peel, pear, thyme, sea breeze, broom blossoms and almond. Pleasant palate: juicy, savory and clean. The finish is long and definitively marine.

---

92   Price B

Cretarossa 2011

100% Aglianico grapes. Garnet. Very distinctive nose of black cherry, cinnamon, black pepper and licorice. The palate is firm, round and supported by good freshness. The tannins are still young and it has a long blueberry and nutty finish.

IL VERRO

Località Acquavalle
Frazione Lautoni
81040 Formicola (CE)
Tel. +39 345 6416200
info@ilverro.it
www.ilverro.it
aziendaagricola.ilverro

YEAR OF FOUNDATION **2003**
NAME OF THE OWNER **Cesare Avenia and Partners**
TOTAL BOTTLES PRODUCED **25,000**
DIRECT SALES

VISITS TO THE WINERY - RESERVATION NEEDED
HECTARES OF VINEYARD 3.5

This tiny winery is not far from Pontelatone which is the home of Casavecchi, an ancient wine that was only recently rediscovered. The area is north of Caserta and near the Colline Caiatine and it was here that Cesare Avenia decided to produce wine using grapes that are not general used or almost forgotten, like Casavecchia, Pallagrello Nero and even the very rare Coda di Pecora which practically only he uses.

☐ 90   👍 Price A
Verginiano 2015

100% Pallagrello Bianco grapes. Matures in stainless steel tanks. Deep Straw yellow. Intense nose of cedar and eucalyptus, then hint of aromatic herbs and yellow blossoms. Gentle and balanced. The palate has good body; great balanced acidity and it delivers what promises on the nose.

☐ 89   Price A
Sheep 2015

100% Coda di Pecora grapes (rare local grapes variety). Matures in stainless steel tanks. Straw yellow. Intense nose of nettle, sage and lemongrass. Savory and firm palate. The palate is pleasant and reminds notes of lemongrass.

LA GUARDIENSE

Località Santa Lucia, 104/105
82034 Guardia Sanframondi (BN)
Tel. +39 0824 864034
Fax +39 0824 864935
info@laguardiense.it
www.laguardiense.it
 Vini-La-Guardiense
 @LaGuardiense

YEAR OF FOUNDATION 1960
TOTAL BOTTLES PRODUCED 3,500,000
DIRECT SALES
VISITS TO THE WINERY - RESERVATION NEEDED
HECTARES OF VINEYARD 1,500
RESTAURANT

Considered one of Italy's best wine cooperatives, this winery produces some excellent wines at excellent prices. It has 1,300 members who have a total of some 1,500 hectares of vine-

yards. The winery has adhered to Riccardo Cotarella's Sfide (Challenge) initiative that aims at producing wines without the use of sulfites.

■ 91   👍 Price A
Sannio Guardia Sanframonti Aglianico Lucchero 2014

100% Aglianico grape. Ages for 6 months in Allier and Tronçais tonneau. Intense ruby. Hints of sour cherry, blueberry, rhubarb and sweet tobacco leaf. The palate is savory, vertical, round and with silky tannins. Good finish with a slightly smoky note.

☐ 89   👍 Price A
Sannio Guardia Sanframonti Falanghina Senete 2015

100% Falanghina grapes. Matures in stainless steel tanks. Straw yellow. Nose of mango, white plum and freesia blossoms. The palate is round, savory and with good acidity. The finish is supple and reminds sea breeze.

☐ 88   👍 Price A
Sannio Falanghina Janare 2015

100% Falanghina grapes. Matures in stainless steel tanks. Floral and fruity nose. The palate is savory, fresh and delivers what promises on the nose. The finish is of a good length on citrusy notes.

★

LA RIVOLTA

Contrada Rivolta
82030 Torrecuso (BN)
Tel. +39 0824 872921
info@fattorialarivolta.com
www.fattorialarivolta.it
 fattorialarivolta1812
 @FattoriaRivolta

YEAR OF FOUNDATION 1997
NAME OF THE OWNER Cotroneo Family
TOTAL BOTTLES PRODUCED 150,000
DIRECT SALES
VISITS TO THE WINERY - RESERVATION NEEDED
HECTARES OF VINEYARD 29
RESTAURANT
CERTIFIED ORGANIC VITICULTURE

This is the best estate in the area of Sannio Beneventano and Taburno in particular. Paolo Cotroneo runs it in a very professional manner together with enologist Vincenzo Mercurio. The estate's top wines are the traditional Aglianico del Taburno and the more innovative Terra di Rivolta Riserva and both are very good. But this year the best has been a white wine.

108

 92   Price A

Sogno di Rivolta 2013

Blend of 50% Falanghina, 25% Fiano and 25% Greco grapes. Matures for 5 months in barrique. Deep Straw yellow.Very captivating and aromatic nose, grapesfruit, tropical fruit, yellow peach and hint of tea leaf. The palate is fresh and supple, savory, elegant and mouth filling. The finish offers a note of Mediterranean scrub.

 90 Price B

Aglianico del Taburno Terra di Rivolta Riserva 2013

100% Aglianico grapes. Matures for 18 months in barriers and tonneau. Ruby with garnet rim. Jammy nose, lightly woody with a hint of sweet spices. Sleek palate with firm and refined tannins, savory, tense. Warm and long finish.

★

LA SIBILLA

Via Ottaviano Augusto, 19
80070 Bacoli (NA)
Tel. +39 081 8688778
info@sibillavini.it
www.sibillavini.it
 La-sibilla

YEAR OF FOUNDATION **1997**
NAME OF THE OWNER **Di Meo Family**
TOTAL BOTTLES PRODUCED **65,000**
DIRECT SALES
VISITS TO THE WINERY - RESERVATION NEEDED
HECTARES OF VINEYARD **9.5**

Vincenzo Di Meo is a young enologist-winegrower who is demonstrating what level of quality can be achieved in a difficult yet unique area like Campi Flegrei, more precisely in Baia. The soil is volcanic and the vineyards are terraced with unique grapes like Marsigliese, Piedirosso, Falanghina and Olivella. It takes a lot of courage to make wine here and protect land and the landscape from real estate speculation and pollution caused by illegal waste disposal.

☐ **90**   Price A

Campi Flegrei Falanghina 2015

100% Falanghina grapes. Matures for 3 months in stainless steel tanks. Warm green yellow. The nose offers very clean notes of citrus, field blossoms and flint. It's savory and fresh, easy drinking with hints of cedar, lemon and aromatic herbs.

■ **89** Price A

Campi Flegrei Piedirosso 2015

100% Piedirosso grapes. Matures for 3 months in stainless steel tanks. Intense ruby. Rustic nose that shows notes of cherry, tomato leaf and blood orange. The palate is savory, warm and long. It has great body and length.

★

LUIGI MAFFINI

Località Cenito
84048 Castellabate (SA)
Tel. +39 0974 966345
info@luigimaffini.it
www.luigimaffini.it
 Luigi-Maffini

YEAR OF FOUNDATION **1996**
NAME OF THE OWNER **Luigi Maffini**
TOTAL BOTTLES PRODUCED **100,000**
DIRECT SALES
VISITS TO THE WINERY - RESERVATION NEEDED
HECTARES OF VINEYARD **15**
CERTIFIED ORGANIC VITICULTURE

The fact Cilento, the southern part of Campania, is a magnificent place can be seen by watching the film Benvenuti al Sud (Welcome to the South) with Claudio Bisi which was shot in Castellabate. This is where Luigi Maffini has his estate and produces some very interesting organic wines.

☐ **93** Price B

Cilento Fiano Pietraincatenata 2014

100% Fiano grapes. The 70% matures for 8 months in barrique. Warm Straw yellow. Intense nose, very clean and with distinctive note of citrus blossoms, sage and then hint of almond, cedar and white pepper. Tense palate, wonderful freshness that makes the wine mouth-watering, sea breeze. The finish is fascinating with note of hawthorn, slim and long finish.

☐ 89   👍 Price A

Paestum Fiano Kratos 2015

100% Fiano grapes. Matures in stainless steel tanks, green yellow. Aromas of camomile, broom blossoms, barley and almond. The palate is pleasantly fresh, savory and with a light flinty note. Long sea breeze finish.

SALVATORE MARTUSCIELLO

Via Spinelli, 4
80010 Quarto (NA)
Tel. +39 081 8766123
🅢 *salvatoremartusciello*
info@salvatoremartusciello.it
www.salvatoremartusciello.it
f *salvatore.martusciello.1*

YEAR OF FOUNDATION 2015
NAME OF THE OWNER Gilda and Salvatore Martusciello
TOTAL BOTTLES PRODUCED 87,000
DIRECT SALES
VISITS TO THE WINERY - RESERVATION NEEDED
HECTARES OF VINEYARD 2

The Martusciello family has the merit of bringing into the spotlight wines like Gragnano and Lettere. In accordance with his family, Salvatore struck out on his own from Grotta del Sole together with his wife Gilda. Few in this area know the land and the wines as much as Salvatore who has focused his new project on the production of Gragnano in order to enhance its quality and tradition.

■ 86   👍 Price A

Penisola Sorrentina Rosso Frizzante Gragnano Ottouve 2015

Blend of 60% Piedirosso, 100% Aglianico and Sciscinoso and 40% of local grapes varieties. Matures in stainless steel tanks. Lively ruby. Crunchy strawberry, red currant and fine herbs. Light foam, fresh and with small tannins. Easydrinking. Long finish.

★★

MASSERIA FELICIA

Località San Terenziano - Frazione Carano
81037 Sessa Aurunca (CE)
Tel. +39 0823 935095

info@masseriafelicia.it
www.masseriafelicia.it
f *Masseria-Felicia*

YEAR OF FOUNDATION 1995
NAME OF THE OWNER Maria Felicia Brini
TOTAL BOTTLES PRODUCED 25,000
DIRECT SALES
VISITS TO THE WINERY - RESERVATION NEEDED
HECTARES OF VINEYARD 5
OLIVE OIL PRODUCTION

This tiny estate is situated in the extreme northwest corner of Campania and was created with determination by Maria Felicia who gave her name to it. For many wine lovers she is the most rigorous producer of Falerno del Massico. Her wines are always original and very territorial also thanks to a soil rich in tuff, ash and pumice.

■ 93   Price B

Falerno del Massico Rosso Etichetta Bronzo 2012

Blend of 80% Aglianico and 20% Piedirosso grapes. Matures in barrique for around 14 months. Wonderful brilliant ruby red. Complex and multi-layered nose: hint of ripe mulberry, blackberry and blueberry; then notes of pencil shavings and flint. The palate is extremely balanced, it's juicy, savory and with a round and refined tannin. Long finish.

☐ 90   👍 Price A

Falerno del Massico Anthologia 2015

100% Falanghina grapes. Matures in stainless steel tanks. Golden yellow. Aromas of pear, lime and broom blossoms. Refined palate, warm yet with refreshing acidity and good body. The finish is long and reminds fruity nose with a distinctive almond hint.

★★★

MASTROBERARDINO

Via Manfredi, 75/81
83042 Atripalda (AV)
Tel. +39 0825 614111
mastro@mastroberardino.com
www.mastroberardino.com
f *MastroberardinoVineyards*
🐦 *@Mastroberardino*

YEAR OF FOUNDATION 1878
NAME OF THE OWNER Piero Mastroberardino

TOTAL BOTTLES PRODUCED 2,000,000
DIRECT SALES
VISITS TO THE WINERY - RESERVATION NEEDED
HECTARES OF VINEYARD 200
HOSPITALITY
RESTAURANT
OLIVE OIL PRODUCTION

Piero Mastroberardino, a cultured top-notch manager, is demonstrating to be a worthy heir of his father Antonio, the father of Irpinia wine and the man who literally invented Fiano di Avellino. For this estate each year is a challenge and the winery is an example of the most authentic winemaking tradition not only in Campania but all of Italy. The elegant and austere style of the wines and their capacity to age as like few others has not changed. The name-brand, known throughout the world, contributes to creating a positive image for all Italian wine.

■ 🍷 95   Price B
Taurasi Radici Riserva 2009

100% Aglianico grapes. Ages for 30 months in barrique. Ruby with garnet rim. Explosive and elegant nose that shows dark fruits: blackcurrant and blackberry; then notes of pencil shavings and light hint of smoke. The palate is rich, powerful with refined tannins; savory and vertical. It has wonderful depth and a very long finish. Outstanding wine.

☐ 90   🍷 Price A
Greco di Tufo Novaserra 2015

100% Greco grapes. Matures in stainless steel tanks. Golden with greenish hues. Multi-layered nose: cedar, anise, white plum, almond and slightly smoky. The palate is vertical, savory and fresh with aftertaste of pine and mint. Long finish.

☐ 89   Price A
Fiano di Avellino Radici 2015

100% Fiano grapes. Matures in stainless steel tanks. Straw yellow. Herbaceous nose that offers hint of tomato leaf, sage and rosemary. Tense palate, marine and with a pleasant acidity; aftertaste of lime and quince. Long and composed finish.

★
MOLETTIERI

Contrada Musanni, 19b
83040 Montemarano (AV)
Tel. +39 0827 63722

info@salvatoremolettieri.it
www.salvatoremolettieri.com
 SalvatoreMolettieri
🐦 @SalvMolettieri

YEAR OF FOUNDATION 1983
NAME OF THE OWNER Salvatore Molettieri
TOTAL BOTTLES PRODUCED 65,000
DIRECT SALES
VISITS TO THE WINERY - RESERVATION NEEDED
HECTARES OF VINEYARD 13

Salvatore Molettieri is one of the fathers of Taurasi, a wine which he has produced and bottled since 1988. He now makes three versions with two using grapes from the historic Cinque Querce vineyards and one with grapes from the Renonno vineyard which was replanted a few years back. His wines have a severe and bold style and are the product of an extremely selective winegrowing approach that produces a very low yield in order to make wines that are full-bodied and can age long.

■ 93   Price C
Taurasi Vigna Cinque Querce Ris. 2009

100% Aglianico grapes, 48 months in barrique and large casks. Deep ruby garnet. Intense, spicy nose of cinnamon, licorice, black pepper, eucalyptus and dried plums. Rich and bold on the palate, sleek, refined tannins and wonderful acidity. Great length with a light tobacco and inky notes. Great Classic.

■ 91   Price B
Taurasi Vigna Cinque Querce 2010

100% Aglianico grapes. Ages for 36 months in barrique and large casks. Ruby with garnet hues. Intense and complex aromas of black cherry, blackcurrant and wet leaves. Savory palate, tense and with great body; youthful tannins yet refined. It's round and rich with a fairly long finish.

MONTEVETRANO

Via Montevetrano, 3
84099 San Cipriano Picentino (SA)
Tel. +39 089 882285
Fax +39 089 882011
info@montevetrano.it
www.montevetrano.it
 Montevetrano

YEAR OF FOUNDATION **1991**
NAME OF THE OWNER **Silvia Imparato**
TOTAL BOTTLES PRODUCED **39,000**
DIRECT SALES
VISITS TO THE WINERY - RESERVATION NEEDED
HECTARES OF VINEYARD **5**

Silvia Imparato is the princess of Campania wine, a cultured and charming woman who was once a successful photographer and has always been passionate about wine. Some 25 years ago, she decided to produce exceptional wine at her family's small estate near Salerno. With the help of famed enologist Riccardo Cotarella, she was able to make her wine known around the world in a short time. Her Montevetrano is an elegant red made with native grapes and is a kind of Campania Sassicaia, which has helped make it famous. Not long ago it has been skirted by the two Core. Maybe simpler but splendid as well. So good that we decided to reward it.

☐ 95   👍 **Price A**

Core Bianco 2015

Blend of 50% Fiano and 50% Greco grapes. Matures for a couple of months in oak barrels then in stainless steel tanks. Intense Straw yellow. Aromas of tropical fruits, white peach, pineapple and fresh almond with a light citrusy hint. The palate shows good body, supple, tense, warm, Mediterranean, mouth filling, wonderful length and structure. 'Dangerously' easy drinking.

---

 93   **Price C**

Montevetrano 2014

Blend of 60% cabernet sauvignon, 30% Aglianico and 20% merlot grapes. Ages for 1 year in barrique. Dark ruby of good depth. Particularly fruity vintage, blueberry, lightly vegetal and woody hints. Medium bodied palate, supple, sleek, with small tannins, good acidity and with a fairly long finish.

---

 90   👍 **Price A**

Core 2014

100% Aglianico grapes. Ages in second fill barrique for 10 months. Very dense ruby. Fragrant and fruity nose, hint of black cherry, mint and tamarind. Supple palate, lightly tannic, well balanced with acidity and a body that reflects the challenging vintage.

 ⭐

NANNI COPÈ

Via Tufo, 3
81041 Vitulazio (CE)
Tel. +39 0823 990529
nc@nannicope.it
www.nannicope.it
🐦 *@NanniCope*

YEAR OF FOUNDATION **2007**
NAME OF THE OWNER **Giovanni Ascione**
TOTAL BOTTLES PRODUCED **6,500**
DIRECT SALES
VISITS TO THE WINERY - RESERVATION NEEDED
HECTARES OF VINEYARD **2.5**

Giovanni Ascione is a winegrower by passion and has a small vineyard of just over two hectares in the area of Caiatina. He makes only one wine, Sabbie di Sopra (Upper Sand), named after the soil composition of his vineyard. In just a few years he has become one of Italy's better-known producers of vins de garage. His is a romantic and poetic story, one full of love for his land and absolute determination.

■ 93   **Price B**

Sabbie di Sopra il Bosco 2014

Blend of 90% Pallagrello Nero, 5% Aglianico and 5% Casavecchia grapes. Ages in tonneau for 1 year. Lively and deep ruby. Distinctive fruity aromas, hints of spice, violet and black berries. The palate is refined, readier to drink, less edgy and bodied than previous vintages, it has a great finish with structure and lively tannins.

OPPIDA AMINEA

Contrada Coluonni, 20
82100 Benevento (BN)
Tel. +39 0824 334061
oppida.aminea@arcipelagomuratori.it
www.arcipelagomuratori.it
📘 *tenutaoppidaaminea*
🐦 *@arcipelagomura*

YEAR OF FOUNDATION **1999**
NAME OF THE OWNER **Muratori Family**
TOTAL BOTTLES PRODUCED **110,000**
DIRECT SALES
VISITS TO THE WINERY - RESERVATION NEEDED

HECTARES OF VINEYARD 25
CERTIFIED ORGANIC VITICULTURE

The Muratori family owns estates in Franciacorta, Tuscany's Maremma district, Ischia and here in Benevento in the old Sannio area. The enologist in charge of all production is the most talented Francesco Iacone, who experiments with new methods even those using no carbon dioxide. Here he has created an extraordinary white without any added sulfites that brings together organoleptic value with greater attention to health, something we feel is important.

□ 91   👍 Price A
Simbiotico 2015

Blend of 40% Fiano 10% Greco and 50% local grapes varieties. Matures in stainless steel tanks without added suphites. Straw yellow; aromas of anise, tilia, thyme and freshly cut grass. Juicy, fresh and savory palate. Round and pleasant finish.

□ 88   👍 Price A
Coda di Volpe 2015

100% Coda di Volpe grapes. Ages in 25hl oak casks. Deep straw yellow. Ripe and candied fruit on the nose, then Mediterranean scrub. On the palate there's balance between ripe fruity notes and a wonderful refreshing acidity. The finish is savory, clean and with good body.

★★
PERILLO

Contrada Valle, 19
83040 Castelfranci (AV)
Tel. +39 0827 72252
cantinaperillo@libero.it
f *Cantina Perillo*

YEAR OF FOUNDATION 1999
NAME OF THE OWNER Michele Perillo
TOTAL BOTTLES PRODUCED 20,000
DIRECT SALES
VISITS TO THE WINERY - RESERVATION NEEDED
HECTARES OF VINEYARD 5

It is a pleasure to be able to present an authentic, small winemaker who produces exceptional and surprising wines. His name is Michele Perillo and he makes Taurasi in Castelfranci, an area particularly favorable for winegrowing, using grapes from old vines and following

traditional methods. His are great and authentic wines that will age long and cost little considering their value. His wines go on the market only after they have aged for years, which makes it difficult to understand which one is the latest. This year we tasted a Taurasi Riserva 2007 which is simply extraordinary and we are convinced it will only get better with age.

■ 🔖 99   Price B
Taurasi Riserva 2007

100% Aglianico grapes, 5 years in different sized casks. Ruby with garnet rim. Austere and multi-layered nose, hint of wet leaves, licorice, ripe red fruit and a light smoky note. The palate is incredibly round and elegant. It's savory, supple and with wonderfully extracted tannins. This is an amazing wine with a long and exciting finish. Red Wine of the Year.

□ 92   👍 Price A
Irpinia Coda di Volpe 2013

100% Coda di Volpe grapes. Stainless steel tanks. Deep golden yellow. Nose of great personality that shows hint of pear, yellow peach, jasmine and fine herbs. Incredibly balanced palate, it shows great savoriness and freshness. Very long finish that offers notes of cedar, eucalyptus and wet leaves.

CIRO PICARIELLO

Contrada Acqua Festa
83010 Summonte (AV)
Tel. +39 0825 702516
ciropicariello@hotmail.com
www.ciropicariello.it
f *AZ-Agricola-CIRO-Picariello*
🐦 *@PicarielloCiro*

YEAR OF FOUNDATION 2004
NAME OF THE OWNER Ciro Picariello
TOTAL BOTTLES PRODUCED 50,000
DIRECT SALES
VISITS TO THE WINERY - RESERVATION NEEDED
HECTARES OF VINEYARD 7

The tiny winery of Ciro and Rita Picariello, two passionate winegrowers sees at work their sons Emma and Bruno as well. Their vocation for producing whites is clear and has placed them among the top producers for quality Fiano di Avellino and one of the leading ones for Greco di Tufo.

☐ 91   Price B

Fiano di Avellino Ciro 906 2012

100% Fiano grapes. Matures for 14 months on the lees in stainless steel tanks. Deep golden yellow. Refined and intense notes of green tea, mint, barley, acacia blossoms honey, mango and flint. The palate offers a refined hint of licorice root, apple and white pepper. It's savory, refreshing and it has a great body. Wonderful and surprising finish.

☐ 90   Price A

Fiano di Avellino 2014

100% Fiano grapes. Matures for 10 months on the lees in stainless steel tanks. Green yellow. Multi-layered nose of citrus, quince, acacia blossoms, thyme and lightly smoky. Slim and balanced on the palate that shows wonderful freshness and a cedar and anise finish.

★★★

PIETRACUPA

Contrada Vadiaperti, 17
83030 Montefredane (AV)
Tel. +39 0825 607418
pietracupa@email.it

YEAR OF FOUNDATION 1992
NAME OF THE OWNER Sabino Loffredo
TOTAL BOTTLES PRODUCED 40,000
DIRECT SALES
VISITS TO THE WINERY - RESERVATION NEEDED
HECTARES OF VINEYARD 7.5

Sabino Loffredo is the epitome of a Campania winemaker. He does everything by himself. He cultivates his vineyards, which are situated at an altitude between 350 and 550m above sea level, and makes and ages his wines with the skill of a craftsman who knows all the latest techniques and technology. His wines are simply exceptional and do honor to him and all of Irpinia and sell like hot cakes worldwide. His great specialty is Fiano di Avellino and sometimes he will produce one that is not DOCG, Cupo, which has proven to be great in the 2013 vintage. He also produces Greco di Tufo and every so often comes out with a Greco di Tufo G.

☐ 🏆 97   Price B

Cupo 2013

100% Fiano grapes. Matures for 10 months on the lees in stainless steel tanks. Green yellow. Multi-layered nose of citrus, quince, acacia blossoms, thyme and lightly smoky. Slim and balanced on the palate, shows wonderful freshness. Cedar and anise finish.

◼ 94   Price B

Taurasi 2011

100% Aglianico grapes. Ages in large casks for 3 years. Intense ruby with garnet hues. Very complex nose, notes of black cherry, wild strawberry, then notes of dark tobacco, violet and blood orange. Tense palate, elegant, silky tannins; supple yet full bodied. It drinks surprisingly well; it almost reminds a "Burgundian" wine for its drinkability, very long finish.

☐ 93   Price A

Greco di Tufo 2015

100% Greco grapes. Matures on the lees in stainless steel. Straw yellow with green hues. Citrusy and sleek nose, almond, lemongrass, fine herbs and wet leaves. The palate is rich and round. Great acidity, elegant and tense. Wonderful sea breeze note on the finish.

☐ 92   Price B

Fiano di Avellino 2015

100% Fiano grapes. Matures on the lees in stainless steel. Straw yellow with green hues. Particularly shiny. Fine and intense notes of oregano, sage, cedar and lemongrass. The palate is vertical, savory with light notes of resin and pencil shavings. Is a slim and supple wine with great acidity; slightly smoky finish.

★★

QUINTODECIMO

Via San Leonardo, 27
83036 Mirabella Eclano (AV)
Tel. +39 0825 449321
info@quintodecimo.it
www.quintodecimo.it
🇫 *www.quintodecimo.it*
🐦 *@info47433170*

YEAR OF FOUNDATION 2001
NAME OF THE OWNER Laura Di Marzio and Luigi Moio
TOTAL BOTTLES PRODUCED 36,000
DIRECT SALES
VISITS TO THE WINERY - RESERVATION NEEDED
HECTARES OF VINEYARD 16

This winery, a small Irpinia 'château', belongs to Maura Di Marzio and Luigi Moio, a professor of enology at the Federico II University in

113

Naples and an extraordinary and technically brilliant person. The wines are excellent and while they may be expensive, they rank among the best for quality in the whole region.

■ 🍷 **96**   Price D

Taurasi Vigna Grande Cerzito Ris. 2010

100% Aglianico grapes. Matures for 2 years in oak casks. Intense ruby-garnet. Elegant and neat aromas of sour cherry, plum and tamarind. The palate shows great structure, savory, tense and with a refined tannins compound; youthful but sleek. The finish is very long. Great wine.

☐ **92**   Price B

Greco di Tufo Giallo di Arles 2015

100% Greco grapes. Part of the wine ages in barrique for 10 months and the rest matures on the lees in stainless steel tanks. Golden yellow. The nose opens to notes of quince, pear, almond and hay. Elegant style, the palate shows lively acidity, vertical with notes of nettle and freshly cut grass. Good length with smoky notes.

☐ **91**   Price B

Fiano di Avellino Exultet 2015

100% Fiano grapes. Part of the wine ages in barrique for 10 months and the rest matures on the lees in stainless steel tanks. Straw yellow with greenish hues. Notes of quince, wild fennel and indian spices. The palate is balanced; aftertaste of sea breeze and Mediterranean scrub. Tense with great acidity.

ROCCA DEL PRINCIPE

S.P. 88, Contrada Arianiello, 9
83030 Lapio (AV)
Tel. +39 0825 1728013
info@roccadelprincipe.it
www.roccadelprincipe.it
🅕 *Rocca-del-Principe*

YEAR OF FOUNDATION **2004**
NAME OF THE OWNER **Aurelia Fabrizio**
TOTAL BOTTLES PRODUCED **30,000**
DIRECT SALES
VISITS TO THE WINERY - RESERVATION NEEDED
HECTARES OF VINEYARD **6.5**
OLIVE OIL PRODUCTION

After years of selling their grapes to others, Ercole Zarrella and his wife Aurelia decide to produce and sell their wines made from grapes

---

grown in Lapio, one of the best areas for Fiano. The estate has ten hectares of which only six are planted with Fiano while the enologist is the talented Carmine Valentino.

☐ 🍷 **95**   Price A

Fiano di Avellino 2014

100% Fiano grapes. Matures in stainless steel for 11 months. Straw yellow. Intense nose of field blossoms, hay, cedar, almond and a hint of petrol. The palate is tense, savory and wonderfully refined. It has great length with notes that remind sage and mediterranean scrub.

ETTORE SAMMARCO

Via Civita, 9
84010 Ravello (SA)
Tel. +39 089 872774
info@ettoresammarco.it
www.ettoresammarco.it
🅕 *Casa-Vinicola-Ettore-Sammarco*

YEAR OF FOUNDATION **1962**
NAME OF THE OWNER **Sammarco Family**
TOTAL BOTTLES PRODUCED **80,000**
DIRECT SALES
VISITS TO THE WINERY - RESERVATION NEEDED
HECTARES OF VINEYARD **11**

At the splendid age of 80, Ettore Sammarco can look back at his success and that of the surrounding winemaking area where he was a pioneer. For some years now he has been joined at the winery by his children Bartolo, Maria Rosaria and Antonella who in this magnificent natural setting continue what Ettore created with passion and professionalism. The winery has always used historic and local native grapes that were considered 'secondary' like Pepella, Ripolo and Serpentaria, which can only be found in small plots spread throughout the Amalfi peninsula, and for this reason Sammarco wines stand out for their typicity and distinct personality.

■ **93**   Price B

Costa d'Amalfi Ravello Rosso Selva delle Monache Riserva 2012

Blend of 70% Aglianico and 30% Piedirosso. Ages in casks for 18 months. Deep ruby. Intense nose of eucaliptus, mint, light wet forrest leaves. The palate is velvety, savory, intense, refreshing. Very long finish.

Costa d'Amalfi Terre Saracene 2015

☐ 91 👍 Price A

Blend of 50% Biancatenera, 30% Pepella, 20% Falanghina grapes. Matures in stainless steel. Straw yellow. Nose of white blossoms, citrus with distinctive note of lemon leaf and hint of almond. The palate is vertical, refreshing, savory and with a wonderful acidity. Juicy and long finish.

SAN PAOLO

Via Aufieri, 25 - Contrada San Paolo
83010 Aiello del Sabato (AV)
Tel. +39 0832 704398
Fax +39 0832 709022
info@cantinasanpaolo.it
www.claudioquarta.it
🅕 *ClaudioQuartaVignaiolo*
🐦 *@ClaudioQuarta-W*

YEAR OF FOUNDATION 1999
NAME OF THE OWNER Claudio Quarta
TOTAL BOTTLES PRODUCED 115,000
DIRECT SALES
VISITS TO THE WINERY - RESERVATION NEEDED
HECTARES OF VINEYARD 21

The estate is part of Claudio Quarta's Magistravini business group and is named after the San Paolo district in the town of Tufo where the winery is located. The 21 hectares of vineyards rise to an altitude of 700m, have a soil composed of clay, chalk and volcanic ash and enjoy great temperature variations between day and night. Aside from Greco, the estate also produces Fiano, Taurasi and Falanghina.

Fiano di Avellino 2015

☐ 91 👍 Price A

100% Fiano grapes. Matures on the lees in stainless steel tanks. Green yellow. Subtle nose of aromatic herbs, musk and lemongrass. The palate is complex, savory, fresh and supple. Long finish.

Greco di Tufo 2015

☐ 90 👍 Price A

100% Greco grapes. Matures on the lees in stainless steel tanks. Fragrant nose of aromatic herbs, white plum and grapesfruit. The palate is fresh, savory with good suppleness. Balanced and clean finish.

Falanghina 2015

☐ 86 👍 Price A

100% Falanghina grapes. Matures on the lees in stainless steel tanks. The nose offers aromas of white stone fruits and white blossoms. The palate is fresh and pleasant. Good length with hay aftertaste.

SARNO 1860

Contrada Serroni, 4/B
83100 Avellino (AV)
Tel. +39 339 7265669
info@tenutasarno1860.it
www.sarno1860.it
🅕 *tenutasarno.tenutasarno*
🐦 *@1860info*

YEAR OF FOUNDATION 2004
NAME OF THE OWNER Maura Sarno
TOTAL BOTTLES PRODUCED 20,000
DIRECT SALES
VISITS TO THE WINERY - RESERVATION NEEDED
HECTARES OF VINEYARD 8
CERTIFIED ORGANIC VITICULTURE

Tenuta Sarno is synonymous with Fiano, the only wine this small, seven-hectare estate produces at its winery in the ancient hamlet of Candida, situated at 600m above sea level. The vineyards are without a doubt the highest in Irpinia to the extent that the wines are referred to as 'mountain' wines. Owner Maura Sarno is constantly working to produce wines that are expressive, typical and have a propensity to age.

Fiano di Avellino Sarno 1860 2011

☐ 92 Price B

100% Fiano grapes. Matures for 8 months on the lees in bottle. Golden yellow. Varietal nose, distinctive tertiary notes of chestnut honey, ripe white plum and lightly smoky notes. Savory, juicy, fresh and long. Minty and round finish.

Fiano di Avellino Sarno 1860 2014

☐ 88 Price B

100% Fiano grapes. Matures in stainless steel. Straw yellow with greenish hues. Nose of yellow flesh fruit, alpine herbs, citrus. Dynamic palate, vertical and savory.

★
LUIGI TECCE

Via Trinità
83052 Paternopoli (AV)
Tel. +39 0827 71375
ltecce@libero.it
f *Luigi-Tecce-Poliphemo*

YEAR OF FOUNDATION 2003
NAME OF THE OWNER Luigi Tecce
TOTAL BOTTLES PRODUCED 10,000
DIRECT SALES
VISITS TO THE WINERY - RESERVATION NEEDED
HECTARES OF VINEYARD 4

Unmistakable with his narrow-brimmed hat, Luigi Tecce is a star, a celebrity of Campania winemaking. But don't let his look fool you for he has a true passion for his vineyard, which is over 80 years old and has vines that are traditionally 'raggiera irpinia' or wheel-spoked trained, and the crafted wines he makes which may seem a bit peasant but are intriguing. If you go and see him you'll know what we mean.

■ 89   Price B
Irpinia Campi Taurasini Satyricon 2012

100% Aglianico grapes. Matures for 1 year in large casks. Deep ruby. Nose of raspberry, currant and sweet spices. Good body, balanced acidity and easy to drink. Savory, good finish that reminds minty notes.

■ 88   Price B
Taurasi Poliphemo 2012

100% Aglianico grapes. Matures for 1 year in different sized casks then is partially matured in stainless steel tanks. Ruby with garnet hues. Nose of cassis, blueberry and light licorice notes. Youthful with fair acidity. good length.

★
TENUTA CAVALIER PEPE

Via Santa Vara
83050 Sant'Angelo All'Esca (AV)
Tel. +39 0827 73766
info@tenutacavalierpepe.it
www.tenutapepe.it
f *Tenuta-Cavalier-Pepe*
y *@TCavalierPepe*

YEAR OF FOUNDATION 2005
NAME OF THE OWNER Milena Pepe
TOTAL BOTTLES PRODUCED 300,000
DIRECT SALES
VISITS TO THE WINERY - RESERVATION NEEDED
HECTARES OF VINEYARD 40
HOSPITALITY
OLIVE OIL PRODUCTION

In 2005, Milena Pepe, a Belgian-Irpinian enologist, returned to the land of her origin and with the help of her father acquired 40 hectares of vineyards and 10 hectares of olive groves, creating an estate that in just a few years achieved excellent heights. The modern winery, which includes a restaurant, is in Sant'Angelo all'Esca and is surrounded by rolling hills of vineyards from which Milena produces wines that are distinguished by their typicity and ability to age.

■ 93   Price B
Taurasi La Loggia dei Cavalieri Ris. 2009

100% Aglianico grapes. Ages in barrique for 18 months. Deep garnet. Incredibly neat nose that shows notes of black pepper, ink, eucalyptus, camphor and sweet spices. Elegant palate, vertical and supple; the tannins are still ripening but are well integrated. Long juicy finish.

□ 92   👍 Price A
Greco di Tufo Nestor 2015

100% Greco grapes. Matures in stainless steel tanks. Straw yellow. Neat and intriguing nose that offers notes of citrus, almonds. The palate is savory, crunchy and with great acidity. Pleasant aftertaste of lemongrass. Elegant and well-structured with good length.

□ 90   Price B
Fiano di Avellino Brancato 2015

100% Fiano grapes. Ages 10 months in barrique. Straw yellow. Notes of pineapple, peach, white almonds, lightly minty. The palate has good body and freshness; good depth and savory finish.

TENUTA SAN FRANCESCO

Via Solficiano, 18
84010 Tramonti (SA)
Tel. +39 089 876748
aziendasanfrancesco@libero.it
www.vinitenutasanfrancesco.it
f *Tenuta-San-Francesco-Winery*

YEAR OF FOUNDATION 2004
NAME OF THE OWNER Chiara Di Palma
TOTAL BOTTLES PRODUCED 40,000
DIRECT SALES
VISITS TO THE WINERY - RESERVATION NEEDED
HECTARES OF VINEYARD 10

This 18th century farm is in Tramonti in the Monti Lattari hills that are a gateway to the Sorrento Peninsula and Amalfi Coast and where the best mozzarella-style cheese using cows' milk is said to be made. Here Gaetano Bove and Chiara Di Palma own a dozen or so hectares of vineyards mostly planted with Tintore di Tramonti, a local grape which for decades was confused with Aglianico. The also make wines from Falanghina and Aglianico but their best is the one per reviewed here. And they themselves refer to it as "E'Iss", which in dialect means 'that's the one'.

 92   Price B
Tintore Prephilloxera E' Iss 2012
100% Tintore grapes. Ages for 2 year in large casks. Intense ruby. Great personality on the nose offering notes of cherry, pomegranate and lightly woody hints. Tense palate, supple, good tannins and balanced acidity. Sea breeze and resin aftertaste. Long finish.

☐ 89   Price A
Costa d'Amalfi Bianco Per Eva 2014
Blend of 65% Falanghina, 30% Ginestra, 5% Pepella grapes. Matures in stainless steel tanks. Golden yellow. Nose of lemongrass, anise, pear and quince. The palate is mouth filling, supple, savory and slim. Very long with smoky hints.

★★
TERRE DEL PRINCIPE

Via SS. Giovanni e Paolo, 30
81010 Castel Campagnano (CE)
Tel. +39 0823 867126
Fax +39 0823 1760571
info@terredelprincipe.com
www.terredelprincipe.com
🅕 *Terre-del-Principe*

YEAR OF FOUNDATION 2003
NAME OF THE OWNER Manuela Piancastelli and Peppe Mancini

TOTAL BOTTLES PRODUCED 55,000
DIRECT SALES
VISITS TO THE WINERY - RESERVATION NEEDED
HECTARES OF VINEYARD 11
HOSPITALITY
RESTAURANT

Manuela Piancastelli and Peppe Mancini are partners in life and on the job and are the 'prophets' of Casavecchia and Pallagrello Nero, two wines that had all but disappeared and which they brought back from near-extinction some 15 years ago. They thus hold a very special place in the world of Campania winemaking and continue to what they do best with passion and determination, turning out wines that can move you year after year.

 95   Price B
Centomoggia 2012
100% Casavecchia grapes. Matures for 1 year in barrique. Intense ruby. Intense nose of myrtle, spices and resin hint. The palate shows youth tannins, firm but not aggressive. Wonderfully long finsh.

 87   Price A
Fontanavigna Pallagrello bianco 2015
100% Pallagrello Bianco grapes. On the lees for 6 months. Straw yellow. Aromas of lemongrass, apricot, field blossoms and anise. The palate shows good body, it's fresh and savory. Long finish.

★★
TERREDORA

Via Serra
83030 Montefusco (AV)
Tel. +39 0825 968215
Fax +39 0825 963022
info@terredora.com
www.terredora.com
🅕 *terredorawine*
🐦 *@Terredorawines*

YEAR OF FOUNDATION 1978
NAME OF THE OWNER Walter Mastroberardino and Sons
TOTAL BOTTLES PRODUCED 1,000,000
DIRECT SALES
VISITS TO THE WINERY - RESERVATION NEEDED
HECTARES OF VINEYARD 200
OLIVE OIL PRODUCTION

This estate was born when Walter Mastroberardino broke away from his family's winery. Today, after the painful and premature death of Walter's son Lucio Mastroberardino, his siblings Daniela and Paolo are in charge of production and with excellent results. The Terradora brand is synonymous with reliability and consistent quality and the wines can be found on all the leading world markets.

■ 91   Price B

Taurasi Fatica Contadina 2010

100% Aglianico grapes. Ages for 18 months in casks. Garnet. Complex fruity nose: plum, black cherry, currant, then lightly minty note, geranium and violet. The palate is smooth, fresh and with small tannins. Good acidity, savory and lightly smoky.

☐ 90   👍 Price A

Fiano di Avellino Ex Cinere Resurgo 2015

100% Fiano grapes. Matures in stainless steel tanks. Straw yellow. Delicate nose of field blossoms, aromatic herbs, sea breeze and golden apple. The palate is dynamic, tense and it reminds sea breeze notes. Vertical and long finish.

☐ 89   Price A

Greco di Tufo Loggia della Serra 2015

100% Greco grapes. Matures in stainless steel tanks. Straw yellow. Fragrant and fruity nose: cedar, yellow plum, peach. Savory and with good body; long and savory finish.

TRAERTE

Contrada Vadiaperti
83040 Montefredane (AV)
Tel. +39 082 5607270
info@vadiaperti.it
www.vadiaperti.it

YEAR OF FOUNDATION 1984
NAME OF THE OWNER Raffaele Troisi
TOTAL BOTTLES PRODUCED 50,000
DIRECT SALES
VISITS TO THE WINERY - RESERVATION NEEDED
HECTARES OF VINEYARD 8

This used to be called Vadiaperti and while today they name has changed, the management and responsibility for the vineyards and the winery remain in the hands of Raffaele Troisi, a visionary and talented winemaker. It is located in Montefredane, an immense cru for Fiano di Avellino but that from time to time also produces a truly 'amazing' other whites as certain Masters of Wine would say.

☐ 90   👍 Price A

Fiano di Avellino 2014

100% Fiano grapes. Matures in stainless steel tanks. Straw yellow. Citrus flavor, floral and hint of petrol. The palate is fresh, savory with a neat minty note. Long and intense finish.

☐ 89   👍 Price A

Irpinia Coda di Volpe 2014

100% Coda di Volpe grapes. Matures in stainless steel tanks. Straw yellow. Varietal nose: pear and yellow blossoms. Savory, fresh and vertical palate. Pleasant sage aftertaste.

VILLA DIAMANTE

Via Toppole, 16
83030 Montefredane (AV)
Tel. +39 0825 670014
Fax +39 0825 22920
villadiamante1996@gmail.com
 Azvinicola-Villa-Diamante

YEAR OF FOUNDATION 1996
NAME OF THE OWNER Diamante Maria Renna
TOTAL BOTTLES PRODUCED 6,000
DIRECT SALES
VISITS TO THE WINERY - RESERVATION NEEDED
HECTARES OF VINEYARD 3.5
CERTIFIED ORGANIC VITICULTURE

It was January 15th when the news of the premature death, at only 60 years of age, of Antoine Gaita, the creator of this small but important Irpinia reality. Antoine was a great person, as well as a fantastic winemaker, and we like to remember him with the last masterpiece he left us, 'his' great wine Fiano Vigna della Congregazione, that in vintage 2014 though has not been produced. We signal another Fiano, the Clos D'Haut 2013.

☐ 88   Price B

Fiano d'Avellino Clous D'Haut 2013

100% Fiano grapes. Matures for 18 months in

stainless steel. Golden yellow. Nose of rosehip, tropical fruits and yeasts. Savory palate, fresh, vertical with a honey and baked apple finish.

months. Ruby with garnet hues. The nose offers nose of resin, red fruits, woody notes and lightly smoky. The palate is supple and has firm tannins; long finish that reminds spices and licorice.

★★
VILLA MATILDE

S.S. Domitiana, 18
81030 Cellole (CE)
Tel. +39 0823 932088
info@villamatilde.it
www.villamatilde.it
villamatilde
@agrvillamatilde

YEAR OF FOUNDATION **1960**
NAME OF THE OWNER **Francesco Paolo, Maria Ida and Salvatore Avallone**
TOTAL BOTTLES PRODUCED **700,000**
DIRECT SALES
VISITS TO THE WINERY - RESERVATION NEEDED
HECTARES OF VINEYARD **120**
HOSPITALITY
RESTAURANT
OLIVE OIL PRODUCTION

Maria Ida and Tani Avallone are the fortunate owners of what is today one of the most complete wineries in Campania. The have vineyards in the province of Casera, in Sannio and Irpinia which allow them to produce almost the full range of wines the region is known for.

█ 92   Price B
Cecubo 2013
Blend of 50% Primitivo, 50% of other indigenous grapes varieties. Ages in barrique for 1 year. Dark ruby. Elegant nose of red fruits and Mediterranean scrub. Powerful and fresh palate, savory; firm and refined tannins. Long sea breeze finish.

☐ 91   👍 Price A
Falerno del Massico Bianco 2015
100% Falanghina grapes (falerna clone). Matures in stainless steel tanks for 3 months. Yellow green. Aromas of citrus, apricot and thyme. Round palate, good acidity. It shows personality, savory with a light sulphur hint. Supple and savory finish.

█ 90   Price B
Taurasi Tenuta di Altavilla 2010
100% Aglianico grapes. Ages in oak barrels for 18

VILLA RAIANO

Via Bosco Satrano, 1 - Località Cerreto
83020 San Michele Di Serino (AV)
Tel. +39 0825 595550
villa.raiano
info@villariano.com
www.villaraiano.com
villaraiano
@villaraiano

YEAR OF FOUNDATION **1996**
NAME OF THE OWNER **Basso Family**
TOTAL BOTTLES PRODUCED **300,000**
DIRECT SALES
VISITS TO THE WINERY - RESERVATION NEEDED
HECTARES OF VINEYARD **23**
CERTIFIED ORGANIC VITICULTURE
OLIVE OIL PRODUCTION

The Basso family has a long history in producing olive oil and in 1996 they also began to produce wine. The winery was built on a hill in the hamlet of Raiano, inside an old factory that was once used to produce and store olive oil. The estate is surrounded by chestnut trees and vineyards with a total of 23 hectares of vineyards which are organic certified and planted only with indigenous varieties.

☐ 91   Price B
Greco di Tufo Contrada Marotta 2013
100% Greco grapes. Matures in stainless steel. Straw yellow. Elegant nose of citrus and tropical fruit. Dynamic palate, savory with great acidity; long smoky finish.

█ 90   👍 Price A
Irpinia Campi Taurasini 2012
100% Aglianico grapes. Matures in concrete and terracotta tanks. Ruby with garnet rim. Very fascinating nose: cardamom, blood orange, mulberry and blackberry. The palate shows slightly grainy tannins, good concentration and freshness. Very long and captivating finish.

EMILIA ROMAGNA

This region was created with the unification of Italy from the ashes of the dukedoms of Parma and Piacenza, Modena, Reggio, Ferrara and the northern holdings of the Papal States. From a winemaking point of view, this brought together all the ancient divisions and created a bridge between the traditions of northern and central Italy. This despite the many different winegrowing areas and types of wines and grapes used, traditions that at times seem distinctly different.

Colli Piacentini is in the northwest and its most representative wine is without a doubt Gutturnio which has a nice body and is made from Barbera and Croatina grapes and is very similar to the Oltrepò Pavese reds. There are some other reds as well as whites of which the most important are Ortrugo, a light and at times sparkling wine made from grapes of the same name; Monterosso Val d'Arda, a blend of Malvasia di Candia, Moscato, Trebbiano Romagnolo and Ortrugo; Trebbianino Val Trebbia, made mostly with Ortrugo; and Val Nure, a light wine made from Malvasia di Candia, Trebbiano Romagnolo, and Ortrugo. There are also varietal Chardonnay, Pinot Grigio and Sauvignon wines. Among the other reds are Bonarda, Barbera and a series of wines made with international grapes including Pinot Nero and Cabernet Sauvignon which are often more modern approach and are aged in French barrique.

The neighboring zone of Colli di Parma is less famous but its wines are very similar. The Rosso has the same blend as Gutturnio, the Malvasia is often sparkling and is a lot like Monterosso Val d'Arda and Val Nure. Sauvignon is the most representative white and is the Parma version of the Colli Piacentini one.

The provinces of Reggio Emilia and Modena are homes to sparkling wines. The first one we deal with is not a Lambrusco and not even a red wine but a white, Bianco di Scandiano, made from Sauvignon grapes which here is called Spergola. It is a light, often sparkling wine from the village of the same name in the province of Reggio Emilia and neighboring towns. The area of Lambrusco begins more to the north, between Montecchio. Gualtieri and Cavriago. The area as well as the towns leading up to Reggio Emilia is where Reggiano is made, which was once called Lambrusco Reggiano, the lightest and most drinkable wine of its kind.

The other Lambrusco are made in the province of Modena. The most famous is probably Lambrusco di Sorbara but the ones with more body and a purple color are Lambrusco Salamino di Santa Croce and Lambrusco Grasparossa di Castelvetro. These are simple yet intriguing wines that have their roots in authentic folk traditions. Lambrusco wines are of historic importance because they helped pave the way for other Italian wines on international markets.

There are two other wines that are similar to Lambrusco: Montuni del Reno, made from Montù grapes and produced primarily in the province of Bologna; and Fortana del Bosco Eliceo, made from Fortana grapes in the area of the Comacchio marshlands.

Colli Bolognesi wines are totally different from the others in the area of Emilia. There are many different types but the most characteristic is Pignoletto, a light and fragrant white which is sometimes sparkling, made from grape of the same name and has been classified DOCG. There are also a host of wines made from the international grapes as well as a Barbera, which recalls those of the northwest, and a Bianco made from Albana and Trebbiano grapes that is similar to those produced in Romagna.

The vineyards of Sangiovese, Trebbiano and Albana are an indication that you are in Romagna where the wines have practically nothing in common with those of Emilia. The grapes and winegrowing methods are those also found in central Italian regions. The most famous wine in this subzone is without a doubt Sangiovese di Romagna, which can also be a Superiore, if it has an alcoholic content above 12%, or a Riserva, if it has aged for at least two years. The best Sangiovese wines from this subzone

are from the hills south of the Via Emilia and hold their own against the best Italian reds. They are divided into a number of appellations including Colli di Imola, Colli di Faenza and Colli di Rimini, where wines can also made be using grapes other than Sangiovese. Under this umbrella is a new DOC Romagna which produces, aside from Sangiovese, the area's second most important red. Cagnina is a rare and sweet red made with grapes of the same name and is similar to Terrano del Carso except with a great sugar content. The most widespread white wine is Trebbiano followed by the lesser known Pagadebit, made with the grape of the same name that is particularly resistant and allows for making wine even in difficult years. This aspect explains its name because it allows you to 'pay your debts' even when there is a poor harvest. And then there is an Albana di Romagna which is also made as a white semi-sweet and Passito dessert wine.

CONTROLLED AND GUARANTEED DESIGNATION OF ORIGIN (DOCG)

- Colli Bolognesi Classico Pignoletto
- Romagna Albana

CONTROLLED DESIGNATION OF ORIGIN (DOC)

- Bosco Eliceo
- Colli Bolognesi, with or without Bologna
- Colli d'Imola
- Colli di Faenza
- Colli di Parma
- Colli di Rimini
- Colli di Scandiano e di Canossa, with or without Classico (only for Bianco)
- Colli Piacentini, with or without Monterosso Val d'Arda, Trebbianino Val Trebbia, Val Nure, Vigoleno (only for the Vin Santo)
- Colli Romagna Centrale
- Gutturnio, with or without Classico (Superiore or Riserva)

- Lambrusco di Sorbara
- Lambrusco Grasparossa di Castelvetro
- Lambrusco Salamino di Santa Croce
- Modena or di Modena
- Ortrugo
- Reggiano
- Reno
- Romagna, with or without Bertinoro, Brisighella, Castrocaro, Cesena, Longiano, Meldola, Modigliana, Marzeno, Oriolo, Predappio, San Vicinio, Serra (only for Romagna Sangiovese)

ARIOLA

Strada della Buca, 5a - Calicella
43010 Langhirano (PR)
Tel. +39 0521 637678
 andreac3rn
info@viniariola.it
www.viniariola.it
 viniariola
 @viniariola

YEAR OF FOUNDATION 1956
NAME OF THE OWNER Marcello Ceci, Andrea Cernuschi, Claudia Ghezzi
TOTAL BOTTLES PRODUCED 1,300,000
DIRECT SALES
VISITS TO THE WINERY
HECTARES OF VINEYARD 70
HOSPITALITY
RESTAURANT

On the beautiful Ariola hills, Marcello Ceci has created a little chateau where sparkling wines are at home. Even if tradition is fundamental, there is space for experimentation and for experimentation we mean international varieties planted to develop themes that are not tied anymore only to local varieties but demonstrate how a great territory can give nice expressions with international varieties as well.

 89 Price A
Lambrusco Marcello 2015
100% Lambrusco Maestri grapes. Charmat method. Deep red with a lot of sparkles. Intense fruitiness with great flowery expression. Black cherry and cherry but very pleasant grape flavors. On the palate it is wide and smooth, nice freshness, extremely gourmand. One of the best versions ever tasted.

 88 Price A
Metodus 2012
Blend of 50% Chardonnay and 50% Pinot Nero grapes. Classic method. Light straw yellow with very thin sparkles. Elegant light fruity notes, citrusy, flowery hint. Briny and fresh on the palate, easy to drink.

 87 Price A
Malvasia Forte Rigoni 2015
100% Malvasia di Candia grapes. Stainlees steel only. Relatively deep yellow color with thin and persistent sparkle. Typical yet not very intense aromas.

Ripe fruit with nice aromatic notes. Tense on the palate with great body and acidity balance which gives freshness and drinkability.

FRANCESCO BELLEI

Via Nazionale, 130/132 - Fraz. Cristo di Sorbara
41030 Bomporto (MO)
Tel. +39 059 902009
Fax +39 059 8070147
info@francescobellei.it
www.francescobellei.it

YEAR OF FOUNDATION 1920
NAME OF THE OWNER Cavicchioli Family
TOTAL BOTTLES PRODUCED 70,000
DIRECT SALES
VISITS TO THE WINERY - RESERVATION NEEDED
HECTARES OF VINEYARD 100

The Cavicchioli family winery is a small gem. Specializing in the production of traditional method bubbly, which is uncommon given the area's vocation for traditional wines, has allowed it to a leader in the trend that is developing in the classic area of Lambrusco. Over the years, their experimentation have allowed them to achieve a quality that was unthinkable in the past.

 89 Price A
Modena Lambrusco Rifermentazione Ancestrale 2015
100% Lambrusco di Sorbara grapes. Re-fermentation in the bottle with indigenous grapes. Almost transparent cherry color with thin but exuberant sparkle. Some light reductions in the beginning then wild flowers and red fruits with vinous hints. Sharp on the palate, very nice balance between strong acidity and structure.

 87 Price B
Brut Extra Cuvée Metodo Classico
Blend of 70% Pinot Nero and 30% Chardonnay grapes. Classic method. Nice bright and transparent golden yellow, rich and persistent sparkles. Light but varied aromas of jasmine, white peach and smoky hint. Incredibly fresh, creamy with a long finish.

 87 Price B
Extra Cuvée Brut Metodo Classico Rosso
100% Lambrusco di Sorbara grapes. Re-fermenta-

tion in bottle for 18 months. Light red color with never overwhelming sparkles. Varied aromas of citrus and black cherry, currant and underbrush. Agile and easy to drink, fresh and extremely clean.

BISSONI

Via Colecchio, 280
47032 Bertinoro (FC)
Tel. +39 0543 460382
info@vinibissoni.com
www.vinibissoni.com
 Cantina-Bissoni

YEAR OF FOUNDATION 1988
NAME OF THE OWNER Raffaella Bissoni
TOTAL BOTTLES PRODUCED 30,000
DIRECT SALES
VISITS TO THE WINERY - RESERVATION NEEDED
HECTARES OF VINEYARD 5
CERTIFIED ORGANIC VITICULTURE

This small estate run by women, which became organic in 2016, is in the town of Bertinoro, one of the historic centers for Sangiovese Romagnolo. Its vineyards are at the right altitude, above the edges of ravines and have a soil that is for the most part sandy and sandstone. They have five hectares of vineyards overlooking their beautiful winery of which four are Sangiovese and one Albana. The cellar is a throwback to the past and may appear to be 'primordial', with not modern gadgets, but everything is clean, above all the old and new barrels. Fermentation takes place under controlled temperatures in stainless steel vats using ripe grapes without excessive macerations, ten days for the Sangiovese.

■ 94   Price B
Romagna Sangiovese Superiore Vigna Collecchio Riserva 2013
100% Sangiovese grapes. Matures in used barrique. Intense and bright ruby red. Excellent on the nose with red cherry, morello cherry and a light smoky hint. Slightly bittering freshness. Very elegant on the palate with good power, nicely integrated tannins and an aftertaste of violets and dark flowers. Elegant and persistent finish.

▪ 88   Price B*
Romagna Albana Passito 2010
100% Albana grapes. Matures in oak and stainless

steel. Golden color. Intense and clean notes of yellow plum, apricot, boxwood and Mediterranean herbs. Elegant on the palate with nice balance between sugars and acidity. Smooth and enveloping, easy to drink with an attractive and relaxed finish. *50 cl bottle.*

■ 85   👍 Price A
Romagna Sangiovese Superiore Girapoggio 2014
100% Sangiovese grapes. Matures in stainless steel. Light ruby red. The nose needs a little oxygenation then it opens on notes of underbrush, fresh hints of blackberries and white cherry. Convincing on the palate, harmonic, easy to drink, balanced tannins and good finish.

CANTINA DELLA VOLTA

Via per Modena, 82
41030 Bomporto (MO)
Tel. +39 059 7473312
Fax +39 059 7473313
 cantinadellavolta
info@cantinadellavolta.com
www.cantinadellavolta.com
 cantina.dellavolta
 @CantinaVolta

YEAR OF FOUNDATION 2010
NAME OF THE OWNER Christian Bellei
TOTAL BOTTLES PRODUCED 100,000
DIRECT SALES
VISITS TO THE WINERY - RESERVATION NEEDED
HECTARES OF VINEYARD 9

The winery's current headquarters is in Bomporto which was once a port in for Modena in the important canal system in the Po River Valley. Even if it is much more recent, the Bellei family's wine history goes far back and they now obtain extraordinary results making bubbly using the traditional method while continuing to pay particular attention to Lambrusco traditions.

▣ 90   👍 Price A
Lambrusco di Sorbara Rimosso 2015
100% Lambrusco di Sorbara grapes. Re-fermentation in the bottle. Very light color, lively sparkles. Nice grape flavor on the nose with a little reduction in the beginning. Then a lot of flowers: violets on top, strawberry and black cherry jam. Very fresh on

123

the palate with an unusual consistence, fruity and high quality finish.

 88   Price B

Il Mattaglio Blanc de Blancs 2011

100% Chardonnay of the Riccò area. Classic method, 60 months on the yeasts and 2016 disgorging. Light straw yellow color, thin sparkles. Intense flowery notes, daisy and gerbera but rennet apple and white melon as well. Very intense. Wide and rich on the palate, good freshness.

🔲 87   Price B

Lambrusco di Sorbara Rosé 2012

100% Lambrusco di Sorbara grapes. Classic method. Matures 8 moths in stainless steel and 40 months on the yeasts. 2015 disgorging. Very light color. Almost wild before oxygenation then notes of wild strawberries and raspberries. Very tense and fresh on the palate, apparently thin but clean and with strong acidity.

CARRA DI CASATICO

Strada della Nave, 10 - Frazione Casatico
43013 Langhirano (PR)
Tel. +39 0521 863510
Fax +39 0521 863510
🅢 *carradicasatico*
info@carradicasatico.com
www.carradicasatico.com
🅵 *AziendaViticolaCarraDiCasatico*

YEAR OF FOUNDATION 1992
NAME OF THE OWNER Bonfiglio Carra
TOTAL BOTTLES PRODUCED 125,000
DIRECT SALES
VISITS TO THE WINERY
HECTARES OF VINEYARD 27
RESTAURANT

The splendid hills overlooking the majestic Castello di Torrechiara are home to the winery of this very skilled family of winemakers, headed by the dynamic Bonfiglio (aka Boni). He is good-natured yet intransigent as is his winemaking philosophy: keep the production chain as short as possible in order to keep everything under control. His wine are thus exasperatingly precise and while attention is paid to the environment, production is quite advanced from the technical point of view.

 88   👍 Price A

Lambrusco Torcularia 2015

100% Lambrusco Maestri grapes. Charmat method. Bright red with violet hues. Rich and persistent sparkles. Morello and cherry on the nose, exuberant flowers with macerated violet in evidence. Sharp, opulent on the palate. Nice grip and exemplar freshness.

 86   👍 Price A

Malvasia Frizzante Extra Dry 2015

100% Malvasia di Candia grapes from 50 years old vines. Charmat method. Deep straw yellow with not aggressive sparkles. Aromatic herbs aromas like sage and thyme, citrusy hints. Balanced and pleasantly refreshing on the palate, even though it has strong body.

CASTELLUCCIO

Via Tramonto, 5
47015 Modigliana (FC)
Tel. +39 0546 942486
info@ronchidicastelluccio.it
www.ronchidicastelluccio.it
🅵 *fiorewines*

YEAR OF FOUNDATION 1980
NAME OF THE OWNER Vittorio Fiore
TOTAL BOTTLES PRODUCED 85,000
DIRECT SALES
VISITS TO THE WINERY - RESERVATION NEEDED
HECTARES OF VINEYARD 14
OLIVE OIL PRODUCTION

The Castelluccio winery is an historic winery in Romagna and the high quality of its wines have made iy point of reference for the area. It is located in the small hill town of Modigliana and originally belonged to the Baldi family before passing to the Fiore family. Vittorio Fiore, who became an eminent enologist, lifted the winery to be among the elite in Italy. For several years now the estate has been run by his son Claudio who continues to produce excellent wines.

 85   👍 Price A

Romagna Sangiovese Superiore Le More 2014

100% Sangiovese grapes. Stainless steel only. Bright ruby red. Fruity and fragrant on the nose with notes of cherry and plum. Tense and briny on the palate, nice acidity. Simple and average length.

CAVICCHIOLI

Via Canaletto, 52
41030 San Prospero (MO)
Tel. +39 059 812411
Fax +39 059 812414
cantina@cavicchioli.it
www.cavicchioli.it

YEAR OF FOUNDATION 1928
NAME OF THE OWNER Gruppo Italiano Vini
TOTAL BOTTLES PRODUCED 10,000,000
DIRECT SALES
VISITS TO THE WINERY - RESERVATION NEEDED
HECTARES OF VINEYARD 90

The Cavicchioli winery stands out for the quantity of wines it produces and far from being an offense it is a clear example of the entrepreneurial spirit that has deep roots in the area. And most of all the quantity in no affects the high quality of their wines that in some cases achieve excellence. The line of production is vast and made with all the classic grapes native to Modena.

回 87   Price A
Lambrusco di Sorbara Vigna del Cristo 2015
100% Lambrusco di Sorbara grapes. Charmat method. Light red color, almost pink as its bubbles. This vintage has a very pleasant aroma of roses and pomegranate, and an intriguing eucalyptus hint. Tense on the palate, good acidity but smooth and easy to drink.

CECI

Via Provinciale, 99/99a
43056 Torrile (PR)
Tel. +39 0521 810252
Fax +39 0521 810134
info@lambrusco.it
www.lambrusco.it
 Cantine-Ceci
 @CantineC

YEAR OF FOUNDATION 1938
NAME OF THE OWNER Ceci Family
TOTAL BOTTLES PRODUCED 2,500,000
DIRECT SALES
VISITS TO THE WINERY - RESERVATION NEEDED

Sandro Ceci is a volcano of ideas and the far-sighted head of his family's estate, where he is assisted by a staff of relatives and friends who make a formidable team that always looks to the future. A communication wizard and among the ambassadors of Lambrusco to the world, he is an example of what this province can do and with his strong sales, which never hurts, he has become a locomotive for the whole area.

回 88   👍 Price A
Otello Nero di Lambrusco 2015
100% Lambrusco Maestri grapes. Stainless steel only. Dark red with intense and very rich sparkles. Exuberant on the nose with notes of Morello cherry and red fruits. Round on the palate (less than other vintages) and stimulating, rich as few Lambrusco. Nice freshness even with powerful structure.

UMBERTO CESARI

Via Stanzano, 1120
40024 Castel San Pietro Terme (BO)
Tel. +39 051 941896
Fax +39 051 944387
info@umbertocesari.it
www.umbertocesari.it
 UmbertoCesari
 @UmbertoCesari

YEAR OF FOUNDATION 1967
NAME OF THE OWNER Umberto Cesari
TOTAL BOTTLES PRODUCED 2,700,000
DIRECT SALES
VISITS TO THE WINERY - RESERVATION NEEDED
HECTARES OF VINEYARD 320

The best definition for this winery is a dream come true. The dream was that of Umberto Cesari who in the 1960s wanted to export Romagna wines all around the world. And he made his dream come true with wines that reflect this international vision. They are technically well-made and keep the consumer in mind while never forgetting their roots.

91   Price B

Tauleto 2011

Blend of 90% Sangiovese and 10% Longanesi grapes. Matures 2 years in barrique and tonneau. Intense, dark ruby red. Still very young on the nose, woody notes and spices, then black cherry and kirsch. Rich, warm, full flavors, very typical with sweet tannins.

CEVICO

Via Fiumazzo, 72
48022 Lugo (RA)
Tel. +39 0545 284711
Fax +39 0545 284931
cevico@cevico.com
www.cevico.com
 GruppoCevicoAnniversario50Anni19632013

YEAR OF FOUNDATION **1956**
NAME OF THE OWNER
TOTAL BOTTLES PRODUCED **26,000,000**
DIRECT SALES
VISITS TO THE WINERY - RESERVATION NEEDED
HECTARES OF VINEYARD **6,600**
CERTIFIED ORGANIC VITICULTURE

Cevico, or rather the Cevico Group, is run with decision and foresight by Ruenza Santandrea, one of the most influential wine women in Italy. She has some 5,000 supplier-partners who produce 130 million kilos of grapes, part of which is used to produce 26 million bottles of wine. It is a giant cooperative that offers well-made wines and at affordable prices. Along with their table wines, Cevico produces – from the 16-hectare Messelina estate – a selection of top quality wines for restaurants.

92   Price B

Romagna Sangiovese Superiore Masselina Riserva 2013

100% Sangiovese grapes. Matures 18 months in barrique. Intense ruby red. On the nose there are continuous alternation of spicy and vanilla notes, then varietal aromas of black cherry, kirsch and red orange. Tense, briny, warm and persistent flavor.

89   Price A

Romagna Sangiovese Superiore Le Rocche Malatestiane I Diavoli 2015

100% Sangiovese grapes. Matures 6 months in con-crete vats and 4 in stainless steel. Intense ruby red. Clear notes of black cherry, cassis and violet. Rich flavor, savory, warm, very pleasant and great persistence.

CLETO CHIARLI

Via Belvedere, 4
41122 Castelvetro di Modena (MO)
Tel. +39 059 3163311
Fax +39 059 313705
italia@chiarli.it
www.chiarli.it
chiarli1860
@chiarli1860

YEAR OF FOUNDATION **2001**
NAME OF THE OWNER **Chiarli Family**
TOTAL BOTTLES PRODUCED **900,000**
DIRECT SALES
VISITS TO THE WINERY - RESERVATION NEEDED
HECTARES OF VINEYARD **100**

The Chiarli family winery is a rare example of one that can that can produce great quantity with a remarkable level of quality that sometimes achieves excellence. The modern methods needed to make such a critical mass surprisingly compliment ancient traditions, one in which flavors are extraordinarily consistent with a land with such a vocation for food.

91   Price A

Lambrusco di Sorbara del Fondatore 2015

100% Lambrusco di Sorbara grapes. Ancestral method. Intense pink color. Very thin and consistent sparkles. Intense notes of strawberry jelly with hints of macerated rose petals. Vigor and acidity on the palate, with a very light intriguing spiciness. Really convincing, probably the positive vintage, favored the structure and consistence on the palate.

88   Price A

Lambrusco di Sorbara Premium Vecchia Modena 2015

100% Lambrusco di Sorbara grapes. Charmat method. Light pink color with intense sparkles. Notes of wild strawberries and raspberries, black cherry and a delicious eucalyptus hint in the finish. Very tense on the palate, extremely fresh due to the strong acidity.

COSTA ARCHI

Via Rinfosco, 1690 - Località Serra
48014 Castel Bolognese (RA)
Tel. +39 338 4818346
Fax +39 0546 656181
aziendacostaarchi@yahoo.it
costaarchi.wordpress.com

YEAR OF FOUNDATION **1960**
NAME OF THE OWNER **Gabriele Succi**
TOTAL BOTTLES PRODUCED **15,000**
DIRECT SALES
VISITS TO THE WINERY - RESERVATION NEEDED
HECTARES OF VINEYARD **13**

Estate owner Gabriele Succi has a passion for wine that few can match. He is always ready to question his decisions, has an almost monastic dedication to his vineyards is hypercritical of his wines and every year strives for perfection. When he fails to achieve the standards he desires, he is open to make changes and even take drastic action. And so this year he decided to concentrate only on a few wines in his line and the results were surprising.

◼ 91	Price B

Sangiovese G&S 2013

100% Sangiovese grapes. Matures 16 months in tonneau. Bright and intense red color. Rich on the nose with notes of underbrush, raspberries and blackberries, humus and bark, hints of tobacco. Warm and wide on the palate, powerful but with incredible elegance and balance. Thick tannins but well integrated.

▣ 86	Price A

Romagna Sangiovese Assiolo Serra 2014

100% Sangiovese grapes. Matures 12 months in used barrique and tonneau. Intense, bright ruby red. Aromas of macerated violets, red fruits, hints of licorice. Strong on the palate, nice freshness, savory with very thin tannins.

DREI DONÀ - LA PALAZZA

Via del Tesoro, 23 - Fraz. Massa di Vecchiazzano
47100 Forlì (FC)
Tel. +39 0543 769371
Fax +39 0543 765049
palazza@dreidona.it

www.dreidona.it
 dreidonatenutalapalazza
 @DreiDonaWinery

YEAR OF FOUNDATION **1927**
NAME OF THE OWNER **Drei Donà Family**
TOTAL BOTTLES PRODUCED **130,000**
DIRECT SALES
VISITS TO THE WINERY - RESERVATION NEEDED
HECTARES OF VINEYARD **30**
CERTIFIED ORGANIC VITICULTURE
OLIVE OIL PRODUCTION

This estate has deep roots in the territory and is a point of reference not only for wine-lovers but also other producers who consider it a model to be imitated. The winegrowing approach is quite adventurous and already in the 1980s the density of the vineyards was unusually high and the care taken in the cellar was similar to that of a Burgundy Chateau. And all this was done to exalt Sangiovese.

◼ 94	Price B

Romagna Sangiovese Superiore Pruno Riserva 2013

100% Sangiovese grapes. Matures 18 months in French oak. Deep ruby red. Smoky notes on the nose that don't cover the red fruits, morello and cherry. Light hints of blackberry and violets. Intense on the palate, young but juicy and dense. It just needs more time in the bottle. Complex in the finish.

◼ 90	Price B

Romagna Sangiovese Superiore Palazza Riserva 2013

Blend of 90% Sangiovese and other grapes. Matures 2 years in oak barrels. Bright ruby. Intense and flowery notes on the nose, then cherry and basil. Young tannins on the palate. Full bodied, powerful but agile. Persistent finish.

FATTORIA NICOLUCCI

Via Umberto I, 21
47016 Predappio (FC)
Tel. +39 0543 922361
Fax +39 0543 922361
casetto@tin.it
www.vini-nicolucci.it
 FattoriaNicolucciPredappio
 @ViniNicolucci

YEAR OF FOUNDATION **1885**
NAME OF THE OWNER **Alessandro Nicolucci**
TOTAL BOTTLES PRODUCED **70,000**
DIRECT SALES
VISITS TO THE WINERY - RESERVATION NEEDED
HECTARES OF VINEYARD **10**

Alessandro Nicolucci is the third generation of his family to make wine and he maintains a very classic style in his wines without any concessions to easy or modern gimmicks. His wines are austere and reflect the area the where the grapes are grown, upper Predappio, and are thus bold with a finesse not found in the harder wines from the lower altitudes.

■ 🍇 **95** Price B
Romagna Sangiovese Predappio di Predappio Vigna del Generale Ris. 2013

100% Sangiovese grapes. Matures 2 years in 30 hl barrels. Intense ruby red. Wide and clear on the nose, good intensity, fruity notes of cherry and morello then smoky hints and flowery puffs. Very classy on the palate, young tannins and thick structure, intense and progressive. Super elegant finish, savory with hints of cocoa.

■ **86** 👍 Price A
Romagna Sangiovese Superiore Tre Rocche 2015

100% Sangiovese grapes. Matures a few months in barrels. Ruby red. Light rustic aromas on the nose together with cherry and spices. Intriguing and savory on the palate, great drinkability.

★★★

FATTORIA ZERBINA

Via Vicchio, 11
48018 Faenza (RA)
Tel. +39 0546 40022
info@zerbina.com
www.zerbina.com
 FattoriaZerbina
🐦 *@FattoriaZerbina*

YEAR OF FOUNDATION **1966**
NAME OF THE OWNER **Cristina Geminiani**
TOTAL BOTTLES PRODUCED **190,000**
DIRECT SALES
VISITS TO THE WINERY - RESERVATION NEEDED
HECTARES OF VINEYARD **29**

In the Colli Romagnoli this estate is an absolute point of reference. Its wines are modern yet reliable, made with a precise style that focuses on the grape without ever being commonplace. All the wines are of top quality and some are among the best in the country. The vineyards are magnificently cared for and in the winery great care is taken not to ruin the grapes. An applause for the dynamic force at Zerbini: Cristina Geminiani.

▣ 🍇 **96** Price B*
Romagna Albana Passito Scaccomatto 2013

*100% Albana grapes. Botrytis. Matures in barrique and stainless steel. Bright golden color. Notes of botrytis on the nose, light iodine and nice sea breeze emphasize the medlar and candied apricot. Elegant light smoky hints. Rich and intense on the palate with balanced, nice sweetness, never sickly. A real champion in the finish. *37.5 cl bottle.*

■ **93** 👍 Price A
Romagna Sangiovese Superiore Terre di Ceparano 2012

Blend of Sangiovese with Syrah, Merlot and Cabernet grapes. Matures in American and French barrels. Dark ruby red. Intense on the nose with hints of citrus, red orange, morello cherry and wild cherry. Elegant eucalyptus hints. Harmonic on the palate and classy with elegant tannins and intense and convincing progression. Elegant and juicy finish.

☐ **87** 👍 Price A
Romagna Albana Secco Bianco di Ceparano 2014

100% Albana grapes. Matures on the lees for few months. Classic straw yellow color. Clean on the nose, intense white fruits and yellow flowers. Tense and intense acidity and nice structure. Easy to drink and good refreshing acidity.

LAMORETTI

Strada della Nave, 6 - Frazione Casatico
43013 Langhirano (PR)
Tel. +39 0521 863590
info@lamoretti.eu
www.lamoretti.eu
 Lamoretti

YEAR OF FOUNDATION **1930**
NAME OF THE OWNER **Lamoretti Family**

Masterpiece

**Premio Speciale
Gran Vinitaly 2016**

Trofeo 2016 "5 Star Wines"

www.vrankenpommery.it

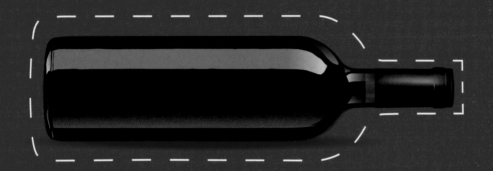

offset print, flat bed uv print, cnc cut
visual design.

ink droplets

PANTONE® P 74-8 C

CSR
Centro Stampa e Riproduzione srl

Via di Salone 131/c | Tecnopolo | 00131 Roma | tel 064182113 | info@csr.it | **www.csr.it**

TOTAL BOTTLES PRODUCED
DIRECT SALES
VISITS TO THE WINERY - RESERVATION NEEDED
HECTARES OF VINEYARD **20**

This historic winery is in a fairy-tale setting on to the Parma hills not far from the Torrechiara farm. The vineyards extend throughout the estate and cover a large hill which has a southeast exposure, overlooking the Torrente Parma Valley, and has an altitude of between 210 and 310m above sea level. The soil has nice drainage and is most clay with a high among of lime which limits the yield of the vines while the grapes are very concentrated.

 85   **Price A**

Colli di Parma Lambrusco Maestri 2015

100% Lambrusco Maestri grapes. Charmat method. Bright red color with violet hues. Abundant and persistent sparkles. Extremely fruity, cherries and strawberries. Evident grape notes. Powerful and agile on the palate, not too long on the finish but very pleasant.

LINI 910

*Via Vecchia Canolo, 7
42015 Correggio (RE)
Tel. +39 0522 690162
info@lini910.it
www.lini910.it*
 LINI 910
 @LINI910

YEAR OF FOUNDATION **1910**
NAME OF THE OWNER **Lini Family**
TOTAL BOTTLES PRODUCED **400,000**
DIRECT SALES
VISITS TO THE WINERY - RESERVATION NEEDED
HECTARES OF VINEYARD **25**

This year we tasted some amazing wines here. The recently disgorged traditional method reserve Lambrusco could be classified as 'wine to study', the kind tasters rarely have an opportunity to try. Always innovative and in love with the Traditional Method, this winery revolutionized the concept of Lambrusco breaking the cliché of it being a simple wine to pair with cold cut and local

cuisine. The selection of grapes for quality is fierce and if the harvest is not good they do not even produce the bubbly.

 95   **Price B**

Rosso In Correggio 2005

100% Lambrusco Salamino grapes. Classic method. I thought that 2004 vintage was the best but this version is even better. Purple red. Sober and light sparkles. Notes of blackberry jam, underbrush, medical herbs and spices. Austere on the palate in the beginning, it opens shameless at a deep and varied pleasure.

 89   **Price A**

Spumante Gran Cuvée di Lambrusco

100% Lambrusco Salamino grapes. Classic method (36 months on the yests). Not too deep color, bright and clear red. Vigorous sparkles. Notes of blackberry and plum jam on the nose. Agile and comforting on the palate, elegant finish.

 88   **Price B**

Metodo Classico Millesimato 2010

100% Pinot Nero grapes. Classic method (48 months on the yeasts). Straw yellow with nice golden hues. White and not too intense sparkles. White fruits, hints of citrus, soft briny aromas on the nose. Great freshness on the palate but full bodied. Opulent and clear finish. Great personality and drinkability.

 85   **Price A**

Lambrusco Rosso Charmat Labrusca

Blend of 80% Lambrusco Salamino and 20% Ancellotta grapes. Charmat method. Bright red with violet hues. Rich and persistent sparkles. A blaze of wild flowers, pansies and strong cherry. Agile, very fresh, extremly pleasant in its simplicity.

LUSENTI

*Località Casa Piccioni, 57 - frazione di Vicobarone
29010 Ziano Piacentino (PC)
Tel. +39 0523 868479
info@lusentivini.it
www.lusentivini.it*
 Lusentivini

YEAR OF FOUNDATION **Inizi 900**
NAME OF THE OWNER **Gaetano and Ludovica Lusenti, Giuseppe Ferri**
TOTAL BOTTLES PRODUCED **100,000**
DIRECT SALES

VISITS TO THE WINERY - RESERVATION NEEDED
HECTARES OF VINEYARD 17

Pietro Lusenti purchased his first farm to cultivate table grapes at the beginning of the 20th century. Today his youngest grandchild Ludovica and her husband Giuseppe manage an estate that is now also producing wine, exclusively from their own grapes. The grapes used are those typical to this part of the Piacenza province: Malvasia di Candia, Ortrugo and Bonarda.

☐ 90　　　　　　　　　　　Price B

Colli Piacentini Malvasia Bianca Regina 2011

100% Malvasia di Candia from 50-60 years old vineyards. Late harvest. Matures 9 months in barrels. Deep golden color with bright hues. Oriental notes, spicy, turmeric, dry flowers, curry and yellow plum. Wide, with glycerin sensations on the palate. Extremely fresh and full bodied. Elegant and agile.

LUSIGNANI

Località Case Orsi, 9
29010 Vernasca (PC)
Tel. +39 0523 895178
m.lusignani@alice.it
www.lusignani.com

YEAR OF FOUNDATION 1946
NAME OF THE OWNER Lusignani Family
TOTAL BOTTLES PRODUCED 8,000
DIRECT SALES
VISITS TO THE WINERY - RESERVATION NEEDED
HECTARES OF VINEYARD 10

A small winery specialized in producing Colli Piacentini wines but that also makes the rare Vin Santo di Vigoleno, an unknown pearl of Italian winemaking. It is one of the few sweet wines made without sulfur dioxide using an ancient method that makes it an authentic cultural treasure as well as a splendid wine. Watching how it is made is a true blast to the past.

▪ 94　　　　　　　　　　　Price C*

Colli Piacentini Vin Santo di Vigoleno 2006

Blend of Beverdino, Santa Maria, Melara, Trebbiano and Ortrugo grapes dried on straw mats for 3 months. Matures 6 months in small durmast caratelli only half filled, than moved into smaller

and smaller containers like for eucalyptus vinegar. Light amber color. Oxidative notes on the nose, tamarind, cocoa and nut liquor. Briny, enveloping, warm, sweet and exceptional persistence. *37.5 cl bottle.*

MEDICI ERMETE

Via I. Newton, 13a - Frazione Gaida
42124 Reggio Emilia (RE)
Tel. +39 0522 942135
info@medici.it
www.medici.it
f *MediciErmete*
𝕩 *ermetemedici*

YEAR OF FOUNDATION 1900
NAME OF THE OWNER Medici Family
TOTAL BOTTLES PRODUCED 800,000
VISITS TO THE WINERY - RESERVATION NEEDED
HECTARES OF VINEYARD 75

Despite coming from an otherwise disastrous year, the wines from this historic Reggio Emilia estate are truly remarkable. By making a rigorous selection grapes and using an avant-garde technical approach, the estate made wines that offer extreme pleasure and nice structure.

▣ 92　　　　　　　　　　　Price B

Granconcerto Metodo Classico 2012

100% Lambrusco Salamino grapes from Tenuta La Rampata. Classic method. We talk again about 2012 vintage while we wait for 2013 not ready yet. One extra year in the bottle gave even more complexity. Still intense red color with purple sparkles. Extremely rich on the nose, eucalyptus, black cherry and cherry jam. Delicious spicy hint. Austere but tense on the palate, fresh and elegant, with great persistence.

▣ 91　　　　　　　　　👍 Price A

Reggiano Lambrusco Concerto 2015

100% Lambrusco Salamino grapes from Tenuta La Rampata. Charmat method. Rich, bright and intense ruby red. Rich and lively sparkles. Intense flowery notes with macerated roses and violets. Easy to drink with smooth fruity sensations.

☐ 87　　　　　　　　　　👍 Price A

Colli di Scandiano e di Canossa Daphne 2015

100% Malvasia di Candia grapes. Natural fermen-

tation. Golden straw yellow. Intense fruity notes of yellow peach, medlar and melon. Slightly sparkling on the palate, very pleasant and refreshing that balances the fruity sweetness. Bright and pleasant.

MONTE DELLE VIGNE

Via Monticello, 22 - Frazione Ozzano Taro
43044 Collecchio (PR)
Tel. +39 0521 309704
mdv@montedellevigne.it
www.montedellevigne.it
f *montedellevigne*
🐦 *@MontedelleVigne*

YEAR OF FOUNDATION 1983
NAME OF THE OWNER Paolo Pizzarotti and Andrea Ferrari
TOTAL BOTTLES PRODUCED 380,000
DIRECT SALES
VISITS TO THE WINERY - RESERVATION NEEDED
HECTARES OF VINEYARD 60

The improvement in quality this winery has made is impressive also considering that its production is one of the highest in the district. In just a few years the initial six hectares of vineyards have become 60 thanks to the great entrepreneurial support offered by Paolo Pizzarotti that included the building of a new, cutting-edge winery which is also environmentally friendly. It is amazing how the wines interpret the land and convey the wonderful subsoil of Ozzano Taro.

 92 Price B
Argille 2012

100% Barbera grapes. Matures 24 months in new allier barrique. Dark ruby red. Notes of black cherries, blackberries, tobacco and chocolate on the nose. Powerful but balanced on the palate. Strong tannins. Great balance between elegance and power. Few bottles produced but excellent quality.

 90 Price B
Nabucco 2012

Blend of 70% Barbera and 30% Merlot grapes. Matures 12 months in new barrique. Intense purple red color. Strong cherry, blackberry, underbrush, humus and licorice notes together with a light and delicious cinchona. Rich and pulpy with thick and pleasant tannins.

 89 Price A
Lambrusco I Salici 2014

100% Lambrusco Maestri. Classic method. Rich red color. Nice, dense and persistent sparkles. Prominent morello cherry, then violet and Vignola cherry. Fresh and rich on the palate but it keeps its virility. Unusual complexity.

☐ **88** Price B
Callas 2013

100% Malvasia di Candia grapes. Stainless steel only. Deep straw yellow with golden hues. Great aromatic aromas with notes of cedar, medical herbs, good briny aromas. Tense, fresh and briny on the palate. Very savory.

★★
PALTRINIERI

Via Cristo, 49 - Località Sorbara
41030 Bomporto (MO)
Tel. +39 059 902047
info@cantinapaltrinieri.it
www.cantinapaltrinieri.it
f *CANTINA-PALTRINIERI*

YEAR OF FOUNDATION 1926
NAME OF THE OWNER Alberto Paltrinieri
TOTAL BOTTLES PRODUCED 95,000
DIRECT SALES
VISITS TO THE WINERY - RESERVATION NEEDED
HECTARES OF VINEYARD 15

The estate of Alberto and Barbara Paltrinieri is in Cristo di Sorbara, in the heart of the appellation, and is an example of how uncompromised craftsmanship, talent and passion can obtain results that are extraordinary to say the least. This from their super selections of Sorbara made with the classic, natural bottle fermentation to the very rare, for the area, Salamino varietal wine. All are a pure expression of a great land that fortunately is in the hands of great producers.

🔲 **94** 👍 Price A
Lambrusco di Sorbara Radice 2015

100% Lambrusco di Sorbara grapes. Light pink color. One of the best versions of this wine, if not the best. Exuberant notes of cherry and wild strawberry together with delicate spicy hits. As usual, austere on the palate, vertical and juicy fruit aromas. Nice briny finish and very easy to drink.

91 👍 Price A

Lambrusco di Sorbara Leclisse 2015

100% Lambrusco di Sorbara grapes. Light ruby red. Spicy aromas and fresh fruits on the nose. Still austere on the palate, but enveloping, great tension. Very long progressive finish.

 88 👍 Price A

Lambrusco di Sorbara Sant'Agata 2015

100% Lambrusco di Sorbara grapes. Light ruby red. Clear notes of cherry and spices on the nose. Agile, dry and edgy on the palate. Pulpy and unusually deep finish.

 88 Price A

Solco 2015

100% Lambrusco Salamino grapes. Dark ruby red. Blueberry and pepper on the nose. Juicy, fresh and easy to drink on the palate.

★

PODERI DAL NESPOLI

Via Villa Rossi, 50 - Località Nespoli
47012 Civitella di Romagna (FC)
Tel. +39 0543 989911
Fax +39 0543 989999
🅢 *poderidalnespoli*
info@poderidalnespoli.com
www.poderidalnespoli.com
🅵 *poderidalnespoli1929*
🐦 *@PdN1929*

YEAR OF FOUNDATION **1929**
NAME OF THE OWNER **Fabio Ravaioli**
TOTAL BOTTLES PRODUCED **700,000**
DIRECT SALES
VISITS TO THE WINERY - RESERVATION NEEDED
HECTARES OF VINEYARD **150**

This important and historic estate in Valle del Bidente has, with its 150 hectares of vineyards, contributed to improving the reputation of this whole winemaking area of Romagna. The soil at the lower altitudes is more clay while higher up it has more marl and is looser. The style of the wines, which are very clean and intense, tends to lean more towards elegance than seeking greater and unnecessary boldness. The estate is run by Fabio Ravaioli, a man who has very balanced and winning ideas.

91 👍 Price A

Romagna Sangiovese Superiore Il Nespoli Riserva 2013

100% Sangiovese grapes. Matures 1 year in barrique. Intense ruby red. Smoky hints on the nose, wide fruity notes of cherry and fresh blackberry. Rich and intense on the palate, very young tannin and thick structure. Juicy and fruity finish.

PODERI MORINI

Via Via Gesuita, 4/B - San Biagio
48018 Faenza (RA)
Tel. +39 0546 638172
info@poderimorini.com
www.poderimorini.com
🅵 *poderimorini*
🐦 *@PoderiMorini*

YEAR OF FOUNDATION **1998**
NAME OF THE OWNER **Alessandro Morini**
TOTAL BOTTLES PRODUCED
DIRECT SALES
VISITS TO THE WINERY - RESERVATION NEEDED
HECTARES OF VINEYARD **40**

The Poderi Morini estate is situated in the Faentini Hills around Torre di Oriolo. There are a total of 40 hectares of vineyards that grow in the classic Romagna 'spungone' rocky soil. Alessandro Morini is a promotor of native Romagnolo grapes: he is part of the Bursòn group and produces four wines from the grape centesimino (a Rosé sparkling wine, a young simple version, one aged in wood and a Passito dessert wine). His estate also produces typical wines from the area: Albana, Sangiovese as well as a Super Romagna. Since 2010 the winemaking consultant is Maurizio Castelli.

 88 Price B

Augusto Bursòn 2009

100% Longanesi grapes, late harvested. 20 months in tonneau barrels. Dark, ruby-red color. The aroma has an intense herbal note typical of the grape, followed by sensations of spice, dried plums and a hint of leather. Rich on the palate, with bold tannins that need a long time to settle. Good persistence.

■ **88** Price A

Traicolli 2011

100% Centesimino grapes. Matures 14 months in

500-liter tonneau then in concrete. Dark ruby color. Its bouquet is a floral explosion of rose, violet, lilacs and wisteria, followed by a little spice and hints of red berries. The mouthfeel is full and rounded, balanced and flavorful with a distinct return of floral notes and spice. The finish has a nice length.

☐ 85   Price A
Romagna Albana Secca Sette Note 2013

100% Albana grapes, grown on small trellises in a clay soil. Bold, straw-yellow color. Clean, floral aroma with notes of hawthorn and white peach. High acidity and saline and yet not aggressive thanks to its fine structure. The flavor is tasty and full of character with some nice fruit in the finish.

RIUNITE

Via G. Brodolini, 24
42040 Campegine (RE)
Tel. +39 0522 905711
comita@riunite.it
www.riunite.it
f *Riunite*
𝕏 *@RiuniteOnIce*

YEAR OF FOUNDATION **1950**
NAME OF THE OWNER **Corrado Casoli, presidente**
TOTAL BOTTLES PRODUCED **65,000,000**
DIRECT SALES
VISITS TO THE WINERY - RESERVATION NEEDED
HECTARES OF VINEYARD **3,700**

Corrado Casoli, the head of this colossal Italian wine cooperative with its 1,500 members, is responsible for exporting millions of bottles around the world, much of which is Lambrusco, making the cooperative one of the biggest exporters in Italy. The cooperative's wines are technically impeccable and offered at reasonable prices. The cooperative has opened the way for the exports of more expensive and famous wines but this in itself only adds to its importance.

回 85   Price A
Lambrusco di Sorbara Metodo Ancestrale Albinea Canali

100% Lambrusco di Sorbara grapes. Ancestral method. Very light ruby red. Yeasts and strawberries on the nose, fragrant and very inviting. Acidity on the palate, tense and juicy, agile, a hint of carbonic. Refreshing finish.

ROMAGNOLI

Via Genova, 20 - Frazione Villò
29029 Vigolzone (PC)
Tel. +39 0523 870904
info@cantineromagnoli.it
www.cantineromagnoli.it
f *Cantine-Romagnoli*
𝕏 *@CantineRomagnol*

YEAR OF FOUNDATION **1857**
NAME OF THE OWNER **Ferrari and Perini Families**
TOTAL BOTTLES PRODUCED **300,000**
DIRECT SALES
VISITS TO THE WINERY - RESERVATION NEEDED
HECTARES OF VINEYARD **50**

This is one of the leading wine estates in Colli Piacentini and is located in Villò di Vigolzone, some 20 km south of Piacenza. Using an organic winegrowing approach, it produces for the most part sparkling wines of excellent quality and great reliability. Its new owners, the Ferrari and Perini families, took over in 2012 and operate with full respect of what nature can offer.

回 93   Price B
Il Pigro Dosaggio Zero 2011

Blend of 70% Pinot Nero and 30% Chardonnay grapes. Classic method. Light straw yellow color, continuous sparkles. Complex and attractive on the nose, re-fermentation notes and fruity of yellow plum and medlar. Agile and elegant on the palate, full bodied, creamy carbonic. Pleasant and persistent finish.

回 91   Price A
Il Pigro 2013

Blend of 70% Pinot Nero and 30% Chardonnay grapes. Classic method. Light yellow color, thick and fast sparkles. Bread crust and slightly smoky hints for the aromas on the nose. Notes of pineapple and yellow plum. Intense and briny on the palate, very pleasant, delicious to drink.

回 87   Price A
Gutturnio Frizzante Sassonero 2015

Blend of 60% Barbera and 40% Bonarda grapes. Charmat method. Violet ruby red. Fragrant, notes of yeasts then raspberries, wild strawberries and plums, all elegant and clear. Dynamic on the palate, nice carbonic hint, tense and fresh.

★★★
SAN PATRIGNANO

Via San Patrignano, 53
47853 Coriano (RN)
Tel. +39 0541 362111
Fax +39 0541 756718
info@sanpatrignano.org
www.sanpatrignano.org
f *comunitasanpatrignano*
🐦 *@San_Patrignano*

YEAR OF FOUNDATION **1978**
NAME OF THE OWNER **Comunità San Patrignano**
TOTAL BOTTLES PRODUCED **500,000**
DIRECT SALES
VISITS TO THE WINERY - RESERVATION NEEDED
HECTARES OF VINEYARD **110**
RESTAURANT
CERTIFIED ORGANIC VITICULTURE
OLIVE OIL PRODUCTION

Founded by Vincenzo Muccioli in 1978, the Community of San Patrignano is the biggest drug rehabilitation center in the world. It has been a worthy yet difficult task that is more important than any other. Winemaking is one of the activities the center offers and they are now producing wines of excellent quality, thanks to the hard work of those participating in the program and the free advice from enologist Riccardo Cotarella.

 95   Price B
Romagna Sangiovese Superiore Avi Riserva 2012

100% Sangiovese grapes. Matures in barrels and barrique. Intense ruby red. Rich and intense ripe red fruit, cherry, wild cherry and blackberry. Elegant spicy note and persistent turmeric, then warmer, blond hints. Slightly smoky and elegant underbrush. Powerful and thick on the palate, never sickly thanks to the young tannins. Coherent and persistent finish.

 85   👍 Price A
Romagna Sangiovese Superiore Ora 2014

100% Sangiovese grapes. Stainless steel only. Bright ruby red. Clear fruity notes, red and black fruits, white fruit hints and freshness. Easy to drink on the palate and complex. Smooth tannins and balanced acidity. Fragrant fruit, perfect to drink.

TENUTA LA VIOLA

Via Colombarone, 888
47032 Bertinoro (FC)
Tel. +39 0543 445496
Fax +39 0543 445496
S *tenutalaviola*
info@tenutalaviola.it
www.tenutalaviola.it
f *Tenuta-La-Viola*
🐦 *@TenutaLaViola*

YEAR OF FOUNDATION **1998**
NAME OF THE OWNER **Gabellini Family**
TOTAL BOTTLES PRODUCED **47,000**
DIRECT SALES
VISITS TO THE WINERY - RESERVATION NEEDED
HECTARES OF VINEYARD **11**
CERTIFIED ORGANIC VITICULTURE
OLIVE OIL PRODUCTION

Located in the town of Bertinoro, this is a modern estate above all due to the attention to detail in producing wine and the constant quest for ways to improve quality. Sangiovese is the principle grape used to make a variety of wines including one made using amphorae. The estate also makes some fine Bordeaux-blend wines and in the cellar are barrels of different sizes and give strong personality to the wines.

■ 90   Price B
Romagna Sangiovese Patri Honori Bertinoro Riserva 2012

100% Sangiovese grapes. Matures in small barrels. Bright ruby red. Intense and dark, austere underbrush notes and the typical cherry aroma. Elegant on the palate with young tannins, nice progression and important structure. Juicy and elegant finish.

■ 89   Price B
Vigna 25 2013

Blend of 45% Cabernet, 45% Merlot and Sangiovese grapes. Matures 14 months in new barrique. Dark ruby red. Il opens slowly on the nose, spices and cardamome, notes of cinchona, red orange and citrus, then black cherry. Average intensity on the palate, good progression. Savory finish.

TRE MONTI

Via Lola, 3
40026 Imola (BO)
Tel. +39 0542 657116
🟢 *tremontiwines*
tremonti@tremonti.it
www.tremonti.it
f *tremontiwines*

YEAR OF FOUNDATION 1971
NAME OF THE OWNER David and Vittorio Navacchia
TOTAL BOTTLES PRODUCED 180,000
DIRECT SALES
VISITS TO THE WINERY - RESERVATION NEEDED
HECTARES OF VINEYARD 40
CERTIFIED ORGANIC VITICULTURE

Owned by the Navacchia family that founded it in the 1970s, this estate has its vineyards in into two separate townships. The first is Serra in the Imola Hillls, which also hosts the winery, and the other is nearer to Forlì in the village of Petrignone. The vineyards were planted in consideration of the soils and so those in Serra grow Albana grapes, which thrive in clay, while Sangiovese is cultivated in Petrignone, where the soil is sandier and full of gravel.

| 89 | Price A |

Romagna Sangiovese Superiore Petrignone Oriolo Riserva 2013

100% Sangiovese grapes. Matures 6 months in barrique. Intense ruby red. Warm on the nose with ripe black fruits, blackberries and wild cherries. Dense, thick and young tannins. Compact and warm finish.

| 86 | 👍 Price A |

Romagna Albana Secco Vigna Rocca 2015

100% Albana grapes. Matures in stainless steel on the lees. Complex on the nose, fresh, eucalyptus hints then classic notes of peach and medlar. Pleasant on the palate with a very interesting savory note. Dense in the finish but very easy to drink due to the acidity.

TRERÈ

Via Casale, 19
48018 Faenza (RA)
Tel. +39 0546 47034
🟢 *trerevini*

trere@trere.com
www.trere.com
f *Trerenonsolovino*
🐦 *@Trerevinoe*

YEAR OF FOUNDATION Inizio anni '60
NAME OF THE OWNER Morena Trerè
TOTAL BOTTLES PRODUCED 200,000
DIRECT SALES
VISITS TO THE WINERY - RESERVATION NEEDED
HECTARES OF VINEYARD 35
HOSPITALITY
RESTAURANT

On the sweet hills that look towards the city of Faenza, in the beginning of the sixties, Vitaliano Trerè had the opportunity to buy the first 14 hectares of the estate. But it was in the mid-seventies when his daughter Morena decided to join the winery that the company improved its quality, opening the farmhouse to guests and the restaurant. The wines are the Docs' of the area and it's ten years that the winemaking consultants are the expert Attilio Pagli and Emiliano Falsini.

| 91 | 👍 Price A |

Romagna Sangiovese Superiore Amarcord d'un Ross Riserva 2013

Blend of Sangiovese with 15% Cabernet Sauvignon grapes. Matures 12 months in barrique. Ruby red color. Clear and intense on the nose, cherry and smoky hints. Intense on the palate with elegant tannins, briny and savory. Average body and great finish.

| 85 | 👍 Price A |

Colli di Faenza Sangiovese Re Nero 2014

100% Sangiovese grapes. Matures 6 months in barrique. Agerage ruby color. Pleasant notes of white cherry, vegetal hints and underbrush. Great drinkability with an attractive rustic note.

VENTURINI BALDINI

Via Filippo Turati, 42 - Frazione Roncolo
42020 Quattro Castella (RE)
Tel. +39 0522 249013
info@venturinibaldini.it
www.venturinibaldini.it
f *VenturiniBaldini*
🐦 *@venturinibaldin*

YEAR OF FOUNDATION **1976**
NAME OF THE OWNER **Iverna Holdings**
TOTAL BOTTLES PRODUCED **100,000**
DIRECT SALES
VISITS TO THE WINERY
HECTARES OF VINEYARD **32**
HOSPITALITY
CERTIFIED ORGANIC VITICULTURE

This Reggio Emilia farm was set up in 1976, in Roncolo di Quattro Castella, but its history is centuries' old, dating back to 1670. It recently changed hands and returned to its origins, a move that allowed its wines to swiftly climb the quality ladder even outside the province. The estate is situated in a fairytale setting with 150 hectares of alternating forests and vineyards in an incredibly beautiful landscape. Production today is exclusively certified organic with an emphasis on sustainability which is not in contrast with the refined and avant-garde winery.

回 **89**　　　　　　　　　　　Price A
Reggiano Lambrusco Spumante Quaranta

Blend of 40% Lambrusco Montericco, 25% Marani, 20% Maestri and Malbo Gentile grapes. Charmat method. Typical, well balanced, local grapes blend. Intense and bright red. Rich sparkles. Exuberant on the nose with notes of morello cherry, wild berries and ripe plum. Coquettish hint of pipe tobacco. Gourmet on the palat, wide and rich, with elegant but vigorous tannins.

回 **88**　　　　　　　　　　 Price A
Reggiano Lambrusco Spumante Rubino del Cerro 2015

Blend of Lambrusco Montericco, Salamino and Grasparossa grapes. Charmat method. Intense and bright ruby red. Rich, thin and persistent sparkles. Morello cherry, plum and ripe cherry on the nose, then leather with a hint of spices. Wide and rich on the palate, dynamic and great freshness.

VILLA DI CORLO

Strada Cavezzo, 200 - Località Baggiovara
41126 Modena (MO)
Tel. +39 059 510736
info@villadicorlo.com
www.villadicorlo.com
 villadicorlo.cantina

YEAR OF FOUNDATION **1998**
NAME OF THE OWNER **Maria Antonietta Munari**
TOTAL BOTTLES PRODUCED **85,000**
DIRECT SALES
VISITS TO THE WINERY - RESERVATION NEEDED
HECTARES OF VINEYARD **25**

The splendid late 17th century Villa di Corlo is in Cavezzo, the home of the celebrated Aceto Balsamic Tradizionale, of which it is a fine producer. It is also specialized in producing Lambrusco Grasparossa di Castelvetro and is considered a leader is producing this wine that is often underappreciated. The results always live up to its fame.

回 **89**　　　　　　　　　　 Price A
Lambrusco Grasparossa di Castelvetro Corleto 2015

100% Lambrusco Grasparossa di Castelvetro from Corlo di Formigine. Stainless steel only. Intense ruby red with abundant sparkles. Very pleasant flowery impact on the nose, then red fruits, plum, and coquettish hint of cherry. Creamy on the palate, rich and intense, you would never get tired of it.

回 **87**　　　　　　　　　　 Price A
Lambrusco Grasparossa di Castelvetro Amabile 2015

100% Lambrusco Grasparossa di Castelvetro from Corlo di Formigine. Charmat method. Dark ruby red with violet hues. Strong fruity notes, plum and Vignola cherry, with very nice raspberry hints. Smooth on the palate, opulent but not too sweet. One of the best of its kind.

★

VILLA PAPIANO

Via Ibola, 24
47015 Modigliana (FC)
Tel. +39 0546 941790
 villapapiano
info@villapapiano.it
www.villapapiano.it
 Villa Papiano

YEAR OF FOUNDATION **2000**
NAME OF THE OWNER **Villa Papiano Società Agricola**
TOTAL BOTTLES PRODUCED **50,000**
DIRECT SALES

VISITS TO THE WINERY - RESERVATION NEEDED
HECTARES OF VINEYARD 10
CERTIFIED ORGANIC VITICULTURE

This pioneering estate is situated at an altitude of 500m above sea level on the slopes of Monte Chioccia where the soil is sandstone and marl. Here the wines must strive to be elegant, with the risk of becoming too thin, and thus the vineyards are dense and a rigorous selection of the grapes must be made in order to obtain great, territorial wines. A moderate use of wood and the right winemaking method make this possible but at a cost of great sacrifice.

94 Price B

Romagna Sangiovese I Probi di Papiano Riserva 2013

100% Sangiovese grapes. Matures in barrique and tonneau. Classic ruby color. Clear and intense aromas of flowers and various types of cherries. A delicate smoky touch and sweet spices. Classy tannins and good acidity sustain the taste on the palate. A very elegant wine, savory and with a very classy finish.

93 Price B*

Romagna Albana Passito Tregenda Riserva 2013

*100% Albana grapes. Matures in small oak barrels. Golden yellow color. Medlar aromas on the nose, then dried apricot, hints of saffron and candied citrus. Very elegant on the palate with strong acidity that makes it easy to drink even considering the sugar content. Wide and intense elegant finish. *50 cl bottle.*

★

VILLA VENTI

Via Doccia, 1442
47020 Roncofreddo (FC)
Tel. +39 0541 949532
 Villa Venti
info@villaventi.it
www.villaventi.it
Villa-Venti
@VillaVenti

YEAR OF FOUNDATION 2002
NAME OF THE OWNER Mauro Giardini and Davide Chiellucci
TOTAL BOTTLES PRODUCED 27,000
DIRECT SALES

VISITS TO THE WINERY - RESERVATION NEEDED
HECTARES OF VINEYARD 7
HOSPITALITY
RESTAURANT
CERTIFIED ORGANIC VITICULTURE

The small estate of Davide Castellucci and Mauro Giardini is in the lovely area of Logiano in the Valle de Rubicone. It is a viable model for those who wish to engage in winemaking that respects nature, the vineyard and the consumer. Their wines are simple in the best sense of the word, the product of a lot of work by hand and impeccable skill. The main wine they produce is Sangiovese di Romagna which comes in several versions and is always expressive and of top quality.

93 Price B

Romagna Sangiovese Superiore Primo Segno 2013

100% Sangiovese grapes. Stainless steel only. Ruby red color. Intense fruity notes enriched with spices and graphite. Austere on the palate, briny, rich and very agile. Juicy, savory and deep finish.

90 Price A

A 2015

100% Centesimino grapes. Ferments and matures in Georgian amphorae. Dark ruby red color. Intense aromas of black pepper and blueberries. Savory, irony, agile and strong volume on the palate. Smooth tannins and very deep finish.

90 Price A

Serenaro 2015

100% Famoso di Cesena grapes. Ferments 4 months on the skins in amphorae and matures in stainless steel. Bright straw yellow color. Notes of white pepper and iodine. Juicy, savory, balanced on the palate. Briny and deep finish.

88 Price B

Romagna Sangiovese Longiano Riserva 2013

100% Sangiovese grapes aged in tonneau. Deep ruby red. Aromas of ripe blackberries, cherry jam and slightly smoky hint. Strong on the palate with a dense beginning but becomes fluid do to the tannins.

FRIULI VENEZIA GIULIA

Although it produces 'only' some one million hectoliters (for the most part DOC and DOCG), Friuli Venezia Giulia is considered one of Italy's most prestigious winemaking regions. This is above all true in regard to its white wines for which this region is avant-garde and produces outstanding versions in diverse areas. The most important of these are the hills along the order with Slovenia where there are two DOC appellations, Collio Goriziano, which is more to the south, and Colli Orientali del Friuli, in the province of Udine, and within these are the DOCG Colli Orientali Picolit, Ramandolo to the north and Rosazzo to the south. The border between them is the Judrio River which up until 1918 was also the border between the Kingdom of Italy and the Austro-Hungarian Empire. The two areas, however, are very similar in that they both have chalky-clay soils and the topography is hilly. At the center of the region is the great alluvial Grave plain that was created over thousands of years by the debris brought down by the Isonzo and Tagliamento Rivers. Today this DOC area is called Friuli Grave and it is the ideal continuation of the neighboring Veneto zones of Piave and Lison (which also extends into Friuli and recently obtained a DOCG classification). Between Grave and the hills is another plain but one that has more clay in the soil and has a greater vocation for red grapes. This is the DOC Friuli Isonzo appellation and is currently the most popular. To the east, between Gorizia and Trieste, is the tiny DOC Carso, while in the southern part of the region and close to the sea are the DOC areas of Aquileia, Annia and Latisana. What makes Friulano zones special is that while their division is quite simple, within each one there are a substantial number of different wines that are also made in the other appellations.

CONTROLLED AND GUARANTEED DESIGNATION OF ORIGIN (DOCG)

- Colli Orientali del Friuli Picolit, with or without Cialla
- Ramandolo
- Rosazzo
- Lison

CONTROLLED DESIGNATION OF ORIGIN (DOC)

- Carso or Carso-Kras
- Collio Goriziano or Collio
- Friuli-Annia
- Friuli Aquileia
- Friuli Colli Orientali, with or without Cialla, Ribolla Gialla di Rosazzo, Pignolo di Rosazzo, Refosco di Faedis, Schioppettino di Prepotto
- Friuli Grave
- Friuli Isonzo or Isonzo del Friuli
- Friuli Latisana
- Lison-Pramaggiore
- Prosecco, with or without provincia di Treviso or Treviso (for Veneto), and provincia di Trieste or Trieste

ANGORIS

Località Angoris, 7
34071 Cormòns (GO)
Tel. +39 0481 60923
info@angoris.it
www.angoris.it
 Tenuta-di-Angoris
 @TenutaDiAngoris

YEAR OF FOUNDATION 1648
NAME OF THE OWNER Locatelli Family
TOTAL BOTTLES PRODUCED 750,000
DIRECT SALES
VISITS TO THE WINERY - RESERVATION NEEDED
HECTARES OF VINEYARD 130

Since 2015 Marta Locatelli has taken over running the estate from her sister Claudia in order to boost this historic Friuli estate even further. The vineyards are still those in the area of Isonzo, in Cormòns, and the annex ones in Colli Orientali and Ipplis, one of the best areas for winegrowing in the whole region. This is an important estate was given by the Emperor of Austria to Locatello Locatelli in 1648.

☐ 90   Price B
Collio Bianco Giulio Locatelli Riserva 2013

Blend of 60% of Friulano, 30% of Sauvignon and 10% of Malvasia Istriana grapes. Stainless steel only on the lees for 10 months. Intense straw yellow color. On The nose complex with scents of yeasts at first, then aromas of white peach and, underneath, fresh almond. Savory, full-bodied, tense taste with long finish and slightly bitter.

☐ 88   👍 Price A
Friuli Isonzo Pinot Bianco Villa Locateli 2015

100% Pinot Bianco grapes. Stainless steel only. Light straw yellow. On the nose floral and fragrant with delicate aromas of hawthorn and white peach. Ttense taste, pleasant very easy to drink and discreetly persistent.

☐ 87   Price A
FCO Ribolla Gialla 2015

100% Ribolla Gialla grapes. Stainlees steel only. Light yellow green color. On the nose fragrant and citrusy, with aromas of cedar, Amalfi lemon and green plums. The taste is delicate but tense, fresh and savory.

AQUILA DEL TORRE

Via Attimis, 25 - Frazione Savorgnano del Torre
33040 Povoletto (UD)
Tel. +39 0432 666428
Fax +39 0432 647942
info@aquiladeltorre.it
www.aquiladeltorre.it
 aquiladeltorre
 @aquiladeltorre

YEAR OF FOUNDATION 1996
NAME OF THE OWNER Claudio Ciani
TOTAL BOTTLES PRODUCED 50,000
DIRECT SALES
VISITS TO THE WINERY - RESERVATION NEEDED
HECTARES OF VINEYARD 18
HOSPITALITY
CERTIFIED ORGANIC VITICULTURE

Set up in 1996, this winery will turn 20 next year which is considerable in an area like Colli Orientali, especially in the northern part of the appellation which only recently has been producing quality wines. The vineyards are lovely and well-kept, situated in a natural amphitheater which seems as if it was created for that purpose.

▪ 93   Price B*
FCO Picolit 2013

*100% Picolit grapes. Matures 1 year in barrique on the yeasts. Intense golden yellow color. On the nose aromas of honey, dry apricot, pineapple in syrup. Sweet but not sickly, agile, with great acidity that balances the sugar, warm and absolutely persistent in the finish. *37.5 cl bottle.*

☐ 91   Price B
Oasi 2014

100% Picolit grapes. Matures 1 year in barrique on the yeasts. Intense straw yellow color. On the nose at first aromas of flowers, hawthorn, then mango, honey, light vanilla, rich and complex. Fresh as well as complex, with a nice acidity, almost crispy. Very persistent in the finish.

◼ 86   Price A
FCO Refosco At 2013

100% Refosco dal Peduncolo Rosso grapes. Stainless steel only for 12 months. Purple ruby color. On the nose full flavored and fruity with aromas of black cherry, red plum, and hints of violet. Firm taste with present but dry tannins, warm with good persistence.

BASTIANICH

Via Darnazzacco, 44/2 – Frazione Gagliano
33043 Cividale del Friuli (UD)
Tel. +39 0432 700943
winery@bastianichwinery.com
www.bastianich.com
f Bastianich
🐦 @BastianichWines

YEAR OF FOUNDATION **1998**
NAME OF THE OWNER **Joseph and Lidia Maticchio Bastianich**
TOTAL BOTTLES PRODUCED **190,000**
DIRECT SALES
VISITS TO THE WINERY - RESERVATION NEEDED
HECTARES OF VINEYARD **34**
HOSPITALITY

Joe Bastianich is a star in the world of entertainment. He is the lead in the Masterchef program in Italy and the United States, a famous and talented restauranteur, most of all in New York, and yet he has not forgotten his roots in Istria and even those that are a bit Friulano. This is why he created a winery near Cividale del Friuli and for a few years now has been producing wines full of personality.

☐ **92** Price B
Vespa 2014

Blend of 45% Chardonnay, 45% Sauvignon and 10% Picolit grapes. The Picolit is vinified in oak barrels. Matures half in tonneau and half in stainless steel on the yeasts. Golden yellow color. On the nose fruity and has less impact than in other versions, hints of vanilla, then white peach, pineapple, wildflowers. The taste is warm, full, well sustained by the acidity. The result of a rainy and fresh season. Less full-bodied and more elegant than usual.

☐ **90** Price B
Plus 2013

100% Friuliano grapes grown in a 60 years old vineyard, 10% withered. Matures for 9 month in stainless steel on the yeasts. Golden yellow color. On the nose aromas of cedar, yellow peach, then strong floral scents but tense and slightly savory, warm, a little diluted and bitter on the finish.

■ **88** Price B
Calabrone 2012

Blend of 70% Refosco and 30% Schioppettino, Merlot and Pignolo grapes, partly withered. Matures 2 years in barrique. Very intense and dark garnet ruby color. On the nose aromas of griottines, cocoa, little berries, vanilla and cardamom. Full taste, tense, lightly tannic, warm and persistent, a little heavy, residual sugars make it sweeter in the finish.

BELADEA

Via Boccaccio, 26
20123 Milano
Tel. +39 335 299409
cantine@beladea.it
www.beladea.it

YEAR OF FOUNDATION **2015**
NAME OF THE OWNER **Toni Cuman**
TOTAL BOTTLES PRODUCED **24,000**

Toni Cuman is a celebrity in the world of Italian wine and food. He is a restauranteur, wine and restaurant critics, salesman and now a selector of Friuli wines that he chooses and has bottled under the Cantine Beladea label. His great expertise ensures these wines are of surprising quality.

☐ **90** 👍 Price A
Collio Bianco 2015

Blend of 50% Friulano, 20% Riesling Renano, 20% Sauvignon, 10% Malvasia Istriana grapes. Stainless steel only. Straw green yellow color. On the nose citrusy and fruity with aromas of cedar, white peach, light fresh almond. The taste is fresh, tense and agile, easy to drink with great acidity. Wwarm and persistent in the finish.

☐ **88** Price A
Ribolla Gialla 2015

100% Ribolla Gialla grapes. Greenish yellow color. Stainless steel only. On the nose aromas of cedar, Amalfi lemon, yellow plum. Savory, tense, very pleasant. A simple wine but delicious to drink, the finish is thin but persistent enough.

☐ **87** Price A
Pinot Grigio 2015

100% Pinot Grigio grapes. Stainless steel only. Intense straw yellow color. On the nose aromas of pear and white peach. On the palate very savory, tense with a good acidity and adequate alcohol content.

★★
BORGO DEL TIGLIO

Via San Giorgio, 71 - Frazione Brazzano
34070 Cormòns (GO)
Tel. +39 0481 62166
Fax +39 0481 630845
info@borgodeltiglio.it
www.borgodeltiglio.it
🐦 *@N_Manferrari*

YEAR OF FOUNDATION 1981
NAME OF THE OWNER Nicola Manferrari
TOTAL BOTTLES PRODUCED 35,000
DIRECT SALES
VISITS TO THE WINERY - RESERVATION NEEDED
HECTARES OF VINEYARD 8.5

Nicola Manferrari is a meticulous wine craftsman, a winemaker who can 'feel' the various moments of a season and interpret them with almost artistic intuitions. You either like his wines or you don't and the same can be said about him because he can stir great antipathy or great passion, the way everyone does who believes in what they do. For sure he produces some real wine pearls which at time reach extreme heights and his ability to make it without question.

☐ 93   Price C
Collio Studio di Bianco 2013

Blend of Friulano, Riseling Renano and Sauvignon Blanc grapes. Matures in barrels for more than 1 year. Intense straw yellow color. On the nose very complex and particular with aromas of peach, juniper, grapefruit, wildflowers and pine resin. On the palate full and agile, very persistent and nicely acidic. Is an outsider wine, almost sperimental, it is made harvesting the grapes all at the same time and then, with the overripe Sauvignon.

★
BORGO SAN DANIELE

Via San Daniele, 28
34071 Cormòns (GO)
Tel. +39 0481 60552

Fax +39 0481 630525
info@borgosandaniele.it
www.borgosandaniele.it
 BorgosanDaniele

YEAR OF FOUNDATION 1990
NAME OF THE OWNER Mauro Mauri
TOTAL BOTTLES PRODUCED 45,000
DIRECT SALES
VISITS TO THE WINERY - RESERVATION NEEDED
HECTARES OF VINEYARD 19
HOSPITALITY

The great passion of siblings Mauro and Alessandra Mauri is making this small estate famous and appreciated by wine lovers around the world. They do not make many bottles and they reach the market more than a year after harvest and are made with grapes from some of the best vineyards in the area of Isonzo, in the eastern part of the Cormòns township.

☐ 90   Price B
Arbis Blanc 2014

40% Sauvignon, 20% Pinot Bianco , 20% Chardonnay, 20% Friulano grapes. Matures for 1 year in oak barrels. Intense straw yellow color. On the nose fruity and lightly vegetal with aromas of white peach and medical herbs. On the palate agile and tense, with a good acidity, savory and pleasant to drink.

☐ 88   Price B
Friuli Isonzo Friulano 2014

100% Friulano grapes. Matures in stainless steel on the lees for 1 year. Straw yellow color. With less impact then other versions, on the nose aromas of white peach and cedar, on the palate savory and tense.

☐ 87   Price B
Friuli Isonzo Malvasia 2013

100% Malvasia Friuliana grapes. Matures in stainless steel on the lees for 1 year. Light golden yellow color. On the nose flowery, lightly aromatic. On the palate savory, agile and slightly bitter in the finish.

CA' BOLANI

Via Ca' Bolani, 2
33052 Cervignano del Friuli (UD)
Tel. +39 0431 32670
Fax + 39 0431 34901

141

info@cabolani.it
www.cabolani.it
f *TenutaCaBolani*
𝕏 *@zonin1821*

YEAR OF FOUNDATION 1970
NAME OF THE OWNER Zonin Family
TOTAL BOTTLES PRODUCED 2,700,000
DIRECT SALES
VISITS TO THE WINERY - RESERVATION NEEDED
HECTARES OF VINEYARD 550

This spectacular estate in the Zonin Group is run with the care and attention of an independent one. It is situated in southern Friuli, nor far from Aquileia and Monfalcone, and is composed of a single 550-hectares vineyard making it the biggest in the region. The estate's specialty are their Refosco and Sauvignon wines.

☐ 93   Price A

Friuli Aquileia Sauvignon Aquilis 2015

100% Sauvigon Blanc grapes. Matures for 8 moth in stainless steel on the lees. Bright green yellow color. On the nose aromas of exotic fruits then nettle and grapefruit. On the palate full, savory, tense and warm. Absolutely persistent.

★★

CASTELLO DI SPESSA

Via Spessa, 1
34071 Capriva del Friuli (GO)
Tel. +39 0481 60445
Fax +39 0481 808124
info@castellodispessa.it
www.castellodispessa.it
f *CastelloSpessa*
𝕏 *@castellospessa*

YEAR OF FOUNDATION 1987
NAME OF THE OWNER **Loretto Pali**
TOTAL BOTTLES PRODUCED 150,000
DIRECT SALES
VISITS TO THE WINERY - RESERVATION NEEDED
HECTARES OF VINEYARD 28
HOSPITALITY
RESTAURANT

Loreto and Barbara Pali are the lucky owners of this castle estate in Capriva del Friuli, more specifically in the area of Spessa from which

the 18th century castle takes its name. The wines produced here are Pinot Bianco, Friulano and Sauvignon and the vineyards look like gardens and the castle has rooms for guests and even a golf course.

☐ 🖼 95   Price B

Collio Sauvignon Segre 2015

100% Sauvignon Blanc grapes. Matures in barrique for 6 months. Green straw yellow color. On the nose different variety of aromas, mango, nettle, with a light spicy scent that make this wine rarely elegant. On the palate tense, warm but agile, savory, easy to drink and very persistent.

■ 91   Price B

Collio Pinot Nero 2014

100% Pinot Nero grapes. Matures 6 months in barrique. Clear light ruby color. On the nose aromas of currant, wild strawberry, light spicy notes with a very surprising range of aromas for a Pinot Nero fromCollio. On the palate agile, crisp, very pleasant, tense and elegant.

☐ 90   Price A

Collio Pinot Bianco 2015

100% Pinot Bianco grapes. Stainless steel only. Light straw yellow color. Very fresh on the nose with aromas of white peach and almond at first, then, hawthorn flowers. On the palate savory, warm, balanced, easy to drink with a full-flavored finish.

★

CASTELVECCHIO

Via Castelnuovo, 2
34078 Sagrado (GO)
Tel. +39 0481 99742
Fax +39 0481 960736
info@castelvecchio.com
www.castelvecchio.com
f *AziendaAgricolaCastelvecchio*

YEAR OF FOUNDATION 1978
NAME OF THE OWNER **Terraneo** Family
TOTAL BOTTLES PRODUCED 180,000
DIRECT SALES
VISITS TO THE WINERY - RESERVATION NEEDED
HECTARES OF VINEYARD 35
HOSPITALITY
OLIVE OIL PRODUCTION

The estate is at the entrance to the Carso (Karst) region, just past the bridge over the Isonzo River that connects Gradisca and Sagrado. There are 35 hectares of vineyards which have a chalky-clay soil and grow different and typical grapes for the area. The vineyards are quite dense, with at least 5,000 vines per hectare, and are in some places quite steep.

 91 — — — — **Price B**

Carso Malvasia Dileo 2015

100% Malvasia Istriana grapes. 6 month in stainless steel on the lees. Bright straw yellow color. On the nose typical floral and aromatic notes, fragrant and clean. On the palate warm, savory, full-flavored, tense with a pleasant bitter finish.

 90 — — — — **Price B**

Carso Cabernet Sauvignon 2012

100% Cabernet Sauvignon grapes. 1 year in barrique. Purple ruby color. On the nose complex ,aromas of black cherry, blueberry at first, then, spices, cassis and smoky tones. On the palate firm, the tannins are present but already integrated. The finish is warm and persistence.

★

COLLAVINI

Via della Ribolla Gialla, 2
33040 Corno di Rosazzo (UD)
Tel. +39 0432 753222
Fax +39 0432 759792
collavini@collavini.it
www.collavini.it
 collavini
 @CollaviniVini

YEAR OF FOUNDATION **1896**
NAME OF THE OWNER **Manlio Collavini**
TOTAL BOTTLES PRODUCED **1,500,000**
DIRECT SALES
VISITS TO THE WINERY - RESERVATION NEEDED
HECTARES OF VINEYARD **173.5**
RESTAURANT

This is one of the best-known wineries in the whole region. For decades now it has been run by Manlio Collavini, one of the leading personalities in Friuli winemaking and the area of Colli Orientali in particular. He is an entrepreneur and former MP who has a special passion

for sparkling wine and his Ribolla Gialla Brut is outstanding, unique, which undergoes secondary fermentation in steel vats for over two years.

 93 — — — — **Price B**

Ribolla Gialla Brut 2011

100% Ribolla Gialla grapes. 50% of the base wine matures for 6 months in barrique. The second fermentation is made in tank for 28 months. Light yellow color with a thick and continuous perlage. On the nose present complex scents, a blend of the varietal notes and the aromas from the fermentation creates aromas on cedar, read crust, hint of smoke and flowers. On the palate creamy, savory, tasty, sensual, of a compelling drinkability. A little gem of its kind.

☐ **92** — — — — **Price B**

Collio Bianco Broy 2015

80% Friuliano and Chardonnay grapes partly withered and 20% of Sauvignon. Matures in stainless steel on yeasts. Green straw yellow color. On the nose fragrant and full-flavored, aromas of citrus, cedar specifically, then exotic fruits. On the palate savory, warm and persistent.

☐ **91** — — — — **Price B**

Collio Sauvignon Blanc Fumat 2015

100% Sauvignon grapes. Stainless steel only. Bright green yellow color. On the nose varietal with aromas of passion fruit, elder flower, with scents of vegetables and tomato leafs. On the palate tense and savory, warm, full bodied but agile and pleasant to drink. The finish is warm and with a good persistence.

★

COLLE DUGA

Località Zegla, 10
34071 Cormòns (GO)
Tel. +39 0481 61177
Fax +39 0481 61177
info@colleduga.com
www.colleduga.com

YEAR OF FOUNDATION **1991**
NAME OF THE OWNER **Damian Princic**
TOTAL BOTTLES PRODUCED **55,000**
DIRECT SALES
VISITS TO THE WINERY - RESERVATION NEEDED
HECTARES OF VINEYARD **10**

The estate is a point of reference for the zone of Cormòns, in the heart of Colle Goriziano. At its helm is Damian Princic, a winemaker in his 40s who for years has been producing excellent wines, especially the whites. His Friulano, in particular, has been among the best in their cateory for some time.

☐ 92   Price A
Collio Friulano 2015

100% Friulano grapes. Stainless steel only. Straw yellow color. On the nose aromas of white peach and almond, very varietal and integrate. On the palate savory, tense, full-bodied with a slightly bitter finish and a good length.

☐ 89   Price A
Collio Pinot Grigio 2015

100% Pinot Grigio grapes. Stainless steel only. Intense straw yellow color. On the nose typical and clear aromas of pear Williams and white peach on the background. On the palate savory, warm, full-bodied , lightly diluted on the finish.

★
DI LENARDO VINEYARDS

Piazza Battisti, 1 - Ontagnano
33050 Gonars (UD)
Tel. +39 0432 928633
info@dilenardo.it
www.dilenardo.it
f *DI-LENARDO-vineyards*

YEAR OF FOUNDATION **1878**
NAME OF THE OWNER **Di Lenardo Family**
TOTAL BOTTLES PRODUCED **600,000**
DIRECT SALES
VISITS TO THE WINERY - RESERVATION NEEDED
HECTARES OF VINEYARD **47**

The Di Lenardo winery is in Gonars, in the heart of the Grave del Friuli appellation. And although they also produce a DOC wine, almost all the other wines are classified IGT Venezia Giulia. The decision to do this was made years ago by Massimo Di Lenardo with the precise aim of promoting the estate brand and the names of the wine as opposed to highlighting their official classification. This has also allowed the estate to produce wines with an excellent price/quality ratio.

☐ 90   Price A
Friuli Grave Friulano Toh! 2015

100% Friulano grapes. Stainless steel only. Intense straw yellow color. On the nose the scents of exotic fruit is strong as well as mature pineapple, then aromas of wildflowers, elder fruit and white peach. On the palate warm, savory, tense, full-bodied, persistent and slightly bitter on the finish. Delicious in is kind.

 88   Price A
Pinot Grigio Ramato Gossip 2015

100% Pinot Grigio grapes. Stainless steel only. Pale coppery color. On the nose strong the scent of wildflowers at first, then wild strawberry and plum. On the palate savory, full-bodied and easy to drink.

★
DRIUS

Via Filanda, 100
34071 Cormòns (GO)
Tel. +39 0481 60998
info@driusmauro.it
www.driusmauro.it
f *driuswine*

YEAR OF FOUNDATION **1950**
NAME OF THE OWNER **Mauro Drius**
TOTAL BOTTLES PRODUCED **50,000**
DIRECT SALES
VISITS TO THE WINERY - RESERVATION NEEDED
HECTARES OF VINEYARD **15**

Mario Drius's estate is just ten meters or so inside the zone of Isonzo. On the other side of the railroad tracks, in fact, is the appellation of Collio but all this means little to him. What is important is that it is in Cormòns and his vineyards are splendid and allow him to make wines with great personality. First among these is his Malvasia which has become a real cult wine.

☐ 92   Price A
Friuli Isonzo Malvasia 2015

100% Malvasia Istriana grapes. Stainless steel only. Straw yellow color. On the nose are predominant the scents of flower with aromas of jasmine, room flower at first, then yellow peach and almond. On the palate warm, full-flavored, savory, very Mediterranean, with a typical slightly bitter finish. This is 'the' Malvasia.

☐ 90   👍 Price A
Friuli Isonzo Bianco Vignis di Siris 2013

Blend of Friulano, Pinot Bianco and Sauvignon grapes. The Friulano grapes mature in stainless steel, the rest mature in barrique for almost 1 year. Straw yellow color. On the nose full-flavored with aromas of white peach, almonds and light vanilla. On the palate full-bodied, savory, rich, with a good sour tension and the finish is warm and persistent.

☐ 88   Price A
Collio Friulano 2015

100% Friulano grapes. Stainless steel only. Straw yellow color. On the nose aromas of white peach and fresh almond at first, then a hint of wildflower. On the palate savory, tense and warm when tasted with a slightly bitter note on the finish.

LIVIO FELLUGA

Via Risorgimento, 1 - Brazzano
34071 Cormòns (GO)
Tel. +39 0481 60203
fax +39 0481 630126
info@liviofelluga.it
www.liviofelluga.it
f *vignemuseum*
🐦 *@LivioFellugaCo*

YEAR OF FOUNDATION 1956
NAME OF THE OWNER Livio Felluga
TOTAL BOTTLES PRODUCED 800,000
DIRECT SALES
VISITS TO THE WINERY - RESERVATION NEEDED
HECTARES OF VINEYARD 170

Livio Felluga is over a century old, an age few people reach. And even Terre Alte, his winery's most prestigious wine than was created in 1980, is reaching a healthy age, the winery marked its 60th anniversary. And so there is a lot to celebrate, including the fact that his wines with the 'geographic map' labels are among the most famous and appreciated Italian whites.

☐ 93   Price C
FCO Rosazzo Bianco Terre Alte 2014

Blend of Friulano, Pinot Bianco and Sauvignon grapes in similar percentage. Matures in oak barrels for 1 year. On the nose intense and slightly smoky with aromas of vanilla and almond at first, *then more vegetal and smoky hints. On the palate tense, savory, polite with a good persistence.*

☐ 92   Price B
FCO Bianco Illivio 2014

Blend of Pinot Bianco, Chardonnay and a little hint of Picolit grapes. Matures in oak barrels for 1 year. Straw yellow color. On the nose aromas of vanilla at first, then almond and slightly citrusy. On the palate savory, warm, full-bodied but not heavy. It is very pleasant, agile, not as full-bodied as other versions but this is not always a negative aspect.

■ 91   Price B
FCO Rosazzo Rosso Sossò Riserva 2012

Blend of Refosco, Merlot and Pignolo grapes. Matures in oak barrels of different capacity for 18 months. Intense and dark ruby color. On the nose clear aromas of cinchona, rhubarb, small berries, and a little hint of mint and eucalyptus. On the palate full tannic, tense and savory. Full-bodied.

☐ 90   Price B
FCO Friulano 2015

100% Friulano grapes. Stainless steel only. Straw yellow color. On the nose very typical with aromas of white peach, alfalfa and almond. On the palate tense, savory, warm and full-bodied. Good length on the finish.

☐ 88   Price A
FCO Pinot Grigio 2015

100% Pinot Grigio grapes. Stainless steel only. Intense straw yellow color with antic gold reflexes. On the nose varietal, fruity with typical aromas of pear Williams and white peach. On the palate savory, warm, very pleasant, slightly diluted on the finish.

MARCO FELLUGA

Via Gorizia, 121
34072 Gradisca d'Isonzo (GO)
Tel. +39 0481 99164
info@marcofelluga.it
www.marcofelluga.it
f *marcofelluga.russizsuperiore*
🐦 *@MarcoFelluga*

YEAR OF FOUNDATION 1956
NAME OF THE OWNER Roberto Felluga
TOTAL BOTTLES PRODUCED 600,000
DIRECT SALES

VISITS TO THE WINERY - RESERVATION NEEDED
HECTARES OF VINEYARD **100**
HOSPITALITY
RESTAURANT

TOTAL BOTTLES PRODUCED **100,000**
DIRECT SALES
VISITS TO THE WINERY - RESERVATION NEEDED
HECTARES OF VINEYARD **25**

The winery of Marco Felluga is also almost 60 years old and it also has a reputation for producing quality wine. His historic was set up long before he started making Russiz Superiore that brought him international recognition. The wines are reliable, well-made, reasonably prices and in some cases are of top quality.

In Colli Orientali it goes without question: the best Friulano is Vigneto Storico from Adriano Gigante, a winery on the road from Corno di Rosazzo towards the Ipplis Hills. But Gigante sometimes pulls out some other gems from the cellar, temonstrating that its vineyard are located in extremely vocated area.

☐ 92   Price B
Collio Bianco Pinot Grigio Mongris Riserva 2013

100% Pinot Grigio grapes. 30% of them matures in oak barrels for some months and the rest in stainless steel. Straw yellow color. On the nose full-flavored and complex with aromas of pear Williams, cedar, slightly smoky due to the yeasts, floral. On the palate savory, tense, elegant and very persistent. Great version.

☐ 89   Price A
Collio Friulano 2015

100% Friulano grapes. Stainless steel only. Light straw yellow color. On the nose fragrant and emblematic with aromas of white peach and a little hint of almond milk and wildflowers. On the palate savory and a little bitter on the finish.

☐ 87   Price A
Collio Ribolla Gialla 2015

100% Ribolla Gialla grapes. Stainless steel only. Light straw yellow color. On the nose fragrant with aromas of wildflowers, cedar, and alfalfa. On the palate tense, fresh and easy to drink.

☐ 94   Price B
FCO Friulano Vigneto Storico 2015

100% Friulano grapes. Stainless steel on the lees for few months. Bright straw yellow color. On the nose extremely typical with aromas of white peach at first, then medlar and slightly smoky due to the yeasts. On the palate savory, firm, full bodied but also agile and very long on the finish. Great version.

☐ 90   👍 Price A
FCO Friulano 2014

100% Friulano grapes. Stainless steel only. Light straw yellow color. On the nose typically fruity with aromas of white peach and fresh almond, floral scents on the background. On the palate savory, juicy, warm with a slightly bitter finish.

☐ 88   Price A
FCO Ribolla Gialla 2015

100% Ribolla Gialla grapes. Stainless steel only. Light yellow color. On the nose aromas of cedar and alfalfa with fragrant and partly fermentative notes. On the palate full, agile ad fresh, very pleasant and easy to drink.

GIGANTE

Via Rocca Bernarda, 3
33040 Corno di Rosazzo (UD)
Tel. +39 0432 755835
info@adrianogigante.it
www.adrianogigante.it
 Adriano-Gigante
 @GiganteVini

YEAR OF FOUNDATION **1957**
NAME OF THE OWNER **Adriano and Giuliana Gigante**

GRADIS'CIUTTA

Località Giasbana, 32a
34070 San Floriano del Collio (GO)
Tel. +39 0481 390237
info@gradisciutta.com
www.gradisciutta.eu
 gradisciutta

YEAR OF FOUNDATION **1997**
NAME OF THE OWNER **Robert Princic**
TOTAL BOTTLES PRODUCED **100,000**
DIRECT SALES
VISITS TO THE WINERY - RESERVATION NEEDED
HECTARES OF VINEYARD **20**

All wine lovers know that San Floriano is one of the best winegrowing areas of all Collio Goriziano. It is here where some of the more famous and charismatic producers have their vineyards. And there are also some relatively new estates like this one, owned by Robert Princic, which is not yet 20 years old but is already making a name for itself thanks to its consistency and reliability.

☐ 90 👍 Price A

Collio Bianco Bratinis 2014

Blend of 45% Chardonnay, 45% Sauvignon with 10% of Ribolla Gialla grapes. Matures in stainless steel on the yeasts. Intense straw yellow color. On the nose intense with aromas of chamomile, alfalfa and white peach. On the palate tense, juicy, not heavy, deliciously savory and easy to drink.

☐ 89 Price A

Collio Friulano 2015

100% Friulano grapes. Stainless steel only. Straw yellow color. On the nose typical with classic aromas of white peach at first, then alfalfa. On the palate savory, hole, full-bodied and with good length.

☐ 88 Price A

Collio Ribolla Gialla 2015

100% Ribolla Gialla grapes. Stainless steel only. Green light yellow color. On the nose aromas of cedar, wildflowers at first, then yellow plum. On the palate agile, full-bodied, savory and tense, easy to drink with a thin finish and a good length.

GRAVNER

Via Lenzuolo Bianco, 9 - Frazione Oslavia
34070 Gorizia (GO)
Tel. +39 0481 30882
Fax +39 0481 548871
info@gravner.it
www.gravner.it
 Josko-Gravner
 @JoskoGravner

YEAR OF FOUNDATION 1901
NAME OF THE OWNER Josko Gravner
TOTAL BOTTLES PRODUCED 38,000
DIRECT SALES
VISITS TO THE WINERY - RESERVATION NEEDED
HECTARES OF VINEYARD 18

Josko Gravner is one of the great winemakers not only in Friuli Venezia Giulia but all of Italy. And he is, above all, an artist is the truest sense as evidenced by his direct and tactile, intimate, visceral and intellectual approach and relationship he has with his land. His wines are imperfect works of art of rare beauty, difficult to understand and interpret. The same can be said of Josko's intense and sharp gaze which makes him seem burly whereas he is actually a little shy and modest as only great people can be.

☐ 🗐 97 Price C

Ribolla Gialla 2008

100% Ribolla Gialla grapes. It does 7 months of long maceration in burried amphorae, then matures for 7 years in big Slavonia durmast barrels. Intese antic gold color. On the nose fantasticly complex with aromas ranging from beeswax to smoke, passing by aromas of spices and dry flowers, little hint of green tea and botrytis. On the palate solid, ery savory, full-bodied but polite, very elegant to be a nonconformity wine, and very persistent. An absolute champion.

☐ 94 Price C

Bianco Breg 2008

Blend of Chardonnay, Sauvignon, Riesling Italico and Pinot Grigio grapes. 7 months of maceration in buried amphorae, then matures 7 year in big Slavonian durmast barrels. Light amber color. On the nose aromas of dry fruits at first, then an hint of smoke, beeswax and Earl Grey tea. On the palate savory, even slightly tannic and full-bodied. Josko Gravner insists calling it 'a white wine' but it looks more like a rosè.

I CLIVI

Località Gramogliano, 20
33040 Corno di Rosazzo (UD)
Tel. +39 328 7269979
iclivi@gmail.com
www.iclivi.it

YEAR OF FOUNDATION 1995
NAME OF THE OWNER Ferdinando and Mario Zanusso
TOTAL BOTTLES PRODUCED 35,000
DIRECT SALES
VISITS TO THE WINERY - RESERVATION NEEDED
HECTARES OF VINEYARD 12
CERTIFIED ORGANIC VITICULTURE

This small, family-run estate practices wine-growing that has a low impact on the environment while the wines have great character and personality and can age for decades. The wines are made using traditional local varieties in the heart of Colli Orientali, not far from the Rosazzo Abbey, from vineyards with a yield that never surpasses 3,000kg per hectare, much like a Burgundy Grand Cru.

☐ 92   Price B
Collio Brazan 2014

Mostly Friulano grapes but with an hint of Malvasia Istrina grapes. Stainless steel only on yeasts for almost 2 years. Straw yellow color. On the nose aromas of wildflowers and little smoky thanks to the yeasts at first, then white peach and fresh almond. On the palate savory, powerful, warm, full-flavored and very persistent.

☐ 90   Price B
Collio Malvasia 80 anni 2015

100% Malvasia Istriana grapes. Stainless steel on the lees only. Intense straw yellow color. On the nose clearly floral with aromas of jasmine, made precious by the smoke aroma thanks to the yeasts. On the palate warm, savory, alcoholic and persistent.

JERMANN

Via Monte Fortino, 21
34070 Farra d'Isonzo (GO)
Tel. + 39 0481 888080
Fax + 39 0481 888512
info@jermann.it
www.jermann.it
 jermann.it

YEAR OF FOUNDATION **1881**
NAME OF THE OWNER **Silvio Jermann**
TOTAL BOTTLES PRODUCED **900,000**
DIRECT SALES
VISITS TO THE WINERY - RESERVATION NEEDED
HECTARES OF VINEYARD **150**

The first Vintage Tunina was a 1975, when Silvio Jermann has just turned 21 and had no idea that this wine would become an icon in the world for Italian winemaking. Tunina has already turned 40 and is a splendid and youthful lady of wine. To keep her company, Silvio

has created a slew of other wines which today make up a formidable line of production for both quality and their ability to age.

☐ 95   Price B
Vintage Tunina 2014

Blend of 40% Sauvignon Blanc and 40% Chardonnay, the rest Malvasia Istriana, Ribolla Gialla and Picolit grapes. A part of the Chardonnay grapes mature in big oak barrels for 3 months and the rest matures in stainless steel on the lees. Light straw yellow color. On the nose present complex aromas of pineapple, rennet apple and cedar. On the palate savory and tense, agile and fresh. Great persistence.

☐ 93   Price B
Capo Martino 2014

Blend of Friulano, Malvasia Istriana, Ribolla Gialla and Picolit grapes. Matures for 1 year in big oak barrels. Light golden yellow color. On the nose aromas of almond, white peach, wildflower and slightly aromatic and fruity. On the palate full but agile, savory, full-bodied. The finish is long and lightly alcoholic.

☐ 90   👍 Price A
Vinnae Ribolla Gialla 2015

Blend of Ribolla Gialla with some Riesling Renano and Friulano grapes. Stainless steel only. Green straw yellow color. On the nose aromas of cedar, grapefruit, rennet apple, wildflower. On the palate agile, fresh an tense, very drinkable and with a thin but long finish.

★★
KANTE

Località Prepotto, 1a
34011 Duino Aurisina (TS)
Tel. +39 040 200255
kante@kante.it
www.kante.it
 KanteAziendaAgricola

YEAR OF FOUNDATION **1980**
NAME OF THE OWNER **Edi Kante**
TOTAL BOTTLES PRODUCED **60,000**
DIRECT SALES
VISITS TO THE WINERY - RESERVATION NEEDED
HECTARES OF VINEYARD **13**

The winery was set up 25 years ago and Edi has been a pioneer in winemaking in Carso using indigenous and international grapes. His wines are distinguished by their elegance, refinedness and great drinkability. The winery is a wonder, craved out of stone, where the temperature and level of humidity are constantly maintained without any consumption of energy and only by the air that filters through the rock walls. All production follows the same rule: one year in barrique, one year in stainless steel vats and then again in the bottle. And the white wines do not macerate on the skins. The wines become Reserves when they are already in the bottle (some 5,000 bottles a year).

☐ **94**   Price C
Vitovska Selezione 2007

100% Vitovska grapes. Matures 1 year in used barrique and stainless steel. Light gold yellow color. On the nose aromas of dry and fresh flowers, spicy aromas of cardamom and ginger, as well we could say. On the palate strong, very savory, full-bodied, very Nordic Mediterranean, unique, deep.

☐ **93**   Price B
Chardonnay La Bora di Kante 2008

100% Chardonnay grapes. Matures in used barrique for 1 year then in stainless steel. Light golden yellow color. On the nose complex as usual with smoky scents and aromas of mature fruits and spices. On the palate savory, tense, almost sharp, great acidity that helps a full-bodied but yet agile structure.

☐ **92**   Price B
Malvasia 2013

100% Malvasia Istriana grapes. Matures for 1 year in used barrique, then 6 motnhs in stainless steel. Light straw yellow color. On the nose fruity with aromas of white peach at first, then jasmine and alfalfa. On the palate savory, very typical, full-bodied and agile with a slightly bitter finish.

★★
EDI KEBER

Località Zegla, 17
34071 Cormòns (GO)
Tel. +39 0481 61184
Fax +39 0481 61184
edi.keber@virgilio.it
www.edikeber.it
 EdiKeber

YEAR OF FOUNDATION **Fine 1700**
NAME OF THE OWNER **Edi Keber**
TOTAL BOTTLES PRODUCED **50,000**
DIRECT SALES
VISITS TO THE WINERY - RESERVATION NEEDED
HECTARES OF VINEYARD **12**
HOSPITALITY

Zega, a sub-zone east of Cormòns, is one of the most suited for winegrowing in all Collio and this is where Edi Keber has his vineyards. He is a very rigorous winemaker who some years ago decided to produce just one wine, Collio Bianco, which as tradition dictates in this area is not made with just one grape variety but is a blend. Friulano dominates a blend that also includes Ribolla Gialla and Malvasia Istriana which are by no means secondary players and in difficult years make an important contribution.

☐ **93**   Price B
Collio Bianco 2015

70% Friulano and 30% of Malvasia Istriana, Ribolla Gialla grapes. It matures for 8 month in concrete vats on the yeasts. The most classic and traditional blend in Collio. Straw yellow color. On the nose intense aromas of peach, wildflowers. On the palate savory, tense, warm, full-bodied and very persistent. A wine that well represents the typicality of the wines in the area.

THOMAS KITZMÜLLER

Via XXIV Maggio, 56 - Frazione Brazzano
34071 Cormòns (GO)
Tel. +39 0481 639636
Fax +39 0481 639636
info@vinikitzmueller.com
www.vinikitzmueller.com

YEAR OF FOUNDATION **1987**
NAME OF THE OWNER **Thomas Kitzmüller**
TOTAL BOTTLES PRODUCED **30,000**
DIRECT SALES
VISITS TO THE WINERY - RESERVATION NEEDED
HECTARES OF VINEYARD **6**
HOSPITALITY

Thomas Kitzmüller, known as Tommy, is a small producer in Brazzano who has vineyards in Collio and some vines in Isonzo. He has been making his own wine since 1987, after he restored an old 18th century farm house and turned it into a winery as well as holiday farm. His specialty is Friulano but all his wines are well-made and economical.

☐ 90   👍 Price A

Collio Friulano 2015

100% Friulano grapes. Stainless steel only. Light straw yellow color. On the nose if pleasant and fragrant with aromas of wildflowers and white peach, on the palate savory with a good body and a nice length.

150

LA BOATINA

Via Corona, 62
34071 Cormòns (GO)
Tel. +39 0481 60445
info@paliwines.com
www.paliwines.com
👍 *La-Boatina*

YEAR OF FOUNDATION 1979
NAME OF THE OWNER Loretto Pali
TOTAL BOTTLES PRODUCED 350,000
DIRECT SALES
VISITS TO THE WINERY - RESERVATION NEEDED
HECTARES OF VINEYARD 80

This is an annex in the area of Isonzo for Castello di Spessa and while they may be only kilometers apart, they are sufficient to change both appellation and landscape. Being on a plain the topography is flat and the wines are more simple and immediate and their quality/price ration is exemplary as is their ability to age.

☐ 87   👍 Price A

Friuli Isonzo Pinot Grigio 2015

100% Pinot Grigio grapes. Stainless steel only. Straw yellow color. On the nose fruity, compact with aromas of summer pear and white peach. On the palate delicate, savory, very pleasant with a discreet body and easy to drink.

☐ 86   👍 Price A

Friuli Isonzo Chardonnay 2015

100% Chardonnay grapes. Stainless steel only. Light gold yellow color. On the nose aromas of white plum, yeasts and wildflowers. Very pleasant and easy to drink. On the palate savory, agile with a good body.

LA DELIZIA

Via Udine, 24
33072 Casarsa Della Delizia (PN)
Tel. +39 0434 869564
Fax +39 0434 868823
info@ladelizia.com
www.ladelizia.com
👍 *Vini-La-Delizia*
🐦 *@ViniLaDelizia*

YEAR OF FOUNDATION 1931
NAME OF THE OWNER
TOTAL BOTTLES PRODUCED 16,000,000
DIRECT SALES
VISITS TO THE WINERY
HECTARES OF VINEYARD 2,000

Almost half of the wine made in Italy is made by cooperatives. And when one comes across a cooperative like La Delizia, which is able to produce a lot of well-made wines at affordable prices, they can only take off their hat. On the verge of bankruptcy only a few years ago, thanks to brilliant administration and capable members the cooperative is now one of the biggest success stories in Friuli winemaking.

◙ 88   👍 Price A

Ribolla Gialla Brut Naonis

100% Ribolla Gialla grapes. Charmat method. Light yellow color with a quick perlage. On the nose fragrant, fermentative with aromas of cedar and yeasts. On the palate lively, acidic, pleasant and easy to drink.

☐ 86   👍 Price A

Friuli Grave Pinot Grigio Vigneti 2015

100% Pinot Grigio grapes. Stainless steel only. Light yellow color. On the nose fruity, lear and fragrant with aromas of fruits and rennet apple, and wild mint. On the palate fresh, acidic, with a decent body and easy to drink. Nice length.

◙ 85   👍 Price A

Prosecco Extra Brut Naonis

100% Glera grapes. Charmant method. Pale yellow color. The perlage is thick and quick. On the nose present classic aromas of yeasts and wisteria flowers. On the palate fresh, lively, light and very easy to drink.

★★
LA TUNELLA

Via del Collio, 14 - Ipplis
33040 Premariacco (UD)
Tel. +39 0432 716030
info@latunella.it
www.latunella.it
 az.agr.latunella

YEAR OF FOUNDATION **1986**
NAME OF THE OWNER **Zorzettig Family**
TOTAL BOTTLES PRODUCED **390,000**
DIRECT SALES
VISITS TO THE WINERY - RESERVATION NEEDED
HECTARES OF VINEYARD **70**

The La Tunella vineyards are located in some of the best areas of the Ipplis district, in the heart of Colli Orientali. The winery, that has entered its third decade of existence, is modern and very functional and produces wines that are at times surprising for both their quality and their correct quality/price ratio.

☐ **93** 👍 **Price A**
FCO Bianco Biancosesto 2014

50% Ribolla Gialla and 50% Friulano grapes. Stainless steel only. Straw yellow color. On the nose more citrusy then other past version with aromas of cedar and lemon grass as well as classic fruity aromas of white peach specifically. On the palate savory, tense, with an evident acidity and not as full-bodied as usual. It is persistent on the finish.

☐ **90** **Price B**
FCO Bianco Lalinda 2014

70% Malvasia Istriana and 30% Ribolla Gialla grapes. Matures for almost 1 year in tonneau. Intense straw yellow color. On the nose present very evident aromas of vanilla and almond milk at first then wildflowers and white peach. On the palate tense, with a good acidity, agile full-bodied and with a long finish.

☐ **89** **Price A**
FCO Friulano Col Livius 2014

100% Friulano grapes. Matures for 10 months in oak barrels on the lees. Straw yellow color with green hues. On the nose very similar to a Sauvignon (infact for the international ampelography the Friulano is called Sauvignon Vert). On the nose aromas of anise at first, then white peach a cedar. On the palate agile, full, just slightly bitter on the finish.

LA VIARTE

Via Novacuzzo, 51
33040 Prepotto (UD)
Tel. +39 0432 759458
laviarte@laviarte.it
www.laviarte.it
 laviarte

YEAR OF FOUNDATION **1973**
NAME OF THE OWNER **Alberto Piovan**
TOTAL BOTTLES PRODUCED **100,000**
DIRECT SALES
VISITS TO THE WINERY - RESERVATION NEEDED
HECTARES OF VINEYARD **26**

Alberto Piovan acquired this splendid estate several years ago from its founder Giulio Ceschin. It has always produced elegant and technically irreproachable wines with a particular predilection for Sauvignon, which here is distinguished by grace and elegance.

☐ **95** **Price B**
FCO Sauvignon Liende 2015

100% Sauvignon grapes. Stainless steel only. Green straw yellow color. On the nose varietal with aromas of tomato leafs and exotic fruits that ar typical, then hint of smoke that prepare for the hydrocarbon. On the palate agile, tense but full-bodied and alcoholic. Very pleasant on the finish.

☐ **92** **Price B**
FCO Friulano Liende 2015

100% Friulano grapes. Stainless steel only. Light gold yellow color. On the nose very varietal with typical and clean aromas of peach and almond, full-flavored and intense. On the palate full, warm, savory, full-flavored and long.

★★
LE DUE TERRE

Via Roma, 68b
33040 Prepotto (UD)
Tel. +39 0432 713189
Fax +39 0432 713189
fortesilvana@libero.it
 le.dueterre
🐦 *@Le_Due_Terre*

YEAR OF FOUNDATION **1984**
NAME OF THE OWNER **Flavio and Silvana Basilicata**

TOTAL BOTTLES PRODUCED **20,000**
DIRECT SALES
VISITS TO THE WINERY - RESERVATION NEEDED
HECTARES OF VINEYARD **5**

The world of wine is filled with good stories and people with great humanity. For sure Silvana and Flavio Basilicata, who created Le Due Terre, are fine examples of this. Their estate and their way of life are intertwined and they have been able over the years to apply all their personal and productive convictions. Their wines are as environmentally friendly as can be imagined and they have always been able to practice a winegrowing method that respects the environment and a 'soft' winemaking approach that uses only indigenous yeasts.

☐ **92**   Price B
FCO Bianco Sacrisassi 2014

Blend of 70% Friulano and 30% Ribolla gialla grapes. Matures for 20 months in tonneau. On the nose floral, spicy lightly smoky due to the yeasts, with aromas of alfalfa and wildflowers. On the palate savory, well conducted by the acid component, less full-bodied that other version but definitely agile and pleasant.

■ **91**   Price B
FCO Rosso Sacrisassi 2014

Blend of 50% Refosco and 50% Schioppettino grapes. Matures in barrique for almost 2 years. Dark garnet ruby color. On the nose presents typical spicy note at first with aromas of dark cherry, cassis, cardamom, rhubarb and cinchona. On the palate firm, tense, less full-bodied then other versions but elegant and agile.

■ **90**   Price B
FCO Merlot 2014

100% Merlot grapes. Matures in barrique barrels for almost 20 months. Intense garnet ruby color. On the nose aromas of wild strawberry and raspberry at first, then hint cocoa, cassis and sweet spices. On the palate full with a nice body, tense and a savory.

★★

LE VIGNE DI ZAMÒ

Via Abate Corrado, 4 - Località Rosazzo
33044 Manzano (UD)
Tel. +39 0432 759693
Fax +39 0432 759884

info@levignedizamo.com
www.levignedizamo.com

YEAR OF FOUNDATION **1978**
NAME OF THE OWNER **Zamò** Family and Oscar Farinetti
TOTAL BOTTLES PRODUCED **280,000**
DIRECT SALES
VISITS TO THE WINERY - RESERVATION NEEDED
HECTARES OF VINEYARD **67**

This estate used to be called Vigna dal Leon and was founded by the unforgettable entrepreneur Tullio Zamò. Today his sons Pierluigi and Silvano are in charge and have taken in as a partner Oscar Farinetti, the now-famous Mr. Eataly. The wines are always interesting and reach the market after they have aged sufficiently in the bottle. But most of all they are reliable with a precise estate style which never disappoints.

☐ 🔲 **95**   Price B
FCO Friulano Vigne Cinquant'Anni 2015

100% Friulano grapes. Matures almost 1 year in stainless steel on the lees. Intense straw yellow color. On the nose aromas of almonds and white peach but also honey, smoke and flint that complete a very complex and convincing olfactory phase. On the palate full, whole, young, very savory, warm and very long on the finish.

☐ **90**   Price B
FCO Friulano No Name 2015

00% Friulano grapes. Stainless steel only. Straw yellow color. On the nose straight forward and fruity with aromas of peach, yellow plum, wildflowers and fragrant on the palate tense with a great acidity, very drinkable, savory with a thin finish just a little bitter. The 'No Name' is because from 2008 is not possible in Italy to use appellation 'Tokai' because of the contentious with Hungary.

☐ **88**   Price A
FCO Rosazzo Ribolla Gialla 2015

100% Ribolla Gialla grapes. Stainless steel only. Light straw yellow color. On the nose aromas of cedar, green plum, alfalfa, very straight forward and fragrant. On the palate tense savory, agile, typical with thin and yet long finish.

★★
LIS NERIS

Via Gavinana, 5
34070 San Lorenzo Isontino (GO)
Tel. +39 0481 80105
lisneris@lisneris.it
www.lisneris.it
Lis-Neris
@LisNeris

YEAR OF FOUNDATION 1879
NAME OF THE OWNER Alvaro Pecorari
TOTAL BOTTLES PRODUCED 400,000
DIRECT SALES
VISITS TO THE WINERY - RESERVATION NEEDED
HECTARES OF VINEYARD 70
HOSPITALITY

When a winery is reliable and professional it can produce small gems even in poor years. This estate is a classic example of this and not even the difficult 2014 harvest posed excessive problems for the crystalline wines of Alvaro Pecorari, an authentic 'vineyard master'. The excellent white wines have great class and the Pinot Grigio Gris is perhaps the best.

☐ 🄖 95   Price B
Friuli Isonzo Pinot Grigio Gris 2014

100% Pinot Grigio grapes. Matures in tonneau for almost 1 year. Intense straw yellow color. On the nose typical aromas of pear Williams and white peach as well as citrus, specifically cedar. On the palate very agile, well sustained by the acid and savory component that balance the body that is strong and full-flavored anyway. A champion for this year.

▪ 94   Price C*
Tal Luc

*Blend of 95% Verduzzo Friulano grapes with an hint of Riesling Renano. Matures in barrique for 6 months. Intense amber color. Being a blend of 2 different harvests this wine does not have the year on the label. On the nose aromas of Acaciàs honey, with botrytis and lightly volatile scents with aromas of saffron and dry grapes. On the palate very sweet but acidic, with a very tasty tense balance. Very long persistence. *50 cl bottle.*

☐ 91   Price B
Friuli Isonzo Friulano La Vila 2014

100% Friulano grapes. Matures in tonneau for al-

most 1 year. Light golden yellow color. On the nose aromas of almond and white peach that are less impactful then other version but lot more fruity and fragrant. On the palate full, savory, pleasant more agile than usual and easier to drink.

★★
LIVON

Via Montarezza, 33
33048 San Giovanni al Natisone (UD)
Tel. +39 0432 757173
Fax +39 0432 757609
info@livon.it
www.livon.it
Livon
@wineclublivon

YEAR OF FOUNDATION 1964
NAME OF THE OWNER Tonino and Valneo Livon
TOTAL BOTTLES PRODUCED 950,000
DIRECT SALES
VISITS TO THE WINERY - RESERVATION NEEDED
HECTARES OF VINEYARD 180
HOSPITALITY

Making wine for 60 years is not a bad record in Italy. And Tonino and Valneo Livon, who are the second generation to run the winery, have been able to get their wines known around the world to the extent that they are almost more popular in the United States and Germany than in Italy, where they are famous. The line of production is quite vast and so it is difficult to decide each year which is the best or most convenient. Some key wines, like Braide Alte, are always a good bet.

☐ 91   Price B
Braide Alte 2014

Blend of 80% of Chardonnay and Sauvignon with 15% of Picolit and 5% of Moscato Giallo grapes. Matures for 8 months in big oak barrels. Light golden yellow color. On the nose less impactful then other versions, polite, rusty with aromas of citrus, on the palate full, savory, agile and of good persistence.

■ 90   Price B
Tiareblu 2013

Blend of Cabernet Sauvignon and Merlot grapes. Matures in barrique for 1 year. Dark and intense ruby color. On the nose intense note of eucalyptus at first, then aromas of cassis, Back currant and tobacco. On the palate full, a little tannic, savory, rich and long.

☐ 88   Price A

Collio Malvasia Soluna 2015

100% Malvasia Istriana grapes. A little part of them matures in barrique for 6 months the rest matures in stainless steel. Straw yellow color. On the nose floral, with aroma of jasmine and linden at first, then yellow peach, on the palate savory, full-bodied, very pleasant to drink with a deliciously bitter finish.

★

LUISA

Via Campo Sportivo, 13
34070 Mariano del Friuli (GO)
Tel. +39 0481 69680
info@tenutaluisa.com
www.tenutaluisa.com
 TENUTA-LUISA
 @Tenutaluisa

YEAR OF FOUNDATION 1927
NAME OF THE OWNER Eddi Luisa
TOTAL BOTTLES PRODUCED 300,000
DIRECT SALES
VISITS TO THE WINERY - RESERVATION NEEDED
HECTARES OF VINEYARD 80
HOSPITALITY

The winery and vineyards are in Isonzo but Collio is very close by. Eddi Luisa and her son Michele run this magnificent estate with managerial flair as well as great passion. They have 80 hectares of vineyards, which is not bad in Friuli, which are for the most part in a single block which extends for as far as the eye can see around their modern and functional winery and headquarters.

☐ 90   Price B

Desiderium I Ferretti 2013

Blend of 50% Chardonnay, 30% Friulano and 20% Sauvignon grapes vinified separately. The Chardonnay matures for 10 month in barrique, another two in stainless steel on the lees, then then get assembled and mature for few month in stainless steel vats. Straw yellow color. On the nose delicate and complex with smoky aromas thanks to the yeasts, then aromas of spices and fruits with pineapple and

white peach. On the palate rich, savory, warm and agile, great persistence.

☐ 88   Price B

Friuli Isonzo Cabernet Sauvignon I Feretti 2011

100% Cabernet Sauvignon grapes. Matures for 18 months in barrique. Dark ruby color. On the nose aromas of blueberries, black current, tobacco and vanilla. On the palate firm, full, lightly tannic, with a very persistent finish.

MAGNÀS

Via Corona, 47
34071 Cormòns (GO)
Tel. +39 0481 60991
info@magnas.it
www.magnas.it

YEAR OF FOUNDATION 1969
NAME OF THE OWNER Fratelli Visintin
TOTAL BOTTLES PRODUCED 25,000
DIRECT SALES
VISITS TO THE WINERY - RESERVATION NEEDED
HECTARES OF VINEYARD 10
HOSPITALITY
RESTAURANT

The estate is situated between Corona and Mariano in one of the most suitable winegrowing areas in the DOC Friuli Isonzo appellation. Here the Visintin brothers produce a few thousands bottles of mostly white wines including a Sauvignon that is considered one of the absolute best.

☐ 93   👍 Price A

Friuli Isonzo Sauvignon 2015

100% Sauvignon Blanc grapes. Stainless steel only. Intense green yellow color. On the nose extremely varietal with aromas of elderflower, tomato leaf and lime. On the palate firm, savory, full-bodied, elegant and refined balance. Top wine of the company.

MASUT DA RIVE

Via Manzoni, 82
34070 Mariano del Friuli (GO)
Tel. +39 0481 69200
Fax +39 0481 697414

info@masutdarive.com
www.masutdarive.com
 masutdarive
@masutdarive

YEAR OF FOUNDATION 1995
NAME OF THE OWNER Fabrizio and Marco Gallo
TOTAL BOTTLES PRODUCED 80,000
DIRECT SALES
VISITS TO THE WINERY - RESERVATION NEEDED
HECTARES OF VINEYARD 20

This winery was once named after its founder Silvano Gallo, the father of the current owners. However, due to a law suit brought by the California winemaking giant Gallo they had to change the name. The wines are well-made and have a good quality/price ratio. The estate is in Mariano del Friuli, in the middle of the Isonzo Valley.

 88   Price B
Friuli Isonzo Pinot Nero 2014

100% Pinot Nero grapes. Matures 1 year in barrique. On the nose fruity and pleasantly varietal with aromas of wild strawberry, and raspberries. On the palate balanced, fresh and fine.

☐ 86   Price A
Friuli Isonzo Rive Alte Pinot Grigio 2015

100% Pinot Grigio grapes. Stainless steel only. Gold straw yellow color. On the nose intense aromas of pear Williams, with fermentative hints. On the palate savory, warm, full-bodied and with a good length.

★★
MEROI

Via Stretta, 7b
33042 Buttrio (UD)
Tel. +39 0432 674025
info@meroidavino.com
www.meroidavino.it
 MeroiDavino

YEAR OF FOUNDATION 1920
NAME OF THE OWNER Paolo Meroi
TOTAL BOTTLES PRODUCED 30,000
DIRECT SALES
VISITS TO THE WINERY - RESERVATION NEEDED
HECTARES OF VINEYARD 15

Buttrio together with Manzano compose the southern sector of the Colli Orientali del Friuli appellation, which is perhaps the most classic, and produce whites with great structure. With his tiny winery, Paolo Meroi is among the best producers there and while his production is limited, with only a few bottle per type of wine, they all have great personality and undisputed character.

 92   Price B
FCO Merlot Ros di Buri 2012

100% Merlot grapes. Matures almost 2 years in barrique. Intense dark ruby color. On the nose very fruity, with aromas of cassis, raspberry, wild strawberries, dark cherry and vanilla. On the palate solid, full-bodied, with the tannins not to aggressive and a very long persistence.

★★★
MIANI

Via Peruzzi, 10
33042 Buttrio (UD)
Tel. +39 0432 674327
miani.buri@libero.it

YEAR OF FOUNDATION
NAME OF THE OWNER Enzo Pontoni
TOTAL BOTTLES PRODUCED 8,000
DIRECT SALES
VISITS TO THE WINERY - RESERVATION NEEDED
HECTARES OF VINEYARD 15

Enzo Potoni's wines are always hard to find because the limited production from his tiny winery Miani sells out almost instantly due the demand for it among wine lovers the world over. Enzo is an authentic wine craftsman who will only bring out a wine if it has convinced him first. His wines, in fact, last only days on the shelves of wine shops lucky to have acquired it. So being able to evaluate five wines is like making a little miracle, waiting at the wineshop to receive the wines beating everyone on time.

 97   Price D
FCO Merlot Filip 2012

100% Merlot grapes from the homonym plot. It is produced only during the years that are considered excellent and in limited edition. Intense light red color, very concentrated. On the nose gorgeous with scents of noble leathers, minced spices and black-berry compote. On the palate majestic, complex with an extraordinary balance between acidity and tannins. Very impressive intensity and persistence. A Merlot with extraordinary characteristic that remind the wine from Bordeaux especially from Pomerol.

☐ 94   Price C

FCO Friulano Buri 2013

100% Friulano grapes. Matures for 1 year in lit-tle oaks barrels. Intense straw yellow color. On the nose complex almost lactic with aromas of flowers, exotic fruits and fresh almond. On the palate savory, warm, rich and full with a great persistence.

■ 94   Price D

FCO Merlot Buri 2012

100% Merlot grapes. Matures 32 months in new French durmast barrels. Limited edition. Intense red color, concentrated. On the nose an explosion of aromas of spice and tobacco, red fruits and blue-berries, cocoa. On the palate very elegant even if it has a great powerfulness. Fresh, aristocratic with very fine tannins that make the whole wine pre-cious. Never-ending.

☐ 92   Price C

FCO Chardonnay 2014

100% Chardonnay grapes. Matures for almost 1 year in barrique. On the nose scents from Bour-gogne, aromas of flint, grilled bread, yellow plum. On the palate tense, full, warm with a good acidity and very long in the finish.

■ 92   Price C

Rosso Miani 2012

Blend of Merlot, Cabernet Franc, Cabernet Sauvi-gnon and Tazzelenghe grapes. Matures for 30-33 months in new French durmast barrels. Full, light red color. On the nose presents intense scents with aromas of fruits, ark cherry, orello and spices. On the palate not as bulky as usual, but tense with some asperity still to be balanced, but very efficient and of a great personality to drink.

PETRUSSA

Via Albana, 49
33040 Prepotto (UD)
Tel. +39 0432 713192
Fax +39 0432 713821
petrussa@petrussa.it
www.petrussa.it

YEAR OF FOUNDATION 1986 Ini
NAME OF THE OWNER Gianni and Paolo Petrussa
TOTAL BOTTLES PRODUCED 50,000
DIRECT SALES
VISITS TO THE WINERY - RESERVATION NEEDED
HECTARES OF VINEYARD 11
HOSPITALITY

Gianni and Paolo took over their family's estate in 1986 against the wishes of their parents who had hoped their children would chose a differ-ent path than the hard life of farming. But their desire to live according to the rhythm of nature was too strong and today the two brothers are convinced more than ever that they made the right choice and their parents are proud of them The estate is situated in Prepotto, an area that is being identified with Schioppettino, an ancient red grape that had virtually disap-peared from the zone and which the Petrussa brothers are doing justice to.

■ 93   Price B

FCO Schioppettino di Prepotto 2013

100% Schioppettino grapes. Matures in barrels of different dimensions. Bright but light ruby color. On the nose very intense with aromas of red fruits and nice spicy notes of white and pink pepper and cherry. On the palate elegant, with an austere class but young and solved tannin. Progressive with a big persistent finish with spicy notes.

☐ 86   Price A

FCO Sauvignon 2015

100% Sauvignon grapes. Stainless steel only. Straw yellow color with green reflexes. On the nose it need to be oxygenated but then the aromas of cedar, passion fruits, citrus and sage come out better. On the palate easy, savory and with a good acidity. Not perfect but definitely pleasant.

PICÉCH

Località Pradis, 11
34071 Cormòns (GO)
Tel. +39 0481 60347
info@picech.com
www.picech.it
 Azienda-Agricola-Picech

YEAR OF FOUNDATION 1920
NAME OF THE OWNER Roberto Picéch

TOTAL BOTTLES PRODUCED 25,000
DIRECT SALES
VISITS TO THE WINERY - RESERVATION NEEDED
HECTARES OF VINEYARD 7
HOSPITALITY

Pradis is a sub-zone of Collio located halfway between Cormòns and Capriva, an area that has always produced the best Pinot Bianco in the appellation. Among the best interpreters of this variety, which unfortunately is slowly disappearing, is Robert Picéch and his historic but tiny winery.

☐ 91   Price A

Collio Pinot Bianco 2015

100% Pinot Bianco grapes. Stainless steel only. Light straw yellow color. On the nose at first result slightly smoky due to the yeasts, then aromas of white peach, light yellow plum and fresh almond. On the palate savory, full-bodied, tense and persistent.

☐ 90   Price A

Collio Friulano 2015

100% Friulano grapes. Stainless steel only. Intense straw yellow color. On the nose aromas of white peach and wildflowers, some smoky hint. On the palate savory, full-bodied, full-flavored, rich and with very long in the finish.

DAMIJAN PODVERSIC

Via Brigata Pavia, 61
34170 Gorizia (GO)
Tel. +39 0481 78217
damijan.go@virgilio.it
www.damijanpodversic.com
 f *damijan.go*
 🐦 *@podversic*

YEAR OF FOUNDATION 1988
NAME OF THE OWNER Damijan Podversic
TOTAL BOTTLES PRODUCED 23,000
DIRECT SALES
VISITS TO THE WINERY - RESERVATION NEEDED
HECTARES OF VINEYARD 10
CERTIFIED ORGANIC VITICULTURE

An experimental, rigorous and passionate winemaker, Damijan Podversic 'lives', is fully immersed in his vineyards and his miniscule winery. His wines, which macerate long on the skins, are small masterpieces of craftsmanship and are made with great respect for the environment. He uses only indigenous yeasts.

☐ 93   Price B

Bianco Kaplja 2012

Blend of 40% Chardonnay, 30% Friulano and 30% Malvasia Istriana grapes. Matures for 2 years in big oak barrels. Opalescent antic gold color (the wine is not filtered). On the nose aromas of black tea, slightly smoky with aromas of walnut. On the palate savory, warm, full-flavored, lightly tannic and very persistent.

☐ 92   Price B

Ribolla Gialla 2012

100% Ribolla Gialla grapes. Matures for 3 years in big oak barrels. Lightly opalescent and gold yellow color. On the nose complex, aromas of aromatic wood, dry fruits and smoky. On the palate savory, warm, slightly tannic with a great persistence.

DORO PRINCIC

Località Pradis
34071 Cormòns (GO)
Tel. +39 0481 60723
Fax +39 0481 6072
doroprincic@virgilio.it

YEAR OF FOUNDATION 1950
NAME OF THE OWNER Sandro Princic
TOTAL BOTTLES PRODUCED 60,000
DIRECT SALES
VISITS TO THE WINERY - RESERVATION NEEDED
HECTARES OF VINEYARD 11

In the heart of Pradis, south of Cormòns, is the winery of Sandro Princic, the son of Doro who set it up more than 60 years ago. Sandri and Grazia have now become institutions and he makes his wines the way he always has and while they may seem a little rustic, they are fascinating. "If it doesn't sell then I'll drink it all with my friends," he loves to say. The fact is that if you are one of his friends and you do go to see him, it is unlikely that you'll leave after only one bottle.

☐ **93**   Price B
Collio Friulano 2015

100% Friulano grapes. Stainless steel only. Light gold yellow color. On the nose aromas of alfalfa, wildflowers, fresh almond, lightly smoky due to the yeasts that is the predominant aroma. On the palate savory, more agile than in other versions, tense, warm, persistent with a typical and delicious bitter finish.

☐ **92**   Price B
Collio Malvasia 2015

100% Malvasia Istriana grapes. Stainless steel only. Gold yellow color. On the nose emblematically floral with aromas of jasmine, alfalfa, full-flavored, lightly aromatic. On the palate warm, savory, alcoholic, powerful with a great length on the finish.

☐ **90**   Price B
Collio Pinot Bianco 2015

100% Pinot Bianco grapes. Stainless steel only. Intense straw yellow color. On the nose aromas of white peach, hawthorn, almond milk. On the palate polite, pleasant, full-bodied and great persistence.

PRODUTTORI DI CORMÒNS

Via Vino della Pace, 31
34071 Cormòns (GO)
Tel. +39 0481 62471
Fax +39 0481 630031
info@cormons.com
www.cormons.com
 cantina.cormons
 @CormonsStyle

YEAR OF FOUNDATION **1968**
NAME OF THE OWNER
TOTAL BOTTLES PRODUCED **2,250,000**
DIRECT SALES
VISITS TO THE WINERY - RESERVATION NEEDED
HECTARES OF VINEYARD **470**
OLIVE OIL PRODUCTION

The Cantina Produttori di Cormòns cooperative has hundreds of members who together own almost 500 hectares of vineyards that produce quality wines that can hold their own on markets around the world. Among the wines they make is Vino della Pace (Peace Wine), made with 500 different grapes which are locally cultivated but originate from all over the world. Every year it has a different label de-

signed by a famous artist and the profits from sales are donated to charity.

☐ **88**   Price D
Vino della Pace 1987

Blend of 500 different grapes vinified in white. Matures 6 months in big oak barrels. Historical version that still keeps well the years. Intense golden yellow color. On the nose evolved aromas of flowers. On the palate savory, with a remarkable acidity.

☐ **87**   👍 Price A
Collio Friulano 2015

100% Friulano grapes. Stainless steel only. Light straw yellow color. Very typical and helped by the great year. On the nose fermentative aromas at first, then white peach and wildflowers. On the palate tense, pleasant and easy to drink.

☐ **86**   👍 Price A
Collio Pinot Grigio 2015

100% Pinot Grigio grapes. Stainless steel only. Straw yellow color. On the nose the yeasts aroma is fragrant with notes of pear Williams. On the palate agile, savory, very pleasant and fresh.

PUIATTI

Località Zuccole, 4
34076 Romans d'Isonzo (GO)
Tel. +39 0481 909608
Fax +39 0481 909608
puiatti@puiatti.com
www.puiatti.com
 Puiatti

YEAR OF FOUNDATION **1967**
NAME OF THE OWNER **Bertani Domains**
TOTAL BOTTLES PRODUCED **400,000**
DIRECT SALES
VISITS TO THE WINERY - RESERVATION NEEDED
HECTARES OF VINEYARD **50**

Today it belongs to Bertani Domains of the Gruppo Angelini but its historic founder was Vittorio Puiatti, an enologist of charisma and producer of immense and infinite talent. His dictates are still followed at the winery, the wines are varietal and no wood is ever used, which has led to the slogan in the US "save a tree, drink Puiatti".

☐ 92   Price B

Ribolla Gialla Archètipi 2014

00% Ribolla Gialla grapes. Stainless steel only. Light straw yellow color. On the nose fruity with aromas of cedar and evident wildflowers. On the palate agile, tense with an excellent fresh acidity that makes if very pleasant and easy to drink.

☐ 91   👍 Price A

Ribolla Gialla Lus 2015

100% Ribolla Gialla. Stainless steel. Light straw yellow color. On the nose citrusy and fragrant with aromas of cedar and Amalfi lemon. On the palate savory, fresh, fine and elegant, tense thin and persistent.

☐ 90   👍 Price A

Sauvignon Fun 2015

100% Sauvignon Blanc grapes. Stainless steel only. Bright greenish yellow color. Extremely varietal on the nose, almost emblematic, with typical aromas of tomato leaf, celery, elderflower and boxwood. On the palate typical, savory, fresh, thin and long.

DARIO RACCARO

Via San Giovanni, 87b
34071 Cormòns (GO)
Tel. +39 0481 61425
az.agr.raccaro@alice.it

YEAR OF FOUNDATION 1928
NAME OF THE OWNER Dario Raccaro
TOTAL BOTTLES PRODUCED 30,000
DIRECT SALES
VISITS TO THE WINERY - RESERVATION NEEDED
HECTARES OF VINEYARD 6

In Cormòns Dario Raccaro is a true leader and is, in fact, the president of the local producers association whose members are all wine growers who meet at the headquarters of Enoteca di Cormòns to taste each other's wines. Dario is also an excellent taster and everyone listens to what he has to say. His own wines always have great character, from his Friulano del Rolat to the last one in his line.

☐ 93   Price B

Collio Friulano Vigna del Rolat 2015

100% Friulano grapes. Matures in stainless steel

on yeasts for some months. Light gold yellow color. On the nose important and complex, slightly rustic, with aromas of yeasts at first, then white peach, plum, fresh almond and alfalfa. On the palate very intense and with a great alcohol, very savory, rich, strong with a typical bitter finish.

☐ 92   Price B

Collio Malvasia 2015

100% Malvasia Istriana grapes. Stainless steel on yeasts. Light gold yellow color. On the nose very typical and varietal with light aromatic and flowery scents with aromas of hawthorn, and specifically jasmine, smoky aromas from the yeasts. On the palate strong, warm, alcoholic, very savory and persistent.

☐ 91   Price B

Collio Bianco 2015

50% Pinot Grigio grapes with Sauvignon and Friulano. Stainless steel only. Intense straw yellow color. On the nose articulate and intense with aromas of white and yellow fruits, mango and fresh almond. On the palate rich and warm, great alcohol content, savory and pleasantly bitter on the finish.

★

PAOLO RODARO

Via Cormòns, 60 - Località Spessa
33043 Cividale del Friuli (UD)
Tel. +39 0432 716066
Fax +39 0432 716066
info@rodaropaolo.it
www.rodaropaolo.it
🟦 rodaropaolo
🐦 @RodaroPaolo

YEAR OF FOUNDATION 1846
NAME OF THE OWNER Paolo Rodaro
TOTAL BOTTLES PRODUCED 250,000
DIRECT SALES
VISITS TO THE WINERY - RESERVATION NEEDED
HECTARES OF VINEYARD 50

This winery was founded some 170 years ago by a man with the same name as the current owner and so here there is Colli Orientali tradition to burn. Then again Paolo Rodaro has always been convinced that any novelty must have a solid foundation. His wines are very territorial and seek to bring out the typicity of each and every grape variety. And he does this quite successfully.

91 Price B
FCO Romain Schioppettino 2011

100% Schioppettino (Ribolla Nera) grapes a little dried firs on the vine then in fruit sheds. Matures almost 2 years in barrique. Very intense ruby color. On the nose aromas of vanilla, cocoa at first, then a lot of berries, especially raspberries. On the palate intense, slightly tannic, with a nice acidic component that makes it fresh and more elegant.

88 Price A
FCO Ribolla Gialla 2015

100% Ribolla Gialla grapes. Stainless steel only. Light straw yellow color. On the nose compact and fragrant with aromas of cedar and wildflowers. On the palate fresh with a good body, agile and savory.

RONCHI RÒ DELLE FRAGOLE

Località Cime di Dolegna, 12
34070 Dolegna del Collio (GO)
Tel. +39 338 5270908
ronchiro.vini@libero.it
www.ronchiro.com
 agriturismo.ronchi.ro

YEAR OF FOUNDATION **2005**
NAME OF THE OWNER **Romeo Rossi**
TOTAL BOTTLES PRODUCED **18,000**
DIRECT SALES
VISITS TO THE WINERY - RESERVATION NEEDED
HECTARES OF VINEYARD **4**
HOSPITALITY

Romeo Rossi is a typical, silent native of Friuli who comes alive when talking about Sauvignon, the principle varietal at his estate and his favorite grape. He only betrays this variety with Friulano given that the estate already had a 50-year-old vineyard with this grape. The estate is in Dolegna and Romeo has just over four hectares of vineyards surrounding his home and estate headquarters. The soil has marl in it. He does not have a winery and his wines are made and age at a friend's home. However, this takes nothing away from Romeo's extreme precision and his estate was added to our guide thanks to the wonderful wines we tasted.

94 Price B
Collio Sauvignon Riserva 2013

100% Sauvignon grapes. Matures 1 year in 5 hl oak

barrels. Bright and medium straw yellow color. On the nose intense and citrusy with aromas of grapefruits, medlar, boxwood and an extremely elegant sandalwood. On the palate acidic, savory, solid with a big full-flavored finish.

91 Price A
Collio Sauvignon 2015

100% Sauvignon grapes. 80% matures in stainless steel and 20% in 5 lt oak barrels. Pale greenish straw yellow color. On the nose complex and wide with aromas of boxwood, passion fruits, eucalyptus, grapefruit, rose and current. On the palate acidic and savory, elegant and tasty with a perfect matching finish.

RONCO BLANCHIS

Via Blanchis, 70
34070 Mossa (GO)
Tel. +39 0481 80519
info@roncoblanchis.it
www.roncoblanchis.it
 Ronco-Blanchis
 @blanchishills

YEAR OF FOUNDATION **1951**
NAME OF THE OWNER **Palla Family**
TOTAL BOTTLES PRODUCED **40,000**
DIRECT SALES
VISITS TO THE WINERY - RESERVATION NEEDED
HECTARES OF VINEYARD **12**

In Friulano dialect, ronco blanchis means 'white hills' and is a reference to the fact that almost all the vineyards there are cultivated with white grapes. This estate is in Mossa, in the southernmost part of Collio Goriziano, a stone's throw from Monfalcone and where the influence of the sea is distinctly felt. Thus the white wines are saline and bold, almost Mediterranean, and are technically crafted by Gianni Menotti, a talented enologist.

96 Price A
Collio Friulano 2015

100% Friulano grapes. Stainless steel only. Light gold yellow color. On the nose floral with aromas of jasmine, rose, yellow peach. Complex and very articulated, even aromatic. On the palate strong, warm, savory, with a great taste impact, strong personality and unmistakable. Very long in the finish.

☐ 93   👍 Price A
Collio Bianco Blanc di Blanchis 2015

Blend of 60% Friulano grapes with Sauvignon, Malvasia Istriana and Chardonnay. Stainless steel only. Intense straw yellow color. On the nose intense, almost ethereal with aromas of mature yellow fruits and fresh almond. On the palate warm, savory, full-bodied, strong and Mediterranean.

★★
RONCO DEI TASSI

*Località Monte, 38
34071 Cormòns (GO)
Tel. +39 0481 60155
info@roncodeitassi.it
www.roncodeitassi.it*

YEAR OF FOUNDATION 1989
NAME OF THE OWNER Fabio Coser
TOTAL BOTTLES PRODUCED 110,000
DIRECT SALES
VISITS TO THE WINERY - RESERVATION NEEDED
HECTARES OF VINEYARD 18

The esteem that Fabio Coser enjoys among Collio producers is a clear indication that his 'Friulization' is complete. This because while he may be native to Veneto, he now knows the vineyards of Cormòns better than many locals. An accomplished enologist, he produces very elegant wines from vineyards situated at high altitudes on the slopes of Monte Quarin. Every once in a while he comes out with a surprising red wines, as he did this year.

☐ 91   👍 Price A
Collio Malvasia 2015

100% Malvasia Istriana grapes. Stainless steel on yeasts. Intense straw yellow. On the nose varietal and elegant, aromas of hawthorn, jasmine, cedar and thyme. On the palate savory, polite, with a good body but yet agile with a warm persistent finish.

☐ 90   👍 Price A
Collio Sauvignon 2015

100% Sauvignon grapes. Stainless steel. Green straw yellow color. On the nose typical but not excessive with aromas of white peach, exotic fruits, on the underneath greener aromas of tomato leaf. On the palate agile and very pleasant, savory and with a good body.

☐ 88   Price A
Collio Pinot Griglio 2015

100% Pinot Grigio grapes. Stainless steel on yeasts. Intense straw yellow color. On the nose fruity and fragrant with aromas of pear Williams and fermentative notes. On the palate warm, savory, pleasant with a good length.

★★
RONCO DEL GELSO

*Via Isonzo, 117
34071 Cormòns (GO)
Tel. +39 0481 61310
Fax +39 0481 634667
info@roncodelgelso.com
www.roncodelgelso.com*
🅕 *roncodelgelso*
🐦 *@RoncodelGelso1*

YEAR OF FOUNDATION 1988
NAME OF THE OWNER Giorgio Badin
TOTAL BOTTLES PRODUCED 150,000
DIRECT SALES
VISITS TO THE WINERY - RESERVATION NEEDED
HECTARES OF VINEYARD 25

Giorgio Badin is a leading figure in Friuli winemaking. A tall man, he has always been measured in his ways, wise and intelligent. All these characteristics are reflected in his wines which are DOC Friuli Isonzo Rive Alte because his vineyards are right on the Collio border. While a specialist with Pinot Grigio, sometimes he will surprise us with a variation on the theme and which this year was a Riesling that was simply amazing and totally unexpected.

☐ 🆔 96   Price B
Friuli Isonzo Rive Alte Pinot Grigio Sot Lis Rivis 2015

100% Pinot Grigio grapes. Stainless steel only. Light gold yellow color. On the nose extremely varietal with aromas of pear Williams, white peach, alfalfa and slightly smoky. On the palate powerful but tense, savory, warm, great personality, with an exceptionally long finish.

☐ 94   👍 Price A
Riesling Schulz 2015

100% Riesling Renano grapes. Stainless steel only.

Gold yellow color. On the nose very typical with clean aromas of hydrocarbon and grapefruit at first, then bitter citrus, and rubber. On the palate tense, savory, full-bodied, with a hint of residual of sugar and a very long finish.

☐ 93   Price B

Friuli Isonzo Rive Alte Friulano Toc Bas 2015

100% Friulano grapes, stainless steel only. Light gold yellow color. On the nose varietal and very characteristic with classic aromas of white peach at first, then smoky notes and almond. On the palate savory, warm, strong with a slightly bitter finish.

RUSSIZ SUPERIORE

Via Russiz, 7
34070 Capriva del Friuli (GO)
Tel. +39 0481 808753
Fax +39 0481 808348
relais@russizsuperiore.it
www.russizsuperiore.it
 marcofelluga.russizsuperiore
 @MarcoFelluga

YEAR OF FOUNDATION **1976**
NAME OF THE OWNER **Roberto Felluga**
TOTAL BOTTLES PRODUCED **200,000**
DIRECT SALES
VISITS TO THE WINERY - RESERVATION NEEDED
HECTARES OF VINEYARD **50**
HOSPITALITY
RESTAURANT

This estate has been one of the points of reference in Collio for almost 40 years. Founded by Marco Felluga, it is professionally run today by his son Roberto. The vineyards are situated in Spessa di Capriva, in the area of Russiz Superiore, on the border with Slovenia. The wines, particularly in recent years, have improved significantly and there may be stars in the future.

☐ 91   Price B

Collio Bianco Col Disore 2013

Blend of Pinot Bianco, Sauvignon, Friulano and Ribolla Gialla grapes. Matures for almost 1 year in oak barrel of different capacity. Intense straw yellow color. On the nose full-flavored and complex with aromas of white peach, vanilla, fresh almond, and alfalfa. On the palate tense, full-bodied, very savory with a great long finish.

☐ 90   Price B

Collio Sauvignon 2015

100% Sauvignon grapes. Stainless steel only. Green straw yellow color. On the nose floral with aromas of exotic fruits and white peach. The palate tense, fresh, savory and full-bodied. Is one of the most classic wine of the company.

☐ 88   Price B

Collio Pinot Bianco 2015

100% Pinot Bianco grapes. Stainless steel only. Light straw yellow color. On the nose very varietal and delicate scents of flowers fresh almond. On the palate savory, polite, very pleasant and easy to drink. The finish is quite long.

SARA & SARA

Via dei Monti, 5 - Savorgnano del Torre
33040 Povoletto (UD)
Tel. +39 0432 3859042
Fax +39 0432 666365
cantinasaraesara@libero.it
www.saraesara.com

YEAR OF FOUNDATION **1964**
NAME OF THE OWNER **Oriana Giordani and Alessandro Sara**
TOTAL BOTTLES PRODUCED **24,000**
DIRECT SALES
VISITS TO THE WINERY - RESERVATION NEEDED
HECTARES OF VINEYARD **7**

The best area in Friuli for sweet wine is the northern part of the Colli Orientali appellation. The zone is more or less that between Faedis, Savorgnano del Torre, Nimis and Ramandolo. Here the Picolit and Verduzzo grapes are king and they are often cultivated to have some botrytis on them, which occurs more consistently there elsewhere. It is here that Oriana and Alessandro produce some of Friuli's besti sweet wine at their tiny winery.

▪ 93   Price B*

FCO Verduzzo Crei 2013

100% Verduzzo Friulano grapes. Matures 1 year in barrique. Strong antic gold color. On the nose aromas of saffron and sea, with peach, apricot, honey and barley sugar. On the palate the taste is sweet but not sickly, the acidity is even more present than in previous versions. Warm, tense, very persistent. *37.5 cl bottle.

☐ · 91   Price B*

Picolit 2011

*100% Picolit grapes. Matures 2 year in barrique. Golden yellow color with topaz hues. On the nose aromas of vanilla, saffron, tea, light almond paste, hints of yellow fruits compote and honey, intense and heretic with a slightly volatile component. The taste on the palate sweet nut not sickly, the acidity is evident and make it fresh, great body, dense and long. *37.5 cl bottle.*

★★★

SCHIOPETTO

*Via Palazzo Arcivescovile, 1
34070 Capriva del Friuli (GO)
Tel. +39 0481 80332
Fax +39 0481 808073
azienda@schiopetto.it
www.schiopetto.it*
f *SchiopettoMario*
🐦 *@schiopetto*

YEAR OF FOUNDATION **1965**
NAME OF THE OWNER **Emilio Rotolo**
TOTAL BOTTLES PRODUCED **180,000**
DIRECT SALES
VISITS TO THE WINERY - RESERVATION NEEDED
HECTARES OF VINEYARD **30**

More than ten years after his death, Mario Schiopetto, one of the key figures in Collio winemaking, remains a significant presence at what was once his estate. Still today, and after it was acquired by Emilio Rotolo the owner of Volpe Pasini, the winery is organized the way Mario wanted and the vineyards are cultivated as if they were gardens, just as he did.

☐ 🍇 98   Price C

Collio Friulano M 2015

Blend of Friulano grapes from the most ancient vineyard of the estate with some Riesling Renano grapes. Stainless steel only. Bright greenish straw yellow color. On the nose compact with aromas of white peach, almond and some citrus. On the palate tense, intense, agile and yet full-bodied, savory, warm and extremely persistent. Great wine.

☐ 🍇 96   Price B

Collio Friulano 2015

100% Friulano grapes. Stainless steel only. Intense straw yellow color. On the nose very varietal with typical aromas of yellow peach and wildflowers. On the palate savory and tense, but also warm and full-bodied, very pleasant, rich full-flavored and with a very long finish.

☐ 94   Price B

Collio Pinot Bianco 2015

100% Pinot Bianco grapes. Stainless steel only. Bright straw yellow color. On the nose fragrant with aromas of white peach and hawthorn. On the palate the taste is full, warm, savory, full-flavored with a very long finish.

☐ 92   Price B

Collio Pinot Griglio 2015

100% Pinot Grigio grapes. Stainless steel only. Intense straw yellow color. On the nose the aromas are typical, pear Williams, fresh almond and yellow peach. On the palate savory, pleasantly drinkable, warm, absolutely ready with a very long finish.

■ 91   Price B

Blumeri 2013

Blend of 50% Merlot, 50% Refosco grapes. Matures 18 months in barrique and tonneau. Intense purple ruby color. On the nose complex with aromas of blueberries, blackcurrant, sour cherry, sweet spices, and black tobacco. On the palate the taste is firm, slightly tannic, warm and very persistent.

★★

ROBERTO SCUBLA

*Via Rocca Bernarda, 22 - Frazione Ipplis
33040 Premariacco (UD)
Tel. +39 0432 716258
info@scubla.com
www.scubla.com*
f *Azienda-Agricola-Roberto-Scubla*

YEAR OF FOUNDATION **1991**
NAME OF THE OWNER **Roberto Scubla**
TOTAL BOTTLES PRODUCED **60,000**
DIRECT SALES
VISITS TO THE WINERY - RESERVATION NEEDED
HECTARES OF VINEYARD **12**

In a world where many producers are a little over the top, Roberto Scubla is a wise and well-mannered man who prefers to speak with facts. His wines, produced with the precious contribution of renowned enologist Gianni Menotti, are always examples of typicity and respect for the land. His vineyards are in Ipplis, next to Rocca Bernarda, in one of Colli Orientali's historic cru.

☐ 95   Price B
FCO Bianco Pomédes 2014
Blend of 65% Pinot Bianco, 25% Friulano, 10% Riesling Renano grapes. Matures 8 months in barrique. Intense straw yellow color. On the nose extremely fruity with aromas of white peach, cedar, fresh almond and light hint of vanilla. On the palate agile, savory, ore tense and crispy than other versions. A very long finish.

☐ 93   👍 Price A
FCO Pinot Bianco 2015
100% Pinot Bianco grapes. Stainless steel only. Light straw yellow color. On the nose present a clear fruity aromas with mature medlar, yellow plums, hawthorn. On the palate full, oft, full-flavored, warm and persistent.

☐ 91   👍 Price A
FCO Friulano 2015
100% Friulano grapes. Stainless steel only. Intense straw yellow color. On the nose aromas of almond and white peach, defined and fragrant. On the palate savory, warm, full-flavored and great to drink.

★★
SKERK

Via Prepotto, 20
34011 Duino Aurisina (TS)
Tel. +39 040 200156
Fax +39 040 200156
info@skerk.com
www.skerk.com
📘 *Skerk*

YEAR OF FOUNDATION **1987**
NAME OF THE OWNER **Skerk Family**
TOTAL BOTTLES PRODUCED **22,000**
DIRECT SALES
VISITS TO THE WINERY - RESERVATION NEEDED
HECTARES OF VINEYARD **7**
CERTIFIED ORGANIC VITICULTURE

These splendid Carso whites are made allowing the musts to macerate on the skins for a period of time that is not long but determined by the quality of the harvest and the variety of grape and all this is done in a magnificent cellar cared out of Karst rock.

☐ 95   Price B
Ograde Bianco 2015
Blend of Vitovska, Malvasia Istriana, Sauvignon and Pinot Grigio grapes. It macerates on the skins for 10 days the matures in big oak barrels for almost 2 years. Lightly opalescent intense coral pink color. On the nose complex with smoky aromas of yeasts, then wildflowers, honey, and fresh almond. On the palate very savory, warm, full and yet agile. Perfect example of macerated wine.

★★
SKERLJ

Via Sales, 44
34010 Sgonico (TS)
Tel. +39 040 229253
info@agriturismoskerlj.com
www.agriturismoskerlj.com

YEAR OF FOUNDATION **1991**
NAME OF THE OWNER **Matej Skerlj**
TOTAL BOTTLES PRODUCED **5,000**
DIRECT SALES
VISITS TO THE WINERY - RESERVATION NEEDED
HECTARES OF VINEYARD **2**
HOSPITALITY

The key words that describes the Carso (Karst) region is biodiversity. And it is here that Matej Skerlj has become one of the producers most attentive to the environment. The small winery turns out 4-5,000 bottles a year which this is one of the highest outputs for indigenous Carso wines. The wines ferment in wood vats for 2-3 weeks. The wine is transferred after aging a year and then ages another year in barrels. His wines recall the northern Bora wind, stone and the sea.

☐ 91   Price B
Vitovska 2014
100% Vitovska grapes. Matures 2 years in big oak barrels. Intense gold yellow color. On the nose smoky, floral with aromas of wild herbs and hints

of candid citrus and licorice. On the palate intense, full, savory, extremely typical, with a warm persistent finish. A very artisanal wine.

☐ 90   **Price B**

Malvasia 2014

100% Malvasia Istriana grapes. Matures 2 years in big oak barrels. Intense golden yellow color. On the nose full-flavored, floral and slightly aromatic with aromas of yellow flowers, candied fruits, hints of flint.

SPECOGNA

Via Rocca Bernarda, 4
33040 Corno di Rosazzo (UD)
Tel. +39 0432 755840
info@specogna.it
www.specogna.it
 specognatoblarwines
 @SpecognaWINEs

YEAR OF FOUNDATION 1963
NAME OF THE OWNER Specogna Family
TOTAL BOTTLES PRODUCED 120,000
DIRECT SALES
VISITS TO THE WINERY - RESERVATION NEEDED
HECTARES OF VINEYARD 18

This is one of the most active wineries in Colli Orientali thanks to the innovative and entrepreneurial spirit of Cristian and Michele Specogna, who are the third generation of their family to run the estate and their efforts are beginning to pay off. The first, tangible example is their Sauvignon 2014 that won the Concours Mondial de Sauvignon 2015. And 2015 vintage is even better.

☐ 94   👍 **Price A**

FCO Sauvignon Blanc 2015

100% Sauvignon grapes. Matures partly in stainless steel on yeasts and partly in big oak barrels for 7 months. Green yellow color. On the nose intense, varietal, with aromas of celery, tomato leaf, kettle, some hints of passion fruits and mango. On the palate tense and agile, great acidic component, fresh, to complete a very characteristic wine, that is difficult not to note.

☐ 93   👍 **Price A**

FCO Friulano 2015

100% Friulano grapes. 20% of the grapes mature

in big oak barrels for few months, the other 80% in stainless steel on yeasts. Straw yellow color. On the nose very fruity with aromas of evident white peach, medlar and fresh almond. On the palate savory, warm, gull with great persistence.*

TIARE

Località Sant'Elena, 3a
34070 Dolegna del Collio (GO)
Tel. +39 0481 62491
info@tiaredoc.com
www.tiaredoc.com
 tiarevini

YEAR OF FOUNDATION 1991
NAME OF THE OWNER Roberto Snidarcig
TOTAL BOTTLES PRODUCED 100,000
DIRECT SALES
VISITS TO THE WINERY - RESERVATION NEEDED
HECTARES OF VINEYARD 10
RESTAURANT

In Friulano dialect tiare means land and Roberto Snidarcig knows what to do with his land and vineyards. The vineyards are in Venco, close to the border with Slovenia, between Ruttars and Dolegna and, in part, Moraro in the area of Isonzo where red grapes are cultivated. However, his specialty is without a doubt Sauvignon and his 2013 was acclaimed by all, while the 2015 convinced us even more. Really a great wine.

☐ 94   **Price B**

Collio Sauvignon 2015

100% Sauvignon grapes. Stainless steel only. Pale straw yellow color with green hues. On the nose intense with aromas of tomato leaf, green tea, cedar and elderflower. On the palate very convincing with nice acidity and very pleasant, on the second time is compact and elegant with a tasty and deep finish.

☐ 93   **Price B**

Collio Malvasia 2015

100% Malvasia grapes. Stainless steel only. Bright straw yellow color, on the nose intense and complex with aromas of violet, star anise and an hint of licorice. On the palate big, savory with a nice salty note. Compact progression and juicy persistent finish.

☐ 90   **Price B**

Collio Friulano 2015

100% Friulano grapes. Stainless steel only. Intense

straw yellow color. On the nose aromas of white and yellow peach an hint of pear and almond. On the palate convincing with is modern style, savory, and slightly green, and his classic style, almond. The finish is very persistent.

FRANCO TOROS

*Località Novali, 12
34071 Cormòns (GO)
Tel. +39 0481 61327
info@vinitoros.com
www.vinitoros.com*
f *AzAgrTorosFranco*

YEAR OF FOUNDATION 1900
NAME OF THE OWNER Franco Toros
TOTAL BOTTLES PRODUCED 50,000
DIRECT SALES
VISITS TO THE WINERY - RESERVATION NEEDED
HECTARES OF VINEYARD 10

The third star was awarded to Franco Toros in recognition of the great reliability and high quality achieved by his wines. His estate is in Novali, east of the town of Cormons and a stone's throw from the border with Slovenia. For centuries this area was part of the Austro-Hungarian Empire where there existed a classification system similar to that in Bordeaux and this particular area was considered a 'Premier Cru'. Toros has sought to bring this back with white wines, made from Friulano and Pinot Bianco, worthy of their prestigious past.

☐ 🔳 95   Price B
Collio Friulano 2015

100% Friulano grapes. Matures in stainless steel on yeasts. Intense straw yellow color. On the nose present very clean and whole aromas of whit peach and rose, with fresh almond. On the palate savory, warm, tense, alcoholic and very persistent.

■ 94   Price C
Collio Merlot Etichetta Rossa 2013

100% merlot grapes. Matures in barrique for almost 18 months. Dark and intense ruby color. On the nose predominant the aromas of vanilla and strawberry, then little berries and berries compote. On the palate warm, savory, tense, lightly tannic with a great persistence. One of the best Merlot in Italy.

☐ 93   Price B
Collio Pinot Bianco 2015

100% Pinot Bianco grapes. Stainless steel only. Bright straw yellow. Floral and complete, notes of wildflowers, then cedar and pineapple hints. Savory and tense flavor, warm, enveloping, solid and of great lenght.

TORRE ROSAZZA

*Località Poggiobello - Frazione Oleis
33044 Manzano (UD)
Tel. +39 0422 864511
info@torrerosazza.com
www.torrerosazza.com*
f *TorreRosazza*
🐦 *@wineinsocial*

YEAR OF FOUNDATION 1984
NAME OF THE OWNER Genagricola
TOTAL BOTTLES PRODUCED 300,000
DIRECT SALES
VISITS TO THE WINERY - RESERVATION NEEDED
HECTARES OF VINEYARD 110

For many years this has been the feather in the cap in the Genagricola winemaking enterprise, owned by the Assicurazioni Generali Insurance group, and over the years, despite management changes, it has always paid the greatest attention to the vineyards, the territory and the men to care for them. This is why the wines are always of the finest quality. The vineyards are in Oleis, an excellent Manzano cru, and the estate's headquarters is in 19th century Palazzo De Marchi.

☐ 92   👍 Price A
FCO Friulano 2015

100% Friulano grapes. Stainless steel. Gold straw yellow color. On the nose very fruity with typical aromas of white peach, wildflowers and light fresh almond. On the palate savory, warm, rich, well sustained by the acidity. Very persistent on the finish.

☐ 91   👍 Price A
FCO Pinot Bianco 2015

100% Pinot Bianco grapes. Stainless steel only. Bright straw yellow color. On the nose very varietal with aromas of hawthorn, jasmine and white peach. On the palate pleasant, savory, soft and warm.

☐ 90 Price A

FCO Ribolla Gialla 2015

100% Ribolla Gialla grapes. Stainless steel only. On the nose aromas of cedar, alfalfa, lemon apple. On the palate savory, tense, very pleasant, easy to drink.

★★★

VENICA & VENICA

*Località Cerò, 8
34070 Dolegna del Collio (GO)
Tel. +39 0481 61264
Fax +39 0481 639906
info@venica.it
www.venica.it*
f *Venica-Venica*

YEAR OF FOUNDATION 1930
NAME OF THE OWNER Gianni and Giorgio Venica
TOTAL BOTTLES PRODUCED 280,000
DIRECT SALES
VISITS TO THE WINERY - RESERVATION NEEDED
HECTARES OF VINEYARD 37
HOSPITALITY

This famous and reliable Dolegna estate in the northern area of Collio received its third star this year. Three decades of serious and professional commitment made it one of the leading players on the Friuli wine scene. Great Sauvignon and Pinot Bianco experts, their white wines have an incredible capacity to age with truly surprising consistency.

☐ 🔢 95 Price B

Collio Sauvignon Ronco delle Mele 2015

100% Sauvignon grapes. 20% of the grapes matures in big oak barrels for 6 months, the rest matures in stainless steel on yeasts for 6 months. Intense green yellow color. On the nose the scents are typical, absolutely varietal with aromas of tomato leaf, nettle, mango and white peach. On the palate agile and tense, fresh with a great acidity but full-bodied and very long. One of the most iconic Sauvignon in Friuli.

☐ 93 Price B

Collio Sauvignon Ronco del Cero 2015

100% Sauvignon blanc grapes. Stainless steel on yeasts only. Intense green yellow color. On the nose very typical and varietal with aromas of tomato

leaf, boxwood, nettle, elderflower and light hints of mango. On the palate tense, great acidity that gives freshness and makes it easy to drink, agile, good body with a thin savory finish.

☐ 92 Price B

Collio Friulano Ronco delle Cime 2015

100% Friulano grapes. Matures in stainless steel. intense straw yellow color. On the nose varietal, emblematic with aromas of white peach and almond at first, then hint of smoke from the yeasts. On the palate warm, tense, savory, full, great body and slightly bitter finish.

☐ 92 Price A

Collio Pinot Bianco Tàlis 2015

100% Pinot Bianco. Stainless steel only. Light straw yellow color. On the nose fragrant and floral aromas of wildflower with little hints of fresh almond and white peach. On the palate savory, polite, tense from the acidity, full-bodied, fine and persistent.

☐ 91 Price A

Collio Ribolla Gialla L'Adelchi 2015

100% Ribolla Gialla grapes. Stainless steel only. Light straw yellow color. On the nose aromas of cedar, wildflower. The citrusy and fragrant note are predominant. On the palate tense, very pleasant and easy to drink, agile, fresh with a good persistence.

★★★

VIE DI ROMANS

*Località Vie di Romans, 1
34070 Mariano del Friuli (GO)
Tel. .+39 0481 69600
viediromans@viediromans.it
www.viediromans.it*

YEAR OF FOUNDATION 1900
NAME OF THE OWNER Gianfranco Gallo
TOTAL BOTTLES PRODUCED 280,000
DIRECT SALES
VISITS TO THE WINERY - RESERVATION NEEDED
HECTARES OF VINEYARD 53

Vie di Romans in Friulano dialect means the Roman Road and it was in ancient times and still is today the one that leads from the sea to the mountains in northern Friuli. On this ancient way, in the town of Mariano del Friuli, which is also known for being the home town of the great goalie Dino Zoff, Gianfranco Gallo has his vineyards and winery. He produces classic Isonzo wines that recall the nearby sea and his specialty is Sauvignon, of which he makes several versions.

☐ 🗋 96   Price B
Friuli Isonzo Sauvignon Piere 2014

100% Sauvignon grapes. Stainless steel on yeasts only. Greenish straw yellow color. In a not easy vintage an amazing Sauvigon, that recover some 'Nordic' aspects as well as typical aromas of exotic fruits. Some scents more vegetal with aromas of elderflower and tomato leaf that make this wine precious. On the palate savory, firm and very long.

☐ 94   Price B
Dut'un 2013

Blend of 50% of Chardonnay and 50% of Sauvignon. Matures 10 months in barrique. Light gold yellow color. Beautiful version from an amazing harvest. On the nose the aromas are complex and of impact with aromas of flint, fresh almond, exotic fruits and white peach. On the palate solid, tense, warm but agile and very long.

☐ 93   Price B
Friuli Isonzo Chardonnay Ciampagnis Vieris 2014

100% Chardonnay grapes. Matures in stainless on yeasts for 6 months. Bright straw yellow color. On the nose great, solid and complex with aromas of flint due to the yeasts, exotic fruits, fresh almond and wildflowers. On the palate savory, tense, good body, not more agile and fine then other versions with a fresh and persistent finish.

☐ 92   Price B
Friuli Isonzo Malvasia Dis Cumieris 2014

100% Malvasia Istriana grapes. Stainless steel only. 6 months on yeasts. Light gold yellow color. On the nose very typical and floral with aromas of jasmine and wildflower at first, then yellow peach and almond. On the palate full, warm, with a nice alcohol component, savory, very pleasant and surprisingly agile. Very long finish.

☐ 92   Price B
Friuli Isonzo Sauvignon Vieris 2014

100% Sauvignon grapes. Matures 8 months in barrique, green gold yellow color. On the nose intense and full-flavored with aromas of milk, vanilla as well as typical varietal notes of exotic fruits. On the palate full, solid, with nice acidity and a savory, warm finish.

VIGNAI DA DULINE

Via IV Novembre, 136
Località Villanova dello Judrio
33048 San Giovanni al Natisone (UD)
Tel. +39 0432 758115
Fax +39 0432 758115
info@vignaidaduline.com
www.vignaidaduline.com
🄵 *vignaidaduline*

YEAR OF FOUNDATION **1997**
NAME OF THE OWNER **Mocchiutti Family**
TOTAL BOTTLES PRODUCED **25,000**
DIRECT SALES
VISITS TO THE WINERY - RESERVATION NEEDED
HECTARES OF VINEYARD **10**
CERTIFIED ORGANIC VITICULTURE

In recent years this small, organic estate has made quite a name for itself. While they produce few wines, they have a gift for Pinot Noir, something rare in these parts, and they are very attached to local tradition, in regard to both winegrowing and winemaking.

■ 93   Price C
FCO Pinot Nero Ronco Pitotti 2012

100% of Pinot Nero from a small plot. Matures for more than 1 year in small oak barrels. Light ruby color. On the nose varietal and clean aromas of currant, wild strawberry, light aromatic wood. On the palate polite, fine, savory, elegant with a good body and a long finish.

VILLA PARENS

Via Dante, 69
34070 Farra d'Isonzo (GO)
Tel. +39 0481 888198
maison@villaparens.com
www.villaparens.com
🄵 *VillaParens*
🐦 *@villaparens*

YEAR OF FOUNDATION **2014**
NAME OF THE OWNER **Giovanni and Elisabetta Puiatti**
TOTAL BOTTLES PRODUCED **50,000**
DIRECT SALES
VISITS TO THE WINERY - RESERVATION NEEDED
HECTARES OF VINEYARD **6**

The offspring of the great Vittorio Puiatti, one of the father of Friuli winemaking, for some years now Giovanni and Elisabetta Puiatti have been cultivating their vineyards and making wine. The production is currently limited but inspired by their father's concept of wine, which centered on an essential interpretation of the varietal without any use of wood and based on the integrity of the fruit.

| 93 | Price C |

Collio Merlot Graf de La Tour 2011

100% Merlot grapes. Matures in small oak barrels for 2 years. Dark ruby color. On the nose intense with aromas of black fruits, currant, blackberry, blueberry, slightly smoky with a blood spiciness. A touch of graphite. On the palate grave rather vertical with a good acidity respect a full and rich body but not sickly. An unexpected, intense, large finish.

☐ 91   Price B

Sauvignon Ruttars 2015

100% Sauvignon grapes. Stainless steel. Greenish yellow color. On the nose extremely typical with aromas of boxwood, elderflower and anise on a lightly smoky base. On the palate tense, harp cause of if pronounced acidity, fresh, agile and very pleasant.

☐ 92   Price B

Collio Sauvignon de La Tour 2015

100% Sauvignon grapes. Stainless steel on yeasts only. Pale straw yellow color with green reflexes. On the nose intense with a large variety of aromas, boxwood, tomato leaf, an hint of grapefruit, medlar and cedar, brackish note. On the palate nervous, with a good acidity and definitely savory with a finish of great personality.

☐ 90   Price B

Ribolla Gialla Ruttars 2015

100% Ribolla Gialla grapes. Stainless steel only. Light straw yellow color. On the nose aromas of cedar, wildflower alfalfa, with a fragrant and clean. On the palate tense, acidic, agile and thin.

☐ 87   Price B

Collio Pinot Bianco 2015

100% Pinot Bianco grapes. Stainless steel on yeasts. Straw yellow color. On the nose clear with aromas of lychee, white fruits and intense floral scents. On the mouth is elegant with a good acidity and a pleasant finish.

★

VILLA RUSSIZ

Via Russiz, 6
34070 Capriva del Friuli (GO)
Tel. +39 0481 80047
Fax +39 0481 809657
villarussiz@villarussiz.it
www.villarussiz.it
 villarussiz
🐦 *@VillaRussiz*

YEAR OF FOUNDATION 1869
NAME OF THE OWNER Fondazione Villa Russiz
TOTAL BOTTLES PRODUCED 220,000
DIRECT SALES
VISITS TO THE WINERY - RESERVATION NEEDED
HECTARES OF VINEYARD 40

An historic winery owned by the foundation of the same name that also runs the Istituto Cerruti, both born from the heredity left by Count Tedodoro de la Tour who originally owned the estate. The vineyards are in Spessa di Capriva, one of the best areas in the Collio appellation, and the wines have always been technically impeccable.

★★

VISTORTA

Via Vistorta, 82
33077 Sacile (PN)
Tel. +39 0434 782490
vistorta@vistorta.it
www.vistorta.it
🅕 *vistorta*
🐦 *@Vistorta*

YEAR OF FOUNDATION 1800
NAME OF THE OWNER Brandino Brandolini d'Adda
TOTAL BOTTLES PRODUCED 250,000
DIRECT SALES
VISITS TO THE WINERY - RESERVATION NEEDED
HECTARES OF VINEYARD 36
CERTIFIED ORGANIC VITICULTURE

Brandino Brandolini d'Addanis a true countryside gentlmenn. He lives at his estate near the border between Veneto and Friuli, has studied agronomy and enology in the US and France and produces wines of rare finesse. His Merlot, in particular, is one of the most 'Bordeaux-esque' in Italy and yet Italian wine critics often undervalue him.

 90   Price B

Friuli Grave Merlot Vistorta 2013

100% Merlot grapes. Matures in barrique barrels for 18 months. Bordeaux style, the color is dark garnet ruby. The nose complex with aromas of leather, blackcurrant, cassis and an hint of Virginia tobacco. On the palate polite, slightly tannic, savory warm and persistent.

170

★★

VODOPIVEC

Località Colludrozza, 4
34010 Sgonico (TS)
Tel. + 39 040 229181
vodopivec@vodopivec.it
www.vodopivec.it
🅵 *Vodopivec-Vini*

YEAR OF FOUNDATION 1994
NAME OF THE OWNER Paolo Vodopivec
TOTAL BOTTLES PRODUCED 12,000
DIRECT SALES
VISITS TO THE WINERY - RESERVATION NEEDED
HECTARES OF VINEYARD 5

Paolo Vodopivec, Vitovska and the Carso, an extraordinary combination that gives us unique, unmistakable wines that are able to transmit the soul of this hard land and its white grape. This is also possible thanks to meticulous work done in the vineyards which are alberello-trained with over 100,000 vines per hectare and have a yield that rarely reach 500g per plant. In the cellar, Paolo uses not only barrels but also amphorae with great technical skill and intellectual honesty. Long maceration gives density and complexity to his wines and takes nothing away from their aromatic intensity and dynamic tension.

☐ 🄰 **97**   Price C

Solo MM12 2012

100% Vitovska grapes. It ferments for 6 months in amphorae and Matures i big oak barrels. Pale straw yellow color. Every year is better, complex, very energetic. On the nose aromas of salt and pepper to introduce an elegant, very fine but pure steel palate. Dizzing verticality.

☐ **93**   Price B

Origine 2012

100% Vitovska grapes. Matures in oak barrels, straw yellow color with green reflexes. On the nose aromas of citrus and fruits. On the palate true fleshy, but very savory and elegant.

☐ **93**   Price B

Vitovska 2012

100% Vitovska grapes. Matures in amphorae. Straw yellow color with green reflexes. On the nose aromas of peat, white peach and plaster. On the palate austere but juicy and impressively savory.

☐ **91**   Price C

Vitovska T 2012

100% Vitovska grapes. It ferments and matures is amphorae. Straw yellow color with green reflexes. On the nose the aromatic range go from spicy aromas to white fruits and salt. On the palate apparently thin but inexpertly tense and deep.

VOLPE PASINI

Via Cividale, 16 - Frazione Togliano
33040 Torreano (UD)
Tel. +39 0432 715151
Fax +39 0432 715438
info@volpepasini.it
www.volpepasini.net
🅵 *VolpePasiniNews*
🐦 *@volpepasinizuc*

YEAR OF FOUNDATION 1596
NAME OF THE OWNER Emilio Rotolo
TOTAL BOTTLES PRODUCED 350,000
DIRECT SALES
VISITS TO THE WINERY - RESERVATION NEEDED
HECTARES OF VINEYARD 52
HOSPITALITY

When the Calabrian real estate entrepreneur Emilio Rotolo 20 years ago acquired the historic Volpe Pasini estate, with its four centuries of history, many thought he was just out to make a profit and would 'flip' it for quick return. But miracles happen in the world of wine and he fell in love with it and today it is one of the most beautiful and important wines estate in all Friuli. Its vineyards are between Togliano and Prepotto and Rotolo has as his enologist the talented Lorenzo Landi. Now that his oldest son Francesco has joined the wine business, he has also bought the Schiopetto winery. Passion has no limits.

TOTAL BOTTLES PRODUCED 25,000
DIRECT SALES
VISITS TO THE WINERY - RESERVATION NEEDED
HECTARES OF VINEYARD 8

□ 🔲 96   Price B
FCO Sauvignon Zuc di Volpe 2015

100% Sauvignon Blanc grapes. Stainless steel only. Greenish yellow color. On the nose varietal with aromas of exotic fruits, grapefruit and elderflower. On the palate tense, agile, savory, with great acidity to help the notable body. The finish is very persistent.

□ 94   Price B
FCO Pinot Bianco Zuc di Volpe 2015

100% Pinot Bianco grapes. Stainless steel only. Intense and bright straw yellow color. On the nose extremely typical with classic aromas of fresh almond, hawthorn, white peach. On the palate savory, fresh, full-bodied and delicious to drink. Fine and elegant finish.

□ 93   Price B
FCO Ribolla Gialla Zuc di Volpe 2015

100% Ribolla Gialla grapes. Stainless steel only. Light yellow color. On the nose fragrant aromas of wildflowers with citric, lean and whole scents. On the palate tense by a great acidity, nice body, very fresh and delicious to drink.

□ 92   Price B
FCO Pinot Grigio Zuc di Volpe 2015

100% Pinot Grigio grapes. Stainless steel only. Intense straw yellow color. On the nose clean and typical aromas of pear Williams, with a hint of white peach and wildflowers. On the palate savory with a good structure, tense, warm, full-flavored and very long.

★★
ZIDARICH

*Località Prepotto, 23
34011 Duino Aurisina (TS)
Tel. +39 040 201223
Fax +39 040 201223
info@zidarich.it
www.zidarich.it*
 Zidarich

YEAR OF FOUNDATION 1988
NAME OF THE OWNER Benjamin Zidarich

The winery of Benjamin Zidarich is one of the most representative and spectacular in Carso. It has five stories carved out of rick than extend 20m underground Only local materials were used inside and it looks like an underground cathedral complete with arches and columns. It now also houses three magnificent Karst stone vats which Benjamin (whose wines all macerate on the skins) uses to macerate Vitovska. The estate's beautiful terrace surrounded by vineyards and with a spectacular view of the sea towards Grado, several weeks a year this same terrace is turned into an osmitza where one can have lunch sampling the tasty local products.

□ 94   Price B
Vitovska Kamen 2014

100% Vitovska grapes. It macerates for 18 days in Carsica stones (Kamen means 'stone' in Slovenian) vats and 2 years in big durmast barrels. Antic golden color. On the nose present smoky aromas due to the yeasts and maceration, then aromas of honey and quince compote. On the palate full, savory, with a hint of citrus, good tannins, great body. One of the best 'orange wines' on the Italian scene.

□ 93   Price B
Prulke 2013

Blend of 60% Sauvignon, 20% Vitovska, 20% Malvasia Istriana grapes. Matures in oak barrels for 18 months. Intense golden yellow color, slightly opalescent. On the nose smoky due to the yeasts, with aromas of white peach and a little hint of citrus. On the palate tense, full-bodied, savory with a light bitter finish.

ZORZETTIG

*Strada Sant'Anna, 37 - Frazione Spessa
33043 Cividale del Friuli (UD)
Tel. +39 0432 716156
Fax +39 0432 716292*
🅢 *Zorzettig.Cav.Giuseppe*
*info@zorzettigvini.it
www.zorzettigvini.it*
f *ZorzettigVini*
🐦 *@ZorzettigVini*

YEAR OF FOUNDATION **1986**
NAME OF THE OWNER **Zorzettig Family**
TOTAL BOTTLES PRODUCED **800,000**
DIRECT SALES
VISITS TO THE WINERY - RESERVATION NEEDED
HECTARES OF VINEYARD **110**
HOSPITALITY
RESTAURANT
OLIVE OIL PRODUCTION

This is a very important Colli Orientali winery about which too little has been said. It offers a vast range of wines the best of which are in the Myò selection, although all the other wines are good and have an excellent quality/price ratio.

☐ 91   Price B
FCO Sauvignon Myò 2015

100% Sauvignon grapes. Matures in stainless steel on the lees for some months. Intense straw yellow color with light green hues. On the nose wide and a mix of aromas of boxwood, sandal wood, tomato leaf, cedar lychee. On the palate wide, savory, very tasty. Progressive sip and a very intense and wide finish.

☐ 88   Price B
FCO Friulano Myò 2015

100% Friulano grapes. Matures in stainless steel on the lees for some months. Intense straw yellow color. On the nose aromas of pear, light hazelnut, medlar and passion fruit. On the palate intense, with good acidity. The finish is intense with an almond aftertaste.

▪ 86   Price B
FCO Pinot Bianco Myò 2015

100% Pinot Bianco grapes. Matures in stainless steel on the lees for some months. Not too intense straw yellow color. On the nose aromas of white flowers, with light notes of anise and apricot. On the palate savory, average density. Sweet in the beginning and finishes with a slightly bitter taste. Average persistence.

ZUANI

Località Giasbana, 12
34070 San Floriano del Collio (GO)
Tel. +39 0481 391432
Fax +39 0481 393783
info@zuanivini.it

---

www.zuanivini.it
 ZuaniWinery

YEAR OF FOUNDATION **2001**
NAME OF THE OWNER **Patrizia, Antonio and Caterina Felluga**
TOTAL BOTTLES PRODUCED **70,000**
DIRECT SALES
VISITS TO THE WINERY - RESERVATION NEEDED
HECTARES OF VINEYARD **12**
HOSPITALITY

Patrizia Felluga, an important name in Friuli winemaking, has been running her father's estate for years. However, in 2001, she set up her own winery in San Floriano del Collio, just north of Gorizia. And she did it the way she wanted it, with great skill and competence and an equal level of entrepreneurial spirit, involving her children Antonio and Caterina. It produces only two wines, both excellent, using a host of different grape varieties, the way wines used to be made here.

☐ 92   Price B
Collio Bianco Riserva 2013

Blend of Friulano, Chardonnay, Sauvignon and Pinot Grigio grapes in equal parts. Matures 8 months in barrique. Light golden yellow color. On the nose aromas of flint, spices with scents of white peach and almond. On the palate savory, tense, full-bodied, warm and very persistent.

☐ 91   Price B
Collio Bianco Vigne 2015

Blend of Friulano, Chardonnay, Sauvignon and Pinot Grigio grapes in equal parts. Matures in stainless steel on the lees. Intense straw yellow color. On the nose aromas of broom, white peach, medlar, fresh almond and alfalfa. On the palate is warm, savory, pleasant and full-flavored.

LAZIO

The history of winemaking in Lazio has been inconsistent over the centuries with periods of great development alternating with those of decline. Today the region is coming back from a period of decline and is again producing prestigious wines.

The hills in Lazio are of volcanic origin as is evidenced by the presence of its many circular lakes - from Bolsena to Vico, Castel Gandolfo to Nemi - which are once craters. The Etruscans were the first use the volcanic soil to produce wine and were followed by the Latins and the ancient Romans.

Today Lazio produces some 1.36 million hectoliters of wine which is around half of what it produced at the end of the 19th century but it is still more than a few decades ago. The region has 27 DOC classified wines and three DOCG.

Among the areas best suited for winegrowing is the Castelli Romani, which has a DOC appellation that calls for using Trebbiano and Malvasia di Candia grape for the white wines and Sangiovese, Cesanese, Montepulciano, Merlot and Nero Buono for the reds. Frascati is the most emblematic wine for the area, a celebrated white made with Malvasia di Candia, Trebbiano Toscano and Greco. Its sweet version is a DOCG – Cannellino di Frascati DOCG – and there is also a Frascati Superiore DOCG.

Similar grapes are used in the same area to make other DOC wines that, except for some minor differences, have the same organoleptic profile. Among these are Colli Lanuvini, Marino, Colli Albani and Montecompatri Colonna. The area of Velletri is an exception in a sub-zone dominated by whites and produces the red wine Velletri Rosso, a blend of Sangiovese, Montepulciano and Cesanese. The southeast area of Castelli Romani produces whites that are similar to Frascati but are a little more acidic and fruity, while more to the east, where the zone of Ciociaria begins, is the important winemaking area of Cesanese which has two DOC wines – Cesanese d'Affile and Cesanese Olevano Romano - and a DOCG Cesanese del Piglio. These are red wines that can be sweet or semi-sweet and often can seem to be a bit rustic but they have an ancient, 'peasant' charm that makes them so recognizable. Towards the sea is the Agro Pontino agricultural plain – between Terracina, Circeo and Anzio – that was once a giant marsh and was drained in the 1930s to create farmland. Here Trebbiano, Sangiovese and Merlot grapes are cultivated and make wines that recall those of Romagna and Veneto, the regions of origin of those who settled here once it became habitable.

North of Rome is the winemaking area of Cerveteri and then that of Tarquinia where, in a DOC appellation, Trebbiano, Malvasia, Sangiovese and Montepulciano are cultivated. The province of Viterbo is now producing wines from international grapes, from Chardonnay to Grenache and Syrah as well as from the local varieties of Trebbiano, Malvasia, Sangiovese and Montepulciano. The province also hosts the DOC appellations of Lago di Bolsena, Aleatico di Gradoli, a red dessert wines that also comes in a liqueur version, and the famous Est! Est! Est! of Montefiascone.

CONTROLLED AND GUARANTEED DESIGNATION OF ORIGIN (DOCG)

- Cannellino di Frascati or Cannellino
- Cesanese del Piglio
- Frascati Superiore

CONTROLLED DESIGNATION OF ORIGIN (DOC)

- Aleatico di Gradoli, also Liquoroso and Liquoroso Riserva
- Aprilia, also Merlot, Sangiovese, Trebbiano
- Atina Rosso, Atina Rosso Riserva, Atina Cabernet, Atina Cabernet Riserva, Atina Semillon
- Bianco Capena, also Superiore
- Castelli Romani Bianco, Rosato and Rosso
- Cerveteri Bianco (anche Amabile, Frizzante, Secco), Rosato (also Frizzante, Amabile), Rosso (also Amabile, Novello, Secco)
- Cesanese di Affile
- Cesanese di Olevano Romano
- Circeo Bianco, Rosato, Rosso (also Novello), Sangiovese (also Rosato) or Trebbiano
- Colli Albani, also Spumante or Superiore
- Colli della Sabina Bianco (also Frizzante or Spumante), Rosato (also Frizzante), Rosso (also Frizzante, Novello or Spumante)
- Colli Etruschi Viterbesi Bianco, Canaiolo, Grechetto Bianco, Grechetto Rosso, Merlot, Moscatello (also Passito), Novello, Procanico, Rosato, Rossetto, Rosso, Sangiovese Rosato, Violone
- Colli Lanuvini, also Superiore
- Cori Bianco or Rosso
- Est! Est!! Est!!! di Montefiascone, also Spumante
- Frascati, also Novello, Spumante or Superiore
- Genazzano Bianco or Rosso
- Marino, also Spumante or Superiore
- Montecompatri Colonna, also Superiore
- Nettuno
- Roma, with or without Classico (except Romanella spumante)
- Tarquinia, Bianco (Secco, Amabile or Frizzante), Rosato, Rosso (Secco, Amabile or Novello)
- Terracina or Moscato di Terracina
- Velletri Bianco (also Superiore) or Rosso (also Riserva)
- Vignanello Bianco (also Superiore), Greco (also Spumante), Rosato, Rosso (also Novello or Riserva)
- Zagarolo, also Superiore

AND ALSO:

- Orvieto, also Classico, Superiore or Classico Superiore, Doc both in Lazio and Umbria

MARCO CARPINETI

S.P. Velletri-Anzio, km 14,300
04010 Cori (LT)
Tel. +39 06 9679860
info@marcocarpineti.com
www.marcocarpineti.com
f MARCO-CARPINETI

YEAR OF FOUNDATION **1986**
NAME OF THE OWNER **Marco Carpineti**
TOTAL BOTTLES PRODUCED **300,000**
DIRECT SALES
VISITS TO THE WINERY - RESERVATION NEEDED
HECTARES OF VINEYARD **52**
CERTIFIED ORGANIC VITICULTURE
OLIVE OIL PRODUCTION

Carpineti's vineyards are in Cori, some 60km from Rome, on the slopes of the Lepini Hills. Together with his son Paolo, Marco Carpinetti produces quality wines following organic and at times biodynamic methods. Their production uses native grapes and care is taken to bring out their best qualities. These include Nero Buono, Greco Moro, Greco and Greco Giallo but most of all Bellone which is today used to make the sparkling wine Kius. From this year they produce a sparkling wine from Nero Buono grapes which becomes an extra brut of great charme: the Kius rosé.

回 **91**　　　　　　　　　　Price B
Kius rosé 2012

100% Nero Buono grapes. Classic method. Extra brut. Light onion peel color. Notes of nuts, incense, candied citrus, powder and medicinal herbs. On the palate it's fresh and full bodied with great agility and savory. Long finish of candied citrus, flint and smoky hints.

回 **90**　　　　　　　　👍 Price A
Kius 2013

100% Bellone grapes. Classic method. Deep straw yellow. Intense notes of herbs and citrus, underbrush and ripe fruits. Great balance and creamy on the palate, fresh and good citrusy and eucalyptus persistence.

☐ **86**　　　　　　　　👍 Price A
Capolemole 2015

Blend of Bellone and Greco Moro grapes. Stainless

steel only. Chalky and intense exotic fruit aromas on the nose, citrus and aromatic herbs, sage on top. Juicy and pleasant on the palate, fresh and easy to drink.

CASALE DEL GIGLIO

Strada Cisterna - Nettuno Km 13
04100 Latina (LT)
Tel. +39 06 92902530
info@casaledelgiglio.it
www.casaledelgiglio.it
f CasaledelGiglioVini
🐦 @CasaleGiglio

YEAR OF FOUNDATION **1967**
NAME OF THE OWNER **Antonio Santarelli**
TOTAL BOTTLES PRODUCED **1,276,600**
DIRECT SALES
VISITS TO THE WINERY - RESERVATION NEEDED
HECTARES OF VINEYARD **164**
OLIVE OIL PRODUCTION

The Casale del Giglio story began in Piazza Caparinica and with a Vini & Olii (wines and Oil) shop and grew to become one of the biggest wine realities in the region with 1.3 million bottles produced a year. The estate was where Antonio Santarelli used to spend his weekends as a boy but it later became his job when, at 25, he joined his father Dino on the farm. Having previous been a swamp, the land had no winemaking past and was virgin territory which allowed them to embark on a vast wine project that included planting some 60 experimental grape varieties with the collaboration of researchers and ampelographers. Enologist Paolo Tiefenthaler was in charge of the winery and production centered on international grapes although in more recent years they have been experimenting with indigenous ones like Biancolla and Bellone.

◼ **91**　　　　　　　　　Price B
Mater Matuta 2013

85% Syrah and 15% Petit Verdot grapes. Matures 22-24 months in new barrique. Dark ruby color. Thick notes of chocolate and cocoa, black cherry and sweet spices. Great structure on the palate but with a fresh and juicy note that makes it dynamic. Eucalyptus, fruity and roasting notes in the long finish.

☐ 88   👍 Price A
Faro della Guardia 2015

100% Biancolella grapes. Stainless steel for 6 months. Intense and fruity aromas, hints of yellow peach, hawthorn and pennyroyal. Briny on the palate, it finishes with a long citrusy trail.

■ 87   Price B
Madreselva 2013

Blend of 40% Cabernet Sauvignon, 30% Petit Verdot, 30% Merlot grapes. Matures 18-20 months in new barrique. Ruby red. Herbs and flowers on the nose. Hints of juniper, herbs and wild cherries. Soft and eucalyptus on the palate with good tannins.

CASALE DELLA IORIA

Piazza R. Margherita, 1
03010 Acuto (FR)
Tel. +39 0775 56031
Ⓢ *p.perinelli*
info@casaledellaioria.com
www.casaledellaioria.com
🅕 *Casale-della-Ioria*
🐦 *@paolo_perinelli*

YEAR OF FOUNDATION **1921**
NAME OF THE OWNER **Paolo Perinelli**
TOTAL BOTTLES PRODUCED **60,000**
DIRECT SALES
VISITS TO THE WINERY - RESERVATION NEEDED
HECTARES OF VINEYARD **38**
OLIVE OIL PRODUCTION

Paolo Perinelli grows his own grapes in Ciociaria, in the heart of the Cesanese appellation, at an altitude of 400m above sea level. His vineyards are surrounded by forests and olive groves and his grandfather was already making wine there in the 1920s. Paolo cultivates local grapes, first among them Cesanese, of which he is a great expert, along with Passerina and Olivella, the latter being a variety that was almost forgotten. This year, together with the Campo Novo, his top Cesanese del Piglio Riserva Torre del Piano is back.

■ 92   Price B
Cesanese del Piglio Superiore
Torre del Piano Riserva 2013

100% Cesanese d'Affile grapes. Matures in durmast

oak barrels. Dark ruby color. Intense, deep and warm notes of roasting, cocoa and tobacco. Rich and juicy on the palate, fresh, good tannins and sweet finish with spicy and fruity hints.

■ 90   Price A
Cesanese del Piglio Superiore
Tenuta della Ioria 2015

100% Cesanese d'Affile grapes. Matures in stainless steel and oak barrels. Bright ruby red. Intense notes of red fruits, wild cherries, violets, wild herbs and cinchona. Balanced, tense, agile and elegant on the palate. Morello cherry and sweet spices. Great progression and good persistent finish.

■ 87   👍 Price A
Cesanese del Piglio Campo Novo 2014

100% Cesanese d'Affile grapes. Stainless steel. Light ruby red. Flowery bouquet, elegant spices, cloves. Agile and tense, fresh and easy to drink.

CASALE MARCHESE

Via di Vermicino, 68
00044 Frascati (RM)
Tel. +39 06 9408932
Fax +39 06 9408932
Ⓢ *casale.marchese*
info@casalemarchese.it
www.casalemarchese.it
🅕 *casale.marchese*
🐦 *@CasaleMarchese*

YEAR OF FOUNDATION **1713**
NAME OF THE OWNER **Carletti Family**
TOTAL BOTTLES PRODUCED **150,000**
DIRECT SALES
VISITS TO THE WINERY - RESERVATION NEEDED
HECTARES OF VINEYARD **40**
OLIVE OIL PRODUCTION

The olive trees and vineyards are over 100 years old, the soil is volcanic and the love for winemaking has been handed down generation to generation. The Carletti family was originally from Orvieto and came here in the 19th century, acquiring an ancient estate that was cited in document from the time of Pope Boniface VII. Although they came from humble origins, their ancestors included two cardinals including Clemente Micara to whom they have dedicated one of their estate's wines, Clemens. Aside from the grapes common to Frascati, they have recently cultivated some international ones, from Chardonnay to Cabernet.

Fabrizio Bono. This year we're missing the top white wine Donna Adriana, still maturing, and the Muffa Nobile.

☐ 87   Price B
Clemens 2014

Blend of Malvasia del Lazio and Chardonnay grapes. Stainless steel. Straw yellow color. Edgy and clear notes of aromatic herbs, ginger and blossoms. Fresh and briny on the palate, dynamic body and herbs on the slightly bitter finish.

☐ 86   Price A
Cannellino di Frascati Cannellino di Frascati 2014

Blend of Malvasia del Lazio and Trebbiano Toscano grapes. Stainless steel. Intense straw yellow. Sweet citrus and peach notes on the nose, wild herbs and ripe yellow fruit. Sweet on the palate but the residual sugar is balanced by the freshness and it finishes with sugary notes, apricot and honey.

■ 89   Price B
I Quattro Mori 2012

Blend of 40% Shiraz, 30% Cabernet Sauvignon, 20% Merlot and 10% Petit Verdot grapes. 18 months in barrique. Light ruby red. Austere and enveloping notes on the nose with eucalyptus hints, mint and eucalyptus, coca, leather and dark fruits. Tannic and velvety on the palate with hints of rhubarb and hummus. Long eucalyptus finish.

☐ 87   Price A
Frascati Superiore 2014

Blend of Malvasia del Lazio, Trebbiano Giallo and Bombino grapes. Intense straw yellow. Ripe fruit, pineapple and ginger, citrusy, chocolate. Fresh, fragrant and briny on the palate with a long ripe fruit finish.

CASTEL DE PAOLIS

Via Val De Paolis, snc
00046 Grottaferrata (RM)
Tel. +39 06 9413648
Fax +39 06 9413648
info@casteldepaolis.it
www.casteldepaolis.it

YEAR OF FOUNDATION **1993**
NAME OF THE OWNER **Giulio and Adriana Santarelli**
TOTAL BOTTLES PRODUCED **80,000**
DIRECT SALES
VISITS TO THE WINERY - RESERVATION NEEDED
HECTARES OF VINEYARD **11**
RESTAURANT
OLIVE OIL PRODUCTION

Castel De Paolis was built on some Roman ruins and still today the aging barrels are kept in what once was an ancient Roman cistern. The estate has expanded, thanks also the research done by Attilio Scienza, and today it is a point of reference in the Lazio winemaking scene as a virtuous example of how to make wines that are clean, full of personality and well-made. The wines are made using both regional varieties and international ones. The estate is owned by Giulio Santarelli and his wife Adriana who are kind and hospitable as is their enologist

CINCINNATO

Via Cori - Cisterna, 23 - Km 2
04010 Cori (LT)
Tel. +39 06 9679380
Fax +39 06 9677473
info@cincinnato.it
www.cincinnato.it
 vinicincinnato
 cincinnatovini

YEAR OF FOUNDATION **1974**
NAME OF THE OWNER
TOTAL BOTTLES PRODUCED **600,000**
DIRECT SALES
VISITS TO THE WINERY
HECTARES OF VINEYARD **400**
HOSPITALITY
RESTAURANT
OLIVE OIL PRODUCTION

The estate's logo is a depiction of Cincinnatus, the Roman consul who after defeating the Aequians rather than exploiting his power and popularity preferred to return to work his land. A virtuous symbol for this cooperative of 255 members that in the area of Cori produces local wines with an eye on maintaining an excellent quality/price ration and using indigenous grapes.

87 👍 Price A
Ercole 2013
100% Nero Buono grapes. Matures in used barrique for 12 months. Dark ruby red. Spicy notes, underbrush and eucalyptus shades, bark and pepper. Rich and juicy on the palate.

☐ **85** 👍 Price A
Castore 2015
100% Bellone grapes. Straw yellow. Flowers and yellow fruit aromas. Elegant flavors and briny on the palate with average freshness. Simple but pleasant.

brush, hummus, ripe red fruits on the nose. Good body and tannin, nice acidity and long fruity finish.

89 👍 Price A
Cesanese di Olevano Romano Superiore Silene 2014
Blend of 70% Cesanese d'Affile, 30% Cesanese comune grapes. Matures 12 months in concrete vats. Ruby red. Intense and sunny on the nose. Notes of sweet blackberry and raspberry, spices and flowers. Tense, juicy and sharp on the palate. It finishes spicy and flowery.

CIOLLI

Via del Corso, snc
00035 Olevano Romano (RM)
Tel. +39 06 9563334
info@damianociolli.it
www.damianociolli.it

YEAR OF FOUNDATION **2000**
NAME OF THE OWNER **Damiano Ciolli**
TOTAL BOTTLES PRODUCED **25,000**
DIRECT SALES
VISITS TO THE WINERY - RESERVATION NEEDED
HECTARES OF VINEYARD **5**

Damiano Ciolli is a winemaker in Olevano Romano who likes to experiment. Olevano is a small medieval village that sits at an altitude of 600m above sea level on Monte Celeste southeast of Rome. And Daniele is also an enterprising young man with clear ideas who in 2001, together with his father Costantino decided to bottle his own wine with grapes from an old vineyard that his grandfather planted in 1953. It is this vineyards that produces the estate cru Cirsium, the older brother of Silene, the second Cesanese d'Affile this small winery makes from its six-hectares of vineyards. They are both examples of authentic Cesanese wine and both distinguished by a rustic elegance, both with a strong and distinguished personality, expression of a territory and of a unique producer like Damiano.

92 Price B
Cesanese di Olevano Romano Cirsium 2012
100% Cesanese d'Affile grapes. Matures 1 year in big barrels, 1 year in concrete. Ruby red. Under-

⭐⭐
COLETTI CONTI

Via Vittorio Emanuele, 116
03012 Anagni (FR)
Tel. +39 389 9009900
coletticonti@gmail.com
www.coletticonti.it
📘 *ColettiI-Conti-Azienda-Agricola*

YEAR OF FOUNDATION **1850**
NAME OF THE OWNER **Anton Maria Coletti Conti**
TOTAL BOTTLES PRODUCED **45,000**
DIRECT SALES
VISITS TO THE WINERY - RESERVATION NEEDED
HECTARES OF VINEYARD **16**

Anton Maria Coletti Conti has a smiling face and a small gift: the ability to immediately put at ease anyone with his anecdotes and stories. With his sunny disposition and exuberant personality, he has decided to tame a grape like Cesanese which can be difficult and unpredictable, sometimes even surly. However, once it has been 'domesticated' it can produce surprising wines that stand out for their elegance and complexity.

90 Price B
Cosmato 2014
100% Cabernet Franc. Matures 15 months in Allier barrique. Dark ruby color. Strawberry jam and vegetal notes on the nose. Juicy and pulpy on the palate with a long finish of wild strawberries, herbs and spices.

89 Price B
Cesanese del Piglio Romanico 2014
100% Cesanese d'Affile grapes. Matures 15 months

in Allier barrique. Bright ruby red. Ripe fruit and herbs on the nose. Warm and full-bodied on the palate, notes of ripe fruits and eucalyptus hints, cassis and black cherries in the finish.

■ 87   Price A
Cesanese del Piglio Superiore Hernicus 2014

100% Cesanese d'Affile grapes. Matures 12 months in Allier barrique. Ruby red. Red rose and red berries, raspberries on top, on the nose. Tense and agile on the palate, with a juicy finish of red berries.

★★
COLLE PICCHIONI

*Via Colle Picchione, 46 - Località Frattocchie
00040 Marino (RM)
Tel. +39 06 93546329*
🅢 *colle picchioni valerio*
info@collepicchioni.it
www.collepicchioni.it
🅕 *Colle-Picchioni*
🐦 *@collepicchioni*

YEAR OF FOUNDATION 1976
NAME OF THE OWNER Armando and Valerio Di Mauro
TOTAL BOTTLES PRODUCED 90,000
DIRECT SALES
VISITS TO THE WINERY - RESERVATION NEEDED
HECTARES OF VINEYARD 10
RESTAURANT

Between the sea and Lake Albano, and thus near Castegandolfo, there is a small plot of land which was acquired by Paola Di Mauro so she could have a weekend retreat to get away from the city. But that plot of land that was only a few kilometers from Rome soon turned into a passion and she left her previous occupation and dedicated herself to making wine. Since 1985, her son Armando has been in charge of the winery and now even her grandson Valerio has entered the family business. This year we're missing their wines Il Vassallo and Le Vignole, both still in barrique: they will be ready to be bottled only in a few months.

■ 90   👍 Price A
Perlaia 2015

Blend of 35% Merlot, 35% Sangiovese, 30% Caber-

net Sauvignon grapes. Dark ruby red, black fruits, blueberries and cherries on the nose. Then eucalyptus notes, mint and cocoa. Warm and juicy on the palate, fresh and of good length with fruits and spices.

☐ 87   👍 Price A
Donna Paola 2015

Blend of 60% Malvasia Puntinata, 20% Trebbiano, 20% Semillon grapes. Stainless steel only. Almost golden straw yellow. Herbs and aromatic notes, hints of maple, boxwood, ginger and wild herbs. Savory and sulphureus on the palate, agile and with a citrusy and herbal finish.

★
COMINIUM

*Via S. Ritinto, snc
03041 Alvito (FR)
Tel. +39 0776 510683
Fax +39 0776 510683
armando@cantinacominium.it
www.cantinacominium.it*
🅕 *cantina.cominium*
🐦 *@cantinacominium*

YEAR OF FOUNDATION 1999
NAME OF THE OWNER Maria and Armando Pinto
TOTAL BOTTLES PRODUCED 90,000
DIRECT SALES
VISITS TO THE WINERY - RESERVATION NEEDED
HECTARES OF VINEYARD 28
CERTIFIED ORGANIC VITICULTURE
OLIVE OIL PRODUCTION

This little gem is in the heart of Val Comino, in lower Lazio. It is a family-run estate and siblings Armando and Maria Pinto run it with passion and have been able to achieve surprising levels of quality. They are also responsible for bringing back the indigenous grape Maturano, which was added to the National Registry of Grape Varieties in 2010. Thanks to the expert advice of enologist Roberto Mazzer, the Pinto family has in a short time become one of the best winemakers in the region.

■ 92   Price B
Atina Cabernet Riserva 2013

Blend of 85% Cabernet Sauvignon and 15% Merlot. Matures in barrique. Intense and multicolored bouquet of black cherry, delicate smoky notes and eu-

calyptus hints. Rich, full bodied on the palate, great progression, red fruits, ripe plum and vegetal hints. Incredibly long finish.

☐ 92   👍 Price A
Maturano 2015

100% Maturano grapes. Stainless steel only. Intense aromas of juicy white peach, medlar, then spicy white pepper and a touch of ginger. Fresh, tense, again white fruits and spicy puffs on the palate. Balanced and savory. Very long finish.

★
PAOLO E NOEMIA D'AMICO

Località Palombaro - Località Vaiano
01024 Castiglione In Teverina (VT)
Tel. +39 06 84561471; Vaiano +39 0761 948034
info@damicowines.it
www.paoloenoemiadamico.it
🔲 Paolo-e-Noemia-dAmico
🐦 @damicowines

YEAR OF FOUNDATION 1985
NAME OF THE OWNER Paolo and Noemia d'Amico
TOTAL BOTTLES PRODUCED 130,000
DIRECT SALES
VISITS TO THE WINERY - RESERVATION NEEDED
HECTARES OF VINEYARD 30
OLIVE OIL PRODUCTION

The beautiful estate of Paolo and Noemia d'Amico is situated at the heart of the Viterbo area of Tuscia, amid cliffs and ravines. Paolo comes from a family of ship owners while she is a Brazilian from Rio de Janeiro and here in this corner of Lazio they created a solid estate in 1985 that each year stands out for producing seductive and excellent quality wines. Calanchi (Ravines) and Falesie (Cliffs) are two excellent Chardonnay that are sulfurous and full of character, true Lazio pearls. Among their reds the Atlante stands out, a Cabernet Franc wine, last wine to be produced in the upper Lazio winery.

☐ 92   👍 Price A
Calanchi 2015

100% Chardonnay grapes. Matures 8 months in stainless steel. Straw yellow color. Stony and citrusy aromas with hints of flint and white pepper, pineapple and yellow fruits. On the palate it's agile and juicy, thin and dynamic, tense and with a long citrusy finish.

☐ 91   Price B
Falesia 2014

100% Chardonnay grapes. Matures for 10 months in new and used barrique. Golden straw yellow color. Notes of candied citrus and papaya, earthy sensations and aromatic herbs. Pulp and structure on the palate, juicy and citrusy with a savory and smoky finish.

■ 89   Price B
Atlante 2012

100% Cabernet Franc grapes. Matures 12 months in barrique. Dark ruby red. Flowery and fruity notes of red berries, hints of marzipan, underbrush and spices. Sumptuous, tannic, herbal and spicy on the palate.

DE SANCTIS

Via Pietraporzia, 50
00100 Frascati (RM)
Tel. +39 340 3962771
desanctisluigi@yahoo.it
www.frascati-wine.com
🔲 De-Sanctis-bio

YEAR OF FOUNDATION 1816
NAME OF THE OWNER De Sanctis Family
TOTAL BOTTLES PRODUCED 100,000
DIRECT SALES
VISITS TO THE WINERY - RESERVATION NEEDED
HECTARES OF VINEYARD 10
CERTIFIED ORGANIC VITICULTURE

This organic estate is only a few kilometers from Rome in the ancient area of Lake Regillo, near Frascati. Luigi De Sanctis and his son Francesco cultivate typical local varieties and produce some excellent Frascati wine. The oldest vines are between 55 and 45 years old while others were planted in 1991. We tasted their 496, named after the year of the battle between the Romans and the Latin League on Lake Regillo, as well as their showcase Frascati, Amacos.

☐ 92   👍 Price A
Amacos 2014

Blend of Malvasia Puntinata and Bombino Bianco grapes. Matures 6 months in used barrique. Golden yellow color. Still a little too woody on the nose but an explosion of sensations: aromatic herbs, honey, beeswax, macaroon, ripe fruit. Savory and fresh on the palate, long tail on citrusy hints and apricot.

☐ 91   👍 Price A

Frascati 496 2015

Blend of Malvasia di Candia and Trebbiano Toscano grapes. Stainless steel only. Straw yellow color. Notes of aromatic herbs, boxwood, laurel and light shades of citrus and white flowers. Juicy on the palate, sharp and savory with a pleasant citrusy finish and light smoky notes.

★★★

FALESCO

S.S. Cassia Nord km 94,155
01027 Montefiascone (VT)
Tel. +39 0761 827032 - +39 0744 9556
Fax +39 0761 827032 - +39 0744 951219
info@falesco.it
www.falesco.it
 FalescoOfficial
🐦 *@FalescoOfficial*

YEAR OF FOUNDATION 1979
NAME OF THE OWNER Renzo and Riccardo Cotarella
TOTAL BOTTLES PRODUCED 3,000,000
DIRECT SALES
VISITS TO THE WINERY
HECTARES OF VINEYARD 390

This is the estate of siblings Renzo and Roberto Cotarella. Neither they nor the colossus they have created between Lazio and Umbria need any introduction. One need only look at Montiano, considered to be one of Italy's greatest Merlot. Then there is Roscetto, a local variety that was brought back through intense research and is now used in a number of wines of which Ferentano is the most famous. Their estate, created in Montefiascone in 1979, now produces a host of different wines and is gradually being taken over by the all-female second generations, Dominga is Riccardo's daughter and Enrica and Marta are Enzo's daughters.

☐ 🔲 95   👍 Price A

Soente 2015

100% Viogner grapes harvested in three different moments of ripeness. Stainless steel only. Bright straw yellow. Attractive on the nose with exotic fruits, light aromatic and smoky hints and some touches of fresh almond. Briny, tense, full-bodied,

very Mediterranean, warm but not heavy, strong and silky at the same time, great personality. Formidable persistent finish.

■ 93   Price B

Montiano 2014

100% Merlot grapes. Matures 12 months in barrique. Bright and intense ruby red. Notes of raspberries and framboise liquor, then hints of cocoa, vanilla and tobacco. Strong and tense flavor, agile, lighter than other vintages but elegant and dynamic. Warm and savory finish.

■ 92   Price B

Marciliano 2012

Blend of 70% Cabernet Sauvignon and 30% Merlot grapes. Matures 18 months in barrique. Very intense ruby red. Typical and clear notes of blackberry, new oak, tobacco and kirsch. Rich flavor, pleasantly briny, tannic and full bodied.

■ 91   👍 Price A

Tellus Syrah 2015

100% Syrah grapes. Matures 5 months in used barrique. Bright and intense ruby red. Delicious aromas of spices and kirsch, light but enveloping notes of cocoa, vanilla and currant. Smooth, pleasant, easy to drink, warm, briny and of great length. A perfect wine for its price category.

■ 88   👍 Price A

Vitiano Rosso 2015

Blend of Sangiovese, Merlot and Cabernet Sauvignon grapes. Matures 3 months in used barrique. Notes of cassis, hints of wet soil and intense and enveloping vanilla shades. Rich flavor, well sustained by acidity, full bodied and progressive.

FEDERICI

Via Santa Apollaria Vecchia, 30
00039 Zagarolo (RM)
Tel. + 39 06 95461022
Fax +39 06 95461184
info@vinifederici.com
www.vinifederici.com
📘 *aziendavinicola.federici*

YEAR OF FOUNDATION 1966
NAME OF THE OWNER Antonio Federici
TOTAL BOTTLES PRODUCED 200,000
DIRECT SALES
VISITS TO THE WINERY - RESERVATION NEEDED
HECTARES OF VINEYARD 35

181

CERTIFIED ORGANIC VITICULTURE
OLIVE OIL PRODUCTION

A Castelli Romani estate in Zagarola, Federici has expanded over the years and improved its products thanks to targeted research aimed at quality using modern machinery while, at the same time, respecting the estate's philosophy: look to the future and innovate with a firm footing in solid and robust traditions. The young Damiano Federici, who represents the new generation, adheres to this philosophy and his Cesanese Nunc is a fine example.

☐ 88   Price B
Cesanese del Piglio Superiore Nunc 2013
100% Cesanese d'Affile grapes. Matures 18 months in barrique. Deep ruby red. Intense aromas of wild berries, spices and eucalyptus notes. Powerful on the palate with coherent sensations with the nose and a cocoa and roasting finish.

★★
FONTANA CANDIDA

Via Fontana Candida, 11
00078 Monte Porzio Catone (RM)
Tel. +39 06 9401881
Fax +39 06 9448591
fontanacandida@giv.it
www.fontanacandida.it
 FontanaCandida
 @FontanaCandida

YEAR OF FOUNDATION 1958
NAME OF THE OWNER Gruppo Italiano Vini SPA
TOTAL BOTTLES PRODUCED 3,700,000
DIRECT SALES
VISITS TO THE WINERY - RESERVATION NEEDED
HECTARES OF VINEYARD 97

Fontana Candida is synonymous with Frascati and has been fundamental in making this wine popular throughout the world. Loved by Marco Porzio Catone and many popes, the wine is the paradigm of Lazio and on special occasions in the past it would flow from Rome's fountains "to the great joy of the people and men and women of all ages who gladly drank their fill from bottles and cups ". This great Lazio producer has given prestige to a wine that until recently was mistreated and improved its image

also thanks to wines of unquestioned quality like Vigneto Santa Teresa and Luna Mater, wine of impressive longevity.

☐ 📷 95   👍 Price A
Frascati Superiore Luna Mater Ris. 2015
Blend of Malvasia di Candia, Malvasia del Lazio, Greco and Bombino grapes. Part of the grapes ferment in oak. Straw yellow color. Mediterranean and aromatic notes with hints of sage, exotic fruit, Williams pear and flowers. Chalky and rich on the palate, savory and fruity with a pleasant bitter finish.

☐ 87   👍 Price A
Frascati Superiore Vigneto Santa Teresa 2015
Blend of Malvasia di Candia, Malvasia Puntinata, Trebbiano and Greco grapes. Stainless steel only. Straw yellow color. Intense notes of ripe fuit. Nice sweet fruits in the mouth and Mediterranean richness. Freshness and exotic fruits in the finish.

GIANGIROLAMI

Via del Cavaliere, 1414 - Borgo Mantello
04100 Latina (LT)
Tel. +39 0773458626
Fax +39 0773458626
info@donatogiangirolami.it
www.donatogiangirolami.it
 AziendaAgricolaDonatoGiangirolami
 AzDGiangirolami

YEAR OF FOUNDATION 1980
NAME OF THE OWNER Donato Giangirolami
TOTAL BOTTLES PRODUCED 80,000
DIRECT SALES
VISITS TO THE WINERY - RESERVATION NEEDED
HECTARES OF VINEYARD 38
HOSPITALITY
CERTIFIED ORGANIC VITICULTURE

The estate of Donato Giangirolami, founded by his father Dante, has been producing organic wines since 1993. It is located in Cori, in the Castelli Romani, and fruit is grown there along with wine grapes. And so you can find kiwi growing next to Malvasia and Grechetto di Todi, as well as some international varieties and all thisn allows him to produce a varied selection of wine of which the whites are the best.

☐ 87   👍 Price A

Propizio 2015

100% Grechetto di Todi grapes. Straw yellow color. Pleasantly aromatic nose with hints of sage and maple, together with jasmine flowers and citrus. Dynamic on the palate, again citrusy notes. Agile, fresh and delicate.

MARCELLA GIULIANI

Via Anticolana - Località Vico
03012 Anagni (FR)
Tel. +39 335 5376977
m.giulianivinibio@libero.it
www.aziendaagricolamarcellagiuliani.it

YEAR OF FOUNDATION **2002**
NAME OF THE OWNER **Marcella Giuliani**
TOTAL BOTTLES PRODUCED **7,000**
VISITS TO THE WINERY - RESERVATION NEEDED
HECTARES OF VINEYARD **10**
CERTIFIED ORGANIC VITICULTURE
OLIVE OIL PRODUCTION

A small farm managed by a lady that strongly feels "the calling of her roots". The farm, in fact, comes from a large estate property of the family since 1870, that slowly refined its own cultivations until specializing prevalently in arboreus cultivations (vineyards, olive plantations) and limited use of phytochemicals and fertilizers, becoming a certified organic farm.

■ 90   Price B

Cesanese del Piglio Dives Riserva 2010

100% Cesanese di Affile grapes. Matures 12 months in new French barrique. Compact ruby red. Intense on the nose, dark, pleasant note of red orange, then the typical wild cherry and plum. Fruity and smooth on the palate, with pleasant spiciness and balanced tannins.

■ 86   Price A

Cesanese del Piglio Superiore Alagna 2015

100% Cesanese di Affile grapes. Stainless steel only. Ruby red. Warm and clean on the nose, nice fruitiness that comes back on the palate. Average body and acidity. Average length in the finish.

★

LA VISCIOLA

Via Carcassano, snc
03010 Piglio (FR)
Tel. +39 0775 501950
macciocca.piero@libero.it

YEAR OF FOUNDATION **2005**
NAME OF THE OWNER **Rosa Alessandri and Piero Macciocca**
TOTAL BOTTLES PRODUCED **6,000**
DIRECT SALES
VISITS TO THE WINERY - RESERVATION NEEDED
HECTARES OF VINEYARD **2**
CERTIFIED BIODYNAMIC VITICULTURE

If there is an authentic 'vigneron de garage' in Lazio then it is Piero Macciocca who produces his small wine gems, obtained through biodynamic winegrowing, is a small winery that looks like an underground garage. He makes several versions of Cesanese del Piglio and a white wine from Passerina, only a thousand or so bottles, perhaps less, of each type. His wines are a find and should be discovered by going to visit him. He and his family are worth meeting.

■ 91   Price B

Cesanese del Piglio Priore Mozzatta 2014

100% Cesanese grapes. Ages in different sized casks. Deep black color. Intense notes of fruit, bergamot and black currant. Not as rich as usual on the palate due to the not easy vintage but elegant and deep anyways.

■ 88   Price B

Cesanese del Piglio Priore Ju Quarto 2014

100% Cesanese grapes. Ages in different sized casks. Deep black color. Delicate fruity notes on the nose almost covered by graphite and cinchona. Fragrant on the palate, savory with nice tannins. Intense citrusy finish.

■ 87   Price B

Cesanese del Piglio Priore Vignali 2014

100% Cesanese grapes. Ages in different sized casks. Deep black color. The aromas are still austere but we can perceive citrus and cinchona. Fresh on the palate, not powerful, agile and with a juicy finish.

★★

SERGIO MOTTURA

Località Poggio della Costa, 1
01020 Civitella D'agliano (VT)
Tel. +39 0761 914533
Fax +39 0761 1810100
vini@motturasergio.it
www.motturasergio.it
 f *motturasergio*
 𝕏 *@MotturaSergio*

YEAR OF FOUNDATION 1933
NAME OF THE OWNER Sergio Mottura
TOTAL BOTTLES PRODUCED **95,000**
DIRECT SALES
VISITS TO THE WINERY - RESERVATION NEEDED
HECTARES OF VINEYARD **37**
HOSPITALITY
RESTAURANT
CERTIFIED ORGANIC VITICULTURE

The historic Mottura estate is situated near the border between Lazio and Umbria, in an area where wine has been made for ages. It is an organic estate and the consistent and consolidated quality of the wines has made it one of the pearls of Lazio. Here in Civitella d'Agliano, Sergio, together with his children and amid the porcupines – the estate's ecological symbol, an icon of an organic and natural habitat – and the tuff stone, he makes his wines and blends his bubbly. This year to gether with the always good Tragugnano, the Orvieto wine of the winery, the La Tour a Civitella (their wood aged grechetto) is back. to pair his stainless steel refined brother, the Poggio della Costa.

☐ 93   Price B
Latour a Civitella 2014

100% Grechetto grapes. Ages 9 months in barrique and 6 months in stainless steel. Intense yellow color. Very intense notes of ripe yellow fruit and nice aromatic bouquet. Full bodied , great impact on the palate and elegant. Savory and long finish.

☐ 91   👍 Price B
Poggio della Costa 2015

100% Grechetto grapes. Stainless steel only. Straw yellow color. Intense notes of fruit and aromatic herbs, peach, apple and sage. Fresh on the palate, great balance ad with a long and pleasant aromatic finish.

ÔMINA ROMANA

Via del Gesù, 62
00186 Velletri (RM)
Tel. 06 9643 0193
Fax 06 9643 0193
info@ominaromana.com
www.ominaromana.com
 f *ominaromana*
 𝕏 *@ominaromana*

YEAR OF FOUNDATION 2007
NAME OF THE OWNER Katharina Börner
TOTAL BOTTLES PRODUCED **120,000**
DIRECT SALES
VISITS TO THE WINERY - RESERVATION NEEDED
HECTARES OF VINEYARD **60**
OLIVE OIL PRODUCTION

A good omen – from the Latin omina – and a phoenix that rises from the ashes compose the estate's logo. The ashes are the volcanic ones of Velletri where entrepreneur Anton Borner had to the intuition to foresee the potential this area had to produce exceptional wines. Cutting-edge technology, experimentation and precise vision are today producing excellent results.

■ 93   Price D
Cabernet Franc 2013

100% Cabernet Franc grapes. Matures 12 months in French oak barrique. Ruby color. Elegant aromas with complex intense spiciness, rhubarb and ripe fruit. Tense, juicy, rich and incredibly long on the palate.

☐ 92   Price C
Chardonnay Ars Magna 2013

100% Chardonnay grapes. Matures 8-10 months in barrique. Straw yellow. Flowery and intense notes of cedar, mimosa, broom and incense. Wide and full bodied on the palate but with a dynamic acidity and savory. Great progression and persistent finish.

☐ 90   Price B
Chardonnay 2014

100% Chardonnay grapes. Ferments and matures part in stainless steel and part in barrique. Straw yellow. Vertical and flowery nose. On the palate it's fresh and tense with notes of ripe fruit and eucalyptus hints. Well supported by good acidity and savory finish.

ANTONELLA PACCHIAROTTI

Via Roma, 65
01025 Grotte Di Castro (VT)
Tel. +39 339 2216719
vinipacchiarotti@gmail.com
www.vinipacchiarotti.it
f Vini-Pacchiarotti

YEAR OF FOUNDATION 1998
NAME OF THE OWNER Antonella Pacchiarotti
TOTAL BOTTLES PRODUCED 10,000
DIRECT SALES
VISITS TO THE WINERY - RESERVATION NEEDED
HECTARES OF VINEYARD 3.5
OLIVE OIL PRODUCTION

Antonello Pacchiarotti has the bright look of someone who tackles life with enthusiasm and good cheer. When she talks about her wines and how she began from nothing she is overflowing with stories and emotions. "After raising my three children, and seeing how I was pretty good at raising things, I looked around for something else to raise". This is how she begins to explain why, one day, she decided to get involved in winemaking. And what she found was a small vineyard that she could manage herself and a grape, Aleatico, which was native to the area of upper Lazio. She uses it to make a white wine, a red and a rosé, in both dry and sweet versions.

☐ 88   Price A
Aleatico di Gradoli Butunì 2012
100% Aleatico grapes. Stainless steel for 8 months. Garnet color. Nuts, almonds and dates on the nose. Then black cherry and red roses. Dynamic on the palate, velvety and with good freshness. Nuts on the finish.

POGGIO ALLA META

Via Valloni, snc
03034 Casalvieri (FR)
Tel. 3356861317 - 3889448420
Fax 0812488351
poggioallameta@gmail.com
www.poggioallameta.it
f Poggio alla Meta

YEAR OF FOUNDATION 2000
NAME OF THE OWNER Nicòtina Family

TOTAL BOTTLES PRODUCED 60,000
DIRECT SALES
VISITS TO THE WINERY - RESERVATION NEEDED
HECTARES OF VINEYARD 9
CERTIFIED ORGANIC VITICULTURE

The small estate of Mariano Nicòtina has from a few years been producing quality wines in Val Comino, in lower Lazio. He uses international grapes like Merlot and Cabernet as well as typical local ones like Passerina, Maturano and Pampanaro. Organic farming methods and a youthful and passionate approach anda lot of experimentation have made this a growing estate and one with great potential.

☐ 89   Price B
Piluc 2015
100% Passerina grapes (Campolese clone). Stainless steel only. Straw yellow color. Briny and flowery nose with shades of mimosa and broom. Full bodied and savory on the palate, good structure and freshness with a pleasant flowery finish, savory and chalky.

▨ 88   Price B
Piluc Etichetta rosa - Orange Wine 2015
100% Passerina grapes (Campolese clone). Stainless steel only. 35 days of maceration on the skins. Biodynamic method. Orange color. Intense nose of dry flowers, rose and fruity hints. Slightly tannic on the palate and with dynamic acidity. Good flowery and fruity persistence.

POGGIO LE VOLPI

Via Colle Pisano, 27
00040 Monte Porzio Catone (RM)
Tel. +39 06 9426980
info@poggiolevolpi.it
www.poggiolevolpi.it

YEAR OF FOUNDATION 1996
NAME OF THE OWNER Felice Mergè
TOTAL BOTTLES PRODUCED 230,000
DIRECT SALES
VISITS TO THE WINERY - RESERVATION NEEDED
HECTARES OF VINEYARD 35
RESTAURANT
OLIVE OIL PRODUCTION

Mergè is a very well-known name in Frascati. The family has always been involved in making wine in Lazio but a little less than 20 years ago, elice Mergè, who represents the latest generation, began producing wines that were of a total different quality than those of the past. The whites are essentially Frascati-style, while the reds are made with grapes cultivated in Colle degli Zingari, in the township of Olevano Romano. In making his wines he benefits from the experience of enologist Riccardo Cotarella.

■ **90** Price B
Baccarossa 2014

100% Nero Buono grapes. Matures 12 months in barrique. Dark ruby red. Foxy and spicy nose, chocolate and ripe red fruit. Smooth and juicy on the palate, fresh and balanced.

☐ **88** Price A
Donnaluce 2015

Blend of 60% Malvasia del Lazio, 30% Greco and 10% Chardonnay grapes. Part matures in stainless steel and part ages in different sized casks. Straw yellow. Elegant nose of flowers broom and blossom, fruity of apricots and white peach. Tense and savory on the palate. Long fruity finish.

★★
PRINCIPE PALLAVICINI

Via Roma, 121
00030 Colonna (RM)
Tel. +39 06 9438816
Fax 06 9438027 - 06 83773838
info@terredeipallavicini.com
www.principepallavicini.com
f *principepallavicini*
🐦 *@TdPallavicini*

YEAR OF FOUNDATION 2012
NAME OF THE OWNER Maria Camilla Pallavicini
TOTAL BOTTLES PRODUCED 550,000
DIRECT SALES
VISITS TO THE WINERY - RESERVATION NEEDED
HECTARES OF VINEYARD 80
OLIVE OIL PRODUCTION

A noble family that has been in Lazio since the 1600s, the Pallavicini have always administered their vast agricultural holdings around Rome. Today these are separated in two different areas. La Tenuta di Cerveteri is in northeastern Lazio and has 15 hectares of vineyards, while their historic estate, which originally began make wine, is Tenuta Colonna with its 65 hectares of vineyards southeast of Rome in the Castelli Romani. Maria Camilla Pallavicini is in charge of production and aside from quality Frascati, she has also created top quality reds.

■ **95** Price B
Casa Romana 2012

Blend of Cabernet Sauvignon and Petit Verdot grapes. Matures 12 months in tonneau. Dark and bright ruby red. Elegant smoky nose with notes of cinchona and pepper, eucalyptus puffs and herbal hints. Complex on the palate, tense and smooth at the same time, powerful still enveloping and with a very long persistence.

☐ **92** 👍 Price A
Frascati Poggio Verde 2015

Blend of 70% Malvasia del Lazio, 30% Greco and Grechetto grapes. Stainless steel only. Light yellow. Delicate nose, slightly aromatic, flowery with notes of wild flowers, jasmine and hints of medlar. Savory, tense, very balanced and complex.

▪ **92** Price B*
Stillato 2014

100% Malvasia Puntinata grapes dried on the shoots for a month. Ferments and matures for 10 months in barrique. Deep golden yellow. Intense and enveloping nose, light botrytis notes, then saffron and iodine, but dry apricot as well. Sweet and warm on the palate with a pleasant bitter finish.
*50 cl bottle.

☐ **90** 👍 Price A
Roma Malvasia Puntinata 2015

100% Malvasia Puntinata grapes. Bright straw yellow. Delicate aromatic notes, sage and jasmine, then cedar, white peach and yellow plum. Very briny and pleasantly easy to drink. Slightly bitter finish.

★★
SAN GIOVENALE

Località La Macchia
01010 Blera (VT)
Tel. +39 06 6877877
Fax +39 06 6832329
info@sangiovenale.it
www.sangiovenale.it

YEAR OF FOUNDATION 2006
NAME OF THE OWNER Emanuele Pancrazi
TOTAL BOTTLES PRODUCED 7,000
DIRECT SALES
VISITS TO THE WINERY - RESERVATION NEEDED
HECTARES OF VINEYARD 10
CERTIFIED ORGANIC VITICULTURE
OLIVE OIL PRODUCTION

Emanuele Pancrazi, the owner of this magnificent estate in Blera in the province of Viterbo, did not start off as a wine producer but once he caught the 'bug' it became his reason for living. He makes one wine that is clearly Rhone-inspired, a blend of Granache, Carignan and Syrah which grow in a vineyard with a density of 13-15,000 vines per hectares, and starting from this year a wonderful Cabernet Franc. The estate sits perfectly in its magnificent surroundings, untamed and beaten by the wind.

 95   Price D

Habemus Etichetta Rossa 2013

100% Cabernet Franc grapes. Matures in barrique. Very dark and deep red color. The new wine of San Giovenale left us with no words. The aromas are complex of cinchona, graphite and black berries. On the palate it is simply sumptuous and has impressive power together with unique balance and freshness. Multicolored and never-ending finish. Too bad only few bottles are produced.

 94   Price C

Habemus 2014

Blend of 40% Granache, 40% Syrah and 20% Carignan grapes. Matures in barrique. Dark red color. Intense notes of garrigues, spices and citrus. Powerful on the palate but with a surprising agility and progression. Silky tannins and a clear and very elegant finish.

SANT'ISIDORO

Località Portaccia
01016 Tarquinia (VT)
Tel. +39 0766 869716
Fax +39 0766 864154
info@santisidoro.net
www.santisidoro.net

YEAR OF FOUNDATION 1938
NAME OF THE OWNER Giovanni Palombi
TOTAL BOTTLES PRODUCED 65,000
DIRECT SALES
VISITS TO THE WINERY - RESERVATION NEEDED
HECTARES OF VINEYARD 57

A large and spectacular estate with over 800 hectares of fields and vineyards near the ancient city of Tarqunia, which once was a key Etruscan center. This is also the Maremma area of the Lazio region and aside from wine they also produce fruits, vegetables, jams and vegetables preserved in oil.

☐ 86   👍 Price A

Tarquinia Chardonnay Forca di Palma 2015

100% Chardonnay grapes. Stainless steel only. Enveloping fruit, immediate, a little simple and fermentative but fragrant and well made. Fresh taste, agile, easy to drink, thin and pleasant.

■ 85   Price B

Soremidio 2012

100% Montepulciano grapes. Matures 18 months in barrique. Dark and intense garnet ruby. Kirsch and wild cherry jam on the nose, vanilla, the wood a little too in evidence. Savory, woody and thick tannins, good body.

 ★★

TENUTA DI FIORANO

Via di Fioranello, 19/31
00134 Roma (RM)
Tel. +39 06 79340093
info@tenutadifiorano.it
www.tenutadifiorano.it
f *Fiorano*
🐦 *@ilFiorano*

YEAR OF FOUNDATION 1940
NAME OF THE OWNER Alessandrojacopo Boncompagni Ludovisi
TOTAL BOTTLES PRODUCED 21,000
DIRECT SALES
VISITS TO THE WINERY - RESERVATION NEEDED
HECTARES OF VINEYARD 11
CERTIFIED ORGANIC VITICULTURE
OLIVE OIL PRODUCTION

This winery off the Appia Antica, on Via di Fioranello, is the story of a prince who was in love with his vineyards and produced wine with personality that in the 1970s seduced Gino Veronelli. Today this passion has been handed down to Alessandrojacopo Boncompagni Ludovisi, the great nephew of Prince Alberico, who with love and dedication has given new life to the great wines of Fiorano. Important and concentrated wines the two Fiorano; agile and dynamic the two Fioranello, all united by a common elegance.

■ 🍷 95   Price C
Fiorano Rosso 2011

Blend of 65% Cabernet Sauvignon and 35% Merlot grapes. Vinification and maturation in 1000 liters Slavonia oak. Intense spiciness and intriguing on the nose, underbrush and eucalyptus notes and blueberries jam. Velvety and sumptuous on the palate, smooth and full bodied, pulpy fruit, elegant tannins and bold acidity. Long, spicy, smoky hints and dark berries in the finish.

☐ 94   Price B
Fiorano Bianco 2014

Blend of 50% Grechetto and 50% Viognier grapes. Vinification and maturation in 1000 liters Slavonian oak. Golden yellow. Sweet citrus, light vanilla hints, aromatic herbs and wild flowers on the nose. Full bodied, fresh with hints of citrus peel, sage and broom complete the very long finish.

☐ 88   Price A
Fioranello Bianco 2015

Blend of 50% Viognier, 50% Grechetto grapes. Stainless steel only. Straw yellow. Aromatic and intriguing aromas, citrus and wild herbs. Juicy and fresh on the palate. Clean and clear finish.

■ 87   Price A
Fioranello Rosso 2014

100% Cabernet Sauvignon grapes. Matures in 500 l. oak barrels. Nice juicy fruit, red currant and pomegranate with a pleasant spice. On the palate it reveals to be agile with light tannins and long persistent finish of fruit and spice.

VALLE VERMIGLIA

Via Antonio Gramsci, 7
00197 Monte Porzio Catone (RM)
Tel. +39 348 7221073
aziendaagricola@vallevermiglia.it
www.eremotuscolano.it
f *eremo.tuscolano*

YEAR OF FOUNDATION **1996**
NAME OF THE OWNER **Mario Masini**
TOTAL BOTTLES PRODUCED **30,000**
DIRECT SALES
VISITS TO THE WINERY - RESERVATION NEEDED
HECTARES OF VINEYARD **8**

The Camaldolese monks have a monastery and vineyards on the slopes of Monte Tuscolo. Although it is just outside Rome, this area is both hidden and uncontaminated, a place for solitude – and the presence of women is only just tolerated. Here Mario Masini has achieved excellent results producing a different Frascati, one distinguished by its elegance and cleanliness.

☐ 90   👍 Price A
Frascati Superiore Eremo Tuscolano 2015

Blend of 60% Malvasia del Lazio, 10% Malvasia di Candia with Trebbiano Giallo, Trebbiano Toscano and Bombino bianco grapes. Stainless steel. Straw yellow. Elegant aromas of citrus and flowers, agile. Savory finish with notes of aromatic herbs and delicate fruits.

VILLA SIMONE

Via Frascati - Colonna, 29
00040 Monte Porzio Catone (RM)
Tel. +39 06 9449717
agricola@pierocostantini.it
www.villasimone.com

YEAR OF FOUNDATION **1982**
NAME OF THE OWNER **Piero Costantini**
TOTAL BOTTLES PRODUCED **200,000**
DIRECT SALES
VISITS TO THE WINERY - RESERVATION NEEDED
HECTARES OF VINEYARD **21**
OLIVE OIL PRODUCTION

Villa Simone is the farm estate of Piero Costantini, the same Costantini of the historic Rome wine shop in Piazza Cavour. The shop is an hour by car from the estate in Monte Porzio Catone. This year we're missing the red Ferro e Seta which are still refining. We have tasted the Frascati Vigneto Filonardi, a single vignard considered the best of the area.

■ 88   👍 Price A

Cesanese del Piglio Piero Costantini 2014

100% Cesanese d'Affile grapes. 6 months in stainless steel. Foxy, eucalyptus and enveloping on the nose. Black cherry, chestnuts and bark. Fresh and juicy on the palate with a good persistent finish.

☐ 87   Price A

Frascati Sup. Vigneto Filonardi 2015

Blend of Malvasia del Lazio, Malvasia di Candia and Grechetto grapes. Matures 6 months in stainless steel. Straw yellow. Intense notes of apple, fruit and white flowers. Then hints of herbs and a fresh and juicy palate with sulphureus and fruity finish.

LIGURIA

Liguria and winemaking have a very close and traditional ties. This small Mediterranean coastal region has hills that seem to almost drop into the sea and this has made farming, above all olive and grape growing, very difficult. Here winegrowing is almost a heroic endeavor with vineyards virtually carved out of the hills and terraced, which means most of the work has to be done by hand given the impossibility of using tractors and other machinery. Cinque Terre, an incredibly picturesque area situated on the coast between La Spezia and Tigullio, is home to one of the most famous wine made from Bosco, Albarola and Vermentino grapes that are harvested with the employment of a monorail that brings the grapes to the nearby roads where they are loaded onto trucks and brought to the winery. This system of production is thus costly and risks driving up the retail products of the wines. Thus it is a challenge to produce a wine like Cinque Terre Sciacchetrà, a very rare and expensive white Passito made with the same grapes and form the same vineyards as the normal wine. Then again, maintaining winemaking is this area is fundamental for the conservation of the landscape which would suffer irreparable damage were cultivation to be abandoned. More simple, but not more so, is the situ-

ation DOC appellation of Colli di Luni that extends through the region's extreme eastern side and the southernmost part of the area of Lunigiana. The hills here are not as steep and border with the province of Lucca that is only a few kilometers away, which means the wines made here are similar to those in neighboring Tuscany. Colli di Luni Bianco is a blend of Vermentino and Trebbiano Toscano and has a medium-structure much like the whites of Montecarlo and Bolgheri produce not far to the south. The varietal Vermentino is perhaps the most typical wine of the area and is more concentrated than the Bianco and is wonderful to pair with the typical plates of the local cuisine, above all testaroli.

Jumping some 200km to the northeast is the Riviera Ligure di Ponente that aside from being a famous for tourism is also home to a vast DOC appellation that produces the region's most popular wines. Vermentino and Pigato are the leading white wines and they are, all things considered, very similar even if Pigato is produced in the district of Albenga and Vermentino in the province of Imperia. Both have structure and softness and seem intentionally made to pair with traditional Liguria cuisine, like pasta al pesto and capon magro. Among the reds is Ormeasco that is made with Dolcetto grapes and resembles its cousins in Piedmont. There is also a rosé version of this wine called Sciac-tra, not to be confused with Sciacchetrà from Cinque Terre.

The red wine Rossese is produced in two DOC appellations, Riviera Ligure del Ponente and the more famous Dolceacqua, in the Ventimiglia hinterland on the Old Salt road. This is a very interesting and characteristic wine that has a nice structure and aromas which recall those of Mediterranean underbrush. It pairs well with mushrooms and white meats.

- Cinque Terre e Cinque Terre Sciacchetrà. Only Cinque Terre can be with or without the sub areas Costa de Sera, Costa de Campu, Costa da Posa
- Colli di Luni
- Colline di Levanto
- Golfo del Tigullio Portofino o Portofino, with or without the sub-area Costa dei Fieschi
- Pornassio o Ormeasco di Pornassio
- Riviera Ligure di Ponente, with or without the sub-areas Riviera dei Fiori (only for Pigato, Rossese, Vermentino), Albenganese (only for Pigato, Rossese, Vermentino), Finalese (only for Pigato, Rossese, Vermentino), Quiliano (only for Granaccia), Taggia (only for Moscato or Moscatello)
- Rossese di Dolceacqua o Dolceacqua, geographic references allowed
- Val Polcèvera, with or without the sub-area Coronata

LAURA ASCHERO

Piazza Vittorio Emanuele II, 7
18027 Pontedassio (IM)
Tel. +39 0183 710307
lauraaschero@uno.it
www.lauraaschero.it
🅵 *Azienda-Agricola-Laura-Aschero*
🐦 *@LauraAschero*

YEAR OF FOUNDATION **1980**
NAME OF THE OWNER **Marco Rizzo**
TOTAL BOTTLES PRODUCED **65,000**
DIRECT SALES
VISITS TO THE WINERY - RESERVATION NEEDED
HECTARES OF VINEYARD **6.5**

This quintessential artisanal and yet modern family winery uses grapes from its own three-hectare vineyard and others that it has leased and benefits from the consultancy of enologist Gianpaolo Ramò. It is now in the hands of the third generation of the family started by Laura and the 2015 harvest confirms an excellent Vermentino and a great level Pigato.

☐ **87**   Price A
Riviera Ligure di Ponente Pigato 2015

100% Pigato grapes. Stainless steel. Light and bright golden yellow. Notes of flowers and a brackish almost seashore hint on the nose. Fresh and inviting acidity on the palate.

☐ **85**   Price A
Riviera Ligure di Ponente Vermentino 2015

100% Vermentino grapes. Stainless steel. Light straw yellow. Wide and large aromas, with aromatic herbs, clear white fruit, agile and citric. Citrus in the vanish with vibrant acidity.

MARIA DONATA BIANCHI

Via Merea, 101
18013 Diano Arentino (IM)
Tel. +39 0183 498233
info@aziendaagricolabianchi.it
www.aziendaagricolabianchi.it
🅵 *Azienda-Agricola-Maria-Donata-Bianchi*

YEAR OF FOUNDATION **1976**
NAME OF THE OWNER **Emanuele Trevia**
TOTAL BOTTLESS PRODUCED **30,000**
DIRECT SALES
VISITS TO THE WINERY - RESERVATION NEEDED
HECTARES OF VINEYARD **4**
HOSPITALITY

Emanuele Trevia runs this tiny estate in an impeccable way and has turned it into little gem also with its delightful holiday farm facility. The wines are very authentic and made more from the heart than from technique but are captivating in their own way.

☐ **90**   👍 Price A
Riviera Ligure di Ponente Vermentino 2015

100% Vermentino grapes. Stainless steel. Very bright but light color. Unusual, smoky nose. Salty and intensely vibrant on the mouth. The finish alternates ripe fruit and sea scents.

☐ **88**   Price A
Riviera Ligure di Ponente Pigato 2015

100% Pigato grapes. Stainless steel. Light and bright color. Elegant aromas, thyme and sage. In the mouth it is balanced with a salty hint, straightforward, strong.

BIOVIO

Via Crociata, 24
17031 Bastia d'Albenga (SV)
Tel. +39 0182 21856
Fax +39 0182 20538
info@biovio.it
www.biovio.it
🅵 *biovio2*

YEAR OF FOUNDATION **1980**
NAME OF THE OWNER **Giobatta Aimone Vio**
TOTAL BOTTLESS PRODUCED **40,000**
DIRECT SALES
VISITS TO THE WINERY - RESERVATION NEEDED
HECTARES OF VINEYARD **7**
CERTIFIED ORGANIC VITICULTURE
OLIVE OIL PRODUCTION

"We produce aromatic herbs," declared minimalist producer Almone Vio and, in fact, his family estate does cultivate sage, rosemary, laurel, thyme, marjoram, mint and parsley. The old folk in Genoa still say "Pigato della Bastia d'Albenga", stressing the name of the location to indicate an ante litteram cru.

■ 88   Price A

Granaccia Colline Savonesi Gigò 2015

100% Granaccia. Stainless steel. Bright ruby red. Intense red fruits dominate the nose. On the palate crunchy cherry made vivid by the biting tannins.

☐ 88   Price A

Riviera Ligure di Ponente Pigato 2015

100% Pigato grapes. Stainless steel. Bright and luminous straw yellow. Intense, unique notes almost pastry on the nose. On the palate it's soft, well balanced by the hint of salt. Long finish of white fruits.

★

BRUNA

Via Umberto I, 81
18020 Ranzo (IM)
Tel. +39 0183 318082
info@brunapigato.it
www.brunapigato.it

YEAR OF FOUNDATION 1970
NAME OF THE OWNER Francesca Bruna
TOTAL BOTTLESS PRODUCED 37,000
DIRECT SALES
VISITS TO THE WINERY - RESERVATION NEEDED
HECTARES OF VINEYARD 7.5

"Pigato is the indigenous grape in which we have invested the most time and energy", this statement sums up how important this white wine is for the Bruna family that has made their Baccan a point of reference for its variety. Since the 1970s, the estate's vineyards have expanded in size but with the Ligurian parsimony: seven and a half hectares. This year Bruna skips the Baccan 2014 but the Pigato Russeghine and the red Pulin are a warranty.

☐ 89   Price A

Riviera Ligure di Ponente Pigato Russeghine 2015

100% Pigato grapes. Stainless steel. Bright golden color. Classy nose, potpourri of aromatic herbs. It

---

is big without being fat. Saline on the palate, with comforting completeness.

■ 89   Price B

Rosso Colline Savonesi Pulin 2014

Granaccia, Syrah and Barbera grapes. 13 months in barrique. Deep ruby. Toasted notes on the nose, cocoa and coffee, then Mediterranean woods and red berries. Long, intense, important on the palate with elegant tannins. Very few bottles produced.

CHEO

Via Brigate Partigiane, 1
19018 Vernazza (SP)
Tel. +39 333 9594758
bartolocheo@gmail.com
 f *Cheo-vini*

NAME OF THE OWNER Bartolomeo Lercari and Lise Bertram
TOTAL BOTTLES PRODUCED 6,500
DIRECT SALES
VISITS TO THE WINERY - RESERVATION NEEDED
HECTARES OF VINEYARD 2

One would think that Bartolomeo Lercari and Lise Bertram chose Vernazza as their retreat were if not for the fact that maintaining a vineyard in Cinque Terra is more like being condemned to hard labor. The vineyard rows are terraced with stone walls overlooking the town and need constant upkeep yet the stubborn vines produce excellent white wines, a little Passito dessert wine and a very original red.

▣ 92   Price C*

Cinque Terre Sciacchetrà 2013

*Vermentino, Bosco and Piccabun grapes. 50% in oak. Dark and bright amber. Intense dry peach and caramel notes. Very long finish where saltiness balances the incredible bitter honey. 200 half bottles produced. *37.5 cl bottle.*

☐ 91   Price B

Cinque Terre 2015

Vermentino, Bosco and Piccabun grapes. Stainless steel. Bright straw yellow. Intense saline note on the nose together with fruit. Balanced, long and seductive on the palate.

FORLINI CAPPELLINI

Via B. Riccobaldi, 45
19010 Manarola (SP)
Tel. +39 0187 920496
forlinicappellini@libero.it

YEAR OF FOUNDATION 1988
NAME OF THE OWNER Germana Forlini and Alberto Cappellini
TOTAL BOTTLES PRODUCED 8,000
DIRECT SALES
VISITS TO THE WINERY - RESERVATION NEEDED
HECTARES OF VINEYARD 1

The low numbers say it all: three people, Germana Forlini, Alberto Cappellini and their son Giacomo work a one-hectare, terraced vineyard on a steep incline above Manarola and produce few thousand bottles of Cinque Terre and a few hundred half-bottles of the very rare Sciacchetrà. An example of heroic winegrowing.

☐ 88 Price B

Cinque Terre 2015

Vermentino, Bosco and Albarola grapes. Stainless steel. Light and bright straw yellow. Wide and surprisingly delicate nose, notes of talc, then crunchy fruit and saline. Thin and legant on the palate.

IL TORCHIO

Via delle Colline, 24
19033 Castelnuovo Magra (SP)
Tel. +39 0187 670101
gildamusetti@gmail.com
www.agriturismolavallesp.it

YEAR OF FOUNDATION 2012
NAME OF THE OWNER Gilda Musetti
TOTAL BOTTLES PRODUCED 60,000
DIRECT SALES
VISITS TO THE WINERY - RESERVATION NEEDED
HECTARES OF VINEYARD 5
HOSPITALITY
RESTAURANT
OLIVE OIL PRODUCTION

Situated in Castellnuovo Magra, in the area of Colli di Luni, the estate has been run since the death of grandfather Giorgio by his grandchildren Gilda and Edorado Musetti with one handling administration and sales and the other responsible for the vineyards and winemaking. The breath of fresh air brought by this new generation has seen investments in the graphics of the labels, designed by the talented figurative Genoa artist Francesco Musante.

■ 89 👍 Price A

Il Nero 2015

100% Vermentino Nero grapes. Stainless steel. Ruby red with violet shades. Fruity nose of morello cherry and black currant, a hint of violet. Fresh, agile and salty on the palate. Thin tannins well balanced by a nice freshness. Wild cherry in the finish.

☐ 89 Price B

Stralunato 2015

100% Vermentino grapes. Maceration on the skins. Few bottles produced. Intense straw yellow with golden shades. Medlar, honey and chamomile flowers, tangerine and then nettle aromas. Fresh, saline, balanced on the palate. Intriguing and easy to drink. Soft and with a citrus peel finish.

☐ 87 👍 Price A

Colli di Luni Vermentino Il Bianco 2015

100% Vermentino grapes. Stainless steel. Straw yellow. Fruity nose of yellow plum then fresh almond and sea breeze. Soft and saline on the palate with a nice freshness. Good persistence and fresh almond on the finish.

★

KA' MANCINÉ

Piazza Ottoluoghi, 36 - Fraz. San Martino
18036 Soldano (IM)
Tel. +39 0184 289089
Fax +39 0184 289089
kamancine@libero.it
www.kamancine.it
www.kamancine.it
@KaMancin

YEAR OF FOUNDATION 1998
NAME OF THE OWNER Roberta Repaci
TOTAL BOTTLES PRODUCED 18,000
DIRECT SALES
VISITS TO THE WINERY - RESERVATION NEEDED
HECTARES OF VINEYARD 3
OLIVE OIL PRODUCTION

This Soldano estate produces some of the most typical Rossese Dolceacqua wines. Since 1998, the family of Maurizio Anfosso has been identified with Italy's most French wine, only geographically speaking given the estate's proximity to the border. Our tastings confirmed that Ka' Maciné is one of the best producers of this wine.

■ 88   Price B
Rossese di Dolceacqua Galeae 2015

100% Rossese grapes. Stainless steel. Bright ruby red. Fruits and spices dominate the nose. Crunchy on the palate, long and macerated flowers in the finish.

☐ 86   Price A
Tabaka 2015

70% Massarda, 30% Vermentino grapes. Stainless steel. Intense straw yellow. Notes of white crunchy apple. Tense on the palate, balanced but still very vivid for acidity.

LA GINESTRAIA

Via Steria
18100 Cervo (IM)
Tel. +39 338 1283229
info@brangero.com
www.brangero.com/az-agr-la-ginestraia-liguria/
 La-Ginestraia
 @LaGinestraia

YEAR OF FOUNDATION **2007**
NAME OF THE OWNER **Marco Brangero**
TOTAL BOTTLES PRODUCED **40,000**
VISITS TO THE WINERY - RESERVATION NEEDED
HECTARES OF VINEYARD **4**

Marco Brangero is an odd Ligurian. Even though he has vineyards that produce great reds between Diano d'Alba and the area of Barolo, he has always pursued a dream: to produce in Liguria those taut and saline white's that can only come from that terroir. In 2007, he finally found an estate to lease and this allowed his dream to come true and his wines, modern yet recognizable, quickly became exemplary.

☐ 90   Price B
Riviera Ligure di Ponente Pigato
Via Maestra 2015

100% Pigato grapes. 6 months in used barrique.

Deep and bright straw yellow. Flowery notes of elder, briny, Mediterranean woods. Pleasantly wide on the palate, ripe white fruit and a hint of vanilla.

☐ 89   Price B
Riviera Ligure di Ponente Pigato
Le Marige 2015

100% Pigato grapes. Stainless steel. Light and bright straw yellow. Irony notes on the nose, then citrusy, grapefruit. An intense briny note on the palate, complex and compact. From a new vineyard on the red soil of Amasco.

OTTAVIANO LAMBRUSCHI

Via Olmarello, 28
19033 Castelnuovo Magra (SP)
Tel. +39 0187 674261
Fax +39 0187 674261
info@ottavianolambruschi.com
www.ottavianolambruschi.com

YEAR OF FOUNDATION **1995**
NAME OF THE OWNER **Ottaviano Lambruschi**
TOTAL BOTTLES PRODUCED **36,000**
DIRECT SALES
VISITS TO THE WINERY - RESERVATION NEEDED
HECTARES OF VINEYARD **5**
OLIVE OIL PRODUCTION

Like father like son, the young Fabio Lambruschi now joins his father Ottaviano in running an estate that only has a few hectares of vineyards and which is almost exclusively dedicated to producing Vermentino that in the appellation of Colli di Luni has unique potential. Their winemaking approach is a mixture of tradition and innovation and has made them a sure bet.

☐ 88   Price B
Colli di Luni Vermentino Costamarina 2015

100% Vermentino grapes. Stainless steel. Intense and bright golden color. Elegant aromas of aromatic herbs, dried flowers. Surprising acidity on the palate. Long finish between briny and ripe white fruits.

☐ 85   Price B
Colli di Luni Vermentino 2015

100% Vermentino grapes. Stainless steel. Intense

straw yellow. Ripe white fruit on the nose. Soft and pleasing on the palate.

LUNAE BOSONI

Via Bozzi, 63
19034 Ortonovo (SP)
Tel. +39 0187 660187
Fax +39 0187 669223
info@cantinelunae.com
www.cantinelunae.com
f *LVNAEBOSONI*
y *@CantineLunae*

YEAR OF FOUNDATION 1970
NAME OF THE OWNER Paolo Bosoni
TOTAL BOTTLES PRODUCED 450,000
DIRECT SALES
VISITS TO THE WINERY - RESERVATION NEEDED
HECTARES OF VINEYARD 65
HOSPITALITY

Colli di Luni is part of a terroir that extends into both Liguria and Tuscany. Bosoni is perfect interpreter of this duality, producing wines that combines the crispy grace of Ligurian wines enriched with the opulence of the Tuscan ones. This modern winery produces precise and rigorous wines.

☐ 89	Price B

Colli di Luni Vermentino Cavagino 2015

100% Vermentino grapes. 60% stainless steel and 40% barrique. Bright golden color. Deep and complex, a nice mix of tropical fruits and briny hints. Wide mouth, appealing, excellent.

☐ 88	Price A

Colli di Luni Vermentino Etichetta Nera 2015

100% Vermentino. Stainless steel. Shiny golden color. Tropical fruit hints on the nose, wide and gritty. On the palate again pineapple. Very pleasant.

LUPI

Corso Mazzini, 9
18026 Pieve di Teco (IM)
Tel. +39 0183 36161

Fax +39 0183 368061
lupi@casalupi.it
www.casalupi.it
f *Casalupi1960*

YEAR OF FOUNDATION 1960
NAME OF THE OWNER Massimo Lupi
TOTAL BOTTLES PRODUCED 160,000
DIRECT SALES
VISITS TO THE WINERY - RESERVATION NEEDED
HECTARES OF VINEYARD 12

In the extreme part of Ponente Ligure, Massimo Lupi produces a vast range of reds (Ormeasco and Rossese) and typical whites, the classic Pigato and Vermentino. Important attention has been paid to enhancing the capacity of the wines to age and this has resulted in, for example, a white Pigato wine, Vignamare, which goes on the market no earlier than three years after it is made and represents a rare exception to the rule. This year the Petraie, in which converged its grapes, is spectacular.

☐ 90	Price B

Riviera Ligure di Ponente Pigato Petraie 2014

100% Pigato grapes. Stainless steel. Golden straw yellow. Wide and powerful aromas of aromatic herbs, thyme and sage. Briny and impressive on the palate and balances the softness in the finish. Made also with the grapes of the Vignamare vineyard, iconic wine of the winey, not produced in the difficult 2014 vintage.

■ 90	Price B

Ormeasco di Pornassio Superiore Braje 2013

100% Ormeasco grapes. 2 years in used barrique. Intense and deep ruby red. Intense notes of licorice and pepper, then aromatic herbs. Rich on the palate, important, elegant tannins and a delicate coffee finish.

MACCARIO DRINGENBERG

Via Torre, 3
18036 San Biagio della Cima (IM)
Tel. +39 0184 289947
maccariodringenberg@yahoo.it
f *Maccario-Dringenberg*

YEAR OF FOUNDATION **2001**
NAME OF THE OWNER **Giovanna Maccario**
TOTAL BOTTLES PRODUCED **25,000**
DIRECT SALES
VISITS TO THE WINERY - RESERVATION NEEDED
HECTARES OF VINEYARD **5**

With his Rossese Classico and single vineyards Luvaira, Posaù and Curli, Maccario Dringenberg has reiterated his position as a point of reference for the whole appellation. This year we remark the new release of Posaù Biamonti, made with the grapes of the centenary vineyard Posaù.

 93   Price B
Rossese di Dolceacqua Luvaira 2014

100% Rossese grapes. 45% on the shoots. Bright red. Splendid notes of spices and a hint of licorice. Tense and lavish elegance on the palate, enchanting with incredible prospective.

 92   Price B
Rossese di Dolceacqua Posaù Biamonti 2014

100% Rossese. Stainless steel. Bright ruby red, lighter on the edges. Elegant nose, red berries then Mediterranean woods. Complex on the palate, briny and fruity on the finish. Very few bottles produced.

 88   Price A
Rossese di Dolceacqua 2015

100% Rossese grapes. Stainless steel. Bright purple color. Soft pepper and red berries on the nose. Agile and tense on the palate. Typical of its kind.

★
POGGIO DEI GORLERI

Via San Leonardo - Località Gorleri
18013 Diano Marina (IM)
Tel. +39 0183 495207
Fax +39 0183 499031
info@poggiodeigorleri.com
www.poggiodeigorleri.com
 PoggioDeiGorleri

YEAR OF FOUNDATION **2003**
NAME OF THE OWNER **Davide Merano**
TOTAL BOTTLES PRODUCED **69,000**
DIRECT SALES
VISITS TO THE WINERY - RESERVATION NEEDED

HECTARES OF VINEYARD **6.5**
HOSPITALITY

This 13-year-old estate is already producing excellent wines, the result of significant investments in a very modern winery and in the vineyards that have been totally replanted. The contribution of enologist Beppe Caviola has exalted the products of this very suited area. Aside from the winery, they also run a Wine Resort, which is much more than just a holiday farm. The wines are all well-made and offered at affordable prices. The estate is worth a visit, also considering that the sea is only a stone's throw away.

☐ **91**   👍 Price A
Riviera Ligure di Ponente Vermentino Vigna Sorì 2015

100% Vermentino grapes. Stainless steel. Bright straw yellow. Powerful mix of briny and Mediterranean woods on the nose. Extremely rich on the palate balanced by the citrusy note.

☐ **87**   Price B
Riviera Ligure di Ponente Pigato Albium 2014

100% Pigato grapes. Stainless steel. Bright golden color. Layered aromas, deep, between aromatic herbs and macerated flowers. Briny on the palate, long, just a hint of maturity.

RONDELLI

Frazione Brunetti, 1
18033 Camporosso (IM)
Tel. +39 328 0348055
cantina@faroi.it
www.faroi.it

YEAR OF FOUNDATION **2009**
NAME OF THE OWNER **Roberto Rondelli**
TOTAL BOTTLES PRODUCED **22,000**
DIRECT SALES
VISITS TO THE WINERY - RESERVATION NEEDED
HECTARES OF VINEYARD **4**
HOSPITALITY
RESTAURANT
OLIVE OIL PRODUCTION

Roberto Rondelli is someone to keep an eye on. The sole-owner of the Migliarina cru, he produces, among other wines, the very good

Rossese di Dolceacqua and the Pigato Vigna Ciotti. The Rossese classico and the Vermentino in 2015 are again at top level.

■ 87   Price A

Rossese di Dolceacqua 2015

100% Rossese grapes. Stainless steel. Deep and bright ruby red. Fragrant aromas of blackberry and a hint of pepper. Elegant on the palate, deep and balanced. Very convincing.

☐ 87   Price A

Riviera Ligure di Ponente Vermentino 2015

100% Vermentino grapes. Stainless steel. Bright, golden straw yellow. Aromatic herbs, flowers and briny on the nose. Saline on the mouth, long finish with fruits and citrusy.

■ 92   Price B

Rossese di Dolceacqua Bricco Arcagna 2014

100% Rossese grapes. Matures in barrique and tonneau. Bright ruby red. Delicate woody nose then red berries. Deep lively fruits. Agile, iridescent wine with a very pleasing finish

☐ 90   👍 Price A

Riviera Ligure di Ponente Vermentino 2015

100% Vermentino grapes. Stainless steel. Intense bright straw yellow. Open on the nose, almost Riesling aromas. Pleasant and attractive on the palate, where the brininess is balanced by the tasty fruit.

★ ★

TERRE BIANCHE

Località Arcagna
18035 Dolceacqua (IM)
Tel. +39 0184 31426
Fax +39 0184 31230
terrebianche@terrebianche.com
www.terrebianche.com
f *Terre-Bianche*
🐦 *@terrebianche*

YEAR OF FOUNDATION **1870**
NAME OF THE OWNER **Nicola Laconi and Filippo Rondelli**
TOTAL BOTTLES PRODUCED **55,000**
DIRECT SALES
VISITS TO THE WINERY - RESERVATION NEEDED
HECTARES OF VINEYARD **8.5**
HOSPITALITY
OLIVE OIL PRODUCTION

The view from up here, overlooking the Val Nervia, is unforgettable and what is most striking is the light color of the clay soil, after which the estate is named (White Lands). Filippo Rondelli, the master of Terre Bianche is also a strong supporter of Menzioni Geographiche Aggiuntive (Additional Geographic Mention). The estate's wines perfectly reflect his passion for his terroir.

LOMBARDY

Lombardy is an important winemaking region that produces some 1.2 million hectoliters a year of which over half are DOC and DOCG-classified. The primary winegrowing areas have always been the mountains and the plains, Oltrpò Pavese, Franciacorta and Valtellina. Added to these is the area near Lake Garda that for thousands of years has been an ideal habitat for grapes. From a climatic point of view, the cold in the Alpine zones, like Valtellina where the vineyards are terraced and sit at an altitude of around 600m above sea level, gradually eases as you go towards the Prealpi foothills and the valleys that host Italy's biggest lakes. The climate then becomes continental in the plains where it is influenced by the Po River. This is the area that has the greatest temperature difference between summer and winter.

All these micro-regions have winemaking traditions that were influenced by the peoples who dominated them over the centuries. The vast area of Oltrepò Pavese, a land of sparkling and vivacious wines as well as excellent whites and reds, was for a long time part of the Savoy Kingdom and winemaking methods and traditions are similar to those of Monferrato and Asti. Valtellina, on the other hand, makes red wines with the Chiavennasca (Nebbiolo) grape in the winemaking tradition of

northern Piedmont. Wines in the provinces of Brescia and Bergamo are similar to those of Verona and Trentino due to the fact that for centuries they were part of the Republic of Venice.

The area which is an exception to the rule is Franciacorta where mostly sparkling wines are made and that was classified DOCG in 1995. Here the greatest influence on winemaking was a modern, entrepreneurial spirit of people who were not necessarily winemakers or growers but also industrialists or operators in related sectors. Gaining major ground, after a few false starts, are the wines from the western banks of Lake Garda. The area and wines were up until now were identified as Riviera del Garda Bresciano with its relative subzones but are gradually being absorbed by a more general DOC appellation that also has a Garda Superiore classification.

Mantua is home to Lambrusco Mantovano and Garda Colli Mantovani, an independent DOC appellation where the Rosso is made with Rondinella, Merlot and Cabernet, a singular synthesis of Lombardy and Veneto winemaking. The Bianco is made using Trebbiano Toscano, Garganega and other local white varieties as well as international ones. An area that decidedly stands out is that of Lugana that made its fortune with a more 'noble' variation of Trebbiano, while today it is successfully producing table wines using international grapes.

On the Prealpi Bergamasche hills, in Valcalepio, producers are making an excellent name for themselves with hearty reds made from Cabernet and Merlot and nice whites from Pint Bianco and Chardonnay. The area has also seen a comeback of a sweet, Passito-type wine, Moscato di Scanzo, which up until a few years ago seem on the road to extinction. The province of Brescia is full of small DOC wines that are the product of local traditions. The whites include Capriano del Colle Trebbiano and San Martino della Battaglia, made from the Friulano grape. The reds are Botticino, Capriano (without Schiava grapes) and Cellatica made with a singular blend of Barbera, Schiava Gentile and Marzemino that can also use Sangiovese to make Botticino and Capriano (without Schiava) and Incrocio Terzi for Cellatica. The Barbera Lombardo-Piemontese, Schiava and Marzemino Trentino grapes make varietal reds that have a medium body and characteristics that do not seem to derive from the variety and are decidedly rustic.

The only DOC wine in the province of Lodi is San Colombano, a red blend of Croatina, Barbera and Uva Rara.

CONTROLLED AND GUARANTEED DESIGNATION OF ORIGIN (DOCG)

- Franciacorta
- Oltrepò Pavese metodo classico
- Scanzo or Moscato di Scanzo
- Sforzato di Valtellina o Sfursat di Valtellina
- Valtellina Superiore, with or without the sub-areas Grumello, Inferno, Maroggia, Sassella, Valgella

CONTROLLED DESIGNATION OF ORIGIN (DOC)

- Bonarda dell'Oltrepò Pavese
- Botticino
- Buttafuoco dell'Oltrepò Pavese or Buttafuoco
- Capriano del Colle (Novello Rosso, Rosso, Rosso Riserva, Trebbiano and Trebbiano Frizzante)
- Casteggio, Designation of 'Vigna' allowed
- Cellatica also Superiore
- Curtefranca
- Garda Colli Mantovani (Bianco, Rosato and Rosso)
- Lambrusco Mantovano, with or without the sub-areas Viadanese-Sabbionetano, Oltre Po Mantovano
- Oltrepò Pavese, even with the names of the varieties: Pinot Grigio, Pinot Nero, Sangue di Giuda
- Riviera del Garda Bresciano or Garda Bresciano
- San Colombano al Lambro or San Colombano
- San Martino della Battaglia
- Terre del Colleoni o Colleoni
- Valcalepio
- Valtellina Rosso o Rosso di Valtellina
- Valtènesi, geographic references allowed

AND ALSO

- Garda, Doc both for Lombardy and Veneto
- Lugana, Doc both for Lombardy and Veneto

★★
ARPEPE

Via del Buon Consiglio, 4
23100 Sondrio (SO)
Tel. +39 0342 214120
Fax +39 0342 1890925
info@arpepe.com
www.arpepe.com
 ARPEPE
 @arpepe1860

YEAR OF FOUNDATION 1860
NAME OF THE OWNER Pelizzatti Perego Family
TOTAL BOTTLES PRODUCED 70,000
DIRECT SALES
VISITS TO THE WINERY - RESERVATION NEEDED
HECTARES OF VINEYARD 13

The name of this important Valtellina estate is an abbreviation Arturo Pellizzatti Perego, the driving force behind the modern winery he set up in 1984 using the experience he gained working at the winery of his father and grandfather. Today his children Guido, Isabella and Emanuele are in charge and run it with great passion and care. The vineyards are dry-wall terraced and grow Chiavennasca (Nebbiolo) grapes the juice from which then macerates long in the skins and ages in large barrels and in the bottle to create wines with a great capacity to age. The wines are at times austere but have their roots in local tradition, a tradition exemplified by the cellar that is carved out of the rock in the Rhaetian Alps.

| 93 | Price C |

Valtellina Superiore Sassella Vigna Regina Riserva 2007

100% Nebbiolo Chiavennasca grapes, from a 50 years old vineyard. It matures 4 years in chestnut wood, durmast and acacia barrels. Bright garnet ruby red color. The nose is very complex with aromas of medicinal herbs, red tea, hyssop, tamarind, currant and sweet spices with an hint of graphite. On the mouth the drink is deep and mentholated, the tannin is rhythmic, soft and silky, stretched with a very good persistence.

| 92 | Price B |

Valtellina Superiore Grumello Buonconsiglio Riserva 2007

100% Chiavennasca Nebbiolo grapes from a 50

years old vineyard. It matures for 4 years in chestnut, durmast, acacia barrels. Garnet ruby red color. On the nose is refined with floral and eucalyptus aromas, gentle notes of jujube under spirits and tamarind with an hint of sweet tobacco. On the mouth is elegant, silky, with a fresh and gentle tannin, very long on the finish.

| 91 | Price B |

Valtellina Superiore Sassella Stella Retica Riserva 2011

100% Chiavennasca Nebbiolo grapes from a 50 years old vineyard. It matures for 2 years in chestnut, durmast and acacia barrels. Light garnet red color. The nose is alive with aromas of flowers as rose bud, hyssop, cedar, crisp cherry and a hint of hematic scent. On the mouth is full and clean, the tannin is alive and definite, very tonic and juicy almost savory.

★
BARONE PIZZINI

Via San Carlo, 14
25050 Provaglio d'Iseo (BS)
Tel. +39 030 9848311
info@baronepizzini.it
www.baronepizzini.it
 baronepizzini
 @PizziniBlog

YEAR OF FOUNDATION 1870
NAME OF THE OWNER Barone Pizzini Family
TOTAL BOTTLES PRODUCED 375,000
DIRECT SALES
VISITS TO THE WINERY - RESERVATION NEEDED
HECTARES OF VINEYARD 47
CERTIFIED ORGANIC VITICULTURE

Among the first Franciacorta producers since it obtained its DOC classification, in 2001 they became the first estate to adopt organic methods for its 47 hectares of vineyards subdivided into 25 parcels between Provaglio d'Iseo, Corte Franca, Adro and Passirano. The winery was rebuilt in 2006 and was designed to be environmentally friendly and foster great quality and thus underscores the estate's attention to the environment, from the head office to the vineyard.

| 90 | Price B |

Franciacorta Naturae Edizione 2012

Blend of 70% Chardonnay and 30% Pinot Nero

grapes. It matures in stainless steel and barrique for 40 months on yeasts. Light straw yellow color and elegant perlage. On the nose delicate aromas of lemon, lime juice thyme and an hint of salt. On the mouth taste of cedar, very fresh and vivid, tense on is vibrant acidity with a very clean and crispy finish.

🔲 89   Price B

Franciacorta Animante Brut

Blend of 78% Chardonnay, 18% Pinot Nero, 4% Pinot Bianco grapes. It matures 24 months in stainless steel on the yeasts. Golden straw yellow color with gentle perlage. On the nose it's fresh and citrusy with aromas of white melon, lychee and a very fresh pink grapefruit. On the mouth sharp and tense, nice savory finish supported by a clean bubble.

★★★

BELLAVISTA

Via Bellavista, 5
25030 Erbusco (BS)
Tel. +39 030 7762000
Fax +39 030 7762110
info@bellavistawine.it
www.bellavistawine.it
f cantinaBellavista
🐦 @BellavistaVino

YEAR OF FOUNDATION 1977
NAME OF THE OWNER Francesca Moretti
TOTAL BOTTLES PRODUCED 1,300,000
DIRECT SALES
VISITS TO THE WINERY - RESERVATION NEEDED
HECTARES OF VINEYARD 190

In the 40 years they have has been in Franciacorta, the Moretti family has focused on expressing their own ideal of wine, one based on energy and innovation and research into the essence of a style that has deep roots in the land and care of the vineyards. The partnership of Vittorio Moretti and enologist Matia Vezzola has produced a series of successful results that unite an avant-garde approach with tradition. Today, Francesca Moretti is in charge of the estate and continues its quest for excellence with passion and determination.

🔲 92   Price B

Franciacorta Pas Operé Extra Brut 2009

Blend of 65% Chardonnay and 35% Pinot Nero

grapes. It partially ferments in oak barrels and matures for 36 months on yeasts. Thick perlage and straw yellow color. On the nose is fragrant with aromas of pear, apple, a hint of hay and tangerine. On the mouth presents good acidity, tense with taste of citrus, agile and alive with a very fresh depth.

☐ 92   Price B

Curtefranca Uccellanda 2013

100% Chardonnay from a single vineyard. It ferments and matures for almost 2 years in white durmast barrique. Light straw yellow color. On the nose aromas of intense white flowers, magnolia and elderflower, white peach and apple with a clean full-flavored wood note. On the mouth the apple and the white peach are intense. Long, satisfactory and elegant on the finish.

🔲 89   Price B

Franciacorta Rosé Brut 2011

Blend of 62% Chardonnay and 38% Pinot Nero grapes. It matures partially in white durmast barrique for at least 5 years on yeasts. Pale antique pink color with a very fine perlage. On the nose aromas of smoke, currant and blood orange. On the mouth is juicy and full-flavored, very pleasant with fresh acidity.

★★

GUIDO BERLUCCHI & C.

Piazza Durati, 4 - Frazione Borgonato
25040 Corte Franca (BS)
Tel. +39 030 984381
Fax +39 030 894293
info@berlucchi.it
www.berlucchi.it
f berlucchi61franciacorta
🐦 @BerlucchiWine

YEAR OF FOUNDATION 1961
NAME OF THE OWNER Ziliani Family
TOTAL BOTTLES PRODUCED 4,500,000
DIRECT SALES
VISITS TO THE WINERY - RESERVATION NEEDED
HECTARES OF VINEYARD 520

In 1961, Guido Berlucchi and his enologist Franco Ziliani created the first traditional method sparkling wine in Franciacorta. Since then this brand has set the standard that the whole appellation respects today. Dedication to achieving excellence in their wines, a pioneering spirit and a strong bond with the territory – Berlucchi is one of the biggest estates in size – are today what guide the efforts of Cristina, Arturo and Paolo Ziliani. The results are many and have brought new challenges, including that of environmental sustainability that involves reducing CO2 emissions through the introduction of alternative energy sources.

 92   Price B
Franciacorta '61 Brut Nature 2009

Blend of 80% Chardonnay and 20% Pinot Nero grapes. It matures on yeasts for 5 years, dosage zero. Bright straw yellow color, fine perlage. Fresh and rich on the nose with aromas of lemon skin, fresh pineapple, hay, spicy biscuits and green apple. On the mouth vertical and crisp, balance freshness and long on the finish.

 91   Price B
Franciacorta '61 Satèn

100% Chardonnay grapes. 24 months on yeasts. Light straw yellow color and thick and delicate perlage. On the nose delicatly floral with aromas of magnolia and wisteria, hints of vanilla, white peach, green tea and light note of white pepper and comfit on the finish. On the mouth soft and fresh, nice detente and dynamic harmony.

★

BERSI SERLINI

Via Cereto, 7
25050 Provaglio d'Iseo (BS)
Tel. +39 030 9823338
info@bersiserlini.it
www.bersiserlini.it
 bersiserlini.franciacorta

YEAR OF FOUNDATION 1886
NAME OF THE OWNER Arturo, Maddalena and Chiara Bersi Serlini
TOTAL BOTTLES PRODUCED 200,000
DIRECT SALES
VISITS TO THE WINERY - RESERVATION NEEDED
HECTARES OF VINEYARD 30
RESTAURANT

This estate is in the Torbiere Nature Reserve in Sebibo and Piero Bersi Serlini is one of its caretakers. Today the historic estate is run by sisters Maddalena and Chiara and thanks to them the level of quality has decidedly increased in recent years. The vineyards have for

some years been organically cultivated and the whole estate has now almost totally been converted. The winery is in a restored 1100 century building set in a suggestive landscape.

 90   Price B
Franciacorta Satèn

100% Chardonnay grapes. 30% matures in barrique and 30 months on yeasts. Bright straw yellow. On the nose is floral with aromas of broom and wisteria, delicate tangerine, verbena and melissa. On the mouth creamy and soft with taste of citrus and mint. On the finish savory and willowy.

 89   Price B
Franciacorta Extra Brut 2012

Blend of 70% Chardonnay and 30% Pinot Bianco. It matures 4 years on yeasts. Golden straw yellow color, thick and fine perlage. Crispy on the nose with aromas of green apple, lime, pennyroyal and lemon thyme. On the mouth is vibrant tense with taste of white peach to make the drink balanced and fresh.

ALESSIO BRANDOLINI

Frazione Boffalora, 68
27040 San Damiano Al Colle (PV)
Tel. +39 0385 75232
info@alessiobrandolini.com
www.alessiobrandolini.com
 AziendaAgricolaAlessioBrandolini

YEAR OF FOUNDATION 1873
NAME OF THE OWNER Alessio Brandolini
TOTAL BOTTLES PRODUCED 70,000
DIRECT SALES
VISITS TO THE WINERY - RESERVATION NEEDED
HECTARES OF VINEYARD 9

Alessio Brandolini is the owner of this small but prestigious estate his family founded five generations ago. The young enologist has an impressive scholastic and employment experience and, aside from acting as a consultant to others, he personally runs the family's winery, which he registered with the Italian Federation of Independent Winemakers (FIVI), producing some top quality wines.

 90   👍 Price A
Malvasia Il Bardughino 2015

100% Malvasia di Candria grapes from a 40 years

old vineyard. Stainless steel only on the lees for 5 months. Straw yellow color. On the nose it's attractive with aromas of gasoline, almost Riesling style, then aromas of wisteria and fruits. On the mouth full, warm, full-flavored, very savory and with great persistence.

BRUNO VERDI

Via Vergonberra 5
27044 Canneto Pavese (PV)
Tel. +39 0385 88023
Fax +39 0385 241623
info@brunoverdi.it
www.brunoverdi.it
Bruno-Verdi-wines
@brunoverdiwines

YEAR OF FOUNDATION 1980
NAME OF THE OWNER Paolo Verdi
TOTAL BOTTLES PRODUCED 100,000
DIRECT SALES
VISITS TO THE WINERY - RESERVATION NEEDED
HECTARES OF VINEYARD 10

Four generations of the Verdi family have worked this land with a rigorous vocation for winegrowing and seeking quality in production based on the fruit of their vineyards, native Oltrepò grapes. Paolo Verdi has taken the heredity from his father and with tenacity transformed it into a solid and interesting winemaking reality, following every phase of production and giving a voice to the DOCG wines with convincing results.

| 92 | Price B |

OP Cavariola Riserva 2012

Blend of 55% Croatina, 25% Barbera and 10%, 10% Ughetta di Canneto grapes. It matures 24 moths in French barrique. Violet ruby red color with garnet hues. On the nose aromas of underbrush, eucalyptus and spicy notes, dry plum, and licorice root, nutmeg and clove. On the mouth it's full and well-structured with thick and tidy tannin.

| 89 | Price A |

OP Barbera Campo del Marrone 2013

100% Barbera grapes from a single vineyard. 12 months in big oak barrels. Bright ruby red color with purple hues. On the nose aromas of red fruits, gardenia and violet, dark cherry and blueberry, licorice and tobacco. On the mouth it's fresh and

savory, with a light alcoholic hint but with very integrated tannins. On the finish is peppery and balanced.

CÀ MAIOL

Via dei Colli Storici, 119
25015 Desenzano Del Garda (BS)
Tel. +39 030 9910006
Fax +39 030 9910014
info@camaiol.it
www.camaiol.it
camaiol
@camaiol

YEAR OF FOUNDATION 1967
NAME OF THE OWNER Patrizia and Fabio Contato
TOTAL BOTTLES PRODUCED 1,500,000
DIRECT SALES
VISITS TO THE WINERY - RESERVATION NEEDED
HECTARES OF VINEYARD 155
HOSPITALITY
CERTIFIED ORGANIC VITICULTURE
OLIVE OIL PRODUCTION

Located on Lake Garda, Cà Maiol (former Provenza) has demonstrated how Trebbiano di Lugana, or better Turbiana, can be a very versatile and expressive grape that can produce rich and pleasing wines depending on the method employed, including the traditional method for sparkling wine. Fabio Contato owns the estate and personally puts his signature on its best wines, as if to underscore the identity and style of this major Garda producer as well as its capacity to produce quality.

| 91 | Price B |

Lugana Fabio Contato 2012

100% Trebbiano di Lugana. It matures in French durmast barrique. Bright golden yellow color. On the nose is attractive and intense with aromas of vanilla and sweet spices, ripe fruits, golden apple, plums, alfalfa and walnut. On the mouth it's full, savory, noble. Buttery on the finish.

| 89 | Price A |

Lugana Molin 2015

100% Trebbiano di Lugana grapes. Stainless steel only. Pale straw yellow color. On the nose aromas of peach, pineapple, flowers as lemon flower and jasmine, tropical scents of mango and fresh almond and agave juice. On the mouth it's light and dynamic, rish taste of fruits. Clear and savory finish.

---

 86   Price B

Lugana Metodo Classico Brut

100% Trebbiano di Lugana grapes. Matures 36 months in stainless steel on the yeasts. Bright straw yellow color with elegant perlage. Fragrant and fruity on the nose, white peach and crunchy pear, medlar and medicinal herbs hint. Clean and agile on the mouth, fruity and brinty in the finish.

★

CA' DEI FRATI

Via dei Frati, 22 - Frazione Lugana
25019 Sirmione (BS)
Tel. +39 030 919468
info@cadeifrati.it
www.cadeifrati.it/
 Ca-dei-Frati
🐦 @CadeiFrati1

YEAR OF FOUNDATION 1969
NAME OF THE OWNER Fratelli Dal Cero
TOTAL BOTTLES PRODUCED 1,400,000
DIRECT SALES
VISITS TO THE WINERY - RESERVATION NEEDED
HECTARES OF VINEYARD 120
HOSPITALITY
RESTAURANT

This lovely estate has made history in Lugana del Garda with well-made and expressive wines, the product of an authentic vocation for quality since 1939, when Felice Dal Cero chose Sirmione has the center of his production having understood its potential for winemaking. In 1969, after 30 years of work in the vineyard and the winery, his son took part in the creation of the DOC appellation and began to produce Lugana Casa dei Frati. Today his children are running the estate respecting the traditions that for decades have tied the Dal Cero family to the land.

☐ 88   Price A

Lugana Brolettino 2014

100% Lugana grapes. It matures in big oak barrels. Strong straw yellow color. On the nose presents smoky scents at first, then yellow flowers, chamomile, broom and an hint of anise. On the mouth the taste is important, juicy with an adequate acidity and a thick body. Tasty on the finish.

☐ 86   👍 Price A

Lugana I Frati 2014

100% Lugana grapes. Stainless steel only. On the nose intense, floral with aromas of yellow peach, anise and tea leafs. On the mouth is light and savory, soft and full-flavored.

★★★

CA' DEL BOSCO

Via Albano Zanella, 13
25030 Erbusco (BS)
Tel. +39 030 7766111
Fax +39 030 7268425
cadelbosco@cadelbosco.com
www.cadelbosco.com
 CaDelBosco
🐦 @Ca_del_Bosco

YEAR OF FOUNDATION 1969
NAME OF THE OWNER Maurizio Zanella, presidente
TOTAL BOTTLES PRODUCED 1,470,000
DIRECT SALES
VISITS TO THE WINERY - RESERVATION NEEDED
HECTARES OF VINEYARD 159

Today the winery run by Maurizio Zanella is one of the leading producers of sparkling wine in Italy with its Cuvée Annamaria Clementi and the Vintage Collection line. In 1962, Albano and Annamaria Clementi bought property in Erbusco that included a farmhouse named Ca' del Bosco that she immediately fell in love with. As soon as the family realized the potential of the land they had acquired, they began to buy adjoining land and soon planted their first vineyards. The watershed moment came after their son Maurizio visited France and came back with the idea of producing quality sparkling wine and towards the end of the 1970s he was experimenting with the Franciacorta traditional method. The aspirations they had then are the same as today: achieving the highest quality in the vineyard and the winery with a style based on elegance, entrepreneurial skill and a propensity for excellence.

---

 96   Price D

Franciacorta Vintage Collection Dosage Zéro Noir Riserva 2007

100% Pinot Nero from the Belvedere vineyard. It

matures at first in barrique, then 8 years on yeasts. Strong golden yellow color with fine perlage. On the nose intense and vivid with aromas of resins and laurel, crispy apple, currant and walnut, bergamot and helichrysum. On the mouth powerful and expressive, great vitality and hint of wine taste, tense and a pervasive savory depth.

 94 Price C

Franciacorta Vintage Collection Brut 2011

Blend of 55% Chardonnay, 30% Pinot Nero, 15% Pinot Bianco grapes. It matures in durmast barrels with 48 moths on yeasts. Bright golden yellow color with a very fine perlage. Fragrant on the nose with aromas of sweet bread and white peach, white melon and candied ginger. On the mouth intense and vibrant with a very well balanced persistence between fruits and acidity.

 92 Price C

Franciacorta Vintage Collection Dosage Zéro 2011

Blend of 65% Chardonnay, 22% Pinot Nero, 13% Pinot Bianco grapes. It ferments is durmast barrels and matures for 48 months on yeasts. Golden straw yellow color with very fine perlage. On the nose is intense and vibrant with citrusy notes and aromas of pink grapefruit and kumquat, sweet bread and ginger on the finish. Fragrant and fresh on the mouth, very good body , tense and with a savory finish.

 90 Price C

Maurizio Zanella 2011

Blend of 50% Cabernet Sauvignon, 25% Merlot , 25% Cabernet Franc. 60% matures in durmast barrels for 14 months. Dark purple red color. On the nose elegant and refined with aromas of crisp blueberry, red apple skin, morello cherry, plum, pepper and cinchona. Mainly fruity on the mouth with harmonic and elegant tannins. On the finish spicy with a distinguished body.

CA' DI FRARA

Località Casa Ferrari, 1
27040 Mornico Losana (PV)
Tel. +39 0383 892299
Fax +39 0383 892752
cadifrara@cadifrara.com
www.cadifrara.com
 cadifrara
 @cadifrara

YEAR OF FOUNDATION **1905**
NAME OF THE OWNER **Luca Bellani**
TOTAL BOTTLES PRODUCED **470,000**
DIRECT SALES
VISITS TO THE WINERY - RESERVATION NEEDED
HECTARES OF VINEYARD **47**

This over 100-year-old winery is emblematic of the appellation and is now run by the third generation of its founders. The estate is situated between the towns of Mornico Losana (in the district of Casa Ferrari which in dialect is called Cà di Frara) and Oliva Gessi and is specialized in Riesling. The soil of the vineyard varies and is chalk-limestone where the white grapes are grown and marl-clay for the reds. This allows the estate to produce some interesting wines that have consistent quality and expressiveness. This is especially true of the Pinot Noir, a varietal that thrives in this area.

■ **88** Price B

OP Il Frater Riserva 2011

Blend of 95% Croatina, 5% Pinot Nero grapes. Stainless steel only. Intense ruby red color with purple reflexes. Eucalyptus on the nose with aromas of blackberry, blueberry, cinchona and mint licorice. On the mouth full and juicy with strong tannin that is balanced by a nice spicy freshness.

☐ **87** Price A

OP Riesling Superiore 2015

100% Riesling Renano. Stainless steel only. Greenish straw yellow color. On the nose it presents fruity, lightly tropical aromas of pineapple, white melon, green apple, banana, thyme and cardamom. Savory, fresh, juicy and dynamic on the mouth.

CAMOSSI

Via Metelli 5
25030 Erbusco (BS)
Tel. 0307268022
azvitcamossi@yahoo.it

YEAR OF FOUNDATION **1996**
NAME OF THE OWNER **Camossi Family**
TOTAL BOTTLES PRODUCED **60000**
VISITS TO THE WINERY - RESERVATION NEEDED
HECTARES OF VINEYARD **30**

Founded in 1989, this estate has been producing Franciacorta Metodo Classico since 1996.

Brothers Claudio and Dario Camossi take special care of production from the vineyard to the bottle and seek to enhance the different traits of grapes from the areas of Erbusco, Paratico and Provaglio d'Iseo. The production style is clean and incisive with characteristics that are beginning to stand out year after year.

 91 Price C

Franciacorta Pietro Camossi Extra Brut Riserva 2008

100% Pinot Nero. It matures on yeasts for more than 60 months. Bright straw yellow with a very fine perlage. On the nose it's delicate and vibrant with fresh aromas of lemon, grapefruit and mint, barley biscuit with a smoky scents. On the mouth vivid and clean, pleasant with a long savory and lively taste, tense and accurate finish.

 88 Price B

Franciacorta Extra Brut 2011

100% Chardonnay grapes. It lies 48 months on yeasts. Golden straw yellow color with fine perlage. On the nose it's fragrant with aromas of bread, blossom honey, peach, lime and kumquats, with a scents of melissa. On the mouth tense and alive, pleasant and dynamic.

CASTELLO DI CIGOGNOLA

Piazza Castello, 1
27040 Cigognola (PV)
Tel. +39 0385 284828
Fax +39 0385 284263
info@castellodicigognola.com
www.castellodicigognola.com
castellodicigognola

YEAR OF FOUNDATION **2000**
NAME OF THE OWNER **Gian Marco Moratti**
TOTAL BOTTLES PRODUCED **90,000**
DIRECT SALES
VISITS TO THE WINERY - RESERVATION NEEDED
HECTARES OF VINEYARD **30**

The property used to belong the Brichetto family of Genoa and it was run by the grandfather of Letizia Moratti, née Brichetto. It was later sold and then in 2000 Gian Marco Moratti, who had married Letizia Brichetto, bought it with the intention of bringing it back to its former glory. Today it is one of the best wine estates in Oltrepò. The vineyards surround its beautiful castle and are cultivated with Barbera and Pinot Nero and the wines they produce are magnificent.

 95 Price B

OP Barbera La Maga 2013

100% Barbera grapes. It matures for 18 mon ths between tonneau and big oak barrels. Very intense ruby color. Clean on the nose with aromas of violet and raspberry at first, then light vanilla and very refined smoky scents on the finish. On the mouth the taste is tense but compound with great acidity that is not aggressive but instead gives it a warm, savory and very persistent finish.

 90 Price B

OP Pinot Nero Pas Dosé 'More Rosé 2012

100% Pinot Nero grapes. Classic Method. Light pinkish color with plentiful and quick perlage. On the nose aromas of yeasts and currant that together create a fragrant and attractive mixture of scents. On the mouth savory, polite, agile, fresh, easy to drink. Persistent finish.

89 Price A

OP Barbera Dodicidodici 2014

100% Barbera grapes. It matures in big oak barrels for 8 months. Bright and vivid ruby color. On the nose aromas of fruits as citrus, blood orange at first, then blackberry and violet. On the mouth it's agile, savory, very pleasant, not as strong as in other versions but very delicious to drink.

CASTELLO DI GUSSAGO

Via Manica 8
25064 Gussago (BS)
Tel. 0302525267
Fax 0302529311
info@castellodigussago.it
www.castellodigussago.it

YEAR OF FOUNDATION **2007**
NAME OF THE OWNER **Gozio Family**
TOTAL BOTTLES PRODUCED **100000**
DIRECT SALES
VISITS TO THE WINERY
HECTARES OF VINEYARD **15**

The Gozio family have been distillers in Franciacorta since 1901 and almost ten years ago began making their own wine after restoring four-hectares of old terraced vineyards surrounding the Santissima monastery as well as another 11 hectares of vineyards around Colle Barbisone, in the town of Gussago. In order to enhance the value of their product, in 2013 they began to convert to organic farming and today have become an interesting and focused reality, one which Sabrina Gozio represents with determination and passion.

 88 Price B

Franciacorta La Santissima Pas Dosé 2011

Blend of 90% Pinot Nero and 10% Chardonnay grapes, 36 months on the yeasts. Pale straw yellow color with a fine perlage. On the nose it presents aromas of jasmine, apple skin, lime and tangerine skin, bread crust and grapefruit juice. On the mouth it results very acidic and full-bodied. Light notes of almond in the finish.

CAVALLERI

Via Provinciale, 96
25030 Erbusco (BS)
Tel. +39 030 7760217
Fax +39 030 7267350
cavalleri@cavalleri.it
www.cavalleri.it
 Cavalleri

YEAR OF FOUNDATION **1967**
NAME OF THE OWNER **Giulia and Maria Cavalleri**
TOTAL BOTTLES PRODUCED **250,000**
DIRECT SALES
VISITS TO THE WINERY - RESERVATION NEEDED
HECTARES OF VINEYARD **44**

They acquired their first vineyard in Erbusco in 1842 and since then the Cavalleri family has been a point of reference in Franciacorta, an appellation of which Giovanni Cavalleri was one of the founders and served as president of the producers' association. Their wines have a well-defined and recognizable style that combines richness and finesse. The Franciacorta is produced exclusively with Chardonnay from the estate's vineyards and special attention is paid not only to the acidity but also to ensure that the grapes reach full phenolic maturity. In

order to highlight distinct personality of the vineyard's plots and exalt the different characteristics of the territory, a vintage Collezione Grandi Cru wine has been created that is only made in the best years.

 92 Price B

Franciacorta Pas Dosé 2011

100% Chardonnay grapes. 15% of the musts lies in durmast barrels and matures 44 months on yeasts. Golden straw yellow color with fine perlage. On the nose presents smoky scents with aromas of vanilla at first, then wild herbs and linden honey. On the mouth it results delicate, fresh and balanced. Very long on the finish.

 90 Price B

Franciacorta Satèn

100% Chardonnay grapes. 30% matures in barrique on yeasts for 30 months. Golden yellow color with a fine perlage. On the nose aromas of fruits such as pineapple, apple pulp, an hint of flowers with aromas of broom and helichrysum and a delicate note of chamomile. On the mouth it's fresh and vivid, creamy with a savory and clean finish.

CONTADI CASTALDI

Via Colzano, 32
25030 Adro (BS)
Tel. +39 030 7450126
Fax +39 030 7450322
contadicastaldi@contadicastaldi.it
www.contadicastaldi.it
 Contadi
 @contadicastaldi

YEAR OF FOUNDATION **1987**
NAME OF THE OWNER **Francesca Moretti**
TOTAL BOTTLES PRODUCED **900,000**
DIRECT SALES
VISITS TO THE WINERY - RESERVATION NEEDED
HECTARES OF VINEYARD **130**

An ancient building that once housed a furnace today hosts the Contadi Castaldi winery, which the eclectic entrepreneur Vittorio Moretti decided to acquire because of the childhood memories his wife Mariella had of the area. Today in its brick-lined halls they age Franciacorta made with grapes grown by neighboring winegrowers. The name dates back to the Middle Ages when the 'contadi' were counties of Franciacorta and the 'castaldi' were those who governed them. The image of the winery, on the other hand, is very modern and Vittorio Moretti has defined it as "the young face of Franciacorta".

🔲 89   Price B
Franciacorta Zero 2012

Blend of 50% Pinot Nero and 50% chardonnay grapes. It matures in stainless steel and barrique for at least 36 months on the yeasts. Bright straw yellow color with golden hues and fine perlage. On the nose it's fresh with aromas of wild herbs, oregano, lime, pineapple juice and grapefruit. Vertical on the mouth with notes of walnut. Savory finish.

🔲 88   Price B
Franciacorta Rosé

Blend of 65% Chardonnay, 35% Pinot Nero grapes. It matures in stainless steel and barrique at least 24 months on yeasts. Powder pink color with fine perlage. On the nose it presents aromas of orange blossom and rosehip, peach and kumquat. On the mouth willowy and balanced with a spicy finish of pink pepper and ginger.

CONTE VISTARINO

Frazione Scorzoletta, 82/84
27040 Pietra De' Giorgi (PV)
Tel. +39 0385 85117
Fax +39 0385 85530
info@contevistarino.it
www.contevistarino.it
🅕 *Cantina-Conte-Vistarino*
🐦 *@ConteVistarino*

YEAR OF FOUNDATION **1674**
NAME OF THE OWNER **Ottavia Giorgi di Vistarino**
TOTAL BOTTLES PRODUCED **400,000**
DIRECT SALES
VISITS TO THE WINERY - RESERVATION NEEDED
HECTARES OF VINEYARD **200**

This splendid 19th century residence represents the origins of the Giorgi di Vistarino family in this area where winegrowing was the most suited activity given its altitude. The decision in the 19th century to cultivate Pinot Nero was quite adventurous for the time but it has continued with dedication through the years by Ottiaviano and Carlo and today by the latest generation with Ottavia Giorgio di Vista-

rino. Their style seeks to create authentic and elegant wines using the capacity of Pinot Nero to convey the character of the land.

🔲 90   Price B
OP Metodo Classico 1865 Brut 2011

Blend of 95% Pinot Nero grapes vinified in white in stainless steel and 5% Chardonnay grapes vinified in oak barrels 36 months on yeasts. Bright straw yellow color with a fine perlage. On the nose fragrant, fresh, floral aromas and a crispy note of dry fruits. On the mouth it's energetic and upbeat but elegant with notes of citrus and an almost almody finish.

⬛ 88   Price B
OP Pinot Nero Pernice 2013

100% Pinot Nero grapes. It matures in oak barrels. Intense ruby red color. On the nose aromas of black cherry and raspberry, clove and violet, cocoa and roast scents. On the mouth it's soft with a light savory and good progression, juicy with a sinuous and delicate tannin.

CORTEAURA

Via Colzano 13
25030 Adro (BS)
Tel. 0307357281
Fax 0305533119
info@corteaura.it
www.corteaura.it
🅕 *Corteaura-Franciacorta*
🐦 *corteaura*

YEAR OF FOUNDATION **2009**
NAME OF THE OWNER **Federico Fossati**
TOTAL BOTTLES PRODUCED **100,000**
DIRECT SALES
VISITS TO THE WINERY
HECTARES OF VINEYARD **5**

A new estate created in Adro by the Fossati family from Veneto with the support of enologist Pierangelo Bonomi, who is specialized in Franciacorta sparkling wine. Its headquarters is in a farm complex where the wine is produced in a simple and traditional way with particular attention paid to the time the wine sits on the lees, which tends to be longer than usual, in order to achieve an agile and quality style. The estate has chosen the turtle as its symbol because it is slow and lives long.

209

90   Price B
Franciacorta Satèn

100% Chardonnay grapes. Stainless steel only with 36 months on yeasts. Golden straw yellow color with a very fine perlage. On the nose it's fresh and floral with aromas of white rose, osmanthus, lemon skin and juice and a hint of fresh herb. On the mouth it's fresh and delicate with a taste of white chocolate in the finish. Intense and persistent.

COSTARIPA

Via della Costa, 1/a
25080 Moniga Del Garda (BS)
Tel. +39 0365 502010
Fax +39 0365 502675
info@costaripa.it
www.costaripa.it
 Costaripa
 @costaripa

YEAR OF FOUNDATION **1936**
NAME OF THE OWNER **Mattia Vezzola**
TOTAL BOTTLES PRODUCED **400,000**
DIRECT SALES
VISITS TO THE WINERY - RESERVATION NEEDED
HECTARES OF VINEYARD **55**
CERTIFIED BIODYNAMIC VITICULTURE

Mattia Vezzola recently completed the total acquisition of this estate and can finally dedicate all his time to his winery, something which obliged us to reinsert it in our guide. Vezzola is a professional with vast experience and we are convinced he will give a new impetus to a line of wines that are already excellent, especially the rosé and sparkling wines.

 92   Price B
Mattia Vezzola Grande Annata Brut 2011

100% Chardonnay grapes. Classic method. Bright greenish yellow color with a thick and persistent perlage. On the nose both aromas of yeasts with clean fruity notes such as hawthorn, white peach and honey. On the mouth is creamy, tense, fresh, pleasantly savory and very persistent.

 88   Price A
Valtènesi Chiaretto RosaMara 2015

Blend of 65% Groppello, 20% Marzemino and a blend of Sangiovese and Barbera grapes. Part of the grapes mature in small white durmast barrels and the rest matures in stainless steel. Light pink color. On the nose aromas of grapefruit and currant, very fragrant and clean. Fresh, savory on the mouth with a good body structure.

DERBUSCO CIVES

Via Provinciale 83
25030 Erbusco (BS)
Tel. +39 030 7731164
info@derbuscocives.com
www.derbuscocives.com
 Derbusco-Cives

YEAR OF FOUNDATION **2005**
NAME OF THE OWNER **Giuseppe and Dario Vezzoli, Luigi Dotti, Giampaolo Brescianini and Giovanni Bordiga**
TOTAL BOTTLES PRODUCED **60,000**
DIRECT SALES
VISITS TO THE WINERY - RESERVATION NEEDED
HECTARES OF VINEYARD **12**
HOSPITALITY

The estate was founded by friends who either shared a passion for winegrowing or winemaking and who were all from Erbusco, which became the center of their production and inspired the name which explains the philosophy behind their project. At first their production was limited and employed the help of experienced collaborators with the aim of creating a new voice for Franciacorta. In a relatively short time they have been able establish a distinct style and recognizable personality not only in their wine but also in their packaging. The selection of the grapes and care taken in the vineyard are followed by the wine macerating long on the lees, never less than 30 months, which brings out the potential and expressiveness of the cuvée.

 92   Price B
Franciacorta Brut 2010

100% Chardonnay grapes. It matures partly in barrique with 44 months on yeasts. Bright golden yellow color with a very fine perlage. On the nose aromas of confectionery, lemon curd and white peach with a hint of tangerine. On the mouth is fresh, pressing and full-flavored with a taste of honey. Balanced on the finish.

89   Price C

Franciacorta Rosé Brut 2011

100% Pinot Nero grapes. It matures partly in barrique 40 months on yeasts. Intense antique pink color and fine perlage. On the nose fragrant aromas of bread and juicy mandarin, red currant and vanilla. On the mouth fresh and savory, very delicate, dynamic with a soft finish.

 88   Price C

Franciacorta Crisalis Blanc de Noir Brut 2010

100% Pinot Nero grapes. It matures partly in barrique 50 months on yeasts. Bright golden yellow color with very fine perlage. On the nose thin and elegant with aromas of medicinal herbs, crisp apple and dark citrus. On the mouth it's tense and vivid, very persistent and tonic with a stretched and rhythmic length and a savory finish.

★★

FAY

Via Pila Caselli, 1 - Frazione San Giacomo
23036 Teglio (SO)
Tel. +39 0342 786071
Fax +39 0342 786058
info@vinifay.it
www.vinifay.it

YEAR OF FOUNDATION 1973
NAME OF THE OWNER Sandro Fay
TOTAL BOTTLES PRODUCED 50,000
DIRECT SALES
VISITS TO THE WINERY - RESERVATION NEEDED
HECTARES OF VINEYARD 14

Sandro Fay has been making his wine in Valtellina for over 40 years using a style geared to exalt the most particular characteristics of the territory. The wines are elegant, essential and age well without any concessions or attempt to appeal to global wine trends. For a few years now he has been joined by his young children with Marco involved in the technical side while Elena handling administration and sales.

 92   Price B

Valtellina Superiore Valgella Ca' Morei 2013

100% Nebbiolo Chiavennasca grapes.1 year in barrique. Intense garnet color. On the nose aromas of macerated black cherry, kirsch, cocoa and vanilla. On the mouth firm, savory, full-bodied, slightly tannic and very long finish.

 91   Price B

Valtellina Superiore Sassella Il Glicine 2013

100% Nebbiolo Chiavennasca grapes. It matures for 1 year in barrique. Very intense garnet color. On the nose aromas of cocoa and black cherry under spirit, tobacco and smoky scents. On the mouth it's full, agile, lightly tannic with a lovely acidity that supports the body. Great length in the finish.

     88   Price B

Valtellina Superiore Valgella Costa Bassa 2013

100% Nebbiolo Chiavennasca grapes. It matures 1 year in big oak barrels. Vivid garnet color. On the nose aromas of small fruits, even as compote, spicy and floral scents. On the mouth is simpler, agile, pleasant to drink, savory and fresh.

★

FERGHETTINA

Via Saline, 11
25030 Adro (BS)
Tel. +39 030 7451212
Fax +39 030 7453528
info@ferghettina.it
www.ferghettina.it
Ferghettina

YEAR OF FOUNDATION 1991
NAME OF THE OWNER Roberto Gatti
TOTAL BOTTLES PRODUCED 400,000
DIRECT SALES
VISITS TO THE WINERY - RESERVATION NEEDED
HECTARES OF VINEYARD 200

The Adro winery was created almost 25 years ago by Roberto Gatti, who previously worked at the Bellavista winery, and has over time the vineyards have expanded in size and today sees the new generation involved in Franciacorta production. The production style involves using only first, soft-pressed must, which has some of the best characteristics of Franciacorta, and the wine is made in stainless steel vats to maintain a clear and fresh flavor.

88 Price B

Franciacorta Extra Brut 2010

Blend of 80% Chardonnay and 20% Pinot Nero grapes. Stainless steel only 69 months on yeasts. Bright straw yellow color with fine perlage. On the nose it's delicate with aromas of elderflower, fresh almond, sweet mandarin and ripe lemon juice. On the mouth is balanced and vivid, creamy and savory in the finish.

86 Price B

Franciacorta Brut

Blend of 95% Chardonnay and 5% Pinot Nero grapes. Stainless steel only 24 months on yeasts. Greenish straw yellow color with fine perlage. On the nose it presents aromas of almond and gooseberry, light scents of confectionary and a scent of mint at the end. On the mouth tense and fresh. Soft in the finish.

FONDO BOZZOLE

Via Bozzole
46025 Poggio Rusco (MN)
Tel. +39 348 3785695
info@fondobozzole.it
www.fondobozzole.it
FondoBozzoleLambrusco

YEAR OF FOUNDATION 1981
NAME OF THE OWNER Franco and Mario Accorsi
TOTAL BOTTLES PRODUCED
DIRECT SALES
VISITS TO THE WINERY - RESERVATION NEEDED
HECTARES OF VINEYARD 8
CERTIFIED ORGANIC VITICULTURE

While the philosophy of the Accorsi brothers may appear to be 'organic without compromise', it disguises a great capacity to integrate with nature and the environment. This is done with low yield (6-7,00kg per hectare which is half what is allowed for the appellation) and maniacal care in the vineyard and the environment it is set in. They have also adopted winegrowing methods that can be considered revolutionary like the Guyot training of the vines, something rare for the varietals and the area.

87 👍 Price A

Lambrusco Mantovano Incantabiss 2015

100% Lambrusco Ruberti grapes. Stainless steel

only. Purple color with a relatively persistent foam. On the nose aromas of underbrush , strawberries and raspberries in evidence. The wine feel, even if it'is a young product, is just hinted. On the mouth clean, very fresh and exuberant.

⭐

FRATELLI BERLUCCHI

Via Broletto, 2 - Frazione Borgonato
25040 Corte Franca (BS)
Tel. +39 030 984451
Fax +39 030 9828209
info@fratelliberlucchi.it
www.fratelliberlucchi.it
AziendaAgricolaFratelliBerlucchi
@FratelBerlucchi

YEAR OF FOUNDATION 1967
NAME OF THE OWNER Fratelli Berlucchi
TOTAL BOTTLES PRODUCED 400,000
DIRECT SALES
VISITS TO THE WINERY - RESERVATION NEEDED
HECTARES OF VINEYARD 70

An ancient, frescoed building is home to this historic winery in Borgonato di Corte Franca that, with its some 70 hectares of vineyards, belongs to the family, or better the five siblings, headed by the 'Lady of Wine' Pia Donata Berlucchi and the new generation is already getting involved. The productive style for their Franciacorta focuses on the wine's freshness and acidic vivacity even in the Brut versions. In the vineyard, the vines are severely pruned for a low yield while in the winery the grapes are soft-pressed. The wines for the Riserva age long and are those of the 'Casa delle Colonne' line, named after the home of childhood memory.

91 Price B

Franciacorta Freccianera Nature 2012

Blend of 85% Chardonnay and 15% Pinot Nero grapes. Matures 45 months on yeasts. Greenish straw yellow color and very fine perlage. Fragrant on the nose with aromas of shortbread, basswood, sage, mandarin skin and white pepper. On the mouth harmonic and deep, savory almost gingery, agile with a clean finish.

89 Price B

Franciacorta Casa delle Colonne 2009

Blend of 80% Chardonnay and 20% Pinot Nero

grapes. 60 months on yeasts. bright golden yellow color with fine perlage. On the nose aromas of lemon flower and thyme, yeasts and almond paste, scents of tropical fruits and golden apple. On the mouth juicy and opulent with a well-balanced freshness, not extremely willowy but with a good length in the finish.

ENRICO GATTI

Via Metelli, 9
25030 Erbusco (BS)
Tel. +39 030 7267999
Fax +39 030 7760539
info@enricogatti.it
www.enricogatti.it
 aziendaagricola.gattienrico

YEAR OF FOUNDATION **1975**
NAME OF THE OWNER **Lorenzo and Paola Gatti, Enzo Balzarini**
TOTAL BOTTLES PRODUCED **120,000**
DIRECT SALES
VISITS TO THE WINERY - RESERVATION NEEDED
HECTARES OF VINEYARD **17**

This estate founded in 1975 is the realization of Enrico Gatti's dream to become a small wine producer. Over the years, his name has become a reference for a winemaker's approach to Franciacorta. In 1984, his son Lorenzo Gatti and his brother-in-law Enzo Balzarini took over and continued the founder's tradition with the same love of the land and the vineyards. The style of their wines seeks to exalt the typicity of the grapes and the territory in order to bring out the personality of the vineyards. In 2005, a new, underground cellar was completed where the wines now complete their aging with excellent results, especially in the better vintage years.

▣ **90** Price B
Franciacorta Nature
Blend of 85% Chardonnay and 15% Pinot Nero grapes. Stainless steel only at least 24 months on yeasts. Bright greenish straw yellow color with fine perlage. On the nose it presents aromas of Mediterranean herbs, thyme, cedar, bergamot and linden flowers. On the mouth tense and fresh with a savory finish.

▣ **88** Price B
Franciacorta Brut
100% Chardonnay grapes. Stainless steel only at least 24 months on yeasts. Light golden straw yellow color with fine perlage. Floral on the nose with aromas of broom and lime, lemon juice and verbena. On the mouth delicate, pleasantly citrusy with a savory and fresh finish.

IL BOSCO

Località il Bosco
27049 Zenevredo (PV)
Tel. +39 038 5245326
Fax +39 038 5245324
info@ilbosco.com
www.ilbosco.com
 TenutaIlBosco
🐦 *@zonin1821*

YEAR OF FOUNDATION **1987**
NAME OF THE OWNER **Zonin Family**
TOTAL BOTTLES PRODUCED **1,000,000**
DIRECT SALES
VISITS TO THE WINERY
HECTARES OF VINEYARD **152**

Expanding the vineyard from 30 to 152 hectares in less than 25 years is evidence of the commitment that the Zonin family has made to this estate, which today is one of the best in the historic area of Oltrepò Pavese. Great attention is paid to the traditional method and the sparkling wines in general but also to the wines made from Riesling, Bonarda and Barbera and, above all, Pinot Nero. The production from the latter grape is proving to be the most interesting, as evidenced by the wine Oltrenero.

▣ **89** Price B
OP Metodo Classico Brut Nature 2010
100% Pinot Nero grapes. Stainless steel and with the 2% maturing in oak barrels 48 months on yeasts. Light straw yellow color with fine perlage. On the nose aromas of green apple, kiwi, aromatic herbs, blond orange, bread crust and elderflower. On the mouth it results firm with a pleasant savory taste that stays clear untill the finish.

▣ **87** Price B
Franciacorta Oltrenero Cruasè
100% Pinot Nero grapes. Stainless steel only with a

light maceration on the skins 24 months on yeasts. Bright salmon pink color with fine perlage. On the nose aromas of strawberries, raspberry and mandarin, with scents of spring flowers and bread crust. On the mouth tonic and fresh, stretched and clean.

LA COSTAIOLA

Via Costaiola, 23
27054 Montebello Della Battaglia (PV)
Tel. +39 0383 83169
Fax +39 0383 693428
info@costaiola.it
www.lacostaiola.it
 lacostaiola.vini

YEAR OF FOUNDATION 1938
NAME OF THE OWNER Rossetti and
Scrivani Families
TOTAL BOTTLES PRODUCED 100,000
DIRECT SALES
VISITS TO THE WINERY - RESERVATION NEEDED
HECTARES OF VINEYARD 7

According to the winery's owners, here technology and tradition go hand in hand and are not in contrast. We believe this is how it should be and is the reason why we included this small and promising estate which in recent years has proved to be reliable with the excellent quality of some of its wines.

██ 88   🖒 Price A
OP Pinot Nero Bricca 2012

100% Pinot Nero grapes. Stainless steel only. Vivid garnet ruby color. On the nose it's varietal with aromas of currant and strawberries. On the mouth it's fresh and pleasantly savory with good body and a long finish.

LE FRACCE

Via Castel del Lupo, 5
27045 Casteggio (PV)
Tel. +39 0383 805769
info@lefracce.com
www.lefracce.com
 lefracce

YEAR OF FOUNDATION 1905
NAME OF THE OWNER Fondazione Bussolera Branca
TOTAL BOTTLES PRODUCED 160,000

DIRECT SALES
VISITS TO THE WINERY - RESERVATION NEEDED
HECTARES OF VINEYARD 40

A classic example of an Oltrepò estate in the truest sense. Founded over a century ago, it still produces wines with uncommon continuity and reliability. Their production includes almost all the wines typical to the area and the winery is situated in an unforgettable location rich in history and set in a beautiful landscape, a vast park with centuries-old trees.

☐ 86   🖒 Price A
OP Pinot Grigio Levriere 2015

100% Pinot Grigio grapes. Stainless steel only on the lees. Straw yellow color. Fruity and citrusy on the nose with aromas of chamomile at first , then cedar and pear Williams. On the mouth savory and tense, very pleasant and easy to drink. On the finish is thin and averagely long.

▣ 85   🖒 Price A
OP Bonarda Frizzante Rubiosa 2015

100% Bonarda grapes. Stainless steel only. Violet ruby color. On the nose it's very fragrant with intense scents of yeasts and strawberry. Vivid and a little tannic on the mouth, surely young but very pleasant to drink.

LE MARCHESINE

Via Vallosa, 31
25050 Passirano (BS)
Tel. +39 030 657005
Fax +39 030 6857933
info@lemarchesine.com
www.lemarchesine.com
 Le Marchesine
 @LeMarchesine

YEAR OF FOUNDATION 1985
NAME OF THE OWNER Biatta Family
TOTAL BOTTLES PRODUCED 375,000
DIRECT SALES
VISITS TO THE WINERY - RESERVATION NEEDED
HECTARES OF VINEYARD 44

This Passirano winery was created in 1985 by Giovanni Biatta, a descendant of a family of winegrowers, and is run today by his son Loris, who in turn is now assisted by his children. It is also one of those that in the past ten years has developed the most in Franciacorta. Although the winery benefits from the family's five-generation tradition and experience in winegrowing, it has a great desire to innovate inspired by the authentic passion that those who have grown up in the vineyards have. The result are wines with a rich and clean style which unite aromatic pleasure and immediacy.

converted to bio-dynamic dictates and in 2011 became Demeter certified. On its label is has a symbol with 15 moons that refers to the phases of the moon that are the natural cycles followed for work in the vineyard and the winery. With nature at the heart of production, the wines are clean, pleasing and very drinkable.

 90 Price C

Franciacorta Secolo Novo Brut 2009

100% Chardonnay grapes. Stainless steel only 48 months on yeasts. Bright straw yellow color and fine perlage. On the nose it's fragrant with aromas of hazelnut paste, elderflower, candied citrus and butter pastry. On the mouth it's full and whole with a good tense and citrusy finish.

 87 Price B

Franciacorta Extra Brut

Blend of 65% Chardonnay, 20% Pinot Bianco, 15% Pinot Nero grapes. Stainless steel only 24 months on yeasts. Golden greenish yellow color with fine perlage. On the nose fresh aromas of melissa and lime, wildflowers, lemon and white peach. On the mouth its' quick, harmonic and with good persistence.

 92 Price B

Garda Zalte 2010

Blend of 70% Cabernet Sauvignon and 30% Merlot grapes. It matures in barrique for 16 months. Dark and intense ruby color. On the nose it's complex with intense aromas of blueberry and black currant at first, then vanilla and hints of tobacco and mint. On the mouth it's firm, with thick but fine tannins, great acidity that support the full body. On the finish warm and persistent.

 90 Price A

Valtènesi Chiaretto 2015

Blend of Groppello, Marzemino, Barbera and Sangiovese grapes. Stainless steel only on the lees. On the nose is very fruity with aromas of currant and cherry with a little hint of yeasts. On the mouth it's fresh, savory, polite and pleasant.

LE SINCETTE

Via Rosario, 44
25080 Polpenazze (BS)
Tel. +39 0365 651471
info@lesincette.it
www.lesincette.it
 LeSincette

YEAR OF FOUNDATION **1978**
NAME OF THE OWNER **Brunori Family**
TOTAL BOTTLES PRODUCED **35,000**
DIRECT SALES
VISITS TO THE WINERY - RESERVATION NEEDED
HECTARES OF VINEYARD **11**
CERTIFIED BIODYNAMIC VITICULTURE
OLIVE OIL PRODUCTION

This small Valtènesi estate, which looks out over the area of Garda Bresciano, belongs to the Brunori family and is run by steel industrialist Ruggero and his winegrower brother-in-law Andrea Salvetti. It is a lovely estate of vineyards and olive groves that in 1998 began to be

LO SPARVIERE

Via Costa 2
25040 Monticelli Brusati (BS)
Tel. +39 030 652382
info@losparviere.com
www.losparviere.it
 losparviere.franciacorta

YEAR OF FOUNDATION **1974**
NAME OF THE OWNER **Gussalli Beretta Family**
TOTAL BOTTLES PRODUCED **150,000**
DIRECT SALES
VISITS TO THE WINERY - RESERVATION NEEDED
HECTARES OF VINEYARD **25**

Situated in the Franciacorta countryside, surrounded by vineyards, fields and forests, this ancient 17th century estate was chosen by the Gussalli Beretta family to host their winery. The name refers to the sparrow hawk on the crest above the fireplace in the manor house's main hall. They cultivate Chardonnay and Pinot Nero to have a low yield and the winemaking approach seeks to create a sartorial and precise style based on balance, purity and typicity.

91   Price B

Franciacorta Extra Brut 2009

100% Chardonnay grapes. It matures partly in stainless steel and partly in barrique 60 months on yeasts. Golden straw yellow color with very fine perlage. On the nose it's intriguing and intense with aromas of ginger cookie, lime, pineapple and yellow peach, graphite and peppery spices. On the mouth it's willowy and tonic, stretched and pleasantly savory.

 88   Price B

Franciacorta Monique Rosé

100% Pinot Nero grapes. It matures both in stainless steel and barrique with 24 months on yeasts. Bright auburn peach pink color with fine perlage. On the nose it's intense with aromas of oriental flowers such as ylan ylang and iris, then black cherry. On the mouth it's fruity with pleasant acidity that is prolonged on the finish that presents citrusy and sweet spicy notes.

MAJOLINI

Via Manzoni, 3 - Località Valle
25050 Ome (BS)
Tel. +39 030 6527378
Fax +39 030 6529800
majolini@majolini.it
www.majolini.it
 Majolini-Franciacorta
 @CantinaMajolini

YEAR OF FOUNDATION 1981
NAME OF THE OWNER Fratelli Maiolini
TOTAL BOTTLES PRODUCED 150,000
DIRECT SALES
VISITS TO THE WINERY - RESERVATION NEEDED
HECTARES OF VINEYARD 24
OLIVE OIL PRODUCTION

Ezio Majolini and his brothers have reinforced the voice of eastern Franciacorta and 'upper' Ome area by carrying a project begun by their father Vincenzo in the 1960s and that was recently culminated by the completion of a new cellar. Their watershed moment came in the early 1990s when they acquired land in a winemaking area known as Camèi, which allowed them to boost the potential of their vineyards. The wines have an intense and winey style but with an interesting saline component.

 88   Price B

Franciacorta Blanc de Noir

100% Pinot Nero grapes. Stainless steel only 24 months on yeasts. Greenish yellow color with fine perlage. On the nose aromas of plaster, herbs , verbena , marjoram, white peach and lime. On the mouth it's creamy and pleasant, stretched with a citrusy finish.

 86   Price B

Franciacorta Brut

Blend of 90% Chardonnay and 10% Pinot Nero grapes. It matures at least 30 months on the yeasts. Golden straw yellow color with fine perlage. On the nose aromas of pineapple, apricot, linden flower and pine resin, yeasts. On the mouth it's fruity and soft, fresh, with not very persistent carbon note .

★★

MAMETE PREVOSTINI

Via Don Primo Lucchinetti, 69
23020 Mese (SO)
Tel. +39 0343 41522
Fax +39 0343 41521
info@mameteprevostini.com
www.mameteprevostini.com
 Mamete-Prevostini-Vini-di-Valtellina
 @M_Prevostini

YEAR OF FOUNDATION 1925
NAME OF THE OWNER Mamete Prevostini
TOTAL BOTTLES PRODUCED 180,000
DIRECT SALES
VISITS TO THE WINERY - RESERVATION NEEDED
HECTARES OF VINEYARD 22,5
RESTAURANT

It was in the beginning of the 20th century that 'Grandpa' Mamete Prevostini began to cultivate grapes to make wine for the clients of his family's tavern in Crotasc, which still exists today. His grandson Mamete inherited not only his name but also the estate which has become a beacon for the appellation and Lombardy wine. This above all thanks to the careful use of small wood barrels and the skill to exalt the characteristics of the local grapes and the typicity of Valtellina wines, which thanks to their elegance and complexity are undoubtedly among the best.

93   Price B
Sforzato di Valtellina Corte di Cama 2012

100% Chiavennasca grapes. It dries in fruit sheds until December. 15 months in big oak barrels. Intense garnet color. On the nose it's whole and elegant with aromas of dried violet and dry plum, then hints of eucalyptus and star anise. Soft and warm on the mouth, velvety and full tannins with a pleasant long finish that reminds of plum and eucalyptus notes.

92   Price C
Sforzato di Valtellina Albareda 2012

100% Chiavennasca grapes. It dries in fruit sheds until the end of January. It matures in durmast barrels for 18 months. Concentrate garnet color. On the nose aromas of dried plum, violet, licorice and sweet tobacco leaf. On the palate presents a good body with velvety tannins and good acidity. Very long with notes of licorice in the finish.

90   Price B
Valtellina Superiore Sassella San Lorenzo 2012

100% Chiavennasca grapes. It matures in durmast vats for 12 months. The vineyard is surrounded by the walls of the San Lorenzo monastery. Bright garnet color. On the nose it's eucalyptus and elegant with aromas of mint, berries at first , then violet and underbrush. On the palate it's soft with tannins well in evidence never aggressive. Lively freshness. On the finish notes of berries and mint.

89   Price B
Valtellina Superiore Sassella Sommarovina 2013

100% Chiavennasca grapes. It matures in durmast vats for 12 months. Garnet color. On the nose intense aromas of jasmine, tobacco leaf at first then violet and sweet licorice. The palate is elegant and full bodied. The tannins are thick and in evidence spuppored by a good acidity. Great persistence that reminds notes of mulberry and licorice.

MIGLIOLI

Via C. Aroldi, 97
46019 Viadana (MN)
Tel. +39 0375 781106
info@lambruscomiglioli.it
www.lambruscomiglioli.it

YEAR OF FOUNDATION 1864
NAME OF THE OWNER Alberto a Andrea Miglioli

TOTAL BOTTLES PRODUCED
DIRECT SALES
VISITS TO THE WINERY - RESERVATION NEEDED
HECTARES OF VINEYARD

This winery is located in Viadena, Mantua area, where the Lambrusco has unique, savory and excellent characteristics that make it entirely different from the neighboring varieties. Ampelographic research have determined that a particular indigenous variety is cultivated in this area: Lambrusco Viadanese. The Miglioli family is a leading producer of wines from this variety which today are, in my opinion, among the most inspired. The history of the Miglioli family dates back to 1864. Today the winery is run by Alberto, enologist and farmer, and is brother Andrea, who takes care of "business matters" and is in charge of the final stages of production, including logistics.

🔲 86   👍 Price A
Lambrusco Mantovano Il Boschetto

100% Lambrusco Viandense grapes. Martinotti method. Vivid red color with persistent and lively foam. On the nose aromas of red fruits such as black cherries and cherry, with scents of cut herb. The mouth is balanced in the union of acidity and tannins, attractive to drink.

★★★
MONSUPELLO

Via San Lazzaro, 5
27050 Torricella Verzate (PV)
Tel. +39 0383 896043
Fax +39 0383 896391
monsupello@monsupello.it
www.monsupello.it
f *MONSUPELLO...dal 1893*

YEAR OF FOUNDATION 1893
NAME OF THE OWNER Boatti Family
TOTAL BOTTLES PRODUCED 300,000
DIRECT SALES
VISITS TO THE WINERY - RESERVATION NEEDED
HECTARES OF VINEYARD 48

This is without a doubt one of the best and most representatives producers of Oltrepò sparkling wine. It has always belonged to the Boatti family and following the death of Carlo, the patriarch and a leading figure in local winemaking, his wife and children Laura and Pierangelo have carried on production.

 93   Price B

OP Metodo Classico Nature

Blend of 90% Pinot Nero and 10% Chardonnay grapes. 50% matures in oak barrels 36 months on yeasts. Bright greenish yellow color with fine perlage. On the nose aromas of lime and lemon, leavened bread, hazelnut and almond paste, white peach. The mouth is fragrant, fresh and tense, good length.

 89   Price B

OP Metodo Classico Brut 2011

Blend of 90% Pinot Nero and 10% Chardonnay grapes. Stainless steel only 55 months on yeasts. Golden straw yellow color with fine perlage. The nose is intense with aromas of flowers, currant, and white mulberry, star anise and sweet spices. On the mouth it's clean and soft with a pleasant freshness.

☐ **88**   👍 Price A

Riesling 2015

100% Riesling Renano grapes. Stainless steel only. Greenish yellow color with golden hues. The nose is intensely varietal with aromas of tropical fruits such as fresh passion fruit and white melon, grapefruit and broom. On the mouth it's quick, clearly savory, citrusy, dynamic and crisp.

★★

MONTE ROSSA

Via Monte Rossa, 1 - Località Bornato
25040 Cazzago San Martino (BS)
Tel. +39 030 725066
Fax +39 030 7750061
info@monterossa.com
www.monterossa.com
🟦 *MonteRossaFranciacorta*

YEAR OF FOUNDATION **1972**
NAME OF THE OWNER **Rabotti Family**
TOTAL BOTTLES PRODUCED **500,000**
DIRECT SALES
VISITS TO THE WINERY - RESERVATION NEEDED
HECTARES OF VINEYARD **70**

The winery as it is today dates back to 1972 when the Rabotti family decided to dedicate themselves to farming by restoring an old estate on the hill of Monte Rossa, in Bornato, where they began to experiment with the traditional method that was being adopted in Franciacorta at the time. Paola Rovetta and her husband Paolo Rabotti became great supporters of this method and were among the founders of the Franciacorta producers' association, of which Paolo was the first president. The rigorous method employed to obtain quality production merged with rural traditions to create an artisanal approach that their son Emanuele continues today with commitment, passion and entrepreneurial spirit. The winemaking style is focused on structure and complexity and uses grapes from different vineyards that have different exposures that helps to exalt the aromatic qualities of the grapes.

 95   Price B

Franciacorta Sansevé Satèn

100% Chardonnay. It matures at least 24 months on yeasts. Golden straw yellow color with fine perlage. On the nose the aromas are slightly smoky with scents of almond paste, hazelnut and barely cookie with an hint of citrus. The mouth is delicate, agile with refined freshness and good persistence.

 89   Price B

Franciacorta Flamingo Rosé

Blend of 60% Chardonnay and 40% Pinot Nero. It matures partly in stainless steel and partly in durmast barrels 24 months on yeasts. Pale pink color with fine perlage. On the nose aromas of orange and pomegranate, lemon verbena leafs, white and red currant. The mouth is precise with a good acidity and agile, savory finish.

MONTELIO

Via Domenico Mazza, 1
27050 Codevilla (PV)
Tel. +39 0383 373090
Fax +39 0383 373083
montelio.gio@alice.it
www.montelio.it
🟦 *MontelioVini*

YEAR OF FOUNDATION **1848**
NAME OF THE OWNER **Caterina and Giovanna Brazzoli**
TOTAL BOTTLES PRODUCED **100,000**
DIRECT SALES
VISITS TO THE WINERY - RESERVATION NEEDED

Sisters Caterina and Giovanna Brazzoli are the seventh generation of a family that over a century and a half ago founded this famous Oltrepò estate. Some of you may remember the enthusiastic reviews Luigi Veronelli wrote about it in the 1970s in his Catalogo Bolaffi dei Vini d'Italia. The estate continues to produce interesting and well-made wines with a particular predilection for Müller Thurgau, which has been their specialty for decades now.

☐ 90   👍 Price A

La Giostra 2013

100% Müller Thurgau overripe grapes. It matures partly in big oak barrels and partly in tonneau for 9 months. Intense straw yellow color. On the nose aromas of flowers such as chamomile at first , then medicinal herbs with hints of ripe Renetta apple. On the mouth the taste is savory, warm but agile, salty, with a good persistence in the finish.

☐ 88   👍 Price A

Müller Thurgau 2015

100% Müller Thurgau grapes. Stainless steel only. The nose is fragrant and lightly aromatic with notes of medicinal herb and Renetta apple, very clean and varietal. On the mouth it's deliciously fresh and savory, good body, pleasant to drink with a thin but long finish.

★★

MOSNEL

Via Barboglio, 14
25040 Passirano (BS)
Tel. +39 030 653117
Fax +39 030 654236
 ilmosnel
info@ilmosnel.com
www.ilmosnel.com
 ilMosnel
 @ilMosnel

YEAR OF FOUNDATION **1836**
NAME OF THE OWNER **Giulio and Lucia Barzanò**
TOTAL BOTTLES PRODUCED **250,000**
DIRECT SALES
VISITS TO THE WINERY - RESERVATION NEEDED
HECTARES OF VINEYARD **35**
HOSPITALITY

Becoming an excellent winegrower and producer is a question of personality and continuity and this small winery in Camignone still has the imprint left by Emanuela Barzanò Barboglo, the mother of Lucia and Giulio who to their credit have perpetuated her approach and style. This was a responsibility they took on not only towards the territory and farmers that worked for them but also towards a family tradition of producing wines that had a precise identity, one based on harmonious flavor, an authentic interpretation of the vineyards and a great capacity to age. Among the first wineries too be classified DOCG Franciacorta, it remains a point of reference for the balance and consistency of their cuvée.

🔲 🔲 96   Price B

Franciacorta EBB Extra Brut 2011

100% Chardonnay grapes. It matures in durmast barrique at least 36 months on yeasts. Bright straw yellow color with golden hues and thick but fine perlage. On the nose aromas of jasmine, linden flowers, grapefruits, almond, candied ginger and fresh passion fruit. The mouth is creamy and present a balance and savory citrusy freshness, dynamic and elegant with a salty depth.

🔲 92   Price B

Franciacorta Satèn Brut 2012

100% Chardonnay grapes. 40% of the musts ferments in barrique and matures 36 months on yeasts. Bright golden yellow color and thin and continuous perlage. The nose is intense with aromas of white tea, jasmine, lemon flower and almond shortbread. On the mouth it's silky and tonic, pleasant, with a savory finish with pastry notes.

🔲 89   Price B

Franciacorta Pas Dosé

Blend of 60% Chardonnay, 30% Pinot Bianco and 10% Pinot Nero grapes. Stainless steel only at least 30 months on yeasts. Light straw yellow color with fine perlage. The nose is refined and clear with aromas of crispy yellow plum, grapefruit, cedar and an hint of mint. On the mouth it's fresh and juicy with a pleasant finish.

219

ALFIO MOZZI

Via Cà Bianca 19
23012 Castione Andevenno (SO)
Tel. +39 0342 358670
alfiomozzi@alice.it
☐ *Azienda-Agricola-Alfio-Mozzi*

YEAR OF FOUNDATION **1998**
NAME OF THE OWNER **Alfio Mozzi**
TOTAL BOTTLES PRODUCED **14,000**
DIRECT SALES
VISITS TO THE WINERY - RESERVATION NEEDED
HECTARES OF VINEYARD **4**

Alfio Mozzi spent much of his childhood among the rocky, terraced vineyards of his grandparents in Valtellina. After working for years as a blacksmith, in 1998 he became a wine producer beginning with his Grisone vineyard to which he later added other plots in the Sassella appellation, situated at an altitude of between 350 and 600m above sea level. His dedication to this area of heroic winemaking reveals an aspect of his interesting talent.

■ **89**   Price B
Valtellina Superiore Grisone 2012

100% Nebbiolo Chiavennasca grapes. It matures in oak barrels for 24 months. Light red color. The nose is sweet and floral with aromas of fruit licor and juniper, tobacco and plum. On the mouth it's agile and fresh, harmonic and fine with pepper, deep and stretched tannins.

NINO NEGRI

Via Ghibellini, 3
23030 Chiuro (SO)
Tel. +39 0342 485211
Fax +39 0342 482235
n.negri@giv.it
www.ninonegri.net
☐ *Nino-Negri*

YEAR OF FOUNDATION **1897**
NAME OF THE OWNER **Gruppo Italiano Vini**
TOTAL BOTTLES PRODUCED **800,000**
DIRECT SALES
VISITS TO THE WINERY - RESERVATION NEEDED
HECTARES OF VINEYARD **36**

Certain wineries play a role that goes beyond simple winemaking. Nino Negri, and its historic director Casimiro Maule, in fact, are an authentic bulwark for Valtellina. They protect the landscape and the territory itself by maintaining their terraced vineyards, the dry walls that support them and growing their vines in a way that respects the environment. As for their wines, they are excellent and offered at reasonable prices considering the difficulty in making them and their production cost.

■ ☐ **97**   Price C
Valtellina Superiore Sfursat 5 Stelle 2013

100% Nebbiolo Chiavennasca grapes that dry naturally for 3 months. It matures in barrique for 18 months. Garnet ruby color. The nose is intense and complex with aromas of spices, floral scents of rosehip and violet, eucalyptus and wood notes. On the mouth it's tense and deep, dry with a warm thin tannin and a noble persistence.

■ **93**   Price B
Valtellina Superiore Sfursat Carlo Negri 2012

100% Nebbiolo Chiavennasca grapes. It matures partly in big oak barrels for 22 months, and partly in barrique for 16 months. Concentrated, intense garnet color. The nose is rich and variegated with aromas of kirsch, cocoa, black cherry under spirit, dry plum. The mouth is warm, alcoholic, well sustained by the acidity with lightly choppy tannins because of the youth and with a great persistent finish.

■ **91**   Price B
Valtellina Superiore Vigneto Fracia 2013

100% Nebbiolo Chiavennasca grapes. It matures in durmast barrique for 15 months. Intense garnet ruby color. On the nose aromas of underbrush and licorice, a smoky hint with scents of spices and leather. The mouth is full-flavored, with a gently warm and stretched tannin.

■ **90**   👍 Price A
Valtellina Superiore Grumello Sassorosso 2013

100% Nebbiolo Chiavennasca grapes. It matures for 2/3 in French durmast barrique. Garnet ruby color. On the nose aromas of dark flower, clove and juniper, cocoa and soft scents. The mouth is persistent and elegant with clean tidy tannins and a savory, almondy finish.

■ 90   Price B

Sassella Le Tense 2013

100% Nebbiolo Chiavennasca grapes. It matures in big oak barrels for 20 months. Intense garnet ruby color. On the nose is very traditional with aromas of black cherry and tamarind at first, then licorice. The mouth is ruffled by a young and strong tannin, great acidity, full-bodied but agile and deep at the same time.

OLMO ANTICO

*Via Marconi, 8
27040 Borgo Priolo (PV)
Tel. +39 0383 872672
info@olmoantico.it
www.olmoantico.it*
�f *olmo.antico*

YEAR OF FOUNDATION 1996
NAME OF THE OWNER Paolo Baggini
TOTAL BOTTLES PRODUCED 52,000
DIRECT SALES
VISITS TO THE WINERY - RESERVATION NEEDED
HECTARES OF VINEYARD 36

Paolo Baggini left a successful career as a director of luxury hotels and restaurants to take over his family's wine estate. At the beginning many has doubts about what they considered to be his drastic decision but his limitless passion soon convinced even the most skeptical. Today Olmo Antico is a prestigious estate that respects the environment and is a reality that Paolo is rightfully proud of.

■ 92   Price B

Barbera 2011

100% Barbera grapes. It matures 2 years in big oak barrels. Intense garnet ruby color. A great wine for class and capability to evolve through time. The nose is complex with a range of aromas that go from floral notes of violet to tamarind, licorice and mint. The mouth is supported by the acidity , tense balance and persistent on the finish.

PERLA DEL GARDA

*Via Fenil Vecchio, 9
25017 Lonato (BS)
Tel. +39 030 9103109*

*Fax +39 030 9103109
info@perladelgardo.it
www.perladelgarda.it*
�f *Perla-del-Garda*
🐦 *@perladelgarda*

YEAR OF FOUNDATION 2000
NAME OF THE OWNER Giovanna and Ettore Prandini
TOTAL BOTTLES PRODUCED 120,000
DIRECT SALES
VISITS TO THE WINERY - RESERVATION NEEDED
HECTARES OF VINEYARD 30

This is a young winery but it is already well-known for its beautiful four hectare, for now, organic vineyards and the unusual shape of their bottles. The Prandini family has from the start focused on the wine that best represented the Garda area, Lugana, and brought it international commercial success thanks to intelligent and efficient marking and impeccably made wines.

☐ 89   Price B

Lugana Superiore Madonna della Scoperta 2013

100% Trebbiano di Lugana grapes. It matures in stainless steel as well as small durmast vats for 29 months. Straw yellow color. On the nose aromas of white pulp fruits and crisp yellow plums, an hint of wildflowers, graphite and spices. On the mouth it presents delicate freshness, pleasant, savory and aromatic herbs in the finish.

▣ 87   Price B

Garda Chardonnay Brut 2008

100% Chardonnay grapes. Stainless steel only 44 months on yeasts. Golden straw yellow color with a quite fine perlage. The nose is fragrant with aromas of yeast and tropical fruits, mango lychee, citrus. On the mouth it's fresh and clean, simple and soft.

★★

QUADRA

*Via S. Eusebio, 1
25033 Cologne (BS)
Tel. +39 030 7157314
info@quadrafranciacorta.it
www.quadrafranciacorta.it*
�f *Tenuta-Quadra-Franciacorta*

YEAR OF FOUNDATION 2003
NAME OF THE OWNER Ghezzi Family
TOTAL BOTTLES PRODUCED 130,000
DIRECT SALES
VISITS TO THE WINERY - RESERVATION NEEDED
HECTARES OF VINEYARD 42
RESTAURANT

Although it officially began operation in 2003, the project for this winery began to take shape already at the beginning of the 1990s. Today it is one of the Franciacorta wineries that is evolving the fastest with a commercial success based on the reliability of its products.

---

 92   Price B

Franciacorta Qzero 2010

Blend of 90% Chardonnay and 10% Pinot Nero grapes. 60% of the musts is vinified in barrique 5 year on yeasts. Golden straw yellow color with fine perlage. On the nose aromas of wild herbs and flowers, mint and salt scents, citrus and white pepper. The mouth is fine and fresh, agile with a good balance.

---

 89   Price B

Franciacorta EretiQ 2011

Blend of 50% Pinot Nero and 50% Pinot Bianco grapes. Stainless steel only 4 years on yeasts. Straw yellow color with fine perlage. The nose is opulent with aromas of magnolia, peony, sweet mandarin. On the mouth at times it's vinous, forthright, very fresh almost almondy.

★
RICCI CURBASTRO

Via Adro, 37
25031 Capriolo (BS)
Tel. +39 030 736094
Fax +39 030 7460558
info@riccicurbastro.it
www.riccicurbastro.it
f Ricci-Curbastro-Azienda-Agricola

YEAR OF FOUNDATION 1885
NAME OF THE OWNER Riccardo Ricci Curbastro
TOTAL BOTTLES PRODUCED 200,000
DIRECT SALES
VISITS TO THE WINERY - RESERVATION NEEDED
HECTARES OF VINEYARD 26,5
HOSPITALITY

An historic Franciacorta estate, to the extent that it even has wine museum, which is the culmination of 30 years of research by Gualberto Ricci Curbastro and represents the evolution of winemaking technology in the appellation. The emphasis on tradition and quality is evident in the estate's latest line, Museum Release, a selection of wines that have aged on the lees for between five and eight years. The rich and ripe style of the wines make it enjoyable wine and is the result of a precise winemaking approach directly monitored by Riccardo Ricci Curbastro, an enologist and agronomist as well as the estate's owner who over the years has carried out a number of initiatives in the winery to make it more environmental friendly.

---

 90   Price B

Franciacorta Museum Release Extra Brut 2007

Blend of 50% Chardonnay, 50% Pinot Nero grapes. It matures partly in oak barrels and partly in stainless steel 7 years on yeasts. Golden straw yellow with persistent perlage. On the nose aromas of dried fruits and smoky scents, powder and sweet spices, apricot compote and golden apple. The mouth is rich and consistent with a good acidity. The finish is savory with good persistence.

回 85   Price B

Franciacorta Extra Brut 2012

Blend of 50% Chardonnay and 50% Pinot Nero grapes. It matures both stainless steel and oak barrels with 36 months on yeasts. Straw yellow color with an exuberant perlage. On the nose aromas of lemon, wild herbs, tamarind skin and white flowers. On the mouth it presents good freshness, very clear with great length.

RONCO CALINO

Via Fenice, 45 - Frazione Torbiato
25030 Adro (BS)
Tel. +39 030 7451073
info@roncocalino.it
www.roncocalino.it
f RoncoCalinoFranciacorta
🐦 @roncocalino

YEAR OF FOUNDATION 1996
NAME OF THE OWNER Paolo Radici
TOTAL BOTTLES PRODUCED 70,000
DIRECT SALES

In 1996, Bergamo industrialist Paolo Radici found in Franciacorta not only a nice country retreat in its hills but also a new passion for winemaking. His scenic estate near Erbusco once belonged to pianist Arturo Benedetti Michelangeli and is surrounded by a vineyards that composes a single cru and this is what inspired his desire to make wine. Over the years, the small Ronco Calino winery has consolidated a style of elegance and aromatic complexity, thanks to a scrupulous approach both in the vineyards and the winery.

🔲 **89**   Price B

Franciacorta Brut Nature 2010

Blend of 80% Chardonnay and 20% Pinot Nero grapes. 70% matures in stainless steel and 30% in French durmast barrique 54 months on yeasts. Bright golden yellow color and fine perlage. On the nose aromas of ripe plums, pineapple and peaches in syrup, fresh tangerine. The mouth is juicy, alive with a delicate finish.

★

SAN CRISTOFORO

Via Via Villanuova, 2
25030 Erbusco (BS)
Tel. +39 333 3397684
info@sancristoforo.eu
www.sancristoforo.eu
🔳 *sancristoforofranciacorta*

YEAR OF FOUNDATION **1992**
NAME OF THE OWNER **Bruno Dotti**
TOTAL BOTTLES PRODUCED **80,000**
DIRECT SALES
VISITS TO THE WINERY - RESERVATION NEEDED
HECTARES OF VINEYARD **10**

Bruno Dotti created this small, family-run winery in 1992 and has personally been involved in both the vineyards and the winery. Over the years he has become a talented winemaker producing interesting wines with an excellent quality/price ratio. All the estate's vineyards are in Erbusco and his straightforward approach is evident in the style of his wines, especially in the non-vintage cuvée that offers immediate satisfaction.

🔲 **89**   Price B

Franciacorta Pas Dosé 2011

100% Chardonnay. It matures for 36 months of yeasts. Light straw yellow color with fine perlage. The nose is citrusy with aromas of flowers, camphorates scents, lime and red apple. On the mouth it's vivid with defined tension and savory finish.

🔲 **87**   Price B

Franciacorta Brut

100% Chardonnay grapes. Stainless steel only 18 months on yeasts. The nose is fresh and citrusy with aromas of crisp yellow plums, golden apple skin. The mouth is balanced with a clear, stretched finish.

SULLALI

Via Costa Sopra, 22
25030 Erbusco (BS)
Tel. +39 393 0206080
info@sullali.com
🔳 *Sullali*

YEAR OF FOUNDATION **2008**
NAME OF THE OWNER **Jessica and Dario Vezzoli**
TOTAL BOTTLES PRODUCED **15,000**
VISITS TO THE WINERY
HECTARES OF VINEYARD **3,5**

Franciacorta is also a reservoir of projects, new experiences and research. A case in point is very young estate of Jessica and Dario Vezzoli who have winemaking in their blood given that their father Giuseppe not only has his own estate but is also a partner in Derbusco Cives. With their estate they have sought to give their wines an imprint as young as they are, wines geared for a market of young people and that offers carefree but well-thought out introduction to Franciacorta.

🔲 **91**   Price B

Franciacorta Extra Brut

100% Chardonnay grapes. Stainless steel only 24 months on yeasts. Straw yellow color with golden reflexes and very fine perlage. The nose is alive and vivid with aromas of lime, fresh ginger and grapefruit, hints of mint and white pepper. On the mouth it's clear and willowy, vibrant and refreshing.

223

TENUTA MAZZOLINO

Via Mazzolino, 34
27050 Corvino San Quirico (PV)
Tel. +39 0383 876122
info@tenuta-mazzolino.com
www.tenuta-mazzolino.com
☐ TenutaMazzolino

YEAR OF FOUNDATION 1984
NAME OF THE OWNER Sandra Braggiotti
TOTAL BOTTLES PRODUCED 130,000
DIRECT SALES
VISITS TO THE WINERY
HECTARES OF VINEYARD 22

Sandra Braggiotti has never hidden her love for French viticulture as inspiration for the production in her winery. In 1980 her father Enrico Braggiotti chose the Oltrpò countryside as the place to reunite his numerous family and enhance his French origins. But it was Sandra to see in the town close to Pavia the promising wine future of the family: she replanted the vineyards and build the winery with the consultancy of French winemakers, creating an interesting farm with the focus on Pinot Nero production.

■ 87 Price B
OP Noir Pinot Nero 2013

100% Pinot Nero grapes. Matures 1 year in barrique. Bright ruby red. Fragrant and intense on the nose with notes of wild strawberries, humus, sweet tobacco and cinnamon, cherry and pepper puffs. Rich on the mouth, polite tannins, harmonic development.

■ 84 Price A
OP Pinot Nero Terrazze 2015

100% Pinot Nero grapes. Stainless steel only. Bright ruby red. Inviting and crunchy on the nose. Notes of wild berries and sweet spices, dark citrus and black cherry. Agile and fruity on the mouth with a light tannin, refreshing and pleasant to drink.

TENUTA MONTENISA - MARCHESE ANTINORI

Via Paolo VI, 62
25046 Cazzago San Martino (BS)
Tel. +39 030 7750838

Fax +39 030 725005
info@montenisa.it
www.montenisa.it

YEAR OF FOUNDATION 2000
NAME OF THE OWNER Marchesi Antinori
TOTAL BOTTLES PRODUCED 3,000,000
DIRECT SALES
VISITS TO THE WINERY - RESERVATION NEEDED
HECTARES OF VINEYARD 60

Located south of Lake Iseo, the estate takes its name from a mountain dear to Bacchus and is comprised of a group of buildings at the center of which is a 17th century manor house with frescoes. It is set between to courtyards closed in by porticos and surrounded by vineyards and there is a small church that is over a thousand years old and hosts the tombs of the local nobility. It now belongs to the Antinori family who in 1999 recognized the great potential of this area to produce intense wines with a style rich in body and finesse. The quest for quality over the years has resulted in harmonious wines with a precise personality, especially for the vintage ones that are made with the estate's best grapes.

▣ 94 Price C
Franciacorta Conte Aimo 2009

100% Pinot Nero grapes. It matures both in stainless steel and barrique 70 months on yeasts. golden Straw yellow color with very fine perlage. The nose is elegant with aromas of elderflower and verbena, linden blossoms and crisp apple, pomegranate and white mulberries. On the mouth it's balanced and complex, harmonic and tense with a savory and clear finish.

▣ 91 Price B
Franciacorta Donna Cora Satèn 2011

100% Chardonnay grapes. It matures in both stainless steel and barrique 40 months on yeasts. Bright straw yellow color with very fine perlage. On the nose aromas of chamomile and verbena, candied lemon skin, fresh almond and laurel. On the mouth is silky and refined, harmonic with a fresh and balanced finish.

▣ 89 Price B
Franciacorta Cuvée Royale Brut

Blend of 78% Chardonnay, 10% Pinot Bianco and 12% Pinot Nero grapes. Stainless steel only 30 months on yeasts. Bright straw yellow color with fine perlage. On the nose aromas of thyme, hay and melissa, cedar and fresh yellow plums. On the mouth presents a good acidity, it's dynamic and savory, pleasantly sharp finish.

TORREVILLA

Via Emilia, 4
27050 Torrazza Coste (PV)
Tel. +39 0383 77520
info@torrevilla.it
www.torrevilla.it

YEAR OF FOUNDATION 1907
NAME OF THE OWNER Cooperativa Torrevilla
TOTAL BOTTLES PRODUCED 3,000,000
DIRECT SALES
VISITS TO THE WINERY - RESERVATION NEEDED
HECTARES OF VINEYARD 650

A great and historic Oltrepò cooperative that has been active for over 100 years. Its vast range of wines all stand out for their reliability and a good quality/price ratio, which is the cooperative's true trademark.

 87   👍 Price A
OP Cortese La Genisia Garlà 2015

100% Cortese grapes. Stainless steel only. Light yellow color. The nose is fruity and fragrant with aromas of yeasts, cedar, fresh almond and peppermint. On the mouth it's attractive, fresh, salty, easy and very pleasant to drink.

TRAVAGLINO

Località Travaglino, 6a
27040 Calvignano (PV)
Tel. +39 0383 872222
info@travaglino.it
www.travaglino.it
 TenutaTravaglino

YEAR OF FOUNDATION 1868
NAME OF THE OWNER Lorella Comi
TOTAL BOTTLES PRODUCED 220,000
DIRECT SALES
VISITS TO THE WINERY - RESERVATION NEEDED
HECTARES OF VINEYARD 80

This estate has been in the Comi family's hands since it was founded almost 150 years ago and

represents a point of reference in Oltrepò. The winery is specialized in producing traditional method sparkling wines but it also makes from good still wines.

 91   👍 Price A
OP Gran Cuvée Brut

100% Pinot Nero grapes vinified in white. Classic method on yeasts for 36 months. Light golden yellow color with thick and quick perlage. On the nose aromas of yeasts at first, then light aromas of white peach, alfalfa and cedar. The mouth is tense, savory, well supported by the acidity with a hint of creamy carbon dioxide. Long and persistent finish.

 88   Price B
OP Pinot Nero Poggio della Buttinera 2012

100% Pinot Nero grapes. It matures in barrique for 10 months. Bright and intense ruby color. On the nose aromas of spices at first, then strawberry and currant. The mouth is warm, lightly tannic, whole, full-bodied with a long full-flavored finish.

 86   👍 Price A
Pernero 2015

100% Pinot Nero grapes. Stainless steel only. Vivid ruby color. The nose is fruity, fragrant, simple but attractive and varietal with aromas of strawberries and fermentative scents. On the mouth it's light, pleasant, easy to drink, savory and fresh.

 ★★
UBERTI

Via Enrico Fermi, 2
25030 Erbusco (BS)
Tel. +39 030 7267476
Fax +39 030 7760455
info@ubertivini.it
www.ubertivini.it
 Uberti-vini

YEAR OF FOUNDATION 1793
NAME OF THE OWNER Uberti Family
TOTAL BOTTLES PRODUCED 180,000
DIRECT SALES
VISITS TO THE WINERY - RESERVATION NEEDED
HECTARES OF VINEYARD 25

This estate has solid historic roots representing a dynasty of winegrowers that dates back to

1793. The latest descendants are sisters Silvia and Francesca and they now work with the person who has made history for the estate, Giovanni Agostino Uberti who was the founder of its modern era together with his wife and 'Lady of Wine' Eleonora. Their vineyards have excellent exposures and soil being pebbly has near perfect drainage and thus allows them to avoid using chemical fertilizers and pesticides and this, in turn, has facilitated converting it to organic farming. Their winemaking style is unusual and several years ago involved bringing in truncated cone-shaped oak vats to produce wines that are even more wrapping and intense that has been winning over countless fans.

回 92   Price B
Franciacorta Comarì del Salem Extra Brut 2009

Blend of 80% Chardonnay and 20% Pinot Bianco grapes. Vinified partly in stainless steel and partly in barrique with at least 48 months on yeasts. Golden straw yellow color with fine perlage. On the nose it presents smoky scents with aromas of vanillaand dry fruits. The mouth is polite and fresh, signs of evolution, great persistence.

回 92   Price D*
Franciacorta Quinque Extra Brut

*100% Chardonnay grapes from 5 different harvest, 2002,2003,2004,2005,2006. It matures in durmast vats with almost 60 months on yeasts. Intense golden yellow color with thin perlage. On the nose aromas of sage, vanilla shortbread, white tea, apple juice and candied ginger. The mouth is long, silky, faceted and attractive. *Only Magnum.*

回 90   Price B
Franciacorta Francesco I Extra Brut

Blend of 75% Chardonnay, 15% Pinot Bianco and 10% Pinot Nero grapes. Stainless steel only with almost 36 months on yeasts. Golden straw yellow color with fine perlage. The nose is intense with aromas of bread crust, dry fruits, citrus, honey and barley. On the mouth it's creamy and delicate with good acidity and an almondy finish.

GIUSEPPE VEZZOLI

Via Costa Sopra 22
25030 Erbusco (BS)
Tel. 030 7267579
Fax 030 7267601

info@vezzolivini.it
www.vezzolivini.it
f *VezzoliVini*
y *@VezzoliVini*

YEAR OF FOUNDATION **1994**
NAME OF THE OWNER **Giuseppe Vezzoli**
TOTAL BOTTLES PRODUCED **180,000**
DIRECT SALES
VISITS TO THE WINERY - RESERVATION NEEDED
HECTARES OF VINEYARD **40**

Giuseppe Vezzoli is a winemaker who with his children Jessica and Dario is making an important contribution to Franciacorta's new territorial identity with clear ideas in regard to productive style and using grapes from vineyards in Erbusco's morainal amphitheater. His children have struck out on their own with their Sullali estate that focuses on innovation and freshness.

回 91   Price B
Franciacorta Nefertiti Dizeta Extra Brut 2010

100% Chardonnay grapes. it matures in barrique with 48 months on the yeasts. Golden straw yellow color and fine perlage. On the nose it's intense with aromas of hazelnut paste, apricot, peach compote, apple and citrus. The mouth is clean and mature, tasty with nice acidity and a savory finish.

回 89   Price B
Franciacorta Dosage Zero

Blend of 50% Chardonnay and 50% Pinot Nero grapes. Stainless steel only 30 months on yeasts. Light straw yellow color with very fine perlage. The nose intensely citrusy with aromas of Amalfi lemon, yeasts, crisp green apple and fresh ginger. On the mouth it presents a juicy, refreshing acidity.

回 89   Price B
Franciacorta Satèn Brut

100% Chardonnay grapes. 70% matures in stainless steel and the 30% in barrique 24 months on yeasts. Bright straw yellow color with fine perlage. On the nose aromas of medicinal herbs, laurel and verbena, grapefruit and an hint of bitter orange marmalade. The mouth is tense and firm with a savory finish.

VILLA

Via Villa 12
25040 Monticelli Brusati (BS)
Tel. +39 030 652329
info@villafranciacorta.it
www.villafranciacorta.it
f *Villa Franciacorta*
𝕏 *@CantinaVilla*

YEAR OF FOUNDATION 1960
NAME OF THE OWNER Alessandro Bianchi
TOTAL BOTTLES PRODUCED 300,000
DIRECT SALES
VISITS TO THE WINERY - RESERVATION NEEDED
HECTARES OF VINEYARD 37
HOSPITALITY
RESTAURANT

This splendid medieval hamlet in the heart of Franciacorta, sought after for centuries because of its agricultural and winegrowing vocation, was acquired in 1960 by Alessandro Bianchi. At the time agricultural production focused on wheat and other grains but soon its vineyards revealed their great potential for producing quality wine and this convinced the owners in the late 1970s to convert the estate to winegrowing and production. They were among the pioneers in adopting the traditional method and rebuilt hamlet to enlarge the underground cellars. They also restored two farmhouse complexes with courtyards that today house holiday farms. The wines are very personal, made with care and refinedness and they have acquired an interesting expressiveness through aging.

🔲 **92**   Price B
Franciacorta Cuvette Brut 2008

Blend of 85% Chardonnay and 15% Pinot Nero grapes. Stainless steel and barrique for 1/3 of the base wines, 7 years on yeasts. Bright golden yellow. The nose is fragrant with aromas of shortbread and Saturnine peaches, plum compote and candied lemon. On the mouth it's harmonic with a polite freshness, soft and with a lightly savory finish.

🔲 **89**   Price B
Franciacorta Emozione Brut 2012

Blend of 85% Chardonnay, 10% Pinot Nero and 5% Pinot Bianco grapes. Stainless steel only, 36 months on yeasts. Golden straw yellow color with fine per-

lage. The nose is fragrant and fresh, vital and pleasant with aromas of citrus and wildflowers. On the mouth it's crisp and fresh, stretched with a slightly eucalyptus finish.

🔲 **89**   Price B
Franciacorta Mon Satèn 2012

100% Chardonnay grapes. Stainless steel only, 36 months on yeasts. Straw yellow color with bright reflexes and a thin perlage. On the nose it presents floral scents with aromas of elderflower and linden, pear Williams, white pepper. On the mouth it's pleasant and silky, dynamic and delicately fresh.

VILLA CRESPIA

Via Valli, 31
25030 Adro (BS)
Tel. +39 030 7451051
villa.crespia@arcipelagomuratori.it
www.arcipelagomuratori.it
f *Villa-Crespia*
𝕏 *@arcipelagomura*

YEAR OF FOUNDATION 1999
NAME OF THE OWNER Muratori Family
TOTAL BOTTLES PRODUCED 350,000
VISITS TO THE WINERY - RESERVATION NEEDED
HECTARES OF VINEYARD 60

While not among the historic estates that formed the producers' association, the Arcipelago Muratori estate in Franciacorta stands out for the commitment the family has shown in working its over 60 hectares of vineyards that are planted with Chardonnay and Pinot Nero subdivided into six units determined by the characteristics they offer. It is an ambitious winemaking reality with large winery in Andro that allows them to produce separate wines from each parcel and store them until the final blending. The wines have a rich and full style and with each year become more convincing and elegant.

🔲 **90**   Price B
Franciacorta Dosage Zero Francesco Iacono Riserva 2008

100% Pinot Nero grapes. Classic method. Light golden yellow color with a fine and persistent perlage. On the nose it's complex with smoky scents from the yeasts at first, then grapefruit and cedar. The mouth is firm, creamy, tense, very fresh and easy to drink with a great persistence on the finish.

MARCHE

For reasons related to different traditions that evolved over the centuries, Marche wines are very different from each other and are particularly tied to specific territorial realities. The conformation of the land would seems tailor-made for the vast development of winegrowing. From above, the Marche region looks like a giant comb facing the Adriatic with rivers and the valleys they created running perpendicular to the coast. These have created an excellent habitat for winegrowing. The only valley that runs parallel to the coast is Matelica, in the region's central interior, but grapes are grown and wine is made everywhere. The climate is amore northern than one would expect because the region is exposed to cold northeast winds and storm fronts from the Balkans. This in part explains the vast presence of white wine grapes. Moving from north to south, the first DOC appellation is Colli Pesaresi which extends from the border with Romagna to the outskirts of Fano and represents a continuation of the winegrowing area in Romagna. Consequently, the wines produced are Sangiovese and Trebbiano, also made in two subzones, Focara for the first and Roncaglia for the second, and they are very similar to their counterparts in Romagna. Further south is the district of Fano that produces a different white than the others. It is Bianchello del Metauro, made with the grape of the same name, and

is a very traditional wine with a fruity aroma and while body is not great, it is a perfect wine to pair with local seafood dishes.

In the province of Ancona, just past Senigallia, is the region's most important winemaking area, the vast area of Verdicchio or better the Verdicchios. This because there are two DOC and DOCG Verdicchio appellations. The first is Verdicchio dei Castelli di Jesi, the larger and more famous one which comprises the whole Ancona province. The second is Verdicchio di Matelica, which is in the interior near the border between the provinces of Ancona and Macerata. Both white wines have an excellent body and are made from the Verdicchio grape which is one of the best (if not the best) indigenous Italian white wine grapes. The fundamental difference between the two wines regards their concentration. In general, Verdicchio dei Castelli di Jesi is more rounded and soft, while Verdicchio di Matelica is more gritty and sometimes even tart, an aspects that lessens with age. Nevertheless, they are both whites of great class, easy to pair with food and which have improved greatly in quality in recent years. Both have Riserva wines that have been given a DOCG classification. Recently, the same area has become home to a new DOC appellation: Esino. The Bianco is made with the grapes not used for the other Verdicchio wines while the Rosso, a blend of Sangiovese and Montepulciano, is a fresh and immediate wine that has always been made in the area. The province of Ancona also produces two other red DOC wines: Lacrima di Morro d'Alba (which has nothing to do with Piedmont but is named after the town Morro d'Alba in the Senigallia hinterland) and Rosso Conero, which is made from select grapes and once aged can qualify as a DOCG. The first is made with Lacrima grapes and is a medium-bodied red. The second is a blend dominated by Montepulciano that is a great to pair with roasts. It is produced in limited quantities along the coast of the Conero Riviera, and the immediate interior areas, and is the region's best red wine. In the province of Macerata can be found the very strange and ultra-typical Vernaccia di Serrapretona, a DOCG sparkling red wine that is often sweet or semi-sweet. It is made with red Vernaccia grapes that are left to raisinate on racks and is rustic yet captivating. On the coast, near Loreto and Recanti, is the heart of the DOC appellation of Colli Maceratesi, the home to a light and pleasing wine made for the most part with Maceratino grapes. Further to the south, in the province of Ascoli, is the appellation for Falerio dei Colli Ascolani, another white wine based on Trebbiano grapes but has in its blend Passerina, Verdicchio and

Pecorino. More important is Rosso Piceno, a wine that can be made throughout this area of the region and is a blend of Sangiovese and Montepulciano. The area between Offida, Ripatransone, San Benedetto del Tronto and another ten neighboring towns, all in the province of Ascoli, can qualify for the appellation Rosso Piceno Superiore on the condition that the wine has an alcoholic content of over 12% and has aged for at least a year. This is a red with a lot more concentration and body that can age in the bottle for at least another four to five years. The name Offida has been given to a new DOCG appellation that includes an Offida Pecorino and an Offida Rosso, the later a blend of 85% Montepulciano and 15% other red grape wines.

CONTROLLED AND GUARANTEED DESIGNATION OF ORIGIN (DOCG)

- Conero
- Castelli di Jesi Verdicchio Riserva with or without the sub-area Classico, geographic references allowed
- Offida
- Verdicchio di Matelica Riserva, geographic references allowed
- Vernaccia di Serrapetrona

CONTROLLED DESIGNATION OF ORIGIN (DOC)

- Bianchello del Metauro
- Colli Maceratesi
- Colli Pesaresi, with or without the sub-areas Focara (for Rosso, Pinot Nero), Parco Naturale Monte San Bartolo (for Sangiovese, Cabernet Sauvignon), Roncaglia (for Bianco, Pinot Nero)
- Esino
- Falerio
- I Terreni di Sanseverino
- Lacrima di Morro o Lacrima di Morro
- d'Alba
- Pergola
- Rosso Conero
- Rosso Piceno
- San Ginesio
- Serrapetrona
- Terre di Offida
- Verdicchio dei Castelli di Jesi, with or without the sub-area Classico, geographic references allowed
- Verdicchio di Matelica, geographic references allowed

★

BELISARIO

Via Aristide Merloni, 12
62024 Matelica (MC)
Tel. +39 0737 787247
belisario@belisario.it
www.belisario.it
 cantinabelisario

YEAR OF FOUNDATION **1971**
NAME OF THE OWNER
TOTAL BOTTLES PRODUCED **850,000**
DIRECT SALES
VISITS TO THE WINERY - RESERVATION NEEDED
HECTARES OF VINEYARD **300**
CERTIFIED ORGANIC VITICULTURE

Even if the area of Matelica has at least two other valid producers, Collestefano and Fattoria La Monacesca (both included in the guide), there is no doubt that the biggest producer is the Bellisario wine cooperatives. Their serious approach and consistency place them on the level of those in Alto Adige. The cooperative produces two top wines: Riserva Cambrugiano, which has a discreet use of wood, and Meridia. All the other wines are impeccable Verdicchio.

☐ 🍇 **95**　　　　　　　　　🖒 **Price A**
Verdicchio di Matelica Cambrugiano Riserva 2013

100% Verdicchio grapes. Ages in barrels and in stainless steel tanks. Straw yellow with golden hues. Aromas of anise, jasmine, white peach and almond, light woody notes. Warm and full bodied, wonderful acidity balanced by well extracted weight on the palate. Exceptional long finish.

☐ **88**　　　　　　　　　　　**Price A**
Verdicchio di Matelica Meridia 2012

100% Verdicchio grapes. Ages 1 year in concrete tanks. Straw yellow with greenish hues. Field blossoms, lightly citrusy and fermentation notes. Tense and juicy, pleasant suppleness, savory and long.

★★★

BUCCI

Via Cona, 30
60010 Ostra Vetere (AN)
Tel. +39 071 964179

Fax +39 071 964179
bucciwines@villabucci.com
www.villabucci.com
 VillaBucci
 @bucciwines

YEAR OF FOUNDATION **1983**
NAME OF THE OWNER **Ampelio Bucci**
TOTAL BOTTLES PRODUCED **120,000**
DIRECT SALES
VISITS TO THE WINERY - RESERVATION NEEDED
HECTARES OF VINEYARD **31**
CERTIFIED ORGANIC VITICULTURE
OLIVE OIL PRODUCTION

Ampelio Bucci is a Verdicchio institution. Then again, as the Latins said nomen omen (destiny is in the name, in this case bucci= skins, ed.note) and àmpelos in Greek means vines. For 30 years he has been producing, with the assistance of the talented enologist Giorgio Grai, some of Italy's best white wines. His Villa Bucci Riserva, in particular, is a masterpiece and 'White Wine of the Year' in this edition of the Guide.

☐ 🍇 **98**　　　　　　　　　　**Price B**
Castelli di Jesi Verdicchio Classico Villa Bucci Riserva 2013

100% Verdicchio grape. Ages 2 years in large casks. Warm and shiny straw yellow. Very complex and captivating nose: jasmine, flint, hint of anise and fine herbs. Mouth filling, wonderful body, savory, well balance fresh tension, full of character and with a very long length. Excellent wine. Best white wine of the year award.

■ **92**　　　　　　　　　　　**Price B**
Rosso Piceno Villa Bucci 2013

Blend of Montepulciano with a small percentage of Sangiovese grape. Ages 1 year in large casks. Intense ruby. Refined nose of black cherry and cassis, then light spicy notes. Savory, velvety, tense, ripe tannins and with a wonderful length.

☐ **91**　　　　　　　　　　🖒 **Price A**
Verdicchio dei Castelli di Jesi Classico Superiore 2015

100% Verdicchio grapes. Ages 6 months in large casks. White blossoms and yeasty notes on the nose, then fine herbs and William pear. Savory and tense, supple, pleasant and captivating. Long and warm finish.

★★
MARIA PIA CASTELLI

Contrada Sant' Isidoro, 22
63813 Monte Urano (FM)
Tel. +39 0734 841774
info@mariapiacastelli.it
www.mariapiacastelli.it
f *mariapia.castelli*
🐦 *ViniMPC*

YEAR OF FOUNDATION **2001**
NAME OF THE OWNER **Maria Pia Castelli**
TOTAL BOTTLES PRODUCED **25,000**
DIRECT SALES
VISITS TO THE WINERY - RESERVATION NEEDED
HECTARES OF VINEYARD **8**

In just a few years, Enrico Bartoletti and Maria Pia Castelli have been able to transform a winery bent on producing quantity to one that exemplified the renaissance of quality Piceno wine. The four wines they produce have unmistakable style and character also thanks to a soil rich in iron and vineyards producing a low yield. The vineyards are organically cultivated and simple winemaking methods are employed in order to exalt the characteristics of the grapes and the territory.

☐ **94** Price B
Stella Flora 2013

Blend of 50% Pecorino, 30% Passerina and 30% Trebbiano grapes. Ages in used barrels. Golden yellow. Explosive nose of citrus, candy barley and peat. Concentrated palate, dense but with a wonderful acidity. Complex finish with notes of tobacco and sea breeze and an incredible depth.

■ **93** Price B
Erasmo Castelli 2012

100% Montepulciano grapes. Ages in barrique. Inky color. Powerful notes of pencil lead, raw meat and black fruits. Austere palate but powerful. Great tannins yet very smooth. Flavorful finish, earthy and the benchmark for these vines is definitively the steely note.

■ **91** 👍 Price A
Orano 2013

100% Sangiovese grapes. Ages in used barrique. light ruby. Intense aromas of white tobacco, wet leaves and dry blossoms. As usual the palate is

sleek, delicate with thin tannins and good suppleness. Vertical finish with a distinctive steely note.

▨ **89** 👍 Price A
Sant'Isidoro 2014

Blend of Montepulciano and Sangiovese grapes. Ages in barrels and stainless steel tanks. Shiny cherry red. Regardless the challenging vintage this rosè is complex and offers notes of wild strawberry, cane sugar and spices. Irresistible palate, chewy, flavorful, mouth-filling but with a wonderful freshness. Very long finish.

★
CIÙ CIÙ

Contrada Ciafone, 106
63073 Offida (AP)
Tel. +39 0736 810001
info@ciuciuvini.it
www.ciuciuvini.it
f *ciuciuvini*

YEAR OF FOUNDATION **1970**
NAME OF THE OWNER **Massimiliano Bartolomei**
TOTAL BOTTLES PRODUCED **800,000**
DIRECT SALES
VISITS TO THE WINERY
HECTARES OF VINEYARD **300**
RESTAURANT
CERTIFIED ORGANIC VITICULTURE
OLIVE OIL PRODUCTION

The estate of the young brothers Massimiliano and Walter Bortolomei has in recent years acquired a number of important vineyards in the towns which are historically the best for wine-growing in the Piceno area, including Offida and Acquaviva Piceno, and this has made them one of the most important wine producers in southern Marche. They cultivate the region's classic grapes – Pecorino, Passerina, Montepulciano and Sangiovese – and their wines are distinguished by technical precision and great respect of the territory. They are assisted by a young and motivated staff that has allowed them to become organically certified and offer an ample line of products at excellent prices.

■ **89** 👍 Price A
Rosso Piceno Superiore Gotico 2013
Blend of 70% Montepulciano and 30% Sangiovese

grapes. Ages in barrels. Deep ruby. Multy-layered nose of ripe fruit, tobacco and fine herbs. Solid structure, notes of pencil lead and wet leaves. Firm tannins and the aftertaste remind notes of pencil lead and wet leaves.

 88   👍 Price A

Offida Pecorino Merlettaie 2015

100% Pecorino grapes. Only stainless steel. Shiny straw yellow. Nose of white stone fruits, blossoms and a delicate sea breeze note. The palate is savory, peaty and with a wonderful finish. Lightly warm.

 87   👍 Price A

Rosso Piceno Bacchus 2015

Blend of Montepulciano and Sangiovese grapes. Only stainless steel. Deep ruby red. Nose of dried blossoms, tobacco and spices. Firm and fresh palate. Juicy and dynamic length.

⭐
COLLESTEFANO

Località Colle Stefano, 3
62022 Castelraimondo (MC)
Tel. +39 0737 640439
info@collestefano.com
www.collestefano.com
f *Collestefano*
🐦 *@Collestefanobio*

YEAR OF FOUNDATION 1978
NAME OF THE OWNER Fabio Marchionni
TOTAL BOTTLES PRODUCED 80,000
DIRECT SALES
VISITS TO THE WINERY - RESERVATION NEEDED
HECTARES OF VINEYARD 15
CERTIFIED ORGANIC VITICULTURE

The organically certified estate of Fabio Marchionni has become over the years the standard-bear of the more citrusy, dry and flavorful side of Verdicchio di Matelica. This has allowed Verdicchio di Collestefano to enter the heats of the more attentive and intransigent wine-lovers. If you can, visit the estate to enjoy a wonderful view of the entire Valle Camertina.

☐ 91   👍 Price A

Verdicchio di Matelica 2015

100% Verdicchio grapes. Only stainless steel. Pale straw yellow. Good aromas profile, very fruity with

distinctive note of white peach. Supple palate, savory, elegant, medium-bodied and decent length.

COLONNARA

Via Mandriole, 6
60034 Cupramontana (AN)
Tel. +39 0731 780273
Fax +39 0731 789610
info@colonnara.it
www.colonnara.it
f *Colonnara*
🐦 *@ColonnaraWines*

YEAR OF FOUNDATION 1959
NAME OF THE OWNER
TOTAL BOTTLES PRODUCED 1,000,000
DIRECT SALES
VISITS TO THE WINERY - RESERVATION NEEDED
HECTARES OF VINEYARD 120

Colonnara is a wine cooperative in Cupramontana that was founded 50 years ago and today has some 100 members. Their success and positive reputation have allowed than to offer their wines with an excellent quality/price ratio. As always the Cuprese is one of the best white wine of the Region. Also their sparkling wine made from Verdicchio is very good.

▣ 91   Price B

Verdicchio dei Castelli di Jesi Metodo Classico Brut Ubaldo Rosi Riserva 2009

100% Verdicchio grapes. Ages on the lees for 60 months. The usual Ubaldo Rosi in a wonderful vintage: shiny green yellow; aromas of licorice and white blossoms; aftertaste of honey, licorice; the bubbles are creamy, plentiful and refined. Floral finish. One of the top Italian sparkling wine.

☐ 88   👍 Price A

Verdicchio dei Castelli di Jesi Classico Superiore Cuprese 2015

100% Verdicchio grapes. Only stainless steel. As always this version of verdicchio from Colonnara ages wonderfully. Greenish yellow. Nose that offers hint of mothballs and delicate white blossoms hint. Light but firm palate, with hint of white blossoms and steely scents. Wonderful but it definitively needs time.

☐ 85   Price A

Verdicchio dei Castelli di Jesi Classico Lyricus 2015

100% Verdicchio grapes. Only stainless steel. Text-book verdicchio: pale straw yellow; aromas of mustard blossoms on the nose and a juicy and almondy palate. Dry finish. Wonderful value for money.

CRESPAIA

Via Prelato, 4
61032 Fano (PU)
Tel. +39 0721 862383
info@crespaia.it
www.crespaia.it
 Crespaia
 @crespaia

YEAR OF FOUNDATION 2011
NAME OF THE OWNER Rossano Sgammini
TOTAL BOTTLES PRODUCED 30,000
DIRECT SALES
VISITS TO THE WINERY - RESERVATION NEEDED
HECTARES OF VINEYARD 5
OLIVE OIL PRODUCTION

This small winery is specialized in producing Sangiovese and Bianchello del Metauro. It is a young estate set up in 2011 in the hills that surround Fano and their vineyards thus benefit from the breezes of the nearby Adriatic. The winery has cutting-edge equipment but this does not interfere with the simple art of wine-making.

☐ 89   👍 Price A

Bianchello del Metauro 2015

100% Biancame grapes. Only stainless steel. Medium straw yellow. Aromas of unripe apricot and cedar peel. Fresh palate, flavorful, citrusy, lightly almondy. Fresh finish. Impeccable and very pleasant.

☐ 87   👍 Price A

Bianchello del Metauro Chiaraluce 2015

100% Biancame grapes. Matures on the lees in stainless steel tanks. Medium straw yellow. Aromas of citrus and light hint of biscuit. It has a bit more weight on the palate than the little brother, yet lesser supple. More complex finish, but a bit warmer. Overall extraordinary.

★★
FAZI BATTAGLIA

Via Roma, 117
60031 Castelplanio (AN)
Tel. +39 0731 81591
info@fazibattaglia.it
www.fazibattaglia.it
 Fazi-Battaglia
 @FaziBattaglia

YEAR OF FOUNDATION 1949
NAME OF THE OWNER Bertani Domains
TOTAL BOTTLES PRODUCED 1,500,000
DIRECT SALES
VISITS TO THE WINERY
HECTARES OF VINEYARD 210

The big news is that this historic and fundamental Castelli di Jesi producer has been acquired by Gruppo Angelini that has placed it in the galaxy of estates that constitute Bertani Domains. They are in good company together with Val di Suga, Trerose and San Leonino in Tuscany, Puiatti in Friuli and Bertani in Veneto. Lorenzo Landi has stayed on as technical consultant and the estate maintains the traditions that have made this a winery that epitomizes the Marche region as few others can.

☐ 91   👍 Price A

Verdicchio dei Castelli di Jesi Classico Superiore Massaccio 2014

100% Verdicchio grapes. Only stainless steel. Greenish yellow. Distinguishing aromas of anise and camphor. Almost (pleasantly) austere on the palate, camphor finish. A wine with great character that will please many Verdicchiòs lovers.

☐ 87   Price A

Verdicchio dei Castelli di Jesi San Sisto Riserva 2014

100% Verdicchio grapes. Ages partially in barrique and stainless steel. Light golden yellow, very bright. Pleasant aromas of lavander, anise, vanilla hint. Thinner palate than usual but still with good weight, with a nice floral finish. Could age and improve a lot.

☐ 82   Price A

Verdicchio dei Castelli di Jesi Classico Titulus 2015

100% Verdicchio grapes. Only stainless steel. As

usual a great wine. Simple but varietal: greenish straw yellow, green almond, a wine with personality and a wonderful almondy finish. Always a great buy.

★★★
GIOACCHINO GAROFOLI

Via Carlo Marx, 123
60022 Castelfidardo (AN)
Tel. +39 071 7820162
mail@garofolivini.it
www.garofolivini.it
 Casa-Vinicola-Garofoli
 @GarofoliVini

YEAR OF FOUNDATION **1901**
NAME OF THE OWNER **Gianfranco and Carlo Garofoli**
TOTAL BOTTLES PRODUCED **2,000,000**
DIRECT SALES
VISITS TO THE WINERY
HECTARES OF VINEYARD **50**
OLIVE OIL PRODUCTION

Garofoli has brought honor to the Marche region for over a century thanks to the quality evident in the one million bottles it produces a year. While it is understandable that wine-lovers will focus their attention on Podium, their select Verdicchio dei Castelli di Jesi, this year we suggest they take their Spumante Riserva 2008 into serious consideration. This not forgetting the value of their top line of wines, Macrina, which is always a sure bet.

☐ 🍷 96   Price B
Verdicchio dei Castelli di Jesi Classico Superiore Podium 2014

100% Verdicchio grapes. Only stainless steel. Straw yellow with greenish hues. White peach, field blossoms, thiolic and smoky hints, wonderful and well defined aromas compound. Great character, tense, good structure, wondeful length. A great classic despite the challanging vintage.

☐ 94   Price B
Verdicchio dei Castelli di Jesi Serra Fiorese Riserva 2012

100% Verdicchio grapes. Ferments and ages in barrique for 1 year with frequent stirring. Lively golden yellow. Well defined nose of pennyroyal, basil, vanilla, white almond. Rich palate, mouth filling but very tense and very lively. Aftertaste of anise,

dry fruits and vanilla, powerful and very long. Amazing wine.

▣ 91   Price C
Verdicchio dei Castelli di Jesi Metodo Classico Brut 2009

100% Verdicchio grapes. On the lees for 48 months. Warm mustard yellow color. Intense nose, complex, fragrant, yeasty, licorice, star anise. Fresh palate, very rich, creamy bubbles and a powerful finish on licorice notes.

☐ 89   👍 Price A
Verdicchio dei Castelli di Jesi Classico Superiore Macrina 2015

100% Verdicchio grapes. Only stainless steel. Pale straw yellow; aromas of tilia, almond and light yeasty hint. Fresh and very flavorful on the palate, long and almondy finish. Impeccable as usual.

★★★
IL POLLENZA

Contrada Casone, 4
62029 Tolentino (MC)
Tel. +39 0733 961989
lacantina@ilpollenza.it
www.ilpollenza.it
 cantina.ilpollenza
 @ilpollenza

YEAR OF FOUNDATION **2000**
NAME OF THE OWNER **Aldo Brachetti Peretti**
TOTAL BOTTLES PRODUCED **300,000**
DIRECT SALES
VISITS TO THE WINERY - RESERVATION NEEDED
HECTARES OF VINEYARD **82**

The winery is spectacular, one of the most beautiful in Italy and set in an exceptional Italian landscape and well-worth a visit. The area was not considered particularly suited one for winegrowing. At least this was the case up until recently, when Aldo Brachetti Peretti, a former oil man who is now a successful wine entrepreneur, decided to change its global image.

■ 🍷 95   Price C
Il Pollenza 2013

Blend of 60% Cabernet Sauvignon, 20% Merlot, 14% Cabernet franc and Petit Verdot grapes. Ages in barrique. Deep ruby. Distinctive nose of ink, to-

bacco and berries. The palate is dense, meaty with well extracted tannins; long and dynamic finish.

 90   **Price B**

Cosmino 2013

Blend of 80% Cabernet Sauvignon and 20% Cabernet Franc grapes. Ages in tonneau. Deep ruby. Elegant and distinctive aromas of leather, tobacco and pencil lead. The palate is chewy, the tannins are elegant and the finish is very long on aromatic herbs.

☐ **89**   **Price A**

Colli Maceratesi Ribona Angera 2015

100% Maceratino grapes. Ages in concrete tanks. Golden yellow. The nose is austere with peaty and spicy notes. The palate is savory, lightly tannic but supple and dynamic with a long and savory finish.

★★
LA MONACESCA

Contrada Monacesca
62024 Matelica (MC)
Tel. +39 0733 672641
info@monacesca.it
www.monacesca.it
 la.monacesca

YEAR OF FOUNDATION 1966
NAME OF THE OWNER Aldo Cifola
TOTAL BOTTLES PRODUCED 200,000
DIRECT SALES
VISITS TO THE WINERY - RESERVATION NEEDED
HECTARES OF VINEYARD 27

Fattoria la Monacesca is an estate that in the past 20 years has done the most to demonstrate the potential of the great area of Matelica, an area with a temperate climate and that is the only valley in the region closed to the sea. This thanks to its owner, the agronomist Aldo Cifola, who was the first to see the potential of using Verdicchio grapes picked just after they have ripened and turning them into one of central Italy's (and not only) greatest whites; Riserva Mirum.

☐ **92**   **Price B**

Verdicchio di Matelica Mirum Riserva 2014

100% Verdicchio grapes. Ages on the lees for 36 months in stainless steel tanks. Golden yellow. The

nose offers a well-defined and a Matelica characteristic note of chestnut honey, then cardamom. Rich and powerful with a precise note of smoked apricot and a very vigorous finish. Lesser fat and refined than usual but very lively. Fantastic.

☐ **85**   **Price A**

Verdicchio di Matelica 2014

100% Verdicchio grapes. Only stainless steel. Straw yellow. Smoky, vegetal and spicy (cardamom) nose with a camomile blossoms background. The palate is rich and tense, with a pleasantly bitter aftertaste on the middle palate and austere finish.

LA STAFFA

Via Castellaretta, 19
60039 Staffolo (AN)
Tel. +39 0731 779810
Fax +39 0731 59007
info@vinilastaffa.it
www.vinilastaffa.it/staffa
 lastaffa.vinidautore

YEAR OF FOUNDATION 1992
NAME OF THE OWNER Riccardo Baldi
TOTAL BOTTLES PRODUCED 30,000
DIRECT SALES
VISITS TO THE WINERY
HECTARES OF VINEYARD 7
CERTIFIED ORGANIC VITICULTURE
OLIVE OIL PRODUCTION

Riccardo Baldi is a young man with clear ideas and a great desire to work. Over the past few years, he has taken control of this small estate that until then was only known to the most passionate wine-lovers. Riccardo has beautiful, garden-like vineyards in the district of Castellaretta, on the road linking Staffolo and Cupramontana. In just a few years, his Verdicchio has become of one the best in the appellation, in part thanks to their uncommon salinity and limpid expression.

☐ **87**   👍 **Price A**

Verdicchio dei Castelli di Jesi Classico Superiore 2015

100% Verdicchio grapes. Only stainless steel. Straw yellow. Subtle aromas, very typical scent of anise blossoms and apricot; the palate offer everything you would expect from an easy drinking Verdicchio:

flavorful attack, almondy notes on the middle palate and a long length on vegetal notes. Impeccable.

⭐

LE CANIETTE

Contrada Canali, 23
63065 Ripatransone (AP)
Tel. +39 0735 9200
Fax +39 0735 91028
Ⓢ *Giovanni Vagnoni*
info@lecaniette.it
www.lecaniette.it
🅕 *Le-Caniette*
🐦 *@lecaniette*

YEAR OF FOUNDATION **1897**
NAME OF THE OWNER **Giovanni and Luigi Vagnoni**
TOTAL BOTTLES PRODUCED **75,000**
DIRECT SALES
VISITS TO THE WINERY
HECTARES OF VINEYARD **16**
CERTIFIED ORGANIC VITICULTURE

The Vagnoni brothers' estate is the result of generations of winemakers who have always worked with the obstinacy and passion that Marche producers are known for. Even though Piceno is an area not well-known among wine lovers, Le Caniette has been able to carve out a national and international Marche niche for itself. They offer a fine line of products with reds made with Montepulciano and Sangiovese, as traditional dictates, representing the lion's share of production although their whites have a lot of personality.

◼ 94   Price D
Cinabro 2012

100% Bordò (grenache) grapes. Ages in barrique. Light ruby red. Sunny version of Cinabro. Mediterranean scrub, spices and dry blossoms. Ample palate, warm and delicate with subtle tannins and incredible depth. Long and elegant finish.

◼ 92   Price B
Rosso Piceno Morellone 2011

Blend of 70% Montepulciano and 30% Sangiovese grapes. Ages in barrique. Deep ruby red. Fascinating and expressive nose. The palate is fresh, meaty with sumptuous and refined tannins; long and dynamic finish.

◼ 92   Price B
Nero di Vite 2009

100% Montepulciano grapes. Ages in barrique. Inky color, very deep. Spices and thyme, ripe black fruits; powerful palate, chewy and with minty notes. Great tannic structure, silky texture with a dynamic and fresh finish.

☐ 92   👍 Price A
Offida Pecorino Io sono Gaia non sono Lucrezia 2015

100% Pecorino grapes. Ages in used barrels and stainless steel tank. Shiny straw yellow. Complex nose of aromatic herbs and peat. Rich palate, solid but supple and with a very long finish on sea breeze notes.

☐ 91   👍 Price A
Offida Pecorino Veronica 2015

100% Pecorino grapes. Only stainless steel, unfiltered. Shiny straw yellow. Lively nose of anise and thyme. The palate is fresh, round and spicy with a savory and harmonic finish.

LE TERRAZZE

Via Musone, 4
60026 Numana (AN)
Tel. +39 071 7390352
info@fattorialeterrazze.it
www.fattorialeterrazze.it
🅕 *Fattoria-Le-Terrazze*

YEAR OF FOUNDATION **1882**
NAME OF THE OWNER **Antonio and Georgina Terni**
TOTAL BOTTLES PRODUCED **90,000**
DIRECT SALES
VISITS TO THE WINERY - RESERVATION NEEDED
HECTARES OF VINEYARD **20**

Antonio Terni is a big fan of Bob Dylan, who he knows personally and never misses a concert, as well as a passionate winemaker who has a lovely artisan's touch. His wines are stylistically modern and the product of rural wisdom and his appropriate interpretation of the land.

◼ 92   Price B
Conero Sassi Neri Riserva 2012

100% Montepulciano grapes. Ages for 18 months in

barrique. Deep inky color. The nose at moment is not extremely characteristic but is very fascinating: black cherry jam, licorice, vanilla, hint of black truffle. Very rich palate, flavorful, with austere tannins. Deep and composed finish.

Purple-violet color with a very fragrant notes of rose, musk and green pepper nose. Very fragrant palate, cold tannins, very varietal, and extremely floral finish. An exquisite wine that should be tried slightly cool.

■ 85   👍 Price A

Rosso Conero 2014

100% Montepulciano grapes. Ages for 1 year in large casks. Medium ruby. Dark nose: leather, licorice and a lightly herbaceous note. The palate shows grainy tannins and a medium finish. A great wine with a little shy fruity compound.

■ 89   Price B

Terre dei Goti 2010

100% Lacrima grapes dried for 4 months. Ages 2 years in barrique and 2 years in tonneau. Inky color with garnet rim. Astonishing varietal aromas, soft and intense: sour cherry, black peppercorn, cardamom; superb. Full bodied palate, very fruity, well extracted tannins, wonderful structure. It lacks a bit of depth but as usual it is a great wine.

MANCINELLI

Via Roma, 62
60030 Morro D'alba (AN)
Tel. +39 0731 63021
info@mancinellivini.it
www.mancinellivini.it
f stefano.mancinelli.7106
𝕏 @SteManci

YEAR OF FOUNDATION 1978
NAME OF THE OWNER Stefano Mancinelli
TOTAL BOTTLES PRODUCED 150,000
DIRECT SALES
VISITS TO THE WINERY - RESERVATION NEEDED
HECTARES OF VINEYARD 25
HOSPITALITY
OLIVE OIL PRODUCTION

Situated a dozen or so kilometers from Ancona, in a beautiful area in the northernmost part of the Castelli di Jesi appellation, Morro d'Alba owes its fame to the grape Lacrima (tear), its name deriving from the fact that the grapes break open and release 'tears' when they fully ripen. There is no doubt that the leading interpreter of this grape and the wine Lacrima di Morro d'Alba is Stefano Mancinelli, a kind and generous man who in 25 years of hard work has made this unusual wine, rich is color and fragrant aromas, known throughout the world. He also makes sweet versions that are also very interesting. All in all a very reliable winery thanks to its consistent quality.

■ 90   👍 Price A

Lacrima di Morro d'Alba Sensazioni di Frutto 2015

100% Lacrima grapes. Full carbonic maceration.

CLARA MARCELLI

Via Fonte Vecchia, 8
63030 Castorano (AP)
Tel. +39 0736 87289
Fax +39 0736 87289
info@claramarcelli.it
www.claramarcelli.it
f Cantina-Clara-Marcelli

YEAR OF FOUNDATION 2005
NAME OF THE OWNER Clara Marcelli
TOTAL BOTTLES PRODUCED 37,000
DIRECT SALES
VISITS TO THE WINERY - RESERVATION NEEDED
HECTARES OF VINEYARD 13
HOSPITALITY
CERTIFIED ORGANIC VITICULTURE
OLIVE OIL PRODUCTION

The young Emanuele and Daniela Colletta have been in the wine business for a few years and their wines are very convincing. Their family estate and vineyards are in the district of Castorano, an area historically suited for wine-growing, and their line of wines make it clear that they are determined to exalt the characteristics of the grapes and the land. The wines are well-made, responsive and technically impeccable.

■ 🍇 95   👍 Price A

K'un 2013

100% Montepulciano grapes. Ages in used barrique. Inky color. Explosive nose of aromatic herbs, spices and crunchy fruity notes. Sumptuous palate, mouth filling and balanced, well-structured chewy tannins, very dynamic. Complex and endless finish.

☐ 93   👍 Price A

Offida Pecorino Irata 2015

100% Pecorino grapes. Only stainless steel. Shiny straw yellow. Intense notes of Mediterranean scrub and sea breeze scent. Explosive palate, supple, very savory. Long and peaty finish.

■ 93   👍 Price A

Rosso Piceno Superiore 2013

Blend of Montepulciano and Sangiovese grapes. Ages in different sized barrels. Deep ruby. Multi-layered nose of black fruits, spice and tobacco. Austere palate, solid, mouth filling with very refined tannins and a fascinating freshness. Long, flavorful and complex finish.

■ 91   👍 Price A

Corbù 2014

Blend of 90% Montepulciano and 10% Cabernet Sauvignon grapes. Ages in different sized barrels and stainless steel tanks. Inky color. Fresh aromas of pencil lead and tobacco. Juicy palate, elegant tannins and good weight with a wonderful and pleasant drinkability.

☐ 89   👍 Price A

Offida Passerina Raffa 2015

100% Passerina grapes. Only stainless steel. Golden yellow. The nose offers rich notes of peat and malt. Austere palate but flavorful and complex; wonderful freshness well balanced by good weight. Long and savory finish.

VALTER MATTONI

Via Pescolla, 1
63030 Castorano (AP)
Tel. +39 0736 87329
info@valtermattoni.it
www.valtermattoni.it
valter.mattoni

YEAR OF FOUNDATION **2006**
NAME OF THE OWNER **Valter Mattoni**
TOTAL BOTTLES PRODUCED **5,500**
DIRECT SALES
VISITS TO THE WINERY - RESERVATION NEEDED
HECTARES OF VINEYARD **3**

Valter Mattoni, known to all as 'Roccia' (Rock), is the son of a family of local farmers in one of the most beautiful and suited areas for wine-growing in the whole region. His overwhelming passion for wine is legendary and his wines perfectly mirror his straightforward and convivial personality. Montepulciano, Trebbiano and the always more famous Bordò (Grenache) are the grapes grown at this small estate that gaining cult status among wine lovers.

■ 95   👍 Price A

Arshura 2014

100% Montepulciano grapes. Ages in barrique. Intense and deep red. Powerful aromas of spices and pencil lead. Vigorous palate, dense, fresh but balanced. Very tight but sweet tannins and an extremely long finish. a great version of this flagship wine.

■ 94   Price C

Rossobordò 2013

100% Bordò (grenache) grapes. Ages in barrique. Light red. Dark notes of tobacco, spices, juniper and black forrest berries. Ample structure, soft tannins and impeccable balance. Powerful finish but supple, savory and with a good depth.

★

MONTE SCHIAVO

Via Vivaio - Località Monteschiavo
60030 Maiolati Spontini (AN)
Tel. +39 0731 700385
Fax +39 0731 700359
Monte Schiavo Vini
info@monteschiavo.it
www.monteschiavo.it
monteschiavovini
@monteschiavo

YEAR OF FOUNDATION **1995**
NAME OF THE OWNER **Pieralisi**
TOTAL BOTTLES PRODUCED **950,000**
DIRECT SALES
VISITS TO THE WINERY - RESERVATION NEEDED
HECTARES OF VINEYARD **105**
OLIVE OIL PRODUCTION

With the arrival last year of renowned enologist and consultant Carlo Ferrini, the quality of the wines has seen a marked increase in quality.

The estate's top wine, Le Giuncare, is excellent as is Pallio di San Florano. This is good news for this important Jesi producer that is part of the Gruppo Pieralisi, which is also known as a producer of presses for oil mills making extra-virgin olive oil.

☐ 91   👍 Price A

Verdicchio dei Castelli di Jesi Classico Superiore Pallio di San Floriano 2015

100% Verdicchio grapes. Ages on the lees for 5 months in stainless steel tanks. Light straw yellow. Intense fruity nose: white peach, almond and hint of anise. Savory palate, mouth filling but supple, easy drinking with a savory and long finish.

☐ 87   👍 Price A

Verdicchio dei Castelli di Jesi Classico Le Coste del Molino 2015

100% Verdicchio grapes. Only stainless steel. Fragrant, fermentative, with distinctive notes of ripe white peach and field blossoms. Savory palate, fresh, very pleasant, thin and with a fair length.

MONTECAPPONE

Colle Olivo, 2
60035 Jesi (AN)
Tel. +39 0731 205761
info@montecappone.com
www.montecappone.com
� vini.dimontecappone
🐦 @montecappone

YEAR OF FOUNDATION 1968
NAME OF THE OWNER Mirizzi Family
TOTAL BOTTLES PRODUCED 150,000
DIRECT SALES
VISITS TO THE WINERY - RESERVATION NEEDED
HECTARES OF VINEYARD 70
OLIVE OIL PRODUCTION

There is no denying that the Mirizzi family, who have a well-known wine shop in Rome, have done great thing in Castelli di Jesi. Their 70 hectares of vineyards are cultivated to produce quality, a quest that in the winery continues with the supervision of enologist Lorenzo Landi. The improvement of their wines, like Verdicchio Riserva Utopia, make this estate worth knowing.

☐ 🔲 95   Price B

Castelli di Jesi Verdicchio Utopia Ris. 2013

100% Verdicchio grapes. Ages on the lees for 1 year in stainless steel tanks. Straw yellow with greenish hues. fascinating, complex and intense; notes of fine herbs, light flint note, cedar and white plum. Mouth filling palate, savory with a wonderful balanced tense acidity; very good weight. Very long finish.

☐ 90   👍 Price A

Verdicchio dei Castelli di Jesi Classico Superiore Federico II 2015

100% Verdicchio grapes. Only stainless steel. Pale yellow. Aromas of loquat, white plum and doughnut peach, citrus hint. Supple, fresh and savory palate, good drinkability despite the good weight. Long finish.

★★

MORODER

Via Montacuto, 121
60129 Ancona (AN)
Tel. +39 071 898232
info@moroder-vini.it
www.moroder-vini.it
🅕 cantinemoroder

YEAR OF FOUNDATION 1984
NAME OF THE OWNER Alessandro and Serenella Moroder
TOTAL BOTTLES PRODUCED 130,000
DIRECT SALES
VISITS TO THE WINERY - RESERVATION NEEDED
HECTARES OF VINEYARD 28
HOSPITALITY
RESTAURANT
CERTIFIED ORGANIC VITICULTURE
OLIVE OIL PRODUCTION

Having witnessed the first steps Sandro and Serenella Morodor made in the world of wine, now 30 years ago, we cannot be but proud of what they have achieved. Today they are a solid point of reference for Conero wines and organic winegrowing in the area, while their wines are one better than the next.

■ 93   Price B

Conero Dorico Riserva 2011

100% Montepulciano grapes. Ages for 36 months in

barrique. Deep and intense garnet. Complex steely notes, cardamom, nutmeg, sea breeze and violet. Austere palate, just as great Conero should be, powerful and flavorful. One of the greatest expressions of the last few years.

■ 91   Price B
Conero Riserva 2012

100% Montepulciano grapes. Ages for 30 months: 50% in 10hl oak casks and 50% in tonneau. Very deep ruby-garnet. Characteristic notes of red blossoms, nutmeg, cardamom. At the moment it is a little bit tight but it has great impact, pleasantly rustic tannins, lightly woody note on the finish alongside floral notes. Excellent.

▨ 88   👍 Price A
Rosa di Moroder 2015

Blend of Montepulciano and Alicante grapes. Cold maceration and ageing for 6 months in stainless steel tanks. Intense pink. Well-defined aromas, very fruity with hint of white and red cherries. Flavorful and mouth-filling palate, savory and with a balanced residual sugar. Delicious.

MURÒLA

Contrada Villamagna, 9
62010 Urbisaglia (MC)
Tel. +39 0733 506843
info@murola.it
www.murola.it
 f *CantinaMurola*

YEAR OF FOUNDATION **1724**
NAME OF THE OWNER **Jurek Mosiewicz**
TOTAL BOTTLES PRODUCED **700.000**
DIRECT SALES
VISITS TO THE WINERY - RESERVATION NEEDED
HECTARES OF VINEYARD **60**

A great winery close to Macerata, where traditions and grape varieties coming from the near by region combine. So if Passerina and Montepulciano come from Ascoli area and Abruzzi, the Grechetto is typically from Umbria like the Trebbiano Spoletino, and the Sangiovese is found in all central Italy regions. Every one is made with an impeccable tecnique.

■ 90   Price B
Camà Sangiovese 2013

100% Sangiovese grapes. Matures 1 year in big

barrels. Bright garnet ruby red. Very typical notes of cherry, black cherry, hints of spices. Clear and pleasant on the nose. Full, warm and clear on the palate, smooth tannins and great persistant finish.

■ 88   Price B
Teodoro Montepulciano 2013

100% Montepulciano grapes. Matures 1 year in barrique. Dark ruby red. Intense and enveloping, notes of kirsch and vanilla on the nose. Warm, rich taste, slight roughness in the tannins, full-bodied, well balanced by the acidity and good length.

☐ 87   Price A
Baccius Trebbiano 2015

100% Trebbiano Spoletino grapes. Stainless steel only on the yeasts. Intense on the nose, cedar and medlar, with hints of yeasts. Briny, fresh, fine on the palate. Very pleasant and discrete persistence.

★★★

OASI DEGLI ANGELI

Contrada Sant'Egidio, 50
63012 Cupra Marittima (AP)
Tel. +39 0735 778569
Fax +39 0735 778569
info@kurni.it
www.kurni.it
 f *Kurni-Az-Oasi-degli-Angeli*

YEAR OF FOUNDATION **1997**
NAME OF THE OWNER **Eleonora Rossi**
TOTAL BOTTLES PRODUCED **7,500**
DIRECT SALES
VISITS TO THE WINERY - RESERVATION NEEDED
HECTARES OF VINEYARD **16**
OLIVE OIL PRODUCTION

Marco Casolanetti and Eleonora Rossi have represented and continue to represent the example of the growing quality of wines from small and medium-sized estates in Piceno. This thanks to their competence, passion and desire to share their experience. Added to that is their exasperated quest for quality using a winegrowing method that calls for a density of between 22,000 and 40,000 rootstocks per hectare and extremely low vineyard yields, along with a refined choice of wood for aging. All this is done to exalt a unique territory for Montepulciano thanks to its loose soil and altitudes that reach 450m above sea level. Marco and Eleonora also have the merit of having rediscovered, brought back and promoted the use of an old variety of Bordò, a Grenache or Cannonau grape variation that had all but disappeared in Piceno.

dynamic dictates and is part of a project that extends into various Italian regions. Their top Marche wine this year was Castelli di Jesi Verdicchio Classico Superiore Dominé that came out well despite the off year.

 98   Price D

Kupra 2013

100% Bordò (grenache) grapes. Ages in barrique. Shiny ruby. Nose and palate are explosive yet very sleek and fresh; without doubt it is a wine that speaks of complexity and terroir. To drink with joy and respect! Marco Casolanetti and Eleonora Rossi, perhaps helped by a blessed vintage for this grape variety, have produced an outstanding version of Kupra.

 96   Price C

Kurni 2014

100% Montepulciano grapes. Ages in barrique. Deep and intense ruby. Sumptuous aromas of spices, tobacco, leather, aromatic herbs and citrus. As usual the palate is dense but with a surprising suppleness: quite unusual for this wine when it is young. Chewy tannins and well defined tense finish; juicy and very long.

★

PIEVALTA

Via Monteschiavo, 18
60030 Maiolati Spontini (AN)
Tel. +39 0731 705199
Fax +39 0731 705199
pievalta@baronepizzini.it
www.pievalta.it
 Pievalta-Azienda-Agricola-Viticoltura-Biodinamica
 @PizziniBlog

YEAR OF FOUNDATION 2002
NAME OF THE OWNER **Barone Pizzini**
TOTAL BOTTLES PRODUCED **110,500**
DIRECT SALES
VISITS TO THE WINERY - RESERVATION NEEDED
HECTARES OF VINEYARD **26.5**
CERTIFIED ORGANIC VITICULTURE
CERTIFIED BIODYNAMIC VITICULTURE
OLIVE OIL PRODUCTION

This is one of the estates belonging to the famous Franciacorta winery Barone Pizzini and, like the others, is cultivated according to bio-

 96   Price A

Castelli di Jesi Verdicchio Classico Riserva 2013

100% Verdicchio grapes. On the lees for 30 months in stainless steel tanks. Shiny straw yellow. Intense, fascinating and refined nose; yeasty hints, then floral and white peach notes, elegant and defined profile. Tense palate, supple, savory, great body, fresh and very long finish.

☐ 90   Price A

Verdicchio dei Castelli di Jesi Classico Superiore Dominé 2015

100% Verdicchio grapes. Only stainless steel. Straw yellow with greenish hues. The nose offers field blossoms, lavender, lemongrass and a light almondy note. Savory palate, firm with a good weight, tense and very long.

★

PODERI CAPECCI

Via Santa Maria in Carro, 13 - Località San Savino
63065 Ripatransone (AP)
Tel. +39 0735 90107
Fax +39 0735 90409
info@sansavino.com
www.sansavino.com
 CIPREA-Offida-Pecorino-Poderi-Capecci-San-Savino

YEAR OF FOUNDATION 1974
NAME OF THE OWNER **Simone Capecci**
TOTAL BOTTLES PRODUCED **120,000**
DIRECT SALES
VISITS TO THE WINERY - RESERVATION NEEDED
HECTARES OF VINEYARD **22**
CERTIFIED ORGANIC VITICULTURE

Simone Capecci is a young winemaker who has already accumulated a great deal of experience. His vineyards of Montepulciano, Sangiovese, Pecorino and Passerina, typical for the area, are in the area of Acquaviva and near Offida. The full line of products has always been focused and defined even if his Pecorino Ciprea is becoming the estate's symbol and one of the most interesting wines of its kind.

☐ 93   👍 Price A

Offida Pecorino Ciprea 2015

100% Pecorino grapes. Only stainless steel. Shiny straw yellow. It is still very young yet complex with note of peat, sea breeze and white pepper. The palate is savory, fresh with an important structure but supple and dynamic. Long finish, sharp and with a great personality.

 90   Price B

Quinta Regio 2012

100% Montepulciano grapes. Ages in barrique. Inky color. Fascinating nose with scents of black fruits and ground beef. Austere palate, powerful but dynamic, supple and with well extracted tannins. Flavorful and deep finish.

■ 87   👍 Price A

Rosso Piceno Superiore Picus 2014

Blend of Montepulciano and Sangiovese grapes. Ages in used barrique. Dark ruby red. Nose of spices and wet leaves. Fruity palate, fresh and supple. Juicy tannins and a long and flavorful palate.

★

PODERI SAN LAZZARO

Via San Lazzaro, 88
63073 Offida (AP)
Tel. +39 335 8252640
info@poderisanlazzaro.it
www.poderisanlazzaro.it
 f *poderi.sanlazzaro*

YEAR OF FOUNDATION **2003**
NAME OF THE OWNER **Elisetta Carosi and Paolo Capriotti**
TOTAL BOTTLES PRODUCED **50,000**
DIRECT SALES
VISITS TO THE WINERY
HECTARES OF VINEYARD **7**
CERTIFIED ORGANIC VITICULTURE
OLIVE OIL PRODUCTION

Paolo Capriotti's wines impeccably express the territory they are from, Piceno, and have an artisanal style that never infringes on technical precision. They are wines that fully respect their appellation to which they add unique

character and style and an economical quality/price ratio. A new winery has given a boost to this estate that has become an authentic jewel for the area.

■ 92   Price B

Bordò 2012

100% Bordò (grenache) grapes. Ages in different sized barrels. Distinctive notes of spices, tobacco and red fruits. Sweet tannins are supported by a good acidity. Long finish with a unique and delicate note of mustard blossoms.

■ 91   👍 Price A

Rosso Piceno Superiore Podere 72 2013

100% Montepulciano grapes. Only stainless steel. Ages in different sized barrels. Deep ruby red. The nose offers floral notes and hint of tobacco. The palate is chewy with a good weight and freshness. The finish plays on mineral and earthy notes.

■ 90   👍 Price A

Polesio 2015

100% Sangiovese grapes. Only stainless steel. Light ruby. Distinctive floral and red fruity notes. The palate is fresh, supple with a chewy, mineral and flavorful finish.

☐ 88   👍 Price A

Offida Pecorino Pistillo 2015

100% Pecorino grapes. Matures in stainless steel and big barrels. Bright straw yellow. Aromati herbs and white fruits introduce a fresh, dynamic, not too powerful palate but agile and juicy.

SARTARELLI

Via Coste del Molino, 24
60030 Poggio San Marcello (AN)
Tel. +39 0731 89732
Fax +39 0731 889902
info@sartarelli.it
www.sartarelli.it

YEAR OF FOUNDATION **1972**
NAME OF THE OWNER **Donatella Sartarelli**
TOTAL BOTTLES PRODUCED **300,000**
DIRECT SALES
VISITS TO THE WINERY
HECTARES OF VINEYARD **55**
OLIVE OIL PRODUCTION

Sartarelli's Verdicchio are recognizable for three reasons: the unconditional respect for the typicity of the grape and how it expresses a territory or vineyard; no use of wood; and the shape of the bottle he himself designed. But these become just side aspects when you taste the wines, three great versions of Verdicchio that are difficult to find from a single producer. Our compliments to the whole estate also for their reasonable prices.

☐ 92   Price B

Verdicchio dei Castelli di Jesi Classico Superiore Balciana 2014

100% late harvested Verdicchio grapes. Only stainless steel. Golden yellow, deep. Powerful, clean and fascinating aromas: tropical fruits, mint, sweet licorice, anise. The palate is irresistible: off-dry but in perfect balance, middle-palate of salted honey, saffron. Powerful and elegant finish. Thinner than previous vintage but very lively. Unmissable.

☐ 89   Price A

Verdicchio dei Castelli di Jesi Classico Superiore Tralivio 2014

100% Verdicchio grapes. Only stainless steel. Lively straw yellow, rich with a textbook nose: apricot, pennyroyal, mustard blossoms, intense and clean. Very rich palate, powerful, deep and with a pleasantly bitter notes. It lacks of depth but it can only be matter of time.

TAVIGNANO

Località Tavignano,10
62011 Cingoli (MC)
Tel. +39 0733 617303
tavignano@libero.it
www.tenutaditavignano.it
f *tenutaditavignano*

YEAR OF FOUNDATION **1974**
NAME OF THE OWNER **Stefano Aymerich**
TOTAL BOTTLES PRODUCED **100,000**
DIRECT SALES
VISITS TO THE WINERY - RESERVATION NEEDED
HECTARES OF VINEYARD **30**
OLIVE OIL PRODUCTION

The Tavignano estate is in the castle of the same name, one of the most beautiful castles in the zone of Castelli di Jesi, and is in the southern part of this large and important appella-

tion. For a long time it belonged to the Castiglioni family before being acquired some 40 years ago by Stefano Aymerich di Laconi, an engineer of noble roots and great foresight. Although unknown to some wine lovers, the estate's Verdicchio stand out for their consistent quality and represent the grape's more somber side.

☐ 89   👍 Price A

Verdicchio dei Castelli di Jesi Classico Superiore Villa Torre 2015

100% Verdicchio grapes. Only stainless steel. Pale greenish yellow; wonderful aromas of yellow blossoms, citrus and camomile. Consistent palate, juicy, simple but very pleasant. Unmissable.

☐ 87   Price A

Verdicchio dei Castelli di Jesi Classico Superiore Misco 2015

100% Verdicchio grapes. Ages on the lees for 1 year in stainless steel tanks. Medium straw yellow. Tight nose, at the moment it is a bit shy; herbaceous palate, dynamic and with great freshness with a relative simple finish. Very typical.

TERRE CORTESI MONCARO

Via Piandole, 7a
60036 Montecarotto (AN)
Tel. +39 0731 89245
b.fabbretti@moncaro.it
www.moncaro.it
f *cantinemoncaro*

YEAR OF FOUNDATION **1964**
NAME OF THE OWNER
TOTAL BOTTLES PRODUCED **7,500,000**
DIRECT SALES
VISITS TO THE WINERY - RESERVATION NEEDED
HECTARES OF VINEYARD **1,200**
RESTAURANT
CERTIFIED ORGANIC VITICULTURE

Virtuos example of how a cooperative winery can produce wines of the utmost quality. The cooperative is in Montecarotto, one of the leading towns for Verdicchio dei Castelli di Jesi production. It has been operative for over 50 years and has always offered well-made wines at convenient prices. In other words, a cooperative of which there should be more of.

243

☐ 93 Price A

Castelli di Jesi Verdicchio Classico Vigna Novali Riserva 2013

100% Verdicchio grapes. A small percentage ages in barrique for 10 months, the rest ages for the same time in stainless steel. Intense straw yellow. Fascinating, complex, with smoky and thiolic notes that remind a Riesling. Then hint of cedar and grapefruit. Firm palate, warm but tense and with a good body.

☐ 90 Price A

Verdicchio dei Castelli di Jesi Classico Superiore Verde Ca' Ruptae 2015

100% Verdicchio grapes. Only stainless steel. Pineapple, passion fruit, white peach and light note of fine herbs on the nose. Savory and tense palate, easy drinking with a fresh and long finish.

☐ 86 Price A

Verdicchio dei Castelli di Jesi Classico Le Vele 2015

100% Verdicchio grapes. Only stainless steel. Greenish yellow. Delicate fermentative notes, peppermint, then pineapple and white peach. Light palate, supple, very drinkable, savory with a medium length.

★★★

UMANI RONCHI

Via Adriatica, 12
60027 Osimo (AN)
Tel. +39 071 7108019
wine@umanironchi.com
www.umanironchi.com
 Umani Ronchi
 @UmaniRonchiVino

YEAR OF FOUNDATION 1955
NAME OF THE OWNER Massimo and Michele Bernetti
TOTAL BOTTLES PRODUCED 2,800,000
DIRECT SALES
VISITS TO THE WINERY
HECTARES OF VINEYARD 230
CERTIFIED ORGANIC VITICULTURE

There is little doubt Umani Ronchi's visibility, clear marketing strategy, global sales and, above all, consistent quality make it, together with Garofoli (an estate with slightly more clas-

sical style), one of the best representatives of Marche's two winemaking territories: Castelli dei Catelli di Jesi for the whites and Conero for the reds. In all our years of tasting, we have never sampled one of their wines that was anything less than excellent and have even had some outstanding ones. This year we included Riserva Campo San Giorgio that is simply one of the greatest Conero wines ever tasted.

■ 95 Price B

Conero Campo San Giorgio Riserva 2011

100% Montepulciano grapes. Ages in barrique and tonneau for 18 months. Intense ruby red. Nose of vanilla, kirsch, black cherry, cocoa and sweet tobacco. Firm palate, rich, tannic, powewful; very warm but with a very tense and savory acidity, very Mediterranean.

☐ 93 Price B

Verdicchio dei Castelli di Jesi Classico Sup. Casal di Serra Vecchie Vigne 2014

100% Verdicchio grapes. Ages on the lees for 10 months in concrete tanks. Intense golden yellow. Very floral nose: field blossoms, then tropical fruit and white peach. Firm and mouth filling palate, savory, full bodied but tense and very long.

☐ 88 Price A

Verdicchio dei Castelli di Jesi Classico Superiore Casal di Serra 2015

100% Verdicchio grapes. Ages on the lees in stainless steel tanks. Greenish straw yellow. Solid and fragrant nose with scents of broom blossoms and camomile, then smoky and yeasty hints. Savory and fresh, easy drinking with a thin and pleasant finish.

★★

VELENOSI

Via dei Biancospini, 11
63100 Ascoli Piceno (AP)
Tel. +39 0736 341218
info@velenosivini.com
www.velenosivini.com
 velenosi.vini
 @VelenosiVini

YEAR OF FOUNDATION 1984
NAME OF THE OWNER Angela and Ercole Velenosi and Paolo Garbini
TOTAL BOTTLES PRODUCED 2,500,000

If Ascoli wines today are internationally known and appreciated, much of the credit goes to the very efficient efforts of Angela Velenosi, who travels the world to promote her wines and has inevitably become an ambassador for her whole area. Thanks to her, Rosso Piceno or Offida DOC are no longer unknown entities, even on the East Asian market.

 96   **Price B**

Rosso Piceno Superiore Roggio del Filare 2013

Blend of 70% Montepulciano and 30% Sangiovese grapes. Ages 1 year in barrique. Deep ruby, intense and lively. Deliciously complex nose, hints of dark cherry and kirsch, then cardamom, vanilla, black pepper and white tobacco. Warm palate, fascinating, with subtle tannins but well balanced by well extracted sweetness. Very long finish.

93   **Price B**

Offida Rosso Ludi 2013

Blend of 85% Montepulciano and 15% Merlot and Cabernet Sauvignon grapes. Ages 1 year in barrique. very concentrated and deep ruby. Notes of kirsch followed by intense spicy hint, light notes of eucalyptus and mint. Firm palate, rich, warm, powerful with thick but refined tannins and a very long finish.

92   👍 **Price A**

Rosso Piceno Superiore Brecciarolo Gold 2013

Blend of 70% Montepulciano and 30% Sangiovese grapes. Ages 18 months in different sized barrels. Very intense ruby. Well defined, fruity and neat aromas of black cherry, spices and white tobacco. The palate is firm and well balanced by good acidity and with a good structured body. Warm and fascinating finish.

88   👍 **Price A**

Rosso Piceno Superiore Brecciarolo Silver 2014

Blend of 70% Montepulciano and 30% Sangiovese grapes. Ages in different sized barrels. Intense ruby. Simple, fruity with notes of black cherry and floral hints. Tense palate, supple and fresh; fair length.

☐ **87**   **Price A**

Offida Pecorino Reve 2014

100% Pecorino grapes. The 50% matures in barrique and the rest in stainless steel tanks. Intense straw yellow. Cedar, light vanilla hint and white peach on the nose. Savory palate, tense, good weight and with a very good acidity.

MARCHE

245

MOLISE

According to the latest data from Federdoc, the association that groups together all Italy's wine associations, the production of DOC and DOCG classified wine in the region of Molise is in the neighborhood of 50,000 hectoliters. A good 37,000 of these are Molise Rosso or Tintilia del Molise, 13,000 are Biferno and just 28,000 are Pentro d'Isernia, which makes it one of Italy's smallest appellations. The main reason for the low level of production is the fact that 55% of the region is mountainous. And while the data cited dates back to 2011, there does not appear to have been any significant increase of late, even if some new producers are appearing on the national winemaking landscape. The most widespread grape grown is Montepulciano, almost half of the total, but its name is not allowed to be on the label because the town of Montepulciano, known for its Vino Nobile, which is made from Sangiovese, would object. This despite the fact that it has been cultivated for years in Abruzzo, Puglia and Marche as well as Molise and used to make wines that have nothing to do with that Tuscan town or its wine. At present, only Abruzzo is allowed to use the name on the labels of its wines. The grapes that can be cited on the labels of Molise wines are Aglianico, which makes some interesting ones, and above all Tintilia, a traditional local grape that is probably not indigenous. Nevertheless, it is almost only found in Molise vineyards and is considered an undisputed regional asset. Most of the white wine grapes have emigrated from neighboring regions like Bombino Bianco from nearby Puglia, and those from the zone of Sannio Beneventano like Falanghina and Greco, as well as Fiano from Avellino.

CONTROLLED DESIGNATION OF ORIGIN (DOC)

- Biferno
- Molise or del Molise
- Pentro di Isernia or Pentro
- Tintilia del Molise

DI MAJO NORANTE

Contrada Ramitelli, 4
86042 Campomarino (CB)
Tel. +39 0875 57208
Fax +39 0875 57379
vini@dimajonorante.it
www.dimajonorante.com
dimajo.norante
@DimajoNorante

YEAR OF FOUNDATION 1968
NAME OF THE OWNER Alessio Di Majo
TOTAL BOTTLES PRODUCED 800,000
DIRECT SALES
VISITS TO THE WINERY - RESERVATION NEEDED
HECTARES OF VINEYARD 120
CERTIFIED ORGANIC VITICULTURE
OLIVE OIL PRODUCTION

If Molise wine is known in the world, much of the credit goes to Alessio di Majo who is constantly on the go to promote his wines. He makes a variety of them, some are truly excellent and others well-made and all of them have an excellent quality/price ratio. His winery is in Campomarino, almost on the border with Puglia, from where you can see the Tremiti Islands and the Gargano peninsula, and he benefits from the consultancy of the famous enologist Riccardo Cotarella.

 92 Price A*
Molise Moscato Apianae 2013

100% Moscato Reale grapes. Matures 18 months in tonneau. Golden yellow. Pleasant notes of honey, apricot and white flowers; fragrant and aromatic it gets better on the palate, giving freshness and with a surprising spicy finish. Pleasant and not too sweet. *50 cl bottle.

 90 Price A
Molise Aglianico Contado Riserva 2013

100% Aglianico grapes. Matures 18 months in tonneau. Intense ruby color. Notes of macerated black cherry and vanilla, then leather. Powerful on the palate, great body and smooth tannins. Strong and enveloping flavor.

 90 Price B
Molise Don Luigi Riserva 2013

Blend of 90% Montepulciano and 10% Aglianico

grapes. Matures 18 months in French barrique. Intense ruby color. Rich nose: eucalyptus notes, vanilla, nuts. On the palate it is rich, enveloping but tense with a strong tannin.

87 Price A
Molise Tintilia 2013

100% Tintilia grapes. Matures 12 months in tonneau. Ruby red with violet hues. Notes of morello cherry and a light spiciness. Briny on the palate, good body and balanced tannin. The finish is not as long as you would expect it to be.

TENIMENTI GRIECO

Contrada Defensola
86035 Portocannone (CB)
Tel. +39 0875 590032
Fax +39 0875 590032
info@tenimentigrieco.it
www.tenimentigrieco.it

YEAR OF FOUNDATION 2015
NAME OF THE OWNER Antonio Grieco
TOTAL BOTTLES PRODUCED 400,000
DIRECT SALES
VISITS TO THE WINERY - RESERVATION NEEDED
HECTARES OF VINEYARD 85

Born from the ashes of Masseria Flocco it immediately becomes one of the leader wineries of the Molise region, both for quantity of vineyards and number of bottles produced. The labels are articulated in various lines, including one called Passo delle Tremiti dedicated to the memory of the famous Italian singer Lucio Dalla who was a fan of these wines.

 90 Price A
Podere di Lenda Aglianico 2014

100% Aglianico grapes. Stainless steel only. Intense ruby red. Clear, with notes of black cherry, cassis, a hint of tamarind. Agile, fresh, not too tannic, easy to drink and good length.

86 Price A
Tintilia del Molise 200 metri 2015

100% Tintilia grapes. Stainless steel only. Bright ruby red. Slightly fermentative, then wild berries and a hint of black cherry. Fresh, pleasant, well sustained by acidity, long and elegant finish.

VINICA

Contrada Costa Bianca, 4
86025 Ripalimosani (CB)
Tel. +39 0874 1866935
Fax +39 338 280 3618
info@agricolavinica.it
www.agricolavinica.it
f *vinica.it*
𝕏 *@vinica_it*

YEAR OF FOUNDATION **2009**
NAME OF THE OWNER **Rodolfo and**
Melanie Gianserra
TOTAL BOTTLES PRODUCED **16,000**
DIRECT SALES
VISITS TO THE WINERY - RESERVATION NEEDED
HECTARES OF VINEYARD **24**
OLIVE OIL PRODUCTION

This is a new winemaking reality which we are sure to hear more about in the future. It is owned by Rodolfo Gianserra and his wife Melanie and they embarked on this project with great ambitions and both a modern and serious approach. At present they are bottling only part of the harvest from their 24-hectare organic vineyard. The bottles are sealed with screw caps to best preserve the wine's primary characteristics. Aside from wine, they also produce olive oil, corn flour and cannellini beans, all top quality.

■ **87**   👍 **Price A**
Tintilia del Molise Lame del Sorbo 2011

100% Tintilia grapes. Stainless steel only. Intense and bright ruby red. Very fruity, black cherry, cassis and anise. Savory and pleasant on the palate, easy to drink and average persistence.

■ **85**   👍 **Price A**
Molise Merlot 2014

100% Merlot grapes. Stainless steel only. Bright ruby red. Very typical, fruity, fragrant and a little simple with notes of raspberry and cassis. Average intensity on the palate but easy to drink.

www.doctorwine.it is the first **totally bi-lingual (Italian-English)** web-magazine published in Italy and thus offers an Italian point of view to a global public. It is not a blog but an authentic **on-line magazine** which deals with wine and related subjects. The magazine was created and is run by **Daniele Cernilli**, internationally considered to be one of Italy's most authoritative wine critics, who used his nickname as the magazine's name.

From February 2016 DoctorWine is on line with a completely new site. We realized we have an impressive archive that is constantly expanding and which we wanted to make as accessible as possible. Thus the key feature in the change is related to the research of information within the site: making it easier for anyone to find a particular wine we have taste.

PIEDMONT

Piedmont is one of Italy's most important regions for quality wine as well as one the most beautiful places on Earth. In fact, in 2014 UNESCO declared the geographic area of Langhe-Roero and Monferrato to be a World Heritage Site. It is a territory that has been recognized for its wine culture that has risen to heights that not even the sophisticated hills of Champagne or Bordeaux have been able to reach- Piedmont has a 'cultural landscape' that is the result of a centuries-old relationship between the generosity of the land and human endeavor that has kept ancient traditional alive and produced wines known around the word. The name Piedmont, this vast region in northwest Italy, refers to its position at the feet of the mountains of the Alps, which to the east and north separate it from France and Switzerland, and the Apennines to the south that divide it from the region of Liguria. In the middle is a vast hilly area that descends softly towards the Po River Valley and a discontinuous pre-Alpine foothill one that is concentric with the mountain chain and where winegrowing at times extends deep in the valleys. These geographic characteristics have had enormous historical importance in the history of the region that since ancient times has been controlled by different peoples.

The Greeks were probably the one who made Piedmont wines known to the Ligurian people but it was surely thanks to the Romans if winegrowing took root in a major way thanks to their method of allowing vines to climb mulberry trees the way the Etruscans did.

Count Camillo Benso of Cavour, the first prime minister of the Kingdom of Italy, gets the credit for the birth of Barolo, one of Italy's greatest red wines, which has exemplified how the history of man and the history of wine often go hand in hand. The wines the region produces now are those than have come down over the past three or four centuries or, in the case of Barolo and Barbaresco, over the past 100 years, at least in the versions we know today. Piedmont grows a vast variety of grapes but the most widespread is Barbera, a grapes that is used to make Barbera d'Alba and d'Asti, dei Colli Tortonesi and del Monferrato. The second leading grapes is Dolcetto, a variety used to wake a host of different denominations: Dolcetto d'Alba, di Diano d'Alba, d Dogliani, di Acqui. di Asti, di Ovada, delle Langhe Monregalesi, del Monferrato, dei Colli Tortonesi, Langhe Dolcetto and Piemonte Dolcetto. The third grape among the reds for cultivation but first for fame and quality, is Nebbiolo. This grape is used to make Nebbiolo d'Alba, Roero, Barolo, Barbaresco, Gattinara and Ghemme as well as lesser known wines from the DOC appellations of Novara and Vercelli like Boca, Bramaterra, Fara, Lessona and Sizzano, as well as Carema which is made in the district of the same name near Ivrea.

And then there is Moscato. In the province of Asti, Moscato is used to make the world's most famous sweet sparkling wine. But there is also a lesser-known still wine, Moscato d'Asti, a very light, sweet and aromatic wine that, as opposed to the sparkling version, is generally made by small producers. When allowed to raisinate, either on the vine or on drying racks, Moscato is used to make Loazzolo, a small and little-known sweet white wine that is among the best of its kind in Italy. Aside from its sparkling white wine, the province of Asti is also home to Brachetto d'Acqui, a sweet and very aromatic red that is usually a sparkling wine and is perfect to pair with a fruit tart. Red Malvasia grapes produce two small, sweet and sparling reds, Malvasia di Casorzo d'Asti and Malvasia di Castelnuovo Don Bosco. These wines are the product of a local rural culture and should be viewed in the contest of the territory and considered a delicious curiosity.

In central Piedmont, where the terrain is flatter – the area east of Turin, north of Asti and west of Novara and Vercelli – aside from the Carema appellation you find Freisa di Chieri, a sparling red made from Freisa grapes that is simple and light and very popular in the area. Central Piedmont also produce Erbaluce di Caluso, a light white made with Erbaluce grapes of which there is also a sweet version made with raisinated grapes called Caluso Passito.

In the northern part of the Alessandria province are two small but important DOC appellations: Gabiano and Rubino di Cantavenna. Both are made using mostly Barbera grapes and are reds that have a medium-body and age well.

Grignolino is a unique grape that only is only cultivated in the area between the provinces of Asti and Alessandria, in southeastern Piedmont. The wines it makes are not concentrated in color and have a sharp tannic-acidic tang. The best-known is probably Grignolino d'Asti but equally good is Grignolino del Monferrato Casalese, produced more to the north and almost on the border with Vercelli province.

The latest DOC appellation to be approved regard vast areas of production distinguished by innovative winegrowing which includes international varieties as well as traditional ones. These DOC are Langhe and Piemonte. The first encompasses almost the whole southeast province of Cuneo. It is a kind of 're-entry' appellation and includes, for example, all the Nebbiolo and Dolcetto-based reds that did not qualify for the other appellations. Among other things, these wines have different aging periods in barrels compared to Barolo or Barbaresco and the aging methods are less traditional. The DOC has also allowed many producers to have their experimental wines recognized, varietals like Chardonnay, Sauvignon and Cabernet Sauvignon. DOC Piemonte encompasses the whole region an can include all the wines made with grapes found in the region (Piemonte Cortese, Piemonte Chardonnay and Piemonte Barbera, for example) with regulations that are less strict than for other appellations. There are also an appellation for those Spumante that did not qualify as DOCG Asti.

Controlled and Guaranteed Designation of Origin (DOCG)

- Alta Langa
- Asti, with or without the sub-areas Canelli or Santa Vittoria d'Alba or Strevi
- Barbaresco, geographic references allowed
- Barbera d'Asti, solo per Barbera d'Asti Superiore with or without the sub-areas Nizza, Tinella, Colli Astiani o Astiano
- Barbera del Monferrato Superiore
- Barolo, geographic references allowed
- Brachetto d'Acqui o Acqui
- Dogliani
- Dolcetto di Diano d'Alba o Diano d'Alba, geographic references allowed
- Dolcetto di Ovada Superiore or Ovada
- Erbaluce di Caluso or Caluso
- Gattinara
- Gavi or Cortese di Gavi, geographic references allowed (except the Riserva and Riserva Spumante Classic Method)
- Ghemme
- Roero
- Ruchè di Castagnole Monferrato

Controlled Designation of Origin (DOC)

- Alba
- Albugnano
- Barbera d'Alba
- Barbera del Monferrato
- Boca
- Bramaterra
- Calosso
- Canavese
- Carema
- Cisterna d'Asti
- Colli Tortonesi, with or without the sub-areas Monleale, Terre di Libarna
- Collina Torinese
- Colline Novaresi
- Colline Saluzzesi
- Cortese dell'Alto Monferrato
- Coste della Sesia
- Derthona
- Dolcetto d'Acqui
- Dolcetto d'Alba
- Dolcetto d'Asti
- Dolcetto di Ovada
- Fara
- Freisa d'Asti
- Freisa di Chieri
- Gabiano
- Grignolino d'Asti
- Grignolino del Monferrato Casalese
- Langhe, with or without the sub-areas Nascetta del Comune di Novello or Nas-cëtta del Comune di Novello
- Lessona
- Loazzolo
- Malvasia di Casorzo d'Asti or Casorzo or Malvasia di Casorzo
- Malvasia di Castelnuovo don Bosco
- Monferrato, with or without the sub-areas Casalese (followed by Cortese variety)
- Nebbiolo d'Alba
- Piemonte, with or without the specific designation Vigneti di Montagna
- Pinerolese
- Rubino di Cantavenna
- Sizzano
- Strevi
- Terre Alfieri
- Valli Ossolane
- Valsusa
- Verduno Pelaverga or Verduno
- Ghemme
- Roero
- Ruchè di Castagnole Monferrato

MARZIANO ABBONA

Borgata San Luigi, 40
12063 Dogliani (CN)
Tel. +39 0173 721317
Fax +39 0173 70999
🔵 *Marziano Abbona*
abbona@abbona.com
www.abbona.com
f *marzianoabbona*

252

YEAR OF FOUNDATION **1970**
NAME OF THE OWNER **Marziano Abbona**
TOTAL BOTTLES PRODUCED **260,000**
DIRECT SALES
VISITS TO THE WINERY - RESERVATION NEEDED
HECTARES OF VINEYARD **45**

A great producer of Dolcetto di Dogliani, or more simply Dogliani as the appellation is now called, Marziano Abbona brings together skill, a nice personality and esthetic taste, as is evidence by the labels of his wines. His top of the line is Papà Celso, a great Dogliani, but one should not pass up his Barolo Ravera and Pressenda, made from grapes grown in the Novello and Monforte cru.

🆔 **95**   👍 **Price A**
Dogliani Papà Celso 2015

100% Dolcetto grapes. Stainless steel on the lees for 10 months. Intense violet ruby red. Enveloping, very fruity with notes of raspberry, black currant, violet, typical and impressive integrity. Warm and tense with a delicious acidic component, savory, young tannins, powerful but with nice involving drinkability. Very long finish.

■ **93**   **Price C**
Barolo Ravera 2012

100% Nebbiolo grapes. Matures 3 years in big barrels. Intense garnet red. Enveloping and very typical notes of alfalfa, violet and hints of currant. Strong flavor, tense acidity, savory, warm, agile, pleasant and very persistent.

■ **90**   **Price B**
Barolo Pressenda 2012

100% Nebbiolo grapes. Matures 3 years in barrels. Clear ruby red. Slightly evolved, notes of licorice, smoky and notes of raspberries and violet. Yong tannins, progressive, lively acidity, a little split. Great persistence.

ORLANDO ABRIGO

Frazione Cappelletto, 5
12050 Treiso (CN)
Tel. +39 0173 630533
Fax +39 0173 630907
info@orlandoabrigo.it
www.orlandoabrigo.it
f *Orlando-Abrigo*

YEAR OF FOUNDATION **1994**
NAME OF THE OWNER **Giovanni Abrigo**
TOTAL BOTTLES PRODUCED **85,000**
DIRECT SALES
VISITS TO THE WINERY - RESERVATION NEEDED
HECTARES OF VINEYARD **20**
HOSPITALITY
RESTAURANT

A small but well-equipped Treiso winery that was founded just over 20 years ago and offers food and lodging at its Foresteria Setteville estate. Splendid vineyards surround the estate and produce a small but prestigious line of wines with the Barbaresco di Treiso 'cru' standing out.

■ **94**   **Price C**
Barbaresco Rongallo Riserva 2011

100% Nebbiolo grapes. Matures in different size barrels for 2 years. Very intense and lively ruby red. Quite modern style, notes of Kirsch, vanilla, tobacco and black cherry. Tense flavor, very well made, full-bodied and agile, young but promising tannins. Great long and enveloping finish.

■ **93**   **Price B**
Barbaresco Rocche Meruzzano 2013

100% Nebbiolo grapes. Matures 15 months in tonneau. Whole notes of currant, spices, Kirsch and a hint of vanilla. Strong flavot, powerful body, thick tannins, abundant, slightly woody and young. Rich and long finish.

LORENZO ACCOMASSO

Frazione Annunziata, 32
12064 La Morra (CN)
Tel. +39 0173 50843

YEAR OF FOUNDATION **1958**
NAME OF THE OWNER **Lorenzo Accomasso**

TOTAL BOTTLES PRODUCED 16,500
DIRECT SALES
VISITS TO THE WINERY - RESERVATION NEEDED
HECTARES OF VINEYARD 3

Elena and Lorenzo Accomasso are part of that authentic rural and artisanal culture that is slowly disappearing. Elio Altare, a very famous producer who is their neighbor, sees them as his true mentors. They are two old Langhe winemakers who make 'soulful wines' with ancient wisdom. Their two cru Rocche and Rocchette are extraordinary. The first has more body while the latter is more elegant. Then there are their Dolcetto and Barbera that are everyday wines that any wine-lover would like to have in their cellar. We have not given them a third star only because it would have embarrassed them.

93   Price C

Barolo Rocche Riserva 2008

100% Nebbiolo grapes. Matures 5 years in big barrels. Intense garnet red. Great farmer's wine, a little reduction notes in the beginning, then violets and licorice, dry flowers and light white truffle. Tannic flavor, tense, more agile compared to last vintage, savory, a little rough but absolutely attractive.

88   Price B

Barbera d'Alba Pochi Filagn 2010

100% Barbera grapes. Matures 2 years in big barrels. Intense ruby red. Less impact compared to 2009 version, due to a fresher vintage. Notes of cherry, violet and slight wet soil. Tense flavor, with an evident acidic component, a little rough and of discrete persistence.

★

GIULIO ACCORNERO & FIGLI

Via Ca' Cima, 1
15049 Vignale Monferrato (AL)
Tel. +39 0142 933317
info@accornerovini.it
www.accornerovini.it
 Azienda-Agricola-Accornero-Giulio-figli

YEAR OF FOUNDATION 1897
NAME OF THE OWNER Giulio Accornero
TOTAL BOTTLES PRODUCED 100,000
DIRECT SALES
VISITS TO THE WINERY - RESERVATION NEEDED

HECTARES OF VINEYARD 22
HOSPITALITY

We lost another piece of Italian winemaking history when Giulio Accornero, one of the noble stalwarts of Barbera and Grignolino, died at the start of 2015. His children are now carrying on a tradition that is over a century old and passed through five generations at the Cascina Ca' Cima estate in Vignale Monferrato. All we can do now is remember a great winemaker with his magnificent wines.

93   Price B

Grignolino del Monferrato Casalese Bricco del Bosco Vecchie Vigne 2011

100% Grignolino grapes. Matures 30 months in tonneau. Intense and lively garnet red. One of the best versions of the last years. Complex smoky and spicy notes, raspberries, pomegranate and rhubarb. Strong, tense, warm, enveloping flavor with tannic hints and extraordinary persistence.

90   Price B

Barbera del Monferrato Bricco Battista 2013

100% Barbera grapes. Matures 18 months in tonneau. Intense and lively ruby red. Violet, cardamom, currant and rhubarb in the nose, with a vanilla and smoky background. Strong flavor, evident acidic tension, some edges due to the youth and nice long and persistent finish.

★★

GIANFRANCO ALESSANDRIA

Località Manzoni, 13
12065 Monforte d'Alba (CN)
Tel. +39 0173 78576
azienda.alessandria@gmail.com
www.gianfrancoalessandria.com

YEAR OF FOUNDATION 1986
NAME OF THE OWNER Gianfranco Alessandria
TOTAL BOTTLES PRODUCED 45,000
DIRECT SALES
VISITS TO THE WINERY - RESERVATION NEEDED
HECTARES OF VINEYARD 7

From his seven hectares of vineyards, Gianfranco Alessandria produces some fantastic wines that can stand up to the more important and famous ones of the region. His Barolo has a modern and captivating style even in off years.

92   Price C
Barolo San Giovanni 2012

100% Nebbiolo grapes. Matures in tonneau. Lively garnet red. Intense warm notes of medical herbs, fresh as well, blond spices and ripe red plums. Intense taste, thick and progressive structure, crunchy tannins but with a very persistent and juicy finish.

87   Price B
Barolo 2012

100% Nebbiolo grapes. Matures in big barrels. Garnet ruby red. To be oxygenated slowly, then notes of herbs and warm flowers. Average structure with a young and slightly invading tannin that makes the drinkability less progressive than usual. Average persistent finish.

GIOVANNI ALMONDO

Via San Rocco, 26
12046 Montà (CN)
Tel. +39 0173 975256
almondo@giovannialmondo.com
www.giovannialmondo.com

YEAR OF FOUNDATION **1978**
NAME OF THE OWNER **Domenico Almondo**
TOTAL BOTTLES PRODUCED **80,000**
DIRECT SALES
VISITS TO THE WINERY - RESERVATION NEEDED
HECTARES OF VINEYARD **15**

Domenico Almondo, the son of Giovanni, is one of the lead players in the glorious revolution taking place in the Langhe and Roero that began at the beginning of the 1980s. It is a revolution that has seen winegrowers take back control of their grapes and produce their own wines without having to sell them to middle men and the big producers. This has allowed many wines to flourish including, in particular, Almondo's Arneis and Roero, which Giovanni is very happy to produce.

91   Price B
Roero Bric Valdiana 2013

100% Nebbiolo grapes. Matures in Slavonia barrique and big barrels. Bright bury red. Enveloping

notes of cherry and cloves. Austere in the mouth, elegant and pulpy, with delicate tannins and discrete tannins. Outstretched finish.

☐ **90**   👍 Price A
Roero Arneis Bricco delle Ciliegie 2015

100% Arneis grapes. Matures 80% in stainless steel and the rest in new barrique. Bright straw yellow. This is a myth single vineyard at 380 meters of altitude on sandy soil rich of limestone. Sumptuous notes of pepper and hawthorn for an elegant, pulpy mouth with a long and fruity finish.

ELIO ALTARE

Frazione Annunziata, 51
12064 La Morra (CN)
Tel. +39 0173 50835
elioaltare@elioaltare.com
www.elioaltare.com
Elio-Altare-La-Morra

YEAR OF FOUNDATION **1976**
NAME OF THE OWNER **Elio Altare**
TOTAL BOTTLES PRODUCED **60,000**
DIRECT SALES
VISITS TO THE WINERY - RESERVATION NEEDED
HECTARES OF VINEYARD **11**

Several years ago, Robert Parker Jr. proclaimed Elio Altare as one of the ten top winemakers of the year. He was surprised and a bit embarrassed by this recognition that seemed to have come out of nowhere. Being a reserved and somewhat philosophical winemaker, America was somewhere far away. He lives for his vineyards, in Annunziata near La Morra, which are in the heart of the area producing Barolo and his rhythm of life follows the seasons. This has allowed him to make extraordinary wines that break with a tradition that is sometimes too archaic. Time has proved him right and today everyone recognizes Elio as a true maestro.

96   Price D
Barolo Brunate 2011

100% Nebbiolo grapes. Matures 2 years in barrique. Intense ruby red with garnet hues. Whole and elegant aromatic profile. Notes of violets, currant, vanilla, mint and Kirsch. Near and tense flavor, very thin, savory, with light tannins and light but very long persistence.

93   Price D
Barolo Arborina 2012
100% Nebbiolo grapes. Matures 2 years in barrique. Intense ruby red with garnet hues. Notes of currant and raspberry then alfalfa, hints of vanilla and mint. Neat and elegant taste, warm, with some young tannic hint, savory and good persistence.

92   Price C
Langhe Larigi 2013
100% Barbera grapes. Matures 18 months in barrique. Vanilla, violet, black cherry and light notes of spices for an elegant and articulated aromatic profile. Full and agile taste, well tense by acidity, not a big body but really elegant.

90   Price B
Barbera d'Alba 2015
100% Barbera grapes. Stainless steel only. Lively and intense ruby red. Black cherrt, red berry, plum, then hints of violets. Fragrant and whole. Acidulous taste, savory, crunchy, delicious drinkability and good length in the finish.

GIACOMO ANSELMA

Piazza Maria Cappellano, 2
12050 Serralunga D'Alba (CN)
Tel. +39 0173 613170
Fax +39 0173 613114
🆂 *anselma.franco*
info@anselmagiacomo.it
www.anselmagiacomo.it
🄵 *anselmagiacomo.aziendaagricola*
🐦 *@AnselmaGiacomo*

YEAR OF FOUNDATION 1920
NAME OF THE OWNER Franco Anselma
TOTAL BOTTLES PRODUCED 15,000
DIRECT SALES
VISITS TO THE WINERY - RESERVATION NEEDED
HECTARES OF VINEYARD 3
HOSPITALITY
RESTAURANT

The true backbone of Langhe winemaking is made up of small winegrowers who used to sell their wines to industrial wineries and who have slowly begun to produce their own wines. The Ansemi family did this many decades ago and today they are a model of how a small vineyard, hard work and research to obtain quality without no shortcuts can produce a master-

piece in a bottle. Their estate is in Serralunga where their cru is Vigna Rionda. Today the Anselma family also has the Italia restaurant-hotel in Serralunga's central square.

93   Price C
Barolo Vignarionda Riserva 2010
100% Nebbiolo grapes. Matures 3 years in big barrels. Intense garnet ruby red. Notes of spices, wet soil, hints of licorice and tamarind. Strong flavor, austere tannins, still young in the mouth but promising, savory, warm and very long.

92   Price B
Barolo Collaretto 2012
100% Nebbiolo grapes. Matures 2 years in big barrels. Intense garnet ruby red. Notes of cassis, roses, spices, then currant and violets. Strong flavor, typical thick tannins of Barolo from Serralunga, good acidity, savory, warm and persistent.

ANTICHI VIGNETI DI CANTALUPO

Via M. Buonarroti, 5
28074 Ghemme (NO)
Tel. +39 0163 840041
info@cantalupo.net
www.cantalupo.net
🄵 *cantalupowines*
🐦 *@CantalupoWines*

YEAR OF FOUNDATION 1977
NAME OF THE OWNER Arlunno Family
TOTAL BOTTLES PRODUCED 200,000
DIRECT SALES
VISITS TO THE WINERY - RESERVATION NEEDED
HECTARES OF VINEYARD 35

Alberto Arlunno is one of the most cinvincing Ghemme producers who has explored all its potential and offers diverse versions of it. The most impressive is Collis Breclemae, which ages long, is incredible for richness of the structure, elegant tannins and long aromatic persistence.

90   Price B
Ghemme Collis Breclemae 2006
100% Nebbiolo grapes. Matures 24 months in big barrels. Iridescent ruby red. Notes of soil and silica,

graphite and smoky, initially austere and dry flowers and delicate spices. Vibrant in the mouth, lively tannins, very long.

ANTONIOLO

Corso Valsesia, 277
13045 Gattinara (VC)
Tel. +39 0163 833612
antoniolovini@bmm.it

YEAR OF FOUNDATION **1948**
NAME OF THE OWNER **Antoniolo Family**
TOTAL BOTTLES PRODUCED **55,000**
DIRECT SALES
VISITS TO THE WINERY - RESERVATION NEEDED
HECTARES OF VINEYARD **15**

Rosanna Antoniolo, with her children Lorella and Alberto, produce some of the best Gattinara that they have subdivided based on the estate cru, taking the old advice given to them by Luigi Veronelli. The result over the years have been such that this extraordinary winery easily sits among the elite in national winemaking.

■ **94**   Price C
Gattinara Osso san Grato 2012

100% Nebbiolo grapes. Matures 3 years in barrels. Bright garnet with orange hues. Intense floral notes, graphite, rhubarb, plums and licorice roots, cassis and a minty hint. Clear in the mouth with neat and elegant tannins, tension and good structure.

■ **93**   Price C
Gattinara San Francesco 2012

100% Nebbiolo grapes. Matures 3 years in different size barrels. Bright ruby red. Intense and austere notes of juniper and cassis, black olives and mint, flowery background of rhododendron and soil. Crunchy and full-bodied in the mouth, savory and notes of underbrush, rich and expressive tannins, pulpy and harmonic.

■ **92**   Price B
Gattinara Le Castelle 2012

100% Nebbiolo grapes. Vinified in barrique. Bright garnet red. Notes of lavender, cherry and macerated medlar, hints of sweet wood and resin, mirth and mint. Spicy and savory in the mouth, eucalyptus notes and fragrant, tasty tannin and long finish.

ODILIO ANTONIOTTI

Frazione Casa del Bosco
13868 Sostegno (BI)
Tel. +39 0163 860309
antoniottiodilio@libero.it
 AziendaAgricolaAntoniottiOdilio

YEAR OF FOUNDATION **1861**
NAME OF THE OWNER **Anoniotti Family**
TOTAL BOTTLES PRODUCED **12,000**
DIRECT SALES
VISITS TO THE WINERY - RESERVATION NEEDED
HECTARES OF VINEYARD **4.8**

Odilio Antoniotti and his young enologist son Mattia have a small farm in Upper Piedmont that has existed since 1861. Their wines have a strong and austere personality, are made in an absolutely traditional manner and have a remarkable stylistic correctness. Spontaneous fermentation takes place in concrete vats, maceration lasts over three weeks and the wine ages for more than three years in large wood barrels in order to produce wines that are frank and sincere with undeniable personality. The estate has 40 hectares of land, mostly chestnut and oak forests, with around five hectares of vineyards situated at an altitude of between 400 and 450m above sea level. The vineyards have a very acidic porphyry soil, good drainage and a southern exposure and benefit from constant breezes and while the soil is weak in organic materials it is rich in mineral salts.

■ **89**   Price B
Bramaterra 2012

Blend of 70% Nebbiolo, 20% Croatina, 7% Vespolina and 3% Uva Rara grapes. Matures in big barrels. Bright ruby red. Austere notes, almost severe of graphite and wet soil. Nervous on the palate, agile with almost aggressive tannins, but well integrated and with great energy in the finish.

■ **88**   Price A
Coste della Sesia Nebbiolo 2013

Blend of 90% Nebbiolo and 10% Croatina grapes. Matures in big barrels. Bright ruby red. Spicy and floral notes in the nose. Juicy, fresh and elegant in the mouth with thin tannins and a long and outstretched finish.

ASCHERI

Via Piumati, 23
12042 Bra (CN)
Tel. +39 0172 412394
ascheri@ascherivini.it
www.ascherivini.it

YEAR OF FOUNDATION 1880
NAME OF THE OWNER Ascheri Family
TOTAL BOTTLES PRODUCED 240,000
DIRECT SALES
VISITS TO THE WINERY - RESERVATION NEEDED
HECTARES OF VINEYARD 40
HOSPITALITY
RESTAURANT

The Ascheri family has been making excellent wine in Barolo for over a century and are also very famous for their hotel, next to the winery, and the truly excellent Osteria Murivecchi restaurant located on the estate, which is in Bra. Highly recommended.

 94   Price B

Barolo Sorano 2012

100% Nebbiolo grapes. Matures more than 2 years in big barrels. Intense garnet red. The quintessence of traditional Serralunga Barolo. Enveloping notes of licorice, hints of mint, then tamarind and violets. The taste is warm, with thick tannins, gritty, still young with great body, savory, rich. We expect a long and slow evolution in time.

AZELIA

Via Alba-Barolo, 143
12060 Castiglione Falletto (CN)
Tel. +39 0173 62859
Fax +39 0173 462070
l.scavino@azelia.it
www.azelia.it

YEAR OF FOUNDATION 1920
NAME OF THE OWNER Luigi Scavino
TOTAL BOTTLES PRODUCED 80,000
DIRECT SALES
VISITS TO THE WINERY - RESERVATION NEEDED
HECTARES OF VINEYARD 16

Castiglione Falletto is at the center of the area producing Barolo and the wines they make there magically blend the finesse of the best cru of La Morra with the great boldness and long life of those of Monforte and Serralunga. In other words, a bit Cannubi and a bit Bussia. And Barolo Bricco Fiasco, made in Castiglione, is exactly that.

 92   Price C

Barolo Bricco Fiasco 2012

100% Nebbiolo grapes. Matures more than 2 years in big barrels. Intense garnet red. Hints of wood, then carob, currant and licorice in the nose. Savory, progressive, agile, a little rough tannins for its great youth, warm and persistent finish.

 91   Price C

Barolo Margheria 2012

100% Nebbiolo grapes. Matures 28 months in big barrels. Clear garnet ruby. Intense notes of currant and vegetal hints. Simple and pleasant taste, some tannic roughness, a little peevish and young.

BARALE FRATELLI

Via Roma, 6
12060 Barolo (CN)
Tel. +39 0173 56127
Fax +39 0173 56350
info@baralefratelli.it
www.baralefratelli.it
 barale.fratelli

YEAR OF FOUNDATION 1870
NAME OF THE OWNER Sergio Barale
TOTAL BOTTLES PRODUCED 80,000
DIRECT SALES
VISITS TO THE WINERY - RESERVATION NEEDED
HECTARES OF VINEYARD 20

We first ran across the Barale wines with their vintages from the 1960s and remember with great nostalgia the 1961 and '64 vintages that were the greatest of that era. Today the winery is run by Sergio Barale, with the help of his daughters Eleonora and Gloria, and it remains a point of reference for all those who love Barolo in its most classic tradition.

 95   Price C

Barolo Bussia Riserva 2010

100% Nebbiolo grapes. Matures 3 years in durmast barrels. Intense garnet ruby. Varied notes of cur-

rant, then wild strawberry, hints of new wood. Savory taste, pleasant, solid tannins but not aggressive.

■ 94 — Price B
Barolo Cannubi 2012
100% Nebbiolo grapes. Matures 3 years in big barrels. Lively garnet ruby. Light wood, then spices, currant, tobacco and cherry. Strong taste, lively tannins, savory, still a little rough but very promising.

■ 91 — Price B
Barbaresco Serraboella 2013
100% Nebbiolo grapes. Matures 2 years in big barrels. Lively garnet ruby. Very clear notes of currant, pomegranate, then hints of wood. Savory taste, pleasant, neat tannins, not enormous body but agile and persistent.

★★
BATASIOLO

Frazione Annunziata, 87
12064 La Morra (CN)
Tel. +39 0173 50130
Fax +39 0173 509258
info@batasiolo.com
www.batasiolo.com
 Batasiolo
 @Batasiolo

YEAR OF FOUNDATION 1978
NAME OF THE OWNER Fratelli Dogliani
TOTAL BOTTLES PRODUCED 2,500,000
VISITS TO THE WINERY - RESERVATION NEEDED
HECTARES OF VINEYARD 108

This great winery is owned by the Dogliani family. Its vineyards are spread out in various towns in the Barolo district, in La Morra and Serralunga in particular which produce the cru Brunate and Corda della Briccolina. They also produce a series of other Piedmont wines that are all well-made and some have an excellent quality/price ratio.

■ 95 — Price C
Barolo Briccolina 2012
100% Nebbiolo grapes. Matures 2 years and more in big barrels. Garnet ruby. Notes of violets, cassis, roses, then spices and new wood. Modern style but

not excessive with very typical notes. Balanced taste, light tannins, good sustained acidity, young but elegant, very persistent.

■ 93 — Price C
Barolo Boscareto 2012
100% Nebbiolo grapes. Matures 2 years in big barrels. Garnet ruby. Floral, notes of violets and roses on top, then tar, Kirsch and currant. Strong taste, savory, slightly tannins, young.

■ 91 — 👍 Price A
Barbera d'Alba Sovrana 2013
100% Barbera grapes. Matures 1 year in barrique. Dark garnet ruby red. Violet and mint notes, then licorice and wildflowers in the nose. Tense acidity in the mouth, rich and solid, with a long finish.

■ 90 — 👍 Price A
Dolcetto d'Alba Bricco Vergne 2015
100% Dolcetto grapes. Stainless steel. Violet ruby red. Blueberry, cranberry, violet in the fragrant and immediate nose. Clear taste, savory, great acidity and very pleasant finish.

BEL SIT

Via Piani, 30
14054 Castagnole Lanze (AT)
Tel. +39 0141 875162
Fax +39 0141 875162
info@belsitvini.com
www.belsitvini.com

YEAR OF FOUNDATION 1860
NAME OF THE OWNER Ezio Rivella
TOTAL BOTTLES PRODUCED 50,000
DIRECT SALES
VISITS TO THE WINERY - RESERVATION NEEDED
HECTARES OF VINEYARD 7

Ezio Rivella is one of the 'founding fathers' of modern Italian wine. Born in 1934, for decades he was president of the enologists association first for Italy and then the world. He created Enoconsult, an international wine consulting firm, and directed the creation of Castello di Banfi in Montalcino where he served as CEO until a few years ago. But he also has a winery in his home town in Astigiano which may be small but it is all his. It is called Bel Sit and produces some excellent Barbera d'Asti.

90   Price A

Barbera d'Asti Superiore Sichivej 2013

100% Barbera grapes. Matures 1 year in tonneau. Intense ruby red. Typical and thin notes of black cherry, violet and slightly smoky notes. Tense and strong in the mouth, good acidic component, savory, good body, warm and persistent.

 85   Price A

Barbera d'Asti La Turna 2015

100% Barbera grapes. Stainlees steel. Intense violet ruby red. Fruity, fragrant, simple and whole, with fermentative notes then cherry and currant. Pleasantly savory taste, nice refreshing acidity, average consistence.

BERA

Località Castellero, 12 - Cascina Palazzo
12050 Neviglie (CN)
Tel. +39 0173 630194
Fax +39 0173 630956
info@bera.it
www.bera.it

YEAR OF FOUNDATION **1950**
NAME OF THE OWNER **Valter Bera**
TOTAL BOTTLES PRODUCED **130,000**
DIRECT SALES
VISITS TO THE WINERY - RESERVATION NEEDED
HECTARES OF VINEYARD **23**

An historic winery for Asti winegrowing and for Moscato grapes, which have been cultivated for centuries. Wine production, however, did not begin until the 1970s and was for the most versions of Asti and Moscato d'Asti, along with a few other wines. Bera's heart and 'mission' remains the aromatic fragrances and effervescence of a wine that is often undervalued yet has made the world envious of Piedmont.

 90   Price A

Asti Moscato Vittorio Bera 2015

100% Moscato Bianco di Canelli grapes. Sweet filtered. Light yellow. Fruity and aromatic, notes of sage, moscato grapes, pink and bergamot. Sweet taste, light, pleasant, elegant, delicious hint of carbonic that tenses the body and makes it easy to drink.

★★

NICOLA BERGAGLIO

Frazione Rovereto - Località Pedaggeri, 59
15066 Gavi (AL)
Tel. +39 0143 682195
nicolabergaglio@alice.it
 Nicola-Bergaglio

YEAR OF FOUNDATION **1946**
NAME OF THE OWNER **Gianluigi Bergaglio**
TOTAL BOTTLES PRODUCED **140,000**
DIRECT SALES
VISITS TO THE WINERY - RESERVATION NEEDED
HECTARES OF VINEYARD **17**

Gianluigi Bergaglio is one of the most classic interpreters of Gavi wines. In his vineyards he only cultivates Cortese grapes and this has been true even since the estate was founded by his father Nicola. His cru wine Minaia is perhaps the most representative and congruent in the district.

☐ 94   Price A

Gavi del Comune di Gavi Minaia 2015

100% Cortese grapes. Matures some months in stainless steel on the lees. Light yellow. Fruity and fragrant notes of cedar, lime, grapefruit and slightly smoky hints from the yeasts. Savory taste, nice body, slightly acidic, elegant and delicious drinkability. Adequate persistent finish.

☐ 91   Price A

Gavi del Comune di Gavi 2015

100% Cortese grapes. Stainless steel. Greenish straw yellow. Very fruity, notes of white peach, lime, cedar and alfalfa in the background. Discrete full taste, savory, fresh, pleasant and persistent.

★★★

BORGOGNO

Via Gioberti, 1
12060 Barolo (CN)
Tel. +39 0173 56108
info@borgogno.com
www.borgogno.com
 Borgogno

YEAR OF FOUNDATION **1761**
NAME OF THE OWNER **Farinetti Family**
TOTAL BOTTLES PRODUCED **110,000**

DIRECT SALES
VISITS TO THE WINERY - RESERVATION NEEDED
HECTARES OF VINEYARD 16

Today this historic and inescapable estate belongs to Oscar Farinetti, Mr. Eataly, and his family who, very intelligently, decided to change little or nothing of the traditional style of its wines. The Barolo are profoundly classic and can age for decades, only getting better with time. The estate's quest is to become an icon for the area and interpret Barolo in the most correct and traditional way possible.

96   Price C
Barolo Liste 2011

100% Nebbiolo grapes. Matures 3 years in big barrels. Bright and intense garnet red. Violets, cassis, licorice, mint and spicy hints and tamarind for the attractive aromatic profile, typical and complex. Elegant and tense taste, with some still evident tannic roughness, very promising even if the vintage was warm and with an enveloping and very long finish.

94   Price C
Barolo Riserva 2009

100% Nebbiolo grapes. Matures 5 years in big barrels. Garnet ruby red. Ethereal, intense, enveloping and complex notes, slightly spicy, with hints of cassis. Rich taste, progressive, warm, agile, juicy and very elegant. Incredibly long finish.

93   Price C
Barolo Cannubi 2011

100% Nebbiolo grapes, 3 years in big barrels. Bright and intense garnet red. Complex and varied notes of violets, pomegranate, current, hints of spices and Kirsch. Warm taste, with alcoholic warmth, savory, young tannins and very persistent finish.

91   Price B
Barbera d'Alba Superiore 2013

100% Barbera grapes. Matures 1 years in big barrels. Intense and bright ruby red. Enveloping notes of wildflowers, Kirsch and slightly spicy. The taste is very tense by the acidity, not without alcoholic warmth, savory and of good length.

88   Price A
Dolcetto d'Alba 2015

100% Dolcetto grapes. Stainless steel. Violet ruby red. Intense fruity notes, simple but fragrant, notes of currant, violet and plums. Savory taste, tense, good body, warm and persistent.

★
BOROLI

Frazione Como, 34
12051 Alba (CN)
Tel. +39 0173 365477
Fax +39 0173 35865
S *boroliachille*
info@boroli.it
www.boroli.it
f *boroli.boroli*
🐦 *@AchilleBoroli*

YEAR OF FOUNDATION 1997
NAME OF THE OWNER Boroli Family
TOTAL BOTTLES PRODUCED 200,000
DIRECT SALES
VISITS TO THE WINERY - RESERVATION NEEDED
HECTARES OF VINEYARD 32
HOSPITALITY
RESTAURANT

When, at the end of the 1990s, Silvano and Elena Boroli decided to do something new the choice almost naturally went in the direction of Langhe wines and soon it became a full-time job. Their Barolo cru are Villero in Castiglione Falletto, Bussia in Monforte and Cerequio in La Morra and one could not be more different than the other. The first two are full-bided and can age long, while the third is more delicate and elegant.

93   Price C
Barolo Villero 2012

100% Nebbiolo grapes. Matures 2 year in small barrels. Intense garnet red. Enveloping notes of tobacco, licorice, pomegranate and vanilla for an elegant and refined aromatic profile. Savory taste, elegant, with velvety and neat tannins, warm and with great persistent.

90   Price C
Barolo Cerequio 2012

100% Nebbiolo grapes. Matures 2 year in small barrels. Intense garnet red. More floral, with hints of carnation, pomegranate, mint, hints of tobacco and tamarind. Savory taste, warm, neat tannins and good length.

LUIGI BOVERI

Via XX Settembre, 6 - Frazione Montale Celli
15050 Costa Vescovato (AL)
Tel. +39 0131 838165
info@boveriluigi.com
www.boveriluigi.com
 Azienda-Agricola-Boveri-Luigi-Michele
 @LuigiBoveriVino

YEAR OF FOUNDATION **1992**
NAME OF THE OWNER **Luigi Boveri**
TOTAL BOTTLES PRODUCED **90,000**
DIRECT SALES
VISITS TO THE WINERY - RESERVATION NEEDED
HECTARES OF VINEYARD **16**

Among those in the 'Tortonesi Clan', Luigi Boveri is perhaps the less showy. He prefers to let his wines speak for him, especially Timorasso, and they are constantly improving. The estate is small and artisanal with red wine grapes growing in a clay soil and the Timorasso planted in a marl-chalk as it should be.

---

 90   Price B

Colli Tortonesi Filari di Timorasso 2013

100% Timorasso grapes. Stainless steel on the lees. Intense straw yellow. Very attractive notes of pineapple, grapefruit, cedar, and smoky hints of yeasts. Warm but savory taste, great body, savory and well sustained acidity. Warm and enveloping finish.

---

 88   Price B

Colli Tortonesi Barbera Vignalunga 2013

100% Barbera grapes. Matures 18 months in barrique. Intense and concentrated ruby red. Enveloping and alcoholic notes of Kirsch, black cherry, vanilla, cocoa and light leather. Powerful taste with and evident acidic component to sustain it, warm, rich, good persistence, maybe a little abundant.

★★

GIACOMO BOLOGNA BRAIDA

Via Roma, 94
14030 Rocchetta Tanaro (AT)
Tel. +39 0141 644113
Fax +39 0141 644584
welcome@braida.it
www.braida.it
 braidawines
 @braidawine

YEAR OF FOUNDATION **1961**
NAME OF THE OWNER **Raffaella and Giuseppe Bologna**
TOTAL BOTTLES PRODUCED **600,000**
DIRECT SALES
VISITS TO THE WINERY - RESERVATION NEEDED
HECTARES OF VINEYARD **60**

In the 1970s, the Bologna family set a new course in Asti winemaking transforming Barbera d'Asti, with the cru Bricco dell'Uccellone, into one of most prestigious wine of the region. The driving force behind this was Giacomo Bologna, a famous winemaker who died some time ago. He has the credit of discovering that Barbera could become, if made and aged with a modern approach, a great red wine. Bricco dell'Uccellone was followed by Bricco della Bigotta and Ai Suma ('we got it') which today are among the region's best wines.

---

 94   Price C

Barbera d'Asti Superiore Ai Suma 2013

100% Barbera grapes. Matures 18 months in barrique. Intense and lively ruby red. Great complexity in the nose, with notes of strawberry, currant, smoky hints, then spices, cocoa, wet soil and violets. Powerful taste, tense acidity, savory, full-bodied and agile, even elegant with outstretched tannins and great persistent, long finish.

---

 90   Price C

Barbera d'Asti Bricco dell'Uccellone 2014

100% Barbera grapes, 12 months in barrique. Bright garnet ruby red. Smoky notes with blood orange and pomegranate, with hints of tobacco in the background. Simpler and more immediate than in other version, great acidity, tense body and savory, good persistence.

---

 85   👍 Price A

Barbera del Monferrato La Monella 2015

100% Barbera grapes. Charmat method for 4 months. Bright ruby, evanescent violet perlage. Delicious. Fragrant, simple, very fruity, notes of strawberry and cherry. Lively taste, acidulous, good body and incredibly easy to drink.

BREMA

Via Pozzomagna, 9
14045 Incisa Scapaccino (AT)
Tel. +39 0141 791982

261

Fax +39 0141 747652
info@vinibrema.com
www.vinibrema.com
🐦 *@vinibrema*

YEAR OF FOUNDATION **1887**
NAME OF THE OWNER **Ermanno Brema**
TOTAL BOTTLES PRODUCED **150,000**
DIRECT SALES
VISITS TO THE WINERY - RESERVATION NEEDED
HECTARES OF VINEYARD **25**

Brema is one of the few estates that can boast an over 100-year history. It is in the area of Nizza and has around 25 hectares of vineyards in the more important towns. The estate's style is decidedly classic and is perpetuated by Umberto who pays keen attention to his vineyards. In the winery they mostly use Slavonian oak barrels but for their showcase wine, Barbera d'Asti Superiore Nizza, they use barrique. The wine is dedicated to Luigi Veronelli who had the intuition to recognize the potential of this grape aging in small barrels.

■ 93   Price B
Barbera d'Asti Superiore Nizza Dedicata a Luigi Veronelli 2013

100% Barbera grapes. Matures in barrique. Intense and dark ruby red. Intense notes of maple and Kirsch with classic hints of wet underbrush and very dark violet. Austere in the mouth with great personality and class, thick structure, high acidity and compelling progression. Very tasty finish.

■ 89   👍 Price A
Barbera d'Asti Ai Cruss 2014

100% Barbera grapes. Matures in barrique. Intense and bright ruby red. Classic notes of red frutis, black cherry, dark flowers hints of violets. Fragrant acidity in the mouth, polite tannins, pleasant and very classy drinkability.

★★
BREZZA

Via Lomondo, 4
12060 Barolo (CN)
Tel. +39 0173 560921
Fax +39 0173 560026
brezza@brezza.it
www.brezza.it

YEAR OF FOUNDATION **1885**
NAME OF THE OWNER **Brezza Family**
TOTAL BOTTLES PRODUCED **80,000**
DIRECT SALES
VISITS TO THE WINERY - RESERVATION NEEDED
HECTARES OF VINEYARD **16**
HOSPITALITY
RESTAURANT

The Brezza family are hoteliers and restaurateurs in Barolo but have also been magnificent wine producers since 1885. They own some of the Barolo vineyards of Sarmassa, Cannubi and Castellero. All their wines are very classic and decidedly traditional to the extent that they exalt the most authentic territorial characteristics of the various cru.

■ 92   Price B
Barolo Cannubi 2012

100% Nebbiolo grapes. Matures 2 years in big barrels. Lively garnet ruby red. Wet soil, light tobacco, currant and pomegranate notes. Enormous in the taste but balanced and neat, with smooth tannins and great persistent.

■ 91   Price B
Barolo Sarmassa 2012

100% Nebbiolo grapes.Matures 2 years in big barrels. Clear garnet ruby red. Wet soil, hints of wood, then violet and pomegranate. Warm, enveloping, slightly evolved, well integrated tannins and good length.

BRIC CENCIURIO

Via Roma, 24
12060 Barolo (CN)
Tel. +39 0173 56317
bric_cenciurio@libero.it
www.briccenciurio.com

YEAR OF FOUNDATION **1996**
NAME OF THE OWNER **Fiorella Sacchetto**
TOTAL BOTTLES PRODUCED **45,000**
DIRECT SALES
VISITS TO THE WINERY - RESERVATION NEEDED
HECTARES OF VINEYARD **15.5**

This estate is just 20 years old but has already made a name for itself in Roero but above all in Barolo, where it uses the grapes from the cru Bricco di Rose, one of the best in the area.

91 — Price B
Barolo Costa di Rose 2012

100% Nebbiolo grapes. Matures in tonneau. Intense smoky notes on a fruity background of red and yellow plums and the dark flowery note of violets. Average structure with classy tannins and good progression. Elegant, savory and persistent finish.

91 — Price C
Barolo Costa di Rose Riserva 2010

100% Nebbiolo grapes.Matures in different size barrels. Garnet ruby red. Classic notes of dark flowers and medical herbs with a touch of wild strawberries. Great elegance in the mouth, outstretched and polite tannins andbalanced and attractive structure. A whispered, very persistent wine.

BRICCO DEI GUAZZI

Via Vittorio Veneto, 23
15030 Olivola (AL)
Tel. +39 0422 864511
Fax +39 0422 864131
info@briccodeiguazzi.it
www.briccodeiguazzi.it

YEAR OF FOUNDATION 1978
NAME OF THE OWNER Genagricola
TOTAL BOTTLES PRODUCED 45,000
DIRECT SALES
VISITS TO THE WINERY - RESERVATION NEEDED
HECTARES OF VINEYARD 40
HOSPITALITY
RESTAURANT

This splendid estate in the heart of Monferrato Casalese is owned by Genagricola and has its headquarters in the wonderful Villa Candiani Guazzo that also hosts the beautiful La Presidenta resort and the Ai Cedri restaurant. While they produce a vast range of wines, their specialty is Albarosa, made from the grape of the same name that is a cross between Nebbiolo and Barbera.

90 — Price A
Piemonte Albarossa 2014

100% Albarossa grapes. Matures 6 months in barrique and 1 year in big barrels. Violet ruby red. Intensely fruity in the nose, plums, pomegranate, blood orange. Rich flavor, smooth, warm, balanced and great persistence.

87 — Price A
Barbera d'Asti 2013

100% Barbera grapes. Matures 1 year in barrique. Intense garnet red. Fruity and smoky in the nose, notes of black cherry and vanilla. Savory taste, full and rich, good length.

FILIPPO BROCCARDO E FRATELLI

Borgata Manzoni, 12
12065 Monforte d'Alba (CN)
Tel. +39 0173 78180
Fax +39 0173 1911005
broccardowines@broccardo.it
www.broccardo.it
 Azienda-Agricola-Filippo-Broccardo-e-Flli
 @AzAgrBroccardo

YEAR OF FOUNDATION 1970
NAME OF THE OWNER Broccardo Family
TOTAL BOTTLES PRODUCED 25,000
DIRECT SALES
VISITS TO THE WINERY - RESERVATION NEEDED
HECTARES OF VINEYARD 7

A surprising, small and fantastic Monforte winery that received high marks from Jancis Robinson and at the Decanter World Awards and that we were able discover during the Nebbiolo Prima event. They make other wines but the two Barolo we reviewed here were truly interesting.

94 — Price C
Barolo I Tre Pais 2012

100% Nebbiolo grapes. Matures 2 years in big barrels. Clear garnet red. Very typical notes of hay, light cassis, dry flowers, hints of licorice. Thin and elegant taste, agile, nice acidity, good body, very persistent.

92 — Price C
Barolo Bricco San Pietro 2012

100% Nebbiolo grapes. More than 2 years in big barrels. Clear garnet red. Enveloping notes of Kirsh, with some rustic alcohol hint. Sumptuous in the mouth, tense, gritty tannins, great acidity, some edges due to the youth but a lot of personality as well, tense body, rich and warm.

★★
BROGLIA

Località Lomellina, 22
15066 Gavi (AL)
Tel. +39 0143 642998
Fax +39 0143 645102
broglia.azienda@tin.it
www.broglia.it
 Broglia-Tenuta-La-Meirana
 @LaMeirana

YEAR OF FOUNDATION 1972
NAME OF THE OWNER Broglia Family
TOTAL BOTTLES PRODUCED 400,000
DIRECT SALES
VISITS TO THE WINERY - RESERVATION NEEDED
HECTARES OF VINEYARD 64
HOSPITALITY

The wonderful estate of Gian Piero Broglia, with its villa that sits above the vineyards, dominates the whole district of Gavi. Thus it is logical for it to produce some of the best whites, from Cortese grapes, that are very appreciated abroad, especially in Britain. However, the wines have almost been forgotten in Italy despite having everything needed to be loved: elegance, delicacy and freshness. The wines definitely deserve to be rediscovered.

☐ 91   Price B
Gavi del Comune di Gavi Bruno Broglia 2014

100% Cortese grapes. Stainless steel on the yeasts for 1 year. Light yellow. More citrusy than in other versions, notes of cedar, lime and Amlfi lemon, notes of yeasts and hawthorn. Acidulous taste, a little sharp, young, very tense, discrete body and of good persistence.

☐ 89   👍 Price A
Gavi del Comune di Gavi La Meirana 2015

100% Cortese grapes. Stainless steel only. Light yellow. Fragrant and very fruity notes of cedar, green plum, pineapple and flowery hints in the background. Tense and savory, agile, fresh and savory. Great length.

★★★
BROVIA

Via Alba-Barolo, 54
12060 Castiglione Falletto (CN)
Tel. +39 0173 62852
gibrovia@tin.it
www.brovia.net
 Brovia

YEAR OF FOUNDATION 1863
NAME OF THE OWNER Elena and Cristina Brovia
TOTAL BOTTLES PRODUCED 60,000
DIRECT SALES
VISITS TO THE WINERY - RESERVATION NEEDED
HECTARES OF VINEYARD 17

An inescapable point of reference for anyone who loves Barolo. The state has existed for 150 years and is currently run by Elena and Cristina Brovia who carry on with great consistency the work of their predecessors. The vineyards are between Castiglione Falletto and Serralunga d'Alba, home to the boldest and long-living Barolo.

■ 92   Price C
Barolo Brea Vigna Ca' Mia 2012

100% Nebbiolo grapes. Matures 2 year in big barrels. Intense garnet red. Very classic and traditional notes of violet, pomegranate and currant, hints of licorice in the background. Thick tannins, of young roughness, warm, savory, very persistent.

■ 91   Price C
Barolo Rocche di Castiglione 2012

100% Nebbiolo grapes. Matures 2 year in big barrels. Intense garnet red. Very complete in the nose and slightly more vanilla hints, notes of currant, raspberry and spices. Savory, young, with some tannic roughness but substantially neat and ready. Enveloping and warm finish.

★
COMM. G.B. BURLOTTO

Via Vittorio Emanuele, 28
12060 Verduno (CN)
Tel. +39 0172 470122
burlotto@burlotto.com
www.burlotto.com
 Burlotto

YEAR OF FOUNDATION 1850
NAME OF THE OWNER Marina Burlotto
TOTAL BOTTLES PRODUCED 90,000
DIRECT SALES
VISITS TO THE WINERY - RESERVATION NEEDED
HECTARES OF VINEYARD 15
HOSPITALITY

There is an air of ancient tradition in the historic winery run today by Fabio Alessandria and it is as if time has stood style. Not due to any refusal of technology nor desire to evolve but for the respect of rites and habits that have given this winery its reputation for quality. Today its wines are a splendid expression of the territory, thanks to the great temperature variations that have created unique microclimates. The consistency in quality, through the various vintages, is surprising.

___

94   Price C
Barolo Monvigliero 2012

100% Nebbiolo grapes. Matures 36 months in big barrels after 60 months of maceration. Intense and lively red. Deep notes of flowers and fruits. Very typical macerated roses, one of the most recognizable Barolo's, notes of cinchona, rhubarb and eucalyptus. Wide and refined in the mouth with very long persistence.

___

93   Price B
Barolo Acclivi 2012

100% Nebbiolo grapes from the areas of Monvigliero North, Rocche Olmo, Neirane and Verdino. Matures 36 months in big barrels. Lively ruby red. Notes of red fruits and macerated violet, hints of cinnamon and licorice in the background. Agile and pleasant in the mouth, difficult to find another Barolo so easy to drink. Very elegant tannins and exemplar freshness.

___

93   Price C
Barolo Cannubi 2012

100% Nebbiolo grapes. Matures 36 months in big barrels. Intense and bright red. Very spicy notes, eucalyptus, bark and cut flowers. Severe mouth but not heavy, austere, evident but balanced tannins. You should wait some years for the perfect balance.

___

90   Price A
Verduno Pelaverga 2015

100% Pelaverga grapes. Light and very bright red. Fragrant fresh fruit, mith on top. Very easy to drink, elegant, fresh and outstretched.

★

PIERO BUSSO

Via Albesani, 8
12052 Neive (CN)
Tel. +39 0173 67156
bussopiero@bussopiero.com
www.bussopiero.com
 Piero-Busso-Wines
 @PierBusso

YEAR OF FOUNDATION 1953
NAME OF THE OWNER Piero Busso
TOTAL BOTTLES PRODUCED 45,000
DIRECT SALES
VISITS TO THE WINERY - RESERVATION NEEDED
HECTARES OF VINEYARD 10

The winery Piero Busso runs together with his wife Lucia and their children Emanuela and Pierguido is a rare example of great artisanal winemaking with a pinch of modernity, above all in regard to promotion. The estate's philosophy is for each vineyard to have a single grape variety and for each wine to be made from a single vineyard. Thus production is subdivided into a series of cru of Barbaresco and Barbera d'Alba, all which represent a specific terroir through the wine they produce. Their is an avant-garde approach and style.

___

92   Price C
Barbaresco Gallina 2012

100% Nebbiolo grapes. Matures 18 months in barrique. Intense garnet ruby red. Enveloping and spicy notes with hints of vanilla, violet and currant. Warm taste, savory, young tannic roughness, very promising and long finish.

___

89   Price B
Barbera d'Alba San Stefanetto 2013

100% Barbera grapes, 14 months in barrique. Intense and lively ruby red. A modern, well-made Barbera with notes of spices, cassis and smoky hints. Tense, acidulous flavor, great body, warm and enveloping.

CA' BIANCA

Località Regione Spagna, 58
15010 Alice Bel Colle (AL)
Tel. +39 0144 745420

Fax +39 0144 745419
cabianca@giv.it
www.gruppoitalianovini.com
f cabianca.aziendavitivinicola

YEAR OF FOUNDATION **1954**
NAME OF THE OWNER **Gruppo Italiano Vini**
TOTAL BOTTLES PRODUCED **650,000**
DIRECT SALES
VISITS TO THE WINERY - RESERVATION NEEDED
HECTARES OF VINEYARD **39**

Ca' Bianca is located near Alessandria and is one of the most important estates of the area. It belongs to Gruppo Italiano Vini and offers wines from Asti, Acqui, along with some Barolo and Gavi. Production is mostly based on two grape varieties, Barbera and Dolcetto, which are the those typical of the two areas they come from.

■ 88   Price B
Barbera d'Asti Superiore Chersì 2013

100% Barbera grapes. Matures 12 months in barrique. Intense ruby red. Ripe red fruits and spices dominate the aromatic bouquet, then Kirsch and vanilla. Powerful taste, alcoholic, light tannins, warm and enveloping in the mouth.

CA' D' GAL

Strada Vecchia di Valdivilla, 1
12058 Santo Stefano Belbo (CN)
Tel. +39 0141 847103
Fax +39 0141 855970
info@cadgal.it
www.cadgal.it
f *Ca-d-Gal*

YEAR OF FOUNDATION **1990**
NAME OF THE OWNER **Alessandro Boido**
TOTAL BOTTLES PRODUCED **60,000**
DIRECT SALES
VISITS TO THE WINERY - RESERVATION NEEDED
HECTARES OF VINEYARD **8**
HOSPITALITY
RESTAURANT

This estate has been producing the best Moscato d'Asti for over 150 years. We feel we can say this because the winery, owned by Alessandro Boido, is not always appreciated for what it is. Here the 'simple' Moscato d'Asti is a very

great wine, Italian to the bone, which can age as long as a great red. The vineyards are in Santo Stefano Belbo, in the area that UNESCO has declared a World Heritage Site.

▫ 93   Price B
Moscato d'Asti Vigna Vecchia 2013

100% Moscato Bianco di Canelli grapes. Sweet filtered. Golden yellow. Explosive aromatic notes of bergamot, candied cedar, tangerine, sage, orange flowers and mango. Lively flavor, sweet, well sustained by acidity, light, easy and involving drinkability. A real champion of its category.

▫ 88   Price A
Moscato d'Asti Lumine 2014

100% Moscato Bianco di Canelli grapes. Sweet filtered. Light yellow. Fragrant aromas of sage, exotic fruit and cedar. Sweet flavor, lively, great and refreshing acidity. Adequate persistent finish.

CA' DEL BAIO

Via Via Ferrere, 33
12050 Treiso (CN)
Tel. +39 0173 638219
cadelbaio@cadelbaio.com
www.cadelbaio.com
f *cadelbaio*

YEAR OF FOUNDATION **1891**
NAME OF THE OWNER **Giulio Grasso**
TOTAL BOTTLES PRODUCED **120,000**
DIRECT SALES
VISITS TO THE WINERY - RESERVATION NEEDED
HECTARES OF VINEYARD **25**

Giulio Grasso, owner of this splendid Treiso estate, in one of the most emblematic areas of Barbaresco, is blissfully surrounded by women. Aside from his wife Luciana, in fact, he works with his three daughters: Paolo, Valentina and Federica. The wines are territorial and the style is for the most part traditional. In one word: excellent.

■ 🍇 96   Price C
Barbaresco Asili Riserva 2011

100% Nebbiolo grapes. Matures 3 years and a half in tonneau. Very intense garnet ruby. Youthful aromatic profile, very promising, initial smoky hints, then currant, spices, tobacco, pomegranate and hints of violets. Strong flavor, still a little tannic, very tense, compact body, rich and a very persistent finish.

 94 **Price B**

Barbaresco Marcarini 2013

100% Nebbiolo grapes. Matures 2 years in big barrels. Bright garnet ruby. Black cherry and currant in the nose, then violets, for an aromatic profile of great integrity and elegance. Thick tannins, youthful, briny notes, agile body, elegant and of great length.

☐ **93** 👍 **Price A**

Langhe Riesling 2014

100% Riesling Renano grapes. Stainless steel on the lees for 1 year. Greenish yellow. Notes of grapefruit, the yeasts and carbonic. Savory, fresh, agile, elegant, very typical, easy to drink and thin persistence.

 92 **Price B**

Barbaresco Asili 2013

100% Nebbiolo grapes. Matures 30 months in different size barrels. Lively garnet ruby. Licorice, mint, smoky hints, violet are the aromatic notes. Tense, youthful in the palate, with some tannic roughness and good length.

★

CA' VIOLA

Borgata San Luigi, 11
12063 Dogliani (CN)
Tel. +39 0173 742535
Fax +39 0173 720921
info@caviola.com
www.caviola.com
 CaViola

YEAR OF FOUNDATION **1991**
NAME OF THE OWNER **Giuseppe Caviola**
TOTAL BOTTLES PRODUCED **60,000**
DIRECT SALES
VISITS TO THE WINERY - RESERVATION NEEDED
HECTARES OF VINEYARD **10**

Enologist Beppe Viola is one of the most famous names in the Piedmont winemaking scene. He started off working in a lab analyzing wines and then become the wine consultant for many estate in the region. Today he has his own

estate and makes his own wines. His Barbera d'Alba Bric du Luvis a small masterpiece.

 90 **Price B**

Barbera d'Alba Bric du Luv 2014

100% Barbera grapes. Matures 18 months in barrique and tonneau. Intense ruby red. Notes of violets and black cherry, fragrant and simpler and more immediate than in other versions. Agile taste, tense by acidity, not enormous body, warm, pleasant.

CANTINA DEL PINO

Strada Ovello, 31
12050 Barbaresco (CN)
Tel. +39 0173 635147
Renato@cantinadelpino.com
www.cantinadelpino.com

YEAR OF FOUNDATION **1997**
NAME OF THE OWNER **Renato Vacca**
TOTAL BOTTLES PRODUCED **35,000**
HECTARES OF VINEYARD **7**

In less than 20 years, Renato Vacca has succeeded in making his wines known and appreciated. Their style is in part traditional, with long maceration, and in part modern, with careful use of small barrels. This means that his Barbaresco wines need time to better express themselves.

▇ **92** **Price C**

Barbaresco Ovello Riserva 2011

100% Nebbiolo grapes. Matures over 2 years in barrique and big barrels. Intense garnet ruby. Modern aromatic profile, very complete and thin. Notes of tobacco, vanilla, spices and hints of currant. Very youthful in the mouth, savory, essential tannins, some woody but very promising, elegant body, thin but long finish.

★

CAPPELLANO

Via Alba, 13
12050 Serralunga D'Alba (CN)
Tel. +39 0173 613103
info@cappellano1870.it
www.cappellano1870.it
 augusto.cappellano

YEAR OF FOUNDATION **1870**
NAME OF THE OWNER **Augusto Cappellano**
TOTAL BOTTLES PRODUCED **20,000**
DIRECT SALES
VISITS TO THE WINERY - RESERVATION NEEDED
HECTARES OF VINEYARD **5**

This is one of the historic estates in the Langhe and Serralunga that has been operating since the second half of the 19th century. Augusto Cappellano, son of the legendary Teobaldo, must carry the weight of a great tradition but does so with confidence and conviction. You can say anything you want about his Barolo except that they are commonplace or made to please. They are, above all, precise expressions of the Vigna Gabutto which is one of the souls of Serralunga.

■ 92   Price C
Barolo Franco 2011

100% Nebbiolo grapes. Matures in big barrels. Bright ruby red. Austere notes of cinchona and graphite. Full structure, balanced with powerful tannins but well extracted.

■ 88   Price B
Piè Rupestris 2011

100% Nebbiolo grapes. Matures in big barrels. Bright ruby red. Mineral notes with some alcohol hints. Nervous in the mouth, strong and slightly dusty tannins.

CASCINA AMALIA

Località Sant'Anna, 85
12065 Monforte d'Alba (CN)
Tel. +39 0173 789013
info@cascinaamalia.it
www.cascinaamalia.com
 Amalia-Cascina-in-Langa-Monforte-dAlba

YEAR OF FOUNDATION **2003**
NAME OF THE OWNER **Paolo Boffa**
TOTAL BOTTLES PRODUCED **60,000**
DIRECT SALES
VISITS TO THE WINERY - RESERVATION NEEDED
HECTARES OF VINEYARD **8**
HOSPITALITY
RESTAURANT

The estate came into being in 2003 after the Boffa family – mother, father and son Paolo, ac-

quired an old farmhouse built in the early 20th century in the hills of Monforte d'Alba. Soon after they built a winery to produce the typical wines of the area but they also made is hospitable and embellished it with works of art. From their original three hectares of vineyards, planted with Dolcetto and Barbera, in a matter of a few years they bought others to bring the total to eight hectares. Today the produce a full line of wines from Nebbiolo, Dolcetto and Barbera grapes as well as a rare white Rossese.

■ 92   Price B
Barolo Le Coste di Monforte 2012

100% Nebbiolo grapes. Matures in tonneau. Intense and slightly garnet ruby red. Intense and rich notes of fresh dark flowers, yellow and violet plums and Mediterranean spices. Rich in the mouth with thick structure and polite tannins. Good progression and juicy and enveloping finish.

■ 88   Price B
Barolo 2012

100% Nebbiolo grapes. Matures in barrels. Garnet ruby. Slightly evolved notes of flowers even dried, medical herbs and hints of tobacco. Slightly aggressive tannins with a wide structure that makes the finish a little elusive even if the substance is good. Nice persistence.

■ 88   🖒 Price A
Dolcetto d'Alba Sant'Anna 2015

100% Dolcetto grapes. Stainless steel only. Lively violet red. Wide notes of red roses, cyclamen and hints of ripe fruits, plums and blueberries as well. Intense in the mouth, savory, smooth and dry, sustained by tannins and freshness. Pleasant, persistent, very convincing.

CASCINA BRUNI

Località Bruni, 6
12050 Serralunga D'Alba (CN)
Tel. +39 0173 613 208
bruni@cascinabruni.it
www.cascinabruni.it
 cascinabruni
 @CascinaBruni897

YEAR OF FOUNDATION **1897**
NAME OF THE OWNER **Cristiano Maria Veglio di Castelletto**
TOTAL BOTTLES PRODUCED **70,000**

DIRECT SALES
VISITS TO THE WINERY - RESERVATION NEEDED
HECTARES OF VINEYARD 12

This Serralunga winery, that dates its origins in the end of the 19th century, was one of the surprises of this year's tastings. Today at its sixth generation with the two brothers Cristiano and Fulvio Veglio di Castelletto, both oenologyst, still helped by their father Giuseppe. The wines are well-made and territorial and several absolutely valid.

 91 Price D
Barolo Batistot Riserva 2009

100% Nebbiolo grapes. Matures 6 years in chestnut big barrels. Garnet ruby. Extremely traditional, enveloping notes of Kirsch, tamarind, hints of white truffle. Rich and full-bodied, warm, with tannins still youthful, savory. Extremely long finish.

90 Price C
Barolo Marialunga 2012

100% Nebbiolo grapes. Matures 3 years in big barrels. Garnet ruby. Spices, tamarind, plums, dry flowers and licorice in the nose for a traditional and varied aromatic profile. Smooth and enveloping taste, thick and neat tannins, warm and very persistent.

88 Price B
Barbera d'Alba Superiore Otin Matè 2012

100% Barbera grapes. Matures 1 year in barrique and 18 months contrete. Intense garnet ruby red. Enveloping notes of vanilla and Kirsch. Rich, full-bodied, tense and great acidity, rich and persistent.

CASCINA CA' ROSSA

Località Cascina Ca' Rossa
12043 Canale (CN)
Tel. +39 0173 98348
Fax +39 0173 968922
angelo.ferrio@gmail.com
www.cascinacarossa.com
 cascina.carossa

YEAR OF FOUNDATION 1995
NAME OF THE OWNER Angelo Ferrio

TOTAL BOTTLES PRODUCED 80,000
DIRECT SALES
VISITS TO THE WINERY - RESERVATION NEEDED
HECTARES OF VINEYARD 13
CERTIFIED ORGANIC VITICULTURE

The straightforward and incredible nice nature of Angelo Ferrio at risks overshadowing his great expertise as a winemaker also due to his great modesty. The wines of Cascina Ca' Rossa are some of the best of the Roero appellation in all their typical expressions, from Arneis to Barbera to Roero. They have a traditional style and an as natural approach has possible, which has allowed them to be certified organic.

 95 Price B
Roero Mompissano Riserva 2013

100% Nebbiolo grapes. Matures in barrels. Great version, maybe the best ever of this Roero Riserva of the likable Angelo Ferrio. Bright ruby red. It has clear notes of cinchona, graphite and spices. Powerful in the mouth, complex, great freshness and elegant tannins. An excellent Roero.

☐ **85** Price A
Roero Arneis Merica 2015

100% Arneis. Stainless steel. Bright straw yellow. Clear notes of white peach and hawthorn. Coherent in the mouth, full and pleasantly juicy.

★
CASCINA CHICCO

Via Valentino, 14
12043 Canale (CN)
Tel. +39 0173 979411
Fax +39 0173 979411
cascinachicco@cascinachicco.com
www.cascinachicco.com
 cascinachicco
 cascinachicco

YEAR OF FOUNDATION 1950
NAME OF THE OWNER Marco ed Enrico Faccenda
TOTAL BOTTLES PRODUCED 300,000
DIRECT SALES
VISITS TO THE WINERY - RESERVATION NEEDED
HECTARES OF VINEYARD 40

Marco and Enrico Faccenda are specialists in making Roero and Barbera d'Alba and sometimes they tried make a traditional method sparkling wine with Nebbiolo. Then in 2007 they embarked on a Barolo adventure and acquired five hectares in the cru Caastelletto sulla Ginestra and the results are something else.

---

92   Price B

Roero Valmaggiore Riserva 2013

100% Nebbiolo grapes. Matures in new and used barrique. Bright ruby red. Enveloping notes of spices, tobacco and cinchona. Juicy on the palate, elegant tannins. Long and refreshing finish.

---

90   Price B

Barolo Ginastra Riserva 2009

100% Nebbiolo grapes. Matures 40 months in barrique. Light ruby red. Intense notes of flowers, spices and tobacco. Pulpy in the mouth, powerful and with a complex finish with hints of eucalyptus.

---

88   Price A

Roero Montespinato 2014

100% Nebbiolo grapes. Matures in different size barrels. Light red color. Notes of flowers and eucalyptus. Thin and elegant mouth-feel with ripe tannins and nice structure. Average length in the finish.

---

86   Price A

Barbera d'Alba Bric Loira 2014

100% Barbera grapes. Matures in barrique. Bright ruby red. Notes of flowers and fruits. Fresh, smooth in the mouth with a tobacco and cinchona finish.

CASCINA DELLE ROSE

Strada Rio Sordo, 58
12050 Barbaresco (CN)
Tel. +39 0173 630322
cascinadellerose@cascinadellerose.it
www.cascinadellerose.it
Cascina-delle-Rose-Barbaresco

YEAR OF FOUNDATION **1974**
NAME OF THE OWNER **Giovanna Rizzolo and Italo Sobrino**
TOTAL BOTTLES PRODUCED **20,000**
DIRECT SALES
VISITS TO THE WINERY - RESERVATION NEEDED
HECTARES OF VINEYARD **3.6**
HOSPITALITY

Giovanna Rizzolo and Italo Sobrino are producers of rare skill and courtesy. Their wines reflect their sober and discreet style to which they add pleasing sensations and territorial expression. Their two Barbaresco, in particular, from important cru in the appellation, Rio Sardo and Tre Stelle, are ideal for those seeking elegant and communicative Nebbiolo wine. Added to all this they have a very correct pricing policy and a lovely holiday farm.

---

92   Price B

Barbaresco Rio Sordo 2013

100% Nebbiolo grapes. Matures in big barrels. Bright ruby red. The clayish soils of this vineyard give enveloping notes of licorice and violets. Pulpy, austere with smooth and juicy tannins and a long, outstretched finish.

---

89   Price B

Barbaresco Tre Stelle 2013

100% Nebbiolo grapes. Matures in big barrels. Light ruby red. The soil of this vineyard is white and the wine results more austere in the aromas of violets and licorice, but it has the same elegant and deep style as the preview.

CASCINA LA BARBATELLA

Strada Annunziata, 55
14049 Nizza Monferrato (AT)
Tel. +39 0141 701434
Fax +39 0141 721550
cascina@labarbatella.com
www.labarbatella.com
cascina.labarbatella

YEAR OF FOUNDATION **1983**
NAME OF THE OWNER **Lorenzo Perego**
TOTAL BOTTLES PRODUCED **22,000**
DIRECT SALES
VISITS TO THE WINERY - RESERVATION NEEDED
HECTARES OF VINEYARD **4**

Four years ago, Angelo Sonvico sold his estate to Lorenzo Perego who has continued with passion and congruency to produce its wines, improving its productive structure and even the quality of the wines. It is located in Nizza Monferrato, in the heart of the best area for Barbera, and this is evident above all in the two cru selections a Vigna dell'Angelo and Sonvico. These are two incredibly complex wines and are among the best in the region.

94 — Price B
Barbera d'Asti Superiore Nizza La Vigna dell'Angelo 2013

100% Barbera grapes. Matures in barrique and tonneau. Intense and dark ruby red. Clear, austere and intense notes of red fruits with black cherry, a smoky hint, dark spices, Kirsch and maple juice. Rich in the mouth, thick structure and marvelous progression. Juicy and pleasing finish.

91 — Price B
Monferrato Rosso Sonvico 2011

Blend of Barbera and Cabernet Sauvignon grapes. Matures in barrique. Dark red with ruby hues. Notes of dark fruits, blueberry, blackberry, wild cherry, a touch of candied orange and smoky hints. Rich in the mouth with attractive tannins and great drinkability and elegance.

88 — 👍 Price A
Barbera d'Asti 2014

100% Barbera grapes. Stainless steel for long on the yeasts. Slightly garnet ruby red. Notes of maple and fresh hints of eucalyptus and blackberries. Nice agility in the mouth and good progression with a very attractive drinkability.

CASCINA LA GHERSA

Regione Chiarina, 2
14050 Moasca (AT)
Tel. +39 0141 856 012
Fax +39 0141 174 5165
info@laghersa.it
www.laghersa.it
 CASCINA-LA-GHERSA
 @MaxPastura

YEAR OF FOUNDATION **1920**
NAME OF THE OWNER **Massimo Pastura**
TOTAL BOTTLES PRODUCED **150,000**
DIRECT SALES
VISITS TO THE WINERY - RESERVATION NEEDED
HECTARES OF VINEYARD **20**

There are some people who have radically changed estates and Massimo Pastura is one of them. He entered his family's estate in 1989 and totally changed its established direction.

He acquired vineyards outside the historic area of Moasca and planted new vines but at the same time made sure he also bought old vineyards in order to produce wines of particular interest like Timorasso. He also made revolutionary changes in the winery using various types of wood and paying maniacal attention to fermentation. All this without turning his back to deep-rooted Nicese traditions which include great attention to grape cultivation. All this has resulted in a solid estate with some very interesting wines.

91 — Price B
Barbera d'Asti Superiore Nizza Vignassa 2013

100% Barbera grapes. Matures in different size barrels. Dark ruby red. Warm notes of red and black fruits, maple juice and a light, not invading toasted note with dark spices. Classic aromas in the mouth with evident acidity and great drinkability and thick structure. Tasty finish.

☐ 90 — Price B
Colli Tortonesi Timorasso Tinian Riserva 2013

100% Timorasso grapes. Stainless steel on the yeasts for 10 months. Intense yellow with green hues. Intense and clear notes of medlar, fresh almond and saffron. Savory taste, progressive and good acidity, tasty finish for this wine of great drinkability.

88 — Price A
Grignolino d'Asti Spineira 2011

100% Grignolino grapes. Matures in wood. Garnet ruby red. Smoky notes, then pomegranate and watermelon. Wide but tasty in the mouth with elegant tannins, the good finish makes it very pleasant.

CASTELLO DI GABIANO

Via San Defendente, 2
15020 Gabiano (AL)
Tel. +39 0142 945004
info@castellodigabiano.com
www.castellodigabiano.com
 CastelloDiGabiano
 @CastelloGabiano

YEAR OF FOUNDATION **XI secolo**
NAME OF THE OWNER **Giacomo Cattaneo and Adorno Giustiniani**

TOTAL BOTTLES PRODUCED 80,000
DIRECT SALES
VISITS TO THE WINERY - RESERVATION NEEDED
HECTARES OF VINEYARD 20
HOSPITALITY
RESTAURANT

The town of Gabiano is on the hills the look out over the Po River, more or less halfway between Casale Monferrato and Chivasso, on the border between the provinces of Alessandria and Turin. The castle, owned by the Marquis Cattaneo Adorno, apparently dates back to the 8th century and the wine aging cellar to 1200. Today the estate is run by Giacomo Cattaneo Adorno Gustiniani, and produces the rare Gabiano DOC from Barbera grapes.

 91 Price B
Gabiano Matilde Giustiniani Riserva 2010

Blend of 95% Barbera and 5% Freisa grapes. Matures 2 years in barrique. Intense and lively ruby red. Nice aromatic profile, clear and elegant notes of black currant, black cherry, violet and plums with a spicy and smoky background. Rich, savory and tense taste, nice acidity, warm, enveloping with a very long finish.

★★
CASTELLO DI NEIVE

Via Castelborgo, 1
12052 Neive (CN)
Tel. +39 0173 67171
info@castellodineive.it
www.castellodineive.it

YEAR OF FOUNDATION 1964
NAME OF THE OWNER Italo Stupino
TOTAL BOTTLES PRODUCED 160,000
DIRECT SALES
VISITS TO THE WINERY - RESERVATION NEEDED
HECTARES OF VINEYARD 27

Italo Stupino makes wine that are as good as they are undervalued by distracted critics. At his Castello di Neive estate, which has some of the best Barbaresco cru, he produces some great reds which at first may seem to be a bit surly but that with time can compete with the best the Langhe can offer.

 93 Price B
Barbaresco Santo Stefano Albesani 2013

100% Nebbiolo grapes. Matures 2 years in big barrels. Classic notes of licorice on top, then floral and smoky hints. Full-bodied, savory, neat, warm, elegant taste and great persistent finish.

★
CASTELLO DI VERDUNO

Via Umberto, 1
12060 Verduno (CN)
Tel. +39 0172 470284
cantina@castellodiverduno.com
www.castellodiverduno.com
f *cantinecastelloverduno*

YEAR OF FOUNDATION 1954
NAME OF THE OWNER Bianco and Burlotto Families
TOTAL BOTTLES PRODUCED 60,000
DIRECT SALES
VISITS TO THE WINERY - RESERVATION NEEDED
HECTARES OF VINEYARD 10
HOSPITALITY
RESTAURANT

The history of Barolo began here in 1838 when King Carlo Alberto of Savoy commissioned a great wine from this estate to be made from Nebbiolo grapes. Time passed with not much happening until a new enologist came in, Mario Andrion. After a little aging in wood and experiments on different vintages the wine became a reality, also thanks to the vineyards having such an incredible exposure. Today the estate makes a Barolo, Monvigliero, and two Barbaresco wines, Rabaja and Faset.

94 Price C
Barolo Monvigliero Riserva 2010

100% Nebbiolo grapes. Matures 3 years and a half in big barrels. Intense garnet. An ode to tradition. Locirice, violet, dry flowers, truffle hints for the aromatic bouquet. Thick tannins, a little youthful roughness, savory, tense and agile, promising and with a warm and enveloping finish.

93 Price C
Barbaresco Rabajà Riserva 2011

100% Nebbiolo grapes. Matures 2 years and a half in big barrels. Intense garnet ruby. Violet, currant, wild berries, aromatic herbs hints in the nose. Very savory, tense with perceivable alcoholic warmth, lively and youthful tannins, enveloping, velvety and very persistent finish.

 92 Price B

Barbaresco Rabajà 2013

100% Nebbiolo grapes. Matures 1 year and a half in big barrels. Lively garnet ruby. Black cherry and currant, then violets and medical herbs with smoky hints in the background. Savory, evident tannins, nice and refreshing acidity. Long finish.

 87 Price A

Verduno Pelaverga Basadone 2013

100% Pelaverga grapes. Stainless steel. Light ruby red. Raspberries, violets, strawberries, fragrant fermentative notes. Almost sharp for acidity, light and agile body, great drinkability. A delicious little wine.

★★
CERETTO

*S.P. Alba - Barolo; Località San Cassiano, 34
12051 Alba (CN)
Tel. +39 0173 282582
ceretto@ceretto.com
www.ceretto.com*
 Ceretto-Winery
 @CerettoWinery

YEAR OF FOUNDATION 1937
NAME OF THE OWNER Bruno and Marcello Ceretto
TOTAL BOTTLES PRODUCED 900,000
DIRECT SALES
VISITS TO THE WINERY - RESERVATION NEEDED
HECTARES OF VINEYARD 110

Bruno and Marcello Ceretto have always been wine entrepreneurs of great intelligence. Today they have passed the baton to the new generation and running the winery is the young Alessandro who has opted to convert to organic methods. The wines have always been examples of style with the Barolo and Barbaresco decidedly traditional, while the other wines are rightfully more modern and in line with the times.

 95 Price D

Barolo Bricco Rocche 2012

100% Nebbiolo grapes. Matures 2 years in tonneau and big barrels. Lively garnet. Extremely elegant

notes of wild strawberries, currant, pomegranate, smoky hints in the background. Savory, tense, very refined, youthful but neat tannins, agile body, aristocratic, not enormous but of unexpected length.

 93 Price C

Barolo Brunate 2012

100% Nebbiolo grapes. Matures 2 years in different size barrels. Bright garnet ruby. Enveloping and complex notes of licorice and violet. Some smoky hints. Savory, pleasant, still young and agile tannins, a very promising wine that closes long and persistent.

 92 Price D

Barbaresco Asili 2013

100% Nebbiolo grapes. Matures 18 months in big barrels. Lively garnet. Traditional profile, notes of violet and licorice in evidence, then wild roses. Neat taste, savory, thick and elegant tannins, agile body and elegant and good persistence.

 88 Price A

Dolcetto d'Alba Rossana 2015

100% Dolcetto grapes. Stainless steel only. Violet ruby red. Fragrant and fruity notes of violets, black cherry, fermentative hints. Deliciously savory, already balanced, simple but very easy and pleasant to drink.

★★
MICHELE CHIARLO

*S.S. Nizza-Canelli, 99
14042 Calamandrana (AT)
Tel. +39 0141 769030
Fax +39 0141 769033
info@chiarlo.it
www.michelechiarlo.it*
 michele.chiarlo.3
 @michelechiarlo

YEAR OF FOUNDATION 1956
NAME OF THE OWNER Michele Chiarlo
TOTAL BOTTLES PRODUCED 1,100,000
DIRECT SALES
VISITS TO THE WINERY - RESERVATION NEEDED
HECTARES OF VINEYARD 100

Michele Chiarlo is an authentic institution in Piedmont. His estate is in Calamandrana, near Asti, but he has always made his wines in the Langhe, in the cru of Cerequio and Cannubi in

La Morra and Barolo, and in the Asili cru in Barbaresco. That not being enough, in Cerequio, amid the vineyards with a breathtaking view, he has created a Relais resort of outstanding beauty, Palas Cerequio.

96   Price C

Barbera d'Asti Superiore Nizza La Court Vigna Veja 2011

100% Barbera grapes. Matures in barrique and tonneau. Dark violet. Intense and clear notes of red fruits with hints of sage and dark spices, maple juice. Strong beginning in the mouth, a champion for progression, nice acidity, very smooth tannins. Enveloping, tasty and very persistent finish.

94   Price B

Barbera d'Asti Superiore Nizza La Court 2013

100% Barbera grapes. Matures in barrique and tonneau. Intense ruby red. Red and black fruity notes with currant and intense balckberry, then violets, a very refreshing eucalyptus note and a smoky and slightly toasted touch. Elegant wine, dense but never sickly thanks to the acidity that makes it always pleasant. Red fruits aromas and juicy finish.

90   Price C

Barolo Cerequio 2012

100% Nebbiolo grapes. Matures in barrique and tonneau. Classic ruby slightly garnet. Light warm notes of yellow peach and black fruits, a little too delicate the classic eucalyptus aroma. Elegant, balanced, thin tannins that sustain the drinkability without prevailing. Again dark fruits in the finish.

★★

QUINTO CHIONETTI & FIGLIO

Borgata Valdiberti, 44
12063 Dogliani (CN)
Tel. +39 0173 71179
Fax +39 0173 71179
chionettiquinto@chionettiquinto.com
www.chionettiquinto.com
 chionetti

YEAR OF FOUNDATION **1912**
NAME OF THE OWNER **Quinto Chionetti**
TOTAL BOTTLES PRODUCED **84,000**
DIRECT SALES
VISITS TO THE WINERY - RESERVATION NEEDED
HECTARES OF VINEYARD **16**

Quinto Chionetti, the patriarch of Dogliani, recently handed the reins of his winery to his grandson Nicola, the son of Andrea who tragically died prematurely in 1988. At the time Quinto, who was already of retirement age, rolled up his sleeves and with the vigor of a young man went back to work also to help overcome such a deep loss. Now that his grandson is almost 30, he can limit himself to offering priceless advice and, from a distance and a protective eye, observe how Nicola carries on over 100 years of family tradition.

92   Price A

Dogliani Briccolero 2014

100% Dolcetto grapes. Stainless steel for 1 year. Intense and dark ruby red with violet hues. Blackberry, black cherry and light rhubarb in the nose. More agile taste than other versions, good body, usual rustic elegance and long finish.

91   Price A

Dogliani San Luigi 2014

100% Dolcetto grapes. Stainless steel for 1 year. Intense violet ruby red. Wild berries on top then violets and wet soil aromas. Strong flavor, tense, slightly tannic, not enormous but savory and pleasant.

PARIDE CHIOVINI

Via Giuseppe Garibaldi, 20
28070 Sizzano (NO)
Tel. +39 339 4304954
 paridechiovini
info@paridechiovini.it
www.paridechiovini.it
 paride.chiovini

YEAR OF FOUNDATION **1997**
NAME OF THE OWNER **Paride Chiovini**
TOTAL BOTTLES PRODUCED **10,000**
DIRECT SALES
VISITS TO THE WINERY - RESERVATION NEEDED
HECTARES OF VINEYARD **3**

Towards the end of the 1970s, Paride Chiovini took over his grandfather's as a hobby. At the time his grandfather had been selling his grapes and bulk wines to producers in the area. Paride became interested in winemaking and after working at a chemical laboratory that worked with wine he decided to turn his hobby into a real job and profession. He firmly believes in the potential of his territory and has exclusively cultivated local grapes. Today he produces some 10,000 bottles a year of wine made for the most part with Spanna, Vespolina and rare grapes.

| 94 | Price B |

Ghemme 2012

100% Spanna grapes. Matures 2 years in different size barrels. Light ruby red with garnet hues. Notes of rosehip, cherry, tobacco and hints of vanilla and eucalyptus. Austere and warm in the mouth, ripe and thick tannins but balanced by good acidity and savory. Notes of cherry and eucalyptus in the finish.

| 88 | Price A |

Colline Novaresi Afrodite 2014

100% Vespolina grapes. Stainless steel only. Light ruby red. Notes of black cherry and black pepper, then eucalyptus hints. Fresh and savory in the mouth, light and soft tannins. Very pleasant to drink and the persistence reminds notes of black cherry and black pepper again.

| 87 | Price A |

Colline Novaresi Briseide 2014

100% Bonarda Novarese or Uva Rara grapes. Stainless steel. Light ruby red. Notes of red blueberry, black berry and hints of licorice and violets. Pleasantly savory in the mouth with thin tannins and good freshness. The finish reminds notes of blackberry and licorice roots.

DOMENICO CLERICO

Località Manzoni, 67
12065 Monforte d'Alba (CN)
Tel. +39 0173 78171
info@domenicoclerico.com
www.domenicoclerico.com
 Domenico-Clerico-Az-Agr

YEAR OF FOUNDATION **1978**
NAME OF THE OWNER **Domenico Clerico**
TOTAL BOTTLES PRODUCED **120,000**
DIRECT SALES
VISITS TO THE WINERY - RESERVATION NEEDED
HECTARES OF VINEYARD **22**

Domenico Clerico is another lead player in the Barolo scene. When he was young he was one of the leaders of the group of the so-called innovators and of 'Langhe In'. Today he continues his activities in his modern winery. His wines are greatly crafted and a personality typical of the great cru of Monforte. He has vineyards in Bussia, Ginestra and Manzoni which allow him to produce great, bold Barolo with a long life.

| 92 | Price C |

Barolo Aeroplan Servaj 2012

100% Nebbiolo grapes. Matures 2 years and a half in barrique. Intense ruby red with garnet hues. In the local dialect the name of the wine means wild airplane and this was the name with which Domenico Clerico was called by his father when he was a baby, for its desire to wonder around and discover things. This wine from the Serralunga vineyards represents an alter ego compared to the other Monforte ones. Intense ruby red with garnet hues. Smoky and spicy notes, strong flavor, impressive, thick tannins and it will last a long.

| 91 | Price C |

Barolo Ciabot Mentin 2011

100% Nebbiolo grapes. Matures 2 years and a half in barrique. Intense garnet ruby red. The most classic among Clerico's crus. Notes of Kirsch, vanilla and mint, with spices in the background. Savory, tense, agile, with youthful tannins but already neat.

ELVIO COGNO

Via Ravera, 2
12060 Novello (CN)
Tel. +39 0173 744006
Fax +39 0173 744921
elviocogno@elviocogno.com
www.elviocogno.com
 Elvio-Cogno
 @elviocogno

YEAR OF FOUNDATION **1991**
NAME OF THE OWNER **Nadia Cogno and Valter Fissore**
TOTAL BOTTLES PRODUCED **70,000**
DIRECT SALES
VISITS TO THE WINERY - RESERVATION NEEDED
HECTARES OF VINEYARD **13**

Nadia Cogno and her husband Valter Fissore are the heirs of Elvio Cogno, recently passed away, who was one of the leading figures in the rebirth of Barolo. Today they run the family winery with great competence. Their wines have a traditional style and are made from grapes from their vineyards in Novello, specifically in the most important cru of this municipality that is Ravera.Together with Barolo and Dolcetto, they also produce a very nice white from the local grape variety Nascetta.

96 | Price C

Barolo Vigna Elena Riserva 2010

100% Nebbiolo rosé variety. Matures 36 months in 40 hl barrels. Intense garnet ruby red. Notes of spices, licorice, and a slight smoky hint, then the classic dark flower and plum. Great taste in the mouth, classy tannins perfectly blended in the wine's elegance. Elegant, juicy and very deep finish.

93 | Price C

Barbera d'Alba Pre-Phylloxera 2014

100% Barbera grapes from a 0,25 ha vineyard. Matures 12 months in Slavonia durmast big barrel. Considering the vintage a true miracle. Intense ruby red. Complex aromas of red plums, a noble touch of wild strawberries and dark fruits. Very beautiful spice note from the wood already well blended. Great persistence in the mouth where elegance and density match together giving great emotions.

88 | 👍 Price A

Dolcetto d'Alba Vigna del Mandorlo 2015

100% Dolcetto grapes. Stainless steel for 6 months. Dark color with magenta hues. Clear and intense notes without the typical reductions. Cherry, wild cherry, blackberry and currant, very intense. Savory, progressive, nice development and a youthful, balanced tannin. Coherent and persistent finish.

87 | Price B

Langhe Nascetta di Novello 2015

100% Nascetta grapes. Stainless steel. Bright and deep straw yellow. Intense notes of citrus and lime. A floral hint of maple flowers and Mediterranean herbs. Pleasant drinkability, savory and progressive. A light briny note makes it easy to match with food.

COLOMBERA & GARELLA

Via Cascina Cottignano, 2
13866 Masserano (BI)
Tel. +39 334 1525151
📘 *ColomberaeGarella*

YEAR OF FOUNDATION 1992
NAME OF THE OWNER Colombera Family and Cristiano Garella
TOTAL BOTTLES PRODUCED 20,000
DIRECT SALES
VISITS TO THE WINERY - RESERVATION NEEDED
HECTARES OF VINEYARD 8

Carlo Colombera does not pass unnoticed given his size but above all contagious charm. In 1992, he stopped working in the rice fields to dedicate himself to winegrowing and bought a one-hectare vineyard in Cascina Cottignano. Today, his estate in the Biella Hills has some eight hectares of vineyards spread out in the towns of Masserano, Roasio and Lessona and he produces two wines: Bramaterra and Coste della Sesia. For the beginning, attention has been focused on bringing back old vines. Nebbiolo and the indigenous grapes Croatina and Vespolina here produce wines that have great finesse and complexity. The arrival at the estate of Carlo's son Giacomo, an enology student, and Cristiano Garella, a young enologist but already with important experience, has given further impetus to one of the most interesting estates in northern Piedmont. The wines produced are typical for the area with their strong character but they also have significant elegance and unusual technical style.

91 | Price B

Lessona 2013

Blend of 95% Nebbiolo and 5% Vespolina grapes. Matures 2 years in tonneau. Bright ruby red. Notes of spices and graphite. Fresh in the mouth, irony of great tension, but elegant and juicy tannins. Deep and long finish.

89 | Price B

Bramaterra 2013

Blend of 70% Nebbiolo, 20% Croatina and 10% Vespolina grapes. Matures in barrels. Bright ruby red. Austere, almost severe aromas but in the mouth it expresses its strong character. Strong tannins but very well made and the tension never stops.

88 | Price A

Coste della Sesia Rosso 2013

Blend of 70% Nebbiolo, 15% Croatina and 15% Vespolina. Aged in wood barrels, the wine has a bright ruby-red color and an aroma with notes of graphite and damp earth. The mouthfeel is meaty and bracingly elegant and has a savory and relaxed aftertaste.

COLOMBO - CASCINA PASTORI

S.R. Cafra, 172b
14051 Bubbio (AT)
Tel. +39 0144 852807
Fax +39 0144 852807
info@colombovino.it
www.colombovino.it
f Colombo-Cascina-Pastori

YEAR OF FOUNDATION 2006
NAME OF THE OWNER Antonio and Andrea Colombo
TOTAL BOTTLES PRODUCED 30,000
DIRECT SALES
VISITS TO THE WINERY - RESERVATION NEEDED
HECTARES OF VINEYARD 10

Aside from being one of Italy's leading cardiologists, Antonio Colombo is also passionate about wine, living a healthy life in the country and, understandably, all things that are good for the heart. Living in the country, he decided to make his own wine in Bubbio, in the Asti zone of Langhe, using Pinot Noir and the results are surprisingly good.

 92   Price B
Piemonte Pinot Nero Apertura 2013

100% Pinot Nero grapes. Matures 18 monts in different size barrels. Lively ruby red. Typical notes of wild strawberries, pink flowers, smoky hints. Enveloping taste, warm but not without agility, savory and of good persistence.

🔲 91   Price B
Alta Langa Rosé Riserva Brut

100% Pinot Nero grapes. Classic method. Onion peel pink, thin and continuous perlage. Great fragrance in the nose with notes of wild strawberries, yeasts and bread crust. Lively taste, creamy, savory and acidulous, very pleasant to drink and of persistent and agile taste.

▫ 90   Price B
Piemonte Moscato Passito Pastù Tardì 2012

*100% Moscato Bianco di Canelli dried grapes. Matures 2 years in barrique. Very attractive aromatic notes then candied fruits, vanilla sugar, peaches in syrup. Sweet but not sickly taste, well sustained and refreshed by acidity. Very long finish. *37.5 cl bottle.*

CONTERNO FANTINO

Via Ginestra, 1
12065 Monforte d'Alba (CN)
Tel. +39 0173 78204
Fax +39 0173 787326
info@conternofantino.it
www.conternofantino.it

YEAR OF FOUNDATION 1982
NAME OF THE OWNER Claudio Conterno and Guido Fantino
TOTAL BOTTLES PRODUCED 140,000
VISITS TO THE WINERY - RESERVATION NEEDED
HECTARES OF VINEYARD 27
CERTIFIED ORGANIC VITICULTURE

Claudio Conterno and Guido Fantino have been running this winery for decades and the result of their collaboration is a line of wines that few can match. Among the best are Barolo Sori Ginestra and Langhe Rosso Monprà, a blend of Nebbiolo and Barbera with a touch of Cabernet Sauvignon.

 92   Price C
Barolo Sorì Ginestra 2012

100% Nebbiolo grapes. Matures 2 years barrique and tonneau. Intense garnet ruby red. Spicy and whole taste with modern style aromas, notes of vanilla, black cherry and pomegranate. Strong flavor, neat, nice velvety tannins, elegant and with a very long finish.

ALDO CONTERNO

Località Bussia, 48
12065 Monforte d'Alba (CN)
Tel. +39 0173 78150
Fax +39 0173 787240
www.poderialdoconterno.com

YEAR OF FOUNDATION 1969
NAME OF THE OWNER Franco, Stefano and Giacomo Conterno
TOTAL BOTTLES PRODUCED 80000
DIRECT SALES
VISITS TO THE WINERY - RESERVATION NEEDED
HECTARES OF VINEYARD 25

Tasting these wines today one cannot help but remember the great Aldo Conterno, who died several years ago. He was an intelligent and courageous man who was open to new ideas and for sure his death was a great loss for Italian wine. The estate is now run by his sons Stefano, Giacomo and Franco and they still have their wonderful Bussia vineyards in Monforte. Because they age so well, many of the wines Aldo made can still be enjoyed today and will help keep his memory alive.

■ 🏷 96 Price E
Barolo Gran Bussia Riserva 2008

100% Nebbiolo grapes. Matures about 32 months in big barrels. Intense garnet ruby red. Great traditional wine. Complex and articulated aromatic profile that goes from licorice notes to dry flowers, currant jam, violet and tobacco. Powerful but elegant flavor, rich, velvety tannins, elegant and tense balance, refined and unique, a real champion for persistence.

■ 92 Price D
Barolo Bussia Colonnello 2012

100% Nebbiolo grapes. Matures 30 months in big barrels. Lively garnet ruby red. Wet soil, violet, Kirsch and tobacco for an elegant and whole aromatic profile. Strong flavor, savory, warm, tannic, with a great persistent finish.

■ 88 Price B
Barbera d'Alba Conca Tre Pile 2013

100% Barbera grapes. Matures 1 year in barrique. Intense ruby red. Notes of Blackberry and Kirsch, then vanilla and sweet spices. Tense flavor, typical acidity a little too evident. Agile and long finish.

★★★
GIACOMO CONTERNO

Località Ornati
12065 Monforte d'Alba (CN)
Tel. +39 0173 78221
conterno@conterno.it
www.conterno.it

YEAR OF FOUNDATION **1900**
NAME OF THE OWNER **Roberto Conterno**
TOTAL BOTTLES PRODUCED **n.d.**
DIRECT SALES
VISITS TO THE WINERY - RESERVATION NEEDED
HECTARES OF VINEYARD **17**

The wines or Roberto Conterno are sought after almost as if they were religious relics. They only reach the market if they have the high quality the estate is recognized for and that consistently make them among the best in the category. The winery was recently modernized and expanded, as was the estate's property. Quality is an obsession for the latest Conterno heir and not just in the vineyard or the winemaking method. The corks are selected one-by-one and the labels, bottles are packaging are never left to chance and must be part of, as he puts it, 'total quality'.

■ 🏷 96 Price D
Barolo Francia 2012

100% Nebbiolo grapes from Francia vineyard in Serralunga. Matures 48 months in big barrels. Bright and light ruby red. Charming floral aromas, classical notes of roses and violets on top. Then sweet tobacco, medical herbs and almost minty. Great energy in the mouth, almost electric for very thick but elegant tannins. Proud and nervous finish. Extraordinary version of great elegance.

■ 94 Price D
Barolo Cerretta 2012

100% Nebbiolo grapes. 48 months in big barrel. Lively and relatively concentrated red, very classic. Less intense than the Francia one but complex as well, with strawberry jam, black pepper, various spices, nice eucalyptus. Elegant in the mouth but strong, almost austere, with not trivial tannic structure and very long finish.

■ 93 Price B
Barbera d'Alba Cascina Francia 2014

100% Barbera grapes. Matures 20 months in big barrels. Lively and bright ruby red. Intense notes of morello and cherry, medlar and underbrush. Wonderful freshness in the mouth, thin tannic structure makes it almost Nebbiolo like, good drinkability. It will last a long time. Considering the difficult vintage, a masterpiece.

■ 91 Price B
Barbera d'Alba Vigna Cerretta 2014

100% Barbera grapes. Matures 20 months in big barrels. Intense red color. Superb aromatic bouquet. Notes of blueberry juice and blackberries, a classic ripe cherry. Tense and solemn in the mouth, wide and fresh. The vintage has been magisterially interpreted.

COPPO

Via Alba, 68
14053 Canelli (AT)
Tel. +39 0141 823146
info@coppo.it
www.coppo.it
COPPO1892
@COPPO1892

YEAR OF FOUNDATION **1892**
NAME OF THE OWNER **Coppo Family**
TOTAL BOTTLES PRODUCED **400,000**
DIRECT SALES
VISITS TO THE WINERY - RESERVATION NEEDED
HECTARES OF VINEYARD **22**

Again this year the Coppo brothers have produced an excellent line of wines. The wines are technically well-made and expressive of the territory, all are top class and among the best in their category. This historic, reliable winery is surely one of the best, if not the best, in the province of Asti and this year is yet another confirmation.

 96   Price D

Barbera d'Asti Superiore Nizza Riserva della Famiglia 2007

100% Barbera grapes. Matures about 18 months in barrique. Dark ruby red with garnet hues. Extremely complex aromatic profile with evolution hints and great freshness with a still evident fruitiness. Blackberry, blueberry and a smoky hint. Absolute value for the taste, great balance between power and elegance with a stratospheric finish and incredible drinkability.

 94   Price B

Barbera d'Asti Pomorosso 2013

100% Barbera grapes. Matures in barrique and tonneau. Intense ruby red. Clear and intense aromatic profile with notes of red citrus, a touch of medical herbs and Mediterranean spices. The fruit is black. Great classy taste, juicy, balanced and with a thick structure and good acidity to sustain it. Rare complexity and length in the finish.

 93   Price B

Riserva Coppo Metodo Classico Brut 2008

Blend of 80% Pinot Nero and 20% Chardonnay grapes. Vinified in wood for 60 months on the yeasts. Bright straw yellow, very thin perlage. Intense notes of medlar, hazelnuts, light yeasts and a various colors flowery notes. Neat taste, savory and with very elegant good acidity. Elegant, wide and very long finish.

CORDERO DI MONTEZEMOLO

Frazione Annunziata, 67
12064 La Morra (CN)
Tel. +39 0173 50344
info@corderodimontezemolo.com
www.corderodimontezemolo.it
cdmwinery

YEAR OF FOUNDATION **1340**
NAME OF THE OWNER **Giovanni, Elena and Alberto Cordero di Montezemolo**
TOTAL BOTTLES PRODUCED **230,000**
DIRECT SALES
VISITS TO THE WINERY - RESERVATION NEEDED
HECTARES OF VINEYARD **35**

This celebrated and historic winery (founded in 1340) is situated in the area of Monfaletto, in La Morra, excellent for Barolo. They have three hectares of vineyards in the cru Villero in Castiglione Falletto which produces another Barolo, Enrico VI, but all their wines are excellent.

 94   Price C

Barolo Enrico VI Villero 2012

100% Nebbiolo grapes. Matures 20 months in barrique and tonneau. Intense garnet ruby. Spices, wet soil, medical herbs, violet and tobacco complete the intense and strong aromatic profile. Youthful taste, thick tannins, good body, warm and good tension, some ripple in the mouth but promising as well.

 91   Price C

Barolo Bricco Gattera 2012

100% Nebbiolo grapes. Matures almost 2 years in barrique and tonneau. Notes of Kirsch, a little penetrating in the nose, then carnation, spices and wet soil. The taste has some very youthful tannic/acidic edges, good structure and great persistence.

87   Price B

Barbera d'Alba Superiore Funtanì 2013

100% Barbera grapes. Matures 15 months in barrique. Blackberry, underbrush, hints of vanilla and licorice, mint in the background. Tense, savory, acidulous and good length.

RENATO CORINO

Frazione Annunziata Pozzo, 49a
12064 La Morra (CN)
Tel. +39 338 7301814
renatocorino@alice.it
www.renatocorino.it

YEAR OF FOUNDATION **2005**
NAME OF THE OWNER **Corino Family**
TOTAL BOTTLES PRODUCED **45,000**
DIRECT SALES
VISITS TO THE WINERY - RESERVATION NEEDED
HECTARES OF VINEYARD **7**

Renato Corino and his son Stefano produce wines that are rich in color, fruit and concentration. This is true of both their Barbera and, above all, Barolo. Barbera d'Alba Vigna Pozzo is a very pleasing drop but in a good year Barolo Vigneto Arborina and Rocche dell'Annunziata, both La Morra cru, are phenomenal.

 93   Price D

Barolo Vigne Vecchie Riserva 2009

100% Nebbiolo grapes. Matures 2 years in barrique. Intense garnet ruby. Modern and elegant, spicy notes, then black cherry, Kirsch and hints of mint. Savory, warm, good body but agile, thin and powerful, with neat tannins and great persistence.

 92   Price C

Barolo Rocche dell'Annunziata 2012

100% Nebbiolo grapes. Matures 2 years in barrique. Intense and lively garnet ruby. Slightly smoky aromas, notes of spices, then black cherry, cassis and tobacco. Savory, neat tannins, elegant, not enormous body but thin and agile.

 88   Price B

Barbera d'Alba Vigna Pozzo 2013

100% Barbera grapes. Matures 18 months in 2/3 used barrique. Intense ruby red. Black cherry, cardamom, vanilla and blood orange in the nose. Tense body, agile, pleasant drinkability.

★★

MATTEO CORREGGIA

Via Santo Stefano Roero, 124
12043 Canale (CN)
Tel. +39 0173 978009
Fax +39 0173 959849
cantina@matteocorreggia.com
www.matteocorreggia.com
MATTEO-CORREGGIA
@Roero_Wine

YEAR OF FOUNDATION **1985**
NAME OF THE OWNER **Ornella Costa**
TOTAL BOTTLES PRODUCED **140,000**
DIRECT SALES
VISITS TO THE WINERY - RESERVATION NEEDED
HECTARES OF VINEYARD **20**

Matteo Correggia died prematurely in 2001 but his wife Ornella Costa is committed to carrying on his work at the estate he founded. And she does this with courage and dedication achieving more than respectable results. Her Roero wines have always stood out for their elegance and Roche d'Ampsej is a small gem.

 92   Price B

Roero Roche d'Ampsej Riserva 2012

100% Nebbiolo grapes. Matures 18 months in barrique. Intense ruby red. Fruity and spicy, smoky notes, then vanilla, black cherry. Savory taste, thick but neat and elegant tannins, whole and tense with great persistence.

 89   Price B

Roero La Val dei Preti 2013

100% Nebbiolo grapes. Matures 18 months in different size barrels. Intense garnet ruby red. Classic notes of violet, black cherry, currant, licorice and vanilla. Youthfut taste, tense, some tannic edge, warm and persistent.

★★

GIUSEPPE CORTESE

Via Rabajà, 80
12050 Barbaresco (CN)
Tel. +39 0173 635131
Fax +39 0173 635131
info@cortesegiuseppe.it
www.cortesegiuseppe.it

YEAR OF FOUNDATION **1971**
NAME OF THE OWNER **Pier Carlo Cortese**
TOTAL BOTTLES PRODUCED **50,000**
DIRECT SALES

VISITS TO THE WINERY - RESERVATION NEEDED
HECTARES OF VINEYARD **8**
HOSPITALITY

Rabajà is, along with Martinenga and, perhas, Asili, an authentic Barbaresco grand cru, the same as Chambertin and Chambertin Clos de Béze in Gevrey Chambertin are. The difference is that in Burgundy this is officially recognized whereas in Italy it almost seems to be a secret among sector operators. The most authentic Rabajà winemaker is Giuseppe Cortese who today is assisted by his children Pier Carlo and Tiziana who are carrying on the family tradition. His Barbaresco Rabajà is tradition in a bottle.

93   Price B
Barbaresco Rabajà 2013

100% Nebbiolo grapes. Matures in big barrels. Bright ruby red. Litterally explosive notes of spices and berries. Powerful on the palate and elegant at the same time with sweet tannins and a never-ending progression with an eucalyptus note in the finish.

87   Price A
Langhe Nebbiolo 2014

100% Nebbiolo grapes. Matures in big barrels. Bright ruby red. Notes of flowers, tobacco and wet soil. Agile, fragrant and a long and savory finish.

★
GIACOMO FENOCCHIO

Località Bussia, 72
12065 Monforte d'Alba (CN)
Tel. +39 0173 78675
Fax +39 0173 787218
info@giacomofenocchio.com
www.giacomofenocchio.com
 GiacomoFenocchio
 @gfenocchio

YEAR OF FOUNDATION **1864**
NAME OF THE OWNER **Claudio and Albino Fenocchio**
TOTAL BOTTLES PRODUCED **90,000**
DIRECT SALES
VISITS TO THE WINERY - RESERVATION NEEDED
HECTARES OF VINEYARD **15**

The winery of Claudio and Albino Fenocchio, the sons of founder Giacomo, is located in Monforte where they own vineyards in Bussia. They also have vineyards in Castiglione Falletto, Villero and Barolo, in the Cannubi cru. Their wines have a traditional style and are available at reasonable prices for these types of wine.

92   Price B
Barolo Villero 2012

100% Nebbiolo grapes. Matures 2 years in big barrels. Lively garnet ruby. Ethereal, a little stingy notes of Kirsch, then spicy aromas, smoky and pomegranate. Savory, youthful tannins, still rough, great body. Very promising. Very long finish.

FERRANDO

Via Torino, 599a
10015 Ivrea (TO)
Tel. +39 0125 633550
Fax +39 0125 633550
info@ferrandovini.it
www.ferrandovini.it

YEAR OF FOUNDATION **1890**
NAME OF THE OWNER **Roberto Ferrando**
TOTAL BOTTLES PRODUCED **45,000**
DIRECT SALES
VISITS TO THE WINERY - RESERVATION NEEDED
HECTARES OF VINEYARD **5**

When it comes to heroic winegrowing, Ferrando is a wine that comes to mind. First of all because this family is one of the reasons why Carema red wine still exists today and then because their dedication goes way back beginning with Giuseppe in the 1950s and then Luigi and Roberto, who runs the winery today. Carema is made from 20 hectares of vineyards, of which they own five, and produces a wine with great personality.

88   Price B
Carema Etichetta Bianca 2012

100% Nebbiolo grapes. Matures 2 years in big barrels. Garnet ruby red. Typical aromas of wild berries, light mint, hints of licorice and spices. Tense flavor, acidulous, a little edgy, agile with average structure and good persistent finish.

281

FONTANAFREDDA

Via Alba, 15
12050 Serralunga D'Alba (CN)
Tel. +39 0173 626111
info@fontanafredda.it
www.fontanafredda.it
f *fontanafreddawine*
𝕏 *@Fontanafredda_*

YEAR OF FOUNDATION **1878**
NAME OF THE OWNER **Oscar Farinetti**
TOTAL BOTTLES PRODUCED **7,500,000**
DIRECT SALES
VISITS TO THE WINERY - RESERVATION NEEDED
HECTARES OF VINEYARD **85**
RESTAURANT

The awarding this year of a third star to Fontanafredda, or better former Savoy Tenimenti di Barolo and Fontanafredda estate, which also includes the historic Langue marque Casa Mirafiore, is in recognition of the distinct improvement achieved in recent years. A prime example of this is their Barolo Riserva 2007 di Mirafiore which here received a Doctor Wine 'faccino' hedcut and won the Platinum Best in Show Award at the Decanter World Winne Awards, the most important wine contest in the world, which has been awarded to only 31 of the some 18,000 wines tasted.

 98   Price C
Barolo Casa Mirafiore Riserva 2007

100% Nebbiolo grapes, 3 years in big barrels and 2 in concrete vats. Intense garnet ruby. Classy notes of plums, spices, light smoky, then violet and licorice for a complex and refined aromatic profile. Velvety flavor, hypnotizing tannins of glycerin smoothness, good body, neat, warm, elegant e very persistent.

 94   Price C
Barolo Riserva 2010

100% Nebbiolo grapes. Matures 3 years in big barrels. Intense garnet ruby. Clear and typical notes of humus, violet, smoky and minty hints. Gritty flavor, savory, youthful tannins but blending in, great body, neat and powerful. A promising wine.

 93   Price B
Barolo Casa Mirafiore Paiagallo 2012

100% Nebbiolo grapes. Matures 1 year in barrique

and 1 year in big barrels. Elegantly spicy in the nose, notes of cardamom and vanilla, then pomegranate and currant. Enveloping flavor, agile, youthful elegance, savory and pleasant to drink. Long and persistent finish.

 92   Price C
Barolo La Rosa 2012

100% Nebbiolo grapes. Matures 2 years in different size barrels. Clear garnet. Typical and traditional in the nose. Dry flowers, medical herbs, then licorice and currant. Strong flavor, classical thick tannins a little drying as Serralunga ones. Powerful, savory, warm and full-bodied.

 90   Price B
Barbera d'Alba Superiore Mirafiore 2012

100% Barbera grapes. Matures 1 year in barrique. Intense ruby red. Black cherry, spices and smoky hints describe the aromatic profile. Strong flavor, savory, acidulous, full-bodied and warm. Very persistent finish.

FRATELLI ALESSANDRIA

Via B. Valfrè, 59
12060 Verduno (CN)
Tel. +39 0172 470113
info@fratellialessandria.it
www.fratellialessandria.it
f *Alessandria-Fratelli*

YEAR OF FOUNDATION **1870**
NAME OF THE OWNER **Fratelli Alessandria**
TOTAL BOTTLES PRODUCED **80,000**
DIRECT SALES
VISITS TO THE WINERY - RESERVATION NEEDED
HECTARES OF VINEYARD **14**

The estate of Alessandro and Gian Battista has rightly earned an important place in the complex Langhe wine world thanks to wines that are very classic but never nostalgic. Monvigliero and San Lorenzo in the township of Verduno and Gramolere in Monforte d'Alba are their Barolo cru that are bottled separately to best express their characteristics.

92   Price B
Barolo Monvigliero 2012

100% Nebbiolo grapes. Matures in tonneau and big barrels. Bright ruby red. Well defined aromatic bouquet with fruity notes, spices and smoky hints. Thin on the palate, but juicy, tonic with sweet tannins and an strong and deep finish.

 90 Price B

Barolo Gramolere 2012

100% Nebbiolo grapes. Matures in tonneau and big barrels. Bright ruby red. Austere notes of cinchona and graphite. Mineral in the mouth, savory with a not very long finish of licorice and spices.

89 Price B

Barolo San Lorenzo di Verduno 2012

100% Nebbiolo grapes. Matures in tonneau and big barrels. Bright ruby red. Elegant notes of blond tobacco and pepper. Elegant in the mouth with sweet tannins and good agility.

88 👍 Price A

Verduno Pelaverga Speziale 2015

100% Pelaverga grapes. Stainless steel. Great version of a wine wrongly considered a little one. Light ruby red. Litterally explosive spicy notes. Juicy on the palate, fruity, fresh and with a pleasing finish.

FRATELLI BIANCO VINI

Viale Umberto I, 6
14049 Nizza Monferrato (AT)
Tel. +39 0141 721108
Fax +39 0141 724791
vini@fllibianco.it
www.fllibianco.it
f Fratelli-Bianco-vini

YEAR OF FOUNDATION **1930**
NAME OF THE OWNER **Fiorella Bianco**
TOTAL BOTTLES PRODUCED **100,000**
DIRECT SALES
VISITS TO THE WINERY - RESERVATION NEEDED
HECTARES OF VINEYARD **16**

We are pleased to have been able to enter this estate in our guide. The charm of Fiorella Bianco and the historic importance of her estate merit it. Set up around the 1930s, the estate underwent an authentic revolution when Fiorella took over and sought to modernize both the estate's image and production. She succeeded in this a few years ago thanks to greater attention paid during the making and aging of their more important wines. Revamping the winery played a key role in this. Hats off.

 94 Price B

Barbera d'Asti Superiore Nizza Carpe Diem 2013

100% Barbera grapes. Matures 1 year in barrique and tonneau. Intense ruby red. Thin and elegant in the nose with classy notes of wild cherries and attractive violets. Elegant touch of wood and light spiciness. Cardamom, Kirsch and maple juice. Intense in the mouth with thick structure and very beautiful acidity that makes it really lovable. Very classy finish.

 89 Price A

Barbera d'Asti Cuntrò Maestra 2015

100% Barbera grapes. Stainless steel on the yeasts. Bright ruby red. Youthful and attractive notes, very intense and clear hints of violets, currant and wild cherry. Attractive taste and pleasant with nice acidity never overwhelming and very pleasant finish.

★★

FRATELLI CAVALLOTTO TENUTA BRICCO BOSCHIS

Via Alba - Monforte, 48
12060 Castiglione Falletto (CN)
Tel. +39 0173 62814
Fax +39 0173 62914
info@cavallotto.com
www.cavallotto.com

YEAR OF FOUNDATION **1948**
NAME OF THE OWNER **Alfio, Giuseppe and Laura Cavallotto**
TOTAL BOTTLES PRODUCED **110,000**
DIRECT SALES
VISITS TO THE WINERY - RESERVATION NEEDED
HECTARES OF VINEYARD **23.5**
CERTIFIED ORGANIC VITICULTURE

The Cavallotto family has been making wine in Castiglione Falletti for almost 70 years. The current heirs, siblings Alfio, Giuseppe and Laura, continue the family traditional with great dedication. Their historic cru is Bricco Boschis and is used to make both a vintage and Riserva wine, the latter with only grapes from the Vigna San Giuseppe parcel and is one of the great, classic-style Barolo wines.

93   Price C
Barolo Bricco Boschis Vigna San Giuseppe Riserva 2010

100% Nebbiolo grapes. Matures 4 years in big barrels. Intense garnet ruby red. Very classic aromatic and traditional prodile, notes of licorice, tamarind, violet and austere, ethereal and complex smoky notes. Powerful taste, thick tannins, warm, enveloping and long persistence.

92   Price C
Barolo Vignolo Riserva 2010

100% Nebbiolo grapes.Matures 4 years in big barrels. Bright garnet ruby red. Complete and elegant notes of black cherry, Kirsch, smoky hints in the background for more modern style aromatic profile. Tense flavor, thick but thin tannins, great body, rich but agile and warm yet very long finish.

90   Price B
Barolo Bricco Boschis 2012

100% Nebbiolo grapes. Matures 3 years in big barrels. Bright garnet ruby red. Very classic notes of black cherry, yellow peach, violets and a slight minty touch in the background. Youthful flavor, still a little rough tannins, savory, warm and enveloping.

FRATELLI CIGLIUTI

Via Serraboella, 17
12052 Neive (CN)
Tel. +39 0173 677185
Fax +39 0173 67142
info@cigliti.it
www.cigliuti.it

YEAR OF FOUNDATION **1964**
NAME OF THE OWNER **Renato Cigliuti**
TOTAL BOTTLES PRODUCED **30,000**
DIRECT SALES
VISITS TO THE WINERY - RESERVATION NEEDED
HECTARES OF VINEYARD **7.5**

Renato Cigliuti is a pioneer among Barbaresco producers. 2014 was his 50th vintage, a very respectful milestone for a winemaker and evidence of experience, an ability to interpret the seasons and great dedication. His best wine has always been the classic Barbaresco from the cru of Serraboella.

93   Price C
Barbaresco Serraboella 2012

100% Nebbiolo grapes, 2 years in different size barrels. Lively garnet ruby red. Classic aromatic profile with violets, hints of licorice, currant and smoky. Savory, with personality, tense, youthful tannins.

92   Price B
Barbaresco Vie Erte 2012

100% Nebbiolo grapes. Matures 2 years in different size barrels. Lively garnet ruby red. Very traditional, almost emblematic in the nose with notes of licorice and slightly smoky hints together with notes of underbrush. Tense flavor, very young tannins, rough but very typical. Warm and savory finish.

89   Price B
Barbera d'Alba Vigna Serraboella 2013

100% Barbera grapes. Matures 18 months in barrique. Intense ruby red. Enveloping notes, smoky, then Kirsch, blackberry and tobacco. The taste is tanse by acidity, powerful, very savory and warm.

GAJA

Via Torino,18
12050 Barbaresco (CN)
Tel. +39 0173 635158
info@gaja.com

YEAR OF FOUNDATION **1859**
NAME OF THE OWNER **Gaja Family**
TOTAL BOTTLES PRODUCED **380,000**
HECTARES OF VINEYARD **92**

You could easily write a book about this winery that for decades has epitomized excellence. It is in Barbaresco where generations of Gaja descendants built a worldwide reputation based on uncompromised quality. Their wines are very elegant and can age decades and while their prices are high, there is always a great demand for them. Many of the wines are made with Nebbiolo, including varietal versions, but the common thread that unites all the wines is the Gaja style. This year we point out two very important news: the first is the return, after twenty years, of the two famous Sorì in the Barbaresco appelation; the second is the increasing involvement of Rossana and Giovanni, sons of Angelo and Lucia, in the family winery.

98   Price E

Barbaresco Sorì San Lorenzo 2013

100% Nebbiolo grapes. Matures 24 months in wood. Dark garnet ruby red. Spicy notes, with violet, licorice and a hint of wood. Neat on the palate, very articulated, savory, warm, enveloping, velvety, thick tannins, never-ending finish. A true masterpiece.

 97   Price E

Barbaresco Sorì Tildin 2013

100% Nebbiolo grapes. Matures 24 months in wood. Intense garnet ruby red. Enveloping notes of currant, violets, licorice and hints of vanilla. Rich in the mouth, pulpy, articulated, perfect tannins, savory, tense, neat, warm and very long finish. It's very young, if you manage to resist wait to drink it for a long time.

■ 93   Price D

Barbaresco 2013

100% Nebbiolo grapes. Matures 12 months in wood. Very clear garnet color. Immediate notes of sweet spices, currant and a hint of vanilla. Long, warm, savory, velvety, outstretched and elegant tannins.

★

ETTORE GERMANO

Località Cerretta, 1
12050 Serralunga D'Alba (CN)
Tel. +39 0173 613528
Fax +39 0173 613593
germanoettore@germanoettore.com
www.germanoettore.com

YEAR OF FOUNDATION **1975**
NAME OF THE OWNER **Sergio Germano**
TOTAL BOTTLES PRODUCED **90,000**
DIRECT SALES
VISITS TO THE WINERY - RESERVATION NEEDED
HECTARES OF VINEYARD **18**
HOSPITALITY

It is hard to find a producer who can offer both excellent whites and reds. Such a miracle takes place in this winery that makes a Barolo of the utmost quality as well as a splendid Riesling. The vineyards for the Barolo are in Serralunga and include the famous cru Cerretta, Prapò and Lazzarito that provide healthy grapes to produce wines with the right classic-mod-

ern balance. The Riesling grapes are from the pre-Alpine zone of Alta Langa, where the winery owns vineyards that are quite old.

■ 94   Price C

Barolo Lazzarito Riserva 2010

100% Nebbiolo grapes. Matures in 2 thousand liters barrels. Made from a really old vineyard it's a magnificent wine. Bright ruby red. Notes of violets, licorice, delicate spices and aromatic herbs. Austere and juicy in the mouth with a deep and explosive finish.

☐ 92   Price B

Langhe Riesling Hérzu 2015

100% Riesling grapes. Stainless steel only. Bright straw yellow with greenish hues. Even if very young there are clear notes of grapefruit and white pepper. Juicy in the mouth, elegant and with great tension. Powerful and vertical finish.

■ 90   Price B

Barolo Prapò 2012

100% Nebbiolo grapes. Matures in different size barrels. From a vineyard of about 45 years. Bright ruby red. The aromatic profile is already well expressed with notes of tobacco, spices and licorice. Juicy in the mouth, very spicy and with an agile finish.

BRUNO GIACOSA

Via XX Settembre, 52
12057 Neive (CN)
Tel. +39 0173 67027
Fax +39 0173 677477
brunogiacosa@brunogiacosa.it
www.brunogiacosa.it

YEAR OF FOUNDATION **1900**
NAME OF THE OWNER **Bruno Giacosa**
TOTAL BOTTLES PRODUCED **400,000**
DIRECT SALES
VISITS TO THE WINERY
HECTARES OF VINEYARD **22**

In Neive we find the homebase of one of the universally renouned masters of Langa. When we talk abut Bruno Giacosa, fot his winemaking and selector abilities, even his collegues go hats off. Historical producer and great excellence researcher, he has produced wines that will remain like milestones in the memory of winelovers. His red lables are a myth, rare and objects of desire. But the extreme difficulty in finding them is widely rewarded by the emotions it is able to give. His entire production though is extremely emotional.

 97   Price E

Barbaresco Asili Riserva 2011

100% Nebbiolo grapes. Matures 60 months in big barrels. Relatively light and bright red. Deep notes of wild strawberries jelly, raspberry jam, musk and juniper underbrush hunts, an almost esoteric eucalyptus aroma. Intense and good. Dense and strong in the mouth with unique balance and elegance.

 95   Price D

Barolo Falletto 2012

100% Nebbiolo grapes. Matures in big barrels. Lively and compact red. For the second year in a row even if we're talking about the 'white label' the emotions are present. Notes of peppermint, strawberries and raspberries, pansy and oriental spices. Great energy in the mouth, thick and strong tannic structure, but the lever of pleasantness has few equals. Very long persistence, great power.

91   Price B

Nebbiolo d'Alba Vigna Valmaggiore 2014

100% Nebbiolo grapes. Matures in big barrels. Relatively light red. Very thin but complex notes of spices (pepper, cinnamon), blackberries and hummus. The berries are well represented. Elegant and incredibly easy to drink. Very pleasing. A great classy Nebbiolo that can compete with many Barolo or Barbaresco.

GIOVANNI BATTISTA GILLARDI

Località Corsaletto
12060 Farigliano (CN)
Tel. +39 0173 76306
gillardi@gillardi.it
www.gillardi.it
 gillardi.az.agr

YEAR OF FOUNDATION **1980**
NAME OF THE OWNER **Giacolino Gillardi**
TOTAL BOTTLES PRODUCED **35,000**
DIRECT SALES
VISITS TO THE WINERY - RESERVATION NEEDED
HECTARES OF VINEYARD **7**

The winery of Giacolino Gillardi, a small, historic producer in Farigliano who is also the technical director at the famous estate of Bruno and Marcello Ceretto, produced only 'one' wine this year. It was his Dogliani Cursalet, his most classic wine, which was really good as you can see from the review.

92   Price A

Dogliani Cursalet 2015

100% Dolcetto grapes. Stainless steel. Violet ruby red. Deliciously fragrant, flowery notes, violet and rose, then blueberry, plum and fermentative hints. Dangerous drinkability, if possible, they should write on the label: 'to drink a full bucket of it'. Savory, warm, tense, maybe a little simple, but there should be more wines like this.

★★★

ELIO GRASSO

Località Ginestra, 40
12065 Monforte d'Alba (CN)
Tel. +39 0173 78491
info@eliograsso.it
www.eliograsso.it

YEAR OF FOUNDATION **1928**
NAME OF THE OWNER **Elio Grasso**
TOTAL BOTTLES PRODUCED **90,000**
VISITS TO THE WINERY - RESERVATION NEEDED
HECTARES OF VINEYARD **18**

This is a small yet prestigious winery in Monforte in the southern part of the Barolo district, home to the cru Ginestra and Gavarini which are among the most suited for this wine, from where you can see the southern side of Serralunga. Here Elio Grasso has developed a very personal style and his wines, while boasting a captivating fruit component and a pleasing drinkability in youth, stand out for their concentration and ability to age. In a way, he put a square peg in a round hole.

92   Price C

Barolo Ginestra Casa Matè 2012

100% Nebbiolo grapes, 30 months in big barrels. Bright garnet ruby. Smoky notes, then Kirsch, blackberry, black cherry, ethereal notes and red fruits. Youthful but complete flavor, thick tannins, alcoholic warmth, great body and very long finish.

91   Price C

Barolo Gavarini Chiniera 2012

100% Nebbiolo grapes. Matures 2 years in big barrels. Garnet ruby red. Ethereal notes of Kirsch and strawberries, then blackberry, wild berries and light tobacco. Strong flavor, savory, tense body, youthfully aggressive tannins and great persistent finish.

PARIDE IARETTI

Via Pietro Micca, 23/b
13045 Gattinara (VC)
Tel. +39 340 319 1157
info@parideiaretti.it
www.parideiaretti.it
 Paride-Iaretti-C-Società-Agricola-Gattinara
 @parideiaretti

YEAR OF FOUNDATION 2000
NAME OF THE OWNER Paride Iaretti
TOTAL BOTTLES PRODUCED 16,000
DIRECT SALES
VISITS TO THE WINERY - RESERVATION NEEDED
HECTARES OF VINEYARD 3

Paride's father, Pietro Iaretti, also made wine but using some rather adventurous methods. When Paride took over production the music changed and today he is one of the best producers in the area of Gattinara and some of his wines are small masterpieces of craft winemaking.

94   Price B

Gattinara Riserva 2007

100% Nebbiolo grapes, more than 4 years in big barrels. Intense garnet red. Enveloping and complex aromatic profile, strawberry jam, mint, rosemary flowers, thyme and marjoram. Powerful in the mouth, warm, savory, very elegant tannins, velvety, great body, agile acidity. Splendid and long finish.

IL CHIOSSO

Viale Marconi, 45
13045 Gattinara (VC)
Tel. +39 0163 826739
info@ilchiosso.it
www.ilchiosso.it
 ilchiosso.cambieriarlunno

YEAR OF FOUNDATION 2007
NAME OF THE OWNER Famiglie Arlunno and Cambieri
TOTAL BOTTLES PRODUCED 80,000
DIRECT SALES
VISITS TO THE WINERY - RESERVATION NEEDED
HECTARES OF VINEYARD 12

There are some passe-partout red wines for all seasons (summer included) and Vespolina from Il Chiosso is undoubtedly one of them. The Il Chiosso winery was started up in 2007 by enologist Marco Arlunno and Carlo Cambieri, an engineer who has always had a passion for wine. The dream the two men were able to achieve was to produce in a single place the best wines of Upper Piedmont: Gattinara on the one hand and Ghemme and Colline Novarese DOC wine on the other. The name Il Chiosso in Upper Piedmont was historically used to define a walled-in vineyard, what the French call a clos. Winegrowers would wall in vineyards to underscore the importance they gave to a particular cru and its propensity to produce unique wines.

92   Price B

Gattinara Galizja 2009

100% Nebbiolo grapes. Matures in durmast barrels. Intense garnet red. Chocolate and mint notes, then clear floral and eucalyptus notes. Wide on the palate, savory, with a nice tannins, compact structure and very persistent finish.

89   Price B

Gattinara 2010

100% Nebbiolo grapes. Matures in big durmast barrels. Light ruby red. Intense notes of fruits, watermelon and pomegranate, then red flowers. Rich on the palate, crunchy, relaxe drinkability and pleasant finish.

88   Price A

Colline Novaresi Vespolina 2012

100% Vespolina grapes. Stainless steel only. Bright ruby red color. The bouquet opens with elegant whiffs of spice and green tea leaves followed by scents small red berries and floral notes, above all miniature roses in a potpourri. The mouthfeel is extremely fresh, taut without ever losing its mellowness. Very good persistence in the finish.

287

★★

LA CAUDRINA

Strada Brosia, 21
12053 Castiglione Tinella (CN)
Tel. +39 0141 855126
romano@caudrina.it
www.caudrina.it
f *Moscato-dAsti-La-Caudrina*
y *@LaCaudrina*

YEAR OF FOUNDATION 1970
NAME OF THE OWNER Romano Dogliotti
TOTAL BOTTLES PRODUCED 200,000
DIRECT SALES
VISITS TO THE WINERY - RESERVATION NEEDED
HECTARES OF VINEYARD 30

Romano Dogliotti has for years been one of the great interpreters of Moscato d'Asti, a great wine that is horribly under-appreciated, even the best ones. And Galesia is one of these.

□ 91   👍 Price A
Asti Moscato La Galeisa 2015

100% Moscato Bianco di Canelli grapes. Sweet filtered. Light golden yellow. Very aromatic, fragrant and typical, classic notes of sage and Moscato grapes, then lime and hints of roses. Sweet flavor, carbonic hint in the entire body making agile and easy to drink.

□ 89   👍 Price A
Asti Moscato 2015

100% Moscato Bianco di Canelli grapes. Sweet filtered. Light golden yellow. Very fragrant and aromatic. Sage, rose, lime, cedar. Sweet and lively flavor, very pleasant and of average consistence.

LA COLOMBERA

S.C. per Vho, 7
15057 Tortona (AL)
Tel. +39 0131 867795
S *la.colomberavini*
info@lacolomberavini.it
www.lacolomberavini.it
f *La-Colombera-Vini*
y *@lacolombera*

YEAR OF FOUNDATION 1937
NAME OF THE OWNER Piercarlo ed Elisa Semino

TOTAL BOTTLES PRODUCED 70,000
DIRECT SALES
VISITS TO THE WINERY - RESERVATION NEEDED
HECTARES OF VINEYARD 20

The Semino family estate has carved out a place for itself in the Tortonese area of the province of Alessandria thanks to wines that are very well made and typical using grapes like Timorasso as well as Barbera and Croatina. Cultivating organically has added to the wine's ability to be expressive and the stylistic definition is the product of the tireless efforts of Pier Carlo and his daughter Elisa, the epitome of a 'mamma winemaker'.

□ 90   Price B
Colli Tortonesi Il Montino Timorasso 2014

100% Timorasso grapes. Stainless steel. Bright straw yellow. Despite the difficult vintage Il Monfortino is very expressive with peaty and thyme notes. Agile in the mouth, agile and savory with good length and a very briny finish.

■ 90   Price B
Colli Tortonesi Rosso Suciaja 2013

100% Nibiò (a sort of Dolcetto) grapes. Matures in barrique and stainless steel. Bright ruby red. Austere spicy and tobacco notes. Agile and juicy in the mouth with a nice, crunchy fruit and a cinchona and graphite finish.

□ 88   Price A
Colli Tortonesi Derthona Timorasso 2014

100% Timorasso grapes. Stainless steel. Bright straw yellow. Made with grapes coming from 4 different parcels this Derthona shows strong peaty and chalky notes. Thin and delicate in the mouth, average length and strong savory finish.

LA RAIA

Strada Monterotondo, 79
15067 Novi Ligure (AL)
Tel. +39 0143 743685
Fax +39 0143 320765
info@la-raia.it
www.la-raia.it
f *LaRaia.it*
y *@LaRaia_Gavi*

IL BOSCARETO

RESORT & SPA
★ ★ ★ ★ ★ L
SERRALUNGA D'ALBA

Away from ordinary,
close to your heart.

ADDING VALUE
TO YOUR
PACKAGING

Luxoro

K_GRAPHIC
bellezza & valore

LOENHARD KURZ EXCLUSIVE AGENT FOR THE ITALIAN MARKET

we taste and evaluate wines, we judge them from an organoleptic point of view, we are 'wine tasters'.

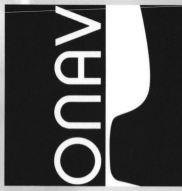

ORGANIZZAZIONE NAZIONA
ASSAGGIATORI DI VIN
The National Wine Tasters' Organizat

Discover your natural skills, learn to evaluate wines and become a **taster**

Sections in all Italian provinces
www.onav.it

WE WILL RECOGNIZE OUR 'FRIENDS' FROM A SIMPLE GESTURE

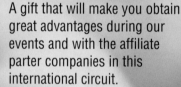

There is a new free card for DoctorWine friends.

A gift that will make you obtain great advantages during our events and with the affiliate parter companies in this international circuit.

Ask for it during our presentations or register using the following link.

http://friends.doctorwine.it

YEAR OF FOUNDATION 2003
NAME OF THE OWNER Giorgio Rossi Cairo
TOTAL BOTTLES PRODUCED 150,000
DIRECT SALES
VISITS TO THE WINERY - RESERVATION NEEDED
HECTARES OF VINEYARD 42
HOSPITALITY
CERTIFIED ORGANIC VITICULTURE
CERTIFIED BIODYNAMIC VITICULTURE

Giorgio Rossi Cairo bought the first vineyards at la Raia, in Novi Ligura, in the upper Gavi appellation area, in 2003 and in a few time it has made a lot of work. There's not only wine in his project but fruit production, vegetables and organic products. The entire estate is organic certified and for the wine production it's biodynamic. Coherent with this credo the farm hosts a Steiner school and a kindergarten.

☐ 91 Price A

Gavi 2015

100% Cortese grapes. Stainless steel. Greenish straw yellow. Really nice version of this apparently simple wine. Fragrant and fruity notes of lime, white peach and medical herbs. Tense, savory, discrete body, agile, very pleasant and delicious drinkability.

★★
LA SPINETTA

Via Annunziata, 17
14054 Castagnole Lanze (AT)
Tel. +39 0141 877396
info@la-spinetta.com
www.la-spinetta.com
 LaSpinetta.Italy
🐦 *@LaSpinettaItaly*

YEAR OF FOUNDATION 1977
NAME OF THE OWNER Bruno, Carlo and Giorgio Rivetti
TOTAL BOTTLES PRODUCED 450,000
DIRECT SALES
VISITS TO THE WINERY - RESERVATION NEEDED
HECTARES OF VINEYARD 100

The Rivetti brothers have one of the most important wineries in Asti and Piedmont in general. Initially, they produced Moscato d'Asti and Barbera, which they continue to do with excellent results, and then they became wine entrepreneurs acquiring vineyards in Langhe, first in Barbaresco and then in Barolo, and Tuscany, in the province of Pisa. They produce wines with a modern style, so much so that Giorgio Rivetti, who runs the winery with his brothers Carlo and Bruno, is considered one of the leaders of the so-called 'modernists' in the Langhe.

■ 94 Price D
Barolo Campè 2012

100% Nebbiolo grapes. Matures 2 years in barrique. Intense garnet ruby red. A very modern style Barolo much loved by American critics. Fruity notes, clear aromas of plum, yellow peach and black cherry over spicy notes of vanilla and smoky hints. Powerful taste, great body, made agile by the good acidity, savory, warm, very long.

■ 93 Price B
Barbera d'Asti Superiore Bionzo 2013

100% Barbera grapes. Matures 18 months in barrique. Intense and lively ruby red. Smoky and spicy hints, then black cherry, yellow peach and violet. Tense flavor, great personality, warm, savory, well sustained by acidity which makes it neat and even elegant. Very long finish.

■ 90 Price B
Barbera d'Asti Ca' di Pian 2012

100% Barbera grapes. Matures 1 year in used barrique. Very intense ruby. Notes of black cherry, plum, vanilla and slightly smoky hints. Enveloping and warm in the mouth, savory, full-bodied, rich and very persistent.

LE CECCHE

Via Moglia Gerlotto, 10
12055 Diano D'alba (CN)
Tel. +39 0173 69 323
🅢 *lececche*
lececche@libero.it
www.lececche.it

YEAR OF FOUNDATION 2001
NAME OF THE OWNER Jan De Bruyne and Paola Invrea
TOTAL BOTTLES PRODUCED 38,000
DIRECT SALES
VISITS TO THE WINERY - RESERVATION NEEDED
HECTARES OF VINEYARD 5.5
HOSPITALITY

289

Diano d'Alba is a small village with wine land extending into the Barolo appellation, although it is above all known for its Dolcetto. In 2001, the Marengo family sold it to Jan De Bruyne and the Marchioness Paola Invrea. He is a Belgian physician with an infinite passion for Italy (before the Langhe he lived in Castellina in Chianti), while she is an aristocrat from the 'magical' city of Turin. In total the estate has 5.5 hectares of vineyards that are in different locations. This includes one in Bossolasco, at an altitude of some 750m above sea level, planted with Riesling, the latest fad in the Langhe. In 2010, they bought a vineyard of Nebbiolo in the zone of Sorano in Serralunga, while the latest acquisition was a vineyard in Grinzane Cavour in 2014, purchased to improve their vintage Barolo.

 94　　　　　　　　　　　　　　　　**Price B**

Barolo Sorano 2012

100% Nebbiolo grapes. Matures 2 years in barrique and tonneau. Clear garnet ruby red. Surprisingly classic aromas of tamarind, plum, licorice and mint. Near and elegant in the mouth, thin and thick tannins, warm, savory, typical and very persistent.

★

LE PIANE

Via Cerri, 10
28010 Boca (NO)
Tel. +39 348 3354185
Fax +41 338470007
info@bocapiane.com
www.bocapiane.com
 bocapiane
 @LePianeBoca

YEAR OF FOUNDATION **1998**
NAME OF THE OWNER **Christoph Künzli**
TOTAL BOTTLES PRODUCED **13,000**
DIRECT SALES
VISITS TO THE WINERY - RESERVATION NEEDED
HECTARES OF VINEYARD **14**
HOSPITALITY

It took the arrival of Cristoph Kunzli from Switzerland to demonstrate to the world the extraordinary potential of Boca. Not the Argentinian soccer team Boca Juniors but a fantastic red wine made mostly with Nebbiolo with a small addition of Vespolina. It is a wine that can

easily represent for Italy and Piedmont what the great Burgundy reds are for France. The estate is in northern Piedmont, in the province of Novara. If you are not careful, the harmony and elegance of a great Boca Le Piane, the latest is an excellent vintage, you could might think it came from Gevrey-Chambertin.

 93　　　　　　　　　　　　　　　　**Price C**

Boca 2012

Blend of 75% Nebbiolo and 15% Vespolina grapes. Matures 3 years in tonneau and big barrels. Intense garnet red. Expressive and whole aroms of wild strawberries, even in aspic, rosehip, slight Maraschino, then hints of vanilla. The taste is neat, warm, smooth, tense, savory, with thick but elegant tannins, nice body and very long finish.

★

MALVIRÀ

Via Case Sparse, 144 - Località Canova
12043 Canale (CN)
Tel. +39 0173 978145
malvira@malvira.com
www.malvira.com
 malvirawinery

YEAR OF FOUNDATION **1982**
NAME OF THE OWNER **Massimo and Roberto Damonte**
TOTAL BOTTLES PRODUCED **340,000**
DIRECT SALES
VISITS TO THE WINERY - RESERVATION NEEDED
HECTARES OF VINEYARD **42**
HOSPITALITY

The estate of brothers Massimo and Roberto Damonte has for some time been one of the top ones for producing Roero. Malvirà has vineyards in some of the most interesting cru of the appellation: Mombeltramo, Renesio, Saglietto, San Michele and Trinità. The vineyards are in the process of becoming organic, the result of research to enhance the value of the land. This goal has included creating excellent hospitality facilities including the Villa Tiboldi relais hotel.

 92　　　　　　　　　　　　　　　　**Price B**

Roero Renesio Riserva 2012

100% Nebbiolo grapes. Matures in new and used barrique. Red with orange hues. Complex notes of violet, cinchona, tobacco and wet soil. Rich in the mouth, still austere but with elegant and juicy tannins with a fresh and earthy finish.

 90   Price B
Roero Trinità Riserva 2012

100% Nebbiolo grapes. Matures in new and used barrique. Red with orange hues. Notes of spices and tobacco. Full structure, juicy with pulpy tannins and a fresh, long, eucalyptus finish.

 88   Price B
Roero Mombeltramo Riserva 2012

100% Nebbiolo grapes. Matures in new and used barrique. Red with orange hues. Notes of flowers and blond tobacco. Thin, smooth, delicate tannins and a good outstretched finish.

★★
MARCARINI

Piazza Martiri, 2
12064 La Morra (CN)
Tel. +39 0173 50222
Fax +39 0173 509035
marcarini@marcarini.it
www.marcarini.it
 Poderi-Marcarini-AzAgr
 @marcariniagrit

YEAR OF FOUNDATION 1961
NAME OF THE OWNER Anna Marcarini Bava
TOTAL BOTTLES PRODUCED 17,000
DIRECT SALES
VISITS TO THE WINERY - RESERVATION NEEDED
HECTARES OF VINEYARD 25
HOSPITALITY

The historic estate of Luisa and Manuel Marchetti has vineyards in the cru of Brunate, La Serra and Boschi di Berri. The first two produce elegant Barolo that ages long, while the last produces an incredibly captivating Dolcetto d'Alba from vines that are over 100 years old and have never been grafted.

 91   Price B
Barolo Brunate 2012

100% Nebbiolo grapes. Matures 2 years in big barrels. Intense garnet red. Very classic notes, even evolved, with carob, tobacco, sweet spices and light smoky hints. Elegant taste, average body, thick

tannins and little drying and youthful and a long enveloping finish.

 88   Price A
Dolcetto d'Alba Boschi di Berri 2013

100% Dolcetto grapes. Stainless steel. Violet ruby red. Fragrant, fruity, typical and simple, notes of blackberry and raspberry, fermentative hints. Fresh flavor, savory, pleasant, warm and with good tension.

MARCHESI ALFIERI

Piazza Alfieri, 28
14010 San Martino Alfieri (AT)
Tel. +39 0141 976015
Fax +39 0141 976288
info@marchesialfieri.it
www.marchesialfieri.it
 marchesialfieri

YEAR OF FOUNDATION 1985
NAME OF THE OWNER Giovanna, Antonella ed Emanuela San Martino
TOTAL BOTTLES PRODUCED 100,000
DIRECT SALES
VISITS TO THE WINERY - RESERVATION NEEDED
HECTARES OF VINEYARD 21
HOSPITALITY

Perhaps because it is because the estate is owned by women, but the fact is that here Barbera, a female name, reaches its peak. The estate is in San Martino Alfieri, the last town in Asti before you enter Roero, in Govone. It is a meeting place for the Barbera's various personalities which Alfieri synthesizes with class into a great, authoritative and indisputable wine.

 90   Price B
Barbera d'Asti Superiore Alfiera 2013

100% Barbera grapes. Matures 18 months in barrique. Dark and intense ruby red. Violet, vanilla, currant and blackberry compose the aromatic profile. Tense flavor, acidulous, with some youthful edge and a very persistent finish.

 85   Price A
Barbera d'Asti La Tota 2014

100% Barbera grapes. Matures 12 months in used barrique and tonneau. Fruity, notes of currant, blood orange and plum. Tense flavor, strong, acidulous and a little edgy. Discrete persistence.

MARCHESI DI BAROLO

Via Roma, 1
12060 Barolo (CN)
Tel. +39 0173 564491
Fax +39 0173 564419
reception@marchesibarolo.com
www.marchesibarolo.com
🅕 marchesidibarolo
🐦 @MarchesiBarolo

YEAR OF FOUNDATION **1807**
NAME OF THE OWNER **Abbona Family**
TOTAL BOTTLES PRODUCED **1,500,000**
DIRECT SALES
VISITS TO THE WINERY - RESERVATION NEEDED
HECTARES OF VINEYARD **195**
RESTAURANT

The novelty this year for this famous and historic Barolo winery is the production of Barbaresco. this was possible thanks to the acquisition from Carlo Balbo of Cascina Bruciata, a tiny yet prestigious estate that is almost 150 years old and has two hectares of vineyards in the cru of Rio Sordo, one of the most important in the area. The Abbona family could not have chosen a better way initiate Barbaresco production.

---

 96   Price C

Barbaresco Rio Sordo Cascina Bruciata Riserva 2011

100% Nebbiolo grapes. Matures 2 years in barrique and 1 in concrete vats. Intense garnet ruby red. Varied notes of Kirsch, black cherry, blackberry, violet and a smoky hint in the background. Full and elegant taste, savory, neat tannins, refined, great body, enveloping and with a spectacular length.

■ **94**   Price C

Barolo Cannubi 2012

100% Nebbiolo grapes. Matures 2 years in different size barrels. Intense garnet ruby red. Thing and whole fruity notes, modern but not modernist style, light smoky note then violet and currant. Savory and tense taste, neat tannins, delicate, very thin, elegant profile, good body and splendid finish of great length.

■ **93**   Price C

Barolo Sarmassa 2012

100% Nebbiolo grapes. Matures 2 years in different size barrels. Intense garnet ruby red. Very fruity notes of plum, cherry, black cherry, then spices and a smoky note for a modern style aromatic profile. Savory in the mouth, with some youthful edgy tannin, then warm and of good length.

■ **91**   Price B

Barolo del Comune di Barolo 2012

100% Nebbiolo grapes. Matures 2 years in different size barrels. Intense ruby red. Very fruity, cherry, black cherry and blackberry for a very complete aromatic profile. Neat and elegant taste, thick and outstretched tannins, warm, savory and persistent.

CLAUDIO MARIOTTO

Strada per Sarezzano, 29
15057 Tortona (AL)
Tel. +39 0131 868500
Fax +39 0131 868500
info@claudiomariotto.it
www.claudiomariotto.it
🅕 Claudio-Mariotto-Vignaiolo-in-Vhò

YEAR OF FOUNDATION **1920**
NAME OF THE OWNER **Claudio Mariotto**
TOTAL BOTTLES PRODUCED **50,000**
DIRECT SALES
VISITS TO THE WINERY - RESERVATION NEEDED
HECTARES OF VINEYARD **26**

The Timorasso 'clan' is composed of a half a dozen winegrowers who operate around Tortona, in the extreme southeast corner of Piedmont near the border with Oltrepò. They are all friends and all produce Timorasso, a full-bodied white made with grapes of the same name that is having a small but important success. Claudio Mariotto is its happy winemaker.

☐ **93**   Price B

Colli Tortonesi Pitasso 2013

100% Timorasso grapes. Stainless steel on the yeasts for 1 year. Intense straw yellow. Very articulated notes of flint, then medlar, medical herbs and wildflowers. Warm and savory taste, good body, enveloping and tense, glycerin, great persistence.

Price A

Colli Tortonesi Derthona Timorasso 2014

100% Timorasso grapes. Stainless steel on the yeasts. Intense straw yellow. Slightly smoky in the nose, then medlar, yeallow peach and wildflowers. Warm taste, savory, good acidity and agile. Adequate persistent finish.

FRANCO M. MARTINETTI

Corso Turati, 14
12128 Torino (TO)
Tel. +39 011 8395937
Fax +39 011 8106598
info@francomartinetti.it
www.francomartinetti.it
f *francomartinettivinicultore*

YEAR OF FOUNDATION 1974
NAME OF THE OWNER Franco Maria Martinetti
TOTAL BOTTLES PRODUCED 140,000
DIRECT SALES
VISITS TO THE WINERY - RESERVATION NEEDED
HECTARES OF VINEYARD 5

A great gourmet, television celebrity and eleveur of great wines, he select grapes from vineyards, with the assistance of his sons Guido and Michele, the way a great chef would select his ingredients. The result are wine pearls from the best area of Piedmont, from Barolo, Asti, Gavi and Colli Tortonesi, examples of which follow.

 Price C

Barolo Marasco 2011

100% Nebbiolo grapes. Matures 2 years in barrique. Intense garnet ruby red. Enveloping, ethereal, spicy, notes of vanilla and cardamom, then black cherry and plums. Warm taste, tense, savory, great body and good acidity. Long and persistent finish.

 Price B

Sul Bric 2012

Blend of 50% Barbera and 50% Cabernet Sauvignon grapes. Matures 18 months in barrique. Dark ruby red. Eucalyptus notes and spicy, intense, enveloping, good articulation. Strong flavor, slightly tannic but already elegant, youthful, warm, savory and long.

 92 **Price B**

Barbera d'Asti Superiore Montruc 2012

100% Barbera grapes. Matures 18 month in barrique. Lively ruby red. Notes of Mon Cherie, sweet spices and underbrush, ethereal, enveloping, typical. Savory and tense, nice body, pleasant drinkability, good warm and persistent finish.

■ 88 **Price A**

Barbera d'Asti Bric dei Banditi 2014

100% Barbera grapes. Matures in concrete vats for almost 1 year. Intense and lively ruby red. Very fruity and fragrant, notes of black cherry and violets, some fermentative hints. Tense and acidulous taste, average body, great drinkability.

★★

GIUSEPPE MASCARELLO & FIGLIO

Strada del Grosso, 1
12060 Castiglione Falletto (CN)
Tel. +39 0173 792126
mauromascarello@mascarello1881.com
www.mascarello1881.com
f *MascarelloGiuseppe*

YEAR OF FOUNDATION 1881
NAME OF THE OWNER Mauro Mascarello
TOTAL BOTTLES PRODUCED 60,000
DIRECT SALES
VISITS TO THE WINERY - RESERVATION NEEDED
HECTARES OF VINEYARD 12.5

Tasting Mauro Mascarello's wines is always an emotional experience. Year after year, true to a traditions from dawn of time, he is able to offer stupendous sensations with wines that are small masterpieces. He has always been linked with the Monprivato vineyard and is able to express its essence in a prodigious way, developing a theme that become the object of admiration of the whole world of wine. And if Monprivato is a magical name, Ca' D'Morissio is a legend, the quintessence of this monument of fine drinking. As all great wines, it has to be waited for and the 2010 vintage, won't be releasad soon.

■ 96 **Price D**

Barolo Monprivato 2011

100% Nebbiolo grapes. Matures in big barrels.

Lively but not very concentrated red. Impressive aromatic profile, complex, great flowery expressions: roses, violets and gerbera. Then currant and black cherry, delicious eucalyptus puffs and strong spiciness. Wine, vigorous palate with strong but never aggressive tannins. Exceptional persistence.

94   Price C
Barolo Perno Vigna Santo Stefano 2011

100% Nebbiolo grapes. Matures in big barrels. Relatively deep red. It's the most unique wine produce by this winery, with attractive licorice notes and bark, extremely minty with hints of bitter cocoa. Powerful, structured and of great impact in the mouth. Very long finish.

93   Price C
Barolo Villero 2011

100% Nebbiolo grapes. Matures in big barrels. Light and bright red. The aromatic profile is played on elegance, notes of raspberry jam, currant jelly, pomegranate. Extremely elegant flowers, thin and fresh tannic structure. Far from austerity.

88   Price A
Langhe Freisa Toetto 2013

100% Freisa grapes. Matures 36 months in big barrels. Deep red. Fruity aromas with still some slightly grapes notes, it's characterized by a very pleasant spiciness. The mouth is not blended in, savory, good energy.

★★★
BARTOLO MASCARELLO

Via Roma, 19
12060 Barolo (CN)
Tel. +39 0173 56125
Fax +39 0173 560826

YEAR OF FOUNDATION 1918
NAME OF THE OWNER Maria Teresa Mascarello
TOTAL BOTTLES PRODUCED 30,000
DIRECT SALES
VISITS TO THE WINERY - RESERVATION NEEDED
HECTARES OF VINEYARD 5

There are some wineries that are one in the same with their winemaker and this is one of them. Bartolo Mascarello was a great rural intellectual who did not found this small winery but created its soul and who became an authentic maître à penser for winemaking in the Langhe from the 1960s up until his death.

Fortunately, sometimes there are people capable of continuing the work of great people and this is a case in point. Bartolo's daughter Maria Teresa Mascarello may not have the charisma of her father but her wines are equally as good, perhaps in some cases better in regard to consistency.

97   Price D
Barolo 2012

100% Nebbiolo grapes. Matures over 2 years in big barrels. Bright garnet red. Extremely typical notes of violet, black cherry, Kirsch, pomegranate and currant. Smoky hints in the background. Exceptional personality in the mouth, tense, savory, thick but not aggressive tannins, warm, velvety and of incredible persistence.

92   Price B
Barbera d'Alba 2013

100% Barbera grapes. Matures 18 months in big barrels. Very typical, notes of violets, black cherry and Kirsch. Savory and tense taste, warm, slightly tannic, great body and long persistence.

91   👍 Price A
Dolcetto d'Alba 2014

100% Dolcetto grapes. Matures 10 months in big barrels. Violet ruby. Fruity and fragrant notes of violet, cassis and slight smoky hint, fermentative. Good structure in the mouth, warm, savory, easy to drink and good persistent finish.

★★★
MASSOLINO

Piazza Cappellano, 8
12050 Serralunga D'Alba (CN)
Tel. +39 0173 613138
Fax +39 0173 613949
massolino@massolino.it
www.massolino.it
 MassolinoVignaRionda
 @MassolinoWinery

YEAR OF FOUNDATION 1896
NAME OF THE OWNER Fratelli Massolino
TOTAL BOTTLES PRODUCED 150,000
DIRECT SALES
VISITS TO THE WINERY - RESERVATION NEEDED
HECTARES OF VINEYARD 23

Brothers Franco and Roberto Massolino appear to have succeeded in giving their estate a style which could be seen as putting a square peg in a round hole. Without betraying a long tradition of macerating long on the skins and using medium and large barrels, they have been able to capture the extraordinary essences of the cru of Serralunga and, more recently, Parusi in Montforte d'Alba. This have also shown great skill and modesty in surrounding themselves with a team of young and talented collaborators who have brought out even more of this estate's extraordinary potential. The result is that their whole line of production is among the absolute best in the Langhe and Italy.

info@massuccovini.com
www.massuccovini.com
 massuccowine
@massuccowine

YEAR OF FOUNDATION 1908
NAME OF THE OWNER Fratelli Massucco
TOTAL BOTTLES PRODUCED 150,000
DIRECT SALES
VISITS TO THE WINERY - RESERVATION NEEDED
HECTARES OF VINEYARD 20
RESTAURANT

A winery of ancient traditions that in recent years made a decisive shift towards producing quality Roero wines. While they produce many wines they are now hosting visits to the winery with tours that that are also educational. Next to the estate's headquarters is the family restaurant that offers classic Piedmont cuisine and Massucco Winne Wellness Center.

■ 🇪 95   Price C
Barolo Parafada 2012

100% Nebbiolo grapes. Matures in big barrels. Bright ruby red. Strong notes of spices and licorice. Dense in the mouth, juicy with clean acidity, smooth tannins and a deep still reserved finish. A great version in a not easy vintage.

■ 93   Price C
Barolo Vigna Rionda Riserva 2010

100% Nebbiolo grapes. Matures in big barrels. It's an important vintage in and Vigna Rionda doesn't disappoint the expectative. Slightly light ruby red. Classic notes of aromatic herbs together with spices and violets. Powerful structure in the mouth, strong tannins but in a very balanced frame. Sweet tannins and it's proverbial depth close the circle.

■ 92   Price C
Barolo Margheria 2012

100% Nebbiolo grapes. Matures in big barrels. Bright ruby red. Blond tobacco and macerated cherry introduce an outstretched palate with elegant tannins. Tense finish, pleasant and of good length.

■ 88   Price B
Barolo 2010

100% Nebbiolo grapes. Matures in big barrels. Bright ruby red. Already very pleasant with delicate notes of spices and aromatic herbs. Full, tonic and pleasant to drink.

MASSUCCO

Via Serra, 21/c - Località San Giuseppe
12050 Castagnito (CN)
Tel. +39 0173 211121

■ 92   Price B
Roero Riserva 2012

100% Nebbiolo grapes. Matures 20 months in barrique. Intense garnet ruby red. Smoky notes, then violet, black cherry and hints of spices. Strong flavor, important tannins, almost Barolo style, youthful, good body, warm, enveloping and long, persistent finish.

MAURO MOLINO

Frazione Annunziata Gancia, 111a
12064 La Morra (CN)
Tel. +39 0173 50814
Fax +39 0173 500035
info@mauromolino.com
www.mauromolino.com
 mauromolinowinery

YEAR OF FOUNDATION 1953
NAME OF THE OWNER Mauro, Matteo and Martina Molino
TOTAL BOTTLES PRODUCED 70,000
DIRECT SALES
VISITS TO THE WINERY - RESERVATION NEEDED
HECTARES OF VINEYARD 12

For many years now Mauro Molino has been making wines with the grapes he used to sell to others. Thanks to the excellent exposure of his vineyards and his great skill, Mauro has achieved significant success especially abroad.

 93 — Price C

Barolo Bricco Luciani 2012

100% Nebbiolo grapes. Matures 18 months in barrique. Intense garnet ruby red. The aromatic profile is dominated by notes of cassis, spices and flowery hints, for a strongly modern style. Velvety taste, pleasant and warm, neat tannins, nice body, elegant and great length.

★

MONCHIERO CARBONE

Via S. Stefano Roero, 2
12073 Canale (CN)
Tel. +39 0173 95568
Fax +39 0173 959063
 Francesco.Moncherio
info@monchierocarbone.it
www.monchierocarbone.com
 Monchiero-Carbone

YEAR OF FOUNDATION **1990**
NAME OF THE OWNER **Francesco Monchiero**
TOTAL BOTTLES PRODUCED **180,000**
DIRECT SALES
VISITS TO THE WINERY - RESERVATION NEEDED
HECTARES OF VINEYARD **15**

Francesco Monchiero is not only the heir of one of the historic families of Canale, he is also a tireless promotors of the Roero appellation. His estate has some of the most beautiful cru of the Canale district including Printi, Monbirone and Renesio, as well as vineyards in Vezza d'Alba for his whites and Pricco for Barbera. The wines are very expressive and have a definite, technical style that respects the characteristics of the grapes and the individual cru.

 95 — Price B

Roero Printi Riserva 2012

100% Nebbiolo grapes. Matures in barrique. 2012 vintage demonstrates to be a really good vintage for Printi. Dark ruby red. Enveloping notes of cinchona, spices and tobacco.Powerful and very mineral with compact but elegant and juicy tannins. Tense and tasty finish.

92 — Price B

Roero Srü 2013

100% Nebbiolo grapes. Matures in barrique. Bright ruby red. The sandy soil of this vineyard expresses clear notes of flowers and spices. Powerful but elegant in the mouth with very thin tannins. Tense, gritty and austere finish.

☐ **90** — Price B

Roero Arneis Cecu d'la Biunda 2015

100% Arneis grapes. Stainelss steel. Straw yellow with golden hues. The Cecu doesn't suffer the warm vintage, strong notes of white peach and pepper and a powerful volume but fresh and balanced at the same time. Long, austere and tasty finish.

90 — Price B

Barbera d'Alba Mombirone 2013

100% Barbera grapes. Matures in barrique. One of the best versions of this Barbera. Bright ruby red. Graphite, spices and small black berries open to a pulpy, powerful but dynamic finish. Very tense finish.

MONTALBERA

Via Montalbera, 1
14030 Castagnole Monferrato (AT)
Tel. +39 011 9433311
Fax +39 011 9434289
montalbera@montalbera.it
www.montalbera.it
 montalbera

YEAR OF FOUNDATION **1980**
NAME OF THE OWNER **Morando Family**
TOTAL BOTTLES PRODUCED **525,000**
DIRECT SALES
VISITS TO THE WINERY - RESERVATION NEEDED
HECTARES OF VINEYARD **170**

The Morando family estate was created in the 1980s when they began to make important acquisitions, something they continue to do. They now have over 170 hectares of vineyards divided between two Piedmont appellations, Monferrato and Langhe. Here we focused on the Monferrato one and on an indigenous varietal that the Morando is using with particular skill: Ruchè. The estate has 80 hectares of this variety, the largest part of the entire appellation.

92   Price B

Ruchè di Castagnole Monferrato Limpronta 2014

100% Ruché grapes. Matures in wood. Light ruby red with garnet hues. Complex version of this wine. Very intense aromatic profile with warmer notes of spices. Thick structure but great persistence and drinkability.

91   👍 Price A

Ruchè di Castagnole Monferrato Laccento 2015

100% Ruché grapes, partially overripe. Stainless steel. Intense ruby red. Explosive notes, attractive with notes of roses, orange peel, also candied, then intense notes pink and black pepper. Very pleasant, relaxed structure, suading, very pleasing. A tiny jem to serve slightly fresh.

FIORENZO NADA

Via Ausario, 12c
12050 Treiso (CN)
Tel. +39 0173 638254
nadafiorenzo@nada.it
www.nada.it

YEAR OF FOUNDATION 1982
NAME OF THE OWNER Bruno Nada
TOTAL BOTTLES PRODUCED 40,000
DIRECT SALES
VISITS TO THE WINERY - RESERVATION NEEDED
HECTARES OF VINEYARD 7

Bruno Nada, the son of Fiorenzo who founded the winery, produces elegant and modern Barbera from the Rombone and Manzola vineyards in Tresio. The first, that surrounds the winery, gives complex wines that age for long, the second elegant ones. The vignards are on slope hills at about 250 meters above sea level, where they grow not only Nebbiolo but Barbera and Dolcetto as well.

 95   Price B

Barbaresco Rombone 2012

100% Nebbiolo grapes. Matures in 25% new barrique. One of the best 2012 from Langhe ever tasted. Bright ruby red. Intense notes of spices and flowers. Full in the mouth, but dynamic, compact and of good freshness with a very tonic finish.

 92   Price B

Barbaresco Manzola 2012

100% Nebbiolo grapes. Matures in different size barrels. Bright ruby red. Outstretched and clear spicy notes. Fruity and vigorous in the mouth with smooth tannins and a convincing finish.

91   Price B

Langhe Rosso Seifile 2012

Blend of 80% Barbera and 20% Nebbiolo grapes. Matures in barrique. Bright ruby red. A lot of fruit and spices in the nose that we find again in the mouth, rich and pulpy, maybe it only lacks the usual propulsion.

90   👍 Price A

Dolcetto d'Alba 2015

100% Dolcetto grapes. Stainless steel. Violet ruby red. Delicious integrity in the nose, very fruity, notes of strawberry, blueberry and black currant on slightly fermentative hints. Savory, intriguing drinkability, pleasant, warm, extremely typical. It makes you think that Treiso deserves a specific DOC for his Dolcetto just like Dogliano or Diano.

ANGELO E FIGLI NEGRO

Frazione Sant'Anna, 1
12040 Monteu Roero (CN)
Tel. +39 0173 90252
negro@negroangelo.it
www.negroangelo.it
 negroangeloefigli
 @NEGROROERO

YEAR OF FOUNDATION 1670
NAME OF THE OWNER Giovanni Negro
TOTAL BOTTLES PRODUCED 350,000
DIRECT SALES
VISITS TO THE WINERY - RESERVATION NEEDED
HECTARES OF VINEYARD 60

Giovanni Negro is a leader figure in Roero. His family has been making since since the 17th century while he for years was the mayor of Monteu Roero. He carries on his family's centuries- old winemaking tradition with some very interesting wines made with a cautiously innovative style using with grapes from Roero as well as Barbaresco, which is right across the Tanaro River.

■ 91   Price B
Roero Sudisfà Riserva 2012
100% Nebbiolo grapes. Matures in different size barrels. Bright ruby red. Elegant notes of spices and flowers. Pulpy in the mouth, thin, fresh with silky tannins and a deep, dynamic finish.

■ 90   Price B
Barbaresco Basarin Riserva 2011
100% Nebbiolo grapes. Matures in different size barrels. Bright ruby red. Thin aromatic profile with notes of flowers and licorice. Coherent in the mouth, delicate with a graphite and aromatic herbs finish.

■ 90   Price B
Roero San Bernardo Riserva 2012
100% Nebbiolo grapes. Matures in different size barrels. Bright ruby red. Expressive notes of spices and flowers. On the palate it has good volume, delicate tannins and a particularly expressive finish.

☐ 86   Price A
Roero Arneis Perdaudin 2015
100% Arneis grapes. Stainless steel. Bright straw yellow. Delicately flowery in the nose with hawthorn aromas. Agile in the moth, fruity and with a tense and savory finish.

NERVI

*Corso Vercelli, 117
13045 Gattinara (VC)
Tel. +39 0163 833228
Fax +39 0163 825746
info@nervicantine.it
www.nervicantine.it*
f *NerviCantine*

YEAR OF FOUNDATION 1906
NAME OF THE OWNER Astrup Family & Co.
TOTAL BOTTLES PRODUCED 100,000
DIRECT SALES
VISITS TO THE WINERY - RESERVATION NEEDED
HECTARES OF VINEYARD 25

This historic estate is over 100 years and, above all, is one of the most important for Gattinara. It produces very traditional wines that macerate long on the skins and age long in large barrels.

■ 92   Price B
Gattinara Valferana 2009
100% Nebbiolo grapes. Matures 4 years in big barrels. Intense garnet red. Enveloping and ethereal notes of carub, wild strawberries and thyme. Warm flavor, rich, enveloping, good body but agile and tense by acidity, neat tannins and great long finish.

ANDREA OBERTO

*Borgata Simane, 11
12064 La Morra (CN)
Tel. +39 0173 50104
Fax +39 0173 500994
obertoandrea@libero.it
www.andreaoberto.com*

YEAR OF FOUNDATION 1978
NAME OF THE OWNER Andrea Oberto
TOTAL BOTTLES PRODUCED 100,000
DIRECT SALES
VISITS TO THE WINERY - RESERVATION NEEDED
HECTARES OF VINEYARD 16

The Barolo of Andrea Oberto, as well as all his wines, are a sure bet. He is a down-to-earth, authentic winemaker and while he may use large barrels as opposed to barrique, the difference is not much. The comprehensible style does not disguise origins nor does not seek to dazzle.

■ 93   Price C
Barolo Rocche dell'Annunziata 2012
100% Nebbiolo grapes. Matures 2 years in barrique and big barrels. Intense garnet ruby red. Violets and smoky hints define the thin and elegant, spicy and modern aromatic profile. Neat flavor, already blended in tannins, good body, great persistent finish.

■ 88   Price A
Dolcetto d'Alba 2015
100% Dolcetto grapes. Stainless steel. Violet ruby red. One of the 'house specialties'. Typical fragrant notes, simple and neat notes of violets and wild berries. Warm flavor, powerful but pleasing and pleasant drinkability, with an enveloping and savory finish.

★★
ODDERO

Frazione S. Maria, 28
12064 La Morra (CN)
Tel. +39 0173 50618
Fax +39 0173 509377
info@oddero.it
www.oddero.it
 Oddero-Poderi-e-Cantine
 @oddero

YEAR OF FOUNDATION 1878
NAME OF THE OWNER Oddero Family
TOTAL BOTTLES PRODUCED 150,000
DIRECT SALES
VISITS TO THE WINERY - RESERVATION NEEDED
HECTARES OF VINEYARD 35

Mariacristina and Mariavittoria Oddero are the heirs of a family winemaking tradition that dates back to the later 19th century. They are also the custodians of a classic, traditional style that imposes long macerations on the skins and the use of big barrels. This means that their Barolo are bold and have a capacity to age long and need time to evolve to perfection. Starting with vintage 2006, their cru Vigna Rionda in Serralunga ages many years in the cellar before going to market. Their other wines age for four to five years, be they from crus like Brunate in La Morra or those from Villero and Rocche di Castiglione.

---

 93   Price C
Barolo Villero 2012

100% Nebbiolo grapes. Matures 30 months in big barrels. Lively and intense ruby red. Complex aromatic profile with notes of Kirsch, violets, black cherry and light tobacco. Savory and agile taste, neat tannins, elegant body, not enormous but thin, nice, balanced and persistent finish.

---

 92   Price C
Barolo Bussia Vigna Mondoca Riserva 2010

100% Nebbiolo grapes. Matures 3 years in big barrels. Lively garnet ruby red. Enveloping and slightly evolved notes of tamarind, wet soil and licorice. Much better in the mouth, tense, with personality savory, outstretched and elegant tannins, full-bodied and very persistent.

---

 91   Price C
Barolo Rocche di Castiglione Falletto 2012

100% Nebbiolo grapes. Matures 30 months in big barrels. Lively and intense ruby red. Initially some smoky hints then spices and ripe red fruits. Savory flavor, well sustained by acidity, slightly woody and youthful tannins, great long and persistent finish.

★★
OLIM BAUDA

Località Regione Prata, 50
14045 Incisa Scapaccino (AT)
Tel. +39 0141 702171
Fax +39 0141 702171
info@tenutaolimbauda.it
www.tenutaolimbauda.it
 Tenuta-Olim-Bauda
 @tenutaolimbauda

YEAR OF FOUNDATION 1961
NAME OF THE OWNER Dino, Diana and Gianni Bertolino
TOTAL BOTTLES PRODUCED 120,000
DIRECT SALES
VISITS TO THE WINERY - RESERVATION NEEDED
HECTARES OF VINEYARD 90

Siblings Diana, Gianni and Dino Bertolino are the fourth generation of their family to work the vineyards. And these are very beautiful vineyards that are cultivated in a sustainable way in the heart of Asti. For all wine-lovers Olim Bauda means great Barbera.

---

  96   Price B
Barbera d'Asti Superiore Nizza 2013

100% Barbera grapes. Matures 18 months in barrique. Intense and dark violet ruby red. Great impact and elegance in the nose with intense notes of red fruits, Kirsch, maple juice, slight smoky and eucalyptus hints. A champion on the palate with thick structure, elegant tannins and very savory that give it an incredible progression and great drinkability that results in a wonderful finish.

---

 85   Price A
Barbera d'Asti Superiore Le Rocchette 2014

100% Barbera grapes. Matures 15 months in 25 hl barrels. Bright ruby red. Fresh and intense notes *of cherry, light maple syrup, very fragrant. Great drinkability, thanks to its lively acidity and a compact but neat structure. Savory finish.*

ORSOLANI

Via Michele Chiesa, 12
10090 San Giorgio Canavese (TO)
Tel. +39 0124 32386
Fax +39 0124 450342
info@orsolani.it
www.orsolani.it
OrsolaniWine

YEAR OF FOUNDATION **1894**
NAME OF THE OWNER **Orsolani Gian Luigi**
TOTAL BOTTLES PRODUCED **150,000**
DIRECT SALES
VISITS TO THE WINERY
HECTARES OF VINEYARD **15**

For almost 120 years, four generations of the Orsolani family has made wine with great respect for and ties with the land and distinguished by an avant-garde, pioneering spirit to develop Erbaluce, a varietal that is not easy to cultivate but is expressively versatile. In the 1960s, father Gian Luigi Orsolani was already making sparkling Caluso wine and with the dry Rustia enhanced the territorial tradition of making Passito dessert wine with nuances from the varietals Caluso, Mazzé and San Giorgio.

🔳 **94**   **Price B**
Erbaluce di Caluso Passito Sulé 2009
*100% Erbaluce di Caluso grapes traditionally vinified in wood. Deep golden yellow. Sweet and solar notes of apricots, candied tangerine, saffron, jasmine, figs and dates. Sweet and soft in the moth, fresh and outstretched, very long and vibrant finish. *37.5 cl bottle.*

🔲 **93**   👍 **Price A**
Erbaluce di Caluso La Rustia 2015
100% Erbaluce di Caluso grapes vinified in stainless steel. Bright straw yellow. Notes of anise, almonds and white plums, sage and a touch of iodine and chalk. Sweet and savory in the mouth, long and tasty, nice acidity and pleasant notes of aromatic herbs, tonic, long and persistent finish with aromas of grapefruit.

🔲 **87**   **Price A**
Caluso Spumante Brut Cuvée Tradizione 2011
100% Erbaluce di Caluso grapes vinified part in wood and part in stainless steel on the yeasts for 60 months. Bright straw yellow, very thin perlage. Fruity notes, bread crust, honey and dry fruits. Pleasant on the palate with delicate freshness and a hay finish.

⭐

PAITIN

Via Serra Boella, 20
12052 Neive (CN)
Tel. +39 0173 67343
info@paitin.it
www.paitin.it
paitinwine

YEAR OF FOUNDATION **1893**
NAME OF THE OWNER **Pasquero-Elia Family**
TOTAL BOTTLES PRODUCED **85,000**
DIRECT SALES
VISITS TO THE WINERY - RESERVATION NEEDED
HECTARES OF VINEYARD **17**
HOSPITALITY

The Pasquero-Elia is one of the oldest producers of Barbaresco with a history that dates back to 1796 with the acquisition of a farm with a winery and vineyards. The first bottle of Barbaresco Sorè Paitin, which is a parcel in the cru of Serraboella, came out in 1893 and laid the foundation for modern Barbaresco. Production today respects tradition and benefits from the wise consultancy of Dante Scaglione.

🔳 **91**   **Price B**
Barbaresco Serraboella 2013
100% Nebbiolo grapes. Matures 2 year in big barrels. Lively ruby red. Hints of wet soil, then pomegranate and violet, some smoky hints in the background. Outstretched in the mouth, neat, balanced, with velvety tannins, good acidic tension and great persistence.

PALLADINO

Piazza Cappellano, 8
12050 Serralunga D'Alba (CN)
Tel. +39 0173 613108

Fax +39 0173 613448
info@palladinovini.com
www.palladinovini.com
f *palladino*

YEAR OF FOUNDATION 1974
NAME OF THE OWNER Palladino Family
TOTAL BOTTLES PRODUCED 230,000
DIRECT SALES
VISITS TO THE WINERY - RESERVATION NEEDED
HECTARES OF VINEYARD 11
HOSPITALITY

The winery is situated in an historic building in the center of Serralunga and wine has been made there for centuries, while the Palladino family only acquired it in 1974. The Nebbiolo grapes used are from excellent cru in Serralunga like Ornato, Parafada, Broglio and San Bernardo and produce wines with a traditional style some of which are very good.

93   Price B
Barolo San Bernardo Riserva 2010
100% Nebbiolo grapes. Matures in big barrels. Intense garnet ruby red. Clear and intense, elegant and classic notes of dark flowers, spices, graceful wild strawberry and watermelon. Relaxed in the mouth but thick structure and very tasty. Balanced and smooth tannins, very persistent. Rare elegance.

91   Price B
Barolo Ornato 2012
100% Nebbiolo grapes. Matures in big barrels. Garnet ruby red. Fragrant notes of red fruits and fresh flowers. Notes of cola. Thick structure, well-articulated with a youthful but well blended tannins. Solid and tasty finish.

ARMANDO PARUSSO

Località Bussia, 55
12065 Monforte d'Alba (CN)
Tel. +39 0173 78257
Fax +39 0173 787276
info@parusso.com
www.parusso.com

YEAR OF FOUNDATION 1985
NAME OF THE OWNER Marco and Tiziana Parusso
TOTAL BOTTLES PRODUCED 120,000
DIRECT SALES
VISITS TO THE WINERY - RESERVATION NEEDED
HECTARES OF VINEYARD 23

Marco and Tiziana Parusso make wine with grapes from vineyards between Castiglione Falletto and Monforte. Those for their Barolo are from the cru Mariondino, in the first town, and Le Coste-Mosconi and Bussia from the second. Their wines, which are loved by international critics but less so by traditionalists, are made with impeccable technical skill and age longer than one would imagine.

301

94   Price D
Barolo Bussia Riserva 2007
100% Nebbiolo grapes. Matures 3 years in barrique and tonneau. Intense garnet ruby red. Enveloping and complex notes of licorice, spices, tobacco, smoky hints in the background. Powerful taste, well integrated tannins, rich, warm, exceptional persistence. It lacks a little agility.

PELASSA

Borgata Tucci, 43
12046 Montà (CN)
Tel. +39 0173 971312
Fax +39 0173 971312
S *pelassa.daniele*
pelassa@pelassa.com
www.pelassa.com
f *AziendaVitivinicolaMarioPelassa*

YEAR OF FOUNDATION 1960
NAME OF THE OWNER Pelassa Family
TOTAL BOTTLES PRODUCED 90,000
DIRECT SALES
VISITS TO THE WINERY
HECTARES OF VINEYARD 14

The Pelassa estate was founded in 1960 when Mario Pelassa returned from military service and began bottling wine and developing a local market. His offspring have expanded the estate and above all given it a decisive visibility on national and international markets. Their vineyards are situated both in Roero, where the estate has its headquarters, and the area of Verduno in the Barolo appellation. The estate's style is solid and decidedly classic. During this year's tastings we were particularly impressed by the wines from Verduno.

■ **91**   Price B

Barolo 2012

100% Nebbiolo grapes. Matures in big barrels. Intense ruby red. Notes of dark plums, violets and medical herbs. Rich, progressive, average body, crunchy tannins but well integrated. Tasty and savory finish.

■ **90**   Price B

Barolo Riserva 2010

100% Nebbiolo grapes. Matures in barrique and tonneau. Bright ruby red. Intense notes of dark flowers, yellow plums and watermelon, medical herbs and lightly smoky. Agile in the mouth, good and thick structure. Youthful but neat tannins and persistent finish.

★★★

PIO CESARE

Via Cesare Balbo, 6
12051 Alba (CN)
Tel. +39 0173 440386
Fax +39 0173 363680
piocesare@piocesare.it
www.piocesare.it
 Vini-Pio-Cesare

YEAR OF FOUNDATION 1881
NAME OF THE OWNER Pio Boffa
TOTAL BOTTLES PRODUCED 400,000
HECTARES OF VINEYARD 70

The owner of some excellent vineyards, Pio Cesare is a great name in Langhe winemaking that has always been able to constantly renew itself. They offer a range of elegant wines, some of the best of which are the Barolo from the Ornato vineyards in Serralunga and the Barbaresco Il Bricco. For years it has been run by Pio Boffa, a descendent of founder Pio Cesare (Pio being the surname and Cesare the name), who has maintained traditional styles and continued to produce wines that age well. Their ancient cellars are the last remaining in the center of the city of Alba.

■ 🖻 **95**   Price C

Barbaresco Il Bricco 2012

100% Nebbiolo grapes. Matures 3 years and a half in different size barrels. Garnet ruby red. Black cherry, pomegranate, smoky notes, very refined,

hints of cinchona. Strong flavor, youthful but promising tannins, savory, full-bodied, warm but not heavy, great length in the finish.

☐ **93**   Price B

Langhe Bianco Piodilei 2014

100% Chardonnay grapes. Matures about 1 year in barrique. Light golden yellow. Classic smoky notes, then grilled bread, fresh almond, vanilla and yellow plum. Tense flavor, great acidity on a more agile body compared to other versions, savory, fresh, pleasant and with good complexity.

■ **93**   Price C

Barolo Ornato 2012

100% Nebbiolo grapes. Matures 3 years and a half in different size barrels. Garnet ruby red. Austere notes of rhubarb, then violets, pomegranate and vanilla. Great impact in the mouth, very youthful, severe and thick tannins, rich and powerful body, warm and very persistent.

■ **92**   Price C

Barbaresco Classico 2012

100% Nebbiolo grapes. Matures 3 years in different size barrels. Intense garnet red. Very typical and traditional notes of violets, currant, smoky hints, light licorice, dry flowers and tobacco. Strong flavor, tannins, youthful, very promising.

■ **91**   Price C

Barolo Classico 2012

100% Nebbiolo grapes. Matures 3 years and a half in big barrels. Lively garnet red. Austere notes of violet, rhubarb, then tobacco, licorice and currant. Strong taste, with some youthful tannic roughness, savory and long.

★★

E. PIRA & FIGLI DI CHIARA BOSCHIS

Via Vittorio Veneto, 1
12060 Barolo (CN)
Tel. +39 0173 56247
Fax +39 0173 56247
info@pira-chiaraboschis.com
www.pira-chiaraboschis.com
 EPiraFigliChiaraBoschis

YEAR OF FOUNDATION 1981
NAME OF THE OWNER Chiara and Giorgio Boschis
TOTAL BOTTLES PRODUCED 30,000

DIRECT SALES
VISITS TO THE WINERY - RESERVATION NEEDED
HECTARES OF VINEYARD **7**
HOSPITALITY

Cannubi and Via Nuova are vineyards in the township of Barolo that produce elegant wines. Mosconi, on the other hand, is in Monforte and the wine is bolder and needs to age, thus we'll check it out next year. Chiara Boschis uses grapes from small parcels in these vineyards to make her magnificent wines. She produces them under the brand of a winery she acquired some 20 or so years ago and which has always represented, since it was founded over a century ago, an ideal reference point for the most authentic Barolo tradition.

 93   Price C

Barolo Cannubi 2012

100% Nebbiolo grapes. Matures 2 years in barrique. Very intense garnet red. Smoky and spicy, then currant, tobacco and violets. Warm and enveloping taste, thick tannins, slightly woody and youthful, good body, savory and with great persistence.

 90   Price A

Dolcetto d'Alba 2015

100% Dolcetto grapes. Matures 9 months in used barrique. Very intense ruby red with violet hues. Great version. Fruity and spicy notes of black currant, violet and smoky hints. Deliciously savory, easy to drink, warm, enveloping, very pleasant.

LUIGI PIRA

Via XX Settembre, 9
12050 Serralunga D'Alba (CN)
Tel. +39 0173 613106
Fax +39 0173 613106
pira.luigi@alice.it

YEAR OF FOUNDATION **1950**
NAME OF THE OWNER **Pira Family**
TOTAL BOTTLES PRODUCED **50,000**
DIRECT SALES
VISITS TO THE WINERY - RESERVATION NEEDED
HECTARES OF VINEYARD **12**

For some 20 years, Giampaolo and Romolo Pira have been bottling wine made from their vine-

yards spread throughout Serralunga. These are austere Barolo that when young can be severe but with age offer great satisfaction. The right balance between the use of small, new wood barrels and big barrels exalt the characteristics of historic cru like Marenca, Margheria and Vigna Rionda.

 90   Price B

Barolo Margheria 2012

100% Nebbiolo grapes. Matures 2 years in big barrels. Intense garnet ruby color. Elegant in the nose with aromas of cassis, rasberry and spices. Polite taste, savory, with a nice acidity, the tannins are slightly woody and youthful, adeguate persistence on the finish.

   88   Price B

Barolo Marenca 2012

100% Nebbiolo grapes. Matures 2 years in barrique and big barrels. Clear garnet ruby color. On the nose is intensely fruity and complex with aromas of cassis, spices, vanilla. A little dry in the mouth due to slightly woody tannins, youthful but still covering. The finish is warm and persistent.

★★

PODERI COLLA

Località San Rocco Seno d'Elvio, 82
12051 Alba (CN)
Tel. +39 0173 290148
Fax +39 0173 441498
🔵 *poderi.colla*
info@podericolla.it
www.podericolla.it

YEAR OF FOUNDATION **1994**
NAME OF THE OWNER **Colla Family**
TOTAL BOTTLES PRODUCED **150,000**
DIRECT SALES
VISITS TO THE WINERY - RESERVATION NEEDED
HECTARES OF VINEYARD **26**

Beppe and Tino Colla, who once owned this historic Prunetto winery, built this winery some 20 years ago using the same principles and approach they used for decades in their previous activity. In a nutshell these are: great respect for winemaking tradition and the territory of the Langhe.

92   Price B
Barolo Bussia Dardi Le Rose 2012

100% Nebbiolo grapes. Matures 2 years in big barrels. Clear garnet red. Notes of currant, strawberry, violet, ethereal and enveloping. Strong flavor, tense, slightly tannic, agile body, good acidity and great promises to last in time.

PODERI EINAUDI

Borgata Gombe, 31/32 - Cascina Tecc
12063 Dogliani (CN)
Tel. +39 0173 70191
info@poderieinaudi.com
www.poderieinaudi.com
 Poderi-Luigi-Einaudi

YEAR OF FOUNDATION 1897
NAME OF THE OWNER Roberta Einaudi, Matteo and Giovanni Sardagna
TOTAL BOTTLES PRODUCED 250,000
DIRECT SALES
VISITS TO THE WINERY - RESERVATION NEEDED
HECTARES OF VINEYARD 52
HOSPITALITY

This once was the estate of former Italian President Luigi Einaudi. His son Guilio Einaudi did not pay much attention to it but he did build an extraordinary publishing house. Today it is in the hands of Matteo Sardagna Einaudi. The winery is in Dogliani but is specialty is also Barolo and it has vineyards in Barolo cru: Cannubi and Terlo Costa Grimaldi. They also have Vigna Tecc which produces their top Dogliani wine.

 91   Price C
Barolo Terlo Vigna Costa Grimaldi 2012

100% Nebbiolo grapes. Matures 30 months in big barrels. Lively garnet. Slightly penetrating notes of Kirsch, then dry and fresh flowers, black cherry and plums. Powerful taste, warm, young but not too aggressive tannins, good, long and enveloping finish.

 90   Price C
Barolo Cannubi 2012

100% Nebbiolo grapes. Matures 30 months in barrique and big barrels. Intense garnet ruby. Neat and fruity in the nose, notes of black cherry, some lactic and spicy hints. Clean and thin taste, not enormous body, thick but not aggressive tannins.

POMODOLCE

Via IV Novembre, 7
15050 Montemarzino (AL)
Tel. +39 0131 878135
info@pomodolce.it
www.pomodolce.it
 Azienda-Agricola-Pomodolce

YEAR OF FOUNDATION 2005
NAME OF THE OWNER Giuseppe Davico
TOTAL BOTTLES PRODUCED 14,000
DIRECT SALES
VISITS TO THE WINERY - RESERVATION NEEDED
HECTARES OF VINEYARD 4
HOSPITALITY
CERTIFIED ORGANIC VITICULTURE

Silvio Davico, the son of Giuseppe and Camilla, restauranteurs and winemakers in Montemarzino, is directly responsible for the family's winemaking activities and is a member of the well-known Timorasso 'clan', a group of winemakers who produce wine from that grape. Along with his two versions of this wine, he also makes an excellent Croatino and other reds.

☐ 87   Price B
Colli Tortonesi Timorasso Diletto 2014

00% Timorasso grapes. Stainless steel on the yeasts for 10 months. Light golden yellow color. On the nose the smoky aromas are evident due to the yeasts lysis, then scents of grapefruit and plum. The mouth is tense, with a good body, more agile then other versions, savory, warm, great drinkability.

PRODUTTORI DEL BARBARESCO

Via Torino, 54
12050 Barbaresco (CN)
Tel. +39 0173 635139
produttori@produttoridelbarbaresco.com
www.produttoridelbarbaresco.com

YEAR OF FOUNDATION 1958
NAME OF THE OWNER
TOTAL BOTTLES PRODUCED 500,000
DIRECT SALES

VISITS TO THE WINERY - RESERVATION NEEDED
HECTARES OF VINEYARD 110

The 52 members of this extraordinary wine co-operative can be very proud of thei work. Not only are they an example for all other cooperatives in Italy, but they also offer some excellent wines at very reasonable prices. When conditions permit, their Barbaresco is made as nine different cru, obviously the most representative of the appellation, which are examples of typicity and respect for tradition.

93   Price B
Barbaresco Pora Riserva 2011

100% Nebbiolo grapes. Matures 3 years in big oak barrels. Intense garnet color. Very typical and classic in the nose, with aromas of violet, pomegranate and currant in evidence for a whole and clear aromatic profile. Savory taste, with thick but young tannins, good body, warm and persistent.

91   Price B
Barbaresco 2013

100% Nebbiolo grapes. Matures almost 2 years in big oak barrels. Vivid garnet color. Very fruity with aromas of cherry, pomegranate, especially currant at first then hints of rose. Agile on the palate, savory, with a good acidic component, easy to drink and with a medium body.

87   Price A
Langhe Nebbiolo 2014

100% Nebbiolo grapes, 6 months in big oak barrels. Bright garnet color. Fruity and whole with aromas of currant, cherry, raspberry and hints of violet. Son of a difficult harvest, on the mouth it is light and with a great acidity that makes it easy to drink and with an agile body.

★★

PRUNOTTO

Corso Barolo, 14
12051 Alba (CN)
Tel. +39 0173 280017
prunotto@prunotto.it
www.prunotto.it

YEAR OF FOUNDATION 1904
NAME OF THE OWNER Marchesi Antinori

TOTAL BOTTLES PRODUCED 700,000
DIRECT SALES
VISITS TO THE WINERY - RESERVATION NEEDED
HECTARES OF VINEYARD 55

This is one of the best-known brands for Barolo and Barbaresco. The winery, today owned by Marchesi Antinori, has at its top of the line Barolo from the cru of Bussia Soprana in Monforte, a good Barbaresco from the Bric Turot vineyards and the Barbera d'Alba Pian Romualdo.

95   Price D
Barolo Bussia Vigna Colonnello Riserva 2010

100% Nebbiolo grapes. It matures for 3 years in big oak barrels. Vivid garnet color. Very traditional with aromas of violet, licorice, mint at first, then currant, cardamom and tobacco. Complex and yet agile in the mouth with a full-body, acidic tension, thick tannins. Great character. Very long finish.

91   Price B
Barbera d'Alba Pian Romualdo 2013

100% Barbera grapes. It matures for 1 year in big oak barrels. Intense garnet ruby color. A great classic of its kind, on the nose it presents typical aromas of violet, black cherry, 'Barolo like'. Tense in the mouth, savory, with great acidity and great but heavy body. Warm and persistent finish.

88   Price B
Barbaresco Bric Turot 2013

100% Nebbiolo grapes. Matures for 15 months in big oak barrels. Vivid garnet color. Classic aromas of currant, violet and tobacco. Not enormous on the palate, with some acidic/tannic edge, good body, agile, savory with a good length.

PUNSET

Via Zocco, 2
12052 Neive (CN)
Tel. +39 0173 67072
Fax +39 0173 677423
punset@punset.com
www.punset.com
 punsetbiowines.punset

YEAR OF FOUNDATION 1964
NAME OF THE OWNER Marina Marcarino
TOTAL BOTTLES PRODUCED 80,000
DIRECT SALES

VISITS TO THE WINERY - RESERVATION NEEDED
HECTARES OF VINEYARD **40**
HOSPITALITY
CERTIFIED ORGANIC VITICULTURE

TOTAL BOTTLES PRODUCED **300,000**
DIRECT SALES
VISITS TO THE WINERY - RESERVATION NEEDED
HECTARES OF VINEYARD **35**

The estate has been a flagbearer of organic winegrowing a long time. Founded 60 years ago, it produces above all various versions of Barbaresco. Their prize possession is the cru Campo Quadro, a vineyard that is only a hectare in size and produces only a few thousand bottles a year.

 93   Price B
Barbaresco Basarin 2011

100% Nebbiolo grapes. It matures 3 years in big oak barrels. Vivid garnet ruby color. On the nose it presents scents of mint at first, then berries, cocoa hints, leather and violet. Full-flavored in the mouth with still young and crinkled tannins, good body, warm, savory and very persistent.

 92   Price B
Barbaresco Campo Quadro Riserva 2010

100% Nebbiolo grapes. It matures for 2 years in barrique and tonneau. Vivid garnet ruby color. Calssic, clear and intense aromas of plum, medicinal herbs, hints of rhubarb and fresh underbrush. Elegant in the mouth, harmonic thanks to great tannins and a medium weft. Long and persistent finish.

 88   👍 Price A
Dolcetto d'Alba 2015

100% Dolcetto grapes. Stainless steel only. Violet ruby color. Fragrant and fruity aromas of black cherry, violet and black currant. On the mouth is simple but easy and delicious to drink, warm, savory and with a good length.

★★
RENATO RATTI

Frazione Annunziata, 7
12064 La Morra (CN)
Tel. +39 0173 50185
Fax +39 0173 509373
info@renatoratti.com
www.renatoratti.com
🐦 *@RenatoRatti*

YEAR OF FOUNDATION **1965**
NAME OF THE OWNER **Pietro Ratti**

Renato Ratti was a man of stature and intelligence who is still remembered today, 25 years after his death. He helped lay the foundation to finally make Barolo the great wine that it is today. He made it known the world over and was the first to separate the appellation into cru. Since 1988, his estate has been in the hands of his son Pietro who runs it with competence and a firm hand to honor the memory of his great father. The wines are still made at Abbazia dell'Annuziata in La Morra and, in the province of Asti, at Villa Pattono.

 92   Price C
Barolo Rocche dell'Annunziata 2012

100% Nebbiolo grapes. It matures 2 years in oak barrels of different sizes. Intense garnet color. On the nose aromas of violet, currant, licorice, little smoky hints. Full-flavored in the mouth, with young but not aggressive tannins, good body, long and persistent with a light dilution on the finish.

 90   Price B
Barolo Marcenasco 2012

100% Nebbiolo grapes. It matures 2 years in barrique and big oak barrels. Intense and vivid garnet color. On the nose light smoky aromas and scents of spices at first, then currant and licorice. In the mouth it is warm, agile, still tannic, savory with a good persistence.

 88   Price A
Dolcetto d'Alba Colombé 2015

100% Dolcetto grapes. Stainless steel only. Violet ruby color. Fragrant and fruity, typical aromas on strawberry, black currant and plum. Savory taste, warm, very pleasant with an attractive drinkability due to its immediatness.

RESSIA

Via Canova, 28
12052 Neive (CN)
Tel. +39 0173 677305
Fax +39 0173 062192
info@ressia.com
www.ressia.com
📘 *aziendaagricola.ressia*

YEAR OF FOUNDATION 1997
NAME OF THE OWNER Fabrizio Ressia
TOTAL BOTTLES PRODUCED 30,000
DIRECT SALES
VISITS TO THE WINERY - RESERVATION NEEDED
HECTARES OF VINEYARD 5.5

A small estate in Neive that produces wine using grapes from the Canova cru of which they own a part. Although the family has been making wine for decades, it was not until Fabrizio, a passionate winemaker as he likes to define himself, entered the estate that the quality of the wines literally took off. They have quite a vast line of production and the showcase wine remains Barbaresco Canova.

 93   Price B

Barbaresco Canova 2013

100% Nebbiolo grapes. It matures for more than 1 year in different size oak barrels of. Intense garnet ruby color. On the nose is slightly smoky at first, then hints of tar, wet soil and currant. Tense on the palate, crispy, savory, well supported by acidity with not too aggressive tannins.

★★

GIUSEPPE RINALDI

Via Monforte, 5
12060 Barolo (CN)
Tel. +39 0173 56156
Fax +39 0173 56156
rinaldimarta@libero.it

YEAR OF FOUNDATION 1890
NAME OF THE OWNER Giuseppe and Marta Rinaldi
TOTAL BOTTLES PRODUCED 35,000
DIRECT SALES
VISITS TO THE WINERY - RESERVATION NEEDED
HECTARES OF VINEYARD 6.5

To write about Beppe 'Citrico' Rinaldi is more difficult than would seem. He is an intelligent man full of charisma and is certainly a farmer, and not just a wine producer, who would just as easily talk to you about his collection of Lambretta scooters as his Barolo. Sometimes he can produce unforgettable wines and others some that are not. This because he seeks to intervene a little as possible and left the wine do the rest and what comes out, comes out. However,

when there is a good year, Beppe and his wines become the stuff of legend.

 93   Price C

Barolo Brunate 2012

100% Nebbiolo grapes. It matures 3 years in big oak barrels. Bright garnet color. Luigi Veronelli would have said that you can feel ' The breath of the Barolo' in it, and if it wasn't for a volatile and rustis scents that fogs the aromatic profile, he would've been right. Ethereal, floral with aromas of black cherry, all the rest is perfect. On the mouth is strong, with vibrant tannins, a tense and savory body, very typical and traditional.

 93   Price C

Barolo Tre Tine 2012

100% Nebbiolo grapes. It matures for 3 years in big oak barrels. Vivid garnet ruby color. Very similar topic. Still a little volatile in the nose with some evolved notes of tamarind and licorice. Extremely tense in the mouth, full of personality with pawing tannins and with the acidity all over the body. Very persistent.

 90   Price A

Dolcetto d'Alba 2014

100% Dolcetto grapes. Stainlees steel only. Intense violet ruby color. Clean, typical and extremely fruity in the nose. Full taste, very pleasant, with no harsh acidity, discreetly alcoholic, great length and dangerous drinkability. A gorgeous wine that will leave you without words. Not a complex wine, of course, but which Dolcetto should be complex? Fragrant, agile and harmonic.

★

SERAFINO RIVELLA

Località Montestefano, 6
12050 Barbaresco (CN)
Tel. +39 0173 635182
Fax +39 0173 635182

YEAR OF FOUNDATION 1967
NAME OF THE OWNER Teobaldo Rivella
TOTAL BOTTLES PRODUCED 12,000
VISITS TO THE WINERY - RESERVATION NEEDED
HECTARES OF VINEYARD 2

Teoblado Rivella and his wife Maria Musso run their tiny estate with an old-fashion lightness that can also be found in each of their wines.

Barbaresco Montestefano and a Dolcetto d'Alba, which unite traditional style with unmistakable character, bold and elegant, pure expressions of an extraordinary territory.

 91 Price B

Barbaresco Montestefano 2012

100% Nebbiolo grapes. It matures in big oak barrels. Bright ruby red color. Delicate aromas of spices and licorice. Very fine in the mouth with sweet and juicy tannins.

 86 👍 Price A

Dolcetto d'Alba 2014

100% Dolcetto grapes. It matures in big oak barrels. Bright ruby red color. Despite the disastrous vintage for this grape variety the nose is lively fruity. Juicy on the palate with a crispy fruit and very pleasant drinkability as usual.

★

RIZZI

Via Rizzi, 5
12050 Treiso (CN)
Tel. +39 0173 638161
Fax +39 0173 638935
cantinarizzi@cantinarizzi.it
www.cantinarizzi.it
🄵 *Azienda-Vitivinicola-Rizzi*

YEAR OF FOUNDATION **1974**
NAME OF THE OWNER **Ernesto Dellapiana**
TOTAL BOTTLES PRODUCED **65,000**
DIRECT SALES
VISITS TO THE WINERY - RESERVATION NEEDED
HECTARES OF VINEYARD **35**
HOSPITALITY

Ernesto Dellapiana founded this estate over 40 years ago. Today it is run by his children Jole and Enrico who have no intention of changing an iota of his winemaking style. Thus their Barbaresco, particularly Pajorè, remain classic and congruent.

 93 Price B

Barbaresco Boito Riserva 2011

100% Nebbiolo grapes. It matures 2 years between concrete vats and big oak barrels. Intense and lively garnet ruby color. On the nose the smoky notes are evident and the it presents aromas of black cher-

ry, kirsch, violet. Very convincing taste, polite, balanced with velvety tannins and elegant body, very persistent.

 92 Price B

Barbaresco Pajorè 2013

100% Nebbiolo grapes. It matures 2 years between concrete vats and big oak barrels. Light garnet ruby color. On the nose it is dominated by the smoky scents at first then ethereal and a little piercing aromas of kirsch and strawberries. Strong taste, with young tannins, full-body, warm and savory.

★★★

ROAGNA I PAGLIERI

Località Paglieri, 9
12050 Barbaresco (CN)
Tel. +39 0173 635109
info@roagna.com
www.roagna.it

YEAR OF FOUNDATION
NAME OF THE OWNER **Alfredo Roagna**
TOTAL BOTTLES PRODUCED **60,000**
HECTARES OF VINEYARD **14**

The wines from this estate are some of the most convincing in the Langhe, cru produced in small quantities and with maniacal care. Again this year Luca has been able to amaze us with a series of wines that will leave you dumbstruck. Over the past 20 years, these wines have had a formidable evolution and now interpret a series of historic cru of both Barbaresco and Barolo in a most remarkable way. Because he is deeply passionate about what he does, Luca's wines continue to evolve and improve, a task made easier thank to a new, modern and efficient winery.

■ 🖻 **99** Price E

Barbaresco Crichet Pajé 2006

100% Nebbiolo grapes from the highest part of the Amphitheater of Paje, owned by the family. It matures for 90 months in big oak barrels. Already extraordinary. Intense garnet color with bright reflexes. On the nose it presents unusual aromas that go from the floral notes (rose and violet) to the less academic sweet tobacco, incense, cinchona, bark and licorice. The intensity is extraordinary. Huge in the mouth, not as much for the structure but for his complexity. The tannins are well integrated with the full-body. Exciting.

96   Price D
Barbaresco Pajé Vecchie Viti 2010

100% Nebbiolo grapes. It matures for 48 months in big oak barrels. Clear, intense and bright red color. On the nose aromas of ripe fruits, wet underbrush. Strict on the palate, strut with firm strong and manly tannins. Very long persistence. A great expression of this historical Cru.

94   Price D
Barbaresco Asili Vecchie Viti 2010

100% Nebbiolo grapes, 48 months in big oak barrels. Vivid red color. Strong eucalyptus and spicy notes with strong floral scents and delicious aromas of licorice in the background. It is a perfect combination of finesse and strength. Austere in the mouth with a very notable tension supported by the alive tannins typical of the cru. We need to wait long years before tasting this wine at its best.

94   Price D
Barbaresco Montefico Vecchie Viti 2010

100% Nebbiolo grapes from 50 years old vineyard. It matures 48 months in big oak barrels. Bright, light red color. On the nose aromas of roses, violet of Parma, licorice. Coquettish the cut tobacco scent. Great eucalyptus notes. Powerful taste, with no hesitations, the tannins are firm but well balanced. Austere. Unforgettable version of this Cru even in a very difficult vintage like this one.

93   Price D
Barolo Pira Vecchie Viti 2010

100% Nebbiolo from a 50 years old vineyard. It matures for 48 months in big oak barrels. Relatively light red color, son of 'high' vineyards and the fresh area of Castiglione Falletto. Ethereal and refined in the nose, complex, diffusely eucalyptus and floral. Silky in the mouth, straight, with a splendid character. Impressive is the inversion of Barbaresco and Barolo in Roagna house: this Barolo is less redundant and organoleptic invasive compared to the monumental Barbaresco of the estate.

YEAR OF FOUNDATION **1978**
NAME OF THE OWNER **Bruno Rocca**
TOTAL BOTTLES PRODUCED **65,000**
DIRECT SALES
VISITS TO THE WINERY - RESERVATION NEEDED
HECTARES OF VINEYARD **15**

Bruno Rocca's Barbaresco express in full the typical characteristics of Nebbiolo from this terroir. They are wines with a complex structure and use elegance as their trump card. Over time he has lifted the finesse of his wines to incredible levels, as is the case with Barbaresco Rabajà, a superlative Barbaresco produced from one of the most extraordinary vineyards in the appellation.

95   Price C
Barbaresco Rabajà 2013

100% Nebbiolo grapes. It matures in barrique. If we still needed a proof that Rabaja is a true Grand Cru, this 2013 version from Bruno Rocca left no doubt. Bright ruby red color. Explosive in the nose, powerful in the mouth. Balanced with simply fantastic tannins, infinite finish, fresh and eucalyptus hints. Do we need something else?

92   Price C
Barbaresco Coparossa 2013

100% Nebbiolo grapes. It matures in tonneau. Garnet ruby color. Classic and slightly warm aromas of alfalfa, spices and fresh and dry red flowers. Very elegant taste with very sober tannins and a wide, voluminous and tasty body. On the finish is classic and persistent.

89   Price B
Barbaresco 2013

100% Nebbiolo grapes. It matures in barrique. Bright ruby red color. Clear and fresh in the nose and on the palate strong but harmonic with soft tannins. Tonic and dynamic finish.

★★
BRUNO ROCCA RABAJÀ

Strada Rabajà, 60
12050 Barbaresco (CN)
Tel. +39 0173 635112
info@brunorocca.it
www.brunorocca.it
 roccarabaja
 roccarabaja

★★
ALBINO ROCCA

Strada Ronchi, 18
12050 Barbaresco (CN)
Tel. +39 0173 635145
Fax +39 0173 635921
roccaalbino@roccaalbino.com
www.albinorocca.com
 daniela.rocca.50

YEAR OF FOUNDATION 1950
NAME OF THE OWNER Daniela, Monica and Paola Rocca
TOTAL BOTTLES PRODUCED 100,000
DIRECT SALES
VISITS TO THE WINERY - RESERVATION NEEDED
HECTARES OF VINEYARD 21

Following the tragic and premature deaths of Angelo Rocca and his wife, their children took over the estate to continue their work. They use old and new barrique and barrels of some 20hl in size depending on what the vintage demands. The style is modern with a spasmodic search for balanced flavor and intense aroma.

---

 96   Price C

Barbaresco Angelo 2013

100% Nebbiolo grapes. It matures in big oak barrels for 20 months. Vivid garnet ruby color. On the nose is full-flavored, young, with aromas of currant and just an hint of smoky scent. On the mouth is elegant, agile, with tangible but not aggressive tannins and great persistence. The grapes that this wine is made of are from the Cru in Ovello, the wine is dedicated to the memory of Angelo Rocca, died prematurely.

---

94   Price D

Barbaresco Ronchi Riserva 2011

100% Nebbiolo grapes. Intense garnet ruby color. It matures for more than 2 years in oak barrels of different sizes. Spicy and complex aromas of violet, black cherry, vanilla and tobacco. Full taste, tense, savory, with a warm but agile body, still young tannins and a great personality.

---

93   Price B

Barbaresco Ronchi 2013

100% Nebbiolo grapes. It matures for 2 years in big oak barrels. Intense ruby color with garnet reflexes. On the nose at first a little smoky, then it presents aromas of black cherry, currant, wheat earth. Fine, savory, gritty, with thick and young tannins, full-bodied, tense and crispy. Very long finish.

GIOVANNI ROSSO

Località Baudana, 6
12050 Serralunga D'Alba (CN)
Tel. +39 0173 613340
Fax +39 0173 613340

elroro@tin.it
www.giovannirosso.com
 giovannirossobarolo

YEAR OF FOUNDATION 1960
NAME OF THE OWNER Giovanni Rosso
TOTAL BOTTLES PRODUCED 53,000
DIRECT SALES
VISITS TO THE WINERY - RESERVATION NEEDED
HECTARES OF VINEYARD 9

This small Serralunga estate is skillfully run by Davide Rosso. He makes wines that are very territorial using grapes from particularly good cru, like La Serra and Cerretta, or with grapes from Vigna Rionda. And there is a Barolo that has everything needed, in his view, to evolve quickly, which of course is relative when you're dealing with a Serralunga Barolo which is perhaps the one that ages the longest.

---

 98   Price E

Barolo Ester Canale Rosso Poderi dell'Antica Vigna Rionda 2012

100% Nebbiolo grapes. It matures for 3 years in big oak barrels. Intense garnet ruby color. Complex alternated aromas of currant and violet at first, then licorice and light mint. Great classy taste, full-bodied, agile and yet strong, perfect tannins, polite, savory, warm, full-flavored with great balance. Gorgeous.

---

91   Price C

Barolo del Comune di Serralunga 2012

100% Nebbiolo grapes. It matures for 2 years and a half in big oak barrels. Intense garnet ruby color. On the nose full-flavored aromas of cassis, spices, smoky scents, and little hints of smoke. Firm taste, with still youthful and woody tannins, crispy and with a very long finish.

★★★

LUCIANO SANDRONE

Via Pugnane, 4
12060 Barolo (CN)
Tel. +39 0173 560023
info@sandroneluciano.com
www.sandroneluciano.com
 Sandrone.Barolo

YEAR OF FOUNDATION 1978
NAME OF THE OWNER Luciano Sandrone

TOTAL BOTTLES PRODUCED 95,000
DIRECT SALES
VISITS TO THE WINERY - RESERVATION NEEDED
HECTARES OF VINEYARD 27

"Sandrone never misses" is what his fellow Barolo winemakers say about him. And, in fact, if he has ever made a mistake, no one knows about it. His wines are all very good above all his two Barolo, Cannubi Boschis, a Barolo cru in every way, and Le Vigne, which is a 'blend' of grapes from the vineyards of Vignane in Barolo, Merli in Novello, Conterni in Monforte and Baudana in Serralunga. This year we limit ourselves to review Cannubi Boschis.

 91   Price D

Barolo Cannubi Boschis 2012

100% Nebbiolo grapes. It matures 2 years and a half in tonneau. Intense garnet ruby color. On the nose it's full-flavored with initial smoky notes, then aromas of violet, black cherry, vanilla and light raspberry. On the mouth is delicate, not huge, thick tannins, pleasantly savory, full-bodied with an agile and persistent finish. Elegant with a medium structure.

PAOLO SARACCO

Via Circonvallazione, 6
12053 Castiglione Tinella (CN)
Tel. +39 0141 855113
Fax +39 0141 855360
info@paolosaracco.it
www.paolosaracco.it
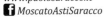 MoscatoAstiSaracco

YEAR OF FOUNDATION 1900
NAME OF THE OWNER Paolo Saracco
TOTAL BOTTLES PRODUCED 600,000
VISITS TO THE WINERY - RESERVATION NEEDED
HECTARES OF VINEYARD 45
HOSPITALITY

For four generations, the Saracco family have been among the absolute best interpreters of Moscato. Paolo Saracco also produces other wines, some quite well-made, but his best remains Moscato d'Autunno, which defines his winery and is among the best Moscato in Piedmont. It is a very Italian and extraordinary wine that he makes with a master's touch.

 91   👍 Price A

Piemonte Moscato d'Autunno 2015

100% Moscato Bianco di Canelli. Sweet filtered. Light golden yellow color. On the nose is aromatic, fragrant, characteristic of Moscato grapes at first, then scents of sage and citrus. On the mouth is lively, with a very evident Co2 note, sweet but well balanced by acidity and by carbonic, light and fine.

⊡ 89   👍 Price A

Moscato d'Asti 2015

100% Moscati Bianco di Canelli grapes. Sweet filtered. Light golden yellow color. Very fragrant aromatic notes and yeasts, aromas of citrus and sage. Sweet taste, lively, fizzy, light, very pleasant and tense.

★

SCAGLIOLA

Via San Siro, 42
14052 Calosso (AT)
Tel. +39 0141 853183
Fax +39 0141 853091
info@scagliolavini.com
www.scagliolavini.com

YEAR OF FOUNDATION 1930
NAME OF THE OWNER Scagliola Family
TOTAL BOTTLES PRODUCED 160,000
DIRECT SALES
VISITS TO THE WINERY - RESERVATION NEEDED
HECTARES OF VINEYARD 35

Barbera d'Asti Superiore Sansi is the pride and joy of the Scagliola family who have been making wine for 80 years in Calosso, at the border between Monferrato and the Langhe. A soil of sand, layers of tuff stone and a nice dose of chalk leave an important imprint on their wines. The estate is at the top of the San Siro hill, surrounded by vineyards, and here aside from classic Barbera and Moscato they also cultivate a limited amounts of Dolcetto, Cortese, Grignolino, Brachetto and Pinot Nero.

■ 92   Price B

Barbera d'Asti Superiore Sansì 2013

100% Barbera grapes. It matures 1 year new partly new barrique. Intense ruby color with garnet reflexes. Complex and typical aromas of violet, cocoa, black cherry, vanilla. Strong taste, with great acid-

ity that supports a full-flavored and warm body. Very long finish. The word 'Sansì' is the contraction of San Siro, a little village near Calosso where the vineyard and the Scala of Italian football are.

 91   Price B

Monferrato Rosso Azord 2013

Blend of the same amount of Barbera, Cabernet Sauvignon and Nebbiolo grapes. It matures 1 year in semi new barrique. Dark, intense ruby color. Very spicy aromas of vanilla at first, then black cherry and blueberry. Full-bodied and savory with polite tannins, still a little young and woody, persistent finish.

★★

PAOLO SCAVINO

Via Alba - Barolo, 157
12060 Castiglione Falletto (CN)
Tel. +39 0173 62850
Fax +39 0173 462042
info@paoloscavino.com
www.paoloscavino.com
f Paolo-Scavino

YEAR OF FOUNDATION 1921
NAME OF THE OWNER Enrico Scavino
TOTAL BOTTLES PRODUCED 120,000
DIRECT SALES
VISITS TO THE WINERY - RESERVATION NEEDED
HECTARES OF VINEYARD 23

For the past 30 years, Enrico Scavino has been one of the leading players on the Barolo scene and his vineyards are spread throughout the appellation. In Castiglione Falletto, the estate has its headquarters, there is Bric del Fiasc, in La Morra Rocche dell'Annunziata, which produces the Riserva of the same name, in Barolo Cannubi and in Verduno Monvigliero. All his wines are cautiously innovative and strive above all to express the typicity of the different cru.

 94   Price D

Barolo Rocche dell'Annunziata Riserva 2010

100% Nebbiolo grapes. It matures in tonneau. Very intense ruby color. On the nose smoky aromas, underbrush, citrus and watermelon, also the classic ripe plum and dry flowers notes. Whole taste, with a thick weft almost muscular. The tannin is young and still needs the bottle but the progression is im-

portant and on the finish it is very persistent and tasty. Warm after-taste.

 90   Price C

Barolo Monvigliero 2012

100% Nebbiolo grapes. It matures in oak barrel and tonneau. Garnt ruby color. Fresh in the nose, with aromas of citrusy, spices and delicate flowers. Thick body, with polite and elegant tannins. Progressive taste, good acidity and tasty.

 89   Price C

Barolo Bric del Fiasc 2012

100% Nebbiolo grapes. It matures in barrique and tonneau. Intense garnet ruby color. Fruity notes with plum and cherry, alfalfa and mulberry. Medium structure in the mouth with balanced and juicy tannins. Tasty and quite complex finish.

★

SCHIAVENZA

Via Mazzini, 4
12050 Serralunga D'Alba (CN)
Tel. +39 0173 613115
Fax +39 0173 613130
schiavenza@schiavenza.com
www.schiavenza.com

YEAR OF FOUNDATION 1956
NAME OF THE OWNER Luciano Pira
TOTAL BOTTLES PRODUCED 40,000
DIRECT SALES
VISITS TO THE WINERY - RESERVATION NEEDED
HECTARES OF VINEYARD 8
RESTAURANT

Luciano Pira, a restauranteur and quality winemaker in Serralunga d'Alba, is a friendly and reliable person. His restaurant offers excellent food and the wines of all the producers of Serralunga, in sign of fair play. These, of course, include his own great Barolo made from famous cru: Prapò, Broglio and Cerretta. These are impeccably intense wines destined to age long.

 93   Price B

Barolo Prapò 2012

100% Nebbiolo grapes. It matures in big oak barrels for 3 years. Intense garnet color. On the nose clear aromas of licorice, violet, spices, and smoky hints for a very typical aromatic profile. Savory taste, austere, with tightened and young tannins, typical of Serralunga, good body. A very promising wine still a little bit behind.

SOCRÉ

Strada Terzolo, 7
12050 Barbaresco (CN)
Tel. +39 348 7121685
info@socre.it
www.socre.it

YEAR OF FOUNDATION 1999
NAME OF THE OWNER Marco Piacentino
TOTAL BOTTLES PRODUCED 30,000
DIRECT SALES
VISITS TO THE WINERY - RESERVATION NEEDED
HECTARES OF VINEYARD 5.5

The Socré estate belongs to Marco Piacentino, a charming and pragmatic architect with great passion and an open mind who produces Barbaresco in the area of Roncaglie. Marco is decidedly talented and his Barbaresco Roncaglie impressed us a lot. From his 5.5 hectares of vineyards, divided for the most part in two sections, he produces two Barbaresco the second of which is made with a selection of the best grapes. The first vintage produced was a 2000. Fermentation takes place in 20hl wood vats and the wine ages in barrique and tonneau barrels of various ages to then be stored in concrete, a technique that rightfully is coming back into fashion.

92   Price B
Barbaresco Roncaglie 2013

100% Nebbiolo grapes. It matures in tonneau. Concentrated ruby color. On the nose is intense and persistent, slightly spicy with aromas of red fruits: the classic scent of plum is evident with hints of mulberry and cherry. Rich taste with a thick body and a good progression, the tannin is young and balanced. Juicy and persistent finish.

91   Price B
Barbaresco 2013

100% Nebbiolo grapes. It matures in 30 hl oak barrels. Bright ruby color. Classic aromas of saffron, red fruits such as plums and a warm scent of rose. Thick structure, with a crispy but not annoying tannin, good progression. Classic notes of herbs in the finish and with a good persistence.

GIOVANNI SORDO

Via Alba – Barolo, 175
12060 Castiglione Falletto (CN)
Tel. +39 0173 62853
Fax +39 0173 462056
info@sordogiovanni.it
www.sordogiovanni.it

YEAR OF FOUNDATION 1900
NAME OF THE OWNER Giorgio Sordo
TOTAL BOTTLES PRODUCED 350,000
DIRECT SALES
VISITS TO THE WINERY - RESERVATION NEEDED
HECTARES OF VINEYARD 53

An historic, very traditional estate that has always been in the hands of the Sordo family and is today run by Giorgio Sordo with the important contribution of the famous, expert enologist Armando Cordero. Their vineyards are spread out through various villages and, aside from Castiglione Falletto, are in Serralunga, with the Gabutti cru, and Monforte with the Perno cru, as well as in Verduno with the Monvigliero cru.

92   Price B
Barolo Perno 2012

100% Nebbiolo grapes. It matures for at least 2 years in big oak barrels. Intense garnet color. On the nose is full-flavored with aromas of black cherry, currant, pomegranate and hints of violet. Full taste, agile, savory, warm and crispy with polite tannins and a persistent finish.

91   Price B
Barolo Rocche di Castiglione 2012

100% Nebbiolo grapes. It matures for at least 2 years in big oak barrels. Very intense garnet ruby color. On the nose it presents smoky notes with hints of wild strawberry and currant for a very elegant aromatic profile. Firm in the mouth, with evident young tannins, savory notes. Very promising even if it is still a little bit behind with the maturation.

90   Price B
Barolo Gabutti 2012

100% Nebbiolo grapes. Limpid garnet color. Very typical aromas with hints of dry flowers and medical herbs, kirsch and black cherry. Agile, savory with a good acid component and tightened and young tannins, typical of Serralunga.

★★

SOTTIMANO

Località Cottà, 21
12052 Neive (CN)
Tel. +39 0173 635186
🆂 *Az.Agr.Sottimano*
info@sottimano.it
www.sottimano.it
🅵 *AziendaAgricolaSottimano*
🐦 *@AzAgr.Sottimano*

YEAR OF FOUNDATION **1971**
NAME OF THE OWNER **Rino Sottimano**
TOTAL BOTTLES PRODUCED **85,000**
DIRECT SALES
VISITS TO THE WINERY - RESERVATION NEEDED
HECTARES OF VINEYARD **18**

In the past ten years, the Sottimano estate in Neive has seen a rise in quality that only those who are unfamiliar with the tenacity, passion and skill of Rino and Andrea would not understand. And the increasingly Burgundy-esque and natural style of wines from the four magnificent cru they own is the result of years of study, experiments and risk-taking both in the vineyards and in the winery. Nevertheless, the results are truly outstanding, Nebbiolo wines with crystalline purity that soar over the Langhe sky.

🔲 🔲 96   Price B
Barbaresco Cottà 2013

100% Nebbiolo grapes. It matures in used barrique. Bright ruby red color. On the nose it present itself with mint, floral scents and aromas of small fruits literally suave. On the mouth it is sweet, elegant with silky tannins and a gritty and deep finish. Gorgeous.

🔲 93   Price B
Barbaresco Fausoni 2013

100% Nebbiolo grapes. It matures in used barrique. The best Fausoni ever. Bright ruby red color. On the nose complex aromas of tobacco, spices and flint. Full taste, elegant, the volume is perfectly balanced and the finish is vibrant and austere.

🔲 93   Price B
Barbaresco Pajorè 2013

100% Nebbiolo grapes. It matures in used barrique. Bright ruby red color. On the nose this 2013 vintage is very Bourgogne style with aromas of spices and

red fruits. Juicy, mineral with very fine tannins that only the Pajore can have. Very long and elegant finish.

🔲 90   Price B
Langhe Nebbiolo 2014

100% Nebbiolo grapes. It matures in used barrique. It is actually a downgraded Barbaresco because of the age of the vineyard (just over 20 years) still not sufficient. Bright ruby red color. Surprisingly expressive aromas but what is attractive is the palate: elegant, agile but very tonic and vibrant.

🔲 90   Price B
Barbera d'Alba Pairolero 2013

100% Barbera grapes. It matures in used barrique. It does 22 days of maceration and 2 years on the lees: a few number to explain that is not a common Barbera. Bright ruby color. Spicy and fruity aromas. Elegant on the palate with the fruit that is mixed with the minerality. The Pairolero 2013 is gorgeous.

TENUTA SANTA CATERINA

Via Guglielmo Marconi, 17
14035 Grazzano Badoglio (AT)
Tel. +39 0141 925 108
info@tenuta-santa-caterina.it
www.tenuta-santa-caterina.it
🅵 *tenutasantacaterina*

YEAR OF FOUNDATION **1737**
NAME OF THE OWNER **Guido Carlo Alleva**
TOTAL BOTTLES PRODUCED **50,000**
DIRECT SALES
VISITS TO THE WINERY - RESERVATION NEEDED
HECTARES OF VINEYARD **23**
HOSPITALITY
RESTAURANT

Set in the Asti part of Monferrato, this splendid estate was totally revamped over the past ten years thanks to its current owner, the Milan attorney Guido Carlo Alleva and his daughter Giulia. They have over 20 hectares of vineyards from which they produce very territorial and well-made wines. Next to the winery is a wonderful resort of the same name.

🔲 91   👍 Price A
Barbera d'Asti Superiore VignaLina 2013

100% Barbera grapes. Stainless steel for 1 year.

Alive and intense ruby color. Very fruity, aromas of black cherry, plum, very fragrant and whole scents. On the mouth is delicious, simple, great and pleasant to drink, good body, tense, savory and with an adequate persistence.

 90　　　　　　　　　　　 **Price A**

Grignolino d'Asti Arlandino 2014

100% Grignolino grapes. Stainless steel only. Clear garnet color. Typical in the nose, fruity with aromas of currant, pomegranate and cherry. Tense in the mouth, fresh, pleasantly savory, great to drink and a good length. Delicious.

★★
TENUTE CISA ASINARI DEI MARCHESI DI GRESY

Strada della Stazione, 21 - Località Martinenga
12050 Barbaresco (CN)
Tel. +39 0173 635222
Fax +39 0173 635187
matilde@marchesidigresy.com
www.marchesidigresy.com
 marchesidigresy

YEAR OF FOUNDATION **1797**
NAME OF THE OWNER **Alberto Cisa Asinari di Gresy**
TOTAL BOTTLES PRODUCED **200,000**
DIRECT SALES
VISITS TO THE WINERY - RESERVATION NEEDED
HECTARES OF VINEYARD **35**

Alberto di Gresy is one of those rare Piedmont aristocrats who has continued his family's winemaking tradition. His family has owned Tenuta Cisa Asinari since 1797 and he has been running it for the past 40 years. The historic cru Martinenga (the name derives from the ancient cult of the god Maris that was celebrated here) is the most prestigious vineyard in the district, while the best parcels are Camp Gros and Gaiun.

96　　　　　　　　　　　**Price C**

Barbaresco Camp Gros Martinenga Riserva 2011

100% Nebbiolo grapes. Matures 30 months in different size barrels. Intense garnet ruby. Very classy notes of licorice, cassis, Kirsch, spicy hints in the background. Compact in the mouth, savory, youthful and strong tannins but well balanced by its smoothness, alcoholic warmth and thin and persistent finish.

92　　　　　　　　　　　**Price C**

Barbaresco Martinenga 2013

100% Nebbiolo grapes. Matures 12 months in different size barrels. Lively garnet ruby red. Wet soil, slighty smoky, then violets and pomegranate. Slightly aggressive tannins, youthful, nice body but not enormous, savory, agile.

 88　　　　　　　　　　　**Price A**

Langhe Sauvignon 2015

100% Sauvignon grapes. Stainless steel. Greenish yellow. Typical notes of exotic fruits and elder. Very pleasant and easy to drink, savory, fresh and of discrete persistence.

★
TENUTE SELLA

Via IV novembre, 128
46310 Lessona (BI)
Tel. +39 015 99455
info@tenutesella.it
www.tenutesella.it

YEAR OF FOUNDATION **1671**
NAME OF THE OWNER **Sella Family**
TOTAL BOTTLES PRODUCED **90,000**
DIRECT SALES
VISITS TO THE WINERY - RESERVATION NEEDED
HECTARES OF VINEYARD **22**

The Sella family are descendants of Quintino Sella who was a textile industrialist and finance minister in the government of Urbano Rattazzi. And it was to their illustrious ancestor that they have dedicated their best wine, Lessona. The estate is in Biella, a town famous for its wool mills and red wines, and has always been a leading producer ever since the winery was created more than 300 years ago.

92　　　　　　　　　　　**Price C**

Lessona Omaggio a Quintino Sella 2009

Blend of 85% Nebbiolo and 15% Vespolina grapes. It matures 48 months in 25 ht Slavonia durmast barrels. Bright garnet red color. Spicy aromas of red fruits and underbrush, hints of leather and eucalyptus. Powerful taste with fine tannins and a nice acidity. On the finish the harmony is all played on the fruitiness.

89   Price B
Bramaterra 2011

Blend of 70% Nebbiolo, 20% Croatina and 10% Vespolina grapes. It matures for 28 months in 10 hl Slavonia durmast barrels. Iridescent ruby color. On the nose aromas of crisp red fruits and spices, an hint of alfalfa and pepper as well. Savory taste with an harmonic tannin and a good development.

★
TORRACCIA DEL PIANTAVIGNA

Via Romagnano, 96a
28074 Ghemme (NO)
Tel. +39 0163 840040
info@torracciadelpiantavigna.it
www.torracciadelpiantavigna.it
 TorracciadelPiantavigna

YEAR OF FOUNDATION **1990**
NAME OF THE OWNER **Alessandro Francoli**
TOTAL BOTTLES PRODUCED **120,000**
DIRECT SALES
VISITS TO THE WINERY - RESERVATION NEEDED
HECTARES OF VINEYARD **40**

The Francoli family planted their first vineyards (in Torraccia di Ghemme) at the end of the 1970s and now have 40 hectares between the provinces of Novara and Vercelli. Over the years, they have become reference points for classic Ghemme and Gattinara wines. More recently, in collaboration with Beppe Caviola, they have developed a line of austere reds that need time to express themselves but have undeniable character.

 ### 96   Price B
Ghemme Vigna Pelizzane 2010

Blend of 90% Nebbiolo and 10% Vespolina grapes. It matures in big oak barrels. A radiant and radiating Nebbiolo. Bright ruby red color. On the nose aromas of spices, cinchona and blond tobacco are predominant with small fruits and eucalyptus notes as support. Sumptuous taste with velvety tannins and a powerful and yet elegant progression.

94   Price B
Ghemme 2011

Blend of 90% Nebbiolo and 10% Vespolina grapes.

It matures in big oak barrels. Bright ruby color. On the nose it is an explosion of aromas of aromatic herbs and spices, powerful and harmonic mouth, fresh and juicy. The usual gorgeous tannins lead to a deep and juicy finish.

GIANCARLO TRAVAGLINI

Strada delle Vigne, 36
13045 Gattinara (VC)
Tel. +39 0163 833588
info@travaglinigattinara.it
www.travaglinigattinara.it
 www.travaglinigattinara.it

YEAR OF FOUNDATION **1958**
NAME OF THE OWNER **Cinzia Travaglini**
TOTAL BOTTLES PRODUCED **250,000**
DIRECT SALES
VISITS TO THE WINERY - RESERVATION NEEDED
HECTARES OF VINEYARD **44**

Giancarlo Travaglini has the undeniable merit of having promoted the noble and austere Piedmont wine Gattinara throughout the world. Over the years, he has been able to renew himself with well-made wines that bring together boldness and rich aromas. His daughter Cinzia has successfully been at the helm of the estate for the past few years and revamped the image of a winery that has been fundamental for the history of Gattinara.

94   Price B
Gattinara Riserva 2010

100% Nebbiolo grapes. Intense garnet color. On the nose aromas of small berries, pomegranate at first, then more austere scents of dry flowers and smoky hints. Savory and tense with a great texture, full-flavored, warm, velvety with polite tannins that are almost completely integrated with the structure of the wine. Very persistent finish.

93   Price C
Il Sogno 2011

100% Nebbiolo grapes left to fade on trellises for a few months. It matures for 40 months on big oak barrels. Intense garnet color. On the nose aromas of tamarind, carob, currant jelly, kirsch that defined a very rich, even alcoholic, aromatic profile. On the mouth warm and full-flavored, savory, with young and thick tannins and an impressive finish.

★★
G. D. VAJRA

Via delle Viole, 25
12060 Barolo (CN)
Tel. +39 0173 56257
Fax +39 0173 56345
info@gdvajra.it
www.gdvajra.it

YEAR OF FOUNDATION 1972
NAME OF THE OWNER Aldo and Milena Vajra
TOTAL BOTTLES PRODUCED 300,000
DIRECT SALES
VISITS TO THE WINERY - RESERVATION NEEDED
HECTARES OF VINEYARD 60

Aldo and Milena Vajra have been making wine in Barolo for 40 years and are now having success thanks to the quality of their wine and their well-mannered, old-fashion ways that are moving. They have vineyards of which Bricco delle Viole and even parcels of Coste and Fossati are used for their Dolcetto. The wines are territorial, elegant, kind and traditional. A few years ago they have also bought the small but prestigious winery of Luigi Baudana, in Serralunga, who owns part of the homonym vineyard.

☐ 95	Price C

Barolo Bricco delle Viole 2012

100% Nebbiolo grapes. It matures in big oak barrels for 42 months. Intense garnet color. From one of the highest vineyards in the village of Barolo. Intense ruby color with light garnet reflexes. On the nose elegant and refined aromas of currant, cardamom, vanilla and kirsch for a young and refined aromatic profile. Savory taste, with a good acidity to support the body that is already agile, the tannins are maybe too young but very promising. Warm and thin finish.

■ 93	Price C

Barolo Baudana 2012

100% Nebbiolo grapes. It matures in big oak barrels for 42 months. Intense garnet ruby color. On the nose aromas of violet, fume scents, austere with light notes of tar on the background. On the mouth it is firm with thick but very pleasant tannins, gritty but not dried, good acidity, a more agile body then usual almost surprising for the finesse. The finish is savory and very long. Very young and promising.

☐ 91	Price B

Langhe Riesling 2015

100% Riesling grapes. Stainless steel only. Greenish straw yellow color. Varietal aromas of grapefruit, cedar, lime and an hint of kerosene. Sharp taste with a very persistent acidity, refreshing, good body, savory and very long.

■ 90	Price C

Barolo Ravera 2012

100% Nebbiolo grapes. It matures for almost 3 years in big oak barrels. Clear garnet ruby color. Intense and delineated in the nose, whole with aromas of currant and raspberry. Tense, savory, crisp, with thick and fine tannins and a good length on the finish.

VIBERTI

Via delle Viole, 30
12060 Barolo (CN)
Tel. +39 0173 56192
info@viberti-barolo.com
www.viberti-barolo.com
 f *cantinaviberti*

YEAR OF FOUNDATION 1923
NAME OF THE OWNER Giovanni and Claudio Viberti
TOTAL BOTTLES PRODUCED 100,000
DIRECT SALES
VISITS TO THE WINERY - RESERVATION NEEDED
HECTARES OF VINEYARD 18
RESTAURANT

This historic Barolo winery has been making vast improvements thanks to Claudio Viberti who has brought back a very traditional and convincing style for his wines. Along with their winemaking activities, the Viberti family also runs a wonderful restaurant in the hamlet of Vergne, Trattoria del Buon Padre, which alone is worth a visit for both the food and the beauty of the landscape.

■ 94	Price C

Barolo La Volta Riserva 2010

100% Nebbiolo grapes. It matures almost 4 years in big oak barrels. Alive and intense garnet ruby color. Whole and clear in the nose, incredibly young, with a well delineated fruity aromas of black cherry at first, then currant and violet. Savory taste and polite with thick tannins, agile, tense, great body, very elegant and definitely promising regarding his evolution in time.

---

 93   Price C

Barolo San Pietro Riserva 2010

100% Nebbiolo grapes. It matures almost 4 years in big oak barrels. Intense ruby color. On the nose aromas of wet soil at first, then currant and pomegranate for a whole and complex aromatic profile. Intense with velvety tannins, and elegant and tense body, young and very promising.

---

 92   Price B

Barolo Buon Padre 2012

100% Nebbiolo grapes. It matures for 3 year in big oak barrels. Intense ruby color. On the nose aromas of plum, medical herb, floral notes of violet, everything very clear. Intense, savory, with thick tannins, rich and with a good persistent finish.

★★★

VIETTI

Piazza Vittorio Veneto, 5
12060 Castiglione Falletto (CN)
Tel. +39 0173 62825
info@vietti.com
www.vietti.com
🐦 *@vietti_vino*

YEAR OF FOUNDATION 1900
NAME OF THE OWNER Krause Holdings
TOTAL BOTTLES PRODUCED 250,000
DIRECT SALES
VISITS TO THE WINERY - RESERVATION NEEDED
HECTARES OF VINEYARD 37

The latest news is that this estate has been sold to an American investment company but there is no need to panic because it will continue to be run by the Currado family. Barolo della Vietti wines are an excellent expression of the terroir of Castiglione Falletto, Serralunga d'Alba and La Morra, interpreted with a cautious and elegantly modern style which rigorously respects the characteristics of the various vineyards. Again this year the estate's wines are of the utmost quality.

---

 95   Price D

Barolo Lazzarito 2012

100% Nebbiolo grapes. It matures in big oak bar-

rels. Light almost garnet ruby color. Intense aromas of plum at first, then scents of austere underbrush and dark flowers. Powerful taste with important but refined tannins that do not interfere with the drinkability. The progression is great and on the finish is of a rare wholeness and tastiness.

---

 94   Price D

Barolo Ravera 2012

100% Nebbiolo grapes. It matures in barrels made with different kind of woods. Intense garnet ruby color. On the nose the modern style overcomes the smoky notes with aromas of black cherry, cassis and spices. Savory and warm taste with thick but still young body. Long persistence.

---

 94   Price C

Barbera d'Asti Scarrone Vigne Vecchie 2013

100% Barbera grapes. It matures in oak barrels. Intense ruby color. In the nose classic aromas of black and red fruits and dark flowers. Very compact taste with a light hint of still young tannins and great personality. Sumptuous finish.

---

 92   Price D

Barolo Rocche di Castiglione 2012

100% Nebbiolo grapes. It matures in oak barrels. Intense ruby color with garnet reflexes. Full-flavored, ethereal, spicy and elegant with floral notes. Elegant in the mouth, soft, slightly warm with a great progression and a very long finish.

★★

VIGNETI MASSA

Piazza G. Casponi, 10
15059 Monleale (AL)
Tel. +39 0131 80302
Fax +39 0131 806565
vignetimassa@libero.it

YEAR OF FOUNDATION 1879
NAME OF THE OWNER Famigli Massa
TOTAL BOTTLES PRODUCED 80,000
DIRECT SALES
VISITS TO THE WINERY - RESERVATION NEEDED
HECTARES OF VINEYARD 22

Walter Massa is a passionate and vivacious man as you will ever met. He is one of the driving forces behind the Federation of Italian Independent Winemakers and, above all,

318

the undisputed leader of the Timorasso 'clan' which he basically founded. His wines are small masterpieces, typical and with a long life that have become authentic reference points for all producers in the area, especially those working with the Timorasso grape.

☐ 🎵 95   **Price B**

Colli Tortonesi Derthona Timorasso Sterpi 2013

100% Timorasso grapes. It matures 18 months in stainless steel on the yeasts. Bright greenish straw yellow color. Very complex aromas of acacia and wisteria flowers at first, then aromas of pear, cedar, grapefruit and smoky hints. Powerful and tense, warm, savory, well supported by the acidity, with a sustained body and a very long persistence.

☐ 93   **Price B**

Colli Tortonesi Derthona Montecitorio 2013

100% Timorasso grapes. It matures 18 months in stainless steel on the yeasts. Greenish golden yellow color. The nose is smoky at first, then it presents aromas of wisteria, grapefruit, plum and pineapple. Warm and full-bodied, very savory with a good acid tension and a great length.

☐ 90   **Price B**

Colli Tortonesi Derthona Timorasso 2014

100% Timorasso grapes. It matures almost 1 year in stainless steel on the yeasts. Greenish straw yellow color. Fruity and citrusy aromas of cedar, grapefruit, pear Williams and light notes of exotic fruits. On the mouth it is more agile and savory of other versions, pleasant to drink with a good persistence in the finish.

VIGNETI VALLE RONCATI

Via Nazionale, 10/a
28072 Briona (NO)
Tel. +39 011 800 5851
Fax +39 011 897 0577
info@vignetivalleroncati.it
www.vignetivalleroncati.it
🆗 *Vigneti-Valle-Roncati*

YEAR OF FOUNDATION 1997
NAME OF THE OWNER Cecilia Bianchi
TOTAL BOTTLES PRODUCED 30,000
DIRECT SALES
VISITS TO THE WINERY - RESERVATION NEEDED
HECTARES OF VINEYARD 10

A tiny estate with only ten hectares of vineyards in northern Piedmont, in the province of Novara, where on clear days it is almost as if you can touch Monte Rosa. This is the Burgundy of Italy except here they mostly cultivate Nebbiolo and Vespolino and not Pinot Noir, Nevertheless, the wines have an elegance and grace comparable to the great French wines and have names like Fara, Ghemme and Sizzano and not Vosne Romanée. Hats off to Cecilia Bianchi who produced this unknown and extraordinary wines that has exceptional success at the 2016 Decanter World Wine Awards.

■ 🎵 96   **Price B**

Ghemme Le Blanque 2011

100% Nebbiolo grapes. It matures in big oak barrels for 38 months. Lively garnet ruby color. Complex and articulated aromas of spices at first, then black cherry, leather, violet, and an hint of licorice. Firm taste, rich, velvety, well supported by the acidity with thick but not aggressive tannins, agile and tense body and a very long finish.

■ 94   **Price B**

Fara Ciada 2010

Blend of 70% of Nebbiolo grapes with Vespolina and Uva Rara. It matures in big oak barrels for 30 months. Lively garnet color. Complex aromas of blackberry, incense, caramel, eucalyptus and violet. Agile, elegant, with good body, nice acidity, very fine tannins. Not an huge wine but very elegant and with a great persistence.

VILLA SPARINA

Frazione Monterotondo, 56
15066 Gavi (AL)
Tel. +39 0143 633835
sparina@villasparina.it
www.villasparina.it
🆗 *VillaSparinaResort*

YEAR OF FOUNDATION 1974
NAME OF THE OWNER Massimo Moccagatta
TOTAL BOTTLES PRODUCED 600,000
DIRECT SALES
VISITS TO THE WINERY - RESERVATION NEEDED
HECTARES OF VINEYARD 70

HOSPITALITY
RESTAURANT

The Moccagatta family are Gavi specialists who, with the consultancy of enologist Beppe Caviola and agronomist Federico Curtaz, are turning this famous estate into an authentic research laboratory. The headquarters are in the 18th century villa once belonged to the Franzoni Marquises of Genoa, as can be seen in the cellars. The antique farm house today houses the splendid Ostelliere hotel.

 93 Price B

Gavi del Comune di Gavi Monterotondo 2012

100% Cortese grapes. It matures 4 months in barrique and 4 months in stainless steel. Light golden yellow color. Complex and faceted aromas of cedar, pear Williams, hints of saffron and honey at first, then more smoky scents from the yeast lysis. Savory, tense, not huge but fine and elegant with a thin and persistent finish. Is one of the bet of this vintage.

 91 👍 Price A

Gavi del Comune di Gavi 2015

100% Cortese grapes. Stainless steel only. Light straw yellow color. Deliciously citrusy aromas of cedar and lime at first, then pear Williams and white peach. Savory taste, great to drink, polite, fine, thin. You could drink a bucket of it!

★

VITE COLTE

Via Bergesia, 6
12060 Barolo (CN)
Tel. +39 0173 564611
info@vitecolte.it
www.vitecolte.it
 ViteColte
 @ViteColte

YEAR OF FOUNDATION **1980**
NAME OF THE OWNER
TOTAL BOTTLES PRODUCED **1,200,000**
DIRECT SALES
VISITS TO THE WINERY - RESERVATION NEEDED
HECTARES OF VINEYARD **300**

For years, Terre da Vino was a point of reference for Langhe and Asti wine production. Under the supervision of Piero Quadrumolo, a great administrator with a deep knowledge of winemaking, it offered wines of good quality at reasonable prices. Today the cooperative has been has split into two. Terra da Vino produces the basic wines, while the experience of the better winemaker-suppliers has given birth to Vite Colte (Cultured Vines). It is a line dedicated to these producers who by working their vineyards and bringing the fruits of their labor to the wine cooperative have passed on to it their wine culture.

 95 Price C

Barolo Essenze Riserva 2007

100% Nebbiolo grapes. It matures for more than 3 years in barrels of different sizes. A small masterpiece, a selection that resumes the best of the cooperative production in the Barolo area. Very intense garnet color. Very articulated aromas of tamarind, licorice, mint, violet and light spices. Full-flavored, rich, warm, with tannins well buffered by the rich glycerol, very typical of the year. Surprisingly long finish.

■ **93** Price B

Barbaresco La Casa in Collina 2013

100% Nebbiolo grapes. It matures for 18 months in oak barrels of different sizes. Intense garnet ruby color. Elegantly fruity and spicy, whole, with aromas of violet and pomegranate. Tense on the palate, with thick and elegant tannins, with an agile body, savory and balanced and persistent.

■ **92** Price B

Barolo del Comune di Barolo Essenze 2012

100% Nebbiolo grapes, 2 years in oak barrels of different sizes. Intense garnet color. On the nose it is ethereal and full-flavored with aromas of kirsch, light tamarind, licorice and rose. Savory taste, with young tannins, a tense body and a good alcoholic component. Great length in the finish.

■ **90** 👍 Price A

Barbera d'Asti Superiore La Luna e i Falò 2014

100% Barbera grapes. It matures for 1 year in barrique. Alive and intense ruby color. On the nose smoky scents at first, then black cherry, violet and vanilla. On the mouth it presents a great tension with the typical acidic component of the Barbera at first, then very soft tannins and an adequate length in the finish.

VOERZIO MARTINI

Strada Loreto, 1
12064 La Morra (CN)
Tel. +39 0173 509194
info@voerziomartini.com
www.voerziomartini.com

YEAR OF FOUNDATION **2011**
NAME OF THE OWNER **Gianni Voerzio, Mirko and
Federica Martini**
TOTAL BOTTLES PRODUCED **60,000**
DIRECT SALES
VISITS TO THE WINERY - RESERVATION NEEDED
HECTARES OF VINEYARD **12**

The new life for Gianni Voerzio's winery began only recently when Mirko and Federica Martini became partners. Production continues to be based on the same wines but are the result of the collaboration and contribution between the three partners. Gianni Voerzio is a wine-grower, Mirko Martini is an enologist and Federica Martini is in charge of running the estate and sales. The first results are amazing to say the least.

---

 94   Price C
Barolo La Serra 2012

100% Nebbiolo grapes. It matures for 2 years in oak barrels of different sizes. Intense ruby color. Clear, full-flavored, spicy with aromas of vanilla, cherry, violet and wildflowers for a refined and young aromatic profile. Tense structure, full-bodied, refined tannins, thick but not aggressive and with a great persistent finish.

★★★
ROBERTO VOERZIO

Località Cerreto, 7
12064 La Morra (CN)
Tel. +39 0173 509196
info@voerzioroberto.it
www.voerzioroberto.it
 RobertoVoerzioLaSerraBarolo

YEAR OF FOUNDATION **1986**
NAME OF THE OWNER **Roberto Voerzio**
TOTAL BOTTLES PRODUCED **50,000**
DIRECT SALES
VISITS TO THE WINERY - RESERVATION NEEDED
HECTARES OF VINEYARD **20**

If anyone represents the figure of a modern winemaker it is Roberto Voerzio. And this not because he is a modernist but because he interprets tradition in an intelligent and substantial way. His wines are the product of hard work in the vineyard and a respectful, light yet technically impeccable winemaking approach. The international success these wines have had reflects this and are a demonstration that you don't need a revolution to be understood.

---

 96   Price D
Barolo Brunate 2012

100% Nebbiolo grapes. It matures 2 years in barrique and big oak barrels. Very fine and articulated with aromas of blackberry, blueberry, currant as well as more sweet scents of vanilla and cocoa. Very intense, with a notable extractive weight, nice alcoholic component, perfectly integrated and polite tannins. Substantially elegant despite the big structure. Very long and warm finish.

---

 93   Price B
Barbera d'Alba Vigneti Cerreta 2013

100% Barbera grapes. It matures in tonneau for 1 year. Very intense ruby color. Extremely whole aromas of raspberry, blackberry, black cherry, plum and violet with a light hint of vanilla and smoky note on the background. Full and deep taste with the acidity that supports the full-body, savory and warm.

---

 92   Price B
Langhe Nebbiolo Fontanazza Vigneti San Francesco 2013

100% Nebbiolo grapes. It matures in tonneau for 1 year than in stainless steel for 9 months. Bright garnet ruby color. On the nose aromas of licorice at first, then plum, light currant, pomegranate and light smoky hints. Warm in the mouth, intense, with thick but not aggressive tannins, great structure with a savory and persistent finish.

■ 91   🖒 Price A
Dolcetto d'Alba Priavino 2015

100% Dolcetto grapes. Stainless steel only. Intense violet ruby color. Very fruity aromas of cherry and blackberry, light fermentative scents and then wildflowers. On the mouth it is delicious, soft, full-flavored, savory and with a good length.

SARDINIA

These wines represent the backbone of winemaking in Sardinia and are the most made, the best known and represent almost all of DOC production. However, other wines do exist and are made in more restricted areas and represent authentic gems of ancient Sardinian traditions. We start with two very particular whites that are produced in the central-western part of the island. They are Vernaccia di Oristano, a dry white with a high alcoholic content, and Malvasia di Bosa, a very rare semi-sweet white produced between Bosa and Planargia in the eastern part of the province of Nuoro. The province of Oristano also produces a red wine from Bovale grapes, Campidano di Terralba, and whites from Trebbiano and Sangiovese di Arborea. Further south, in the area of Sulcis, is the wonderful Carignano del Sulcis, a soft and wrapping red that is as good as it is unknown. At the heart of the island, around Sorgono, is the zone where they produce another red made with Bovale and Cannonau grapes, Mondrolisai. To the far north, between Olbia and Sassari, is where they produce Moscato di Sorso-Sennori, a sweet, slightly aromatic white. And then there is the relatively new DOC Alghero appellation which is the monopoly of Sella & Mosca and the Santa Maria La Palma wineries where, among the other wines, they produce the rare Torbato di Alghero, an excellent white, as well as Sauvignon, Chardonnay, Cabernet and Sangiovese. Together all these wines mirror the different climates and soils as well as the wealth of grape varieties the region possesses.

This region produces less wine than one would have imagined. At the same time, it is also the one in the southern Mezzogiorno region that is moving the fastest to improve the quality of its wines. The awarding of a DOCG classification to Vermentino di Gallura, one region's most representative whites, and the presence in different areas on the island of first-rate cooperatives and private estates is doing the rest. There is no doubt that wine in Sardinia today is far better than it was in the past. There are now many wines that are classified DOC and other qualify for the regional appellation. This occurs when the name of a region is indicated on the label together with that of the grape variety used. Thus from Cagliari to Sassari, from Olbia to Carbonia they are producing Cannonau, Monica, Moscato, Vermentino and Sardinia DOC wines. The first two are reds and the other whites.

In the province of Cagliari alone, on the other hand, (where the term 'di' or from Cagliari is used on the label), they produce Monica, a dry Rosso, Nasco Moscato, Malvasia and Girò, semi-sweet or sweet wines at times produced as a sweet or dry liqueur. And then there is Nuragus, a dry white that is very well-known and popular.

Vini a Denominazione di origine controllata e garantita

- Vermentino di Gallura

Vini a Denominazione di origine controllata

- Alghero
- Arborea
- Cagliari
- Campidano di Terralba o Terralba
- Cannonau di Sardegna, accompagnata o no dalle sottozone Classico o Oliena o Nepente di Oliena o Capo Ferrato o Jerzu
- Carignano del Sulcis
- Girò di Cagliari
- Malvasia di Bosa
- Mandrolisai
- Monica di Sardegna
- Moscato di Sardegna, accompagnata o no dalle sottozone Tempio Pausania o Tempio o Gallura (per la tipologia spumante)
- Moscato di Sorso-Sennori o Moscato di Sorso o Moscato di Sennori
- Nasco di Cagliari
- Nuragus di Cagliari
- Sardegna Semidano, accompagnata o no dalla sottozona Mogoro
- Vermentino di Sardegna
- Vernaccia di Oristano

★★★
ARGIOLAS

Via Roma, 28
09040 Serdiana (CA)
Tel. +39 070 740606
info@argiolas.it
www.argiolas.it
f ArgiolasWinery
y @ArgiolasWinery

YEAR OF FOUNDATION **1938**
NAME OF THE OWNER **Franco and Giuseppe Argiolas**
TOTAL BOTTLES PRODUCED **2,000,000**
DIRECT SALES
VISITS TO THE WINERY - RESERVATION NEEDED
HECTARES OF VINEYARD **230**
OLIVE OIL PRODUCTION

Argiolas represents a kind of model for a family estate even if it is so large. The new generation at the helm is professional and passionate and have the fortune of benefitting from the advice of an enologist who is as modest as he is expert, Mariano Mauro. All their hard work has resulted in a slew of recognitions for Arigiolas on both a national and international level over the past years. No small feat considering how difficult is to operate in a region like Sardinia with all its social and economic problems. The estate uses a modern approach to traditional style and thus focuses much of its production on the region's traditional grapes. They to this using modern techniques, perhaps sometimes too much, without ever allowing the wines to lose their originality.

■ 91 Price B
Korem 2013

Blenf of 55% Bovale, 35% Cannonau and 20% Carignano grapes. Ages in barrique. Very deep ruby. Fascinating nose of pencil lead, ink and light wild notes. The palate is rich, tense, with very firm tannins and a lively dynamism. Deep and tense finish.

■ 91 Price B
Turriga 2012

Blend of Cannonau (85%), Bovale, Carignano and Malvasia Nera grapes. Ages in barrique. Dark ruby. Intense and defined aromas of mediterranean scrub and spices. The palate is elegant, supple, medium-bodied and overall with a good balance. Long and supple finish.

■ 90 Price B
Cannonau di Sardegna Senes Ris. 2012

100% Cannonau grapes. Ages in barrique. Deep ruby. Fascinating nose with notes of spices and sweet tobacco. Soft palate with very elegant tannins; meaty and warm finish.

★
AUDARYA

S.S. 466, km 10,100
09040 Serdiana (CA)
Tel. +39 070 740437
info@audarya.it
www.audarya.it
f Audarya
y @AUDARYAVINI

YEAR OF FOUNDATION **2014**
NAME OF THE OWNER **Enrico Pala**
TOTAL BOTTLES PRODUCED **50,000**
DIRECT SALES
VISITS TO THE WINERY - RESERVATION NEEDED
HECTARES OF VINEYARD **37**

Serdiana is the area with the most vineyards on the island and is home to the great and historic Sardinian estates. Salvatore and Nicoletta Pala are very young leading figures in this new and ambitious estate that was set up in 2014. Their 37 hectares of vineyards are cultivated with maniacal care and a technical staff of the highest level is obtaining results that from the first wine they put on the market would seem surprising except to those who are unfamiliar with the overwhelming passion driving this young couple. Production is purposely and exclusively concentrated on the typical grapes of the zone.

■ **95** Price B
Nuracada 2014

100% Bovale grapes. Ages in barrique. Inky color. Expressive nose of ink, clove and a lightly citrusy note. Powerful palate, firm tannins but with a wonderful suppleness and vigour. Tense and savory finish.

☐ 93 **👍 Price A**
Vermentino di Sardegna Camminera 2015

100% Vermentino grapes. Stainless steel only. Golden yellow with green hues. Explosive nose of aromatic herbs and white pepper. Rich palate, juicy with good tension and a deep savory finish.

☐ **90** 👍 Price A

Nuragus di Cagliari 2015

Nuragus grapes. Stainless steel. Straw yellow with greenish hues. Expressive nose of Mediterranean scrub and smoky hints. The palate is rich, savory, vertical and with an expressive and peat finish.

☐ **87** 👍 Price A

Vermentino di Sardegna 2015

100% Vermentino grapes. Stainless steel. Straw yellow with greenish hues. Fruity nose with hint of white pepper. The palate is juicy, fresh and supple. Long and chalky finish.

CANTINA DI OLIENA

Via Nuoro, 112
08025 Oliena (NU)
Tel. +39 0784 287509
info@cantinasocialeoliena.it
www.cantinasocialeoliena.it
🅕 *Cantina-Sociale-Oliena*

YEAR OF FOUNDATION 1950
NAME OF THE OWNER
TOTAL BOTTLES PRODUCED 350,000
DIRECT SALES
VISITS TO THE WINERY - RESERVATION NEEDED
HECTARES OF VINEYARD 100

Established in 1950, is situated in the heart of Barbaglia, that is synonymous with Cannonau. What is unusual here is that the DOC Cannonau has been called, since 1972, Nepente di Oliena. This small cooperative, with some 100 members, appears to be making a comeback, after apparently losing direction, under the management of Daniele Manca. Its wines are traditional but produced using topnotch modern technology and methods in the vineyard and the winery. The first results are more than encouraging.

■ **89** 👍 Price A

Cannonau di Sardegna Nepente di Oliena 2014

100% Cannonau grapes. Ages in concrete tanks. Shiny ruby. Fascinating nose of Mediterranean herbs and nutmeg. Elegant palate, well-structured and with a good tension. Smooth tannins and juicy sip.

■ **87** Price A

Lanaitto 2014

Blend of Cannonau and other indigenous grape varieties. Concrete tanks. Shiny ruby. Distinctive notes of tobacco, blueberry and spices. Austere palate with notes of pencil lead and ink; dynamic and supple; fresh and juicy finish.

★

CANTINA DI SANTADI

Via Cagliari, 78
09010 Santadi (CI)
Tel. +39 0781 950127
info@cantinadisantadi.it
www.cantinadisantadi.it
🅕 *cantinadisantadi*
🐦 *@CantinaSantadi*

YEAR OF FOUNDATION 1960
NAME OF THE OWNER
TOTAL BOTTLES PRODUCED 1,700,000
DIRECT SALES
VISITS TO THE WINERY - RESERVATION NEEDED
HECTARES OF VINEYARD 600

This cooperative winery in the area of Sulcis has represented and continues to represent a model for the whole region on how quality can be achieved even by a cooperative. It operates in a unique area and can count on a slew of vineyards, obviously cultivated with Carignano grapes, which are extraordinary for their age and beauty. The range of wines produces is vast and on an average very good even if their standard-bearer remains Carignano del Sulcis Terre Brune, which represents the history of this winery and this type of wine.

⬚ **88** Price B

Latinia 2010

1005 Nasco overripe grapes. Ages in barrique. Warm amber, fascinating nose of dates and dried apricot. Concentrated palate, rich, sweet and balanced. Warm and juicy finish.

■ **87** Price C

Carignano del Sulcis Superiore Terre Brune 2012

100% Carignano grapes. Ages in barrique. Deep ruby. Nose of dried blossoms and Mediterranean scrub. Medium-bodied and supple palate, ripe tannins and the finish shows a light developed note.

CANTINA GIBA - 6 MURA

Via Ciusa, 16
09131 Cagliari (CA)
Tel. +39 0781 689718
info@cantinagiba.it
www.cantinagiba.it
 CantinaGiba
🐦 @CantinaGiba

YEAR OF FOUNDATION **2000**
NAME OF THE OWNER
TOTAL BOTTLES PRODUCED **150,000**
DIRECT SALES
VISITS TO THE WINERY - RESERVATION NEEDED
HECTARES OF VINEYARD **20**
OLIVE OIL PRODUCTION

Although just over ten years of age, Cantina di Giba has risen up the quality ladder in Sardinia. Located in the heart of Sulcis, its Carignano vineyards are in a place of extraordinary beauty. Their wines have a modern style but are extremely respectful of the land and the varietal and are among the best in their category. They also produce a Vermentino di Sardegna which has a very strong Mediterranean character.

■ **94**   Price B
Carignano del Sulcis 6Mura 2011

100% Carignano grapes. Ages in different sized barrels. Dark red. Complex nose of spices, tobacco and Mediterranean scrub. Meaty palate, sleek and with refined and chewy tannins; juicy acidity. Deep finish with notes of licorice and citrus. Amazing.

☐ **93**   Price B
Vermentino di Sardegna 6Mura 2015

100% Vermentino grapes. Stainless steel only. Shiny golden yellow. The nose is still austere and shows captivating notes of aromatic herbs. Wonderful palate, very good weight, savory and wonderfully dynamic. Powerful and very savory finish.

■ **90**   👍 Price A
Carignano del Sulcis Giba 2013

100% Carignano grapes. Stainless steel only. Deep ruby. Intense nose of citrus and Mediterranean scrub. Fresh palate, supple and with good structure. Crunchy tannins with a long, juicy and savory finish.

CANTINA IL NURAGHE DI MOGORO

S.S. 131, km 62
09095 Mogoro (OR)
Tel. +39 0783 990285
cantina@ilnuraghe.it
www.cantinadimogoro.it
🅕 cantinadimogoroilnuraghe
🐦 @CantinaDiMogoro

YEAR OF FOUNDATION **1956**
NAME OF THE OWNER
TOTAL BOTTLES PRODUCED **850,000**
DIRECT SALES
VISITS TO THE WINERY - RESERVATION NEEDED
HECTARES OF VINEYARD **600**

Cantina Il Nuraghe di Mogoro was founded in 1956 and for a long time was considered one of the most avant-garde estates in Sardinia before falling on difficult times. In recent years, and under the management of the young expert Daniele Manca, its wines have rebounded from a quality and sales point of view and it now offers some ambitious products. The key to its recovery was to enhance the value of local varietals beginning with Semidano di Mogoro, a variety that has 'northern' characteristics and a distinct personality. Their whole line of production is distinguished by a technical cleanliness and attention to bringing out the traits of the grapes being used. The wines also have an excellent quality/price ratio.

☐ **94**   👍 Price A
Semidano di Mogoro Superiore Puistèris 2013

100% Semidano di Mogoro grapes. Stainless steel only. Wonderful version of this very rare Sardinian white. Intense nose of sea breeze, Mediterranean scrub and peat. Austere and rich palate, sharp and tense. Very long finish.

■ **92**   Price B
Cavaliere Sardo Riserva 2013

100% Bovale grapes. Ages in used barrels. Ink color. This new wine shows notes of bay leaf and spices. Rich palate, thick but ripe tannins and with a wonderful balanced acidity. Long and expressive finish.

☐ 90   Price B

Mora Bianca 2015

100% Monica Bianca grapes. Stainless steel only. Golden yellow. This is an old Sardinian grape variety recently discovered by Daniele Manca. Distinctive notes of white pepper and wild strawberry. The palate is meaty, savory and with a finish already complex and expressive.

■ 89   Price B

Cannonau di Sardegna Riserva Chio 2011

Blend of 90% Cannonau and 10% Bovale grapes. Ages in different sized casks. Shiny ruby. Subtle spicy notes, then Mediterranean scrub. The palate is dense, fascinating but also fresh and consistent. Elegant and flavorful finish.

☐ 88   👍 Price A

Semidano di Mogoro Anastasia 2015

100% Semidano di Mogoro grapes. Stainless steel only. Shiny straw yellow. Fragrant nose withy notes of spices, sweet tobacco and citrus. Juicy and fruity palate with notes that reminds white peach. Vibrant finish, supple and savory.

★

CANTINE DI ORGOSOLO

Via Ilole
08027 Orgosolo (NU)
Tel. +39 0784 403096
 nicola.corria
info@cantinediorgosolo.it
www.cantinediorgosolo.it
🅕 *cantinediorgosolo*
🐦 *@info70014082*

YEAR OF FOUNDATION 2007
NAME OF THE OWNER
TOTAL BOTTLES PRODUCED 17,000
DIRECT SALES
VISITS TO THE WINERY - RESERVATION NEEDED
HECTARES OF VINEYARD 16

It was only ten years ago that this tiny cooperative winery began to bottle its own wines, which were exclusively made with Cannonau. In this short period of time they have been able to attract the attention of the wine-consuming public and wine lovers with wines capable of bringing together respect for tradition with

necessary technical skill. The results are bold, warm wines that are harmonious and rich in personality. Considering the outstanding potential of their magnificent vineyards we can only expect them to make even further and important improvements.

■ 93   Price B

Cannonau di Sardegna Urùlu 2014

100% Cannonau grapes. Ages in wooden tanks. Lively ruby. Well defined nose of Mediterranean scrub and spices. Mouth-filling palate, rich and with firm tannins and wonderfully balanced structure. Very agile and long finish.

■ 90   👍 Price A

Cannonau di Sardegna Neale 2014

Blend of 85% Cannonau and 15% Bovale grapes. Stainless steel only. Shiny ruby. Well-defined notes of tobacco and ink. The palate is juicy, tense and with a crunchy fruit aftertaste. Elegant, tense and flavorful finish.

■ 88   Price A

Cannonau di Sardegna Luna Vona 2015

100% Cannonau grapes. Ages in chestnut casks and stainless steel tanks. Light ruby. Delicate nose of Mediterranean scrub and spices; warm and supple palate. Meaty and long finish.

★★

CAPICHERA

Strada Arzachena-S. Antonio, km 3.5
07021 Arzachena (OT)
Tel. +39 0789 80612
info@capichera.it
www.capichera.it
🅕 *amicidicapichera*

YEAR OF FOUNDATION 1978
NAME OF THE OWNER Ragnedda Brothers
TOTAL BOTTLES PRODUCED 250,000
DIRECT SALES
VISITS TO THE WINERY - RESERVATION NEEDED
HECTARES OF VINEYARD 50

The Ragnedda family made winemaking history in Sardinia but most of all they played a major role to allow Vermentino, especially that of Gallura, to achieve a success that was difficult to imagine. Their extraordinary vineyards with the

327

typical Gallura granite soil, surrounded in lush Mediterranean brush, have for years offered us unique wines of great class and undeniable skill. They are wines that boldly challenge time and in recent years have seen a marked improvement in regard to freshness and elegance.

☐ 🄖 95	Price B

Capichera 2014

100% Vermentino grapes. Ages in barrels and stainless steel. Golden yellow. Expressive nose of white stone fruit and Mediterranean scrub. Meaty and dense palate, balanced, fresh and wonderfully dynamic. The endless finish is very savory, reminds sea breeze.

■ 94	Price D

Albòri di Lampada 2009

100% Syrah grapes. Ages in barrique and large casks. Deep ruby. The nose offers notes of spices and citrus. Full bodied palate, dense and with firm tannins yet surprisingly fresh and balanced. Wonderful depth and well defined finish.

■ 93	Price B

Assajè 2012

Blend of 95% Carignano and 5% Syrah grapes. Ages in barrique. Deep ruby. Intense nose of tobacco and ripe fruit. The palate is meaty, warm but elegant; juicy tannins and a long and firm finish.

☐ 93	Price B

Vermentino di Gallura Vigna Angena 2014

100% Vermentino grapes. Stainless steel only. Straw yellow with golden hues. intense nose of aromatic herbs and sea breeze. Juicy palate, vertical and with a wonderful dynamism. The aftertaste remind sea breeze notes; tense and long finish.

☐ 93	Price B

VT 2014

100% Vermentino grapes. Matures 6-8 months in barrique. Golden yellow. Fascinating nose of anise, pear and aromatic herbs. The palate is dense, creamy and lightly tannic. Warm, savory finish, very long finish.

★★
DETTORI

Località Badde Nigolosu
07036 Sennori (SS)
Tel. +39 079 512772

info@tenutedettori.it
www.tenutedettori.it
f *TenuteDettori*
🐦 *@TenuteDettori*

YEAR OF FOUNDATION **1998**
NAME OF THE OWNER **Dettori Family**
TOTAL BOTTLES PRODUCED **40,000**
DIRECT SALES
VISITS TO THE WINERY - RESERVATION NEEDED
HECTARES OF VINEYARD **22**
HOSPITALITY
RESTAURANT
CERTIFIED BIODYNAMIC VITICULTURE

It is difficult to explain the wines of the Dettori family if you have never been to Badde Nigolosu, near Sennori. It is unique place, 250m above sea level, with a view of the sea and wild beauty that is both violent and hypnotizing. The wines produced here perfectly mirror these characteristics as well as the tenacity and stubbornness with which Alessandro produces his traditional wines according to biodynamic dictates. "I don't follow market trends, I make wines I like, the wines of my land, Sennori wines". Not everyone may like his wines but for sure they leave no one indifferent. Estate of the Year in 2016 edition.

■ 🄖 97	Price B

Tenores 2012

100% Cannonau grapes. Ages in concrete tanks. Lively ruby. A "sunny wine" with aromas of Mediterranean scrub, ink and wild strawberry. The palate is juicy, sleek, with silky tannins and incredible suppleness. The length offers a multi-layered spectrum of spicy aromas and aromatic herbs. Incredible long length.

■ 94	Price C

Dettori 2012

100% Cannonau grapes. Ages in concrete tanks. Shiny ruby. Fascinating nose with notes of tobacco, ripe fruits and spices. Mouth-filling palate, dense, wonderfully balanced with a great depth. Chewy tannins and wonderfully long finish.

☐ 91	Price B

Dettori Bianco 2015

100% Vermentino grapes. Ages in concrete tanks. Golden yellow. Intense nose of marjoram, rosemary and apricot. Savory palate, lightly tannic, powerful but well balanced. The finish offers notes of sea breeze and with a unique character.

FRADILES

Via Sandro Pertini, 2
08030 Atzara (NU)
Tel. +39 333 1761683
info@fradiles.it
www.fradiles.it
 f *Fradiles-vitivinicola*
 🐦 *@Fradiles*

YEAR OF FOUNDATION 2004
NAME OF THE OWNER Paolo Savoldo, Giuseppe Fiore
TOTAL BOTTLES PRODUCED 15,000
DIRECT SALES
VISITS TO THE WINERY - RESERVATION NEEDED
HECTARES OF VINEYARD 14

This small Atzara estate is run by Paolo Savoldo who with his hard work and passion is bringing out the enormous potential of the area of Mandrolisai, in the shadows too long. His wines have a distinct personality and are made with a sure hand and courageous determination.

---

 90   Price A
Mandrolisai Fradiles 2014

Blend of Bovale sardo, Cannonau and monica grapes. Stainless steel only. Shiny ruby. Captivating aromas of Mediterranean scrub and red fruit. Juicy palate, supple and with a very good drinkability.

GABBAS

Via Trieste, 59
08100 Nuoro (NU)
Tel. +39 0784 33745
info@gabbas.it
www.gabbas.it

YEAR OF FOUNDATION 1974
NAME OF THE OWNER Giuseppe Gabbas
TOTAL BOTTLES PRODUCED 80,000
DIRECT SALES
VISITS TO THE WINERY - RESERVATION NEEDED
HECTARES OF VINEYARD 20
RESTAURANT
OLIVE OIL PRODUCTION

Giuseppe Gabbas is a spirited and laid-back winemaker of few words and the ironic look of someone who has seen it all during his life and is not surprised by many things anymore. His estate is in the heart of Sardinia and a few kilometers from Oliena on the slopes of Monte Corrasi, in an uncontaminated almost disturbingly powerful place. His winery produces three of the most elegant and refine versions of a grape that defines the region: Cannonau. The wines are fresh and Mediterranean and yet austere, magnificently drinkable and have an unmistakable personality. Over the past four-five years the stylistic definition of these wines has increased in an amazing way.

■ 🏆 96   Price B
Cannonau di Sardegna Classico Dule 2013

100% Cannonau grapes. Ages in used barrique. Shiny ruby. Wonderful vintage that offers notes of spices, tobacco and ink. Mouth-filling palate, aristocratic with silky tannins and a long vertical finish. Amazing.

■ 93   Price B
Cannonau di Sardegna Arbore Riserva 2013

Blend of 90% Cannonau and 10% Bovale grapes. Ages in used barrique. deep ruby red. Fascinating nose of rosemary, tobacco and light wild notes. Mouth-filling palate, austere, firm and meaty. Firm and chewy tannins but with a good tension and vertical finish.

■ 88   👍 Price A
Cannonau di Sardegna Lillovè 2014

Blend of Cannonau with small percentage of international grape varieties. Ages in barrels. Shiny red. Fascinating nose of spices and tobacco. Juicy palate, supple, thin and with a captivating finish.

□ 87   👍 Price A
Vermentino di Gallura Manzanile 2015

100% Vermentino grapes. Stainless steel only. Straw yellow. Floral and white peach nose. meaty palate, round but with a pleasant push on finish.

MONTISCI

Via Asiago, 7b
08024 Mamoiada (NU)
Tel. +39 328 0193273
 Ⓢ *giovannimontisci*

giovannimontisci@tiscali.it
giovannimontisci.centovigneitalia.com
f *Cantina-Giovanni-Montisci*

YEAR OF FOUNDATION 2003
NAME OF THE OWNER Giovanni Montisci
TOTAL BOTTLES PRODUCED 5,000
DIRECT SALES
VISITS TO THE WINERY - RESERVATION NEEDED
HECTARES OF VINEYARD 2

Giovanni Montisci's wines seem to be created to be talked about. The have force, character and at times are totally unpredictable and are never boring. His tiny production is divided into two products made from the magnificent Cannonau vineyards in Mamoiada. The wines have no additional sulfites and almost always are able to maintain significant integrity and express a style in which finesse, nicely paired with a high alcohol content, is its trademark. With the right harvest, Giovanni's wines are of the utmost quality.

■ 94   Price C
Cannonau di Sardegna Franziska Riserva 2014
100% Cannonau grapes. Ages in barrels. Light ruby. Rich and well-defined nose of licorice, ink and spices, fascinating palate with silky tannins and extremely elegant structure. The finish is tense, flavorful and very long.

EMIDIO OGGIANU

Località Badde Nuraghe - Strada Vicinale Pischina
08010 Magomadas (NU)
Tel. + 39 0785 359329
info@malvasiaoggianu.it
www.malvasiaoggianu.it
f *Malvasia-Oggianu*

YEAR OF FOUNDATION 1956
NAME OF THE OWNER Emidio Oggianu
TOTAL BOTTLES PRODUCED 5,000
DIRECT SALES
VISITS TO THE WINERY - RESERVATION NEEDED
HECTARES OF VINEYARD 4

Emidio Oggianu is an 80-year-old former station master who has brought the maniacal precision of that profession to his Malvasia di Bosa wines. His small Badde Murage vineyard is neat and the vines are between 22 and 55 years of age. His wines reach the market five years after harvest and they are not filtered nor are selected yeasts used. Harvest takes place in three stages in order pick the grapes when they are perfectly ripe. His aim is to produce a concentrated yet fresh Malvasia that is elegant and has no notes of oxidation.

▪ 94   Price B
Malvasia di Bosa Vigna Badde Nuraghe Riserva 2011
Malvasia di Bosa grapes. Ages in barrels. Golden yellow. Explosive nose with notes of Mediterranean scrub, dates, spices and candied citrus. Very concentrated palate but perfectly balanced; it delivers what promises on the palate. Wonderful depth; long, fresh and fulfilling finish.

OLIANAS

Località Purruddu
08030 Gergei (CA)
Tel. +39 055 8300411
olianas@olianas.it
www.olianas.it
f *Olianas-vini*
🐦 *@TenutaOlianas*

YEAR OF FOUNDATION 2000
NAME OF THE OWNER Artemio Olianas, Stefano Casadei and Simone Mugnaini
TOTAL BOTTLES PRODUCED 60,000
DIRECT SALES
VISITS TO THE WINERY
HECTARES OF VINEYARD 15
CERTIFIED ORGANIC VITICULTURE

The farm was set up in 2000 by three friends-partners – Artemio Olianas, Stefano Casadei and Simone Mugnaini – who had different backgrounds but shared a passion for Sardinia and winemaking. The estate, which also cultivates almonds, olives and figs, is on a plateau 400m above sea level that is rich in Mediterranean vegetation and is some 60km from Cagliari. Wine production focuses on the island's typical grapes made with an approach to the vineyard and cellar that is modern but not interventionist.

☐ 90 👍 Price A

Vermentino di Sardegna 2015

100% Vermentino grapes. Ages in amphora. Shiny straw yellow. Well-defined nose with hint of sea breeze and white peach. Dry palate, tense and savory. Very vertical finish, lightly tannic and definitively savory.

ORGOSA

Località Lucuriò
08027 Orgosolo (NU)
Tel. +39 339 7784958
mgorgosolo@tiscali.it
Cantina-Orgosa

YEAR OF FOUNDATION 2002
NAME OF THE OWNER Giuseppe Musina
TOTAL BOTTLES PRODUCED 9,000
DIRECT SALES
VISITS TO THE WINERY - RESERVATION NEEDED
HECTARES OF VINEYARD 2

Giuseppe Musina di Orgosolo is a winemaker of few words and a subtle sense of humor. Like many other Sardinians he travelled the world before settling back in his homeland to care for his family's vineyards. The old Cannonau vines are alberello-trained in a sandy soil with love and respect for nature and cultivated according to biodynamic principles, without being certified as such, and no sulfites are used. The estate is tiny with its just over two hectares of vineyards producing around 9,000 bottles of two types of wine. The wines are basic, juicy and made with a surprising amount of modern technology considering the winery doesn't even have electricity. But above all the wines have unquestionable character and charm.

■ 90 👍 Price A

Cannonau di Sardegna Orgosa 2014

100% Cannonau grapes. Stainless steel only. Shiny ruby. Captivating nose of licorice, spices and candied orange rind. The palate is juicy, elegant and with a sweet delicate tannins. Pleasant and vertical with a wonderful structure; very good depth with a mineral and chewy finish.

FAMIGLIA ORRO

Via Giuseppe Verdi
09070 Tramatza (OR)
Tel. +39 347 7526617
info@famigliaorro.it
www.famigliaorro.it
FAMIGLIA-ORRO
FamigliaOrro

YEAR OF FOUNDATION 2006
NAME OF THE OWNER Davide Orro
TOTAL BOTTLES PRODUCED 20,000
DIRECT SALES
VISITS TO THE WINERY - RESERVATION NEEDED
HECTARES OF VINEYARD 5
OLIVE OIL PRODUCTION

Davide Orro is a brave winemaker who is striving to keep alive one of the most extraordinary wines in Italy: Vernaccia di Oristano. At a time when many are uprooting these vines and planting others, he is keeping his and plans to plant another ten hectares in the coming years. This is not the dream of a madman but the plan of a cultured, expert and passionate businessman who has total faith in this wine. He not only makes wine but also some wonderful vegetable preserves.

⊡ 93 Price B

Vernaccia di Oristano 2009

Vernaccia di Oristano grapes. Ages in chestnut casks. Dark amber. Fascinating nose of Mediterranean scrub, dates, caramel and walnut husk. The palate is austere, aristocratic, rich but wonderfully balanced. Long and citrusy finish.

⊡ 93 Price B

Passentzia 2013

Dried vernaccia di Oristano grapes. Ages in chestnut casks. Amber yellow. Rich aromas of dates and dried apricots. Dense palate but fresh and dynamic. The finish is dry, long and vertical.

★★

PALA

Via Verdi, 7
09040 Serdiana (CA)
Tel. +39 070 740284
info@pala.it

www.pala.it
f *pala.vini*
y *@palavini*

YEAR OF FOUNDATION **1950**
NAME OF THE OWNER **Mario Pala**
TOTAL BOTTLES PRODUCED **450,000**
DIRECT SALES
VISITS TO THE WINERY - RESERVATION NEEDED
HECTARES OF VINEYARD **98**

In recent years, the estate of Mario Pala has had increasing success in Italy and abroad. The reasons for this are relatively simple: hard work and insisting on using traditional grapes even when other were switching to other varieties. Thus along with the classic Cannonau and Vermentino, he also uses the almost-extinct Nuragus and Bovale. His wines have a defined style and an efficient technical approach that is never invasive and geared to maintain the characteristic of the grapes.

☐ 🔲 **95**   Price B
Stellato Nature 2015
100% Vermentino grapes. Unfiltered. Shiny straw yellow. Generous aromas of white peach and field herbs. Mouth-filling palate, juicy and fragrant. Good depth, vertical and tense with fresh and definitively savory finish.

■ **93**   🖒 Price A
Cannonau di Sardegna Riserva 2014
100% Cannonau grapes. Ages in barrels. Deep ruby. Complex nose of spices, ink and aromatic herbs. Chewy palate, fulfilling, with juicy tannins and a fresh drinkability. The finish is savory and tense.

☐ **91**   🖒 Price A
Entemari 2014
Blend of Malvasia Sarda, Chardonnay and Vermentino grapes. Stainless steel only. Shiny straw yellow. Fascinating nose of white peach, quince and star anise. Rich palate, juicy, flavorful and vertical. Mouth-filling and savory finish.

☐ **90**   🖒 Price A
I Fiori 2015
Nuragus grapes. Stainless steel only. Shiny straw yellow. Austere nose of peat and sea breeze. The palate is dry, flavorful and full of personality. Sea breeze aftertaste and savory finish.

PUTZOLU

Via Eleonora, 8
09070 Baratili San Pietro (OR)
Tel. +39 333 2855632
mauroputzolu@tiscali.it

YEAR OF FOUNDATION **1997**
NAME OF THE OWNER **Mauro Domenico Putzolu**
TOTAL BOTTLES PRODUCED **1,000**
DIRECT SALES
VISITS TO THE WINERY - RESERVATION NEEDED
HECTARES OF VINEYARD **1.7**
OLIVE OIL PRODUCTION

Mauro Putzolu is a surveyor by profession but as soon as he speaks you know where his heart lies: his home in the area of Oristano and the grape that defines it: Vernaccia. And he will not accept the unexplainable yet understandable decline it has seen. His vineyards are Baratili San Pietro in what one could define as a kind of Vernaccia di Oristano Grand Cru. It is an area where the desert, among the biggest in Europe, co-exists with Mediterranean brush, the sea and vineyards, a bold, wild and unique land. The estate has only 1.5 hectares of vineyards which are worked by the whole family.

▪ **93**   Price B
Vernaccia di Oristano S'Anatzu Riserva 1998
Vernaccia di Oristano grapes. Ages in barrels. Deep amber. Mediterranean aromas: orange peel, dates, thyme and walnut husk. The palate is austere, mouth-filling and wonderfully balanced with a tense, vibrant and very long finish. A great hand-crafted wine.

GIUSEPPE SEDILESU

Via Adua, 2
08024 Mamoiada (NU)
Tel. +39 0784 56791
giuseppesedilesu@tiscali.it
www.giuseppesedilesu.com
f *cantinagiuseppes*
y *@CantinaSedilesu*

YEAR OF FOUNDATION **2001**
NAME OF THE OWNER **Salvatore Sedilesu**

TOTAL BOTTLES PRODUCED 100,000
DIRECT SALES
VISITS TO THE WINERY - RESERVATION NEEDED
HECTARES OF VINEYARD 17
CERTIFIED ORGANIC VITICULTURE
CERTIFIED BIODYNAMIC VITICULTURE

YEAR OF FOUNDATION 1899
NAME OF THE OWNER Gruppo Campari
TOTAL BOTTLES PRODUCED 6,700,000
DIRECT SALES
VISITS TO THE WINERY
HECTARES OF VINEYARD 541

The Mamoiada estate of the Sedilesu family has seen a leap in quality in recent years that is unmatched in Sardinia and elsewhere. His Cannonau wines are for the most part made with grapes from old vines and thy have acquired a style that perfectly complements tradition in a quest for freshness and elegance. The family recently bought another old vineyard and a fantastic plot of some ten hectares where they planted Cannonau, which is naturally alberello-trained.

With an annual production of almost seven million bottles, this is Sardinia's biggest wine producer. Owned by the Campari group, in recent years the quality of its wines has improved and production has centered above all on white wine made from traditional grapes and on quality reds. The white wines are made with Vermentino and the rare Torbato grapes, while Cannonau, Monica and Carignano are used for the reds. They also produce one of the most important Italian Cabernet Sauvignon: Marchese di Villamarina.

---

 95   👍 Price A

Mamuthone 2014

100% Cannonau grapes. Ages in concrete tanks and barrels. Shiny ruby. Fragrant and fascinating notes of licorice and ink. Juicy palate, mouth-filling and very elegant. The palate shows silky tannins and the wonderful acidity gives an incredible drinkability to a wine with such complexity. Very long and fulfilling tail.

☐ 93   Price B

Perda Pintà 2014

Granazza di Mamoiada grapes. Stainless steel only. Golden yellow. Intense notes of aromatic herbs and yellow fresh fruits. Powerful palate, warm but balanced and with great agility. Very good depth and distinctive sea breeze finish.

☐ 91   👍 Price A

Granazza 2015

Granazza di Mamoiada grapes. Stainless steel only. Shiny straw yellow. Light version of this local grape variety. Surprising and complex notes of cherry, apricot and pear. The palate is austere, lightly tannic, but with a wonderful freshness and length.

★★

SELLA & MOSCA

*Località I Piani
07041 Alghero (SS)
Tel. +39 079 997700
welcome@sellaemosca.com
www.sellaemosca.com*

---

 95   Price B

Alghero Marchese di Villamarina 2011

Cabernet Sauvignon grapes. Ages in barrique. Deep ruby. Generous notes of tobacco, ink and licorice. Sumptuous palate: sleek and dense. Wonderful tannins, smooth and juicy and with a great firm depth; austere and very long finish.

■ 93   Price B

Alghero Anghelu Ruju Riserva 2005

100% Cannonau grapes. Ages in barrels. Inky color. Literally explosive nose offering notes of Mediterranean scrub and spices. The palate is warm, captivating and of a wonderful complexity. Juicy and flavorful sip with a great length.

☐ 93   👍 Price A

Alghero Terre Bianche Cuvée 161 2015

Torbato grapes. Ages in barrique and stainless steel tanks. Shiny straw yellow. Austere nose, still very young with aromas of sea breeze, peat and cherry. Powerful palate, tense, lightly tannic and wonderfully fresh. Very long finish that reminds notes of sea breeze.

☐ 88   👍 Price A

Vermentino di Sardegna Cala Reale 2015

100% Vermentino grapes. Stainless steel only. Straw yellow with greenish hues. Lightly savory and definitively fruity nose. Fresh palate, juicy and vertical with a pleasant and savory finish.

SIDDÙRA

Località Siddùra
07020 Luogosanto (OT)
Tel. +39 079 6573027
Fax +39 079 9570860
info@siddura.com
www.siddura.com
 siddura
 siddurasrl

YEAR OF FOUNDATION 2008
NAME OF THE OWNER
TOTAL BOTTLES PRODUCED 150,000
DIRECT SALES
VISITS TO THE WINERY - RESERVATION NEEDED
HECTARES OF VINEYARD 37

The Siddùra estate was set up in 2008 in the heart of Gallura in a setting of incomparable natural beauty. Two entrepreneurs are behind it, a Sardinian and a German, who have very clear ideas on what they want to do and share a love of this land. Thanks to their first-rate staff, the result came quickly. They produce classic Gallura wines with a modern style, in the best sense of the word, which totally respects the nature of the grapes and the land.

☐ 91   👍 Price A
Vermentino di Gallura Spèra 2015

100% Vermentino grapes. Stainless steel only. Straw yellow with greenish hues. Fragrant nose of white peach and aromatic herbs. The palate is fresh, savory and captivating.

◼ 89   Price B
Bacco 2014

Cagnulari grapes. Ages in barrels. Deep ruby. Balm, licorice and very fruity aromas. The palate is still young, but with solid structure and well extracted tannins. Fresh and juicy finish.

◼ 89   Price B
Cannonau di Sardegna Fòla 2014

100% Cannonau grapes. Ages in barrels and stainless steel tanks. Shiny ruby. Well-defined notes of red fruit and spices. Fresh, juicy and supple palate.

◼ 88   Price A
Erema 2014

Blend of Sardinian grapes. Stainless steel only. Lively ruby. Fragrant and fruity nose. The palate is juicy, pleasant and with a juicy tannins. It has a wonderful and pleasant drinkability.

SURRAU

Località Chilvagghja - S.P. Arzachena-Porto Cervo
07021 Arzachena (OT)
Tel. +39 0789 82933
 vigne.surrau
info@surrau.it
www.vignesurrau.it
 VIGNE-SURRAU
 @VSurrau

YEAR OF FOUNDATION 2004
NAME OF THE OWNER
TOTAL BOTTLES PRODUCED 200,000
DIRECT SALES
VISITS TO THE WINERY - RESERVATION NEEDED
HECTARES OF VINEYARD 43

This important winery in the Arzachena area of Gallura has for a few years now been producing wines with an elegant style and that respect an area which mostly has a vocation for whites, although they are also making some interesting reds. The wines are intelligently modern while the classic granite soil of Gallura offer them a truly unique finesse.

◼ 88   Price B
Cannonau di Sardegna Sincaru Riserva 2013

100% Cannonau grapes. Ages in casks. Lively ruby. Aromas of spices and ink. Balanced palate, mouth-filling and with firm tannins. Juicy and pleasant finish.

◼ 87   Price B
Surrau 2013

Blend of 45% Cannonau, 45% Carignano and 10% Muristellu grapes. Stainless steel only. Fragrant nose of red fruit and thyme. Supple, balanced and pleasant palate.

SICILY

I n his *Italian Journey*, Goethe saw Sicily as the clue to everything. While he was referring to ancient civilization, the same could be applied to the world of wine. Sicily, in fact, is one of the homelands of Italian wine and with its six million hectoliters a year it is one of the most produce regions in Italy. Those who have been to Sicily know that in the countryside grape vines are as much of the landscape as olives and fig trees. Before we get into the various DOC appellations and wines they produce, it should be noted that only recently was a regional DOC Sicilia appellation created that serves as a legal umbrella for a large part of the island's production. Although this has only just begun, it is clear that it represents a revolution. The province of Messina in eastern Sicily is the home of Faro, a red wine made from Nerello Mascalese and Nerello Cappuccio. Unfortunately, it is a wine at risk of extinction that only a couple of wineries produce and in limited quantities. The grapes are from the eastern foothills of the Peloritani mountains between Messina and Taormina. On the island of Salina, one of the largest in the Aeolian archipelago, they produce small quantities of a delicious and aromatic white, Malvasia delle Lipari, which exists both as a normal wine and as a Passito with unmistakable aromas of dried apricot. In the province of Catania is the vast winegrowing area of Etna where the vineyards climb up the volcano to as high as 1,000m above sea level and have a soil rich in ash and potassium. Here they produce Etna Bianco, made from Carricante and Catarratto grapes, and Etna Rosso, from mostly Nerello Mascalese grapes. The first can also be a Superiore if it has an alcoholic content of at least 12%. These latter wines are complex and elegant, rich in particular aromas that recall mountain herbs and flowers. To the south are the provinces of Siracusa and Ragusa with their rare Moscato di Siracusa and Moscato di Noto, sweet wines that are practically impossible to find outside the area. But above all the area produces Eloro, a wine made in different variations. One that stands out is Eloro Pachino, an explosive, dense and full-bodied red made from Nero d'Avola grown on alberello-trained vines in the district of Pachino south of Noto. This is an area of extraordinary importance for the future of winemaking in Sicily and in coming years many great wines will come from here, you can bet on it. At present, the most representative wine for the southeast Sicily is Cerasuolo di Vittoria, made from Frappato and Nero d'Avola, which here is called Calabrese. It is a soft and wrapping red that can have a high alcoholic content and is classified DOCG. The southern coastal area of Sicily produces wines but none are classified until you get to Agrigento, Menfi, Sambuca di Sicilia and Santa Margheria del Belice, areas where Grecanico, Catarratto and Inzolia are used to make white wines and, for the most part, Nero d'Avola, and Perricone for the reds. However, this is also an area where the cultivation of non-native grapes is producing extraordinary results from Chardonnay, Merlot, Cabernet Sauvignon and Syrah. A phenomenon in this area is Settesoli, a giant cooperative

335

which by itself produces more wine than all of Basilicata and over a host of fine wines. Between southern Sicily and the province of Palermo are two Doc appellations which are equally new and interesting: Contessa Entellina and Contea di Sclafani. They were created to provide a legal umbrella and regulate the production of two important wineries in two respective zones: Tenuta di Donnafugata and the estate of Tasca d'Almerita, best known for its wine Regaleali. In both cases, together with traditional grapes like Ansonica or Inzolia and Grecanico, wines can be produced using the so-called international grapes (Cabernet, Merlot, Syrah, Pinot Noir, Chardonnay and so on). These wines have allowed these two important Sicilian wines to achieve international success. Off the coast of the provinces of Agrigento and Trapani is the island of Pantelleria, the home to one of Italy's best sweet white wines: Moscato di Pantelleria. It is made from Zibibbo grapes cultivated on low vines that are very difficult to work. There is also a Passito version that has an extraordinary sugar and aromatic concentration and when produced with almond paste it simply delicious. Between the provinces of Palermo and Trapani is the DOC Alcamo or Bianco d'Alcamo appellation which exclusively produces wine with Catarratto grapes. Masala is a legendary wine in Sicily that in recent years has been somewhat mistreated but remains a point of reference for traditional winemaking in the area. The Marsala we know today was invented by the English. Before the 18th century, Marsala was a rustic and very strong, alcoholic wine, a blend of three local grapes: Grillo, Catarratto and Inzolia. In order to facilitate shipping this wine to England, two English merchants, Woodhouse and Ingham, added a little alcohol to keep the wine from refermenting or turning sour before it reached destination. The success of this Marsala on the English market convinced other producers, Florio and Pellegrino first among them, to fortify their wines and soon Marsala was famous around the world. Today, Marsala does not enjoy the popularity it had 20 or 30 years ago, when it was considered 'the' dessert wine or after-dinner drink. But while the quantity of the wine has declined in recent years, its quality has decidedly improved and those available now are among the best ever made. In 1969, Marsala was given a DOC classification and since then production has been regulated. The principle types of Marsala are Fino and Superiore, both made with the traditional practice of adding alcohol. The most appreciated version among experts, however, is Vergine that is made without adding alcohol. It is a dry Marsala with an amber color and a distinct flavor that is particularly suited to pair with sweets with intense or concentrated flavors like marron glacés or Sicilian marzapane. It is also good with bold desserts, unlike many other wines, including chocolate cakes and cookies.

CONTROLLED AND GUARANTEED DESIGNATION OF ORIGIN (DOCG)

- Cerasuolo di Vittoria, with or without the sub-areas Classico

CONTROLLED DESIGNATION OF ORIGIN (DOC)

- Alcamo, with or without the sub-areas Classico
- Contea di Sclafani
- Contessa Entellina
- Delia Nivolelli
- Eloro, with or without the sub-areasPachino
- Erice
- Etna, geographic references allowed
- Faro
- Malvasia delle Lipari
- Mamertino di Milazzo or Mamertino
- Marsala
- Menfi, with or without the sub-areas Feudo dei Fiori or Bonera
- Monreale
- Noto
- Moscato di Pantelleria and Passito di Pantelleria or Pantelleria
- Riesi
- Salaparuta
- Sambuca di Sicilia
- Santa Margherita di Belice
- Sciacca, with or without the sub-areas Rayana (mandatory to mention Riserva before)
- Sicilia
- Siracusa
- Vittoria

AUGUSTALI

*S.S. 113 Alcamo-Partinico km 318,700 - Contrada
Bosco Falconeria
90047 Partinico (PA)
Tel. +39 339 6132334
fattoriaugustali@gmail.com
www.augustali.com*
 augustali.aziendaagricola

YEAR OF FOUNDATION **1960**
NAME OF THE OWNER **Vincenzo Bambina**
TOTAL BOTTLES PRODUCED **27,000**
DIRECT SALES
VISITS TO THE WINERY - RESERVATION NEEDED
HECTARES OF VINEYARD **12**
RESTAURANT
OLIVE OIL PRODUCTION

The estate is on a plain between Alcamo and
Partinico and winemaking is part of an inter-
disciplinary project. Aside from vineyards for
wine production, there are also citrus and olive
groves, honey is produced and there is even an
area for animals at risk of extinction. Wine production is in the hands of Vincenzo Bambina, a
well-known enologist even outside Sicily, and
while the choice of grapes was classic, at the
same time it was extremely innovative. The red
wine is classic and is made with Nero d'Avola,
while the white wine is innovative and is made
mostly from Vermentino with a small addition
of Catarratto.

90 👍 **Price A**
Terza Nota 2015

*Blend of Merlot and Nero d'Avola grapes. Matures
in concrete vats. Intense ruby red with violet hues.
Notes of red fruits, morello and cherry. Aromas
of pomegranate and sweet spices. Fresh sip, thin,
sweet finish, very pleasant. Long and fruity finish.
To drink a little cool. Nice quality/price ratio.*

☐ **89** **Price A**
Contrasto del Bianco 2013

*Blend of Vermentino and Catarratto grapes. Ma-
tures in concrete vats. Light golden yellow. Notes of
Mediterranean herbs, clean and intense. Yellow and
wildflowers. Fresh and structured sip. Again yellow
fruits. Good persistence.*

☐ **88** 👍 **Price A**
Terza Nota Bianco 2015

Blend of Catarratto and Vermentino grapes. Ma-

*tures in concrete vats. Straw yellow with golden
hues. Notes of yellow flowers, honey and baked
sweets. Fresh on the mouth and good structure,
clear, long finish with a bitter almond tail.*

BAGLIO DEL CRISTO DI CAMPOBELLO

*S.S. 123 km 19,200 - Contrada Favarotta
92023 Campobello Di Licata (AG)
Tel. +39 0922 877709 - 883214
Fax +39 0922 883788
mail@cristodicampobello.it
www.cristodicampobello.it*
 cristodicampobello
 @campobello_wine

YEAR OF FOUNDATION **2000**
NAME OF THE OWNER **Bonetta Family**
TOTAL BOTTLES PRODUCED **300,000**
VISITS TO THE WINERY - RESERVATION NEEDED
HECTARES OF VINEYARD **30**

In a short period of time this winery has become a point of reference for many wine lovers. One of things that makes the estate particular is the significant presence of chalk in the
hills that host its vineyards. Domenico Bonetta,
one of its owners, was an untiring worker and
personality in the Sicilian wine world but he
passed away just over a year ago. Despite this
irreplaceable loss the estate has continue to
produce wine thanks to the constant commitment, pride and passion of all those involved
who make up a large family. There is also the
important contribution of Riccardo Cotarella.
The quality of both the white and red wines is
excellent and they share a common trait of having a perfect combination of incisiveness and
capacity to please.

92 **Price B**
Sicilia Lu Patri 2014

*100% Nero d'Avola grapes. Matures 14 months in
barrique. Very dark ruby red. Intense notes of red
fruits, morello and spices. Great balance on the
mouth, structured. Wide variety of aromas on the
mouth and long persistence.*

91 **Price A**
Sicilia Adènzia 2014

Blend of 50% Nero d'Avola and 50% Syrah grapes.

Matures 10 months in French durmast big barrels and stainless steel. Purple red with violet hues. Elegant on the nose with notes of sweet spices. Fresh sip, balanced, elegant tannins and good length.

tense ruby red. Complex and intriguing on the nose. Red fruits and sweet spices in evidence. Eucalyptus aromas. Warm, rich and good balance on the mouth. Great persistence. Evident eucalyptus tail.

☐ 91   Price A
Sicilia Lalùci 2015

100% Grillo grapes. Matures 4 months in stainless steel. Straw yellow with greenish hues. Citrus notes on the nose, bergamot on top. Nice freshness and savory with a not too long finish bur gradual.

☐ 87   Price A
Sicilia Ficiligno 2015

Blend of 70% Viognier and 30% Insolia grapes. Matures 4 months in stainless steel. Straw yellow color. Notes of white pulp fruits and aromatic herbs. Nice freshness. Average saltiness. Gradual finish.

■ 87   Price B
Sicilia Ramione 2013

Blend of Nero d'Avola and Merlot grapes. Mature 14 months in barrique. Intense ruby red. Notes of red fruits and macerated fruits. Eucalyptus aromas. Smooth on the mouth, nice freshness, savory at times. Good persistence.

BAGLIO DI PIANETTO

Via Francia - Località Pianetto
90030 Santa Cristina Gela (PA)
Tel. +39 0444 323688
Fax +39 0444 323407
🅢 agrirelais
info@bagliodipianetto.com
www.bagliodipianetto.com
🅕 Baglio-di-Pianetto
🐦 @BaglioPianetto

YEAR OF FOUNDATION 1997
NAME OF THE OWNER Paolo Marzotto Family
TOTAL BOTTLES PRODUCED 550,000
DIRECT SALES
VISITS TO THE WINERY - RESERVATION NEEDED
HECTARES OF VINEYARD 104
HOSPITALITY
RESTAURANT
CERTIFIED ORGANIC VITICULTURE
OLIVE OIL PRODUCTION

The most recent novelty here was the change at the helm at the Sicilian estate of Count Paolo Marzotto. Renato De Bartoli stepped down as CEO of this renovated family estate to pursue other interests and his position was filled by Alberto Buratto who works alongside the count's granddaughter Ginevra Notabartolo. The change resulted in the need for a new strategy in regard to both production and sales. The wines are very interesting but need a little more personality. We'll see.

■ 91   Price B
Sicilia Cembali 2012

100% Nero d'Avola grapes. Matures 8 months in barrique and 10 months in 2.500 litres barrels. In-

BARONE DI VILLAGRANDE

Via del Bosco, 25
95025 Milo (CT)
Tel. +39 095 708 2175
Fax +39 095 7082175
info@villagrande.it
www.villagrande.it
🅕 Barone-di-Villagrande
🐦 @Villagrandewine

YEAR OF FOUNDATION 1727
NAME OF THE OWNER Carlo Nicolosi Asmundo
TOTAL BOTTLES PRODUCED 180,000
DIRECT SALES
VISITS TO THE WINERY - RESERVATION NEEDED
HECTARES OF VINEYARD 19
HOSPITALITY
RESTAURANT
CERTIFIED ORGANIC VITICULTURE

This splendid estate has its headquarters on the eastern slopes of Mt Etna and offers a spectacular view of the countryside and the coast. Carlo Nicolosi has restored prestige to his family's old winery which was once one of the most famous in the area.

☐ 91   👍 Price A
Etna Bianco Superiore 2015

100% Carricante grapes. Stainless steel on the lees

for 6 months. Bright straw yellow. Cedar, lime, smoky hints, hawthorn and lemon apple on the nose. Fragrant and citrusy. Tense, savory, good acidity on the mouth with a more polite and rich body compared to other versions. Long finish.

BENANTI

Via Garibaldi, 361
95029 Viagrande (CT)
Tel. +39 095 7893399
benanti@vinicolabenanti.it
www.vinicolabenanti.it
⬛ benantiwinery
🐦 @BenantiWines

YEAR OF FOUNDATION **1988**
NAME OF THE OWNER **Benanti Family**
TOTAL BOTTLES PRODUCED **145,000**
DIRECT SALES
VISITS TO THE WINERY - RESERVATION NEEDED
HECTARES OF VINEYARD **24**
OLIVE OIL PRODUCTION

Antonio and Salvino Benati have for some years now have been working with their father Giuseppe in running this estate demonstrating great professionalism and sincere passion for the world of wine. This is an estate to which winemaking in Sicily and above all on Etna owe much. And while Salvo Foti has left the winemaking helm to Michele Bean, the winery has not rested on its laurels but is in constant evolution. What has not changed is the quality of the wines and the image of a name that remains fundamental for Etna winemaking.

☐ 📄 95   Price B

Etna Bianco Superiore Pietra Marina 2012

100% Carricante grapes. Matures 30 months in stainless steel, 24 of which on the lees. Deep straw yellow. Intense, complex and citrusy notes on the nose, grapefruit, aromatic herbs and hazelnut. Very fresh on the mouth, sharp, great energy. Very long finish.

⬛ 93   Price B

Etna Rosso Rovittello 2012

Blend of 90% Nerello Mascalese and 10% Nerello Cappuccio grapes. Matures about 18 months in 1.500 liters French durmast barrels. Average in-

tensity ruby red. Elegant on the nose with red fruits and complex and elegant spiciness with hints of flowers. Fresh on the mouth, balanced, sober with strong but well integrated tannins. Long finish.

⬛ 92   Price B

Etna Rosso Serra della Contessa 2012

Blend of 80% Nerello Mascalese and 20% Nerello Cappuccio grapes. Matures about 18 months in 1.500 liters French durmast barrels. Light ruby red with garnet hues. Macerated red fruits on the nose, sweet spices and a hint of eucalyptus. Still austere on the mouth with powerful and velvety tannins. Great persistence.

CIRO BIONDI

Corso Sicilia, 20
95039 Trecastagni (CT)
Tel. +393921179746
🅢 cirobiondi
ciro@levignebiondi.it
www.ibiondi.com
⬛ ciro.biondi.59
🐦 @levignebiondi

YEAR OF FOUNDATION **1900**
NAME OF THE OWNER **Ciro and Stephanie Biondi**
TOTAL BOTTLES PRODUCED **22,000**
DIRECT SALES
VISITS TO THE WINERY - RESERVATION NEEDED
HECTARES OF VINEYARD **6.8**

The story of Ciro and Stephanie Biondi is one of consistency, determination and, above all, wine. He has always been on Etna and is from a family of successful winemakers that began with his great uncle Salvatore, while she is an English woman who came to the volcano for love and wine. Thus this small estate has deep roots in the eastern slopes of Etna which are home to true cru in the various farms and where unique pedoclimatic conditions can produce intense reds and very refined whites.

⬛ 91   Price B

Etna Rosso Outis 2014

Blend of Nerello Mascalese and Nerello Cappuccio grapes. Matures in barrique and tonneau. Ruby red color. Deep on the nose with notes of red fruits and intense spiciness, black pepper on top. Warm, enveloping on the mouth with good body and well extracted tannins. Great persistence.

☐ 87   Price B

Etna Bianco Outis 2015

Blend of 90 % Carricante with Catarratto and Min-nella grapes. Stainless steel only. Delicate aromas of wild herbs and white fruits. Fresh on the mouth, balanced, savory and of good length.

CALCAGNO

Via Regina Margherita,153 – Frazione Passopisciaro
95012 Castiglione di Sicilia (CT)
Tel. +39 338 7772780
info@vinicalcagno.it
www.vinicalcagno.it
 ViniCalcagno
 @VinoCalcagno

YEAR OF FOUNDATION 2006
NAME OF THE OWNER Giuseppina Calcagno
TOTAL BOTTLES PRODUCED 15,000
DIRECT SALES
VISITS TO THE WINERY - RESERVATION NEEDED
HECTARES OF VINEYARD 3

The Calcagno family has been winegrowers for four generations. Their vineyards are between 70 and 90 years old and are situated in the districts of Arcuria and Feudo di Mezzo in Passopisciaro, in the municipality of Castiglione di Sicilia. The vineyards are cultivated with respect of the environment without any use of chemical products, only manure and a lot of hand labor. All this to obtain authentic wines that are rich in personality and faithfully express the land and the harvest. The results are very good and there is a firm commitment to continue to improve. A new winery will soon be completed and will certainly help improve quality even further.

■ 90   Price B

Etna Feudo di Mezzo 2013

Blend of Nerello Mascalese with a small percentage of Nerello Cappuccio grapes. Matures about 1 year in barrique. Light ruby red. Aromas of berries and light spiciness with an irony hint. Clear on the mouth with nice progression and fresh tannins. Persistent.

■ 90   Price B

Etna Rosso Arcuria 2013

Blend of Nerello Mascalese with a small percentage

of Nerello Cappuccio grapes. Matures about 1 year in barrique. Light ruby red. Notes of red fruits with a hint of spices and roots. Fresh on the mouth, harmonic, savory, soft tannins and good length.

▨ 88   Price B

Etna Rosato Arcuria 2015

Blend of Nerello Mascalese and Nerello Cappuccio grapes. Matures 7 months in stainless steel. Nice intense pink with orange hues. Clean on the nose with strawberries and raspberries aromas. Agile, fresh, savory and fruity on the mouth. Easy to drink and good persistence.

CANTINE CUPPARI
ISTITUTO AGRARIO MINUTOLI

Contrada San Placido Calonerò
98138 Messina (ME)
Tel. +39 090 685800
info@cantinecuppari.it
www.cantinecuppari.it

YEAR OF FOUNDATION 2000
NAME OF THE OWNER Istituto Agrario Minutoli
TOTAL BOTTLES PRODUCED 10,000
DIRECT SALES
VISITS TO THE WINERY - RESERVATION NEEDED
HECTARES OF VINEYARD 4.5

This agrarian institute just outside Messina in the DOC Faro appellation has an exemplary and unique history. The institute was set up in a 13th century Benedictine monastery with a breathtaking view of the Messina Strait that alone is worth a visit. Some 30 years ago they decided to plant vineyards in with DOC accepted grapes like Nerello Mascalese, Nerello Cappuccio, Nocera and limited amounts of Nero d'Avola and Sangiovese. The upper classmen take part in all phases of wine production, from pruning the vines to bottling the wine. Today they produce 10,000 bottles a year which are for the most part sold abroad. The consulting enologist is Nicola Centonze.

■ 93   Price B

Faro San Placido 2012

Blend of Nerello Mascalese, Nerello Cappuccio, Nocera and a bit of Nero d'Avola grapes. Matures 12/18 months in tonneau. Ruby red with orange hues. Intriguing and complex on the nose with evident notes of red fruits, Mediterranean woods, coffe with milk and licorice. Intense on the mouth, thick with a fresh and long finish. Again underbrush and eucalyptus notes. This wine will have a long life even though it's already very good.

CARAVAGLIO

Via Provinciale, 3 3
98050 Malfa (ME)
Tel. +39 090 9844093
caravagliovini@virgilio.it
www.caravaglio.it

342

YEAR OF FOUNDATION 1992
NAME OF THE OWNER Nino Caravaglio
TOTAL BOTTLES PRODUCED 45,000
DIRECT SALES
VISITS TO THE WINERY - RESERVATION NEEDED
HECTARES OF VINEYARD 16
HOSPITALITY
CERTIFIED ORGANIC VITICULTURE

Nino Caravaglio has for some time now been reaping the fruits of his entrepreneurial mission. And he was one of the few inhabitants on the island of Salina who over 20 years ago put his cards on Malvasia and the typicity of the Eolie Islands. More recently, he was among the first to diversify production and to also make a dry Malvasia and, more important, red wines. His Corinto Nero varietal is surprisingly good considering that this ancient grape rich in history had up to now had been used to blend with the sweet Malvasia wines these islands are famous for. Caravaglio also produces some excellent capers.

☐ 93   Price B*
Malvasia delle Lipari Passito 2015
Blend of Malvasia with a small percentage of Corinto Nero grapes dried for 1 month on straw mats. Stainless steel only for 1 year. Intense golden yellow. Rich on the nose with notes of candied apricot, marzipan, Maditerranean woods, thyme and mint. Intense and balanced on the mouth. The sweet note doesn't prevail on the freshness and aromas. Never sickly. Great persistence. *50 cl bottle.

■ 90   👍 Price A
Nero du Munti 2014
100% Corinto Nero grapes. Part matures in stainless steel and part for 1 year in durmast barrels. Very dark ruby red. Red fruit jam on the nose and

Mediterranean herbs. Rich, fruity and full bodied on the mouth with a pleasant bitter hint.

☐ 87   Price A
Infatata 2015
100% Malvasia delle Lipari grapes. Stainless steel for 6 months. Deep straw yellow. Rich and clean of Mediterranean herbs on the nose. Agile, fresh, tense and averagely deep on the mouth. Aromatic tail.

CASTELLUCCI MIANO

Via Sicilia, 1
90029 Valledolmo (PA)
Tel. +39 0921 542385
info@castelluccimiano.it
www.castelluccimiano.it
f CastellucciMiano

YEAR OF FOUNDATION 2005
NAME OF THE OWNER
TOTAL BOTTLES PRODUCED 135,000
DIRECT SALES
VISITS TO THE WINERY - RESERVATION NEEDED
HECTARES OF VINEYARD 105
CERTIFIED ORGANIC VITICULTURE

The 'mountain' wines of this estate are the product of grapes grown in vineyards on the slopes of the Madonie Mountains that range in altitude of between 650 and 1,050m above sea level and that are divided into 84 plots. The vines have an average age of between 30-40 years, are for the most part alberello-trained and the grape varieties are Catarratto and Perricone. Among the wines produced, two whites stand out for quality, both are made from Catarratto, and their amazing capacity to age.

☐ 93   Price B
Sicilia Shiarà 2015
100% Catarratto grapes cultivated at about 1000 mt of altitude. Stainless steel for 6 months. Bright straw yellow. Fresh and elegant on the nose with notes of white fruits, wild herbs, exotic fruits, lemon and cedar. Dense and fresh on the mouth, great balance. Again fruity and citrusy notes. Savory and very long. It confirms to be a very pleasant white wine, ready to drink now but with a long life ahead.

■ 90   Price B
Sicilia PerricOne 2014
100% Perricone grapes. Matures 1 year in bar-

rique. Intense ruby red. Elegant notes of wild berries, licorice and laurel on the nose. Intense, savory on the mouth with fruity notes and eucalyptus tail. Long persistence.

---

 89   Price A

Sicilia Miano 2015

100% Catarratto grapes. Stainless steel for 4 months. Deep straw yellow. Fresh and fruity on the nose with aromas of exotic fruits and pineapple. Fresh and smooth on the mouth, again notes of exotic fruits. Savory and gradual finish.

★

COS

S.P. 3 Acate-Chiaromonte, km 14,300
97019 Vittoria (RG)
Tel. +39 0932 876145
🅢 cosvittoria
info@cosvittoria.it
www.cosvittoria.it
🅕 cosvittoria

YEAR OF FOUNDATION 1980
NAME OF THE OWNER Gianbattista Cilia and Giusto Occhipinti
TOTAL BOTTLES PRODUCED 190,000
DIRECT SALES
VISITS TO THE WINERY - RESERVATION NEEDED
HECTARES OF VINEYARD 34
HOSPITALITY
CERTIFIED ORGANIC VITICULTURE

There is no doubt that this winery is a model of consistency and the evolution of winemaking in southeast Sicily. Giusto Occhipinti and Titta Cilia have been friends forever and they produce wine using amphorae, making them a point of reference for other winemakers who are intrigued by this method. In recent years, Cos has downsized their productive ambitions in order to restore a more territorial character to their wines made in the only DOCG appellation in Sicily, Cerasuolo di Vittoria.

■ 94   Price B

Cerasuolo di Vittoria Classico 2013

Blend of 60% Nero d'Avola and 40% Frappato grapes. Matures 12 months in durmast barrels. Bright ruby red. Elegant Mediterranean aromas on the nose, with floral notes, thyme and savory, balanced tannin, fresh and enveloping finish.

■ 93   Price B

Sicilia Pithos Rosso 2014

Blend of 60% Nero d'Avola and 40% Frappato grapes. Matures in amphorae. Bright ruby red. Warm, deep and enveloping aromas of lavender and olive tapenade, verbena and rosemary, iodine, and Provence see shore hints. Soft and sensual on the mouth, clean tannins, fresh and long spicy finish.

☐ 89   Price A

Sicilia Ramì 2014

Blend of Grecanico and Inzolia grapes. Matures in concrete vats. Deep straw yellow with golden hues. Pleasant on the nose with notes of almond and fennel, citrus and crunchy apricot, honey and blossom. ripe cedar and sage. Agile and tense on the mouth, structured and sharp.

COTTANERA

S.P. 89 - Contrada Iannazzo
95030 Castiglione di Sicilia (CT)
Tel. +39 0942 963601
Fax +39 0942 963706
staff@cottanera.it
www.cottanera.it
🅕 cottanera
🐦 @Cottanera

YEAR OF FOUNDATION 2000
NAME OF THE OWNER Cambria Family
TOTAL BOTTLES PRODUCED 300,000
DIRECT SALES
VISITS TO THE WINERY - RESERVATION NEEDED
HECTARES OF VINEYARD 55

We like to underline the total, all-encompassing passion with which siblings Mariangela, Emanuele and Francesco are involved in very sector and phase of winemaking: from winegrowing, to winemaking to marketing and sales. Most of all they decided to give their all to a unique and extraordinary territory like Etna.

■ 🔲 97   Price C

Etna Rosso Zottorinoto Riserva 2012

100% Nerello Mascalese from the homonymous single vignard. Matures 18 months in barrique. Bright and lively garnet ruby red. Elegant and clear on the nose with notes of wild strawberries, wildflowers,

343

raspberries and spices, vanilla and cardamom. Tense, briny, nice acidity to sustain the elegant and aristocratic body, where no element prevails on the other and all of them are very classy. Light tannins and incredibly long finish. Great wine.

☐ 🏵 96   Price B
Etna Bianco Contrada Calderara 2014

100% Carricante grapes. Here there is also a little wood passage, 6 months in barrique, to make the scene more complex and articulated. It is the first release of this wine but we must say that a star is born. Marvellous. Light straw yellow. Flint, white peach, citrus aromas on the nose. Tense, rich on the mouth, alternating alcoholic warmth and the freshness of the acidity, to make this wine almost sensual and for sure of involving drinkability. Very persistent finish.

☐ 93   👍 Price A
Etna Bianco 2015

Blend of 90% Carricante and 10% Catarratto grapes. Stainless steel on the lees. Intense greenish straw yellow. Very fruity on the nose with notes of lime, ginger, cedar, green plum and alfalfa. Fresh and savory flavor, delicious and elegant drinkability with a tense finish of good length.

■ 93   Price B
Etna Rosso 2013

Blend of 90% Nerello Mascalese and 10% Nerello Cappuccio grapes. Matures 7 months in barrique and tonneau. Intense garnet ruby red. Red berries in the nose, then spices and blond tobacco. Strong flavor, slightly tannic, with some edge due to the youngness to smoothen in and with great persistence.

■ 90   👍 Price A
Etna Rosso Contrada Diciassettesalme 2014

Blend of 90% Nerello Mascalese and 10% Nerello Cappuccio grapes. Matures 9 months in big barrels. Intense and clear ruby red. Smoky hints, then wild berries and black cherry on the nose. Savory, warm, pleasant and with elegant persistence in the mouth.

CURTO

*S.S. Ispica-Rosolini, km 358 - Contrada Sulla
97014 Ispica (RG)
Tel. +39 0932 950161
info@curto.it
www.curto.it*

YEAR OF FOUNDATION 1670
NAME OF THE OWNER Giombattista Curto
TOTAL BOTTLES PRODUCED 70,000
DIRECT SALES
VISITS TO THE WINERY - RESERVATION NEEDED
HECTARES OF VINEYARD 25
OLIVE OIL PRODUCTION

The Curto family has a long history and have been winegrowers for centuries. Today their estate is run by Francesca Curto, a very dynamic woman who is very tied to her land. She worked with her father for years and even did nternships with important Bordeaux producers like Chateau Villemaurine, Chateau Timberlay and Chateau Clos Fourtet. The vineyards are in southeast Sicily in the area of Ispica, on the border between the provinces of Ragusa and Siracusa and in the farming area of Pachina. The soil here is light, very calcareous with tuff stone and marl. The climate is hot, sunny, with little rainfall and benefits from refreshing sea breezes. The wines produced have strong personalities and unique characteristics.

■ 91   Price B
Eloro Fontanelle 2011

100% Nero d'Avola grapes. Matures 8 months in barrique and tonneau. Deep ruby red. Intense and complex notes of ripe fruits, plum on top. evident aromas of carob, licorice hint and eucalyptus notes. Fresh on the mouth then rich and with great balance. Long finish. Territorial.

■ 90   Price B
Krio 2012

100% Syrah grapes. Matures 6-8 months in barrique. Ruby red with purple hues. Intense on the nose with aromas of wild berries, vanilla and an elegant spiciness with black pepper on top. Fresh and rich on the mouth with well extracted tannins and a sweet and long finish.

■ 88   👍 Price A
Eloro 2013

100% Nero d'Avola grapes. Stainless steel only. Ruby red. Notes of red fruits, cherry on top with hints of chocolate. Rich taste, good freshness, structure and good harmony with a sweet note and great persistence. Typical.

CUSUMANO

Contrada San Carlo - Via Bisaccia
90047 Partinico (PA)
Tel. +39 091 8908713
Fax +39 0918907933
cusumano@cusumano.it
www.cusumano.it
 cantinecusumano
@cusumanowinery

YEAR OF FOUNDATION 2000
NAME OF THE OWNER Diego and Alberto
Cusumano
TOTAL BOTTLES PRODUCED 2,500,000
DIRECT SALES
VISITS TO THE WINERY - RESERVATION NEEDED
HECTARES OF VINEYARD 465

Over the past 15 years Diego and Alberto Cu-sumano followed a real virtuous path. They created a brand and an efficient winery that are more unique than rare. The success they achieved is the result of an entrepreneurial foresight that is difficult to match in Italy. This year we add on our guide the wines from the Etna winery Alta Mora, built by the Cusumano family in the last years and that is revealing to be very promising.

 95   Price B
Sicilia Sàgana 2014
100% Nero d'Avola grapes. Mature 1 year in different types of wood. Intense and dark ruby red. Black cherry, light caper, spicy notes of vanilla and pepper, hints of mint dominate the articulated and refined nose. Tense, savory, agile even with a big body, light tannins and warm finish. Enveloping and very long finish.

94   👍 Price A
Etna Rosso Alta Mora 2014
100% Nerello Mascalese grapes. Matures 1 year in big barrels. Attractive and elegant, with notes of wild strawberries, carnation, cassis, vanilla and light spicy hints in the background. Velvety, almost silky on the palate, well sustained by acidity, polite, agile and very long.

93   Price B
Sicilia Noà 2014
Blend of 40% Nero d'Avola and 60% Cabernet Sau-

vignon and Merlot grapes. 1 year in barrique. Dark and concentrated ruby red. As usual very spicy on the nose, vanilla, light black pepper, then smoky hints, black cherry, cassis and wild berries. Warm, enveloping, full-bodied on the mouth, still young tannins and promising aromas. Long finish.

 91   Price A
Etna Bianco Alta Mora 2014
100% Carricante grapes. Stainless steel on the lees. Bright straw yellow. Lime, cedar, alfalfa, wildflowers on the nose. Savory and tense on the palate, very pleasant and easy to drink. Thin and persistent finish.

 88   Price A
Nero d'Avola 2015
100% Nero d'Avola grapes. Stainless steel on the lees. Intense ruby red. Typical and fragrant, classic notes of capers then black currant and hints of black cherry. Savory taste well sustained by pleasant acidity, warm, enveloping and good length in the finish.

MARCO DE BARTOLI

Contrada Fornara Samperi, 292
91025 Marsala (TP)
Tel. +39 0923 962093
info@marcodebartoli.com
www.marcodebartoli.com
 marco.debartoli
@MarcoDeBartoli

YEAR OF FOUNDATION 1980
NAME OF THE OWNER Renato, Sebastiano and
Giuseppina De Bartoli
TOTAL BOTTLES PRODUCED 100,000
DIRECT SALES
VISITS TO THE WINERY - RESERVATION NEEDED
HECTARES OF VINEYARD 17
HOSPITALITY
RESTAURANT
CERTIFIED ORGANIC VITICULTURE
OLIVE OIL PRODUCTION

Renato, Sebastiano and Giuseppina De Barto-li are carrying on the mission left to them by their father Marco, a man who literally re-invented Marsala wine as well as those of Pantelleria and whose only fault is that he left us too soon. He created Vecchio Samperi and although it was exactly what a great Marsala Vergine should be, he refused to call it that because he disagreed with the regulations governing its production and the big industrialists who he felt were destroying Marsala. And he produced Bukkuram, a top quality Passito di Pantelleria, when the market was flooded with horrible sweet liqueur wines. This was all now some 40 years ago and one must recognize that his efforts and his work was not in vain for saving and relaunching a great Sicilian product like Marsala. From this year the winery is lead by Sebastiano and Giuseppina De Bartoli. Renato, thus remaining the owner, decided to accept to become CEO of Baglio di Pianetto. If this is a good bye to the Marsale, we'll soon know.

⬛ 🄶 98   Price B
Vecchio Samperi

100% Grillo grapes. Matures in durmast and walnut barrels for 20 year with the addition of 5% of the younger wine every year according to the perpetual traditional method. Amber with topaz hues. Cristal clear aromas on the nose. A wine of rare intensity. Very complex and varied: nuts, dry figs, eucalyptus, mirth. Extremely elegant sip, fresh and balanced. Again toasted notes on the mouth, hazelnuts and almonds. Neverending. A masterpiece. Sweet Wine of the Year.

⬛ 94   Price B*
Marsala Superiore Riserva 10 anni

*100% Grillo grapes. Matures over 10 years in different sizes durmast barrels. Intense amber color. Complex aromas of nuts, candied apricot, dry figs, iodine hints and Mediterranean herbs in the background. Powerful mouth, rich, with evident notes of toasted hazelnuts. Very long. *50 cl bottle.*

☐ 88   Price B
Grappoli del Grillo 2014

100% Grillo grapes. Matures 12 months in 10 hl barrels and tonneau. Intense light straw yellow. Notes of thyme, chamomile and briny. The sip is divided between savory and freshness, good structure. Easy to drink.

▣ 87   Price B
Terzavia Metodo Classico Brut Nature 2013

100% Grillo grapes. Matures 12 months in barrique and stainless steel. Average perlage. Laurel, lemongrass and aromatic herbs aromas. Good intensity, a little edgy, fresh and nice length. Original.

★★

DONNAFUGATA

Via Sebastiano Lipari, 18
91025 Marsala (TP)
Tel. +39 0923 724200
Fax +39 0923 722042
info@donnafugata.it
www.donnafugata.it
🄵 *DonnafugataWine*
🐦 *@DonnafugataWine*

YEAR OF FOUNDATION **1983**
NAME OF THE OWNER **Rallo Family**
TOTAL BOTTLES PRODUCED **2,100,000**
DIRECT SALES
VISITS TO THE WINERY
HECTARES OF VINEYARD **338**
OLIVE OIL PRODUCTION

Even though Giacomo Rallo was like a giant for the winery, after his death (in May 2016) the lead of the company is in the hands of his sons Antonio (Director of the Sicilia Doc Consortium as well) and José. Both have inheried from their father a great business sense (rare in this region) and an incredible love for their land from their mother Gabriella. What distinguishes this family is their incredible and the fact that their linear, well-made wines mirror the history, culture and diversity of Sicily. All this is Donnafugata.

⬛ 🄶 95   Price C
Contessa Entellina Mille e una notte 2011

Blend of mostly Nero d'Avola and other varieties. Matures 16 months in barrique. Dark and very concentrated ruby red. Intense and clear aromas of red fruits, orange even candied and cedar. Hints of blueberry and graphite with a warm and deep spice. Intense and thick flavor. Good acidity. Important progression and very persistent finish.

⬛ 92   Price C
Pantelleria Passito Ben Ryé 2014

100% Zibibbo grapes. Mature at leat 7 months in vats. Antique and intense golden yellow. Metiterranean aromas with apricot, even dehydrated, dates, green candied fruits and Mediterranean woods hints. Intense and savory on the month, less intense structure but nice saltiness. Always intriguing finish.

88 Price B

Tancredi 2012

Blend of Cabernet and Nero d'Avola with some other varieties. Matures 14 months in barrique. Deep and intense color. Warm notes of blackberry and small red fruits. Light and intense spiciness. Rich on the palate, muscular, good tannins and average acidity. Thick structure and savory finish.

★★
DUCA DI SALAPARUTA

S.S. 113 - Via Nazionale
90014 Casteldaccia (PA)
Tel. +39 091 945201
Fax +39 091 953227
info@duca.it
www.duca.it
 GruppoDucaSalaparuta
@CorvoWines

YEAR OF FOUNDATION 1824
NAME OF THE OWNER Illva Saronno Holding -
Reina Family
TOTAL BOTTLES PRODUCED 10,000,000
VISITS TO THE WINERY - RESERVATION NEEDED
HECTARES OF VINEYARD 1,550

This great producer has its headquarters in Casteldaccia, some 20 kilometers from Palermo, but they produce wine from their own grapes and those of suppliers all over Sicily. Known for its Corvo brand, used for most classic and best-selling wines, they also have the merit of having produced the first great wine from Nero d'Avola, Duca Enrico, which was first produced with grapes from the 1984 harvest and still represents an emblem of style.

 93 Price C

Duca Enrico 2011

100% Nero d'Avola grapes. Matures at least 18 months in durmast barrels. Deep ruby red. Powerful aromas of ripe fruits, licorice and orange marmelade. Rich flavor, structured but agile and balanced at the same time. Long fruity finish.

89 Price A

Lavico 2013

100% Nerello Mascalese grapes. Matures 1 year in barrique. Light ruby red. Average intensity aromas of small red fruits, sweet spices and smoky hints.

Agile and fresh on the palate with fruity notes and a well-integrated tannin.

☐ **86** Price B

Bianca di Valguarnera 2013

100% Inzolia grapes. Matures at least 8 months in barrique. Light straw yellow with greenish hues. Good intense aromas of hazelnut, yellow fruits and sweet durmast. Good structure, rich and good length.

FEUDI DEL PISCIOTTO

Contrada del Pisciotto
93015 Niscemi (CL)
Tel. +39 0933 1930280
info@castellare.it
www.castellare.it
 Wine-Relais-Feudi-del-Pisciotto
@CastellareWines

YEAR OF FOUNDATION 2002
NAME OF THE OWNER Paolo Panerai
TOTAL BOTTLES PRODUCED 250,000
DIRECT SALES
VISITS TO THE WINERY - RESERVATION NEEDED
HECTARES OF VINEYARD 33
HOSPITALITY
RESTAURANT

Feudi del Pisciotto is the Sicilian winery of the publisher of the magazine Class, Paolo Panerai, and is his third after Castellare in Castellina in Chianti and Rocca di Frassinello in Maremma. It sits at an altitude of some 250m and is six kilometers from the sea as the crow flies. This estate is a perfect combination of history and cutting-edge technology. Its labels, all different, are designed by Italy's top fashion designers, from Dolce&Gabbana to Versace to Missoni. The estate also hosts a very elegant and suggestive Wine Relais resort created in the part of the largest 18th century palmento winery in Sicily.

90 Price B

Nero d'Avola Versace 2014

100% Nero d'Avola grapes. Matures 1 year in barrique, half new. Intense ruby red. Very varietal on the nose, the typical caper then black cherry and cassis. Enveloping flavor, smooth but well sustained by a light and constant acidity. Warm and persistent finish.

88   Price B
Cabernet Sauvignon Missoni 2014

100% Cabernet Sauvignon grapes. Matures 1 year in barrique, half new. Intense and deep ruby red. Typical notes of blueberry and black currant on the nose, then cassis and kirsch. Briny and complete in the mouth, warm, enveloping and a little bittering in the finish.

87   Price B
Frappato Carolina Marengo per Kisa 2014

100% Frappato grapes. Matures 1 year in barrique, half new. Intense garnet red. Very fruity, strawberry, currant, pomegranate and kirsch. Smooth taste, savory, light tannins and good length in the finish.

FEUDO DISISA

Contrada Disisa - SP 30, km 6
90046 Monreale (PA)
Tel. +39 091 6127109
info@vinidisisa.it
www.vinidisisa.it
Feudo-Disisa
@Feudodisisa

YEAR OF FOUNDATION 2005
NAME OF THE OWNER Di Lorenzo Family
TOTAL BOTTLES PRODUCED 100,000
DIRECT SALES
VISITS TO THE WINERY - RESERVATION NEEDED
HECTARES OF VINEYARD 130
OLIVE OIL PRODUCTION

For years this estate used to sell its grapes but then decided to bottle its own wines around the last turn of the century. The winery is efficient and functional using modern technology and a vast collection of barrels ranging from barrique to classic, medium-sized barrels. Recent changes in the technical staff, with Tonino Guzzo being put in charge, lifted the already high quality level of the wines, by now especially in the production of the white wines that are for the most part produced with native grapes. The estate also produces some lovely, aromatic olive oil that purists may turn their noses up at but which your taste buds will thoroughly enjoy. The baglio farmhouse is very lovely and used to serve as the estate's headquarters.

☐ 92   👍 Price A
Chara 2015

Equal blend of Catarratto Lucido and Inzolia that ferments and ages in stainless steel. It has an intense color with luminous reflections and a strong bouquet of medlar, gooseberry, Mediterranean brush herbs and yellow flowers. The whole aroma is refreshed by a slightly eucalyptus note of wild asparagus and wild fennel. The mouthfeel is tasty and balanced and extremely drinkable despite the pronounced density. The finish is unexpectedly deep.

☐ 91   👍 Price A
Sicilia Terre delle Fate 2015

100% Fiano grapes. It has a tenuous, straw-yellow color with green reflections and a complex aroma of citrus notes like lime and grapefruit along with a vein of yellow flowers and notes of fresh medicinal herbs. The mouthfeel stands out with its high acidity and strong yet balanced salty streak. A gelid and almost mountain wine. The finish is intense, tasty and very long.

☐ 86   👍 Price A
Sicilia Grillo 2015

100% Grillo white with a bright, straw-yellow color and an intriguing aroma with floral notes of lavender along with hints of passion fruit and medlar. The mouthfeel is as intense as the aroma and has a nice salty note and countervailing acidity. Suave balances grace to the finish.

FEUDO MACCARI

S.P. Pachino-Noto, km 13,500
96017 Noto (SR)
Tel. +39 0575 477857
info@feudomaccari.it
www.feudomaccari.it
FeudoMaccari
@FeudoMaccari

YEAR OF FOUNDATION 2000
NAME OF THE OWNER Moretti Cuseri Family
TOTAL BOTTLES PRODUCED 230,000
DIRECT SALES
VISITS TO THE WINERY - RESERVATION NEEDED
HECTARES OF VINEYARD 51
OLIVE OIL PRODUCTION

Antonio Maccari does not bother with cost. The vineyard at his Feudo Maccari estate, in the sunniest part of Italy between Noto and Pachino, is a sight to see. The vines are, as the terroir dictates, alberello-trained which is more expensive to manage but worth it. A fashion industrialists as well as a wine producer in Valdano di Sopra and Bolgheri, Moretti has joined the growing number of people investing in Sicilian wine. Although this enterprise got off to a shaky start, it is now better achieving its objectives and potential. Wheat is Moretti's latest hobby and he is producing past of the highest quality.

☐ 🏆 95   Price B

Sicilia Saia 2014

100% Nero d'Avola grapes. Matures 12-14 months in barrique. Deep ruby red. Intense and complex notes of cherry, spices, citrusy hints and licorice. Fresh and savory in the mouth, balanced, rich and very pleasant sip. Velvety tannins and very long persistence.

☐ 91   Price B

Sicilia Maharis 2014

100% Syrah grapes. Matures 14-16 months in barrique. Deep ruby red with purple hues. Clean aromas of berries, vanilla and pepper. Wide, powerful, smooth and long, gradual, fruity finish. Elegant tannins.

☐ 86   Price B

Family & Friends 2015

100% Grillo grapes. Matures 6 months in tonneau. Light golden yellow. Good, intense notes of aromatic herbs on a yellow fruit background. Nice freshness in the mouth, clear, great aromatic impact and good persistence.

FEUDO MONTONI

Contrada Montoni Vecchi
92022 Cammarata (AG)
Tel. +39 091 513106
🌐 *feudo.montoni.sicily.wines*
info@feudomontoni.it
www.feudomontoni.it
f *Feudo.Montoni.Fabio.Sireci*

YEAR OF FOUNDATION **1469**
NAME OF THE OWNER **Fabio Sireci**
TOTAL BOTTLES PRODUCED **190,000**
DIRECT SALES
VISITS TO THE WINERY - RESERVATION NEEDED

HECTARES OF VINEYARD **30**
HOSPITALITY
RESTAURANT
CERTIFIED ORGANIC VITICULTURE
OLIVE OIL PRODUCTION

The estate is in central Sicily in the area of Cammarata and the vineyards are situated at altitudes of between 500 and 700m above sea level. The climate is temperate-warm with ample rainfall and significant temperature variations between day and night, both in the vineyards and in the winery. The vineyards are cultivate with great respect for nature and great care is taken to ensure the wines best mirror the characteristics of the terroir. The result are truly excellent, quality wines in which typicity and character unite in richness and incisiveness and an excellent balance.

349

☐ 93   Price B

Vrucara 2012

100% Nero d'Avola grapes. Matures 40 months in concrete vats and 4 months in durmast barrels. Very intense ruby red. Complex and deep notes of morello, wild berries, sweet spices, black pepper and evident eucalyptus. Powerful, rich, harmonic with thin tannins. Very long.

☐ 90   👍 Price A

Sicilia Nero d'Avola Lagnusa 2014

100% Nero d'Avola grapes. Matures 20 months in concrete vats and 2 months in durmast barrels. Intense aromas of red fruit, spices and a pleasant eucalyptus note. Fresh in the mouth, fruity, good structure and length. Pleasant and easy to drink.

☐ 87   Price A

Sicilia Catarratto del Masso 2015

100% Catarratto grapes. Matures 12 months in concrete vats on the lees. Aromatic herbs, laurel and eucalyptus aromas. Great freshness and good structure in the mouth. Great progression and long finish.

FEUDO PRINCIPI DI BUTERA

Contrada Deliella
93011 Butera (CL)
Tel. +39 0934 347726
Fax +39 0934 347851
info@feudobutera.it

350

www.feudobutera.it
f *PrincipiDiButera*
y *@cvzonin*

YEAR OF FOUNDATION **1997**
NAME OF THE OWNER **Zonin Family**
TOTAL BOTTLES PRODUCED **900,000**
DIRECT SALES
VISITS TO THE WINERY - RESERVATION NEEDED
HECTARES OF VINEYARD **180**
OLIVE OIL PRODUCTION

The Sicilian estate of the Zonin family is in an area of the island blessed by nature with plenty of sun, a nice breeze and a terrain that creates a host of microclimates in the 180 hectares of vineyards. With such wealth one needs to know what to focus on and what to discard. This task has been left to Claudio Galosi, the young director of Feudo Principi di Buttera as well as head of production. The results are beginning to appear and this is just the start.

■ 89	Price B

Symposio 2014

Blend of 65% Cabernet Sauvignon, 30% Merlot and 5% Petit Verdot grapes. Matures 18 months in tonneau and big barrels. Very deep ruby red. Intense notes of wild berries, tobacco and mint. Powerful in the mouth, great structure, present tannins but not overwhelming, very long.

■ 88	Price B

Sicilia Deliella 2014

100% Nero d'Avola grapes. Matures 18 months in big barrels. Deep ruby red. Rich notes of ripe fruit, plums and cherry together with sweet spices. Smooth, structured, great aromatic intensity on the palate and very long persistence.

☐ 84	Price B

Sicilia Serò 2015

100% Inzolia grapes. Matures 8 months in stainless steel on the lees. Light straw yellow. Average intensity for the aromas of white peach, pear and floral hint. Discrete freshness, good balance and correspondence between nose aromas and taste.

FINA

Contrada Bausa
91025 Marsala (TP)
Tel. +39 0923 733070

Fax +39 0923 733070
info@cantinefina.it
www.cantinefina.it
f *cantine.fina.7*

YEAR OF FOUNDATION **2005**
NAME OF THE OWNER **Fina Family**
TOTAL BOTTLES PRODUCED **200,000**
DIRECT SALES
VISITS TO THE WINERY - RESERVATION NEEDED
HECTARES OF VINEYARD **320**
RESTAURANT

More than ten years ago, Bruno Fina and his wife Mariella, inspired by the late, great enologist Giacomo Tachis, decided to make their dream come true and created a modern and efficient winery. Their dream was a success and their wines, almost all international blends, have conquered markets the world over. Visits to the winery are organized in every detail offering various options including lunch.

■ 90	Price B

Caro Maestro 2012

Blend of 60% Cabernet Sauvignon, 30% Merlot and 10% Petit Verdot grapes. 2 year in barrique. Great red wine Bordeaux style dedicate to Giacomo Tachis. Intense and dark ruby color. Classic aromas, blueberry, black currant then caramel, cocoa and hints of spices and mint. Full, rich taste, nice tannins, warm and persistent.

☐ 88	Price A

Kiké 2015

Blend of Traminer Aromatico and Sauvignon Blanc. Stainless steel. Intense straw yellow. Typical, very clear and pleasant aromatic notes, roses, lychee, mango. Savory, warm taste with a slightly bittering finish.

★★
FIRRIATO

Via Trapani, 4
91027 Paceco (TP)
Tel. +39 0923 882755
Fax +39 0923 883266
S *firriatoexport*
info@firriato.it
www.firriato.it
f *firriato*
y *@firriato*

YEAR OF FOUNDATION 1985
NAME OF THE OWNER Salvatore and Vinzia Di Gaetano
TOTAL BOTTLES PRODUCED 4,250,000
DIRECT SALES
VISITS TO THE WINERY - RESERVATION NEEDED
HECTARES OF VINEYARD 320
HOSPITALITY
CERTIFIED ORGANIC VITICULTURE
OLIVE OIL PRODUCTION

Salvatore and Vinzia Di Gaetano began by investing in the island of Favignana and on Etna, then they created a wine tourism activity with two small centers, one in Baglio Soria near the headquarters of their winery in Paceco and the other in Verzella amid their vineyards on Etna. And then they decided to convert everything to organic farming, no small task for an enterprise the size of theirs. To help them out their daughter Irene and son-in-law Federico have joined them which has allowed them more time to strive for excellence both in the vineyards and in the winery.

☐ 92   Price B
Etna Cavanera Ripa di Scorciavacca 2014

Blend of Carricante and Catarratto grapes. 6 months on the lees. Intense yellow. Notes of summer fruits, wild yellow flowers and cut herbs. Clear, elegant and attractive in the mouth with long, fresh, balanced and savory persistence.

■ 91   Price B
Camelot 2011

Blend of 60% Cabernet Sauvignon and 40% Merlot grapes. Matures 9 months in barrique. Dark garnet ruby red. Very Mediterranean aromas with notes of blood orange, raspberries, spices, vanilla and light hints of tamarind and thyme. Impressive, warm, smooth, enveloping and savory. Great persistence.

■ 91   Price B
Etna Cavanera Rovo delle Coturnie 2014

Blend of Nerello Mascalese and Nerello Cappuccio. Matures 12 months in Slavonia durmast barrels. Light ruby red. Spicy notes and wild berries in the nose, with hints of flowers and irony puffs. Intense, smooth, exuberant and extremely pleasant.

■ 88   Price B
Harmonuim 2013

100% Nero d'Avola grapes. Matures 1 year in barrique and big barrels. Intense and lively ruby color.

Toasted notes of coffee, then vanilla, capers, wild cherry jam. Savory taste, slightly tannic, good body and acidity, warm. Good persistence.

FLORIO

Via Vincenzo Florio, 1
91025 Marsala (TP)
Tel. +39 0923 781111
info@duca.it
www.cantineflorio.it
 GruppoDucaSalaparuta
 @CorvoWines

YEAR OF FOUNDATION 1833
NAME OF THE OWNER Illva Saronno Holding - Reina Family
TOTAL BOTTLES PRODUCED 3,000,000
DIRECT SALES
VISITS TO THE WINERY - RESERVATION NEEDED
HECTARES OF VINEYARD 590

This historic Marsala estate now, along with Duca di Salaparuta, is part of the Saronno group. The cellars and winery are extremely beautiful, an example of winemaking archeology with barrels of Riserva wine aging there for decades. Here Marsala and its history are the name of the game because it is here that its fame began. Great care continues to be paid to the production of the many versions of this wine that is known and appreciated the world over.

▪ 92   Price B
Marsala Superiore Semisecco Donna Franca Riserva

100% Grillo grapes. Blend of wines matured from 15 to 30 years in durmast barrels. Very intense amber color. Rich and powerful in the nose with aromas of candied fruit, dates and toasted almonds that prevail on the oxidation component. Wide, strong in the mouth with the sweet note balanced by the other elements. Very long.

▪ 91   👍 Price A
Marsala Vergine Terre Arse 2002

100% Grillo grapes. Matures 8 years in big barrels. Intense amber. Notes of nuts and dry figs together with elegant oxidation aromas. Smooth, rich on the palate with an evident toasted component. Great persistence.

★ GRACI

Contrada Arcuria - Frazione Passopisciaro
95012 Castiglione di Sicilia (CT)
Tel. +39 348 7016773
info@graci.eu
www.graci.eu
f *Graci.Vini.Etna*
𝕏 *@AlbertoGraci*

YEAR OF FOUNDATION 2004
NAME OF THE OWNER Alberto Aiello Graci and
Emiliano Falsini
TOTAL BOTTLES PRODUCED 80,000
DIRECT SALES
VISITS TO THE WINERY - RESERVATION NEEDED
HECTARES OF VINEYARD 20
CERTIFIED ORGANIC VITICULTURE
OLIVE OIL PRODUCTION

Alberto Graci Aiello is a native of Catania who moved to Milan before he was 30 to follow a career in finance and banking. But his passion for wine got the better of him and he returned to Sicily in 2004 to make wine at his small estate on Etna and since then his determination has made him one of the most respected young producers in the area. His wines already have a very personal style based on the pleasure and tension the local grapes can offer. To his credit, he has also brought back an old vineyards on Etna at an altitude of 1,000m that has become a cru.

■ 94	Price B

Etna Rosso Arcurìa 2014

100% Nerello Mascalese grapes, 24 months in 42 hl barrels. Ruby red with garnet hues. Thin, clear notes of wild berries, eucalyptus and underbrush. Wide, elegant, direct, well-articulated. Smooth tannins. Great persistence and expression of the terroir.

■ 92	Price B

Etna Rosso Feudo di Mezzo 2014

Blend of Nerello Mascalese and Nerello Cappuccio grapes. Matures 24 months in 10 and 15 hl barrels. Dark ruby with garnet hues. Delicate aromas of red fruits, wet soil and musk. Wide, fresh, tannic but never overwhelming. Juicy. Great length.

☐ 89	Price B

Etna Bianco Arcurìa 2014

100% Carricante grapes. Matures part in concrete

vats and part 12/14 months in 10 hl barrels. Golden straw yellow. Notes of citrus, grapefruit, flint and wild herbs. Fresh, agile and a little thin in the mouth but long and balanced. Citrusy finish.

★ GULFI

Contrada Patria
97012 Chiaramonte Gulfi (RG)
Tel. +39 0932 921654
info@gulfi.it
www.gulfi.it
f *Gulfi-Wines*
𝕏 *@ViniGulfi*

YEAR OF FOUNDATION 1996
NAME OF THE OWNER Vito Catania
TOTAL BOTTLES PRODUCED 250,000
DIRECT SALES
VISITS TO THE WINERY - RESERVATION NEEDED
HECTARES OF VINEYARD 70
HOSPITALITY
RESTAURANT
CERTIFIED ORGANIC VITICULTURE
OLIVE OIL PRODUCTION

Vito Catania, the owner of this model winery in the Iblei Hills, is not one to cut corners when it comes to winemaking and the results are here to see, or better drink. This because his Nero d'Avola are among the best ever made. Oddly enough, his wines have never received the attention they deserve. He offers a nice range of wines including, for the moment, four cru wines plus other reds that are more accessible. There are also some other wines that will be ready to be tasted in the near future. This because one of the traits of this estate is that their wines reach the market sometimes as much as 4-5 years after they were made. The estate also hosts a nice restaurant run by the talented chef Giuseppe Causarano and has guest facilities. The restaurant is now lead by a very good and young chef: Ninni Radicini.

■ 94	Price B

NeroBufaleffj 2011

100% Nero d'Avola grapes from one of the winery's single vignards. Matures 24 months in tonneau and barrique. Very dark ruby red. Intense and complex aromas of red berries, white pepper, oregano, aromatic herbs. Full, warm, powerful and agile at the same time. Great balance, velvety and elegant. Very long.

 90 Price B

Reseca 2011

100% Nerello Mascalese grapes. Matures 24 months in barrique. Ruby red. Intense notes of red fruits, raspberries and strawberries. Great balance in the mouth, full, smooth and good persistent finish.

 89 Price B

Cerasuolo di Vittoria Classico 2014

Blend of 70% Nero d'Avola and 30% Frappato grapes. Matures 1 year in 500 liters barrels. Intense ruby red. Deep aromas of ripe fruit, laurel, sage and notes of bitter chocolate. Rich and fruity sip. Again notes of ripe fruit. Good length a little atypical.

★

HAUNER

Via Umberto I - Località Lingua
98050 Santa Marina Salina (ME)
Tel. +39 090 6413029
info@hauner.it
www.hauner.it
f *Hauner-Winery*

YEAR OF FOUNDATION 1968
NAME OF THE OWNER Carlo Hauner
TOTAL BOTTLES PRODUCED 100,000
DIRECT SALES
VISITS TO THE WINERY - RESERVATION NEEDED
HECTARES OF VINEYARD 20

It would be wrong to equate this winery just with its very good sweet wines. Today, Carlo Hauner Jr. is focusing great attention also to other types of wine and the possibility of producing whites and reds that can convey the Aeolian Islands and this involves identifying their diversities and capacity to please. It is not by chance that most of his winemaking activities take place on the island of Vulcano, at Punta dell'Ufala, a beautiful place where he has a vineyards that look out at the sea. But we still remain dazzled by his Malvasia delle Lipari which his father, with foresight and courage, began to produce 50 years ago and amazed the world.

▣ **93** Price C

Malvasia delle Lipari Passito Selezione Carlo Hauner 2013

Blend of 95% Lipari and 5% Corinto Nero grapes. Matures in barrique. Light amber color. Opulent notes of apricot, peach in syrup, Mediterranean herbs and hints of marzipan.

■ **87** Price B

Rosso Antonello 2012

Blend of 60% Calabrese, 30% Sangiovese and 10% Corinto Nero grapes. Matures in barrique. Very deep ruby red. Delicate notes of ripe fruit, plums on top. Full, good structure, fruity and long.

□ **86** Price A

Iancura 2015

Blend of 90% Malvasia delle Lipari and 10% Inzolia grapes. Stainles steel only. Deep straw yellow with golden hues. Notes of exotic fruits and Mediterranean woods. Fresh, agile, pleasant and savory on the palate with a gradual finish of aromatic notes.

I CUSTODI DELLE VIGNE DELL'ETNA

Contrada Moganazzi - Frazione Solicchiata
95012 Castiglione di Sicilia (CT)
Tel. +39 393 1898430
Fax +39 095 7374379
info@icustodi.it
www.icustodi.it
f *ICustodi*
🐦 *@icustodi*

YEAR OF FOUNDATION 2007
NAME OF THE OWNER Mario Paoluzi
TOTAL BOTTLES PRODUCED 50,000
DIRECT SALES
VISITS TO THE WINERY - RESERVATION NEEDED
HECTARES OF VINEYARD 13
CERTIFIED ORGANIC VITICULTURE

A young estate that was born from the passion and determination of its owner, Mario Paoluzi, who in a short period of time has been able to produce top quality wines that have a strong tie to the land. The vineyards, some of which are over 100 years old, are on the northern and eastern sides of Mt. Etna and are alberello-trained and have a high density of between 8,500 and 10,000 vines per hectare. Salvo Foti, who knowns and interprets this area well, has made an important contribution to the wines while the vines are cared for by Vigneri, a group of highly specialized winegrowers. Work in the vineyards respects nature and is for the most part done by hand following local tradition. The wines are decidedly Etna-esque.

☐ 93   Price B

Etna Bianco Ante 2014

Blend of Carricante, Grecanico and Minnella grapes. Matures 12 months in stainless steel. Straw yellow with greenish hues. Clean and elegant in the nose with notes of citrus, grapefruit, white fruits, aromatic herbs and a touch of eucalyptus. Very fresh sip, agile but full at the same time. Briny note together with the very long finish.

■ 93   Price B

Etna Rosso Aetneus 2009

Blend of Carricante, Grecanico and Minnella grapes. Matures 12 months in stainless steel. Straw yellow with greenish hues. Clean and elegant in the nose with notes of citrus, grapefruit, white fruits, aromatic herbs and a touch of eucalyptus. Very fresh sip, agile but full at the same time. Briny note together with the very long finish.

■ 89   Price B

Etna Rosso Pistus 2014

Blend of Nerello Mascalese and Nerello Cappuccio grapes. Stainless steel for 12 months. Average intensity ruby red. Notes of berries, wet soil and a spicy hint in the nose. Fresh, good tannins and nice persistence.

I VIGNERI

Largo Signore Pietà, 17
95036 Randazzo (CT)
Tel. +39 0933 982942
Fax +39 0933 983264
info@ivigneri.it
www.@ivigneri.it
 ivignerietna
 @ivignerietna

YEAR OF FOUNDATION 2009
NAME OF THE OWNER Salvo e Simone Foti
TOTAL BOTTLES PRODUCED 8,000
VISITS TO THE WINERY - RESERVATION NEEDED
HECTARES OF VINEYARD 5.5
OLIVE OIL PRODUCTION

Salvo Foti is the real prophet of Etna winemaking and his winemaking can be considered heroic. Aften many consultancies, here is an authonomus project, run with the help of his son Simone. Everything is inspired by the respect of the vines, cultivated at extreme altitudes, the are over 70 years old and have ungrafted roots and are planted at a density of 10 thousand plants per hectar. Furthermore there is no use of chemical products in the vineyards nor in the cellar. The result are wines with slight imperfections, really excusable, but with an unforgetteble charm.

 92   Price C

Etna Rosso Vinupetra 2013

Blend of Nerello Mascalese and a little Nerello Cappuccio, Alicante and Francisi grapes. Matures in big barrels for 2 years. Bright ruby red. Complex and deep aromas with a bit of volatile and notes of wild berries, wildflowers and pomegranate. Gritty taste, tense, savory, of great personality. A rustic yet charming wine from ungrafted vines over 100 years old.

★

MORGANTE

Contrada Racalmare
92020 Grotte (AG)
Tel. +39 0922 945579
Fax +39 0922 946084
 morgantevini
info@morgantevini.it
www.morgantevini.it
 Morgante.Fratelli
 @MorganteVini

YEAR OF FOUNDATION 1998
NAME OF THE OWNER Morgante Family
TOTAL BOTTLES PRODUCED 310,000
DIRECT SALES
VISITS TO THE WINERY - RESERVATION NEEDED
HECTARES OF VINEYARD 60
OLIVE OIL PRODUCTION

Few can make Nero d'Avola wine the way the Morgante family can. Here Sicily's banner grape becomes a deep and important wine and its various versions have, over the years, have become increasingly linear and full of personality. Their estate is in the hills in the province of Agrigento, in southern Sicily. The wines are sunny, Mediterranean, bold and never commonplace.

 91 Price B

Sicilia Don Antonio 2013

100% Nero d'Avola grapes. Matures 1 year in new barrique. Very deep ruby red. Notes of berries, leather and sweet spices. Great taste in the mouth, complex, powerful with a sweet note of vanilla and pleasant savory. Thick tannins and very long finish.

 89 Price A

Sicilia Nero d'Avola 2014

100% Nero d'Avola grapes. Matures for a small period in used barrique. Deep ruby red. Intense notes of red fruits, cherry on top and light spices. Smooth and fresh in the mouth. Persistent.

MURGO

Via Zafferana, 13
95010 Santa Venerina (CT)
Tel. +39 095 950520
Fax +39 095 954713
info@murgo.it
www.murgo.it
 CantineMurgo

YEAR OF FOUNDATION 1860
NAME OF THE OWNER Manuele Scammacca del Murgo
TOTAL BOTTLES PRODUCED 250,000
DIRECT SALES
VISITS TO THE WINERY - RESERVATION NEEDED
HECTARES OF VINEYARD 30
HOSPITALITY
RESTAURANT
OLIVE OIL PRODUCTION

An historic Etna estate situated in the southern part of the volcano's eastern side. The estate has become a reference point for sparkling Sicilian wines, a type of wine the owners have always believed in and were among the first to produce on the island. The vineyards are cultivated in respect of nature and aside from native varieties also include some French varietals. The aim of the estate is to produce wines that have the characteristics of the terroir and are original and pleasing.

 90 Price B

Murgo Extra Brut 2009

100% Nerello Mascalese grapes. Matures 6 months on the lees. Light golden yellow. Thin and persistent perlage. Intense notes of flowers, grapefruit and almond. Very fresh sip, tense, with a long and pleasantly briny finish.

 88 Price A

Murgo Brut Rosè 2012

100% Nerello Mascalese grapes. Pink with orange hues. Thin and persistent perlage. Rich notes of raspberry, strawberry and a hint of cinnamon. Fresh on the palate with fragrant fruity notes and good persistence.

 86 Price B

Etna Rosso Tenuta San Michele 2014

100% Nerello Mascalese grapes. Matures in stainless steel and 15 months in tonneau. Intense notes of cherry in the nose. Fresh, good structure, good tannins and long finish.

OCCHIPINTI

S.P. 68 Vittoria-Pedalino, km 3,300
97019 Vittoria (RG)
Tel. +39 0932 1865519
info@agricolaocchipinti.it
www.agricolaocchipinti.it
 az.agr.ariannaocchipinti
 @CCHRNN

YEAR OF FOUNDATION 2004
NAME OF THE OWNER Arianna Occhipinti
TOTAL BOTTLES PRODUCED 120,000
DIRECT SALES
VISITS TO THE WINERY - RESERVATION NEEDED
HECTARES OF VINEYARD 18
CERTIFIED ORGANIC VITICULTURE
OLIVE OIL PRODUCTION

Right after earning her degree in enology, Arianna Occhipinti went to work to apply her conviction that the land and the grapes are what make a wine. An her feminine tenacity together with her strong conviction pumped new blood into winegrowing in Vittoria, an area of untapped potential which is for the moment the only DOCG appellation in Sicily. Arianna's center of operation is a new winery in Bombolieri, a restored ancient 'baglio' farm complex where an ageing cellar has been dug out of the chalky earth close to the vineyards, which have always been organically cultivated. With her boundless energy she has transformed it into a media attraction to promote Sicilian wine, especially abroad, as well as Sicily's pride in excellence.

 92   Price B
Il Frappato 2014

100% Frappato grapes. Ferments in concrete vats and matures 18 months in concrete but 50% of the wine matures 12 months in big barrels. Ruby red. Delicate aromas of macerated fruits and soil. Rich and intense in the mouth with average structure. Tense and fresh. Pleasantly briny touches. Very long.

 91   Price B
Siccagno 2013

100% Nero d'Avola grapes. Matures 22 months in 25 hl Slavonian durmast barrels. Purple red. Sweet notes of fruits, morello on top. Nice freshness, wide, great correspondence between taste and nose, long fruity finish.

☐ **89**   Price A
Sp 68 Bianco 2015

Blend of Moscato d'Alessandria and Albanello grapes. Matures 6 months in concrete vats. Aromas of medical herbs, chamomile and roseship. Fresh sip with nice correspondence between taste and nose. Average persistence.

 85   Price A
Sp 68 Rosso 2015

Blend of 70% Frappato and 30% Nero d'Avola grapes. Matures 7 months in concrete vats. Grape aromas with hints of red fruits in the nose. Good intensity in the mouth, fragrant, fruity. Good persistence.

PALARI

Contrada Barna - Frazione S. Stefano Briga
98137 Messina (ME)
Tel. +39 090 630194
Fax +39 090637247
info@palari.it
www.palari.it
f *Azienda-Agricola-Palari*

YEAR OF FOUNDATION **1990**
NAME OF THE OWNER **Salvatore Geraci**
TOTAL BOTTLES PRODUCED **36,000**
VISITS TO THE WINERY - RESERVATION NEEDED
HECTARES OF VINEYARD **7**

Salvatore 'Turi' Geraci is a well-known architect from Messina, as well as an old acolyte of Luigi Veronelli, who at a certain point in his life decided to go back to producing at his family's estate. His first attempt date back to 1990 but his first real wine did not come out until five years later. It was a Faro, an ancient wine that at the time had all but disappeared. It was produced after a period of "experimentation" during which time it was tasted and criticized by himself and his friends. When he got serious about it, however, he produced some true masterpieces, extraordinary wines that were deeply Mediterranean and made with grapes vines that were over 100 years old and looked out over the Messina Strait towards Reggio Calabria.

■ 🖩 **97**   Price C
Faro Palari 2011

Blend of 50% Nerello Mascalese, 40% Nerello Cappuccio and 10% Nocera grapes. 2 years in barrique. Intense and bright ruby red. Complex and articulated on the nose, spicy notes, then cassis, wild strawberry, wet soil, cardamom, carob and vanilla hints. Polite and balanced in the mouth, warm, elegant, harmonic and impressive persistence. Great wine.

■ **93**   Price B
Rosso del Soprano 2014

Blend of 50% Nerello Mascalese, 40% Nerello Cappuccio and 10% Nocera grapes. Barrique for 18 months. Lively ruby red. Spices and berries dominate the nose aromas, notes of cassis and roses in the background. Smooth and agile, warm, elegant on the palate, with velvety tannins and great persistence.

PALMENTO COSTANZO

Contrada Santo Spirito - Passopisciaro
95012 Castiglione di Sicilia (CT)
Tel. +39 334 6779915 - +39 335 7861686
info@palmentocostanzo.com
www.palmentocostanzo.com
f *palmentocostanzo*

YEAR OF FOUNDATION **2011**
NAME OF THE OWNER **Mimmo Costanzo and Valeria Agosta**
TOTAL BOTTLES PRODUCED **50,000**
DIRECT SALES
VISITS TO THE WINERY - RESERVATION NEEDED
HECTARES OF VINEYARD **9**
CERTIFIED ORGANIC VITICULTURE

Mimmo Costanzo is an entrepreneur who comes from the world of public works and infrastructures but has embarked on an ambitious project from his beautiful vineyards between Passopisciaro and Randazzo. He and his wife Valeria Agosta have invested in both wine and the territory and their new winery has been finished recently and in the near future they plan to create a tasting room and guest facilities. With their 2014 they also brought in a new and renowned winemaker, Donato Landini, and the first results are in the glass.

 92 Price B
Etna Rosso Nero di Sei 2012

100% Nerello Mascalese grapes, 15 months in barrique and tonneau. Ruby red with garnet hues. Complex notes, red fruits, bark and cardamom. Wide and complex in the mouth with clear aromas. Good tannins. Long and gradual finish. It will have a long life.

 90 Price B
Etna Bianco di Sei 2014

Blend of 70% Carricante and 30% Catarratto grapes. Matures 15 months in barrique and tonneau. Golden yellow. Elegant notes of flowers, straw and sage with hints of eucalyptus in the nose. Full, fresh, savory in the mouth with a nice briny finish.

 90 👍 Price A
Etna Rosso Mofete 2012

Blend of Nerello Mascalese and Nerello Cappuccio grapes, 1 year in barrique and tonneau. Ruby red with garnet hues. Good intensity, small wild berries, lava rock and soil aromas. Wide, enveloping, light tannins and nice freshness on the palate. Long finish.

PASSOPISCIARO

Contrada Guardiola
95012 Castiglione di Sicilia (CT)
Tel. +39 0942 983225

info@passopisciaro.com
www.passopisciaro.com
 PassopisciaroWinery
 @Passopisciaro1

YEAR OF FOUNDATION **2001**
NAME OF THE OWNER **Andrea Franchetti**
TOTAL BOTTLES PRODUCED **75,000**
DIRECT SALES
VISITS TO THE WINERY - RESERVATION NEEDED
HECTARES OF VINEYARD **25**

More ten years ago, Andrea Franchetti and Vincenzo Lo Mauro were among the first to see the enormous potential of the Etna area. They adopted an extreme approach to bring out the best from each vineyard, even if they were a few kilometers apart, and then highlighted their incredible differences by accentuating their elegance and the allure of imperfection. All this thanks to an indigenous and capricious grapes like Nero Mascalese.

 93 Price B
Contrada S 2014

100% Nerello Mascalese grapes from Contrada Sciaranuova at 900 meters of altitude. Matures 18 months in big barrels. Excellent notes of red fruits, wild cherry, underbrush, hay and flint. Long and rich in the mouth, intense, great balance and incredible persistence.

 92 Price B
Contrada C 2014

100% Nerello Mascalese grapes from Contrada Chappemacine at 550 meters of altitude. Matures 18 months in big barrels. Clear and intense red. Not immediate in the nose with typical notes of volcanic soils, flint and red fruits in the finish. Intense and fruity in the mouth, velvety and with nice smoothness. Incredibly long and pleasant finish.

 90 Price B
Contrada R 2014

100% Nerello Mascalese grapes from Contrada Rampante 100 year old single vignard at 1000 mt of altitude. Matures 18 months in durmast big barrels. Ruby red. Irony notes and red fruits in the nose. Good acidity, again clear fruit notes, well balanced by freshness.

★
PELLEGRINO

Via del Fante, 39
91025 Marsala (TP)
Tel. +39 0923 719911
info@carlopellegrino.it
www.carlopellegrino.it
f *cantinepellegrino*
🐦 *PellegrinoWine*

YEAR OF FOUNDATION 1880
NAME OF THE OWNER Pellegrino Family
TOTAL BOTTLES PRODUCED 6,500,000
DIRECT SALES
VISITS TO THE WINERY - RESERVATION NEEDED
HECTARES OF VINEYARD 157
RESTAURANT
CERTIFIED ORGANIC VITICULTURE

During these 140 years of history, the maternal lineage of the Pellegrino family has brought new links with the Alagna, Tumbarello, Renda and Bellina families that are presently leading the company. It has always been a reference point for Marsala and in recent years they have also concentrated on making wine using native grapes. Today, aside from their Marsala, they offer white and red wines representative of the territory and at reasonable prices. Aside from wine, they have also have a vocation for wine tourism and they recently inaugurated a new hotel with a view over the Egadi Islands where you can taste their wines, visit the historic cellars and even enjoy an aperitif and a fine meal.

■ 91   Price B
Tripudium Rosso 2013
Blend of Nero d'Avola and Syrah grapes. Stainless steel. Matures 1 year in 20 hl barrels. Intense ruby red. Elegant and deep notes of red fruits, spices, white pepper. Dense, smooth and briny on the palate. Again spices. Very persistent.

▣ 89   Price B*
Passito di Pantelleria Nes 2014
*100% Zibibbo grapes. Double vinification. The first one with the fresh grapes, the second with the dried grapes on the straw mats. Bright amber color. Very intense and complex notes of dates, candied apricot and honey. Fresh, sweet, savory and capers on the palate. Very balanced. Great persistence. *50 cl bottle.*

☐ 87   👍 Price A
Tripudium Bianco 2015
100% Catarratto grapes. Stainless steel. Straw yellow color. Notes of white fruits, herbs, Mediterranean woods. Fresh, intense, smooth and savory in the mouth. Good persistence.

PIANO DEI DAINI

S.P. 64 - Frazione Solicchiata
95012 Castiglione di Sicilia (CT)
Tel. +39 095 7086583
info@pianodeidaini.it
www.pianodeidaini.it
f *pianodeidaini*
🐦 *@pianodeidaini*

YEAR OF FOUNDATION 2010
NAME OF THE OWNER Sofia Bosco
TOTAL BOTTLES PRODUCED 25,000
DIRECT SALES
VISITS TO THE WINERY - RESERVATION NEEDED
HECTARES OF VINEYARD 9

A young estate but one with clear ideas focused on producing quality wines that express the rich terroir of Etna. Sofia and Concetto Bosco began this endeavor with great passion and dedication. Helping them are agronomist Salvo Giuffrida and enologist Carlo Ferrini. The vineyards are located in two areas in the zone of Castiglione di Sicilia, one in Solicchiata, where the winery is located, and the other in Passopisciaro, which has the estate's jewel, Vigna Vico, made up of centuries-old, ungrafted vines that date back to be from the phylloxera plague and are terraced on a mountainside. The wines are already very good and we expect them to improve in coming years.

■ 92   Price B
Etna Rosso Vigna Vico 2013
Blend of 90% Nerello Mascalese and 10% Nerello Cappuccio grapes. Matures 12-14 months in 700 liters French durmast tonneau. Light ruby red. Deep and elegant in the nose with flowery hints, red fruits, bark and spices. Great energy in the mouth, not based on power but on balance between freshness, velvety tannins and very long finish.

■ 89   Price B
Etna Rosso Piano dei Daini 2014
Blendo of 90% Nerello Mascalese and 10% Nerello

Cappuccio grapes. Matures 10-12 months in 300 to 700 liters French durmast tonneau. Light ruby red. Elegant in the nose with hints of spices in the background. Full in the mouth, with smooth tannins, savory and long fruity finish.

---

 88   **Price B**

Etna Bianco Piano dei Daini 2015

Blend of 90% Carricante with Catarratto, Grecanico and Inzolia grapes. 50% matures in stainless steel and 50% in 500 liter French durmast tonneau for 4 months. Straw yellow. Clean in the nose, average intensity with notes of white peach and flowers. Fresh on the palate, agile and savory. Great drinkability.

★

PIETRADOLCE

Contrada Rampante - Frazione Solicchiata
95012 Castiglione di Sicilia (CT)
Tel. +39 348 4005913
info@pietradolce.it
www.pietradolce.it

YEAR OF FOUNDATION 2005
NAME OF THE OWNER Michele and Mario Faro
TOTAL BOTTLES PRODUCED 48,500
HECTARES OF VINEYARD 13
OLIVE OIL PRODUCTION

They were already an established and historic nursery, one of the largest in Europe, and then they caught the winegrowing and winemaking bug. Today the Faro family, brothers Mario and Michele together with their father Venerano, are full-fledged members of the Sicilian quality wine club and this thanks above all to Etna and the capacity of this area to produce elegant wines. Their estate is not large but can boast vineyards that are at least 40 years old including, especially in the Contrada Barbaglia where they there is a wonderful alberello-trained, pre-phylloxera vineyard that has vines between 80-100 years of age. The vineyards are a treasure and are being run by the talented agronomist Giuseppe Parlavecchio and together with enologist Carlo Ferrini they produce authentic red and white wines that are among the best in Sicily.

☐ **92**   **Price B**

Etna Bianco Archineri 2015

100% Carricante grapes. Stainless steel only. Light

straw yellow. Elegant notes of white fruits, hawthorn and eucalyptus. Fresh, intense, savory in the mouth, a wine of great tension. Very persistent.

■ **91**   **Price B**

Etna Rosso Contrada Rampante 2014

100% Nerello Mascalese grapes. Matures 14 months in French durmast tonneau. Very clear ruby red. Intense and polite aromas of wild berries, spicy notes and nutmeg. Fresh and winde in the mouth with present tannins but never overwhelming. Great persistence. It will have a long life.

■ **90**   **Price B**

Etna Rosso Archineri 2014

100% Nerello Mascalese grapes. Matures 14 months in French durmast tonneau. Light ruby red. Clear in the nose, good intensity with red fruits, elegant spiciness and earthy notes. Fresh on the palate, good structure, strong tannins and long finish.

 ★★★

PLANETA

Contrada Dispensa
92013 Menfi (AG)
Tel. +39 091 327965
Fax +39 091 6124335
planeta@planeta.it
www.planeta.it
 planetawinery
 @PlanetaWinery

YEAR OF FOUNDATION 1995
NAME OF THE OWNER Alessio, Santi and Francesca Planeta
TOTAL BOTTLES PRODUCED 2,300,000
VISITS TO THE WINERY - RESERVATION NEEDED
HECTARES OF VINEYARD 370
HOSPITALITY
OLIVE OIL PRODUCTION

This producer symbolizes the new-found success of Sicilian wines. It was set up exactly 20 years ago and from the beginning was run a family of young, then, entrepreneurs – Alessio, Santi and Francesca Planeta – who immediately ushered in an extraordinary and efficient wind of change. Today Planeta have five wineries, in different areas of Sicily, but their enthusiasm and passion remain the same and are evident in all their wines.

☐ 🔲 96   👍 Price A
Sicilia Carricante Eruzione 1614 2015

Blend of Carricante with a little Riesling grapes from the Feudo di Mezzo Etna estate. Stainless steel on the lees. Bright straw yellow. Notes of lime, flowers, cedar and grapefruit on the elegant nose. Strong, tense, fresh, agile in the mouth with a very long finish. Splendid and not at all expensive considering the high quality of this wine.

☐ 93   Price B
Sicilia Cometa 2014

100% Fiano grapes. Stainless steel on the lees. Bright straw yellow. A lot of exotic fruits on the nose, pineapple, mango then cedar, yellow peach and wildflowers. Warm, savory, enveloping, great body but with a good acidity to sustain it. Very persistent finish.

■ 91   Price B
Noto Santa Cecilia 2012

100% Nero d'Avola grapes. Matures 14 months in used barrique. Dark and concentrated ruby red. Caper and mint on the nose, eucalyptus, small fruits and spices. Strong flavor, some roughness due to the young tannins, good acidity and warm and persistent finish.

■ 90   👍 Price A
Etna Rosso 2014

100% Nerello Mascalese grapes. Stainless steel. Bright and luminous ruby red. Very fruity on the nose, notes of red currant, wild strawberry and wildflowers hints. Fresh flavor, agile, pleasantly savory, not too full-bodied but of 'dangerous' drinkability.

☐ 88   👍 Price A
Alastro 2015

Blend of 70% Grecanico, 15% Grillo and 15% Sauvignon Blanc grapes. Stainless steel. Bright straw yellow. Fruity and fragrant on the nose with notes of white peach, wildflowers, lime and cedar. Fresh flavor, polite, savory, easy to drink and good length.

www.rapitala.it
f *tenutarapitala*

YEAR OF FOUNDATION **1977**
NAME OF THE OWNER **GIV and de la Gatinais Family**
TOTAL BOTTLES PRODUCED **2,800,000**
DIRECT SALES
VISITS TO THE WINERY - RESERVATION NEEDED
HECTARES OF VINEYARD **175**

Originally owned by de la Gatinais counts, some 15 years ago it became part of Gruppo Italiano Vini. The vineyards are in the area of Alcamo, in northwest Sicily, and produce a vast range of wines made from local varieties as well as some international ones. It is one of the few Sicilian producers that can boast high sales on the Italian market, the result of past investments to enhance quality and build a brand that had great success among both consumers and wine lovers.

■ 90   Price B
Solinero 2013

100% Syrah grapes. Matures 18 months in barrique. Very deep ruby red. Intense nose, a little complex, notes of spices and cocoa. Powerful sup, warm, structured and with great balance. Very persistent.

■ 87   Price A
Sicilia Alto Nero d'Avola 2014

100% Nero d'Avola grapes. Matures 5 months in barrique and 7 months in 30 and 50 hectoliters barrels. Intense ruby color. Notes of ripe fruit and spices. Average body, fresh and fruity. Good length.

■ 87   Price A
Sicilia Nuhar 2014

Blend of Pinot Nero and Nero d'Avola grapes. Matures 9 months in barrique. Intense ruby red. Average intensity aromas mostly flowery and fruity. Good fresh sip, structure and a sweet note. Again fruit aromas and good persistence.

★
RAPITALÀ

Contrada Rapitalà
90043 Camporeale (PA)
Tel. +39 0924 37233
Fax +39 0924 36115
rapitala@giv.it

★
GIROLAMO RUSSO

Via Regina Margherita, 78 - Frazione
Passopisciaro
95012 Castiglione di Sicilia (CT)
Tel. +39 328 3840247
Fax +39 0942 897042

info@girolamorusso.it
www.girolamorusso.it
f Azienda-Girolamo-Russo

YEAR OF FOUNDATION **2005**
NAME OF THE OWNER **Giuseppe Russo**
TOTAL BOTTLES PRODUCED **70,000**
DIRECT SALES
VISITS TO THE WINERY - RESERVATION NEEDED
HECTARES OF VINEYARD **15**
CERTIFIED ORGANIC VITICULTURE
OLIVE OIL PRODUCTION

Giuseppe Russo earned a fine arts degree and started off as a music teacher before he became a winemaker, by circumstance. His father, on the other hand, worked the vineyards in Passopisciaro di Castiglione di Sicilia, on the northern slopes of Mt Etna. It was the latter's premature death in 2003 that prompted Giuseppe to devote himself to their vineyards and with the help of enologist Emiliano Falsini soon became one of the most appreciated Etna producers. Only grapes native to the volcano are used and they produce extraordinary reds, with each plot vinified separately The single vignard wine, usually excellent for elegance and typicality, in 2014 vintage seemed to us less territorial, more muscular, with riper and warmer notes. Very good as usual but not up to the levels reached in the past..

■ 🇬 95   Price B
Etna Rosso Feudo di Mezzo 2014

100% Nerello Mascalese grapes. Matures 16 months in wood. Light ruby red with garnet hues. Warm and intense notes of wild berries, blackberries, jasmine and raspberries. Then flowers and spices. Nice freshness on the palate, harmonic and velvety tannins. Long and elegant finish.

■ 92   Price B
Etna Rosso 'A Rina 2014

Blend of 95% Nerello Mascalese and 5% Nerello Cappuccio grapes. Matures 6 months in concrete vats and 6 months in wood. Light ruby red. Notes of red fruit and flowery hints, elegant spiciness and hints of lava rock. Fresh on the palate, clean, good tannins and nice progression. Long finish.

■ 90   Price B
Etna Rosso Feudo 2014

Blend of 95% Nerello Mascalese and 5% Nerello Cappuccio grapes. Matures 16 months in wood.

Light garnet color. Notes of ripe fruits, licorice and spices. Powerful month with enveloping tannins. Great persistence.

SETTESOLI

S.S. 115
92013 Menfi (AG)
Tel. +39 0925 77111
🅢 *cantine.settesoli*
info@cantinesettesoli.it
www.cantinesettesoli.it
f *Cantine-Settesoli*
🐦 *@CantineSettesol*

YEAR OF FOUNDATION **1958**
NAME OF THE OWNER
TOTAL BOTTLES PRODUCED **20,000,000**
DIRECT SALES
VISITS TO THE WINERY - RESERVATION NEEDED
HECTARES OF VINEYARD **6,000**
OLIVE OIL PRODUCTION

With some 20 million bottles produced a year, this cooperatives is not only the biggest producer in Sicily but also one of the most important cooperatives in southern Italy. It is run by Vito Varvaro who believes in teamwork and producing quality. The acquisition of new vineyards and recruiting new members is not as important as improving the quality of production. This is done both in the vineyard and by producing a line of wines from the best grape.

■ 92   Price B
Sicilia Carthago 2014

100% Nero d'Avola grapes. Matures 12 months in barrique. Intense ruby red. Notes of ripe red fruits, plums and morello. Powerful on the palate, structured and agile. Well made. Long finish.

■ 86   🖒 Price A
Mandrarossa Timperosse 2015

100% Petit Verdot grapes. Stainless steel. Ruby red with violet hues. Elegant nose, exotic yellow fruit and spicy hint. Fresh sip, a little salty, easy to drink and average persistence.

☐ 86   🖒 Price A
Sicilia Urra di Mare 2015

100% Sauvignon Blanc grapes. Stainless steel only.

Greenish yellow. Intense and vegetal nose with hints of sage and citrus. Nice acidity, savory, agile and fresh. Good persistence.

★★★
TASCA D'ALMERITA

Tenuta Regaleali
90020 Sclafani Bagni (PA)
Tel. +39 091 6459711
🔊 *tascadalmerita*
info@tascadalmerita.it
www.tascadalmerita.it
📘 *TascadAlmerita*
🐦 *@TascaWine*

YEAR OF FOUNDATION 1830
NAME OF THE OWNER Tasca d'Almerita Family
TOTAL BOTTLES PRODUCED 3,000,000
DIRECT SALES
VISITS TO THE WINERY - RESERVATION NEEDED
HECTARES OF VINEYARD 420
HOSPITALITY
OLIVE OIL PRODUCTION

One of Italy's most famous and prestigious wineries is today run by Giuseppe and Albert Tasca d'Almerita who are the offspring of Lucio and grandchildren of founder Giuseppe Sr., aka Conte Tasca. They have a vast and established line of production and use both native and international grapes which are interpreted with great skill and talent by enologist Laura Orsi with the consultancy of winemaker Carlo Ferrini.

■ 🗋 97   Price B
Contea di Sclafani Rosso del Conte 2012

Blend of 63% Nero d'Avola with Perrione and other red grapes. Matures 18 months in barrique. Intense ruby red. Notes of cassis, mulberry, raspberry, blackberry, eucalyptus and light smoky hints complete the elegant and varied nose. Clean flavor, savory, full-bodied with a little roughness due to the young tannins. Exceptional persistent finish. Great wine.

■ 93   Price B
Contea di Sclafani Cabernet Sauvignon 2013

100% Cabernet Sauvignon grapes. Matures 18 months in barrique. Intense and deep ruby red. Blueberry and blackberry jam on the nose, then mint and eucalyptus, smoky hints on the nose. Rich flavor, thick tannins but not aggressive, great body and long and enveloping finish.

☐ 92   Price B
Contea di Sclafani Chardonnay 2014

100% Cabernet Sauvignon grapes. Matures 18 months in barrique. Intense and deep ruby red. Blueberry and blackberry jam on the nose, then mint and eucalyptus, smoky hints on the nose. Rich flavor, thick tannins but not aggressive, great body and long and enveloping finish.

☐ 89   Price A
Dydime Tenuta Capofaro 2015

100% Malvasia grapes from Salina island. Stainless steel only. Straw yellow with golden hues. Notes of ripe fruit, peach, apricot together with medical herbs and wildflowers. Rich on the palate, dry but smooth, pleasantly salty, with a savory crescendo finish. A great version.

☐ 88   Price A
Mozia Grillo Fondazione Whitaker 2015

100% Grillo grapes from Mozia island organic alberello vines. Matures 5 months on the yeasts. Straw yellow with greenish hues. Pear and white peach on the nose, aromatic herbs and smoky hints. Very fresh and savory, sharp, vertical, easy to drink and salty finish. A wine of sea and wind.

TENUTA DI FESSINA

S.S. 120 - Via Nazionale, 22
95012 Castiglione di Sicilia (CT)
Tel. +39 329 9714353
fessina@tenutadifessina.com
www.tenutadifessina.com
📘 *tenutadifessina*
🐦 *@tenutadifessina*

YEAR OF FOUNDATION 2007
NAME OF THE OWNER Silvia Maestrelli
TOTAL BOTTLES PRODUCED 65,000
DIRECT SALES
VISITS TO THE WINERY - RESERVATION NEEDED
HECTARES OF VINEYARD 9
HOSPITALITY
OLIVE OIL PRODUCTION

After latest year's important change that saw the arrival of Giandomenico Negro to replace Federico Curtaz, the estate has moved forward

362

without interruption and the 2015 harvest will all be expressions of this new direction. Although a native of Piedmont, Negro knows the area of Etna well having collaborated with Benanti 25 years ago, when the area's rebirth was beginning. The vineyards are located in various places: Rovittello in the township of Castiglione di Sicilia and in the district of Feudo in Randazzo, both on the northern side; in Milo on the eastern side of the volcano; and Santa Maria di Licodia on the southeastern side. The wines are a rich expression of the land, intriguing, nicely made and with a great propensity to age.

☐ 94   Price B

Etna Bianco A'Puddara 2014

100% Carricante grapes. Ferments 9 months in durmast barrels. Straw yellow with greenish hues. Fine and complex aromas of Granny Smith apples, oregano, sage, baby powder and pepper puffs. Fresh, sharp, edgy on the palate, great saltiness and length.

■ 93   Price B

Etna Rosso Il Musmeci Riserva 2011

100% Nerello Mascalese grapes. Matures 18 months in big barrels and tonneau. Light ruby red. Complex aromas of flowers, nutmeg, cloves and a hint of pepper. Agile sip, balanced with silky tannins and never-ending length.

■ 87   Price B

Etna Rosso Erse 2015

100% Nerello Mascalese grapes. Matures 18 months in big barrels and tonneau. Light ruby red. Complex aromas of flowers, nutmeg, cloves and a hint of pepper. Agile sip, balanced with silky tannins and never-ending length.

TERRAZZE DELL'ETNA

Contrada Bocca d'Orzo
95036 Randazzo (CT)
Tel. +39 091 6236343
Fax +39 091 6236326
info@terrazzedelletna.it
www.terrazzedelletna.it
f *Terrazze-dellEtna*
🐦 *@TerrazzeEtna*

YEAR OF FOUNDATION 2008
NAME OF THE OWNER Antonio Bevilacqua
TOTAL BOTTLES PRODUCED 120,000

DIRECT SALES
VISITS TO THE WINERY - RESERVATION NEEDED
HECTARES OF VINEYARD 24

For some time now Nino Bevilacqua, who runs one of Italy's most important engineering firms, has been making wine on Etna where bought some panoramic vineyards and planted new ones, all in the countryside of Solicchiata and Randazzo. The technical side of winemaking is handled by renowned enologist Riccardo Cotarella and the result are wines that reflect the identity of the territory as well as appeal to international tastes by polishing the rustic edges off the wine.

■ 91   👍 Price A

Etna Rosso Carusu 2013

Blend of 80% Nerello Mascalese and 20% Nerello Cappuccio grapes. Matures 6 months in big barrels. Bright ruby. Typical aromas of wild strawberry, pomegranate, red mirth and spicy notes in the underground. Savory and agile, elegant body, well sustained by acidity and good length in the finish.

TORNATORE

Via Pietramarina, 8/a - Località Verzella
95012 Castiglione di Sicilia (CT)
Tel. +39 095 7563542
Fax +39 095 7133777
info@tornatorewine.com
www.tornatorewine.com

YEAR OF FOUNDATION 1865
NAME OF THE OWNER Francesco Tornatore
TOTAL BOTTLES PRODUCED 84,000
DIRECT SALES
VISITS TO THE WINERY - RESERVATION NEEDED
HECTARES OF VINEYARD 46
OLIVE OIL PRODUCTION

Francesco Tornatore, an entrepreneur who heads various manufacturing enterprises in Italy and China, has return to his family's ancient mission: winemaking. This is an old family vocation and Tornatore is Etna through and through and with his family background he had to get into winemaking. His aim is to run an estate with the greatest number of vineyards in the DOC appellation. His first wines are very promising with good stock wines and showcase ones that demonstrate that he has 'got' the uniqueness of Etna. The winery's enologist is Vincenzo Bàmbina.

93   Price B
Etna Rosso Trimarchisa 2014

100% Nerello Mascalese grapes. Matures in concrete and oak barrels. Ruby red with light garnet hues. Warm on the nose, elegant and complex: wild berries, spices, nutmeg, musk, underbrush notes. Wide, dense, smooth, fresh and savory on the palate. Ready but with a long life ahead. Expression of the territory. Very long.

91   👍 Price A
Etna Rosso 2014

100% Nerello Mascalese grapes. Matures in big barrels. Ruby red with garnet hues. Notes of wild berries, evident spices, hints of wet soil and lava rock. Rich, full, fresh on the palate, good integrated tannins, territorial. Balanced and of great length.

89   Price B
Etna Bianco Pietrarizzo 2015

100% Carricante grapes. Matures 5 months in barrels. Deep straw yellow color. Intense notes of yellow fruits, nuts and aromatic herbs. Full, rich, wide on the mouth, nice aromatic impact and good persistence.

★
VALLE DELL'ACATE

Contrada Bidini
97011 Acate (RG)
Tel. +39 0932 874166
Fax +39 0932 875114
🅢 *valle.dellacate*
info@valledellacate.it
www.valledellacate.com
🅕 *Valle-dellAcate*
🐦 *@VdaWinery*

YEAR OF FOUNDATION **1981**
NAME OF THE OWNER **Jacono and Ferreri Families**
TOTAL BOTTLES PRODUCED **450,000**
DIRECT SALES
VISITS TO THE WINERY - RESERVATION NEEDED
HECTARES OF VINEYARD **100**

Gaetana Jacono and Francesco Ferreri are the heart and soul of this winery that is one of the most representative of the area of Vittoria, home to Sicily's only DOG appellation: Cerasuo-

lo di Vittoria. They also represent the alliance of two families that own the estate that today produces consistent and modern wine that don't try to be fancy and are often economical. Gaetana was also a brand ambassador for the We-Women initiative at Milan's Expo 2015 world's fair, while Francesco is president of Assovini Sicilia, an association that represents the island's leading wineries.

91   👍 Price A
Cerasuolo di Vittoria Classico 2014

Blend of Nero d'Avola and Frappato grapes. Matures 12 months in barrels and tonneau. Bright red color. Notes of ripe red fruits, macerated cherry, dry plums and delicate spices like black pepper and licorice. Enveloping and elegant on the palate. Again notes of red fruits and spices with a nice eucalyptus hint.

88   👍 Price A
Vittoria Il Frappato 2015

Blend of Nero d'Avola and Frappato grapes. Matures 12 months in barrels and tonneau. Bright red color. Notes of ripe red fruits, macerated cherry, dry plums and delicate spices like black pepper and licorice. Enveloping and elegant on the palate. Again notes of red fruits and spices with a nice eucalyptus hint.

ALDO VIOLA

Via per Camporeale, 18/C
91011 Alcamo (TP)
Tel. +39 0924 27 998
info@viniviola.it
www.viniviola.it
🅕 *alessandro.viola.9862*

YEAR OF FOUNDATION **1999**
NAME OF THE OWNER **Viola Family**
TOTAL BOTTLES PRODUCED **25,000**
DIRECT SALES
VISITS TO THE WINERY - RESERVATION NEEDED
HECTARES OF VINEYARD **10**
CERTIFIED ORGANIC VITICULTURE

The wines from this tiny estate with its vineyards on the Trapani hills are complex, particular and increasingly expressive. Aldo Viola studied enology in Marsala and has a French mother and these factors alone were enough to convince him to become a winemaker.

☐ 92   Price B

Crimiso 2015

100% Catarratto grapes from a single vignard. Maceration on the skins for 5 months. Straw yellow color with golden hues. Deep and complex notes of yellow fruits, honey and pleasant hints of Mediterranean woods. Great balance on the palate between acidity and the sweet hint. Enveloping. Again ripe fruits. Savory and very long finish.

■ 90   Price B

Guarini Plus 2015

100% Syrah grapes, alberello grown. Matures 11 months in 8 hl French durmast barrels. Violet red color. Notes of small ripe fruits. Powerful in the mouth with nice freshness and structure. Well extracted tannins. Good persistence.

☐ 87   Price B

Egesta 2015

100% Grillo grapes. Matures 6 months stainless steel. Golden yellow with topaz hues. Notes of pear and aromatic herbs on the nose. Dense and fruity in the mouth. Gradual lengt. Original.

■ 87   Price A

Moretto 2015

Blend of Nerello Mascalese, Perricone and Syrah grapes. Matures 6 months in stainless steel and used tonneau. Violet red with purple hues. Red and macerated fruits in the nose. Fragrant, rich and with nice acidity in the mouth. Slightly savory. Present tannins. Long.

365

Every **MONDAY**
Editor Speak by
DANIELE CERNILLI

www.doctorwine.it

Technical and thoughtful opinion of one of Italy's most authoritative wine critics

TRENTINO

Archeological finds have discovered that winemaking in Trentino dates by to the V-VI century BC. One of these was an Etruscan Situla, a copper pail with inscriptions praising the cult of Bacchus that was found towards the middle of the 19th century in Val di Cembra. The Romans, too, were known to have appreciated and encouraged winemaking in the area. In the Middle Ages and up to 1145, the Augustine monks of the Abbey of San Michele all'Adige documented with their 'charter rules' winemaking methods, harvest dates, controls on production and even wine prices. All this helps to give a picture of the importance winemaking has had through the ages. In more recent times the history of Trentino wines was told by Michelangelo Mariani, the historian of the Council of Trent, who towards the middle of the 14th century described the various types of wine and grapes used in the Trentino area. The annexation of the region into the Hapsburg Austro-Hungarian Empire coincided with the official recognition of Trentino wines to the extent that in 1874, the Istituto Agrario di San Michele all'Adige, built on the site of the ancient abbey, was given the task of coordinating regional wine production and training enologists and agronomists. This is a function the institute still performs today preparing scores of top spe-

cialized experts who go on to work for the most part in the region.

From a winemaking point of view, but not only, Trentino and Alto Adige (South Tyrol) are to totally distinct realities. In the province of Trentino, the influence from neighboring Veneto is very strong and this is evident in their wine production. The vineyards are for the most part located along the Valle dell'Adige with the sole exception of Isera, the home of Marzemino, a medium-body and fragrant red, that was even cited by Lorenzo Da Ponte in his libretto for Mozart's Don Giovanni. The rest are between Avio and Mezzolombardo where the vineyards follow the course of the river and, at times, the narrow valley it has created. Winegrowing here is very difficult and the vineyards are often terraced on steep slopes with the vines trained using the pergola Trentina method, which makes them look like an upside down '7'. At one time the most widespread grape was Nosiola, a white variety that was all but wiped out during the phylloxera plague at the start of the 20th century. It can still be found but it is rarely used. Today the prominent grape is Chardonnay which is used to make a fruity white with not much body, Trentino Chardonnay, as well as traditional method sparkling wines that today have a Trento Classico Doc appellation, commonly referred to as Trentodoc, and include some of Italy's best bubbly. The most famous produces of this sparkling wine are Ferrari, Cavit and Mezzocorona. The rest of production, 60% of which is doc Trentin, is for the most part wine made with the so-called international varieties including Müller Thurgau, Pinot Grigio, Sauvignon, Cabernet Sauvignon, Merlot and Pinot Nero. But there are still some traditional varietal wines, like Nosiola or Sorni, both Rosso and Bianco. No matter who is the producer, the wines are all distinguished by their technical quality that is guaranteed by the experts trained at the Fondazione Edmund Mach-Istituto Agrario di San Michele all'Adige.

The vast majority of Trentino wines are produced by large and modern cooperatives, Cavit being the best example, which can boast a very respectable average level of quality. These wines are well-made, perhaps a bit simple but almost most always with an excellent quality-price ratio. Since there is an exception to every rule, there is a DOC red wine that contrasts with the others of the Trentino appellation. It is Teroldego Rotaliana and is made from Teroldego grapes cultivated on the Piana Rotaliana, the only plain in the whole province. It is a great wine with enormous potential that ages with class, never has the aggressiveness of a Barolo nor the elegance of a Pinot Noir, and yet its spicy aromas and its remarkable balance make in one of the most interesting reds in the area. It should be served at 18°C in broad glasses and paired with typical, local cuisine including mushrooms. Casteller also has a separate DOC and is a red made from Schiava grapes.

The differences in altitudes and the exposures of the vineyards, along with their positions, create a variety of microclimates that make winegrowing easy in some areas and difficult in others. The area more to the south, which benefit from the influence of Lake Garda, even have olive and palm trees and thus have an almost Mediterranean climate. More to the north, where the mountain peaks tower over the towns of Mezzolombardo and Mezzocorona, it seems more like being on the banks of the Moselle River and even a precocious grape like Chardonnay has trouble ripening.

The soils of the province in the other hand, are more uniform. Around the Valle dell'Adige the soil is sandy and pebbly with only a small presence of chalk here and there. Vine training methods are also similar and almost everyone uses the pergola trentina style. However, here as in other regions, a growing number of new vineyards are being planted with low, Guyot-trained vines. This is especially the case where estates are striving for extreme quality.

CONTROLLED DESIGNATION OF ORIGIN (DOC)

- Casteller
- Teroldego Rotaliano
- Trentino, with or without the sub-areas Sorni or Bianco di Sorni or Rosso di Sorni (only for Trentino Bianco and Trentino Rosso), Isera or d'Isera (only for Trentino Marzemino Superiore), Ziresi or dei Ziresi (only for Trentino Marzemino Superiore), Castel Beseno or Beseno (only for Trentino Superiore)
- Trento
- Valdadige or Etschaler
- Valdadige Terradeiforti or Terradeiforti, geographic references allowed

★

ABATE NERO

Sponda Trentina, 45
38121 Trento (TN)
Tel. +39 0461 246566
spumante@abatenero.it
www.abatenero.it
 abatenero.trentodoc

YEAR OF FOUNDATION 1973
NAME OF THE OWNER Eugenio De Castel Terlago,
Luciano Lunelli
TOTAL BOTTLES PRODUCED 55,000
DIRECT SALES
VISITS TO THE WINERY - RESERVATION NEEDED
HECTARES OF VINEYARD 8

368

Today as yesterday, the leitmotif of the Abate Nero estate in Trento is always the same: utmost care beginning on the plant where the grape are carefully chosen for the base musts to make classic sparkling wine. Their first cuvée was created in 1975 almost as a challenge involving the estate's two owners, Luciano Lunelli and Eugenio De Castel Terlago, and a group of friends all involved in the world of wine. This challenge then transformed into a productive reality and each of the winery's bubblies represents a clear and original example of Trentodoc.

---

 90   Price B
Trentodoc Domini Brut 2010
100% Chardonnay grapes. Classic method. Intense straw yellow color. Light and fast perlage. Smooth notes of yeasts then yellow plum and wildflowers. Tense on the mouth, acidulous, very briny, creamy and good length.

BALTER

Via Vallunga II, 24
38068 Rovereto (TN)
Tel. +39 0464 430101
info@balter.it
www.balter.it
 BalterAziendaAgricola
 @Balter_az_agr

YEAR OF FOUNDATION 1990
NAME OF THE OWNER Nicola Balter

TOTAL BOTTLES PRODUCED 80,000
DIRECT SALES
VISITS TO THE WINERY - RESERVATION NEEDED
HECTARES OF VINEYARD 10

The Balter family has owned this winery since 1875. In the 1960s, the estate shifted away from growing grapes for sale to making their own wines. Today. Nicola Balter puts his signature on every wine the estate makes, assisted by his daughter Clementina who handles external relations. The estate is composed of 10 hectares of vineyards and a small castle with a 16th century turret that is situated on a hilltop about three km from Rovereto. The winery is underground and its tasting rooms welcomes wine lovers from around the world.

---

 90   Price B
Trentodoc Rosé Brut
Blend of 80% Pinot Nero and 20% Chardonnay grapes. Classic method. Deep antique pink, fast and light perlage. Complex on the nose, smoky hints, enveloping, raspberry aromas. Creamy on the mouth, balanced and polite, great persistence.

---

 87   Price B
Trentodoc Brut
100% Chardonnay grapes. Greenish straw yellow color. Slow and light perlage. Fragrant on the nose with notes of yeasts and bread crust. Light flavor on the mouth, acidulous, pleasantly briny, not too big structure and adequate length.

BELLAVEDER

Località Maso Belvedere
38100 Faedo (TN)
Tel. +39 0461 650171
info@bellaveder.it
www.bellaveder.it
 bellaveder

YEAR OF FOUNDATION 2004
NAME OF THE OWNER Tranquillo Lucchetta
TOTAL BOTTLES PRODUCED 80,000
DIRECT SALES
VISITS TO THE WINERY - RESERVATION NEEDED
HECTARES OF VINEYARD 12

The estate is set in a magnificent position with a breathtaking view over the Rotaliana Valley and has a single, 12-hectare vineyard above the town of San Michele all'Adige on the Faedo hill, an area that is historically apt for winegrowing. In 2003, next to the farmstead, known as Mansum Bellavedere in 1780 registry records, is a modern underground winery that uses technology which is compatible with craft winemaking. The wine is made by Luca Gasperinatti.

☐ **92** 👍 **Price A**
Trentino Müller Thurgau San Lorenz 2015

100% Müller Thurgau grapes. Straw yellow color. Notes of elder together with hints of sage. Nice body, not too persistent but very pleasant to drink.

■ **91** **Price B**
Trentino Lagrein Dunkel Mansum 2012

100% Lagrein grapes. Matures 2 years in barrique. Intense and dark ruby red with violet bright hues. Intense notes of ripe blackberry, cocoa and nigritella. Powerful body, clean and tense, excellent persistence.

▣ **90** **Price B**
Trentodoc Brut Nature Riserva 2011

100% Chardonnay grapes, the best of the estate. On the yeasts for 60 months. Light greenish yellow. Light and continuous perlage. Notes of yellow plum, golden apple, cedar, yeasts. Fresh and easy to drink on the mouth, agile and clear. Great body and persistence.

CANTINA ROTALIANA

Via Trento 65/b
38017 Mezzolombardo (TN)
Tel. +39 0461 601010
🅢 *cantina.rotaliana*
info@cantinarotaliana.it
www.cantinarotaliana.it

YEAR OF FOUNDATION 1931
TOTAL BOTTLES PRODUCED 1,000,000
DIRECT SALES
VISITS TO THE WINERY - RESERVATION NEEDED
HECTARES OF VINEYARD 330

This is one of the best cooperatives in Trentino. It is located on the Piana Rotaliana, the undisputed home the region's most noble red Teroldego. For over 80 years they have been producing excellent grapes and wines.

■ **92** **Price B**
Teroldego Rotaliano Clesurae 2012

100% Teroldego grapes. Matures 2 years in barrique. Dark and intense violet ruby red. On the nose typical, rich and articulated notes of blueberry, blackberry, ink, vanilla, pepper, cardamom, black currant. Strong taste, nice savory note, young tannins, warm and very persistent.

▣ **87** **Price B**
Trentodoc Redor Brut

100% Chardonnay grapes. Stainless steel only. Intense greenish yellow with light perlage. Fragrant and fruity notes on the nose with gooseberry aromas and fresh almond, wildflowers and yeasts. Fresh and balanced on the mouth, pleasantly briny finish.

⭐⭐⭐
CANTINE FERRARI

Via Ponte di Ravina, 15
38123 Trento (TN)
Tel. +39 0461 972311
info@ferraritrento.it
www.ferraritrento.it
🅕 *FerrariTrento*
🐦 *@FerrariTrento*

YEAR OF FOUNDATION 1902
NAME OF THE OWNER Lunelli Brothers
TOTAL BOTTLES PRODUCED 4,650,000
DIRECT SALES
VISITS TO THE WINERY - RESERVATION NEEDED
HECTARES OF VINEYARD 120
RESTAURANT

This is simply the best producer of sparkling wine in Italy. It belongs to the Lunelli family who have transformed it into a true jewel both for the quality of its products and the way they have managed it to achieve great economic and financial success. Their top product, Giulio Ferrari Collezione, is a sparkling wine that does not come out every year but tbut the winery is always able to place its other products to the highest categories.

▣ 🄶 **97** **Price C**
Trentodoc Giulio Ferrari Riserva del Fondatore 2005

100% Chardonnay grapes from Maso Pianizza

single vineyard. 10 years on the yeasts. Straw yellow with bright golden hues. Very elegant perlage. Classy notes of jasmine and osmanthus, hints of citrus and fresh herbs, ginger and honey, gingerbread and white pepper. Sophisticated and complex on the mouth, vibrant tension, pulpy and elegant finish, harmonic and incredibly long. Sparkle Wine of the Year.

◎ 94   Price C

Trentodoc Lunelli Extra Brut Riserva 2008

100% Chardonnay grapes from Villa Margon vineyards. Matures in Austrian durmast barrels and 7 years on the yeasts. Bright straw yellow with very elegant perlage. Aristocratic on the nose, yeasts and iodine sensations, fragrant of yellow plums and cedar. Full and agile on the mouth, enveloping and tasty, persistent finish.

◎ 91   Price B

Trentodoc Ferrari Perlé Rosé 2010

Blend of 80% Pinot Nero and 20% Chardonnay grapes. Matures 5 years on the yeasts. Cameo pink color with elegant perlage. Notes of rosehip and rhododendron, smoky hint and then raspberries and red berries, blood orange and sweet spices. Creamy on the mouth, fresh and savory. Nice development.

◎ 90   Price C

Trentodoc Ferrari Perlé Nero 2009

100% Pinot Nero, vinified in white. Stainless steel and matures 6 years on the yeasts. Bright golden yellow with very elegant perlage. Notes of anise, almond and bread crust, apple and barley, light toasted hints and briny. Aristocratic and full bodied on the mouth, complex and dynamic, balanced and savory.

CANTINE MOSER

Via Castel di Gardolo, 5
38121 Trento (TN)
Tel. 0461990786
info@cantinemoser.com
www.cantinemoser.com

YEAR OF FOUNDATION 1979
NAME OF THE OWNER Moser Family
TOTAL BOTTLES PRODUCED
DIRECT SALES
VISITS TO THE WINERY - RESERVATION NEEDED
HECTARES OF VINEYARD 15

Winemaking in Trentino has a convincing example in the Moser family estate which is imposing its new identity thanks to the latest generation led by Carlo, who studied economics and was the first to get involved; the agronomist Ignazio, who has a flare for sales; and Francesca who is in charge of hospitality; while Matteo and Leonardo help out in the vineyards and the winery. The estate was established in Val di Cembra in 1979, where their grandfather had vineyards, and the winery is in Palù di Giovo. In the 1990s, the winery was moved to Maso Villa Warth, a former bishop's residence in Gardolo di Mezzo. The children of cycling legend Francesco Moser took complete control of the estate 2008 but continue to work with their cousin Matteo who sells them his grapes.

◎ 87   Price B

Trentino 51,151 Brut

100% Chardonnay grapes. Matures in stainless steel and a small part for 30 months on the yeasts. Greenish yellow with golden hues and elegant perlage. Fruity on the nose with nice citrusy and iodine notes, verbena, mauve and white peach pulp. Agile on the mouth, nice balance between maturity, freshness and savory.

CAVIT

Via del Ponte, 31/33
38123 Trento (TN)
Tel. +39 0461 381711
cavit@cavit.it
www.cavit.it
🇫 cavitwines
🐦 @CavitWines

YEAR OF FOUNDATION 1950
TOTAL BOTTLES PRODUCED 62,000,000
DIRECT SALES
VISITS TO THE WINERY
HECTARES OF VINEYARD 5,500

A great, second tier cooperative that sells and in produces wines from the grapes of its thousands of members which include individual winegrowers and seven smaller Trentino cooperatives. Cavit is an authentic, regional productive juggernaut and its modern winery processes three quarters of the wine Trentino produces and provides the livelihood for thousands of families. The wine, especially the sparkling ones, are at the least good and at times extraordinary. This thanks to the fact that they can selected the best from the some 80,000,000kg of grapes they have available. Co-operation Prize.

回 匀 **95**   Price B

Trentodoc Altemasi Graal Brut Riserva 2009

Blend of 70% Chardonnay and 30% Pinot Nero grapes. Classic method, 72 month on the lees. Intense golden yellow, thick perlage, elegant and continuous. Nice and complex on the nose with notes of almond, white peach, yeasts, grilled bread and wildflowers. Enveloping flavor, great body, agile, briny, creamy, polite and incredibly long.

■ **94**   Price B

Trentino Superiore Rosso Quattro Vicariati 2012

Blend of Cabernet Sauvignon, Cabernet Franc and Merlot. Matures 18 months in barrique. Dark and intense ruby. Very 'Bordeaux style' nose with notes of black currant, blueberry, vanilla and spicy hints. Enveloping taste, smooth, well integrated tannins, warm, rich and very pleasant.

☐ **93**   Price B

Maso Torresella Cuvée 2014

Blend of Sauvignon and Chardonnay with Riestling Renano and Gewürztraminer. Part of the Chardonnay matures in oak, the rest in stainless steel on the lees for 1 year. Bright straw yellow. Clear notes of Sauvignon like mango and elder, then aromas of flowers and white peach. Intense on the mouth, savory, great acidity that makes it agile and elegant.

■ **92**   Price B

Teroldego Rotaliano Maso Cervara 2012

100% Teroldego grapes. Matures 1 year in barrique. Intense and dark ruby red. Very typical notes of blueberry, ink and black currant, then vanilla and smoky hints. Clear, savory and full-bodied on the mouth, light tannins and alcoholic heat in the finish.

回 **91**   👍 Price A

Trentodoc Altemasi Brut Riserva 2011

100% Chardonnay grapes. Classic method, 48 months on the lees. Abundant and continuos perlage. Light straw yellow color. Cedar, yeasts, bread crust, yellow plum, alternating fragrant and fruity

notes on the nose. Savory on the mouth, tense, acidulous and refreshing, pleasant to drink with a long and thin finish.

CEMBRA CANTINA DI MONTAGNA

Viale IV Novembre, 76 - Frazione Cembra
38034 Cembra (TN)
Tel. +39 0461 680010
info@cembracantinadimontagna.com
www.cembracantinadimontagna.it
🔲 *lavis*
🐦 *cantinalavis*

YEAR OF FOUNDATION 1952
NAME OF THE OWNER Gruppo La-Vis
TOTAL BOTTLES PRODUCED 300,000
DIRECT SALES
VISITS TO THE WINERY - RESERVATION NEEDED
HECTARES OF VINEYARD 300

Currently part of the Cantina Lavis group, the Cembra winery is one of the best examples of quality high altitude winemaking in Trentino. The vineyards are situated at between 550 and 900m above sea level, have a loose porphyry soil and produce wines that have great structure and complex aromas of ripe fruit and mineral stones.

回 匀 **95**   Price B

Trentodoc Ororosso Dosaggio Zero

100% Chardonnay grapes. 60 months on the yeasts. Intense straw yellow, thin and fast perlage. Complex notes of almond on the nose, then cedar, peach and yeasts. On the mouth it has great structure and fragrance, impressive persistence.

☐ **93**   Price B

Trentino Müller Thurgau Vigna delle Forche 2015

100% Müller Thurgau grapes. Bright straw yellow with greenish hues. Clear on the nose with intense notes of elder, sage and flint. Wide, savory on the mouth, very complex and great persistence.

CESARINI SFORZA

Via Stella, 9
38123 Trento (TN)

Tel. +39 0461 382200
Fax + 39 0461 382222
info@cesarinisforza.com
www.cesarinisforza.com
🐦 @CesariniSforza

YEAR OF FOUNDATION 1974
NAME OF THE OWNER Gruppo La-Vis
TOTAL BOTTLES PRODUCED 1,300,000
DIRECT SALES
VISITS TO THE WINERY - RESERVATION NEEDED
HECTARES OF VINEYARD 1,000

The winery was born in 1974 thank to an initiative by a group of Trentino wine entrepreneurs, including Giuseppe Andreaus, a strong promotors of regional sparkling wines. It takes its name from Count Lamberto Cesarini Sforza and its historic brand is closely tied to the area's identity. Tridentum and Aquila Reale are not only the winery's top products but also a celebration of the city of Trento. Since 2001, it has been part of the Gruppo La-Vis. Technology, innovation and a lot of tradition are the components that Giorgia Brugnara, the enologist and head of production, uses to crate the whole line of sparkling wines.

回 90   Price B
Trentodoc Tridentum Rosé Brut 2010
100% Pinot Nero grapes. Classic method, 60 months on the lees. Bright pink, thin and fast perlage. Notes of strawberry and yeasts, hints of bread crust and raspberries on the nose. Savory, agile and easy to drink. Not too full-bodied, creamy Co2 component and adequate persistence in the finish.

回 89   Price B
Trentodoc Tridentum Extra Brut 2009
100% Chardonnay grapes. Classic method, 72 months on the lees. Light straw yellow, thin and fast perlage. Notes of yeasts and bread crust, then flowers and fruits like yellow plum on the nose. Thin on the mouth, the acidity stands out, refreshing and citrusy, savory and persistent.

DE VESCOVI ULZBACH

Piazza Garibaldi,12
38016 Mezzocorona (TN)
Tel. +39 0461 605648
info@devescoviulzbach.it
www.devescoviulzbach.it

YEAR OF FOUNDATION 1708
NAME OF THE OWNER Giulio de Vescovi
TOTAL BOTTLES PRODUCED 60,000
DIRECT SALES
VISITS TO THE WINERY - RESERVATION NEEDED
HECTARES OF VINEYARD 7.5

Towards the middle of the 17th century, Viglilio de Vescovi, a doctor of philosophy and economic adviser to the Prince Bishop of Trento, deacon of Alto Adige, apostolic protonotary and delegate to the Diet in Innsbruck for the prince, moved his family estate from Vermiglio in the upper Val di Sole valley to the Rotaliana Plain. The two areas are connected by the Noce River that begins in Val di Sole and ends in Campo Rotaliano, which at the time had the German name Ulzbach. The estate still carries his name and the wine is made by Giulio de Vescovi.

■ 93   Price B
Teroldego Rotaliano Vigilius 2013
100% Teroldego grapes. Matures 1 year in small durmast barrels. Intense ruby red with garnet hues. Notes of nigritella and eucalyptus hints, tense on the mouth, enveloping and with notes of ripe blackberries, nice balance between acidity and structure, very long finish.

☐ 91   👍 Price A
Sauvignon Blanc 2015
100% Sauvignon grapes. Bright straw yellow with greenish hues. Intense elder notes, sage, tomato leaf, ripe grapefruit and pomegranate. Nice balance between structure and acidity. Great persistence.

DORIGATI

Via Dante, 5
38016 Mezzocorona (TN)
Tel. +39 0461 605313
Fax +39 0461 605830
vini@dorigati.it
www.dorigati.it
📘 Cantina-DORIGATI
🐦 @CantinaDorigati

YEAR OF FOUNDATION 1858
NAME OF THE OWNER Paolo, Michele and Franco Dorigati

TOTAL BOTTLES PRODUCED 100,000
DIRECT SALES
VISITS TO THE WINERY - RESERVATION NEEDED
HECTARES OF VINEYARD 10

Founded in 1858 by Luigi Dorigati, the estate today is run by the fifth family generation represented by Paolo and Michele, cousins and enologists, together with their Uncle Franco. They produce still wines and only one traditional method sparkling one. Methius Riserva was created in 1986 by two enologists: Carlo Dorigati (Paolo's father) and Enrico Paternoster. It is the winery's prime product and one of the most representative Trentodoc wines. The winery is in the center of the town of Mezzocorona and extends on three levels and was rebuilt in 1998.

 90   Price B
Trentodoc Methius Brut Riserva 2010
Blend of Chardonnay and Pinot Nero. Classic method, 72 months on the lees. Greenish yellow color. Continuous perlage. Very fragrant on the nose, evident notes of yeasts, then yellow plum and floral hints. Delicate flavor, thin, less structured then in other versions but elegant and with good length.

 88   Price B
Teroldego Rotaliano Superiore Diedri Riserva 2012
100% Teroldego grapes. 12 months in barrique. Dark and concentrated ruby red. Notes of black cherry, blueberry and spices on the nose. Slightly tannic on the mouth, then velvety, savory and warm.

FONDAZIONE EDMUND MACH

Via E. Mach, 1
38010 San Michele all'Adige (TN)
Tel. +39 0461 615252
Fax +39 0461 650218
cantina@fmach.it
www.fmach.it
 fondazionemach
@Fondazione_Mach

YEAR OF FOUNDATION 1874
TOTAL BOTTLES PRODUCED 250,000
DIRECT SALES

VISITS TO THE WINERY - RESERVATION NEEDED
HECTARES OF VINEYARD 60

The true institution of Trentinos' wine once known as Istituto Agrario San Michele all'Adige. This school of enology and agronomy every years turns out highly trained experts who quickly find jobs. The students also produce wine under the supervision of winery director Enrico Paternoster, a recognized Italian wine genus, a great teacher and an extraordinary enologist. Their top wine is Trento Mach Riserva del Fondatore and is made with Chardonnay and Pinot Nero cultivated in Maso Togn, near Faedo, at an altitude if 700m above sea level.

 90   Price B
Trentodoc Mach Riserva del Fondatore 2010
Blend of 50% Chardonnay and 50% Pinot Nero grapes. Classic method. Light yellow, thin and abundant perlage. A lot of aromas, yeasts on top, fragrant, enveloping, yellow plum, gooseberry and cedar. Savory, creamy, acidulous, tense, very pleasant, fresh, thin and long.

FORADORI

Via Damiano Chiesa, 1
38017 Mezzolombardo (TN)
Tel. +39 0461 601046
Fax +39 0461 603447
info@elisabettaforadori.com
www.elisabettaforadori.com
 elisabettaforadori
 @AzAgrForadori

YEAR OF FOUNDATION 1939
NAME OF THE OWNER Elisabetta Foradori
TOTAL BOTTLES PRODUCED 160,000
DIRECT SALES
VISITS TO THE WINERY - RESERVATION NEEDED
HECTARES OF VINEYARD 26
CERTIFIED ORGANIC VITICULTURE
CERTIFIED BIODYNAMIC VITICULTURE

The world of wine and Teroldego, in particular, owe a lot to Elisabetta Foradori and if this wine has the wine lovers talking the credit in large part goes to the extraordinary work of his woman winemaker. Over the past ten years,

Elisabetta has progressively reconverted her vineyards to biodynamic farming and for a few seasons now has also been experimenting with using amphorae to make her wines. They are very expressive, not always perfect but never nondescript.

92   Price C
Granato 2013

100% Teroldego grapes. Matures 15 months in big barrels. Very intense and dark ruby red. Notes of ink, blueberry, raspberry and slight spicy hints. Agile and savory on the mouth, less full-bodied then in other versions but incredibly pleasant and of good elegance.

90   Price B
Teroldego 2014

100% Teroldego grapes. Matures 1 year in big barrels. Intense violet ruby. Very fruity, clear and intense notes of blueberry, blackberry and black raspberry. Tense and full-bodied on the mouth, pleasantly savory, warm and easy to drink.

LA-VIS

Via del Carmine, 7
38015 Lavis (TN)
Tel. +39 0461 440111
Fax +39 0461 440244
cantina@la-vis.com
www.la-vis.com

YEAR OF FOUNDATION **1948**
TOTAL BOTTLES PRODUCED **1,000,000**
DIRECT SALES
VISITS TO THE WINERY - RESERVATION NEEDED
HECTARES OF VINEYARD **850**

A pearl in the somewhat sleepy Trentino wine scene, the cooperative was founded in 1945 and has always had a vocation for quality. The cooperative now has some 800 members who account for practically all the vineyards in the region. The interesting studies they have made of the terroir over the past 30 years have allowed then to choose the right grape for the right soil based on the concept of "every variety has it favorite soil". Ritratti is the cooperative's top line and includes wines that have a great propensity to age and excellent personality.

■ 91   👍 Price A
Trentino Cabernet Ritratti 2012

100% Cabernet Sauvignon grapes. Matures 1 year in tonneau and barrique. Intense, dark ruby red. Very fruity, notes of blueberry, black raspberry, blackberry and smoky hints. Young but promising tannins, savory, tense, good body and great persistence.

☐ 90   👍 Price A
Trentino Sauvignon Maso Tratta 2015

100% Sauvignon Blanc grapes. A small part matures 4 months in big barrels, the rest in stainless steel. Greenish yellow color. Typical, intense notes of elder, passion fruit and hints of tomato leaf. Fresh flavor, tense, very briny and very easy to drink. Thin and persistent finish.

☐ 88   👍 Price A
Trentino Müller Thurgau 2015

100% Müller Thurgau. Stainless steel only. Light greenish yellow. Aromatic and fruity on the nose, notes of merdical herbs, lime, cedar and hints of fresh almond. Acidulous taste, tense, savory and of good lengh.

LETRARI

Via Monte Baldo, 13/15
38068 Rovereto (TN)
Tel. +39 0464 480200
Fax +39 0464 401451
🅢 *letrarivini*
info@letrari.it
www.letrari.it
🅕 *letrari*
🐦 *@lucialetrari*

YEAR OF FOUNDATION **1976**
NAME OF THE OWNER **Letrari Family**
TOTAL BOTTLES PRODUCED **160,000**
DIRECT SALES
VISITS TO THE WINERY - RESERVATION NEEDED
HECTARES OF VINEYARD **20**
OLIVE OIL PRODUCTION

The Letrari estate has been in production since 1976 but its founder, Leonello, was making wine long before that. He is considered to be one of the fathers of Trentino wine who was the first to make an Italian 'barriccato' (Fojaneghe

1961) and Equipe 5, one of the best-known Spumante of the 1960s. To drink with him is like taking a stroll through time and the history of sparkling wine production in Italy. Today it is above all his daughter Lucia, the chef de cave at Letrari, who is giving that magic touch to their Trentodoc bubbly. The estate produces over 20 sparkling and still wines.

 93   Price C

Trentodoc 976 Riserva del Fondatore Brut 2006

Blend of Chardonnay and Pinot Nero grapes. Classic method, 120 months on the lees. Bright golden yellow, thin and continuous perlage. Notes of yeasts, buttery hints, then melon, yellow plum, cedar, grilled bread and smoky aromas. Creamy on the mouth, rich and warm, clear and attractive extractive sweetness. Savory and persistent finish.

 91   Price B

Trentodoc Letrari Rosé Brut 2011

Blend of 70% Chardonnay and 30% Pinot Nero grapes. Classic method, 48 months on the lees. Light antique pink, thin and fast perlage. Fragrant notes of yeasts and raspberries. Savory flavor, crunchy, agile, very pleasant and with nice body.

★

MASO MARTIS

Via dell'Albera, 52 - Località Martignano
38121 Trento (TN)
Tel. +39 0461 821057
Fax +39 0461 426773
 masomartis
info@masomartis.it
www.masomartis.it
 masomartis
 @masomartis

YEAR OF FOUNDATION **1990**
NAME OF THE OWNER **Roberta and Antonio Stelzer**
TOTAL BOTTLES PRODUCED **60,000**
DIRECT SALES
VISITS TO THE WINERY - RESERVATION NEEDED
HECTARES OF VINEYARD **12**
CERTIFIED ORGANIC VITICULTURE

A small, family-run estate, Maso Matis has cut out a place for itself among the elite of sparkling wine producers in Trentino and thus

in Italy. Situated on a hill above Trento, at an altitude of 450m above sea level, it produces some 60,000 bottles of wine of which 45,000 are Trentodoc that are distinguished by their elegance, technical cleanliness and sharpness typical of Italian Spumante.

 93   Price C

Trentodoc Madame Martis 2006

Blend of 70% Pinot Nero, 25% Chardonnay and 5% Pinot Meunier grapes. Classic method, 9 years on the lees. Straw yellow with rich and fast perlage. Clear, thin and fragrant on the mouth, complex, notes of yeasts and yellow fruit, hints of almond. Creamy flavor, elegant, evident acidity to balance the big structure. Warm and enveloping finish.

 91   Price B

Trentodoc Dosaggio Zero Riserva 2011

Blend of 70% Pinot Nero and 30% Chardonnay grapes. Intense greenish straw yellow. Thin and fast perlage. Enveloping notes of yeasts and exotic fruits on the nose, with notes of pineapple on top. Agile, thin, savory, fresh, elegant and easy to drink.

OPERA VITIVINICOLA IN VALDICEMBRA

Via III Novembre 8
38030 Giovo (TN)
Tel. 0461684302
info@operavaldicembra.it
www.operavaldicembra.it

YEAR OF FOUNDATION **2007**
NAME OF THE OWNER **Alfio Gazzetti and Bruno Zanotelli**
TOTAL BOTTLES PRODUCED **60,000**
DIRECT SALES
VISITS TO THE WINERY
HECTARES OF VINEYARD **15**

This small sparkling wine reality has already stood out for the quality of its wines made from vineyards in the mountains between Lavis and Val di Fiemme, in Val di Cembra. Alfio Gazzetti and Bruno Zanotelli are two friends who chose to use the traditional method for their wine benefitting from the experience of enologists Paolo Tiefenthaler and Mattia Clementi. They reconstructed the oldest winery in the valley, founded in the 1800s, and chose Opera as its

375

name because in Latin it means work and their work has been to develop a style of high quality exalting the particular characteristics of the local grapes.

 90 Price B

Trentodoc Opera Brut 2011

100% Chardonnay grapes. Matures 36 months on the yeasts. Light straw yellow with thin perlage. Fruity notes on the nose of yellow plum and citrus, graphite and refreshing notes. Agile and fresh with nice progression.

88 Price B

Trentodoc Opera Nature Riserva 2009

100% Chardonny grapes. Stainless steel, 72 months on the yeasts. Straw yellow with greenish hues. Thin perlage. Citrusy on the nose, notes of cedar and tangerine, apple and ripe apricot, bakery aromas and slightly spicy finish. Fresh and balanced on the mouth, good distension and easy to drink, slightly almondy finish.

PEDROTTI SPUMANTI

Via Monte Corona, 2
38060 Nomi (TN)
Tel. +39 0464 835111
info@pedrottispumanti.it
www.pedrottispumanti.it
PedrottiTrentodoc
PedrottiWinery

YEAR OF FOUNDATION 1901
NAME OF THE OWNER Paolo Pedrotti
TOTAL BOTTLES PRODUCED 40,000
DIRECT SALES
VISITS TO THE WINERY - RESERVATION NEEDED
HECTARES OF VINEYARD

Since the beginning of the last century the Pedrotti family has been committed to exalting Trentino's potential. Thanks to the contribution of enologist Paolo, a member of the family's third generation, the estate began producing sparkling wine and today his daughters Donatella and Chiara have with passion and determination gotten involved in the estate's evolution. The estate is situated in the heart of Vallagarina, in the small medieval village of Nomi, which has a castle and is worth a visit to see the suggestive natural cave where the bottles age and where you can taste the wines.

92 Price B

Trentodoc Pas Dosé Riserva 111 2009

Blend of 90% Chardonnay and Pinot Nero grapes. 72 months on the yeasts. Golden straw yellow. Abundant and fast perlage. Intense on the nose with notes of yeasts, green plum and almond. Fresh on the mouth, savory and agile, great body and enveloping finish.

90 Price B

Trentodoc Bouquet Brut

100% Chardonnay grapes. 32 months on the yeasts. Straw yellow with bright greenish hues. Thin and fast perlage. Notes of yellow plum and hints of almond. Enveloping on the mouth, savory and persistent.

89 Price C

Brut Riserva 12

Blend of 90% Chardonnay and 10% Pinot Nero grapes. Classic method, 12 years on the yeasts. Deep straw yellow. Deep straw yellow. Clear notes of yeasts but not too strong. Ripe golden apple, bread crust, ripe yellow plum, gooseberry. On the mouth the structure is well sustained by the good acidity. Great persistence.

PISONI DAL 1852

Via San Siro, 7/a
38076 Lasino (TN)
Tel. +39 0461 564106
info@pisoni.it
www.pisoni.it
Distilleriapisoni
@grappapisoni

YEAR OF FOUNDATION 1852
NAME OF THE OWNER Pisoni Family
TOTAL BOTTLES PRODUCED 40,000
DIRECT SALES
VISITS TO THE WINERY - RESERVATION NEEDED
HECTARES OF VINEYARD 12

It seams that since 17th century the Pisoni family gave its wines to Cristoforo Madruzzo, the Prince Archbishop Cardinal. Since then, the family has always made spirits and wines but it's the spirits production that takes over in the last centuries and specially in the 20th century after the wars. In the beginnig of the new millennium though the new generation of Pisoni, Elio and Giuliano together with the cousings

Andrea and Franco, take the lead of the winery giving it new impulse, with a special eye on the sparkling wine production followed by Andrea Pisoni.

 93   **Price B**

Trentodoc Pisoni Riserva 90 mesi 2008

Blend of 85% Chardonnay and 15% Pinot Nero from the best vineyards of Valle dei Laghi. On the lees. Light straw yellow with fast perlage. Enveloping notes of almond and white peach. Great structure on the mouth and very persistent.

 90   **Price B**

Pisoni Brut Nature 2012

100% Chardonnay grapes. Matures 33 months on the lees. Straw yellow with greenish hues. Very thin and abundant perlage. Notes of green plum, gooseberry and yeasts on the nose. Nice acidity, fresh and creamy on the mouth with good persistence.

 88   **Price B**

Pisoni Brut Rosè 2012

100% Pinot Nero grapes. 34 months on the lees. Intense antique pink color. Thin and slow perlage. Notes of yeasts, plum and ripe peach. Slightly foamy but pleasant. A little briny.

POJER & SANDRI

Località Molini, 4
38010 Faedo (TN)
Tel. +39 0461 650342
Fax +39 0461651100
info@pojeresandri.it
www.pojeresandri.it
 Pojer-e-Sandri
 @pojeresandri

YEAR OF FOUNDATION **1975**
NAME OF THE OWNER **Mario Pojer and Fiorentino Sandri**
TOTAL BOTTLES PRODUCED **250,000**
DIRECT SALES
VISITS TO THE WINERY - RESERVATION NEEDED
HECTARES OF VINEYARD **26**
HOSPITALITY
CERTIFIED ORGANIC VITICULTURE

Everything that can be said has been said about Mario Pojer and Fiorentino Sandri. Their partnership has lasted 40 years and to mention one without the other would be like mentioning Oliver without Hardy. Their wines continue to be the product of very technical and focused research and experimentation. The results are often noteworthy.

 94   **Price B**

Dolomiti Rosé Brut

Blend of Pinot Nero and Chardonnay of 2011 and 2012 harvest. Antique pink color. Thick and continuous perlage. Very attractive aromas of almond, wild strawberry, white peach, medical herbs and toasted aromas on the background. Creamy flavor, savory, polite, very pleasant and great persistence.

☐ **90**   👍 **Price A**

Müller Thurgau Palai 2015

100% Müller Thurgau grapes. Stainless steel only. Hyper-reduction vinification. Greenish yellow color. Typical notes of medical herbs then cedar and green apple. Tense on the palate, great, refreshing acidity, thin and elegant.

PRAVIS

Località Le Biolche, 1
38076 Lasino (TN)
Tel. +39 0461 564305
Fax +39 0461 564565
info@pravis.it
www.pravis.it
 AziendaAgricolaPravis

YEAR OF FOUNDATION **1974**
NAME OF THE OWNER **Giovanni Chistè, Domenico Pedrini, Mario Zambarda**
TOTAL BOTTLES PRODUCED **210,000**
DIRECT SALES
VISITS TO THE WINERY - RESERVATION NEEDED
HECTARES OF VINEYARD **32**

For these three winemaking friends, vines are life, experimentation and tradition. The have many small vineyards plots spread out in the suggestive Valle dei Laghi, kissed by the Ora del Garda wind and situated between medieval castles, lakes and the Brenta Dolomite mountains. Both winemakers and distillers, they have cultivated several grape varieties at risk of extinction including: Nosiola, Negrara and Gropello di Revò. At their modern winery, at the feet of Castel Madruzzo and completely undergound, the grapes are turned into free run juice to give quality to their wines.

☐ 93   Price B
Stravino di Stravino 2013

Blend of Riesling Renano, Incocio Manzoni, Kerner, Chardonnay and Sauvignon grapes, partially dried on the vines and partially on straw mats. Vinified separately part in oak and part in stainless steel. Intense straw yellow color. Exotic fruit, quince jam, honey, flowery notes make up the unique bouquet. Full-bodied and rich on the mouth, savory, warm and with great persistence.

☐ 89   Price A
Müller Thurgau San Thomà 2015

100% Müller Thurgau grapes. Stainless steel only. Typical notes of medical herbs and cedar. Savory, fresh, very pleasant and easy to drink with a thin, long finish.

REDONDÈL

Via Roma, 28
38017 Mezzolombardo (TN)
Tel. +39 0461 605861
info@redondel.it
www.redondel.it
 redondel-piccola-azienda-agricola

YEAR OF FOUNDATION **2001**
NAME OF THE OWNER **Paolo Zanini**
TOTAL BOTTLES PRODUCED **9,500**
DIRECT SALES
VISITS TO THE WINERY
HECTARES OF VINEYARD **3**
CERTIFIED ORGANIC VITICULTURE

Paolo Zanini is an authentic winemaker and his tiny estate in Campo Rotaliano is both his passion and reason to exist. His has a strict respect for nature and its rhythms and an equal and religious respect for his grapes. His wines, Teroldego, naturally, mirror his productive philosophy and are thus straightforward, tasty and generous.

◼ 92   Price B
Beatome 2009

100% Teroldego grapes from 70 year-old vines. Matured in various sized barrels. Prplish red. In-

tense flavor of ripe fruit, spices and minerals. Good acidity and creamy on the palate, very easy to drink. Long and lovely finish.

◼ 90   👍 Price A
Teroldego Rotaliano Dannato 2010

100% Teroldego grapes. Matured in various sized barrels. Ruby-purple red. Flavor of quinine and graphite. Juicy tannins and liveliness on the palate with a along and crispy finish.

REVÌ

Via Pascoli, 10
38060 Aldeno (TN)
Tel. +39 0461 843155
info@revispumanti.com
www.revispumanti.com
 ReviTrentodoc

YEAR OF FOUNDATION **1982**
NAME OF THE OWNER **Malfer Family**
TOTAL BOTTLES PRODUCED **35,000**
DIRECT SALES
VISITS TO THE WINERY - RESERVATION NEEDED
HECTARES OF VINEYARD **3.5**

It has been Paolo Malfer, founder of the winery in 1982, feeling after years of experiments and tests to perfect techniques he learned from textbooks to be ready to start his own activity based on sparkling wines. The name refers to that of the area of production which legend says once produced grapes to make a superior, regal wine, 'Re Vin' (King Wine) hence Revì. In more recent years, the passion which led to the estate's creation has been contagious in the family and resulted in higher production and different wine variations. Today, Revìn continues its mission and is synonymous with excellent Trentodoc.

▣ 93   Price B
Trentodoc Cavaliere Nero Rosè Extra Brut Riserva 2009

100% Pinot Nero grapes. Antique pink color with thin and persistent perlage. Slightly toasted notes on the nose, bread crust, berries, strawberry, raspberry, red berry, blueberry and cherry. A unique flowery note of nigritella with hints of chocolate and vanilla. Fragrant and complex. Wide and juicy on the mouth. Great harmony and persistence with a nice savory note.

91   **Price B**

Trentodoc Revì Dosaggio Zero Millesimato 2012

Blend of 75% Chardonnay and 25% Pinot Nero grapes. Straw yellow color and thin, persistent perlage. Fragrant on the nose, thin with notes of fruit, fresh flowers and a delicate yeasts hint. Intense on the mouth where freshness and savory blend together in harmony and elegance.

 88   **Price C**

Trentodoc Paladino Millesimato 2010

100% Chardonnay grapes. Straw yellow with golden hues. Thin and persistent perlage. Fruity and flowery notes on the nose, with clear aromas of flint. Enveloping and silky on the mouth, pleasant and intense aromas. Great savory and eucalyptus notes that makes it pleasant to drink.

★
ROSI

Via Tavernelle, 3b
38060 Volano (TN)
Tel. +39 340 0611047
Fax +39 0464 461375
rosieugenio.viticoltore@gmail.com
f *eugenio.rosiviticoltoreartigiano*

YEAR OF FOUNDATION 1997
NAME OF THE OWNER Eugenio Rosi
TOTAL BOTTLES PRODUCED 25,000
DIRECT SALES
VISITS TO THE WINERY - RESERVATION NEEDED
HECTARES OF VINEYARD 8.5

Eugenio Rosi is an eclectic personality in the Vallagarina wine scene who defines himself as a wine craftsman. He loves to work on his own and broke away from the traditional winemaking conventions of the time. His wines reflect his stubborn personality and his determination to achieve results even using unconventional methods. The wines are very interesting and distinct and stand out for their boldness.

 93   **Price B**

Dòron

100% dried Marzemino grapes. Dark ruby red. Clear and intense smoky notes, spicy and roses, not at all sickly on the mouth. Slightly tannins and good persistence.

■ 92   **Price B**

Pojema 2013

100% partly dried Marzemino grapes. Matures in durmast, cherry and chestnut tonneau. Dark and intense ruby red with violet hues. Intense notes of morello, macerated cherry, light spices and cinnamon. Slightly tannic on the mouth, it seems like chewing rose petals, very fruity, average persistence.

□ 90   **Price B**

Anisos 2013

Blend of 50% Nosiola, 20% Chardonnay and Pinot Bianco grapes. Matures in 500 liter durmast barrels. Golden yellow color. It's a non-filtered white of great personality. On the nose evident notes of sea breeze and peat. Tense and lightly fruity with an important progression.

ROTARI - MEZZACORONA

Via del Teroldego, 1e
38016 Mezzocorona (TN)
Tel. +39 0461 616399
Fax +39 0461 616315
info@mezzacorona.it
www.mezzacorona.it
f *MezzacoronaIT*
🐦 *@MezzacoronaIT*

YEAR OF FOUNDATION 1904
TOTAL BOTTLES PRODUCED 45,000,000
DIRECT SALES
VISITS TO THE WINERY - RESERVATION NEEDED
HECTARES OF VINEYARD 2,800

The Rotari winery is the feather in the Gruppo Mezzacorona cap and it is one of the biggest Italian producers of sparkling wine. The group was set up in 1904 and has 2,800 hectares of vineyards and 1,600 members spread out in the areas of Piana Rotaliana and the valleys of Cembra, Adige, Laghi and Garda as well as in Sicily with Feudo Arancio. They produce and market a vast and varied line of production and at competitive prices.Technology is used at the service of the territory in the production of Trentodoc and still wines.

回 91   **Price B**

Trentodoc Rotari Brut Flavio 2008

100% Chardonnay grapes. Matures 60 months on

the yeasts. Intense golden straw yellow color with thin perlage. Notes of candied citrus, appeal and mountain herbs, rhododendron honey, hazelnuts and eucalyptus hints. Structured on the mouth, with balanced and savory finish.

🔲 86   Price A

Trentodoc Cuvée 28+ Brut

100% Chardonnay grapes. Matures 36 months on the yeasts. Light straw yellow with thin perlage. Fruity notes on the nose of yellow plum and citrus, graphite and refreshing notes. Agile and fresh with nice progression.

380

★★★

SAN LEONARDO

Località San Leonardo
38060 Avio (TN)
Tel. +39 0464 689004
Fax +39 0464 682200
info@sanleonardo.it
www.sanleonardo.it
f tenutasanleonardo
🐦 @San_Leonardo

YEAR OF FOUNDATION 1724
NAME OF THE OWNER Carlo Guerrieri Gonzaga
TOTAL BOTTLES PRODUCED 180,000
DIRECT SALES
VISITS TO THE WINERY - RESERVATION NEEDED
HECTARES OF VINEYARD 25

It is almost as if the aristocratic manner, gentle ways and old-fashion kindness of Carlo Guer-riero Gonzaga somehow ends up in his wines. There must be magic at San Leonardo, a place with an endless past that once marked the Hapsburg Austro-Hungarian side of its border with the Republic of Venice, and thus Italy. Car-lo, whose family name is full of history, tends to downplay this and always seems surprised when you say his wines are extraordinary. And his son Anselmo has the same aristocratic el-egance.

🔲 97   Price C

San Leonardo 2011

Blend of 60% Cabernet Sauvignon, 15% Caber-net Franc, 15 Carmenere and 10% Merlot grapes. Matures 18 months in barrique. Dark and intense ruby red. Classic notes of blueberry, raspberry, then hints of vanilla, mint, pine resin. Silky on the mouth,

thick and thin tannins, elegant, aristocratic, har-monious balance with a warm and very persistent finish. Great wine.

◼ 93   Price B

Villa Gresti 2011

Blend of 90% Merlot and 10% Carmenere grapes. Matures 1 year in barrique. Bright garnet ruby. The aromas are so clear and distinguished that it seems like smelling a basket of raspberries with a couple of mint leaves on top. Tense, savory, very pleasant on the mouth, warm but not heavy, with great per-sistence.

⬜ 92   👍 Price A

Vette di San Leonardo 2015

100% Sauvignon Blanc grapes. Stainless steel only. Greenish straw yellow. Emblematic, typical, notes of white peach and mango then hints of elder. Deli-cious to drink, clear, savory and elegant. Thing and long finish.

⬜ 91   Price B

Riesling 2014

100% Riesling Renano grapes. Stainless steel only on the lees. Light greenish straw yellow. Notes of grapefruit, kerosene hints then medical herbs and wildflowers. Tense on the mouth, acidulous, very typical, not too big structure but elegant and agile. Thin and very persistent finish.

◼ 90   👍 Price A

Terre di San Leonardo 2013

Blend of 90% Merlot and 10% Carmenere grapes. Matures 1 year in barrique. Garnet ruby red. Notes of red berry, cassis, cocoa and light vanilla on the nose. Savory, tense, good body and nice length on the mouth.

TENUTE LUNELLI - TENUTA MARGON

Via Ponte di Ravina 15
38123 Trento (TN)
Tel. +39 0461 972311
Fax +39 0461 913008
margon@tenutelunelli.it
www.tenutelunelli.it
f TenuteLunelli
🐦 @TenuteLunelli

YEAR OF FOUNDATION 1986
NAME OF THE OWNER Lunelli Family

TOTAL BOTTLES PRODUCED 119,150
DIRECT SALES
VISITS TO THE WINERY - RESERVATION NEEDED
HECTARES OF VINEYARD 29
RESTAURANT

In the 1980s, after producing sparkling wines for over a century, the Lunelli family decided to also produce still wines. The Trentino-based Tenuta Lunelli, which also as an estate in Umbria a stone's throw from Montefalco, created Tenuta Margon in the foot hills of the mountains around Trento and here produce Chardonnay and Pinot Noir at an altitude of 350-600m above sea level.

 90 Price B
Trentino Maso Montalto 2013
100% Pinot Nero grapes. 12 months in durmast barrels. Transparent ruby red. Sharp notes of wild berries and smoky hints. Sweet spices both on the nose and on the mouth. Fresh and good spicy persistent finish.

 88 Price A
Trentino Villa Margon 2014
100% Chardonnay grapes. Matures part in stainless steel and part for 10-12 months in oak. Intense on the nose, smoky notes on a citrusy and minty background. Nice body and freshness on the mouth, long smoky persistence and vanilla pods.

ZENI

Via Stretta, 2
38010 San Michele all'Adige (TN)
Tel. +39 0461 650456
Fax +39 0461 650748
info@zeni.tn.it
www.zeni.tn.it
 zenivignaioliedistillatori
 @Zeni_az_agr

YEAR OF FOUNDATION 1882
NAME OF THE OWNER Roberto and Andrea Zeni
TOTAL BOTTLES PRODUCED 160,000
DIRECT SALES
VISITS TO THE WINERY - RESERVATION NEEDED
HECTARES OF VINEYARD 16
CERTIFIED ORGANIC VITICULTURE

The Zemi family in Grumo, on the right bank of the Adige River, are at the same wine wine-makers, distillers and sparkling wine producers. They thus interpret all aspects of their territory. Their vineyards are next to the estate headquarters as well as on the hill above Lavis, between Pressano and Faedo. Teroldego, Nosiola, Pinot Grigio, Müller Thurgau, along with Chardonnay and Pinot Nero are among the grapes brothers Andrea and Roberto have been making wine with for the past 40 years. They have transmitted their work ethic and passion for winemaking to their children, involving them in new wine projects centered on their Trentodoc.

 91 Price B
Trentodoc Maso Nero Rosé Brut Riserva 2010
Blend of Pinot Nero and Chardonnay. Classic method, 60 months on the lees. Light antique pink, thin and fast perlage. Notes of yeasts and bread crust, then raspberries, wild strawberry and plum. Lively flavor, savory, tense, with evident Co2 that gives freshness and drinkability. Long and persistent finish.

TUSCANY

Tuscany is Italy's most important winemaking region for sales and exports and 95% of its production is classified. It has 11 DOCG classified wines that are known worldwide including Brunello di Montalcino, Chianti and Chianti Classico, Vernaccia di San Gimignano, Morellino di Scansano and Vino Nobile di Montepulciano. There are also 39 prestigious DOC appellations from Bolgheri to Montecarlo, from Montecucco to Pomino, from Rosso di Montalcino to Montepulciano and, more recently, Maremma Tuscany. And these are just the better-known ones. Together they offer a virtuous selection that, thanks to the producers who are particularly skilled at both interpreting the territory as well as exploiting Tuscany's reputation and image, has lifted regional wine production to the very top on an international level, alongside Bordeaux, Burgundy and parts of California.

Tuscany has a vast range of pedoclimatic conditions as is the case in the world's other leading winemaking areas.

The coastal zone, which includes the area around Bolgheri and most of the Maremma coast in the province of Grosseto, has a decidedly Mediterranean climate with mild winters and long, hot and often dry summers. The soils vary even if they are for the most part sandy and chalky, above all near the sea and rivers. Winemaking there, especially to the north, follows very innovative methods.

The central part of Tuscany is the most important wine-wise. This includes the area of Montalcino, in the southernmost part of the province of Siena, which has a clay and chalky soil that is particularly suited for cultivating Sangiovese. The climate is for the most part Mediterranean but in some areas conditions are more continental, with colder winters and summers that in some years is hotter than on the coast, although Mount Amiata helps to lessen any extreme heat. Montepulciano has a more continental climate due to its altitude and the fact that it is further away from the sea, which can result in harsh winters. The vast area of Chianti Classico has very diverse conditions and the soil tends to have more clay to the south and more lime in the north. In general, the climate is Mediterranean-continental with dry summers and harsh winters. Here Sangiovese is the most used grape for winemaking and it is cultivated in vineyards that have a density of between 3-4,000 vines per hectare. The situation is similar more to the north, above all in Carmignano and Rufina, except that here factors relayed to higher altitudes come into play given the proximity to the Apennine Mountains.

The first documentation of winemaking in Tuscany dates back to between the VII and V BC when the current region of Tuscany was part, along with Umbria, northern Lazio and parts of Emilia and Marche of the land known as Etruria. And it was the Etruscans, in fact, who began to systematically cultivate grapes in order to make wine, none of which were apparently on the level of quality of the more celebrated wines of the times like Falerno. Quality wine in Tuscany began to emerge during the Renaissance with the production of Vernaccia di San Gimignano and Montepulciano red. The year 1282 saw the foundation of the Arte dei Vinattieri (winemakers' guild) in Florence while Chianti wine was first mentioned in 1398, although it referred to a white wine. Chianti later changed color and in 1872, Baron Bettino Ricasoli, after years of experimentation, formulated his celebrated blend. However, already in the 18th century there was an ample market for wines from Chianti, Carmignano, Rufina and Valdarno di Sopra. And in 1888, the Biondi Santi winery came out with the first 'official' Brunello di Montalcino.

The so-called 'promiscuous' cultivation method of wine grapes in Tuscany lasted for almost 3,000 years. The vines climbed up fruit and olive trees and the wines they made were primarily for local consumption and more than often just for those who owned the land.

'Modern' winemaking in Tuscany developed in earnest about a half a century ago and involved most of the producers on the market today.

There is a phenomenon in Tuscany, however, that no other region has seen. It is the one of the so-called Super Tuscan wines, red wines that were developed towards the end of the 1970s and during the 1980s as experiments in making top quality red wines made with grapes different from those typical to the region. These wines, which are often of the utmost quality, were for years denied any DOC recognition and were classified as IGT geographic appellations, the one above table wine. This represented a typical Italian contradiction with Italian legislators and authorities totally incapable of regulating wines that were among the best produced in Italy. This included Sassicaia, which now has its own Bolgheri Sassicaia DOC appellation, Tignanello from Antinori, Ruffino's Cabreo (today part of Tenute Folonari), Vigorello San Felice and Fontallora from Fattoria di Fel-

sina. But even if from a legislative point of view these wines were, and in large part still are, in a 'second division' market, some Super Tuscans are selling at prices far above those for the DOC and DOCG wines from the same area. These wines use Cabernet Sauvignon and Merlot either to blend with Sangiovese or to make varietal wines and that age in French oak barrique in order to make products that can be appreciated everywhere. For a while now the phenomenon appears to have waned somewhat, although this is not the case for the more famous wines. In other appellations, Chianti Classico first among them, there have been some important novelties regarding classification and the recent creation of Gran Selezione is the most recent example.

383

CONTROLLED AND GUARANTEED DESIGNATION OF ORIGIN (DOCG)

- Brunello di Montalcino
- Carmignano
- Chianti, with or without the sub-areas Colli Aretini, Colli Fiorentini, Colline Pisane, Colli Senesi, Montalbano, Montespertoli and Rufina
- Chianti Classico
- Elba Aleatico Passito or Aleatico Passito dell'Elba
- Montecucco Sangiovese, geographic references allowed
- Morellino di Scansano
- Rosso della Val di Cornia or Val di Cornia Rosso
- Suvereto
- Vernaccia di San Gimignano
- Vino Nobile di Montepulciano

CONTROLLED DESIGNATION OF ORIGIN (DOC)

- Ansonica Costa dell'Argentario, geographic references allowed
- Barco Reale di Carmignano, Rosato di Carmignano, Vin Santo di Carmignano, Vin Santo Carmignano Occhio di Pernice
- Bianco dell'Empolese
- Bianco di Pitigliano, geographic references allowed
- Bolgheri, Bolgheri Sassicaia
- Candia dei Colli Apuani
- Capalbio
- Colli dell'Etruria Centrale
- Colline Lucchesi
- Colli di Luni
- Cortona
- Elba
- Grance Senesi
- Maremma Tuscany, geographic references allowed
- Montecarlo
- Montecucco
- Monteregio di Massa Marittima, geographic references allowed
- Montescudaio
- Moscadello di Montalcino
- Orcia
- Parrina
- Pomino
- Rosso di Montalcino
- Rosso di Montepulciano
- San Gimignano
- Sant'Antimo
- San Torpè, geographic references allowed
- Sovana, geographic references allowed
- Terratico di Bibbona
- Terre di Casole
- Terre di Pisa, geographic references allowed
- Val d'Arbia
- Val d'Arno di Sopra o Valdarno di Sopra, with or without the sub-areas Pietraviva and Pratomagno
- Val di Cornia
- Valdichiana Tuscany
- Valdinievole, geographic references allowed
- Vin Santo del Chianti, with or without the sub-areas Colli Aretini, Colli Fiorentini, Colli Senesi, Colline Pisane, Montalbano, Montespertoli and Rufina
- Vin Santo del Chianti Classico
- Vin Santo di Montepulciano

AMIATA

Località Montebendico, Frazione Montegiovi
58030 Castel del Piano (GR)
Tel. +39 348 5714219 - 339 6902444
info@amiatavini.it
www.amiatavini.it
f AmiataIViniDelVulcano
𝕏 @Amiatavini

YEAR OF FOUNDATION 2001
NAME OF THE OWNER Stefano and Simona Toninelli
TOTAL BOTTLES PRODUCED 8,000
VISITS TO THE WINERY - RESERVATION NEEDED
HECTARES OF VINEYARD 3
OLIVE OIL PRODUCTION

Stefano and Simona Toninelli firmly believe in the potential of the volcanic area that hosts their small estate. And although the volcano that created Monte Amiata has been extinct for thousands of years, it has left its unmistakable imprint on the surrounding land. Their passion for this land came from their farmer grandparents who knew its value well. The estate sits at an altitude of 400m above sea level and the principle grape they cultivate is Sangiovese.

---

 90   Price B
Montecucco Sangiovese Cenere Ris. 2010

100% Sangiovese grapes. Ages 24 months in 25hl barrel. Intense ruby garnet. The nose, fairly developed, offers notes of licorice, wet leaves, leather and dry prunes. The palate is mouth filling and warm, medium acidity, firm and sweet tannins. Lightly youthful finish but good length.

---

 89   👍 Price A
Lapillo 2012

Blend of 90% Sangiovese and 10% Cabernet Sauvignon grapes. Ages 6 months in tonneau of 6hl. Austere nose and of medium intensity, dark fruit, forest berries, black cherry and floral hints. The palate has medium body and good acidity, firm tannins and a long fruity finish.

---

 88   Price A
Montecucco Sangiovese Lavico 2011

100% Sangiovese grapes. Ages in 25hl barrels for 18 months. Deep ruby with garnet rim. The nose offers sweet fruity notes with a light hint of eucalyptus and notes of ink. Full bodied palate, it is a bit rustic with slightly dry but not aggressive tannins. Good fruity finish.

 ★★★
ANTINORI

Via Cassia per Siena, 133 - Località Bargino
50026 San Casciano in Val di Pesa (FI)
Tel. +39 055 23595
antinori@antinori.it
www.antinori.it
www.antinorichianticlassico.it
f MarchesiAntinori
𝕏 @AntinoriFamily

YEAR OF FOUNDATION 1385
NAME OF THE OWNER Antinori Family
DIRECT SALES
VISITS TO THE WINERY - RESERVATION NEEDED
HECTARES OF VINEYARD 2,400
RESTAURANT

Antinori is one of the most famous producers of Italian wine and has a glorious history of winemaking that is over a century old. At the helm is Piero Antinori who has Renzo Cotarella as his enologist and CEO and is assisted by his daughters Albiera, Allegra and Alessia. They have own a total of some 2,400 hectares of vineyards which are divided among the various estates that compose the Antinori galaxy. Aside from the original one in San Casciano Val di Pesa, in Chianti, and Badia in Passignano, these include Guado al Tasso in Bolgheri, Pian delle Vigne in Montalcino and Braccesca between Montepulciao and Cortona. Outside Tuscany they own Castello della Sala in Umbria, Prunetto in Piedmont, Montenisia in Franciacorta and Tormaesca in Puglia.

🔲 🗺 97   Price E
Solaia 2013

Blend of 75% Cabernet Sauvignon, 20% Sangiovese and 5 % Cabernet Franc grapes, 18 months in new barrique. Intense and dark ruby. Complex and wonderfully refined nose, spicy notes then hint of blueberry, blackcurrant and leather on a minty background. Very elegant palate, silky tannins, tense and refined acidity, typical for this vintage that makes the palate supple and "crunchy". Incredibly long finish.

🔲 🗺 95   Price C
Tignanello 2013

Blend of 80% Sangiovese, 15% Cabernet Sauvugnon and 5% Cabernet Franc grapes. Ages for 18 months in barrique. Elegant notes of dark cherry, tobacco and spices, floral hints on the background. tense palate with lively acidity to balance the structure. Very young but very promising.

94   Price B
Chianti Classico Gran Selezione Badia a Passignano 2011

100% Sangiovese grapes. Ages for 1 year in Hungarian barrels. Intense and shiny ruby garnet. Complex and elegant nose with notes of violet, sweet tobacco, black cherry, cassis and a hint of prune. Savory palate, lightly tannic, mouth filling, warm and a very long finish.

93   Price B
Chianti Classico Podere Tignanello Riserva 2013

Blend of 90% Sangiovese and 10% Cabernet Sauvignon grapes. Ages for 1 year in barrique. Intense ruby garnet. Refined and captivating nose that offers notes of black cherry, cassis, and sweet spices. Very balanced palate with firm tannins but not aggressive and a warm and very long length.

91   Price B
Chianti Classico Villa Antinori Ris. 2013

Blend of 90% Sangiovese and 10% Cabernet Sauvignon. The 60% ages in large casks while the rest ages in second fill barrique. Lively and intense ruby with garnet rim. Very fruity nose: black cherry, cassis then notes of tobacco and violet. Mouth filling and supple palate, good acidity and good length.

ARGENTIERA

Via Aurelia, 412/a - Località Pianali - Frazione Donoratico
57022 Castagneto Carducci (LI)
Tel. +39 0565 773176
info@argentiera.eu
www.argentiera.eu
 TenutaArgentiera
 @Argentiera_Vini

YEAR OF FOUNDATION **1999**
NAME OF THE OWNER **Stanislaus Turnauer, Corrado and Marcello Fratini**
TOTAL BOTTLES PRODUCED **450,000**
DIRECT SALES
VISITS TO THE WINERY - RESERVATION NEEDED
HECTARES OF VINEYARD **75**
OLIVE OIL PRODUCTION

The lovely estate is set on the plateau that for kilometers on end dominates the coastline south of Bolgheri. It was once owned by the historic Serristori family and is today in the hands of brothers Corrado and Marcello Fratini with Stanislaus Turnauer. Of the estate's 500 hectares, 75 are cultivated with specializes grapes and are planted with, depending on the soil composition, Cabernet Sauvignon, Cabernet Franc, Merlot and Syrah. Its cellars hold 1,200 French oak barrique to give the estate's wines their modern style.

93   Price C
Bolgheri Superiore Argentiera 2013

Blend of Cabernet Sauvignon, Merlot and Cabernet Franc grapes. Ages 18 months in barrique. Dense and deep ruby, the nose offers notes of resin and spices then a wonderful notes of raspberry and black cherry. The palate is fresh and flavorful, mouth filling, velvety tannins, ample, elegant and long. 10th anniversary edition.

93   Price D
Bolgheri Superiore Opheliah Maria 2012

100% Cabernet Sauvignon grapes. Ages 24 months in barrique. Deep and intense ruby. Complex nose with notes of pencil lead and coffee, smoky hints and then herbaceous and floral notes. Very rich palate, mouth filling and fresh, youthful and agile tannins. Intense and flavorful, long fruity tail.

90   Price B
Bolgheri Villa Donoratico 2013

Blend of Cabernet Sauvignon, Cabernet Franc, Merlot and Petit Verdot grapes, 12 months in barrique. Deep ruby red. Intense nose; sweet spices then fruity notes and cypress berries. Mouth filling palate, flavorful, sleek and well developed. Flavorful finish.

ARGIANO

Località S. Angelo in Colle
53024 Montalcino (SI)
Tel. +39 0577 844037
argiano@argiano.net
www.argiano.net
 argiano
 @Argianowinery

YEAR OF FOUNDATION **1980**
NAME OF THE OWNER **Andrè Esteves**

TOTAL BOTTLES PRODUCED **330,000**
DIRECT SALES
VISITS TO THE WINERY - RESERVATION NEEDED
HECTARES OF VINEYARD **51**
HOSPITALITY
OLIVE OIL PRODUCTION

VISITS TO THE WINERY - RESERVATION NEEDED
HECTARES OF VINEYARD **62**
HOSPITALITY
RESTAURANT
CERTIFIED ORGANIC VITICULTURE
OLIVE OIL PRODUCTION

This beautify and historic estate in the southern part of the appellation was recently acquired by a foreign group. Its headquarters is in the magnificent Argiano castle, which in reality was a 'grancia' or grain silo, and the winery was recently restructured into a modern structure that allows for total control over humidity levels and temperatures during the various winemaking stages and aging.

Reliability and an excellent quality/price ratio are the strongpoints of this famous Chianti Classico estate owned by the Stucchi family. Its products, made under the technical supervision of enologist Maurizio Castelli, have a nice structure and are easy to drink. Thus they are typical Chianti reds that are particularly easy to pair with food.

 95   **Price D**
Brunello di Montalcino Riserva 2010

100% Sangiovese grapes. Ages in different sized Slavonian and French barrels. Intense ruby with a lighter rim. Multi-layered nose of cherries, yellow peach, hint of pencil lead and a white spice. Rich and ample palate, wonderful balance between acidity and very sleek tannins. Flavorful and long finish. This wine is a wonderful example of a new era for the winery.

 93   **Price C**
Brunello di Montalcino 2011

100% Sangiovese grapes. Ages in different sized barrel. Dark and deep ruby. Intense nose of blackberry, undergrowth, intense but not overwhelming spicy note, overall intense and clean nose. Warm and well balanced youthful tannin on the palate. Wonderful drinkability despite the vintage and the hot area where it comes from. Wonderful finish.

★★

BADIA A COLTIBUONO

Località Badia a Coltibuono
53013 Gaiole in Chianti (SI)
Tel. +39 0577 74481
marketing@coltibuono.com
www.coltibuono.com
 badiaa.coltibuono
@coltibuono

YEAR OF FOUNDATION **1057**
NAME OF THE OWNER **Stucchi Prinetti Family**
TOTAL BOTTLES PRODUCED **750,000**
DIRECT SALES

 92   **Price B**
Chianti Classico Riserva 2012

Blend of Sangiovese, Canaiolo, Colorino and Ciliegiolo grapes. Ages for 2 years in French and Austrian oak barrel. Ruby. Floral notes of lavender then fruity hints of raspberry and strawberry. Crunchy tannins, flavorful, impressive. The house style succeeds in this challenging vintage.

 88   **Price C**
Montebello 2012

Blend of ancient Chianti varieties: Mammolo, Ciliegiolo, Pugnitello, Colorino, Sanforte, Malvasia Nera, Canaiolo, Fogliatonda and Sangiovese grapes. Ages for 16 months in large cask. Intense ruby. Rich and multi-layered nose. Juicy palate, savory, pleasant, lightly rough tannins, pleasant and intriguing but with plenty of warm and ripe notes.

 87   **Price A**
Chianti Classico 2014

Blend of 90% Sangiovese and 10% of Canaiolo, Colorino and Ciliegiolo grapes. Shiny ruby. Warm fruity nose, strawberry and raspberry, forest berries. Precise palate with a good tannin and freshness.

BADIA DI MORRONA

Via di Badia, 8 – Località Morrona
56030 Terricciola (PI)
Tel. +39 0587 656013
Fax +39 0587 655162
cantina@badiadimorrona.it
www.badiadimorrona.it
BadiadiMorrona

YEAR OF FOUNDATION **1939**
NAME OF THE OWNER **Filippo Gaslini Alberti**
TOTAL BOTTLES PRODUCED **350,000**
DIRECT SALES
VISITS TO THE WINERY
HECTARES OF VINEYARD **105**
HOSPITALITY
RESTAURANT
OLIVE OIL PRODUCTION

Badia di Morrona is an important, large and beauty estate with its some 550 hectares of land including over 100 of vineyards and around 40 of olive groves. It is situated between Pisa and Volterra and includes an old religious complex that first belonged to the Benedictine order and later the Camaldoli one. For several years now, Filippo Gaslini Alberti has taken over running the estate from his father and the change is most evident in a better definition of the fruit in the wines, which was also thanks to greater attention in the vineyard and the completion of a new winery. They have also built a modern oil mill which has lifted the quality level of the whole estate.

■ 93   Price B*
Vin Santo del Chianti 2010

*Blend of 40% Trebbiano, 30% Malvasia and 30% Colombana grapes. Ages at least 4 years in 110 litres barrel. Intense golden yellow. Captivating aromas of dry apricot, sultanas and a hint of candied orange. The palate is dense, wonderful balance between sugar and acidity, with a long length that reminds notes of apricot and almond. *50 cl bottle.*

■ 90   Price B
N'Antia 2013

Blend of 50% Cabernet Sauvignon, 30% Cabernet Franc and 20% Merlot grapes. Ages for 15 months in barrique. Intense dark ruby. Light herbaceous notes, eucalyptus then cedar, currant and a hint of face powder. Ample and mouth filling palate with firm and well integrated tannins, long finish with notes of fine herbs.

■ 85   Price A
Chianti I Sodi del Paretaio 2015

Blend of 85% Sangioveseand 15% of Cabernet Sauvignon, Merlot and Syrah grapes. Ages 10 months in concrete tank. Ruby red. Fresh and fruity nose with notes of red cherry and a light floral hint. The palate is simple and easy drinking, fruity and crunchy.

ERIK BANTI

Località Fosso Dei Molini
58054 Scansano (GR)
Tel. +39 0564 508006
Fax +39 0564 508019
info@erikbanti.com
www.erikbanti.com
f *morellino.banti*
🐦 *@ErikBantiMorell*

YEAR OF FOUNDATION **1981**
NAME OF THE OWNER **Erik Banti**
TOTAL BOTTLES PRODUCED
DIRECT SALES
VISITS TO THE WINERY - RESERVATION NEEDED
HECTARES OF VINEYARD **24.5**
OLIVE OIL PRODUCTION

Maremma was a sleepy coastal area before Erik Banti erupted on the scene in the mid-1980s. At the time this Italian-Danish former tour operator in Rome was 40 years old and had decided to move to Maremma, to dedicate himself full-time to the vineyards and tiny winery he had set up over the years. When he came, Morellino di Scansano was unknown to both the locals and the area's holiday-goers and totally unknown outside the area. To his credit, Erik believed in this wine and worked to make it known first in Rome and then the rest of Italy and the world. Thus he can be considered one of Morellino's Founding Fathers,

■ 88   Price A
Morellino di Scansano Carato 2013

Blend of 85% Sangiovese, 10% Ciliegiolo and 5% Merlot grapes. Ages in American and Slavonian oak barrique for 8 months. Ruby. The nose offers woody notes then aromatic herbs like rosemary and thyme then black cherry and dark spices. On the palate the woody notes are quite prominent but they will integrate as per the good body, the medium freshness and the fruity compound.

■ 85   👍 Price A
Morellino di Scansano 2015

Blend of 85% Sangiovese, 10% Alicante and 5% Merlot grapes. Only stainless steel. Dark ruby. Warm nose; notes of dark cherry, also dark cherry jam, sweet spices, cinnamon and a floral hint. The palate is juicy, fruity and a lightly tannic finish; medium length.

★★★
BARONE RICASOLI · CASTELLO DI BROLIO

Località Madonna a Brolio
53013 Gaiole in Chianti (SI)
Tel. +39 0577 7301
barone@ricasoli.it
www.ricasoli.it
 baronericasolispa
🐦 *@barone_ricasoli*

YEAR OF FOUNDATION **1141**
NAME OF THE OWNER **Barone Francesco Ricasoli**
TOTAL BOTTLES PRODUCED **2,500,000**
DIRECT SALES
VISITS TO THE WINERY - RESERVATION NEEDED
HECTARES OF VINEYARD **230**
RESTAURANT

After falling into obscurity for several decades, for some years now Brolio has gotten back in the game with both determination and the ambition to regain the leading role it had in Chianti for centuries. The driving force behind this is Francesco Ricasoli who overcame thousands of difficulties and polemics to get control of what had always been his family's estate. The wine he now offers are often exceptional.

■ 🍷 96   Price B
Chianti Classico Gran Selezione Castello di Brolio 2013
Blend of 80% Sangiovese, Cabernet Sauvignon and Merlot grapes. Ages for 2 years in barrique and tonneau. Intense ruby garnet. Spicy, captivating, waxy notes, dark cherry, kirsch, tobacco and vanilla. Firm palate, tense, savory, rich, warm, lightly tannic, definitively refined and very long.

■ 93   Price B
Chianti Classico Brolio Bettino 2013
Blend of 90% Sangiovese and 10% other grape varieties. Ages for 18 months in large cask. Very intense ruby. Typical and traditional nose: black cherry and violet then a hint of tobacco and kirsch. Warm but tense palate, mouth filling, savory and with a wonderful length.

■ 93   Price B
Casalferro 2013
100% Merlot grapes. Ages for 18 months in barrqiue. Very intense ruby. Clean fruity nose, hint of sour

cherry then spicy and lightly woody notes. Savory palate, tense, supple, wonderful acidity and a thin but long finish.

■ 92   Price B
Chianti Classico Brolio Riserva 2013
Blend of 80% Sangiovese, 15% Merlot and 5% Cabernet Sauvignon grapes. Ages for 16 months in barrique and tonneau. Intense ruby garnet. Captivating nose with notes of kirsch and vanilla; savory palate, it is still a bit tannic and youthful; very promising.

■ 87   Price A
Chianti Classico Brolio 2014
Blend of 80% Sangiovese and 20% of Merlot and Cabernet Sauvignon grapes. Ages for 9 months between used barrique and tonneau. Intense Ruby. Fruity nose, black cherry and prune, then a hint of green note such as cardamom. Fresh palate, good acidity, tense and medium bodied.

BELMESSERI

Via Case Sparse, 4 - Molino La Serra
54010 Pontremoli (MS)
Tel. + 39 335 7752116
cantinebelmesseri@gmail.com
www.cantinebelmesseri.it
 Cantine-Belmesseri

YEAR OF FOUNDATION **2008**
NAME OF THE OWNER **Giuseppe Balestra**
TOTAL BOTTLES PRODUCED **6,500**
DIRECT SALES
VISITS TO THE WINERY - RESERVATION NEEDED
HECTARES OF VINEYARD **2**

Around 15 years ago, Paolo Balestra embarked on a project to bring back the vineyards of the farm in Serra where the physician-philosopher-poet Paolo Belmesseri was born in the 16th century and name a wine estate after him. The vineyards are only two hectares in size, both have southeast and southwest exposures and sit at an altitude of 280m above sea level and have a clay-sand soil with a deep subsoil of lime and which is rich in minerals.

■ 88   Price A
Belmesseri 2014
Blend of 60% Merlot, 20% Pollera, 10% Cabernet Sauvignon and 10% Syrah grapes. Stainless steel.

Ruby red. The nose is mainly floral with notes of rose and geranium, then a hint of wild strawberry and aromatic herbs. Mouth filling, flavorful and ample palate. Well integrated tannins. Medium finish.

BINDELLA

*Via delle Tre Berte, 10a
53045 Montepulciano (SI)
Tel. +39 0578 767777
Fax +39 0578 767255
info@bindella.it
www.bindella.it*
 bindellavallocaia

YEAR OF FOUNDATION **1984**
NAME OF THE OWNER **Rudi Bindella**
TOTAL BOTTLES PRODUCED **150,000**
DIRECT SALES
VISITS TO THE WINERY - RESERVATION NEEDED
HECTARES OF VINEYARD **40**
OLIVE OIL PRODUCTION

Swiss-native Rudi Bindella fell in love with this area and here decided to set up his own estate. In just a few years his winery has become one of the most important points of reference for Montepulciano. The area is that of Argiano, one of the most suited in the district, and the wines are the product of a modern approach with an excellent use of technology in the winery and great attention in the vineyard. The principle grape used in Sangiovese (Prugnolo Gentile) together with some Colorino and Mammolo that are used for the Nobile.

■ 90   Price B
Vino Nobile di Montepulciano I Quadri 2013

100% Sangiovese grapes. Ages in tonneau. Deep ruby. Intense nose, almost dark, notes of ink and citrus, then spicy, sweet and fruity notes. Smoky notes. The palate is still young and the tannin is a bit aggressive but not bitter. Firm palate, good weight and full finish.

■ 87   Price A
Vino Nobile di Montepulciano 2013

Blend of Sangiovese and other indigenous grape varieties. Ages in barrel. Ruby red. The nose is not well defined yet and offers notes of red fruit like

sour cherry and blossoms. Supple palate, pleasant balance. The tannins are a bit edgy but are well balanced by the acidity. Good finish.

BIONDI SANTI
TENUTA IL GREPPO

*Villa Greppo, 183
53024 Montalcino (SI)
Tel. +39 0577 848087
Fax +39 0577 849396
biondisanti@biondisanti.it
www.biondisanti.it*
 biondisantiofficial
🐦 *@BiondiSanti_*

YEAR OF FOUNDATION **1888**
NAME OF THE OWNER **Jacopo Biondi Santi**
TOTAL BOTTLES PRODUCED **85,000**
DIRECT SALES
VISITS TO THE WINERY - RESERVATION NEEDED
HECTARES OF VINEYARD **25**
HOSPITALITY
OLIVE OIL PRODUCTION

The great history of Brunello di Montalcino began in 1888. It was here at this estate that Ferruccio Biondi- Santi decided to make a varietal wine from the Sangiovese grape known as Brunello. The estate has since been handed down to the fourth generation and Jacopo Biondi Santi, together with his young children who are learning the trade, is following in his ancestors' footsteps. Tradition here, however, is not written in stone and clones are used from the estate's best vines, particular attention is paid to the use of indigenous yeasts (selected and reproduced) and studies are made on the contribution of fine lees. These are the three aspects that Tenuta Il Greppo focuses on with extreme care.

■ 🔲 99   Price E
Brunello di Montalcino Greppo Riserva 2010

100% Sangiovese grapes. Ages in casks. Ruby red with garnet rim. The nose offers a wonderful fruity note then tobacco and a floral hint. The powerful palate is well balanced by an extraordinary elegance. Amazing palate with a wonderful tannic structure and an incredible depth with the acidity to support and drive the length. The finish is mouth filling and of extraordinary length. Precise and unique style. This is the 'house style' since 1800, austere and very recognisable, it doesn't follow fashion and trend and is everlasting.

 94   Price D

Brunello di Montalcino Il Greppo 2011

100% Sangiovese grapes. Ages in barrel. Ruby color with garnet rim; very fruity nose, more captivating than usual, the 'creamy' tannin reflects the warm vintage but it has an excellent drinkability and length. Something is changing in the house philosophy but always following the tradition.

 89   Price B

Rosso di Montalcino 2013

100% Sangiovese grapes. Ages in different sized barrels. Ruby. Lightly warm aromas with notes of fine herbs, tobacco, red fruit. Firm palate with a young tannin and a subtle acidity. A different version of Rosso di Montalcino that well understand the vintage.

★★

BOSCARELLI

Via di Montenero, 28
53045 Montepulciano (SI)
Tel. +39 0578 767277
🅢 *boscarellipoderi*
info@poderiboscarelli.com
www.poderiboscarelli.com
🅕 *Boscarelliwines*

YEAR OF FOUNDATION 1962
NAME OF THE OWNER Paola De Ferrari Corradi
TOTAL BOTTLES PRODUCED 100,000
DIRECT SALES
VISITS TO THE WINERY - RESERVATION NEEDED
HECTARES OF VINEYARD 16
OLIVE OIL PRODUCTION

The estate was founded in 1966 by Paolo Corradi who inherited her passion for this land from her father and passed it on to her sons Luca and Nicolò who now run the Poderi Boscarelli estate, now one of the leading ones in the area. The vineyards are in the wonderful zone of Cervognano and the wines have unique style and personality. They age in both 30hl barrels and barrique and blend is the key moment to maintain their famous style.

 92   Price B

Vino Nobile di Montepulciano Sottocasa Riserva 2011

Blend of Sangiovese and small percentage of Merlot and Cabernet grapes. Ages in tonneau and barrique. Dark ruby red. Nose of red and black fruits, then a light hint of ink and pencil lead. The palate offers refined and young tannins, firm but with a good drinkability, sleek; the finish is flavorful and it has a wonderful length.

 91   Price C

Vino Nobile di Montepulciano Il Nocio 2012

100% Sangiovese grapes. Ages for 2 years in oak barrel. Intense ruby. Captivating nose, warm, spicy and lightly smoky. Well-structured palate, firm, lively tannin and good weight but it doesn't overwhelm the tannic structure. Flavorful but subtle finish.

89   Price B

Vino Nobile di Montepulciano 2013

Blend of Sangiovese and Ciliegiolo grapes. Ages in different sized barrels. Dark, deep and shiny ruby red. Very intense nose with warm notes, intense red fruit aromas, ripe prune and dark blossoms. Elegant palate, balanced and with good depth, young and austere tannin, wonderful drinkability. Flavorful finish.

★

BRANCAIA

Località Poppi
53017 Radda in Chianti (SI)
Tel. +39 0577 742007
Fax +39 0577 742010
brancaia@brancaia.it
www.brancaia.com
🅕 *Brancaia*
🐦 *@CasaBrancaia*

YEAR OF FOUNDATION 1981
NAME OF THE OWNER Bruno and Brigitte Widmer
TOTAL BOTTLES PRODUCED 475,000
DIRECT SALES
VISITS TO THE WINERY - RESERVATION NEEDED
HECTARES OF VINEYARD 65
OLIVE OIL PRODUCTION

This famous Chianti estate groups brings diverse territorial areas in that the wine grapes come from vineyards in Brancaia (in the township of Castellina in Chianti), Poppi (Radda in Chianti) and several hectares in Maremma, which produce the grapes that in part make Tre and Ilatraia, a few kilometers from the sea. The winery was created in 1981 after Swiss-natives Brigitte and Bruno Widmer fell in love with and acquired Brancaia a Castellina, an estate that was in a state of abandon. Since 1998, Barbara Widmer, an enologist and daughter of the owners, has been in charge of production and all three vineyards of all three with the assistance of enologist Carlo Ferrini.

93   Price B
Ilatraia 2013

Blend of 40% Cabernet Sauvignon, 40% Petit Verdot and 20% Cabernet Franc grapes grown in Maremma. Ages for 18 months in barrique. Dark and intense ruby garnet. Well-defined nose with hint of blueberry, vanilla and sweet spices. Tense, savory, elegant, full bodied, warm and with a very long finish.

89   Price C
Il Blu 2012

Blend of 50% Cabernet Sauvignon, 45% Merlot and 5% Cabernet Franc grapes. Ages for 20 months in barrique. Intense ruby garnet. Developed nose, tamarind, prune and spicy hint, then eucalyptus and licorice. Savory palate, warm and with a slightly dry tannins.

BRUNI

*Strada Vicinale Migliorina - Località La Marta,
6 - Fonteblanda
58015 Orbetello (GR)
Tel. +39 0564 885445
info@aziendabruni.it
www.aziendabruni.it*
 Azienda-Bruni

YEAR OF FOUNDATION **1974**
NAME OF THE OWNER **Marco and Moreno Bruni**
TOTAL BOTTLES PRODUCED **350,000**
DIRECT SALES
VISITS TO THE WINERY - RESERVATION NEEDED
HECTARES OF VINEYARD **40**
OLIVE OIL PRODUCTION

The Bruni estate in is Fonteblanda, Maremma, and the winery was founded in 1974. This was the same year that saw the birth of the Bruni twins, Moreno and Marco, who 20 years later took over the estate. Today, Bruni has 40 hectares of vineyards and produces over 350,000 bottles a year. Most of production is of Morellino di Scansano but they also make wine with Vermentino, Cabernet and other international varieties.

88   Price B
Morellino di Scansano Laire Riserva 2013

Blend of 85% Sangiovese grapes with small percentage of Syrah. Ages for 12 months in barrique. The nose offers toasted notes, then fruity hint of black cherry. The palate has character, full bodied, with oaky aftertaste notes and a sweet fruity finish.

87   Price B
Oltreconfine 2014

100% Grenache grapes. Ages in barrels. Purple ruby color. Refined nose, lightly spicy, then fruity notes of wild strawberry, floral hint and subtle aromas of fresh basil. The palate delivers what promises on the nose, well balanced oaky notes, medium bodied and well balanced.

85   Price A
Vermentino 2015

Blend of Vermentino and a small percentage of other allowed grapes. Stainless steel. Warm straw yellow. Smoky notes then fresh aromas of elderflower and lychee. Tense palate, supple and savory with a lightly sweet note on the finish.

★★
CA' MARCANDA

*Località Santa Teresa, 272
57022 Castagneto Carducci (LI)
Tel. +39 0565 763809
info@camarcanda.com
www.camarcanda.com*

YEAR OF FOUNDATION **1996**
NAME OF THE OWNER **Gaja Family**
TOTAL BOTTLES PRODUCED **380,000**
VISITS TO THE WINERY - RESERVATION NEEDED
HECTARES OF VINEYARD **100**

Angelo Gaja does not really need any introduction. It is a pleasure to hear him tell his long story of how he acquired this lovely estate in Bolgheri, upper Maremma. He fell in love with it and, as he did with Pieve Santa Restituta, in Montalcino, in the end bought it, investing a lot to make it the way he wanted. Naturally, the vineyards are primarily planted with international varieties, certainly not uncommon in this district.

 95 Price D

Bolgheri Camarcanda 2013

Blend of Merlot, Cabernet Sauvignon and Cabernet Franc grapes. Ages for 18 months in oak barrels. Very dark and intense ruby color. Intense and captivating nose, developed notes then fruity aromas of blackcurrant, blueberry, sweet spices and tobacco. The palate is savory and warm, firm and well extracted tannins, very elegant and with a very long finish.

 90 Price B

Bolgheri Magari 2014

Blend of Merlot, Cabernet Sauvignon and Cabernet Franc grapes. Ages for 12 months in oak barrel. Very dark ruby. Fruity nose, blueberry then well-defined notes of eucalyptus on a background of sweet spice aromas. Mouth filling palate, savory, firm tannins. Simpler and lighter version than usual.

CAMPO ALLA SUGHERA

Località Caccia al Piano - Bolgheri
57020 Castagneto Carducci (LI)
Tel. +39 0565 766936
Fax +39 0565 766938
info@campoallasughera.com
www.campoallasughera.com
 CampoAllaSughera
 @CampoSughera

YEAR OF FOUNDATION **1998**
NAME OF THE OWNER **Knauf Family**
TOTAL BOTTLES PRODUCED **100,000**
DIRECT SALES
VISITS TO THE WINERY - RESERVATION NEEDED
HECTARES OF VINEYARD **16.5**
OLIVE OIL PRODUCTION

If you exclude the famous producers, this is one of the most important estates in Bolgheri. From the start it was organized with Teutonic precision (it is owned by the Knauf family, world leaders in the production of construction materials) both in the vineyards, which are meticulously cultivated, and the winery. The wines have a modern style and the quality is always reliable.

 93 Price B

Bolgheri Superiore Arnione 2013

Blend of 40% Cabernet Sauvignon, 20% Cabernet Franc, 20% Merlot and 20% Petit Verdot grapes. Ages between 18 and 20 months in mostly new barrique. Ruby color with purple hues. Nose of black fruit, jelly black fruit, spices and eucalyptus, the palate is vertical and austere, dense and fresh, velvety tannins. Good depth and fruity finish.

91 Price B

Bolgheri Adeo 2013

Blend of 60% Cabernet Sauvignon and 40% Merlot grapes. Ages for 12 months in barrique. Dark ruby of good depth. The nose fashions aromas of powder gun, sweet spices, pencil lead and blackcurrant. Full bodied and flavorful palate, firm and austere tannins. Good length.

★

CANALICCHIO DI SOPRA

Località Casaccia, 73
53024 Montalcino (SI)
Tel. +39 0577 848316
Fax +39 0577 846221
info@canalicchiodisopra.com
www.canalicchiodisopra.com
 CANALICCHIODISOPRA
 @canalicchiosopr

YEAR OF FOUNDATION **1962**
NAME OF THE OWNER **Francesco, Marco and Simonetta Ripaccioli**
TOTAL BOTTLES PRODUCED **70,000**
DIRECT SALES
VISITS TO THE WINERY - RESERVATION NEEDED
HECTARES OF VINEYARD **15**
HOSPITALITY
OLIVE OIL PRODUCTION

The winery of the three, young and skilled Ripaccioli siblings is quickly climbing the ladder in Montalcino thanks the reliability and quality of their wines. The vineyards are very well cared for in the prestigious zone of Canalicchi, an historic cru on the northern side if Montalcino. Their approach to winemaking can be defined as 'neo-classical' in the sense that while attention is paid to tradition in regard to style, they also employ modern technology. Decisions made in regard to the harvest and estate strategy are all geared for quality.

 95   Price D

Brunello di Montalcino Riserva 2010

100% Sangiovese grapes. Ages in barrels. Ruby red with garnet rim. Good complexity on the nose with hint of citrus, undergrowth and fine herbs. Wonderful palate with a firm and well integrated tannins; flavorful. The finish offers austere and dark notes.

91   Price B

Brunello di Montalcino 2011

100% Sangiovese grapes. Ages in large cask. Ruby red. Intense and fresh fruity notes of prune and cherry then hint of wild herbs. Intense, flavorful and balanced palate. The finish is citrusy but ample and with good weight. The north facing vines helped in this warm vintage.

eastern European oak which best suited the estate's philosophy that seeks to makes wines that can age long.

 97   Price C

Brunello di Montalcino Riserva 2010

100% Sangiovese grapes. Ages in barrel. Intense ruby with garnet hues. Intense and very clean nose of black fruits, blackberry, red plum, cherry. Wonderful spicy hints that reminds sweet tobacco. Lively palate, austere tannin but well extracted and firm, never tiring. Very long finish. 'Baffo' get a bull's eye with this wonderful Riserva.

 92   Price A

Moscadello di Montalcino Vendemmia Tardiva 2012

100% Moscadello grapes. Ages in small barrel. Intense straw yellow. Nose of mandarin, eucalyptus, sea breeze and apricot. Amazing palate with a wonderful acidity and a never tiring sweetness, well balanced. The finish offers floral hints, still subtle but very lively and elegant. A classic Moscadello.

★★
CAPANNA

Località Capanna, 333
53024 Montalcino (SI)
Tel. +39 0577 848298
Fax +39 0577 1652
info@capannamontalcino.com
www.capannamontalcino.com
 Capanna-Montalcino-Italy

YEAR OF FOUNDATION **1958**
NAME OF THE OWNER **Benito Cencioni & Figli**
TOTAL BOTTLES PRODUCED **70,000**
DIRECT SALES
VISITS TO THE WINERY
HECTARES OF VINEYARD **19.5**
OLIVE OIL PRODUCTION

This beautiful winemaking reality has for years benefited from the sure hand and dynamic personality of Patrizio Cencioni. Located in the northern area of Montalcino, at the feet of Montosoli, the estate offers classic wines that are quite bold with tannins that need to be tamed by rigorous choices made at harvest time. The winery has recently replaced its store of barrels that remain medium-sized ones (30hl) of

★
CAPARSA

Via Caparsa, 47
53017 Radda in Chianti (SI)
Tel. +39 0577 738174
caparsa@caparsa.it
www.caparsa.it
 caparsa
 @PaoloCianferoni

YEAR OF FOUNDATION **1965**
NAME OF THE OWNER **Paolo Cianferoni**
TOTAL BOTTLES PRODUCED **20,000**
DIRECT SALES
VISITS TO THE WINERY - RESERVATION NEEDED
HECTARES OF VINEYARD **11**
HOSPITALITY
CERTIFIED ORGANIC VITICULTURE
OLIVE OIL PRODUCTION

Paolo Cianferoni is a stubborn and courageous winemaker who says what he thinks and cultivate his grapes with passion. His vineyards are in Radda and have various exposures and soil. The wines are authentic and rebellious and do not seek to please everyone but which are easy to fall in love with if they have aged properly.

91   Price B
Chianti Classico Doccio a Matteo Riserva 2012

Blend of Sangiovese, Colorino and Ancellotta grapes; single vineyard. Ages for 18 months in large casks of 500 – 1000 litres capacity. Light ruby. Vibrant and floral, lavender, violet and iris, fresh and under spirit fruity notes. Balanced and very fresh palate, clean, precise and characterful. Lively but never overwhelming tannin with an intriguing outlook.

90   Price B
Chianti Classico Caparsino Riserva 2012

100% Sangiovese grapes. Ages for 30 months in large cask of 18 hl capacity. Ruby. Classic and elegant, rustic but fascinating nose of violet, red and black currant, then spicy hint of tobacco and bay leaf. Mouth filling and vibrant palate, good acidity with a ripe and well balanced tannin. It won't last as long as a previous vintage yet is very enjoyable.

88   Price A
Rosso di Caparsa

Non vintage as it is a blend of 85% Sangiovese grapes from 2014 and 15% Sangiovese grapes 2011. Ages in concrete tanks. Intense nose, full and flavorful. "Double face" wine, the freshness comes from the younger vintage while the structure and the weight comes from the 2011 vintage. The palate is ample but dynamic and the finish reminds notes of cherry and raspberry.

★
CAPARZO

S.P. del Brunello, km 1,700 - Località Caparzo
53024 Montalcino (SI)
Tel. +39 0577 848390
info@caparzo.com
www.caparzo.com
🐦 *@CaparzoWines*

YEAR OF FOUNDATION 1970
NAME OF THE OWNER Elisabetta Gnudi
TOTAL BOTTLES PRODUCED 500,000
DIRECT SALES
VISITS TO THE WINERY
HECTARES OF VINEYARD 81
HOSPITALITY

A brand on the up-and-up thanks to significant investments made in recent years. The aging barrels have all been replaced, a new outside consultant has been brought in to handle winemaking and some of the vineyards have been renovated. The vineyards are for the most part in northeast Montalcino but the estate also has some vineyards in the more prestigious cru. These include in Montosoli in the north, Castelgiocondo with its wonderful tufaceous soil and a few hectares in the fantastic zone of Sesta. The wines alternate from being traditional and classic ones to being innovative, as is the case with Brunello La Casa, truly outstanding.

90   Price C
Brunello di Montalcino La Casa 2011

Sangiovese grapes. Ages in tonneau and barrique. Intense and shiny ruby red. Clean and intense notes of red fruits, never overripe. Light notes of eucalyptus, then smoky hints, mint and lychee. The palate is typical from northern climate and from gravelly soil, with a wonderful acidity. Captivating and elegant finish. Historical Cru of Montosoli that also in a challenging vintage has the edge over.

86   Price B
Brunello di Montalcino 2011

100% Sangiovese grapes. Ages in barrel. Light and shiny ruby. Warm nose with notes of undergrowth and cola. Fruity hint of mulberry and ripe cherry. Balanced palate, good balanced and good drinkability with a refined balanced between tannin and acidity. Ample finish even if not extremely long.

84   Price A
Rosso di Montalcino 2013

100% Sangiovese grapes. Ages in barrel. Medium ruby. Nose of toffee then warm red fruit aromas. Simple palate, tense but overall it has good drinkability.

★★★
CAPEZZANA

Via Capezzana, 100
59015 Carmignano (PO)
Tel. +39 055 8706005
Fax +39 055 8706673
capezzana@capezzana.it
www capezzana.it
📘 *Capezzana*
🐦 *@Capezzana1*

YEAR OF FOUNDATION 804
NAME OF THE OWNER Contini Bonacossi Family

TOTAL BOTTLES PRODUCED **500,000**
DIRECT SALES
VISITS TO THE WINERY - RESERVATION NEEDED
HECTARES OF VINEYARD **100**
HOSPITALITY
RESTAURANT
OLIVE OIL PRODUCTION

The Capezzana estate is on the northern border of Carmignano and is owned by the Contini Bonacossi family who are great antique collectors who have made important donations to the Uffizi gallery. Their tendency to collect is also evident at their estate which has a collection of historic vintages dating back to 1925, thanks to the meticulous work done by the late Count Ugo who transformed this historic estate into a modern enterprise.

■ 🍇 98   Price C
Ugo Contini Bonacossi 2013

100% Sangiovese grapes. Ages for 18 months in tonneau. Intense ruby. Multi layered and complex nose; black cherry, undergrowth and field blossoms. The palate is tense, essential, firm and very elegant, young and firm tannins; the acidity is well balanced by aristocratic and sleek structure; one of the stars of the Tuscan wine scene. This is an amazing wine dedicated to the person that relaunched the Carmignano in the Gotha of Tuscan wines.

▪ 94   Price B
Vinsanto di Carmignano 2009

Blend of Trebbiano and Colombano grapes dried until February. Ages for 5 years in small barrels. Amber color. Intense and well defined notes of walnut, tobacco, cedar and peach. Dense palate, firm, velvety, rich but with wonderful freshness. Very long apricot finish.

■ 90   Price B
Carmignano Trefiano Riserva 2012

Blend of Sangiovese with small percentage of Cabernet Sauvignon and Canaiolo grapes. Ages for 16 months in tonneau. Dense ruby color. Classic and traditional nose, fruity, hint of citrus and spices, tea leaf. Dense, mouth filling and rich palate with firm and round tannins and a fruity aftertaste.

■ 89   Price B
Carmignano Villa di Capezzana 2013

Blend of 80% Sangiovese and Cabernet Sauvignon grapes. Ages for 14 months in tonneau. Dark and dense ruby. Fruity notes of blueberry, blackberry,

also jammy notes then dark notes of ink and rhubarb. The palate is rich, ample, juicy, licorice aftertaste with well extracted tannins and a flavorful finish.

CAPITONI

Podere Sedime, 63
53026 Pienza (SI)
Tel. +39 338 8981597
Fax +39 0578 748436
info@capitoni.eu
www.capitoni.eu
🄵 *Marco Capitoni*

YEAR OF FOUNDATION **1993**
NAME OF THE OWNER **Marco Capitoni**
TOTAL BOTTLES PRODUCED **20,000**
DIRECT SALES
VISITS TO THE WINERY - RESERVATION NEEDED
HECTARES OF VINEYARD **5**
OLIVE OIL PRODUCTION

The Sedime farm, home to the Capitoni estate in near Pienza, is named after the place where farmers would come set down their tools. 50-year-old Marco Capitoni is a man with old fashioned manners and the product of a forgotten rural culture. He was born where he now lives and works with his wife Antonella and son Angelo. From his few hectares of Sangiovese and some Merlot he makes two wines with meticulous care: Capitoni and Frasi Orcia DOC. He third wine is the newborn Troccolone, Orcia Sangiovese Doc, vinified in handmade terracotta jars.

■ 89   Price A
Orcia Capitoni Riserva 2012

Blend of 80% Sangiovese and 20% Merlot grapes. Ages in barrique. Dark ruby with garnet rim. Intense and deep nose wonderfully balanced between fruity aromas of ripe cherry, spices and tertiary notes of sweet tobacco and hint of chocolate and mint, benchmark for this wine. The palate is balanced and fresh and it has a very good structure. Great vintage.

■ 87   👍 Price A
Orcia Sangiovese Troccolone 2015

100% Sangiovese grapes. Only stainless steel then ages in 5hl terracotta amphora. Light ruby, shiny and textbook for shades. Small red berries notes, raspberry and currant then lightly unripe black cherry, clean and defined. Fresh palate and smooth tannins, mellow finish with black cherry aftertaste. A unique Sangiovese.

CAPRILI

Podere Caprili, 268
53024 Montalcino (SI)
Tel. +39 0577 848566
 azcaprili
info@caprili.it
www.caprili.it
CapriliWinery
@Caprili

YEAR OF FOUNDATION 1965
NAME OF THE OWNER Fratelli Bartolommei
TOTAL BOTTLES PRODUCED 75,000
DIRECT SALES
VISITS TO THE WINERY - RESERVATION NEEDED
HECTARES OF VINEYARD 18
OLIVE OIL PRODUCTION

Set in the area surrounding the Santa Restituta Church, one of the most fascinating places in Montalcino both for its history and vocation for winegrowing, the state of Giacomo Bartolommei has in the past ten years made a remarkable leap in quality. Rigorous selections during harvest and extreme care taken in the vineyards have resulted in wines that are very representative of the area. They have a neo-classic style and aromas that lean towards fruit but without significantly compromising the structure which is always bold. The wines are a nice combination of boldness and elegance.

 97   Price C
Brunello di Montalcino Riserva 2010
100% Sangiovese grapes. Ages in barrel. Ruby color. The nose is clean and defined with notes of sour cherry then tobacco, eucalyptus and an austere note of licorice. The palate reminds the great old Brunellos, everything is balanced and the acidity is well integrated in the structure. The finish is solid, powerful and very long.

90   Price B
Brunello di Montalcino 2011
100% Sangiovese grapes. Ages in barrels. Clean, intense and warm notes of cherry, sour cherry and a blackberry/mulberry hint. Rich palate with earthy

notes, solid tannin and a youthful acidity; amazingly flavorful and long finish.

 89   Price B
Rosso di Montalcino 2014
100% Sangiovese grapes. Ages in barrels. Ruby color. Ripe cherry and eucalyptus. Young palate and lively tannin, good weight and depth, pleasantly unexpected. A miracle in this challenging vintage.

 ★★
CARPINETA FONTALPINO

Località Podere Carpineta
53019 Castelnuovo Berardenga (SI)
Tel. +39 0577 369219
office@carpinetafontalpino.it
www.carpinetafontalpino.it
Fattoria-Carpineta-Fontalpino

YEAR OF FOUNDATION 1965
NAME OF THE OWNER Filippo and Gioia Cresti
TOTAL BOTTLES PRODUCED 100,000
DIRECT SALES
VISITS TO THE WINERY - RESERVATION NEEDED
HECTARES OF VINEYARD 23

This this farm has been home to the Cresti family since the 1960s but wine has been produced here since 1800. Today enologist Gioia is in charge of producing all the wines while Filippo handles sales and marketing. The wines have a modern style but constant attention is paid to exalting the potential of Sangiovese, both when uses to make a varietal wine or when blended, from their most simple Colli Senesi right up to the top IGT wine.

 95   Price B
Do ut des 2013
Blend of Merlot, Sangiovese and Cabernet Sauvignon grapes. Ages for 18 months in barrique. Intense ruby. Nose of lavander and violet, mustard and spices, cardamom and anise. The palate is firm, juicy, balanced and harmonic, supple palate thanks to a good acidity that balances the rich finish of forest fruits and Asian spices.

 91   Price B
Chianti Classico Fontalpino Riserva 2013
100% Sangiovese grapes. Ages for 1 year in tonneau. Red color with garnet rim. Developed and

spicy notes. Tangy and robust, aftertaste of mustard and woody notes, it is a still young and at the moment lacks of depth but it will refine with the time.

■ 88   Price A
Chianti Colli Senesi 2014

Mainly Sangiovese grapes, 10 months in barrique. Very light ruby. Lively floral and intriguing notes. Vibrant palate, fresh and with a fruity depth.

CASALE FALCHINI

*Via di Casale, 40
53037 San Gimignano (SI)
Tel. +39 0577 941305
casalefalchini@tin.it
www.casale-falchini.it*
f *Azienda-Agricola-Casale-Falchini*

YEAR OF FOUNDATION 1964
NAME OF THE OWNER Michael and Christopher Falchini
TOTAL BOTTLES PRODUCED 280,000
DIRECT SALES
VISITS TO THE WINERY
HECTARES OF VINEYARD 35

The estate was founded in the 1960s and in recent years has seen a significant leap in quality. It is located near the town and has a clay and sandstone soil that is more or less compact. The main grape here is naturally Vernaccia di San Gimignano but they also cultivate red varieties like Sangiovese. Care in the vineyard and, especially, in the winery has made this year's wines very interesting.

☐ 92   👍 Price A
**Vernaccia di San Gimignano
Vigna a Solatio 2012**

100% Vernaccia grapes from the oldest vineyard with south aspect, hence the name. Ages in stainless steel and tonneau. Light straw yellow. Nose of eucalyptus then floral hints of hawthorn, fruity notes of loquat and a subtle nettle aroma. Rich and supple palate.

☐ 87   Price A
**Vernaccia di San Gimignano Ab Vinea
Doni 2014**

Blend of Vernaccia and small percentage of Char-

donnay grapes. Ages in stainless steel and part in barrique. Shiny straw yellow. Complex nose: floral, hint of olive, yellow fruit like loquat and a hint of anise. Savory palate, good depth and good finish.

CASALOSTE

*Via Montaglieri, 32 - Frazione Panzano
50022 Greve in Chianti (FI)
Tel. +39 055 852725*
S *casaloste*
*casaloste@casaloste.com
www.casaloste.com*
f *fattoria.casaloste*
🐦 *@Casaloste*

YEAR OF FOUNDATION 1992
NAME OF THE OWNER Giovanni ed Emilia d'Orsi
TOTAL BOTTLES PRODUCED 50,000
DIRECT SALES
VISITS TO THE WINERY - RESERVATION NEEDED
HECTARES OF VINEYARD 10
HOSPITALITY

Neapolitan-born Giovanni d'Orsi found a new home in the Chianti Classico hills, more precisely in Casaloste not far from the village of Panzano. Here he makes his splendid wine from grapes from his vineyards of breathtaking beauty.

■ 92   Price B
Chianti Classico Riserva 2011

100% Sangiovese grapes. Ages for 15 months in barrique. Floral, lavender and currant, strawberry, sweet raspberry and caramel, barley and sour cherry. Savory but fruity palate, good suppleness and finish. Good distinctive tannin.

■ 90   Price B
Rosso Maniero 2014

Blend of 70% Sangiovese and 30% Canaiolo grapes. Ages for 1 year in oak barrel. Ruby red. Nose of capers, olive and salt. Supple palate, less powerful than the nose, elegant with a spicy note of juniper and mint; long and aromatic finish.

■ 89   Price B
Inversus 2013

Blend of Sangiovese and Merlot grapes. Ages in barrique. Deep and dark ruby. The nose is very oaky and offers hint of spices, mint and salty notes. Firm and tangy palate, generous tannin, lightly aggressive and woody but the structure is fascinating and very 'Panzano style' on the finish.

 87 — Price A

Chianti Classico 2014

100% Sangiovese grapes, 12 months in small oak barrels. Powerful nose of cherry, floral notes of lavende. Rich and warm palate, vibrant and lightly rustic tannin. Wonderful personality.

★★★

CASANOVA DI NERI

Podere Fiesole
53024 Montalcino (SI)
Tel. +39 0577 834455
info@casanovadineri.com
www.casanovadineri.com

YEAR OF FOUNDATION 1971
NAME OF THE OWNER Giacomo Neri
TOTAL BOTTLES PRODUCED 275,000
DIRECT SALES
VISITS TO THE WINERY - RESERVATION NEEDED
HECTARES OF VINEYARD 65
OLIVE OIL PRODUCTION

Over the past 20 years this estate has climbed to the top in Montalcino. It has 65 hectares of vineyards situated in different locations in the area and a cutting-edge winery that is a model for the others with its various sizes of barrels for aging Brunello. Giacomo Neri is the man who has allowed this estate to become one of the best in the world. The winery produces three Brunello using different styles but always in respect of their roots. Etichetta Bianca is made with grapes from the cooler Tenuta Nuova vineyard which is more to the south and the estate cru Cerretalto is made with grapes from a single, unique vineyard.

 99 — Price E

Brunello di Montalcino Cerretalto 2010

100% Sangiovese grapes. Ages in barrique and tonneau. Sometimes it is very difficult to describe some great wines as there are not words that could possibly describe perfectly the emotions and the sensations that they can offer. This wine it is definitivily a benchmark for the style. Extraordinary. Don't be intimidated by the light sediment.

 93 — Price D

Brunello di Montalcino Tenuta Nuova 2011

100% Sangiovese grapes. Ages in tonneau and barrique. Shiny ruby with 'pigeon's blood' hues. Very clean and well defined nose of red fruit, dark cherries, sour cherry, jammy notes, Mediterranean herbs, hint of cinnamon. Great palate and depth, young tannins and a subtle acidity as per the warm vintage; complex and elegant depth. Good intensity and length.

88 — Price C

Brunello di Montalcino 2011

100% Sangiovese grapes. Ages in barrels. Ruby. Wonderful nose of cherries and a hint of tobacco. Elegant and flavorful wine, balanced acidity, harmonic and long finish with a classic aftertaste.

CASTELGIOCONDO

Località Castelgiocondo
53024 Montalcino (SI)
Tel. +39 0577 84131
info@frescobaldi.it
www.frescobaldi.it

YEAR OF FOUNDATION 1989
NAME OF THE OWNER Marchesi de' Frescobaldi
TOTAL BOTTLES PRODUCED
VISITS TO THE WINERY - RESERVATION NEEDED
HECTARES OF VINEYARD 235
RESTAURANT

The ancient fortress of Castelgiocondo was built in the 1100s to protect the road that connected Siena to the sea. Today the hamlet still towers over this estate in Montalcino that Frescobaldi acquired in 1989 to expand their production of the best wines Tuscany produces. The very big 815-hectare estate includes some 150 hectares of Brunello vineyards and it is situated in southeastern part of Montalcino at an altitude of around 300m above sea level and the mixed soil gives the grapes a thousand different nuances.

94 — Price C

Brunello di Montalcino Ripe al Convento 2010

100% Sangiovese grapes. Ages in small sized oak barrel. Intense fruity note of blackberry, ripe cherry, mulberry. Earthy notes then citrus and spices. Rich palate, well defined, firm and elegant tannins, good acidity and very captivating finish.

 91   Price B

Brunello di Montalcino 2011

100% Sangiovese grapes. Ages in different sized barrels. Deep ruby. Intense and well defined nose, light hint of citrus and red fruit then tobacco and fine herbs. The palate shows a youth tannin but it is well defined and flavorful. Good depth and firm finish.

★★

CASTELL'IN VILLA

Località Castell'in Villa
53019 Castelnuovo Berardenga (SI)
Tel. +39 0577 359074
Fax +39 0577 359222
info@castellinvilla.com
www.castellinvilla.com

YEAR OF FOUNDATION 1971
NAME OF THE OWNER Coralia Pignatelli
TOTAL BOTTLES PRODUCED
DIRECT SALES
VISITS TO THE WINERY - RESERVATION NEEDED
HECTARES OF VINEYARD 54
HOSPITALITY
RESTAURANT
OLIVE OIL PRODUCTION

This is undoubtedly one of the most magical places in Chianti Classico. Here Princess Coralia Pignatelli della Leonessa cares for a structure built in 1200 that is in the middle of 298 hectares of property that includes 54 hectares of vineyards. One never gets tired of these classic wines that live long in the bottle and, after a glass, in memory.

94   Price B

Chianti Classico 2011

100% Sangiovese grapes. Ages in large casks. It's a textbook for the interpretation of the vintage for elegance and power. Generous aromas of ripe fruit and spices. Great acidity and umami character on the palate. Long finish and depth.

★★★

CASTELLARE DI CASTELLINA

Località Castellare
53011 Castellina in Chianti (SI)
Tel. +39 0577 742903
Fax +39 0577 742814
info@castellare.it
www.castellare.it
f CastellarediCastellina
🐦 @CastellareWines

YEAR OF FOUNDATION 1978
NAME OF THE OWNER Paolo Panerai
TOTAL BOTTLES PRODUCED 200,000
DIRECT SALES
VISITS TO THE WINERY - RESERVATION NEEDED
HECTARES OF VINEYARD 32
OLIVE OIL PRODUCTION

All the Castellare Chianti Classico have the most noble characteristics of Castellina wines, including their drinkability and ability to charm and seduce from the first sip. The same is true of the I Sodi di San Niccolò, a red wine made from Sangiovese and Malvasia Nera that ages in small kegs.

96   Price C

I Sodi di San Niccolò 2012

Blend of Sangiovese and Malvasia Nera grapes. Ages for 18 months in barrique. Floral, fresh and savory notes; tense and traditional palate and the altitude of the vines give the right acidity to compensate the warm vintage. Citrusy and strawberry notes. Firm palate, distinctive, very pleasant, old style, wonderful depth with sweet notes but very savory, fresh and with a harmonious finish.

91   Price B

Chianti Classico Riserva 2012

Blend of Sangiovese and Canaiolo grapes. Ages for 1 year in barrique. Ruby red. Courious smoky note then floral and forest berries hint. Agile and supple palate, tense but elegant and refined; good weight but fresh and lively.

87   Price C

Poggio ai Merli 2014

100% Merlot grapes. Ages for 18 months in barrique. Intense ruby. Quince juice, caramel, raspberry. Spicy palate, intriguing, citrusy and pleasant, strawberry relish; good finish.

86   Price A

Chianti Classico 2014

Blend of Sangiovese and Canaiolo grapes. Ages in large casks. Classic ruby. Floral and hay notes, olive, black cherry and a note of under spirit fruit. Good fruity palate but it lacks a bit of suppleness.

★★

CASTELLO BANFI

*Castello di Poggio alle Mura
53024 Montalcino (SI)
Tel. +39 0577 840111
Fax +39 0577 840444
banfi@banfi.it
www.castellobanfi.it*
f *CastelloBanfi*
🐦 *@CastelloBanfi*

YEAR OF FOUNDATION **1978**
NAME OF THE OWNER **Mariani Family**
TOTAL BOTTLES PRODUCED **10,500,000**
DIRECT SALES
VISITS TO THE WINERY - RESERVATION NEEDED
HECTARES OF VINEYARD **850**
HOSPITALITY
RESTAURANT
OLIVE OIL PRODUCTION

Without any doubts Castello Banfi is one of the most important winery in Montalcino history, What is most striking about the Banfi estate is its productive thoroughness. All their wines are well-made and are consistently among the best in their respective categories. And there is no lack of excellence. The wines most connected with Montalcino, the Poggio alle Mura line, are made with grapes from the vineyards closest to the castle, and continue to gain consistency and personality thanks to a modern approach that never infringes on tradition.

 96   Price D

Brunello di Montalcino Poggio all'Oro Riserva 2010

100% Sangiovese grapes. Ages in different sized barrel. A great return for this classic Brunello. Well defined, intense and austere nose with notes of sour cherry and red cherry; citrus, undergrowth and dark spices. Sleek palate, ample, austere with well extracted tannins, firm and with an outstanding finish.

94   Price C

Brunello di Montalcino Poggio alle Mura Riserva 2010

100% Sangiovese grapes. Ages in tonneau. Intense ruby. The nose offers intense fruity nose, modern with a defined spicy-fruity aromas. Powerful palate, firm but never tiring thank to a good tannic structure. Medium acidity and very pleasant palate. Juicy finish.

93   Price B

Excelsus 2012

100% Cabernet Sauvignon grapes. Ages in barrique. Very dark color. Complex nose of ink, cedar, currant, blueberry and pencil lead. Intense palate, firm structure, balanced tannin and a deep finish.

88   Price B

Brunello di Montalcino Poggio alle Mura 2011

100% Sangiovese grapes. Ages in small barells. Ruby color with garnet hues. Traditional nose of tobacco and Mediterranean herbs. Excessively young tannin that makes the palate slightly unbalanced. Firm and with a jammy aftertaste.

★★

CASTELLO D'ALBOLA

*Via Pian d' Albola, 31
53017 Radda in Chianti (SI)
Tel. +39 0577 738019
Fax +39 0577 738793*
S *castellodalbola*
*info@albola.it
www.albola.it*
f *Castello-dAlbola*
🐦 *@zonin1821*

YEAR OF FOUNDATION **1979**
NAME OF THE OWNER **Zonin Family**
TOTAL BOTTLES PRODUCED **600,000**
DIRECT SALES
VISITS TO THE WINERY - RESERVATION NEEDED
HECTARES OF VINEYARD **150**
HOSPITALITY
OLIVE OIL PRODUCTION

Castello d'Albola is set in one of the most beautiful locations in Chianti Classico and has one of the loveliest countrysides in the world. For sure this was one of the factors that convinced

Zonin family to buy it years ago and restore it to its ancient splendor. The modern winery was built with care not to spoil the landscape and the wines it produces are gaining attention in Italy and abroad thanks to their surprising quality, especially those in the new Grand Selezione classification.

■ 🗗 95   Price B
Chianti Classico Gran Selezione Solatìo 2012

100% Sangiovese grapes. Ages for 24 months in large barrels. Light ruby red. Elegant and complex nose, refined, rich and spicy. 'Radda' style, well balanced tannins, citrusy finish. Refreshing and savory palate; stylish even if a bit richer than previous vintages but it still has a very good drinkability.

■ 90   Price A
Chianti Classico 2013

Blend of Sangiovese and Canaiolo grapes. Ages for 12 months in oak barrels. Ruby color. Nose of strawberry, black pepper, currant and blueberry. Savory palate, pleasant, round, young tannins yet well integrated.

■ 88   Price B
Chianti Classico Riserva 2012

Blend of Sangiovese and Canaiolo grapes. Ages for 2 years in oak barrels. Ruby color with garnet rim. Developing nose of prune, cinnamon, woody notes, vanilla and jam. The palate is a bit heavy even if rich and complex with firm tannins, also oak tannins.

■ 87   Price B
Acciaiolo 2013

Blend of Sangiovese and Cabernet Sauvignon grapes. Ages for 20 months in barrique. Intense ruby. Oaky nose, strawberry and mothballs. The palate shows vibrant tannin; lightly warm, a bit rustic with wild notes and a good structure.

★

CASTELLO DEL TERRICCIO

Via Bagnoli, 16 - Località Terriccio
56040 Castellina Marittima (PI)
Tel. +39 050 699709
info@terriccio.it
www.terriccio.com
 castellodelterriccio
🐦 *@terriccio*

YEAR OF FOUNDATION 1921
NAME OF THE OWNER Gian Annibale Rossi di Medelana Serafini Ferri
TOTAL BOTTLES PRODUCED 150,000
DIRECT SALES
VISITS TO THE WINERY - RESERVATION NEEDED
HECTARES OF VINEYARD 50
OLIVE OIL PRODUCTION

Of the estate's 1,500 hectares, only 50 or so are vineyards. The castle's lucky proprietor is Gian Annibale Rossi di Medelana, Pucci Rossi for his friends, who runs the estate with decision and great personality and benefits from the consultancy of enologist Carlo Ferrini.

■ 🗗 96   Price C
Castello del Terriccio 2011

Blend of 50% Syrah and 25% Petit Verdot grapes with small percentage of other grape varieties. Ages for 18 months in barrique. Dark and dense ruby. Intense nose of fine herbs and eucalyptus, black fruits and spicy hints. Rich and balanced palate, velvety, ample and elegant with a long and eucalyptus finish.

■ 94   Price D
Lupicaia 2012

Blend of 90% Cabernet Sauvignon and small percentage of Petit Verdot grapes. Ages for 18 months in tonneau. Deep ruby. Austere nose, almost earthy, classic eucalyptus hint then pencil lead, blueberry, cedar peel. The palate is young, dense with a good depth, velvety with well refined tannin. Long, ample and lasting finish.

☐ 90   👍 Price A
Con Vento 2015

Blend of Sauvignon Blanc and Viognier grapes. Only stainless stell. Straw yellow. Good intensity on the nose that offers hint of anise and elderflower. Tomato leaf and floral notes. The palate is fresh, tense and fragrant with smoky and yeasty notes. Long and flavorful finish.

■ 90   Price B
Tassinaia 2012

Blend of Cabernet Sauvignon and Merlot grapes. Ages for 14 months in Allier barrique (part in second fill barrique). Ruby red. Intense and defined nose of red plum, cherry and floral notes. Very flavorful, fresh, good depth, good tannins and with a flavorful and ample finish.

⭐⭐⭐ CASTELLO DI AMA

Località Ama - Frazione Lecchi in Chianti
53013 Gaiole in Chianti (SI)
Tel. +39 0577 746031
info@castellodiama.com
www.castellodiama.com
🅕 *castellodiama.chianticlassico*
🐦 *@CastellodiAma*

YEAR OF FOUNDATION 1972
NAME OF THE OWNER Sebasti, Carini, Tradico Families
TOTAL BOTTLES PRODUCED 400,000
DIRECT SALES
VISITS TO THE WINERY - RESERVATION NEEDED
HECTARES OF VINEYARD 85
RESTAURANT
OLIVE OIL PRODUCTION

Castello di Ama is one of the leading estates in Chianti. This was thanks to wines that to define as convincing would be an understatement. Lorenza Sebasti and Marco Pallanti, partners in life and on the job, have for almost 30 years run this winery and can be proud of what they have achieved.

92 — Price C
Chianti Classico Gran Selezione San Lorenzo 2013

Blend of Sangiovese and other grapes for 24 months in large casks and barrique. Intense floral nose, warm note and intense fruity aromas. The palate is a bit exuberant but it has good weight and it will be balanced by the great acidity. Eucalyptus and savory finish.

90 — Price B
Chianti Classico Ama 2013

Blend of Sangiovese and small percentage of Merlot grapes. Ages for 12 months in barrique. Fascinating nose, floral notes of violet, rose and lavender. The palate is very savory; long and very fresh finish.

CASTELLO DI BOLGHERI

Via Lauretta 7 - Bolgheri
57022 Castagneto Carducci (LI)
Tel. +39 0565 762110
Fax +39 0565 762116
info@castellodibolgheri.eu
www.castellodibolgheri.eu
🅕 *Castello-di-Bolgheri*

YEAR OF FOUNDATION 1986
NAME OF THE OWNER Federico Zileri Dal Verme
TOTAL BOTTLES PRODUCED 100,000
DIRECT SALES
VISITS TO THE WINERY - RESERVATION NEEDED
HECTARES OF VINEYARD 53
HOSPITALITY
OLIVE OIL PRODUCTION

At the end of the famous tree-line road celebrated by Carducci is the small town of Bolgheri which is dominated by the old castle of the della Gheradesca counts. The castle and surround land was inherited by its current owners, the Zileri Dal Verme counts, who are directly involved in running the agricultural activities. The vineyards were planted in 1997 with grapes recognized for the appellation: Cabernet Sauvignon, Cabernet Franc, Merlot, Syrah and Petit Verdot. The winery is in town and uses cement vats and barrique.

92 — Price C
Bolgheri Superiore Castello di Bolgheri 2013

Blend of Cabernet Sauvignon, Merlot, Cabernet Franc and Petit Verdot grapes from the best plots around the Castle. Ages for 20 months in barrique and tonneau. Intense dark and deep ruby. Fresh and well defined nose: dark notes of coffee, pencil lead, basil and peach. Good palate, fresh and flavorful, ample and intense; long and with a good depth.

CASTELLO DI BOSSI

Località Bossi in Chianti
53019 Castelnuovo Berardenga (SI)
Tel. +39 0577 359330
Fax +39 0577 359048
🅢 *castello.di.bossi*
info@castellodibossi.it
www.castellodibossi.it
🅕 *CastellodiBossi*

YEAR OF FOUNDATION 1983
NAME OF THE OWNER Marco and Maurizio Bacci
TOTAL BOTTLES PRODUCED 687,000
DIRECT SALES
VISITS TO THE WINERY - RESERVATION NEEDED

HECTARES OF VINEYARD **124**
HOSPITALITY
OLIVE OIL PRODUCTION

info@castellodicacchiano.it
www.castellodicacchiano.it
🅕 castello.di.cacchiano

The Bacci family has vineyards in many different areas of Tuscany but the productive heart of their enterprise is in southern Chianti Classico, in Castello Berardenga, Castello di Bossi. Their wines have won many recognitions and are known throughout the world and are made with close attention to expression and modern tastes while never straying far from the typical way Tuscan wines respect their terroir.

YEAR OF FOUNDATION **1974**
NAME OF THE OWNER **Giovanni Ricasoli-Firidolfi**
TOTAL BOTTLES PRODUCED **120,000**
DIRECT SALES
VISITS TO THE WINERY - RESERVATION NEEDED
HECTARES OF VINEYARD **31**
HOSPITALITY
OLIVE OIL PRODUCTION

92 — Price C
Girolamo 2012

100% Merlot grapes. Ages for 24 months in barrique. Intense ruby red. Spicy nose with mulberry, strawberry jam, pepper, steely and minty notes. Good acidity on the palate with vibrant tannin: savory and pleasant.

92 — Price B
Il Grido Tenuta di Renieri 2012

100% Merlot grapes. Ages for 24 months in barrique. Notes of licorice, caramel and black cherry. Very pleasant palate, the fruity compound is balanced by the tannin, pleasantly fresh and finish with notes of blackberry and orange.

92 — Price A
Chianti Classico Tenuta di Renieri 2013

100% Sangiovese grapes. Ages for 12 months in large cask and barrique. Very interesting nose: fruity and smoky, spices and umami notes. Red and black fruit aftertaste, good acidity that enhance the juiciness; rich but not heavy.

90 — Price B
Chianti Classico Riserva Berardo 2012

100% Sangiovese grapes. Ages for 2 years in barrique. Toasted notes, red currant and strawberry. Juicy palate, warm and tense; pleasant and distinctive drinkability, captivating, classical and 'warm vintage' tannin that makes the wine supple yet with elegance and structure.

Castello di Cacchiano, owned by the Ricasoli-Firidolfi family, is an historic name in Chianti Classico and is one of the few estates that can boast centuries of winemaking tradition. Production is in the hands of Giovanni Ricasoli-Firidolfi, a very talented wine sector manager, while the wines have a traditional style.

92 — Price B
Chianti Classico Gran Selezione Millennio 2006

100% Sangiovese grapes. Ages for 2 years in barrique. Toasted notes, red currant and strawberry. Juicy palate, warm and tense; pleasant and distinctive drinkability, captivating, classical and 'warm vintage' tannin that makes the wine supple yet with elegance and structure.

90 — 👍 Price A
Chianti Classico 2011

100% Sangiovese grapes. Ages for 18 months in large casks. Ruby red. Raspberry, currant and mint, blood orange and tobacco. Juicy, fruity and full bodied palate. Wonderful supple finish.

88 — Price B
Fontemerlano 2014

100% Merlot grapes. Ages for 18 months in barrique. Dark ruby red. Light notes of resin and nail polish, oaky. On the palate offers dark fruit and good attack, evident tannin, decent depth with a continuous and defined fruity hint.

★
CASTELLO DI CACCHIANO

Località Cacchiano
53013 Gaiole in Chianti (SI)
Tel. +39 0577 787018

★★★
CASTELLO DI FONTERUTOLI

Via Ottone III di Sassonia, 5 - Località Fonterutoli
53011 Castellina in Chianti (SI)
Tel. +39 0577 73571

Fax +39 0577 735757
mazzei@mazzei.it
www.mazzei.it
marchesimazzei
@MarchesiMazzei

YEAR OF FOUNDATION 1435
NAME OF THE OWNER Marchesi Mazzei
TOTAL BOTTLES PRODUCED 700,000
DIRECT SALES
VISITS TO THE WINERY - RESERVATION NEEDED
HECTARES OF VINEYARD 117
HOSPITALITY
RESTAURANT
OLIVE OIL PRODUCTION

Fonterutoli today is owned by the by the Mazzei family and is one of the Chianti Classico wineries that has seem the greatest improvements in recent years. For some 25 years now it has been going through a kind of winemaking revolution that has focused on selecting Sangiovese clones. Also in Tenuta Belguardo, winery in Maremma bought in the '90s by the Mazzei family, they have demonstrated to be able to produce at high level quality. The same in Tenuta Zisola, in South-East Sicily.

97   Price B
Chianti Classico Gran Selezione Castello di Fonterutoli 2012

Blend of 92% Sangiovese and 8% of Colorino and Malvasia Nera grapes. Ages for 20 months in barrique. Deep and lively ruby red. Very refined nose: licorice, sweet spices, black cherry and subtle hint of vanilla. Tense palate, refined, thin and essential, extremely elegant and wonderful length.

93   Price D
Siepi 2013

Blend of Sangiovese and Merlot grapes. Ages for 20 months in barrique. Dark ruby red. Complex nose: woody and spicy notes then raspberry, kirsch and sweet tobacco. Mouth filling palate, tense, full bodied, warm, lightly tannic, wonderful length.

91   Price B
Chianti Classico Ser Lapo 2013

Blend of 90% Sangiovese and 10% Merlot grapes. Ages for 1 year in barrique of which 50% are new. Lively ruby garnet. Fragrant and defined nose of black cherry, vanilla and subtle aromas of tobacco. Tense and full bodied palate, warm but supple and with a good length.

88   Price A
Chianti Classico Fonterutoli 2014

Blend of 90% Sangiovese grapes with small percentage of Malvasia Nera, Colorino and Merlot. Ages for 1 year in different sized oak barrel. Lively ruby. Fragrant, fruity, a bit simple with notes of black cherry and blood orange. Tense palate, pleasantly savory, good body.

87   Price A
Morellino di Scansano Tenuta Belguardo Bronzone Riserva 2013

100% Sangiovese grapes. Ages for 14 months in 40% new barrique. Ruby red. Well defined nose; spicy and sweet forest fruit aromas. Full bodied, captivating, velvety with ripe tannins and a good finish.

CASTELLO DI MELETO

Località Castello di Meleto
53013 Gaiole in Chianti (SI)
Tel. +39 0577 749217
Fax +39 0577 749762
castellodimeleto
market@castellomeleto.it
www.castellomeleto.it
castello.meleto
@castellomeleto

YEAR OF FOUNDATION 1968
NAME OF THE OWNER Viticola Toscana
TOTAL BOTTLES PRODUCED 600,000
DIRECT SALES
VISITS TO THE WINERY - RESERVATION NEEDED
HECTARES OF VINEYARD 125
HOSPITALITY
RESTAURANT
OLIVE OIL PRODUCTION

At the center of this vast estate is a castle of outstanding beauty which has been surrounded by vineyards since the end of the 13th century. The lion's share of the vineyards, mostly planted with Sangiovese together with some other varieties, date back to the 1990s and are reaching their expressive peak. It should be noted that a decisive shift towards quality in recent years has restored value and dignity to the Sangiovese and indigenous grapes used to make wines in large barrels.

93   Price B
Chianti Classico Gran Selezione 2012

100% Sangiovese grapes. Ages for 2 years different sized barrels. Intense ruby garnet. Captivating and lightly developed nose, kirsch and black cherry notes, hint of cocoa on the background. Tense and savory palate, wonderful body yet supple with refined tannins and long finish.

88   Price A
Chianti Classico 2013

Blend of 80% Sangiovese, 15% Cabernet Sauvignon and 5% Syrah grapes. Ages for 1 year in different sized barrel. Shiny ruby red. Smoky nose then classical notes of black cherry, small berries and sweet spices. Savory palate, tense and with a good length.

★★★
CASTELLO DI MONSANTO

Via Monsanto, 8
50021 Barberino Val d'Elsa (FI)
Tel. +39 055 8059000
monsanto@castellodimonsanto.it
www.castellodimonsanto.it
 castello.dimonsanto
 @castelmonsanto

YEAR OF FOUNDATION 1962
NAME OF THE OWNER Fabrizio Bianchi
TOTAL BOTTLES PRODUCED 450,000
DIRECT SALES
VISITS TO THE WINERY - RESERVATION NEEDED
HECTARES OF VINEYARD 72
OLIVE OIL PRODUCTION

This wine estate is now over 50 years old and was founded by a very young Fabrizio Bianchi. For a few years now he has been assisted by his daughter Laura who shares his passion for wine and the vineyards. Castello di Monsanto today is a pillar of Chianti Classico tradition and its reserves, bold and able to age, are famous around the world.

93   Price B
Nemo 2012

100% Cabernet sauvignon grapes. Ages for 18 months in barrique. Intense ruby purple. Rich and developing nose, meaty and 'sunny': blueberry, blackberry, strawberry and vanilla. Good tension on the palate, complex and pleasant length.

92   Price C
Chianti Classico Il Poggio Riserva 2011

Blend of Sangiovese, Canaiolo and Colorino grapes from a 310m altitude. Ages for 20 months in French barrique. The nose is rather warm with eucalyptus and Mediterranean notes, bay leaf, sour cherry and myrtle. Spicy palate, vanilla, mint and rose aftertaste; good weight. The oaky notes are quite upfront and the finish offers developing tannin.

91   👍 Price A
Chianti Classico 2014

100% Sangiovese grapes. Ages for 15 months in different sized barrel. Ruby red. Floral and savory nose, strawberry and black cherry, tobacco and spices. Full and dynamic palate despite the challenging vintage.

90   Price B
Chianti Classico Riserva 2013

Blend of Sangiovese, Canaiolo and Colorino grapes. Ages for 34 months in different sized barrel. Vibrant and intense nose, aromatic and fruity then a light warm note might add weight to a palate that offers a spicy tannin and a savory acidity that enhance a citrusy and sour cherry finish.

87   Price C
Sangioveto 2009

Blend of Sangiovese, Canaiolo and Colorino grapes. Ages for 34 months in different sized barrel. Vibrant and intense nose, aromatic and fruity then a light warm note might add weight to a palate that offers a spicy tannin and a savory acidity that enhance a citrusy and sour cherry finish.

★★
CASTELLO DI QUERCETO

Via Alessandro François, 2
50022 Greve in Chianti (FI)
Tel. +39 055 85921
Fax +39 055 5892200
querceto@castellodiquerceto.it
www.castellodiquerceto.it
 Castello-di-Querceto
 @CastQuerceto

YEAR OF FOUNDATION 1897
NAME OF THE OWNER Alessandro François
TOTAL BOTTLES PRODUCED 600,000
DIRECT SALES
VISITS TO THE WINERY - RESERVATION NEEDED

HECTARES OF VINEYARD **60**
HOSPITALITY
OLIVE OIL PRODUCTION

Alessandro François has been producing his austere wines in Lucolena, at the northeast border of Chianti Classico, for dozens of years. His wines have a great capacity to age and are the product quality winegrowing and a very traditional approach in the winery.

 94   Price B
Chianti Classico Gran Selezione Il Picchio 2012

Blend of Sangiovese and Canaiolo grapes. Ages for 2 years in barrique. Ruby red. Very fruity and defined nose with notes of coffee and eucalyptus. Well-structured body with great tannins, dense fruity finish with light bitter notes that stimulates and refreshes the palate.

91   Price B
Il Cignale 2012

Blend of Cabernet Sauvignon and Merlot grapes. Ages for 24 months in barrique. Dark ruby red. Balanced and vibrant nose, savory and fresh red fruit notes. On the palate citrus and raspberry aftertaste, fresh and savory, rich, smooth and refined tannins.

91   Price B
Chianti Classico Riserva 2013

Blend of Sangiovese, Canaiolo and Colorino grapes. Ages for 20 months in barrique. Austere, ripe and firm, licorice, red and black currant. The palate is livelier on the palate, precise tannins, tense and with a long and fulfilling finish.

87   Price A
Chianti Classico 2014

Blend of Sangiovese and Canaiolo grapes. Ages for 10 months in large casks. Intense and rich nose, red and black fruits, flavorful tannin that ease the drink.

CASTELLO DI RADDA

Località Il Becco, 101a
53017 Radda in Chianti (SI)
Tel. +39 0577 738992
info@castellodiradda.com
www.castellodiradda.it
castelloradda
@CastellodiRadda

YEAR OF FOUNDATION **2003**
NAME OF THE OWNER Gussalli Beretta Family
TOTAL BOTTLES PRODUCED **150,000**
DIRECT SALES
VISITS TO THE WINERY - RESERVATION NEEDED
HECTARES OF VINEYARD **32**

This relatively new estate (2003) was a challenge taken up by the Gussalli Beretta family using vines of a certain age and they quickly carved out a niche in the excellent Radda in Chianti area, perhaps the Chianti Classico area that has stood out the most in recent years.

91   Price B
Chianti Classico Riserva 2012

Blend of Sangiovese and Canaiolo grapes. Ages for 10 months in large casks. Intense and rich nose, red and black fruits, flavorful tannin that ease the drink.

88   Price A
Chianti Classico 2014

Blend of Sangiovese and small percentage of other grape varieties. Ages for 12 months in large cask. Eucalyptus, floral, crunchy and savory; slightly thin but with a citrusy and intriguing finish.

CASTELLO DI VERRAZZANO

Via Citille, 32a - Località Greti
50022 Greve in Chianti (FI)
Tel. +39 055 854243
Fax +39 055 854241
info@verrazzano.com
www.verrazzano.com
castellodiverrazzano
@StaffVerrazzano

YEAR OF FOUNDATION **1958**
NAME OF THE OWNER Luigi Giovanni Cappellini
TOTAL BOTTLES PRODUCED **300,000**
DIRECT SALES
VISITS TO THE WINERY - RESERVATION NEEDED
HECTARES OF VINEYARD **52**
HOSPITALITY
OLIVE OIL PRODUCTION

The winery has its headquarters in te castle that once belonged to Giovanni de Verrazzano, the great navigator who for first entered the New York Bay and after whom the bridge linking Brooklyn to Staten Island is named. Today this manor and is vineyards are owned by Luigi Cappellini who honors its great past by producing excellent wines. The estate is situated in the northern part of the Chianti Classico district, an area that is home to elegant and balanced reds.

■ 90   Price B
Chianti Classico Gran Selezione Sassello Vigneto Querciolina 2012

100% Sangiovese grapes. Ages for 2 years in different sized barrel. Lively ruby garnet. Nose of under spirit black cherry, violet, light spicy notes and subtle woody hints. Tense palate, typical, composed, warm with still young tannins and good length.

■ 87   Price A
Chianti Classico 2013

Blend of Sangiovese grapes with small percentage of Canaiolo grapes. Ages for 18 months in large French cask. Lively ruby red. Fruity, defined and clean nose: typical notes of black cherry and light spicy hints. Thin palate, tense and very pleasant, medium bodied and decent length.

★★
CASTELLO DI VOLPAIA

Località Volpaia
53017 Radda in Chianti (SI)
Tel. +39 0577 738066
Fax +39 0577 738619
S *volpaia.*
info@volpaia.com
www.volpaia.com
f *volpaia*
🐦 *@volpaia*

YEAR OF FOUNDATION **1966**
NAME OF THE OWNER **Giovanna Stianti**
TOTAL BOTTLES PRODUCED **200,000**
DIRECT SALES
VISITS TO THE WINERY
HECTARES OF VINEYARD **46**
HOSPITALITY
RESTAURANT
OLIVE OIL PRODUCTION

The wines of Castello di Volpaia have always had their own style determined for the most part by the fact that the vineyards sit at a high altitude and thus produce reds that do not have

excessive body and are very fragrant. The 12th century fortified hamlet is well worth a visit as are the cellars that were carved out of the rock.

■ 93   Price B
Chianti Classico Coltassala Riserva 2012

100% Sangiovese grapes. Ages for 18 months in barrique. Ample nose, delicate, opulent but very elegant: fruity notes and eucalyptus hints. Firm and classic palate with continuous fruity aromas that remind sour cherry, bay leaf, mint and cardamom. Lively but not aggressive tannin.

■ 90   👍 Price A
Chianti Classico 2014

100% Sangiovese grapes. Ages for 12 months in large casks. Luminous, delicate and thin; the palate is subtle but well executed. An elegant Sangiovese that makes the most out of a challenging vintage.

■ 87   Price B
Balifico 2012

Blend of Sangiovese and Cabernet Sauvignon grapes. Ages for 18 months in barrique. Dark and rich; sweet fruity notes and Asian spices hint. Firm palate with a long fruity aftertaste balanced by good tannin.

CASTELLO ROMITORIO

Località Romitorio, 279
53024 Montalcino (SI)
Tel. +39 0577 847212
Fax +39 0577 847110
info@castelloromitorio.com
www.castelloromitorio.com
f *Castello-Romitorio*

YEAR OF FOUNDATION **1985**
NAME OF THE OWNER **Sandro Chia**
TOTAL BOTTLES PRODUCED **150,000**
DIRECT SALES
VISITS TO THE WINERY - RESERVATION NEEDED
HECTARES OF VINEYARD **25**
HOSPITALITY
OLIVE OIL PRODUCTION

This estate belongs to Sandro Chia who is one of Italy's leading artists. More than a castle, it reminds the manor of Don Rodrigo in The Betrothed but when you go inside this impression quickly vanishes when you see his works of art that depict scenes between dreams and reality.

The estate this year is once again offering top quality wines after a few years that were under par and we are glad to see this. The wines have a personal style with one eye on classic tradition and the other looking forward and this tension has resulted in very good wine and that is all that matters.

 96   Price D

Brunello di Montalcino Riserva 2010

100% Sangiovese grapes. Ages in tonneau and other oak barrel. Intense and shiny ruby. Intense nose of citrusy notes, lightly earthy then classic red fruit hint and sweet spices. Extremely elegant palate, very refined tannins and a very long finish.

90   Price C

Brunello di Montalcino Filo di Seta 2011

100% Sangiovese grapes. Ages in tonneau and barrique. Intense ruby red. Aromas of ink, pencil lead and light citrusy notes and black cherry. Balanced palate; elegant and with good depth, firm tannins and good savoriness.

86   Price B

Brunello di Montalcino 2011

100% Sangiovese grapes. Ages in oak barrels. Classic ruby red with garnet rim. Developed nose of tobacco and fresh fine herbs. Very balanced palate, good depth and finish.

CASTELLO VICCHIOMAGGIO

Via Vicchiomaggio, 4
50022 Greve in Chianti (FI)
Tel. +39 055 854079
Fax +39 055 853911
info@vicchiomaggio.it
www.vicchiomaggio.it
 Castello-Vicchiomaggio
 @vicchiomaggio

YEAR OF FOUNDATION **1965**
NAME OF THE OWNER **John F. Matta**
TOTAL BOTTLES PRODUCED **400,000**
DIRECT SALES
VISITS TO THE WINERY - RESERVATION NEEDED
HECTARES OF VINEYARD **32**
HOSPITALITY
RESTAURANT
OLIVE OIL PRODUCTION

This fairy tale castle of John Matta every year produces an always more reliable line of wines. Since a couple of years it has included a Gran Selezione that has given prestige to the estate's Sangiovese. Together with it, a series of wines of great level among which the famous Ripa delle More, a classic Supertuscan.

93   Price B

Ripa delle More 2013

Blend of Sangiovese, Cabernet Sauvignon and Merlot grapes, 20 months in barrique. Well defined fruity nose then delicate notes of spices and oak. Tannins and acidity balanced by great structure, fruity aftertaste: long and fresh, caramel, forest berries and a flavorful finish.

91   Price D

FSM 2012

100% Merlot grapes, 16 months in new barrique. Evolved fruity notes on the nose, sweet aromas of jam, apple tart, almonds and figs. Complex, tense and fresh on the palate, pleasant tannins.

91   Price B

Chianti Classico Gran Selezione La Prima 2011

Blend of Sangiovese and Merlot, 18 months in barrique. Notes of peach and strawberries, intense and rich. Nice on the palate with a deep and attractive fruit, agile and rocky tannins, acidity and structure.

CASTIGLION DEL BOSCO

Località Castiglion del Bosco
53024 Montalcino (SI)
Tel. +39 0577 1913750
wine@castigliondelbosco.com
www.castigliondelbosco.com

YEAR OF FOUNDATION **1888**
NAME OF THE OWNER **Massimo Ferragamo**
TOTAL BOTTLES PRODUCED **250,000**
DIRECT SALES
VISITS TO THE WINERY - RESERVATION NEEDED
HECTARES OF VINEYARD **62**
HOSPITALITY
RESTAURANT
OLIVE OIL PRODUCTION

The major overhaul embarked upon by the Ferragamo family is just about finished. The restoration of the ancient hamlet of Castiglion del Bosco was completed a few years ago and while the golf course still needs some finishing touches, the work done to the vineyards and winery are producing more than satisfying results. The ample spaces, cutting-edge technology and the definition of the wines were achieved thanks to the estate's enologist Cecilia Leoneschi. The vineyards, of which 50 hectares are registered Brunello, have all been divided into parcels and are harvested separately. The winery is very beautiful but above all functional with barrels of various sized barrels and vats that are totally controlled. This year they presented a limited edition of a new Brunello named 1100 in homage to Montalcino tradition.

---

 93   Price D

Brunello di Montalcino 1100 Ris.2010

100% Sangiovese grapes. Ages in 30 hl barrel. Ruby red with garnet hues. Classic aromas of black cherry and white cherry, undergrowth, ink, tobacco and a hint of licorice. Austere and elegant palate, very flavorful and with a good depth. Very sleek but still young tannin. Austere and tense wine but with a great character.

---

 91   Price C

Brunello di Montalcino Campo del Drago 2010

100% Sangiovese grapes. Ages in barrique and tonneau. Intense and shiny ruby. Intense and modern nose with defined fruity and spicy notes. Very good palate. Cherry, blackcurrant, citrusy and pleasant then Mediterranean spices. Intense palate with tense acidity, developed tannin, firm and flavorful finish.

---

 85   Price B

Brunello di Montalcino 2011

100% Sangiovese grapes. Ages in different sized barrel. Dark ruby. Classic nose of yellow peach, very floral with a hint of tobacco and dried herbs. Balanced palate, good weight but the finish is slightly short for its vibrant tannins.

---

www.cecchi.net
f CecchiWinery
🐦 @cecchiwinery

YEAR OF FOUNDATION 1893
NAME OF THE OWNER Cecchi Family
TOTAL BOTTLES PRODUCED 7,200,000
VISITS TO THE WINERY - RESERVATION NEEDED
HECTARES OF VINEYARD 292

It can happen that someone who is not an expert in winegrowing and enology will produce a few thousand bottles of good wine. But to produce millions of them is quite another matter, especially if the wines are distinguished by their consistency and reliability. This is the case of Cecchi di Castellina, a big and famous winery that for some years has with great determination embarked on the road towards quality.

---

 92   Price B

Chianti Classico Riserva di Famiglia 2013

Blend of 90% Sangiovese and 10% of other grape varieties. Ages for 1 year in barrique and tonneau. Classic ruby red. Mobern but very interesting, savory balance, rich dark fruit, mint, bay leaf, raspberry and strawberry. Ample and aromatic, flavorful tannin.

---

 90   Price A

Chianti Classico 2014

Blend of Sangiovese with small percentage of Colorino grapes. Ages for 1 year in small barrels. Nice fruity aromas of raspberry and blackberry. Exuberant palate, flavorful and fruity; nice finish on black pepper and spicy notes.

---

 88   Price B

Chianti Classico Villa Cerna Riserva 2013

Blend of Sangiovese with small percentage of Colorino grapes. Ages for 14 months in different sized barrel. Body, weight and tension; acidity, flavorful palate with rich fruity notes; developing but intriguing tannin.

★★

CECCHI

Località Casina dei Ponti, 56
53011 Castellina in Chianti (SI)
Tel. + 39 0577 54311
cecchi@cecchi.net

★★★

CERBAIONA

Via Cerbaia, 146
53024 Montalcino (SI)
Tel. +39 0577 848660
cerbaiona@alice.it

YEAR OF FOUNDATION 1977
NAME OF THE OWNER Gary Rieschel
TOTAL BOTTLES PRODUCED 16,000
DIRECT SALES
VISITS TO THE WINERY - RESERVATION NEEDED
HECTARES OF VINEYARD 3

The change at Cerbaiona has been epochal to say the least. Diego and Nora Molinari sold the estate to a foreign investment company and the estate is now run by Matthew Fioretti. The first changes he made were to change enologist and uproot the Toscana IGT vineyard. Soon the olive groves will also be uprooted to make from for more vineyards. Brunello 2011 is thus the last wine to be bottled by the previous owners.

 94   Price C

Brunello di Montalcino 2011

100% Sangiovese grapes. Ages in barrels. Ruby with a garnet rim. Classic cherry note, sour cherry and dark tobacco hint. Firm palate, well integrated tannins and juicy acidity. Elegant depth, medium weight and wonderful length for this vintage.

 90   Price B

Rosso di Montalcino 2013

100% Sangiovese grapes. Ages in barrels. Warm nose with spicy and herbaceous notes, dark cherry. The palate is a bit tight with a young tannins but it has a good length.

CESANI

Località Pancole, 82/D
53037 San Gimignano (SI)
Tel. +39 0577 955084
info@cesani.it
www.cesani.it

YEAR OF FOUNDATION Inizio anni '50
NAME OF THE OWNER Cesani Family
TOTAL BOTTLES PRODUCED 40,000
DIRECT SALES
VISITS TO THE WINERY - RESERVATION NEEDED
HECTARES OF VINEYARD 19
CERTIFIED ORGANIC VITICULTURE
OLIVE OIL PRODUCTION

This estate was set up in the 1950s based on the common model for the time with various cultivations which are still being produced today, including saffron and olive oil. It modern-

ized with the creation of holiday accommodations some 15 years ago. The estate is only six kilometers from the splendid town of San Gimignano and they have around 20 hectares of vineyards. Wine production is mostly centered on Vernaccia for the whites and Sangiovese for the red wines. Letizia Cesani, heir of the founder and president of the Consorzio di Tutela producer association, has vastly improved the estate and lifted the Sanice cru Vernaccia to a high level. The winery is modern and well-equipped while the wines became certified organic in 2012.

☐ 91   👍 Price A

Vernaccia di San Gimignano Sanice 2013

100% Vernaccia grapes. Partially aged in different sized barrels. Shiny straw yellow. Well defined smoky notes, intense floral and fruity notes of loquat, hint of anise and aromatic herbs. Rich palate, intense and savory; good weight. Complex and pleasant drinkability enhanced by captivating pink salt aromas.

☐ 86   👍 Price A

Vernaccia di San Gimignano 2015

100% Vernaccia grapes. Stainless steel. Straw yellow. Well defined and intense nose: fresh fruit and a hint of undergrowth. Balanced palate with good acidity and decent structure. Flavorful and floral finish.

CIACCI PICCOLOMINI D'ARAGONA

Località Molinello - Frazione Castelnuovo dell'Abate
53024 Montalcino (SI)
Tel. +39 0577 835616
info@ciaccipiccolomini.com
www.ciaccipiccolomini.com
ciaccipiccolominidaragona
@cpdavini

YEAR OF FOUNDATION 1985
NAME OF THE OWNER Paolo and Lucia Bianchini
TOTAL BOTTLES PRODUCED 200,000
DIRECT SALES
VISITS TO THE WINERY - RESERVATION NEEDED
HECTARES OF VINEYARD 40
OLIVE OIL PRODUCTION

A beautiful reality in the hamlet of Castelnuovo dell'Abate, in the southwest corner of Montalcino. The old cellar under an historic building is amazing but the productive winery is now closer to the vineyards which are situated in the subzone of Sesta, an authentic Montalcino cru. The new winery uses wood vats for fermentation and 20 to 50-hectoliter barrels for aging. The wines have a classic style and are bold with a great capacity to age with little concession to fads and immediate drinkability. While bold, these wines have refined tannins and a rather austere aroma.

YEAR OF FOUNDATION **1998**
NAME OF THE OWNER **Donatella Cinelli Colombini**
TOTAL BOTTLES PRODUCED **160,000**
DIRECT SALES
VISITS TO THE WINERY - RESERVATION NEEDED
HECTARES OF VINEYARD **33**
HOSPITALITY
RESTAURANT
OLIVE OIL PRODUCTION

Donatella Cinelli Colombini, who was recently made a 'Knight of the Republic', runs her estate with great skill and professionalism. Casato Prime Donne is all run by women with its headquarters and some of its vineyards in the northern zone of Montalcino. The wines have changed in style in recent years to reflect more the traits of elegance and distinct acidity found in the grapes from northern area. She uses different aging methods for the two Brunello she produces. Prime Donne ages in small French barrels, while her vintage wine uses big barrels.

 97   Price D

Brunello di Montalcino Vigna di Pianrosso Santa Caterina d'Oro Ris. 2010

100% Sangiovese grapes. Ages in barrel. Ruby. Dark nose with floral notes then fruity hint of sour cherry and black cherry. Powerful palate, dense and with a young tannin. Balanced acidity. Austere and powerful depth. It will age wonderfully for a long time.

90   Price B

Brunello di Montalcino 2011

100% Sangiovese grapes. Ages in barrel. Ruby. Clean and warm notes of under spirit cherry and hint of jam, myrtle. Good palate with a good depth on fresh but intense notes. Flavorful finish.

88   Price A

Rosso di Montalcino 2014

100% Sangiovese grapes. Ages in barrels. Shiny ruby. Defined nose, lightly herbaceous, black cherry and Mediterranean herbs. Medium bodied, the tannin is a bit tight but it has a good depth and good drinkability.

⭐

DONATELLA CINELLI COLOMBINI

Località Casato, 17
53024 Montalcino (SI)
Tel. +39 0577 849421
Fax +39 0577 849353
vino@cinellicolombini.it
www.cinellicolombini.it
f *Donatella-Cinelli-Colombini*
🐦 *@news_donatella*

88   Price B

Brunello di Montalcino 2011

100% Sangiovese grapes. Ages in different sized barrel. Ruby. Warm nose, fruity and floral with a light leafy hint. The palate is still young but the tannin is not bitter but vibrant. Firm palate and decent weight but the depth is limited. Flavorful finish on dark notes.

 ★★

COL D'ORCIA

Via Giuncheti
53024 Montalcino (SI)
Tel. +39 0577 80891
Fax +39 0577 844018
S *Coldorcia*
info@coldorcia.it
www.coldorcia.it
f *coldorcia.montalcino*
🐦 *@coldorcia*

YEAR OF FOUNDATION **1973**
NAME OF THE OWNER **Francesco Marone Cinzano**
TOTAL BOTTLES PRODUCED **800,000**
DIRECT SALES
VISITS TO THE WINERY - RESERVATION NEEDED
HECTARES OF VINEYARD **142**
HOSPITALITY

RESTAURANT
CERTIFIED ORGANIC VITICULTURE
OLIVE OIL PRODUCTION

YEAR OF FOUNDATION **1998**
NAME OF THE OWNER **Franca Luana Buzzegoli**
TOTAL BOTTLES PRODUCED **80,000**
DIRECT SALES
VISITS TO THE WINERY - RESERVATION NEEDED
HECTARES OF VINEYARD **13**

This magnificent estate extends on the southern side of Montalcino up to the hamlet of Sant' Angelo in Colle. It is run by Francesco Marone Cinzano and has one of the few cellars with bottles from the mid-1970s. The Brunello has an extremely classic style and ages long in large barrels made of Slovenian wood. The estate owns one of the most famous vineyards in the whole appellation, Poggio al Vento, which produces the grapes for their most important wine and that carries its name and its only produced in the best vintages.

Visiting the Uccellina Nature Park in Maremma is a wonderful experience, a habitat full of Mediterranean colors and aromas. On the outskirts of the park, some 15km from the sea, is the 18-hectare hillside estate of Alberto Carnasciali and his wife Franca Buzzegoli. The estate has some 13 hectares of vineyards planted with grapes typical to the area, which is the DOC Morellino di Scansano appellation, and thus include Sangioves together with some Vermentino to make a fresh and easy to drink white. They also cultivate Merlot and Cabernet Sauvignon to make their classic IGT wine.

 95   Price B
Olmaia 2012

100% Cabernet Sauvignon grapes. Ages for 2 years in barrique. Intense nose: blueberry, blackberry then a hint of pencil lead and cedar, also candied cedar. Classic palate with young but harmonious and well integrated tannins. The finish is very elegant and complex.

88   Price A
Morellino di Scansano 2015

Blend of 90% Sangiovese with small percentage of other allowed grapes. Ages for 4 months in used barrique. Ruby with violet hues. Intense and fruity nose, cherry and black cherry. The palate is full, warm, low acidity but good depth. Long and fruity finish.

91   Price C
Brunello di Montalcino Nastagio 2011

100% Sangiovese grapes. Ages in tonneau and different sized barrels. The latest wine of the winery has its debut in a challenging vintage but it performed well. Ruby with garnet hue. Classic nose of spices, fine herbs, yellow peach and sweet tobacco. Elegant and firm palate, pleasant and fulfilling palate with refined tannin.

87   Price B
Morellino di Scansano Rovente Riserva 2013

Blend of 90% Sangiovese and Syrah grapes. Ages for 12 months in tonneau. Ruby garnet. The nose offers notes of sweet spices and light vegetal notes, while the fruity compound is a bit subtle. Meaty and rich palate, sweet oaky notes, ripe and smooth tannins, vanilla aftertaste.

87   Price B
Brunello di Montalcino 2011

100% Sangiovese grapes. Ages in barrels. Ruby garnet. Intense nose with warm notes of red fruit and a hint of blackberry and prune. Light eucalyptus aromas, convincing and classical palate.

COLLE BERETO

Località Colle Bereto
53017 Radda in Chianti (SI)
Tel. +39 0577 738083
Fax +39 0577 738083
colle.bereto@collebereto.it
www.collebereto.it

COL DI BACCHE

Strada di Cupi Montiano
58051 Magliano in Toscana (GR)
Tel. +39 0564 589538
 carna.azienda
info@coldibacche.com
www.coldibacche.com
 ColDiBaccheAziendaAgricola
🐦 *@ColDiBacche*

YEAR OF FOUNDATION
NAME OF THE OWNER **Pinzauti Family**
TOTAL BOTTLES PRODUCED **20,000**
DIRECT SALES

VISITS TO THE WINERY - RESERVATION NEEDED
HECTARES OF VINEYARD 15
OLIVE OIL PRODUCTION

The estate of the Pinzauti family, entrepreneurs in the fashion sector, is an act of love towards Chianti Classico and its magnificent landscape. They pay the same attention to their vineyards and the estate as they do to the creations they sell around the world. The details are what make the difference and they are slowing adopting the typical patience farmers have in waiting for the harvest and for results. Their enologist consultant is Nicolò d'Affittò.

90   Price B

Il Tocco 2014

100% Merlot grapes. Ages for 18 months in barrique. Intense ruby. Nose of raspberry, currant and mint. Rich and mouth filling wine, caramel and resin, well integrated woody notes, citrus, red pepper. Savory palate, good grip and flavorful tannins, elegant and refined finish.

89   Price B

Il Cenno 2014

100% Pinot Noir grapes. Ages for 15 months in barrique. Light color. Refined and distinctive, red and black forest berries, lavender and juniper. Dry palate, note very long but pleasantly smooth with refined tannin and fresh notes of cherry and black pepper.

88   Price B

Chianti Classico Riserva 2013

Blend of Sangiovese and other grape varieties. Ages for 18 months in barrique. Meaty and sweet notes, black pepper and blueberry. The palate is delicate, captivating and with very ripe fruity notes, powerful and savory.

COLLE SANTA MUSTIOLA

Via delle Torri, 86/a
53043 Chiusi (SI)
Tel. +39 0578 20525
info@poggioaichiari.it
www.poggioaichiari.it
ColleSantaMustiola

YEAR OF FOUNDATION **Inizio Novecento**
NAME OF THE OWNER **Fabio Cenni**
TOTAL BOTTLES PRODUCED **18,000**

DIRECT SALES
VISITS TO THE WINERY - RESERVATION NEEDED
HECTARES OF VINEYARD 5

Fabio Cenni was a physician and a passionate wine lover. At the beginning of the 1990s he planted a vineyard and restored some old ones (some still with ungrafted vines along with clones from older vines) and began to make wine. His estate is in the Chiusi township in a lovely position at around 300m above sea level and here he produced his first estate wine, Poggio ai Chiari. Even more beautiful and evocative was his first cellar that was an Etruscan tomb that proved to be perfect in regard to average annual temperature and relative humidity.

94   Price B

Poggio ai Chiari 2009

100% Sangiovese grapes. Ages at least 2 years in tonneau and 20hl barrels. Intense ruby. Intense nose with hint of sour cherry, white spices and tobacco then eucalyptus and very refined floral notes. Intense, elegant and austere palate, firm, juicy depth, very long finish. The winning choice was to release this wine after 7 years.

90   Price B

Vigna Flavia 2010

Blend of 97% Sangiovese and 3% Colorino grapes. Ages in tonneau and large cask. Intense and shiny ruby. Well defined and intense nose with fruity notes. Austere fruity hints of cherry and black cherry. Intense and elegant palate, firm, elegant thank to a much defined tannin and to a balanced acidity. Flavorful finish with good depth.

★★

COLLEMASSARI

Località Poggi del Sasso
58044 Cinigiano (GR)
Tel. +39 0564 990496
info@collemassari.it
www.collemassari.it
ColleMassari
@ColleMassari

YEAR OF FOUNDATION **1998**
NAME OF THE OWNER **Maria Iris Tipa Bertarelli and Claudio Tipa**
TOTAL BOTTLES PRODUCED **600,000**
DIRECT SALES

VISITS TO THE WINERY - RESERVATION NEEDED
HECTARES OF VINEYARD 110
HOSPITALITY
CERTIFIED ORGANIC VITICULTURE
OLIVE OIL PRODUCTION

Claudio Tipa continues undaunted in his quest to boost the entire Montecucco appellation by drawing attention to it with the quality of his own wines and vineyards. His style is modern from a technical point but his choice of grapes is traditional and he mostly uses Sangiovese, although he does not snub other red variety. His modern and efficient winery has a cellar where the wood barrels are no larger than 40hl.

95   Price B
Montecucco Sangiovese Poggio Lombrone Riserva 2012

100% Sangiovese grapes from a 45 years old single vineyard. Ages for 2 years in 40hl Slavonian oak casks. Ruby with garnet hues. intesnse and defined nose, sweet cherry and black cherry notes then blackberry jam and eucalyptus hints. Mouth filling and smooth palate, juicy, fruity and captivating with firm tannins and a balanced and elegant finish.

90   Price B
Montecucco Rosso ColleMassari Riserva 2013

Blend of 80% Sangiovese, 10% Ciliegiolo and Cabernet Sauvignon grapes. Ages for 18 months in oak barrel and tonneau. Intense ruby red. Intense ruby. Intense and open nose with aromas of cherry and blackberry and floral and eucalyptus hints. Intense palate, with a juicy and fruity aftertaste, good tannic structure with evident and firm tannins. Very long finish.

88   Price A
Montecucco Vermentino Melacce 2015

100% Vermentino grapes. Ages for 5 months in stainless steel. Straw yellow. Floral nose: broom blossoms, field blossoms then fruity nose of yellow peach and a hint of spices. Fresh and savory palate, fragrant with a pleasant almond finish.

COLLEVERDE

Frazione Matraia
55018 Capannori (LU)
Tel. +39 0583 402310

Fax +39 0583 402313
info@colleverdevineyards.com
www.colleverdevineyards.com
Colleverdevineyard

YEAR OF FOUNDATION 1989
NAME OF THE OWNER Piero Tartagni and Francesca Partini
TOTAL BOTTLES PRODUCED 40,000
DIRECT SALES
VISITS TO THE WINERY - RESERVATION NEEDED
HECTARES OF VINEYARD 7
HOSPITALITY
CERTIFIED ORGANIC VITICULTURE
OLIVE OIL PRODUCTION

Piero Tartagni and Francesca Partini came to the Colle Lucchesi 25 years ago answering the call to 'come back to the land' and Francesca's great desire to take charge of her family's 16th century hamlet. In the years that followed, they became totally involved in the project creating one of the best country holiday resorts in the province of Lucca and bio-dynamically cultivating the vineyards to produce wines with a nice personality as well as olive oil from their 3,000 century-old trees.

93   Price C
Sinopia 2012

100% Cabernet Franc grapes. Wild yeast. Ages for 20 months in barrique. Deep ruby red. Intense and generous nose, smoky and eucalyptus notes then intense dark fruit aromas. Mouth filling, elegant, good depth and with a fruity and intense finish.

91   Price B
Nero della Spinosa 2013

100% Syrah grapes. Wild yeast. Ages for 20 months in barrique. Deep ruby-purple color. Spicy nose that fashions hint of turmeric, cinnamon and black pepper. Floral and fruity with notes of cherry and mulberry. Ample palate, rich, balanced tannins, captivating, intense and very long finish.

88   Price B
Brania delle Ghiandaie 2013

Blend of 80% Sangiovese and 20% of Syrah grapes. Wild yeast. Ages for 20 months in barrique. Light ruby. Intriguing nose of blood orange, cherry and some fresh notes of watermelon. The palate is fresh, supple, tense, flavorful and with a good tannin. Fruity finish.

★

DEI

Via di Martiena, 35
53045 Montepulciano (SI)
Tel. +39 0578 716878
Fax +39 0578 758680
info@cantinedei.com
www.cantinedei.com
 Cantine-Dei

YEAR OF FOUNDATION 1985
NAME OF THE OWNER Dei Family
TOTAL BOTTLES PRODUCED 200,000
DIRECT SALES
VISITS TO THE WINERY - RESERVATION NEEDED
HECTARES OF VINEYARD 55
HOSPITALITY
OLIVE OIL PRODUCTION

This classic estate has been run for years with great class and skill by Caterina Dei. She recently built a new, uniquely beautify winery to improve her wines. The vineyards are situated in magnificent locations and the best cru, Bossona, which produce her Riserva di Nobile. The estate only uses Sangiovese (Prugnolo Gentile) for the Nobile and adds a little indigenous grapes for Sancta Catherina.

■ 91 　　　　　　　　　　　　　　Price B

Sancta Catharina 2010

Blend of Sangiovese, Cabernet, Syrah and 10% Petit Verdot grapes. Ages for 12 months in new barrique. Very deep ruby-violet. Interesting nose with aromas of blueberry, raspberry, black pepper, cinnamon and hints of blood orange and cedar. Intense and firm palate, good depth, wonderful tannin and with a good acidity to balance the structure. The finish is solid, ample and very long.

■ 85 　　　　　　　　　　　　　　Price B

Vino Nobile di Montepulciano 2013

100% Sangiovese grapes. Ages in different sized barrel. Ruby garnet. Dark notes on the nose: dark spices and ink. The palate highlights a good drinkability, harmonious and with a young tannin. The finish is pleasant and of medium intensity.

★

DIEVOLE

Via Dievole, 6 - Località Vagliagli
53019 Castelnuovo Berardenga (SI)
Tel. +39 0577 322613
Fax +39 0577 322574
info@dievole.it
www.dievole.it
 dievole
 @dievole

YEAR OF FOUNDATION 1979
NAME OF THE OWNER Alejandro Pedro Bulgheroni
TOTAL BOTTLES PRODUCED 80,000
DIRECT SALES
VISITS TO THE WINERY
HECTARES OF VINEYARD 80
CERTIFIED ORGANIC VITICULTURE
OLIVE OIL PRODUCTION

In 2013 Dievole, located in one of the best positions of the entire Siena Chianti Classico and where it's 2000 years they produce wine, has been bought by Alejandro Pedro Bulgheroni, a millionaire from Argentina, that bought it from Schwemm family. Unlikely from what we would've expected, instead of producing wines according to international winemaking styles, he chose Alberto Antonini a very traditional style consultant and from 2013 vintage the difference from the past has become evident. Not only big barrels, environmentally conscious agriculture, extraordinary wines that make you jump in the past with the knowledge of modern winemaking techniques.

■ 🗟 95 　　　　　　　　　　　　　Price B

Chianti Classico Novecento Riserva 2013

Blend of 90% Sangiovese with small percentage of Colorino and Canaiolo grapes. Ages for 1 year in large casks. Intense and shiny ruby. Extremely typical aromas of black cherry, violet and light hint of currant. Tense palate, firm, good body but supple, savory and with a subtle tannins. Warm, captivating and long finish. Outstanding example of terroir.

■ 90 　　　　　　　　　　　　🖒 Price A

Chianti Classico 2014

Blend of Sangiovese with small percentage of Canaiolo and Colorino grapes. Ages for 14 months in large cask. Lively ruby. One of the rarest example of good quality red wine of 2014 vintage. Very fruity,

BRUNELLO
DI MONTALCIN

WE LOVE OLTREPÒ

Foto di Alessandro Anglisani - www.alessandroanglisani.it

Oltrepò Pavese has an ancient tradition of wine-making, with the first written documents dating back to Pliny the Elder and Strabo who, in 40 BC, wrote 'fine wine, friendly people, and large wooden barrels'. The mission of the Consortium for the Protection of Oltrepò Pavese Wines is to safeguard and promote one of the top five historical Italian Wine Denominations, with its 13,500 hectares of vineyards. The most representative varieties of the Pavian hills are: Croatina, Barbera, Pinot nero, Riesling and Moscato. Our flagship wine is 'Cruasé', a collective brand exclusive to Consortium members which identifies Oltrepò Pavese traditional method DOCG rosé sparkling wines made with Pinot Noir grape.
Come and discover Oltrepò Pavese, its territory, its wines, its people and say: "**We love Oltrepò!**".

Discover
Oltrepò Pavese

CAMPAGNA FINANZIATA AI SENSI DEL REG. CE. N. 1308/2013 - CAMPAIGN FINANCED ACCORDING TO (EC) REGULATION N. 1308/2013

#weloveoltrepo
www.weloveoltrepo.it

fragrant and defined notes: black cherry, prune and currant. Tense palate, supple, savory, medium bodied but with a wonderful drinkability.

★★
DUEMANI

Località Ortacavoli
56046 Riparbella (PI)
Tel. +39 0583 975048
Fax +39 0583 974675
🔵 *duemani-elena*
info@duemani.eu
www.duemani.eu
📘 *duemani.aziendavitivinicola*
🐦 *@DuemaniToscana*

YEAR OF FOUNDATION 2000
NAME OF THE OWNER Luca D'Attoma ed Elena Celli
TOTAL BOTTLES PRODUCED 40,000
DIRECT SALES
VISITS TO THE WINERY - RESERVATION NEEDED
HECTARES OF VINEYARD 10
CERTIFIED ORGANIC VITICULTURE
CERTIFIED BIODYNAMIC VITICULTURE

This is one of those biodynamic estate we would like to see more of. And for this reason we have awarded a second star to the small yet extraordinary winery of Luca D'Attoma, a talented enologist with a prestigious past as a consultant but who is now making his own wine.

 96   Price D
Duemani 2013

100% Cabernet Franc grapes. Ages for 1 year in barrique. Intense ruby-violet. Varietal nose of raspberry then kirsch, cassis, hint of cardamom and refined oaky notes, very refined and elegant. Refined and balanced palate, velvety tannins, almost silky and a good body balanced by good acidity. Very long finish.

 94   Price D
Suisassi 2013

100% Syrah grapes. Ages for 1 year in barrique. Very intense and deep ruby. Initially it is a bit reduced on the nose then offers defined notes of spices and raspberry. Impressive palate, rich and captivating, warm and full bodied, good acidity and savoriness with a wonderful length.

FANTI

Località Podere Palazzo, 14 - Castelnuovo dell'Abate
53024 Montalcino (SI)
Tel. +39 0577 835795
🔵 *tenuta.fanti*
info@tenutafanti.it
www.tenutafanti.it
📘 *tenuta.fanti*
🐦 *@tenutafanti*

YEAR OF FOUNDATION 1800
NAME OF THE OWNER Filippo Baldassarre Fanti
TOTAL BOTTLES PRODUCED 200,000
DIRECT SALES
VISITS TO THE WINERY - RESERVATION NEEDED
HECTARES OF VINEYARD 60
OLIVE OIL PRODUCTION

This estate now has over 60 hectares of Brunello grapes and the great strides made in just 20 years are thanks to the skill of its volcanic owner-operator 'Sarrino' Fanti. Its two-room winery has become the estate's wonderful headquarters where the quest for quality is paramount. This involves attention to detail during both the fermentation and aging in wood and a non-orthodox estate style using barrels of various shapes and sizes and origin. The fermentation method is innovative and seeks to minimize any contact of the wine with the grape seeds.

 92   Price C
Brunello di Montalcino Vigna Le Macchiarelle Riserva 2010

100% Sangiovese grapes. Ages in different sized barrels, barrique and tonneau. Intense ruby. Dark notes of black pepper, tobacco, dark fruits and spices. Intense palate, thin and flavorful. Good tannin and weight with a good depth on the finish. Convincing debut for this new-born Riserva.

▪ 87   Price B
Brunello di Montalcino 2011

100% Sangiovese grapes. Ages in barrel. Nose of eucalyptus, fennel seeds, black pepper, fruity hints of blackberry. The palate offers good weight and slightly rough tannins; it still needs time in bottle to refine. The finish is juicy even if not in perfect balance.

FATTOI

Podere Capanna, 101 – Località Santa Restituta
53024 Montalcino (SI)
Tel. +39 0577 848613
info@fattoi.it
www.fattoi.it
 Fattoi-Ofelio-e-figli-viticoltori

YEAR OF FOUNDATION **1964**
NAME OF THE OWNER **Fattoi Family**
TOTAL BOTTLES PRODUCED **50,000**
DIRECT SALES
VISITS TO THE WINERY - RESERVATION NEEDED
HECTARES OF VINEYARD **10**
OLIVE OIL PRODUCTION

A winery that has been around for many years producing reliable products at very interesting prices. The style of the wines is neoclassic with the aim to not be too aggressive in regard to extracts and color. An interesting change came in 2008 when they started using barrels that were less than 10hl in size for aging. The area where it is located is quite renowned, on the southeast side of the Santa Restituta promontory, one of the most important cru in Montalcino.

■ 93   Price C
Brunello di Montalcino Riserva 2010

100% Sangiovese grapes. Ages in different sized barrel. Ruby with garnet rim. Intense floral nose, red and black fruits: classic black cherry and blackberry. Hint of tobacco and citrus. Intense palate, good depth, firm and with good drinkability thank to a wonderful support of the acidity-tannin component. Classy finish.

■ 90   Price C
Brunello di Montalcino 2011

100% Sangiovese grapes. Ages in barrel. Ruby garnet. Nose of coffee then red fruits, ripe cherry, undergrowth and hint of spices. Rich and tense palate, young and well integrated tannins, well balanced savoriness. Vigorous and relaxed finish.

■ 88   Price A
Rosso di Montalcino 2014

100% Sangiovese grapes. Ages in different sized oak barrel. Ruby red. Lightly smoky notes, white cherry and undergrowth aromas. Good palate, flavorful and with a great drinkability.

FATTORIA AMBRA

Via Lombarda, 85
59015 Carmignano (PO)
Tel. +39 055 8719049
Fax +39 055 8719049
fattoria.ambra@alice.it
www.fattoriaambra.it
f *FattoriaAmbra*
y *@FattoriaAmbra*

YEAR OF FOUNDATION **1955**
NAME OF THE OWNER **Romei Rigoli Family**
TOTAL BOTTLES PRODUCED **80,000**
DIRECT SALES
VISITS TO THE WINERY - RESERVATION NEEDED
HECTARES OF VINEYARD **20**

Carmignano wines were the first to qualify as DOCG and yet they are not that well known. Tradition (and regulations) dictates that the wine be a blend, a mix of Tuscan Sangiovese grapes with the 'French grapes' brought to Tuscany by Caterina de' Medici: Cabernet Sauvignon. Fattoria Ambra respects tradition also by letting the blend age in wood, be it French or Slavonian barrel. The vineyards, where integrated pest management (IPM) is practiced, are situated in four restored cru in the zone of Carmignano: the Montalbiolo hill, Elzana, Santa Cristina in Pilli and Montefortini.

■ 90   Price B
Carmignano Elzana Riserva 2012

Blend of 90% Sangiovese and Cabernet Sauvignon. Ages for 12 months in French oak barrel and other 12 months in Slovenian oak barrel. Dark ruby. Shy nose, then offers fruity and toasted notes. The palate is mouth filling and elegant, harmonious and with a good length.

■ 89   Price B
Carmignano Le Vigne Alte Montalbiolo Riserva 2012

Blend of 70% Sangiovese, 20% Canaiolo Nero and Cabernet Sauvignon grapes. Ages for 12 months in tonneau and 12 months in Slovenian oak barrel. Dark ruby. Intense nose of cherry and blackcurrant, with light floral hints. Austere palate, vertical, firm tannins. Fruity and spicy finish.

▪ 88   Price B
Vinsanto di Carmignano 2008

Blend of 90% Trebbiano and San Colombano

grapes. Ages for 5 years in 50lt and 100lt barrel. Light golden yellow. Very bright. Intriguing nose of prickly pear, pear, peanut, walnut husk. Sweet and flavorful. A well-made Vin Santo.

FATTORIA DEI BARBI

Località Podernovi, 170
53024 Montalcino (SI)
Tel. +39 0577 841111
info@fattoriadeibarbi.it
www.fattoriadeibarbi.it
fattoriabarbi
@FATTORIABARBI

YEAR OF FOUNDATION 1790
NAME OF THE OWNER Stefano Cinelli Colombini
TOTAL BOTTLES PRODUCED 600,000
DIRECT SALES
VISITS TO THE WINERY
HECTARES OF VINEYARD 66
HOSPITALITY
RESTAURANT
OLIVE OIL PRODUCTION

This is another historic Montalcino winery that has been producing Brunello since the mid-20th century. It is on the road to Castelnuovo dell'Abate and is a typical old Tuscan farm. Up until recently it was possible to by its products other than wine. After a lull the estate is returning to form offering classic wines that are well-made and with a style that is more elegant than bold and nicely mirrors the area. The estate also has an interesting museum.

| 89 | Price B |

Brunello di Montalcino Riserva 2010

100% Sangiovese grapes. Ages in barrels. Traditional ruby garnet. Citrusy nose with lightly developed notes of tobacco and leather. The palate is elegant with crunchy tannins and a good weight. A wine that needs more time to refine in bottle.

FATTORIA DI LAMOLE

Via di Lamole, 70
50022 Greve in Chianti (FI)
Tel. +39 055 8547065

Fax +39 055 8547065
info@fattoriadilamole.it
www.fattoriadilamole.it
Fattoria-di-Lamole

YEAR OF FOUNDATION 1862
NAME OF THE OWNER Paolo Socci
TOTAL BOTTLES PRODUCED 6,000
DIRECT SALES
VISITS TO THE WINERY - RESERVATION NEEDED
HECTARES OF VINEYARD 15.5
HOSPITALITY
CERTIFIED ORGANIC VITICULTURE
OLIVE OIL PRODUCTION

419

This young estate recently appeared in the limelight thanks to its very classic and energetic wines. Its vineyards are in Lamole on historic terraces that were restored with great effort and today are an example of the determination of the people of Lamole. Paolo Socci runs this estate that may be ambitious but has deep roots in Sangiovese tradition.

 94 | Price C

Le Viti di Livio 2012

Selection of old pre-phylloxera Sangiovese vines. Ages for 24 months in large oak casks. Deep red, light and bright. Nose of raspberry, blackberry, lavender and juniper. Dusty palate but stylish and classy, firm and intense with a very long finish that highlights a great tannic structure, firm and elegant. Muscle, class and charm of the old vines renewed in a modern feeling.

 92 | Price C

Chianti Classico Gran Selezione Lama della Villa 2012

100% Sangiovese grapes. Ages for 18 months in tonneau. Floral notes of rose and iris, strawberry and raspberry. Mouth filling and fresh palate, crunchy, rich of spicy and captivating notes.

FATTORIA DI MAGLIANO

Località Sterpeti, 10
58051 Magliano in Toscana (GR)
Tel. +39 0564 593040
fattoriadimagliano
info@fattoriadimagliano.it
www.fattoriadimagliano.it
fattoriadimagliano
@FattdiMagliano

YEAR OF FOUNDATION 1988
NAME OF THE OWNER Agostino Lenci
TOTAL BOTTLES PRODUCED 300,000
DIRECT SALES
VISITS TO THE WINERY - RESERVATION NEEDED
HECTARES OF VINEYARD 53
HOSPITALITY
RESTAURANT
CERTIFIED ORGANIC VITICULTURE
OLIVE OIL PRODUCTION

Lucca entrepreneur Agostino Lenci came to Magliano in Toscana, in Maremma, towards the end of the 1990s with the intention of making great wines and focused his whole estate on producing quality. We can now say that he achieved his goal.

■ 89   Price B

Poggio Bestiale 2013

Blend of 35% Merlot, 35% Cabernet Sauvignon, 25% Cabernet Franc and Petit Verdot grapes. Ages for 12 months in new and used barrique. Ruby red with violet hues. Intense and warm nose, spicy hints, slightly smoky, blackcurrant and mulberry. The palate is fresh, medium weight, evident but not aggressive tannins. Good palate.

■ 88   Price B

Maremma Toscana Perenzo 2013

100% Syrah grapes. Ages for 1 year in new barrique. Dark and deep ruby. Classic spicy notes then kirsch and warm notes. Warm palate, firm tannins, rich body, great weight but lacks a bit of suppleness. Wonderful length.

★★
FATTORIA LA MASSA

Via Case Sparse, 9 - Frazione Panzano
50022 Greve in Chianti (FI)
Tel. +39 055 852722
info@fattorialamassa.com
www.lamassa.com
f *Fattoria-La-Massa*
y *@FattoriaLaMassa*

YEAR OF FOUNDATION 1992
NAME OF THE OWNER Giampaolo Motta
TOTAL BOTTLES PRODUCED 160,000
DIRECT SALES
VISITS TO THE WINERY - RESERVATION NEEDED
HECTARES OF VINEYARD 27

Neapolitan Giampaolo Motta came to Tuscany in 1990. He began his career in wine working in the winery and vineyard of John Dunkley in Riecine, at Zonin's Castello d'Albola and for Alceo di Napoli at Castello dei Rampolla. He then found an estate in Panzano and went into debt to buy it and begin making his own wine there in the heart of Chianti Classico.

■ 91   Price A

La Massa 2013

Blend of 60% Sangiovese, 20% Merlot and 20% Cabernet Sauvignon. Ages for 1 year in barrique. Intense ruby. Very 'Chianty style' nose, despite the use of international grape varieties. Black cherry and violet then oaky notes and spicy hints on the background. Supple and tense palate, savory, very pleasant and with a good length.

FATTORIA LA TORRE

Via Provinciale di Montecarlo, 7
55015 Montecarlo (LU)
Tel. +39 0583 22981
info@fattorialatorre.it
www.fattorialatorre.it
f *TorreMontecarlo*
y *@TorreMontecarlo*

YEAR OF FOUNDATION 1994
NAME OF THE OWNER Marco Celli
TOTAL BOTTLES PRODUCED 35,000
DIRECT SALES
VISITS TO THE WINERY - RESERVATION NEEDED
HECTARES OF VINEYARD 7
HOSPITALITY
RESTAURANT
OLIVE OIL PRODUCTION

The village of Montecarlo di Lucca, a medieval jewel, has always had a reputation for being suitable for being a good place to make wine. The Celli family, aside from managing the Borgo La Torre resort and restaurant, also makes wine and is restoring their vineyard - replanted with a density of 7,000 vines per hectare – and restructuring the winery and cellar. Their consultant is enologist Valentino Ciarla.

■ 89   Price B

Esse 2013

100% Syrah grapes. Ages for 18 months in bar-

rique. Dark ruby red. Intense nose, smoky hints and caramel then dark spices and fruity aromas of blackberry. Round tannins, decent acidity and good depth. The palate is elegant and young with still evident oaky notes.

☐ 88   👍 Price A

Altair 2015

Blend of Vermentino and Viognier grapes. Vinified and aged partially in stainless steel and partially in barrique. Lively straw yellow. Fresh and fruity notes of peach, lychee, passion fruit and fine herbs. Full and fresh palate, fruity and well executed. Fruity and savory finish.

FATTORIA LAVACCHIO

Via Montefiesole, 55
50065 Pontassieve (FI)
Tel. +39 055 8317472
gabriele@fattorialavacchio.com
www.fattorialavacchio.com
🅵 fattorialavacchio
🐦 @lavacchio

YEAR OF FOUNDATION 1978
NAME OF THE OWNER Lottero Family
TOTAL BOTTLES PRODUCED 100,000
DIRECT SALES
VISITS TO THE WINERY - RESERVATION NEEDED
HECTARES OF VINEYARD 22
HOSPITALITY
RESTAURANT
CERTIFIED ORGANIC VITICULTURE
OLIVE OIL PRODUCTION

Entering Rufina from the direction of Florence is this estate that dates back to the 18th century and that was brought back to life by the Lottero family of Genoa who acquired it in 1978.

■ 91   Price B

Chianti Rufina Cedro Riserva 2009

Blend of 90% Sangiovese and 10% Merlot. Ages for 18 months in different sized barrel. Very lively ruby. Captivating nose, berries, black cherry and violet. Tense palate, supple, firm but not aggressive tannins, aristocratic and elegant palate balanced by good acidity. Good length.

■ 87   👍 Price A

Chianti Rufina Cedro 2014

Blend of 90% Sangiovese with 10% of Canaiolo and

Ciliegiolo grapes. Ages for 24 months in 35 and 70 hl French oak barrels and concrete tanks. Light ruby red. Red fruit on the nose: cherry and orange then resin and incense. Medium bodied, integrated tannins and good depth with a fruity and medium length finish.

★★

FATTORIA LE PUPILLE

Località Piagge del Maiano, 92/a - Frazione Istia d'Ombrone
58100 Grosseto (GR)
Tel. +39 0564 409517
Fax +39 0564 409519
info@fattorialepupille.it
www.fattorialepupille.it
🅵 Fattoria-Le-Pupille
🐦 @FPupille

YEAR OF FOUNDATION 1978
NAME OF THE OWNER Elisabetta Geppetti
TOTAL BOTTLES PRODUCED 450,000
DIRECT SALES
VISITS TO THE WINERY - RESERVATION NEEDED
HECTARES OF VINEYARD 75
OLIVE OIL PRODUCTION

Elisabetta Geppetti in one of those producers who has been able to leave their mark on the winemaking history of their territory. She began running her family's small estate when she was very young and over the years had expanded it and, above all, drew attention to Scansano and Morellino as no one had been able to before. The estate's top wine is Saffredi, one of the so-called Super Tuscans, while care and attention have lifted Morellino Poggio Valente to the highest levels with tis modern style.

■ 🍷 96   Price C

Saffredi 2013

Blend of Cabernet Sauvignon, Merlot and Syrah grapes. Ages in barrique. Dark ruby. Defined nose, rich and intense notes of dark fruit: blackberry, blueberry and currant then hints of candied cedar and pencil lead. Classy palate, firm and long; silky tannins and elegant depth. Great and refined finish.

☐ 90   👍 Price A

Poggio Argentato 2015

Blend of Traminer and Sauvignon Blanc grapes. Stainless steel and barrel. Shiny straw yellow. Intense fruity nose of loquat and peach, yellow blossoms, smoky hints, citrus and tomato. Rich palate, supple and flavorful, very savory and balanced acidity. The finish is very long and flavorful.

 90   Price B
Morellino di Scansano Riserva 2013

Blend of 90% Sangiovese and 10% Cabernet Sauvignon. Ages for 15 months in 10-20-50 hl barrel. Light ruby. Varietal nose of black cherry then spicy notes and fresh basil. The palate is full bodied, flavorful with a black cherry aftertaste. The palate is elegant and with refined tannins with a black cherry finish.

FATTORIA SARDI

Via della Maulina 747
55100 Lucca (LU)
Tel. +39 0583 341230
fattoriasardi@gmail.com
www.fattoriasardi.com
f FattoriaSardiGiustiniani
🐦 @FattoriaSG

YEAR OF FOUNDATION **2000**
NAME OF THE OWNER **Matteo Giustiniani**
TOTAL BOTTLES PRODUCED **105,000**
DIRECT SALES
VISITS TO THE WINERY - RESERVATION NEEDED
HECTARES OF VINEYARD **17**
HOSPITALITY
CERTIFIED ORGANIC VITICULTURE
CERTIFIED BIODYNAMIC VITICULTURE
OLIVE OIL PRODUCTION

It is unusual to find an estate producing mostly rosé in the province of Lucca. And while the choice made by Matteo Giustiniani and his wife Mina may seem extravagant, it was made taking into consideration the area the estate is located in. The family estate, which first began producing wine in 1929, is located between the Freddana and Serchio Rivers where the loose, lime-sand soil has gravel in it and this has proved to be ideal to produce Provence-style rosé wine that is popular abroad. The young couple, who both studied enology in Bordeaux, practice biodynamic farming.

🖋 90   Price B
Le Cicale 2015

Blend of Sangiovese and Vermentino grapes. Fer-

mented and aged in barrels for 8 months on the lees. Onion skin color. Defined nose, delicate and refined, fruity notes of peach, lightly citrusy and floral. The palate is fresh and savory, full, fragrant and fruity, flavorful finish.

 86   Price A
Rosé 2015

Blend of Sangiovese, Ciliegiolo and Malvasia Bianca grapes. 4 months on the lees. Onion skin color. Fresh nose, fruity aromas of white peach and melon, rose petals hints. The palate is fresh and savory, simple, tense and fairly long.

★★
FÈLSINA

Via del Chianti, 101
53019 Castelnuovo Berardenga (SI)
Tel. +39 0577 355117
Fax +39 0577 355651
info@felsina.it
www.felsina.it
f felsina
🐦 @felsinawines

YEAR OF FOUNDATION **1966**
NAME OF THE OWNER **Poggiali Family**
TOTAL BOTTLES PRODUCED **480,000**
DIRECT SALES
VISITS TO THE WINERY - RESERVATION NEEDED
HECTARES OF VINEYARD **94**
HOSPITALITY
OLIVE OIL PRODUCTION

If there is a there is a winery in Tuscany that has truly impressed us with the constant improvements it has made in recent years then it is Fèlsina. The overall level of their production, from their stock wine to their most select Riserva, is always of the highest order, even when the year was not exceptional. Among their best wines are Chianti Classico Rancia Riserva and Fontalloro, reds made with only Sangiovese grapes and that both age in small, French oak barrels.

■ 🗖 96   Price C
Fontalloro 2013

100% Sangiovese grapes. Ages for 20 months in barrique. Deep ruby. Nose of eucalyptus, pepper and plum, loquat and filed blossoms, forest berries and undergrowth. The tannin is still vibrant but already shows its potential on a very long and harmonious finish; great progression that support the palate and the pleasure.

 92   Price B
Chianti Classico Rancia Riserva 2013

100% Sangiovese grapes. Ages for 18 months in barrique. Shiny ruby red. Classic, aromatic, undergrowth and Mediterranean Scrub. Vibrant and crunchy, savory with sea breeze aftertaste, earthy, steely, vibrant tannin with a long and dark citrus finish of blood orange and bergamot.

 91   Price B
Maestro Raro 2013

100% Cabernet Sauvignon grapes. Ages for 12 months in barrique. Notes of blood orange, strawberry, celery and horseradish, chestnut honey and mustard. The palate fashions good freshness and savoriness, the length shows balance between savoriness and sweetness of the fruit, precise tannins.

 88   Price A
Chianti Classico Berardenga 2014

100% Sangiovese grapes. Ages for 12 months in larges casks and used barrique. Ruby garnet. Delicate floral notes but intense and fascinating, forest fruits, light rustic notes and eucalyptus. Fresh palate, dynamic and with a wonderful depth.

 88   Price C
Chianti Classico Gran Selezione Colonia 2012

100% Sangiovese grapes. Ages for 24 months in different sized oak barrel. Dark ruby. Elegant and rich, oaky, black pepper, peach juice and red apple, strawberry. Meaty and full palate, slightly rough tannins but with developing dynamic savoriness and acidity.

★★
AMBROGIO E GIOVANNI FOLONARI

Via di Nozzole, 12 - Località Passo dei Pecorai
50022 Greve in Chianti (FI)
Tel. +39 055 859811
Fax +39 055 859823
 tenute.folonari
folonari@tenutefolonari.com
www.tenutefolonari.com
 folonaritenute
 @FolonariTenute

YEAR OF FOUNDATION **2000**
NAME OF THE OWNER **Ambrogio and Giovanni Folonari**
TOTAL BOTTLES PRODUCED **1,400,000**
DIRECT SALES
VISITS TO THE WINERY - RESERVATION NEEDED
HECTARES OF VINEYARD **200**
HOSPITALITY
OLIVE OIL PRODUCTION

This estate is composed of a pool of smaller ones spread throughout Tuscany. From Nozzole, in Greve in Chianti, comes Pareto, a varietal Cabernet Sauvignon that is one the best 'innovative' wines in the region and can stand up to the best made not only in Tuscany but also California and Bordeaux. The nearby Cabreo estate produces Folonari's other famous IGT wines.

93   Price B
Cabreo Il Borgo 2013

Blend of 70% Sangiovese and 30% Cabernet Sauvignon grapes. Ages for 18 months in tonneau. Intense and dark ruby. Captivating and defined nose, classic aromas of berries and black cherry supported by elegant spices and oaky notes. Tense and savory palate, upfront tannins but not aggressive with warm and captivating finish.

92   Price B
Il Pareto 2013

100% Cabernet Sauvignon grapes. Ages for 18 months in barrique. Intense and dark ruby. Very varietal nose: blueberry, black currant, ink, oaky and lightly minty notes. Firm palate, firm tannins and wonderful long finish. Historically one of the best Tuscan Bordeaux blend, produced at Tenuta di Nozzole in the northern part of Chianti Classico area.

90   Price B
Chianti Classico Gran Selezione La Forra 2012

Blend of 90% Sangiovese and 10% other red grape varieties. Ages for 15 months in barrique. Intense ruby garnet. Typical nose, black cherry and prune with oaky notes on the background. Savory palate, good body but supple, warm finish, very pleasant.

★★★
FONTODI

Via San Leolino, 89 - Frazione Panzano
50022 Greve in Chianti (FI)
Tel. +39 055 852005
Fax +39 055 852537
fontodi@fontodi.com
www.fontodi.com
f *Az-Agr-Fontodi*

YEAR OF FOUNDATION **1968**
NAME OF THE OWNER **Giovanni and Marco Manetti**
TOTAL BOTTLES PRODUCED **300,000**
DIRECT SALES
VISITS TO THE WINERY - RESERVATION NEEDED
HECTARES OF VINEYARD **85**
OLIVE OIL PRODUCTION

Year after year, this estate continues to be among the best wineries in the area. Much of the credit for this goes to its dynamic owner, Giovanni Manetti, who over the past 30 years has literally shot his estate to the top in regard to quality in Chianti. Flaccianello delle Pieve is a great classic and Vigna del Sorbo, now classified Grand Selezione, is absolutely one of the best wines of its kind.

■ 🍷 **95** Price C
Flaccianello della Pieve 2013

100% Sangiovese grapes. It matures 24 month in barrique. Dark ruby red color. On the nose scents of pepper and cinnamon, meat and blood, mint and cardamom. On the mouth is clean and long, savory, with a lot of substance, fruity and with a thick tannins. It is a young wine but with a brilliant future in front of it that is worth following.

■ **90** Price C
Chianti Classico Gran Selezione Vigna del Sorbo 2013

100% Sangiovese grapes. It matures 12 months in big barrels. Bright purple color. On the nose aromas of matures fruits and meat. On the mouth presents a vivid tannin with taste of raspberry and currant and a refreshing finish.

■ **89** Price B
Chianti Classico 2013

Blend of 50% Sangiovese and 50% Cabernet Sauvignon grapes. It matures 2 years in barrique. Dark ruby color. On the nose is intense with aromas of

dark cherry, mint and black cherry. On the mouth persists the sensation of woody tannins that are anyway softened by the intense taste of fruit. In the finish is slightly arid but well persistent with a eucalyptus note that make it fresh to drink.

■ **88** Price B
Pinot Nero Case Via 2014

100% Pinot Nero grapes. It matures 12 months in barrique. Garnet ruby color. On the nose intense and original aromas of berries, wildflower, tobacco and ginger. On the mouth is agile and polite, savory, very fresh. 2014 is been the right year to try this wine in Panzano...

★★
FRESCOBALDI

Via Santo Spirito, 11
50125 Firenze (FI)
Tel. +39 055 27141
Fax +39 055 289546
info@frescobaldi.it
www.frescobaldi.it
f *FrescobaldiVini*
🐦 *@FrescobaldiVini*

YEAR OF FOUNDATION **1300**
NAME OF THE OWNER **Marchesi de' Frescobaldi**
TOTAL BOTTLES PRODUCED **6,000,000**
DIRECT SALES
VISITS TO THE WINERY - RESERVATION NEEDED
HECTARES OF VINEYARD **1,200**
OLIVE OIL PRODUCTION

This fundamental Tuscan winery has vineyards in different areas of the region. Its primary estate is in Rufina, northeast of Florence, and includes vineyards in the area that produces Pomino. Then there is Castelgiocono in Montalcino, one of the biggest estate in the district, Ornellaia in Bolgheri and even Attems in Collio. Together they demonstrate Frescobaldi's desire to represent the many sides of Italian winemaking. Today they possess over 1,000 hectares of vineyards and are one of the most famous Italian wine brands in the world.

■ **94** Price B
Montesodi Castello Nipozzano 2013

100% Sangiovese grapes. It matures for 2 years in barrique. Very intense garnet ruby color. On the nose is very powerful with aromas of violet and kirsch supported by more smoky and spicy note underneath. On the mouth is powerful, with a great body, plentiful, warm, thick and young tannins, very rich partly because of the acidity. Very long in the finish.

■ 91   Price B
Chianti Rufina Nipozzano Vecchie Viti Riserva 2013

Blend of mostly Sangiovese with Colorino, Cannaiolo and Malvasia grapes. It matures 2 years in big oak barrels. Intense garnet ruby color. The most traditional wine product by this estate. On the nose aromas of violet, currant, black cherry with little smoky scents and notes of blood orange. On the mouth is tense and agile, very pleasant, savory and persistent.

■ 89   Price D
Brunello di Montalcino Luce 2011

100% Sangiovese grapes. It matures in both barrique and tonneau. Deep intense ruby color. On the nose is clean and intense with aromas of red fruit, morello and sour cherry with scents of blond spices. On the mouth is thick , in progression with a polite tannin. In the finish is juicy and relaxed.

☐ 88   Price C
Gorgona 2015

Blend of Vermentino and Ansonica grapes. It matures 7 years both stainless steel and barrique. Golden yellow color. On the nose is varietal with aromas of anise and broom, alfalfa and a light vanilla. On the mouth is rich and full-flavored, averagely acidic and very savory. This wine is the result of the Frescobaldi social project for the island of Gorgona in collaboration with the penitentiary: the wine is made by the prisoners.

FULIGNI

Via Soccorso Saloni, 33
53024 Montalcino (SI)
Tel. +39 0577 848710
Fax +39 0577 848710
❸ *fuligni*
info@fuligni.it
www.fuligni.it

YEAR OF FOUNDATION 1923
NAME OF THE OWNER Maria Fuligni
TOTAL BOTTLES PRODUCED 55,000
DIRECT SALES
VISITS TO THE WINERY - RESERVATION NEEDED

HECTARES OF VINEYARD 12
OLIVE OIL PRODUCTION

This historic Montalcino label has been run for some years now by Roberto Guerrini, a man held in high regard in the town. Music is a passion for him and he has connections with some of the leading orchestras in the world being a professor and assistant chancellor at the University of Siena. This passion is also found in his wines which are elegant, never loud and always of great class. The vineyards are situated in the upper area of Canalicchi and thus on the north side of Montalcino. The estate's wines have a neo-classical style with a moderate use of tonneau barrels, especially for the Brunello reserve.

■ 94   Price D
Brunello di Montalcino Riserva 2010

100% Sangiovese grapes. It matures both in oak barrels and tonneau. Bright ruby color with a light garnet reflex. On the nose is intense, complex and clean with aromas of citrus, red fruit, humus and an hint of light tobacco. On the mouth it presents refined tannins and a fresh acidity that makes it easy to drink. In the finish is juicy and elegant.

■ 90   Price C
Brunello di Montalcino 2011

100% Sangiovese grapes. It matures in oak barrels. Garnet ruby color. On the nose is firm with smoky scents and an hint of blond spices, cherries and blackberry. On the nose is vivid with a good acidity with a young tannin balanced by the full flavored body. Tasty in the finish.

GIODO

Località Poderino
53024 Montalcino (SI)

YEAR OF FOUNDATION 2003
NAME OF THE OWNER Carlo Ferrini
TOTAL BOTTLES PRODUCED 8,000
HECTARES OF VINEYARD 3

The first vintage was already fantastic and the second is a great wine. The small estate has three-hectares of Sangiovese vineyards in the wonderful area of Sesta Nobile amid Mediterranean brush and holm oak trees. It is owned by a renowned enologist who uses cement and stainless steel vats and barrels of various sizes to achieve a neo-classic style. All this excellence result in wines of great quality.

 95   Price D

Brunello di Montalcino 2011

100% Sangiovese grapes. It matures both in tonneau and 700 l oak barrels for 2 years. Bright intense ruby color. On the nose is neat and intense with aromas of blackberry, morello and light dark spices with smoky notes. On the mouth is rich, intense, progressive without excesses. Thick body and a good tannin that make it elegant and important to drink.

★★
GRATTAMACCO

Località Lungagnano, 129
57022 Castagneto Carducci (LI)
Tel. +39 0565 765069
info@collemassari.it
www.collemassari.it
 ColleMassari
 @ColleMassari

YEAR OF FOUNDATION 1977
NAME OF THE OWNER Maria Iris Tipa Bertarelli and Claudio Tipa
TOTAL BOTTLES PRODUCED 85,000
DIRECT SALES
VISITS TO THE WINERY - RESERVATION NEEDED
HECTARES OF VINEYARD 13
CERTIFIED ORGANIC VITICULTURE
OLIVE OIL PRODUCTION

The estate is almost 40 years ago and started when Pier Mario Meletti Cavallari, a manager and wine shop owner from Bergamo, decided to make wine in Bolgheri. Fifteen years ago his estate was acquired by Claudio and Iris Tipa, who today also own ColleMassari in Montecucco and Poggio di Sotto in Montalcino. The change in ownership had no effect on the style of the wines because Maurizio Castelli stayed on to supervise production as he has done from the very beginning.

 97   Price C

Bolgheri Superiore Grattamacco 2013

Blend of 65% Cabernet Sauvignon, 20% Merlot and 15% Sangiovese grapes. It matures for 18 months

in barrique. Very intense ruby color. Great version. On the mouth is elegant, clean, whole with specific aromas of currant, raspberry and light black cherry. Simply perfect the smoky note of the wood, polite and fine. On the mouth is balanced and tense with a great acidity to makes it agile and savory. The tannin is velvety an in the finish it results aristocratic and long.

 94   Price C

Bolgheri Superiore L'Alberello 2013

Blend of 70% Cabernet Sauvignon, 25% Cabernet Franc and 5% Petit Verdot. It matures for almost 18 month in barrique. Very intense ruby color. On the nose is spicy with aromas of cassis, cardamom, black currant and light scents of smoke underneath. On the mouth is firm, warm, the tannin results a little strong due to the youth. Already and elegant wine that will evolve well with time.

☐ 91   Price B

Bolgheri Vermentino Grattamacco 2014

100% Vermentino grapes. It matures for almost 8 months in barrique. Greenish straw yellow color. On the nose is fruity with aromas of plum and citrus at first, then light aromas of smoke due to the yeast, hints of aromatic wood underneath. On the mouth is strong, with a great acidic freshness that doesn't result aggressive. In the finish is agile and pleasant.

 90   Price A

Bolgheri 2014

Blend of 60% Cabernet Sauvignon, 20% Cabernet Franc, 10% Merlot and 10% Sangiovese grapes. It matures for 10 months in barrique. Dark ruby color. On the nose is dark and varietal and eucalyptus with aromas of alfalfa and light fruits. On the mouth is nicely fresh and balances, compact and quite silky.

★★
GUADO AL TASSO

Località Belvedere - Frazione Bolgheri
57020 Castagneto Carducci (LI)
Tel. +39 0565 74735
Fax +39 0565 749707
antinori@antinori.it
www.antinori.it
 MarchesiAntinori
 @AntinoriFamily

YEAR OF FOUNDATION 1934
NAME OF THE OWNER Antinori Family

TOTAL BOTTLES PRODUCED 1,300,000
DIRECT SALES
VISITS TO THE WINERY - RESERVATION NEEDED
HECTARES OF VINEYARD 300

Antinori's vast estate in Montalcino has existed for 80 years and it is more than just a simple annex for the family because, being related to the Gherardesca family, they have family root here. The wines here have a strict Bolgheri, or if you prefer neo-Bordeaux, style. These include a true masterpiece, Matarocchio, of which only a few thousand bottles are produced and that is not only one of the producer's top wines for quality but also for Italy's.

 96   Price E
Matarocchio 2012

100% Cabernet Franc grapes. It matures in barrique for 18 months. Dark intense ruby color. On the nose results very complex with aromas of black currant at first, then mint, pine resin, wild strawberry and light cassis. On the mouth is polite and velvety, very fine with enchanted tannins die to the sweetness and an incredible persistence.

92   Price D
Bolgheri Superiore 2013

Blend of 55% Cabernet Sauvignon, 25% Merlot, 18% Cabernet Franc and Petit Verdot grapes. It matures in barrique for 18 months. Whole dark ruby red color. On the nose aromas of medicinal herbs, Mediterranean maquis, black spices and a hint ok black fruits. On the mouth is fresh, dynamic and tasty with fine tannins and a good persistence.

89   Price B
Bolgheri Superiore Il Bruciato 2014

Blend of 55% Cabernet Sauvignon, 30 % Merlot, 15% Syrah grapes. It matures in barrique. Dark, intense ruby color. On the nose a mix of fruity scents of the currant and eucalyptus notes of the aromatic herbs with an hint of floral. On the mouth is very savory, with a taste of fruit and a lot of licorice. The tannins, well integrated, support the finish.

GUICCIARDINI STROZZI
FATTORIA CUSONA

Località Cusona, 5
53037 San Gimignano (SI)
Tel. +39 0577 950028

Fax +39 0577 950260
tenuteguicciardinistrozzi
info@guicciardinistrozzi.it
www.guicciardinistrozzi.it
TenuteGuicciadiniStrozzi
@TGStrozzi

YEAR OF FOUNDATION 994
NAME OF THE OWNER Girolamo Strozzi
TOTAL BOTTLES PRODUCED 750,000
DIRECT SALES
VISITS TO THE WINERY - RESERVATION NEEDED
HECTARES OF VINEYARD 115

427

Vernaccia di San Gimignano was probably invented here. Vernaccia is mentioned in the Divine Comedy and in the Decameron and Cusona is always cited. Historical evidence shows that Cusona existed as a military tower before the year 1000. The Guicciardini Strozzi family acquired in 1500 and in modern times commercial wine production began in 1970 with Prince Girolamo. The wines are very traditional as is the magnificent cellar under the villa. But in the past two years we have seen, with joy, the influence of the pas de bourrée renovator Natalia.

☐ 88   Price A
Vernaccia di San Gimignano Cusona 1933 2014

100% Vernaccia grapes. Stainless steel. Intense straw yellow color. On the nose it presents very intense floral scents such as broom, elderflower meanwhile on the fruity side is light on the aromas of yellow fruits. On the mouth has a good impact, not too strong but savory and easy to drink. The body is tasty and in the finish it presents note of flowers.

I GIUSTI E ZANZA

Via Puntoni, 9
56043 Fauglia (PI)
Tel. +39 0585 44354
Fax +39 0585 489912
igiustiezaza
info@igiustiezanza.it
www.igiustiezanza.it
IGiustieZanzaVigneti

YEAR OF FOUNDATION 1995
NAME OF THE OWNER Giusti Family

TOTAL BOTTLES PRODUCED 100,000
DIRECT SALES
VISITS TO THE WINERY - RESERVATION NEEDED
HECTARES OF VINEYARD 17
CERTIFIED ORGANIC VITICULTURE

The approach of Paolo Giusti, an engineer working in agriculture, is quite modern with great attention to clean aromas and an ample use of small French barrels. His estate is in the hills of Fauglia, in the province of Pisa, a cold area with soils that range from sandy to compact marl. There are some 17 hectares of vineyard and the varieties cultivated are Cabernet Sauvignon, Syrah, Merlot and Sangiovese. The density of the vineyards is very high and reachs 9,000 vines per hectare, while yield is very low and this generally produces decidedly rich wines.

■ 89   Price B
Dulcamara 2013

Blend of 70% Cabernet Sauvignon, 25% Merlot and 5% Petit Verdot grapes. It matures for 18-24 months in French durmast tonneau. Intense purple ruby color. On the nose is typical with eucalyptus notes and aromas of graphite, an hint of smoke, sweet spices and fruity scents such as blackberry and currant. On the mouth is strong, full-bodied, with a good progression and integrated tannins. Very consistent in the finish.

I VERONI

Via Tifariti, 5 - Località I Veroni
50065 Pontassieve (FI)
Tel. +39 055 8368886
Fax +39 055 8323715
info@iveroni.it
www.iveroni.it

YEAR OF FOUNDATION 1897
NAME OF THE OWNER **Lorenzo Mariani**
TOTAL BOTTLES PRODUCED 110,000
DIRECT SALES
VISITS TO THE WINERY - RESERVATION NEEDED
HECTARES OF VINEYARD 21
HOSPITALITY
OLIVE OIL PRODUCTION

This estate is in Rufina, geographically a stone's throw from Florence, but in an almost mountainous area that is very different from the rest

of Chianti. The vineyards of I Veroni are situated as high as 350m above sea level and very near Pieve di Sanmartino in Quona. Of the estate's 70 hectares, close to a third are vineyards and a major replanting begun in the 1990s involves boosting the density to 5,000 vines per hectare. The grapes are select Sangiovese clones. They also have 4,000 olive trees of the Frantoio, Moraiolo and Leccino varieties that are being converted to organic farming.

■ 93   Price B
Chianti Rufina Riserva 2013

100% Sangiovese grapes. It matures in oak barrels and tonneau. Bright intense ruby color. On the nose is whole with scents of pink fruits even mature one and light spices very intense and attractive. The smoky touch with cinnamon and light caramel is perfectly dosed. On the mouth is elegant with persistent but very polite and almost refined tannins. The acidy is elegant and will give the wine a long life and with a great persistent in the finish.

■ 85   Price A
Chianti Rufina 2014

100% Sangiovese grapes. It matures in medium size oak barrels. Light ruby color. On the nose is clean with aromas on white cherry, an hint of smoke and fresh bramble. On the mouth is ruled by the freshness of the acidity and by the very polite tannin. In the finish presents slightly green notes.

★
IL BORRO

Località Borro, 1 - Frazione San Giustino Valdarno
52024 Loro Ciuffenna (AR)
Tel. +39 055 977053
Fax +39 055 977864
vino@ilborro.it
www.ilborro.it
 IlBorro
 @Il_Borro

YEAR OF FOUNDATION 1993
NAME OF THE OWNER **Ferruccio Ferragamo**
TOTAL BOTTLES PRODUCED 160,000
DIRECT SALES
VISITS TO THE WINERY - RESERVATION NEEDED
HECTARES OF VINEYARD 45
HOSPITALITY
RESTAURANT
OLIVE OIL PRODUCTION

The property that once belonged to Amedeo Savoia-Aosta was acquired in 1993 by Ferruccio Ferragamo who has turned it into a small paradise on Earth. The hamlet is simply stupendous and wine production, from vineyards that became bio-dynamic inn 2012, benefits from the consultancy of Stefano Chioccioli.

92   Price C
Il Borro 2012

Blend of 50% Merlot, 35% Cabernet Sauvignon and 15% Syrah grapes. It matures in barrique for 18 months. Intense, dark ruby color. On the nose aromas of raspberry, black currant, vanilla and blood orange. On the mouth is very rich but agile, consistent with thick young tannins. In the finish is very worm and full-flavored, very long.

88   Price A
Pian di Nova 2013

Blend of 75% Syrah and 25% Sangiovese grapes. It matures in barrique for 9 months. Intense, alive ruby color. On the nose it results very fruity with aromas of cassis and black cherry at first, then black pepper and cardamom. On the mouth is savory, agile, well supported by the acidic component.

★★
IL CARNASCIALE

Località Podere Il Carnasciale
52020 Montevarchi (AR)
Tel. +39 055 9911142
Fax +39 055 992957
contact@caberlot.eu
www.caberlot.eu
 Caberlot

YEAR OF FOUNDATION 1986
NAME OF THE OWNER Bettina Rogosky
TOTAL BOTTLES PRODUCED 3,500
VISITS TO THE WINERY - RESERVATION NEEDED
HECTARES OF VINEYARD 5

When he died a few years ago, Wolf Rogosky left his wife Bettina a small farm in Mercatale Valdarno and an extraordinary wine he began to produce towards the end of the 1980s. Carnasciale's Caberlot was born from the idea of planting a vineyard with a very rare grape that agronomist Remigio Bordoni had discovered on the Colli Euganei. The grape is most likely a cross of Cabernet Franc and Merlot, hence the name. This wine the Caberlot hasn't been released on time for the guide. We console ourselves with its little brother Rosso Carnasciale.

91   Price C
Rosso Carnasciale 2013

100% Caberlot grapes (cross of Cabernet Franc and Merlot grapes). It matures for 22 months in barrique. Dark ruby color. On the nose aromas of blackberry, black currant at first, then hints of resin and mint. On the mouth is firm, the tannins are very young but with a bright future, savory, worm and persistent.

IL CERCHIO

Via Valmarina, 24
58011 Capalbio (GR)
Tel. +39 0564 898856
ilcerchio@ilcerchiobio.it
www.ilcerchiobio.it

YEAR OF FOUNDATION 1989
NAME OF THE OWNER Beniamino Podestà and Corinna Vicenzi
TOTAL BOTTLES PRODUCED 16,000
DIRECT SALES
VISITS TO THE WINERY - RESERVATION NEEDED
HECTARES OF VINEYARD 5
CERTIFIED ORGANIC VITICULTURE
OLIVE OIL PRODUCTION

As often happens, Corinna Vincenza and her husband did not intend to become wine producers. The Milan natives had an established architectural and urban design firm and for them Maremma was just their favorite holiday destination. Then they bought a small farm near Capalbio as a vacation home and a new life began for them, at first schizophrenic, as farmers. In the end they definitively moved there and got their son Beniamino, who had since grown, involved in the estate.

89   👍 Price A
Ansonica Costa dell'Argentario 2015

Blend of Ansonica and Vermentino grapes. Stainless steel. Golden straw yellow color. On the nose is clean and fruity with aromas of yellow pulp fruit with an hint of herbs. On the mouth is full-bodied, fresh, savory, easy to drink with a salty and long finish. A great wine, an Ansonica like this is not easy to find.

89   Price A

Maremma Toscana Valmarina 2014

Blend of mainly Sangiovese grapes with an hint of Alicante Grapes. stainless steel for 1 year. Clear not too intense ruby color. On the nose is quite intense with aromas of fruits such as cherry and cedar, little hints of spices as well. On the mouth is tasty, rich, with a pleasant note of rose, thick and well integrated tannins. In the finish it's whole and balanced.

★

IL COLOMBAIO
DI SANTA CHIARA

Località Racciano, 9
53037 San Gimignano (SI)
Tel. +39 347 8655490
🛇 *alessio.logi*
info@colombaiosantachiara.it
www.colombaiosantachiara.it
🅕 *colombaio.santachiara*

YEAR OF FOUNDATION **2000**
NAME OF THE OWNER **Alessio Logi**
TOTAL BOTTLES PRODUCED **85,000**
DIRECT SALES
VISITS TO THE WINERY - RESERVATION NEEDED
HECTARES OF VINEYARD **12**
HOSPITALITY
OLIVE OIL PRODUCTION

This young estate has a solid winemaking foundation with vineyards that have excellent exposures and are cultivated with great care. The Logi brothers produce modern Vernaccia. The fermentation procedure is innovative, the use of wood is very limited with the Riserva and the technical staff is excellent and benefits from the contribution of the talented Caciornia who has added an Alto Adige touch. The new winery, practically completed, has allowed them to take further steps forward. Research on the use of new yeasts will result in a new wine which could be defined as ancestral.

☐ 🗐 95   Price B

Vernaccia di San Gimignano Albereta Riserva 2013

100% Vernaccia grapes. It matures in oak barrels. Intense straw yellow color with light reflexes. On

the nose is intense and complex with a great scent of smoke and aromas of saffron and yellow flower such as broom. On the mouth is intense with a good acidity and savory. Wonderful to drink even if full-bodied. Amazing in the finis.

☐ 93   👍 Price A

Vernaccia di San Gimignano Campo della Pieve 2014

100% Vernaccia grapes. It matures partly in stainless steel on yeast and partly in big oak barrels. Bright straw yellow color. On the mouth aromas of cedar, light citrus, nettle and a classic flower. On the mouth it's very elegant, with a classic tannin and a modest acidity, savory and with a great taste.

☐ 86   👍 Price A

Vernaccia di San Gimignano Selvabianca 2015

100% Vernaccia grapes. Stainless steel only. Pale straw yellow color. On the nose aromas of fresh fruits, eucalyptus notes and cedar. On the mouth is firm, savory and with a good acidity. Gradual and tasty finish.

IL CONVENTINO

Via della Ciarliana, 25b
55045 Montepulciano (SI)
Tel. +39 0578 715371
info@ilconventino.it
www.ilconventino.it
🅕 *ilconventino.aziendaagricola*

YEAR OF FOUNDATION **2003**
NAME OF THE OWNER **Fratelli Brini**
TOTAL BOTTLES PRODUCED **100,000**
DIRECT SALES
VISITS TO THE WINERY - RESERVATION NEEDED
HECTARES OF VINEYARD **20**
HOSPITALITY
CERTIFIED ORGANIC VITICULTURE

The estate has its headquarters in an old monastery and in recent years important renovations were carried out both in the winery and the cellar in regard to the barrels. The new owners have embraced organic methods and the vineyards are for the most part in the extremely suited enclaves of Bossona and Ciarliana. The estate's style is neo-classic but what is most impressive is the constant improvement of the wines' quality.

91   Price B
Vino Nobile di Montepulciano 2013

Blend of mostly Sangiovese grapes with little hint of authorized grapes. It matures in oak barrels and tonneau. Dark ruby color. On the nose after an initial reduction comes out scents of intense fruits, hints of sage and underbrush and a great quality spiciness. On the mouth is extremely firm, progressive and tasty. In the finish is very persistent with a quality tannin.

★

IL MARRONETO

Località Madonna delle Grazie, 306
53024 Montalcino (SI)
Tel. +39 0577 849382
Fax +39 0577 846075
info@ilmarroneto.it
www.ilmarroneto.com
 BrunelloIlMarroneto
 @IlMarroneto

YEAR OF FOUNDATION 1974
NAME OF THE OWNER Alessandro Mori
TOTAL BOTTLES PRODUCED 28,000
DIRECT SALES
VISITS TO THE WINERY - RESERVATION NEEDED
HECTARES OF VINEYARD 6

Alessandro Mori has dedicated years to his family's old estate, sacrificing his brilliant career as a lawyer. His passion for wine is contagious and for him totally absorbing. The winery has existed since the 1970s but it has only been with Alessandro that it has returned to producing excellent quality. The estate's style ranges from extremely classic for its vintage Brunello to imperiously modern for the cru Madonna delle Grazie. This wine reflects Alessandro's truly extroverted, joyous and captivating personality. It is a wine with a nice impact, distinct fruit sensations and a nice acidity.

94   Price C
Brunello di Montalcino Madonna delle Grazie 2011

100% Sangiovese grapes. It mautres in different kind of wood barrels. Garnet ruby color. On the nose results complex with strong fruity notes, aromas of red fruits such as sour cherry and aromas of black fruits such as blackberry. Good the part with scents

of spices and citrus. On the mouth is very strong without smudges thanks to the high savories. The tannin is still young but the body is full so is difficult to notice. In the finish is very juicy.

87   Price B
Brunello di Montalcino 2011

100% Sangiovese grapes. It matures in oak barrels. Not too strong garnet ruby color. On the nose worm aromas of morello, sour cherry, humus and medicinal herbs. On the mouth is wide but tasty with typical notes and crisp tannins. In the finish is flavored on dark notes.

★

IL MOLINO DI GRACE

Località Il Volano Lucarelli
50020 Greve in Chianti (FI)
Tel. +39 055 8561010
Fax +39 055 8561942
info@ilmolinodigrace.it
www.ilmolinodigrace.com
 ilmolino.grace
 @Ilmolinodigrace

YEAR OF FOUNDATION 1999
NAME OF THE OWNER Frank C. Grace
TOTAL BOTTLES PRODUCED 200,000
DIRECT SALES
VISITS TO THE WINERY - RESERVATION NEEDED
HECTARES OF VINEYARD 36

This estate only makes Sangiovese Panzano wine and it must be tasted if one want to understand the potential of this grape grown around the legendary Conca d'Oro, an area known to produce explosive wines that are full of personality. Frank Grace continues to expand, assisted by Franc Bernabei, and last year his production included a Gran Selezione, which was almost an immediate hit in the new classification.

93   Price B
Chianti Classico Gran Selezione Il Margone 2012

100% Sangiovese grapes. It matures in barrique for 22 months. Intense garnet ruby color. On the nose is very refined articulate with aromas of black cherry, spices and vanilla. On the mouth is savory, slightly crispy due to the young tannins, good acidity and great persistence on the finish.

■ **91**   Price B
Gratius 2012

Blend of 95% Sangiovese with Cannaiolo and Corolino grapes. It matures in barrique for 22 months. Intense garnet ruby color. On the nose the aromas of fruits are clear with scents of black cherry and blackberry, deeper scents of vanilla and incense. On the mouth is firm with the tannins still in evidence, good acidity and persistent in the finish.

■ **89**   Price A
Chianti Classico 2014

100% Sangiovese grapes. It matures for 12 months in stainless steel, Slavonia durmast barrels, barrique and tonneau. Clear ruby color. On the nose aromas of sour cherry, raspberry, chili and pepper. On the mouth is agile and firm, the tannins are crisp, good freshness and very intense.

IL POGGIONE

Località Sant'Angelo in Colle
53024 Montalcino (SI)
Tel. +39 0577 844029
Fax +39 0577 844165
info@ilpoggione.it
www.tenutailpoggione.it
 ilpoggione
 @IlPoggioneWines

YEAR OF FOUNDATION **Fine Ottocento**
NAME OF THE OWNER **Leopoldo and Livia Franceschi**
TOTAL BOTTLES PRODUCED **500,000**
DIRECT SALES
VISITS TO THE WINERY - RESERVATION NEEDED
HECTARES OF VINEYARD **125**
HOSPITALITY
OLIVE OIL PRODUCTION

The Franceschi family owns this wonderful estate that has its administrative headquarters in the medieval hamlet of Sant'Angelo in Colle, which once hosted the winery and cellars. Everything now has been moved outside the town's walls to a modern and efficient winery with all the latest technology at hand. The complex also includes an equally modern oil mill. The vast vineyards are spread out around the village with some having excellent exposures. The estate stands out for the consistency of its

wines and their excellent quality/price ratio even if we believe their potential is far greater than what has been seen so far.

■ **92**   Price C
Brunello di Montalcino Vigna Paganelli Riserva 2010

100% Sangiovese grapes. It matures in oak barrels. Lightly garnet ruby color. On the nose is classic with evolved aromas of tobacco and herbs, attractive the floral and fruity notes. On the mouth is balanced, fluent with a full body and a convincing finish.

■ **87**   Price B
Brunello di Montalcino 2011

100% Sangiovese grapes. It matures in oak barrels. Pale ruby color. On the nose warm notes lightly earthy with a hint of sour cherry. On the mouth is intense with a good thick body, the tannin is evident but in the finish is quite relaxed.

★★★
ISOLE E OLENA

Località Isole, 1
50021 Barberino Val d'Elsa (FI)
Tel. +39 055 8072283
Fax +39 055 8072236
office@isoleolena.it
www.isoleolena.it

YEAR OF FOUNDATION **1956**
NAME OF THE OWNER **De Marchi Family**
TOTAL BOTTLES PRODUCED **200,000**
DIRECT SALES
VISITS TO THE WINERY - RESERVATION NEEDED
HECTARES OF VINEYARD **50**

Paolo De Marchi's Isole and Olena estate is a beacon for wine production in Chianti. His Chianti Classico is among the best and most reliable, even in off years, while his innovative wines are a point of reference. The Cabernet Sauvignon is among the five best in Italy, while his Cepparello, a varietal Sangiovese, and varietal Syrah sometimes even surpass it.

■ 96   Price C
Syrah Collezione de Marchi 2009

100% Syrah grapes. It matures 18 months in barrique. Great color for persistence and freshness.

On the nose is intense and very rich with aromas of blackberry, currant, plum and raspberry. On the mouth is juicy with a persistent palate, the pulp is supported by the acidity and the tannin is in great shape. Wonderful.

92   Price B
Chianti Classico 2014

Blend of Sangiovese, Cannaiolo and Syrah grapes. It matures in big oak barrels. Clean ruby color. On the nose aromas of iris and red flowers, whole typical fruits, tobacco, licorice and wildflowers. On the mouth is savory and tense, crisp, good body. The difficult year refine the drinkability, less powerful respect other years but easy to drink with an harmonic and eucalyptus finish.

91   Price C
Cepparello 2013

100% Sangiovese grapes. It matures in barrique and big oak barrels. Garnet ruby color. On the nose results very mature and evolved with aromas of syrup peach very rich and intense. On the mouth the fruit is very energetic, intense and warm, the drink is very rich and disruptive with taste of juniper, laurel and carnation.

ISTINE

Strada del Chianti
53017 Radda in Chianti (SI)
Tel. +39 0577 733684
info@istine.it
www.istine.it
istineraddainchianti

YEAR OF FOUNDATION 2009
NAME OF THE OWNER Anna Fronti
TOTAL BOTTLES PRODUCED 5,000
DIRECT SALES
VISITS TO THE WINERY - RESERVATION NEEDED
HECTARES OF VINEYARD 20
OLIVE OIL PRODUCTION

This young winemaking reality in Radda is Angela Fronti's dream come true. After promoting a number of Tuscan wine estates, she decided to work for herself and make wine from the grapes her family's estate had previously sold to other wineries. Her wines have a feminine touch and are elegant and pleasing while, at the same time, deeply rooted in the Radda terroir, which is mineral and rocky, and she has strived to exalt each single cru.

91   Price B
Chianti Classico Vigna Istine 2014

100% Sangiovese grapes from the homonym cru in Radda. It matures 12 months in 20 l durmast barrels. Good ruby color. On the nose is calm, attractive and thoughtful, aromatic and eucalyptus. On the mouth is savory, with taste of citrus and sage, lavender and cherry. Great tannins.

89   Price B
Chianti Classico Vigna Cavarchione 2014

100% Sangiovese from the homonym vineyard in Gaiole. It matures 12 months in 20 l Slavonia durmast barrels. Intense ruby color. On the nose aromas of sour cherry in spirit, black cherry, tobacco and licorice. On the mouth the tannin is sharp but pleasant, savory in the finish, very fruity balanced with the rest. A very modern wine but yet elegant.

88   Price B
Chianti Classico 2014

Blend of Sangiovese and Merlot grapes. It matures 12 months in big oak barrels. Alive ruby color. On the nose presents classic aromas of black cherry, smoky, raspberry, strawberry and mint. On the mouth is savory but fresh even if not very long with wood notes well integrated.

LA FORNACE

Podere Fornace, 154/a
53024 Montalcino (SI)
Tel. +39 0577 848465
info@agricola-lafornace.it
www.agricola-lafornace.it
brunellolafornace
@la_fornace_wine

YEAR OF FOUNDATION 1964
NAME OF THE OWNER Fabio Giannetti
TOTAL BOTTLES PRODUCED 18,000
DIRECT SALES
VISITS TO THE WINERY - RESERVATION NEEDED
HECTARES OF VINEYARD 4.5
OLIVE OIL PRODUCTION

Fabio Giannetti is bringing his family estate to new heights. This in regard to the overall quality and potential of their vineyards, situated in the area of Fornaci on the eastern side of Montalcino and close to the town. The estate's wines are classic in the use of 10 and 25hl bar-

433

rels for aging while fermentation takes place for the most part in stainless steel under temperature-controlled conditions.

 92 Price C

Brunello di Montalcino Riserva 2010

100% Sangiovese grapes. It matures in different kind of wood barrels. Well maintained ruby color. On the nose is complex with fruity aromas such as cherry, blackberry, warm spice and a delicate eucalyptus sweetness. On the palate is tasty, rich and elegant with tannins already sorted and a good acidity.

91 Price B

Brunello di Montalcino 2011

100% Sangiovese grapes. It matures in different kind of wood barrels. Garnet ruby color. On the nose is intense with warm aromas of peach and a light floral note well integrated with the red fruit. on the mouth is impactful and complex with soft tannins and a good progression.

★

LA FORTUNA

Località La Fortuna, 83
53024 Montalcino (SI)
Tel. +39 0577 848308
Fax +39 0577 846463
info@tenutalafortuna.it
www.tenutalafortuna.it
 La-Fortuna-Azienda-Agricola

YEAR OF FOUNDATION **1965**
NAME OF THE OWNER **Zannoni Family**
TOTAL BOTTLES PRODUCED **85,000**
DIRECT SALES
VISITS TO THE WINERY - RESERVATION NEEDED
HECTARES OF VINEYARD **18**
OLIVE OIL PRODUCTION

While the estate is just over 100 years old, wine production is more recent and later exploded under the guidance of Gioberto Zannoni and his son Angelo. The estate is on the northwest side of Montalcino where the clay soil begins to become less fertile and thinner. Over the years they have acquired vineyards in the southern part of town in order to have greater flexibility in making their Brunello Riserva. In the cellar they use barrels of various sizes, from barrique to 35hl Slovenian oak barrels. From last

year they came out a new wine, Giobi Brunello di Montalcino, made with a selection of Sangiovese from both the upper area of Canalicchi to the northeast, and, above all, the vineyards in Castelnuovo dell'Abate.

 95 Price C

Brunello di Montalcino Riserva 2010

100% Sangiovese grapes. It matures in different kind of wood barrels. Concentrated ruby color. On the nose aromas of clean and intense fruits such as cherry in front, the elegant spiciness make it a lot more complex. On the mouth is progressive with a second taste well balanced between tannins and acidity meanwhile in the finish is wide and deep to makes it very pleasant.

88 Price B

Brunello di Montalcino 2011

100% Sangiovese grapes. It matures in different kind of wood barrels. Classic blend of the estate, it result a very good product even this year. On the nose the warmer notes are stronger and even the color is less bright than usual without exceed on the garnet shade. On the nose the mature fruit doesn't bring up the usual notes of compote but remain more on earthy and spicy scents well supported by the mature cherry. On the mouth is clean and savory with an intense finish and sorted tannins.

85 Price A

Rosso di Montalcino 2014

100% Sangiovese grapes. It matures in oak barrels. Bright red color. On the nose it presents fresh and vegetal aromas at first , then scents of white cherry and flowers. On the mouth is soft with a fresh acidic note even if not very wide.

LA GERLA

Località Canalicchio
53024 Montalcino (SI)
Tel. +39 0577 848599
lagerla@tin.it
www.lagerlamontalcino.com

YEAR OF FOUNDATION **1978**
NAME OF THE OWNER **Eredi Sergio Rossi**
TOTAL BOTTLES PRODUCED **80,000**
DIRECT SALES
VISITS TO THE WINERY - RESERVATION NEEDED
HECTARES OF VINEYARD **11.5**
OLIVE OIL PRODUCTION

La Gerla is an estate with a great tradition. Founded by Sergio Rossi, who recently passed away, its Brunello has always had a traditional blend. The acquisition a few years ago of vineyards in the area of Castenuovo dell'Abate has allowed it to have greater leeway in interpreting the territory. The backbone of their production remains in the northern area of Canalicchi.

93 — Price C
Brunello di Montalcino Riserva degli Angeli 2010

100% Sangiovese grapes. It matures in oak barrels and tonneau. Bright garnet ruby color. On the nose intense aromas of black and red fruit such as blackberry, cherry, mulberry and with fresh flower scents. Nice delicate and elegant spiciness. On the mouth is elegant, full-bodied with well integrated tannins. Good acidity and tasty progression. Deep in the finish.

88 — Price C
Brunello di Montalcino 2011

100% Sangiovese grapes. It matures in oak barrels of different sizes. Garnet ruby color. On the nose is traditional with aromas of cherry, and black spices, little hint of compote scent. On the mouth is quite full-bodied with an exuberant but not unpleasant tannin. Relaxed and quite consistent in the finish.

LA LASTRA

Via L. de Grada, 9
53037 San Gimignano (SI)
Tel. +39 0577 941781
Fax +39 0577 941781
staff@lalastra.it
www.lalastra.it

YEAR OF FOUNDATION 1994
NAME OF THE OWNER Renato Spanu
TOTAL BOTTLES PRODUCED 39,000
DIRECT SALES
VISITS TO THE WINERY - RESERVATION NEEDED
HECTARES OF VINEYARD 5
HOSPITALITY

This estate makes a very particular Vernaccia, the product of the exposure and soil the grapes grown in. The vineyards are at a slightly higher altitude in an extremely hard and poor terrain, dominated by a wall of alberese limestone (lastra being slab). The grapes are sharp

and the estate exploits this by making wines which have a great capacity to age and have a very distinct acidity and mineral salinity. When young the wines can seem a bit surly but they are dynamic and with age…

89 — Price A
Vernaccia di San Gimignano Riserva 2014

100% Vernaccia grapes. It matures in big oak barrels. Straw yellow color. On the nose aromas of bramble, an hint of dark and yellow flowers, smoky and tea scents. On the mouth is intense, firm but tasty with polite fresh notes in accordance with the body of the wine.

86 — 👍 Price A
Vernaccia di San Gimignano 2015

100% Vernaccia grapes. It matures in stainless steel on yeast. pale straw yellow color. A slightly different version with wormer notes than usual. On the mouth is clean with aromas of black and green tea, oleander and in the finish candid citrus. On the mouth is morbid and tasty, with a controlled acidity. Savory in the finish.

LA SALA

Via Sorripa, 34
50026 San Casciano in Val di Pesa (FI)
Tel. +39 055 8240013
Fax +39 055 8240013
info@lasala.it
www.lasala.it
f *lasalavini*

YEAR OF FOUNDATION 1981
NAME OF THE OWNER Rossi Ferrini Family
TOTAL BOTTLES PRODUCED 40,000
VISITS TO THE WINERY - RESERVATION NEEDED
HECTARES OF VINEYARD 28
HOSPITALITY
OLIVE OIL PRODUCTION

An historic estate from the golden years of Chianti Classico that used to be owned by Laura Baronti, who died prematurely. It was acquired in 2014 by the Rossi Ferrini family who had been in Chianti for generations at their Azienda Agricola del Torriano estate. La Sala is the result of an important project involving plots of land with various exposures and altitudes and of its 68 hectares, 28 are vineyards and of these

27.6 registered Chianti Classico. The vineyards are situated at altitudes ranging from 150 to 310 meters above sea level in the districts of Torriano (Montefiridolfi which has a red soil and produce wines that are more structured and have intense colors) and San Casciano (where the soil has alberese limestone that gives elegance and freshness to the wine).

■ 90   👍 Price A
Chianti Classico 2013

Blend of 85% Sangiovese and 15% Merlot grapes. It matures for 12 months in stainless steel and big oak barrels on the nose is fine, polite and floral. On the mouth little hint of wood, elegant and discreet, good body with a fruity freshness that end with a savory taste. Funny, modern but yet a classic wine.

■ 88   Price B
Campo all'Albero 2012

Blend of Cabernet and Merlot gapes. It matures 18 months in barrique. Dark color. On the nose presents a bright and energetic fruit with aromas of pepper, ginger and citrus. On the mouth the tannin is mature, fresh and with a good length but not very agile to drink.

■ 88   Price B
Chianti Classico Riserva 2012

Blend of 85% Sangiovese and 15% Cabernet Sauvignon grapes. It matures 18 months between barrique and big oak barrels. Intense and load ruby color. On the nose deep aromas of blueberry, pepper and ginger. On the mouth is dark, peppery with notes of berries and an hint of toasted taste. on the nose is rich with an alcoholic trace.

LA SALCETA

Località Campogialli, 101
52028 Terranuova Bracciolini (AR)
Tel. +39 344 0109342
Fax +39 0557 471323
🅢 *lasalceta*
mail@lasalceta.it
www.lasalceta.it
🅕 *La-Salceta-organic-winery*
🐦 *@lasalceta*

YEAR OF FOUNDATION **1986**
NAME OF THE OWNER **Ettore Ciancico**
TOTAL BOTTLES PRODUCED **10,000**
DIRECT SALES

VISITS TO THE WINERY - RESERVATION NEEDED
HECTARES OF VINEYARD **4**
CERTIFIED ORGANIC VITICULTURE
OLIVE OIL PRODUCTION

La Salceta is a small winery in Valdarno di Sopra (which now DOC appellation) that has organic vineyards run by Ettore Ciancico, an ex-unionist and now passionate winemaker who is a big supporter of the new appellation. His wines are fresh, very pleasing and well-made.

■ 91   👍 Price A
Val d'Arno di Sopra Ruschieto 2013

Blend of 90% Sangiovese and 10% Cannaiolo grapes. Stainless steel only. Bright, alive ruby color. On the nose fruity aromas of cherry, plum and black cherry. On the mouth present an attractive drinkability, is tense, agile, fresh, savory and very pleasant. If there was a category called 'drink no stop' it would be perfect for this amazing wine from Val D'Arno.

▨ 88   Price A
Val d'Arno di Sopra Rosato Osato 2015

100% Cabernet franc grapes. stainless steel only. Intense pinkish color. On the nose is fragrant and deeply fruity with aromas of strawberry, plum and carnation. On the mouth is thin, fresh, delicious to drink with a medium-body and a good length.

LA TOGATA

Via del Colombaio, località Sant'Angelo in Colle
53024 Montalcino (SI)
Tel. +39 06 68803000
Fax +30 06 68134047
🅢 *latogata*
info@brunellolatogata.com
www.brunellolatogata.com
🅕 *brunello.latogata*

YEAR OF FOUNDATION **1990**
NAME OF THE OWNER **Danilo Tonon**
TOTAL BOTTLES PRODUCED **100,000**
DIRECT SALES
VISITS TO THE WINERY - RESERVATION NEEDED
HECTARES OF VINEYARD **15**

It seems like yesterday that this estate's first Brunello came out, whereas it has be 25 years. The volcanic lawyer who runs the estate, Danilo Tonon, has continually expanded it by acquiring plots in various areas of Montalcino in order to have a 'palette' of richer and varied grapes. The estate's headquarters and winery are between Argiano and Tavernelle on the southern side of Montalcino. The winery is modern but what is most surprising is that some of the aging barrels are kept in a temperature-controlled room in the manor house.

 94   Price C

Brunello di Montalcino La Togata dei Togati 2011

100% Sangiovese grapes. It matures in different kind of wood barrels. On the nose is classic and complex with aromas of spices, tobacco and leather, then intense blood orange, and morello with a great eucalyptus hint. On the mouth is important but relaxed, juicy, wide and progressive with a full-body. Deep and wide in the finish.

87   Price B

Brunello di Montalcino 2011

100% Sangiovese grapes. It matures in oak barrels. Intense garnet ruby color. On the nose presents at first eucalyptus scents and then cola and dark spices. The fruits are worm and mature. On the mouth is important with warm notes and a little rustic tannin but with a compact body. Slightly warm in the finish but tasty.

LAMOLE DI LAMOLE

Località Lamole
50022 Greve in Chianti (FI)
Tel. +39 055 9331411
Fax +39 055 8547014
info@lamole.com
www.lamole.com
 LamoleDiLamole
 @lamoledilamole

YEAR OF FOUNDATION 1974
NAME OF THE OWNER Gruppo Santa Margherita
TOTAL BOTTLES PRODUCED 242,000
DIRECT SALES
VISITS TO THE WINERY - RESERVATION NEEDED
HECTARES OF VINEYARD 57
OLIVE OIL PRODUCTION

The estate is in one of the most prestigious higher areas of Chianti Classico. The microclimate and a unique subsoil of rock and marl give

the wines salinity and intense floral aromas. It is an historic estate dear to Tuscans and when it became part of the Santa Margherita group became known worldwide. Great attention is paid to Sangiovese, its clones and to how it can grow in the vineyard.

93   Price B

Chianti Classico Gran Selezione Campolungo 2011

Blend of mainly Sangiovese grapes with an hint of Cabernet Sauvignon. It matures in big oak barrels and barrique. Garnet ruby color. On the nose aromas of laurel, black tea with hints of cherry. On the mouth is sweet with a finish of rose water and Alchermes, the tannin is very refined and spicy. Long and fresh in the finish.

92   Price B

Chianti Classico Riserva 2012

100% Sangiovese grapes. It matures 18 months in big oak barrels. Bright ruby color. On the nose is fresh with aromas of berries, laurel and tobacco. On the mouth is classic with a vivid tannin that close sweet and refined. Good classic style with a fresh imprint for the year.

91   👍 Price A

Chianti Classico Chianti Classico 2013

Blend of mainly Sangiovese grapes with hints of Cannaiolo. It matures in big oak barrels. Bright ruby color. A fine, sharp, distinctive wine with a sweet taste but savory, rocky and pleasant, good rhythm and attractive.

LANCIOLA

Via Imprunetana per Pozzolatico, 210
50023 Impruneta (FI)
Tel. +39 055 208324
info@lanciola.it
www.lanciola.it
 AziendaAgricolaLanciola

YEAR OF FOUNDATION 1978
NAME OF THE OWNER Andrea Guarnieri
TOTAL BOTTLES PRODUCED 200,000
DIRECT SALES
VISITS TO THE WINERY - RESERVATION NEEDED
HECTARES OF VINEYARD 40
HOSPITALITY
RESTAURANT
OLIVE OIL PRODUCTION

Andrea and Elisa Dabizzi's estate is not far from Florence and produces a Chianti Classico that is always recognizable and elegant. They also produce a number of quality table wines (their Chianti Colli Fiorenitni is a model for many) as well as personal wines with character that are always worth drinking like Terricci, a blend of Sangiovese with other varieties,

 92   Price B

Terricci 2012

Blend of 80% Sangiovese grapes with the rest 20% of Cabernet Franc and Cabernet Sauvignon. It matures 18 months in oak barrels of different sizes. Very intense ruby color. On the nose aromas of black cherry, currant and kirsch at first, then hints of spices and resin. On the mouth is full, warm, rich with still young tannins and a great length.

LE BERTILLE

Via San Bartolomeo, 1
53040 Montepulciano (SI)
Tel. +39 0578 758330
Fax +39 0578 758330
info@lebertille.com
www.lebertille.com
lebertille

YEAR OF FOUNDATION **2001**
NAME OF THE OWNER **Olimpia Roberti**
TOTAL BOTTLES PRODUCED **48,000**
DIRECT SALES
VISITS TO THE WINERY - RESERVATION NEEDED
HECTARES OF VINEYARD **10**
HOSPITALITY
OLIVE OIL PRODUCTION

This young and dynamic estate sits just bellows the San Biago Church and produces traditional wine. Acquired in 1971 by the Roberti family, it began bottling its own wines in the new millennium and their first Vino Nobile was 2006. Some of their vineyards have old vines that are in perfect balance with the land. This has allowed this estate to climb the ladder to become one of the wineries that 'count' thanks to the quality of their wines. The estate is run by Olimpia Roberti who left her law career to dedicate herself to her vineyards and wines.

 92   👍 Price A

Vino Nobile di Montepulciano 2013

Blend of Sangiovese grapes with hints of indigenous grapes. It matures in 25-30 lt oak barrels. Bright ruby color. On the nose is austere with aromas of underbrush, lightly smoky, floral and fruity with classic aromas of intense cherry and an hint of currant. On the mouth is elegant and intense with a good progression and a present but elegant tannin. In the finish is stretch, savory with a good taste of violet and very persistent.

LE CHIUSE

Località Pullera, 228
53024 Montalcino (SI)
Tel. +39 338 1300380
lorenzo.magnelli
info@lechiuse.com
www.lechiuse.com
azagr.lechiuse
@AzAgrLeChiuse

YEAR OF FOUNDATION **1987**
NAME OF THE OWNER **Simonetta Valiani**
TOTAL BOTTLES PRODUCED **27,000**
DIRECT SALES
VISITS TO THE WINERY - RESERVATION NEEDED
HECTARES OF VINEYARD **8**
HOSPITALITY
CERTIFIED ORGANIC VITICULTURE
OLIVE OIL PRODUCTION

This ancient estate was once part of the Biondi-Santi holdings but in 1986, Elisabetta Valiani decided to strike out on her own, after she inherited it from the female side of the family, and began producing Brunello. There are some eight hectares of vineyards on the eastern side of Montalcino in the direction of Siena. The vineyards are lovely and some of the vines are also very old. The exposure and position favor making traditional wines using 30 to 50hl barrels. The estate's wines, especially the reserves, are best in hotter years.

 87   Price B

Brunello di Montalcino 2011

100% Sangiovese grapes. It matures in oak barrels. Garnet ruby color. On the nose presents smoky notes and a vegetal scent with warm aromas of underbrush that create a nice contradiction. On the

mouth is fluent with sorted tannins and an average density. Fresh in the finish.

 86   Price B

Rosso di Montalcino 2014

100% Sangiovese grapes. It matures in oak barrels. Bright ruby color. On the nose is clean and intense with aromas of pale cherry, and fresh notes. On the mouth is fluent, elegant with a sorted tannin. Good acidity and tasty in the finish.

★

LE CINCIOLE

Via Case Sparse, 83 - Frazione Panzano
50022 Greve in Chianti (FI)
Tel. +39 055 852636
info@lecinciole.it
www.lecinciole.it
 Podere-Le-Cinciole

YEAR OF FOUNDATION 1991
NAME OF THE OWNER Luca and Valeria Orsini
TOTAL BOTTLES PRODUCED 42,000
DIRECT SALES
VISITS TO THE WINERY - RESERVATION NEEDED
HECTARES OF VINEYARD 13
CERTIFIED ORGANIC VITICULTURE
OLIVE OIL PRODUCTION

The ancient 'Lands of Quintius' today host one of the most famous and known estates in Conca d'Oro di Panzano, Podere Le Cinciole. Luca and Valeria Orsini have been running it for years with their passion for wine and have always played an important role in the local producers' association which seeks to promote the Panzano area.

 92   👍 Price A

Chianti Classico 2014

100% Sangiovese grapes. It matures 18 months in oak barrels of different sizes. Ruby red color. On the nose it present a good distinctive, savory fruit such as black cherry and cassis. On the mouth is pleasant, full-bodied but tasty. In the finish is quite long and salty and the drink is surprisingly alive.

 92   Price B

Chianti Classico Aluigi Riserva 2012

100% Sangiovese grapes. It matures 24 months in oak barrels. Ruby color with garnet reflexes. On the

nose is elegant and measured, spicy with aromas of incense and powder, raspberry and currant. On the mouth is vivid and firm, taste of citrus and strawberry, the tannin is spicy with a light alcohol trace with a great structure and substance kept together by a great freshness that is difficult to find in this terroir and during this particular year.

 91   Price B

Camalaione 2012

Blend of Cabernet, Merlot and Syrah grapes. It matures 20 months in barrique. Impressing and dark color. On the nose aromas of strawberry and raspberry. On the mouth is savory rich with a great body, citrusy, fresh and long with a very light pleasant bitter note.

★★

LE MACCHIOLE

Via Bolgherese, 189a - Frazione Bolgheri
57022 Castagneto Carducci (LI)
Tel. +39 0565 766092
info@lemacchiole.it
www.lemacchiole.it
 le.macchiole
 @LMacchiole

YEAR OF FOUNDATION 1983
NAME OF THE OWNER Cinzia Merli
TOTAL BOTTLES PRODUCED 140,000
VISITS TO THE WINERY - RESERVATION NEEDED
HECTARES OF VINEYARD 22

This estate was set up in Bolgheri before the area became famous and Eugenio Campolmi and his wife Cinzia Merli have always made sure the emphasis was on elegance. Great attention is paid to the vineyards and each parcel is processed separately. After the untimely death of Eugenio, Cinzia has continued to run the estate with determination.

 📷 95   Price C

Paleo Rosso 2013

100% Cabernet Franc grapes. 75% maures in new barrique and 25% matures in 20 years old one for 20 months. Compact and dark ruby color. On the nose is spicy with aroma of red fruit at first, then scents of Mediterranean maquis and an attractive hint of cedar. On the mouth is very rich, dense and wide but still very fresh. Good tannic trace and very long in the finish.

92 Price B

Bolgheri 2014

Blend of Merlot, Cabernet and Syrah grapes. 80% matures in used barrique and 20% in concrete vat for 11 months. Dense and dark ruby color. On the nose is intense, spicy and austere with aromas of cinchona and graphite. Austere as well on the mouth, fresh and tasty with hints of licorice. The tannin is crisp and is persistent in the finish.

 92 Price D

Messorio 2013

100% Merlot grapes.75% of it matures in new barrique and 25% of it in second passage ones for 20 months. Compact and intense ruby color. On the nose remind of sweet scents with aromas of berries and compote, black cherry, maple syrup, blueberry pie. On the mouth is beautiful, tasty, whole with tannins just evident due to the youth. Spicy notes that make the finish very long.

★★

LE POTAZZINE

Località Le Prata, 262
53024 Montalcino (SI)
Tel. +39 0577 846168
Fax +39 0577 847974
tenuta@lepotazzine.it
www.lepotazzine.it
f *Tenuta-Le-Potazzine*
🐦 *@LePotazzine*

YEAR OF FOUNDATION **1993**
NAME OF THE OWNER **Giuseppe Gorelli and Gigliola Giannetti**
TOTAL BOTTLES PRODUCED **38,000**
DIRECT SALES
VISITS TO THE WINERY - RESERVATION NEEDED
HECTARES OF VINEYARD **4.6**
RESTAURANT

Giuseppe Gorelli and his wife Gigliola are two, fun and excellent entrepreneurs and their bistro restaurant is one of the most reliable in Montalcino. Their wine estate, Le Potazzine, was founded at the start of the 1990s on the ashes of the old one that belonged to Giuseppe's father and which had been named Due Portine and was cited by critics for the quality of its wines. Giuseppe built a winery near the vineyards, in the upper part of Montalcino, and expanded the estate by buying a few hectares in the area of Sant'Angelo in Collle, where a different microclimate added vigor to their wines.

 95 Price C

Brunello di Montalcino 2011

100% Sangiovese grapes. It matures in oak barrels. Garnet ruby color. On the nose it present complex and fresh scents with aromas of white and black cherry, lightly eucalyptus with notes if cinchona and blond tobacco, pale and clean. On the mouth is completely vertical with acidity and tannin already sorted meanwhile the wide body doesn't affect the progression. Savory and persistant in the finish.

★

LE RAGNAIE

Località Le Ragnaie
53024 Montalcino (SI)
Tel. +39 0577 848639
Fax +39 0577 848758
info@leragnaie.com
www.leragnaie.com
f *leragnaie*
🐦 *@LeRagnaie*

YEAR OF FOUNDATION **1996**
NAME OF THE OWNER **Riccardo Campinoti**
TOTAL BOTTLES PRODUCED **70,000**
DIRECT SALES
VISITS TO THE WINERY - RESERVATION NEEDED
HECTARES OF VINEYARD **15.5**
HOSPITALITY
RESTAURANT
OLIVE OIL PRODUCTION

2011 has been a complex vintage for the winery guided by Riccardo Campinoti: his Brunello's are good as always but they are a little too 'Burgundy style' that doesn't go well with Montalcino in this particular vintage. The style of the winery is solid and very recognizable with a very nice aromatic profile, very territoria and nice for the vintage.

◼ **89** Price D

Brunello di Montalcino Fornace 2011

100% Sangiovese grapes. It matures in oak barrels. Typical color, a not too intense ruby. On the nose is classic, slightly evolved with aromas of violet that finish on notes of dark tobacco, hints of alfalfa. On the mouth is strong with a mature tannin well integrate in the warm structure of the wine. Remind of floral notes in the finish.

86   Price B

Rosso di Montalcino 2012

100% Sangiovese grapes. It matures in oak barrels. Unexposed ruby color. On the nose is balanced and fresh with aromas of white cherry and rose with a eucalyptus note. On the mouth is elegant and savory with sorted tannins and a good acidity.

86   Price D

Brunello di Montalcino V.V. 2011

100% Sangiovese grapes. It matures in oak barrels. Clean garnet color. On the nose aromas of licorice, tobacco, peach and a light spicy note. On the mouth is elegant with a balanced acidity. Even is the floral notes come back on the palate, is still not convincing.

LENZINI

*Via della Chiesa, 44 - Località Gragnano
55012 Capannori (LU)
Tel. +39 0583 974037 - +39 340 1820713
Fax +39 0583 974514
tenuta@tenutalenzini.it
www.tenutalenzini.it*
f *TenutaLenzini*

YEAR OF FOUNDATION 1993
NAME OF THE OWNER Lenzini Family
TOTAL BOTTLES PRODUCED 50,000
DIRECT SALES
VISITS TO THE WINERY - RESERVATION NEEDED
HECTARES OF VINEYARD 13
HOSPITALITY
CERTIFIED ORGANIC VITICULTURE
OLIVE OIL PRODUCTION

The Lenzini estate in Gragnano, in the province of Lucca, dates back to the 16th century. It is currently run by Elisabetta, the daughter of Franco Lenzini who acquired the estate at the end of the 1970s, and her husband Michele Guarino. The vineyards are mostly composed of indigenous grapes to underscore the ancient trade ties with France (the Via Francigena pilgrim road passes through here). The style of the wines is modern with an extensive use of small, French oak barrels.

90   Price B

Poggio de' Paoli 2012

Blend of Cabernet Sauvignon, Cabernet Franc, Alicante Bouschet and Syrah grapes. It matures 2 years in big oak barrels. Dark ruby color. On the nose is pleasant with aromas of almond that brings with it scents of dark fruit and graphite. On the mouth is dense and fresh with velvety tannins and a tasty finish.

87   👍 Price A

Colline Lucchesi Merlot Casa e Chiesa 2014

100% Merlot grapes. stainless steel only for 2 years. Violet ruby color. On the nose aromas of red plum, blueberry, currant, and an hint of spices. On the mouth is balanced and pleasant with a good acidity and nice drinkability.

★★

LILLIANO

*Via Lilliano, 8
53011 Castellina in Chianti (SI)
Tel. +39 0577 743070
Fax +39 0577 743036*
S *tenutadililliano*
*info@lilliano.it
www.lilliano.it*
f *Tenuta-di-Lilliano*

YEAR OF FOUNDATION 1920
NAME OF THE OWNER Giulio and Pietro Ruspoli
TOTAL BOTTLES PRODUCED 150,000
DIRECT SALES
VISITS TO THE WINERY - RESERVATION NEEDED
HECTARES OF VINEYARD 45
HOSPITALITY
OLIVE OIL PRODUCTION

Another medieval village with a long history and another magical place to visit. Adding to this tourist attraction in recent years is the estate of Giulio Ruspoli who has turned Lilliano into a great Chianti wine destination. His wines, from Chianti Classico to the vintage Riserva and Anagallis, are always dependable.

94   Price B

Chianti Classico Gran Selezione 2012

Blend of 80% Sangiovese with hints of Corolino and Merlot. It matures for 2 years in big oak barrels. In-

tense and alive ruby color. On the nose is extremely typical, is the emblem of the Chianti Classico from Castellina, with aromas of black cherry, violet and tobacco. On the nose is savory, full=bodied, warm but agile and with a great persistence.

 92   🖒 Price A

Chianti Classico 2013

Blend of 80% Sangiovese and other red berry grapes. Pale ruby color. It matures for almost 1 year in big oak barrels. On the nose is fragrant and fruity with aromas of violet, cherry, light cassis and carnation. On the mouth is fresh, savory, very pleasant and averagely long.

442

★★

LISINI

Podere Casanova - Località Sant'Angelo in Colle
53024 Montalcino (SI)
Tel. +39 0577 844040
azienda@lisini.com
www.lisini.com
🅵 AziendaAgrariaLisini

YEAR OF FOUNDATION Inizi 1600
NAME OF THE OWNER Lisini Family
TOTAL BOTTLES PRODUCED 80,000
DIRECT SALES
VISITS TO THE WINERY - RESERVATION NEEDED
HECTARES OF VINEYARD 20
OLIVE OIL PRODUCTION

This historic Montalcino estate is situation in one of the most suited areas in the whole district. Sesta is where every producer would like to have a vineyard because of the excellent and healthy way the grapes ripen here. At Lissini they are bringing back some very old vines that have never been grafted and are in an isolated vineyards that has a sandy soil. Another estate cru is Ugolaia that also produces Brunello but only in the best years. The wines are bold and intense and age in both barrique and 30hl barrels.

 97   Price C

Brunello di Montalcino Ugolaia 2010

100% Sangiovese grapes. It matures in barrels made with woods. Garnet ruby color. On the nose is intense with aromas of underbrush, morello, cinchona and citrus. very intense. On the mouth is powerful and elegant thanks to the strong but el-

egant tannin. A progressive wine with a thick body and a compact and complex finish. A great version of this great classic wine from the area of Sesta.

■ **87**   Price B

Brunello di Montalcino 2011

100% Sangiovese grapes. It matures in oak barrels. Well maintained garnet ruby color. On the nose it presents warm and dark aromas such as cherry under spirit and an hint of chocolate and notes of smoke and cinchona. On the mouth is tasty supported by the alcohol and the polite tannin. Avaragely long in the finish.

MANTELLASSI

Località Banditaccia, 26
58051 Magliano in Toscana (GR)
Tel. +39 0564 592037
info@fattoriamantellassi.it
www.fattoriamantellassi.it
🅵 Fattoria-Mantellassi
🐦 @FattMantellassi

YEAR OF FOUNDATION 1960
NAME OF THE OWNER Aleardo and Giuseppe Mantellassi
TOTAL BOTTLES PRODUCED 980,000
DIRECT SALES
VISITS TO THE WINERY - RESERVATION NEEDED
HECTARES OF VINEYARD 100
OLIVE OIL PRODUCTION

This historic winery in the area of Scansano produces wines with a classic style using large barrels and traditional winemaking methods involving long and cold maceration. Its many vineyards produce not only the classic Morellino grape, made in various versions, but also an intriguing Alicante wine that ages long in the bottle. The wines are a homage to the land with a tartness that gives them a distinct personality and a long aftertaste.

■ **89**   Price B

Quercliolaia 2010

100% Alicante grapes. It matures in different kind of wood barrels for q6 months. Garnet color. On the nose is clear and intense with aromas of spices, flowers such as rose, alfalfa and an hint of graphite. On the mouth is simply elegant and clean, fruity and juicy, soft and relaxed with a good tannin and a fruity finish. A classic wine from the Maremma.

89   Price B
Morellino di Scansano Sentinelle Riserva 2011

Blend of 85% Sangiovese and 15% Alicante grapes. It matures for 18 months in barrique and big oak barrels. Garnet color. On the nose is intense and very traditional with aromas of tobacco, red fruits like black cherry and orange skin. On the mouth is dense with the sweetness of the fruit that work very well with the mature tannin. Fruity in the finish.

86   Price A
Morellino di Scansano San Giuseppe 2013

Blend of 85% Sangiovese grapes with Cabernet Sauvignon and Cannaiolo Nero . It matures 6 months in oak barrels. Ruby color. On the nose aromas of dry cherry tomato with more classic floral notes such as cherry and black cherry, lightly eucalyptus. On the mouth is fruity with a slightly aggressive tannin but at the end it results very fluent.

MAREMMALTA

Località Casteani
58023 Gavorrano (GR)
Tel. +39 0566 80049
🔵 *maremmalta*
info@maremmalta.it
www.maremmalta.it
📘 *MaremmAlta*
🐦 *@MaremmaltaRizzi*

YEAR OF FOUNDATION **2006**
NAME OF THE OWNER **Stefano Rizzi**
TOTAL BOTTLES PRODUCED **50,000**
DIRECT SALES
VISITS TO THE WINERY - RESERVATION NEEDED
HECTARES OF VINEYARD **10**
CERTIFIED ORGANIC VITICULTURE

This young and tiny estate is near Gavorrano, in the Monteregio area of Massa Marittima. It is here that Stefano Rizzi, an authentic wine professional who has worked as a salesman in Italy and the United States and produced wine in Maremma, has created his retreated. The organic wines are craft-made and very interesting.

☐ 88   👍 Price A
Vermentino Micante 2015

Blend of 90% Vermentino and 10% Sauvignon

Blanc grapes. stainless steel only for 5 months. Bright straw yelllow color.on the nose is fruity with aromas of cedar and white peach, light smoky scents due to the yeasts. On the mouth is fresh, savory, tense, thin, very pleasant and with an average persistence.

★★
MASTROJANNI

Podere Loreto e San Pio
53024 Monticiano (SI)
Tel. +39 0577 835681
info@mastrojanni.com
www.mastrojanni.com
📘 *MastrojanniWine*
🐦 *@MastrojanniWine*

YEAR OF FOUNDATION **1975**
NAME OF THE OWNER **Gruppo Illy**
TOTAL BOTTLES PRODUCED **100,000**
DIRECT SALES
VISITS TO THE WINERY - RESERVATION NEEDED
HECTARES OF VINEYARD **24**

Being acquired by the Illy Group has given a great boost to this beautiful estate that gave prestige to the area of Castelnuovo dell'Abate at the beginning of the 1980s. Continuity has been ensured by Andrea Machetti who has always worked at the winery. A total renewal of the store of aging barrels and the vineyards, which is still in progress, have given the wines great quality and excellent stylistic definition. Restructuring the winery, on the other hand, made it more productive and easy to work in.

🈂 95   Price D
Brunello di Montalcino Vigna Schiena d'Asino 2010

100% Sangiovese grapes. It matures in oak barrels. Garnet ruby color. On the nose dark notes both spiced and fruity with aromas of blackberry and classic morello. On the mouth is predominant the youth of the tannin even if well integrated in the thick body. Progression and finish of great impact.

94   Price C
Brunello di Montalcino Vigna Loreto 2011

100% sangiovese grapes. It matures in oak barrels. Classic ruby color not too strong. On the nose is clean with aromas of ancient morello, blackberry and a good underbrush, warm spices. On the mouth is great with a slightly relaxed tannin and a good but never sickly density. In the finish the warm notes come back.

■ 88   Price B
Brunello di Montalcino 2011

100% Sangiovese grapes. It matures in oak barrels. Garnet ruby color. On the nose classic aromas of blond tobacco and leather that rules on the yellow fruits and an hint of cherry. On the mouth is dense with a sorted tannin and a medium acidity that support the warm flavor. Classic in the finish.

GIORGIO MELETTI CAVALLARI

*Via Bolgherese - Località Vallone
57022 Castagneto Carducci (LI)
Tel. +39 0565 775620
Fax +39 0565 775620
info@giorgiomeletticavallari.it
www.giorgiomeletticavallari.it*
f *giorgiomeletticavallari*

YEAR OF FOUNDATION **2002**
NAME OF THE OWNER **Giorgio Meletti Cavallari**
TOTAL BOTTLES PRODUCED **50,000**
DIRECT SALES
VISITS TO THE WINERY - RESERVATION NEEDED
HECTARES OF VINEYARD **7**
HOSPITALITY

Giorgio is the son of Giovanni Meletti Cavallari who in the 1980s came out with one of the first Bolgheri wines with an international style, Grattamacco (later acquired by Claudio Tipa of ColleMassari). He has followed in his father's footsteps with his small estate, in Bolgheri, that he founded in 2002 when he was 24 years old. He achieved his goal of upmost quality with an extraordinary Bolgheri Superiore, Impronte.

■ 92   Price B
Bolgheri Superiore Impronte 2013

Blend of 70% Cabernet Sauvignon and 30% Cabernet Franc grapes. It matures for 14 months in new barrique. Very dark ruby color. On the nose initial aromas of coffee followed by red and black fruits, graphite, an hint of pepper and a blow of flowers. On the mouth is elegant and austere, savory with an hint of tannins and a good freshness. In the finish is tense and tasty.

■ 87   Price A
Bolgheri Borgeri 2014

Blend of 40% Cabernet Sauvignon, 40% Merlot and 20% Syrah grapes. It matures for 8 months in barrique. Not too dense ruby color. On the nose is fruity with an hint of citrus and aromas of spices and graphite. On the mouth is full, peppery, quite fresh with good tannins. Pleasant even if a little simple.

★★
MELINI

*Località Gaggiano
53036 Poggibonsi (SI)
Tel. +39 0577 998511
Fax +39 0577 989002
melini@giv.it
www.cantinemelini.it*
f *melinichianti*
🐦 *@melinichianti*

YEAR OF FOUNDATION **1705**
NAME OF THE OWNER **Gruppo Italiano Vini**
TOTAL BOTTLES PRODUCED **4,000,000**
DIRECT SALES
VISITS TO THE WINERY - RESERVATION NEEDED
HECTARES OF VINEYARD **145**
OLIVE OIL PRODUCTION

Here we unite the presentations of Melini and Machiavelli because they both belong to Gruppo Italiano Vini and have the same technical staff. Melini is based in Poggibonsi where its Granaio vineyard is located. But their most prestigious vineyard is La Selvanella, in Lucarelli, just past Panzano and in the village of Radda by just a few meters. The name of this cru was the first to be cited on the label of a Chianti Classico back in 1969. It is a spectacular, single vineyard of about 50 hectares on the brow of a hill that is some 500m above sea level. Machiavelli's winery and vineyards, on the other hand, are in Sant'Andrea in Percussina in the northwest sector of Chianti Classico and its historic cru, Vigna di Fontalle, it there.

■ 🍇 95   Price B
Chianti Classico Vigneto La Selvanella Riserva 2012

100% Sangiovese grapes. It matures for 3 years in big oak barrels. Intense garnet ruby color. On the nose aromas of violet, black cherry with light notes of smoke and hints of berries. On the mouth is tense, savory, very elegant, with just a little hint of tannins and a fresh acidity that remind the altitude of the vineyard. It close thin and very persistent. Typically emblematic.

93 Price B
Chianti Classico Gran Selezione Terra Rossa 2012

Blend of 85% Sangiovese and 15% Merlot grapes. It matures 6 months in barrique and then for 2 years in big oak barrels. Very intense ruby color. On the nose aromas of black cherry, raspberry, vanilla and kirsch. On the mouth is full-flavored with thick but integrated tannins, savory and persistent.

89 Price A
Il Principe Machiavelli 2013

Blend of 83% Cabernet Sauvignon and 17% Sangiovese grapes. It matures 1 year in barrique. Very intense ruby color. On the nose aromas of black currant, raspberry, light black cherry, sweet spice. On the mouth is tense, with great acidity, medium body and a finish with a little aggressive tannins.

MONTECHIARI

Via di Montechiari, 27
55015 Montecarlo (LU)
Tel. +39 0583 22189
info@montechiari.com
www.montechiari.it
FattoriaDiMontechiari

YEAR OF FOUNDATION 1978
NAME OF THE OWNER Moreno Panattoni
TOTAL BOTTLES PRODUCED 45,000
DIRECT SALES
VISITS TO THE WINERY - RESERVATION NEEDED
HECTARES OF VINEYARD 10
CERTIFIED ORGANIC VITICULTURE
OLIVE OIL PRODUCTION

Not many people know that the so-called international grapes have always been cultivated in the province of Lucca and, in particular, in Montecarlo. Moreno Panattoni and his wife have dedicated themselves to these French varieties from the beginning and have, with the consultancy of enologist Stefano Chioccioli, achieved quality results. This is especially true of their Cabernet that stands always out for its splendid characteristics.

90 Price B
Cabernet 2013

Blend of Cabernet Sauvignon and Cabernet Franc from a 30 years old vineyard. It matures in barrique for 20 months. Worm red ruby color. On the nose the range of aromas go from scents of graphite , laurel to the black currant. On the mouth is savory, with a young but elegant tannin, tasty and progressive and intense and fulfilling in the finish.

86 Price B
Merlot 2013

100% Merlot grapes. It matures for 16 months in barrique. Bright ruby color. On the nose is wide and fruity with aromas of currant and red berry, light smoky note. On the mouth is fresh and not too heavy with a nice tannin. Fruity in the finish.

MONTENIDOLI

Località Montenidoli
53037 San Gimignano (SI)
Tel. +39 0577 941565
S elisabetta.montenidoli
montenidoli@valdelsa.net
www.montenidoli.com

YEAR OF FOUNDATION 1965
NAME OF THE OWNER Elisabetta Fagiuoli
TOTAL BOTTLES PRODUCED 120,000
DIRECT SALES
VISITS TO THE WINERY - RESERVATION NEEDED
HECTARES OF VINEYARD 25
HOSPITALITY
CERTIFIED ORGANIC VITICULTURE
OLIVE OIL PRODUCTION

The fact that 25 hectares produce 120,000 bottles of wine says a lot about the maniacal care Elisabetta Fagiuoli takes in selecting grapes first and then the musts. She is a strong-willed woman who is sometimes a bit testy but she has made Vernaccia a great wine and the territory more important. There is no precise estate style but a perfect combination of Elisabetta's vision and the land through. Her wine Fiore highlights the freshness and floral nature of Vernaccia; Tradizionale the tradition of aging on the skins; and Carato is an example of extreme aging and the use of wood. Three ways to interpret a territory.

445

☐ 86   Price A

Vernaccia di San Gimignano Fiore 2014

100% Vernaccia grapes. stainless steel only. Intense straw yellow color. Traditional wine that presents on the nose floral aromas of dry flowers, mature fruits and an hint of star anise. On the mouth is rich, intense almost tannic.

MONTERAPONI

*Località Monteraponi
53017 Radda in Chianti (SI)
Tel. +39 0577 738208
Fax +39 0577 541120*
🆂 *monteraponi*
mail@monteraponi.it
www.monteraponi.it
🅵 *Monteraponi*
🐦 *@Monteraponi*

YEAR OF FOUNDATION **1974**
NAME OF THE OWNER **Braganti Family**
TOTAL BOTTLES PRODUCED **45,000**
DIRECT SALES
VISITS TO THE WINERY - RESERVATION NEEDED
HECTARES OF VINEYARD **10**
HOSPITALITY
CERTIFIED ORGANIC VITICULTURE
OLIVE OIL PRODUCTION

Michele Braganti's estate has new vineyards on the horizon and he is paying greater attention to the estate's cru and to a Chianti Classico that is a model of reliability. Very interesting also a Trebbiano white in Bourgogne style. Michele is a good producer and optimistic about the future.

 96   Price B

Chianti Classico Il Campitello Riserva 2013

Blend of Sangiovese, Cannaiolo and Colorino grapes from the homonym vineyard in the woods. It matures 26 months in big oak barrels. Intense ruby color. On the nose the fruit is energetic and results salty yet sweet with aromas of currant, raspberry, pepper, sour cherry and tobacco. On the mouth the tannins are well integrated and matures ti support a vibrant and very fresh palate with an always fresh and refreshing fruit. in the finish is long and exiting.

■ 93   Price C

Baron'Ugo 2012

Blend of Sangiovese, Cannaiolo and Colorino grapes form the homonym vineyard at 500 m above sea level. It matures for 36 months in Slavonia or French oval barrel. From Chianti Classico Riserva it began IGT during a particular year. On the nose intense aromas of spices and freshness, mint. On the mouth the acidity give a nice sharpness to the wine with taste of blood orange, is savory with a strong pace and a savory finish that persist very long.

■ 91   👍 Price B

Chianti Classico 2014

Blend of Sangiovese and Cannaiolo grapes. It matures for 16 months in big oak barrels. The difficult year bring the grapes of the Baron'Ugo to benefit the Chianti Classico and the wine present the energy of the cru vineyard that usually is vinified separately. Pale ruby color. On the nose is sumptuous and firm with aromas of fresh flower and fruits. On the mouth is savory and proud with floral and citrusy notes, the tannin is very pleasant and the acidity is sustained but well integrated.

MONTETI

*Strada Della Sgrilla, 6
58011 Capalbio (GR)
Tel. +39 0564 896160
Fax +39 0564 896160*
🆂 *tenutamonteti*
info@tenutamonteti.it
www.tenutamonteti.it

YEAR OF FOUNDATION **2001**
NAME OF THE OWNER **Paolo Baratta**
TOTAL BOTTLES PRODUCED **102,000**
DIRECT SALES
VISITS TO THE WINERY - RESERVATION NEEDED
HECTARES OF VINEYARD **28**

In only a few years Paolo Baratta has created an estate that stands out for its quality, management of the vineyards and attention to detail, all of which have made Monteti not only an already reliable estate but one with a bright future. The wines are not many but are distinguished by their structure, intensity and salinity that allow them to age well and precisely express the terroir of Capalbio and neighboring areas.

91   Price B

Caburnio 2012

50% Cabernet Sauvignon, 25% Merlot, 15% Alicante and the rest Cabernet Franc and Petit Verdot grapes. It matures for 12 months half in stainless steel half in barrique. Dark ruby color. On the nose is intense with aromas of rose, cherry and pyridine notes, spicy and a little eucalyptus. On the mouth is intense, full-bodied, tasty but a little nervous cause of the young tannin. Good in the finish.

MONTEVERRO

*Villa Villaggio Capalbio
58011 Capalbio (GR)
Tel. +39 0564 890721
info@monteverro.com
www.monteverro.com*
🅵 *monteverrowines*
🐦 *@Monteverro*

YEAR OF FOUNDATION **2008**
NAME OF THE OWNER **George Weber**
TOTAL BOTTLES PRODUCED **200,000**
DIRECT SALES
VISITS TO THE WINERY - RESERVATION NEEDED
HECTARES OF VINEYARD **50**
OLIVE OIL PRODUCTION

At his estate in Capalbio, Georg Weber shows no signs to slow down and relax. On the contrary, he continues to incessantly explore the Maremma terroir maintaining separate harvest for tiny plots, using natural fermentation, making separate vinification and experimenting with different wood barrels.

93   Price D

Monteverro 2013

Blend of Cabernet Sauvignon, Cabernet Franc and Merlot with an hint of Petit Verdot grapes, 2 years in barrique. An authentic "Tuscan Bordeaux". Dark ruby color. On the nose is full-flavored with aromas of Mediterranean maquis close to classic scents of blueberry, cassis and vanilla. On the mouth is full-flavored, silky tannins, great finish. Everything is perfect but not too close the territory, obviously.

☐ **91**   Price C

Chardonnay 2013

100% Chardonnay grapes. 75% Of the grapes matures in barrique for 14 months and the rest in con-

crete vats. Light golden yellow color. On the nose intense aromas of exotic fruits at first, then aromas of vanilla and saffron. On the mouth is warm, polite but not heavy. Very persistent.

★★

MONTEVERTINE

*Località Montevertine
53017 Radda in Chianti (SI)
Tel. +39 0577 738009
info@montevertine.it
www.montevertine.it*
🅵 *Montevertine*
🐦 *@pergole_torte*

YEAR OF FOUNDATION **1967**
NAME OF THE OWNER **Martino Manetti**
TOTAL BOTTLES PRODUCED **80,000**
VISITS TO THE WINERY - RESERVATION NEEDED
HECTARES OF VINEYARD **18**
OLIVE OIL PRODUCTION

Like his father Sergio before him, Montevertine owner Martino Manetti by choice does not produce Chianti Classico DOCG to protest the regulations for its production that he does not agree with. But he does make some fantastic wines from only Sangiovese grapes which achieve, even in off years, surprising levels of quality. The jewel in his productive crown is Le Pergole Torte, a famous wines that is appreciated in Italy for its finesse and balance that few can match.

94   Price C

Le Pergole Torte 2013

100% Sangiovese grapes. Ages for 18 months in Slavonian oak and 6 months in Allier barrique. Ruby garnet. Multi dimensional wine, fresh, violent but also soft and gentle. Intense fruity notes of raspberry and currant, tobacco and bay leaf, anise. Developing tannin yet the palate is explosive and it reflects the vintage: generous and fresh.

90   Price B

Montevertine 2013

Blend of 90% Sangiovese, Canaiolo and Colorino grapes. Ages for 24 months in Slavonian oak barrels. Lively ruby. This wine shows power and cleanness, body and juice, cherry and black cherry. The palate offers citrusy flavors, weight, very long and supple despite the weight, good structured tannins even if they need time to refine.

★

MORISFARMS

Località Cura Nuova - Fattoria Poggetti
58024 Massa Marittima (GR)
Tel. +39 0566 919135
Fax +39 0566 919380
🅢 *morisfarms*
morisfarms@morisfarms.com
www.morisfarms.com
🔗 *morisfarms*
🐦 *@Morisfarms*

YEAR OF FOUNDATION **1971**
NAME OF THE OWNER **Moris Family**
TOTAL BOTTLES PRODUCED **300,000**
DIRECT SALES
VISITS TO THE WINERY - RESERVATION NEEDED
HECTARES OF VINEYARD **70**
HOSPITALITY
OLIVE OIL PRODUCTION

The winery founded by Gualtiero Moris and lead by his son-in-law, Adolfo Parentini, represents one of the stronghold of Maremma. Divided betrween Massa Marittima andScansano it has always presented wines of great personality and high quality. The style is modern-classic style with a very laic use of wood in wines. Here was born the Avooltore, one of the iconic wines of Maremma. In the last years with the arrival of his son Guilio, the winery has taken a moderate modernist style with a more fruity aromatic profile. The falcon (locally called 'avvoltore') continues to fly high.

■ **89**   Price B
Morellino di Scansano Riserva 2012

Blend of 90% Sangiovese, Cabernet and Merlot grapes. Ages for 1 year in used barrique. Deep and dark ruby. Classic nose of Meremma sangiovese with violet blossoms and blackberry jam, spicy notes of black pepper. The palate is dense, smooth, flavorful, well made, with a medium sweet finish.

NITTARDI

Località Nittardi
53011 Castellina in Chianti (SI)
Tel. +39 0577 740269
🅢 *fattoria.nittardi*

info@nittardi.com
www.nittardi.com
🔗 *fattoria.nittardi*
🐦 *@nittardi*

YEAR OF FOUNDATION **1980**
NAME OF THE OWNER **Leon Femfert and Stefania Canali**
TOTAL BOTTLES PRODUCED **94,000**
DIRECT SALES
VISITS TO THE WINERY - RESERVATION NEEDED
HECTARES OF VINEYARD **29**
HOSPITALITY
OLIVE OIL PRODUCTION

Peter Femfert and Stefania Canali have for a few years now passed the helm of the estate to their son Leon, who has embraced his work with the enthusiasm and determination that only the young have. It helps, of course, to have grown up in Nittardi, an idyllic place between Castellini and Panzano. Under his guidance the wines seem to have bloomed again and all seems to be going for the best even in the Maremma winery.

■ **94**   Price B
Chianti Classico Riserva 2013

Blend of 95% Sangiovese and 5% Merlot grapes. Ages for 2 years in barrique and tonneau. Very intense ruby. Captivating and spicy on the nose, elegant, refined, with notes of cassis and violet. Warm palate, full bodied yet supple, savory and well balanced by the acidity.

■ **92**   Price B
Nectar Dei 2013

Blend of 50% Cabernet Sauvignon with Merlot, Petit Verdot and Syrah grape from the Mongibello della Mandorlaia property in Maremma. Ages for 18 months in barrique. Intense ruby garnet. Captivating nose, intense notes of cassis, blueberry, raspberry, vanilla and violet. Savory palate, well-executed, firm but refined tannins, elegant and long.

■ **89**   Price A
Chianti Classico Bel Canto 2014

Blend of 90% Sangiovese, Malvasia Nera, Colorino and Canaiolo grapes. Ages for 1 year in tonneau. Lively ruby. Definitively fruity, violet, black cherry, prune and a hint of vanilla on the nose. Medium bodied, crunchy acidity, savory, tense, very pleasant.

ORMA

Via Bolgherese
57022 Castagneto Carducci (LI)
Tel. +39 0575 477857
dd@ormabolgheri.it
www.ormabolgheri.com
 f *OrmaBolgheri*
 y *@OrmaBolgheri*

YEAR OF FOUNDATION 2005
NAME OF THE OWNER Antonio Moretti
TOTAL BOTTLES PRODUCED 30,000
VISITS TO THE WINERY
HECTARES OF VINEYARD 5

Aside from this estate in Bolgheri, Antonio Moreti owns the Tenuta Sette Ponti estate near Arezzo and Feudo Maccari near Noto, both included in this guide. Here he makes only one wine, Orma, a classic Bordeaux-style, 'rive droit' red.

---

 96   Price C

Orma 2013

Blend of 50% Merlot, 30% Cabernet Sauvignon and 20% Cabernet Franc grapes. Ages for 15 months in barrique. Intense ruby with violet hues. Very impressive nose, raspberry, spices, cassis on a lightly oaky background well balanced and integrated with the nose profile. Sleek palate, composed, savory, supple despite the good body and with a very long finish.

ORMANNI

Località Ormanni
53036 Poggibonsi (SI)
Tel. +39 0577 937212
info@ormanni.it
www.ormanni.net
 f *Ormanni*

YEAR OF FOUNDATION 1818
NAME OF THE OWNER Paolo Brini Batacchi
TOTAL BOTTLES PRODUCED 75,000
DIRECT SALES
VISITS TO THE WINERY - RESERVATION NEEDED
HECTARES OF VINEYARD 60
HOSPITALITY

Paolo Brini Batacchi has been running this estate between Poggibonsi and Castellina in Chianti for years. His wines have a long life, a classic style and are dry and rigorous, the product of decades of tasting with the legendary Giulio Gambelli. He has always worked with Sangiovese with passion and respect but has also experimented with international grapes for his different wines. But the great terroir is obviously best expressed in his Chianti Classico and the famous Riserva Borro del Diavolo.

■ 92   Price B

Chianti Classico Gran Selezione Etichetta Storica 2011

100% Sangiovese grapes. Ages for 24 months in large casks. Ruby garnet. A classic. Well-defined nose of lavender, red currant, strawberry jam, black pepper and tobacco. Ample palate, sleek yet fresh and flavorful, long and elegant.

■ 90   Price A

Chianti Classico 2013

Blend of Sangiovese and Canaiolo grapes. Ages in large casks. Light ruby. Lavander, currant and raspberry, fresh and classic. A safe bet.

■ 87   Price B

Chianti Classico Borro del Diavolo Riserva 2012

100% Sangiovese grapes. Ages in partially new barrique. Shiny ruby. Lightly overripe nose but refined and lively. Spiky and pleasant palate with savoriness and floral aftertaste; flavorful finish.

SIRO PACENTI

Località Pelagrilli
53024 Montalcino (SI)
Tel. +39 0577 848662
Fax +39 0577 846935
 S *siro.pacenti*
info@siropacenti.it
www.siropacenti.it

YEAR OF FOUNDATION 1970
NAME OF THE OWNER Pacenti Family
TOTAL BOTTLES PRODUCED 80,000
DIRECT SALES
VISITS TO THE WINERY - RESERVATION NEEDED
HECTARES OF VINEYARD 22

Giancarlo Pacenti is a very important figure in the evolution of Brunello's history. He was the first to explore the potential of using barrique and because of this is considered the leader of the 'modernists'. His estate is very beautiful; the cellar with its barrels is magnificent; in the fermentation area where they also studiy fermentation agents; and his vineyards are on two opposite sides of Montalcino. Giancarlo recently created a new Brunello using only grapes from his northern vineyard and larger barrels for aging.

■ 🔲 96   Price D
Brunello di Montalcino PS Riserva 2010

100% Sangiovese grapes. Ages in barrique and tonneau. Deep and shiny ruby. Ample nose, intense and refined, classic note of cherry and a hint of eucalyptus and spices, then dark fruits. Very classy palate with smooth tannins yet still young but elegant. Very consistent finish.

■ 94   Price B
Brunello di Montalcino Vecchie Vigne 2011

100% Sangiovese grapes. Ages in tonneau and barrique. Intense ruby. Ample nose with intense fruity notes of cherry, lightly spicy. Balanced palate, flavorful and captivating with very well extracted tannins and an intense and long finish.

■ 90   Price B
Rosso di Montalcino 2013

100% Sangiovese grapes. Ages in different sized oak barrels. Intense ruby. Clean and defined nose with notes of cherry and smoky hint. Rich palate with a wonderful balanced acidity that eases the drink. Juicy finish. As usual a very complex Rosso di Montalcino for Giancarlo Pacenti.

PALAGETTO

Via Racciano, 10
53037 San Gimignano (SI)
Tel. +39 0577 943090
Fax +39 0577 943249
info@palagetto.it
www.palagetto.it
🅕 *palagettosrl*

YEAR OF FOUNDATION **1991**
NAME OF THE OWNER **Sabrina Niccolai**
TOTAL BOTTLES PRODUCED **400,000**

DIRECT SALES
VISITS TO THE WINERY - RESERVATION NEEDED
HECTARES OF VINEYARD **44**
HOSPITALITY
RESTAURANT
OLIVE OIL PRODUCTION

This all-female estate is run by Sabrina Niccolai, a renowned entrepreneur in the camper sector. Passion, strength and determination are the characteristics she applies to winemaking. The vineyards are spread out around the area of San Gimignano and are constantly being 'tweaked' with the older vines kept if they are productive and non-productive vines replaced no matter what their age. In the winery, which has just been restored, technology is welcome as long as it does not alter the estate's style and only improves it.

□ 88   👍 Price A
Vernaccia di San Gimignano Santa Chiara 2015

100% Vernaccia grapes. Only stainless steel. Straw yellow. Intense and defined nose of yellow flower such as broom blossoms, hint of saffron and loquat. Good firm palate with balanced acidity. Good weight and a long finish.

□ 88   Price B
Vernaccia di San Gimignano Ventanni 2014

100% Vernaccia grapes. Only stainless steel. Straw yellow. Multi-layered nose: reductive notes and warm hint of honey, fruity aromas of ripe loquat and apricot. Rich and intense palate. Smooth but subtle. Controvertial wine in different tastings.

PANZANELLO

Via Case Sparse, 86 - Località Panzano
50022 Greve in Chianti (FI)
Tel. +39 055 852470
Fax +39 055 8549090
🅢 *andrea-panzanello*
commerciale@panzanello.it
www.panzanello.it
🅕 *PanzanelloWinery*

YEAR OF FOUNDATION **1964**
NAME OF THE OWNER **Andrea Sommaruga**
TOTAL BOTTLES PRODUCED **80,000**
DIRECT SALES

VISITS TO THE WINERY - RESERVATION NEEDED
HECTARES OF VINEYARD 16
HOSPITALITY
RESTAURANT
CERTIFIED ORGANIC VITICULTURE
OLIVE OIL PRODUCTION

Andrea and Iole Sommaruga have been running their family estate for some 15 years during which time they have transformed themselves from super-Roman city folk to passionate and competent winemakers. The recent history of the Panzanello estate, with its vineyards on the hills overlooking the village, as well as its wines is also that of their new life and while their Roman accents may come out every once in a while, this is all they retain from their past life.

 91   Price B
Il Manuzio 2010
Blend of Sangiovese and Merlot grapes. Ages for 2 years in barrique. Dark ruby garnet. Captivating and slightly developed nose. Aromas of sour cherry and tamarind then kirsch. The palate is well balanced by the acidity; full bodied but supple and with a refined tannin. Warm and long finish.

88   Price A
Chianti Classico 2014
Blend of Sangiovese with a small percentage of Merlot grapes. The 60% ages in third fill French oak barrels, the 40% in stainless steel. Lively ruby, violet then hint of black cherry and berries. Savory and tense palate, very typical, supple, medium bodied with a thin and long finish.

★
PETRA

*Località S. Lorenzo Alto, 131
57028 Suvereto (LI)
Tel. +39 0565 845308
info@petrawine.it
www.petrawine.it*
 petrawine

YEAR OF FOUNDATION 1997
NAME OF THE OWNER Francesca Moretti
TOTAL BOTTLES PRODUCED 350,000
DIRECT SALES
VISITS TO THE WINERY - RESERVATION NEEDED
HECTARES OF VINEYARD 94
OLIVE OIL PRODUCTION

This Suvereto winery first became the talk of the town for architectural reasons, the spectacular and futuristic winery design by Swiss architect Mario Botta, and then for the challenge Vittorio Moretti, a great entrepreneur in Franciacorta, made over ten years ago to produce a red wine that could stand up with the best. The Maremma estate now has over 100 hectares of vineyards that practically surround the winery that is just a few kilometers from the sea. Mostly Cabernet Sauvignon, Merlot and Sangiovese are cultivated and production is in the firm and competent hand of Francesca Moretti.

89   Price C
Petra Rosso 2012
Blend of 70% Cabernet Sauvignon and 30% Merlot grapes. Ages for 18 months in barrique. Intese and dark ruby. Warm nose, ripe red fruits, mulberry and blueberry, then a citrusy hint of blood orange and aromatic herbs. The palate is rich and opulent, powerful and fruity.

★★
PETROLO

*Via di Petrolo, 30
52021 Bucine (AR)
Tel. +39 055 9911322
petrolo@petrolo.it
www.petrolo.it*
 Tenuta.Petrolo

YEAR OF FOUNDATION 1947
NAME OF THE OWNER Lucia Bazzocchi, Luca and Maria Sanjust
TOTAL BOTTLES PRODUCED 70,000
DIRECT SALES
VISITS TO THE WINERY - RESERVATION NEEDED
HECTARES OF VINEYARD 31
HOSPITALITY

The Galatrona Tower, which for centuries has dominated the landscape in Valdarno, is part of the Petrolo estate and lends its name to its top wine. Luca Sanjust has always produced wine of the utmost quality there with the help of Carlo Ferrini. This year saw the debut of Campolusso, a Cabernet Sauvignon that joins Bòggina (and Bòggina Anfora) and, above all, Galatrona which has become Vigna Galtrona Valdarno Superiore DOC. The appellation is an important development for the area and followed the great 'inArno' initiative in which grapes of from producers through the area were blended together to create a true territorial wine from the bottom.

 95   Price C

Val d'Arno di Sopra Sangiovese Vigneto di Bòggina 2013

100% Sangiovese grapes. Matures 18 months in different size barrels. Intense and dark ruby red. Incredibly expressive notes of black cherry and violet, very classic, together with very refined notes of resin and tobacco. Savory and tense in the mouth, with light tannins and an agile and tense body, a wine of great elegance but not without muscles.

91   Price B

Val d'Arno di Sopra Pietraviva Torrione 2013

Blend of 80% Sangiovese, with Merlot and Cabernet Sauvignon grapes. Matures 15 months in barrique. Intense garnet ruby red. Intense and enveloping notes of Kirsch, black berry, raspberry and spicy hints in the background. Some youthful tannins edge, acceptable, with some roughness and a warm, persistent finish.

★

PIAGGIA

Via Cegoli, 47
59016 Poggio a Caiano (PO)
Tel. +39 055 8705401
🅢 *piaggia*
info@piaggia.com
www.piaggia.com
f *PIAGGIA*
🐦 *@vinipiaggia*

YEAR OF FOUNDATION 1990
NAME OF THE OWNER Silvia Vannucci
TOTAL BOTTLES PRODUCED 75,000
DIRECT SALES
VISITS TO THE WINERY - RESERVATION NEEDED
HECTARES OF VINEYARD 15
OLIVE OIL PRODUCTION

In a little more than 20 years, the Vannucci family has built up a winery in Poggio a Caiano, in the heart of Carmignano, which has taken center stage. The wines are bold, full of per-

sonality and have a capacity to age. In short, they're very good.

91   Price B

Poggio de' Colli 2014

100% Cabernet Franc grapes. Ages for 15 months in barrique. Dark ruby. Defined and intense fruity nose of candied cedar, than red currants, mulberry and eucalyptus. Good weight on a palate, fruity, soft and silky tannins and elegant finish.

87   Price B

Carmignano Riserva 2013

Blend of 70% Sangiovese and 30% Cabernet Sauvignon and Merlot grapes. Ages for 18 months in barrique. Intense ruby. Tight nose, then shows fruity aromas of cassis and then a hint of chestnut. The palate is savory, full and juicy, with firm tannins and a good acidity. Velvety finish.

PIANCORNELLO

Località Piancornello
53024 Montalcino (SI)
Tel. +39 3396886671
piancornello@libero.it

YEAR OF FOUNDATION 1990
NAME OF THE OWNER Caludio Monaci
TOTAL BOTTLES PRODUCED 30,000
DIRECT SALES
VISITS TO THE WINERY - RESERVATION NEEDED
HECTARES OF VINEYARD 7

Claudio Monaci is a serious, well-mannered and somber person who before he was swept away by Brunello had a lovely career as a doctor behind him. He works his small estate, on the southeastern edge of Montalcino overlooking Monte Amiata, with enthusiasm and his vineyards are in a plot of land on the Orcia stream which marks the town's border. Some difficult years and the painful (for the estate's production) separation from his sister hurt the quality of his wines but he is back on top with his 2011 Brunello. The winery's style is neo-classic with a moderate use of wood and fermentation.

92   Price B

Brunello di Montalcino 2011

100% Sangiovese grapes. Ages in casks and tonneau. Intense ruby. Nose of ripe fruits, mulberry, sour cherry and black cherry; then refreshing nose of eucalyptus, cedar and Mediterranean herbs. Wonderful palate and depth with tannin that eases the drink. The finish is flavorful, juicy and of great personality.

PIANDACCOLI

Via di Piandaccoli, 7 - Frazione Malmantile
50055 Lastra a Signa (FI)
Tel. +39 055 0750005
Fax +39 055 0750004
info@piandaccoli.it
www.piandaccoliwine.com
 f *Piandaccoli*
 𝕏 *@PiandaccoliWine*

YEAR OF FOUNDATION 2004
NAME OF THE OWNER Giampaolo Bruni
TOTAL BOTTLES PRODUCED 80,000
DIRECT SALES
VISITS TO THE WINERY - RESERVATION NEEDED
HECTARES OF VINEYARD 20
HOSPITALITY
OLIVE OIL PRODUCTION

Giampaolo Bruni has made his dream come true in Lastra a Signa. A splendid estate with holiday farmhouse and winery where he started producing wines of great interest. We must point out the recovery of an ancient and almost forgotten indigenous grape: Foglia Tonda. This was a cultural and well as winemaking feat and our compliments go out to Giampaolo Bruni.

 93   Price B
Foglia Tonda 2013

100% Foglia Tonda grapes. Ages for 15 months in tonneau. Intense and lively ruby. Very particular nose with notes of wild strawberries and cassis. Floral aromas of violet and rose. Spicy and vanilla hints on the background. Deliciously tense palate. Good structure but supple and crunchy, slightly edgy acidity. Very long finish.

 90   👍 Price A
Chianti Cosmus Riserva 2012

100% Sangiovese grapes. Ages for 1 year in large casks. Lively ruby. Fragrant and fruity, not very complex but pleasant. Notes of black cherry and violet. Agile and savory palate, good body and easy drinking. Unpretentious but well made.

PIETROSO

Podere Pietroso, 257
53024 Montalcino (SI)
Tel. +39 0577 848573
Fax +39 0577 848573
info@pietroso.it
www.pietroso.it
 f *pietrosomontalcino*

YEAR OF FOUNDATION 1970
NAME OF THE OWNER Gianni Pignattai and Cecilia Brandini
TOTAL BOTTLES PRODUCED 30,000
DIRECT SALES
VISITS TO THE WINERY - RESERVATION NEEDED
HECTARES OF VINEYARD 6
OLIVE OIL PRODUCTION

This family-run estate has some four hectares registered as Brunello denomination that are in vineyards located in three different areas of Montalcino, the preferred being the ones at the higher altitude. Few months ago Gianni and Cecilia acquired the vineyard in Montasoli, they used to rent, and new land not far from the cellar. The estate's style is quite classic with long maceration on the skins and long aging in medium-sized barrels (30hl). Special attention is paid to fermentation which take place in both stainless steel and wood vats in order to best maintain the estate's style that is all geared for excellence.

 93   Price B
Villa Montosoli 2012

Blend of Sangiovese with small percentage of indigenous grapes. Ages in barrels. Shiny ruby. Intense and defined nose: fruity notes of cherry, blackberry and mulberry; elegantly spicy, subtle warm notes. Very intense palate, flavorful with good weight and smooth and classy tannins. Intense and elegant finish.

 89   Price B
Brunello di Montalcino 2011

100% Sangiovese grapes. Ages in casks. Ruby with garnet hues. Dark nose with fruity aromas of blackberry and prune. Medium intensity palate, elegant, developed tannin, despite being young it is well integrated with the body of the wine.

★★
PIEVE DI SANTA RESTITUTA

Località Chiesa di Santa Restituta
53024 Montalcino (SI)
Tel. +39 0577 848610
info@pievesantarestituta.com

YEAR OF FOUNDATION 1994
NAME OF THE OWNER Angelo Gaja
TOTAL BOTTLES PRODUCED
VISITS TO THE WINERY - RESERVATION NEEDED
HECTARES OF VINEYARD

The Montalcino winery of Angelo Gaja is incredibly beautiful with its ancient church, wonderful vineyards and incredible winery-cellar that is totally underground. It was carved out of the rock and is embellished with works of art and he interior is all made out of steel, iron and wood.

| 93 | Price D |

Brunello di Montalcino Sugarille 2011

100% Sangiovese grapes from a single vineyard. Quite dark and shiny color. Multi-layered nose: leather, blossoms and ripe fruits. Captivating palate, warm, serious: aftertaste of ripe cherry and chocolate, then refined and elegant tannins that enhance the drink sip after sip. Textbook length.

| 91 | Price D |

Brunello di Montalcino Rennina 2011

100% Sangiovese grapes, blend of 3 vineyard. Very dark color, almost inky with violet hues. Generous nose of forest fruits, tobacco and wet leaves; than offers hint of violet and spicy aromas. Firm palate with well defined tannins, quite elegant and refined. Good depth and notable length.

PODERE ALBIANO

Via Podere Albiano, 42 - Località Petroio
53020 Trequanda (SI)
Tel. +39 0577 665386
🄢 poderealbiano
info@poderealbiano.it
www.poderealbiano.it
🅵 Podere-Albiano

YEAR OF FOUNDATION 2002
NAME OF THE OWNER Alberto Turri

TOTAL BOTTLES PRODUCED 20,000
DIRECT SALES
VISITS TO THE WINERY - RESERVATION NEEDED
HECTARES OF VINEYARD 4

Alberto Turri, a born and raised Milan businessman, first fell in love with Anna Becheri, agricultural expert, and then with the Tuscan countryside in Val d'Orcia. In 2000, he took the plunge and built a wine estate in Albiano from nothing. It is situated at the feet of the enchanting village of Petroio, north of Pienza, and the vineyard was planted in 2002 in the soon-to-be DOC Orcia appellation. Its four hectares are most of all Sangiovese and with the consultancy of enologist Paolo Vagaggini and agronomist Laura Bernini and the first vintage produced was 2009.

| 90 | Price B |

Orcia Rosso Tribolo 2011

100% Sangiovese grapes. Ages for 30 months in 10hl Slavonian oak barrels. Ruby garnet. Elegant and intense fruity nose of cherry and plum; face powder and vanilla aromas enrich the floral notes. Fresh palate, long and well structured. Lightly almond finish. Top class wine.

PODERE ASSOLATI

Località Podere Assolati
58033 Castel del Piano (GR)
Tel. +39 349 2241055 (Luca)
info@assolati.it
www.assolati.it

YEAR OF FOUNDATION
NAME OF THE OWNER Loriano Giannetti
TOTAL BOTTLES PRODUCED 20,000
DIRECT SALES
VISITS TO THE WINERY - RESERVATION NEEDED
HECTARES OF VINEYARD 5
HOSPITALITY
OLIVE OIL PRODUCTION

Never has a name (Sunny Farm) been more appropriate. The farmhouse at the center of the estate receives sun all day long and from it there is a magnificent 360° view of the landscape. Luca and Silvia Gianetti are young but they had to take over running the estate after their father was killed in an accident. They gave it their heart and soul and have achieved excellent results with an increasing level of quality. Aside from wine, the production of which is still limited, they also raise Chianina cattle, grow wheat and produce olive oil.

 92   👍 **Price A**

Montecucco Sangiovese Assolati 2013

Blend of 95% Sangiovese and 5% of Colorino and Canaiolo grapes. Ages for 8-12 months in different sized oak barrel from barrique to 20 hl barrels. Light ruby. Austere nose, notes of licorice and a well defined fruity aromas. Mouthfilling, fresh and savory, very youthful with firm but still vibrant tannins.

 90   **Price B**

Montecucco Sangiovese Assolati Riserva 2013

100% Sangiovese grapes. Ages for 18 months in barrique. Ruby with garnet rim. The nose initially a bit tight, than offers foxy notes, spices and fruity nose of cherry. The palate is fresh, full, very fruity with still evident tannins, highlighted specially in the dry finish.

PODERE CAPACCIA

Località Capaccia
53017 Radda in Chianti (SI)
Tel. +39 0577 738385
capaccia@chianticlassico.com
www.poderecapaccia.com
❤ *Podere-Capaccia*

YEAR OF FOUNDATION Inizio anni '70
NAME OF THE OWNER Herman De Bode
TOTAL BOTTLES PRODUCED 25,000
VISITS TO THE WINERY - RESERVATION NEEDED
HECTARES OF VINEYARD 4
CERTIFIED ORGANIC VITICULTURE

The estate of Belgian Herman De Bode is situated on one of the highest hills in Radda and his wines have undergone a slight change in style with a more pronounced use of Sangiovese and greater territorial expression. Aside from Sangiovese, the estate also cultivates Canaiolo and traditional grapes like Ancellotta. The soils of the vineyards are assorted with marl, alberese limestone and tuff stone and are located just north of the town of Radda, an area particularly suited for winegrowing and home to a number of illustrious estates.

 91   **Price B**

Chianti Classico Riserva 2012

Blend of Sangiovese with small percentage of Ancellotta grapes. Ages for 24 months in barrique. Dark ruby. Notes of rhubarb and blossoms, then ink, rose, violet and incense. Vibrant tannins, fresh; aromatic and strawberries aftertaste, the finish reminds notes of eucalyptus and spices.

 90   **Price B**

Podere Capaccia 2012

100% Sangiovese grapes. Ages for 18 months in barrique. Ruby garnet. Intense, savory and chalky, fruity and spicy, black pepper and resin. Flavorful and very intense palate, firm tannins with decent body and a citrusy finish; good depth.

★

PODERE FORTE

Località Petrucci
53023 Castiglione d'Orcia (SI)
Tel. +39 0577 888510
Fax +39 0577 888721
podereforte@podereforte.it
www.podereforte.it
❤ *PodereForte*
🐦 *@podereforte*

YEAR OF FOUNDATION 1997
NAME OF THE OWNER Pasquale Forte
TOTAL BOTTLES PRODUCED 24,000
DIRECT SALES
VISITS TO THE WINERY - RESERVATION NEEDED
HECTARES OF VINEYARD 14
CERTIFIED ORGANIC VITICULTURE
CERTIFIED BIODYNAMIC VITICULTURE
OLIVE OIL PRODUCTION

For Pasquale Forte, a famous entrepreneur with a passion for wine and the country, this is a dream come true. His estate is in a simply wonderful place and the result of a careful restoration of the building and the magnificent landscape. The wines are excellent and made with impeccable skill from grapes that were cultivated according to bio-dynamic methods.

🟥 93   **Price C**

Orcia Petrucci 2012

100% Sangiovese grapes. Ages for 16 months in barrique. Very intense ruby. The nose is still oaky, sweet spices, black cherry, kirsch and sweet tobac-co. Great palate, rich, captivating, still a bit tannic, youthful and very promising. Warm and long finish.

■ 91   Price B
Orcia Petruccino 2013

Blend of 70% Sangiovese and 30% Merlot grapes. Ages for 14 months in barrique. Intense and live-ly ruby. captivating nose, fruity and spicy. Savory palate, tense, good body, velvety tannins with warm and a good length finish.

PODERE LA REGOLA

Località San Martino
56046 Riparbella (PI)
Tel. +39 0588 81363
Fax +39 0588 90378
info@laregola.com
www.laregola.com
f *Podere-La-Regola*
🐦 *@LRegola*

YEAR OF FOUNDATION 1990
NAME OF THE OWNER Flavio and Luca Nutti
TOTAL BOTTLES PRODUCED 90,000
DIRECT SALES
VISITS TO THE WINERY - RESERVATION NEEDED
HECTARES OF VINEYARD 20
OLIVE OIL PRODUCTION

Brothers Luca (agronomist) and Flavio (law-yer) are among the most active producers seeking to promote the area of Riparbella and the wine it produces: Montescudaio, one of the many DOC appellations of the Tuscan coast. Their estate is a few kilometers from the sea in the valley created by the Cecina River and a stone's throw from the splendid Etruscan city of Volterra. Their production line is very vast – offering dozens of wines to satisfy every taste – and is personally monitored by Luca with the assistance of consultant Luca D'Attoma.

■ 90   Price B
La Regola 2013

Blend of 85% Cabernet Franc, Merlot and Petit Verdot grapes. Ages for 12 months in new barrique. Dark ruby. Very varietal nose, fine herbs, pencil lead, black forest fruits. Dense palate, firm, good weight with silky tannins; ample and long finish.

PODERE LE RIPI

Località Le Ripi
53024 Montalcino (SI)
Tel. +39 0577 835641
S *podere.le.ripi.*
info@podereleripi.it
www.podereleripi.it
f *Podere-Le-Ripi*
🐦 *@PodereLeRIpi*

YEAR OF FOUNDATION 2003
NAME OF THE OWNER Francesco Illy
TOTAL BOTTLES PRODUCED 30,000
DIRECT SALES
VISITS TO THE WINERY - RESERVATION NEEDED
HECTARES OF VINEYARD 13
CERTIFIED ORGANIC VITICULTURE
CERTIFIED BIODYNAMIC VITICULTURE
OLIVE OIL PRODUCTION

Francesco Illy is a creative man full of original ideas that may seem to go against the grain. At his estate on the southeastern side of Montal-cino he had increased the density of his vine-yards which has begun to produce some inter-esting results. The density is 12,000 to 60,000 vines, in his already famous bonsai vineyard, and the grapes are mostly Sangiovese. In order to better understand the fermentation process and the convection of the musts, he had a trans-parent vat built as well as truncated cones. Var-ious sizes of barrels are used for aging and he is experimenting with other containers.

■ 93   Price C
Rosso di Montalcino Amore e Magia 2011

100% Sangiovese grapes. Ages in different sized oak barrels. Intense ruby with garnet hues. Red fruit nose, spices, eucalyptus. Very impressive pal-ate for intensity and drinkability, great tannins and good depth. A great Rosso even in this version.

■ 93   Price D
Brunello di Montalcino Lupi e Sirene Riserva 2010

100% Sangiovese grapes. Ages in different sized oak barrels. Intense ruby with garnet hues. Defined nose of cherries and sour cherries, hint of tobacco, leather and citrusy aromas. Great personality on the palate, rich, dynamic and juicy. Very long finish.

★★
PODERE SAPAIO

Località Lo Scopaio, 212
57022 Castagneto Carducci (LI)
Tel. +39 0565 765187/239
info@sapaio.it
www.sapaio.it
 Podere-Sapaio

YEAR OF FOUNDATION 1999
NAME OF THE OWNER Massimo Piccin
TOTAL BOTTLES PRODUCED 90,000
VISITS TO THE WINERY - RESERVATION NEEDED
HECTARES OF VINEYARD 25
OLIVE OIL PRODUCTION

This is a relatively young estate in Bolgheri and an extremely dynamic one. For the beginning it has attracted the attention of consumers and critics thanks to the boldness, concentration and characteristics of their wines, which with age obtain elegance and an ability to age. Massimo Piccin's aim is to achieve quality through experimentation and he is assisted in this by Carlo Ferrini.

90	Price C

Bolgheri Superiore 2013

Blend of 70% Cabernet Sauvignon, 20% Petit Verdot and 10% Cabernet Franc grapes, 18 months in barrique. Dark and deep ruby with violet hues. Warm and intense nose with oaky notes and sweet spices, black fruit and a hint of Virginia tobacco. Mouth filling palate, almost opulent, slightly aggressive tannins, still a bit young. Very warm finish.

87	Price B

Bolgheri Volpolo 2014

Blend of 70% Cabernet Sauvignon, 15% Merlot and 15% Petit Verdot grapes. Ages for 14 months in barrique and tonneau. Deep purple ruby. The nose is still very oaky, then it opens to spicy and floral notes. Mouth filling palate, good tannins, good freshness and length.

PODERE TORCILACQUA

Strada Greve, 8 - Località Badia a Passignano
50028 Tavarnelle Val Di Pesa (FI)
Tel. +39 055 8071598
Fax +39 055 8071598
info@torcilacqua.it

www.torcilacqua.it
 PodereTorcilacqua

YEAR OF FOUNDATION
NAME OF THE OWNER Mauro Bianchi
TOTAL BOTTLES PRODUCED 10,000
DIRECT SALES
VISITS TO THE WINERY - RESERVATION NEEDED
HECTARES OF VINEYARD 7
HOSPITALITY
OLIVE OIL PRODUCTION

The estate of agronomist Mauro Bianchi can boast to having some of the most panoramic Sangiovese vineyards in the Florentine side of Chianti Classico given that they overlook the beautiful Passignano Abbey. The great boldness and energy of the wines always maintain a somber elegance fully respecting the spirit of the terroir of an area that many producers are rediscovering.

93	Price B

Chianti Classico Gran Selezione 2013

100% Sangiovese grapes. Ages for 24 months in used barrique. Shiny ruby. Notes of fresh raspberry, currant, under spirit fruit, vanilla and a sweet tobacco. Well-balanced palate, spicy and vanilla aftertaste, smooth tannins, good depth and freshness that eases the drink.

91	Price A

Chianti Classico 2013

100% Sangiovese grapes. Ages for 1 year in barrique. Ruby garnet. Very traditional nose, thin without being weak, black pepper, smoky, intense, interesting and flavorful fruity aromas. Very unique palate with delicate tannin and a citrusy, mint and eucalyptus finish.

##
POGGIO AL TESORO

Via Bolgherese, 189B - Frazione Bolgheri
57022 Castagneto Carducci (LI)
Tel. +39 0565 765245
info@poggioaltesoro.it
www.poggioaltesoro.it
 AllegriniEstates
 @AllegriniWine

YEAR OF FOUNDATION 2002
NAME OF THE OWNER Allegrini Family

TOTAL BOTTLES PRODUCED 283,000
DIRECT SALES
VISITS TO THE WINERY - RESERVATION NEEDED
HECTARES OF VINEYARD 60

A 70-hectare estate with vineyards that are on hillsides as well as near the sea creating a zone that can best bring out the 'soul' of Bolgheri. This was the intent of Walter Allegrini when he decided to expand from his property in Valpolicella and invest in Bolgheri. He currently has four parcels of vineyards: two along the Via Bolgherese road, another and the largest in the district of Le Sondraie, very close to the sea, and the fourth in the town of Bibbona. The vineyards were the soil is sandy and rich in rock fragments are planted with Cabernet and Petit Verdot to bring out their boldness and concentration, while Merlot is grown in soil rich in minerals and clay to give it elegance and fragrance.

94 Price C
Bolgheri Superiore Dedicato a Walter 2013
100% Cabernet Franc grapes. Ages for 18 months in new barrique. Very dark, intense and deep ruby. very complex and intense nose: pencil lead, cedar, green peppercorn, dark fruits and herbaceous notes. Very rich palate, balanced acidity, velvety and captivating, powerful and supple.

92 Price B
Bolgheri Superiore Sondraia 2013
Blend of Cabernet Sauvignon, Merlot and Cabernet Franc grapes. Ages for 18 months in barrique (50% new). Ruby with purple rim. Ecalyptus nose, Mediterranean Scrub then pencil lead, black spices and a hint of raspberry. The palate is fresh, mouth filling, with sweet fruit and bell pepper aftertaste; powerful finish.

POGGIO AL VENTO

Via Poggio al Vento, 7
53023 Castiglione d'Orcia (SI)
Tel. +39 347 1806276
info@poggioalvento.net
www.poggioalvento.net
 f famigliaMascelloni

YEAR OF FOUNDATION 1961
NAME OF THE OWNER Roberto Mascelloni
TOTAL BOTTLES PRODUCED 15,000

DIRECT SALES
VISITS TO THE WINERY - RESERVATION NEEDED
HECTARES OF VINEYARD 4.5
HOSPITALITY
CERTIFIED ORGANIC VITICULTURE
OLIVE OIL PRODUCTION

A three-time archery champion during the famous Barbarossa historical re-enactment that has taken place every year since 1957 in San Quirico d'Orcia, Roberto Mascelloni has dedicate these victories to his showcase wine Arcere, where he hit the bullseye with an excellent Sangiovese that incarnates the purest Val d'Orcia tradition. Poggio al Vento is a family-run farm estate that also has holiday accommodation and produces not only wine but some excellent olive oil as well. It is surrounded by a breathtaking landscape and is caressed by the breezes from Valle del Fiume Orcia.

88 Price A
Orcia Sangiovese Arcere 2012
Blend of Sangiovese, Merlot and Foglia Tonda grapes. Ages for 2 years in barrique and tonneau. Dark and intense ruby. intense and fruity, then captivating foxy notes; it is still young and shows spicy notes of vanilla and clove. Meaty palate, juicy and fulfilling fruity aftertaste.

POGGIO ANTICO

Località Poggio Antico
53024 Montalcino (SI)
Tel. +39 0577 848044
 poggioanticomarketing
mail@poggioantico.com
www.poggioantico.com
 f PoggioAnticoMontalcino

YEAR OF FOUNDATION 1976
NAME OF THE OWNER Gloder Family
TOTAL BOTTLES PRODUCED 128,000
DIRECT SALES
VISITS TO THE WINERY - RESERVATION NEEDED
HECTARES OF VINEYARD 32.5
RESTAURANT
OLIVE OIL PRODUCTION

A great, classic Montalcino estate run by the legendary Paola Gloder, who came here from

Milan many years ago. The estate offers wines of great quality made with different styles, exemplifying their great ability to interpret the territory. The vineyards are well-cared for as is the winery-cellar which is totally air conditioned and extremely efficient. They make three Brunello; the classic using 30-40hl barrels for aging; Altero which ages in barrique and tonneau barrels; and a Riserva in a good year.

![] 90   Price C
Brunello di Montalcino Riserva 2010

100% Sangiovese grapes. Ages in different sized barrels. Deep and intense ruby. Intense nose of red fruit and spicy hint, then aromas of leather and tobacco. The palate offers refined tannins, medium weight and a flavorful finish.

![] 89   Price B
Brunello di Montalcino 2011

100% Sangiovese grapes. Ages in different sized barrels. Ruby with garnet rim. Warm notes of jam on the nose, undergrowth and hint of almond. Warm palate, rich and captivating with slightly rough tannin.

★★★
POGGIO DI SOTTO

Località Castelnuovo dell'Abate
53024 Montalcino (SI)
Tel. +39 0577 835502
Fax +39 0577 835509
🅢 *palmucci_montalcino*
info@poggiodisotto.it
www.collemassari.it
🅕 *ColleMassari*
🐦 *@ColleMassari*

YEAR OF FOUNDATION 1989
NAME OF THE OWNER Claudio Tipa
TOTAL BOTTLES PRODUCED 40,000
DIRECT SALES
VISITS TO THE WINERY - RESERVATION NEEDED
HECTARES OF VINEYARD 16
CERTIFIED ORGANIC VITICULTURE
OLIVE OIL PRODUCTION

This estate has a large following and was recently acquired by Claudio Tipa and thus entered group headed by ColleMassari. The

change of ownership has not changed anything although the quantity of wines has diminished further. To make up for this, some beautiful neighboring vineyards have been acquired. The style of the wines is extremely classic with long maceration on the skins and aging in large oak barrels. In the best years a Riserva is also made while the Rosso di Montalcino is award-winning.

![] 93   Price B
Rosso di Montalcino 2013

100% Sangiovese grapes. Ages in casks. Intense ruby garnet. The nose offers warm notes of herbs and sour cherry under spirit, white spices a hint of strawberry tree. Rich palate, elegant and intense with very refined tannins and a very flavorful finish.

![] 92   Price E
Brunello di Montalcino Riserva 2010

100% Sangiovese grapes. Ages in barrels. Deep garnet. Developed nose: warm notes of spices and the traditional aroma of tobacco. The palate offers very refined tannins and good weight, good acidity and the finish reminds the warm traditional notes.

POGGIO GRANDE

Podere Poggio Grande, 11
53023 Castiglione d'Orcia (SI)
Tel. +39 0577 897390
info@aziendapoggiogrande.it
www.aziendapoggiogrande.it
🅕 *Azienda Poggio Grande*

YEAR OF FOUNDATION 1999
NAME OF THE OWNER Luca Zamperini
TOTAL BOTTLES PRODUCED 18,000
DIRECT SALES
VISITS TO THE WINERY - RESERVATION NEEDED
HECTARES OF VINEYARD 4
OLIVE OIL PRODUCTION

The bubbly and passionate Luca Zamperini and his dynamic daughter Giulitta have come out with a new 'baby', Tagete, a white wine made from the French grapes Marsanne and Roussanne, and have once again amazed us with what they can bring out of this area of Ripa. Among the reds their Sesterzo remains the best, a 100% Sangiovese from a single vineyards near Montalcino. The 2013 vintage was the first from the new enologist Maurizio Saettini.

■ 90   Price B
Orcia Sangiovese Sesterzo 2013

100% Sangiovese grapes. Ages for 24 months in French tonneau. Ruby with garnet rim. The nose is elegant as usual: undergrowth, mushroom, tobacco and toasty notes alongside flavor of black cherry and citrusy hints. Solid palate, harmonic, gentle freshness and smooth tannin. Long, savory and silky finish.

POGGIO SCALETTE

*Via Barbiano, 7 - Località Ruffoli
50022 Greve in Chianti (FI)
Tel. +39 055 8546108
Fax +39 055 8546589*
🅢 *poggioscalette*
*info@poggioscalette.it
www.poggioscalette.it*

YEAR OF FOUNDATION 1991
NAME OF THE OWNER Adriana Assjé di Marcorà and Vittorio Fiore
TOTAL BOTTLES PRODUCED 55,000
DIRECT SALES
VISITS TO THE WINERY - RESERVATION NEEDED
HECTARES OF VINEYARD 22

The estate is in the middle of the high Ruffoli hills, right in front of Lamole. It is also the retreat of Vittorio Fiore, a famous enologist and the father of many important wines, especially Tuscan ones. Everyone once in a white he makes his own wine and has chosen to do so in one of the most beautiful places in the area.

■ 93   Price B
Piantonaia 2013

100% Merlot grapes. Ages for 18 months in barrique. Intense ruby. Reductive nose at the beginning then it opens to notes of raspberry and oaky hints, youthful. Tense and warm palate, captivating body, good acidity and definitively a long finish.

■ 92   Price B
Il Carbonaione 2013

100% Sangiovese grapes. Ages for 14 months in tonneau. Intense and lively ruby. Solid and multi-layered nose: black cherry and violet then notes of vanilla, cardamom and blood orange. Very tense palate, refined, elegant, medium bodied but supple and with a thin and long finish.

★★★
POLIZIANO

*Via Fontago, 1
53045 Montepulciano (SI)
Tel. +39 0578 738171
Fax +39 0578 738752
info@carlettipoliziano.com
www.carlettipoliziano.com*
🅕 *PolizianoAz.Agr*
🐦 *@PolizianoAzAgr*

YEAR OF FOUNDATION 1961
NAME OF THE OWNER Federico Carletti
TOTAL BOTTLES PRODUCED 800,000
DIRECT SALES
VISITS TO THE WINERY - RESERVATION NEEDED
HECTARES OF VINEYARD 140

Federico Carletti is the force behind this estate. When he took over it had only 18 hectares of vineyards and today, between the DOC and DOCG ones, there are 140. The vineyards are spread throughout the area and many have exceptional exposures, like Caggiole and those in Argiano. Sangiovese (Prugnolo Gentile) is not the only grape cultivated and 15% of the vineyards have alternative varieties. The estate has a modern style with ample use of small wood barrels of different ages. What is important for Polizano wines it that they have strong personality and represent their territory.

■ 🄖 97   Price B
Vino Nobile di Montepulciano Asinone 2012

Blend of Sangiovese with small percentage of Merlot grapes. Ages for 18 months in barrique. Dark and shiny color. Very complex nose of red and black fruit, cherry, blackberry, currant and blueberry. Red citrus and elegant spicy flavor; eucalyptus. Muscular palate but with a wonderful drinkability thank to a refined balanced; textbook depth and finish.

■ 93   Price B
Le Stanze del Poliziano 2012

100% Cabernet grapes. Ages for 18 – 24 months in barrique. Very inky color with violet hues. Nose of cedar, black fruit, eucalyptus, pencil lead, hint of candied orange. Extremely elegant and powerful palate, refined tannins and wonderful drinkability despite the weight. A forgotten wine, it's a must-try wine!!!

92 Price B

Vino Nobile di Montepulciano 2013

100% Sangiovese grapes. Ages in barrels and barrique. Intense and shiny ruby. Lightly smoky nose then flavors of fruit and spice, warm notes. Cherry, violet, black pepper and citrus. Ample palate, dense and flavorful, muscular but never tiring thank to a great balance. Very long and pleasant finish.

★★

PRINCIPE CORSINI
FATTORIA LE CORTI

Via San Piero di Sotto, 1
50026 San Casciano in Val di Pesa (FI)
Tel. +39 055 829301
Fax +39 055 8290089
info@principecorsini.com
www.principecorsini.com
 principe.corsini.1427
 @PrincipeCorsini

YEAR OF FOUNDATION 1427
NAME OF THE OWNER Duccio Corsini
TOTAL BOTTLES PRODUCED 250,000
DIRECT SALES
VISITS TO THE WINERY - RESERVATION NEEDED
HECTARES OF VINEYARD 50
HOSPITALITY
RESTAURANT
OLIVE OIL PRODUCTION

One of the most beautiful villas in Chianti Classico is that of Fattoria delle Corti of the Corsini princes. Up until a few years ago it was also the estate's main attraction. For some time now, however, things have been rapidly changing and the credit goes to Duccio Corsini who has become seriously involved in the estate's winemaking activities. His best wines are Chianti Classico Don Tommaso and Cortevecchia, which is a Riserva. But great results are coming from the Maremma estate, La Marsiliana, as well.

 94 Price B

Chianti Classico Gran Selezione Don Tommaso 2012

Blend of Sangiovese and Merlot grapes. Ages for 18 months in barrique. Dark ruby. A classic wine for style, personality and grace. Eucalyptus nose, black fruit and ripe cherry, woody notes. Evident and firm tannin, intense fruity aftertaste. It need more time than other version but it will definitively deliver with the time.

 91 Price B

Marsiliana 2012

Blend of Cabernet Sauvignon, Merlot and Petit Verdot grapes from Maremma. Ages for 15 months in new barrique. Deep, very dark and almost inky color. Multi-layered nose: floral hint of rose then fruity flavor of cassis, blackberry and blackcurrant. Hint of eucalyptus, scrub and spices. The palate is flavorful and elegant, rich and round.

 88 Price A

Chianti Classico 2014

Blend of Sangiovese, Canaiolo and Colorino grapes. Ages for 1 year in tonneau. Elegant floral and citrusy notes. The palate offers aftertaste of raspberry and currant, vibrant and lively tannin, pleasant and ready.

QUERCIABELLA

Via di Barbiano, 17
50022 Greve in Chianti (FI)
Tel. +39 055 85927777
Fax +39 055 85927778
info@querciabella.com
www.querciabella.com
 querciabella
 @Querciabella

YEAR OF FOUNDATION 1974
NAME OF THE OWNER Sebastiano Cossia Castiglioni
TOTAL BOTTLES PRODUCED 260,000
DIRECT SALES
VISITS TO THE WINERY - RESERVATION NEEDED
HECTARES OF VINEYARD 106
CERTIFIED BIODYNAMIC VITICULTURE

Querciabella was the dream of Pepito Castiglioni, a great international entrepreneur who died more than ten years ago. Today this magnificent estate is in the hands of his son Sebastiano Cossia Castiglioni who is assisted by enologist by Guido De Santi, while Roberto La Sorte handles the business side. The wines, the product and vegan-biodynamic dictates, are exceptional and inspired by the strictest attention to environmental sustainability. This

461

year, aside from two gems making their debut, we re-present two wines that are available on the market.

 99   Price C

Chianti Classico Riserva 2013

100% Sangiovese grapes. Ages for 15 months in barrique. Intense and shiny ruby. The nose is very precise and it is very fruity and essential: black cherry, violet, hint of cardamom, vanilla and blood orange. Varietal and elegant. Youthful, tense and aristocratic palate; great tense body, subtle tannins, lively and refined with a thin and very long finish. A perfect Chianti Classico!

 91   Price B

Chianti Classico 2014

100% Sangiovese grapes. Ages for 1 year in large casks and barrique. Lively ruby. Very rich and ripe but savory and balanced, lively, firm; very fresh palate yet flavorful.

 90   Price D

Camartina 2012

Blend of Cabernet Sauvignon and Sangiovese grapes. Ages for 18 months in barrique. Intense and dark ruby. Warm nose with vegetal and fruity notes: bell pepper and mint. A bit overextracted palate with firm and slightly rough tannins, wonderful weight that will refine with time.

 90   Price B

Mongrana 2013

Blend of 50% Sangiovese, Cabernet and Merlot grapes from Maremma. Ages for 18 months in barrique. Ruby. The nose offers floral notes of violet and lavender, black pepper and currant, salt and plum. Firm and structured with young tannins that are still slightly overwhelming the structure. Elegant finish.

 ★★

RIECINE

Località Riecine
53013 Gaiole in Chianti (SI)
Tel. +39 0577 749098
Fax +39 0577 744935
info@riecine.it
www.riecine.it
 Riecine
🐦 *@RIECINE*

YEAR OF FOUNDATION **1971**
NAME OF THE OWNER
TOTAL BOTTLES PRODUCED **65,000**
DIRECT SALES
VISITS TO THE WINERY - RESERVATION NEEDED
HECTARES OF VINEYARD **15**
CERTIFIED ORGANIC VITICULTURE
OLIVE OIL PRODUCTION

Created in 1971 John Dunkley, an important British marketing expert, Riecine is situated at an altitude of 400m above sea level and above Gaiole in Chianti, with a southern exposure and protected from intemperate wines by the nearby Monti del Chianti. Following the death of its founder, the estate was acquired by an important Russian businessman. Acting as the trait d'union is Sean O'Callaghan, an enologist who is in charge of production and is a refined taster and expert on world wines.

 92   Price C

Riecine 2012

100% Sangiovese grapes. Ages for 2 years in barrique. Intense ruby garnet. Precise and well-defined notes of black cherry, prune and violet. Savory palate, elegant, supple, balanced acidity, refined, fairly thin but with great length.

■ **91**   Price C

La Gioia 2012

100% Sangiovese grapes. Ages for 2 years in barrique. Intense garnet. Very varietal with notes of black cherry, blackberry and currant. Refined and thin palate, supple, structured, with partially integrated tannins and a warm and long finish.

■ **90**   Price B

Chianti Classico 2013

100% Sangiovese grapes. Ages for 18 months in barrique. Lively and shiny ruby. Fragrant and fruity, very varietal, currant, strawberry then vanilla. Tense palate, savory, medium bodied, supple, very pleasant, simple and with a good length.

★★

ROCCA DELLE MACÌE

Località Le Macìe, 45
53011 Castellina in Chianti (SI)
Tel. +39 0577 7321
Fax +39 0577 743150

info@roccadellemacie.com
www.roccadellemacie.com
 roccadellemacie
@roccadellemacie

YEAR OF FOUNDATION 1973
NAME OF THE OWNER Zingarelli Family
TOTAL BOTTLES PRODUCED 4,500,000
DIRECT SALES
VISITS TO THE WINERY - RESERVATION NEEDED
HECTARES OF VINEYARD 210
HOSPITALITY
RESTAURANT
OLIVE OIL PRODUCTION

The wines of Rocca della Macìe are famous for being the standard-bearer for a traditional winemaking style that is much appreciated in Italy and abroad and produces reds that are soft with wrapping aromas. The wines exalt those Chianti characteristics that are defined as 'palatable' and refers those that make the wine easy to drink and gives is a rounded and balanced flavor. Of all their wines, check out Gran Selezione Sergio Zingarelli.

 97   Price B

Chianti Classico Gran Selezione Sergio Zingarelli 2012

Blend of 90% Sangiovese and 10% Colorino grapes. Ages for 2 years in large casks and barrique. Intense ruby garnet. The nose opens to notes of black cherry and blood orange then prune, vanilla and a hint of tobacco. Warm, captivating, balanced, well integrated tannins, wonderful acidity, tense body and a long and elegant finish.

93   Price B

Chianti Classico Gran Selezione Fizzano 2013

Blend of 95% Sangiovese and 5% Merlot grapes. Ages for 2 years mainly in large casks and only for a short percentage in barrique. Intense ruby garnet. Aromas of Prune, black cherry, hint of tamarind and spices. Warm, captivating, good tannins and long length.

90   Price A

Chianti Classico Tenuta Sant'Alfonso 2014

100% Sangiovese grapes. Ages for 1 year in large casks. Lively ruby garnet. Very fruity: prune, black cherry, hint of leather. The palate is fresh and agile, very pleasant with good body and good length.

ROCCA DI CASTAGNOLI

Località Castagnoli
53013 Gaiole in Chianti (SI)
Tel. +39 0577 731004
Fax +39 0577 731050
roccadicastagnoli
info@roccadicastagnoli.com
www.roccadicastagnoli.com
RoccadiCastagnoli
@Roccacastagnoli

YEAR OF FOUNDATION 1981
NAME OF THE OWNER Calì Family
TOTAL BOTTLES PRODUCED 350,000
DIRECT SALES
VISITS TO THE WINERY - RESERVATION NEEDED
HECTARES OF VINEYARD 132
HOSPITALITY
RESTAURANT
OLIVE OIL PRODUCTION

Owned by the Calì family, Rocca has its headquarters in a small medieval village in Gaiole in Chianti which is surrounded by forests, olive groves and Cyprus trees. The estate owns some 850 hectares of land that has altitudes ranging from 860m (Colle di Monte Luca) to 380m above sea level. These include 132 hectares of vineyards which are mostly Sangiovese with some estate clones that produce a vast and varied line of wines that always have a high level of quality.

90   Price B

Chianti Classico Tenuta di Capraia Riserva 2013

Blend of Sangiovese and Colorino grapes. Ages for 24 months in large casks. Ruby garnet. Spiky and dynamic, floral notes of lavender and broom blossoms. Very crunchy palate with aftertaste of raspberry and yoghurt but also myrtle, bay leaf and mustard, celery and light vegetal notes. Decise and complex, great length.

89   Price A

Chianti Classico 2014

Blend of Sangiovese with small percentage of Canaiolo and Colorino grapes. Shiny ruby. Aromatic, savory palate, good length and with a wonderful juicy and fruity drinkability.

87   Price A
Chianti Classico Tenuta di Capraia 2014

Blend of Sangiovese with small percentage of Colorino grapes. Ages in large casks. Light ruby. Savory and intriguing, lively and racy, it is a bit short but it has good weight.

★
ROCCA DI FRASSINELLO

Località Giuncarico
58023 Gavorrano (GR)
Tel. +39 0566 88400
 roccadifrassinello
info@castellare.it
www.roccadifrassinello.it
RoccadiFrassinello
CastellareWines

YEAR OF FOUNDATION 1999
NAME OF THE OWNER Paolo Panerai
TOTAL BOTTLES PRODUCED 300,000
DIRECT SALES
VISITS TO THE WINERY - RESERVATION NEEDED
HECTARES OF VINEYARD 80

This estate is becoming something more than just a simple annex to Paolo Panerai's Castellare one. And this beginning with the spectacular winery designed by Renzo Piano, an extraordinary work of art dedicated to the world of wine. Then there are the wines which are all good and are consistently getting better as the vineyards get older.

 92   Price D
Maremma Toscana Baffonero 2014

100% Merlot grapes. Ages for 15 months in barrique. Very intense ruby. Definitively varietal nose, raspberry, kirsch, notes of spices and undergrowght, oaky hints. Mouth filling palate, youthful, slightly rough tannin; warm but with decent balanced acidity. Very long.

90   Price B
Maremma Toscana Le Sughere di Frassinello 2014

Blend of 50% Sangiovese, Merlot and Cabernet Sauvignon grapes., one year in barrique. Intense ruby. Black cherry, cassis, spices, resin hint, smoky notes; wonderful nose. The palate is a bit tannic, savory, pleasent, warm and with a decent length finish.

 87   Price B
Maremma Toscana Rocca di Frassinello 2014

Blend of 60% Sangiovese, Merlot and Cabernet Sauvignon grapes. Ages for 14 months in barrique. Amongst the three is the one that suffered the most the challenging vintage. Intense and dark ruby. Oaky nose then notes of kirsch and tobacco. The tannins are a bit dry, firm and young; decent body and good length finish.

★
ROCCA DI MONTEGROSSI

Località San Marcellino - Monti in Chianti
53013 Gaiole in Chianti (SI)
Tel. +39 0577 747977
roccadimontegrossi@chianticlassico.com
www.roccadimontegrossi.it
Rocca-di-Montegrossi

YEAR OF FOUNDATION 1981
NAME OF THE OWNER Marco Ricasoli Firidolfi
TOTAL BOTTLES PRODUCED 60,000
DIRECT SALES
VISITS TO THE WINERY - RESERVATION NEEDED
HECTARES OF VINEYARD 20
CERTIFIED ORGANIC VITICULTURE
OLIVE OIL PRODUCTION

From a descendent of the historic Baron Bettino Ricasoli one would have expected respect for tradition and conviction in the choices made. What Marco Ricasoli-Firidolfi has done has gone far beyond this with the way he is committed to rediscovering the territory and the force of Chianti Classico. A demonstration of this is constant and in-depth research to produce wines from both indigenous grapes - like the Pugnitello used to make a DOCG - and international ones – Merlot and Cabernet – used for wines other than Chianti Classico. The splendid Romanesque Pieve di San Marcellino Church gives its name to the estate's Riserva which each year reveals evermore intriguing nuances.

94   Price B
Chianti Classico Gran Selezione San Marcellino 2012

Blend of Sangiovese and small percentage of Pugnitello grapes. Single vineyard. Ages for 24 months in small and large oak barrels. Intense ruby. Nose of carnation flower, cardamom and black cherry. Structured and intriguing palate with good grip tannins even if they need time to refine but they alredy show firmness and quality; savory and crunchy, classic and stylish.

---

93   *Price B*

Chianti Classico 2014

Blend of Sangiovese with small percentage of Canaiolo and Colorino grapes. Ages for 12 months in large casks. Ruby. Generous nose of red and black fruit, black pepper, spices and eucalyptus. Racy palate, very savory, juicy and stimulating tannin with a red citrus finish.

---

87   *Price B*

Geremia 2012

Blend of Merlot and Cabernet Sauvignon grapes. Ages for 24 months in barrique. Dark and ripe nose: black pepper, prune, vanilla and anise. Full bodied palate, vanilla aftertaste, slightly rough tannins but with wonderful length.

ROCCAPESTA

Località Macereto, 9
58054 Scansano (GR)
Tel. +39 0564 599252
Fax +39 0564 1900030
info@roccapesta.it
www.roccapesta.com
[f] roccapesta
[tw] @Roccapesta

YEAR OF FOUNDATION 2003
NAME OF THE OWNER Leonardo and Alberto Tanzini
TOTAL BOTTLES PRODUCED 100,000
DIRECT SALES
VISITS TO THE WINERY - RESERVATION NEEDED
HECTARES OF VINEYARD 20

In the beginning of the year 2000, Maremma has represented a little Italian California, a really suited area of Tuscany where it seemed possible to start the production of great Sangiovese base red wines, but different from the usual appellations areas. Here, under the Morellino di Scanzano appellation, Leonardo and Alberto Tanzini bought their estate, taking over exiting vineyards (like the Calestaia one, planted in 1974) and planted new ones, 90% of them with Sangiovese but with Pugnitello and

Alicante as well. If Maremma has lost his Eldorado fame with the year, Tanzini's work didn't stop, and is still giving some nice productive surprises.

---

91   *Price B*

Morellino di Scansano Calestaia Riserva 2010

100% Sangiovese grapes from an old single vineyard. Ages in 25hl barrels. Ruby with garnet rim. Dark nose, earthy, lively and fragrant fruity aromas. Good weight on the palate, flavorful, firm tannins, long sweet fruity finish.

---

89   *Price A*

Morellino di Scansano Roccapesta 2013

Blend of 96% Sangiovese and 4% Ciliegiolo grapes. Ages in 500 – 600 litres casks. Ruby with a light garnet rim. Intense nose, blackberry and ripe cherry with a spicy hint. Black cherry aftertaste, good freshness, the tannins are integrated depite being young; good finish.

RUFFINO

Piazzale Ruffino, 1
50065 Pontassieve (FI)
Tel. +39 055 83605
Fax +39 055 8313677
info@ruffino.it
www.ruffino.com
[f] ruffinowines
[tw] @RuffinoWines

YEAR OF FOUNDATION 1877
NAME OF THE OWNER Constellation Brands
TOTAL BOTTLES PRODUCED 17,000,000
DIRECT SALES
VISITS TO THE WINERY - RESERVATION NEEDED
HECTARES OF VINEYARD 550
OLIVE OIL PRODUCTION

This leading national wine producer was sold several years ago by the Folonari family to the American conglomerate Constellation Brands. The progress its production has made over the past decades may seem miraculous but is the result of serious and professional efforts to transform an ultra-commercial producer into a modern estate capable of offering high-level wines to any market sector.

93   Price B
Chianti Classico Gran Selezione Riserva Ducale Oro 2012

Blend of 85% Sangiovese, 10% Merlot and 5% Cabernet Sauvignon grapes. Ages for 2 years in barrique and large casks. Intense ruby garnet. Black cherry, leather and small berries on the nose then hints of kirsch and vanilla. Firm palate, wonderful body, savory and very warm. Very long finish.

91   👍 Price A
Chianti Classico Riserva Ducale 2012

Blend of 80% Sangiovese and other red grape varieties. Ages for 18 months in different sized barrels. Lively ruby garnet. Very typical, black cherry, violet, hint of tobacco, kirsch and berries. Savory palate, lightly tannic, pleasant drinkability and good length. A textbook wine.

90   👍 Price A
Santedame 2014

Blend of 80% Sangiovese and 20% of Merlot, Colorino and other grape varieties. Ages for 8 months in barrique. Intense and lively ruby. Floral and fruity nose: violet, currant and vanilla. Tense palate, savory, simple but pleasant, refreshing acidity and thin length.

SALCHETO

Via di Villa Bianca, 15
53045 Montepulciano (SI)
Tel. +39 0578 799031
info@salcheto.it
www.salcheto.it
 Salcheto
 @SalchetoWinery

YEAR OF FOUNDATION **1987**
NAME OF THE OWNER **Michele Manelli**
TOTAL BOTTLES PRODUCED **230,000**
DIRECT SALES
VISITS TO THE WINERY - RESERVATION NEEDED
HECTARES OF VINEYARD **50**
RESTAURANT
CERTIFIED ORGANIC VITICULTURE

The winery became operative in the mid-1980s and was quickly producing quality wine. In 1997, Michele Manelli joined the estate and this led to significant grown both in regard to the vineyards, thanks to acquisitions, and the winery which was first expanded and then to-tally rebuilt based on a project that had a low environmental impact that won praised from various international organs. Production is modern in method and classic in style.

93   Price C
Salco 2123

Blend of Sangiovese from 2012 and 2013 vintage. Ages in different sized oak barrels. Intense and dark ruby. intense and well defined nose, black cherry, violet, white spices and Kentucky tobacco leaf. Defined palate, good depth, agile and tense. Young tannin and balanced finish.

92   Price B
Vino Nobile di Montepulciano Salco 2011

100% Sangiovese grapes. Ages in tonneau and barrique. Ruby with dark garnet rim. Very classy nose: peach, plum and black cherry then floral aromas of violet and rose. Smoky notes, spices and sweet tobacco. Very intense and complex. Very elegant palate, great depth, delicate and with a good depth rather than being powerful; very long finish. A wine with great personality.

86   Price B
Vino Nobile di Montepulciano 2013

Blend of Sangiovese with a small percentage of indigenouse grape varieties. Ages in barrels and barrique. Ruby with garnet hues. The nose is a bit shy then opens to undergrowght and leaves. Dark red blossoms notes. The palate it is still young with a vibrant tannin that slightly unease the drink. Flavorful and medium length finish.

SALUSTRI

Via La Cava, 5 - Località Poggi del Sasso
58040 Cinigiano (GR)
Tel. +39 0564 990529
info@salustri.it
www.salustri.it

YEAR OF FOUNDATION **1996**
NAME OF THE OWNER **Salustri Family**
TOTAL BOTTLES PRODUCED **100,000**
DIRECT SALES
VISITS TO THE WINERY - RESERVATION NEEDED
HECTARES OF VINEYARD **20**
HOSPITALITY
CERTIFIED ORGANIC VITICULTURE
OLIVE OIL PRODUCTION

The estate is in Poggi del Sasso, near Cinigiano, on the slopes of Monte Amiata. Here the Salustri family has always cultivated grapes and olives and they even brought back a Sangiovese sub-variety clone that has the family's name. The vines are old and the vineyards organic which brings out the differences of the Sangiovese cru produce. In the winery fermentation takes place in wood which is also used for aging and great attention is paid to the type and size of the barrels as well as the time the wines age.

92   Price B
Montecucco Sangiovese Grotte Rosse 2013

100% Sangiovese grapes (Clone Salustri). Ages for 24 months in 25 hl oak barrels. Dark ruby. Classic nose of black cherry and cherry, floral notes of violet, very varietal but not well defined. Medium bodied, fair freshness with black cherry aftertaste; good depth and still young tannins. Warm and defined finish.

89   Price A
Montecucco Sangiovese Santa Marta 2013

100% Sangiovese grapes (Clone Salustri). Single vineyard. Ages for 24 months in 25 hl oak casks. Ruby. fruity nose of cherry then sweet spices,. Mouth filling palate, slightly dry tannin, almond aftertaste. Slightly rough finish.

★★
SALVIONI - CERBAIOLA

Piazza Cavour, 19
53024 Montalcino (SI)
Tel. +39 0577 848499
Fax +39 0577 848499
info@aziendasalvioni.com
www.aziendasalvioni.com
🅕 *Salvioni*

YEAR OF FOUNDATION 1985
NAME OF THE OWNER Giulio Salvioni
TOTAL BOTTLES PRODUCED 12,000
VISITS TO THE WINERY - RESERVATION NEEDED
HECTARES OF VINEYARD 4

In the mid-1990s, Giulio Salvioni and his wife Mirella, also known as 'hail' for her drastic

pruning of the vine leaves, created a new style of Brunello. It is an elegant Brunello distinguished by its refined tannins and aroma of white peach and floral scents. The vineyards are on the eastern side of Montalcino at an altitude of over 400m above sea level. The wine is made in stainless steel and aged in classic, 30hl Slovenian oak barrels. The winery is in the town of Montalcino and is a destination for the many fans of this estate.

93   Price D
Brunello di Montalcino 2011

100% Sangiovese grapes. Ages in barrels. Ruby with garnet hues. Nose of peach, red cherry, and fine herbs, tobacco and dark spices. Very classy tannin, youthful, great weight and a juicy and ample finish.

88   Price B
Rosso di Montalcino 2014

100% Sangiovese grapes. Ages in 20 and 30 hl barrels. Shiny ruby. Fresh fruity nose, eucalyptus, yellow peach. Intense palate, good weight, crunchy tannin and a surprising finish.

★★
SAN FABIANO CALCINAIA

Località Cellole
53011 Castellina in Chianti (SI)
Tel. +39 0577 979232
Fax +39 0577 979455
info@sanfabianocalcinaia.com
www.sanfabianocalcinaia.it
🅕 *SanFabianoCalcinaia*
🅧 *@InfoCalcinaia*

YEAR OF FOUNDATION 1983
NAME OF THE OWNER Guido Serio
TOTAL BOTTLES PRODUCED 160,000
DIRECT SALES
VISITS TO THE WINERY - RESERVATION NEEDED
HECTARES OF VINEYARD 45
HOSPITALITY
RESTAURANT
OLIVE OIL PRODUCTION

This estate is situated amid the highest hills in Castellina in Chianti and its vineyards in Cellole reach an altitude of 450m above sea level. Here Guido Serio, a finance expert and owner

468

of the estate, offers well-made Chianti Classico and his Gran Selezione, made with grapes from higher Cellole vineyards, is excellent.

 90   Price B
Chianti Classico Gran Selezione Cellole 2013

Blend of 90% Sangiovese with small percentage of Colorino and Merlot grapes. Ages for 18 months in barrique. Very intense ruby. captivating nose, very spicy, blackcurrant, black cherry, vanilla and leather. Firm palate, the tannins are still a bit young and aggressive, warm, rich and promising.

 87   Price A
Chianti Famalgallo 2015

Blend of 80% Sangiovese, Cabernet Sauvignon and other grape varieties. Ages for 8 months in stainless steel and 8 months in barrique. Lively garnet. Typical nose: fragrant, solid, floral note of violet, cherry, prune and black cherry. Tense palate, lightly tannic, very youthful, simple but very pleasant.

★★
SAN FELICE

Località San Felice
53019 Castelnuovo Berardenga (SI)
Tel. +39 0577 3991
Fax +39 0577 359223
info@agricolasanfelice.it
www.agricolasanfelice.it
 AgricolaSanFelice
 @AgricolaSFelice

YEAR OF FOUNDATION **1968**
NAME OF THE OWNER **Gruppo Allianz**
TOTAL BOTTLES PRODUCED **900,000**
DIRECT SALES
VISITS TO THE WINERY - RESERVATION NEEDED
HECTARES OF VINEYARD **140**
HOSPITALITY
RESTAURANT
OLIVE OIL PRODUCTION

The challenge in the name of tradition to bring back and make wine from a host of grape varieties that were thought lost started from the restored ancient hamlet of Berardenga. Great attention was also paid to the estate's vineyards and plots. The Sangiovese grown in the vineyards of Chiesamonti, Colti and Pianacci

which, together with the Abrusco, Pugnitello, Malvasia Nera, Ciliegiolo and Mazzese grapes provide the excellent prime materials for a vast production of wine that is always of guaranteed quality.

 94   Price C
Brunello di Montalcino Campogiovanni Il Quercione Riserva 2010

100% Sangiovese grapes. Ages for 2 years in different sized barrels. Deep and shiny ruby. Complex nose of cherry, sour cherry and black cherry and a captivating white spiciness. Intense palate, rich and juicy, classy tannins; elegant and very long finish.

 92   Price B
Chianti Classico Gran Selezione Il Grigio 2013

Blend of 80% Sangiovese and 20% of Arbusco, Ciliegiolo, Pugnitello, Malvasia Nera and Mazzese grapes. Ages for 24 months in barrique and large casks. Intensity and flavor, firm and crunchy tannins, sweet fruity length. The nose offers notes of bay leaf, licorice, cardamom, raspberry jam, violet, spices and black pepper. Precise palate.

 92   Price C
Chianti Classico Gran Selezione Poggio Rosso 2011

100% Sangiovese grapes. Ages for 26 months in large casks and barrique. The return to a monovarietal brings territorial notes and savoriness, fruity and earthy nose. Intense and fresh palate, vibrant and long, bizarre and with carachter but also multy-layered and with eucalyptus notes.

 91   Price B
Vigorello 2011

Blend of Pugnitello, Cabernet Sauvignon, Merlot and Petit Verdot grapes. Ages for 20 months in barrique. Sweet and ample palate, warm and rich, dark spices, blueberry and black pepper. Racy palate, intriguing tannin and a sour cherry and eucalyptus finish.

 90   🍶 Price A
Chianti Classico 2013

Blend of Sangiovese, Colorino and Pugnitello grapes. Ages for 12 months in Slavonian large casks. Ruby. Notes of plum, redcurrant and strawberry; firm and crunchy palate with savory and dark fruit; juicy finish with a classic and flavorful tannin.

SAN FILIPPO

Strada Consorziale dei Comunali - Località San Filippo, 134
53024 Montalcino (SI)
Tel. +39 0577 847176
Fax +39 0577 847213
info@sanfilippomontalcino.com
www.sanfilippomontalcino.com

YEAR OF FOUNDATION **1972**
NAME OF THE OWNER **Roberto Giannelli**
TOTAL BOTTLES PRODUCED **80,000**
DIRECT SALES
VISITS TO THE WINERY - RESERVATION NEEDED
HECTARES OF VINEYARD **10**
HOSPITALITY
RESTAURANT

An historic Montalcino estate that came back from the ashes thanks to Roberto Gianelli who acquired it at the end of the 1990s. Heavy investments were made in in the winery and at the estate which became a beautiful holiday farm. The style of the wines is extremely traditional and they age long in 30-40hl barrels. The vines are of various ages and are as old as 40 years and situated in the zone of eastern Cerbaie, known for producing Brunello that are a perfect blend of boldness and elegance.

| 94 | Price C |

Brunello di Montalcino Le Lucere 2011

100% Sangiovese grapes. Ages in barrels. Dark ruby. Classic nose of yellow and red notes, lightly warm notes but never overwhelming. Great depth and tannin. Wonderful savory note; classic. Flavorful and captivating finish.

| 93 | Price D |

Brunello di Montalcino Le Lucere Riserva 2010

100% Sangiovese grapes. Ages in barrels. Ruby garnet. Classic nose with aromas of ink, herbs, white spices, sweet tobacco and cinnamon; hint of cinnamon. Very elegant and classic palate, good weight, flavorful and tasty. Very refined tannin; austere finish with undergrowth notes.

★★
SAN GIUSTO A RENTENNANO

Località San Giusto a Rentennano
53013 Gaiole in Chianti (SI)
Tel. +390577 747121
Fax +390577 747109
info@fattoriasangiusto.it
www.fattoriasangiusto.it

YEAR OF FOUNDATION **1914**
NAME OF THE OWNER **Martini di Cigala Family**
TOTAL BOTTLES PRODUCED **80,000**
DIRECT SALES
VISITS TO THE WINERY - RESERVATION NEEDED
HECTARES OF VINEYARD **31**
CERTIFIED ORGANIC VITICULTURE
OLIVE OIL PRODUCTION

469

Despite the fact that the past hot summers have put their capacity to express elegance to the test, the innate class and vocation of this area of Etruscan tradition is still evident in the more classic wines of this denomination. This estate has 32 hectares of vineyards and continues to be run by the Fratelli Martini di Cigala. The various compositions of the soil hold up well even in difficult years like 2014.

| 93 | Price B |

Chianti Classico 2014

100% Sangiovese grapes, 12 months in large oak barrels. Ruby garnet. Well defined fruity notes, very harmonic and juicy, firm and ready palate but doesn't lack for body, tannin and satisfaction.

SAN LEONINO

Località I Cipressi
53011 Castellina in Chianti (SI)
Tel. +39 0577 743108
info@tenimentiangelini.it
www.tenimentiangelini.it
 sanleonino

YEAR OF FOUNDATION **1994**
NAME OF THE OWNER **Bertani Domains**
TOTAL BOTTLES PRODUCED **230,000**
DIRECT SALES
VISITS TO THE WINERY - RESERVATION NEEDED
HECTARES OF VINEYARD **45**
OLIVE OIL PRODUCTION

San Leonino estate in Chianti is part of the Bertani Domains galaxy owned by the Angelini group. Forty-five of its 100 hectares are vineyards and produce traditional Chianti Classico. However, the Monsenese cru is a different story and offers a more modern and international vision using French oak barrels for aging.

■ **88**   Price B
Chianti Classico Monsenese Riserva 2012
Blend of 90% Sangiovese and Cabernet Sauvignon grapes. Ages for 18 months in barrique. Lively ruby garnet. Well-defined and captivating nose, notes of kirsch, a bit pungent, then black cherry and vanilla. Savory palate, young tannins, warm and lightly diluted finish.

SANLORENZO

Podere Sanlorenzo, 280
53024 Montalcino (SI)
Tel. +39 339 6070930
Fax +39 0577 832965
info@poderesanlorenzo.net
www.sanlorenzomontalcino.it
🅕 *Sanlorenzo.Montalcino*
🐦 *@_Sanlorenzo_*

YEAR OF FOUNDATION 1998
NAME OF THE OWNER Luciano Ciolfi
TOTAL BOTTLES PRODUCED 16,000
DIRECT SALES
VISITS TO THE WINERY - RESERVATION NEEDED
HECTARES OF VINEYARD 4.5
CERTIFIED ORGANIC VITICULTURE
OLIVE OIL PRODUCTION

This young estate owes its boost in quality to its current owner Luciano Ciolfi. He began bottling his first Brunello with vintage 2003 and it immediately stood out. The style is modern with attention paid to maintaining the integrity of the fruit. The vineyards are at quite a high altitude, 450m above sea level, where the soil is loose and full of marl. The Brunello ages in 30hl barrels while barrique and tonneau barrels are used for the Rosso.

■ **91**   Price B
Brunello di Montalcino Bramante 2011
100% Sangiovese grapes. Ages in 20 and 30 hl

barrels. Ruby garnet. Floral nose of violet and red field blossoms. Neat cherry note and undergrowth aromas. Elegant and 'relaxed' palate, developed tannins, good acidity; medium weight but very flavorful.

SASSOTONDO

Località Pian di Conati, 52 - Frazione Sovana
58010 Sorano (GR)
Tel. +39 0564 614218
Fax +39 0564 617714
🆂 *sassotondo*
info@sassotondo.it
www.sassotondo.it
🅕 *sassotondo*

YEAR OF FOUNDATION 1990
NAME OF THE OWNER Carla Benini ed Edoardo Ventimiglia
TOTAL BOTTLES PRODUCED 50,000
DIRECT SALES
VISITS TO THE WINERY - RESERVATION NEEDED
HECTARES OF VINEYARD 12

The estate of Carla Bernini and Edoardo Ventimiglia is lovely place to return to. They always welcome you back and have some "vulcanic" ideas. The estate is located in the middle of the Etruscan zone of Maremma, not far from Pitigliano. This is a volcanic area as evidenced by the cellar carved out of tuff stone and the expressive wines. Such as the pure Ciliegiolo cru San Lorenzo, or the Bianco di Pitigliano Isolina. The owners are helped in the production of the wines by the consultant enologist Attilio Pagli.

■ **91**   Price B
San Lorenzo 2013
100% Ciliegiolo grapes. Matures 18 months in big barrels and barrique. Lively garnet red. Nice version. Spivy notes of pepper, wet soil, underbrush and black cherry. Elegant flavor, thick but thin tannins, full, warm, enveloping and long.

☐ **87**   Price A
Bianco di Pitigliano Isolina 2015
Blend of 70% Trebbiano Toscano, 15% Sauvignon, 10% Greco and 5% other grapes. Stainless steel. Intense staw yellow. Very clear and clean in the nose, with notes of yellow plum and wildflowers. Savory, simple and with an average body.

86   **Price A**
Maremma Toscana Ciliegiolo 2015

Blend of 90% Ciliegiolo and 10% Alicante grapes. Stainless steel. Lively and bright ruby red. Very fruity, fragrant, simple and immediate in the nose with notes of plums and black cherry. Fresh flavor, savory, pleasant and easy to drink.

★★
MICHELE SATTA

Località Vigna al Cavaliere, 61
57022 Castagneto Carducci (LI)
Tel. +39 0565 773041
Fax +39 0565 773944
🅢 *michelesatta55*
info@michelesatta.com
www.michelesatta.com
🅕 *michelesattawines*
🐦 *@MicheleSatta1*

YEAR OF FOUNDATION 1984
NAME OF THE OWNER Michele Satta
TOTAL BOTTLES PRODUCED 180,000
DIRECT SALES
VISITS TO THE WINERY - RESERVATION NEEDED
HECTARES OF VINEYARD 23
OLIVE OIL PRODUCTION

Michele Satta is one of the most active producers in the DOC Bolgheri appellation, someone who for 30 years has worked to draw attention to his territory, the potential of which he firmly believes in. He is also one of the few who, knowing the soils of is estate as he does, cultivates Sangiovese in Bolgheri that makes IGT wine that can certainly stand beside his Bolgheri Superiore.

 89   **Price C**
Bolgheri Superiore I Castagni 2012

Blend of 70% Cabernet Sauvignon, Syrah and Teroldego grapes. Ages for 2 years in 60% new barrique. Very dark ruby. Asutere and subtle nose, dark notes of Mediterranean scrub and dark fruits. The palate is a bit rough, good body. Youthful tannins and long finish.

 87   **Price B**
Bolgheri Superiore Piastraia 2012

Blend of equal part of Cabernet, Merlot, Syrah and Sangiovese grapes. Ages for 12 months in oak barrels. Dark, deep and shiny ruby. The nose offers notes of eucalyptus and cypress, cherry and a hint of peach. Rich palate and medium acidity, good tannins for a perhaps simple but pleasant wine.

★★
SELVAPIANA

Località Selvapiana, 45
1827 Rufina (FI)
Tel. +39 055 8369848
Fax +39 055 8316840
🅢 *fattoria.selvapiana*
info@selvapiana.it
www.selvapiana.it
🅕 *Fattoria-Selvapiana*

YEAR OF FOUNDATION 1827
NAME OF THE OWNER Franco Giuntini
TOTAL BOTTLES PRODUCED 220,000
DIRECT SALES
VISITS TO THE WINERY - RESERVATION NEEDED
HECTARES OF VINEYARD 66

Few know where Rufina exactly is in Tuscany. Even fewer know that this zone northeast of Florence produces some of the absolutely best Chianti and that it is a product of ancient tradition. A custodian of this tradition is Federico Giuntini that continues the work of his fahter Francesco with dedication.

92   **Price B**
Chianti Rufina Bucerchiale Riserva 2012

100% Sangiovese grapes. Ages for 1 year and a half in barrique. Intense ruby garnet. Captivating and floral nose, typical violet notes then forest fruits and a hint of black cherry. Elegant and firm palate, warm, savory, good tension and a thin but long length.

91   👍 **Price A**
Pomino Rosso Villa di Petrognano 2011

Blend of Sangiovese, Merlot and Cabernet Sauvignon grapes. The Sangiovese ages for 2 years in large casks and the Merlot and Cabernet also for 2 years in barrique. Intense and lively ruby. Very defined notes of violet, blackcurrant and raspberry then sweet spices on the background. Tense and elegant palate, savory, well integrated tannins and very long length.

SERPAIA DI ENDRIZZI

Via Goldoni, 15/B - Località Fonteblanda
58010 Magliano in Toscana (GR)
Tel. +39 0461 650129
Fax +39 0461 650043
info@endrizzi.it
www.endrizzi.it
f *CantinaEndrizzi*
🐦 *@CantinaEndrizzi*

YEAR OF FOUNDATION 2000
NAME OF THE OWNER Paolo and Christine Endrici
and Thomas Kemmler
TOTAL BOTTLES PRODUCED 120,000
DIRECT SALES
VISITS TO THE WINERY - RESERVATION NEEDED
HECTARES OF VINEYARD 30

The name Endrizzi is well-known to those who love Trentino wine but the talent of Paolo and Christine Endrici is not limited to their San Michele all'Adige estate but has extended to Maremma where, near Magliano, the family acquired 30 hectares of land in 2000. Here they cultivate Sangiovese on sunny hills to make Morellino and typical international varietals for the young DOC Maremma appellation. The soil is mostly clay and the vineyards are cultivated using integrated eco-sustainable methods.

90   Price B
Morellino di Scansano Riserva Dono 2010

100% Sangiovese grapes. Ages for 12 months in barrique and 8 months in large casks. Dark ruby with garnet hues. Wonderful austere nose, dark fruit notes such as black cherry and blackberry, hint of eucalyptus. Good weight on the palate, ample and intense, good sweetness of fruit. Firm tannins and warm and fruity finish.

89   Price B
Mèria 2011

Blend of Merlot, Cabernet Sauvignon, Sangiovese and Petit Verdot grapes. The grapes age separately in barrique for 1 year then the final cuvee ages in large oak casks for 8 months. Ruby garnet. Very fruity nose, cherry, black cherry, mulberry, under spirit black cherry, fine herbs and a hint of pencil lead. Dense palate, structured, balanced acidity, firm tannins, flavorful, fruity and juicy finish.

87   Price A
Serpaiolo 2014

Blend of Merlot, Cabernet Sauvignon and Sangiovese grapes. Ages for 8 months in Slavonian oak barrels. Ruby. Intense and refined nose, fruity and spicy with undergrowth, tobacco and leather notes. Good palate, firm, rich and fruity. Firm and youthful tannins, flavorful finish.

SESTI - CASTELLO DI ARGIANO

Castello di Argiano
53024 Montalcino (SI)
Tel. +39 0577 843921
Fax +39 0577 843921
elisa@sesti.net
www.sestiwine.com

YEAR OF FOUNDATION 1985
NAME OF THE OWNER Elisa and Giuseppe Sesti
TOTAL BOTTLES PRODUCED 60,000
DIRECT SALES
VISITS TO THE WINERY - RESERVATION NEEDED
HECTARES OF VINEYARD 9.3
OLIVE OIL PRODUCTION

The Argiano tower that identifies this estate was part of a defensive line for the Republic of Siena. The Sesti family has owned the estate since the 1970s and the work in the vineyards and the cellar follows a lunar calendar due to the owner's passion for astronomy. The vineyards used to produced Brunello are at an altitude of some 350m and the estate's style is classic with the use of 15-35hl barrels.

94   Price C
Brunello di Montalcino Phenomena Riserva 2010

100% Sangiovese grapes. Ages in barrels and tonneau. Classic ruby. Intense, ample and well-defined nose: undergrowth, fresh fine herbs and ripe black cherry. Young but rich and firm palate, vibrant and wonderful quality tannin, good weight and great depth, very intense finish.

88   Price B
Rosso di Montalcino 2014

100% Sangiovese grapes. Ages in large casks. Classic house style, tobacco and dark notes. Intense palate with elegant tannins and flavorsome drinkability.

█ 87   Price C
Brunello di Montalcino 2011

100% Sangiovese grapes. Ages in different sized barrels. Ruby garnet. Classic notes of tobacco, leather and slightly developed herbaceous notes. Flavorful palate, very classic, good weight and depth and a medium flavorful finish.

STELLA DI CAMPALTO

S.P. 55 Della Badia di Sant'Antimo, km 10,2
53024 Montalcino (SI)
Tel. +39 0577 835754
Fax +39 0577 835754
info@stelladicampalto.it
www.stelladicampalto.it
🅵 *Stella-di-Campalto*
🐦 *@SdiCampalto*

YEAR OF FOUNDATION Anni '90
NAME OF THE OWNER Stella di Campalto
TOTAL BOTTLES PRODUCED 15,000
DIRECT SALES
VISITS TO THE WINERY - RESERVATION NEEDED
HECTARES OF VINEYARD 7
HOSPITALITY
CERTIFIED ORGANIC VITICULTURE
CERTIFIED BIODYNAMIC VITICULTURE

The estate is in the southern part of Montalcino, more precisely Castelnuovo dell'Abate, overlooking Monte Amiata. Stella is a young woman who fell in love with Brunello in the 1990s and by the end of that decade was successfully producing wine and her reds from the early 2000s are famous. The estate became certified organic in 1992 and in 2005 all her some seven hectares of registered Brunello vineyards were certified biodynamic. Production varies significantly year by year given that only the best wine is bottled as Brunello and so while in 2009 some 20,000 bottles were produced, in 2014 only 3,000 were made. The wines have a classic style and age in wood often at controlled temperatures.

█ 93   Price C
Brunello di Montalcino Podere San Giuseppe Riserva 2010

100% Sangiovese grapes. Vinified and aged in oak barrels. Shiny ruby. Well-defined and intense nose of classic notes of cherry, lightly smoky, white spices

and red citrus. Very pleasant palate, good weight and classy tannins, juicy and austere finish; very long.

TASSI

Viale P. Strozzi, 1/3
53024 Montalcino (SI)
Tel. +39 0577 846147
info@tassimontalcino.com
www.tassimontalcino.com

YEAR OF FOUNDATION 2004
NAME OF THE OWNER Franca Franci
TOTAL BOTTLES PRODUCED 25,000
VISITS TO THE WINERY - RESERVATION NEEDED
HECTARES OF VINEYARD 4

Fabio Tassi is a well-known Montalcino entrepreneur. His activities all center around wine, first with a wine shop and later a restaurant. He also has vineyards on the southeaster side of Montalcino, some four hectares of which 2.5 are registered Brunello, and they are all becoming organic. After several years of research with alternating results, he hit the bullseye with his 2011 vintage. Aside from wine Fabio is also an accomplished beekeeper who has won several prizes for his honey.

█ 93   Price C
Brunello di Montalcino Franci 2011

100% Sangiovese grapes. Ages for 3 years in 20 hl barrels. Ruby with garnet hues. Intense and well-defined nose of yellow peach, and an intense floral aromas, lychee. Elegant and dynamic palate, good depth and weight, flavorful, classy tannins, vertical. Very long finish.

TENUTA DELL'ORNELLAIA

Via Bolgherese, 191 - Frazione Bolgheri
57022 Castagneto Carducci (LI)
Tel. +39 0565 71811
info@ornellaia.it
www.ornellaia.it
🅵 *OrnellaiaWinery*
🐦 *@Ornellaia*

YEAR OF FOUNDATION 1981
NAME OF THE OWNER Marchesi de' Frescobaldi

TOTAL BOTTLES PRODUCED 832,000
VISITS TO THE WINERY - RESERVATION NEEDED
HECTARES OF VINEYARD 97

Frescobaldi's flagship estate is going through a new phase following the departure of Leonardo Raspini. Nevertheless, they have many ambitious projects as demonstrated by the building of the Masseto winery that perhaps already by 2017 will become totally. Their Ornallaia white is ready, made from a parcel of Sauvignon Blanc, while the overall quality of all the estate's wines remains, as always, very high.

---

 97   Price E

Masseto 2013

100% Merlot grapes. Ages for 24 months in barrique. Intense and dark ruby. Complex and intense fruity nose of cherry, blackberry, currant and blueberry, then dark and austere notes. Fairly austere palate, elegant, firm and structured with a wonderful depth and a wonderful long finish.

---

 95   Price D

Bolgheri Superiore Ornellaia 2013

Blend of 53% Cabernet Sauvignon, 39% Merlot, Cabernet Franc and Petit Verdot grapes. Ages for 18 months in barrique. Deep and dark ruby. Elegant oaky note then citus flavor of cedar and blood orange, mulberry and blackcurrant, gentle floral hints and tobacco. The palate is rich, dense, intense with a wounderful sweetness of fruit. Captivating and long finish.

☐ 90   Price D

Ornellaia Bianco 2014

Blend of Sauvignon Blanc and Viognier grapes. Ferment and ages for 12 months in 30% new and 70% used barrique. Intense straw yellow with green hues. Rich and intense nose, white and yellow blossoms then white stone fruit and a hint of eucalyptus, spicy notes on the background. The palate is lively and ample, very elegant and long length.

---

 89   Price B

Bolgheri Le Serre Nuove 2014

Blend of 57% Merlot, 17% Cabernet Sauvignon, 14% Petit Verdot and Cabernet Franc grapes. Ages for 2 years in barrique. Deep and dark ruby. Multi-layered nose: notes of Mediterranean scrub and fine herbs then fruity flavor of cassis and raspberry. Fresh palate that reminds fruity and licorice aromas, fairly elegant.

TENUTA DI ARCENO

Località Arceno San Gusmè
53010 Castelnuovo Berardenga (SI)
Tel. +39 0577 359346
info@tenutadiarceno.com
www.tenutadiarceno.com

YEAR OF FOUNDATION 1994
NAME OF THE OWNER Jackson Family
TOTAL BOTTLES PRODUCED 300,000
DIRECT SALES
VISITS TO THE WINERY - RESERVATION NEEDED
HECTARES OF VINEYARD 92
OLIVE OIL PRODUCTION

Tenuta di Arceno is situated in the southern part of Chianti Classico in the town of Castelnuovo Berardenga, near the hamlet of San Gusmè. It has around 1,000 hectares of land of which some 92 are vineyards and another 50 or so used for olive production. The property also has about 30 farm houses and a beautiful manor house that is the estate's headquarters. It is owned by the American Kendall Jackson Group, one of the most important on the worldwide wine scene. The estate was acquired in 1994 and after initially focusing on international varieties they have shifted more to a Chianti spirit and now produce a Chianti the latest of which stand out for their austerity.

---

 93   Price C

Arcanum 2010

Blend of Cabernet Franc, Cabernet Sauvignon and Merlot grapes. Ages in barrique. Dark color. Rich palate, eucalyptus, intense black fruit aromas: mulberry, currant and blackberry. Very classy palate for weight and depth. Wonderful tannin and a length that reminds eucalyptus notes.

■ 93   Price B

Chianti Classico Strada al Sasso Riserva 2010

100% Sangiovese grapes. Ages in barrique and tonneau. Ruby with light garnet hues. Dark nose of undergrowth and black fruits, dark blossoms. Vibrant palate with great acidity, youthful tannin and a good weight but with great and flavorful depth. Extremely long finish.

■ 90   Price B

Chianti Classico Riserva 2012

Blend of Sangiovese with small percentage of Cab-

ernet grapes. Ages for 12 months in barrique. Deep ruby. Intense and austere nose, notes of black cherry and a hint of tobacco, sage and a light eucalyptus. Rich palate with good weight, well defined and balanced thank to the wonderful acidity and to a savory note that gives a wonderful elegant depth. Intense and flavorful finish.

★★
TENUTA DI GHIZZANO

Via della Chiesa, 4 - Frazione Ghizzano
56037 Peccioli (PI)
Tel. +39 0587 630096
info@tenutadighizzano.com
www.tenutadighizzano.com
 TenutadiGhizzano
🐦 @Ghizzano_Wines

YEAR OF FOUNDATION 1370
NAME OF THE OWNER Ginevra Venerosi Pesciolini
TOTAL BOTTLES PRODUCED 80,000
DIRECT SALES
VISITS TO THE WINERY - RESERVATION NEEDED
HECTARES OF VINEYARD 20
HOSPITALITY
CERTIFIED ORGANIC VITICULTURE
OLIVE OIL PRODUCTION

There are some Italian winemaking areas that owe a lot to very few people. The area of Pisa owes a great deal to Ginevra Venerosi Pescioli-ni who over the years has produced important wines with a clear style for this area. Great care is taken in the vineyards where the yield is reduced and while the winery is old in structure, modern in ideas there ensured that Veneroso, made mostly from Sangiovese, and Nambrot, made from Merlot, have forced their way to be among the elite wines in Tuscany.

 95   Price B
Terre di Pisa Nambrot 2013
Blend of 60% Merlot, Cabernet Franc and Petit Verdot grapes. Ages for 1 year in barrique. Very intense ruby with violet hues. Intense fruity nose, blackberry, blueberry, currant, kirsch and oaky hint. Very good palate, fresh, balanced and elegant; ample and flavorful finish, very long.

 90   Price B
Terre di Pisa Veneroso 2013
Blend of 70% Sangiovese and 30% Cabernet Sau-

vignon grapes. Ages for 18 months in Frech oak barrels. Dark ruby. The nose plays on ripe fruity notes with prune and cherry, floral notes of violet then oaky notes. The palate is fresh, savory, elegant, vertical with a fruity finish.

 86   👍 Price A
Il Ghizzano 2014
Blend of Sangiovese with small percentage of Merlot grapes. Ages in stainless steel and concrete tanks. Ruby. Intense fruity nose, raspberry and cherry, hint of spices. The palate is fresh and savory, simple and easy drinking, good tannins and fruity finish. A wine with wonderful drinkability.

★★
TENUTA DI VALGIANO

Via di Valgiano, 7
55018 Capannori (LU)
Tel. +39 0583 402271
Fax +39 0583572141
info@valgiano.it
www.valgiano.it
 tenutadi.valgiano
🐦 @Lauracollobiano

YEAR OF FOUNDATION 1993
NAME OF THE OWNER Moreno Petrini
TOTAL BOTTLES PRODUCED 70,000
DIRECT SALES
VISITS TO THE WINERY - RESERVATION NEEDED
HECTARES OF VINEYARD 20
CERTIFIED ORGANIC VITICULTURE
CERTIFIED BIODYNAMIC VITICULTURE
OLIVE OIL PRODUCTION

Moreno Petrini and Saverio Petrilli create wines that are very clean and consistent with their territory and this has made their winery one of the most important in the province of Lucca. The wines are the product of bio-dy-namic farming methods and are technically very expressive and become sublime thanks to aging in barrels in the old and confused cellar of the manor house. The vineyards sit at different altitudes and have been replanted in recent years to offer an enviable palette of grapes.

■ 93   Price C
Colline Lucchesi Tenuta di Valgiano 2013
Blend of Sangiovese, Merlot, Syrah and other grape varieties. Ages for 12 months in barrique and con-

475

TUSCANY

crete tank. Dark ruby. Initially the nose is shy then shows its potential with notes of blood orange, bay leaf and a cold territorial note. Spicy palate, wonderful acidity, integrated tannins, vertical. Long and flavorful finish.

88 — Price B
Colline Lucchesi Palistorti di Valgiano 2013

Blend of Sangiovese, Syrah, Merlot and other grape varieties. Ages for 12 months in barique. Dark ruby. medium intensity on the nose, fruity (white cherry), floral (violet), lightly spicy. Medium bodied, good acidity, good depth, the finish offers fruity notes of cherry.

TENUTA POGGIOVENTOSO

Strada Terenzana 5
56046 Pisa (PI)
Tel. +39 392 9084949 / +39 393 8973677
Fax +39 0565 1761038
info@poggioventoso.wine
www.poggioventoso.wine
f Poggioventoso-Vini

YEAR OF FOUNDATION 2004
NAME OF THE OWNER Maricla Affatato
TOTAL BOTTLES PRODUCED 26,000
DIRECT SALES
VISITS TO THE WINERY - RESERVATION NEEDED
HECTARES OF VINEYARD 6
HOSPITALITY
RESTAURANT
CERTIFIED ORGANIC VITICULTURE
CERTIFIED BIODYNAMIC VITICULTURE
OLIVE OIL PRODUCTION

In Riparbella, in the province of Pisa, Maricla Affatato and her filmmaker husband Enzo d'Alò have with great passion and enthusiasm created their Poggioventoso (Windy Hill) estate. And on this truly windy hill they cultivate mostly Merlot which year after year keeps getting better also thanks to the consultancy of an enologist of the caliber of Lorenzo Landi.

90 — Price B
Fuochi 2013

Blend of Merlot, Sangiovese, Petit Verdot and Cabernet Sauvignon grapes. Ages for 10-12 months in barique. Ruby. Captivating nose with flavors of fruits and herbs, toasty notes and tobacco, dark

spices. Meaty palate, fresh and long finish with a spicy and toasted aftertaste.

☐ 87 — Price B
Poetico 2015

Blend of Vermentino, Malvasia di Candia and Petit Manseng. Stainless steel. Straw yellow. Nose of sweet citrus and fine herbs. Juicy and intense palate, see breeze and fruity notes.

TENUTA SAN GUIDO

Località Le Capanne, 27 - Frazione Bolgheri
57022 Castagneto Carducci (LI)
Tel. +39 0565 762003
Fax +39 0565 762017
info@tenutasanguido.com
www.tenutasanguido.com
www.sassicaia.com
🐦 @InfoSassicaia

YEAR OF FOUNDATION 1940
NAME OF THE OWNER Marchesi Incisa della Rocchetta
TOTAL BOTTLES PRODUCED 740,000
VISITS TO THE WINERY - RESERVATION NEEDED
HECTARES OF VINEYARD 90
OLIVE OIL PRODUCTION

This estate is right next to the Cyprus tress that Carducci said "run in rows to San Guido". Everyone identifies this estate with Sassicaia, an icon of Italian winemaking. It is owned by Nicolò Incisa della Rocchetta, a noble but more important gentleman of Piedmont origin transplanted in Tuscany. His father Mario invented Sassicaia as well as the horse breed Dormello Olgiata that he raised and trained, together with Federico Tesio, and produced, among others, Ribot. Nicolò has continued his father's work with intelligence and humility, as the great man his is.

98 — Price D
Bolgheri Sassicaia 2013

Blend of 85% Cabernet Sauvignon and 15% Cabernet Franc grapes. Ages for 2 years in barrique. Intense and lively ruby. Complex nose, well-defined and very refined with notes of blackcurrant, tobacco, raspberry, leather and a hint of vanilla and pine resin on the background. Elegant and tense palate, crunchy acidity, savory, refined and

velvety tannins, and with an exeptional length. A
great wine!

91   Price B
Guidalberto 2014

Blend of 60% Cabernet Sauvignon and 40% Merlot grapes. Ages for 1 year in barrique. Intense and lively ruby. Despite the challenging vintage, the aroma profile seems solid and fruity, simpler than other vintages but crunchy and with notes of blueberry and raspberry. Supple palate, decent body, subtle tannins and good length.

88   Price B
Le Difese 2014

Blend of 70% Cabernet Sauvignon and 30% Sangiovese grapes. Ages for 1 year in barrique. Lively ruby. Nose of forest fruits, pine resin, hint of Mediterranean scrub and black cherry. Agile palate, medium weight, simple and pleasantly savory, fair length.

★★★

TENUTA SETTE PONTI

Via Sette Ponti, 71
52029 Castiglion Fibocchi (AR)
Tel. +39 0575 477857
Fax +39 0575 431542
🅢 tenuta.sette.ponti
tenutasetteponti@tenutasetteponti.it
www.tenutasetteponti.it
🅕 Tenuta-Sette-Ponti
🐦 TenSettePonti

YEAR OF FOUNDATION 1998
NAME OF THE OWNER Moretti Family
TOTAL BOTTLES PRODUCED 185,000
DIRECT SALES
VISITS TO THE WINERY - RESERVATION NEEDED
HECTARES OF VINEYARD 50
OLIVE OIL PRODUCTION

Wine lovers are always a bit skeptical when someone from another profession decides to make wine. Antonio Moretti, a textile industrialist from Arezzo, is a happy exception to this rule. For some years now he has been producing great quality wines in Valdarno di Sopra, Bolgheri and in Sicily, near Noto. His base, however, is Tenuta Sette Ponti, a magnificent estate immersed in the beautiful Arezzo countryside. And his wines are marvelous.

94   Price C
Val d'Arno di Sopra Vigna dell'Impero 2013

100% Sangiovese grapes. Ages for 18 months in barrique. Very intense ruby. Well-defined and multi-layered nose, notes of cocoa, kirsch and vanilla. Firm and well-structured palate, youthful but not aggressive tannins, wonderful body, savory, tense, good length.

92   Price C
Oreno 2014

Blend of 50% Merlot, 40% Cabernet Sauvignon and 10% Petit Verdot grapes. Ages for 18 months in barrique. Very intense and dark ruby. developed notes of kirsch, lightly pungent then vanilla, blackcurrant and raspberry. Agile palate, crunchy, medium to full-bodied, pleasant and with a good length.

88   Price B
Poggio al Lupo 2014

100% Cabernet Sauvignon from Maremma vineyard. Ages for 18 months in barrique. Intense ruby with violet hues. Light vegetal notes on the nose then blueberry, blackcurrant and vanilla. Medium weight, supple, youthful and still lively tannins.

TENUTA TRE ROSE

Via della Stella, 3 - Frazione Valiano
53045 Montepulciano (SI)
Tel. +39 0578 72491
info@borgotrerose.it
www.borgotrerose.it
🅕 Hotel-Borgo-Tre-Rose-Montepulciano-Siena
🐦 @Borgo_Tre_Rose

YEAR OF FOUNDATION 1994
NAME OF THE OWNER Bertani Domains
TOTAL BOTTLES PRODUCED 345,000
DIRECT SALES
VISITS TO THE WINERY - RESERVATION NEEDED
HECTARES OF VINEYARD 78
HOSPITALITY
RESTAURANT

This historic estate is situated around the ancient 12th century hamlet Borgo Tre Rose that has a tower that looks out over the countryside. The hamlet was restored to become a country 'hotel de charme' and the surrounding vineyards produce a series of territorial wines that, according to a precise style, age in large oak

TUSCANY

477

barrels and barrique. The main wine is Simposio, a Vino Nobile di Montepulciano, produced with only Sangiovese grapes from the historic vineyards.

478

■ 🖻 95   Price B
Vino Nobile di Montepulciano Simposio 2011

100% Sangiovese grapes. Ages in tonneau and barrique. Lively ruby garnet. Classic nose of white spices, herbs, black cherry, sour cherry, undergrowth, intense and lightly smoky. Refined and elegant palate thank to wonderful tannic structure; very classy. Firm attack, medium weight and great depth with a very intense and long finish.

■ 92   Price B
Vino Nobile di Montepulciano Villa Romizi 2012

Blend of Sangiovese and other international grape varieties. Ages in tonneau. The nose offers fruity aromas of cherry and prune, also jammy. The palate shows great depth and dynamism thank to youthful tannin that gives agility to a firm structure. The licorice aftertaste enhances the flavorful finish.

■ 91   Price B
Vino Nobile di Montepulciano Santa Caterina 2013

Blend of Sangiovese and other allowed grape varieties. Ages in barrels and tonneau. Ruby with garnet hues. Very elegant nose on classic notes of yellow fruit: peach and a hint of citrus: orange. The palate is not muscular but very classic, lightly developed notes, well-integrated tannins, good weight, agile but supple. Surpising finish.

★★
TENUTE DEL CERRO

Via Grazianella, 5 - Frazione Acquaviva
53045 Montepulciano (SI)
Tel. +39 0578 767722 - 767700
Fax +39 0578 768040
info@tenutedelcerro.it
www.tenutadelcerro.it
 Saiagricola
🐦 *@Saiagricola*

YEAR OF FOUNDATION **1978**
NAME OF THE OWNER **Gruppo Unipol**
TOTAL BOTTLES PRODUCED **1,500,000**
DIRECT SALES

VISITS TO THE WINERY - RESERVATION NEEDED
HECTARES OF VINEYARD **180**
HOSPITALITY
RESTAURANT
OLIVE OIL PRODUCTION

This is the largest, privately-owned estate producing Nobile, with almost 100 hectares registered for the DOCG classification, as well as a leading wine group with other estates in Tuscany and Umbria. This sizes allows it to have a vast selection of grapes to maintain a constant estate style each year. The style of the estate's wines is modern but centered on Sangiovese. The use of aging barrels of various sizes help to define the style.

■ 92   Price B*
Moscadello di Montalcino 2014

*100% Moscadello grapes. Ages in barrique and stainless steel. Intense yellow with green hues. Intense sea breeze notes, yellow orange and blossoms, lavender and a hint of cedar. The palate shows balance between sweetness and acidity and a unique drinkability. A benchmark wine! *37.5 cl bottle.*

■ 92   Price B
Vino Nobile di Montepulciano Antica Chiusina 2013

100% Sangiovese grapes. Ages in small barrels. Ruby. Very defined nose of cherry then floral aromas of violet and field blossoms, green tea. Well-structured palate, refined tannin, great weight and an extremely long finish.

■ 88   Price A
Vino Nobile di Montepulciano 2013

Blend of Sangiovese and other allowed grape varieties. Ages in different types of barrels. Deep ruby. Intense notes, eucalyptus, classic red and yellow fruit aromas, ink. Elegant palate, flavorful, 'relaxed' and balanced thank to refined tannin. Good finish.

■ 87   Price B
Brunello di Montalcino 2011

100% Sangiovese grapes. Ages in barrels. Ruby. Fruity nose of ripe cherry and blackberry, hint of herbs and white spices. Good palate with smooth tannins and medium weigth. Flavorful finish.

TENUTE SILVIO NARDI

Casale del Bosco
53024 Monticiano (SI)
Tel. +39 0577 808269
🅢 *tenute.silvio.nardi*
info@tenutenardi.com
www.tenutenardi.com
🅕 *tenutenardi*
🐦 *@TenuteNardi*

YEAR OF FOUNDATION 1950
NAME OF THE OWNER Emilia Nardi
TOTAL BOTTLES PRODUCED 250,000
DIRECT SALES
VISITS TO THE WINERY - RESERVATION NEEDED
HECTARES OF VINEYARD 80
OLIVE OIL PRODUCTION

This estate has finally achieved productive continuity thanks to Emilia Nardi, a dynamic businesswoman who has run this family enterprise for some years now. While it has a long history, the estate had slipped a bit in quality but over the past 15 years Emilia has made significant investments and redefined the estate's standards, efforts that are now producing positive results.

⬛ 89   Price B
Brunello di Montalcino 2011

100% Sangiovese grapes. Ages in barrels. A new era statement for the winery. Classic nose of tobacco and undergrowth then fruity aromas of cherry, blackberry and a hint of almond. Firm palate, good acidity that eases the drink; developed tannin; good weight but elegance and drinkability are the best qualities of this wine with a flavorful finish.

⬛ 87   Price A
Rosso di Montalcino 2014

100% Sangiovese grapes. Ages in barrels. Light ruby. Very fresh nose with fruity aromas of cherry. The palate is fresh and offers great drinkability. Fragrant and pleasant wine.

TERENZI

Località Montedonico
58054 Scansano (GR)
Tel. +39 39 0564 599601
info@terenzi.eu
www.terenzi.eu
🅕 *societaagricolaterenzi*

YEAR OF FOUNDATION 2001
NAME OF THE OWNER Terenzi Family
TOTAL BOTTLES PRODUCED 350,000
DIRECT SALES
VISITS TO THE WINERY - RESERVATION NEEDED
HECTARES OF VINEYARD 75
HOSPITALITY
RESTAURANT
OLIVE OIL PRODUCTION

In 2001, the Terenzi family decided to make a total life change and dedicate themselves to winemaking. It was a bold decision which began as a dream with a splendid Maremma estate and just over a hectare of vineyards. But their passion, credibility and experience grew rapidly as did the size of their vineyards and production of Morellino di Scansano. Today the estate owns 60 hectares of vineyards, leases another 15 and produces some 350,000 bottles a year.

⬛ 92   👍 Price A
Morellino di Scansano Purosangue Riserva 2013

100% Sangiovese grapes. Ages in tonneau. Intense ruby. Intense and clean nose with upfront fruity compound of cherry and black cherry, warm and subtle blackberry and sweet spice note. Rich palate, intense and with a youthful tannin to support the good weight. Juicy and flavorful finish.

☐ 88   Price B
Maremma Toscana Viognier Montedonico 2015

100% Viognier grapes. Ages on the lees in stainless steel tanks. Very intense straw yellow. Nose of loquat, white peach and hint of anise. Savory palate, balanced. A very flavorful Mediterranean wine.

⬛ 87   Price B
Morellino di Scansano Madrechiesa Riserva 2013

100% Sangiovese grapes. Ages in oak barrels. Lively ruby. The nose offer notes of blueberry candy and a slightly overwhelming spicy note. Convincing palate, firm but well integrated tannin and a good depth thank to balanced acidity.

★

TERENZUOLA

Via Vercalda, 14
54035 Fosdinovo (MS)
Tel. +39 0187 670387
Fax +39 0187 670387
info@terenzuola.it
www.terenzuola.it
 terenzuola.ivangiuliani

YEAR OF FOUNDATION 1993
NAME OF THE OWNER Ivan Giuliani
TOTAL BOTTLES PRODUCED 80,000
DIRECT SALES
VISITS TO THE WINERY - RESERVATION NEEDED
HECTARES OF VINEYARD 15

Brining back, in a winemaking sense, the ancient area of Lunigiana, including the Cinque Terre, had always been the dream of Ivan Giuliani, who for over 20 years has been making wine there between the regions of Liguria and Tuscany. His estate is old, dating back to 1930, but the 'new path' Ivan embarked on in 1993 is now producing excellent results.

☐ 93 👍 Price A

Colli di Luni Vermentino Fosso di Corsano 2015

100% Vermentino grapes. Ages for 6 months on the lees in stainless steel tanks. Straw yellow with green hues. Complex nose, smoky yeasty notes then hint of cedar, loquat and green apple. Tense palate, great character, savory, with a light and gentle fizzness to enrich the freshness; agile, good body and a great length.

★

TOLAINI

S.P. 9 di Pievasciata, 28
53019 Castelnuovo Berardenga (SI)
Tel. +39 0577 356972
Fax +39 0577356701
info@tolaini.it
www.tolaini.it
 Tolaini-Wine
 @TolainiWines

YEAR OF FOUNDATION 1999
NAME OF THE OWNER Pier Luigi Tolaini

TOTAL BOTTLES PRODUCED 230,000
DIRECT SALES
VISITS TO THE WINERY - RESERVATION NEEDED
HECTARES OF VINEYARD 50

Pier Luigi Tolaini is a great entrepreneur who made his fortune in Canada. When he returned to Italy he wanted to have a place all his own where he could enjoy country life and make quality wine. He found it and some 15 years ago bought Castelnuovo Berardenga. The rest is history. Today it is a splendid estate producing excellent wines. From a man like this, who could expect less?

■ 91 Price B

Valdisanti 2011

Blend of 75% Cabernet Sauvignon, 20% Sangiovese and Cabernet Franc grapes. Ages for 16 months in barrique. Very dark ruby. Rich nose of currant and blueberry, light eucalyptus note with warm spices and blood orange aromas. Powerful palate, dense, muscular depth, wonderful tannin. The finish offers a warm pencil lead aftertaste and a jammy notes.

■ 85 Price B

Al Passo 2011

Blend of 80% Sangiovese and 20% Merlot grapes. Ages in second and third fill barrique and tonneau. Dark ruby. Weel-defined nose of spices and red fruits, redberry and black cherry, hint of turmeric and carob. The palate shows great drinkability and balance with a smooth and flavorful finish. Even if it is labelled as IGT it can be a Chianti Classico, but the winery prefers a 100% Sangiovese for their Chianti Classico.

★★

TRINORO

Via Val d'Orcia, 15
53047 Sarteano (SI)
Tel. +39 0578 267110
Fax +39 0578 267303
 tenutaditrinoro
info@trinoro.it
www.trinoro.it
 TenutadiTrinoro
 @TenutadiTrinoro

YEAR OF FOUNDATION 1995
NAME OF THE OWNER Andrea Franchetti
TOTAL BOTTLES PRODUCED 80,000

DIRECT SALES
VISITS TO THE WINERY - RESERVATION NEEDED
HECTARES OF VINEYARD 22

Among the first to go to the slopes of Mt. Etna, in Passopisciaro, Andrea Franchetti applied his ambition and skill to this estate in Val d'Orcia which was in an area where no one had planted vineyards nor with such density. Harvest is a key element in production and grapes are picked at ten to as many 20 different periods to ensure they are perfect for winemaking.

 93   **Price D**
Tenuta di Trinoro 2014

Blend of 39% Cabernet Franc, 39% Merlot, 11% Cabernet Sauvignon and 11% Petit Verdot grapes. Ages for 18 months in barrique. Intense and dark ruby. Captivating nose of blackberry, blueberry, blackcurrant, also jammy notes, and a hint of vanilla. Savory, youthful, smooth tannins and good length.

TUA RITA

Località Notri, 81
57028 Suvereto (LI)
Tel. +39 0565 829237
Fax +39 0565 827864
info@tuarita.it
www.tuarita.it
rita.tua.35

YEAR OF FOUNDATION 1984
NAME OF THE OWNER Rita Tua
TOTAL BOTTLES PRODUCED 250,000
DIRECT SALES
VISITS TO THE WINERY - RESERVATION NEEDED
HECTARES OF VINEYARD 35
CERTIFIED ORGANIC VITICULTURE

This estate also began as a country retreat. Rita and Virgilio found this corner of Val di Cornia to be the ideal location to relax in nature and then, as often occurs, they caught the wine-making bug. Their first bottles came out almost in secret and were few in number considering they only had two hectares of vineyards. Since then the estate has expanded and today Tua Rita is justly considered, on an international level, to be one of the leasing Tuscan producers.

 94   **Price C**
Giusto di Notri 2010

Blend of 60% Cabernet Sauvignon, 30% Merlot and Cabernet Franc grapes. Ages for 18 months in barrique. Dark ruby. Intense nose, pencil lead, fruity aromas of mulberry and blackberry, wonderful spicy notes. Elegant and powerful, flavorful, well balanced. Long finish.

 89   **Price A**
Rosso dei Notri 2014

Blend of 50% Sangiovese and 50% of Cabernet Sauvignon, Merlot and Syrah grapes. The Sangiovese ages in stainless steel and the other grapes in barrique. Lively ruby. Very fruity nose with cherry, black cherry and strawberry, clean and defined. Pleasant palate, fresh and easy drinking with a very fruity finish. A simple and very pleasant wine.

★
UCCELLIERA

Podere Uccelliera, 45 - Frazione Castelnuovo dell'Abate
53024 Montalcino (SI)
Tel. +39 0577 835729
Fax +39 0577 835729
ancomontalcino
anco@uccelliera-montalcino.it
www.uccelliera-montalcino.it

YEAR OF FOUNDATION 1986
NAME OF THE OWNER Andrea Cortolesi
TOTAL BOTTLES PRODUCED 60,000
DIRECT SALES
VISITS TO THE WINERY - RESERVATION NEEDED
HECTARES OF VINEYARD 6.3
RESTAURANT
OLIVE OIL PRODUCTION

The estate was founded by Andrea Cortonesi in the mid-1980s and its vineyards were in an unusual location. It is located in Castelnuovo dell'Abate, between the abbey and the former onyx mine where the soil is a clay marl rich in pebbles. The first Brunello produced was a 1993 and the quality of the estate's products allowed it to shoot up to be among the top in Montalcino. The style of the wine is modern but not excessively so and the approach is not fundamentalist. Andrea is constantly striving for perfection, experimenting with the fermen-

481

tation and aging depending on the quality of the harvest.

 🔲 97   Price D*

Costabate 2010

*100% Sangiovese grapes. Ages in tonneau. Intense and dark ruby. Intriguing and well defined typical notes from the 'Southern side': black cherry, blood orange, smoky notes and Mediterranean spices. Great weight, dense, wonderful and elegant depth. Youthful and subtle tannin, very classy finish! *Only Magnum.*

🔲 94   Price D

Brunello di Montalcino Riserva 2010

100% Sangiovese grapes. Ages in different types of oak barrels. Intense ruby. Complex and ample palate that offers warm spicy notes, intense fruity aromas of cherry, blackberry and black cherry. Good spicy and austere hints. Powerful palate with great weight, savory and youthful tannins. The finish is firm, rich and juicy.

USIGLIAN DEL VESCOVO

Via Usigliano, 26
56036 Palaia (PI)
Tel. +39 0587 622138
Fax +39 0587 629795
🔵 *usigliandelvescovo*
e.disessa@usigliandelvescovo.it
www.usigliandelvescovo.it
🔘 *Usiglian-del-Vescovo*
🔵 *@UdelV*

YEAR OF FOUNDATION 2001
NAME OF THE OWNER Final Spa
TOTAL BOTTLES PRODUCED 150,000
DIRECT SALES
VISITS TO THE WINERY - RESERVATION NEEDED
HECTARES OF VINEYARD 28
OLIVE OIL PRODUCTION

A lot is going on in Palaia, in the province of Pisa, and this estate is an example. In a cellar of this lovely medieval village are the barrique aging wines made from very dense vineyards, 5-6,000 vines per hectare, and with sandy soils that have little clay. The grapes are for the most part indigenous with a small presence of Sangiovese and the wine making approach is modern with fermentation in wood and cement and aging in 250 and 500-liter barrels.

🔲 90   Price B

Barbiglione 2013

Blend of 70% Syrah and 30% of Cabernet Sauvignon, Sangiovese and Merlot grapes. Ages for 12 months in barrique and tonneau. Dark and deep ruby. Fruity nose with aromas of cherry and blackberry, white pepper and rose, lightly smoky. Fresh palate, round and harmonious, balanced and velvety.

🔲 87   Price A

Il Grullaio 2015

Blend of Cabernet Sauvignon, Merlot and Sangiovese grapes. Ages for 6 months in stainless steel. Ruby purple red. Intense and fruity aromas of cherry, blueberry and a hint of violet. The palate is fresh, savory, crunchy and fruity with a blueberry aftertaste.

🔲 87   Price A

Chianti Superiore 2014

Blend of Sangiovese and small percentage of other grape varieties. Ages for 6 months in 18 hl barrels. Shiny ruby. Cherry color such as the fruity aroma on the nose, then notes of wet leaves and spices. The palate is fresh and rich with crunchy tannins and a flavorful finish.

VAL DELLE CORTI

Casali Val delle Corti, 141
53017 Radda in Chianti (SI)
Tel. +39 0577 738215
info@valdellecorti.it
www.valdellecorti.it
🔘 *valdellecorti*
🔵 *@ValdelleCorti*

YEAR OF FOUNDATION 1974
NAME OF THE OWNER Roberto Bianchi
TOTAL BOTTLES PRODUCED 7,000
DIRECT SALES
VISITS TO THE WINERY - RESERVATION NEEDED
HECTARES OF VINEYARD 4
CERTIFIED ORGANIC VITICULTURE
OLIVE OIL PRODUCTION

From Milan to Radda without looking back. Roberto Bianchi's wines are 'rural' yet very elegant. Stubborn and determined, Roberto Bianchi continuous following his father's footsteps when in the Sixties he started to work in the family's winery. His wines are always genuine and direct with a unique character that makes them recognizable and enthusiastic.

 97   **Price B**

Chianti Classico Riserva 2013

100% Sangiovese grapes. Ages in large casks. Light ruby. Impressive nose of sage, redcurrant, strawberry and steely notes. Agile palate, steely and precise, aftertaste of lavender and currant; balanced, savory, perfect tannin: refined and juicy with a lot potential. Wonderful finish.

 94   👍 **Price A**

Chianti Classico 2014

Blend of Sangiovese and Canaiolo grapes. Ages in large casks. Light ruby, transparent, burgundian. Nose of currant, raspberry, salt, sea breeze, and steely notes. Thin, solid, incredibly long with character and personality. Very good drinkability.

VAL DELLE ROSE

Località Poggio la Mozza
58100 Grosseto (GR)
Tel. +39 0564 409062
info@valdellerose.it
valdellerose.it/
 CecchiWinery
 @cecchiwinery

YEAR OF FOUNDATION **1996**
NAME OF THE OWNER **Cecchi Family**
TOTAL BOTTLES PRODUCED **1,500,000**
DIRECT SALES
VISITS TO THE WINERY - RESERVATION NEEDED
HECTARES OF VINEYARD **105**

The investment the Cecchi family has made in Maremma has risen significantly over the years. In 2011, they completed the construction of a new winery and aging facility which are fully equipped and connected with a new hospitality area – inaugurated in 2016 – which Andrea Cecchi intends to use to enhance appreciation of the area and of his wines.

 89   **Price B**

Maremma Toscana Aurelio 2013

Blend of Merlot and small percentage of Cabernet Franc grapes, 12 months in barrique. Dark ruby. Intense and clean nose with flavor of dark forest fruits,

spicy hint of green peppercorn and eucalyptus. Rich and flavorful palate, with firm but smooth tannins, good extraction and flavorful finish. First vintage for this wine dedicated to the Aurelia Road.

■ 87   **Price A**

Morellino di Scansano Poggio al Leone Riserva 2013

Blend of Sangiovese and other international grape varieties. Ages for 12 months in barrique. Ruby with garnet hues. International style nose, ripe black fruits, pencil lead, paprika and green peppercorn. Very dense palate, captivating, sweet fruit character, silky tannins, very harmonic finish.

□ 85   👍 **Price A**

Maremma Toscana Litorale 2015

Blend of 90% of Vermentino and other grape varieties. Only stainless steel. Straw yellow with warmer hues. The nose is fruity with yellow peach, apple, loquat and a refreshing sage hint. The palate is fresh and round, good structured and fruity.

VAL DI SUGA

Località Val di Cava
53024 Montalcino (SI)
Tel. +39 0577 804101
info@tenimentiangelini.it
www.valdisuga.it

YEAR OF FOUNDATION **1969**
NAME OF THE OWNER **Bertani Domains**
TOTAL BOTTLES PRODUCED **270,000**
DIRECT SALES
VISITS TO THE WINERY - RESERVATION NEEDED
HECTARES OF VINEYARD **52**

This beautiful estate has its headquarters in the northern zone of Montalcino but its vineyards are spread throughout the district. It recently entered the galaxy of Bertani Domains which has allowed it to accelerate its return to its former glory. It has two very lovely vineyards that are the envy of all: Vigna del Lago, in front of the estate's headquarter, and Spuntali on the south side of Montalcino. The latter was one of the first to be high density even if only a small part of it reached 6,000 vines per hectare. The estate's latest acquisition is in an area that has a great future on the eastern side known as Poggio al Granchio.

483

■ 93   Price C
Brunello di Montalcino Vigna del Lago 2010

100% Sangiovese grapes. Ages in tonneau and casks. Dark ruby. Defined and fresh nose of red fruit, light citrus and white spices; developing. Firm palate, not muscular but elegant and juicy with a flavorful and captivating finish. Good expression of this Cru that produced great wines in the 90's.

★★
VALDICAVA

Via Tenuta Valdicava
53024 Montalcino (SI)
Tel. +39 0577 848261
fuinde2001@gmail.com
www.valdicava.it

YEAR OF FOUNDATION **1968**
NAME OF THE OWNER **Vincenzo Abbruzzese**
TOTAL BOTTLES PRODUCED **80,000**
DIRECT SALES
VISITS TO THE WINERY - RESERVATION NEEDED
HECTARES OF VINEYARD **27**

Vincenzo Abbruzzese has two great passions, Brunello and horses, and you can often see him riding through his vineyards and even in town. His estate has some 27 hectares of vineyards all located in northern Montalcino, from the foot of the legendary Montosoli to the small Madonna del Piano church, an area that produces his Riserva del Brunello. It would be wrong to define him as a modernist because he uses classic 35-40hl barrels. Maniacal care is taken in the vineyard in selecting the grapes and during maceration which may be somewhat extreme. The wines are solid yet elegant.

■ 🔲 97   Price D
Brunello di Montalcino Madonna del Piano 2010

100% Sangiovese grapes. Ages in different types of oak barrels. Shiny ruby. The nose is extremely clean and offers intense notes of dark cherry, fresh herbs, red blossoms and sweet tobacco. The palate is very well balanced, integrated tannins and refresing acidity. Good middle palate and very exciting finish.

■ 90   Price C
Brunello di Montalcino 2011

100% Sangiovese grapes. Ages in barrels. Dark ruby color. Initially the nose is subtle then offers dark notes and undergrowth. Convincing palate even if the tannin is still young and lightly aggressive.

VALLEPICCIOLA

Località Pievasciata
53019 Castelnuovo Berardenga (SI)
Tel. +39 0577 357539
info@vallepicciola.com
www.vallepicciola.com
🅕 *vallepicciola*

YEAR OF FOUNDATION **2006**
NAME OF THE OWNER **Bruno Bolfo**
TOTAL BOTTLES PRODUCED **300,000**
DIRECT SALES
VISITS TO THE WINERY - RESERVATION NEEDED
HECTARES OF VINEYARD **65**
HOSPITALITY
RESTAURANT

A star is born in Pievasciata, one of the most beautiful areas in the province of Siena. It is named Vallepicciola and is simply a corner of paradise created by Bruno Bolfo which aside from a winery also hosts a wonderful, five-star hotel called La Fontanelle. The wines, especially the Chianti Classico and Quercegrosse Merlot, are truly becoming very interesting and production has great growth potential. We will hear a lot about this estate in the future but in the meantime we have given this magnificent reality this year's 'rising star' award.

■ 93   Price C
Quercegrosse Merlot 2015

100% Merlot grapes, 1 year in barrique. Very intense and dark ruby. Tasted before bottling the wine showed immediately its great potential. Raspberry and framboise on the nose, lightly oaky, cassis, tobacco hint of leather and field blossoms; rich and youthful aroma profile. Powerful, smooth, very subtle tannins balanced by the great weight. Warm and very long finish.

■ 92   Price B
Chianti Classico Riserva 2013

100% Sangiovese grapes. Ages for 15 months in

large casks. Lively ruby garnet. Very refined and varietal nose with notes of black cherry and violet, then tobacco, vanilla and hint of leather. Tense and savory palate, great body but supple, warm, captivating; good length.

 90 Price B

Chianti Classico 2014

100% Sangiovese grapes. Ages for 1 year in large casks. Intense ruby. One of the best Chianti Classico 2014. Very varietal on the nose with notes of black cherry and prune. Tense and supple palate, balanced acidity, savory, firm but not aggressive tannins; good length.

★

VIGNAMAGGIO

Via Petriolo, 5
50022 Greve in Chianti (FI)
Tel. +39 055 854661
prodotti@vignamaggio.com
www.vignamaggio.com
f vignamaggio
🐦 @vignamaggio

YEAR OF FOUNDATION 1987
NAME OF THE OWNER Patrice Taravella
TOTAL BOTTLES PRODUCED 200,000
DIRECT SALES
VISITS TO THE WINERY - RESERVATION NEEDED
HECTARES OF VINEYARD 40
HOSPITALITY
RESTAURANT
OLIVE OIL PRODUCTION

The change in ownership that saw it pass into the hands of Patrice Taravella, an architect of Italian origin who lived in France for a long period, gave this estate a significant boost and a change in pace with important acquisitions around Greve in Chianti. The Chianti Classico are always of excellent quality with Monna Lisa now smiling about her Gran Selezione classification. A legend talks about Leonardo da Vinci painting Monna Lisa in one of Villa Vignamaggio rooms and the landscape around the villa reminds that painting.

90 Price B

Chianti Classico Gherardino 2012

Blend of 90% Sangiovese and 10% Merlot grapes. Ages for 18 months in large casks. Deep ruby. Good

powerful structure: rich and opulent nose, palate with youthful but not dry tannins, good weight and balance; dark fruit and eucalyptus.

88 Price B

Chianti Classico Gran Selezione Monna Lisa 2013

Blend of Sangiovese, Cabernet Sauvignon and Merlot grapes. Ages for 30 months in large casks and barrique. Dark ruby. Rich fruity nose even if very ripe, mint, spice, licorice, soy sauce, umami. Lightly rough and drying tannins with good freshness that makes the wine very pleasant.

87 Price A

Chianti Classico Terre di Prenzano 2014

100% Sangiovese grapes. Ages for 1 year in large casks. Light ruby. Steely and savory nose; pleasant and flavorful palate, a bit edgy acidity but well interprate the challenging vintage.

VILLA DEL CIGLIANO

Via Cigliano 16
50026 San Casciano in Val di Pesa (FI)
Tel. +39 055 820033
info@villadelcigliano.it
www.villadelcigliano.it
f VilladelCigliano

YEAR OF FOUNDATION 1600
NAME OF THE OWNER Niccolò and Elisabetta Montecchi
TOTAL BOTTLES PRODUCED 18,000
DIRECT SALES
VISITS TO THE WINERY - RESERVATION NEEDED
HECTARES OF VINEYARD 25
CERTIFIED ORGANIC VITICULTURE
OLIVE OIL PRODUCTION

This ancient and historic estate has been in the same family for over 500 years and is today run by its latest descendants, siblings Niccolò and Elisabetta Montecchi. In line with the latest trends, they are striving for freshness and austerity in their wine and doing this from the terroir of San Casciano, one of the least typical areas for this in the appellation, with elegance.

92 Price B

Chianti Classico Riserva 2013

Blend of Sangiovese and small percentage of Merlot grapes. Ages for 18 months in new barrique. Ruby

485

garnet. Sweet fruity notes, vanilla and an oaky hint but good depth and juice: long, good acidity, good and well extracted tannin: balanced.

and floral aromas with walnut and mustard; juicy and precise palate, very satisfying.

■ 90   👍 Price A
Chianti Classico 2014

Blend of Sangiovese and small percentage of Merlot grapes. Ages for 12 months in large casks. Light ruby. Fresh, pleasant and well-made wine. Fruity

■ 88   Price B
Nettuno 2012

100% Cabernet Sauvignon grapes. Ages for 18 months in barrique. Dark ruby. Nose of mustard, red and black fruit, undergrowth, resin and mint, intense and long fruit aftertaste; rocky tannins.

UMBRIA

E ven if it is a small, interior region, Umbria in recent years has been carving out an important place for itself in the production of high quality Italian wine. The region currently produces some 600,000 hectoliters of wine a year of which 40% is DOC classified. Two DOCG wines are produced: Torgiano Rosso Riserva and Sagrantino di Montefalco. These are two full-bodied reds, authentic gems that can age long and are produced in the hilly area at the center of the region. There are a number of well-made DOC wines including a true phenomenon in regards to sales, Orvieto, while certain Umbria IGT wines are for this region what the Super Tuscans are for Tuscany. These include Cervaro della Sala, made from Chardonnay and Grechetto and produced by Antinori's Castello della Sala estate, which is one of Italy best whites and does well in international competitions.

Northern Umbria is occupied by three, territorially vast DOC appellations which have only been partially exploited by producers, above all cooperatives that dominate production in the area. They are Colli Altotiberrini, Colli del Trasimeno and Colli Perugini. With only few exceptions, wine production here leans more towards quantity than quality. The wines produced in all three zones are Bianco, made from Trebbiano grapes, and Rosso, which is for the most part made from Sangiovese. Only Colli di Trasimeno Rosso can be made with a small addition of Gamay, a grape typical to Beaujolas in France that no one knows how it got to the heart of Umbria.

Past Perugia is the appellation of Torgiano which is among the best in the whole region. Here they produce many types of wines and the winemaking scene is dominated by an almost legendary winery, Lungarotti. Torgiano Rosso Riserva was the first to obtain a DOCG classification, in 1990, and is made with Sangiovese grapes with a little Canaiolo and must age in barrels for at least three years. Its leading perhaps only real producer is Lungarotti that has a versions that come out on the market no earlier than six years after harvest. It is a wine with intense and evolved aromas and has an exemplary softness. It is a great wine to pair with roasts and with dishes prepared with black truffle. There is also a DOC Torgiano Bianco, made with Trebbiano and Grechetto, which can age for several years, as well as Torgiano Rosso, made with Sangiovese and Canaiolo. A series of other wines, created as experiments, have also been given DOC classification: Chardonnay, Pinot Grigio and Riesling Italico among the whites and Cabernet Sauvignon and Pinot Nero among the reds. Chardonnay and Pinot Nero are also used to make a traditional method Torgiano Spumante which is not bad at all.

Futher south towards Foligno is the zone of Montefalco, another pillar of quality winemaking in Umbria. This is home to the region's other DOCG wine, Sagrantino di Montefalco, a great red made from the grape of the same name. Once it was only a sweet wines whereas now it is almost always a dry red capable of aging long. The best producer of this wine is the passionate winemaker Marco Caprai, who in recent years has been coming out with some spectacular Sagrantino. There is also a traditional Passito dessert wine but it is getting rarer to find and is more expensive. A Bianco is also produced in Montefalco, made with Grechetto and Trebbiano, along with a surprising Rosso, a blend of Sangiovese and Sagrantino. And there is even a sub-zone Grechetto di Todi, the last word in whites in those parts. Aside from these rather full-bodied and distinct wines, one can also find Colli Martani Sangiovese and Colli Martani Trebbiano which are the backbone of production in that zone.

In the southern part of the region is the province of Terni. Here the winemaking scene is dominated by a very famous and ancient wine: Orvieto. It is made with Trebbiano, Verdello and Grechetto grapes in an area that also boasts a Classico zone.

The most common Orvieto is the Secco (dry) but it is not unusual to find an Abboccato (medium-sweet), Amabile (semi-sweet) and Dolce (sweet). Orvieto has for years been the leading wine produced in Umbria and several important Chianti wineries used to produce buy it to be able to offer a white with their line of reds. This was the case up until at least the 1970s when Galestro was created to take the place of Orvieto. Following several years of decline, many wineries are now once again offering quality Orvieto.

The last DOC zone, and the southernmost, is Amelia in the area of Colli Amerini. Here whites are made with Trebbiano or Grechetto, while the reds, including reserves, are made with Sangiovese, Ciliegiolo or Merlot. There is also some Tuscan-style Vin Santo and a pleasing Malvasia which is terms of flavor and texture recall the wines of neighboring northern Lazio.

CONTROLLED AND GUARANTEED DESIGNATION OF ORIGIN (DOCG)

- Montefalco Sagrantino
- Torgiano Rosso Riserva

CONTROLLED DESIGNATION OF ORIGIN (DOC)

- Amelia
- Assisi
- Colli Altotiberini
- Colli del Trasimeno or Trasimeno
- Colli Martani, with or without Todi (only for Grechetto) and Cannarra (only for Vernaccia); geographic references allowed
- Colli Perugini
- Lago di Corbara
- Montefalco
- Orvieto, with or without Classico
- Rosso Orvietano or Orvietano Rosso
- Spoleto
- Todi
- Torgiano

★
ADANTI

Via Belvedere, 2
06031 Bevagna (PG)
Tel. +39 0742 360295
info@cantineadanti.com
www.cantineadanti.com
f *Azienda Agricola Adanti*

YEAR OF FOUNDATION 1974
NAME OF THE OWNER Pietro, Daniela and
Donatella Adanti
TOTAL BOTTLES PRODUCED 160,000
DIRECT SALES
VISITS TO THE WINERY - RESERVATION NEEDED
HECTARES OF VINEYARD 30
OLIVE OIL PRODUCTION

Character, character and then more character. Thus sums up the red wines offered by Pietro, Daniela and Donatella who are carrying on the work begun by Domenico some 50 years ago. Adanti has always been a point of reference in the terroir of Sagrantino where it has 30 or so hectares of vineyards on the hills of Bevagna, in the northernmost part of the appellation. The approach in the winery is classic with spontaneous fermentation, long maceration and aging in big barrels. A word of warning: in order to love the reds from this estate, as well as the land and food, you have to love tannins.

| 94 | Price B |

Montefalco Sagrantino Arquata 2010

100% Sagrantino grapes. Two years in big barrels. Dark ruby red with violet hues. Elegant nose, flowery and spicy with pepper hints, rind and red orange. Full bodied, powerful and elegant, thick tannins and ripe fruit and spices in the finish.

| 90 | Price B |

Arquata 2010

Blend of 40% Cabernet Sauvignon, 40% Merlot, 20% Barbera grapes. Matures 24 months in barrique and tonneau. Red ruby color with garnet hues. Elegant on the nose with ripe wild berries, raspberries and spices, herbs. Smooth on the palate, full bodied, eucalyptus finish.

| 88 | 👍 Price A |

Montefalco Rosso Arquata 2012

Blend of 70% Sangiovese with Sagrantino, Barbera,

Merlot and Cabernet grapes. Matures 1 year in big oak barrels. Ruby red. Fruity, full and juicy on the nose, light spices and pepper. Balanced and spicy on the palate, elegant in its simplicity.

★★
ANTONELLI SAN MARCO

Località San Marco, 60
06036 Montefalco (PG)
Tel. +39 0742 379158
info@antonellisanmarco.it
www.antonellisanmarco.it
f *Cantina Antonelli*

YEAR OF FOUNDATION 1881
NAME OF THE OWNER Filippo Antonelli
TOTAL BOTTLES PRODUCED 350,000
DIRECT SALES
VISITS TO THE WINERY - RESERVATION NEEDED
HECTARES OF VINEYARD 50
HOSPITALITY
RESTAURANT
CERTIFIED ORGANIC VITICULTURE
OLIVE OIL PRODUCTION

Filippo Antonelli has a smiling face that immediately makes you like him. He has been running his family's historic estate since 1986 and it has some 50 hectares in a single vineyard that is at a rather high altitude. This may be the reason why their Sagrantino are never too strong and maintain an excellent drinkability without losing any of the extraordinary structural characteristics the wine is known for. We suggest a visit to the estate which also has holiday farm facilities where you can spend a few days relaxing and tasting the area's specialties and the friendly family atmosphere.

| 92 | Price B |

Montefalco Sagrantino Chiusa di Pannone 2009

100% Sagrantino grapes. Matures in oak barrels for 30 months and another 6 months in concrete tanks. Dark ruby red. Intense notes of strong spices, roasting, juniper and red orange. Full bodied and compact on the palate with a long spicy finish.

| 89 | Price B |

Montefalco Sagrantino 2011

100% Sagrantino grapes. Matures in 500 litres oak

barrels for 6 months, then in bigger barrels for 24 months and another 18 months in concrete tanks. Ruby red color. Notes of spices, aromatic herbs, anise, plum and red orange. Smooth tannins and average freshness on the palate. Aromatic herbs in the finish.

490

☐ 88   Price A
Trebium 2015

100% Trebbiano Spoletino grapes. Ferments and matures in 25 hl oak barrels for 6 months. Straw yellow color. Herbs and citrus with sage hints on the nose, white pepper, citrus and pink grapefruit. Juicy and citrusy on the palate, agile with a pleasant aromatic herbs finish.

★

BARBERANI

Località Cerreto
05023 Baschi (TR)
Tel. +39 0763 341820
barberani@barberani.it
www.barberani.it
 barberani
 @barberani

YEAR OF FOUNDATION 1961
NAME OF THE OWNER Luigi A. Barberani
TOTAL BOTTLES PRODUCED 350,000
DIRECT SALES
VISITS TO THE WINERY
HECTARES OF VINEYARD 60
HOSPITALITY
CERTIFIED ORGANIC VITICULTURE
OLIVE OIL PRODUCTION

Barberani has been making wine for over 50 years in the 'Classico' area of the appellation, a few kilometers from Orvieto, along the Tiber River and on the hills overlooking Lake Corbara. The chalky-clay soil, microclimate softened by the lake and years of experience allow for the production of quality wine made mostly from local grapes like Grechetto, Trebbiano, Procanico and Sangiovese.

☐ 93   Price C*
Orvieto Classico Superiore Muffa Nobile Calcaia 2013

Blend of 80% Grechetto, 20% Procanico, both with botrytis. Stainless steel only. Bright yellow color. Apricot and aromatic herbs on the nose, saffron

and yellow peach jam. Agile and tense on the palate with sweet fruity aromas, cane sugar and fresh, very long finish. *50 cl bottle.

☐ 91   Price B
Orvieto Classico Superiore Luigi e Giovanna 2013

Blend of 90% Grechetto and 10% Procanico grapes. Matures in big barrels. Straw yellow color. Grapefruit sensations on the nose, then vanilla, lime and aromatic herbs on the background. Nice progression on the palate, full body and fresh with a long citrusy finish.

■ 89   Price B
Lago di Corbara Polvento 2010

Blend of 95% Sangiovese Grosso with Merlot and Cabernet Sauvignon. Matures 24 months in barrique. Briny on the nose with semi-dried cherry tomatoes, elegant spices, red flowers and intense notes of incense, vanilla and cocoa. Rich and fresh on the palate with a long briny and morello cherry finish.

BIGI

Località Ponte Giulio
05018 Orvieto (TR)
Tel. +39 0763 315888
bigi@giv.it
www.cantinebigi.it

YEAR OF FOUNDATION 1880
NAME OF THE OWNER Gruppo Italiano Vini
TOTAL BOTTLES PRODUCED 4,000,000
DIRECT SALES
VISITS TO THE WINERY - RESERVATION NEEDED
HECTARES OF VINEYARD 248

Bigi is one of the oldest wine producer in the area and has a total of 248 hectares of vineyards in the classic zone of Orvieto that have altitudes ranging between 150 and 450m above sea level. For the past 40 years it has been part of Gruppo Italiano Vini and produces good quality wines at reasonable prices. Aside from classic Orvieto they also make red wines from Sangiovese and produce olive oil.

■ 87   Price A
Sartiano 2014

Blend of 60% Sangiovese and 40% Merlot grapes. Matures 10 months in barrique. Garnet ruby red.

Spicy and eucalyptus notes with ripe fruits almost jammy. Dark spices and pepper. Fresh on the palate, smooth tannins, toasted notes of tobacco, dark fruits and bark in the finish.

☐ 86   👍 Price A
Orvieto Classico Vigneto Torricella 2015

Blend of 40% Trebbiano Toscano, 40% Verdello and Grechetto, 20% Malvasia Toscana and Drupeggio grapes. Stainless steel only. Straw yellow color. Notes of herbs and flowers, ripe fruit and medlar on the nose. Sweet and aromatic on the palate, average freshness.

BOCALE

Via Fratta Alzatura
Località Madonna della Stella
06036 Montefalco (PG)
Tel. +39 0742 399233
Fax +39 0742 718052
info@bocale.it
www.bocale.it
❦ Bocale Vini
🐦 @Bocalevini

YEAR OF FOUNDATION 2002
NAME OF THE OWNER Valentini Family
TOTAL BOTTLES PRODUCED 28,000
DIRECT SALES
VISITS TO THE WINERY
HECTARES OF VINEYARD 5.2
OLIVE OIL PRODUCTION

Bocale is a small family estate created in 2002 but which has its roots in farming and wine, which Grandfather Valentino was making already back in 1927. His friends would call him Bocale because they would go to him for two-liter boccale bottles of wine. The name stuck and was given to the new estate. While not certified organic, they adhere to this philosophy and use no chemical products and only natural indigenous yeasts are employed. Emiliano Falsini is the enologist consultant.

▪ 90   Price B
Montefalco Sagrantino Passito 2008

100% dried Sagrantino grapes. Matures 2 years in barrique. Garnet color. Aromas of carob and cinchona on the nose, sweet but balanced on the palate with a dynamic and long fruity finish.

▪ 87   Price A
Montefalco Rosso 2013

Blend of 70% Sangiovese, 15% Sagrantino, 10% Merlot and 5% Colorino grapes. Matures 12 months in oak barres. Ruby red. Great intense spiciness on the nose and red berries. Fresh and juicy on the palate. Long persistence.

LEONARDO BUSSOLETTI

Strada delle Pretare, 62
05035 Narni (TR)
Tel. +39 0744 715687
Ⓢ leo.bussoletti
info@leonardobussoletti.it
www.leonardobussoletti.it
❦ Leonardo Bussoletti Viticoltore in Narni
🐦 InfoBussoletti

YEAR OF FOUNDATION 2008
NAME OF THE OWNER Leonardo Bussoletti
TOTAL BOTTLES PRODUCED 32,000
VISITS TO THE WINERY - RESERVATION NEEDED
HECTARES OF VINEYARD 9
CERTIFIED ORGANIC VITICULTURE
OLIVE OIL PRODUCTION

The Bussoletti estate was founded in Narni in 2008 by Leonardo Bussoletti who decided to produce quality wines with the local Ciliegiolo grape. He went on to organize the Narni Association of Ciliegiolo Producers in order to create a team to make the grape better known. Up until then the varietal was mostly used to blend with other wines even if on its own it produce a very descent wine.

■ 90   Price B
Vigna Vecchia 2014

100% Ciliegiolo grapes. Matures in different types of oak barrels for 12 months. Ruby red color. Intense and spicy on the nose, underbrush and ripe fruits. Juicy and spicy on the palate, fresh and balanced. Long spicy persistence.

☐ 88   Price A
Colle Murello 2015

100% Trebbiano Spoletino grapes. Matures 7 months in big barrels. Straw yellow color. Elegant and aromatic on the nose with white rose and sweet citrus. Fresh and tense on the palate. Long aromatic and citrusy persistence.

☐ 88   👍 Price A
Colle Ozio 2014

100% Grechetto grapes. Stainless steel for 6 months. Deep yellow color. Intense and richy on the nose, aromatic herbs and flowers. On the palate it has body and freshness. Citrus and sweet fruits on the finish.

CANTINA NINNÌ

Via F. Morvillo, 11
06049 Spoleto (PG)
Tel. +39 335 5450523
info@cantinaninnispoleto.com
www.cantinaninnispoleto.com
👍 *Cantina-Ninni-Spoleto*

YEAR OF FOUNDATION 2012
NAME OF THE OWNER Gianluca Piernera
TOTAL BOTTLES PRODUCED 12,000
DIRECT SALES
VISITS TO THE WINERY - RESERVATION NEEDED
HECTARES OF VINEYARD 3.2

Gianluca Piernera could be considered a winemaker 'by chance' given that he is by trade an electrician. He built his family home on land that included an old vineyard and after meeting Marco Casolanetti he was bitten by the winemaking bug. Since 2012 he has been bottling his first wines. His vineyard's yield is very low and he uses no chemical treatments in it, while in the winery he uses only indigenous natural yeasts. One of his vineyard's strongpoints is its Trebbiano Spoletino, a white wine grape that is now having the success it deserves.

■ 90   Price B
Diavolacciu 2013

Blend of Sangiovese, Merlot, Barbera, Montepulciano and Aleatico grapes. Matures in stainless steel and barrique. Dark red color. Still a little austere on the nose with notes of graphite and cinchona. Rich on the palate but agile with smooth tannins and a long, dynamic, fruity finish.

☐ 90   👍 Price A
Misluli Bianco 2013

Blend of Trebbiano Spoletino and Malvasia Lunga di Candia. Ages in stainless steel vats. The wine has a bright yellow color and a complex aroma of spices and iodine. The mouthfeel is bold, slightly tannic yet juicy and the finish is long and brackish.

☐ 89   Price A
Trebbiano Spoletino Poggio del Vescovo 2015

100% Trebbiano Spoletino grapes. Matures in stainless steel tanks. Straw yellow with green hues. Notes of sea breeze and white fruits. Briny, vibrant on the palate with a long savory finish.

ARNALDO CAPRAI

Località Torre
06036 Montefalco (PG)
Tel. +39 0742 378802
Fax +39 0742 378422
info@arnaldocaprai.it
www.arnaldocaprai.it
👍 *Arnaldo Caprai Viticoltore*
🐦 *@arnaldocaprai*

YEAR OF FOUNDATION 1971
NAME OF THE OWNER Arnaldo Caprai
TOTAL BOTTLES PRODUCED 750,000
DIRECT SALES
VISITS TO THE WINERY - RESERVATION NEEDED
HECTARES OF VINEYARD 136
OLIVE OIL PRODUCTION

The paradigm of Sagrantino, the Caprai estate has played a fundamental and incomparable role in developing this wine and making it famous and appreciated the world over. The credit goes to Marco Caprai, an entrepreneur and passionate winemaker who was able to rediscover the wealth of this land and, with a modern and innovative approach as well as constant research, achieve exceptional results. His avant-garde methods are aimed at sustainability as well as boosting value not only to a land that is rich from a winemaking point of view but that also has a cultural heritage and tradition that are worth preserving.

■ 🍇 95   Price C
Montefalco Sagrantino 25 Anni 2012

100% Sagrantino grapes. Matures 24 months in barrique. Ruby red color. Eucalyptus nose, strong ripe fruit aromas, black cherry and cloves. Rich on the palate, thick and elegant tannins, notes of nutmeg and ripe fruits in the very long finish.

■ 92   Price B
Montefalco Sagrantino Collepiano 2012

100% Sagrantino grapes. Matures 22 months in barrique. Dark ruby red color. Notes of cocoa, cinchona and underbrush on the nose, pleasant briny sensations of semi-dried cherry tomatoes. Powerful on the palate, thick and elegant tannins. Long cocoa and eucalyptus finis.

■ 91   Price B
Montefalco Sagrantino Vigna del Lago 2012

100% Sagrantino grapes. Matures 24 months in barrique. Dark ruby red. Very ripe on the nose, fruit jam, ripe blackberries, spices, pepper, dark tobacco. Rich and tannic on the palate, licorice and spices in the finish.

■ 90   Price B
Montefalco Rosso Riserva 2011

Blend of 70% Sangiovese, 15% Sagrantino and 15% Merlot grapes. Matures 20 months in barrique. Ruby red color. Notes of macerated cherry, herbal notes, spices, nutmeg. Elegant tannins on the palate and long spicy and fruity finish.

★★★
CASTELLO DELLA SALA

Località Sala
05016 Ficulle (TR)
Tel. +39 0763 86127
Fax +39 0763 86491
castellodellasala@antinori.it
www.antinori.it
f *MarchesiAntinori*
🐦 *@AntinoriFamily*

YEAR OF FOUNDATION **1940**
NAME OF THE OWNER **Antinori Family**
TOTAL BOTTLES PRODUCED **750,000**
DIRECT SALES
VISITS TO THE WINERY - RESERVATION NEEDED
HECTARES OF VINEYARD **140**
OLIVE OIL PRODUCTION

The Castello is a 15th century Monaldeschi fortress that today belongs to the Antinori family who have turned it into a pearl of winemaking in Italy. Here tradition and innovation coexist in a virtuous circle that results in well-made wines that have character and long life. The

wines are famous all over the world, especially Cervaro della Sala. The vineyards have a chalky soil, which is well-suited for white wines, and are in a perfect position to benefit from the temperature variations between day and night in the period leading up harvest.

☐ 🖻 98   Price B
Cervaro della Sala 2014

Blend of 90% Chardonnay and 10% Grechetto that ages in barrique for at least a year. The 2014 wine has less structure and more acidity while the color is less bright then usual. The aromas range from flint to citrus fruit with some yellow plum sensations. The mouthfeel is briny, agile, fresh and very elegant with a subtle yet very long finish. In my view, this was the best vintage ever.

☐ 92   Price B
Bramìto 2015

100% Chardonnay grapes. Part ferments in French barrique. Straw yellow color. Intense fruity nose, pineapple and yellow peach, aromatic herbs and toasted sensations. Juicy and rich on the palate, sustained by great freshness.

★
CASTELLO DELLE REGINE

Via Ortana vecchia, 2/V San Liberato
05035 Narni (TR)
Tel. +39 0744 702005
info@castellodelleregine.com
www.castellodelleregine.com
f *Aziendacastellodelleregine*
🐦 *Castello delle Regine*

YEAR OF FOUNDATION **1998**
NAME OF THE OWNER **Paolo Nodari**
TOTAL BOTTLES PRODUCED **500,000**
DIRECT SALES
VISITS TO THE WINERY - RESERVATION NEEDED
HECTARES OF VINEYARD **80**
HOSPITALITY
RESTAURANT
OLIVE OIL PRODUCTION

The estate of Paolo and Livia Nodari started when the celebrated Milan lawyer acquired a few hectares of land in Umbria. Today these hectares have risen to 385 of which 80 are planted with vineyards and 20 or so with olives, while the estate also hosts a restaurant and holiday farm. It is a paradise created with care by its owners who, thanks also to the contribution of enologist Franco Bernabei, produce quality wine.

86 ✋ Price A
Rose delle Regine 2015

100% Montepulciano grapes. Stainless steel only. Intense pink color. Delicate flowery aromas and fruity with hints of cherry and violet on the nose. Fresh and juicy on the palate with strawberry notes in the finish.

494

85 ✋ Price A
Poggio delle Regine Bianco 2015

Blend of 70% Grechetto, 30% Malvasia and Trebbiano grapes. Matures in stainless steel. Delicate straw yellow color. Notes of citrus and stones. Nice acidity on the palate and fruity finish.

CASTELLO DI CORBARA

Località Corbara
05018 Orvieto (TR)
Tel. +39 0763 304035
info@castellodicorbara.it
www.castellodicorbara.it

YEAR OF FOUNDATION 1997
NAME OF THE OWNER Fernando Patrizi
TOTAL BOTTLES PRODUCED 200,000
DIRECT SALES
VISITS TO THE WINERY
HECTARES OF VINEYARD 100
OLIVE OIL PRODUCTION

This is one of the most beautiful estates in the district of Orvieto which at the beginning of the 20th century belonged to Banca Romana, while the castle was that of the Montemarte, the Counts of Corbara. Since 1997 it has belonged to Fernando Patrizi. The vineyards total some 100 hectares and are situated on the hills along the Tiber River near the man-made reservoir of Lake Corbara where the soil is in part volcanic and in part gravelly.

91 Price B
Lago di Corbara Calistri 2013

100% Sangiovese grapes. Matures 18 months in new barrique. Ruby red with garnet hues. Foxy notes and tobacco, sweet spices and licorice root on

the nose. Savory and juicy on the palate, fresh and agile with a pleasant finish of red orange.

☐ 87 Price A
Orzalume 2015

Blend of Grechetto and Sauvignon grapes. Matures 5 months in new barrique. Light straw yellow color. Aromatic herbs on the nose, herbal notes and white fruits. Juicy, savory and minty on the palate. Herbs and eucalyptus finish.

CASTELLO DI MAGIONE

Viale Cavalieri di Malta, 31
06063 Magione (PG)
Tel. +39 075 5057319
segreteria@sagrivit.it
www.sagrivit.it

YEAR OF FOUNDATION 1200
NAME OF THE OWNER Sagrivit
TOTAL BOTTLES PRODUCED 180,000
DIRECT SALES
VISITS TO THE WINERY - RESERVATION NEEDED
HECTARES OF VINEYARD 44
OLIVE OIL PRODUCTION

The castle dates back to the mid-12th century and for many years was a welcoming station for pilgrims travelling the via Francigena. Today it belongs to the Knights of Malta who, as they do in Rocca Bernarda in Friuli, also produce wine. The wines are well-made and have an excellent quality/price ratio.

☐ 90 Price B
Colli del Trasimeno Vin Santo 2008

Blend of 50% Trebbiano and 50% Grechetto grapes. Matures 3 years in 114 liters barrels. Intense amber color. Aromas of nuts and dried citrus peel on the nose. Enveloping, juicy, warm but with nice acidity on the palate. Notes of ancient wood and dates in the finish.

89 Price A
Colli del Trasimeno Morcinaia 2011

Blend of 40% Merlot, 40% Cabernet Sauvignon and 20% Sangiovese grapes. Matures 10 months in barrique. Ruby red, garnet hues. Austere on the nose, notes of see breeze, spices, cloves and eucalyptus puffs. Nice body, juicy and fresh, long spicy, ripe fruit finish.

⭐⭐⭐
CÒLPETRONE

Via Ponte la Mandria, 8/1 - Frazione Marcellano
06035 Gualdo Cattaneo (PG)
Tel. +39 0742 99827
info@tenutedelcerro.it
www.tenutedelcerro.it
f *Colpetrone*

YEAR OF FOUNDATION 1995
NAME OF THE OWNER Tenute del Cerro
TOTAL BOTTLES PRODUCED 230,000
DIRECT SALES
VISITS TO THE WINERY - RESERVATION NEEDED
HECTARES OF VINEYARD 63

All the Tenuta del Cerro estats belong to the Unipol Insurance Group. This one in Umbria is one of the most interesting producers of Sagrantino. Last year their labels were totally resigned to be more modern and minimalist, even if a bit less recognizable. What can always be distinguished is the quality of the line of Montefalco wines, from Rosso to Sagrantino to the top of the line cru, Sacer Sagrantino.

◼ 93	Price C

Montefalco Sagrantino Sacer 2009

100% Sagrantino grapes. Matures 18 moths in new and used French oak barrique. Garnet ruby red color. Great elegance on the nose, light spices and fragrant, intense fruits. It keeps the same elegance on the palate, rich and smooth with thick tannins and a very long black cherry and spicy finish.

◼ 89	Price B

Montefalco Sagrantino 2010

100% Sagrantino grapes. Matures 12 months in barrique. Flowery and elegant spiciness on the nose. Then eucalyptus notes and old wood, underbrush. Full bodied and nice, elegant tannins and nice spicy and fruity finish.

◼ 87	Price A

Montefalco Rosso 2013

Blend of 70% Sangiovese, 15% Merlot and 15% Sagrantino grapes. Matures 12 months in used French oak barrique. Ruby red color. Red fruits and spices on the nose, berries and eucalyptus hints. Crunchy on the palate, fresh and tense with an elegant finish.

⭐⭐
DECUGNANO DEI BARBI

Località Fossatello, 50
05018 Orvieto (TR)
Tel. +39 0763 308255
Fax +39 0763 308118
info@decugnano.it
www.decugnanodeibarbi.com
f *decugnanodeibarbi*

YEAR OF FOUNDATION 1973
NAME OF THE OWNER Claudio and Enzo Barbi
TOTAL BOTTLES PRODUCED 120,000
DIRECT SALES
VISITS TO THE WINERY - RESERVATION NEEDED
HECTARES OF VINEYARD 32
OLIVE OIL PRODUCTION

Decugnano dei Barbi is one of the most important and classic producers in the area of Orvieto. Their vineyards grow in the sandy soil of Fossatello di Corbara while the cellars are carved out of tuff stone. The estate and cellars are well-worth a visit with their stunning beauty and timeless atmosphere. Claudio Barbi begin to buy his first vineyards in 1973 and in 1978 came out with Umbria's first traditional method bubbly, while in 1981 he produced the first Italian wine made with botrytis grapes, those with so-called noble rot, Pourriture Noble.

▫ 🎦 95	Price B

Orvieto Classico Superiore Pourriture Noble 2014

Blend of 55% Grechetto, 35% Sauvignon Blanc, 5% Procanico and 5% Semillon grapes. Botrytis. Stainless steel only. Golden color. The nose is typical of botrytis wines and opens with a briny explosion and notes of saffron together with flowers and delicate honey, curry and apricots. Sweet on the palate but sustained by nice acidity and briny that makes it dynamic and agile. Incredibly long and elegant finish.

☐ 91	👍 Price A

Maris 2014

100% Chardonnay grapes. Stainless steel only. Straw yellow color. Elegant and graphite notes on the nose with intriguing and clear hints of saffron. On the palate it is savory – its name comes from the underground soil of oyster fossils on which the vineyard grows – then again the strong saffron note and pleasant flower notes in the long finish.

□ 90   👍 Price A
Orvieto Classico Villa Barbi Bianco 2015

Blend of 50% Grechetto, 20% Vermetino, 20% Sauvignon Blanc and 10% Procanico grapes. Stainless steel only. Light straw yellow color. Intense and chalky on the nose with citrus and white flower notes. Very fresh on the palate and extremely great savory. Citrusy and spicy finish.

FRATELLI PARDI

Via Giovanni Pascoli, 7/9
06036 Montefalco (PG)
Tel. +39 0742 379023
info@cantinapardi.it
www.cantinapardi.it

YEAR OF FOUNDATION **1919**
NAME OF THE OWNER **Famiglia Pardi**
TOTAL BOTTLES PRODUCED **55.000**
DIRECT SALES
VISITS TO THE WINERY - RESERVATION NEEDED
HECTARES OF VINEYARD **11**

The story of entrepreneur Francesco Pardi, a well-known textile producer from Umbria, is a lovely Italian success story. And yet he is the first to point out that his family were originally farmers and their first success was in the wine sector. The winery is more rational and functional than beautiful. Inside there are excellent thermo-controlled vats that range between 25 to 50 hectoliters in size, in order to keep the various musts separate and allow the estate to better understand the differences between the various grape varieties and soils. The soils, in fact, differ in regard to both the lay of the land and altitude.

■ 92   Price B
Sacrantino 2011

100% Sagrantino grapes. Matures 18 months in barrique. Dark ruby color and an aroma with slightly warm scents of maple sap, violet and a lovely note of lavender followed by those of mulberry and a little blood orange. The mouthfeel is rich and intense with evident but top quality tannins. The finish is very rewarding.

□ 88   👍 Price A
Trebbiano Spoletino 2011

100% Trebbiano Spoletino grapes. Stainless steel

only. Bright and lively straw-yellow color. Broad and complex aromas, slightly smoky, medlar in the bouquet along with an aromatic sensation that recalls Pastis, white peach hints. The mouthfeel is distinguished by its density and persistence with notes of gooseberry and basil in the finish.

LA CARRAIA

Località Tordimonte, 56
05018 Orvieto (TR)
Tel. +39 0763 304013
Fax +39 0763 304048
info@lacarraia.it
www.lacarraia.it
🅵 *lacarraia*

YEAR OF FOUNDATION **1988**
NAME OF THE OWNER **Mauro Gialletti**
TOTAL BOTTLES PRODUCED **580,000**
DIRECT SALES
VISITS TO THE WINERY - RESERVATION NEEDED
HECTARES OF VINEYARD **50**

La Carraia began as a collaboration between the Gialetti and Cotarella families who for the past 20 years have been running this winery together. The mixture of tradition and innovation, the passion for wine of hôtelier Odoardo Gialetti and his fortuitous meeting with Riccardo Cotarella did the rest. They produce a full line of clean, well-made wines, both whites and reds including Fobiano and Tizzonero.

■ 88   👍 Price A
Tizzonero 2014

Blend of Sangiovese and Montepulciano grapes. Matures 8 months in barrique. Light ruby red color. Juicy and intense notes of cherry and spicy, cloves and tobacco. Fresh and nicely tannic. Rich of ripe cherry on the palate.

■ 87   Price B
Fobiano 2014

Blend of Merlot and Cabernet Sauvignon grapes. Ruby red color. Vanilla, roasting and tobacco notes with a slightly eucalyptus hints on the nose. Fresh and rich on the palate, smooth and clear notes of spices and vanilla.

□ 86   👍 Price A
Orvieto Class. Sup. Poggio Calvelli 2015

Blend of 60% Grechetto and Procanico with oth-

er grapes. Stainless steel only. Deep straw yellow. Sweet aromatic spectrum, yellow plum, white peach, ripe pear, citrus and apple. Aromatic herbs puffs on the palate together with citrus and average freshness. Good length in the finish.

LA MADELEINE

Strada Montini, 38
05035 Narni (TR)
Tel. +39 345 3208914
contatti@cantinalamadeleine.it
www.cantinalamadeleine.it
La-Madeleine

YEAR OF FOUNDATION 2008
NAME OF THE OWNER Giulia and Francesco d'Alema
TOTAL BOTTLES PRODUCED 38,000
DIRECT SALES
VISITS TO THE WINERY - RESERVATION NEEDED
HECTARES OF VINEYARD 6.5

Linda Giuva and her husband Massimo D'Alema have now also become winemakers but not out of snobbery or because it creates a positive image for a leading politician like D'Alema. The fact is they simply fell in love with the world of wine and have approached it with humility and dedication. Their tiny winery is in Narni, near the border between Umbria and Lazio, and their wines are beginning to be recognized, even by political rivals, because first of all they are good and then because they are "D'Alema's wines". And that is a good thing. We will limit ourselves to a basic evaluation of his wines, as should be the case with any wine, without any prejudice one way or the other.

91	Price B

Pinot Nero 2014

100% Pinot Nero grapes. Matures 16 months in French barrique. Light ruby red color. Unusual on the nose, ripe red fruits, slightly flowery, spices and vanilla. Full bodied on the palate, flowers and eucalyptus notes on the finish.

90	Price B

NarnOt 2013

100% Cabernet Franc grapes. Matures 18 months in French barrique. Ruby red with garnet hues. Notes of plums and underbrush, tobacco and rhubarb, roots and dried red flowers. Tannic and structured on the palate, herbaceous.

87	Price A

Sfide 2014

100% Cabernet Franc grapes. Matures 10-14 months in French oak barrique. Intense purple ruby red. Ink, dark aromas of underbrush, bark and soil on the nose. Clean, fresh and easy to drink. Nice tannins and notes of macerated wild berries in the finish.

LA PALAZZOLA

Località Vascigliano, 45
05039 Stroncone (TR)
Tel. +39 0744 609091
info@lapalazzola.it
www.lapalazzola.it
lapalazzola

YEAR OF FOUNDATION 1922
NAME OF THE OWNER Stefano Grilli
TOTAL BOTTLES PRODUCED 150,000
DIRECT SALES
VISITS TO THE WINERY - RESERVATION NEEDED
HECTARES OF VINEYARD 27

At his estate in Vascigliano di Stroncone, with its vineyards and geese, Stefano Grilli has embarked on an unusual path composed of changes in direction and research into grapes of the most diverse variety in a quest for quality through experimentation. This former nuclear engineer began with the humble idea of making a simple yet pleasing wine in an area considered unsuitable but then things go out of hand. A passionate experimenter, he produces some excellent traditional method bubbles.

91	Price B

La Palazzola Bianco Brut 2011

Blend of Vermentino and other grape varieties. Ancestral Classic Method. Golden color. Intense and aromatic on the nose, notes of papaya and eucalyptus hints. Structured and fresh on the palate with a very long passion fruit finish.

91	Price B

Riesling Brut 2012

100% Riesling grapes. Ancestral Classic Method. Enveloping eucalyptus notes, aromatic herbs, citrus and hydrocarbons on the nose. Creamy on the palate, elegant sparkles, rich and fresh. Long, citrusy and papaya in the finish.

☐ 87   Price B

Verdello 2014

100% Verdello vinified in oak barrels. Matures 2 months in terracotta cruses. Intense, almost golden, straw yellow. Gooseberry, bread crust and yellow flowers on the nose. Intense on the palate, deep and slightly spicy. Rustic but unique.

LE VELETTE

Località Le Velette, 23
05018 Orvieto (TR)
Tel. +39 0763 29090
tenuta.le.velette@llibero.it
www.levelette.it
 Tenuta Le Velette

YEAR OF FOUNDATION 1965
NAME OF THE OWNER Corrado Bottai
TOTAL BOTTLES PRODUCED 280,000
DIRECT SALES
VISITS TO THE WINERY - RESERVATION NEEDED
HECTARES OF VINEYARD 124
OLIVE OIL PRODUCTION

The story of this winery, today owned by Corrado Bottai and his daughter Cecilia, is that of the past 150 years of Orvieto history. Originally, it belonged to the church and then, after the unification of Italy, it was expropriated by the town and in 1887 was acquire by Felici, a family of Orvieto bankers. But it did not become an operating winery until 1950, when Florence native Marcello Bottai married a Felici daughter and decided to produce wine. In a short time, Orvieto Le Velette became one of the most prestigious wines in the area. Today this tradition is being continued by Corrado and Cecilia Bottai and Le Velette remains a most beautiful place that produces wines that are extremely territorial.

☐ 89   Price A

Orvieto Classico Superiore Lunato 2015

Blend of 50% Grechetto, 20% Trebbiano, 15% Malvasia, with Verdello, Drupeggio and other varieties. Matures 6 months in stainless steel. Straw yellow color. Flint and aromatic herbs on the nose. Briny, fresh and agile on the palate. Citrus and herbs in the finish.

■ 89   Price B

Gaudio 2012

100% Merlot grapes. Matures 12 months in bar-

rique. Very rich ruby color. Ripe fruit aromas of blackberries and raspberries on a spicy background. Full bodied and fresh on the palate. Red fruits in the finish.

LUNGAROTTI

Viale Giorgio Lungarotti, 2
06089 Torgiano (PG)
Tel. +39 075 988661
 zz_d_valeriemore
lungarotti@lungarotti.it
www.lungarotti.it
 lungarotti
 lungarottiwine

YEAR OF FOUNDATION 1962
NAME OF THE OWNER Lungarotti Family
TOTAL BOTTLES PRODUCED 2.500,000
DIRECT SALES
VISITS TO THE WINERY
HECTARES OF VINEYARD 250
HOSPITALITY
RESTAURANT
OLIVE OIL PRODUCTION

Founded in the 1960s, this estate in Torgiano is a true Umbrian jewel. The credit goes to Giorgio Lungarotti, an inspired businessman who more than half a century ago created this splendid winery and literally invented Torgiano wine. He died in 1999 at almost 90 years of age and the estate passed into the hands of his wife Maria Grazia and their daughters Maria Teresa and Chiara, who have carried on the family business with great competence. In the small hamlet of Torgiano they have also built wonderful hotel, Le Tre Vaselle, as well as the most beautiful wine museums in Italy. The estate has a vast line of production that always maintains an exceptionally high level of quality, from Vigna al Pino, to reds like Rubesco and the estate's stratospheric cru Vigna Monticchio, wines made with the brilliant consultancy of Lorenzo Landi.

■ 🔖 96   Price B

Torgiano Rosso Vigna Monticchio Riserva 2011

100% Sangiovese grapes. Matures 12 months in big barrels. Multi colored and elegant on the nose with aromas of wild berries, flowers and eucalyptus hints, cinchona and turmeric. Juicy, tense and agile on the palate with nice tannins and very long persistence in the finish.

---

93   Price B
San Giorgio 2006

Blend of Cabernet Sauvignon, Sangiovese and Canaiolo grapes. Matures in barrique. The label represents Saint George on the dragon. Dark ruby red with garnet hues. Great impact on the nose with roasting notes, cinchona, rhubarb, dark and ripe fruits, briny hints and eucalyptus puffs. Full body and velvety on the palate, rich and elegant with long persistence.

---

88   👍 Price A
Torgiano Bianco Torre di Giano 2015

Blend of 50% Vermentino,with Trebbiano and Grechetto grapes. Stainless steel on the yeasts. Straw yellow color. Herbs and flowers on the nose, stony and fruity. Rich and fresh on the palate with a long fruity finish on peach and medlar notes.

MILZIADE ANTANO FATTORIA COLLEALLODOLE

Via Colle Allodole, 3
06031 Bevagna (PG)
Tel. +39 0742 361897
info@fattoriacolleallodole.com
www.fattoriacolleallodole.com
🟦 Milziade-Antano-Fattoria-Colleallodole
🐦 @MilziadeAntano

YEAR OF FOUNDATION 1967
NAME OF THE OWNER Francesco Antano
TOTAL BOTTLES PRODUCED 70,000
DIRECT SALES
VISITS TO THE WINERY
HECTARES OF VINEYARD 20
OLIVE OIL PRODUCTION

Around the end of the 1960 Cavaliere Milziade Antano, main character of Sagrantino's history, gives birth to the winery that still carries his name. Today, Francesco, his son, leads the company with the same passion. The name Colleallodole is inspired by the migration of larks (*Allodole* in Italian), which every October fly over the hills of the area. Other producers make fun of Francesco saying he's not good in hunting larks but he surly is great in making wines.

---

94   Price C
Montefalco Sagrantino Colleallodole 2012

100% Sagrantino grapes. Matures 37 months of which 16-18 months in big barrels. Garnet ruby color. Complex and powerful on the nose, elegant, flowery and spicy. Sumptuous on the palate, see breeze notes with nice tannins, powerful body but perfectly sustained by acidity. Juicy and very long finish with spices and aromatic herbs.

---

90   Price B
Montefalco Sagrantino 2012

100% Sagrantino grapes. Matures 37 months of which 16-18 months in big barrels. Ruby red color. Toasted notes on the nose, eucalyptus and bark, hematic sensations. Thick tannins and nice freshness, long and elegant on the palate with eucalyptus finish.

---

88   Price B
Montefalco Rosso Riserva 2013

Blend of 65% Sangiovese, 15% Sagrantino, 15% Merlot and 5% Cabernet grapes. Matures 36 months of which 12-15 months in big barrels. Ruby red color. Sharp on the nose, delicate spices, underbrush, roasting and coffee powder. Juicy and rich on the palate, full bodied and average freshness.

★★
PALAZZONE

Località Rocca Ripesena, 68
05019 Orvieto (TR)
Tel. +39 0763 344921
Fax +39 0763 394833
info@palazzone.com
www.palazzone.com
🟦 palazzone
🐦 winePalazzone

YEAR OF FOUNDATION 1968
NAME OF THE OWNER Giovanni Dubini
TOTAL BOTTLES PRODUCED 130,000
DIRECT SALES
VISITS TO THE WINERY - RESERVATION NEEDED
HECTARES OF VINEYARD 24
HOSPITALITY
RESTAURANT
OLIVE OIL PRODUCTION

At the end of the 1960, the Dubini family bought the Palazzone estate in Rocca Ripesena, near Orvieto. Today, Palazzone not only hosts a winery but also is an historic residence and it all sits on the tuff rock typical of Orvieto. Giovanni Dubini's wines are impeccably made but need to breath in the glass a few minutes before they can 'communicate'. Once they are a few years old they acquire exceptional aromas and flavor. Our advice is to try them on-site at the winery together with the gourmet dishes prepared by the restaurant's chef and with a breathtaking panorama over the vineyards and surrounding countryside.

500

☐ 92   Price B
Orvieto Classico Superiore Campo del Guardiano 2014

Blend of 50% Procanico, 30% Grechetto and 20% Verdello, Malvasia Toscana and Drupeggio grapes. Stainless steel. Straw yellow color. Pleasant notes of flowers, mimosa, blossom and aromatic herbs. Savory and herbal on the palate, nice tense and fresh body with a good bittering note on the finish.

☐ 90   Price B
Musco 2013

Blend of 50% Procanico, 30% Verdello and 20% Malvasia grapes. Matures 1 year in chestnuts barrels. Amber yellow color. Oxidative notes, macerated flowers, ripe fruits, quince, dried citrus peels, bitter honey, resin and medicinal herbs. Slightly tannic on the palate, coherent with the nose and a long quince and herbal finish.

■ 89   Price B
Armaleo 2013

Blend of 95% Cabernte Sauvignon and 5% Cabernet Franc grapes. Matures 12 months in small oak barrels. Bright ruby red. Spicy, compact and peppery on the nose with notes of roasting and coffee powder. Fresh on the palate, red fruits and persistent spiciness in the finish.

★★

PERTICAIA

Località Casale
06036 Montefalco (PG)
Tel. +39 0742 379014
Fax +39 0742 371014
info@perticaia.it
www.perticaia.it
 PerticaiaWinery
🐦 *@PerticaiaWinery #perticaia*

YEAR OF FOUNDATION **2000**
NAME OF THE OWNER **Guido Guardigli**
TOTAL BOTTLES PRODUCED **120,000**
DIRECT SALES
VISITS TO THE WINERY - RESERVATION NEEDED
HECTARES OF VINEYARD **16**
OLIVE OIL PRODUCTION

The Perticaia estate is one of the best in the district and its wines are distinguished by their elegance and balance. It is owned by Guido Guardigli who, after running a famous wine estate in Montepulciano for 15 years, decided to set up his own in Montefalco. Perticaia is a word that in the archaic dialect of Umbria means plow, a symbol that Guardigli chose for the name of his enterprise to underscore the unbreakable and deep link between man and the land.

■ 91   Price B
Montefalco Sagrantino 2012

100% Sagrantino grapes. Matures 12 months in barrique and 12 months in stainless steel. Ruby red color. Spices and red fruits, cocoa and cassis on the nose. Tannic and full bodied on the palate, fresh and persistent. Long finish with cassis and spicy hints.

■ 89   Price B
Montefalco Rosso Riserva 2011

Blend of 70% Sangiovese, 20% Sagrantino and 10% Colorino grapes. Matures 12 months in barrique and 12 months in stainless steel. Light ruby red with garnet hues. Peppery and enveloping on the nose. Smoky, smooth and warm on the palate. Long fruity finish and nice acidity to support the power.

☐ 87   Price A
Spoleto Trebbiano Spoletino 2015

100% Trebbiano Spoletino grapes. Matures 7 months in stainlees steel tanks. Deep yellow color. intense notes of citrus and herbs on the nose. Fresh and pulpy on the palate. Long bittering finish.

ROCCAFIORE

Vocabolo Collina 110/A
06059 Todi (PG)
Tel. +39 0758942746
🔵 *luca.baccarelli*
info@roccafiorewines.com
www.roccafiorewines.com
🔷 *Cantina Roccafiore*
🐦 *@roccafiorewines*

YEAR OF FOUNDATION 2000
NAME OF THE OWNER Luca Baccarelli
TOTAL BOTTLES PRODUCED 120,000
DIRECT SALES
VISITS TO THE WINERY - RESERVATION NEEDED
HECTARES OF VINEYARD 15
HOSPITALITY
RESTAURANT
OLIVE OIL PRODUCTION

Situated on a hill in front of Todi, Roccafiore is the estate of Luca Baccarelli, a young and dynamic producer with clear ideas who is achieving excellent result with the Grechetto grape. The estate also produces wine using other local varietals like Trebbiano Spoletino as well as Sagrantino, Sangiovese and Montepulciano. The advising enologist is Hartmann Donà.

☐ 90   Price B
Fiorfiore 2014

100% Grechetto di Todi grapes. Matures 12 months in big Slavonian oak barrels. Intense straw yellow color. Blossom and aromatic herbs on the nose, yellow peach and stony hints. Tasty, juicy on the palate with a long herbal and yellow fruit finish.

■ 87   Price A
Il Roccafiore 2013

100% Sangiovese grapes. Matures 24 months in Slavonian oak barrels. Fruity and spicy on the nose with toasted hints. Elegant both on the nose and on the palate where it is rich and smooth. Nice finish.

⭐
GIAMPAOLO TABARRINI

Frazione Turrita
06036 Montefalco (PG)
Tel. +39 0742 379351
info@tabarrini.com
www.tabarrini.com
Tabarrinimontefalco
@tabarrini

YEAR OF FOUNDATION 1996
NAME OF THE OWNER Giampaolo Tabarrini
TOTAL BOTTLES PRODUCED 70,000
DIRECT SALES
VISITS TO THE WINERY - RESERVATION NEEDED
HECTARES OF VINEYARD 18
OLIVE OIL PRODUCTION

The Tabarrini estate is more than just well worth a visit. From its terrace garden you can see vineyards extend 180° forever with Montefalco on the horizon. It is a pleasure to meet the young Giampaolo Tabarrini because while some dogs look like their masters, in this case it is his wines that have all adopted his enthusiasm and vital energy.

■ 94   Price C
Montefalco Sagrantino Colle alle Macchie 2012

100% Sagrantino grapes. Matures 3 years in big barrels. Ruby garnet color. Spicy and eucalyptus notes on the nose, underbrush and bark. Tense on the palate, tannic and fresh, full bodied and rich with very long persistence. Among the three company cru this is the one with most personality, elegance and terroir correspondence.

☐ 91   Price B
Adarmando 2014

100% Trebbiano Spoletino grapes. Matures 1 year on the yeasts. Deep yellow color. Great personality on the nose, with intense notes of citrus and flowers. Full bodied and creamy on the palate, briny and stony, with a long aromatic finish.

■ 91   Price B
Montefalco Sagrantino Campo alla Cerqua 2012

100% Sagrantino grapes. Matures 3 years in big barrels. Ruby garnet color. Dark notes of plums, rhubarb and bark. Powerful on the palate with underbrush aromas, average freshness and very thick tannins.

TENUTA BELLAFONTE

Via Colle Nottolo, 2
06031 Bevagna (PG)
Tel. 0742 710019
info@tenutabellafonte.it
www.tenutabellafonte.it
Tenuta Bellafonte

YEAR OF FOUNDATION 2008
NAME OF THE OWNER Peter Heilbron
TOTAL BOTTLES PRODUCED 19,000
DIRECT SALES
VISITS TO THE WINERY - RESERVATION NEEDED
HECTARES OF VINEYARD 10.5
HOSPITALITY
OLIVE OIL PRODUCTION

Tenuta Bellafonte is a stone's throw from Bevagna, near the tiny hamlet of Torre del Colle, in a magnificent and uncontaminated place. The Heilbron family built a totally underground winery here that fits right into the landscape with limited energy needs and a very low environmental footprint. They take great care of the vineyards and have a rare sensitivity in their approach to the countryside and in the winery (where the grapes are not pressed but squeezed) and this has made their Sagrantino winery to be one of the most prestigious in the appellation.

naldo Pomodoro. It is shaped like a turtle, a symbol of long life and stability, and is intriguing for the way artistic language is expressed in architecture, for the symbolism related to the turtle and the way the shell-shaped construction, like the shell on the animal, protects another living element, in this case the wine that is conserved in its underground belly.

■ 89	Price B*

Montefalco Sagrantino Passito 2012

*100% Sagrantino grapes dried on straw mats. Ruby red color. Little red berries and gingerbread on the nose. Sweet and fresh on the palate. Long and juicy finish with nuts and spicy notes. *37.5 cl bottle.*

■ 93	Price B

Montefalco Sagrantino Collenottolo 2012

100% Sangrantino grapes. Matures 36 months in Slavonian oak barrels. Bright ruby red. Great elegance on the nose with hints of flowers and spices, notes of cherry and cinchona, red citrus. Clear and soft on the palate, thin elegance and light tannins with a nice progression.

☐ 90	Price B

Arnèto 2014

100% Trebbiano Spoletino grapes. Matures 6 months in big barrels. Deep yellow color. Rich on the nose with notes of quince, honey and beeswax with aromatic herbs and sweet citrus. Creamy and complex on the palate, nice saltiness and length.

TENUTA CASTELBUONO

Vocabolo Castellaccio, 9 - Località Cantalupo
06031 Bevagna (PG)
Tel. +39 0742 361670
Fax +39 0742 362060
carapace@tenutelunelli.it
www.tenutelunelli.it
🅵 *TenuteLunelli*
🐦 *@TenuteLunelli*

YEAR OF FOUNDATION 2001
NAME OF THE OWNER Lunelli Family
TOTAL BOTTLES PRODUCED 113,000
DIRECT SALES
VISITS TO THE WINERY - RESERVATION NEEDED
HECTARES OF VINEYARD 32
CERTIFIED ORGANIC VITICULTURE

This estate in Bevagna, a few kilometers from Montefalco, is also home to the Carapace (tortoise shell) structure created by sculptor Ar-

VALLE D'AOSTA

Valle d'Aosta is Italy's smallest region covering just 3,263 square kilometers and with a population of around 126,000. It is mostly mountainous region where the Dora Baltea River, one of the tributaries of the Po River, has created a central valley that is practically the only area that allows winegrowing. The vineyards are for the most part terraced on the slopes of the mountains that dominate the valley and from a distance almost appear to be vertical.

The most recent data available states that only 208 hectares of vineyards are classified DOC with production in the neighborhoods of 11,000 hectoliters of wine.

There is only one appellation and it has the name of the region, Valle d'Aosta/Vallée d'Aoste, which is in both Italian and French in accordance with the laws governing this autonomous and bilingual region. A large part of wine production is of different types of wines from different areas and that use different grapes varieties (see the following description).

In the northernmost part of the region, below Monte Bianco, the vineyards are situated at an altitude of around 1,000m above sea level and produce Blanc de Morgex e de La Salle, made with white grapes of the same name. It is a very light wine that is difficult to find outside the region.

Further south, mostly red wines are produced the main ones being Arnad-Montjover and Donnas that have more body and are made mostly from Nebbiolo grapes (the same used for Barolo and Barbaresco) which is locally called Picoutener.

Chambave Rosso/Rouge, Nus, Torrette and Enfer d'Arvier are wines made for the most part from Petit Rouge.

Among the dessert wines, which are rare and expensive, the most typical are Chambave Moscato/Muscat and Nus Malvoisie, the latter a blend of Pinot Grigio and Malvoise.

As you can observe, all these wines take their names from specific geographic locations. There are some Valle d'Aosta DOC wines that alongside the name of the regional appellation also have the names of the grapes used. Thus one finds Valle d'Aosta Müller Thurgau, Pinot Grigio/Gris, Chardonnay, Gamay, Pinot Nero/Noir, Petite Arvine, Petite Rouge, Premetta and Fumin.

These are wines that are cultivated in different parts of the region or that come from area with no specific subzone. In any case, they are all difficult to find outside the region. Keep in mind that all Valle d'Aosta wines are 'mountain wines'.

The whites have tenuous and aromatic bouquets and light bodies and are distinguished by an acidic note.

The reds tend to have a medium body, a rather pale color and are not bold and do they age well.

503

CONTROLLED DESIGNATION OF ORIGIN (DOC)

- Valle d'Aosta / Vallée d'Aoste
  wines general also carry the names of the grape variety:
  - Müller Thurgau
  - Gamay
  - Pinot nero / Pinot noir
  - Pinot grigio / Pinot gris
  - Pinot bianco / Pinot blanc
  - Chardonnay
  - Mayolet
  - Petite Arvine
  - Merlot
  - Fumin
  - Syrah
  - Cornalin
  - Nebbiolo
  - Petit rouge
  - Prëmetta
  - Moscato bianco / Muscat petit grain
  - Traminer aromatico / Gewürztraminer
  - Gamaret
  - Vuillermin

  or one of the following geographic references:
  - Donnas
  - Arnad-Montjovet
  - Chambave
  - Chambave Moscato / Chambave Muscat
  - Nus
  - Nus Malvoisie
  - Torrette
  - Enfer d'Arvier
  - Blanc de Morgex et de La Salle

or one of the following color indications:
  - bianco / blanc
  - rosso / rouge
  - rosato / rosé

  or one of the following winemaking methods:
  - novello / nouveau
  - Chambave Moscato Passito / Chambave Muscat Flétri
  - Nus Malvoise Passito / Nus Malvoisie Flétri
  - Moscato bianco Passito / Muscat petit grain Flétri
  - Traminer aromatico Passito / Gewürztraminer Flétri
  - Passito / Flétri

★
ANSELMET

Frazione Vereytaz, 30
11018 Villeneuve (AO)
Tel. +39 0165 904851
Fax +39 0165 904851
info@maisonanselmet.it
www.maisonanselmet.it
f *maison.anselmet.1*
𝕏 *@MaisonAnselmet*

YEAR OF FOUNDATION 1978
NAME OF THE OWNER Giorgio Anselmet
TOTAL BOTTLES PRODUCED 70,000
DIRECT SALES
VISITS TO THE WINERY - RESERVATION NEEDED
HECTARES OF VINEYARD 9

A small, family-run winery which for decades has been run by Giorgio Anselmet in Villeneuve, southwest Aosta. They produce a vast number of wines in small quantities for the most part made with traditional grapes. Their flagship wine is Le Prisonnier, a red made from grapes from a terraced vineyard situated at 800m above sea level on a steep slope.

| 93 | Price C |

Le Prissonier 2013 ·

Blend of 40% Petit Rouge, 35% Cornalin, 20% Fumin, 5% Mayolet. Matures 18 months in barrique. Dark ruby red. Spicy on the nose, notes of cardamom and vanilla, then berries, roses and violets. Tense and agile on the palate, good body but not heavy, nice acidity and light tannins. Great version.

| 91 | Price B |

Nix Nivis

100% Riesling Renano grapes. Stainless steel on the lees. Light greenish yellow color. Typical notes on the nose, classic thiol notes of kerosene, the grapefruit and alfalfa. Classic tension on the palate, briny, fresh, great personality and good length.

| 90 | Price B |

Valle d'Aosta Chardonnay élevé en fût de chêne 2014

100% Chardonnay grapes. Matures 1 year in barrique. Bright straw yellow. Evident notes of cedar and alfalfa on the nose with hints of vanilla and smoky puffs. Fresh taste, tense by the acidity, agile, good body and average length in the finish.

LA CROTTA DI VEGNERON

Piazza Roncas, 2
11023 Chambave (AO)
Tel. +39 0166 46670
Fax +39 0166 46543
info@lacrotta.it
www.lacrotta.it
f *lacrotta.divegneron*

YEAR OF FOUNDATION 1980
NAME OF THE OWNER
TOTAL BOTTLES PRODUCED 200,000
DIRECT SALES
VISITS TO THE WINERY - RESERVATION NEEDED
HECTARES OF VINEYARD 33
RESTAURANT

Some 120 supplier-members annually bring their grapes to this small Valle d'Aosta cooperative that produces just over 200,000 bottles of wine, not even 2,000 per member. We point this out because is exemplifies the small and artisanal style of winegrowing practices in Val d'Aosta. The vineyards from a distance seem like they are vertical. Several varieties wines are produced and here are a few.

| 91 | Price B |

Valle d'Aosta Chambave Muscat Attente 2009

100% Muscat Petit Grains grapes. Matures 40 months in stainless steel on the lees. Aromatic and flowery with notes of rose, sage and grapefruit. Slightly sweet taste, warm, enveloping, briny and well sustained by acidity and with a very pleasant drinkability.

| 89 | Price B |

Valle d'Aosta Fumin Esprit Follet 2013

100% Fumin grapes. Matures 1 year in different types of wood. Intense ruby red. Mostly spicy, cardamom, vanilla, then pomegranate, raspberries and red berries. Tense and pleasant on the palate, savory, light tannins and good length.

| 87 | 👍 Price A |

Valle d'Aosta Müller Thurgau 2015

100% Müller Thurgau grapes. Stainless steel only. Citrus and alfalfa on the nose, then hints of fresh almond. Tense, acidulous on the palate, discrete body, thin and with good persistence.

LA VRILLE

Località Hameau du Grangeon, 1
11020 Verrayes (AO)
Tel. +39 0166 543018
Fax +39 0166 543018
lavrille@gmail.com
www.lavrille.it
 AgriturismoViniLaVrille

YEAR OF FOUNDATION 2005
NAME OF THE OWNER Hervé Daniel Deguillame
TOTAL BOTTLES PRODUCED 18,000
DIRECT SALES
VISITS TO THE WINERY - RESERVATION NEEDED
HECTARES OF VINEYARD 2
HOSPITALITY
RESTAURANT

This little winery, which has also a very cute farmhouse with six guestrooms, and a high level restaurant (one of the reasons to visit the winery), produces one of the best Italian sweet wines, the Chambave Muscat Fletri, available with the 2013 vintage at last. Just a few half bottles, but it's really worth trying it.

---

 93   Price B*
Chambave Muscat Fletri 2013

*100% dried Muscat Petit Grain grapes. Stainless steel only. Golden yellow color. Citrusy and aromatic on the nose, notes of rose jam, grapefruit, dry apricots, honey and peaches in syrup. Sweet taste, tense by the acidity, elegant, very persistent and simply delicious. *37.5 cl bottle.*

LES CRÊTES

Località Villetos, 50
10010 Aymavilles (AO)
Tel. +39 0165 902274
 les-cretes
info@lescretes.it
www.lescretes.it
 lescretes
 @lescreteswinery

YEAR OF FOUNDATION 1989
NAME OF THE OWNER Charrère Family
TOTAL BOTTLES PRODUCED 200,000

DIRECT SALES
VISITS TO THE WINERY - RESERVATION NEEDED
HECTARES OF VINEYARD 20

Costantino Charrère is a key figure in this small region's winemaking scene who set up his winery 25 years ago and since then has made it one of the best in Italy. He has 20 hectares of vineyards, some of which he owns and the others he leases, and produces around 200,000 bottles, which is quite a lot for Valle d'Aosta.

---

 93   Price A
Valle d'Aosta Chardonnay 2015

100% Chardonnay grapes. Stainless steel only. Light greenish straw yellow color. Very fruity. Notes of yellow plum, pineapple, wild flowers and hints of fresh almond. Tense on the palate, with nice acidity that makes it lively and agile, savory, pleasant and good length.

---

 91   Price B
Valle d'Aosta Chardonnay Cuvée Bois 2014

100% Chardonnay grapes. Matures 1 year in barrique. Straw yellow color. Very fruity on the nose, white peach, wild flowers, fresh almond and pineapple. A little diluted and simple on the palate, agile, savory but with average persistence.

---

 90   Price A
Valle d'Aosta Torrette 2015

Blend of 70% Petit Rouge and other local red grapes. Matures 8 months in stainless steel. Bright ruby red. Deliciously fruity, raspberries and red berries, then flowery and slightly spicy. Agile, savory and tense, pleasant to drink, fresh and with good length.

LO TRIOLET

Località Junod, 7
11010 Introd (AO)
Tel. +39 0165 95437
lotriolet@vievini.it
www.lotriolet.vievini.it
 lo.triolet

YEAR OF FOUNDATION 1993
NAME OF THE OWNER Marco Martin
TOTAL BOTTLES PRODUCED 42,000
DIRECT SALES

VISITS TO THE WINERY - RESERVATION NEEDED
HECTARES OF VINEYARD 5
HOSPITALITY

The small winery of Marco Martin is now over 20 and is located in Introd, near Villeneuve, in southwest Aosta. He is a great Pinot Gris specialist and some of his versions, especially those made in wood, are among the best in the region for this variety.

☐ 91   Price B
Valle d'Aosta Rosso Coteau Barrage 2014
Blend of 80% Syrah, 20% Fumin grapes. 60% of the mass matures 1 year in barrique, the rest in stainless steel. Intense violet ruby. Spices and little berries on the nose, clear and fragrant. Enveloping and smooth on the palate with tannins well slacken by the good alcoholic warmth.

☐ 90   Price B
Valle d'Aosta Pinot Gris 2015
100% Pinot Grigio grapes. Stainless steel only. Light straw yellow color. Clear and fragrant notes of pear Williams and fresh almond on the nose, then alfalfa and wild flowers. Nice tension given by the acidity to sustain a pleasantly savory structure with a discrete alcoholic warmth. Good length in the finish.

★

ELIO OTTIN

Frazione Porossan Neyves, 209
11100 Aosta (AO)
Tel. +39 347 4071331
elio.ottin@gmail.com
www.ottinvini.it
 elio.ottin

YEAR OF FOUNDATION 2007
NAME OF THE OWNER Elio Ottin
TOTAL BOTTLES PRODUCED 25,000
DIRECT SALES
VISITS TO THE WINERY - RESERVATION NEEDED
HECTARES OF VINEYARD 4

The winey is recent but in just a few years it has won prizes and captured the attention of the wine-loving public. Elio Ottin produces small quantities of excellent wines and excels with his Petite Arvine made from the grape of the same name.

☐ 91   👍 Price A
Valle d'Aosta Petite Arvine 2015
100% Petite Arvine grapes. Stainless steel only. Greenish straw yellow. Notes of cedar, yellow plum and wild herbs. Tense and elegant on the palate, essential and agile, pleasant and easy to drink. Good persistence.

■ 88   Price B
Torrette Superieur 2014
Blend of 80% Petit Rouge, 10% Cornalin and 10% Fumin grapes. Matures 8 months in stainless steel. Bright and typical violet ruby red. Notes of raspberries, red berries and fermentative hints. Slightly tannic on the palate, tense by acidity, savory and persistent.

ERMES PAVESE

Strada Pineta, 26
11017 Morgex (AO)
Tel. +39 0165 800053
Fax +39 0165 800053
pavese@vievini.it
www.pavese.vievini.it
🅵 *aziendavitivinicola.paveseermes*

YEAR OF FOUNDATION 1999
NAME OF THE OWNER Ermes Pavese
TOTAL BOTTLES PRODUCED 35,000
DIRECT SALES
VISITS TO THE WINERY
HECTARES OF VINEYARD 5

His vineyards are small strips of land near mountain tops at altitudes between 900 and 1,200 meters above sea level and his tiny winery is as well-kept as a living room. All this makes Ermes Pavese and his family the epitome of mountain winemakers. His leading wine is Nathan, a white made from Prié Blanc grapes grown on 60-year-old vines and fermented in barrique.

☐ 93   Price B
Valle d'Aosta Blanc de Morgex e de la Salle Nathan 2015
100% Prié Blanc grapes. 70% of the mass is matured in barrique, the rest in stainless steel. Light golden yellow. Very fruity on the nose, notes of white peach, apricot, cedar and alfalfa. Strong flavor on the palate, savory, tense, warm and very persistent.

507

VENETO

Veneto is can be divided into two district regions: the plains between the provinces of Verona, Treviso and Venice; and the hilly, mountainous area that start from Lake Garda and climbs up to the border with Trentino. Together they comprise a vast and diverse territory with various pedoclimatic zones from Mediterranean, to continental to Alpine that have allowed for the cultivation of a host of different grapes. All this explains why Veneto is the leading Italian region for quantity of grapes produced but also why it produces wines that are famous around with the world with some even exemplifying Italian wine.

The region has some 80,000 hectares of vineyards that produce almost nine million hectoliters of wine, including Prosecco that has become a phenomenon on markets at home and abroad. With its 7,900 hectares of vineyards in the hills in the eastern part of the province of Verona, Soave is Europe's "biggest vineyard" and produces grapes for a vast number different wines and types of wine.

Grapes have been present in the region of Veneto since the dawn of time and the wine Retico originated in the hilly area of the provinces of Vernon and Trentino right up to Valtellina. Acinaticum, from Valpolicella, was a concentrated and elegant Passito made with red grapes of which there is detailed evidence and that has been handed down in traditions. Recioto della Valpolicella and Recioto Soave (the later a technical description being made with white grapes) are its direct descendants.

During the Middle Ages the best winegrowing areas and they best grapes continued evolve and the dual personality of the region's wines began to emerge with the plains producing undistinguished wines while those from the mountains were good enough to be exported. Between the 14th and 15th centuries a wine trade flourished and was legally regulated. Venice was full of places where one could have a glass of wine. They were called 'bacari' and the smallest amount served was called 'ombra' (shadow) because the leading wine market took place under the 'shadow' of the bell tower in St. Mark's Square. At the time, the most cultivated grapes were Bianchetta, Trevigiana, Verdiso and Vespaiolo among the white grapes and Marzemino and Raboso among the reds. Many of these grapes were exterminated in the devastating 1709 cold snap that destroyed a large part of the vineyards in the region. Only those grapes that were the most resistant to cold survived and they are among those found today, along with others brought in after the phylloxera plague. Today, the prominent grapes are Garganega, Glera, Friulano (ex-Tocai), Verduzzo and Trebbiano di Soave among the whites, and the reds Corvina, Rondinella, Raboso and Negara, Merlot and Cabernet.

The region's best-known reds are Valpolicella, Amarone and Recioto della Valpolicella, the grapes for which grow a few kilometers north of Verona where the Monti Lessini Hills descend into the plains. These are great reds, the latter a sweet one, blends of Corvina Veronese, Rondinella and Molinara and if the grapes come from a designated area they can be labeled Superiore. Southeast of Verona is the home of Soave, probably the most famous Italian white in the world which is made from Garganega grapes. This, too, can be a Superiore, if the grapes are from the most suited area, as well as a sweet wine, Recioto di Soave, and there are also two sparkling versions, one of Soave and the other Recioto, the latter obviously sweeter.

Bardolino, the red and the rosé, the famous Chiaretto, and Bianco di Custoza come from the shores of Lake Garda and use the same grapes as Valpolicella and Soave. These wines are lighter and enticing.

Colli Eugeni is a small area in the province of Padua, and zone that does not stand out for quality with only this exception. The volcanic hill stick up in the plains as if they were islands in the sea. The wines made here are all good and perhaps the most representative is Fior d'Arancio, which is one of best Moscato d'Italian wines.

The province of Vicenza is less known that that of Verona for winemaking and yet it does produce some interesting wines of excellent quality. The best-known DOC wine is probably Gambellara, produced in the more western part of the province. The Classico come from a more restricted and traditional area. Gambellara Recioto is a sweet wine, similar to Recioto di Soave, and can also be a sparkling wine. There is also a Gambellara Vin Santo. To the south of Vicenza is the DOC appellation of Colli Berici which includes a vast number of wines almost all made with non-native grapes. The only exception is Garganega, a light white wine similar to others in the region made with the same grape. Below Colli Berici is the recently-created DOC appellation Bagnoli di Sopra that produces a Bianco, a Rosso and several varietal wines, including Raboso, from of a dozen or so towns in the province of Padua.

North of Vicenza is the very interesting zone of Breganze where the classic grape is Vespaiolo that produces a fruity and pleasing white called, appropriately, Breganze Vespaiolo. Torcolato di Breganze is among the most interesting and prestigious Italian sweet wines. Breganze Tai is a made with the Friulano grape (which is also 50% of the blend of Breganze Bianco) and varietal whites include Pinot Bianco, Pinot Grigio, Sauvignon and Chardonnay. The appellations reds are also very good and include Breganze Rosso, which is in fact a Merlot, and the Cabernet and Pinot Nero are excellent.

Western Veneto has a host of appellations, starting with from Montello and Colli Asolani, on the right bank of the Piave River, which produces a slew of varietals, a Bianco and a Rosso and a Prosecco Spumante. The other side of the river marks the beginning of the area of Conegliano Valdobbiadene, another kingdom of Prosecco, as well as the more recent DOC Colli Conegliano for still wines. In regard to Prosecco and the appellations of Montello and Colli Asolani and Conegliano-Valdobbiadene, in 2008 a reform established a DOCG appellation with the indication of Treviso (and Trieste) for nine winemaking areas in nine province in the Regions of Veneto and Friuli.

Further down the river is the appellation of Piave and the DOC of Lison Pramaggiore. These are plain areas that are rich in alluvial sediments. Here production is concentrated on technically well-made varietals that are distinguished by a good quality/price ratio. Merlot and Cabernet are the most cultivated in the first area and Friulano and Pinot Grigio and Bianco in the second.

Controlled and Guaranteed Designation of Origin (DOCG)

- Amarone della Valpolicella, with or without the sub-areas Classico and Valpantena
- Bagnoli Friularo or Friularo di Bagnoli, with or without the sub-area Classico
- Bardolino Superiore, with or without the sub-area Classico
- Colli Asolani Prosecco or Asolo Prosecco
- Colli di Conegliano, with or without the sub-areas Refrontolo (also Passito), Torchiato di Fregona (only Passito)
- Colli Euganei Fior d'Arancio or Fior d'Arancio Colli Euganei
- Conegliano Valdobbiadene Prosecco or Conegliano Prosecco or Valdobbiadene Prosecco, with or without the sub-area Superiore di Cartizze (only for Spumante wine). Allowed only for Spumante variety reffering to the name of the location with the word "Rive"
- Lison, with or without the sub-area Classico
- Montello rosso and Montello
- Piave Malanotte or Malanotte del Piave
- Recioto della Valpolicella, with or without the sub-areas Classico and Valpantena. Spumante variety with or without Valpantena sub-area
- Recioto di Gambellara
- Recioto di Soave, with or without the sub-area Classico (except Spumante variety)
- Soave Superiore, with or without the sub-area Classico

Controlled Designation of Origin (DOC)

- Arcole
- Bagnoli di Sopra or Bagnoli, with or without the sub-area Classico
- Bardolino, anche Chiaretto, with or without the sub-area Classico
- Bianco di Custoza o Custoza
- Breganze, with or without the traditional reference Torcolato for the dried Vespaiola, or from the specific varieties
- Colli Berici, with or without the sub-area Barbarano (Barbarano Rosso or Barbarano)
- Colli Euganei
- Corti Benedettine del Padovano
- Gambellara, with or without the sub-area Classico (Gambellara Classico, Gambellara Classico Vin Santo)
- Garda
- Lessini Durello or Durello Lessini
- Lison-Pramaggiore
- Lugana
- Merlara
- Montello Colli Asolani, with or without the sub-area Venegazzù
- Monti Lessini
- Piave
- Prosecco, with or without the geographic references provincia di Treviso or Treviso, provincia di Trieste or Trieste
- Riviera del Brenta
- San Martino della Battaglia
- Soave, with or without the sub-area Classico and Colli Scaligeri
- Valdadige
- Valdadige Terradeiforti or Terradeiforti Valdadige
- Valpolicella, with or without the sub-areas Classico and Valpantena
- Valpolicella Ripasso, with or without the sub-areas Classico and Valpantena
- Venezia
- Vicenza
- Vigneti della Serenissima or Serenissima

STEFANO ACCORDINI

Località Camparol, 10 - Frazione Cavalo
37022 Fumane (VR)
Tel. +39 045 7760138
Fax +39 045 6845199
info@accordinistefano.com
www.accordinistefano.it

YEAR OF FOUNDATION 1900
NAME OF THE OWNER Accordini Family
TOTAL BOTTLES PRODUCED 130,000
DIRECT SALES
VISITS TO THE WINERY - RESERVATION NEEDED
HECTARES OF VINEYARD 17

Tiziano Accordini is an example of what a small winemaker should be today. He is a craftsman, a custodian of the land and the environment as well as a refined technician. His two Amarone are precise reflections of this, especially the one from the Il Fornetto vineyard, which only comes out in the best years.

93	Price D

Amarone della Valpolicella Classico Vigneto Il Fornetto 2010

Blend of 75% Corvina and 25% Corvinone grapes. Matures 3 years in barrique. Garnet ruby red. Complex aromas, good and wine notes of macerated black cherry, cocoa, spices and eucalyptus woods. Structured, very good and elegant tannins.

91	Price B

Amarone della Valpolicella Classico Acinatico 2012

Blend of 75% Corvina, 20% Rondinella and 5% Molinara grapes. Matures 28 months in barrique. Ruby red with garnet hues. Sweet notes of vanilla and black cherry jam, then spices, tobacco and cocoa. Wide, smooth, soft tannins and persistent in the mouth.

88	Price B

Valpolicella Ripasso Classico Superiore Acinatico 2013

Blend of 60% Corvina, 20% Rondinella, 15% Corvinone and 5% Molinara grapes. Matures 10 months in barrels. Ruby red. Intense notes of black cherry, plums, tobacco and spices. Smooth sip, round tannins and adequate structure.

ADAMI

Via Rovede, 27 - Frazione Colbertaldo
31020 Vidor (TV)
Tel. +39 0423 982110
Fax +39 0423 982130
info@adamispumanti.it
www.adamispumanti.it

YEAR OF FOUNDATION 1933
NAME OF THE OWNER Armando and Franco Adami
TOTAL BOTTLES PRODUCED 700,000
DIRECT SALES
VISITS TO THE WINERY - RESERVATION NEEDED
HECTARES OF VINEYARD 13

In 1920, Abele Adami acquired from Count Balbi Valier a lovely and promising vineyard on the Marca Trevigiana hills, just below the first Dolomite peaks. The vineyard immediately proved to be most suited for high quality grapes and resulted in Abele and his son Adriano creating the estate's Prosecco. Today Armando and Franco Adami, both enologists, are carrying on the family's tradition renewing their passion and benefitting from the experience of their forefathers while using a modern approach and new technology.

92	Price B

Conegliano Valdobbiadene Prosecco Superiore Rive di Colbertaldo Vigneto Giardino Dry 2015

100% Glera grapes. Charmant method. Light straw yellow. Thick and abundant perlage. Intense fruity notes of fruit salad, hints of yeasts. Delicate flavor, creamy, briny, smooth and of good length.

90	Price B

Conegliano Valdobbiadene Prosecco Superiore Rive di Farra di Soligo Col Credas Brut 2015

100% Glera grapes. Charmant method. Light straw yellow. Fast and abundant perlage. Notes of cedar, lemon apple, fragrant aromas of yeasts in the characteristic and whole nose profile. Lively flavor, savory with nice acidity and thin finish.

★★★
ALLEGRINI

Via Giare, 5
37022 Fumane (VR)
Tel. +39 045 6832011
Fax +39 045 7701774
info@allegrini.it
www.allegrini.it
 AllegriniEstates
 @AllegriniWine

YEAR OF FOUNDATION 1854
NAME OF THE OWNER Marilisa and Franco Allegrini
TOTAL BOTTLES PRODUCED 900,000
DIRECT SALES
VISITS TO THE WINERY - RESERVATION NEEDED
HECTARES OF VINEYARD 105

This is a great brand for Verona wines and offers a vast selection of wines. Their top produces are Amarone Classico, the red La Poja, made from only Covina grapes, and La Grola, blend of Corvina and Oseleta grapes, riche and enveloping. The family estate includes a splendid Renaissance villa, Villa della Torre, which is worth a visit.

---

 91   Price C
Amarone della Valpolicella Classico 2012

Blend of 90% Corvina, 5% Oseleta and 5% Rondinella grapes. Matures 18 months in barrique. Intense ruby red. Austere notes of black cherry jam, cocoa, nuts and iodine. Strong body, smoothness not always on top and good impact. Persistent.

---

 91   Price C
La Poja 2012

100% Corvina slightly overripe grapes. Matures 20 months in barrique. Very dark ruby red. Intense aromas of spices, notes of blackberry and black cherry jam. Compact in the mouth, dense and with evident tannins. Fruity and spicy finish.

---

 88   Price B
La Grola 2013

Blend of 90% Corvina and 10% Oseleta grapes. Matures 16 months in barrique. Aromas of spices, pepper on top. red fruits in syrup and eucalyptus hints. Savory in the mouth, nice freshness and plenty but smooth tannins.

★★
ROBERTO ANSELMI

Via San Carlo, 46
37032 Monteforte d'Alpone (VR)
Tel. +39 045 7611488
anselmi@anselmi.eu
www.anselmi.eu

YEAR OF FOUNDATION 1948
NAME OF THE OWNER Roberto Anselmi
TOTAL BOTTLES PRODUCED 600,000
VISITS TO THE WINERY - RESERVATION NEEDED
HECTARES OF VINEYARD 70

After he finished university, Roberto Anselmi closed down his father's business – due to the post-war crisis he had sold his vineyards and became a wine merchant – and bought some vineyards of his own. He then meticulously planned the realization of his childhood dream, selecting the right Garganega clones, cultivating them with a high density per hectare and following a winemaking approach aimed at achieving quality. Today his wines are of great prestige but are not DOC Soave because he disagrees with its regulations.

---

 95   Price B*
I Capitelli 2012

*100% Garganega grapes partly with botrytis. Barrique for 10 months. Lively golden yellow. Very complex notes of saffron, iodine, fresh mushroom and caramel, with hints of peach in syrup and pastries. Sweet taste but well sustained by a sharp and refreshing acidity that makes the taste elegant and aristocratic. Very long finish. *37,5 cl bottle.*

---

 92   Price B
Capitel Croce 2014

100% Garganega grapes. Matures 8 months in barrique. Intense straw yellow. Very fruity, notes of cedar and grapefruit, then rennet, wildflowers, light vanilla and hints of flint. Agile taste, lighter than in other versions, savory, tense and good structure.

---

 91   Price A
Capitel Foscarino 2015

Blend of 90% Garganega and 10% Chardonnay grapes. Stainless steel on the lees for 6 months. Exotic and slightly smoky with notes of pineapple, fresh almond and wildflowers. Savory, full, smooth and tense, very pleasant and easy to drink but not trivial.

ASTORIA

Via Crevada
31020 Refrontolo (TV)
Tel. +39 0423 6699
Fax +39 0423 665077
info@astoria.it
www.astoria.it
 f *astoria.wines*
 🐦 *@Astoria_Wines*

YEAR OF FOUNDATION **1987**
NAME OF THE OWNER **Paolo and Giorgio Polegato**
TOTAL BOTTLES PRODUCED **1,500,000**
DIRECT SALES
VISITS TO THE WINERY - RESERVATION NEEDED
HECTARES OF VINEYARD **40**

The historic headquarters of the Astoria estate, Tenuta Val De Brum, is in the heart of the DOCG Conegliano-Valdobbiadene appellation and was started up in 1987 by Paolo and Giorgio Polegato. Their 40 hectares of vineyards produce top quality sill and sparkling wines but the estate's focus is on Prosecco. In fact, one of the family's two jewels is the vintage Prosecco Millesimato. The extreme attention paid to packaging underscores the estate's fashionable style.

回 **90**   👍 **Price A**

Conegliano Valdobbiadene Prosecco Superiore Cuvèe Tenuta Val de Brun Extra Dry 2015

100% Glera grapes. Charmat method. Light yellow, thin and continuous perlage. Flowery notes of wisteria, then a lot of white and yellow fruit, hints of wild herbs. Soft, fresh, savory, creamy and good length.

回 **88**   **Price A**

Conegliano Valdobbiadene Prosecco Superiore Casa Vittorino Brut 2015

100% Glera grapes. Charmat method. Light yellow, thin and fast perlage. Fragrant notes of yeasts then flowery and fruity. Savory, fresh, agile, creamy, thin but persistent taste.

LORENZO BEGALI

Via Cengia, 10
37029 San Pietro in Cariano (VR)
Tel. +39 045 7725148

Fax +39 045 7725148
tiliana@tiscali.it
www.begaliwine.it

YEAR OF FOUNDATION **1943**
NAME OF THE OWNER **Lorenzo, Giordano and Tiliana Begali**
TOTAL BOTTLES PRODUCED **74,000**
DIRECT SALES
VISITS TO THE WINERY - RESERVATION NEEDED
HECTARES OF VINEYARD **10**

The estate is located in San Pietro in Cariano, at the beginning of the Fumane Valley and in the southwest part of the Valpolicella appellation. Here Lorenzo Begali cultivates his ten hectares of vineyards with the discipline of a great wine artisan. His Amarone Vigneto Monte Ca' Bianca is one of the great classic of the area.

■ 🍇 **95**   **Price C**

Amarone della Valpolicella Classico Monte Ca' Bianca 2011

Blend of 45 Corvina, 35% Corvinone, 20% Rondinella and Oseleta grapes. Matures 40 months in different size barrels. Dense garnet ruby red. Intense and strong notes of black cherry, violets, chocolate, tobacco and spices. Class and power on the palate for a tasty ensemble with aristocratic tannins.

■ **90**   **Price B**

Amarone della Valpolicella Classico 2012

Blend of 60% Corvina, 30% Rondinella and other grapes. Matures 30 months in different size barrels. Deep ruby red. Spicy in the beginning, with black cherry, cocoa and tobacco. Dense in the mouth, smooth tannins, adequate structure, moderate alcoholic content.

BELLENDA

Via Giordano, 90
31029 Vittorio Veneto (TV)
Tel. +39 0438 920025
Fax +39 0438 920015
info@bellenda.it
www.bellenda.it
 f *Bellenda1986*
 🐦 *@bellenda1986*

YEAR OF FOUNDATION **1986**
NAME OF THE OWNER **Umberto Cosmo**

TOTAL BOTTLES PRODUCED 1,100,000
DIRECT SALES
VISITS TO THE WINERY - RESERVATION NEEDED
HECTARES OF VINEYARD 105
HOSPITALITY
OLIVE OIL PRODUCTION

Situated at the feet of the Vittorio Veneto hills, Bellenda is known above all for the vast range of Prosecco it offers, even if the estate also produces a Colli di Conegliano DOC and other wines typical to the area of Marca Trevigiana. The estate's philosophy can be summed up as "the plants come before we do".

---

 89   Price A

Conegliano Valdobbiadene Prosecco Superiore San Fermo Brut 2015

100% Glera grapes. Charmat method. Light yellow. Thick and fast perlage. Very fruity, notes of pear Williams, cedar and white peach, then fragrant notes of yeasts. Fresh taste, savory, creamy, elegantly citric.

回 87   Price A

Conegliano Valdobbiadene Prosecco Superiore Miraval Extra Dry 2015

100% Glera grapes. Charmat method. Intense straw yellow. Abundant perlage. Fragrant, bread crust, ruscks, white peach and cedar. Lively taste, smooth, savory, agile and thin.

★★

CECILIA BERETTA

Strada della Giara, 10
37131 Verona (VR)
Tel. +39 045 8432111
Fax +39 045 8432211
info@pasqua.it
www.ceciliaberetta.it
 Cecilia-Beretta

YEAR OF FOUNDATION 1980
NAME OF THE OWNER Pasqua Family
TOTAL BOTTLES PRODUCED 350,000
DIRECT SALES
VISITS TO THE WINERY - RESERVATION NEEDED
HECTARES OF VINEYARD 89

The estate of Cecilia Beretta was started in the 1980s by the Pasqua family but the Mizzole,

Mattaranetta and San Felice vineyards date back to the 1940s. The estate's name originated from Villa Beretta, the 17th century residence east of Valpolicella of Count Giuseppe Beretta, who governed Verona and was both an agronomist and a country poet. The estate's aim it to being back and restore value to traditional grape varieties through a production independent of the activities of the Pasqua family.

---

 92   Price C

Amarone della Valpolicella Terre di Cariano Riserva 2011

Blend of 60% Rondinella, 25% Corvinone and 15% Croatina and Oseleta grapes. Matures 2 years in barrique and tonneau. Intense and deep ruby red. Macerated cherry, strawberry, notes of aromatic wood, vanilla and tobacco for the elegant and typical aromatic profile. Strong taste, powerful body but well sustained by acidity. Very persistent finish.

★★★

BERTANI

Via Asiago, 1
37023 Grezzana (VR)
Tel. +39 045 8658444
Fax +39 045 8658400
bertani@bertani.net
www.bertani.net
 cantine.bertani

YEAR OF FOUNDATION 1857
NAME OF THE OWNER Bertani Domains
TOTAL BOTTLES PRODUCED 2,000,000
DIRECT SALES
VISITS TO THE WINERY - RESERVATION NEEDED
HECTARES OF VINEYARD 200
OLIVE OIL PRODUCTION

The Bertani brothers decided to get involved in the world of wine in 1857. In the almost 100 years that followed, experience, entrepreneurial skill and history has consolidated into an estate that has expanded its boundaries, making wines known throughout the world thanks to a business sense that existed from the start. Today they own vineyards in Valpantena, in the Villa Novare estate in Valpolicella, in Soave and in the area of Lake Garda. The headquarters are in the original estate in Grezzana, which still has the historic vineyards.

▪ 🎏 97   Price C
Amarone della Valpolicella Classico 2008

Blend of 80% Corvina and 20% Rondinella grapes. Matures 6 years in big barrels. In iconic classic Amarone. Intense garnet ruby red. Wide aromas of black cherry, Maraschino, cocoa, black tobacco, cardamom and mint. Powerful taste, warm, enveloping, polite tannins, savory and almost never-ending finish. Great wine.

▪ 🎏 95   👍 Price A
Secco Bertani Original Vintage 2013

Blend of 80% Corvina and 20% of Sangiovese, Syrah and Cabernet Sauvignon grapes. Matures 1 year in big walnut and cherry barrels. Garnet ruby red. Attractive nose profile, good complexity, smoky hints, then wild cherry, cocoa and Kirsch. Rich, full taste, powerful but with nice acidity, well balanced tannins and long persistence.

▪ 92   Price B
Amarone della Valpolicella Valpantena Villa Arvedi 2013

Blend of 80% Corvina and 20% Rondinella grapes. Matures 30 months in big barrels. Very intense garnet ruby red. Enveloping and ethereal in the nose, notes of cocoa, Maraschino and macerated black berries. Warm, rich, with some ripple due to the tannins, very long persistence.

☐ 90   👍 Price A
Soave Cavalier GB Bertani 2014

100% Garganega grapes. Stainless steel on the yeasts for 1 year. Intense greenish straw yellow. Wildflowers, medlar, cedar, smoky hints aromas. Tense, savory taste, thinner than in previews versions, elegant and thin.

▪ 90   👍 Price A
Valpolicella Classico Superiore Vigneto Ognisanti 2013

Blend of Corvina and a little Rondinella grapes. Matures in barrique 18 months. Intense garnet ruby red. Ethereal and enveloping notes of black berry and Maraschino. Savory, warm, young tannins and good persistence.

★★
BISOL

Via Follo, 33 - Frazione Santo Stefano
31049 Valdobbiadene (TV)
Tel. +39 0423 900138

Fax +39 0423 900577
🔵 *bisol.bisol*
info@bisol.it
www.bisol.it
f *bisol.prosecco*
🐦 *@BisolProsecco*

YEAR OF FOUNDATION 1875
NAME OF THE OWNER Bisol and Lunelli Families
TOTAL BOTTLES PRODUCED 2,500,000
DIRECT SALES
VISITS TO THE WINERY - RESERVATION NEEDED
HECTARES OF VINEYARD 55

The Bisol family was already cited in a 1542 document of the Republic of Venice as being winegrowers working the land of the Pola Counts. Their winemaking vocation emerged in the 19th century with a prosperous business that has continued to today offering top quality wines. All their vineyards are situated at an altitude between 250 and 300m above sea level, subdivided into 20 plots with different soils that produce grapes with unique characteristics. All the wines are the product of constant research to achieve the utmost quality, from the vineyards to the glass, and this had made the brand one of the most known and representative at home and abroad.

▥ 93   Price B
Conegliano Valdobbiadene Prosecco Superiore Cartizze Private Non Dosato 2013

100% Glera grapes. Classic method. Straw yellow and thin, thick and continuous perlage. Very articulated in the nose where the notes of yeasts blend with the aromas of white fruit, almond and wisteria flowers. Creamy, elegant, tense, fresh, very dry and great persistence.

▥ 90   👍 Price A
Conegliano Valdobbiadene Prosecco Superiore Crede Brut 2015

Blend of 85% Glera and 15% Verdiso grapes. Charmat method. Straw yellow, thick and abundant perlage. Notes of yeasts, then wisteria flowers, cedar and lime. Pleasant taste, creamy, savory and of good length.

★★
BOLLA

Via Alberto Bolla, 3
37029 San Pietro in Cariano (VR)
Tel. +39 045 6836555
Fax +39 045 6836556
bolla@giv.it
www.bolla.it
 bollawine
 @BollaWine

YEAR OF FOUNDATION **1883**
NAME OF THE OWNER **Gruppo Italiano Vini**
TOTAL BOTTLES PRODUCED **10,000,000**
DIRECT SALES
VISITS TO THE WINERY - RESERVATION NEEDED
HECTARES OF VINEYARD **350**

This historic Veneto wine producer has the merit of producing the very first Amarone. Relaunched by Gruppo Italia Vini, today it offers a full range of reliable and affordable wines. Try their Soave Classico and Valpolicella Ripasso Le Poiane.

  90   Price A
Valpolicella Ripasso Classico Superiore Le Poiane 2014

Blend of 70% Corvina and 30% Rondinella grapes. Matures 18 months in barrels. Dense ruby red. Fruity notes of black berry, yellow plum, black cherry and cocoa hints. Balanced sip. pleasantly fruity and smooth tannins.

☐ 85   Price A
Soave Classico Superiore Tufaie 2015

Blend of 85% Garganega and Trebbiano di Soave grapes. Stainless steel only. Straw yellow. Fragrant notes of white flowers, citrus and yellow plums. Fresh, savory, agile taste and light body.

★
BORTOLOMIOL

Via Garibaldi, 142
31049 Valdobbiadene (TV)
Tel. +39 0423 974911
info@bortolomiol.com
www.bortolomiol.com
 BortolomiolProseccoSuperioreValdobbiadene
 @BortolomiolDOCG

YEAR OF FOUNDATION **1949**
NAME OF THE OWNER **Bortolomiol Family**
TOTAL BOTTLES PRODUCED **1,800,000**
DIRECT SALES
VISITS TO THE WINERY - RESERVATION NEEDED
HECTARES OF VINEYARD **170**
RESTAURANT
CERTIFIED ORGANIC VITICULTURE

Even if its roots date back to the 18th century, this estate came into its own after the Second World War. It was then that Giuliano Bortomomio, a graduate of the prestigious Scuola di Enologia di Conegliano, became interested in revamping the vineyards of the area and turning Prosecco from a simple, local product first into a nationally known sparkling wine and then into an international phenomenon. He became a master of the Martinotti-Charmat Method and was, in fact, the first to create a Prosecco Brut. Today his four children are running the estate maintaining intact the principles of tradition, quality and territory.

  91   Price A
Conegliano Valdobbiadene Prosecco Superiore Ius Naturae Brut 2015

100% Glera grapes. Charmat method. Light yellow, thick perlage. Very fragrant in the nose, notes of yeasts, the wisteria flowers and white peach. Deliciously savory, fresh, agile, easy to drink and of good length.

 88   Price A
Conegliano Valdobbiadene Prosecco Superiore Banda Rossa Extra Dry 2015

100% Glera grapes. Charmat method. Light yellow, abundant and fast perlage. Notes of yeasts, then flowery hints and wisteria flowers. Savory, pleasant, fresh, smooth and discrete structure.

★
BRIGALDARA

Via Brigaldara, 20
37029 San Pietro in Cariano (VR)
Tel. +39 045 7701055
 brigaldara
info@brigaldara.it
www.brigaldara.it
 Brigaldara
 @Brigaldarawines

YEAR OF FOUNDATION 1979
NAME OF THE OWNER Stefano Cesari
TOTAL BOTTLES PRODUCED 250,000
DIRECT SALES
VISITS TO THE WINERY - RESERVATION NEEDED
HECTARES OF VINEYARD 50
OLIVE OIL PRODUCTION

The Brigaldara winery is in the heart of Valpolicella in the Valla di Marano north of Verona,
one of the four valleys that constitute the classic area of Valpolicella. Amarone is their top
product, in particular the Riserva, and they also
produce olive oil and black truffles.

---

 94   Price C
Amarone della Valpolicella Riserva 2007

*Blend of 40% Corvina, 30% Corvinone, 15% Rond-
inella and 15% of other grape varieties. Matures
5 years in barrique and big barrels. A great modern style Amarone. Articulated ethereal aromas,
macerated black cherry, Maraschino, cocoa and
tobacco. Powerful taste, rich, warm, overwhelming
persistence.*

BRUNELLI

Via Cariano, 10
37029 San Pietro in Cariano (VR)
Tel. +39 045 7701118
info@brunelliwine.com
www.brunelliwine.com
f *amaronewine*

YEAR OF FOUNDATION **1936**
NAME OF THE OWNER **Luigi Brunelli**
TOTAL BOTTLES PRODUCED **120,000**
DIRECT SALES
VISITS TO THE WINERY
HECTARES OF VINEYARD **14**
HOSPITALITY

Since the end of the Second World War, the
Brunelli name has been a reference point for
wines in the area of San Pietro in Cariano, in
the heart of Valpolicella Classico. The calcareous soil, which is often rich in gravel, together with the balanced temperatures during the
time the grapes ripen make wines from this
area of the appellation particularly rich and
bold and give a softness to the mouthfeel and
variety to the aroma. These characteristics of
the terroir have defined the style of the nectars

from Luigi Brunelli, above all the Amarone,
wines that symbolize the rapport between man
and nature.

---

 91   Price C
**Amarone della Valpolicella Classico
Campo del Titari Riserva 2011**

*Blend of 75% Corvina and Corvinone, 15% Rond-
inella and 10% Sangiovese grapes. Matures 36
months in barrique. Powerful and articulated notes
of black cherry and blackberry, hints of cocoa, tobacco and spices. Sumptuous taste, rich, warm and
pleasantly chocolaty.*

---

89   Price B
**Amarone della Valpolicella Classico
2012**

*Blend of 65% Corvina, 25% Rondinella and 10%
Corvinone grapes. Matures 24 months in barrique
and tonneau. Deep ruby red. Rich, fruity, spicy and
hints of eucalyptus. Smooth on the palate, great
body and compact tannins even though thin. Cocoa
in the finish.*

BUGLIONI

Via Campagnole, 55 - Località Corrubbio
37020 San Pietro in Cariano (VR)
Tel. +39 045 6760681
S *mariano.buglioni*
buglioni@buglioni.it
www.buglioni.it
f *cantine.buglioni*

YEAR OF FOUNDATION 1993
NAME OF THE OWNER Mariano Buglioni
TOTAL BOTTLES PRODUCED 180,000
DIRECT SALES
VISITS TO THE WINERY - RESERVATION NEEDED
HECTARES OF VINEYARD 48
HOSPITALITY
RESTAURANT

Mariano Buglioni became involved in winemaking in Valpolicella, where his family had
vineyards, after a successful career in his
family's clothing business bringing with him
his know-how from the fashion world and its
attention to detail and brand image. Since his
experience was in a different area, he brought
in expert agronomists and enologists from the
Istituto Agrario d San Michele all'Adige-Fonda-
zione Edmund Mach to handle the winemaking

517

aside and set out to humbly learn from them. The wines are good and the estate has a promising future.

93   Price D

Amarone della Valpolicella Classico Superiore Il Lussurioso 2011

Blend of 60% Corvina, 15% Corvinone, 10% Rondinella, 10% Oseleta and 5% Croatina grapes. The grapes are dried on straw mats until January and the wine matures in barrique for 2 years. Powerful and wide notes of black cherry jam, cocoa and spices. Dense, smooth, tasty and persistent.

88   Price B

Valpolicella Ripasso Classico Superiore Il Bugiardo 2013

Blend of 60% Corvina, 20% Corvinone, 10% Rondinella and 10% Croatina and Oseleta grapes. Matures 12 months in tonneau. Dense ruby red. Intense notes of ripe red fruits and hints of spices. Balanced taste, fresh, thin tannins and smooth.

CA' DEI ROTTI

Località Rotti, 69
37012 Bussolengo (VR)
Tel. +39 347 8863666
Fax +39 045 7170744
info@cantinacadeirotti.com
www.cantinacadeirotti.com

YEAR OF FOUNDATION 1980
NAME OF THE OWNER Alessandra Castellani
TOTAL BOTTLES PRODUCED 18,000
DIRECT SALES
VISITS TO THE WINERY - RESERVATION NEEDED
HECTARES OF VINEYARD 5

This small estate has been run for the past few years by Alessandra Castellani, together with her uncle Gianluca, after the deaths of her father Carlo and grandfather Natale, who founded the estate in the 1970s. It is located in Bassolengo, a border area between several appellations around Lake Garda in the province of Verona. They have five hectares of vineyards producing Rondinella, Corvina, Molinara and Turbiana (Trebbiano di Lugana). The Bardolino 2015 came out particularly well and earned a place in our guide. This could be a sign of things to come.

89   Price A

Bardolino 2015

Blend of Corvina, Rondinella and Molinara with a little Sangiovese grapes. Stainless steel only. Intense ruby red. Rich, intense, wide with notes of wild strawberries, yellow and dark flowers and hints of peach. Intense and relaxed on the palate, slightly savory, average intensity and enveloping structure, tasty.

85   Price A

Bardolino Chiaretto 2015

Blend of Corvina, Rondinella and Molinara grapes. Stainless steel only. Light cherry color. Intense spicy notes, pepper, wild herbs, hints of white fruits. Agile in the mouth, good acidity, fresh and nice drinkability.

CA' LA BIONDA

Via Bionda, 4 - Frazione Valgatara
37020 Marano Di Valpolicella (VR)
Tel. +39 045 6801198
Fax +39 045 9587131
info@calabionda.it
www.calabionda.it
Azienda-Agricola-Cà-La-Bionda

YEAR OF FOUNDATION 1902
NAME OF THE OWNER Pietro Castellani
TOTAL BOTTLES PRODUCED 150,000
DIRECT SALES
VISITS TO THE WINERY - RESERVATION NEEDED
HECTARES OF VINEYARD 29
CERTIFIED ORGANIC VITICULTURE

The estate was founded in 1902 by Pietro Castellani, the same name of its current owner his great-great-grandson. Since then it has produced wines in the heart of Valpolicella Classica, in the district of Marano. This is a traditional estate where the vineyards are cultivated organically and they are experts in drying the grapes on mats for their Amarone which is made with great care.

93   Price C

Amarone della Valpolicella Classico Vigneti di Ravazzol 2011

Blend of 70% Corvina, 20% Corvinone, 10% Rondinella and Molinara grapes. Intense ruby red. Evolved and enveloping notes of wild cherry jam, dry plums, Maraschino, cocoa and tamarind. Rich and powerful taste, warm, enveloping, thick and polite tannins and great acidity. Very long finish.

CA' LOJERA

Via Bella Italia, 30
37019 Peschiera del Garda (VR)
Tel. +39 045 7551901
Fax +39 045 6409280
info@calojera.com
www.calojera.com
🟦 Ca-Lojera

YEAR OF FOUNDATION
NAME OF THE OWNER Franco and Ambra Tiraboschi
TOTAL BOTTLES PRODUCED 120,000
DIRECT SALES
VISITS TO THE WINERY - RESERVATION NEEDED
HECTARES OF VINEYARD 18
HOSPITALITY
RESTAURANT

When a work project is also that of one's life then this can cement the relationship between couples. At least this was the case with the Tiraboschi family who have dedicated their lives to their estate on Lake Garda. He handles production while she is the heart and soul of the household and a perfect hostess for those visiting the estate. The vineyards are on a plain with a compact, clay soil with typical varietals for producing Lugana while imported varieties are grow in the hills.

☐ 90   👍 Price A

Lugana Riserva del Lupo 2014

100% Turbiana grapes with botrytis. Stainless steel for 2 years. Light and bright straw yellow. Intense and clear notes of saffron, coffee powder and gooseberry. Fresh and very savory in the mouth, agile and of great satisfaction with a nice briny and tasty finish.

☐ 85   Price A

Lugana 2015

100% Turbiana grapes. Stainless steel only. Light straw yellow with some greenish hues. Ripe fruits, yellow flowers and sweet hints in the nose. Fresh and savory in the mouth with fruity notes and licorice hints in the finish.

CA' LUSTRA

Via S. Pietro, 50 - Frazione Faedo
35030 Cinto Euganeo (PD)
Tel. +39 0429 94128
Fax +39 0429 644111
info@calustra.it
www.calustra.it
🟦 CaLustraVinoDegliEuganei
🐦 @CaLustraEuganei

YEAR OF FOUNDATION 1965
NAME OF THE OWNER Zanovello Family
TOTAL BOTTLES PRODUCED 170,000
DIRECT SALES
VISITS TO THE WINERY - RESERVATION NEEDED
HECTARES OF VINEYARD 25
CERTIFIED ORGANIC VITICULTURE
OLIVE OIL PRODUCTION

This organic Colli Eugeni estate was acquired by Angelo Zanovello in the 1960s. It started as a country home to pass some time with his large family but then, in consideration of the interest shown by his son Franco, it became an operating wine estate. Today it is run by Franco and his son Marco and they are aware of their responsibility in cultivating inside the Colli Eugeni Nature Park and acting as caretakers of a unique environment.

▣ 92   👍 Price A*

Colli Euganei Fior d'Arancio Passito Zanovello 2010

*100% Moscato Fior d'Arancio grapes dried for 4 month on straw mats. Matures 2 years in small barrels. Ethereal aromatic and typical notes, then spices and blossom flowers. Sweet taste, full, rich, warm and extremely long. *50 cl bottle.*

CA' OROLOGIO

Via Ca' Orologio, 7a
35030 Baone (PD)
Tel. +39 0429 50099
Fax +39 0429 610875
info@caorologio.com
www.caorologio.com
🟦 caorologio

YEAR OF FOUNDATION 1995
NAME OF THE OWNER Maria Gioia Rosellini
TOTAL BOTTLES PRODUCED 24,000
DIRECT SALES
VISITS TO THE WINERY - RESERVATION NEEDED
HECTARES OF VINEYARD 12
HOSPITALITY

Maria Gioia Rosellini, an urban mother with a love for the country, found Ca' Oroligio in 1995 when she was looking for a country home with her husband Nicola. Acquiring this 16th century villa was the first step towards a new life which saw her begin to produce wines in 2002 in this enchanting place amid the hills and vineyards where she has now also created a holiday farm.

■ 91   Price B
Relogio 2013

Blend of 80% Carménère and 20% Cabernet Franc grapes. Matures 1 year in barrique. Intense and dark ruby red with violet hues. Notes of eucalyptus, mint, pine resin, blueberry, cassis, mint truffles. Exotic and unique bouquet. Tense, good acidity, neat tannins and good persistence.

CA' PIGNETO

Via Pignetto, 1
37024 Negrar (VR)
Tel. +39 045 7513790
Fax +39 045 7513790
info@capigneto.com
www.capigneto.com
f *capigneto.it*

YEAR OF FOUNDATION 1980
NAME OF THE OWNER Paola Augusta Serenelli
TOTAL BOTTLES PRODUCED 75,000
DIRECT SALES
VISITS TO THE WINERY - RESERVATION NEEDED
HECTARES OF VINEYARD 8
OLIVE OIL PRODUCTION

This corner of paradise near Negar, famous for its wines as well as the centuries old Lebanon cedar trees, belongs to the Countess Paolo Serenelli and her husband, the surgeon Carlo Adami. The wine is made under the supervision of Giancarlo and Giuseppe Nicolis, two famous local winemakers.

⊡ 91   Price C
Recioto della Valpolicella Classico 2011

Blend of Corvina, Rondinella and Molinara grapes. Matures 8 months in barrels. Very dark ruby red. Intense and rich notes of flowers, cocoa, eucalyptus hints, spices, tobacco and black cherry. Sweet taste, smooth, silky tannins and balanced alcoholic notes. Long and persistent.

■ 88   Price B
Valpolicella Ripasso 2013

Blend of Corvina and Rondinella grapes. Matures 18 months in barrels. Deep ruby red. Intense notes of black cherry, tobacco and spices. Warm, smooth taste, elegant tannins and silky structure.

CA' RUGATE

Via Pergola, 36
37030 Montecchia Di Crosara (VR)
Tel. +39 045 6176328
S *carugate.aziendaagricola*
carugate@carugate.it
www.carugate.it
f *carugate.aziendaagricola*

YEAR OF FOUNDATION 1986
NAME OF THE OWNER Tessari Family
TOTAL BOTTLES PRODUCED 550,000
DIRECT SALES
VISITS TO THE WINERY - RESERVATION NEEDED
HECTARES OF VINEYARD 58
OLIVE OIL PRODUCTION

Ca' Rugate has a century of history, the history of the Tessari family who began selling wine from a rented tavern in Presina at the start of the 20th century to then, from father to son, hectare by hectare, become the big quality wine producer they are today.

☐ 🄖 95   👍 Price A
Soave Classico Monte Fiorentine 2015

100% Garganega grapes. Stainless steel. Light greenish yellow. Fragrant and elegantly fruity. Cedar, pineapples, yellow plum, fresh almond, then flint in the background, all of this of incredible integrity. Deliciously savory taste, tense but neat, fresh, good body, attractive and of dangerous drinkability. Elegant and long finish. Splendid version.

☐ 93   Price B
Soave Classico Monte Alto 2014

100% Garganega grapes. Vinified in wood and matured for 8 months in big barrels. Straw yellow. Fresh almond, flint hints, white peach, wildflowers for an extremely rich nose profile considering the vintage. Savory and agile, thinner than other versions, with good refreshing acidity on a good body and elegant persistence.

CANTINA DEL CASTELLO

*Corte Pittora, 5
37038 Soave (VR)
Tel. +39 045 7680093
Fax +39 045 6190099*
🅢 *cantinacastellosoave*
cantinacastello@cantinacastello.it
www.cantinacastello.it
🄵 *soavecastello*
🐦 *@soavecastello*

YEAR OF FOUNDATION 1961
NAME OF THE OWNER Arturo Stocchetti
TOTAL BOTTLES PRODUCED 130,000
DIRECT SALES
VISITS TO THE WINERY - RESERVATION NEEDED
HECTARES OF VINEYARD 12

The winery is in the town of Soave, below the Castello Scaligero, to which it seems it as connected by a tunnel. They have been operating since the 1960s but it was only with Arturo Stocchetti that is assumed its current capacity. His goal is to express the terroir and the aroma of the Garganega and Trebbiano di Soave grapes and convey in his wine the fruit of the sweet hills that embrace Soave and its castle.

☐ 92   👍 Price A
Soave Classico Il Castello 2015

Blend of Garganega with a little Trebbiano di Soave grapes. Stainless steel. Very fruity, notes of white peach, apricot, yellow plum, simple but fragrant and very clear. Savory taste, good body, well balanced by the acidity that gives tension and freshness. Very pleasant drinkability. Good length in the finish.

CANTINA DI SOAVE

*Viale Vittoria, 10
37038 Soave (VR)
Tel. +39 0456539811
Fax +39 045 7681203*
🅢 *cdssac01*
cantina@cantinasoave.it
www.cantinasoave.it
🄵 *CANTINADISOAVE*
🐦 *@CantinaDiSoave*

YEAR OF FOUNDATION 1898
NAME OF THE OWNER
TOTAL BOTTLES PRODUCED 30,000,000
DIRECT SALES
VISITS TO THE WINERY - RESERVATION NEEDED
HECTARES OF VINEYARD 6,000

This is one of the largest wine cooperatives in Veneto. Production totals close to 30 million bottles subdivided into all the leading Verona DOC appellations as well as some sparkling wines. It has six winery-cellars, the latest of which was Rocca Sveva that was inaugurated ten years ago.

☐ 86   👍 Price A
Soave Classico Rocca Sveva 2015

100% Garganega grapes. Stainless steel. Greenish straw yellow. Fragrant, fruity, simple and whole in the nose. Fresh, savory, very pleasant and easy to drink. Light body and thin finish.

CANTINA DI VALPOLICELLA NEGRAR

*Via Ca' Salgari
37024 Negrar (VR)
Tel. +39 045 6014300
Fax +39 045 6014399
info@cantinanegrar.it
www.cantinanegrar.it*
🄵 *Cantina-Valpolicella-Negrar*
🐦 *@CantinaNegrar*

YEAR OF FOUNDATION 1933
NAME OF THE OWNER
TOTAL BOTTLES PRODUCED 7,000,000
DIRECT SALES
VISITS TO THE WINERY - RESERVATION NEEDED
HECTARES OF VINEYARD 600

Not only is this one of the more important wine cooperatives in the area, it is also one of the best. This in part thanks to Daniele Accordini, an expert winemaker who runs the winery in the best way imagnable. The Domini Veneti line can compete with the best wines in the area and with the advantage of having competitive prices.

 92   Price D

Amarone della Valpolicella Classico Riserva Mater Domìni Veneti 2010

Blend of 60% Corvina, 15% Corvinone, 15% Rondinella and 10% other grapes. Matures 60 months in barrels. Very compact ruby red. Powerful and direct notes of red and black fruits in syrup, chocolate, spices, iodine and eucalyptus puffs. Pulpy and structured on the palate, dense and with compact but velvety tannins.

 90   Price B

Amarone della Valpolicella Classico Vigneti di Jago Domìni Veneti 2010

Blend of 60% Corvina, 15% Corvinone, 15% Rondinella and 10% other grapes. Matures 3 years in wood. Intense ruby red. Intriguing and articulated notes of pepper, black cherry in syrup, humus and tobacco introduce a smooth and pulpy sip marked by evident tannins but always in good balance with the taste.

 90   Price B

Recioto della Valpolicella Classico Vigneti di Moron Domìni Veneti 2010

Blend of 70% Corvina, 15% Corvinone and 15% Rondinella grapes. Matures 18 months in barrels. Very dark ruby red. Intense notes of violets, black cherry, cassis, spices and tobacco with chocolate finish. Sweet on the palate, smooth, caressing, velvety tannins and of good alcoholic tension.

 87   Price B

Valpolicella Ripasso Superiore Classico La Casetta Domìni Veneti 2013

Blend of 70% Corvina, 15% Corvinone and 15% Rondinella grapes. Matures 2 year in big barres. Bright ruby red. Clear notes of black cherry, spices and hints of cocoa. Smooth taste, thin but present tannins, and adequate body.

CARPENÈ MALVOLTI

Via Antonio Carpenè, 1
31015 Conegliano (TV)
Tel. +39 0438 364611
info@carpene-malvolti.com
www.carpene-malvolti.com
 Carpene1868
 @CarpeneMalvolti

YEAR OF FOUNDATION **1868**
NAME OF THE OWNER **Etile Carpenè**
TOTAL BOTTLES PRODUCED **5,300,000**
VISITS TO THE WINERY - RESERVATION NEEDED

In 1869, four partners – Carpenè, Caccianiga, Malvolti and Vianello – formed a company that over the years evolved into Carpenè Malvolti. Thanks to Antonio Carpenè's dream, sparkling wine began to be produced in Italy and the estate was the first to use the name Prosecco. But his dreams did not end there and he became a driving force behind the one of Italy's most prestigious wine institute, the Scuola Enologica Conegliano. Four generations of Carpenè, now Etile Jr and his family, have made this brand famous in Italy and the world.

 90   Price B

Spumante Metodo Class. Millesimato 2009

100% Chardonnay grapes. Classic method. Intense straw yellow, thin and continuous perlage. Dominant notes of yeasts, then yellow plum, white peach, fresh almond. Creamy flavor, savory, tense, good body, very elegant and of great length.

 89   Price B

Superiore di Cartizze 1868 Dry

100% Glera grapes. Charmat method. Bright straw yellow, fast and abundant perlage. A lot of yeasts in the nose, then wisteria flowers and hawthorn, winter melon, white peach. Lively flavor, smooth, creamy, fresh and slightly sweet finish.

 87   👍 Price A

Conegliano Valdobbiadene Prosecco Superiore 1868 Extra Dry

100% Glera grapes. Charmat method. Light straw yellow, thin and fast perlage. Notes of wisteria, underbrush and gooseberry. Agile, savory, smooth taste, not enormous and easy to drink.

CASA COSTE PIANE

Località Santo Stefano - Strada Coste Piane, 2
31049 Valdobbiadene (TV)
Tel. +39 0423 900219
Fax +39 0423 900671
info@casacostepiane.it
www.casacostepiane.it

YEAR OF FOUNDATION 1994
NAME OF THE OWNER Loris Follador
TOTAL BOTTLES PRODUCED 60,000
VISITS TO THE WINERY - RESERVATION NEEDED
HECTARES OF VINEYARD 6

The Follador family estate started up in 1997 even if they have always produced a Prosecco with natural, secondary fermentation in the bottle. They have six hectares of vineyards, many of which are quite old, subdivided into various plots, all on steep hills. Loris and his sons Adelchi and Raffaele cultivate their vineyards in respect of nature and no chemical products are used in the vineyard and only the bare minimum in the cellar to exalt as much as possible the potential of the land.

 91 Price A
Brichet
100% Glera grapes. Referents in bottle with indigenous yeasts. Characterized by notes of white peach, medlar and hawthorn. Absolutely dry in the mouth and expresses the usual tonicity and verticality what sustains the good structure.

 89 Price A
Conegliano Valdobbiadene Prosecco
100% Glera grapes. Referents in bottle with indigenous yeasts. Austere notes of white peach and pepper. Tense, sharp and good length in the mouth.

CAVALCHINA

Via Sommacampagna, 7 - Frazione Custoza
37066 Sommacampagna (VR)
Tel. +39 045 516002
 cavalchina.piona
cavalchina@cavalchina.com
www.cavalchina.it
 CavalchinaWineries
 @CavalchinaWine

YEAR OF FOUNDATION 1900
NAME OF THE OWNER Giulietto Piona
TOTAL BOTTLES PRODUCED 450,000
DIRECT SALES
VISITS TO THE WINERY - RESERVATION NEEDED
HECTARES OF VINEYARD 40

The estate has existed since 1800 and was known for the quality of its vineyards. It took on its modern structure in the 1960s and were the first to use the name Custoza for the local white wine. The style is classic but with great attention paid to the vineyard and experimentation in the winery.

☐ 90 Price A
Custoza Superiore Amedeo 2014
Blend of 40% Garganega, 30% Bianca Fernanda, 15% Trebbianello and 15% Trebbiano Toscano grapes. Partially matured in wood. Intense straw yellow. Clear and intense fruity notes with yellow flowers and aromatic herbs, a touch of cedar and slightly smoky. Tasty in the mouth with good acidity and thick structure and savory. Consistent finish.

 87 Price A
Bardolino Chiaretto 2015
Blend of 55% Corvina, 35% Rondinella and 10% Molinara grapes. Stainless steel only. Antique pink color. Notes of saffron, slightly smoky and yellow fruits. Good acidity and fragrant in the mouth, savory and fresh finish.

☐ 83 Price A
Bardolino 2015
Blend of 60% Corvina, 30% Rondinella, 10% Molinara grapes. Matures in stainless steel. Light ruby red. Simple notes of fruits like strawberries and plums. Balanced and wide structures, extremely drinkable even if not very complex.

CAVAZZA

Contrada Selva, 22
36054 Montebello Vicentino (VI)
Tel. +39 0444 649166
info@cavazzawine.com
www.cavazzawine.com
 AziendaAgricolaCavazza
 @CavazzaWine

YEAR OF FOUNDATION 1928
NAME OF THE OWNER Cavazza Family

TOTAL BOTTLES PRODUCED **600,000**
DIRECT SALES
VISITS TO THE WINERY - RESERVATION NEEDED
HECTARES OF VINEYARD **150**

This Vicenza winery has almost 100 years of history and the history of the vineyards and the land is intertwined with that of the Cavazza family. It all began in 1928 when Giovanni Cavazza, a native of Montecchia di Crosara, acquired his first vineyards in Selva di Montebello. Today the estate is run by his children who thanks to their vast experience in winemaking follow in their father's footsteps with dedication and sincerity.

☐ 88   👍 Price A
Gambellara Classico Creari 2012
100% Garganega grapes. Stainless steel on the yeasts. Intense straw yellow. Pleasant notes of anise and yellow pulp fruits. Nice structure in the mouth, full taste, savory and pleasantly persistant.

■ 86   Price B
Colli Berici Cicogna Merlot 2013
100% Merlot grapes. Matures 1 year in small French durmast barrels. Light ruby red. Intense notes of fruits and spices. Balanced structure, notes of spices, slightly structured tannins and average persistence in the finish.

☐ 86   👍 Price A
Gambellara Classico Bocaria 2015
100% Garganega grapes. Stainless steel. Light straw yellow color. Light and clean in the mouth with fresh wildflowers notes and mint. Balanced and pleasant to drink.

★★
COFFELE

Via Roma, 5
37038 Soave (VR)
Tel. +39 045 7680007
Fax +39 045 6198091
info@coffele.it
www.coffele.it
 Coffele

YEAR OF FOUNDATION **1971**
NAME OF THE OWNER **Coffele Family**
TOTAL BOTTLES PRODUCED **120,000**

DIRECT SALES
VISITS TO THE WINERY - RESERVATION NEEDED
HECTARES OF VINEYARD **30**
HOSPITALITY

This 17th century winery in the center of Soave and has been run with passion generation after generation. It is run by Alberto Coffele who today works alongside his children Chiara and Giuseppe. The vineyards are in Castelcerino, on the hills north of Soave, and are cultivated with Garganega as well as Trebbiano di Soave and some international varieties. With the acquisition of vineyards in Valpolicella, the estate has been able to enrich its line of products.

☐ 90   👍 Price A
Soave Classico Ca' Visco 2015
Blend of 75% Garganega and 25% Trebbiano di Toscana grapes. Stainless steel. Cedar, white peach, wildflowers for an attractive and whole nose profile. Savory taste, nice body, tense, easy to drink and good length.

☐ 88   👍 Price A
Soave Classico 2015
Blend of 75% Garganega and 25% Trebbiano di Soave grapes. Stainless steel. Light straw yellow. Fragrant, fruity, simple nose, with notes of fruit salad and mint hints. Light flavor, pleasantly savory, very easy to drink.

CORTE GARDONI

Località Gardoni, 5
37067 Valeggio Sul Mincio (VR)
Tel. +39 045 7950382
info@cortegardoni.it
www.cortegardoni.it

YEAR OF FOUNDATION **1980**
NAME OF THE OWNER **Piccoli Family**
TOTAL BOTTLES PRODUCED **200,000**
DIRECT SALES
VISITS TO THE WINERY - RESERVATION NEEDED
HECTARES OF VINEYARD **25**

Situated in Valeggio sul Mincio, on the southern side of lower Garda, the estate is slowly renovating all its vineyards to be Guyot-trained with a density of 5,500 vines per hectare. The renovation is paying special attention to the biotypes of the variations that already existed and which provide the basis for both their Bianco di Custoza and Bardolino, in which Corvina plays an important role.

 92   👍 Price A

Custoza Mael 2015

Blend of 40% Garganega, 20% Trebbiano Toscano, 20% Trebbianello, 20% Riesling grapes. Matures in stainless steel on the yeasts for 6 months. Deep straw yellow with green hues. Intense and varied notes of cedar, citrus, alfalfa and a smoky touch. Agile, young on the palate, tense acidity with a tasty and persistent finish. A wine that will age for long.

 86   Price B

Becco Rosso 2014

100% Corvina grapes. Matures in barrique. Light ruby red. Notes of spices, black and white pepper, cherry hints. Very elegant in the mouth, a little light but savory and tasty.

 85   👍 Price A

Bardolino Le Fontane 2014

Blend of Corvina and Molinara grapes. Matures in stainless steel. Light ruby red, Notes of red fruits, white cherry, saffron and elegant green notes. Relaxed, soft and attractive taste.

CORTE SANT'ALDA

Via Capovilla, 28 - Località Fioi
37030 Mezzane Di Sotto (VR)
Tel. +39 045 8880006
info@cortesantalda.it
www.cortesantalda.com
 Corte-SantAlda
 @CorteSantAlda

YEAR OF FOUNDATION 1986
NAME OF THE OWNER Marinella Camerani
TOTAL BOTTLES PRODUCED 80,000
DIRECT SALES
VISITS TO THE WINERY - RESERVATION NEEDED
HECTARES OF VINEYARD 19
HOSPITALITY
CERTIFIED ORGANIC VITICULTURE
CERTIFIED BIODYNAMIC VITICULTURE
OLIVE OIL PRODUCTION

"Don't worry, those who don't even try don't make mistakes". This was what Marinella Cam-

erani said to us after we told her that by mistake we gave a 'faccino' Doctor Wine hedcut to her Amarone Mithas 2007, which had not come out yet, instead of the 2006. We apologize again to her and our readers. This time we make no mistake in regard to her and her wines when we say they are a small winemaking wonder in the area of Verona, thanks to winemaking methods that are truly compatible with and respectful of the environment and her enormous passion for what she does. The wine are unforgettable.

■ 💷 96   Price D

Amarone della Valpolicella Mithas 2010

Blend of 35% Corvina, 35% Rondinella and 30% Corvinone grapes. Matures 4 years in different size barrels. Intense and concentrated garnet ruby red. A real myth as the sound of the name may recall. Expressive and articulated notes of black cherry, spices, licorice, orange peel covered with chocolate, Kirsch. Strong and austere flavor, rich, warm, with tannins hypnotized by the big body. Very long persistence.

■ 93   Price B

Valpolicella Ripasso Superiore Campi Magri 2013

Blend of 40% Corvina, 40% Corvinone, 20% Rondinella grapes. Matures 2 in cherry big barrels. Intense and concentrated ruby red. Smoky hints, then Kirsch, black cherry, hints of cassis, clear and whole. Tense flavor, alcoholic, warm, rich, with perfectly integrated tannins and long persistence.

■ 93   Price B

Valpolicella Superiore Mithas 2012

Blend of 50% Corvinone, 40% Corvina and 10% Rondinella grapes. Matures 2 years in mostly used tonneau. Intense garnet ruby red. Smoky hints on wild cherry and Kirsch, spices in the underground. Warm taste, savory, great body, neat tannins, velvety, very long finish.

■ 90   Price B

Valpolicella Ca' Fiui 2015

Blend of 50% Corvinone, 30% Corvina and 20% Rondinella and Molinara grapes. Matures 8 months in big barrels. Lively ruby red. Clear fruits, cherry, black cherry, plums in the nose, all particularly neat. Tense and pleasantly savory taste, warm, easy to drink but not trivial.

VALENTINA CUBI

Via Casterna, 60
37022 Fumane (VR)
Tel. +39 045 7701806
Fax +39 045 6834022
info@valentinacubi.it
www.valentinacubi.it
 f *valentinacubi2015*

YEAR OF FOUNDATION 1969
NAME OF THE OWNER Valentina Cubi
TOTAL BOTTLES PRODUCED 40,000
DIRECT SALES
VISITS TO THE WINERY
HECTARES OF VINEYARD 10
HOSPITALITY
CERTIFIED ORGANIC VITICULTURE
OLIVE OIL PRODUCTION

Fumane and San Pietro in Cariano are the two Valpolicella 'terroir' where Valentina Cubi has her vineyards. The vines of Corvina, Corvinone, Rondinella and Molinara have their roots in soil rich in gravel in the plots of Rasso, Monte Tenda and Monte Crosetta, perfect habitats to make the red typical wines of the appellation. The vineyards are organic and production of this small and talented winery rarely surpasses 40,000 bottles. The style of the Amarone, as well as her other nectars, stands out for the clarity of the aromas and how clean the flavor is, exalting to the utmost the exceptional prime ingredients.

■ 92	Price C

Amarone della Valpolicella Classico Morar 2010

Blend of 65% Corvina, 25% Corvinone and 15% Rondinella grapes. Matures 36 months in barrels. Garnet red. Intense and articulated notes of cherry, violets, red fruits jam, tobacco and eucalyptus. Round and balanced in the mouth, thin tannins on a powerful body but never redundant.

■ 88	Price B

Valpolicella Ripasso Classico Superiore Arusnatico 2013

Blend of 65% Corvina, 25% Rondinella and 15% Molinara grapes. Matures 12 months in tonneau. Ruby red. Fruity and spicy notes of cherry, vanilla and pepper. Smooth in the mouth, round tannins, fruity and discrete persistence.

 ★★★

ROMANO DAL FORNO

Località Lodoletta - Frazione Cellore
37031 Illasi (VR)
Tel. +39 045 7834923
Fax +39 045 6528364
info@dalfornoromano.it
www.dalforno.net
 f *Dal-Forno-Romano*

YEAR OF FOUNDATION 1983
NAME OF THE OWNER **Romano Dal Forno**
TOTAL BOTTLES PRODUCED 45,000
DIRECT SALES
VISITS TO THE WINERY - RESERVATION NEEDED
HECTARES OF VINEYARD 25

2010 was a very important year for this estate, not because of the harvest, which was not exceptional, but because it marked the beginning of the third phase of Romano Dal Forno's winemaking history. I would define this phase as 'post-modern', a new definition of the parameters to interpret Valpolicella and Amarone. This new interpretation derives from profound technical skills and a hyper-technological winery all reflecting Romano's vision. A drastic reduction of sugar residue through an extremely controlled raisinating period and almost maniacal care in the vineyard resulted in wines that are incredibly well-made and unimaginably drinkable. A new style.

■ 🍷 97	Price E

Amarone della Valpolicella Vigneto di Monte Lodoletta 2010

Blend of 60% Corvina, 20% Rondinella and 20% Croatina and Oseletta grapes, dried on straw mats. Matures in barrique. Dark ruby red. Marvelous nose, very complex, great black fruits, intense, then eucalyptus and smoky notes make the profile precious without covering the freshness of the fruit, a touch of rosemary. Fantastic in the mouth for complexity and pleasant to drink with a never-ending finish.

■ 94	Price C

Valpolicella Superiore Vigneto di Monte Lodoletta 2010

Blend of 70% Corvina and Corvina Grossa, 20% Rondinella and 10% Croatina and Oseleta grapes dried for 40 days. Intense ruby red. Intense and

clean notes of cherry and wild berries, light spices and a hint of cocoa. Compact beginning, very good progression, fresh and with elegant tannins and great classy finish.

★★
FOLLADOR

Via Gravette, 42 - Frazione Col San Martino
31010 Farra Di Soligo (TV)
Tel. +39 0438 898222
Fax +39 0438 989520
info@folladorprosecco.com
www.folladorprosecco.com
 folladorprosecco
@folladorwines

YEAR OF FOUNDATION 1970
NAME OF THE OWNER Italia Libera Rossi
TOTAL BOTTLES PRODUCED 1,000,000
DIRECT SALES
VISITS TO THE WINERY - RESERVATION NEEDED
HECTARES OF VINEYARD 40
RESTAURANT

The Follador estate is Col San Martini, on the 'wine trail' that leads from Conegliano to Valdobbiadene. The family has been making wines for centuries and in 1769 Giovanni Follador received special recognition from the Doge of Venice for the quality of his wine. Since 1970, however, they have almost exclusively been producing Prosecco Spumante. Gianfranco is the descendent of Giovanni and together with his wife Italia Libera, nicknamed Rita, and their daughters Mariacristina, Francesca and Emanuela represent the estate's beating heart.

回 92   Price B
Conegliano Valdobbiadene Prosecco Sup. Cuvée Torri di Credazzo Extra Dry
100% Glera grapes. Charmat method. Light yellow, thin and fast perlage. A lot of yeasts in the nose, evident bread crust, wisteria flowers, cedar, yellow plum. Lively flavor, creamy, pleasantly savory, fresh and of good length.

回 91   Price B
Conegliano Valdobbiadene Prosecco Superiore Extra Dry 2015
100% Glera grapes. Charmat method. Light yellow, abundant and fast perlage. Fragrant and fruity,

notes of yeasts then white peach, wildflowers, citrus hints. Lively flavor, slightly sweet, smooth, savory and very pleasant.

★★
GINI

Via Matteotti, 42
37032 Monteforte d'Alpone (VR)
Tel. +39 045 7611908
Fax +39 045 6101610
info@ginivini.com
www.ginivini.com
 GiniViticoltori
@GiniVini

YEAR OF FOUNDATION 17th Century
NAME OF THE OWNER Sandro and Claudio Gini
TOTAL BOTTLES PRODUCED 200,000
DIRECT SALES
VISITS TO THE WINERY - RESERVATION NEEDED
HECTARES OF VINEYARD 56

The Gini estate is in Monteforte d'Alpone, in the Soave Classico zone, and has always been run by brothers Claudio and Sandro. With an eye on the future, they are following in the footsteps of their ancestors who worked the same vineyards for four centuries ago. Their very precise and natural approach involves a 'traditional' winemaking style with the use of indigenous yeasts and no chemical additives. Since 1985 their Soave Classico La Froscà has been bottled without any sulfites.

□ 94   Price B
Soave Classico La Froscà 2015
100% Garganega grapes. Stainless steel on the yeasts for 6 months. Bright straw yellow. It's the quintessence of traditional Soave Classico. Fruity notes, white peach, fresh almond, wildflowers. Tense, deliciously savory, good body, enveloping, fresh, very pleasant to drink and unexpected long finish.

□ 91   👍 Price A
Soave Classico 2015
100% Garganega grapes. Stainless steel. Greenish straw yellow. Fragrant and fruity, complete, pleasant, cedar, wildflowers and white peach. Savory taste, good body but agile and easy to drink but not trivial.

VENETO

527

★

GUERRIERI RIZZARDI

Strada Campazzi, 2
37011 Bardolino (VR)
Tel. +39 045 7210028
Fax +39 045 6212254
mail@guerrieri-rizzardi.it
www.guerrieri-rizzardi.it
f guerrieririzzardi
𝕏 @RizzardiEstates

YEAR OF FOUNDATION 1914
NAME OF THE OWNER Rizzardi Family
TOTAL BOTTLES PRODUCED 700,000
DIRECT SALES
VISITS TO THE WINERY - RESERVATION NEEDED
HECTARES OF VINEYARD 100
OLIVE OIL PRODUCTION

This historic Veneto producer was created by the union of two aristocratic families (and their wine estates): the Guerrieri, who for over a century had a wine estate in Bardolino; and the Rizzardi, vineyard owners in Negrar since 1678. The winery's philosophy of exalting the terroir above all is evident in its four estates: in Bardolino, Soave, Valpolicella and Valdadige.

■ 92   Price C
Amarone della Valpolicella Classico Calcarole 2011

Blend of 60% Corvina, 17% Corvinone, 10% San-giovese, 10% Barbera and 3% Rondinella grapes. Matures 1 year in tonneau and 2 years in barrels. Garnet ruby red. Intense and powerful notes on macerated morello cherry, chocolate, tobacco and gunpowder. Balanced and pleasant in the mouth, full and persistent.

☐ 88   Price B
Soave Classico Ferra 2014

Blend of 90% Garganega and 10% Chardonnay grapes. Matures 12 month in barrels. Golden color. Intense notes of wisteria, Mediterranean fruits and smoky hints. Dense, savory and fresh taste with ripe fruits.

■ 87   Price A
Valpolicella Ripasso Classico Superiore Pojega 2014

Blend of 45% Corvina, 45% Corvinone, 10% Merlot, Rondinella and Molinara grapes. Matures 1 year in

barrels. Ruby red. Fruity notes of cherry, then dried violets and eucalyptus hints. Smooth on the palate, soft and well blended tannins.

I STEFANINI

Via Crosara, 21
37032 Monteforte d'Alpone (VR)
Tel. +39 045 6175249
Fax +39 045 4851828
francesco@istefanini.it
www.istefanini.it
f I-Stefanini

YEAR OF FOUNDATION 2003
NAME OF THE OWNER Francesco Tessari
TOTAL BOTTLES PRODUCED 90,000
DIRECT SALES
VISITS TO THE WINERY - RESERVATION NEEDED
HECTARES OF VINEYARD 17

The estate's strange names derives from that of a distant ancestor, a certain Stefano, and became the nickname of the Tessari family and later the brand of their wine estate. It is a relatively young estate but has roots in the 19th century, with its 17 hectares of vineyards passing down from father to son. They make a homemade Vin Santo (note for sale) and still have bottles of it from 1948. Among the Soave wines they produce for sale is the very good and paradigmatic Monte di Fice.

☐ 92   👍 Price A
Soave Superiore Monte di Fice 2015

Blend of 45% Corvina, 45% Corvinone, 10% Merlot, Rondinella and Molinara grapes. Matures 1 year in barrels. Ruby red. Fruity notes of cherry, then dried violets and eucalyptus hints. Smooth on the palate, soft and well blended tannins.

☐ 91   👍 Price A
Soave Classico Monte de Toni 2015

100% Garganega grapes. Stainless steel only. Greenish yellow. Fragrant, fruity, pineapple, medlar and hints of white flowers. Agile taste, savory, easy to drink but not trivial with a thin finish.

★★

INAMA

Località Biacche, 50
37047 San Bonifacio (VR)
Tel. +39 045 6104343
Fax +39 045 6131979
inama@inamaaziendaagricola.it
www.inamaaziendaagricola.it
Inama-Azienda-Agricola
@InamaAziendaAgr

YEAR OF FOUNDATION 1967
NAME OF THE OWNER Inama Family
TOTAL BOTTLES PRODUCED 450,000
DIRECT SALES
VISITS TO THE WINERY - RESERVATION NEEDED
HECTARES OF VINEYARD 62
CERTIFIED ORGANIC VITICULTURE

The paradigmatic Inama estate needs no introduction having distinguished itself for many years with the great quality of their wines. The decision to make wine with Sauvignon was almost casual and came about in 1991 when the quality of Soave was at a low ebb. Grown in Soave, Sauvignon produced a wine that conveyed the characteristics of the land more than the varietal. They did not abandon Soave, however, and the following year came out with a Soave Classico Vin Soave.

■ 90 Price B

Bradisismo 2013

Blend of 70% Cabernet Sauvignon and 30% Carmenére grapes. Matures in part new barrique for 1 year. Intense and dark ruby red. Fruity and spicy, classic notes of blueberry, black currant, then mint, cocoa and pine resin. Compact, full taste, discrete agility even if with big body, polite tannins and long enveloping finish.

□ 88 Price A

Soave Classico Vin Soave 2015

100% Garganega grapes. Stainless steel. Straw yellow. Deliciously fruity, simple, fragrant, notes of cedar, white peach and wildflowers. Savory taste, easy to drink, nice acidic tension and clean finish of good length.

★

LA MONTECCHIA CONTE EMO CAPODILISTA

Via Montecchia, 16
35030 Selvazzano Dentro (PD)
Tel. +39 049 637294
Fax +39 049 8055826
lamontecchia
vino@lamontecchia.it
www.lamontecchia.it
lamontecchia

YEAR OF FOUNDATION 1100
NAME OF THE OWNER Umberto Emo Capodilista
TOTAL BOTTLES PRODUCED 130,000
DIRECT SALES
VISITS TO THE WINERY - RESERVATION NEEDED
HECTARES OF VINEYARD 20
HOSPITALITY

La Montecchia is 15 kilometers from Padua, on the border with the Colli Euganei Regional Park and in the area of Palladio's villas. Its 45 hectares of vineyards are for the most part red grapes: Cabernet Sauvignon and Cabernet Franc, Merlort, Carmenère and Raboso. All these grapes produce varietal wines while the white wines are made with Moscato Giallo Fior d'Arancio , an estate favorite. Aside from winemaking, the estate hosts a holiday farm spread out in various locations of the property.

▣ 92 Price B*

Colli Euganei Fior d'Arancio Moscato Passito 2013

*100% Moscato Giallo grapes. Stainless steel only. Amber color. Notes of dates and dry apricots, some alcohol hints that don't prevail on the noble aromas. Very sweet, tense acidity, well-structured and impressive persistent length. *37.5 cl bottle.*

■ 89 Price B

Colli Euganei Cabernet Sauvignon Ireneo 2013

Blend of 90% Cabernet Sauvignon and 10% of Merlot and Carménere grapes. Barrique for 1 year. Very intense ruby red. A lot of wood in the beginning, young and a little overwhelming, then minty notes, pine resin, tobacco and blueberries. Still a little uneven taste, thick tannins, savory, well sustained by acidity. Still not ready but promising.

★

LE FRAGHE

Località Colombare, 3
37010 Cavaion Veronese (VR)
Tel. +39 0457 236832
info@fraghe.it
www.fraghe.it
 Le-Fraghe

YEAR OF FOUNDATION **1984**
NAME OF THE OWNER **Matilde Poggi**
TOTAL BOTTLES PRODUCED **90,000**
DIRECT SALES
VISITS TO THE WINERY - RESERVATION NEEDED
HECTARES OF VINEYARD **28**
HOSPITALITY

Matilde Poggi is the head of the Italian Federation of Independent Winemakers. This is an important group of quality wine producers who have made craftsmanship and respect of the environment their credo. Her estate is in Cavaion Veronese where she is one of the best Bardolino producers.

■ **88**   Price A
Bardolino 2014

Blend of Corvina and Rondinella grapes. Stainless steel only. Bright ruby red. Clear and intense notes of red fruits, cherry, lily of the valley and violets. Great balance and flavor in the mouth with thick and agile structure and refined and flavored, high quality finish.

---

 85   Price A
Bardolino Chiaretto Rodòn 2015

Blend of Rondinella and Corvina grapes. Stainless steel only. Very light pink, almost red gold color. Spicy notes, green and white pepper, white fruit hints. Savory, good acidity and fresh finish.

★

LE RAGOSE

Località Le Ragose, 1 - Frazione Arbinazzo
37024 Negrar (VR)
Tel. +39 045 7513241
Fax +39 045 7513171
leragose@leragose.com
www.leragose.com
 Le-Ragose

YEAR OF FOUNDATION **1969**
NAME OF THE OWNER **Marco and Paolo Galli**
TOTAL BOTTLES PRODUCED **120,000**
DIRECT SALES
VISITS TO THE WINERY - RESERVATION NEEDED
HECTARES OF VINEYARD **18**
OLIVE OIL PRODUCTION

Le Ragose is in the heart of the classic area of Valpolicella, in the town of Megrar. The winery is run by Marco and Paolo Galli, who have inherited the estate and passion for winemaking from their enologist father Arnaldo and are carrying on his project. Their vineyards are planted with Corvina, Corvinone and Rondinella and the family motto is: "The quality of a wine is indivisible from the origin of the grapes and the people who make it".

■ **91**   Price C
Amarone della Valpolicella Classico Caloetto 2007

Blend of 50% Corvina, 20% Corvinone, 20% Rondinella and other grapes varieties. Matures 3 years in barrels. Garnet ruby red. Wide and articulated notes of macerated black cherry, cocoa, spices and toasted hints. Dense sip, severe and powerful.

---

 88   Price B
Recioto della Valpolicella Classico 2013

Blend of 50% Corvina, 20% Corvinone, 20% Rondinella and other grape varieties. Matures in stainless steel vats for over 2 years. Compact ruby red. Sweet and eucalyptus notes, then black cherry and blackberry jam, mint truffles. Sweet on the palate, gentle tannins and powerful structure.

■ **86**   Price B
Valpolicella Ripasso Superiore Le Sassine 2012

Blend of 50% Corvina, 20% Corvinone, 20% Rondinella and other grape varieties. Matures in barrels. Ruby red. Fuity, spicy, intense notes of black cherry and licorice. Savory, pleasant and smooth tannins.

★

LE VIGNE DI SAN PIETRO

Via San Pietro, 23
37066 Sommacampagna (VR)
Tel. +39 045 510016
Fax +39 045 8960701

info@levignedisanpietro.it
www.levignedisanpietro.it
 levignedisanpietro

YEAR OF FOUNDATION 1980
NAME OF THE OWNER Carlo Nerozzi
TOTAL BOTTLES PRODUCED 70,000
DIRECT SALES
VISITS TO THE WINERY - RESERVATION NEEDED
HECTARES OF VINEYARD 10

Over 30 years ago, Sergio and Franca Nerozzi fell in love with the hills around Lake Garda and bought a small estate in Sommacampagna on the San Pietro Hill, from the top of which there is a commanding view of the Verona plan. In 1980, their son Carlo set up a small winery with his father. This then grew in proportion to his passion and while production may still be limited, it is constantly increasing in quality.

86   🖒 **Price A**
Bardolino 2014
Blend of Corvina, Rondinella and Merlot grapes. Stainless steel for 6 months. Intense ruby red. Slight tendency to green notes, fresh and eucalyptus notes, then red fruit not too ripe and watermelon. Elegant in the mouth, lively acidity and great drinkability.

★★
MACULAN

Via Castellotto, 3
36042 Breganze (VI)
Tel. +39 0445 873733
Fax +39 0445 300149
info@maculan.net
www.maculan.net
 Cantina-Maculan

YEAR OF FOUNDATION 1946
NAME OF THE OWNER Maculan Family
TOTAL BOTTLES PRODUCED 700,000
DIRECT SALES
VISITS TO THE WINERY - RESERVATION NEEDED
HECTARES OF VINEYARD 40
OLIVE OIL PRODUCTION

Fausto Maculan's estate is in Breganze, a small town tucked into the Prealpi Veneto zone, and is a point of reference in the area. He has dedicated his life to this estate where he began to

work at 14. This love has only grown over the years and this is evident in the increasing quality of production. Today he is assisted by his daughters Angela and Maria Vittoria.

92   **Price C**
Fratta 2012
Blend of 65% Cabernet Sauvignon and 35% Merlot grapes. Matures 1 year in barrique. Intense and dark ruby red. Articulated notes, eucalyptus aromas, slightly minty, then blueberry, red currant and vanilla for a classic Bordeaux style profile. Full taste, tense body, good acidity, slightly tannic and young, with great length.

90   **Price B**
Breganze Cabernet Sauvignon Palazzotto 2013
100% Cabernet Sauvignon grapes. Matures 1 year in barrique. Very intense and dark ruby red. Fruity and spicy notes of blueberry, black currant, pine resin, hints of vanilla. Full and agile taste, laid back and polite tannins, nice body, elegant and not heavy, good length in the finish.

MARION

Via Borgo, 2 - Località Marcellise
37036 San Martino Buon Albergo (VR)
Tel. +39 045 8740021
info@marionvini.it
www.marionvini.it

YEAR OF FOUNDATION 1994
NAME OF THE OWNER Stefano Campedelli
TOTAL BOTTLES PRODUCED 25,000
DIRECT SALES
VISITS TO THE WINERY - RESERVATION NEEDED
HECTARES OF VINEYARD 6

Marcellise is northeast of Verona, at the beginning of the Mezzane Valley, and while it is just outside the Valpolicella appellation this does not mean that its wines are in any way inferior. For sure not the wines of Stefano and Nicoletta Campedelli, a couple in life and on the job who offer us authentic artisanal wine gems.

90   **Price C**
Amarone della Valpolicella 2012
100% Cabernet Sauvignon grapes. Matures 1 year in barrique. Very intense and dark ruby red. Fruity

531

and spicy notes of blueberry, black currant, pine resin, hints of vanilla. Full and agile taste, laid back and polite tannins, nice body, elegant and not heavy, good length in the finish.

MASI - SEREGO ALIGHIERI

Via Monteleone, 26 - Frazione Gargagnago
37015 Sant'Ambrogio di Valpolicella (VR)
Tel. +39 045 6832511
masi@masi.it
www.masi.it
🅵 MasiWineExperience
🐦 @MrAmaroneMasi

YEAR OF FOUNDATION 1772
NAME OF THE OWNER Boscaini Family
TOTAL BOTTLES PRODUCED 4,200,000
DIRECT SALES
VISITS TO THE WINERY - RESERVATION NEEDED
HECTARES OF VINEYARD 640
HOSPITALITY

Masi owner Sandro Boscaini has one the most lucid minds in the word of Italian wine and has been able to turn Masi into a successful international brand with a top image. The Amarone Costasera, Campolongo di Torbe and Vaio Armaron from subsidiary Serego Alighieri are monuments of Italian winemaking.

 96   Price D
Amarone della Valpolicella Mazzano 2009

Blend of 70% Corvina, 25% Rondinella and 5% Molinara grapes. Matures 3 years in different size bottles. Deep and intense garnet ruby red. When you will taste it you will think that it is the prototype of Amarone you have always had in mind. Macerated black cherry, cocoa, light leather notes, tobacco, hints of Kirsch, licorice and After Eight (mint truffles). Powerful taste, warm, rich, nice body and very long persistence.

93   Price C
Amarone della Valpolicella Vajo Amaron 2010

Blend of 65% Corvina, 20% Rondinella, 15% Molinara grapes. Matures 3 years in cherry wood barrels. Intense garnet ruby red. Maybe less precise than the previews but typical and traditional. Maraschino, Mon Cherie truffle, light notes of cassia,

licorice and mint. Warm taste, slightly crimped by young tannins and great length.

92   Price C
Amarone della Valpolicella Costasera Riserva 2011

Blend of 70% Corvina and 30% Rondinella, Oseleta and Molinara grapes. Matures 40 months in different size barrels. Lively garnet ruby red. Smoky in the beginnins, spicy, modern, notes of wild cherry jam, cooca and vanilla. The taste is warm but agile, savory, rich and has great persistence.

89   Price B
Brolo di Campofiorin Oro 2012

Blend of 80% Corvina and 20% Oseleta and Rondinella grapes. Matures 2 years in big barrels. Lively garnet ruby. Enveloping notes, spicy and slightly smoky, very precise. Warm and tens, full, very persistent.

MENTI

Contrada Selva, 2a
36054 Montebello Vicentino (VI)
Tel. +39 0444 440117
info@mentivini.it
www.mentivini.it
🅵 Menti-Cantina-Vini

YEAR OF FOUNDATION 2002
NAME OF THE OWNER Agostino Menti
TOTAL BOTTLES PRODUCED 25,000
DIRECT SALES
VISITS TO THE WINERY
HECTARES OF VINEYARD 8
OLIVE OIL PRODUCTION

Agostino Menti is the heir of a family that began making wine in Gambellara, in the western part of Vicenza province, over a century ago. Together he works with his children Nicola and Michaela, a passionate sommeliers, who are ensuring the estate's continuity. Their Vin Santo di Gambellara is excellent and must be tasted.

 96   Price B
Gambellara Classico Vin Santo Nostra Historia 2010

100% Garganega grapes. Amber color with bright antique gold hues. Rare complexity for the nose bouquet: nut kernel and dates, very long and intense, then aromas of candied cedar, slightly toasted almond and hints of blond tobacco. Wonderful on the palate for its compact structure and elegance. The high acidity sustains the never sickly sweetness, even too easy to drink for its refined progression. Never-ending finish.

☐ 86   👍 Price A

Gambellara Classico Rivalonga 2014

100% Gambellara grapes. Stainless steel. Straw yellow with greenish hues. Intense in the nose with fresh lowery notes, lily of the valley and lavender. Then the classic white peach and hydrocarbon hint. Easy to drink, wide but salty and savory.

MERONI

Via Roma, 16a
37015 Sant'Ambrogio di Valpolicella (VR)
Tel. +39 045 6861783
Fax +39 045 7731238
info@vinimeroni.com
www.vinimeroni.com
f *ViniMeroni*
🐦 *@Amarone_M*

YEAR OF FOUNDATION 1935
NAME OF THE OWNER Carlo and Katia Meroni
TOTAL BOTTLES PRODUCED 50,000
DIRECT SALES
VISITS TO THE WINERY - RESERVATION NEEDED
HECTARES OF VINEYARD 15
OLIVE OIL PRODUCTION

Carlo and Katia Meroni inherited a family estate and work it with passion. The winery is in the town of Sant'Ambrogio, in the westernmost part of Valpolicella, between two cru: Sengia and Grola, the last hill in Valpolicella, where the soil is a chalk-clay mix. They only make wine with their own grapes and even if they adhere to organic methods they are still not certified.

◼ 93   Price B

Amarone della Valpolicella Classico Il Velluto Riserva 2008

100% Glera grapes. Charmat method. Matures 6 years in big barrels. Bright and average garnet red. Complex and elegant notes of dry plums, macerated cherry, tobacco and leather, dry violets and smoky hints. Long finish of macerated black cherry and cherry.

☐ 90   Price B

Recioto della Valpolicella Classico Il Velluto 2013

100% Glera grapes. Charmat method, 6 years in big barrels. Bright and average garnet red. Complex and elegant notes of dry plums, macerated cherry, tobacco and leather, dry violets and smoky hints. Long finish of macerated black cherry and cherry.

◼ 89   Price B

Valpolicella Classico Superiore Il Velluto 2009

Blend of Corvina, Rondinella and Molinara grapes dried for 1 month. Matures 24 months in big barrels. Bright ruby red with garnet hues. Notes of black cherry and dry plums, pomegranate and violet. Delicately warm on the palate, well extracted tannins and balanced acidity. The finish has notes of cherry and plums.

MONTE DEL FRÀ

Strada Custoza, 35
37066 Sommacampagna (VR)
Tel. +39 045 510490
🅢 monte.del.fra
info@montedelfra.it
www.montedelfra.it
f Monte-del-Frà

YEAR OF FOUNDATION 1958
NAME OF THE OWNER Eligio, Claudio and Marica Bonomo
TOTAL BOTTLES PRODUCED 1,000,000
DIRECT SALES
VISITS TO THE WINERY - RESERVATION NEEDED
HECTARES OF VINEYARD 172
OLIVE OIL PRODUCTION

This estate dates back to the 1950s and has 172 hectares of vineyards spread out between Lake Garda and Valpolicella Classica. The estate's style changes depending on the wine but is congruent with the terroir the grapes were grown in thanks to rigorous choice made in the vineyard and in the cellar to exalt the qualities of the cru.

◼ 89   👍 Price A

Bardolino 2014

Blend of 65% corvina, 30% Rondinella, 5% Sangiovese grapes. A part of it matures in stainless steel and a part in oak barrels. Bright ruby color. On the nose is intense with aromas of saffron, red fruit, cherry, fresh balckberry and an hint of floral. On the mouth is pleasant, full-flavored and juicy with a thick body and a tasty progression. On the finish is persuasive and persistant.

☐ 88   Price A
Custoza Superiore Ca' del Magro 2015

Blend of 40% Garganega, 20% Trebbiano Toscano, 15% Incrocio Manzoni, 5% Tocai Friulano, 10% Bianca Fernanda, chardonnay, risling Italico and 10% Malvasia grapes. Stainless steel only. Intense straw yellow color. On the nose is clean with aromas of yellow flowers and white peach with an hint of cedar and hydrocarbon. On the mouth is relaxed, pleasant, elegant with yellow notes on the finish. Tasty.

 85   👍 Price A
Bardolino Chiaretto 2015

Blend of 65% Corvina, 30% Rondinella and 5% Sangiovese grapes. Stainless steel only. Antique pinkish color with red gold riflexes. On the nose is clean and quite intese with aromas of mint, aromatic herbs and peach. On the mouth is fresh and with a great drinkability.

MONTE ZOVO

Località Zovo, 23/a
37013 Caprino Veronese (VR)
Tel. +39 045 7281301
info@montezovo.com
www.montezovo.com
🇫 MonteZovo
🐦 @monte_zovo

YEAR OF FOUNDATION 2000
NAME OF THE OWNER Diego Cottini
TOTAL BOTTLES PRODUCED 500,000
DIRECT SALES
VISITS TO THE WINERY - RESERVATION NEEDED
HECTARES OF VINEYARD 140
HOSPITALITY

More than an estate this could be defined as a constellation of wineries. Aside from Monte Zovo, in fact, there are Palazzo Maffei, with an adjoining Country House, Villa Annaberta and La Sagara. The wineries are in Caprino Veronese and San Pietro in Cariano, in other words respectively just to the south of Monte Baldo and in the middle of Valpolicella. There

are also vineyards in Val d'Illasi and in the district of Lugana. A truly striking winemaking reality.

■ 91   Price C
Amarone della Valpolicella 2012

80% Corvina grapes with a belnd of Rondinella and Orsoleta grapes. It matures for 28 months in Barrique and Tonneau. Intense garnet ruby color. On the nose is very young, heteral, penetrating with aromas of Maraschino, balck cherry, cocoa and aromatic wood. On the mouth is strong, still tannic rich, full-flavored and with a great duration.

■ 90   Price B
Ca' Linverno Rosso 2012

Blend of 75% Corvina and Corvinone grapes, 15% Rondinella and for the rest a belnd of Cabernet Sauvignon and Croatina grapes. It fades in cassette for 1 month then it mautres for 18 months in oak barrels of different sizes. Intense ruby color. On the nose is hetereal, alcoholic and full-flavored with aromas of black cherry under spirit and cocoa. On the mouth is full- bodied, with thick but polite tannins, warm and persistant.

☐ 88   Price B
Lugana Le Civaie 2012

100% Turbiana grapes. Stainless steel only on yeast for 4 months. Light straw yellow color. On the nose aromas of exotic fruits, pineapple at first, then lime, cedar and wildflowers. On the mouth is pleasant, savory, full-fodied, soft, easy to drink with a good duration.

MONTETONDO

Via San Lorenzo, 89
37038 Soave (VR)
Tel. +39 045 7680347
info@montetondo.it
www.montetondo.it
🇫 MonteTondo
🐦 @MonteTondo

YEAR OF FOUNDATION 1979
NAME OF THE OWNER Gino Magnabosco
TOTAL BOTTLES PRODUCED 200,000
DIRECT SALES
VISITS TO THE WINERY - RESERVATION NEEDED
HECTARES OF VINEYARD 32
HOSPITALITY
OLIVE OIL PRODUCTION

The Magnabosco family has been working their vineyards for three generations. Today, Gino and Luca offer some very interesting Soave Classico and while the top of the line is their Foscarin Slavinus, of which we're waiting the release of the 2015 vintage, still not available, but alsa their basic Soave Montetondo is very good and is priced right.

 90   👍 Price A

Soave Classico Montetondo 2015

100% Garganega grapes. Stainless steel only. Greenish yellow color. On the nose the fragrant and fruity notes such as cedar, lime, white peach and wildflowers are predominant. On the mouth is delightfuly savory, tense, agile, with a gorgeous drinkability and a young elegance. On the finish is light and pleasant. A very good wine, in is kind.

MUSELLA

Via Ferazzette, 2
37036 San Martino Buon Albergo (VR)
Tel. +39 045 973385
maddalena@musella.it
www.musella.it
 Musella-Winery-Relais

YEAR OF FOUNDATION 1995
NAME OF THE OWNER Emilio, Maddalena and Graziella Pasqua
TOTAL BOTTLES PRODUCED 250,000
DIRECT SALES
VISITS TO THE WINERY - RESERVATION NEEDED
HECTARES OF VINEYARD 40
HOSPITALITY
CERTIFIED ORGANIC VITICULTURE
CERTIFIED BIODYNAMIC VITICULTURE
OLIVE OIL PRODUCTION

A few kilometers from Verona there is an ancient and tree-filled 16th century estate inside a large natural park. This is where Maddelena Pasqua producers her excellent Amarone made with bio-dynamically-grown grapes. The results are very interesting as you can read here.

■ 91   Price B

Amarone della Valpolicella 2011

85% blend of Corvina and Corvinone, 15% Blend of Rondinella and Oseleta grapes. It matures for 2 years in tonneau. On the nose is complex with aro-

mas of Maraschino, cocoa, sour cherry jelly, smoky and spicy scents for a whole and modern nose profile. On the mouth is warm, full-flavored with a great acidity to support a nice full-bodied.

NINO FRANCO

Via Garibaldi, 147
31049 Valdobbiadene (TV)
Tel. +39 0423 972051
info@ninofranco.it
www.ninofranco.it
 ProseccoNinoFranco
🐦 *@NinoFranco1919*

YEAR OF FOUNDATION 1919
NAME OF THE OWNER Primo Franco
TOTAL BOTTLES PRODUCED 1,000,000
DIRECT SALES
VISITS TO THE WINERY - RESERVATION NEEDED
HECTARES OF VINEYARD 2.5

Primo Franco is a noble pioneer of Prosecco. It was he, in fact, who had his family's estate, created by his grandfather in 1919, concentrate on Glera grapes and the terroir of Valdobbiadene. A graduate of the Conegliano Veneto wine institute, he has since the 1970s dedicated himself with great enthusiasm to developing the estate's production and well as boosting its sales abroad.

 95   Price B

Grave di Stecca Brut 2012

100% Glera grapes. Long Charmant Method. Light golden yellow color with a fine and moderate perlage. On the nose is exceptionally complex in relation of the type of wine, elegant smoky aromas for the yeast lysis at first, then wisteria flowers, cedar, winter melon and medlar. On the mouth is sensual, creamy with a fine and well blended carbonic that teases the palate and the tongue, savory, tense, drinkable and with a great persistence.

回 92   👍 Price A

Conegliano Valdobbiadene Prosecco Superiore Vigneto della Riva di San Floriano Brut 2015

100% Glera grapes. Charmant method. Light yellow color with a quick and plentiful perlage. On the nose the aromas of yeast and yellow plum are predominant, then it presents scents of wisteria flowers, winter melon and cedar. On the mouth is lively, tense, acidic with an easy and pleasant finish.

 90   👍 Price A

Conegliano Valdobbiadene Prosecco Superiore Primo Franco Dry 2015

100% Glera grapes. Charmant method. Light yellow color with a slow plentiful perlage. On the nose is aromatic and fruity with aromas of white peach, jasmine and sweet citrus. On the mouth is slightly sugary, pleasant, full-flavored, savory and long.

★★

PASQUA

Via Belvedere, 135
37131 Verona (VR)
Tel. +39 045 8432111
info@pasqua.it
www.pasqua.it

YEAR OF FOUNDATION 1925
NAME OF THE OWNER Pasqua Family
TOTAL BOTTLES PRODUCED 14,500,000
DIRECT SALES
VISITS TO THE WINERY - RESERVATION NEEDED
HECTARES OF VINEYARD 200

Few great wineries in Italy are changing as much as the one of the Pasqua brothers, later the cousins. This important estate, which produces almost 15 million bottles a year, has been placed in the hands of the new generation composed of Giovanni, Riccardo and Cecilia, all in their 30s and 40s, and they are all very motivated and the innovations they have made are already producing results. Bravo.

■ 91   Price B

Amarone della Valpolicella Classico Famiglia Pasqua 2012

Blend of 60% Corvina, 25% Rondinela and 15% of Croatina, Corvinone and Oseleta grapes, 20 months in barrique and tonneau. Intense ruby color. On the nose is ethereal with aromas of kirsch, black cherry, cocoa, tobacco and dry plum. On the mouth is typical, warm, rich and with a great persistence.

■ 88   Price A

Valpolicella Ripasso Superiore Famiglia Pasqua 2014

Mostly Corvina grapes. It matures in barrique for

---

8 months. Lively ruby color. On the nose is intense with aroma of black cherry, Maraschino at first, then cocoa. On the mouth is full and polite, with an agile body not enormous, warm and with an average length.

PIEROPAN

Via Camuzzoni, 3
37038 Soave (VR)
Tel. +39 045 6190171
info@pieropan.it
www.pieropan.it
 pieropan.viticoltori.in.Soave
 @Pieropan_Soave

YEAR OF FOUNDATION 1880
NAME OF THE OWNER Leonildo Pieropan
TOTAL BOTTLES PRODUCED 500,000
DIRECT SALES
VISITS TO THE WINERY - RESERVATION NEEDED
HECTARES OF VINEYARD 45
CERTIFIED ORGANIC VITICULTURE
OLIVE OIL PRODUCTION

Nino and Teresita Pieropan are modern wine artisans. For the most part they produce Soave Classico, a stock version and the vineyard cru Calvarino and La Rocca. They are delicious white wines that can age and are offered at a very reasonable price given their high quality. Nino and Teresity acquired their Cellore d'Illasi estate in 1999 and today their sons Andrea and Dario are working there with their same passion and have decided to expand red wine production.

☐ Ⓖ 95   Price B

Soave Classico Calvarino 2014

Blend of 70% Garganega and 30% Soave grapes. It matures for almost 1 year on concrete vats on yeast. bright greenish yellow color. On the nose is complex and elegant with aromas of lime and cedar at first, the wildflowers, flint for the yeast lysis and white peach. On the mouth is not too full, tense and savory, gritty, with young style, exuberant and yet refined, deliciously to drink and with a great long finish.

☐ 93   👍 Price A

Soave Classico 2015

Blend of 90% Garganega and Trebbiano di Soave grapes. It matures for few months in concrete vats on yeast. greenish yellow color. On the nose is fragrant, clean, fine with aromas of lime, cedar, wildflowers, lemongrass and Renetta apple. On the mouth is tense, agile, juicy, savory, fresh, with a young style. On the finish is thin and persistent.

☐ 92   Price B

Soave Classico La Rocca 2014

100% Garganega grapes. It matures 1 year in oak barrels of different sizes on yeast. intense straw yellow color. On the nose is complex, with evolved scents of honey and mature fruits and aromas of flint and fresh almond. On the mouth is savory, agile, less powerful of other version but whole and persistence.

ALBINO PIONA

Località Casa Palazzina di Prabiano, 2
37069 Villafranca di Verona (VR)
Tel. +39 045 513055
info@albinopiona.it
www.albinopiona.it
 Azienda-Agricola-Albino-Piona

YEAR OF FOUNDATION 1893
NAME OF THE OWNER Fratelli Piona
TOTAL BOTTLES PRODUCED 350,000
DIRECT SALES
VISITS TO THE WINERY - RESERVATION NEEDED
HECTARES OF VINEYARD 77

Situated inside two important Veneto and Garda appellations, Custoza and Bardolino, this estate maintains a basic traditional approach but with some more modern approaches especially in regard to the land that has resulted in several wines that exalt the cru. Some modern concepts have also been applied in the winery and produced new and captivating results. Constant research and a propensity to experiment efficiently sum up the traditional philosophy handed down from father Albino Piona.

▣ 90   Price B

Gran Cuvée

Blend of Corvina, Garganega and Trebbiano grapes. Classic method with 60 months on yeast. intense straw yellow color with a very fine perlage. On the nose is clear with floral scents, an hint of red fruits, smoky aromas and very intense. On the mouth presents a good acidity, the perlage is still very fine and the body is elegant and juicy supported by the acidity.

■ 85   👍 Price A

Bardolino 2015

Blend of mainly Corvina with hints of Rondinella and Molinara grapes. Stainless steel only. Pale ruby color. On the nose is open with aromas of yellow peach and light cherry, saffron and flowers. On the mouth is elegant and soft, not very muscular with floral notes on the finish.

☐ 85   👍 Price A

Custoza 2015

Blend of 40% Garganega, 10% Trebbiano, 20% Tai, 20% Bianca Fernanda and 10% Riesling Renano, Pinot Bianco and Chardonnay grapes. Stainless steel only. Bright straw yellow color. On the nose is clear, intense with aromas of yellow flowers, tropical fruits and lavender. On the mouth is tasty with a great drinkability and a wide body.

POGGIO DELLE GRAZIE

Via Milano, 199
37014 Castelnuovo Del Garda (VR)
Tel. +39 347 8608785
info@poggiodellegrazie.com
www.poggiodellegrazie.it
 poggiodellegrazie

YEAR OF FOUNDATION 2014
NAME OF THE OWNER Massimo and Stefano Brutti
TOTAL BOTTLES PRODUCED 60,000
DIRECT SALES
VISITS TO THE WINERY - RESERVATION NEEDED
HECTARES OF VINEYARD 15

The name Poggio della Grazie derives from a small chapel the local population built on a small hill (poggio) near Castelnuovo del Garda for having avoided destruction during the Second World War. It is here that this winery was created in 2014 by siblings Stefano and Massimo Brutti when they decided to stop selling their grapes and to bottle their own wine. Their 15 hectares of vineyards are spread out in the areas of Bardolino and Custoza and produce some 60,000 bottles a year. The vines are trained in different ways and the winery is modern.

■ 87   👍 Price A

Bardolino 2015

Blend of 70% Corvina and 30% Rondinella grapes. Stainless steel. Bright ruby color. On the nose is com-

plex with a light reduction. Aromas of pink and black pepper, red fruits, cherry and violet. On the mouth is thick with a good acidity, tasty progression. On the finish is persistent with a nice taste of dark spices.

%%% 87   👍 Price A
Bardolino Chiaretto 2015

Blend of 70% Corvina and 30% Rondinella grapes. Stainless steel on yeast for 3 months. Bright antic pink color. On the nose is clear with intense floral notes and aromas of watermelon with an hint of spices. On the mouth is elegant, relaxed, complex. The body is wide but tasty and very good to drink.

★★
PRÀ

Via della Fontana, 31
37032 Monteforte d'Alpone (VR)
Tel. +39 045 7612125
info@vinipra.it
www.vinipra.it
f *Azienda-Agricola-Prà*

YEAR OF FOUNDATION 1980
NAME OF THE OWNER Graziano Prà
TOTAL BOTTLES PRODUCED 220,000
DIRECT SALES
VISITS TO THE WINERY - RESERVATION NEEDED
HECTARES OF VINEYARD 20

Graziano Pra' was born with a vocation for white wine which he fulfills cultivating Garganega in Soave, a passion he inherited from his father. But this is only one side of the estate's productive coin because he also has a vineyard in Valpolicella, La Morandina, which produces a red Graziano that he defines as the "new Burgundy".

☐ 93   Price B
Soave Classico Monte Grande 2015

Blend of 85% Garganega and 15% Trebbiano di Soave grapes. It matures for few months in barrique. Bright straw yellow color. On the nose is attractive and fruity with aromas of cedar, fresh almond, white peach, grapefruit and wildflower. On the mouth is savory, warm, good body and great persistence on the finish.

☐ 90   👍 Price A
Soave Classico Otto 2015

Blend of 85% Garganega and 15% Trebbiano di

Soave grapes. Stainless steel only. On the nose is fragrant and fruity, clean, whole with specific aromas of cedar and white peach at first, then hints of lime, wildflowers and light mint. On the mouth is tense and agile, pleasantly savory, fresh and easy to drink, with a thin but long finish.

★★★
GIUSEPPE QUINTARELLI

Via Cerè, 1
37024 Negrar (VR)
Tel. +39 045 7500016
giuseppe.quintarelli@tin.it

YEAR OF FOUNDATION Early 1900
NAME OF THE OWNER Quintarelli Family
TOTAL BOTTLES PRODUCED 60,000
DIRECT SALES
VISITS TO THE WINERY - RESERVATION NEEDED
HECTARES OF VINEYARD 12

Giuseppe Quintarelli is no longer with us but his presence is still felt in the winery, where his heirs are seeking to maintain a great tradition that involves not just the wine but the image of the 'Supreme Amarone Craftman'. It is always an emotional experience to wander through the estate's historic cellar, amid the memories and old bottles that are still splendidly conserved and full of potential and imaginable pleasure. Not all the varieties of wine are regularly bottled given that only the vintages consider up to standard can carry the estate's label.

▪ 🍷 97   Price E
Recioto della Valpolicella 2004

Blend of 55% Corvina, 30% Rondinella , Cabernet Sauvignon, Croatina, Nebbiolo and Sangiovese grapes. It matures in medium size oak barrels. Very intense red color, almost transparent. On the nose amazing scents of soft spices, cinnamon, juniper, dates, but also aromas of milk chocolate, bark and china. On the mouth is gorgeous for strength and personality, never sickly and well supported by a pulsating acidity.

■ 🍷 96   Price E
Amarone della Valpolicella 2007

Blend of 55% Corvina, 30% Rondinella, Cabernet, Croatina, Nebbiolo and Sangiovese grapes. It matures in big oak barrels for 7 years, then 36 months in bottles. Intense but not too concentrated red col-

or, with little orange reflexes. On the nose is aristo-cratic and elegant, even if still chained by a matter that is going to be revealed with the years, it presents aromas of chocolate, fine herbs, licorice and flint. On the mouth is powerful but very big with a great balance between acidity and tannin. An unusual Amarone that is been create on the nobility of the structure.

| 94 | Price E |
Alzéro 2006
Bland of Cabernet Franc, Cabernet Sauvignon and Merlot is different quantity depending by the year. It matures 30 months in barrique and 30 months in big oak barrels. Relativly lighter color respect the standard of this wine. On the nose is definitely eucalyptus with no pyridine notes and extremely clean even if very warm. It presents aromas of underbrush berries jelly, cut tobacco, juniper berries. On the mouth is warm but virtuous with very thick tannins and a great persistence. The most elegant Alzero ever.

| 89 | Price C |
Valpolicella Superiore 2008
Blend of 55% Corvina, 30% Rondinella , Cabernet, Croatina, Nebbiolo and Sangiovese grapes. It matures in medium size oak barrels. The color is almost lunar, with is crepuscular garnet red. On the nose is still a little compressed cause of his youth, it presents aromas of soft beech wood, leather, salt with a light spiciness, not too evident and an attractive aroma of nutmeg. On the mouth is still hard and need to be softened, supported by an austere but firm matter. A very conceptual Valpolicella.

ROCCOLO GRASSI

Via San Giovanni di Dio, 19
37030 Mezzane Di Sotto (VR)
Tel. +39 045 8880089
 roccolo.grassi
info@roccolograssi.it
www.roccolograssi.it
 roccolograssi

YEAR OF FOUNDATION 1996
NAME OF THE OWNER Marco and Francesca Sartori
TOTAL BOTTLES PRODUCED 48,000
VISITS TO THE WINERY - RESERVATION NEEDED
HECTARES OF VINEYARD 14

The estate run by Marco Sartori is now firmly among the best in Valpolicella in regard to quality. In his revamped cellar he keeps and ages his extraordinary wines that are the product of technically sensible winemaking as well as a terroir that has a vocation to product bold yet balanced reds. This is especially true in the area of Rocco Grassi, which gives the estate's its name, which has a soil of volcanic-basalt origin.

| 96 | Price C |
Amarone della Valpolicella 2012
Blend of 60% Corvina, 20% Rondinella, 15% Corvinone and 5% Croatina grapes. It matures for 26 months in semi-new barrique. Bright and intense ruby red color. On the nose is wide and rich with aromas of radish, blackberry jelly, bitter cocoa, a good blend of spices and a great eucalyptus note. On the mouth is powerful but very elegant, warm, soft and full-flavored ,kept together by a very rare equilibrium for this kind of wine. One of the best interpretation of the year.

| 91 | Price B |
Valpolicella Superiore 2012
Blend of 60% Corvina, 20% Rondinella, 15% Corvinone and 5% Croatina grapes. It matures for 20 months in 15-22 hl oak barrels. Intense garnet red color. On the nose aromas of cherry, morello, leather and hides. On the mouth is very rich with very fine but remarked tannins. Almost a little Amarone, for the structure, but more austere of the 2011 one.

| ☐ 90 | 👍 Price A |
Soave La Broia 2014
100% Garganega grapes from La Broia vineyard. 80% matures in new barrique and 20% in stainless steel, then matures in old barrique. Pale straw yellow color. On the nose intense aromas of flowers, broom, walnut and ginger. On the mouth is tense, fresh with a great body and a great drinkability strain. A masterly interpretation of a very favorable year.

RUGGERI

Via Prà Fontana, 4
31049 Valdobbiadene (TV)
Tel. +39 0423 9092
Fax +39 0423 973304
ruggeri@ruggeri.it
www.ruggeri.it
 RuggeriProseccoDiValdobbiadene

YEAR OF FOUNDATION 1950
NAME OF THE OWNER Paolo, Giustino and Isabella Bisol
TOTAL BOTTLES PRODUCED 1,000,000
DIRECT SALES
VISITS TO THE WINERY - RESERVATION NEEDED
HECTARES OF VINEYARD 17

Giustino Bisol founded this winery in 1950 and it was first located in Santo Stefano before moving to Valdobbiadene where it is today. The Bisol family can be considered as the forefathers of Prosecco and can boast a centuries-old tradition as well as roots in local wine culture. In Chartice or in Gardizze, as the area of what is now called Cartizze was once called, documents show that the Bisol family was already growing grapes in 1542. Paolo Bisol runs the estate today together with his children Giustino and Isabella.

🔲 92   Price B

Conegliano Valdobbiadene Prosecco Superiore Giustino B Extra Dry 2015

100% Grera grapes. Charmat method. Light straw yellow color with a persistant and fine perlage. On the nose aromas of yeast, bread crust at first, then wisteria, lavender, white peach, lime and cedar. On the mouth is lively, creamy, soft and yet agile, slightly sugary and very pleasant.

🔲 90   Price B

Conegliano Valdobbiadene Prosecco Superiore Vecchie Viti Brut 2015

Blend of mainly Glera grapes with hints of Verdiso, Bianchetta and Perera grapes. Charmat method. Light straw yellow color with a quick fine perlage. On the nose aromas of yeast at first, then floral and citrusy notes such as wildflower and cedar. Fume' hints. On the mouth is tense and agile supported by the acidity, creamy with a not too heavy body and with a good length.

SANTA MARGHERITA

Via Ita Marzotto, 8
30025 Fossalta di Portogruaro (VE)
Tel. +39 0421 246111
santamargherita@santamargherita.com
www.santamargherita.com
 ViniSantaMargherita
 ViniSMargherita

YEAR OF FOUNDATION 1935
NAME OF THE OWNER Marzotto Family
TOTAL BOTTLES PRODUCED 13,500,000
DIRECT SALES
VISITS TO THE WINERY - RESERVATION NEEDED
HECTARES OF VINEYARD 50

Textile tycoon Count Gaetano Marzotto founded Santa Margherita in 1935. It was conceived as a "humanist enterprise", as the Count defined it, designed to create a new conception of farming in which the product, the typicity of the grape and the land it was grown in combine into a single entity. The epic story of Pinot Grigio began here in 1960 when this estate began to produce a wine that in a few years would become the most famous Italian white wine in the world, creating a fad that 50 years later is still going strong. Santa Margherita is currently the leading producer of Pinot Grigio in Italy and elsewhere and its 'mother' estate is Villanova di Fossalta di Portogruaro. The Santa Margherita 'empire', however, also includes the estates Lamole di Lamole, Vistarenni and Tenuta di Sassoregale in Tuscany, Kettemeir in Alto Adige and Terreliade in Sicily.

⬜ 93   👍 Price A

Alto Adige Pinot Grigio Impronta del Fondatore 2015

100% Pinot Grigio grapes. Stainless steel only on yeast for few months. Nright straw yellow color. This is the wine that most of the consumers all around the world believe it to be a Quality Pinot Grigio. On the nose aromas of pear Williams, cedar, white peach, light almond and wildflowers. On the mouth is savory and agile, very easy drinking but not trivial, fresh, with a good body, tense by the acidity and with a good persistence.

🔲 88   Price B

Conegliano Valdobbiadene Prosecco Sup. 52 Rive di Refrontolo Brut 2015

100% Glera grapes. Charmat method with 3 months on yeast. light straw yellow color with a fine and quick perlage. On the nose is quite complex with aromas of yeast at first, then wisteria flowers and white peach. On the mouth is lively, savory, fresh, thin and easy drinking.

⬛ 86   Price A

Lison Pramaggiore Malbech Impronta del Fondatore 2013

100% Malbech grapes. It matures in barrique for

10 months. Dark ruby color with purpleish reflexes. On the nose aromas of blueberry, black currant, pine resin, hints of mint and vanilla, refined the aromatic profile. On the mouth is young with still lively tannins, good acidity, good body and a good length on the finish.

SANTA SOFIA

Via Ca' Dedé, 61 - Frazione Pedemonte di Valpolicella
37029 San Pietro in Cariano (VR)
Tel. +39 045 7701074
Fax +39 045 7703222
info@santasofia.com
www.santasofia.com
 SantaSofiaWines
 @SANTASOFIAwines

YEAR OF FOUNDATION **1811**
NAME OF THE OWNER **Giancarlo Begnoni**
TOTAL BOTTLES PRODUCED **550,000**
DIRECT SALES
VISITS TO THE WINERY - RESERVATION NEEDED
HECTARES OF VINEYARD **38**
OLIVE OIL PRODUCTION

The estate's headquarters is in a Palladian villa in Pedemonte, a clear indication that this is an historic estate. For almost 50 years it has belonged to Giancarlo Begnoni who now runs it with his children Luciano and Patrizia. Needless to say the estate's style is classic and traditional but it could not be anything different.

 93   Price C
Amarone della Valpolicella Classico Gioè 2011

Blend of 70% Corvina and Corvinone, 25% Rondinella and Molinara grapes. Fading of the grapes for 100 days at first and then it mautres for 2 years in oak barrels and 18 months in barrique. Garnet ruby color. On the nose is powerful with aromas of black cherry compote, cocoa, spices and a eucalyptus hint. On the mouth is elegant, complete and persistent.

 91   Price B
Amarone della Valpolicella Classico 2011

Blend of 70% Corvina and Corvinone, 25% Rondinella and Molinara. It matures for 3 years in big oak barrels. Garnet ruby color. On the nose is rich and intense with aromas that go from black cherry to chocolate, and scents of spices and an hint of eucalyptus note. On the mouth is perfect for the refinement, with a balanced structure and thin tannins.

 85   Price A
Valpolicella Classico 2014

Blend of 70% Corvina and Corvinone, 30% Rondinella grapes. It matures in stainless steel only. Ruby color. On the nose is fresh and light with aromas of flowers and red fruits. On the palate is quick pleasantly fruity and easy drinking.

SANTI

Via Ungheria, 33
37031 Illasi (VR)
Tel. +39 045 6269600
Fax +39 045 7235772
santi@giv.it
www.carlosanti.it

YEAR OF FOUNDATION **1843**
NAME OF THE OWNER **Gruppo Italiano Vini**
TOTAL BOTTLES PRODUCED **1,200,000**
DIRECT SALES
VISITS TO THE WINERY - RESERVATION NEEDED
HECTARES OF VINEYARD **70**

This famous and historic winery has for decades been part of Gruppo Italiano Vini. Attilio Carlo Santi started to produce typical wines of the Verona area in the first half of XIX century, selecting the best grapes from his vineyards. From then on, it offers a vast range of wines the best being their Amarone Proemio and Valpolicella Ripasso Solane. Santi has three vinification cellars at Tenuta Pule, San Pietro Incariano and Tenuta Preella, a maturation cellar and a bottling plant equipped with state-of-the-art technology at Pedemonte.

    89   Price B
Amarone della Valpolicella Classico 2011

Blend of 75% Corvina and 25% Rondinella grapes. It matures in oak barrel for 24 months and 12 months in barrique. Dark ruby color. On the nose aromas of plum jelly and black cherry at first, then spices and an hint of cocoa. On the mouth is soft, warm with an always adequate body.

88   Price A

Valpolicella Ripasso Classico Superiore Solane 2014

Blend of 70% Corvina and 30% Rondinella grapes. It matures for 18 months in oak barrels. On the nose aromas of violet and black cherry with a thin background of spices and eucalyptus notes. On the mouth is soft with complete tannins, alcohol very well balanced by the evident freshness.

★★
SERAFINI & VIDOTTO

Via Luigi Carrer, 8
31949 Nervesa Della Battaglia (TV)
Tel. +39 0422 773281
Fax +39 0422 879069
serafinievidotto@serafinievidotto.com
www.serafinievidotto.it
 serafinivididotto

YEAR OF FOUNDATION 1986
NAME OF THE OWNER Francesco Serafini and Antonello Vidotto
TOTAL BOTTLES PRODUCED 200,000
DIRECT SALES
VISITS TO THE WINERY - RESERVATION NEEDED
HECTARES OF VINEYARD 25

Francesco Serafini and Antonello Vidotto are the driving forces behind this Nervesa della Battaglia estate, in the area of Montello Colli Asolani DOC. It is situated in an historic place surrounded by the ruins of the abbey that had hosted Giovanni Della Casa when he wrote his Galateo: The Rules of Polite Behavior between 1551 and 1555. Here the two enologist-farmers produce some excellent reds.

95   Price B

Montello Colli Asolani Il Rosso dell'Abazia 2011

Blend of 45% Cabernet Sauvignon, 30% Merlot and 25% Cabernet Franc grapes. It matures for 2 years in barrique. Concentrated and dark ruby color. On the nose present the classic "Neo Bordolese" aromatic profile with aromas of blueberry, black currant, vanilla, cocoa, an hint of mint, pine resin and cardamom. On the mouth is tense and full-bodied, with polite tannins, savory, warm, elegant and with a great length.

88   Price A

Asolo Prosecco Superiore Bollicine di Prosecco Extra Dry 2015

100% Glera grapes. Charmat method. Light yellow color with a plentiful and quick perlage. On the nose is very varietal with aromas of wisteria flowers and lavender at first, then yeast and little hints of white peach. On the mouth is lively, pleasantly savory, easy and delicious to drink with a discreet and thin length.

LINO SORDATO

Via Contrada Selva, 26
36054 Montebello Vicentino (VI)
Tel. +39 0444 649156
Fax +39 0444 649156
sordato@sordatovini.it
www.sordatovini.it
 sordato.vini

YEAR OF FOUNDATION 1938
NAME OF THE OWNER Sordato Family
TOTAL BOTTLES PRODUCED 60,000
DIRECT SALES
VISITS TO THE WINERY - RESERVATION NEEDED
HECTARES OF VINEYARD 25

The estate was founded by Lino's father Basilio who acquired his first vineyards in Selva di Montebello in 1938. Lino then took over and already in 1970 he joined the association to protect and promote Gambellara wine. It is now in the hands of the fourth generation with grandson Lino who, like his grandfather, continues to produce traditional wines with pride and passion: Gambellara, Gambellara Classico, Recioto and Vin Santo.

87   Price A

Gambellara Classico 2015

100% Garganega grapes. Stainless steel only. Pale straw yellow color. On the nose is clean and intense with aromas of citrus and green such as asparagus, light hydrocarbon and eucalyptus and then the classic peach. On the mouth the impact is average with a wide but tasty weft, very pleasant with hints of pink pepper.

SORELLE BRONCA

Via Martini, 20 - Frazione Colbertaldo
31020 Vidor (TV)
Tel. +39 0423 987201
Fax +39 0423 989329
 sorellebronca
info@sorellebronca.com
www.sorellebronca.com
sorellebroncawines
@SorelleBronca

YEAR OF FOUNDATION 1959
NAME OF THE OWNER Ersiliana and Antonella
Bronca
TOTAL BOTTLES PRODUCED 280,000
DIRECT SALES
VISITS TO THE WINERY - RESERVATION NEEDED
HECTARES OF VINEYARD 25
OLIVE OIL PRODUCTION

Ersiliana and Antonella are the Sorelle Bronca (Bronca Sisters), legendary Prosecco producers in Colbertaldo di Vidor, where they have lovely vineyards on steep hills between San Pietro di Feletto and Vidor. They make several versions of Valdobbiadene Prosecco Superiore and here we present the most interesting.

---

90   Price B

Conegliano Valdobbiadene Prosecco Superiore Particella 68 Brut

Blend of 90% Glera grapes with hints of Bianchetta and Perera. Charmat method. Light yellow color with a quick ant thick perlage. On the nose is very fragrant with aromas of bread crust at first, then wisteria flowers, lavender, lime, aromatic herbs. On the mouth is tense, with a good acidic component, creamy, lively and very pleasant. On the finish is savory and thin.

---

89   Price A

Conegliano Valdobbiadene Prosecco Superiore Extra Dry

100% Glera grapes. Charmat method. Light yellow color with a fine and persistent perlage. On the nose is more floral with aromas of hawthorn, wisteria and lavender at first, then yellow plum and winter melon. On the mouth is balanced, with sugary hints, lively,, creamy, savory and with a good persistence.

★★
SPERI

Via Fontana, 14 - Frazione Pedemonte
37029 San Pietro in Cariano (VR)
Tel. +39 045 7701154
Fax +39 045 7704994
info@speri.com
www.speri.com
speri.viticoltori

YEAR OF FOUNDATION 1874
NAME OF THE OWNER Speri Family
TOTAL BOTTLES PRODUCED 350,000
DIRECT SALES
VISITS TO THE WINERY - RESERVATION NEEDED
HECTARES OF VINEYARD 50

This is a classic estate but one that cautiously adds a sensible touch of innovation to keep it up with the times. It is rigorously family-run with Alberto Speri in charge of the winery and the production of its many fine wines. The most prestigious are from the Vigneto Monte Sant'Urbano in the town of Fumane, a prestigious cru in the area.

---

93   Price C

Amarone della Valpolicella Classico Vigneto Monte Sant'Urbano 2012

Blend of 70% Corvina and Corvinone, 25% Rondinella and Molinara grapes. It matures for 30 months in oak barrels of different sizes. Garnet ruby color. On the nose is firm and elegant with aromas of black currant, sour cherry, pepper, licorice and aromatic herbs. On the mouth is refined, powerful with thin tannins. Persistent.

---

90   Price B

Valpolicella Classico Superiore Vigneto Monte Sant'Urbano 2013

Blend of 70% Corvina and Corvinone, 25% Rondinella and Molinara grapes. It matures fir 18 months in tonneau. Dense ruby color. On the nose is powerful with aromas of violet, black cherry, blueberry, alfalfa and toasted scent hints. On the mouth is soft and yet savory, warm and full-bodied.

---

89   Price B

Recioto della Valpolicella Classico La Roggia 2013

Blend of 70% Corvina and 25% Rondinella grapes. It matures in barrique for 2 years. Deep ruby color.

On the nose present extensive aromas of black cherry and plums at first, then chocolate with an hint of eucalyptus scent. On the mouth is sweet, savory with velvety tannins.

★★
SUAVIA

Via Centro, 14 - Frazione Fittà
37038 Soave (VR)
Tel. +39 045 7675089
Fax +39 045 7675991
info@suavia.it
www.suavia.it
 SuaviaVini
 @SuaviaWine

YEAR OF FOUNDATION 1982
NAME OF THE OWNER Valentina Tessari
TOTAL BOTTLES PRODUCED 130,000
DIRECT SALES
VISITS TO THE WINERY - RESERVATION NEEDED
HECTARES OF VINEYARD 15
OLIVE OIL PRODUCTION

An all-girl winery run by Meri, Valentina and Alessandra Tessari, daughters of founders Giovanni and Rosetta. They produce white wines from Garganega and Trebbiano di Soave distinguished by the way they convey the territory.

☐ 91   Price B
Soave Classico Monte Carbonare 2014
100% Garganega grapes. It matures for 15 months in stainless steel on yeast. straw yellow color. On the nose it presents smoky aromas due ti the yeast lysis that is prevalent at first (The producer says that it smell like the wet earth from the first rain in autumn.) , then cedar and lime and flowery notes on the background. On the mouth is tense, acidic, gritty, thinner than other version with a light and agile body and thin finish and a good length.

★
TAMELLINI

Via Tamellini, 4
37038 Soave (VR)
Tel. +39 045 7675328
Fax +39 045 7675328
piofrancesco.tamellini@tin.it

YEAR OF FOUNDATION 1998
NAME OF THE OWNER Gaetano and Pio Francesco Tamellini
TOTAL BOTTLES PRODUCED 250,000
DIRECT SALES
VISITS TO THE WINERY - RESERVATION NEEDED
HECTARES OF VINEYARD 23

The winery of Pio Francesco and Gaetano Tamellini is among those that has seen the most important improvements in producing Soave Classico and today they are consistently among the best for quality.

☐ 90   👍 Price A
Soave Classico 2015
100% Garganega grapes. Stainless steel only. Greenish yellow color. On the nose is delineated and fragrant, whole and clear with aromas of fruits and flowers, scents of wildflowers and eucalyptus notes. On the mouth is deliciously savory, easy to drink, good body , balanced and with a good persistence.

★★
TEDESCHI

Via G. Verdi, 4 - Frazione Pedemonte
37029 San Pietro in Cariano (VR)
Tel. +39 045 7701487
tedeschi@tedeschiwines.com
www.tedeschiwines.com
 TedeschiWines
 @TedeschiWines

YEAR OF FOUNDATION 1630
NAME OF THE OWNER Tedeschi Family
TOTAL BOTTLES PRODUCED 500,000
DIRECT SALES
VISITS TO THE WINERY - RESERVATION NEEDED
HECTARES OF VINEYARD 46
OLIVE OIL PRODUCTION

The Tedeschi family has owned vineyards in Valpolicella since 1630 and have been making wine for Corvina, Rondinella and Molinara grapes. Today they organically cultivate their vineyards and some even adhere to bio-dynamic dictates, even if this is not certified, with the vines trained on the pergola veronese. Among the best wines is the cru Capitel Monte Olmi, made from grapes from the vineyard of the same name in Pedemont Valpolicella.

■ 🇬 96   Price D

Amarone della Valpolicella Classico La Fabriseria Riserva 2011

Blend of 35% Corvina, 30% Corvinone, 30% Rondinella and 5% Oseleta grapes. It matures for 4 years in oak barrel. Very dark ruby color. On the nose is more toasted then Monte Olmi, is intense with aromas of black cherry and cocoa. On the mouth is full-bodied, soft, powerful, fruity and very long.

■ 94   Price C

Amarone della Valpolicella Classico Capitel Monte Olmi Riserva 2010

Blend of 30% Corvina, 30% Corvinone, 10% Oseleta and the rest Negrara, Dindarella, Croatina and Forselina grapes. It matures for 4 years in oak barrel. Deep ruby color. On the nose is satisfied with his elegant aromas of black cherry, currant, spices, smoky hints and cocoa. On the mouth is delicious with thin tannins and velvety softness.

 91   Price B

Recioto della Valpolicella Classico Capitel Fontana 2011

Blend of 35% Corvina, 30% Corvinone, 30% Rondinella and Rossignola. It matures for 24 months in oak barrels. Garnet ruby color. On the nose is complex with aromas of black cherry under spirit, blueberry, cakes and toasted scents. On the mouth is sweet, pleasantly tannic, balanced and fruity.

■ 90   Price B

Valpolicella Superiore Maternigo 2013

Blend of 40% Corvina, 30% Corvinone and 30% Rondinella grapes. The grapes are ripeness and the mature in oak barrel for 14 months. Ruby color. On the nose is eucalyptus and fruity with aromas of black cherry and spices. On the mouth is soft, balanced with silky tannins.

★★

TENUTA SANT'ANTONIO

Via Ceriani, 23
37030 Colognola ai Colli (VR)
Tel. +39 045 7650383
info@tenutasantantonio.it
www.tenutasantantonio.it
 TenutaSantAntonio
🐦 *@TenutaSAntonio*

YEAR OF FOUNDATION 1995
NAME OF THE OWNER Castagnedi Family

TOTAL BOTTLES PRODUCED 700,000
DIRECT SALES
VISITS TO THE WINERY - RESERVATION NEEDED
HECTARES OF VINEYARD 100

This is an up-and-coming winery thanks to the experience the four brothers gained working as consultants at other estates. Their top wines are Amarone Campi dei Gigli, a truly great wine, and a surprising Amarone without added solfites. It's the flagship of Télos project, which aims to develop a production process characterized by the analysis of the must of each vineyard, by the exclusion of copper as a plant protection element and the choice not to add sulfites during the wine making.

■ 🇬 95   Price C

Amarone della Valpolicella Campo dei Gigli 2012

Blend of 70% Corvina, 25% Rondinella and 5% Croatina and Oseleta grapes. It matures for 3 years in tonneau. Very dark ruby color. On the nose is firm and powerful with eucalyptus notes at first, then aromas of syrup black cherry, chocolate, spices and tobacco. On the mouth it present a full-bodied, it is dense and with velvety tannins.

■ 91   Price B

Amarone della Valpolicella Télos 2011

Blend of 70% Corvina, 25% Rondinella and 5% Croatina and Oseleta grapes. It matures 16 months in oak barrels. Clear ruby color. On the nose is complex and floral with aromas of red fruit jelly, spices, and gunpowder. On the mouth is balanced with a clear softness, delicate tannins and an evident full-bodied.

□ 90   👍 Price A

Soave Vecchie Vigne 2014

100% Garganega grapes. It matures for 6 months in tonneau. Bright gold color. On the nose is intense with aromas of citrus and tropical fruit at first, then peach, apricot and a more sweet finish of cookie. On the mouth is soft, savory, freash and pleasant. Fruity on the finish.

TENUTA SANT'ANNA

Via P. L. Zovatto, 71
30020 Annone Veneto (VE)
Tel. +39 0422 864511
Fax +39 0422 864164

info@tenutasantanna.it
www.tenutasantanna.it

YEAR OF FOUNDATION 1972
NAME OF THE OWNER Genagricola
TOTAL BOTTLES PRODUCED 2,500,000
DIRECT SALES
VISITS TO THE WINERY - RESERVATION NEEDED
HECTARES OF VINEYARD 140

546

This estate represents the debut of the Assicurazioni Generali insurance giant in winemaking. It is visible from the Venice-Trieste motorway in the heart of the Lison Pramaggiore appellation that runs along the coast and into the hinterland of the province of Vicenza to the east. The vineyards extend endlessly and production is vast and reliable, as one would expect from an insurance group.

☐ 86   👍 Price A
Lison Classico 2015

100% Tai (Tocai Friulano) grapes. Stainless steel only. Light straw yellow color. On the nose fragrant aromas of yeast with notes of Golden apple, peppermint and light almond. On the mouth is simple, savory, polite and with a great drinkability.

☐ 85   👍 Price A
Pinot Grigio 2015

100% Pinot Grigio grapes. Stainless steel only. Light golden yellow color. On the nose is fruity and varietal with aroma of pear Williams that are whole and pleasant. On the mouth is savory, fresh, easy to drink with a thin finish.

☐ 85   👍 Price A
Traminer 2015

100% Traminer Aromatico grapes. Stainless steel only. Light golden yellow color. On the nose is varietal with aromas of rose, lychee and yellow peach. On the mouth is savory, soft, tense with a discrete persistence on the finish.

★

TRABUCCHI D'ILLASI

Località Monte Tenda, 3
37031 Illasi (VR)
Tel. +39 045 7833233
Fax +39 045 6528112
 trabucchi.illasi

azienda.agricola@trabucchidillasi.it
www.trabucchidillasi.it
f *trabucchi.dillasi*
🐦 *@TrabucchidIllas*

YEAR OF FOUNDATION 1924
NAME OF THE OWNER Giuseppe Trabucchi
TOTAL BOTTLES PRODUCED 150,000
DIRECT SALES
VISITS TO THE WINERY - RESERVATION NEEDED
HECTARES OF VINEYARD 25
CERTIFIED ORGANIC VITICULTURE
OLIVE OIL PRODUCTION

Val d'Illasi is northeast of Verona outside the classic area of Valpolicella and on the border with the Soave appellation. Contrary to what one may think, this area produces some Amarone that have rare elegance. Giuseppe Trabucchi is one of those who produces such wines, assisted by the expert winemaker Franco Bernabei.

■ 🗲 95   Price D
Amarone della Valpolicella Riserva Cent'anni 1907 Alberto Trabucchi 2008

Blend of 40% Corvina, 40% Corvinone, 10% Rondinella, 5% Croatina and Oseleta grapes. It matures in barrique and oak barrels for 30 months. Very intense ruby color. On the nose presents very intense and complex aromas of fruit jelly, cocoa, licorice and tobacco. On the mouth is soft, complete, balanced, sensual and with a long persistence.

▪ 91   Price B
Recioto della Valpolicella 2007

Blend of 40% Corvina, 40% Corvinone, 10% Rondinella and Oseleta grapes. It matures for a long time in barrique. Garnet color. On the nose is wide and intense with aromas of blackberry jelly, violet, cocoa, spices and eucalyptus notes. On the mouth is sweet nd full-bodied with soft tannins and persistent.

■ 88   Price B
Valpolicella Superiore Terra del Cereolo 2008

Blend of 40% Corvina, 40% Corvinone, 15% Rondinella and Oseleta grapes. It does a short fading of the grapes and then it matures in barrique for 18 months, deep ruby color. On the nose aromas of black cherry, currant and violet at first, then spices, very intense all together. On the mouth is savory, full-bodied with thin tannins.

VENTURINI

Via Semonte, 20 - Località San Floriano
37029 San Pietro in Cariano (VR)
Tel. +39 045 7701331
info@viniventurini.com
www.viniventurini.com

YEAR OF FOUNDATION **1963**
NAME OF THE OWNER **Daniele, Mirco and Giuseppina Venturini**
TOTAL BOTTLES PRODUCED **90,000**
DIRECT SALES
VISITS TO THE WINERY - RESERVATION NEEDED
HECTARES OF VINEYARD **12**

Siblings Daniele, Mirco and Giuseppina Venurini are now in charge of their family's winery and are continuing a tradition that has existed for 50 years and involved three generations. It is located in San Floriano, a neighborhood in San Pietro in Cariano, but is not far from Negrar. Here they produce their Amarone, first among them Campomasua, which are good and affordable.

93 Price D
Amarone della Valpolicella Classico Riserva 2005

Blend of 70% Corvina, 25% rondinella and 5% Molinara grapes. It matures for 60 months in oak barrel. Garnet ruby color. On the nose is powerful and complex with aromas of black cherry, cocoa, tobacco and very strong eucalyptus scents. On the mouth is soft, whole, greedy, fruity with thin tannins. Long persistence.

88 Price B
Recioto della Valpolicella Classico Le Brugnine 2011

Blend of 70% Corvina, 25% Rondinella and Molinara grapes. It matures in stainless steel for 2 years. Deep ruby color. On the nose firm aromas of violet at first, then black cherry, chocolate and eucalyptus notes on the finish. On the mouth is dynamic, with a discreet freshness and with turned tannins.

AGOSTINO VICENTINI

Via Cesare Battisti, 62
37030 Colognola ai Colli (VR)
Tel. +39 045 7650539

vicentini@vicentini.com
www.vinivicentini.com
 Azienda-Agricola-Vicentini-Agostino

YEAR OF FOUNDATION **1990**
NAME OF THE OWNER **Agostino Vicentini**
TOTAL BOTTLES PRODUCED **100,000**
DIRECT SALES
VISITS TO THE WINERY - RESERVATION NEEDED
HECTARES OF VINEYARD **20**

Agostino inherited few but essential elements from his father Francesco: 15 hectares of vineyards, the secrets from 40 years of winemaking and a passion for the land. Today he has expanded his vineyards and cultivates grapes in Valle dei Ciliegi with its expressive volcanic soil.

90 Price A
Soave Superiore Il Casale 2014

100% Garganega grapes. It matures in stainless steel for 1 year. Straw yellow color. On the nose it presents hints of exotic fruit, citrus, pineapple, cedar lime aromas at first, then smoky scents due to the yeast lysis. On the mouth is tense, elegant, acidic, less powerful then other versions with a quite persistent finish.

VIGNALTA

Via Scalette, 23
35032 Arqua' Petrarca (PD)
Tel. +39 0429 777305
 societa.agricola.vignalta
info@vignalta.it
www.vignalta.it
 vignaltacantina.collieuganei
 @Vignalta

YEAR OF FOUNDATION **1980**
NAME OF THE OWNER **Lucio Gomiero, Paolo Guzzo, Luciano Salvagnin**
TOTAL BOTTLES PRODUCED **250,000**
DIRECT SALES
VISITS TO THE WINERY - RESERVATION NEEDED
HECTARES OF VINEYARD **50**
OLIVE OIL PRODUCTION

Lucio Gomiero, co-owner of this Colli Euganei winery with Paolo Guzzo and Luciano Salvagnin, is a formidable agricultural entrepreneur.

For at least 20 years he was 'Mr. Radish' in California where he had great success with this vegetable. Today he is in charge of a wine estate and has proved to be a great wine expert. This year we were most impressed by their Moscato Fior d'Arancio, the best of its kind.

⊡ 93   Price B*

Colli Euganei Fior d'Arancio Moscato Passito Alpianae 2013

*100% Moscato Giallo grapes called Fior D'Arancio. It matures for 1 year in oak barrels of different sizes and 6 months in stainless steel. bright golden yellow color. On the nose is complex, still very young, with aromatic aromas of orange blossom, dry apricot, mango and rosehip. On the mouth is sweet but tense with a great acidity, very persistent and slightly bitter on the aftertaste. *37.5 cl bottle.*

■ 93   Price B

Colli Euganei Rosso Gemola 2011

Blend of 70% Merlot and 30% Cabernet Franc grapes. It matures for 2 years in tonneau. Dark ruby color. On the nose is spicy and eucalyptus with aromas of aromatic herbs, berries, cardamom and vanilla. On the mouth is tense, elegant, velvety, not too full-bodied, and a great length finish.

☐ 88   👍 Price A

Colli Euganei Pinot Bianco 2015

100% Pinot Bianco grapes. Stainless steel only. Straw yellow color. On the nose is very floral with aromas of hawthorn and wildflowers at first, then fresh almond and medlar. On the mouth is savory, warm, very pleasant and full-flavored with and adequate persistence.

VIGNATO

Via Guizza, 14
36053 Gambellara (VI)
Tel. +39 0444 444262
Fax +39 0444 444262
info@vinivignato.com
www.virgiliovignato.it

YEAR OF FOUNDATION **1955**
NAME OF THE OWNER **Vignato Family**
TOTAL BOTTLES PRODUCED **25,000**
DIRECT SALES
VISITS TO THE WINERY - RESERVATION NEEDED
HECTARES OF VINEYARD **20**
OLIVE OIL PRODUCTION

Virgilio Vignato's estate has some 20 hectares of vineyards, both owned and leased, that stretch across the whole southern slope of the Gambellara Hill. Virgilio works the vineyards with his son Vincenzo who is also involved in production and wants to experiment with Garganega even making a late-harvest version. With his other son Illario, who handles sales and communication, Virgilio has created a team for which experience, innovation and enthusiasm are guarantees for always producing quality wines.

⊡ 93   👍 Price A*

Gambellara Recioto Passito 2011

*100% Garganega grapes. Stainless steel first and then matures in barriue for 12 months. Golden red color. On the nose is intense with aromas of saffron at first then the warm and slightly dried scent of the muddler and apricot even candied. Light walnut notes. On the mouth is rich and intense , the body is compact but never sickly thanks to the acidity that gives it an elegant progression. *37.5 cl bottle.*

☐ 92   👍 Price A

Gambellara Classico Capitel Vicenzi 2013

100% Garganega grapes. Stainless steel on yeasts for 1 year. Intense straw yellow color. On the nose is slightly savory at first, then it presents aromas of mudler and apricot, very clean and intense. On the mouth it present a thick and definitely savory weft with an attractive progression that gives it an intense, persistent, tasty finish.

★

VILLA SANDI

Via Erizzo, 112b
31035 Crocetta Del Montello (TV)
Tel. +39 0423 665033
info@villasandi.it
www.villasandi.it
 VillaSandi.it
🐦 *@VillaSandi_it*

YEAR OF FOUNDATION **1975**
NAME OF THE OWNER **Giancarlo Moretti Polegato**
TOTAL BOTTLES PRODUCED **4,500,000**
DIRECT SALES
VISITS TO THE WINERY - RESERVATION NEEDED
HECTARES OF VINEYARD **450**
HOSPITALITY
RESTAURANT

Immersed in the green Marca Trevigiana hills, Villa Sandi is an elegant, Palladian-style estate built in 1692. The Moretti Polegato family has owned it for several generations and it is the headquarters of the winery of the same name. Villa Sandi encompasses the culture and history of wine in a place that has a glorious and aristocratic past, one tied to illustrious people including Napoleon Bonaparte. Giancarlo Moretti Polegato has a profound knowledge of winemaking and continues his family's tradition.

🔲 93   Price C
Opere Riserva Amalia Moretti
Blend of Chardonnay and Pinot Bero grapes. Classic method with 7 years on yeast. intense straw yellow color with a fine and persistent perlage. On the nose is complex with aromas of bread crust followed by scents of yellow plum, fresh almond and wildflowers. On the mouth is firm, creamy, lively with a great sharp acidity that support an excellent body .

🔲 92   Price B
Conegliano Valdobbiadene Prosecco Superiore di Cartizze Vigna La Rivetta Brut
100% Glera grapes. Charmat method. Light yellow color with a thick and fine perlage. It comes from the owned homonym vineyard. On the nose it presents fragrant and fruity aromas of yeast at first, then pear Williams, wisteria flowers and lavender. On the mouth is dry, unlike other Cartizze, lively, creamy, fresh and with a good persistence.

🔲 88   Price B
Corpore Merlot 2012
100% Merlot grapes. It matures for 1 year in barrique. Dark and intense ruby color. On the nose is classic with varietal aromas of raspberry, wild strawberry at first, then hints of mint and pine resin. On the mouth is firm, with young and pawing tannins, good body and a discreet persistence on the finish.

★★
VIVIANI

Via Mazzano, 8 - Località Fane
37020 Negrar (VR)
Tel. +39 045 7500286
Fax +39 045 7500286
viviani@cantinaviviani.com
www.cantinaviviani.com

YEAR OF FOUNDATION 1936
NAME OF THE OWNER Claudio Viviani
TOTAL BOTTLES PRODUCED 80,000
DIRECT SALES
VISITS TO THE WINERY - RESERVATION NEEDED
HECTARES OF VINEYARD 10

Claudio Viviani is without a doubt one of the best producers of Amarone. His winery is in Negrar but his vineyards are in Marano, which sits at an altitude of at least 200m above sea level. This is important because it produces a greater level of acidity in the grapes which survives after they have raisinated and gives the wine elegance and a taut balance.

---

 94   Price C
Amarone della Valpolicella Classico della Casa dei Bepi 2010
Blend of 70% Corvina and 30% Rondinella grapes. It matures for 3 years in new barrique. Intense garnet color. On the nose is very complex with classic aromas of black cherry and Maraschino at first, then cocoa, mint, an hint of licorice, tobacco and vanilla. On the nose is powerful but not heavy, warm, full-flavored, savory, full-bodied and with a great length on the finish.

★
ZARDETTO

Via Martiri delle Foibe, 18
31015 Conegliano (TV)
Tel. +39 0438 394969
Fax +39 0438 394970
info@zardettoprosecco.com
www.zardettoprosecco.com
 ZardettoWinery
 @ZardettoWinery

YEAR OF FOUNDATION 1969
NAME OF THE OWNER Fabio Zardetto
TOTAL BOTTLES PRODUCED 2,000,000
DIRECT SALES
VISITS TO THE WINERY - RESERVATION NEEDED
HECTARES OF VINEYARD 25
OLIVE OIL PRODUCTION

The late, great Treviso sparkling wine giant Pino Zardetto has been gone for several years now. In a previous guide we wrote how while some people may have a green thumb, he had a 'sparkling wine' thumb and all he had to do was touch a stainless steel vat and the wine would magically get bubbles in it. His enormous talent has been fully inherited by his son Fabio who runs the estate today in an efficient and modern way and each year enchants us with his delicious wines.

550

🔲 92   Price B
Conegliano Valdobbiadene Prosecco Superiore di Cartizze Dry 2015

100% Glera grapes. Charmat method. Light yellow color with a persistent and fine perlage. On the nose is very typical with aromas of yeast at first, then winter melon, wisteria flowers and light vanilla sugar. On the mouth is soft, just a little sugary, full-flavored, fresh with a pleasant and good persistence.

🔲 91   Price A
Conegliano Valdobbiadene Prosecco Superiore Rive di Ogliano Brut 2015

100% Glera grapes. Charmat method. Light straw yellow color with a quick and fine perlage. On the nose is polite and varietal with wisteria flowers, yeast, cedar, medical herb. On the mouth is firm, savory, fresh, lively, easy to drink and with a thin and elegant finish.

🔲 90   Price A
Conegliano Valdobbiadene Prosecco Extra Dry

100% Glera grapes. Charmat method. Light yellow color with a persistent and thick perlage. On the nose aromas of yeast, wisteria flowers and jasmine. On the mouth is almost sensual, soft, lightly sugary, creamy, full-flavored, not great but dangerous drinkability.

★★
ZENATO

Via San Benedetto, 8
37019 Peschiera del Garda (VR)
Tel. +39 045 7550300
info@zenato.it
www.zenato.it
🔲 *Zenato-Winery*
🐦 *@nadiazenato*

YEAR OF FOUNDATION 1960
NAME OF THE OWNER Zenato Family

TOTAL BOTTLES PRODUCED **2,000,000**
DIRECT SALES
VISITS TO THE WINERY - RESERVATION NEEDED
HECTARES OF VINEYARD **75**
OLIVE OIL PRODUCTION

Alberto and Nadia Zenato have followed in the footsteps of their illustrious father Sergio Zenato with great dedication and commitment. They produce Amarone and Lugana Riserva, which carries the father's name, as well as a fragrant and very pleasing Valpolicella Ripasso.

🔲 95   Price C
Amarone della Valpolicella Classico Sergio Zenato Riserva 2010

Blend of 80% Corvina, 10% Rondinella and 10% Oseleta grapes. It matures for 48 months in oak barrels. Garnet ruby color. On the nose is powerful and complex with aromas of cocoa, spices, black cherry, eucalyptus wood and leather. On the mouth is rich, complex, pleasant, soft and with a great aromatic progression.

🔲 92   Price B
Lugana Sergio Zenato Riserva 2010

100% Turbiana grapes. It matures in oak barrel for 6 months. Bright gold color. On the nose is intense and greedy with aromas of peach, vanilla and citrus. On the mouth is fresh, creamy, fulfilling, balanced, savory and fruity.

🔲 90   Price B
Amarone della Valpolicella Classico 2011

Blend of 80% Corvina, 10% Rondinella and 10% Oseleta and Croatina grapes. It matures for 36 months is oak barrel. Deep ruby color. On the nose intense and complex aromas of black cherry under spirit, eucalyptus notes, cocoa and spices. On the mouth is soft with a compact but thin tannin and a little bit toasted finish.

★★
ZONIN 1821

Via Borgolecco, 9
36053 Gambellara (VI)
Tel. +39 0444 640111
info@zonin.it
www.zonin.it
🔲 *zonin*
🐦 *@cvzonin*

YEAR OF FOUNDATION 1821
NAME OF THE OWNER Zonin Family
TOTAL BOTTLES PRODUCED 38,000,000
DIRECT SALES
VISITS TO THE WINERY - RESERVATION NEEDED
HECTARES OF VINEYARD 2,000

A great winery that together with his mass production of wines produces quality wines in severeal beautiful estates, located in different Italian region, from Veneto to Sicily. Leading the company is now the 7th generation of the Zonin family, represented the three brothers Domenico, Francesco and Michele, to ensure continuity. The heart of Zonin company is in Gambellara where they produce the Veneto wines Amarone, Gambellara Classico Il Giangio and Berengario, a red blend of Cabernet Sauvignion and Merlot.

---

90 Price B
Amarone della Valpolicella 2012

Blend of 60% Corvina, 35% Rondinella and 5% Molinara grapes. It matures for 2 years in oak barrel. Garnet ruby color. On the nose intense aromas of black cherry in syrup, blueberry, cocoa and different spices. On the mouth is soft, pleasantly fruity and spicy with gentle tannins and a well-balanced alcoholic vein.

---

88 Price B*
Recioto di Gambellara Classico Podere il Giangio 2011

*100% Garganega grapes. fading of the grapes for 4 months the wine matures in barrique and tonneau for 2 years. Bright gold color. On the nose fruity aromas of peach melon, candid citrus at first, then honey and hints of herb scent. On the mouth is sweet, savory with a honey finish. *37.5 cl bottle.*

---

86 Price A
Valpolicella Ripasso Superiore 2014

Blend of 70% Corvina, 20% Rondinella and 10% Molinara grapes. It matures in oak barrel for 12 months. Whole ruby color. On the nose aromas of fruits, especially black cherry, at first, then pepper and cocoa. On the mouth it present a medium body, is soft with the tannins well balanced with the other fundamental gustative aspects.

---

85 Price A
Gambellara Classico Il Giangio 2015

100% Garganega grapes. Stainless steel only. Straw yellow color. On the nose suddenly present aromas of white flowers, acacia, citrus, peach and

---

almond. On the mouth is fresh and savory with a slender structure and a citrusy finish.

ZYMÈ

Via Cà del Pipa, 1
37029 San Pietro in Cariano (VR)
Tel. +39 045 7701108
Fax +39 045 6831477
info@zyme.it
www.zyme.it
 zymewines

YEAR OF FOUNDATION 2003
NAME OF THE OWNER Celestino Gaspari
TOTAL BOTTLES PRODUCED 30,000
DIRECT SALES
VISITS TO THE WINERY - RESERVATION NEEDED
HECTARES OF VINEYARD 16
OLIVE OIL PRODUCTION

This history of this winery began 25 years ago. Celestino Gaspari's adventure in wine started at a very early age in Val d'Illasi where he worked the land alongside his parents and studied agriculture. The watershed moment, however, took place when he was 20 and met Mariarosa and his future father-in-law Giuseppe Quintarell. He worked for 11 years at the Quintarelli state before becoming a consultant for a dozen or so wineries in the area. All this culminated in his own estate, he can put into practice his philosophy of tradition expressed though innovative technology and take advantage of all the experience he has gained.

---

96 Price E
Amarone della Valpolicella La Mattonara Riserva 2006

Blend of 40% Corvina, 30% Corvinone, 15% Rondinella, 10% Oseleta and 5% Croatina grapes. It fades for 3 months and then it matures for at least 9 year in big Slavonia durmast barrel and tonneau. Strong but not dark garnet red color. On the nose it presents very rare aromas, from the fruits in jelly to dry flowers and bitter radish, to the fungal and underbrush, very attractive. Very important is the eucalyptus component. On the mouth is very wide, absolutely rich supported by powerful and thick tannins as well as a soufflé boise'. Powerful but with a supreme elegance, for this kind of wine.

93   Price C

Amarone della Valpolicella Classico 2009

Blend of 40% Corvina, 30% Corvinone, 15% Rondinella, 10% Oseleta and 5% Croatina grapes. It fades for 3 months, then it matures for at least 5 years in Slavonia durmast barrel. Deep, alive red color. It incredibly balanced on the nose with aromas of cherry compote, sour cherry under spirit, plum jelly. Embellish the set the aromas of tobacco and chocolate. On the mouth is sublime, rich, soft but well supported by the very fine and silky tannins.

89   Price A

Valpolicella Reverie 2015

Blend of 40% Corvina, 30% Corvinone, 25% Rondinella, 5% Oseleta grapes. Stainless steel only. Light but bright red color. On the nose aromas of red fruits and an hint of delicious grape taste at first, then a little spices that embellishes the set. On the mouth is perfectly fresh, graceful and clean. Of extraordinary drinkability.

---

www.doctorwine.it is the first **totally bi-lingual (Italian-English)** web-magazine published in Italy and thus offers an Italian point of view to a global public. It is not a blog but an authentic **on-line magazine** which deals with wine and related subjects. The magazine was created and is run by **Daniele Cernilli**, internationally considered to be one of Italy's most authoritative wine critics, who used his nickname as the magazine's name.

From February 2016 DoctorWine is on line with a completely new site. We realized we have an impressive archive that is constantly expanding and which we wanted to make as accessible as possible. Thus the key feature in the change is related to the research of information within the site: making it easier for anyone to find a particular wine we have taste.

PRODUCERS IN ALPHABETICAL ORDER

558

N - O

P

W - Z

PRODUCERS BY REGION

573

580